ENVIRONMENTAL AND NATURAL RESOURCES LAW

Second Edition

By

Eric Pearson
Professor of Law
Creighton University School of Law

LexisNexis™

Library of Congress Cataloging-in-Publication Data

Pearson, Eric, Professor.
  Environmental and natural resources law / by Eric Pearson.--2nd ed.
      p. cm.
  Includes index.
  ISBN 0-8205-6241-6 (hardbound)
  1. Environmental law--United States. 2. Natural resources--Law and legislation--United States. I. Title.
KF3775.P43 2005
344.7304'6--dc22

2005001210

Editorial Offices
744 Broad Street, Newark, NJ 07102 (973) 820-2000
201 Mission St., San Francisco, CA 94105-1831 (415) 908-3200
701 East Water Street, Charlottesville, VA 22902-7587 (804) 972-7600
www.lexis.com

(Pub.3145)

For my wife, Lorraine,
and for our children, Scott and Julia

Preface

Taken in its expansive sense, "environmental and natural resources law" encompasses pollution control law, energy allocation and conservation law, species and habitat protection, common law property rights, and a host of other areas. Often, this massive body of legal material is divided into two courses, the environmental law course dealing primarily with pollution control and the natural resources law course covering the rest. This textbook combines the two. The combination comes with benefits and detriments. The obvious detriment is time-related: a single three or four credit course offers precious little time to mull, compare and contrast, and otherwise absorb this broad range of material. The benefits, however, can be substantial. As a survey course, the expansion of subject matter coverage allows the student a fuller understanding of the "playing field" and the generic issues that arise across this wide spectrum of material. The wider coverage, moreover, should suit both students who want a once-through general understanding of this area of law as well as those seeking a foundation for more intense future study.

Accordingly, the goal of these materials is to teach the structure and operation of the law of environmental and natural resources protection, to see how the pieces fit together, and to understand how those pieces share common design. In the author's view, the goal is more readily achieved if the book is used in conjunction with a statutory supplement.

Chapters 1 through 3 are what might be termed "foundational" materials. Chapter One presents a thumbnail sketch of the environmental movement that has led to the current array of legal controls, and offers some theory and perspective not only on the movement but on the use of regulation to promote environmental quality. Chapter 2 examines how the common law has dealt with pollution and resource allocation problems. This material is important because common law mechanisms remain to this day effective tools for resolving environmental disputes. A review of the strengths and weaknesses of the common law as a method to protect the environment also sheds light on why this area of law is now dominated by statutes and administrative regulations. Chapter 3 introduces the federalist dynamic of environmental and natural resources law. As we shall see, both the federal government and the fifty states have become significant actors in this area of law. Each has enacted laws to regulate behavior to protect the environment and conserve natural resources, and each actively enforces its laws. Two masters entering the same arena is both an opportunity for progress through cooperation and a formula for conflict. Chapter 3 endeavors to explore the federal-state relationship. It concludes with coverage of constitutional takings issues. Since virtually every environmental protection and resource use restriction affects the use and marketability of property, takings principles are ever relevant.

Chapters 4 through 8 presents the natural resource law coverage. Chapter 4, examining the National Environmental Policy Act ("NEPA"), discusses the federal government's attempts to put its own house in order. NEPA requires the federal government to take issues of environmental harm into account across the span of its endeavors. Chapter 5, dealing with public lands, tells the story of the federal government's historical disposition and governance of its own storehouse of natural resources. Chapter 6 discusses the public trust doctrine, a principle in the common law rooted in history but growing in prominence. Chapter 7 offers a look at the Endangered Species Act, by design and impact one of the most significant resource protection measures in history. And Chapter 8 overviews the law of water rights. Issues of rights to water are critical to environmental quality, especially in western states, and students are well served by having some familiarity with these legal principles.

Chapters 9 through 12 conclude the text with an examination of the major federal pollution control and remediation statutes. Chapters 9, 10, and 11 review the Clean Air Act, the Clean Water Act, and the Resource Conservation and Recovery Act, respectively. Chapter 12 presents the book's coverage of the significant "Superfund law," formally known as the Comprehensive Environmental Response, Compensation, and Liability Act ("CERCLA"). This statute is the federal government's pathbreaking effort at remediation of hazardous waste contamination. CERCLA has taken on infamous importance in the regulatory world because of its far-reaching liability structure.

Despite its breadth of coverage, this book does not address several areas of law important for the practicing natural resource/environmental lawyer. Two, at least, deserve mention. A critical area of law not covered in these materials, which is addressed frequently in other environmental and natural resources law texts, is Administrative Law. Administrative Law, the study of government agencies, is central to environmental and natural resources law because government agencies have assumed a dominant role in this field. This material is omitted here for two reasons. First is the author's bias that Administrative Law is better learned in a separate course specifically devoted to the subject area. Derivative coverage is simply insufficient. The second reason, of course, is time management. There is simply no opportunity in a broad survey course to squeeze in the additional complexity that is Administrative Law. Any student who envisions a career in environmental and natural resource law is strongly advised to partake of the main course.

A second area not covered is environmental litigation. Environmental litigation courses deal with an array of issues typically found in Civil Procedure, Trial Tactics, and Federal Courts courses, among others. This material, like Administrative Law, is essential groundwork for environmental lawyers, or at least those who expect to enter the courtroom, but is best left to a course devoted exclusively to those purposes.

Eric Pearson

January 2005

NOTE ON ADMINISTRATIVE LAW

As the reader progresses through the coverage of this book, it will become readily apparent that Environmental and Natural Resources Law is a field dominated by legislation and administrative regulation. Consequently, it is imperative for the lawyer practicing in this area to be fully conversant with legislation and regulation. The legislation comes from both the Congress and state legislatures. The regulations, on the other hand, issue from federal agencies, such as the U.S. Environmental Protection Agency, or companion state agencies charged with the responsibility of translating complex federal or state statutory directives into on-the-ground working programs. The following brief and general discussion is for those who have not studied Administrative Law. It is offered merely as a framework to render the material in this book more understandable.

In the current day, programs to reduce or eliminate pollution or conserve natural resources overwhelmingly find their origins in statutory law. A statute is nothing more than an enforceable expression of legislative will established to accomplish some approved end. In the context of Environmental and Natural Resources Law, statutes establish the goals for regulatory programs. They also empower and obligate agencies to achieve those goals, as well as establish in many particulars the means agencies must implement (or not) in doing so. In some cases, statutes can be quite precise in their requirements but in many cases they are not.

The first task confronting a regulatory agency is to determine precisely what the legislature has required. The agency must begin by discerning exactly what authority has been afforded to it by the enabling legislation. For an agency has only the powers statutes give it, either by clear expression or by necessary implication. Once the agency understands the breadth and limit of its powers, it can get about the task of constructing a program to accomplish the legislative end. The agency may choose to implement the statute by initiating a series of enforcement actions against purported violators of the statute's requirements (assuming, of course, that it has the authority to both make the choice and proceed in this way; *see supra*). If that is the agency's approach, there will be built over time a body of case law, emerging either from agency tribunals or from state or federal courts, that sheds light on the meaning of the statute the agency is charged with administering.

More commonly, however, a regulatory agency will choose not to initiate a series of enforcement actions against purported violators until it has made more specific the requirements stipulated by the governing legislation. Typically, it does this by promulgating "rules and regulations" (statutes are *enacted*; regulations are *promulgated*). (Note again that the governing statute must supply the agency with the power to promulgate regulations for it to do so. This authority is known as "rulemaking" authority.) Regulations can be thought of as "little statutes" enacted by agencies to subdefine statutory terms and otherwise make more concrete and understandable the requirements of governing legislation. Once a regulation is promulgated and effective, typically it is enforceable as if it were part of the statute itself. Federal regulations may be found in the Code of Federal Regulations, or "C.F.R."

Agencies do not have an entirely free hand in setting regulatory standards. The precise standards set in regulations must operate within the bounds of the statute authorizing the regulations; a regulation which exceeds the reach of its governing statute is *ultra vires*, and is, thereby, invalid. Agencies, moreover, must follow established procedures when they promulgate regulations. Failure to follow necessary procedures can also result in invalidation.

Once the rules are in place and have survived judicial review, the agency is ready to engage in enforcement. Of course, agency enforcement activities must also accord with the governing statute. In the normal case, the statute will empower the administrative agency to undertake enforcement by filing suits in equity, by issuing administrative orders, by levying civil penalties, and by instituting criminal actions. Often agencies will have adjudicative tribunals within their organizations. These tribunals can serve to hear enforcement cases brought by agency lawyers against purported violators.

Depending on the statute, an agency might also institute a permit system for regulatory, record-keeping, and enforcement purposes. The purpose of such a system is to provide each regulated entity with a formal document outlining the array of particular requirements applicable to it. A violation of a permit condition typically constitutes a violation of the statute.

Courts often review the rulemaking and enforcement activities of agencies to assure no constitutional or statutory transgressions have taken place. Typically, they will reverse agency actions that fail to follow required procedural requirements. When a court is reviewing the substance of an agency's decision (as distinct from the procedures implemented by the agency as it progressed toward its decision) it will not, at least as a general matter, simply determine whether the agency was right or wrong in what it decided. In other words, a court will not overturn an agency's substantive choice merely because it would have chosen differently were it the agency. Rather, courts will uphold agency substantive decisions unless by some measure they are affirmatively unreasonable, or, in the conventional parlance, are "arbitrary and capricious." This so-called "deferential" review standard is founded on two principles: as a constitutional matter, it is not for courts to usurp agencies' designated administrative roles, and, as a prudential matter, it is not for courts to lightly ignore the expertise of agencies in understanding the refinements and necessities of their own regulatory programs.

SUMMARY TABLE OF CONTENTS

TABLE OF CONTENTS

Chapter 1

INTRODUCTION

"Nothing in the world, not all the armies, is so powerful as an idea whose time has come." *Victor Hugo*

A. BACKGROUND

In the 1960s, there was no isolated field of law known as Environmental and Natural Resources Law. There surely is one now, for reasons finding their root in history and common sense.

The major reason laws are in place in the current day to conserve natural resources is because use patterns have threatened their continued availability. Similarly, the major reason laws are in place in the current day to deter pollution of air, water, and land is because pollution has become a widespread phenomenon. In short, environmental and natural resources law came into being because of a commonly held need for it.

Why has society changed so to create a press on natural resources and a decline in environmental quality? The cause of this development, at bottom, is the "population explosion" (to use Paul and Anne Ehrlich's term). In 1900, the population of this nation was about 76 million; in 1960, it had risen to 180 million or so; in 1990, it was up to 250 million; and in 2000, the count reached 281 million. (Global trends have followed the same path: now over 5 billion in number, the global population is surging rapidly toward 8 billion.)

But sheer numbers do not tell the whole story. A good deal of the harm visited upon the environment over the centuries is directly traceable to more mundane sources, such as ignorance and omission. The first European settlers of America viewed the vast frontier of America as essentially unlimited bounty. It was the promise of a new and better life, a blessing and a fortune awaiting the first comer. This understanding of the world would fuel a systematic and massive transformation and subjugation of the land, a practice that reflected an ethic far afield from that of hunter-gatherer Indian populations previously in residence.

For settlers, dominion was Manifest Destiny. Wildlife, foliage, water, and soil were there to be used, not sanctified. That the natural world may have limits was largely unnoticed. This same lack of appreciation characterized the

1

Industrial Revolution of the nineteenth century. This period of national history saw massive numbers of people relocate into great and increasingly crowded cities,[1] to take up residence among smelters, open hearths, trains, steamboats, and the other machinery of the new age. Smokestacks belched pollution into the air, sewers emptied into the waters, and people went to work. The negative quality-of-life implications of all this were viewed as unavoidable trade-offs, not as environmental problems. After all, "one's bread is more important than landscape or clear skies." *Versailles Borough v. McKeesport Coal & Coke Co.*, 83 Pitt. L.J. 375, 379 (1935).

Thus did the nineteenth century lay the groundwork for a conservation movement. The process gained momentum when people like Henry David Thoreau ("Thank God men cannot as yet fly and lay waste the sky as well as the earth") began to see in nature an inherent value unrelated to its service as a source of material benefits. An early expression of this emerging ethic was the setting aside of Yellowstone National Park in 1872, soon to be followed by other national parks, by Central Park in Manhattan, and even by national forests. In the early twentieth century, men such as Gifford Pinchot and John Muir advanced the cause as well. During a long night by a campfire at Yosemite National Park, Muir persuaded President Theodore Roosevelt to join his cause. Roosevelt turned out to be a valuable ally — during his term the amount of federal land brought under governmental protection expanded exponentially. The former big-game hunter made natural resource conservation a centerpiece of national policy.

The conservation movement of these years ultimately matured into the environmental movement of the current era. In the 1950s and 1960s, enlivened by such seminal works as *Silent Spring* by Rachel Carson and *The Population Bomb* by Paul Ehrlich, the public health implications of degradation rose in prominence. People came to understand that environmental quality was more than merely a matter of aesthetics. When a major river caught on fire and temperature inversions trapped people in hazardous air, the call went out for pollution controls. States took the lead at first, but their attempts to curb air and water contamination were largely ineffective. Ignorance was one reason: little was known about the adverse health consequences, if any, of long-term exposure to specific pollutants. Little was understood as well about how best to abate the release of pollutants into the environment. Politics would prove to be a barrier to effective state regulation as well because the objects of regulation, frequently important industrial entities, resisted assiduously the enactment of such laws.

So states had a tall order, too tall as it turned out. For effective environmental protection, it became clear to many that a determined national involvement was essential. How the long road to comprehensive national regulation was traveled is a rich and interesting story, too extensive to bear recitation here. (For readers interested in this history, an interesting book is Philip Shabecoff, *A Fierce Green Fire: The American Environmental Movement,* Hill and Wang, 1993.) There was, however, one event that, more than any other, came to symbolize the national public concern about environmental degradation. The

---

[1] The concentration of populations has continued to this day — the 2000 census found that 80% of the nation's population, or about 219 million people, resided in metropolitan areas.

single day that most enlivened what is now known as the environmental movement was Earth Day, April 22, 1970. The day began inauspiciously, and its huge and unforeseen political success serves as a testament to the impact a single person with a single idea can work upon society:

GEORGE LOBSENZ, WASHINGTON NEWS (UPI) (April 21, 1990)*

You know Mother Nature, she of the unpredictable floods, earthquakes and hurricanes. Now meet the "Father of Earth Day," a soft-spoken former U.S. senator from Wisconsin by the name of Gaylord Nelson.

While organizers in 135 nations prepare to throw an environmental anniversary party of unprecedented proportions on April 22, Nelson has been happily holding court, recalling for reporters how he came up with the idea for the first Earth Day 20 years ago.

It is clearly a gratifying time for the folksy Nelson, 73, who now works for the environment from underneath an enormous schefflera tree at the Washington headquarters of the Wilderness Society, where he is senior counselor.

"The guys who tend our office plants can't believe how big this thing is," Nelson told a visitor eyeing the 8-foot tree in his office. "They want to know what my secret is."

Nelson's green thumb is not surprising in view of his lifetime commitment to a cleaner environment, a commitment nurtured during his childhood in the small Wisconsin town of Clear Lake, where "the only entertainment to be had was the outdoors."

His interest in the issue grew during his tenure as governor of Wisconsin from 1958 to 1962 and then blossomed after he was elected to the Senate in 1962.

However, throughout the 1960s Nelson was a voice crying in the political wilderness as he tried with little success to focus official Washington's attention on the threat posed by pollution.

He thought he had achieved a breakthrough in 1963 when he persuaded President Kennedy to take a nationwide speaking tour devoted to conservation issues, the first such effort by a president.

The trip went well enough until Salt Lake City, where Kennedy made headline-grabbing remarks about foreign policy.

"I've forgotten what it was he said, but it got big notice," Nelson said. "That was the end of the conservation tour. Obviously, this was more important news."

Nelson spent the next six years traveling the country making speeches about the environment and "trying to figure out how the hell do you get Congress interested."

---

* Copyright 1990 by United Press International. Reprinted with permission.

Then, in the summer of 1969, came a brainstorm that changed the nation.

It occurred on a flight from Los Angeles to San Francisco, where he was to address a conservation forum at the University of California at Berkeley.

"On the way up, I read an article in Ramparts Magazine — you're probably too young to remember that," he says, kidding an interviewer with a grandfatherly twinkle about the now-defunct radical journal.

"Anyway, I read this article on the anti-war teach-ins and as I was reading the phrase 'anti-war Vietnam teach-in' — Bang! I thought, 'That's it. We'll have a nationwide environmental teach-in.'"

Nelson formally proposed the idea of a national Earth Day celebration in a speech in Seattle in September 1969.

"By the time I got back to Washington a couple of days later, the phone was ringing off the hook and I was getting called off the floor of the Senate to take all the calls," he said. "Within three months, it had grown so big I had to get it out of my (senatorial) office."

While Americans took to the idea, Nelson's colleagues in Congress were less enthusiastic. Nelson remembers he could not persuade the Senate even to pass a resolution commemorating the event.

But as the day approached and congressmen began receiving invitations to speak at Earth Day rallies, Nelson was besieged by lawmakers wanting copies of his environmental speeches.

"They wanted to know, 'What the hell do you say at an occasion like this?'" he said.

When the first Earth Day finally took place on April 22, 1970, it surpassed all of Nelson's expectations, with an estimated 20 million Americans attending rallies, concerts and tree-plantings.

"I wanted a demonstration big enough to capture the attention of the politicians and force the issue to become part of the political dialogue," he said. "It did that. From that day on, it was a political issue. It achieved everything I had hoped for, and more."

In the years that followed, Nelson helped shepherd a host of environmental bills through a newly awakened Congress, including the Clean Air Act Amendments of 1970, the Clean Water Act of 1972 and the Endangered Species Act of 1973.

Nelson lost his seat in 1980 to Republican Robert Kasten, but he has continued to be a major voice in the environmental movement.

As for Earth Day 1990, Nelson hopes that, above all else, it helps implant "a conservation ethic" in the minds of the nation's children.

"We are not going to make real progress until we raise a generation imbued in its heart and soul and bones with a conservation ethic," he said. "No president, if he wants to be a leader, can get followers to go along if they don't understand it.

"I was asked in New York last week, if I could wave a wand, what's the most important environmental law I would pass," Nelson said.

"I said, very simply, I'd pass a law requiring every single school in America to have environmental education in the curriculum. Then we'll raise the generation we have to have."

* * * * * *

Earth Day is to environmentalism what Dr. Martin Luther King's "I Have A Dream" oration at the Lincoln Memorial is to civil rights. The day saw a national outpouring of concern for environmental quality by millions of Americans across the country. On that day, education programs were presented in thousands of schools, and hundreds of thousands of students took time to collect litter from parks, schoolgrounds, and neighborhoods. Throngs of concerned people demonstrated in major cities such as Philadelphia, Washington, D.C., Chicago, and New York City. Manhattan banned traffic in part of its downtown area. Not unexpectedly, Congress took up the banner as well. It adjourned to let its members attend and participate in rallies across the land. Earth Day brought home in undeniable fashion the enormity of political support for environmental protection. That popular call for environmental protection ultimately translated into a national political movement.

The movement, in turn, became the driving force in the creation of this area of law.

B. SOME THEORY AND PERSPECTIVE

Before beginning the formal study of environmental and natural resources law, it is useful to review, if only in a cursory fashion, its theoretical and philosophical underpinnings. Following are five (mercifully edited) articles. The initial three selections approach issues of environmental policy from distinct perspectives. The first takes an ethics-based approach, the second a purely economic approach, and the third discusses the effect of unrestrained self-interest on the sustainability of natural resources. These three classic articles are considered to be foundational contributors to the formation of environmental policy. The philosophical approaches embodied in these articles, moreover, are reflected in numerous legislative initiatives. The final two pieces offer diametrically different views on the severity of the environmental "crisis" facing the global community. They demonstrate, among other things, the dependence of environmental and natural resources law on scientific disciplines.

ALDO LEOPOLD, A SAND COUNTY ALMANAC, pp. 203-04
(Oxford University Press, ed. 1968)*

All ethics so far evolved rest upon a single premise: that the individual is a member of a community of interdependent parts. His instincts prompt him

---

* From A SAND COUNTY ALMANAC: AND SKETCHES HERE AND THERE by Aldo Leopold, Copyright 1949, 1977 by Oxford University Press, Inc. Used by permission of Oxford University Press, Inc.

to compete for his place in that community, but his ethics prompt him also to cooperate (perhaps in order that there be a place to compete for).

The land ethic simply enlarges the boundaries of the community to include soils, waters, plants, and animals, or collectively: the land.

This sounds simple: do we not already sing our love for and obligation to the land of the free and the home of the brave? Yes, but just what and whom do we love? Certainly not the soil, which we are sending helter-skelter downriver. Certainly not the waters, which we assume have no function except to turn turbines, float barges, and carry off sewage. Certainly not the plants, of which we exterminate whole communities without batting an eye. Certainly not the animals, of which we have already extirpated many of the largest and most beautiful species. A land ethic of course cannot prevent the alteration, management, and use of these "resources," but it does affirm their right to continued existence, and, at least in spots, their continued existence in a natural state.

In short, a land ethic changes the role of Homo sapiens from conqueror of the land-community to plain member and citizen of it. It implies respect for his fellow-members, and also respect for the community as such.

NOTE AND QUESTION

Compare the foregoing with the Bible: According to the Book of Genesis, man should have "dominion over the fish and the sea, and over the fowl of the air, and over the cattle, and over all the earth and over every creeping thing that creepeth upon the earth." (I:26). Another directive: "Be fruitful and multiply and replenish the earth and subdue it." (I:28). Are the Almanac and the Bible compatible or incompatible?

RONALD H. COASE, THE PROBLEM OF SOCIAL COST
3 Journal of Law and Economics 1 (1960) *

The Problem to Be Examined

This paper is concerned with those actions of business firms which have harmful effects on others. The standard example is that of a factory the smoke from which has harmful effects on those occupying neighbouring properties. The economic analysis of such a situation has usually proceeded in terms of a divergence between the private and social product of the factory, in which economists have largely followed the treatment of Pigou in *The Economics of Welfare*. The conclusions to which this kind of analysis seems to have led most economists is that it would be desirable to make the owner of the factory liable for the damage caused to those injured by the smoke, or alternatively, to place a tax on the factory owner varying with the amount of smoke produced and equivalent in money terms to the damage it would cause, or finally, to exclude the factory from residential districts (and presumably from other areas in

---

which the emission of smoke would have harmful effects on others). It is my contention that the suggested courses of action are inappropriate, in that they lead to results which are not necessarily, or even usually, desirable.

The Reciprocal Nature of the Problem

The traditional approach has tended to obscure the nature of the choice that has to be made. The question is commonly thought of as one in which A inflicts harm on B and what has to be decided is: how should we restrain A? But this is wrong. We are dealing with a problem of a reciprocal nature. To avoid the harm to B would inflict harm on A. The real question that has to be decided is: should A be allowed to harm B or should B be allowed to harm A? The problem is to avoid the more serious harm. I instanced in my previous article the case of a confectioner the noise and vibrations from whose machinery disturbed a doctor in his work. To avoid harming the doctor would inflict harm on the confectioner. The problem posed by this case was essentially whether it was worth while, as a result of restricting the methods of production which could be used by the confectioner, to secure more doctoring at the cost of a reduced supply of confectionery products. Another example is afforded by the problem of straying cattle which destroy crops on neighbouring land. If it is inevitable that some cattle will stray, an increase in the supply of meat can only be obtained at the expense of a decrease in the supply of crops. The nature of the choice is clear: meat or crops. What answer should be given is, of course, not clear unless we know the value of what is obtained as well as the value of what is sacrificed to obtain it. To give another example, Professor George J. Stigler instances the contamination of a stream. If we assume that the harmful effect of the pollution is that it kills the fish, the question to be decided is: is the value of the fish lost greater or less than the value of the product which the contamination of the stream makes possible. . . .

NOTE AND QUESTION

The Coase theorem replaces fault with utility as the significant component in the calculation of legal remedy. At its root is the notion that the purpose of law is to assure effective resource allocation rather than to remedy "wrongs" imposed by some persons upon others. Do you view this disregard of considerations of morality to be appropriate?

GARRETT HARDIN, THE TRAGEDY OF THE COMMONS, 83 Science 1234–38 (1968)*

The tragedy of the commons develops in this way. Picture a pasture open to all. It is to be expected that each herdsman will try to keep as many cattle as possible on the commons. Such an arrangement may work reasonably satisfactorily for centuries because tribal wars, poaching, and disease keep the numbers of both man and beast well below the carrying capacity of the land. Finally, however, comes the day of reckoning, that is, the day when the

---

long-desired goal of social stability becomes a reality. At this point, the inherent logic of the commons remorselessly generates tragedy.

As a rational being, each herdsman seeks to maximize his gain. Explicitly or implicitly, more or less consciously, he asks, "What is the utility to me of adding one more animal to my herd?" This utility has one negative and one positive component.

1. The positive component is a function of the increment of one animal. Since the herdsman receives all the proceeds from the sale of the additional animal, the positive utility is nearly + 1.

2. The negative component is a function of the additional overgrazing created by one more animal. Since, however, the effects of overgrazing are shared by all the herdsmen, the negative utility for any particular decision-making herdsman is only a fraction of − 1.

Adding together the component partial utilities, the rational herdsman concludes that the only sensible course for him to pursue is to add another animal to his herd. And another, and another. . . . But this is the conclusion reached by each and every rational herdsman sharing a commons. Therein is the tragedy. Each man is locked into a system that compels him to increase his herd without limit — in a world that is limited. Ruin is the destination toward which all men rush, each pursuing his own best interest in a society that believes in the freedom of the commons. Freedom in a commons brings ruin to all.

Some would say that this is a platitude. Would that it were! In a sense, it was learned thousands of years ago, but natural selection favors the forces of psychological denial. The individual benefits as an individual from his ability to deny the truth even though society as a whole, of which he is a part, suffers. Education can counteract the natural tendency to do the wrong thing, but the inexorable succession of generations requires that the basis for this knowledge be constantly refreshed. . . .

A simple incident that occurred a few years ago in Leominster, Massachusetts, shows how perishable the knowledge is. During the Christmas shopping season the parking meters downtown were covered with plastic bags that bore tags reading "Do not open until after Christmas. Free parking courtesy of the mayor and city council." In other words, facing the prospect of an increased demand for already scarce space, the city fathers reinstituted the system of the commons. (Cynically, we suspect that they gained more votes than they lost by this retrogressive act.)

In an approximate way, the logic of the commons has been understood for a long time, perhaps since the discovery of agriculture or the invention of private property in real estate. But it is understood mostly only in special cases which are not sufficiently generalized. Even at this late date, cattlemen leasing national land on the western ranges demonstrate no more than an ambivalent understanding, in constantly pressuring federal authorities to increase the head count to the point where overgrazing produces erosion and weed-dominance. Likewise, the oceans of the world continue to suffer from the survival of the philosophy of the commons. Maritime nations still respond automatically to the shibboleth of the "freedom of the seas." Professing to believe in the "inexhaustible resources of the oceans," they bring species after species of fish and whales closer to extinction.

The national parks present another instance of the working out of the tragedy of the commons. At present, they are open to all, without limit. The parks themselves are limited in extent — there is only one Yosemite Valley — whereas population seems to grow without limit. The values that visitors seek in the parks are steadily eroded. Plainly, we must soon cease to treat the parks as commons or they will be of no value to anyone.

What shall we do? We have several options. We might sell them off as private property. We might keep them as public property, but allocate the right to enter them. The allocation might be on the basis of wealth, by the use of an auction system. It might be on the basis of merit, as defined by some agreed-upon standards. It might be by lottery. Or it might be on a first-come, first-served basis, administered to long queues. These, I think are all the reasonable possibilities. They are all objectionable. But we must choose — or acquiesce in the destruction of the commons that we call our national parks. . . .

The long-term disadvantage of an appeal to conscience should be enough to condemn it; but it has serious short-term disadvantages as well. If we ask a man who is exploiting a commons to desist "in the name of conscience," what are we saying to him? What does he hear? — not only at the moment but also in the wee small hours of the night when, half asleep, he remembers not merely the words we used but also the nonverbal communication cues we gave him unawares? Sooner or later, consciously or subconsciously, he senses that he has received two communications, and that they are contradictory: (i) (intended communication) "If you don't do as we ask, we will openly condemn you for not acting like a responsible citizen"; (ii) (the unintended communication) "If you do behave as we ask, we will secretly condemn you for a simpleton who can be shamed into standing aside while the rest of us exploit the commons."

Every man then is caught in what Bateson has called a "double bind." Bateson and his coworkers have made a plausible case for viewing the double bind as an important causative factor in the genesis of schizophrenia. The double bind may not always be so damaging, but it always endangers the mental health of anyone to whom it is applied. "A bad conscience," said Nietzsche, "is a kind of illness."

To conjure up a conscience in others is tempting to anyone who wishes to extend his control beyond the legal limits. Leaders at the highest level succumb to this temptation. Has any president during the past generation failed to call on labor unions to moderate voluntarily their demands for higher wages, or to steel companies to honor voluntary guidelines on prices? I can recall none. The rhetoric used on such occasions is designed to produce feelings of guilt in noncooperators.

For centuries it was assumed without proof that guilt was a valuable, perhaps even an indispensable, ingredient of the civilized life. Now, in this post-Freudian world, we doubt it. . . .

The society arrangements that produce responsibility are arrangements that create coercion, of some sort. Consider bank-robbing. The man who takes money from a bank acts as if the bank were a commons. How do we prevent such action? Certainly not by trying to control his behavior solely by a verbal appeal to his sense of responsibility. Rather than rely on propaganda we follow Frankel's lead and insist that a bank is not a commons; we seek the definite social arrangements that will keep it from becoming a commons. That we thereby infringe on the freedom of would-be robbers we neither deny nor regret. . . .

Coercion is a dirty word to most liberals now, but it need not forever be so. As with the four-letter words, its dirtiness can be cleansed away by exposure to the light, by saying it over and over without apology or embarrassment. To many, the word coercion implies arbitrary decisions of distant and irresponsible bureaucrats; but this is not a necessary part of its meaning. The only kind of coercion I recommend is mutual coercion, mutually agreed upon by the majority of the people affected.

To say that we mutually agree to coercion is not to say that we are required to enjoy it, or even to pretend we enjoy it. Who enjoys taxes? We all grumble about them. But we accept compulsory taxes because we recognize that voluntary taxes would favor the conscienceless. We institute and (grumblingly) support taxes and other coercive devices to escape the horror of the commons.

An alternative to the commons need not be perfectly just to be preferable. With real estate and other material goods, the alternative we have chosen is the institution of private property coupled with legal inheritance. Is this system perfectly just? As a genetically trained biologist I deny that it is. It seems to me that, if there are to be differences in individual inheritance, legal possession should be perfectly correlated with biological inheritance — that those who are biologically more fit to be the custodians of property and power should legally inherit more. But genetic recombination continually makes a mockery of the doctrine of "like father, like son" implicit in our laws of legal inheritance. An idiot can inherit millions, and a trust fund can keep his estate intact. We must admit that our legal system of private property plus inheritance is unjust — but we put up with it because we are not convinced, at the moment, that anyone has invented a better system. The alternative of the commons is too horrifying to contemplate. Injustice is preferable to total ruin. . . .

Perhaps the simplest summary of this analysis of man's population problems is this: the commons, if justifiable at all, is justifiable only under conditions of low-population density. As the human population has increased, the commons has had to be abandoned in one aspect after another.

First we abandoned the commons in food gathering, enclosing farm land and restricting pastures and hunting and fishing areas. These restrictions are still not complete throughout the world.

Somewhat later we saw that the commons as a place for waste disposal would also have to be abandoned. Restrictions on the disposal of domestic sewage are widely accepted in the Western world; we are still struggling to close the commons to pollution by automobiles, factories, insecticide sprayers, fertilizing operations, and atomic energy installations. . . .

Every new enclose of the commons involves the infringement of somebody's personal liberty. Infringements made in the distant past are accepted because no contemporary complains of a loss. It is the newly proposed infringements that we vigorously oppose; cries of "rights" and "freedom" fill the air. But what does "freedom" mean? When men mutually agreed to pass laws against robbing, mankind became more free, not less so. Individuals locked into the logic of the commons are free only to bring on universal ruin; once they see the necessity of mutual coercion, they become free to pursue other goals. I believe it was Hegel who said, "Freedom is the recognition of necessity."

NOTES AND QUESTIONS

1. The idea of a commons is directly related to, indeed, is premised on, the notion of economic externalities. "An economic externality may be viewed as an economic gain or loss accruing to one or more recipient agents as a result of an economic action initiated by another agent — with the gain or loss not being reflected in the market price. The initiating or the recipient economic agent may be either a producer or consumer." Jeffrey L. Harrison, *Law and Economics: in a Nutshell* 31, 32, *citing* Bernard Huber, 1979:36 (West Pub. Co. 1995). In laymen's terms, an externality is created when a person uses a resource for his or her own benefit, but imposes the burden, or cost, of that use on third persons. A classic example of an economic externality is a factory that pollutes. The factory provides a benefit for its owner — the production of goods results in a profit for the owner — but by polluting the countryside, it imposes a significant cost on persons external to the actor, nearby residents. The public, in effect, is made to subsidize the production of goods in the form of a reduced quality of life. Economic theory suggests the producer who enjoys the profits ought to "internalize" these costs by removing the pollution.

The objection to externalities goes beyond these considerations of distributive justice. Externalities, it is argued, tend to promote the misuse of resources, that is, to encourage the use of property in less than optimal ways, at least as viewed from the public perspective. One who can externalize costs may well make different choices about how to use land than one who cannot. She might be willing, for example, to use land for a minimal personal gain, even if the use imposes a substantial burden on others, simply because the burden is, in fact, placed on others. Alternatively, she might be unwilling to change a current land use to a more benign form because the removal of externalized costs inures to the public, not to her.

Notably, it is not only costs that can be externalized. Benefits can be externalized as well. Suppose an individual constructs a residence of high artistic and architectural value, so that the residence becomes a landmark attraction enjoyed by the public at large. By so doing, the individual has externalized the benefits of his labor. Later, he wishes to alter the residence to make it more personally useful. Should the prevailing legal regime prevent a person from eliminating this benefit? Few people would argue the legitimacy of a law that requires the internalization of a cost, but how many would find legitimate a law requiring the externalization of a benefit? In this regard, see *Penn Central Transportation Co. v. City of New York*, 438 U.S. 104, 98 S. Ct. 1646 (1978) (*see* Chapter 3, *infra*).

2. Three approaches to avoid the tragedy of the commons are: (a) privatize the commons; (b) unitize the commons (i.e., employ a single operator to manage the commons for the benefit of all); and (c) regulate the commons (i.e., use the force of law to restrict access to the commons). In practice, it has been politically difficult to implement these alternatives. *See, e.g.,* Barton H. Thompson, Jr., *Tragically Difficult: The Obstacles to Governing the Commons,* 30 ENVT'L LAW 241 (2000). Thompson discusses three examples of tragedies dilemmas: depletion of world fisheries, overdraft of groundwater, and global warming. *Id.*

3. There has emerged a theory of the anticommons. *See* Heller, *The Tragedy of the Anticommons: Property in the Transition of Marx to Markets,* 111 HARV. L. REV. 621 (1998). As you might expect, an anticommons is the opposite of a commons. In a commons, the problem is too many persons with use rights and no persons with rights to exclude others from use. The result is overexploitation. In an anticommons, the problem is too many persons having rights to exclude, and the result is underexploitation — the tragedy of the anticommons. This phenomenon is seen in Russia, notes Heller, where storefronts have been empty of consumer goods. In a typical Moscow storefront, one "owner" has the right to sell, another the right to revenues from sale, another the right to lease, another to occupy. And any single "owner" can block all others from using the property productively. Hence, Moscow has seen a proliferation of sidewalk kiosks, typically brimming with items for sale. Anticommonses in property are curable if the prevailing legal system allows individuals to assemble a collection of property rights sufficient to put property to productive use.

AL GORE, EARTH IN THE BALANCE: ECOLOGY AND THE HUMAN SPIRIT, pp. 29–30, 40 (Penguin Books, 1992)[*]

Global warming is also a strategic threat. The concentration of carbon dioxide and other heat-absorbing molecules has increased by almost 25 percent since World War II, posing a worldwide threat to the earth's ability to regulate the amount of heat from the sun retained in the atmosphere. This increase in heat seriously threatens the global climate equilibrium that determines the pattern of winds, rainfall, surface temperatures, ocean currents, and sea level. These in turn determine the distribution of vegetative and animal life on land and sea and have a great effect on the location and pattern of human societies.

In other words, the entire relationship between humankind and the earth has been transformed because our civilization is suddenly capable of affecting the entire global environment, not just a particular area. All of us know that human civilization has usually had a large impact on the environment; to mention just one example, there is evidence that even in prehistoric times, vast areas were sometimes intentionally burned by people in their search for food. And in our own time we have reshaped a large part of the earth's surface with concrete in our cities and carefully tended rice paddies, pastures, wheatfields, and other croplands in the countryside. But these changes, while sometimes appearing to be pervasive, have, until recently, been relatively trivial factors in the global ecological system. Indeed, until our lifetime, it was always safe to assume that nothing we did or could do would have any lasting effect on the global environment. But it is precisely that assumption which must now be discarded so that we can think strategically about our new relationship to the environment.

Human civilization is now the dominant cause of change in the global environment. Yet we resist this truth and find it hard to imagine that our effect on the earth must now be measured by the same yardstick used to calculate the strength of the moon's pull on the oceans or the force of the wind against the mountains. And if we are now capable of changing something so basic as the relationship between the earth and the sun, surely we must acknowledge a new responsibility to use that power wisely and with appropriate restraint. So far, however, we seem oblivious of the fragility of the earth's natural systems. . . .

The insistence on complete certainty about the full details of global warming — the most serious threat that we have ever faced — is actually an effort to avoid facing the awful, uncomfortable truth: that we must act boldly, decisively, comprehensively, and quickly, even before we know every last detail about the crisis. Those who continue to argue that the appropriate response is merely additional research are simply seeking to camouflage timidity or protect their vested interest in the status quo.

NOTE

For a rejoinder to this point of view, see *Environmental Gore – A Constructive Response to "Earth In The Balance,"* John A. Baden, ed. (Pacific Research Institute for Public Policy, 1994).

GREGG EASTERBROOK, A MOMENT ON THE EARTH, THE COMING AGE OF ENVIRONMENTAL OPTIMISM, pp. xvii–xviii (Viking, 1991)*

Ecorealism will be the next wave of environmental thinking. The core principles of ecorealism are these: that logic, not sentiment, is the best tool for safeguarding nature; that accurate understanding of the actual state of the environment will serve the Earth better than expressions of panic; that in order to form a constructive alliance with nature, men and women must learn to think like nature.

The coming wave of ecorealism will enable people and governments to make rational distinctions between those environmental alarms that are genuine and those that are merely this week's fad. Once rational decision-making becomes the rule in environmental affairs, the pace of progress will accelerate.

Essential to the ecorealist awakening will be the understanding that in almost every ecological category, nature has for millions of centuries been generating worse problems than any created by people.

Consider, for example, that today U.S. factories, power plants, and vehicles emit about 19 million tons per year of sulfur dioxide, the chief cause of acid rain. That level is far too high. Yet in 1991, the Mount Pinatubo eruption in the Philippines emitted an estimated 30 million tons of sulfur dioxide in just a few hours. Less spectacular, ongoing natural processes such as volcanic outgassing and ocean chemistry put about 100 million tons of sulfur dioxide into the atmosphere annually.

That nature makes pollutants in no way excuses the industrial variety. The comparison simply points to an important aspect of the environment, understanding of which is absent from current debate: that nature has spent vast spans of time learning to cope with acid rain, greenhouse gases, climate change, deforestation, radiation, species loss, waste, and other problems we humans so quaintly believe ourselves hurling at the environment for the first time. This knowledge suggests that environmental mischief by women and men will harm the Earth much less than popular culture now assumes. It further suggests that if people have the sense to stop the pollution they make today, and clean up that which they made in the past, the environment will regenerate in an amazingly short time by nature's standards.

NOTE

1. A thematic cousin to the Easterbrook book is *The Skeptical Environmentalist — Measuring the Real State of the World,* by Bjorn Lomborg (Cambridge University Press, 2001). In this book, Lomborg, a professor of statistics in Denmark who describes himself as an "old left-wing Greenpeace member," (*Id.* at xix), painstakingly reviews hard data on both the state of the world and the prospects for continued human survival. Comparing that data with what Lomborg calls the "litany" (i.e. the conventional wisdom of doom and gloom), the author concludes that things are getting better, not worse. Complete with a bibliography seventy-one pages in length, the book calls into question the rigor and urgency of environmental protection regulation. Not unexpectedly, the publication engendered a firestorm of controversy. *See, e.g., Symposium on Bjorn Lomborg's "The Skeptical Environmentalist,"* Case Western Reserve L.R., Vol. 53 (Winter, 2002).

2. It was estimated early in the last decade by the United Nations International Children's Emergency Fund ("UNICEF") that each day in the 1990s 27,000 people, mostly children, would die from treatable diseases, "many of which result from dirty water, the world's most truly murderous environmental problem." Christopher D. Stone, *The Gnat is Older than Man — Global Environment and the Human Agenda,* at xviii (Princeton University Press, 1993).

Chapter 2

COMMON LAW CONSIDERATIONS

"[The American lawyer] . . . views the great judge as one who has the intelligence to discern the best rule of law for the case at hand and then the skill to perform the broken-field running through earlier cases that leaves him free to impose that rule: distinguishing one prior case on the left, straight-arming another one on the right, high-stepping away from another precedent about to tackle him from the rear, until (bravo!) he reaches the goal — good law." Antonin Scalia, *A Matter of Interpretation* 9 (1997).

A. INTRODUCTION

We begin coverage of substantive legal materials with a look at the common law. Both property and tort law can serve to address disputes over environmental degradation and resource use. We should pay attention to these areas for several reasons. First, much of the regulatory regime we will examine finds its underlying rationale in common law theory. Second, environmental and natural resource lawyers continue to rely on the common law, even in this day of high profile and comprehensive regulation. Their use of common law moreover, is not limited to small disputes; major controversies have been resolved on these bases as well. *See, e.g., Suit Against Refinery Divides Quiet Town Into Bitter Battlefield,* Wall Street Journal, Sept. 17, 1990, p. 1, col. 1 (discussing how a nuisance judgment against an oil refinery for $10 million disrupted the peaceful lives of residents in a Kentucky town). Last, the inadequacies of common law as a vehicle for protecting the environment and conserving natural resources help to explain why this field of law has been overtaken by statutory and regulatory controls.

B. PROPERTY LAW: THE LAW OF WASTE

One area of common law that can address environmental and natural resource issues is the law of waste. Narrow in application, this is the area of law that determines rights of persons who share title to the same parcel of land. In the typical scenario, the plaintiff in a "waste case" is a future interest holder who objects to "waste" of a parcel by a present possessor defender. The question in these cases invariably is how much the present use of land should be restricted, if at all, for the benefit of the future interest holder.

The matter is not always simple. "Waste" can be "voluntary" (i.e., caused by actions which are deliberate) or "permissive" (i.e., caused by the failure to act in violation of a duty owed to the future interest holder). "Waste" can also be "innocent" (i.e., caused by acts of a third person when the possessory tenant is without fault). Liability for innocent waste is rarely found in the present day.

With respect to voluntary waste, the old English approach was quite solicitous of the rights of the future interest holder. The party in possession was prohibited from cutting timber, for example, except as needed for necessities, such as repairs or fuel. Similarly, she or he was not permitted to mine the land, unless the mine was in operation when the possession began, in which case the possessor could extract minerals without restriction. Furthermore, possessors were not to demolish any structures on the land, even if the demolition would increase land value.

In this country, while this rigid approach may still be followed in some places with respect to mining rights, it has largely been replaced by test of reasonableness. Present possessors may use land so long as the use is "reasonable." Predictably, what constitutes reasonable use of land is debatable.

What factors enter into a determination whether a person's use of land is reasonable vis-a-vis the remainderman or reversioner? The character and intensity of use is obviously relevant. Also relevant is whether the use is a common one in the neighborhood. The use's impact on the market value of the affected parcel is important as well. In assessing reasonableness, courts are often inclined to compare the current use to that which the future interest holder would devote the property upon assuming possession. By this measure, for example, a proposed demolition of a building might be allowed because the future interest holder intends to construct a new home on the land upon receiving possession. Finally, the likelihood of the plaintiff's securing possession of the parcel in the future is significant. A plaintiff with only a remote chance of coming into possessory title has a similarly remote chance of prevailing in a waste case.

With respect to permissive waste, the possessory tenant has the duty to make repairs and pay all charges on the property. This includes property taxes, as failure to pay these could result in forfeiture of the estate. The possessor typically must pay amounts due on outstanding mortgages as well, at least if the mortgage was taken out by that person; if the mortgage predated the possession, its payment might be apportioned between the parties. The possessor must pay special assessments for public improvements to the extent that the benefit of the public improvements are enjoyed by that person. Generally, the possessor is under no burden to assume costs of this sort to the extent those costs exceed the economic benefits supplied by the land itself.

When waste has occurred, and the plaintiff is a proper party to sue, available remedies include damages and injunctive relief. In some cases, courts have placed property in receivership to assure that repairs are made and that moneys received are devoted to such repairs.

C. TORT LAW: THE LAW OF NUISANCE

More important than property law in these respects is tort law. The areas of tort theory most closely related to environmental and natural resources law are strict liability, negligence, trespass, and nuisance. The law of *strict liability* applies when a defendant engages in ultrahazardous activity. In such cases, defendants are held liable for injuries regardless of considerations of standard of care — the simple fact of injury to a plaintiff is sufficient for a *prima facie* case. The law of *negligence* assesses liability upon a finding of (a) a standard of care (b) breached by a defendant so as to (c) proximately cause (d) an injury to a plaintiff (subject to defenses such as contributory negligence and assumption of risk). Negligence law addresses the legal sufficiency of actions that produce unintended consequences. Negligence law reaches a wide range of disputes, the vast majority of which have nothing to do with environmental and natural resources law. The law of *trespass* comes into play when a defendant intended an act that interferes with another's possessory interest in land. A technical trespass is deemed to occur even when the intended act causes no harm or damage to the land.

While these areas of law are important, in the interest of time, we merely mention them here. The most significant common law theory for our purposes, and the one which will command our attention, is the law of nuisance. "There is perhaps no more impenetrable jungle in the entire law than that which surrounds the word 'nuisance.'" William L. Prosser, *The Law of Torts* 592 (West Pub. Co., 1964). "Nuisance" is defined as the actionable interference with the use and enjoyment of rights in land. Like strict liability, negligence, and trespass, the law of nuisance springs from tort concepts (although early judicial opinions often characterized nuisance in terms of property rights). Nuisances are divisible into two types, public and private. As one might expect, public nuisances are those that interfere with rights of the public. Cases involving air and water pollution, slaughterhouses, storing hazardous or combustible materials so to create undue risk, maintaining gambling establishments, and the like are often common law public nuisance cases. Private nuisances are those that affect persons in their individual capacities. Cases involving dust, smoke, odors, noise, light, and electromagnetic fields are often common law private nuisance cases. A single pattern of conduct can qualify as both a public and private nuisance.

MORGAN v. HIGH PENN OIL CO.

238 N.C. 185, 77 S.E.2d 682 (1953)

[This case was a civil action to recover damages and injunctive relief for a private nuisance. Plaintiffs owned a nine-acre tract of residential land upon which was located their dwelling house, a restaurant, and accommodations for thirty-two trailers. About one thousand feet away, the defendant operated an oil refinery. The evidence showed that the refinery emitted "nauseating gases and odors . . . in such amounts and densities as to render persons of ordinary sensibilities uncomfortable and sick; that the operation of the oil refinery thus substantially impaired the use and enjoyment of the nine acres by the plaintiffs and their renters; and that the defendants failed to put an end to the atmospheric pollution arising out of the operation of the oil refinery after notice and demand from the plaintiffs to abate it." The jury found the refinery to be a nuisance. Entering a judgment to that effect, the trial judge awarded damages in the amount of $2500 and issued an injunction.]

Opinion: Ervin, J.

. . . .

The High Penn Oil Company contends that the evidence is not sufficient to establish either an actionable or an abatable private nuisance. This contention rests on a twofold argument somewhat alternative in character. The High Penn Oil Company asserts primarily that private nuisances are classified as nuisances per se or at law, and nuisances per accidens or in fact; that when one carries on an oil refinery upon premises in his rightful occupation, he conducts a lawful enterprise, and for that reason does not maintain a nuisance per se or at law; that in such case the oil refinery can constitute a nuisance per accidens or in fact to the owner of neighboring land if, and only if, it is constructed or operated in a negligent manner; that there was no testimony at the trial tending to show that the oil refinery was constructed or operated in a negligent manner; and that consequently the evidence does not suffice to establish the existence of either an actionable or an abatable private nuisance. The High Penn Oil Company insists secondarily that the plaintiffs in a civil action can recover only on the case presented by their complaint; that the complaint in the instant action states a cause of action based solely on negligence; that there was no testimony at the trial indicating that the oil refinery was constructed or operated in a negligent manner; and that consequently the evidence is not sufficient to warrant the relief sought and obtained by the plaintiffs, even though it may be ample to establish a nuisance.

The case on appeal discloses some substantial reasons for contesting the soundness of the thesis of the High Penn Oil Company that there was no testimony at the trial tending to show that the oil refinery was constructed or operated in a negligent manner. Even expert witnesses for the defendants testified in substance on cross-examination that the oil refinery would not emit gases or odors in annoying quantities if it were "operated properly." We would be compelled, however, to reject the argument of the High Penn Oil Company on the present aspect of the appeal even if we should accept at face value its thesis that there was no testimony at the trial tending to show that the oil refinery was constructed or operated in a negligent manner.

The High Penn Oil Company asserts with complete correctness that private nuisances may be classified as nuisances per se or at law, and nuisances per accidens or in fact. A nuisance per se or at law is an act, occupation, or structure which is a nuisance at all times and under any circumstances, regardless of location or surroundings. . . . Nuisances per accidens or in fact are those which become nuisances by reason of their location, or by reason of the manner in which they are constructed, maintained, or operated. . . . The High Penn Oil Company also asserts with complete correctness that an oil refinery is a lawful enterprise and for that reason cannot be a nuisance per se or at law. . . . The High Penn Oil Company falls into error, however, when it takes the position that an oil refinery cannot become a nuisance per accidens or in fact unless it is constructed or operated in a negligent manner.

Negligence and nuisance are distinct fields of tort liability. . . . While the same act or omission may constitute negligence and also give rise to a private nuisance per accidens or in fact, and thus the two torts may coexist and be practically inseparable, a private nuisance per accidens or in fact may be created or maintained without negligence. . . . Most private nuisances per accidens or in fact are intentionally created or maintained, and are redressed by the courts without allegation or proof of negligence.

The law of private nuisance rests on the concept embodied in the ancient legal maxim *Sic utere tuo ut alienum non laedas*, meaning, in essence, that every person should so use his own property as not to injure that of another. . . . As a consequence, a private nuisance exists in a legal sense when one makes an improper use of his own property and in that way injures the land or some incorporeal right of one's neighbor. . . .

Much confusion exists in respect to the legal basis of liability in the law of private nuisance because of the deplorable tendency of the courts to call everything a nuisance, and let it go at that. . . . The confusion on this score vanishes in large part, however, when proper heed is paid to the sound propositions that private nuisance is a field of tort liability rather than a single type of tortious conduct; that the feature which gives unity to this field of tort liability is the interest invaded, namely, the interest in the use and enjoyment of land; that any substantial non-trespassory invasion of another's interest in the private use and enjoyment of land by any type of liability-forming conduct is a private nuisance; that the invasion which subjects a person to liability for private nuisance may be either intentional or unintentional; that a person is subject to liability for an intentional invasion when his conduct is unreasonable under the circumstances of the particular case; and that a person is subject to liability for an unintentional invasion when his conduct is negligent, reckless or ultrahazardous.

An invasion of another's interest in the use and enjoyment of land is intentional in the law of private nuisance when the person whose conduct is in question as a basis for liability acts for the purpose of causing it, or knows that it is resulting from his conduct, or knows that it is substantially certain to result from his conduct. . . . A person who intentionally creates or maintains a private nuisance is liable for the resulting injury to others regardless of the degree of care or skill exercised by him to avoid such injury. . . . One of America's greatest jurists, the late Benjamin N. Cardozo, made this illuminating observation on this aspect of the law: "Nuisance as a concept of the law has more meanings than one. The primary meaning does not involve the element of negligence as one of its essential factors. One acts sometimes at one's peril. In such circumstances, the duty to desist is absolute whenever conduct, if persisted in, brings damage to another. Illustrations are abundant. One who emits noxious fumes or gases day by day in the running of his factory may be liable to his neighbor though he has taken all available precautions. He is not to do such things at all, whether he is negligent or careful." *McFarlane v. City of Niagara Falls*, 247 N.Y. 340, 160 N.E. 391.

When the evidence is interpreted in the light most favorable to the plaintiffs, it suffices to support a finding that in operating the oil refinery the High Penn Oil Company intentionally and unreasonably caused noxious gases and odors to escape onto the nine acres of the plaintiffs to such a degree as to impair in a substantial manner the plaintiffs' use and enjoyment of their land. This being so, the evidence is ample to establish the existence of an actionable private nuisance, entitling the plaintiffs to recover temporary damages from the High Penn Oil Company. . . . When the evidence is taken in the light most favorable to the plaintiffs, it also suffices to warrant the additional inferences that the High Penn Oil Company intends to operate the oil refinery in the future in the same manner as in the past; that if it is permitted to carry this intent into effect, the High Penn Oil Company will hereafter cast noxious gases and odors onto the nine acres of the plaintiffs with such recurring frequency and in such annoying density as to inflict irreparable injury upon the plaintiffs in the use and enjoyment of their home and their other adjacent properties; and that the issuance of an appropriate injunction is necessary to protect the plaintiffs against the threatened irreparable injury. This being true, the evidence is ample to establish the existence of an abatable private nuisance, entitling the plaintiffs to such mandatory or prohibitory injunctive relief as may be required to prevent the High Penn Oil Company from continuing the nuisance. . . .

The contention of the High Penn Oil Company that the complaint states a cause of action based solely on negligence is untenable. To be sure, the plaintiffs assert that the defendants were "negligent and careless" in specified particulars in constructing and operating the oil refinery. When the complaint is construed as a whole, however, it alleges facts which show a private nuisance resulting from an intentional and unreasonable invasion of the plaintiffs' interest in the use and enjoyment of their land. . . .

For the reasons given, the evidence is sufficient to withstand the motion of the High Penn Oil Company for a compulsory nonsuit. . . .

NOTES

1. The judge who decided *High Penn* was Sam Ervin, later to represent North Carolina in the United States Senate and best known for his major role in the Watergate investigations of President Richard Nixon.

2. For an actionable nuisance, the harm visited upon the plaintiff must be unreasonable. Unreasonableness depends less on the conduct of the defendant

than upon the harm that conduct causes. Accordingly, otherwise socially acceptable conduct, such as manufacturing, may be viewed as unreasonable for nuisance purposes if it causes an undue unreasonable harm to the land of a plaintiff. To be unreasonable, a harm must be more than minimal (in *High Penn*, the defendant had "impair[ed] in a *substantial* manner the plaintiffs' use and enjoyment of their land.") (emphasis added). Other factors that influence the determination of reasonableness of harm include the character of the neighborhood, the intensity and duration of the interference, and prevailing customary uses of land.

In some cases, the social utility of a defendant's activities may have a significant bearing on choices of remedy and determinations of liability. *See, e.g., Kuper v. Lincoln-Union Elec. Co.*, 557 N.W.2d 748 (S.D. 1996) (suggesting that a public utility, stray voltage from which substantially interfered with a nearby dairy operation, cannot be a nuisance).

WEINHOLD v. WOLFF

555 N.W.2d 454 (Iowa 1996)

JUDGES: Andreasen, J., concurred in part and dissented in part with Neuman and Ternus, JJ., joining the concurrence and dissent.

OPINION: Considered en banc.

Landowners in close proximity to a commercial hog feeding and hog confinement facility sued the owner of the facility. The landowners alleged nuisance and negligence and prayed for damages and injunctive relief. The facility owner answered, asserted affirmative defenses, and counterclaimed. The parties tried the case to the court solely on the landowners' nuisance claim. Following trial, the district court concluded the landowners had proven the facility was a temporary nuisance.

Iowa Code section 352.11(1) (1993) grants a defense against nuisance suits to owners of farmland approved as agricultural land. The district court refused to apply section 352.11(1) to the unique facts of this case. The court concluded that section 352.11(1) would work an unconstitutional taking of the landowners' preexisting nuisance claim. . . .

The court awarded the landowners $ 45,000 in damages for their pain and suffering, but refused to grant them injunctive relief. The damage award was in two parts. In part one, the court awarded the landowners $ 9000 for pain and suffering that occurred before the county approved the facility's land as an agricultural area. In part two, the court awarded the landowners $ 36,000 for pain and suffering that occurred after approval and through the end of trial. The facility owners appealed, and the landowners cross-appealed.

As discussed in detail in the analysis of these issues, we affirm as modified in part, reverse in part, and remand for further proceedings.

Background Facts.

In 1977 Dennis and Ruth Weinhold purchased about four acres of real property in Buena Vista County for $ 8000. They have lived on this acreage since the purchase. They raise various breeds of alternative livestock such as deer, emu, rhea, antelope, and occasionally elk.

In February 1974 Norman and Pam Wolff purchased an eighty-acre tract of land approximately one-half mile directly south of the Weinholds' land. The Wolffs originally planted all the land with grain. Since November 1990 the Wolffs have operated a commercial hog feeding and confinement facility on part of this land, which they commute to from their home located about two and one-half miles away.

The facility is substantial and occupies about four acres of the eighty-acre tract. The Wolffs have run the facility at full capacity since its inception and finish about 2080 hogs per year. The building used to house the hogs is approximately forty-one feet by one hundred sixty-one feet. About 6256 square feet are devoted to hog production. The building runs east and west.

An integral part of the facility is a 500,000-gallon, uncovered, earthen, waste collection basin. The basin is located to the east of the building used to house the hogs. The basin is 130-feet long, 110-feet wide, and 14.5-feet deep.

The hogs are kept within pens located over a slatted floor. The waste falls through the slats and into two-foot pits underneath the hog confinement building. When waste accumulation in the pits reaches sixteen inches, a plug is pulled. The waste flows through an eight-inch diameter underground pipe east to the outside of the building where the waste enters the bottom of the earthen basin.

The pits are emptied every four weeks on an alternating basis. Each time the pits are emptied, about 10,000 to 15,000 gallons of waste are deposited into the basin. Twice a year, the waste is emptied from the basin and applied to area fields as fertilizer. This waste is often applied to fields near the Weinholds' property.

In the fall of 1991, the Wolffs and several farmers neighboring the facility applied for an "agricultural area" designation for the land on which the facility sits. The Wolffs filed the application with the Buena Vista County Board of Supervisors pursuant to what is now Iowa Code section 352.6. The board approved the application on October 8. This was about a year after the Wolffs began the hog feeding and confinement operation.

Background Proceedings.

On July 29, 1992, the Weinholds filed a two-count petition at law. Count I alleged the Wolffs' commercial hog feeding and confinement operation was a nuisance because it created noxious and offensive odors that pervaded the Weinholds' property. The Weinholds asked for money damages and injunctive relief to abate the nuisance. Count II alleged the noxious odors emanating from the Wolffs' hog feeding and confinement operation were the proximate result of the Wolffs' negligence. In this count, the Weinholds asked for money damages.

The Wolffs answered, denied liability, asserted an affirmative defense, and counterclaimed. The Wolffs asserted the affirmance [sic] defense under what is now Iowa Code section 352.11.

The Wolffs' counterclaim alleged the Weinholds' suit was frivolous and caused the Wolffs' mental anguish, inconvenience, and expense. The Wolffs asked for damages that would fairly compensate them for the harm resulting from the Weinholds' actions.

Although the case contained both legal and equitable issues, the parties agreed before trial to try the case in equity. During trial, the Weinholds withdrew their negligence claim. The Wolffs withdrew their counterclaim at the close of the evidence.

In their appeal, the Wolffs challenge the district court's finding that the facility (1) constituted a nuisance and (2) did not have the section 352.11 defense against nuisance suits. The Wolffs also challenge the damage award.

The Weinholds challenge the district court's finding that the nuisance was temporary and not permanent. The Weinholds also complain because the court did not award for (1) the diminished market value of their real property, (2) special damages occurring after trial, and (3) injunctive relief to abate the nuisance.

. . . .

The Issues.

Nuisance. The first issue we consider is whether the Wolffs' hog feeding and confinement operation was a nuisance.

Applicable law. Under Iowa Code section 657.1,

> *whatever* is injurious to health, indecent, or *offensive to the senses*, or an obstruction to the free use of property, so *as essentially to interfere with the comfortable enjoyment of life or property, is a nuisance*, and a civil action by ordinary proceedings may be brought to enjoin and abate the same and to recover damages sustained on account thereof.

(Emphasis added.)

Additionally, under Iowa Code section 657.2,

> the following are nuisances: . . . using any building or other place for the exercise of any trade, . . . which, by occasioning noxious exhalations, offensive smells, or other annoyances, becomes injurious and dangerous to the health, comfort, or property of individuals. . . .

These statutory provisions do not modify the common-law's application to nuisances. *Bates v. Quality Ready-Mix Co.*, 261 Iowa 696, 703, 154 N.W.2d 852, 857 (1967). These provisions are skeletal in form, and the courts look to the common law to fill in the gaps.

A private nuisance is "an actionable interference with a person's interest in the private use and enjoyment of the person's land." *Id.* Parties must use their own property in such a manner that they will not unreasonably interfere with or disturb their neighbor's reasonable use and enjoyment of the neighbor's property. *Id.*

Whether a lawful business is a nuisance depends on the reasonableness of conducting the business in the manner, at the place, and under the circumstances in question. *Id.* Thus the existence of a nuisance does not depend on the intention of the party who created it. *Patz v. Farmegg Prods., Inc.*, 196 N.W.2d 557, 561 (Iowa 1972). Rather, it depends on the following three factors: priority of location, the nature of the neighborhood, and the wrong complained of. *Id.* From this discussion it is clear that whether a party has created and maintained a nuisance is ordinarily a factual question. *Bates*, 261 Iowa at 704, 154 N.W.2d at 857.

A fact finder uses the normal person standard to determine whether a nuisance involving personal discomfort or annoyance is significant enough to constitute a nuisance. *Patz*, 196 N.W.2d at 561. The normal-person standard is an objective standard and is explained in comment d to section 821F of the Restatement (Second) of Torts (1977):

> When [an invasion] involves . . . personal discomfort or annoyance, it is sometimes difficult to determine whether the invasion is significant [enough to constitute a nuisance]. The standard for the determination of significant character is the standard of normal persons or property in the particular locality. If normal persons living in the community would regard the invasion in question as definitely offensive, seriously annoying or intolerable, then the invasion is significant. If normal persons in that locality would not be substantially annoyed or disturbed by the situation, then the invasion is not a significant one, even though the idiosyncracies of the particular plaintiff may make it unendurable to him.

The merits.

[The court noted that for a three year period, the hog confinement operation caused a significant burden on nearby residents. The smells were distinguishable and substantially more intrusive than those from a "more traditional hog operation." The court reviewed three factors to determine the presence of an actionable nuisance: (a) the nature of the neighborhood (here, the neighborhood, while agricultural, was also residential); (b) the wrong complained-of (here, the odors were persistent and "close to intolerable to a person of ordinary or normal sensibility"); and (c) priority of location (here, the plaintiffs had acquired their farm and had taken up occupancy before the offending sewage lagoon was constructed. The court found this latter factor "weighed heavily in favor of the [plaintiff] on the nuisance issue.").]

Defense to nuisance suits provided by Iowa Code section 352.11(1).

Applicable law. Iowa Code section 352.11(1) provides:

> *Nuisance restriction.* A farm or *farm operation located in an agricultural area shall not be found to be a nuisance regardless of the established date of operation or expansion of the agricultural activities of the* farm or *farm operation.* The subsection does not apply if the nuisance results from the negligent operation of the farm or farm operation. *This subsection does not apply to actions or proceedings arising from injury or damage to person or property caused by the* farm or *farm operation before the creation of the agricultural area.*

(Emphasis added.)

Under Iowa Code section 352.6, an agricultural area is created by the owner submitting a proposal to the county board for the creation of an agricultural area within the county. . . . The proposal shall include a description of the proposed area, including its boundaries. The territory shall be as compact and as nearly adjacent as feasible. Land shall not be included in an agricultural area without the consent of the owner. Agricultural areas shall not exist within the corporate limits of the city. . . . Agricultural areas may be created in a county which has adopted zoning ordinances. Except as provided in this section, the use of the land in agricultural areas is limited to farm operations.

The merits.

The Wolffs maintain that the language of section 352.11(1) is clear on its face and requires no interpretation by us. The statute, they say, prohibits any award for damages for nuisance actions after the affected property has been included in an agricultural area as defined by section 352.6.

The Wolffs do not dispute that the district court's $ 9000 award to the Weinholds for special damages occurring before October 8, 1991, was proper. (On October 8, 1991, the county board of supervisors approved the Wolffs' property as an agricultural area.)

The Wolffs do, however, contend the $ 36,000 award for special damages occurring on and after October 8, 1991, was improper. The $ 36,000 award is improper, the Wolffs assert, because those damages occurred after the county had approved the Wolffs' property as an agricultural area. The Wolffs insist the legislature intended that a party should not recover for nuisance damages which occur after the county has approved the property as an agricultural area.

The Weinholds agree section 352.11(1) is clear on its face, but they argue the statute plainly favors their claim. The Weinholds contend their nuisance action arose out of "injury created and damage sustained" before the county approved the Wolffs' property as an agricultural area. In short, the Weinholds rely on the following language in section 352.11(1): "This subsection does not apply to actions or proceedings arising from injury or damage to person or property caused by the farm or farm operation before the creation of the agricultural area."

Section 352.11(1) is a "right to farm" law designed to protect agricultural operations by giving those operations meeting the statutory requirements a defense to nuisance actions. *See* Neil D. Hamilton, *A Livestock Producer's Legal Guide to: Nuisance, Land Use Control, and Environmental Law* 21 (1992). All fifty states have enacted right to farm laws in various forms. *Id.*

Negligent operation of the farm resulting in the nuisance defeats the defense. Additionally, the defense does not apply to actions or proceedings arising from injury or damage to property caused by the farm operation before the agricultural area is established.

Our interpretation suggests that the legislature has determined that farming operations like the Wolffs' are sufficiently important to the state to warrant protective state laws like section 352.11(1). The practical effect of these laws, of course, is to limit the ability of persons affected by the operation to sue operators for nuisance.

The purpose clause of Iowa Code chapter 352 supports our interpretation. *See* Iowa Code § 352.1. Section 352.1 states in pertinent part:

> *The general assembly recognizes the importance of preserving the state's finite supply of agricultural land.* Conversion of farmland to urban development, and other nonfarm uses, reduces future food production capabilities and may ultimately undermine agriculture as a major economic activity in Iowa. *It is the intent of the general assembly to provide local citizens and local governments the means by which agricultural land may be protected from nonagricultural development pressures.* This may be accomplished by . . . establishment of agricultural areas in which substantial agricultural activities are encouraged, so that land inside these areas . . . is conserved for the production of food, fiber, and livestock, *thus assuring the preservation of agriculture as a major factor in the economy of this state.*

(Emphasis added.)

The problem in this case is that the Wolffs started their operation about a year before their land was approved as an agricultural area. As we see it, the parties' contentions are resolved by whether the nuisance was permanent or temporary. Before beginning our analysis, we need to distinguish between these types of nuisances.

The distinction has been explained this way:

> An action in damages may be maintained for the creation of a nuisance and a subsequent and separate action may be maintained for the continuance of such nuisance. The determination of whether a single right of action or successive rights are created by a nuisance for damages depends primarily upon whether the cause of injury is permanent or temporary. The nature of the damages, as being temporary or permanent, is determined by the character of the nuisance to which the land is subjected and not by the quantity of resultant damages. The question generally is one of fact for the jury. If injuries from a nuisance are of a permanent character and go to the entire value of the estate, there can be but one action, and all damages — past, present, and future — are recoverable therein; in such a case, one recovery is a grant or license to continue the nuisance, and there can be no second recovery for its continuance. Stated otherwise, damages for permanent nuisances are not dependent upon any subsequent use of the property but are complete when the nuisance comes into existence. . . . Where the injury from the alleged nuisance is temporary in its nature, or is of a continuing or recurring character, the damages are ordinarily regarded as continuing, and one recovery against the wrongdoer is not a bar to successive actions for damages thereafter accruing from the same wrong. In such a case, every day's continuance is a new nuisance. That is, each repetition of the nuisance creates further liability, and gives rise to a new cause of action. If the nuisance does not involve the entire destruction of the estate or its

beneficial use, but may be apportioned from time to time, separate actions must be brought for each recurring injury, and recovery may be had for damages sustained within the period of the statute of limitations applicable to the action. That is, where a nuisance is temporary, damages to property affected by the nuisance are recurrent and may be recovered from time to time until the nuisance is abated. A temporary nuisance may in some circumstances give rise to permanent damages, as well as temporary damages. . . . The rule applicable where the nuisance is permanent has been applied in cases where the court does not deem it just and equitable to order the thing which causes the injury to be removed, although it is removable, since, under such circumstances, the plaintiff must in one action recover his damages and the defendant must pay all the damages suffered, both past and present, unless the defendant removes the thing before the time of trial, in which case damages are recoverable only up to the time of such removal.

58 Am. Jur. 2d *Nuisances* §§ 273–75 (1989).

For reasons that follow, we think — contrary to the district court — the *unique* facts of this case dictate that we consider the nuisance permanent. We characterize the facts here as unique to emphasize that

the terms "permanent" and "temporary" are somewhat nebulous in that they have practical meaning only in relation to particular fact situations and can change in characterization from one set of facts to another.

Mel Foster Co. Properties v. American Oil Co., 427 N.W.2d 171, 175 (Iowa 1988) (quoting Note, *Stream Pollution — Recovery of Damages*, 50 Iowa L. Rev. 141, 153 (1964); holding that chemical contamination of land encompassed aspects of both a temporary and permanent nuisance; injury was temporary in the sense that the cause of pollution had been discovered and abated, and harmful effects would eventually dissipate; injury was permanent in the sense that it constituted damage to ground itself and would continue for an indefinite but significant period of time; court used measure of damages applicable to permanent nuisance).

First, there is no record evidence that, short of shutting down the operation, the Wolffs can or will abate the nuisance in the future. The district court speculated that technology would eventually solve the odor problem. There was, however, no record evidence that odor control breakthroughs were near. A knowledgeable expert in this area testified that more research was necessary on how to detect and control odor.

Mr. Wolff testified he used an odor control additive in the waste basin. He also testified, however, that he stopped using the additive because the additive was ineffective.

The engineer who designed the waste system for the Wolffs offered no evidence that there were any technological breakthroughs on the horizon to control odor.

We agree with the Weinholds' assessment of the district court's finding on this issue: "The court's rationale that the nuisance was not permanent due to rapidly developing technology that would 'hopefully' aid in the control of odor was unsupported by anything other than wishful thinking."

Moreover, the Wolffs offered no evidence that they intended to cease the operation in the foreseeable future. The evidence, in fact, points the other way because the Wolffs built the waste basin with the capacity to double its current holdings. *See Mel Foster Co. Properties*, 427 N.W.2d at 175 (permanent in legal sense does not mean forever — indefinitely long is sufficient); *Patz*, 196 N.W.2d at 562 (permanent easement is one of such character that it will be reasonably certain to continue in the future).

Second, we can abate the odor by ordering closure of the earthen basin. This is not an equitable and practical solution because our closure order would result in closing the whole operation. *See* 58 Am. Jur. 2d *Nuisances* § 275 ("The rule applicable where the nuisance is permanent has been applied in cases where the court does not deem it just and equitable to order the thing which causes the injury to be removed, although it is removable. . . ."). In addition, such a result would be contrary to the spirit and purpose of chapter 352.

Last, without the removal order, the Wolffs would have, in effect, a license to continue the nuisance. *See* 58 Am. Jur. 2d *Nuisances* § 274. Because of the section 352.11(1) defense against nuisance suits, the Weinholds would have no corresponding right to recover for the continuing nuisance. In these unique circumstances, equity dictates that the Weinholds recover in this action all of their past, present, and future damages. *See Wesley v. City of Waterloo*, 232 Iowa 1299, 1303, 8 N.W.2d 430, 432 (1943) (in the case of a permanent nuisance, plaintiff may maintain only one action; plaintiff is therefore allowed to recover all damages — past, present, and future — in the one action).

We reach the critical issue in this case: Did the legislature intend to cut off the Weinholds' cause of action to recover damages because of a permanent nuisance? We think not. Our conclusion is borne out by the plain language of section 352.11(1). As mentioned, section 352.11(1) gives owners of operations within approved agricultural areas a defense against nuisance suits. The defense does not, however, "apply to actions or proceedings arising from injury or damages to person or property caused by the . . . farm operation before the creation of the agricultural area." Iowa Code § 352.11(1).

Iowa Code section 352.2(9) defines "nuisance action or proceeding" to mean "an *action*, claim, or proceeding, whether brought at law, in equity, or as an administrative proceeding, which is based on *nuisance*." (Emphasis added.) An "action" in its usual legal sense means "a lawsuit brought in a court; . . . the legal and formal demand of one's right from another person or party made and insisted on in a court of justice." Black's Law Dictionary 28 (6th ed. 1990). The Weinholds' lawsuit meets the definition of "nuisance action" in section 352.2(9). This lawsuit is an action because they brought it in a court and are demanding their right to relief for damages from the Wolffs. Additionally, the Weinholds' lawsuit is based on nuisance.

Under Iowa law, causes of actions accrue when the wrongful act produces loss or damage to the claimant. *McKiness Excavating & Grading, Inc. v. Morton Bldgs., Inc.*, 507 N.W.2d 405, 408 (Iowa 1993). Here the nuisance created by the Wolffs' operation caused the Weinholds damage long before the county approved the Wolffs' land as an agricultural area. Because the nuisance is a permanent one, the Weinholds' damages were complete at the time the nuisance arose. This is so because a permanent nuisance "contemplates that [the nuisance] is at once necessarily productive of all the damages that can ever result from it." *Patz*, 196 N.W.2d at 562 (citation omitted). *See also Wesley*, 232 Iowa at 1303, 8 N.W.2d at 432 (in the case of a permanent nuisance, plaintiff may maintain only one action; plaintiff is therefore allowed to recover all damages — past, present, and future — in one action).

We have held that we should not construe a statute "as taking away common law rights existing at the time of enactment unless that result is imperatively required." *Ford v. Venard*, 340 N.W.2d 270, 273 (Iowa 1983) (citation omitted). Our interpretation that section 352.11(1) does not take away the Weinholds' nuisance action is consistent with this rule of statutory construction.

Moreover, we see evidence in Iowa Code chapter 352 to support our interpretation. Iowa Code section 352.6(1)(a) provides that "nonconforming pre-existing residences may be continued in residential use" in an approved agricultural area. So not only was the legislature concerned about conserving farmland for agricultural purposes, it was also concerned about preserving private residential property. Our interpretation allowing the Weinholds to recover all of the damages they are entitled to strikes a balance between these two competing interests. Finally, our interpretation would not affect the overall legislative scheme in chapter 352 because, as the Weinholds point out, it is unlikely that many hog farms are nuisances before farmland is approved as an agricultural area.

We hold therefore that section 352.11(1) did not afford the Wolffs a defense to the Weinholds' nuisance action for past, present, and future damages.

[The portion of the opinion dealing with calculations of damages is omitted]

Injunctive relief: whether the district court should have granted injunctive relief and ordered abatement of the nuisance.

Applicable law.

In determining whether to grant injunctive relief to abate a nuisance, courts employ a balancing test incorporating the following factors: (a) the character of the interest to be protected, (b) the relative adequacy to the plaintiff of injunction and of other remedies, (c) plaintiff's delay in bringing suit, (d) plaintiff's misconduct, (e) the relative hardship likely to result to defendant if injunction is granted and to plaintiff if it is denied, (f) the interests of third persons and of the public, and (g) the practicality of framing and enforcing the order or judgment. *Helmkamp v. Clark Ready Mix Co.*, 214 N.W.2d 126, 130 (Iowa 1974). The decision is a judgment call. *Id.*

The merits on the injunctive relief issue. The final issue concerns whether the district court should have granted the Weinholds injunctive relief and ordered an abatement of the nuisance. The Weinholds contend the court should have. The Wolffs, of course, contend otherwise.

In applying the balancing factors in *Helmkamp*, we conclude we should deny the Weinholds injunctive relief. We do so for the following reasons.

First, we have already determined that the Weinholds should have special damages. Additionally, the district court may on remand award damages to the Weinholds for diminution of the market value of their property. We think such damages provide the Weinholds an adequate remedy.

Second, as we mentioned, to abate the nuisance, we would need to order removal or closure of the basin. As we also mentioned, this is not an equitable and practical solution because such relief would result in closing the operation. Closing the operation would be contrary to the spirit and purpose of Iowa Code chapter 352.

Last, because closing the operation would be contrary to the legislature's goal of protecting farming operations, the public's interest is directly implicated.

Disposition.

In summary, we conclude as follows. First, the Wolffs' facility constitutes a nuisance. Second, contrary to the district court's finding, the nuisance is permanent rather than temporary. Third, Iowa Code section 352.11(1) afforded the Wolffs no defense to the Weinholds' nuisance action. Fourth, we award the Weinholds $ 45,000 for all past, present, and future special damages. This is in contrast to the district court's award of $ 45,000 for such damages through the trial date. Fifth, the district court on remand shall determine on the record the amount, if any, the Weinholds shall receive for diminution in market value of their land. Last, we refuse to grant the Weinholds any injunctive relief.

In view of the above conclusions, we need not address other issues raised by the parties.

We therefore affirm as modified in part, reverse in part, and remand for further proceedings.

AFFIRMED AS MODIFIED IN PART; REVERSED IN PART; REMANDED FOR FURTHER PROCEEDINGS.

All justices concur except Andreasen, Neuman, and Ternus, JJ., who concur in part and dissent in part.

[Additional opinions omitted].

NOTES AND QUESTIONS

1. As *Weinhold* shows, Iowa has enacted statutes to address the common law of nuisance. All states, in fact, have done so. Statutes can interact with the common law in various ways. In some cases, statutes operate to replace and make null and void the common law. The federal Clean Water Act, for example, was found to preempt the federal common law of nuisance for water pollution in certain respects. *Milwaukee v. Illinois*, 451 U.S. 304, 101 S.Ct. 1784 (1981); *International Paper Co. v. Ouellette*, 479 U.S. 481, 107 S.Ct. 805 (1987). *See also San Diego Gas & Elec. Co. v. Superior Court*, 13 Cal. 4th 893, 920 P.2d 669 (1996) (nuisance claim found to be inconsistent with an agency regulation). On other occasions, statutes create independent causes of action

unrelated to the common law. In such a case, to put forth a *prima facie* case, a plaintiff need only show the defendant has violated the statute (e.g., defendant ran a brothel); no showing of harm is necessary. In other instances, statutes operate not to supplement the common law but to codify it. Such is the case with Iowa's § 657.1; accordingly, plaintiffs still have to show harm under common law standards to prevail. In still other instances, statutes affirmatively modify the common law. Because it supplies a defense unavailable at common law, Iowa's § 352.11 (the "right-to-farm" provision) is an example of this sort of provision.

Notably, statutes can have an impact beyond their formal interplay with the common law. In *Weinhold,* the court used the right-to-farm statute as a partial justification for its decision to deny injunctive relief. *See supra.* Even though inapplicable to the merits of the case, the court found the statute influential on the issue of remedy.

2. On the liability issue, the defendant in *Weinhold* was denied the use of the statutory defense. Similarly unavailable was the "moving to the nuisance" defense. Recall that in *Weinhold* the plaintiffs had acquired their farm before the defendants began their hogfeeding operation, a fact the court found "weighed heavily in favor of the [plaintiff]." Suppose the converse were true, that plaintiffs had moved in *after* the hogfeeding operation began? Would this fact weigh heavily in favor of the defendant? Should whether the plaintiff "moved to the nuisance" have anything to do with determinations of liability?

Note that in some states, the moving to the nuisance defense has been enshrined by statute. See, for example, Nebraska's version of a right-to-farm law:

A farm or farm operation shall not be found to be a public or private nuisance if the farm or farm operation existed before a change in the land use or occupancy of land in and about the locality of such farm or farm operation and before such change in land use or occupancy of land the farm or farm operation would not have been a nuisance.

Neb. Rev. Stat § 2-4403.

3. Permanent nuisances may not be abated; only damages are available. Continuing nuisances, to the contrary, may be abated, but it is the plaintiffs' burden to prove that abatement is possible at some reasonable cost by some reasonable means. This can be a difficult burden. For a case in which the court determined that the nuisance was not continuing because it was not reasonably abatable, see *Mangini v. Aerojet-General*, 40 Cal. App 4th 303, 912 P.2d 1220 (1994).

Did the finding of a permanent nuisance in *Weinhold* determine the available remedy, or did the available remedy determine the finding of a permanent nuisance?

Note that the permanent nuisance determination in *Weinhold* was important for an additional reason: the statutory defense was deemed inapplicable because the nuisance was a permanent one. The distinction between permanent and continuing nuisance can be critical also with respect to the statute of limitations. For permanent nuisances, persons are generally required to bring a single lawsuit for all injuries, past, present, and future, within a time certain after the permanent nuisance commences. Failure to bring suit in a timely manner precludes relief. By contrast, with a continuing nuisance, lawsuits for damages can be brought successively until abatement is secured. *See, e.g., Baker v. Burbank-Glendale-Pasadena Airport Authority*, 39 Cal. 3d 862, 705 P.2d 866 (1985). When the nuisance in permanent, the damages are deemed complete at the time the interference began; a typical measure of damages is the diminution in market value of the burdened land. Is this an appropriate measurement?

If nuisance behavior causes harm that is unreasonable by definition, should it not always be abatable?

4. To determine the availability of equitable relief, the court in *Weinhold* engaged in the longstanding practice of "balancing the equities." Balancing the equities is a highly subjective weighing process designed to find a remedy that will occasion the least overall harm. The idea is to avoid a remedy that harms the defendant more than it helps the plaintiff. The result of this exercise can be the award of complete or limited injunctive relief, or, alternatively, a complete denial of any relief. For a famous case in which the court allowed permanent damages in lieu of injunctive relief, see *Boomer v. Atlantic Cement Co.*, 26 N.Y.2d 219, 257 N.E.2d 870 (N.Y. Ct. App. 1970). In an arguably even more famous case, the court ordered the defendant to relocate, so its nuisance behavior would no longer interfere with the plaintiff (plaintiff won?), but the plaintiff was ordered to pay for the relocation (defendant won?). *Spur Industries, Inc. v. Del E. Webb Dev't Co.*, 108 Ariz. 178, 494 P.2d 700 (1972).

There are several arguments against balancing the equities. First is the simple observation that persons should not be forced to endure significant burden simply because the cure is even more burdensome. Under this theory, considerations of relative fault place the responsibility for repairing the harm directly, and exclusively, upon the tort-feasors, regardless of other considerations. Second is the matter of legitimization: as noted above, judicial refusal to order abatement can be seen as a licensing of the injury-causing behavior. Third is the matter of equality: balancing equities often results in different actors receiving disparate judicial treatment for what is essentially the same behavior. When engaging in balancing, courts will be more willing to shut down a mom-and-pop operation, for example, than a major employer. Last, as noted above, refusals to enjoin nuisance behavior can disincent tort-feasors from curing the problems they cause in the future, despite the arrival of a cost-effective, technological solution.

Proponents of balancing, however, assert that much so-called nuisance behavior finds its root in unhappy circumstances. What were once perfectly valid pursuits become "incompatible land uses" as greater numbers of people take up residence proximate to those uses; since there is no "wrongdoer" in the classic sense, the theory goes, courts should accommodate as much as possible the interests of all contestants in a lawsuit.

How would Aldo Leopold, Garrett Hardin, and Ronald H. Coase (*see* Chapter 1, *supra*) view the practice of "balancing the equities"?

5. Do you suspect the common law of nuisance law is moribund in the now-statutorily-driven world of environmental and natural resources law?

Consider the following: eight states and New York City filed suit in July, 2004, against five of the nation's largest power companies to force reductions in the companies' carbon dioxide air emissions. The lawsuit seeks to curb global warming, mainly because the federal government has declined to take up the cause. *See* Chapter 9, *infra.* The legal grounds for the action? You guessed it: public nuisance. *See A Novel Tactic on Warming,* N. Y. Times (July 28, 2004). http://www.nytimes.com/2004/07/28/opinion/28wed1.html?th

A NOTE ON *RESERVE MINING CO. v. HERBST*

Since the law of strict liability, negligence, trespass and nuisance are available to injured litigants in every state, why is it that federal and state statutes have so permeated environmental and natural resources law? The famous *Reserve Mining* litigation (256 N.W.2d 808 (Minn. 1977)) sheds light on this issue. The Reserve Mining Company operated a taconite mining and processing operation from the mid-1940s into the 1970s at a site along Lake Superior near Silver Bay, Minnesota. Taconite is a substance marketable for its iron ore content, but processing the material results in the generation of waste material known as "tailings." For many years, Reserve disposed of tailings by dumping them into Lake Superior. So much entered the lake that an enormous delta formed. The delta was visible even on the relatively crude satellite photography of the time.

While this disposal activity was ongoing, the thought was that the tailings would sink to the bottom of a 900-foot trough in the Lake and be forever gone. In the 1960s, however, it was determined that fibers from the tailings in the Lake were making their way into the drinking water of the residents of Silver Bay, and that fibers from the Reserve site itself, blown by the wind, were lodging in the breathing passages of nearby residents. The fight was on.

The case was litigated in a variety of courts, state and federal, and on a variety of issues, including whether Reserve's mining site should be closed, whether the tailings were dangerous to health, how much exposure to tailings was tolerable, and whether Reserve should dispose of its tailings on land. Finally, in 1977, fully 30 years after Reserve had first been granted permission to dump into the Lake, the formal legal battles drew to a close with a final judicial opinion issued by the Minnesota Supreme Court. Requiring Reserve to dispose of its tailings in a land site known as Mile Post 7, the court paused to reflect on the lessons of the case.

> This case should serve as an example to future generations for several lessons:
>
> (1) Man has been a wasteful user of natural resources. He has been the most rapacious animal ever to walk the face of the earth. Greater controls must be exercised in the future in selecting the location for large industrial complexes.
>
> (2) There is an absolute necessity that there be established uniform national air and water quality standards, and that those standards be uniformly enforced throughout the nation to prevent industry from blackmailing one state into lowering its standards with the threat it will move elsewhere if the state fails to comply.

(3) A decision other than that made in this case would not penalize Reserve as much as the public in general. If Reserve left the state, how would the lake cleanup begin? With the taxpayers footing the costs? Reserve is paying a heavy price for its past practices. It is being compelled to spend hundreds of millions of dollars for tailings disposal and to cease the use of Lake Superior as a dumping area. It can be forced to pay damages for any violation of its permits. It has had to accept a site originally strongly opposed by it and has had conditions imposed on its use of Mile Post 7 which are very stringent and will be constantly monitored. Their permit is for an initial 5-year period only.

This is the fourth time in the past 5 years that the Reserve problem has been before this court . . . . This court has been briefed on the facts in dispute and on the issues raised by all appeals since the initial stages of the appeal from the administrative agencies in the summer of 1976. Due to the time limitations decreed in Federal orders, a large portion of the physical resources of this court has been diverted from our regular calendar to this case for a period of over 9 months so that we would be fully cognizant of all facets of the case prior to oral argument . . . and be able to make an early decision. This court has done all that it can to apply law and reason to find a solution to this long drawn out and acrimonious dispute. In the clouds of smoke generated by all of the litigation, it appears at times that many have forgotten that the objective of getting Reserve out of Lake Superior onto a suitable on-land disposal site is within reach. I believe this decision is consistent with that objective.

Reserve Mining Co. v. Herbst, 256 N.W.2d 808, 852 (Minn. 1977) (Yetka, J., concurring).

Do you think the Minnesota Supreme Court was accurate in its view that uniform regulatory standards are necessary? Is not common law nuisance doctrine a sufficient tool to clean the environment? In this regard, see *Diamond v. General Motors*, 20 Cal. App. 3d 374 (1971). The named plaintiff, representing over 7 million California residents, brought a public nuisance action against 293 corporate defendants for air pollution from automobiles, petroleum refining, and other industrial activities affecting the Los Angeles air basin. The complaint, which alleged no violations of existing air pollution controls laws or regulations, sought billions of dollars in damages and injunctive relief. The court held the cause of action could not proceed for procedural reasons: defendants were not all similarly situated; the injuries to the real parties in interest, if any, varied substantially; and joinder of all parties was impossible. In addition, the plaintiff was unable to show an injury special to himself, a requirement to maintain a public nuisance action under the California Civil Code. More significantly, the court thought itself unable, and it certainly was unwilling, to undertake "judicial regulation" of major industries, a task better left to the other branches of government: "The plaintiff has paid the court an extravagant compliment in asking it to supersede the legislative and administrative regulation in this critical area, but [there is] greater wisdom in declining the tender." *Id.* at 383.

For an argument that common law is well-suited to handle environmental disputes, see Terry L. Anderson and Donald R. Leal, *Free Market Environmentalism* (rev. ed. 2001).

D. CONSERVATION AND PRESERVATION SERVITUDES

We have seen in the preceding sections that common law mechanisms can serve to protect environmental quality, albeit with mixed results. But common law can also serve to assure land will remain in pristine condition on a permanent basis, regardless of changes in ownership.

One way to do this is to simply donate a fee simple interest in land, during life or by will, to an organization pledged to conservation purposes. While this might accomplish the desired end, the approach presents two shortfalls. First, since the transferee organization is clothed with a fee interest, it is not legally bound to honour the intentions of the donation. Second, the donor loses all property rights in the donated parcel at the time of the transfer. For these reasons, a better option would be to transfer an interest less than a fee simple absolute. A fee simple defeasable might work, but more useful are conservation and preservation servitude.

The first servitude interest of this sort was created in the 1880s to protect parkways in and around Boston. The widespread use of these mechanisms, however, triggered by the enactment of the federal Tax Reform Act of 1976, which made them tax-deductible, is far more recent. In the current day, many states have enacted statutes to expedite the use of such servitude interests. A typical provision can be found in the statutory code of Nebraska, which defines a conservation easement as:

> a right, whether or not stated in the form of an easement, restriction, covenant, or condition in any deed, will, agreement, or other instrument executed by or on behalf of the owner of an interest in real property imposing a limitation upon the rights of the owner or an affirmative obligation upon the owner appropriate to the purpose of retaining or protecting the property in its natural, scenic, or open condition, assuring its availability for agricultural, horticultural, forest, recreational, wildlife habitat, or open space use, protecting air quality, water quality, or other natural resources, or for such other conservation purpose as may qualify as a charitable contribution under the Internal Revenue Code of 1954, as amended.

R.R.S. Neb. § 76-2, 111(1).

That same code defines a preservation easement as:

> a right, whether stated in the form of an easement, restriction, covenant, or condition in any deed, will, agreement, or other instrument executed by or on behalf of the owner of an interest in real property imposing a limitation upon the rights of the owner or an affirmative obligation upon the owner appropriate to the purpose of preserving the historical, architectural, archaeological, or cultural aspects of real property, or for such other historic preservation purpose

as may qualify as a charitable contribution under the Internal Revenue Code of 1954, as amended.

R.R.S. Neb. § 76-2, 111(2).

In order to "minimize conflicts with land use planning," these easements must be approved by the appropriate governing body. Once created, they may be released to the holder of the servient estate, if approved. R.R.S. Neb. § 76-2, 113 However, they can also be assigned to any governmental body or charitable corporation or to a trust authorized to secure such an easement. They can be modified or terminated upon a showing that they are no longer "in the public interest" or no longer serve the conservation or preservation purpose for which they were created. R.R.S. Neb. § 76-2, 114.

The increasingly popular use of conservation and preservation servitudes has encouraged a proliferation of "land trusts." Land trusts are not "trusts" in the conventional sense of the term. Rather, they are organizations, funded primarily by private donations, that protect land and water by buying or accepting donations of land or development rights in land. The majority of the more than 1200 land trusts in existence, more than a third of which are located in New England, are local and run by volunteers. Local and regional land trusts have protected approximately five million acres around the country. A group known as the Nature Conservancy is the largest land trust in the nation. A non-profit organization founded in 1951 and supported financially by approximately one million members and 1,900 foundations and corporations, this national organization has protected more than 117 million acres of habitat around the world, about 15.24 million of which are in the United States. It currently manages about 1400 preserves, the largest system of private nature sanctuaries in the world. The Nature Conservancy can be found on the web at *www.tnc.org*.

In place to lend assistance to the many land trusts and to act as an umbrella organization for them is an entity known as the Land Trust Alliance. Founded in 1982, the Land Trust Alliance may be found on the web at *www.lta.org*.

Chapter 3

CONSTITUTIONAL CONSIDERATIONS

". . . [T]he Framers split the atom of sovereignty. It was the genius of their idea that our citizens would have two political capacities, one state and one federal, each protected from incursion by the other." *U.S. Term Limits, Inc. v. Thornton*, 514 U.S. 779, 838, 115 S. Ct. 1842, 1872 (1995) (Kennedy, J., concurring).

A. INTRODUCTION

Common law shines as a mechanism to solve narrow disputes between small numbers of persons. It does so because it can focus on the peculiarities of each dispute, and craft precisely tailored remedies to resolve those disputes. But common law falls short when called upon to advance a social agenda. The same features that allowed common law to excel in some contexts — its decentralized, case-by-case approach to dispute resolution — largely disable it as a tool to promote public welfare. This shortcoming became starkly clear in the 1950s and 1960s with respect to environmental protection and natural resource conservation. In those decades, America was rapidly getting unhealthier, dirtier, and less pleasant to live in. Common law mechanisms, primarily the law of nuisance and waste, were not reversing these trends.

What was needed was a uniform and rigorous federal and state commitment to clean the environment and arrest wasteful resource use. That commitment, moreover, would have to take the form of statute, regulation, and ordinance. In the 1970s, the "environmental decade," that is precisely what happened. Enacted during that time was what remains to this day the flagships of environmental and natural resources law. Included among the federal statutes enacted in those years are: the National Environmental Policy Act (1970); Clean Air Act (1970); the Clean Water Act (1972); the Federal Insecticide, Fungicide, and Rodenticide Act (1972); the Marine Protection, Research, and Sanctuaries Act (the "Ocean Dumping Act") (1972); the Noise Control Act (1972); the Endangered Species Act (1973); the Forest and Rangeland Renewable Resources Planning Act (1974); the Safe Drinking Water Act (1974); the Federal Land Policy and Management Act (1976); the Resource Conservation and Recovery Act (1976); the Toxic Substances Control Act (1976); the Surface Mining Reclamation and Control Act (1977); and the Comprehensive Environmental Response, Compensation and Liability Act (the "Superfund" law) (1980). We will begin reviewing much of this statutory material soon, but as a prelude to that endeavor, it is well to first examine the foundational issues raised by the emergence of a two-tiered regulatory state.

We begin, as we must, by reviewing the relationship between the federal and state governments as established by the federal Constitution. This area of law is loosely referred to as the law of federalism. First, we will look at the constitutional authorities vested in the federal and state governments respectively. Then, we will examine the problems that can arise when those powers are exercised. The subject areas reviewed are: the Tenth Amendment to the federal Constitution, which comes into play when the exercise of federal power interferes with state interests; preemption issues, which come into play when both federal and state powers are exercised to the same end; and the dormant Commerce Clause, which comes into play when the exercise of state power interferes with federal interests.

Thereafter, we turn to the rights of the individual, who, we should not forget, is the focus of this vast regulatory enterprise. We will limit our review to an examination of rights of the individual in her or his capacity as a holder of property rights. This inquiry starts with a look at eminent domain authority as a limitation on rights in private property. It concludes with a review of the Takings Clause of the federal Constitution. As we will discover shortly, takings issues are endemic in environmental and natural resources law.

B. ENUMERATED AND SOVEREIGN POWERS

As every law student knows, both the federal and state governments enjoy substantial constitutional power. The federal power is best exemplified by the far-reaching Commerce Clause of the federal Constitution. U.S. Constitution, Art I, § 8, cl.3. State authority is found in what is known as the "police power." (Note that, except for "home rule" municipalities, which secure authority directly from state constitutions, local governments typically have no constitutional power. Their authorities, rather, derive from delegations from the states in which they are located. Local governments, therefore, are largely irrelevant for constitutional federalism purposes.)

The bedrock of the federalism relationship is state sovereignty. States are the constitutional true sovereigns. This means that states are clothed with a broad and generally undifferentiated police power, which allows them to regulate the broad sweep of matters that affect life within their borders. States have police power simply because they exist. In fact, it is this amorphous and all-consuming authority that itself defines a state as a state: any entity without such a power cannot lay claim to that status. This inherent power stems from a general grant of authority from the governed to the state government. The federal government, by contrast, is not a true sovereign despite the grating tendency of some courts and commenters to speak of a "federal police power," which does not exist. Justice Powell explains:

GARCIA v. SAN ANTONIO METROPOLITAN TRANSIT AUTHORITY

469 U.S. 528, 570-72, 105 S. Ct. 1005, 1027-28 (1985)

Powell, J. (dissenting):

The Framers had definite ideas about the nature of the Constitution's division of authority between the Federal and State Governments. In The Federalist No. 39, for example, Madison explained this division by drawing a series of contrasts between the attributes of a "national" government and those of the government to be established by the Constitution. While a national form of government would possess an "indefinite supremacy over all persons and things," the form of government contemplated by the Constitution instead consisted of "local or municipal authorities [which] form distinct and independent portions of the supremacy, no more subject within their respective spheres to the general authority, than the general authority is subject to them, within its own sphere." *Id.*, at 256 (J. Cooke ed. 1961). Under the Constitution, the sphere of the proposed government extended to jurisdiction of "certain enumerated objects only, . . . [leaving] to the several States a residuary and inviolable sovereignty over all other objects." *Ibid.*

Madison elaborated on the content of these separate spheres of sovereignty in The Federalist No. 45:

> "The powers delegated by the proposed Constitution to the Federal Government, are few and defined. Those which are to remain in the State Governments are numerous and indefinite. The former will be exercised principally on external objects, as war, peace, negotiation, and foreign commerce. . . . The powers reserved to the several States will extend to all the objects, which, in the ordinary course of affairs, concern the lives, liberties and properties of the people; and the internal order, improvement, and prosperity of the State."

Id., at 313 (J. Cooke ed. 1961).

Madison considered that the operations of the Federal Government would be "most extensive and important in times of war and danger; those of the State Governments in times of peace and security." *Ibid.* As a result of this division of powers, the state governments generally would be more important than the Federal Government. *Ibid.*

The Framers believed that the separate sphere of sovereignty reserved to the States would ensure that the States would serve as an effective "counterpoise" to the power of the Federal Government. The States would serve this essential role because they would attract and retain the loyalty of their citizens. The roots of such loyalty, the Founders thought, were found in the objects peculiar to state government. For example, Hamilton argued that the States "[regulate] all those personal interests and familiar concerns to which the sensibility of individuals is more immediately awake. . . ." The Federalist No. 17, p. 107 (J. Cooke ed. 1961). Thus, he maintained that the people would perceive the States as "the immediate and visible guardian of life and property," a fact which "contributes more than any other circumstance to impressing upon the minds of the people affection, esteem and reverence towards the government." *Ibid.* Madison took the same position, explaining that "the people will be more familiarly and minutely conversant" with the business of state governments, and "with the members of these, will a greater proportion of the people have the ties of personal acquaintance and friendship, and of family and party attachments. . . ." The Federalist No. 46, p. 316 (J. Cooke ed. 1961). Like Hamilton, Madison saw the States' involvement in the everyday concerns of the people as the source of their citizens' loyalty. *Ibid.* *See also* Nagel, *Federalism as a Fundamental Value:* National League of Cities *in Perspective,* 1981 S. Ct. Rev. 81.

NOTES AND QUESTIONS

1. Thus, states have inherent authorities while the federal government has enumerated powers, themselves voluntarily relinquished to the federal government by the people. Enumerated powers are external to the federal government and are textually narrow in reach. By comparison, the state police power is internal to state governments and is broad in reach. For obvious reasons, the federal government could lose its constitutional authority. An amendment to the federal Constitution would accomplish that. It would seem axiomatic, however, that a state could not lose its police power by any mechanism for any reason. If it did, the state would cease to be a state.

Could the federal government by a voluntary unilateral action abdicate an enumerated power? In *Zabel v. Tabb*, 430 F.2d 199 (5th Cir. 1970), the issue was whether Congress's enactment of the Submerged Lands Act of 1953 ("SLA") accomplished that result. The SLA transferred title to submerged coastal lands from the federal government to the states. *See* Chapter Five, *infra.* The statute contained the following express language: ". . . [subject to certain exceptions] the right and power to manage, administer, lease, develop, and use the [transferred] lands and natural resources all in accordance with applicable State law [shall] be, and they are . . . recognized, confirmed, established, and vested in and assigned to the respective States . . ." 43 U.S.C.A. § 1311(a). Based on this text, the argument was made that Congress had stripped itself of powers to regulate the use of the transferred property. Examining the text and legislative history, the Fifth Circuit Court of Appeals found that what was lost to the federal government was title, not power. Notably, however, the Court did not object to the idea that, had the facts been different, an abdication could have taken place.

2. As a matter of constitutional theory, is the federal government or are the states better suited to take on the task of protecting natural resources and environmental quality? Do you think the Framers intended federal regulation to extend to matters of health, safety, and welfare?

3. All powers necessarily have limits. What are the limits of the reach of the police power? Importantly, who has the power to declare what those limits are? For insight on this question, *see, e.g., Berman v. Parker*, 348 U.S. 26, 75 S. Ct. 98 (1954).

*   *   *   *   *   *

Of all the enumerated powers supplied to the federal government in the United States Constitution, surely the most important in terms of raw empowerment is the "affirmative" Commerce Clause. The Clause provides that "The Congress shall have Power . . . [t]o regulate Commerce with foreign Nations, and among the several States, and with the Indian Tribes." U.S. Constitution, Article I, § 8, cl. 3. As you know, Congress has relied on this Clause more than any other as authority for its regulatory activity.

When examining the question of the reach of the Commerce Clause, courts used to issue the equivalent of a blank check. Without pause, they routinely found the Clause to justify federal regulation in areas only distantly related to interstate commercial activity. In more recent times, however, the courts have begun to focus on the issue.

GIBBS v. BABBITT

214 F.3d 483 (4th Cir. 2000)

JUDGES: Before WILKINSON, Chief Judge, and LUTTIG and MICHAEL, Circuit Judges. Chief Judge Wilkinson wrote the majority opinion, in which Judge Michael joined. Judge Luttig wrote a dissenting opinion.

WILKINSON, Chief Judge:

In this case we ask whether the national government can act to conserve scarce natural resources of value to our entire country. Appellants challenge the constitutionality of a Fish and Wildlife Service regulation that limits the taking of red wolves on private land. The district court upheld the regulation as a valid exercise of federal power under the Commerce Clause. We now affirm because the regulated activity substantially affects interstate commerce and because the regulation is part of a comprehensive federal program for the protection of endangered species. Judicial deference to the judgment of the democratic branches is therefore appropriate.

I.

A.

In response to growing concern over the extinction of many animal and plant species, Congress enacted the Endangered Species Act of 1973 (ESA), Pub. L. 93-205, 81 Stat. 884 (codified as amended at 16 U.S.C. §§ 1531–44 (1994 & Supp. III 1997)). Congress found that many of the species threatened with extinction are of "esthetic, ecological, educational, historical, recreational, and scientific value to the Nation and its people." 16 U.S.C. § 1531(a)(3) (1994). Congress also found that "various species of fish, wildlife, and plants in the United States have been rendered extinct as a consequence of economic growth and development untempered by adequate concern and conservation." *Id.* § 1531(a)(1). To address these national concerns, the ESA sets forth a comprehensive regulatory scheme to conserve these species and the ecosystems upon which they depend. The Act provides, inter alia, for the listing of "endangered" and "threatened" species, *id.* § 1533, and various recovery plans for the "conservation and survival" of listed species, *id.* § 1533(f).

The cornerstone of the statute is section 9(a)(1), which prohibits the taking of any endangered species without a permit or other authorization. *Id.* § 1538(a)(1)(B). The term "take" is defined as "to harass, harm, pursue, hunt, shoot, wound, kill, trap, capture, or collect, or to attempt to engage in any such conduct." *Id.* § 1532(19). The ESA also authorizes the Fish and Wildlife Service (FWS) to issue any necessary regulations for the conservation of threatened species. *Id.* § 1533(d). Finally, in keeping with its commitment to species conservation, the ESA states that a state law may be more restrictive than the provisions of the Act, but not less. *Id.* § 1535(f).

In order to increase the Service's flexibility in reintroducing endangered species into portions of their historic range, Congress amended the ESA in 1982, Pub. L. 97-304, 96 Stat. 1426. Prior to 1982, reintroduced species were treated the same as any other endangered species. *See id.* § 1536 & 1538(a) (providing for stringent consultation and reporting requirements and a near absolute prohibition on the taking of endangered species). These strict limits led to significant local opposition to the reintroductions. In response to these problems, Congress added section 10(j), which allows the FWS to designate as "experimental" some reintroduced populations of endangered or threatened species. *Id.* § 1539(j). Under the looser standards of section 10(j), members of an experimental population are generally to be treated as threatened rather than endangered. *Id.* § 1539(j)(2)(C). This means that protective regulations may be established for their conservation. *See id.* at 1533(d). By promulgating special rules for an experimental population the Service can determine which prohibitions and exceptions shall apply. *See* 50 C.F.R. § 17.82 (1998).

A population may be designated as "experimental" only after the Service determines that it is not "essential" to the continuation of the species. *Id.* § 1539(j)(2)(B). An experimental population located on private land can be exempt from some of the more stringent requirements for endangered species. *See id.* § 1539(j)(2)(C)(i). If a population is found to be "non-essential" and is designated as "experimental," the FWS can develop "special regulations for each experimental population that will address the particular needs of that population." H.R. Rep. No. 97-567, at 34 (1982), *reprinted in* 1982 U.S.C.C.A.N. 2807, 2834. Furthermore, "there will be instances where the regulations allow for the incidental take of experimental populations." *Id.* Thus, under section 10(j), the FWS has the authority to promulgate regulations allowing the taking of experimental reintroduced populations under limited circumstances.

B.

The red wolf, Canis rufus, is an endangered species whose protection is at issue in this case. The red wolf was originally found throughout the southeastern United States. It was once abundant in the "riverine habitats of the southeast," and was especially numerous near the "canebrakes" that harbored large populations of swamp and marsh rabbits, the primary prey of the red wolf. 51 Fed. Reg. 41,790, 41,791 (1986). The FWS found that "the demise of the red wolf was directly related to man's activities, especially land changes, such as the drainage of vast wetland areas for agricultural purposes . . . and predator control efforts at the private, State, and Federal levels." *Id.*

Activities such as wetlands drainage, dam construction, and hunting reduced the red wolf to such meager numbers that it was listed as endangered in 1976. *See* 32 Fed. Reg. 4001 (1976). Because of the paucity of animals left in the wild, their poor physical condition, and the threats posed by inbreeding, the FWS decided to trap the remaining red wolves in the mid-1970s and place them in a captive breeding program. *See* 51 Fed. Reg. at 41,791. The breeding program anticipated the eventual reintroduction of some red wolves into the wild. *Id.*

In 1986, the FWS issued a final rule outlining a reintroduction plan for red wolves in the 120,000-acre Alligator River National Wildlife Refuge in eastern North Carolina. *See* 51 Fed. Reg. 41,790. This area was judged the ideal habitat within the red wolf's historic range. *Id.* at 41,791. Between 1987 and 1992, a total of 42 wolves were released in the Refuge. In 1993, the reintroduction program was expanded to include the release of red wolves in the Pocosin Lakes National Wildlife Refuge in Tennessee. Since reintroduction, some red wolves have wandered from federal refuges onto private property. From available data, as of February 1998 it was estimated that about 41 of the approximately 75 wolves in the wild may now reside on private land.

This case raises a challenge to 50 C.F.R. § 17.84(c), a regulation governing the experimental populations of red wolves reintroduced into North Carolina and Tennessee pursuant to section 10(j). The FWS has extended the takings prohibitions of section 9(a)(1) to the experimental red wolf populations with certain exceptions. *See* 50 C.F.R. § 17.84(c) (1998). As noted above, the taking provision of section 9(a)(1) prevents landowners from harassing, harming, pursuing, hunting, shooting, wounding, killing, trapping, capturing, or collecting any endangered species. *See* 16 U.S.C. § 1532(19). However, in order to insure that other agencies and the public would accept the proposed reintroduction, the FWS relaxed the taking standards for wolves found on private land under its authority over experimental populations.

Section 17.84(c) allows a person to take red wolves on private land "provided that such taking is not intentional or willful, or is in defense of that person's own life or the lives of others." *Id.* § 17.84(c)(4)(i). Private landowners may also take red wolves on their property "when the wolves are in the act of killing livestock or pets, Provided that freshly wounded or killed livestock or pets are evident." *Id.* § 17.84(c)(4)(iii). A landowner may also "harass red wolves found on his or her property. . . . Provided that all such harassment is by methods that are not lethal or injurious to the red wolf." *Id.* § 17.84(c)(4)(iv). Finally, landowners may take red wolves after efforts by Service personnel to capture such animals have been abandoned, and such taking has been approved in writing. *Id.* § 17.84(c)(4)(v). All of these exceptions to the taking prohibition are subject to a 24-hour reporting requirement. *Id.* § 17.84(c)(4).

C.

In October 1990, plaintiff Richard Lee Mann shot a red wolf that he feared might threaten his cattle. The federal government prosecuted Mann under § 17.84(c), and Mann pled guilty. . . .

Appellants Charles Gibbs, Richard Mann, Hyde County, and Washington County filed the instant action challenging the federal government's authority to protect red wolves on private land. . . .

II.

We consider this case under the framework articulated by the Supreme Court in *United States v. Lopez,* 514 U.S. 549, 131 L. Ed. 2d 626, 115 S. Ct. 1624 (1995), and *United States v. Morrison,* 120 S. Ct. 1740, 146, L. Ed. 2d 658 (2000), *aff'g Brzonkala v. Virginia Polytechnic Institute and State University,* 169 F.3d 820 (4th Cir. 1999). While Congress's power to pass laws under the Commerce Clause has been interpreted broadly, both Lopez and Morrison reestablish that the commerce power contains "judicially enforceable outer limits." *See Lopez,* 514 U.S. at 566; *Morrison,* 2000 WL 574361, at 6. It is essential to our system of government that the commerce power not extend to effects on interstate commerce that are so remote that we "would effectually obliterate the distinction between what is national and what is local." *National Labor Relations Board v. Jones & Laughlin Steel Corp.,* 301 U.S. 1, 37, 81 L. Ed. 893, 57 S. Ct. 615 (1937). Indeed, the judiciary has the duty to ensure that federal statutes and regulations are promulgated under one of the enumerated grants of constitutional authority. It is our further duty to independently evaluate whether "a rational basis exists for concluding that a regulated activity sufficiently affects interstate commerce." *Lopez,* 514 U.S. at 557. . . .

The *Lopez* Court recognized three broad categories of activity that Congress may regulate under its commerce power. 514 U.S. at 558. "First, Congress may regulate the use of the channels of interstate commerce. Second, Congress is empowered to regulate and protect the instrumentalities of interstate commerce, or persons or things in interstate commerce, even though the threat may come only from intrastate activities. Finally, Congress' commerce authority includes the power to regulate those activities having a substantial relation to interstate commerce, i.e., those activities that substantially affect interstate commerce." *Id. at* 558–59 (citations omitted).

Section 17.84(c) is "not a regulation of the use of the channels of interstate commerce, nor is it an attempt to prohibit the interstate transportation of a commodity through the channels of commerce." *Lopez,* 514 U.S. at 559. The term "channel of interstate commerce" refers to, inter alia, "navigable rivers, lakes, and canals of the United States; the interstate railroad track system; the interstate highway system; . . . interstate telephone and telegraph lines; air traffic routes; television and radio broadcast frequencies." *United States v. Miles,* 122 F.3d 235, 245 (5th Cir. 1997). This regulation of red wolf takings on private land does not target the movement of wolves or wolf products in the channels of interstate commerce.

This case also does not implicate *Lopez*'s second prong, which protects things in interstate commerce. Although the Service has transported the red wolves interstate for the purposes of study and the reintroduction programs, this is not sufficient to make the red wolf a "thing" in interstate commerce. *See, e.g., Lopez,* 514 U.S. at 559 (rejecting application of prong two to Gun-Free School Zones Act, despite the fact that the regulated guns likely traveled through interstate commerce); *National Assoc. of Home Builders v. Babbitt,* 327 U.S. App. D.C. 248, 130 F.3d 1041, 1046 (D.C. Cir. 1997) ("NAHB") (rejecting notion that Delhi Sands Flower-Loving Fly was a "thing" in interstate commerce). Therefore, if 50 C.F.R. § 17.84(c) is within the commerce power, it must be sustained under the third prong of *Lopez*.

Under the third *Lopez* test, regulations have been upheld when the regulated activities "arise out of or are connected with a commercial transaction, which viewed in the aggregate, substantially affects interstate commerce." *Lopez,* 514 U.S. at 561. In *Morrison,* the Supreme Court noted, "In every case where we have sustained federal regulation under *Wickard*'s aggregation principle, the regulated activity was of an apparent commercial character." *Morrison,* 2000 WL 574361, at 37 n.4. The Court in *Lopez* likewise placed great emphasis on the "commercial concerns that are central to the Commerce Clause." *Lopez,* 514 U.S. at 583 (Kennedy, J., concurring); *see also Hoffman v. Hunt,* 126 F.3d 575, 586–87 (4th Cir. 1997) (noting the importance of the distinction between "the regulation of, on the one hand, those activities that are commercial or economic in nature . . . and, on the other hand, those activities that are not").

Although the connection to economic or commercial activity plays a central role in whether a regulation will be upheld under the Commerce Clause, economic activity must be understood in broad terms. Indeed, a cramped view of commerce would cripple a foremost federal power and in so doing would eviscerate national authority. The *Lopez* Court's characterization of the regulation of home-grown wheat in *Wickard v. Filburn,* 317 U.S. 111, 87 L. Ed. 122, 63 S. Ct. 82 (1942), as a case involving economic activity makes clear the breadth of this concept. The Court explained that "even *Wickard,* which is perhaps the most far reaching example of Commerce Clause authority over intrastate activity, involved economic activity in a way that the possession of a gun in a school zone does not." *Lopez,* 514 U.S. at 560; *accord Morrison,* 2000 WL 574361, at 7. *See also Brzonkala,* 169 F.3d at 835 (explaining that the Court has a "relatively broad understanding of such [economic] activity"). In fact, our understanding of commerce may not be limited to its "18th-century" forms. *See Lopez,* 514 U.S. at 574 (Kennedy, J., concurring). While we must enforce meaningful limits on the commerce power, we must also be mindful of the "Court's relatively generous conception of economic activity." *Brzonkala,* 169 F.3d at 835.

Lopez and *Morrison* rest on the principle that where a federal statute has only a tenuous connection to commerce and infringes on areas of traditional state concern, the courts should not hesitate to exercise their constitutional obligation to hold that the statute exceeds an enumerated federal power. Respect for our federal system of government was integral to those decisions. *See Lopez,* 514 U.S. at 561 n.3; *Morrison,* 2000 WL 574361, at 11. Yet *Lopez* also counsels that "where economic activity substantially affects interstate commerce, legislation regulating that activity will be sustained." 514 U.S. at 560. In enforcing limits on the Congress, we must be careful not to overstep the judicial role. To strike down statutes that bear substantially upon commerce is to overstep our own authority even as we fault Congress for exceeding limits on its power. The irony of disregarding limits on ourselves in the course of enforcing limits upon others will assuredly not be lost on those who look to courts to respect restraints imposed by rules of law.

With these basic principles in mind, we consider appellants' challenge to § 17.84(c).

III.

Appellants argue that the federal government cannot limit the taking of red wolves on private land because this activity cannot be squared with any of the three categories that Congress may regulate under its commerce power. Appellants assert that 50 C.F.R. § 17.84(c) is therefore beyond the reach of congressional authority under the Commerce Clause.

We disagree. It was reasonable for Congress and the Fish and Wildlife Service to conclude that § 17.84(c) regulates economic activity. The taking of red wolves implicates a variety of commercial activities and is closely connected to several interstate markets. The regulation in question is also an integral part of the overall federal scheme to protect, preserve, and rehabilitate endangered species, thereby conserving valuable wildlife resources important to the welfare of our country. Invalidating this provision would call into question the historic power of the federal government to preserve scarce resources in one locality for the future benefit of all Americans.

A.

To fall within Congress' commerce power, this regulation must have a "substantial relation to interstate commerce" — it must "substantially affect interstate commerce." *Lopez,* 514 U.S. at 559. The Supreme Court recently emphasized that "in those cases where we have sustained federal regulation of intrastate activity based upon the activity's substantial effects on interstate commerce, the activity in question has been some sort of economic endeavor." *Morrison,* 2000 WL 574361, at 8. Intrastate activities may be subject to federal regulation if they have a "meaningful connection with a particular, identifiable economic enterprise or transaction." *Brzonkala,* 169 F.3d at 834. We therefore must consider whether the taking of red wolves on private land is "in any sense of the phrase, economic activity." *Morrison,* 2000 WL 574361, at 9.

Unlike the Violence Against Women Act (VAWA) in Morrison and the Gun-Free School Zones Act (GFSZA) in *Lopez,* § 17.84(c) regulates what is in a meaningful sense economic activity. The Court in Morrison explained that both the VAWA and the GFSZA involved activity that was noneconomic and only tenuously linked to interstate commerce. 2000 WL 574361, at 7-9. Yet the taking of a red wolf on private land is unlike gender-motivated violence or guns near schools. The protection of commercial and economic assets is a primary reason for taking the wolves. Farmers and ranchers take wolves mainly because they are concerned that the animals pose a risk to commercially valuable livestock and crops. Indeed, appellants' arguments focus quite explicitly on these economic concerns — they want freer rein to protect their property and investments in the land [citation omitted]; *id.* at 12.

The relationship between red wolf takings and interstate commerce is quite direct — with no red wolves, there will be no red wolf related tourism, no scientific research, and no commercial trade in pelts. We need not "pile inference upon inference," *Lopez,* 514 U.S. at 567, to reach this conclusion. While a beleaguered species may not presently have the economic impact of a large commercial enterprise, its eradication nonetheless would have a substantial effect on interstate commerce. And through preservation the impact of an endangered species on commerce will only increase.

Because the taking of red wolves can be seen as economic activity in the sense considered by *Lopez* and *Morrison,* the individual takings may be aggregated for the purpose of Commerce Clause analysis. *See Morrison,* 2000 WL 574361, at 37 n.4. While the taking of one red wolf on private land may not be "substantial," the takings of red wolves in the aggregate have a sufficient impact on interstate commerce to uphold this regulation. This is especially so where, as here, the regulation is but one part of the broader scheme of endangered species legislation.

Further, § 17.84(c) is closely connected to a variety of interstate economic activities. Whether the impact of red wolf takings on any one of these activities qualifies as a substantial effect on interstate commerce is something we need not address. We have no doubt that the effect of the takings on these varied activities in combination qualifies as a substantial one. The first nexus between the challenged regulation and interstate commerce is tourism. The red wolves are part of a $29.2 billion national wildlife-related recreational industry that involves tourism and interstate travel. *See Heart of Atlanta Motel,* 379 U.S. at 256 (finding it is well-established that "commerce among the States . . . consists of intercourse and traffic between their citizens" (internal quotation marks omitted)). Many tourists travel to North Carolina from throughout the country for "howling events" — evenings of listening to wolf howls accompanied by educational programs. These howlings are a regular occurrence at the Alligator River National Wildlife Refuge. According to a study conducted by Dr. William E. Rosen of Cornell University, the recovery of the red wolf and increased visitor activities could result in a significant regional economic impact. *See* William E. Rosen, Red Wolf Recovery in Northeastern North Carolina and the Great Smoky Mountains National Park: Public Attitudes and Economic Impacts (unpublished, Joint Appendix at 633). Rosen estimates that northeastern North Carolina could see an increase of between $39.61 and $183.65 million per year in tourism-related activities, and that the Great Smoky Mountains National Park could see an increase of between $132.09 and $354.50 million per year. This is hardly a trivial impact on interstate commerce. Appellants understandably seek to criticize the Rosen study, but concede that the howling events attract interstate tourism and that red wolf program volunteers come from all around the country.

While there are no formal congressional findings that the ESA affects interstate commerce, such findings are neither necessary nor sufficient to sustain a statute or regulation. In *Lopez,* the Court said that "Congress normally is not required to make formal findings as to the substantial burdens that an activity has on interstate commerce." 514 U.S. at 562; *see also Perez v. United States,* 402 U.S. 146, 156, 28 L. Ed. 2d 686, 91 S. Ct. 1357 (1971) (particularized findings are not necessary for Congress to legislate). Further, in *Morrison,* the Court emphasized in the face of voluminous congressional findings that "the existence of congressional findings is not sufficient, by itself, to sustain the constitutionality of Commerce Clause legislation." 2000 WL 574361, at 10.

In evaluating whether there is a rational basis for the promulgation of a statute or regulation under the commerce power, we often consider congressional committee findings. *See Lopez,* 514 U.S. at 562. Here, Congress has provided numerous sources of informal findings. Committee reports and legislative debates have emphasized the importance of endangered species to interstate commerce. We independently evaluate the constitutionality of this regulation, but we also take account of congressional judgment and the judgment of the agency designated to implement the statute.

Appellants argue that the tourism rationale relates only to howling events on national park land or wildlife refuges because people do not travel to private land. They reason that without tourism on private land the regulated activity does not substantially affect interstate commerce. Yet this argument misses the mark. Since reintroduction, red wolves have strayed from federal lands onto private lands. Indeed, wolves are known to be "great wanderers." *See* 60 Fed. Reg. 18,940, 18,943 (1995). In 1998, it was estimated that 41 of the 75 wolves in the wild now live on private land. Because so many members of this threatened species wander on private land, the regulation of takings on private land is essential to the entire program of reintroduction and eventual restoration of the species. Such regulation is necessary to conserve enough red wolves to sustain tourism. Appellants in fact seem unmindful of the history of endangered species regulation. The Endangered Species Acts of 1966 and 1969 initially targeted conservation efforts only on federal lands, but they met with limited success. *See Note, Evolution of Wildlife Legislation in the United States: An Analysis of the Legal Efforts to Protect Endangered Species and the Prospects for the Future,* 5 Geo. Int'l Envtl. L. Rev. 441, 449–53 (1993). The Endangered Species Act of 1973 was motivated in part by the need to extend takings regulation beyond the limited confines of federal land. *See id.* at 556. The prohibition of takings on private land was critical to the overall success of the ESA in halting and reversing the near extinction of numerous species. *See* 16 U.S.C. § 1538(a)(1). The success of many commercial enterprises depends on some regulation of activity on private land, and interstate tourism is no exception.

Tourism, however, is not the only interstate commercial activity affected by the taking of red wolves. The regulation of red wolf takings is also closely connected to a second interstate market — scientific research. Scientific research generates jobs. It also deepens our knowledge of the world in which we live. The red wolf reintroduction program has already generated numerous scientific studies. For example, the red wolf is used as a model for other carnivore reintroductions. *See* Donald E. Moore III & Roland Smith, *The Red Wolf as a Model for Carnivore Re-introductions,* 62 Symp. Zool. Soc. Lond. 263 (1990). Scientists have also studied how the red wolf affects small mammal populations and how the wolves interact with the ecosystem as a whole. *See, e.g.,* Bryan T. Kelly, Alligator River National Wildlife Refuge Red Wolf (Canis Rufus) Scat Analysis: Preliminary Analyses of Mammalian Prey Consumed by Year, Season, Pack, Sex, and Age (April 1994) (unpublished, Joint Appendix at 942). By studying the effects of red wolves on the ecosystem, scientists learn about the interdependence of plants and animals, as well as how other threatened species may be reintroduced in the future. Scientific research can also reveal other uses for animals — for instance, approximately 50 percent of all modern medicines are derived from wild plants or animals. *See* Norman Myers, A Wealth of Wild Species: Storehouse for Human Welfare 4 (1983). Protection of the red wolves on private land thus encourages further research that may have inestimable future value, both for scientific knowledge as well as for commercial development of the red wolf.

The anti-taking regulation is also connected to a third market — the possibility of a renewed trade in fur pelts. Wolves have historically been hunted for their pelts. *See* Stanley P. Young & Edward A. Goldman, The Wolves of North America I, 165–70 (1964). Congress had the renewal of trade in mind when it enacted the ESA. The Senate Report noted that the protection of an endangered species "may permit the regeneration of that species to a level where controlled exploitation of that species can be resumed. In such a case businessmen may profit from the trading and marketing of that species for an indefinite number of years, where otherwise it would have been completely eliminated from commercial channels." S. Rep. No. 91-526, at 3 (1969), *reprinted in* 1969 U.S.C.C.A.N. 1413, 1415. The American alligator is a case in point. In 1975, the American alligator was nearing extinction and listed as endangered, but by 1987 conservation efforts restored the species. Now there is a vigorous trade in alligator hides. *See* Catharine L. Krieps, *Sustainable Use of Endangered Species Under CITES: Is it a Sustainable Alternative?*, 17 U. Pa. J. Int'l Econ. L. 461, 479–80 (1996) (explaining that many environmentalists are now encouraging the purchase of alligator products to create an incentive for protecting alligators and their habitats). Although alligator hides have more recently been a part of interstate commercial trade and red wolves were sold for their pelts primarily in the nineteenth century, this temporal difference is beside the point. It is not for the judiciary to move from species to species, opining that species A possesses great commercial potential, but species B does not. Assessing the relative scientific value and commercial impact of alligators and red wolves is for Congress and the FWS, informed as they are by biologists, economists, and others whose expertise is best delivered to the political branches, not the courts.

Finally, the taking of red wolves is connected to interstate markets for agricultural products and livestock. For instance, appellant landowners find red wolves a menace because they threaten livestock and other animals of economic and commercial value. By restricting the taking of red wolves, § 17.84(c) is said to impede economic development and commercial activities such as ranching and farming. This effect on commerce, however, still qualifies as a legitimate subject for regulation. It is well-settled under Commerce Clause cases that a regulation can involve the promotion or the restriction of commercial enterprises and development. Indeed, "the motive and purpose of a regulation of interstate commerce are matters for the legislative judgment." *United States v. Darby*, 312 U.S. 100, 115, 85 L. Ed. 609, 61 S. Ct. 451 (1941). We recognize that "Congress can regulate interstate commerce for any lawful motive." *United States v. Soderna*, 82 F.3d 1370, 1374 (7th Cir.

1996). The regulation here targets takings that are economically motivated — farmers take wolves to protect valuable livestock and crops. It is for Congress, not the courts, to balance economic effects — namely whether the negative effects on interstate commerce from red wolf predation are outweighed by the benefits to commerce from a restoration of this species. To say that courts are ill-suited for this act of empirical and political judgment is an understatement.

It is anything but clear, for example, that red wolves harm farming enterprises. They may in fact help them, and in so doing confer additional benefits on commerce. For instance, red wolves prey on animals like raccoons, deer, and rabbits — helping farmers by killing the animals that destroy their crops. *See* Robert J. Esher & Theodore R. Simons, Red Wolf Propagation on Horn Island, Miss.: Red Wolf Ecological Studies 13-16 (Sept. 1993) (unpublished, Joint Appendix at 890). On Horn Island, for instance, researchers found evidence of increased shore bird nesting, likely due to the reduction in raccoon predation. *See id.* at 15. In *Tennessee Valley Authority v. Hill ("TVA")*, the Supreme Court recognized that one of Congress' primary concerns in enacting the ESA was "the unknown uses that endangered species might have and about the unforeseeable place such creatures may have in the chain of life on this planet." 437 U.S. 153, 178–79, 98 S. Ct. 2279, 57 L. Ed. 2d 117 (1978). It is within the power of Congress to regulate the coexistence of commercial activity and endangered wildlife in our nation and to manage the interdependence of endangered animals and plants in large ecosystems. It is irrelevant whether judges agree or disagree with congressional judgments in this contentious area. Given the existing economic and commercial activity involving red wolves and wildlife generally, Congress could find that conservation of endangered species and economic growth are mutually reinforcing. It is simply not beyond the power of Congress to conclude that a healthy environment actually boosts industry by allowing commercial development of our natural resources.

Section 17.84(c) aims to reverse threatened extinction and conserve the red wolf for both current and future use in interstate commerce. Congress is entitled to make the judgment that conservation is potentially valuable, even if that value cannot be presently ascertained. The Supreme Court has held that the congressional decision to maintain abandoned railroad track is reasonable "even if no future rail use for it is currently foreseeable." *Preseault v. ICC*, 494 U.S. 1, 19, 108 L. Ed. 2d 1, 110 S. Ct. 914 (1990). The Court reasoned that "given the long tradition of congressional regulation of railroad abandonments, that is a judgment that Congress is entitled to make." *Id.* (citations omitted). Similarly, Congress has long been involved in the regulation of scarce and vital natural resources. The full payoff of conservation in the form of tourism, research, and trade may not be foreseeable. Yet it is reasonable for Congress to decide that conservation of species will one day produce a substantial commercial benefit to this country and that failure to preserve a species will result in permanent, though unascertainable, commercial loss.

When enacting the ESA, various legislators expressed these exact concerns, namely that species be conserved for future scientific development:

The value of this genetic heritage is, quite literally, incalculable. . . . From the most narrow possible point of view, it is in the best interests of mankind to minimize the losses of genetic variations. The reason is simple: they are potential resources. . . . Who knows, or can say, what potential cures for cancer or other scourges, present or future, may lie locked up in the structures of plants which may yet be undis-covered, much less analyzed? . . . Sheer self-interest impels us to be cautious.

H.R. Rep. No. 93-412, at 4–5 (1973). Extinction, after all, is irreversible. If a species becomes extinct, we are left to speculate forever on what we might have learned or what we may have realized. If we conserve the species, it will be available for the study and benefit of future generations. In any event, it is for Congress to choose between inaction and preservation, not for the courts.

Courts have uniformly upheld endangered species legislation after *Lopez* based on many of the same current and future connections to interstate commerce articulated here. In fact, no case has been brought to our attention that invalidates any endangered species regulation for exceeding the com-merce power. . . .

The protection of the red wolf on both federal and private land substantially affects interstate commerce through tourism, trade, scientific research, and other potential economic activities. To overturn this regulation would start courts down the road to second-guessing all kinds of legislative judgments. There is a "rational basis" as defined by *Lopez* for sustaining this regulation. We therefore hold that the anti-taking provision at issue here involves regulable economic and commercial activity as understood by current Com-merce Clause jurisprudence.

B.

This regulation is also sustainable as "an essential part of a larger regula-tion of economic activity, in which the regulatory scheme could be undercut unless the intrastate activity were regulated." *Lopez*, 514 U.S. at 561. The Supreme Court in *Hodel v. Indiana* stated: "A complex regulatory program . . . can survive a Commerce Clause challenge without a showing that every single facet of the program is independently and directly related to a valid congressional goal. It is enough that the challenged provisions are an integral part of the regulatory program and that the regulatory scheme when consid-ered as a whole satisfies this test." 452 U.S. 314, 329 n.17 (1981).

The FWS issued this regulation pursuant to the provisions of the Endan-gered Species Act, a comprehensive and far-reaching piece of legislation that aims to conserve the health of our national environment. Congress undoubt-edly has the constitutional authority to pass legislation for the conservation of endangered species. . . .

Appellants repeatedly argue that individual takings of red wolves have only an insubstantial effect on interstate commerce and therefore that the applica-tion of the regulation to private landowners is invalid. But we emphasize that the effect on commerce must be viewed not from the taking of one wolf, but from the potential commercial differential between an extinct and a recovered species. A single red wolf taking may be insubstantial by some measures, but that does not invalidate a regulation that is part of the ESA and that seeks conservation not only of any single animal, but also recovery of the species as a whole. The Supreme Court in *Lopez* was emphatic on this point: " 'where a general regulatory statute bears a substantial relation to commerce, the de minimis character of individual instances arising under that statute is of no consequence.' " 514 U.S. at 558 (alteration in original) (quoting *Maryland v. Wirtz,* 392 U.S. 183, 197 n.27, 20 L. Ed. 2d 1020, 88 S. Ct. 2017 (1968)); *see also Perez v. United States,* 402 U.S. 146, 154, 28 L. Ed. 2d 686, 91 S. Ct. 1357 (1971) ("Where the class of activities is regulated and that class is within the reach of federal power, the courts have no power to excise, as trivial, individual instances of the class." (internal quotation marks omitted)).

Once a species has been designated as endangered, there are by definition only a few remaining animals. Therefore, the effects on interstate commerce should not be viewed from the arguably small commercial effect of one local taking, but rather from the effect that single takings multiplied would have on advancing the extinction of a species. Each taking impacts the overall red wolf population, which has an effect on many dimensions of commerce between the states. As the Supreme Court has stated, "if it is interstate commerce that feels the pinch, it does not matter how local the operation which applies the squeeze." *Heart of Atlanta Motel,* 379 U.S. at 258 (internal quotation marks omitted). Section 17.84(c) must thus be evaluated against the overall congressional goal of restoring red wolves and endangered species generally. It would be perverse indeed if a species nearing extinction were found to be beyond Congress's power to protect while abundant species were subject to full federal regulatory power. Yet under appellants' theory, the more endangered the species, the less authority Congress has to regulate the taking of it. According to this view, endangered species would lie beyond congressional protection because there are too few animals left to make a commercial difference. Such reasoning would eviscerate the comprehensive federal scheme for conserving endangered species and turn congressional judgment on its head.

Appellants protest they do not ask us to overturn the ESA. They simply want us to excise as unconstitutional a disfavored provision that places a strain on their agricultural activities. But given that Congress has the ability to enact a broad scheme for the conservation of endangered species, it is not for the courts to invalidate individual regulations. If appellants think this regulation unwise, they must make their plea to Congress. * * *

IV.

Upholding this regulation is consistent with the "first principles" of a Constitution that establishes a federal government of enumerated powers. *See Lopez,* 514 U.S. at 552. *Lopez* and *Morrison* properly emphasize that we must carefully evaluate legislation in light of our federal system of government. "The Constitution requires a distinction between what is truly national and what is truly local." *Morrison,* 2000 WL 574361, at 11. We must particularly scrutinize regulated activity that "falls within an area of the law where States historically have been sovereign and countenance of the asserted federal power would blur the boundaries between the spheres of federal and state authority." *Brzonkala,* 169 F.3d at 837 (internal quotation marks omitted).

A.

It is imperative to set forth at the outset the historic roles of federal and state authority in this area. The regulated activity at issue here does not involve an "area of traditional state concern," one to which "States lay claim by right of history and expertise." *Lopez,* 514 U.S. at 580, 583 (Kennedy, J., concurring).

Appellants argue that the regulation infringes on the traditional state control over wildlife. We are cognizant that states play a most important role in regulating wildlife — many comprehensive state hunting and fishing laws attest to it. State control over wildlife, however, is circumscribed by federal regulatory power. In *Minnesota v. Mille Lacs Band of Chippewa Indians,* the Supreme Court recently reiterated that "although States have important interests in regulating wildlife and natural resources within their borders, this authority is shared with the Federal Government when the Federal Government exercises one of its enumerated constitutional powers." 526 U.S. 172, 204, 119 S. Ct. 1187, 143 L. Ed. 2d 270 (1999). In *Mille Lacs,* the Court upheld Chippewa Indian rights under an 1837 treaty that allowed the Chippewa to hunt, fish, and gather free of territorial, and later state, regulation. *Id.* These Indian treaty rights were found to be "reconcilable with state sovereignty over natural resources." *Id.* at 205.

It is true that in the nineteenth century courts followed the legal precept that wildlife was the property of the state. *See Geer v. Connecticut,* 161 U.S. 519, 40 L. Ed. 793, 16 S. Ct. 600 (1896) (upholding a Connecticut statute that prohibited the interstate transportation of game birds that had been killed within the state). But the principles in *Geer* were modified early in the twentieth century. *See Hughes v. Oklahoma,* 441 U.S. 322, 329, 60 L. Ed. 2d 250, 99 S. Ct. 1727 (1979) ("The erosion of *Geer* began only 15 years after it was decided."). *Geer* was finally overruled in 1979 by *Hughes v. Oklahoma,* which held that states do not own the wildlife within their borders and that state laws regulating wildlife are circumscribed by Congress's commerce power. 441 U.S. at 326, 335. In light of *Mille Lacs* and *Hughes,* the activity regulated by § 17.84(c) — the taking of red wolves on private property — is not an area in which the states may assert an exclusive and traditional prerogative in derogation of an enumerated federal power.

Appellants next argue that the application of this regulation to private land intrudes on the state's traditional police power to regulate local land use. Of course, states and localities possess broad regulatory and zoning authority over land within their jurisdictions. *See Village of Euclid v. Ambler Realty Co.,* 272 U.S. 365, 71 L. Ed. 303, 47 S. Ct. 114 (1926). It is well established, however, that Congress can regulate even private land use for environmental and wildlife conservation. * * *

Given the history of federal regulation over wildlife and related environmental concerns, it is hard to imagine how this anti-taking regulation trespasses impermissibly upon traditional state functions — either control over wildlife or local land use. *Lopez* and *Morrison* properly caution that States should receive judicial protection from unconstitutional federal encroachments on state matters. Yet endangered wildlife regulation has not been an exclusive or primary state function. * * *

D.

Unlike the statutes in *Lopez* and *Brzonkala,* § 17.84(c) can be upheld while observing principled limitations on federal power. The regulation applies only to a single limited area — endangered species. It does not in any way grant Congress "an unlimited police power inconsistent with a Constitution of enumerated and limited federal powers." *Brzonkala,* 169 F.3d at 852. Nor does the regulation "obliterate the Constitution's distinction between national and local authority." *Morrison,* 2000 WL 574361, at 10. In *Lopez,* the Court rejected the "costs of crime" and "national productivity" justifications for the GFSZA, because under these theories it was "difficult to perceive any limitation on federal power, even in areas such as criminal law enforcement or education where States historically have been sovereign." 514 U.S. at 564.

But these concerns are simply not implicated by § 17.84(c). Rather, the ESA and this regulation in particular permit the exercise of federal power only to conserve those species that are "endangered" or "threatened." The Secretary must determine whether a species is endangered or threatened "solely on the basis of the best scientific and commercial data available to him after conducting a review of the status of the species." 16 U.S.C. § 1533(b)(1)(A). Only after determining that a species is endangered or threatened can Congress regulate it. The rationale for upholding § 17.84(c), and the ESA generally, is restricted to the special relationship between endangered species and interstate commerce as drawn in Part III. It is not a connection that can be drawn outside of the endangered species context to support federal regulation of just any local or intrastate object with a medical, scientific, or economic value.

The rationale for this regulation thus stops far short of conferring upon Congress a broad police power. It is instead appellants' arguments for invalidating this regulation that go too far. If the federal government cannot regulate the taking of an endangered or threatened species on private land, its conservation and preservation efforts would be limited to only federal lands. A ruling to this effect would place in peril the entire federal regulatory scheme for wildlife and natural resource conservation.

[The remainder of this majority opinion responds to the dissent. This portion and the dissenting opinion are omitted].

AFFIRMED.

NOTES AND QUESTIONS

1. *Accord National Association of Home Builders v. Babbitt*, 130 F.3d 1041 (D.C. Cir. 1997). In *Home Builders,* the Circuit Court for the District of Columbia reviewed the constitutionality of ESA applicability to the New Delhi Sands Fly, which was found to occupy a small regional area in California. Unlike the wolves in *Gibbs,* these flies did not wander from state to state or from habitat to habitat, nor did they attract tourists, nor was there any pro-spective market in them. Nonetheless, the court, in another 2-1 decision, found the regulation to satisfy both the first and third prongs of *Lopez.* The measure qualified as a regulation of the channels of interstate commerce, held the court, because the statute served:

to prevent the eradication of an endangered species by a hospital that is presumably being constructed using materials and people from outside the state and which will attract employees, patients, and students from both inside and outside the state. Thus, like regulations preventing racial discrimination or labor exploitation, regulations preventing the taking of endangered species prohibit interstate actors from using the channels of interstate commerce to "promote or spread[] evil, whether of a physical, moral or economic nature." (citation omitted).

Id. at 1048.

In addition, the court found that the regulated activity substantially affected interstate commerce, for two reasons. First, the loss of the species would deprive interstate commerce of "an important natural resource — biodiversity." *Id.* at 1054. Second, "[t]he taking of the Fly and other endangered animals can also be regulated by Congress as an activity that substantially affects interstate commerce because it is the product of destructive interstate competition. It is a principle deeply rooted in Commerce Clause jurisprudence that Congress is empowered to act to prevent destructive interstate competition." *Id.* at 1054.

Judge Wald's majority opinion prompted a vigorous dissent by Judge Sentelle, the first analytical paragraph of which follows:

> The proposition that the federal government can, under the Interstate Commerce Clause, regulate an activity which is neither interstate nor commerce, reminds me of the old chestnut: If we had some ham, we could fix some ham and eggs, if we had some eggs. With neither ham nor eggs, the chances of fixing a recognizable meal requiring both amount to nil. Similarly, the chances of validly regulating something which is neither commerce nor interstate under the heading of the interstate commerce power must likewise be an empty recitation. I recognize that for some decades of jurisprudential development, the Commerce Clause has been used as the justification for the regulation of a plethora of activities not apparently within its text. *See, e.g., Wickard v. Filburn,* 317 U.S. 111, 87 L. Ed. 122, 63 S. Ct. 82 (1942) (regulating the consumption of home-grown wheat). So wide-ranging has been the application of the Clause as to prompt one writer to "wonder why anyone would make the mistake of calling it the Commerce Clause instead of the 'hey-you-can-do-whatever-you-feel-like clause.'" Judge Alex Kozinski, *Introduction to Volume 19,* 19 HARV. J. L. PUB. POL. 1, 5 (1995). However, in 1995, the Supreme Court brought an end to the galactic growth of the Clause's application and reminded Congress that the words of that Clause, like the rest of the Constitution, have content, in *United States v. Lopez,* 514 U.S. 549, 131 L. Ed. 2d 626, 115 S. Ct. 1624 (1995). While I would have found the present application of the ESA to be outside the enumerated powers of Congress under the Commerce Clause even in the world before *Lopez,* after that controlling decision, I think there can be no doubt.

Id. at 1061.

Judge Sentelle went on to argue that speculation about the potential value of specific species for medicinal purposes or otherwise is merely that, speculation, and is insufficient as a justification for Commerce Clause regulation. Moreover, he asserted, the Commerce Clause authorizes regulation of commerce, not as here, the regulation of ecosystems.

2. Commerce Clause issues arise frequently with respect to regulation of wetlands. Loosely defined, wetlands are saturated areas that support water-dependent vegetation. Wetlands can be small or large (consider the Everglades). The dredging and filling of wetlands is regulated by Section 404 of the Clean Water Act. *See* Chapter 10, *infra*. In one noteworthy case, EPA brought an action against a developer for filling in a soybean field. *Hoffman Homes v. U.S. Environmental Protection Agency* ("*Hoffman Homes II*"), 999 F.2d 256 (7th Cir. 1993). The developer defended on Commerce Clause grounds because the soybean field, while falling under the definition of "wetland," was only one acre in size, was isolated, had no interstate commercial significance, and was not even used by migratory birds. In EPA's view, regulation was constitutionally warranted because there existed a theoretical possibility that migratory birds would use the wetland (the "migratory bird rule"). In the agency's view, so long as the wetland constituted a suitable habitat for migratory birds before it was filled in, even if migratory birds had not actually used it, Clean Water Act regulation of it was constitutional. The Seventh Circuit ruled against EPA on evidentiary grounds: as no migratory birds had, in fact, used the wetland, the court was unconvinced the wetland was a suitable habitat for migratory birds. *Accord Leslie Salt Co. v. United States*, 896 F.2d 354 (9th Cir. 1990); *Utah v. Marsh*, 740 F.2d 799 (10th Cir. 1984).

The 7th Circuit considered EPA's migratory bird rule in a later case presenting slightly different facts: in *Solid Waste Agency v. U.S. Army Corps of Engineers*, 191 F.3d 845 (7th Cir. 1999), *rev'd on other grounds*, 531 U.S. 159, 121 S. Ct. 675 (2001) (*see* Chapter 10, Part E., *infra*), the wetland had actually been used by a plethora of migratory birds. For that reason, the court found the Commerce Clause warranted the regulation. Relying on the "cumulative impact doctrine" set forth in *Wickard v. Filburn*, 317 U.S. 111, 87 L. Ed. 122, 63 S. Ct. 82 (1942), the Court argued:

> The relevant legal question for our case is whether the destruction of the natural habitat of migratory birds in the aggregate "substantially affects" interstate commerce. We observed in *Hoffman Homes, Inc. v. EPA*, 999 F.2d 256 (7th Cir. 1993), that "throughout North America, millions of people annually spend more than a billion dollars on hunting, trapping, and observing migratory birds. Yet the cumulative loss of wetlands has reduced the populations of many species and consequently the ability of people to hunt, trap, and observe those birds." *Id.* at 261. Statistics produced by the U.S. Census Bureau reveal that approximately 3.1 million Americans spent $1.3 billion to hunt migratory birds in 1996, and that about 11 percent of them traveled across state lines to do so. Fish & Wildlife Service, U.S. Dep't of the Interior & Bureau of the Census, U.S. Dep't of Commerce, 1996

National Survey of Fishing, Hunting, and Wildlife-Associated Recreation 25 (November 1997). Another 17.7 million people spent time observing birds in states other than their states of residence; 14.3 million of these took trips specifically for this purpose; and approximately 9.5 million traveled for the purpose of observing shorebirds, such as herons. *Id.* at 45. There is no need to dally on this point: we find (once again) that the destruction of migratory bird habitat and the attendant decrease in the populations of these birds "substantially affects" interstate commerce. The effect may not be observable as each isolated pond used by the birds for feeding, nesting, and breeding is filled, but the aggregate effect is clear, and that is all the Commerce Clause requires.

Id. at 849–50.

C.   CONSIDERATIONS OF FEDERALISM

In the preceding section, we discussed federal and state empowerment. Now we turn to some of the core limitations placed on the *exercise* of governmental powers in a federalist system.

[1]   THE TENTH AMENDMENT

The Tenth Amendment is a brief epistle of enormous significance. Stating merely that "[T]he powers not delegated to the United States by the Constitution, nor prohibited by it to the States, are reserved to the States respectively, or to the people[,]" the measure has provoked quarrels in the Supreme Court and an inconsistent jurisprudence from it. A core question is whether the Tenth Amendment has any content. Is it merely a sum-up provision that states the obvious, or does it by affirmative force specify the relationship of the federal government with the states?

NEW YORK v. UNITED STATES

505 U.S. 144, 112 S. Ct. 2408 (1992)

JUDGES: O'CONNOR, J., delivered the opinion of the Court, in which REHNQUIST, C.J., and SCALIA, KENNEDY, SOUTER, and THOMAS, JJ., joined, and in Parts III-A and III-B of which WHITE, BLACKMUN, and STEVENS, JJ., joined. WHITE, J., filed an opinion concurring in part and dissenting in part, in which BLACKMUN and STEVENS, JJ., joined. STEVENS, J., filed an opinion concurring in part and dissenting in part.

OPINION: JUSTICE O'CONNOR delivered the opinion of the Court.

This case implicates one of our Nation's newest problems of public policy and perhaps our oldest question of constitutional law. The public policy issue involves the disposal of radioactive waste: In this case, we address the constitutionality of three provisions of the Low-Level Radioactive Waste Policy Amendments Act of 1985, Pub. L. 99-240, 99 Stat. 1842, 42 U.S.C. § 2021b et seq. The constitutional question is as old as the Constitution: It consists of discerning the proper division of authority between the Federal Government and the States. We conclude that while Congress has substantial power under the Constitution to encourage the States to provide for the disposal of the radioactive waste generated within their borders, the Constitution does not confer upon Congress the ability simply to compel the States to do so. We therefore find that only two of the Act's three provisions at issue are consistent with the Constitution's allocation of power to the Federal Government.

I

We live in a world full of low level radioactive waste. Radioactive material is present in luminous watch dials, smoke alarms, measurement devices, medical fluids, research materials, and the protective gear and construction materials used by workers at nuclear power plants. Low level radioactive waste is generated by the Government, by hospitals, by research institutions, and by various industries. The waste must be isolated from humans for long periods of time, often for hundreds of years. Millions of cubic feet of low level radioactive waste must be disposed of each year.

Our Nation's first site for the land disposal of commercial low level radioactive waste opened in 1962 in Beatty, Nevada. Five more sites opened in the following decade: Maxey Flats, Kentucky (1963), West Valley, New York (1963), Hanford, Washington (1965), Sheffield, Illinois (1967), and Barnwell, South Carolina (1971). Between 1975 and 1978, the Illinois site closed because it was full, and water management problems caused the closure of the sites in Kentucky and New York. As a result, since 1979 only three disposal sites — those in Nevada, Washington, and South Carolina — have been in operation. Waste generated in the rest of the country must be shipped to one of these three sites for disposal. *See* Low-Level Radioactive Waste Regulation 39–40 (M. Burns ed. 1988).

In 1979, both the Washington and Nevada sites were forced to shut down temporarily, leaving South Carolina to shoulder the responsibility of storing low level radioactive waste produced in every part of the country. The Governor of South Carolina, understandably perturbed, ordered a 50% reduction in the quantity of waste accepted at the Barnwell site. The Governors of Washington and Nevada announced plans to shut their sites permanently. . . .

Faced with the possibility that the Nation would be left with no disposal sites for low level radioactive waste, Congress responded by enacting the Low-Level Radioactive Waste Policy Act, Pub. L. 96-573, 94 Stat. 3347. Relying largely on a report submitted by the National Governors' Association, . . . Congress declared a federal policy of holding each State "responsible for providing for the availability of capacity either within or outside the State for the disposal of low-level radioactive waste generated within its borders," and found that such waste could be disposed of "most safely and efficiently . . . on a regional basis." § 4(a)(1), 94 Stat. 3348. The 1980 Act authorized States to enter into regional compacts that, once ratified by Congress, would have the authority beginning in 1986 to restrict the use of their disposal facilities to waste generated within member States. § 4(a)(2)(B),

94 Stat. 3348. The 1980 Act included no penalties for States that failed to participate in this plan.

By 1985, only three approved regional compacts had operational disposal facilities; not surprisingly, these were the compacts formed around South Carolina, Nevada, and Washington, the three sited States. The following year, the 1980 Act would have given these three compacts the ability to exclude waste from nonmembers, and the remaining 31 States would have had no assured outlet for their low level radioactive waste. With this prospect looming, Congress once again took up the issue of waste disposal. The result was the legislation challenged here, the Low-Level Radioactive Waste Policy Amendments Act of 1985.

The 1985 Act was again based largely on a proposal submitted by the National Governors' Association. In broad outline, the Act embodies a compromise among the sited and unsited States. The sited States agreed to extend for seven years the period in which they would accept low level radioactive waste from other States. In exchange, the unsited States agreed to end their reliance on the sited States by 1992.

The mechanics of this compromise are intricate. The Act directs: "Each State shall be responsible for providing, either by itself or in cooperation with other States, for the disposal of . . . low-level radioactive waste generated within the State," 42 U.S.C. § 2021c(a)(1)(A), with the exception of certain waste generated by the Federal Government, §§ 2021c(a)(1)(B), 2021c(b). The Act authorizes States to "enter into such [interstate] compacts as may be necessary to provide for the establishment and operation of regional disposal facilities for low-level radioactive waste." § 2021d(a)(2). For an additional seven years beyond the period contemplated by the 1980 Act, from the beginning of 1986 through the end of 1992, the three existing disposal sites "shall make disposal capacity available for low-level radioactive waste generated by any source," with certain exceptions not relevant here. § 2021e(a)(2). But the three States in which the disposal sites are located are permitted to exact a graduated surcharge for waste arriving from outside the regional compact — in 1986-1987, $ 10 per cubic foot; in 1988-1989, $ 20 per cubic foot; and in 1990-1992, $ 40 per cubic foot. § 2021e(d)(1). After the seven-year transition period expires, approved regional compacts may exclude radioactive waste generated outside the region. § 2021d(c).

The Act provides three types of incentives to encourage the States to comply with their statutory obligation to provide for the disposal of waste generated within their borders.

1. Monetary incentives. One quarter of the surcharges collected by the sited States must be transferred to an escrow account held by the Secretary of Energy. § 2021e(d)(2)(A). The Secretary then makes payments from this account to each State that has complied with a series of deadlines. By July 1, 1986, each State was to have ratified legislation either joining a regional compact or indicating an intent to develop a disposal facility within the State. §§ 2021e(e)(1)(A), 2021e(d)(2)(B)(i). By January 1, 1988, each unsited compact was to have identified the State in which its facility would be located, and each compact or stand-alone State was to have developed a siting plan and taken other identified steps. §§ 2021e(e)(1)(B), 2021e(d)(2)(B)(ii). By January

1, 1990, each State or compact was to have filed a complete application for a license to operate a disposal facility, or the Governor of any State that had not filed an application was to have certified that the State would be capable of disposing of all waste generated in the State after 1992. §§ 2021e(e)(1)(C), 2021e(d)(2)(B)(iii). The rest of the account is to be paid out to those States or compacts able to dispose of all low level radioactive waste generated within their borders by January 1, 1993. § 2021e(d)(2)(B)(iv). Each State that has not met the 1993 deadline must either take title to the waste generated within its borders or forfeit to the waste generators the incentive payments it has received. § 2021e(d)(2)(C).

2. Access incentives. The second type of incentive involves the denial of access to disposal sites. States that fail to meet the July 1986 deadline may be charged twice the ordinary surcharge for the remainder of 1986 and may be denied access to disposal facilities thereafter. § 2021e(e)(2)(A). States that fail to meet the 1988 deadline may be charged double surcharges for the first half of 1988 and quadruple surcharges for the second half of 1988, and may be denied access thereafter. § 2021e(e)(2)(B). States that fail to meet the 1990 deadline may be denied access. § 2021e(e)(2)(C). Finally, States that have not filed complete applications by January 1, 1992, for a license to operate a disposal facility, or States belonging to compacts that have not filed such applications, may be charged triple surcharges. §§ 2021e(e)(1)(D), 2021e(e)(2)(D).

3. The take title provision. The third type of incentive is the most severe. The Act provides: "If a State (or, where applicable, a compact region) in which low-level radioactive waste is generated is unable to provide for the disposal of all such waste generated within such State or compact region by January 1, 1996, each State in which such waste is generated, upon the request of the generator or owner of the waste, shall take title to the waste, be obligated to take possession of the waste, and shall be liable for all damages directly or indirectly incurred by such generator or owner as a consequence of the failure of the State to take possession of the waste as soon after January 1, 1996, as the generator or owner notifies the State that the waste is available for shipment." § 2021e(d)(2)(C).

These three incentives are the focus of petitioners' constitutional challenge.

In the seven years since the Act took effect, Congress has approved nine regional compacts, encompassing 42 of the States. All six unsited compacts and four of the unaffiliated States have met the first three statutory milestones.

New York, a State whose residents generate a relatively large share of the Nation's low level radioactive waste, did not join a regional compact. Instead, the State complied with the Act's requirements by enacting legislation providing for the siting and financing of a disposal facility in New York. The State has identified five potential sites, three in Allegany County and two in Cortland County. Residents of the two counties oppose the State's choice of location.

Petitioners — the State of New York and the two counties — filed this suit against the United States in 1990. They sought a declaratory judgment that the Act is inconsistent with the Tenth and Eleventh Amendments to the Constitution, with the Due Process Clause of the Fifth Amendment, and with the Guarantee Clause of Article IV of the Constitution. The States of Washington, Nevada, and South Carolina intervened as defendants. The District Court dismissed the complaint. 757 F. Supp. 10 (NDNY 1990). The Court of Appeals affirmed. 942 F.2d 114 (CA2 1991). Petitioners have abandoned their Due Process and Eleventh Amendment claims on their way up the appellate ladder; as the case stands before us, petitioners claim only that the Act is inconsistent with the Tenth Amendment and the Guarantee Clause.

II

A

In 1788, in the course of explaining to the citizens of New York why the recently drafted Constitution provided for federal courts, Alexander Hamilton observed: "The erection of a new government, whatever care or wisdom may distinguish the work, cannot fail to originate questions of intricacy and nicety; and these may, in a particular manner, be expected to flow from the establishment of a constitution founded upon the total or partial incorporation of a number of distinct sovereignties." The Federalist No. 82, p. 491 (C. Rossiter ed. 1961). Hamilton's prediction has proved quite accurate. While no one disputes the proposition that "the Constitution created a Federal Government of limited powers," *Gregory v. Ashcroft*, 501 U.S. 452, 457 (1991); and while the Tenth Amendment makes explicit that "the powers not delegated to the United States by the Constitution, nor prohibited by it to the States, are reserved to the States respectively, or to the people"; the task of ascertaining the constitutional line between federal and state power has given rise to many of the Court's most difficult and celebrated cases. At least as far back as *Martin v. Hunter's Lessee*, 1 Wheat. 304, 324 (1816), the Court has resolved questions "of great importance and delicacy" in determining whether particular sovereign powers have been granted by the Constitution to the Federal Government or have been retained by the States.

These questions can be viewed in either of two ways. In some cases the Court has inquired whether an Act of Congress is authorized by one of the powers delegated to Congress in Article I of the Constitution. *See, e.g., Perez v. United States*, 402 U.S. 146 (1971); *McCulloch v. Maryland*, 4 Wheat. 316 (1819). In other cases the Court has sought to determine whether an Act of Congress invades the province of state sovereignty reserved by the Tenth Amendment. *See, e.g., Garcia v. San Antonio Metropolitan Transit Authority*, 469 U.S. 528 (1985); *Lane County v. Oregon*, 7 Wall. 71 (1869). In a case like this one, involving the division of authority between federal and state governments, the two inquiries are mirror images of each other. If a power is delegated to Congress in the Constitution, the Tenth Amendment expressly disclaims any reservation of that power to the States; if a power is an attribute of state sovereignty reserved by the Tenth Amendment, it is necessarily a power the Constitution has not conferred on Congress. *See United States v. Oregon*, 366 U.S. 643, 649 (1961); *Case v. Bowles*, 327 U.S. 92, 102 (1946); *Oklahoma ex rel. Phillips v. Guy F. Atkinson Co.*, 313 U.S. 508, 534 (1941).

It is in this sense that the Tenth Amendment "states but a truism that all is retained which has not been surrendered." *United States v. Darby*, 312 U.S. 100, 124 (1941). As Justice Story put it, "this amendment is a mere affirmation of what, upon any just reasoning, is a necessary rule of interpreting the constitution. Being an instrument of limited and enumerated powers, it follows irresistibly, that what is not conferred, is withheld, and belongs to the state authorities." 3 J. Story, Commentaries on the Constitution of the United States 752 (1833). This has been the Court's consistent understanding: "The States unquestionably do retain a significant measure of sovereign authority . . . to the extent that the Constitution has not divested them of their original powers and transferred those powers to the Federal Government." *Garcia v. San Antonio Metropolitan Transit Authority, supra*, at 549 (internal quotation marks omitted).

Congress exercises its conferred powers subject to the limitations contained in the Constitution. Thus, for example, under the Commerce Clause Congress may regulate publishers engaged in interstate commerce, but Congress is constrained in the exercise of that power by the First Amendment. The Tenth Amendment likewise restrains the power of Congress, but this limit is not derived from the text of the Tenth Amendment itself, which, as we have discussed, is essentially a tautology. Instead, the Tenth Amendment confirms that the power of the Federal Government is subject to limits that may, in a given instance, reserve power to the States. The Tenth Amendment thus directs us to determine, as in this case, whether an incident of state sovereignty is protected by a limitation on an Article I power.

The benefits of this federal structure have been extensively catalogued elsewhere, *see, e.g., Gregory v. Ashcroft*, 501 U.S. at 457-460; Merritt, *The Guarantee Clause and State Autonomy: Federalism for a Third Century*, 88 Colum. L. Rev. 1, 3-10 (1988); McConnell, *Federalism: Evaluating the Founders' Design*, 54 U. Chi. L. Rev. 1484, 1491–1511 (1987), but they need not concern us here. Our task would be the same even if one could prove that federalism secured no advantages to anyone. It consists not of devising our preferred system of government, but of understanding and applying the framework set forth in the Constitution. "The question is not what power the Federal Government ought to have but what powers in fact have been given by the people." *United States v. Butler*, 297 U.S. 1, 63 (1936).

This framework has been sufficiently flexible over the past two centuries to allow for enormous changes in the nature of government. The Federal Government undertakes activities today that would have been unimaginable to the Framers in two senses; first, because the Framers would not have conceived that any government would conduct such activities; and second, because the Framers would not have believed that the Federal Government, rather than the States, would assume such responsibilities. Yet the powers conferred upon the Federal Government by the Constitution were phrased in language broad enough to allow for the expansion of the Federal Government's role. Among the provisions of the Constitution that have been particularly important in this regard, three concern us here.

First, the Constitution allocates to Congress the power "to regulate Commerce . . . among the several States." Art. I, § 8, cl. 3. Interstate commerce

was an established feature of life in the late 18th century. *See, e.g.,* The
Federalist No. 42, p. 267 (C. Rossiter ed. 1961) ("The defect of power in the
existing Confederacy to regulate the commerce between its several members
[has] been clearly pointed out by experience"). The volume of interstate
commerce and the range of commonly accepted objects of government regulation have, however, expanded considerably in the last 200 years, and the
regulatory authority of Congress has expanded along with them. As interstate
commerce has become ubiquitous, activities once considered purely local have
come to have effects on the national economy, and have accordingly come
within the scope of Congress' commerce power. *See, e.g., Katzenbach v.
McClung,* 379 U.S. 294 (1964); *Wickard v. Filburn,* 317 U.S. 111 (1942).

Second, the Constitution authorizes Congress "to pay the Debts and provide
for the . . . general Welfare of the United States." Art. I, § 8, cl. 1. As
conventional notions of the proper objects of government spending have changed
over the years, so has the ability of Congress to "fix the terms on which it
shall disburse federal money to the States." *Pennhurst State School and
Hospital v. Halderman,* 451 U.S. 1, 17 (1981). *Compare, e.g., United States
v. Butler, supra,* at 72–75 (spending power does not authorize Congress to
subsidize farmers), *with* South *Dakota v. Dole,* 483 U.S. 203 (1987) (spending
power permits Congress to condition highway funds on States' adoption of
minimum drinking age). While the spending power is "subject to several
general restrictions articulated in our cases," *id.,* at 207, these restrictions
have not been so severe as to prevent the regulatory authority of Congress
from generally keeping up with the growth of the federal budget.

The Court's broad construction of Congress' power under the Commerce and
Spending Clauses has of course been guided, as it has with respect to
Congress' power generally, by the Constitution's Necessary and Proper Clause,
which authorizes Congress "to make all Laws which shall be necessary and
proper for carrying into Execution the foregoing Powers." U.S. Const., Art.
I., § 8, cl. 18. *See, e.g., Legal Tender Case (Juilliard v. Greenman),* 110 U.S.
421, 449–450 (1884); *McCulloch v. Maryland,* 4 Wheat., at 411–421.

Finally, the Constitution provides that "the Laws of the United States . . .
shall be the supreme Law of the Land . . . any Thing in the Constitution or
Laws of any State to the Contrary notwithstanding." U.S. Const., Art. VI, cl.
2. As the Federal Government's willingness to exercise power within the confines of the Constitution has grown, the authority of the States has corre-
spondingly diminished to the extent that federal and state policies have
conflicted. *See, e.g., Shaw v. Delta Air Lines, Inc.,* 463 U.S. 85 (1983). We have
observed that the Supremacy Clause gives the Federal Government "a decided
advantage in the delicate balance" the Constitution strikes between State and
Federal power. *Gregory v. Ashcroft,* 501 U.S. at 460.

The actual scope of the Federal Government's authority with respect to the
States has changed over the years, therefore, but the constitutional structure
underlying and limiting that authority has not. In the end, just as a cup may
be half empty or half full, it makes no difference whether one views the
question at issue in this case as one of ascertaining the limits of the power
delegated to the Federal Government under the affirmative provisions of the
Constitution or one of discerning the core of sovereignty retained by the States

under the Tenth Amendment. Either way, we must determine whether any of the three challenged provisions of the Low-Level Radioactive Waste Policy Amendments Act of 1985 oversteps the boundary between federal and state authority.

B

Petitioners do not contend that Congress lacks the power to regulate the disposal of low level radioactive waste. Space in radioactive waste disposal sites is frequently sold by residents of one State to residents of another. Regulation of the resulting interstate market in waste disposal is therefore well within Congress' authority under the Commerce Clause. *Cf. Philadelphia v. New Jersey*, 437 U.S. 617, 621–623 (1978); *Fort Gratiot Sanitary Landfill, Inc. v. Michigan Dept. of Natural Resources*, 504 U.S. 353, 359 (1992). Petitioners likewise do not dispute that under the Supremacy Clause Congress could, if it wished, pre-empt state radioactive waste regulation. Petitioners contend only that the Tenth Amendment limits the power of Congress to regulate in the way it has chosen. Rather than addressing the problem of waste disposal by directly regulating the generators and disposers of waste, petitioners argue, Congress has impermissibly directed the States to regulate in this field.

Most of our recent cases interpreting the Tenth Amendment have concerned the authority of Congress to subject state governments to generally applicable laws. The Court's jurisprudence in this area has traveled an unsteady path. *See Maryland v. Wirtz*, 392 U.S. 183 (1968) (state schools and hospitals are subject to Fair Labor Standards Act); *National League of Cities v. Usery*, 426 U.S. 833 (1976) (overruling *Wirtz*) (state employers are not subject to Fair Labor Standards Act); *Garcia v. San Antonio Metropolitan Transit Authority*, 469 U.S. 528 (1985) (overruling *National League of Cities*) (state employers are once again subject to Fair Labor Standards Act). *See also New York v. United States*, 326 U.S. 572 (1946); *Fry v. United States*, 421 U.S. 542 (1975); *Transportation Union v. Long Island R. Co.*, 455 U.S. 678 (1982); *EEOC v. Wyoming*, 460 U.S. 226 (1983); *South Carolina v. Baker*, 485 U.S. 505 (1988); *Gregory v. Ashcroft, supra*. This case presents no occasion to apply or revisit the holdings of any of these cases, as this is not a case in which Congress has subjected a State to the same legislation applicable to private parties. *Cf. FERC v. Mississippi*, 456 U.S. 742, 758–759 (1982).

This case instead concerns the circumstances under which Congress may use the States as implements of regulation; that is, whether Congress may direct or otherwise motivate the States to regulate in a particular field or a particular way. Our cases have established a few principles that guide our resolution of the issue.

1

As an initial matter, Congress may not simply "commandeer the legislative processes of the States by directly compelling them to enact and enforce a federal regulatory program." *Hodel v. Virginia Surface Mining & Reclamation Assn., Inc.*, 452 U.S. 264, 288 (1981). . . .

. . . While Congress has substantial powers to govern the Nation directly, including in areas of intimate concern to the States, the Constitution has never been understood to confer upon Congress the ability to require the States to govern according to Congress' instructions. *See Coyle v. Oklahoma*, 221 U.S. 559, 565 (1911). The Court has been explicit about this distinction. "Both the States and the United States existed before the Constitution. The people, through that instrument, established a more perfect union by substituting a national government, acting, with ample power, *directly upon the citizens*, instead of the Confederate government, which acted with powers, greatly restricted, only upon the States." *Lane County v. Oregon*, 7 Wall., at 76 (emphasis added). The Court has made the same point with more rhetorical flourish, although perhaps with less precision, on a number of occasions. In Chief Justice Chase's much-quoted words, "the preservation of the States, and the maintenance of their governments, are as much within the design and care of the Constitution as the preservation of the Union and the maintenance of the National government. The Constitution, in all its provisions, looks to an indestructible Union, composed of indestructible States." *Texas v. White*, 7 Wall. 700, 725 (1869). *See also Metcalf & Eddy v. Mitchell*, 269 U.S. 514, 523 (1926) ("neither government may destroy the other nor curtail in any substantial manner the exercise of its powers"); *Tafflin v. Levitt*, 493 U.S. 455, 458 (1990) ("under our federal system, the States possess sovereignty concurrent with that of the Federal Government"); *Gregory v. Ashcroft*, 501 U.S. at 461 ("the States retain substantial sovereign powers under our constitutional scheme, powers with which Congress does not readily interfere").

Indeed, the question whether the Constitution should permit Congress to employ state governments as regulatory agencies was a topic of lively debate among the Framers. [At this juncture, the Court undertakes a discussion of constitutional history]. . . .

In the end, the Convention opted for a Constitution in which Congress would exercise its legislative authority directly over individuals rather than over States. . . .

In providing for a stronger central government, therefore, the Framers explicitly chose a Constitution that confers upon Congress the power to regulate individuals, not States. As we have seen, the Court has consistently respected this choice. We have always understood that even where Congress has the authority under the Constitution to pass laws requiring or prohibiting certain acts, it lacks the power directly to compel the States to require or prohibit those acts. *E.g.*, *FERC v. Mississippi*, 456 U.S., at 762–766; *Hodel v. Virginia Surface Mining & Reclamation Assn.*, Inc., 452 U.S., at 288–289; *Lane County v. Oregon*, 7 Wall., at 76. The allocation of power contained in the Commerce Clause, for example, authorizes Congress to regulate interstate commerce directly; it does not authorize Congress to regulate state governments' regulation of interstate commerce.

2

This is not to say that Congress lacks the ability to encourage a State to regulate in a particular way, or that Congress may not hold out incentives to the States as a method of influencing a State's policy choices. Our cases have identified a variety of methods, short of outright coercion, by which Congress may urge a State to adopt a legislative program consistent with federal interests. Two of these methods are of particular relevance here.

First, under Congress' spending power, "Congress may attach conditions on the receipt of federal funds." *South Dakota v. Dole,* 483 U.S. at 206. Such conditions must (among other requirements) bear some relationship to the purpose of the federal spending, *id.,* at 207–208, and n. 3; otherwise, of course, the spending power could render academic the Constitution's other grants and limits of federal authority. Where the recipient of federal funds is a State, as is not unusual today, the conditions attached to the funds by Congress may influence a State's legislative choices. *See Kaden, Politics, Money, and State Sovereignty: The Judicial Role,* 79 Colum. L. Rev. 847, 874–881 (1979). *Dole* was one such case: The Court found no constitutional flaw in a federal statute directing the Secretary of Transportation to withhold federal highway funds from States failing to adopt Congress' choice of a minimum drinking age. Similar examples abound. *See, e.g., Fullilove v. Klutznick,* 448 U.S. 448, 478–480 (1980); *Massachusetts v. United States,* 435 U.S. 444, 461–462 (1978); *Lau v. Nichols,* 414 U.S. 563, 568–569 (1974); *Oklahoma v. Civil Service Comm'n,* 330 U.S. 127, 142–144 (1947).

Second, where Congress has the authority to regulate private activity under the Commerce Clause, we have recognized Congress' power to offer States the choice of regulating that activity according to federal standards or having state law pre-empted by federal regulation. *Hodel v. Virginia Surface Mining & Reclamation Assn., Inc.,* 456 U.S. at 288. *See also FERC v. Mississippi,* 452 U.S. at 764–765. This arrangement, which has been termed "a program of cooperative federalism," *Hodel,* 456 U.S. at 289, is replicated in numerous federal statutory schemes. These include the Clean Water Act, 86 Stat. 816, as amended, 33 U.S.C. § 1251 et seq., *see Arkansas v. Oklahoma,* 503 U.S. 91, 101 (1992) (Clean Water Act "anticipates a partnership between the States and the Federal Government, animated by a shared objective"); the Occupational Safety and Health Act of 1970, 84 Stat. 1590, 29 U.S.C. § 651 et seq., see *Gade v. National Solid Wastes Management Assn.,* 505 U.S. at 97 (1992); the Resource Conservation and Recovery Act of 1976, 90 Stat. 2796, as amended, 42 U.S.C. § 6901 et seq., *see United States Dept. of Energy v. Ohio,* 503 U.S. 607, 611-612 (1992); and the Alaska National Interest Lands Conservation Act, 94 Stat. 2374, 16 U.S.C. § 3101 et seq., *see Kenaitze Indian Tribe v. Alaska,* 860 F. 2d 312, 314 (CA9 1988), *cert. denied,* 491 U.S. 905 (1989).

By either of these two methods, as by any other permissible method of encouraging a State to conform to federal policy choices, the residents of the State retain the ultimate decision as to whether or not the State will comply. If a State's citizens view federal policy as sufficiently contrary to local interests, they may elect to decline a federal grant. If state residents would prefer their government to devote its attention and resources to problems other than those deemed important by Congress, they may choose to have the Federal Government rather than the State bear the expense of a federally mandated regulatory program, and they may continue to supplement that program to the extent state law is not preempted. Where Congress encourages state regulation rather than compelling it, state governments remain responsive to the local electorate's preferences; state officials remain accountable to the people.

By contrast, where the Federal Government compels States to regulate, the accountability of both state and federal officials is diminished. If the citizens of New York, for example, do not consider that making provision for the disposal of radioactive waste is in their best interest, they may elect state officials who share their view. That view can always be preempted under the Supremacy Clause if is contrary to the national view, but in such a case it is the Federal Government that makes the decision in full view of the public, and it will be federal officials that suffer the consequences if the decision turns out to be detrimental or unpopular. But where the Federal Government directs the States to regulate, it may be state officials who will bear the brunt of public disapproval, while the federal officials who devised the regulatory program may remain insulated from the electoral ramifications of their decision. Accountability is thus diminished when, due to federal coercion, elected state officials cannot regulate in accordance with the views of the local electorate in matters not pre-empted by federal regulation. *See* Merritt, 88 Colum. L. Rev., at 61–62; La Pierre, *Political Accountability in the National Political Process — The Alternative to Judicial Review of Federalism Issues,* 80 Nw. U. L. Rev. 577, 639–665 (1985).

With these principles in mind, we turn to the three challenged provisions of the Low-Level Radioactive Waste Policy Amendments Act of 1985.

III

The parties in this case advance two quite different views of the Act. As petitioners see it, the Act imposes a requirement directly upon the States that they regulate in the field of radioactive waste disposal in order to meet Congress' mandate that "each State shall be responsible for providing . . . for the disposal of . . . low-level radioactive waste." 42 U.S.C. § 2021c(a)(1)(A). Petitioners understand this provision as a direct command from Congress, enforceable independent of the three sets of incentives provided by the Act. Respondents, on the other hand, read this provision together with the incentives, and see the Act as affording the States three sets of choices. According to respondents, the Act permits a State to choose first between regulating pursuant to federal standards and losing the right to a share of the Secretary of Energy's escrow account; to choose second between regulating pursuant to federal standards and progressively losing access to disposal sites in other States; and to choose third between regulating pursuant to federal standards and taking title to the waste generated within the State. Respondents thus interpret § 2021c(a)(1)(A), despite the statute's use of the word "shall," to provide no more than an option which a State may elect or eschew.

The Act could plausibly be understood either as a mandate to regulate or as a series of incentives. Under petitioners' view, however, § 2021c(a)(1)(A) of the Act would clearly "commandeer the legislative processes of the States by directly compelling them to enact and enforce a federal regulatory program." *Hodel v. Virginia Surface Mining & Reclamation Assn., Inc.,* 452 U.S. at 288. We must reject this interpretation of the provision for two reasons.

First, such an outcome would, to say the least, "upset the usual constitutional balance of federal and state powers." *Gregory v. Ashcroft*, 501 U.S. at 460. "It is incumbent upon the federal courts to be certain of Congress' intent before finding that federal law overrides this balance," *ibid.* (internal quotation marks omitted), but the Act's amenability to an equally plausible alternative construction prevents us from possessing such certainty. Second, "where an otherwise acceptable construction of a statute would raise serious constitutional problems, the Court will construe the statute to avoid such problems unless such construction is plainly contrary to the intent of Congress." *Edward J. DeBartolo Corp. v. Florida Gulf Coast Building & Construction Trades Council*, 485 U.S. 568, 575 (1988). This rule of statutory construction pushes us away from petitioners' understanding of § 2021c(a)(1)(A) of the Act, under which it compels the States to regulate according to Congress' instructions.

We therefore decline petitioners' invitation to construe § 2021c(a)(1)(A), alone and in isolation, as a command to the States independent of the remainder of the Act. Construed as a whole, the Act comprises three sets of "incentives" for the States to provide for the disposal of low level radioactive waste generated within their borders. We consider each in turn.

[In the next several sections of the opinion, the Court finds the monetary incentives and the access incentives to be constitutional under the Tenth Amendment. It then discusses the "take title" provision]:

The take title provision is of a different character. This third so-called "incentive" offers States, as an alternative to regulating pursuant to Congress' direction, the option of taking title to and possession of the low level radioactive waste generated within their borders and becoming liable for all damages waste generators suffer as a result of the States' failure to do so promptly. In this provision, Congress has crossed the line distinguishing encouragement from coercion. . . .

The take title provision offers state governments a "choice" of either accepting ownership of waste or regulating according to the instructions of Congress. Respondents do not claim that the Constitution would authorize Congress to impose either option as a freestanding requirement. On one hand, the Constitution would not permit Congress simply to transfer radioactive waste from generators to state governments. Such a forced transfer, standing alone, would in principle be no different than a congressionally compelled subsidy from state governments to radioactive waste producers. The same is true of the provision requiring the States to become liable for the generators' damages. Standing alone, this provision would be indistinguishable from an Act of Congress directing the States to assume the liabilities of certain state residents. Either type of federal action would "commandeer" state governments into the service of federal regulatory purposes, and would for this reason be inconsistent with the Constitution's division of authority between federal and state governments. On the other hand, the second alternative held out to state governments — regulating pursuant to Congress' direction — would, standing alone, present a simple command to state governments to implement legislation enacted by Congress. As we have seen, the Constitution does not empower Congress to subject state governments to this type of instruction.

Because an instruction to state governments to take title to waste, standing alone, would be beyond the authority of Congress, and because a direct order to regulate, standing alone, would also be beyond the authority of Congress, it follows that Congress lacks the power to offer the States a choice between the two. Unlike the first two sets of incentives, the take title incentive does not represent the conditional exercise of any congressional power enumerated in the Constitution. In this provision, Congress has not held out the threat of exercising its spending power or its commerce power; it has instead held out the threat, should the States not regulate according to one federal instruction, of simply forcing the States to submit to another federal instruction. A choice between two unconstitutionally coercive regulatory techniques is no choice at all. Either way, "the Act commandeers the legislative processes of the States by directly compelling them to enact and enforce a federal regulatory program," *Hodel v. Virginia Surface Mining & Reclamation Assn., Inc., supra,* at 288, an outcome that has never been understood to lie within the authority conferred upon Congress by the Constitution. . . .

VII

Some truths are so basic that, like the air around us, they are easily overlooked. Much of the Constitution is concerned with setting forth the form of our government, and the courts have traditionally invalidated measures deviating from that form. The result may appear "formalistic" in a given case to partisans of the measure at issue, because such measures are typically the product of the era's perceived necessity. But the Constitution protects us from our own best intentions: It divides power among sovereigns and among branches of government precisely so that we may resist the temptation to concentrate power in one location as an expedient solution to the crisis of the day. The shortage of disposal sites for radioactive waste is a pressing national problem, but a judiciary that licensed extra-constitutional government with each issue of comparable gravity would, in the long run, be far worse.

States are not mere political subdivisions of the United States. State governments are neither regional offices nor administrative agencies of the Federal Government. The positions occupied by state officials appear nowhere on the Federal Government's most detailed organizational chart. The Constitution instead "leaves to the several States a residuary and inviolable sovereignty," The Federalist No. 39, p. 245 (C. Rossiter ed. 1961), reserved explicitly to the States by the Tenth Amendment.

Whatever the outer limits of that sovereignty may be, one thing is clear: The Federal Government may not compel the States to enact or administer a federal regulatory program. The Constitution permits both the Federal Government and the States to enact legislation regarding the disposal of low level radioactive waste. The Constitution enables the Federal Government to pre-empt state regulation contrary to federal interests, and it permits the Federal Government to hold out incentives to the States as a means of encouraging them to adopt suggested regulatory schemes. It does not, however, authorize Congress simply to direct the States to provide for the disposal of the radioactive waste generated within their borders. While there may be many constitutional methods of achieving regional self-sufficiency in radioactive waste disposal, the method Congress has chosen is not one of them. The judgment of the Court of Appeals is accordingly

Affirmed in part and reversed in part.

[Concurring and Dissenting opinions omitted.]

NOTES

1. The *New York* case provides the constitutional basis for "cooperative federalism," a central feature of federal pollution control statutes. Those statutes provide for state enforcement of federal standards, but they take care not to coerce states. If a state fails to abide by a federal statutory directive, there is no penalty, save the fact that the federal government will implement those standards on its own and thereafter maintain a more robust presence in the state. In many instances, states would rather take the lead in environmental enforcement than endure the federal presence. *See* Chapters 9–11, *infra*.

2. The principles in *New York* have been affirmed by the United States Supreme Court in non-environmental contexts. *See, e.g., Printz v. United States*, 521 U.S. 898, 117 S. Ct. 2365 (1997) (the Brady Act case). In *Printz*, the Court reviewed a federal statute which required states, *inter alia,* to participate in the administration of the federal handgun control program. Under the terms of the Brady Act, state chief law enforcement officers were required to accept forms sent to them by gun dealers and exercise "reasonable efforts" within five days to determine whether the sales described in the submitted forms were lawful. Justice Scalia, in a 5-4 opinion, found the Brady Act to violate the Tenth Amendment. In his words, "[I]t is an essential attribute of the States' retained sovereignty that they remain independant and autonomous within their proper sphere of authority." *Id*. at 928. Moreover, Justice Scalia considered it insignificant that the Brady Act directed its mandates at individuals (law enforcement officers) rather than the state itself. "While the Brady Act is directed to 'individuals,' it is directed to them in their official capacities as state officers; it controls their actions, not as private citizens, but as the agents of the State." *Id*. at 930.

Justice Stevens, with Justices Souter, Ginsburg, and Breyer, dissented on the ground that "[w]hen Congress exercises the powers delegated to it by the Constitution, it may impose affirmative obligations on executive and judicial officers of state and local governments as well as ordinary citizens." *Id*. at 939.

3. On October 26, 1987, President Ronald Reagan issued an Executive Order, entitled "Federalism," to formally establish the position of the executive branch on matters of federal and state power. Exec. Order No. 12612, 52 Fed. Reg. 41685 (Oct. 30, 1987). The Order provided, in relevant part, that "[i]n the absence of clear constitutional or statutory authority, the presumption of sovereignty should rest with the individual States. Uncertainties should be resolved against regulation at the national level." *Id*. at § 2(i). The Order further directed that "[f]ederal action limiting the policymaking discretion of the States should be taken only where constitutional authority for the action is clear and certain and the national activity is necessitated by the presence of a problem of national scope." *Id*. at § 3(b).

4. A major generator of low level radioactive waste are utilities, which produce waste material ranging from spent resins to radiation-exposed clothing. Other generators include medical facilities, agricultural and scientific research institutions, and providers of consumer products and services. Low level "radwastes" take on a variety of physical and chemical forms and vary in degree of contamination. Supposedly, the best method of disposing of such wastes is in above-ground concrete vaults designed to resist erosion, cracking, and even tornadoes and earthquakes. The vaults can be large: one is 30 feet tall, 650 feet long, 25 feet wide, and contains 12 cells. When filled, such vaults can be sealed with additional concrete and capped. The more usual disposal method is in trenches.

The U.S. Environmental Protection Agency has estimated that, between the years 1990 and 2010, commercial facilities will generate about 326,000 cubic meters of low level wastes, and the Department of Energy will generate an additional 1.8 million cubic meters. This total amount represents about one percent of the national generation of hazardous wastes.

5. With respect to federalism, consider the issue of unfunded federal mandates. The federal government over the last several decades has taken to shifting governmental responsibilities to states, but often without paying the costs. To put it mildly, the states have not been pleased by this trend. Their vociferous objections finally resulted in enactment of The Unfunded Mandates Reform Act of 1995, 2 U.S.C. § 1501 et seq. (and elsewhere in the federal code). The Act is an attempt to reduce financial burdens on states. Defining a mandate as "any provision in statute or federal court ruling that imposes an enforceable duty upon state, local, or tribal governments including a condition of Federal assistance or a duty arising from participation in a voluntary Federal program. . . ." 2 U.S.C. § 1555, the statute provides that "it shall not be in order in the Senate or the House of Representatives to consider . . . any bill, joint resolution, amendment, motion, or conference report" that would impose more than $50 million in costs of compliance on state and local governments, unless the federal government provides full funding. 2 U.S.C. § 658d(a). Any objection made on this basis within either legislative chamber can be waived, however, by simple majority. The legislation also establishes a regulatory process for federal agencies, to assure that their actions are only taken with due regard to the costs those actions might impose upon states. *See* §§ 1532–35.

Has the UMRA worked? According to a report from the National Conference of State Legislatures, the cost to state governments of implementing federally mandated programs will reach more than $29 billion in fiscal year 2004.

[2] PREEMPTION

"This Constitution, and the Laws of the United States which shall be made in Pursuance thereof; and all Treaties made, or which shall be made, under the authority of the United States, shall be the Supreme Law of the Land; and the Judges in every State shall be bound thereby, any Thing in the Constitution or Laws of any State to the Contrary notwithstanding." U.S. Constitution, art. VI, cl. 2.

FEIKEMA v. TEXACO, INC.

16 F.3d 1408 (4th Cir. 1994)

JUDGES: Before MURNAGHAN and NIEMEYER, Circuit Judges, and YOUNG, Senior United States District Judge for the District of Maryland, sitting by designation.

NIEMEYER, Circuit Judge:

The question of first impression presented on this appeal is whether the Resource Conservation and Recovery Act, 42 U.S.C. § 6901 et seq., or an administrative order entered pursuant to it, preempts state common law causes of action for nuisance and trespass. Several homeowners in Fairfax, Virginia, filed a complaint in March 1993 against Texaco, Inc. and Star Enterprises (collectively "Texaco"), alleging that a plume of oil which leaked from a nearby petroleum distribution terminal owned by Texaco damaged and continues to damage their properties. The complaint requested injunctive relief and demanded damages in an unspecified amount. The district court dismissed the complaint on preemption grounds, and the homeowners appealed. Concluding that the claims for injunctive relief are preempted but that claims for state law damages are not, we vacate the judgment and remand the case for further proceedings consistent with this opinion.

I

Texaco owns and operates a petroleum distribution terminal located at 3800 Pickett Road in Fairfax, Virginia. The terminal, also known as the Tank Farm, consists of office and warehouse facilities, a truck loading rack, nine above-ground storage tanks with a total storage capacity of over 17 million gallons, and eleven underground storage tanks with a total capacity of 40,000 gallons. The Tank Farm is located above a "recharge" area of an aquifer, which is a major underground water source for nearby creeks and streams. It is also near residential properties owned by the homeowners in this case and by others.

Beginning sometime in 1988, petroleum products, consisting of diesel fuel, aviation fuel and gasoline, leaked into the soil and groundwater at the Tank Farm and the surrounding land, and an oil plume began moving toward the properties of the homeowners. Some constituent parts of these petroleum products are toxic and, under certain conditions, constitute a health hazard. Sometime in September 1990, visible petroleum products appeared in Crook Branch Creek which flows near and along the homeowners' properties. The Virginia State Water Control Board ("the State Board") investigated the leak. Pursuant to the direction of the State Board, Texaco conducted tests on the tanks and the lines, installed on-site and off-site monitoring wells, and installed an oil recovery trench along a portion of the Tank Farm. Although almost 7,000 gallons of oil were recovered by these means, the State Board concluded that leaking was continuing and that the appropriate control or elimination of such release had not been implemented. In May 1991, the State Board requested that the United States Environmental Protection Agency (the "EPA") assume responsibility for investigating the oil leak and recovering the released products. In response, the EPA created an interagency task force to take further steps.

Proceeding under the authority granted by section 311(c) of the Clean Water Act, 33 U.S.C. § 1321(c), section 1431 of the Safe Drinking Water Act, 42 U.S.C. § 300i, and section 7003 of the Resource Conservation and Recovery Act ("RCRA"), 42 U.S.C. § 6973, the EPA conducted an investigation, held a hearing, and negotiated an administrative consent order (the "Consent Order") with Texaco, which was entered on September 23, 1991. The EPA found, as a basis for the Consent Order, that if proper measures were not implemented, petroleum would continue to move under the Tank Farm with the natural ground water flow and would migrate to and enter sanitary and storm sewer pipes, eventually entering the basements of residences in the immediate vicinity of the Tank Farm. The EPA also determined that the plume might present an imminent and substantial endangerment to health or the environment within the meaning of section 7003(a) of the RCRA, 42 U.S.C. § 6973(a).

The Consent Order required Texaco to place booms on Crook Branch Creek to contain the oily sheen on the surface, and to use sorbent to collect and clean up the oil. The EPA also ordered Texaco to excavate and remove soils contaminated with oil, to operate an emergency measures pumping system, and to monitor weekly wells and storm sewers for the presence of oil. In addition, the EPA put forth an "Emergency Measures Plan," requiring Texaco, inter alia, to develop an appropriate corrective actions plan to eliminate the leaks; to submit this plan to EPA for review and approval; and to implement EPA-approved corrective actions under an EPA-approved schedule. While the order addressed measures to eliminate the causes of the leaking and to neutralize the adverse effects of the oil plume, it recognized that the response action might not address all contamination and that additional long-term measures might be required. The order was scheduled to terminate when its directives were met to the EPA's satisfaction. Since the entry of the order, Texaco has undertaken the corrective steps as required, and there is no evidence in the record that it is not complying with the terms of the order, which still remains in effect.

In March 1993, the homeowners filed a complaint against Texaco under the district court's diversity jurisdiction, alleging claims for nuisance and trespass under Virginia common law. In their complaint, the homeowners alleged that "even under a Consent Order with and under the direction of the Environmental Protection Agency," Texaco has failed to remedy the leaking, and that they "have had, and continue to be threatened with actual petroleum pollution from the Tank Farm in the soils of the creeks on or near their property." The complaint further alleged that the pollution confronts them with a nuisance that "threatens the destruction of their property and danger to their health," and that "direct and actual pollution of the creek beds and the flow of globules of free phase hydrocarbons under their property constitute a trespass" upon their properties. The homeowners requested permanent injunctive relief for greater remedial measures than those included in the Consent Order, and they demanded "such damages, interest and costs to which the Plaintiffs may be justly entitled."

On Texaco's motion to dismiss the complaint under Federal Rule of Civil Procedure 12(b)(6), the district court dismissed the action on preemption grounds. The court stated:

> I think the injunctive relief of the type the plaintiffs seek here would conflict with and frustrate probably the purpose of Congress in its EPA remediation efforts under the RCRA. Even though the plaintiffs do not purport to bring their action under that, I think that Act and the action taken here with the remediation effort and order preempts this field, and I think that any injunction I would issue would conflict with that.

This appeal followed. * * *

III

We now turn to the principal question presented on appeal, whether the RCRA, or the administrative order entered pursuant to it, preempts state common law causes of action. A review of the applicable preemption principles is useful.

The Supremacy Clause of the United States Constitution mandates that "the Laws of the United States . . . shall be the supreme Law of the Land; and the Judges in every State shall be bound thereby, any Thing in the Constitution or Laws of any State to the Contrary notwithstanding." U.S. Const. art. VI, § 2. Thus, federal legislation, if enacted pursuant to Congress' lawful authority, can nullify conflicting state or local actions. *See M'Culloch v. Maryland,* 17 U.S. (4 Wheat.) 316, 427, 4 L. Ed. 579 (1819); *Worm v. American Cyanamid Co.,* 970 F.2d 1301, 1304–05 (4th Cir. 1992).

There are two ways for preemption to occur. First, Congress may expressly provide that federal law supplants state authority in a particular field, or its intent to preempt may be implicit in regulating so pervasively in the field as not to leave any room within which a state may act. *See Rice v. Santa Fe Elevator Corp.,* 331 U.S. 218, 230, 91 L. Ed. 1447, 67 S. Ct. 1146 (1947); *Worm,* 970 F.2d at 1304. And second, even absent an express or implied congressional intent to preempt state authority in a field, state law is preempted to the extent that it actually conflicts with federal law. *See Pacific Gas & Elec. Co. v. State Energy Resources Conservation & Dev. Com.,* 461 U.S. 190, 204, 75 L. Ed. 2d 752, 103 S. Ct. 1713 (1983).

As the Supreme Court recently instructed, "consideration of issues arising under the Supremacy Clause 'starts with the assumption that the historic police powers of the States are not to be superseded by . . . Federal Act unless that [is] the clear and manifest purpose of Congress.'" *Cipollone v. Liggett Group, Inc.,* 120 L. Ed. 2d 407, 112 S. Ct. 2608, 2617 (1992) (quoting *Rice v. Santa Fe Elevator Corp.,* 331 U.S. 218, 230, 91 L. Ed. 1447, 67 S. Ct. 1146 (1947)). Moreover, in deciphering congressional intent, we are guided by principles of federalism. Where "the regulated conduct touched interests so deeply rooted in local feeling and responsibility, . . . in the absence of compelling congressional direction, [the court] could not infer that Congress had deprived the States of the power to act." *San Diego Bldg. Trades Council v. Garmon,* 359 U.S. 236, 244, 3 L. Ed. 2d 775, 79 S. Ct. 773 (1959).

Particularly with respect to the potential preemption of common law actions, the Supreme Court has instructed,

> A common-law right, even absent a saving clause, is not to be abrogated "unless it be found that the preexisting right is so repugnant to the statute that the survival of such right would in effect deprive the subsequent statute of its efficacy; in other words, render its provisions nugatory."

Nader v. Allegheny Airlines, Inc., 426 U.S. 290, 298, 48 L. Ed. 2d 643, 96 S. Ct. 1978 (1976) (quoting *Texas & Pacific R. Co. v. Abilene Cotton Oil Co.,* 204 U.S. 426, 437, 51 L. Ed. 553, 27 S. Ct. 350 (1907)). The ultimate touchstone of preemption analysis is the purpose of Congress. *See Malone v. White Motor Corp.,* 435 U.S. 497, 504, 55 L. Ed. 2d 443, 98 S. Ct. 1185 (1978). When Congress' intent regarding preemption is unclear, state law must nevertheless yield when it conflicts with federal law. In making the determination of whether state law conflicts with federal law, the test to apply is whether "it is impossible to comply with both state and federal law" or whether "the state law stands as an obstacle to the accomplishment of the full purposes and objectives" of federal law. *Silkwood v. Kerr-McGee Corp.,* 464 U.S. 238, 248, 78 L. Ed. 2d 443, 104 S. Ct. 615 (1984); *see also Worm,* 970 F.2d at 1305.

With such principles at hand, we now turn to the facts to see whether the RCRA, or the administrative consent order entered in this case under section 7003 of the RCRA, preempts state law trespass or nuisance actions.

A

The RCRA contains no provision which mandates comprehensive preemption of all state laws in the field of hazardous waste removal being regulated by the Act. The task, therefore, is to determine whether the regulatory scheme is so comprehensive in that field as to leave no room within which the states may act, or whether any provisions in the Act actually conflict with the state causes of action.

Although the RCRA is national in scope and universal in coverage, we believe that its provisions do not regulate so pervasively as to occupy the field completely. Any doubt on this point is removed by the explicit provisions in the Act which reveal a contrary intent. First, even though the RCRA declares that it is a "national policy of the United States that, wherever feasible, the generation of hazardous waste is to be reduced or eliminated as expeditiously as possible," 42 U.S.C. § 6902(b), a separate provision also states that it is the will of Congress that the RCRA guide "a cooperative effort among the Federal, State, and local governments and private enterprises." 42 U.S.C. § 6902(a)(11). In addition, provisions in the RCRA allow states to run their own waste management programs, although the Act does require federal approval of such state plans. *See* 42 U.S.C. § 6943. Thus, the legislation seems to contemplate state law action, rather than preempt it in its entirety.

The homeowners argue that the general savings clause found in the RCRA is conclusive of Congress' intent to preserve state common law actions. That clause states:

(f) Other Rights Preserved:

Nothing in this section shall restrict any right which any person (or class of persons) may have under any statute or common law to seek enforcement of any standard or requirement relating to the management of solid waste or hazardous waste, or to seek any other relief (including relief against the Administrator or a State agency).

42 U.S.C. § 6972(f). Although the Supreme Court has acknowledged that a savings clause such as § 6972(f) does "negate[] the inference that Congress 'left no room' for state causes of action," *International Paper Co. v. Ouellette*, 479 U.S. 481, 492, 93 L. Ed. 2d 883, 107 S.Ct. 805 (1987), that negation, standing alone, is not determinative of the preemption analysis. In *Ouellette*, the Supreme Court found that a similar savings clause found in the Clean Water Act did not compel the finding that there was no preemption, stating, "[the savings clause] merely says that 'nothing in this section,' i.e., the citizen-suit provisions, shall affect an injured party's right to seek relief under state law; it does not purport to preclude pre-emption of state law by other provisions of the Act." 479 U.S. at 493. The same conclusion is therefore reached under the RCRA, because 42 U.S.C. § 6972(f) also is found in a general citizen-suit provision of the RCRA. The natural reading of the phrase, "nothing in this section shall restrict" does not preclude preemption by other sections of the RCRA. The Supreme Court in Ouellette also cautioned against giving too much meaning to such savings clauses:

> The fact that the language of [the saving clause] is repeated in haec verba in the citizen-suit provisions of a vast array of environmental legislation . . . indicates that it does not reflect any considered judgment about what other remedies were previously available or continue to be available under any particular statute.

479 U.S. at 494 n.14 (citation omitted). Notwithstanding these admonitions, when we consider the entire legislative scheme of the RCRA together with the language of 42 U.S.C. § 6972(f), we are led to conclude that the RCRA does not preempt by implication the field staked out by the Act's regulation. Nevertheless, it remains to be determined whether state common law actions are preempted by an actual conflict with some provision of the Act.

B

Texaco contends that the relief requested by the homeowners in their common law claims would conflict with the EPA's authority under section 7003 of the RCRA to act on "imminent hazards," or with the Consent Order entered pursuant to section 7003. Texaco maintains that it was the intent of Congress that once the EPA acts under the imminent hazard provision, it has the exclusive authority to remedy the hazard.

Section 7003 of the RCRA, as amended in 1984, states:

Imminent Hazard:

(a) Authority of Administrator

Notwithstanding any other provision of this chapter, upon receipt of evidence that the past or present handling, storage, treatment, transportation or disposal of any solid waste or hazardous waste may present an imminent and substantial endangerment to health or the environment, the Administrator may bring suit on behalf of the United States in the appropriate district court against any person . . . who has contributed or who is contributing to such handling, storage, treatment, transportation or disposal to restrain such person. . . . The Administrator may also, after notice to the affected State, take other action under this section including, but not limited to, issuing such orders as may be necessary to protect public health and the environment.

42 U.S.C. § 6973(a).

We find nothing in section 7003 that gives the EPA exclusive authority to act, nor do we find anything to suggest such a conclusion in the legislative history. . . .

. . . On the contrary, the legislative history recited indicates that while Congress intended for the EPA to have broad authority to act in an imminent hazard situation, it also intended such action to complement other efforts and remedies. Finding nothing in the language of the Act or in its legislative history which confers on the EPA the exclusive authority to act in such situations, we conclude that section 7003, which authorizes the EPA to act, does not, in the absence of some EPA action, conflict with the state law causes of action asserted by the homeowners.

Our conclusion does not end our preemption analysis, however. We must still examine whether the Consent Order, entered pursuant to the EPA's authority under § 7003, preempts the homeowners' state law claims on the ground that any state law remedy would conflict with the Consent Order.

C

Texaco argues that homeowners are, through their state law actions for nuisance and trespass, seeking injunctive relief that would conflict with the existing Consent Order between Texaco and the EPA. Texaco argues further that complying with any court order based on state law would force Texaco to violate the Consent Order's requirement that any corrective action be submitted to and approved by the EPA. Thus, Texaco maintains that any such state law remedies are preempted by the Consent Order.

Article VI of the Constitution provides for the supremacy of federal laws over "anything" in the constitution or laws of the states that conflict. Although the issue is not explicitly raised by the homeowners in this case, we must first establish that the EPA's Consent Order may derive rights of supremacy from the clause that elevates federal laws.

The Supreme Court has held that federal regulations issued by agencies have "no less pre-emptive effect than federal statutes." *Capital Cities Cable, Inc. v. Crisp,* 467 U.S. 691, 699, 81 L. Ed. 2d 580, 104 S. Ct. 2694 (1984) (quoting *Fidelity Federal Savings & Loan Assn. v. De la Cuesta,* 458 U.S. 141, 153, 73 L. Ed. 2d 664, 102 S. Ct. 3014 (1982)). Indeed, even if an agency, rather than Congress, resolves to preempt an area, its determination will be enforced to preempt conflicting state regulations so long as the determination represents "a reasonable accommodation of conflicting policies that are within the agency's domain." *Capital Cities,* 467 U.S. at 700. The court's role in that case is to determine only whether the agency exceeded its statutory authority or acted arbitrarily. *See Fidelity Federal,* 458 U.S. at 153.

Accordingly, we hold that when the EPA, acting within valid statutory authority of the RCRA and not arbitrarily, enters into a consent order, that order will also preempt conflicting state regulation, including a federal court order based on state common law. *See United States v. Akzo Coatings of America, Inc.,* 949 F.2d 1409, 1454–57 (6th Cir. 1991) (holding that consent decree entered into between the EPA and defendants to engage in remedial cleanup of hazardous waste pursuant to CERCLA preempted further state law actions seeking injunctive and declaratory relief that would conflict with the consent decree); *cf. Colorado v. Idarado Mining Co.,* 916 F.2d 1486 (10th Cir. 1990) (holding that states may not obtain an order under CERCLA apart from the terms of a valid administrative consent order obtained by the EPA under CERCLA), *cert. denied,* 499 U.S. 960, 113 L. Ed. 2d 648, 111 S. Ct. 1584 (1991).

We have previously held that the test for determining whether state law conflicts with federal law is whether "it is impossible to comply with both state and federal law" or whether "the state law stands as an obstacle to the accomplishment of the full purposes and objectives" of federal law. *Worm,* 970 F.2d at 1305 (quoting *Silkwood,* 464 U.S. at 248). The same test applies in determining whether a state-ordered injunction would conflict with the EPA's Consent Order.

The Consent Order entered on September 23, 1991, required Texaco to implement certain immediate remedial measures, to submit to the EPA emergency measures plans for EPA review and selection, and once a plan is selected, to implement the plan under an EPA-approved schedule. While the immediate requirements have been satisfied, the record does not reveal the status of the plan because the complaint in this case was dismissed at an early stage. There is, however, no evidence that the EPA is, to date, in any way dissatisfied with Texaco's progress.

In these circumstances, the injunctive relief requested by the homeowners from the court would conflict with the remedial measures selected and supervised by the EPA. The homeowners, in their complaint, have asked the district court to order excavation, treatment and replacement of contaminated soil to a specified depth and over a specified area; they have requested that the court direct "enhanced ground water extraction and bio-remediation to reduce the off-site contamination"; and they have requested the construction of a "free phase hydrocarbon trench removal system across the water table." The EPA order addresses the same site and conditions covered by the homeowners' suit and provides its mandatory response, as authorized by § 7003 of the RCRA. Not only would the court, if it granted the relief, be substituting its judgment for the authorized judgment of the EPA, the court also would be usurping the review role given by statute to the EPA. *See* 42 U.S.C. § 6973.

Accordingly, we hold that the homeowners' claims with respect to the contamination described in the complaint, to the extent they seek injunctive relief before the EPA's Consent Order is fulfilled and terminated, are preempted by the EPA's Consent Order. . . .

IV

. . . .

Texaco conceded at oral argument that if the complaint were construed as one for damages as well as for injunctive relief, they would agree that the RCRA does not preempt the damages claims. We think the law confirms its position.

The Supreme Court has held repeatedly that state law damages claims are not necessarily preempted by federal statutes that regulate the same field. For instance, in *Cipollone [v. Liggett Group, Inc.,* 112 S. Ct. 2608 (1992)], the Supreme Court held that a federal warning label requirement on cigarette packages does not preempt state common law damage actions. In *Silkwood [v. Kerr-McGee. supra]*, the Supreme Court also held that federal statute regulating nuclear safety did not preempt state law tort suits seeking damages. Similarly, we held in *Worm v. American Cyanamid Co. [supra]* that the Federal Insecticide, Fungicide and Rodenticide Act did not preempt state tort actions seeking damages for breach of federally-imposed standards.

Moreover, state law damages claims would not conflict with the Consent Order, which makes no provision for the payment of damages to the homeowners. Indeed, section 7003, the provision under which the order was entered, gives the EPA authority to seek injunctive relief but no authority to seek damages on behalf of private parties.

V

[Remainder of majority opinion, and the concurring opinion, are omitted].

NOTE

When Congress enacted its fleet of pollution control statutes, it did not seek to supplant state law-based pollution control statutes. On the contrary, it wanted to preserve state law. It also wanted to empower citizens to help out. To promote this latter interest, it placed in each of the federal pollution control statutes a "citizen suit" provision, designed to allow private individuals to file lawsuits to enforce the federal provisions themselves. *See, e.g.,* 33 U.S.C. § 1365 (Clean Water Act); 42 U.S.C. § 7604 (Clean Air Act); 42 U.S.C. § 6972 (Resource Conservation and Recovery Act); 16 U.S.C. § 1540 (Endangered Species Act); 42 U.S.C. § 9659 (Comprehensive Environmental Response, Compensation, and Liability Act). Under typical citizen suits provisions, an individual may file a cause of action against a polluter if the Environmental Protection Agency has failed to do so, but only after providing notice to the EPA of his or her intent to take up the matter. As we have seen in *Feikema*, these citizen suit provisions may contain savings clauses preserving the rights of federal citizen suit plaintiffs to proceed under state or common law. *See, e.g.*, 33 U.S.C. § 1365(e) (Clean Water Act); 42 U.S.C. § 7604(e) (Clean Air Act); 42 U.S.C. § 6972(f) (Resource Conservation and Recovery Act); 42 U.S.C. § 9659(h) (Comprehensive Environmental Response, Compensation, and Liability Act). It may well be that these rights to pursue relief by non-federal action would remain even in the absence of the savings clauses. The statutory provisions, at least, dispense with any ambiguity. They leave open for litigation, however, questions of scope. As seen in *Feikema*, the question often is whether to read these savings clauses broadly or narrowly.

Federal pollution control statutes may contain other savings clause provisions as well. Not tied to citizen suit provisions, these provisions bear on the question of overall preemptive effect. See, in this regard, § 510 of the Clean Water Act:

> **State authority**. Except as expressly provided in this chapter, nothing in this chapter shall (1) preclude or deny the right of any State or political subdivision thereof or interstate agency to adopt or enforce (A) any standard or limitation respecting discharges of pollutants, or (B) any requirement respecting control or abatement of pollution; except that if [a federal water pollution restriction] is in effect . . ., such State or political subdivision or interstate agency may not adopt or enforce any [state law-based water pollution restriction] which is less stringent than the [counterpart federal restriction]. . . .

33 U.S.C. § 1370. *See also* 16 U.S.C. § 1535(f) (Endangered Species Act); 42 U.S.C. § 6991g (Resource Conservation and Recovery Act (relating to regulation of underground storage tanks)); 42 U.S.C. § 9658 (Comprehensive Environmental Response, Compensation, and Liability Act).

By allowing the preemption of less stringent state laws, these savings clauses establish the federal standard as legal floor below which no pollution control measure may fall.

[3] DORMANT COMMERCE CLAUSE

"The Congress shall have Power . . . To regulate Commerce with foreign Nations, and among the several States, and with the Indian Tribes." U.S. Constitution, Article I, § 8, cl. 3. "Although the Commerce Clause is by its text an affirmative grant of power to Congress to regulate interstate and foreign commerce, the Clause has long been recognized as containing a self-executing negative command prohibiting states from taking certain actions respecting interstate commerce even in the absence of federal action." *CTS Corp. v. Dynamics Corp. of Am.*, 481 U.S. 69, 87, 107 S. Ct. 1637 (1987); *see also Oregon Waste Sys. v. Department of Envtl. Quality*, 114 S. Ct. 1345, 1349 (1994). This limitation is known as the dormant Commerce Clause.

C & A CARBONE, INC. v. TOWN OF CLARKSTOWN, NEW YORK

511 U.S. 383, 114 S. Ct. 1677 (1994)

JUDGES: KENNEDY, J., delivered the opinion of the Court, in which STEVENS, SCALIA, THOMAS, and GINSBURG, JJ., joined. O'CONNOR, J., filed an opinion concurring in the judgment. SOUTER, J., filed a dissenting opinion, in which REHNQUIST, C.J., and BLACKMUN, J., joined.

As solid waste output continues apace and landfill capacity becomes more costly and scarce, state and local governments are expending significant resources to develop trash control systems that are efficient, lawful, and protective of the environment. The difficulty of their task is evident from the number of recent cases that we have heard involving waste transfer and treatment. See *Philadelphia v. New Jersey*, 437 U.S. 617 (1978); *Chemical Waste Management, Inc. v. Hunt*, 504 U.S. 334 (1992); *Fort Gratiot Sanitary Landfill, Inc. v. Michigan Dept. of Natural Resources*, 504 U.S. 353 (1992); *Oregon Waste Systems, Inc. v. Department of Environmental Quality of Oregon, ante*, p. 93. The case decided today, while perhaps a small new chapter in that course of decisions, rests nevertheless upon well-settled principles of our Commerce Clause jurisprudence.

We consider a so-called flow control ordinance, which requires all solid waste to be processed at a designated transfer station before leaving the municipality. The avowed purpose of the ordinance is to retain the processing fees charged at the transfer station to amortize the cost of the facility. Because it attains this goal by depriving competitors, including out-of-state firms, of access to a local market, we hold that the flow control ordinance violates the Commerce Clause.

The town of Clarkstown, New York, lies in the lower Hudson River valley, just upstream from the Tappan Zee Bridge and by highway minutes from New Jersey. Within the town limits are the village of Nyack and the hamlet of West Nyack. In August 1989, Clarkstown entered into a consent decree with the New York State Department of Environmental Conservation. The town agreed to close its landfill located on Route 303 in West Nyack and build a new solid waste transfer station on the same site. The station would receive bulk solid waste and separate recyclable from nonrecyclable items. Recyclable waste would be baled for shipment to a recycling facility; nonrecyclable waste, to a suitable landfill or incinerator.

The cost of building the transfer station was estimated at $1.4 million. A local private contractor agreed to construct the facility and operate it for five years, after which the town would buy it for one dollar. During those five years, the town guaranteed a minimum waste flow of 120,000 tons per year, for which the contractor could charge the hauler a so-called tipping fee of $81 per ton. If the station received less than 120,000 tons in a year, the town promised to make up the tipping fee deficit. The object of this arrangement was to amortize the cost of the transfer station: The town would finance its new facility with the income generated by the tipping fees.

The problem, of course, was how to meet the yearly guarantee. This difficulty was compounded by the fact that the tipping fee of $ 81 per ton exceeded the disposal cost of unsorted solid waste on the private market. The solution the town adopted was the flow control ordinance here in question, Local Laws 1990, No. 9 of the Town of Clarkstown. The ordinance requires all nonhazardous solid waste within the town to be deposited at the Route 303 transfer station. *Id.* § 3.C (waste generated within the town), § 5.A (waste generated outside and brought in). Noncompliance is punishable by as much as a $1,000 fine and up to 15 days in jail. § 7.

The petitioners in this case are C & A Carbone, Inc., a company engaged in the processing of solid waste, and various related companies or persons, all of whom we designate Carbone. Carbone operates a recycling center in Clarkstown, where it receives bulk solid waste, sorts and bales it, and then ships it to other processing facilities — much as occurs at the town's new transfer station. While the flow control ordinance permits recyclers like Carbone to continue receiving solid waste, § 3.C, it requires them to bring the nonrecyclable residue from that waste to the Route 303 station. It thus forbids Carbone to ship the nonrecyclable waste itself, and it requires Carbone to pay a tipping fee on trash that Carbone has already sorted.

In March 1991, a tractor-trailer containing 23 bales of solid waste struck an overpass on the Palisades Interstate Parkway. When the police investigated the accident, they discovered the truck was carrying household waste from Carbone's Clarkstown plant to an Indiana landfill. The Clarkstown police put Carbone's plant under surveillance and in the next few days seized six more tractor-trailers leaving the facility. The trucks also contained nonrecyclable waste, originating both within and without the town, and destined for disposal sites in Illinois, Indiana, West Virginia, and Florida.

The town of Clarkstown sued petitioners in New York Supreme Court, Rockland County, seeking an injunction requiring Carbone to ship all nonrecyclable waste to the Route 303 transfer station. Petitioners responded by suing in United States District Court to enjoin the flow control ordinance. On July 11, the federal court granted Carbone's injunction, finding a sufficient likelihood that the ordinance violated the Commerce Clause of the *United States Constitution. C. A. Carbone, Inc. v. Clarkstown*, 770 F. Supp. 848 (SDNY 1991).

Four days later, the New York court granted summary judgment to respondent. The court declared the flow control ordinance constitutional and enjoined petitioners to comply with it. The federal court then dissolved its injunction.

The Appellate Division affirmed. 182 App. Div. 2d 213, 587 N.Y.S.2d 681 (2d Dept. 1992). The court found that the ordinance did not discriminate against interstate commerce because it "applies evenhandedly to all solid waste processed within the Town, regardless of point of origin." *Id.*, at 686. The New York Court of Appeals denied petitioners' motion for leave to appeal. 80 N.Y.2d 760, 605 N.E.2d 874 (1992). We granted certiorari, 508 U.S. 938 (1993), and now reverse.

At the outset we confirm that the flow control ordinance does regulate interstate commerce, despite the town's position to the contrary. The town says that its ordinance reaches only waste within its jurisdiction and is in practical effect a quarantine: It prevents garbage from entering the stream of interstate commerce until it is made safe. This reasoning is premised, however, on an outdated and mistaken concept of what constitutes interstate commerce.

While the immediate effect of the ordinance is to direct local transport of solid waste to a designated site within the local jurisdiction, its economic effects are interstate in reach. The Carbone facility in Clarkstown receives and processes waste from places other than Clarkstown, including from out of State. By requiring Carbone to send the nonrecyclable portion of this waste to the Route 303 transfer station at an additional cost, the flow control ordinance drives up the cost for out-of-state interests to dispose of their solid waste. Furthermore, even as to waste originant in Clarkstown, the ordinance prevents everyone except the favored local operator from performing the initial processing step. The ordinance thus deprives out-of-state businesses of access to a local market. These economic effects are more than enough to bring the Clarkstown ordinance within the purview of the Commerce Clause. It is well settled that actions are within the domain of the Commerce Clause if they burden interstate commerce or impede its free flow. *NLRB v. Jones & Laughlin Steel Corp.*, 301 U.S. 1, 31 (1937).

The real question is whether the flow control ordinance is valid despite its undoubted effect on interstate commerce. For this inquiry, our case law yields two lines of analysis: first, whether the ordinance discriminates against interstate commerce, *Philadelphia*, 437 U.S. at 624; and second, whether the ordinance imposes a burden on interstate commerce that is "clearly excessive in relation to the putative local benefits," *Pike v. Bruce Church, Inc.*, 397 U.S. 137, 142 (1970). As we find that the ordinance discriminates against interstate commerce, we need not resort to the *Pike* test.

The central rationale for the rule against discrimination is to prohibit state or municipal laws whose object is local economic protectionism, laws that would excite those jealousies and retaliatory measures the Constitution was designed to prevent. *See* The Federalist No. 22, pp. 143–145 (C. Rossiter ed. 1961) (A. Hamilton); Madison, Vices of the Political System of the United States, in 2 Writings of James Madison 362–363 (G. Hunt ed. 1901). We have interpreted the Commerce Clause to invalidate local laws that impose commercial barriers or discriminate against an article of commerce by reason of its origin or destination out of State. *See, e.g., Philadelphia, supra* (striking down New Jersey statute that prohibited the import of solid waste); *Hughes v. Oklahoma*, 441 U.S. 322 (1979) (striking down Oklahoma law that prohibited the export of natural minnows).

Clarkstown protests that its ordinance does not discriminate because it does not differentiate solid waste on the basis of its geographic origin. All solid waste, regardless of origin, must be processed at the designated transfer station before it leaves the town. Unlike the statute in *Philadelphia*, says the town, the ordinance erects no barrier to the import or export of any solid waste but requires only that the waste be channeled through the designated facility.

Our initial discussion of the effects of the ordinance on interstate commerce goes far toward refuting the town's contention that there is no discrimination in its regulatory scheme. The town's own arguments go the rest of the way. As the town itself points out, what makes garbage a profitable business is not its own worth but the fact that its possessor must pay to get rid of it. In other words, the article of commerce is not so much the solid waste itself, but rather the service of processing and disposing of it.

With respect to this stream of commerce, the flow control ordinance discriminates, for it allows only the favored operator to process waste that is within the limits of the town. The ordinance is no less discriminatory because in-state or in-town processors are also covered by the prohibition. In *Dean Milk Co. v. Madison*, 340 U.S. 349 (1951), we struck down a city ordinance that required all milk sold in the city to be pasteurized within five miles of the city lines. We found it "immaterial that Wisconsin milk from outside the Madison area is subjected to the same proscription as that moving in interstate commerce." *Id.*, at 354, n. 4. Accord, *Fort Gratiot Sanitary Landfill, Inc. v. Michigan Dept. of Natural Resources*, 504 U. S. at 361 ("Our prior cases teach that a State (or one of its political subdivisions) may not avoid the strictures of the Commerce Clause by curtailing the movement of articles of commerce through subdivisions of the State, rather than through the State itself").

In this light, the flow control ordinance is just one more instance of local processing requirements that we long have held invalid. *See Minnesota v. Barber*, 136 U.S. 313 (1890) (striking down a Minnesota statute that required any meat sold within the state, whether originating within or without the State, to be examined by an inspector within the State); *Foster-Fountain Packing Co. v. Haydel*, 278 U.S. 1 (1928) (striking down a Louisiana statute that forbade shrimp to be exported unless the heads and hulls had first been removed within the State); *Johnson v. Haydel*, 278 U.S. 16 (1928) (striking down analogous Louisiana statute for oysters); *Toomer v. Witsell*, 334 U.S. 385 (1948) (striking down South Carolina statute that required shrimp fishermen to unload, pack, and stamp their catch before shipping it to another State); *Pike v. Bruce Church, Inc.*, 397 U.S. 137 (1970) (striking down Arizona statute that required all Arizona-grown cantaloupes to be packaged within the State prior to export); *South-Central Timber Development, Inc. v. Wunnicke*, 467 U.S. 82 (1984) (striking down an Alaska regulation that required all Alaska timber to be processed within the State prior to export). The essential vice in laws of this sort is that they bar the import of the processing service. Out-of-state meat inspectors, or shrimp hullers, or milk pasteurizers, are deprived of access to local demand for their services. Put another way, the offending local laws hoard a local resource — be it meat, shrimp, or milk — for the benefit of local businesses that treat it.

The flow control ordinance has the same design and effect. It hoards solid waste, and the demand to get rid of it, for the benefit of the preferred processing facility. The only conceivable distinction from the cases cited above is that the flow control ordinance favors a single local proprietor. But this difference just makes the protectionist effect of the ordinance more acute. In *Dean Milk,* the local processing requirement at least permitted pasteurizers within five miles of the city to compete. An out-of-state pasteurizer who wanted access to that market might have built a pasteurizing facility within the radius. The flow control ordinance at issue here squelches competition in the waste-processing service altogether, leaving no room for investment from outside.

Discrimination against interstate commerce in favor of local business or investment is per se invalid, save in a narrow class of cases in which the municipality can demonstrate, under rigorous scrutiny, that it has no other means to advance a legitimate local interest. *Maine v. Taylor*, 477 U.S. 131 (1986) (upholding Maine's ban on the import of baitfish because Maine had no other way to prevent the spread of parasites and the adulteration of its native fish species). A number of *amici* contend that the flow control ordinance fits into this narrow class. They suggest that as landfill space diminishes and environmental cleanup costs escalate, measures like flow control become necessary to ensure the safe handling and proper treatment of solid waste.

The teaching of our cases is that these arguments must be rejected absent the clearest showing that the unobstructed flow of interstate commerce itself is unable to solve the local problem. The Commerce Clause presumes a national market free from local legislation that discriminates in favor of local interests. Here Clarkstown has any number of nondiscriminatory alternatives for addressing the health and environmental problems alleged to justify the ordinance in question. The most obvious would be uniform safety regulations enacted without the object to discriminate. These regulations would ensure that competitors like Carbone do not underprice the market by cutting corners on environmental safety.

Nor may Clarkstown justify the flow control ordinance as a way to steer solid waste away from out-of-town disposal sites that it might deem harmful to the environment. To do so would extend the town's police power beyond its jurisdictional bounds. States and localities may not attach restrictions to exports or imports in order to control commerce in other states. *Baldwin v. G. A. F. Seelig, Inc.*, 294 U.S. 511 (1935) (striking down New York law that prohibited the sale of milk unless the price paid to the original milk producer equalled the minimum required by New York).

The flow control ordinance does serve a central purpose that a nonprotectionist regulation would not: It ensures that the town-sponsored facility will be profitable, so that the local contractor can build it and Clarkstown can buy it back at nominal cost in five years. In other words, as the most candid of amici and even Clarkstown admit, the flow control ordinance is a financing measure. By itself, of course, revenue generation is not a local interest that can justify discrimination against interstate commerce. Otherwise States could impose discriminatory taxes against solid waste originating outside the State. *See Chemical Waste Management, Inc. v. Hunt*, 504 U.S. 334 (1992) (striking down Alabama statute that imposed additional fee on all hazardous waste generated outside the State and disposed of within the State); *Oregon Waste Systems, Inc. v. Department of Environmental Quality of Oregon, ante*, p.93 (striking down Oregon statute that imposed additional fee on solid waste generated outside the State and disposed of within the State).

Clarkstown maintains that special financing is necessary to ensure the long-term survival of the designated facility. If so, the town may subsidize the facility through general taxes or municipal bonds. *New Energy Co. of Indiana v. Limbach*, 486 U.S. 269, 278 (1988). But having elected to use the open market to earn revenues for its project, the town may not employ discriminatory regulation to give that project an advantage over rival businesses from out of State.

Though the Clarkstown ordinance may not in explicit terms seek to regulate interstate commerce, it does so nonetheless by its practical effect and design. In this respect the ordinance is not far different from the state law this Court found invalid in *Buck v. Kuykendall*, 267 U.S. 307 (1925). That statute prohibited common carriers from using state highways over certain routes without a certificate of public convenience. Writing for the Court, Justice Brandeis said of the law: "Its primary purpose is not regulation with a view to safety or to conservation of the highways, but the prohibition of competition. It determines not the manner of use, but the persons by whom the highways may be used. It prohibits such use to some persons while permitting it to others for the same purpose and in the same manner." *Id.*, at 315–316.

State and local governments may not use their regulatory power to favor local enterprise by prohibiting patronage of out-of-state competitors or their facilities. We reverse the judgment and remand the case for proceedings not inconsistent with this decision.

It is so ordered.

[Appendix to opinion omitted].

[JUSTICE O'CONNOR, concurred on the basis that the ordinance violates the dormant commerce clause because it imposes an excessive burden on interstate commerce]

JUSTICE SOUTER, with whom The CHIEF JUSTICE and JUSTICE BLACKMUN join, dissenting.

The majority may invoke "well-settled principles of our Commerce Clause jurisprudence," *ante*, at 1, but it does so to strike down an ordinance unlike anything this Court has ever invalidated. Previous cases have held that the "negative" or "dormant" aspect of the Commerce Clause renders state or local legislation unconstitutional when it discriminates against out-of-state or out-of-town businesses such as those that pasteurize milk, hull shrimp, or mill lumber, and the majority relies on these cases because of what they have in common with this one: out-of-state processors are excluded from the local market (here, from the market for trash processing services). What the majority ignores, however, are the differences between our local processing cases and this one: the exclusion worked by Clarkstown's Local Law 9 bestows no benefit on a class of local private actors, but instead directly aids the government in satisfying a traditional governmental responsibility. The law does not differentiate between all local and all out-of-town providers of a service, but instead between the one entity responsible for ensuring that the job gets done and all other enterprises, regardless of their location. The ordinance thus falls outside that class of tariff or protectionist measures that the Commerce Clause has traditionally been thought to bar States from enacting against each other, and when the majority subsumes the ordinance within the class of laws this Court has struck down as facially discriminatory (and so avails itself of our "virtually per se rule" against such statutes, see

Philadelphia v. New Jersey, 437 U.S. 617, 624 (1978)), the majority is in fact greatly extending the Clause's dormant reach.

There are, however, good and sufficient reasons against expanding the Commerce Clause's inherent capacity to trump exercises of state authority such as the ordinance at issue here. There is no indication in the record that any out-of-state trash processor has been harmed, or that the interstate movement or disposition of trash will be affected one whit. To the degree Local Law 9 affects the market for trash processing services, it does so only by subjecting Clarkstown residents and businesses to burdens far different from the burdens of local favoritism that dormant Commerce Clause jurisprudence seeks to root out. The town has found a way to finance a public improvement, not by transferring its cost to out-of-state economic interests, but by spreading it among the local generators of trash, an equitable result with tendencies that should not disturb the Commerce Clause and should not be disturbed by us. * * *

The Commerce Clause was not passed to save the citizens of Clarkstown from themselves. It should not be wielded to prevent them from attacking their local garbage problems with an ordinance that does not discriminate between local and out-of-town participants in the private market for trash disposal services and that is not protectionist in its purpose or effect. Local Law 9 conveys a privilege on the municipal government alone, the only market participant that bears responsibility for ensuring that adequate trash processing services continue to be available to Clarkstown residents. Because the Court's decision today is neither compelled by our local processing cases nor consistent with this Court's reason for inferring a dormant or negative aspect to the Commerce Clause in the first place, I respectfully dissent.

NOTES AND QUESTIONS

1. The Supreme Court has identified "discrimination" for purposes of the dormant Commerce Clause to be "differential treatment of in-state and out-of-state economic interests that benefits the former and burdens the latter." *Oregon Waste Systems, Inc. v. Dep't of Environmental Quality*, 511 U.S. 93, 99, 114 S.Ct. 1345, 1350 (1994). *Carbone* held that Clarkstown's flow control ordinance violated this constitutional restriction against discriminatory legislation. In the view of the majority, the ordinance was particularly offensive, and its discriminatory impacts were "more acute," because it discriminated against both in-state and out-of-state actors in favor of a single local proprietor. Still, lower courts have refused to read *Carbone* as a flat ban on such schemes. In *United Haulers Ass'n v. Oneida-Herkimer Solid Waste Mgm't. Authority*, 2001 U.S. App. LEXIS 16919 (2d Cir. 7/27/01), the Court of Appeals for the Second Circuit found no discrimination against interstate commerce where the scheme required all waste generated within municipal borders be processed at one of several publicly owned facilities. In *Maharg, Inc. v. Van Wert Solid Waste Mgm't Dist.*, 249 F.3d 544 (6th Cir. 2001), the Court of Appeals for the Sixth Circuit found no constitutional infirmity where participation in the waste disposal plan was voluntary. In *U & I Sanitation v. City of Columbus*, 205 F.3d 1063 (8th Cir. 2000), the Court of Appeals for the Eighth Circuit found no discrimination against interstate commerce where

the local government effectively eliminated the entire market for waste disposal. The *U&I Sanitation* court, however, did find this arrangement to constitute an undue burden on interstate commerce.

Perhaps this unwillingness among lower courts to apply *Carbone* more broadly has its genesis in the Supreme Court itself. The Supreme Court in *Reeves, Inc. v. Stake*, 447 U.S. 429, 100 S. Ct. 2271 (1980), has advised against imposing the dormant Commerce Clause too strictly, for to do so can

> [I]nterfere significantly with a State's ability to structure relations exclusively with its own citizens. It would also threaten the future fashioning of effective and creative programs for solving local problems and distributing governmental largesse. A healthy regard for federalism and good government renders us reluctant to risk these results.
>
> > To stay experimentation in things social and economic is a grave responsibility. Denial of the right to experiment may be fraught with serious consequences to the Nation. It is one of the happy incidents of the federal system that a single courageous State may, if its citizens choose, serve as a laboratory; and try novel social and economic experiments without risk to the rest of the country.
>
> *New State Ice Co. v. Liebmann*, 285 U.S. 262, 311 (1932) (Brandeis, J., dissenting).

Id. at 441, 100 S.Ct. at 2279-80.

2. A statute or ordinance need not discriminate in an overt, facial way to violate the dormant Commerce Clause. It is enough if a non-facially discriminatory provision discriminates in practical effect. *See, e.g., Waste Management Holdings, Inc. v. Gilmore*, 252 F.3d 316 (4th Cir. 2001): When legislators in the State of Virginia learned that New York City planned to be sending 14,000 tons of solid wastes per day to Virginia landfills, and fearing Virginia would "drown in a sea of garbage," they passed a statute capping the amount of garbage that landfills in the State could receive. *Id.* at 327. This statute obviously did not discriminate in any facial way against interstate commerce (as compared with intrastate commerce), but the court found it did so in practical effect. Buttressing the court's decision was its finding that the statute was enacted for a discriminatory purpose. In reaching its conclusion, the court identified probative factors for determining discriminatory intent:

> (1) evidence of a "consistent pattern" of actions by the decisionmaking body disparately impacting members of a particular class of persons; (2) historical background of the decision, which may take into account any history of discrimination by the decisionmaking body or the jurisdiction it represents; (3) the specific sequence of events leading up to the particular decision being challenged, including any significant departures from normal procedures; and (4) contemporary statements by decisionmakers on the record or in minutes of their meetings.

Id. at 336.

Should discriminatory intent, without more, cause a statute to violate the dormant Commerce Clause?

3. In 1994, both the Senate and the House passed bills to overturn *Carbone.* The Senate bill as it emerged from the Environment and Public Works Committee would have allowed governors to freeze imports of garbage from other states at 1993 levels. It would also have required large exporting states to reduce their exports on a sliding scale over the next six years. At present, forty-two states import garbage and forty-three export it. The House bill, passed on September 28, 1994, varied in some important particulars. Objections by Senator John Chafee of Rhode Island killed any chance of enacting compromise legislation. The final compromise measure failed by a single vote one hour before the Congress adjourned on October 8, 1994.

The loss of flow control authority has had a negative effect on the financing of waste management facilities, according to a spokesperson for Moody's Investors Service. Landfills and waste-to-energy facilities have been losing money, and municipalities may find it difficult to sell bonds to finance them.

4. Discriminations against interstate commerce by the exercise of state taxation authority are unconstitutional. *New Energy Company of Indiana v. Limbach,* 486 U.S. 269, 108 S.Ct. 1803 (1988). Accordingly, a state may not tax a transaction or incident more heavily when it crosses state lines than when it occurs entirely within the state. *Armco, Inc. v. Hardesty,* 467 U.S. 638, 104 S. Ct. 2620 (1984).

SPORHASE v. NEBRASKA

458 U.S. 941, 102 S. Ct. 3456 (1982)

JUSTICE STEVENS delivered the opinion of the Court.

Appellants challenge the constitutionality of a Nebraska statutory restriction on the withdrawal of ground water from any well within Nebraska intended for use in an adjoining State. The challenge presents three questions under the Commerce Clause (1) whether ground water is an article of commerce and therefore subject to congressional regulation; (2) whether the Nebraska restriction on the interstate transfer of ground water imposes an impermissible burden on commerce; and (3) whether Congress has granted the States permission to engage in ground water regulation that otherwise would be impermissible.

Appellants jointly own contiguous tracts of land in Chase County, Nebraska, and Phillips County, Colorado. A well physically located on the Nebraska tract pumps ground water for irrigation of both the Nebraska tract and the Colorado tract. Previous owners of the land registered the well with the State of Nebraska in 1971, but neither they nor the present owners applied for the permit required by Neb. Rev. Stat. § 46-613.01 (1978). That section provides

> "Any person, firm, city, village, municipal corporation or any other
> entity intending to withdraw ground water from any well or pit located
> in the State of Nebraska and transport it for use in an adjoining state
> shall apply to the Department of Water Resources for a permit to do
> so. If the Director of Water Resources finds that the withdrawal of
> the ground water requested is reasonable, is not contrary to the

conservation and use of ground water, and is not otherwise detrimental to the public welfare, he shall grant the permit if the state in which the water is to be used grants reciprocal rights to withdraw and transport ground water from that state for use in the State of Nebraska."

I

Appellee brought this action to enjoin appellants from transferring the water across the border without a permit. The trial court rejected the defense that the statute imposed an undue burden on interstate commerce and granted the injunction. The Nebraska Supreme Court affirmed. 208 Neb. 703, 305 N.W.2d 614 (1981). It held that, under Nebraska law, ground water is not "a market item freely transferable for value among private parties, and therefore [is] not an article of commerce." *Id.*, at 705, 305 N.W.2d, at 616. The Chief Justice, while agreeing that the statutory criteria governing the transfer of water to an adjoining State did not violate the Commerce Clause, dissented on the narrow ground that appellee violated both the Federal and Nebraska Constitutions by attempting "to absolutely prohibit the transfer of water, without regard to its need or availability, based solely upon the acts of another state over which citizens of this state have no control." *Id.*, at 713, 305 N.W.2d, at 620.

In holding that ground water is not an article of commerce, the Nebraska Supreme Court and appellee cite as controlling precedent *Hudson County Water Co. v. McCarter*, 209 U.S. 349 (1908). In that case a New Jersey statute prohibited the interstate transfer of any surface water located within the State. The Hudson County Water Co. nevertheless contracted with New York City to supply one of its boroughs with water from the Passaic River in New Jersey. The State Attorney General sought from the New Jersey courts an injunction against fulfillment of the contract. Over the water company's objections that the statute impaired the obligation of contract, took property without just compensation, interfered with interstate commerce, denied New York citizens the privileges afforded New Jersey citizens, and denied New York citizens the equal protection of the laws, the injunction was granted. This Court, in an opinion by Justice Holmes, affirmed.

Most of the Court's opinion addresses the just compensation claim. Justice Holmes refused to ground the Court's holding, as did the New Jersey state courts, on "the more or less attenuated residuum of title that the State may be said to possess." *Id.*, at 355. For the statute was justified as a regulatory measure that, on balance, did not amount to a taking of property that required just compensation. Putting aside the "problems of irrigation," the State's interest in preserving its waters was well within its police power. That interest was not dependent on any demonstration that the State's water resources were inadequate for present or future use. The State "finds itself in possession of what all admit to be a great public good, and what it has it may keep and give no one a reason for its will." *Id.*, at 357.

Having disposed of the just compensation claim, Justice Holmes turned very briefly to the other constitutional challenges. In one paragraph, he rejected the Contract Clause claim. In the remaining paragraph of the opinion, he rejected all the other defenses. His treatment of the Commerce Clause challenge consists of three sentences "A man cannot acquire a right to property by his desire to use it in commerce among the States. Neither can he enlarge his otherwise limited and qualified right to the same end. The case is covered in this respect by *Geer v. Connecticut*, 161 U.S. 519 [(1896)]."

While appellee relies upon *Hudson County*, appellants rest on our summary affirmance of a three-judge District Court judgment in *City of Altus v. Carr*, 255 F. Supp. 828 (WD Tex.), *summarily aff'd*, 385 U.S. 35 (1966). The city of Altus is located near the southern border of Oklahoma. Large population increases rendered inadequate its source of municipal water. It consequently obtained from the owners of land in an adjoining Texas county the contractual right to pump the ground water underlying that land and to transport it across the border. The Texas Legislature thereafter enacted a statute that forbade the interstate exportation of ground water without the approval of that body. The city filed suit in Federal District Court, claiming that the statute violated the Commerce Clause. . . .

In summarily affirming the District Court in *City of Altus*, we did not necessarily adopt the court's reasoning. Our affirmance indicates only our agreement with the result reached by the District Court. *Metromedia, Inc. v. San Diego*, 453 U.S. 490, 499 (1981). That result is not necessarily inconsistent with the Nebraska Supreme Court's holding in this case. For Texas law differs significantly from Nebraska law regarding the rights of a surface owner to ground water that he has withdrawn. According to the District Court in *City of Altus*, the "rule in Texas was that an owner of land could use all of the percolating water he could capture from the wells on his land for whatever beneficial purposes he needed it, on or off the land, and could likewise sell it to others for use on or off the land and outside the basin where produced, just as he could sell any other species of property." 255 F. Supp., at 833, n. 8. Since ground water, once withdrawn, may be freely bought and sold in States that follow this rule, in those States ground water is appropriately regarded as an article of commerce. In Nebraska the surface owner has no comparable interest in ground water. As explained by the Nebraska Supreme Court, " 'the owner of land is entitled to appropriate subterranean waters found under his land, but he cannot extract and appropriate them in excess of a reasonable and beneficial use upon the land which he owns, especially if such use is injurious to others who have substantial rights to the waters, and if the natural underground supply is insufficient for all owners, each is entitled to a reasonable proportion of the whole.' " 208 Neb., at 705, 305 N.W.2d, at 617 (quoting *Olson v. City of Wahoo*, 124 Neb. 802, 811, 248 N.W. 304, 308 (1933)).

City of Altus, however, is inconsistent with *Hudson County*. For in the latter case the Court found *Geer v. Connecticut, supra*, to be controlling on the Commerce Clause issue. *Geer*, which sustained a Connecticut ban on the interstate transportation of game birds captured in that State, was premised on the theory that the State owned its wild animals and therefore was free to qualify any ownership interest it might recognize in the persons who capture them. One such restriction is a prohibition against interstate transfer of the captured animals. This theory of public ownership was advanced as a defense in *City of Altus*. The State argued that it owned all subterranean water and therefore could recognize ownership in the surface owner who withdraws the water, but restrict that ownership to use of the water within the State. That theory, upon which the Commerce Clause issue in *Hudson County* was decided, was rejected by the District Court in *City of Altus*. In expressly overruling *Geer* three years ago, this Court traced the demise of the public ownership theory and definitively recast it as " 'but a fiction expressive in legal shorthand of the importance to its people that a State have power to preserve and regulate the exploitation of an important resource.' " *Hughes v. Oklahoma*, 441 U.S. 322, 334 (1979) (quoting *Toomer v. Witsell*, 334 U.S. 385, 402 (1948)). *See also Baldwin v. Montana Fish and Game Comm'n*, 436 U.S. 371, 384–387 (1978); *Douglas v. Seacoast Products, Inc.*, 431 U.S. 265, 284–285 (1977). In *Hughes* the Court found the State's interests insufficient to sustain a ban on the interstate transfer of natural minnows seined from waters within the State.

Appellee insists, however, that Nebraska water is distinguishable from other natural resources. The surface owner who withdraws Nebraska ground water enjoys a lesser ownership interest in the water than the captor of game birds in Connecticut or minnows in Oklahoma or ground water in Texas, for in *Geer, Hughes*, and *City of Altus* the State permitted intrastate trade in the natural resources once they were captured. Although appellee's greater ownership interest may not be irrelevant to Commerce Clause analysis, it does not absolutely remove Nebraska ground water from such scrutiny. For appellee's argument is still based on the legal fiction of state ownership. The fiction is illustrated by municipal water supply arrangements pursuant to which ground water is withdrawn from rural areas and transferred to urban areas. Such arrangements are permitted in Nebraska, *see Metropolitan Utilities District v. Merritt Beach Co.*, 179 Neb. 783, 140 N.W.2d 626 (1966), but the Nebraska Supreme Court distinguished them on the ground that the transferor was only permitted to charge as a price for the water his costs of distribution and not the value of the water itself. 208 Neb. at 708, 305 N.W. 2d, at 618. Unless demand is greater than supply, however, this reasoning does not distinguish minnows, the price of which presumably is derived from the costs of seining and of transporting the catch to market. Even in cases of shortage, in which the seller of the natural resource can demand a price that exceeds his costs, the State's rate structure that requires the price to be cost-justified is economically comparable to price regulation. A State's power to regulate prices or rates has never been thought to depend on public ownership of the controlled commodity. It would be anomalous if federal power to regulate economic transactions in natural resources depended on the characterization of the payment as compensation for distribution services, on the one hand, or as the price of goods, on the other. *Cf. In re Rahrer*, 140 U.S. 545, 558 (1891).

The second asserted distinction is that water, unlike other natural resources, is essential for human survival. Appellee, and the *amici curiae* that are vitally interested in conserving and preserving scarce water resources in the arid Western States, have convincingly demonstrated the desirability of state and local management of ground water. But the States' interests clearly have an interstate dimension. Although water is indeed essential for human survival, studies indicate that over 80% of our water supplies is used for agricultural purposes. The agricultural markets supplied by irrigated farms are worldwide. They provide the archetypical example of commerce among the several States for which the Framers of our Constitution intended to authorize federal regulation. The multistate character of the Ogallala aquifer — underlying appellants' tracts of land in Colorado and Nebraska, as well as parts of Texas, New Mexico, Oklahoma, and Kansas — confirms the view that there is a significant federal interest in conservation as well as in fair allocation of this diminishing resource. *Cf. Arizona v. California*, 373 U.S. 546 (1963).

The Western States' interests, and their asserted superior competence, in conserving and preserving scarce water resources are not irrelevant in the Commerce Clause inquiry. Nor is appellee's claim to public ownership without significance. Like Congress' deference to state water law, *see infra*, these factors inform the determination whether the burdens on commerce imposed by state ground water regulation are reasonable or unreasonable. But appellee's claim that Nebraska ground water is not an article of commerce goes too far: it would not only exempt Nebraska ground water regulation from burden-on-commerce analysis, but would curtail also the affirmative power of Congress to implement its own policies concerning such regulation. *See Philadelphia v. New Jersey*, 437 U.S. 617, 621–623 (1978). If Congress chooses to legislate in this area under its commerce power, its regulation need not be more limited in Nebraska than in Texas and States with similar property laws. Ground water overdraft is a national problem and Congress has the power to deal with it on that scale.

II

Our conclusion that water is an article of commerce raises, but does not answer, the question whether the Nebraska statute is unconstitutional. For the existence of unexercised federal regulatory power does not foreclose state regulation of its water resources, of the uses of water within the State, or indeed, of interstate commerce in water. *Southern Pacific Co. v. Arizona ex rel. Sullivan*, 325 U.S. 761, 766–767 (1945); *United States v. South-Eastern Underwriters Assn.*, 322 U.S. 533, 548–549 (1944); *Cooley v. Board of Wardens*, 12 How. 299, 319 (1852). Determining the validity of state statutes affecting interstate commerce requires a more careful inquiry.

"Where the statute regulates evenhandedly to effectuate a legitimate local public interest, and its effects on interstate commerce are only incidental, it will be upheld unless the burden imposed on such commerce is clearly excessive in relation to the putative local benefits. If a legitimate local purpose is found, then the question becomes one of degree. And the extent of the burden that will be tolerated will of course depend on the nature of the local interest involved, and on whether it could be promoted as well with a lesser impact on interstate activities." *Pike v. Bruce Church, Inc.*, 397 U.S. 137, 142 (1970) (citation omitted).

The only purpose that appellee advances for § 46-613.01 is to conserve and preserve diminishing sources of ground water. The purpose is unquestionably legitimate and highly important and the other aspects of Nebraska's ground water regulation demonstrate that it is genuine. Appellants' land in Nebraska is located within the boundaries of the Upper Republican Ground Water Control Area, which was designated as such by the Director of the Nebraska Department of Water Resources based upon a determination that there is "[a]n inadequate ground water supply to meet present or reasonably foreseeable needs for beneficial use of such water supply." Neb. Rev. Stat. § 46-658(1) (Supp. 1981); see App. 56–60. Pursuant to § 46-666(1), the Upper Republican Natural Resources District has promulgated special rules and regulations governing ground water withdrawal and use. See App. 61–82. The rules and regulations define as "critical" those townships in the control area in which the annual decline of the ground water table exceeds a fixed percentage; appellants' Nebraska tract is located within a critical township. The rules and regulations require the installation of flow meters on every well within the control area, specify the amount of water per acre that may be used for irrigation, and set the spacing that is required between wells. They also strictly limit the intrastate transfer of ground water: transfers are only permitted between lands controlled by the same ground water user, and all transfers must be approved by the District Board of Directors. Id., at 68–69.

The State's interest in conservation and preservation of ground water is advanced by the first three conditions in § 46-613.01 for the withdrawal of water for an interstate transfer. Those requirements are "that the withdrawal of the ground water requested is reasonable, is not contrary to the conservation and use of ground water, and is not otherwise detrimental to the public welfare." Although Commerce Clause concerns are implicated by the fact that § 46-613.01 applies to interstate transfers but not to intrastate transfers, there are legitimate reasons for the special treatment accorded requests to transport ground water across state lines. Obviously, a State that imposes severe withdrawal and use restrictions on its own citizens is not discriminating against interstate commerce when it seeks to prevent the uncontrolled transfer of water out of the State. An exemption for interstate transfers would be inconsistent with the ideal of evenhandedness in regulation. At least in the area in which appellants' Nebraska tract is located, the first three standards of § 46-613.01 may well be no more strict in application than the limitations upon intrastate transfers imposed by the Upper Republican Natural Resources District.

Moreover, in the absence of a contrary view expressed by Congress, we are reluctant to condemn as unreasonable measures taken by a State to conserve and preserve for its own citizens this vital resource in times of severe shortage. Our reluctance stems from the "confluence of [several] realities." Hicklin v. Orbeck, 437 U.S. 518, 534 (1978). First, a State's power to regulate the use of water in times and places of shortage for the purpose of protecting the health of its citizens — and not simply the health of its economy — is at the core of its police power. For Commerce Clause purposes, we have long recognized a difference between economic protectionism, on the one hand, and health and safety regulation, on the other. See H. P. Hood & Sons v. Du Mond, 336 U.S. 525, 533 (1949). Second, the legal expectation that under certain circumstances each State may restrict water within its borders has been fostered over the years not only by our equitable apportionment decrees, see, e.g., Wyoming v. Colorado, 353 U.S. 953 (1957), but also by the negotiation and enforcement of interstate compacts. Our law therefore has recognized the relevance of state boundaries in the allocation of scarce water resources. Third, although appellee's claim to public ownership of Nebraska ground water cannot justify a total denial of federal regulatory power, it may support a limited preference for its own citizens in the utilization of the resource. *See Hicklin v. Orbeck, supra*, at 533–534. In this regard, it is relevant that appellee's claim is logically more substantial than claims to public ownership of other natural resources. *See supra*, at 950–951. Finally, given appellee's conservation efforts, the continuing availability of ground water in Nebraska is not simply happenstance; the natural resource has some indicia of a good publicly produced and owned in which a State may favor its own citizens in times of shortage. *See Reeves, Inc. v. Stake*, 447 U.S. 429 (1980); *cf. Philadelphia v. New Jersey*, 437 U.S. at 627–628, and *Baldwin v. Montana Fish and Game Comm'n*, 436 U.S. 371 (1978). A facial examination of the first three conditions set forth in § 46-613.01 does not, therefore, indicate that they impermissibly burden interstate commerce. Appellants, indeed, seem to concede their reasonableness.

Appellants, however, do challenge the requirement that "the state in which the water is to be used grants reciprocal rights to withdraw and transport ground water from that state for use in the State of Nebraska" — the reciprocity provision that troubled the Chief Justice of the Nebraska Supreme Court. Because Colorado forbids the exportation of its ground water, the reciprocity provision operates as an explicit barrier to commerce between the two States. The State therefore bears the initial burden of demonstrating a close fit between the reciprocity requirement and its asserted local purpose. *Hughes v. Oklahoma*, 441 U.S., at 336; *Dean Milk Co. v. City of Madison*, 340 U.S. 349, 354 (1951).

The reciprocity requirement fails to clear this initial hurdle. For there is no evidence that this restriction is narrowly tailored to the conservation and preservation rationale. Even though the supply of water in a particular well may be abundant, or perhaps even excessive, and even though the most beneficial use of that water might be in another State, such water may not be shipped into a neighboring State that does not permit its water to be used in Nebraska. If it could be shown that the State as a whole suffers a water shortage, that the intrastate transportation of water from areas of abundance to areas of shortage is feasible regardless of distance, and that the importation of water from adjoining States would roughly compensate for any exportation to those States, then the conservation and preservation purpose might be credibly advanced for the reciprocity provision. A demonstrably arid State conceivably might be able to marshal evidence to establish a close means-end relationship between even a total ban on the exportation of water and a purpose to conserve and preserve water. Appellee, however, does not claim that such evidence exists. We therefore are not persuaded that the reciprocity requirement — when superimposed on the first three restrictions in the statute — significantly advances the State's legitimate conservation and preservation interest; it surely is not narrowly tailored to serve that purpose. The reciprocity requirement does not survive the "strictest scrutiny" reserved for facially discriminatory legislation. *Hughes v. Oklahoma, supra*, at 337.

III

[The final portion of the opinion, in which the state of Nebraska argued that the Congress had authorized the states to impose burdens on interstate commerce in groundwater, is omitted.]

The reciprocity requirement of Neb. Rev. Stat. § 46-613.01 violates the Commerce Clause. We leave to the state courts the question whether the invalid portion is severable. The judgment of the Nebraska Supreme Court is reversed, and the case is remanded for proceedings not inconsistent with this opinion.

It is so ordered.

DISSENT: JUSTICE REHNQUIST, with whom JUSTICE O'CONNOR joins, dissenting.

. . . .

. . . [A] State may so regulate a natural resource as to preclude that resource from attaining the status of an "article of commerce" for the purposes of the negative impact of the Commerce Clause. It is difficult, if not impossible, to conclude that "commerce" exists in an item that cannot be reduced to possession under state law and in which the State recognizes only a usufructuary right. "Commerce" cannot exist in a natural resource that cannot be sold, rented, traded, or transferred, but only *used*.

Of course, a State may not discriminate against interstate commerce when it regulates even such a resource. If the State allows indiscriminate intrastate commercial dealings in a particular resource, it may have a difficult task proving that an outright prohibition on interstate commercial dealings is not such a discrimination. I had thought that this was the basis for this Court's decisions in *Hughes v. Oklahoma*, 441 U.S. 322 (1979), *Pennsylvania v. West Virginia*, 262 U.S. 553 (1923), and *West v. Kansas Natural Gas Co.*, 221 U.S. 229 (1911). In each case, the State permitted a natural resource to be reduced to private possession, permitted an intrastate market to exist in that resource, and either barred *interstate* commerce entirely or granted its residents a commercial preference.

By contrast, Nebraska so regulates ground water that it cannot be said that the State permits any "commerce," intrastate or interstate, to exist in this natural resource. As with almost all of the Western States, Nebraska does not recognize an absolute ownership interest in ground water, but grants landowners only a right *to use ground water on the land from which it has been extracted*. Moreover, the landowner's right to use ground water is limited. Nebraska landowners may not extract ground water "in excess of a reasonable and beneficial use upon the land in which he owns, especially of such use is injurious to others who have substantial rights to the waters, and if the natural underground supply is insufficient for all owners, each is entitled to a reasonable proportion of the whole." *Olson v. City of Wahoo*, 124 Neb. 802, 811, 248 N.W. 304, 308 (1933). With the exception of municipal water systems, Nebraska forbids any transportation of ground water off the land owned or controlled by the person who has appropriated the water from its subterranean source. 208 Neb. 703, 710, 305 N.W.2d 614, 619 (1981). *See* App. 68–69.

Nebraska places additional restrictions on ground-water users within certain areas, such as the portion of appellants' land situated in Nebraska, where the shortage of ground water is determined to be critical. Water users in appellants' district are permitted only to irrigate the acreage irrigated in 1977, or the average number of acres irrigated between 1972 and 1976, whichever is greater, and must obtain permission from the water district's board before any additional acreage may be placed under irrigation. The amount of ground water that may be extracted is strictly limited on an acre-inch-per-irrigated-acre basis. There are also detailed regulations as to the spacing of wells and the use and operation of flow meters. *Id.*, at 71–82.

Since Nebraska recognizes only a limited right to use ground water on land owned by the appropriator, it cannot be said that "commerce" in ground water exists as far as Nebraska is concerned. Therefore, it cannot be said that Neb. Rev. Stat. § 46-613.01 (1978) either discriminates against, or "burdens," interstate commerce. Section 46-613.01 is simply a regulation of the landowner's *right to use* ground water extracted from lands he owns within Nebraska. Unlike the Court, I cannot agree that Nebraska's limitation upon a landowner's right to extract water from his land situated in Nebraska *for his own use* on land he owns in an adjoining State runs afoul of Congress' unexercised authority to regulate interstate commerce.

NOTES AND QUESTIONS

1. For dormant Commerce Clause purposes, "the practical effect of [a] statute must be evaluated not only by considering the consequences of the statute itself, but also by considering how the challenged statute may interact with the legitimate regulatory regimes of other States and what effect would arise if not one, but many or every, State adopted similar legislation." *Healy v. The Beer Institute, Inc.*, 491 U.S. 324, 336, 109 S. Ct. 2491 (1989).

2. An interesting wrinkle on the dormant Commerce Clause is the "market participant doctrine." Under the doctrine, sometimes called the market participation "exception," when a state or municipality is only participating as a private actor in a market, as distinct from regulating the market, the dormant Commerce Clause is inapplicable. Accordingly, when a state is merely spending its own funds or selling or purchasing a product, its actions are free from constitutional scrutiny on commerce clause grounds. *See, e.g., Reeves Inc. v. Stake*, 447 U.S. 429, 100 S. Ct. 2271 (1980) (a state regulation which restricted cement sales to in-state residents when the cement was produced in a state-owned plant did not violate the dormant Commerce Clause because the state was acting as a market participant). As a market participant, a governmental entity may impose burdens on interstate commerce, so long as the imposition is incidental to its commercial activity. Accordingly, a state's refusal to sell an item in the marketplace would not trigger dormant Commerce Clause invalidation. *See, e.g., South-Central Timber Dev., Inc. v. Wunnicke*, 467 U.S. 82 (1984) ("[T]he limit of the market participant doctrine must be that it allows a state to impose burdens on commerce within the market in which it is a participant, but allows it to go no further.").

The market participation doctrine is especially apt in flow control cases because municipalities often establish their waste disposal programs by entering into contractual arrangements with solid waste haulers or processors. Municipalities thereby participate in the market. The core question is whether a governmental entity's use of a contract as the mechanism to accomplish a governmental duty, as distinct from using an ordinance or statute, relieves the governmental entity from dormant Commerce Clause restraints. The Court of Appeals for the Second Circuit held that it could. *Incorporated Villages of Rockville Centre v. Town of Hempstead*, 196 F.3d 395 (2d Cir. 1999) (use of contracts held to constitute market participation, even if the contracts were formed because of municipalities' threats of regulation); *accord, SSC Corp v. Town of Smithtown*, 66 F.3d 502 (2d Cir. 1995) (a municipality's contractual arrangement with private haulers to take all garbage to the municipal incinerator, the tipping fee from which would go to the haulers, was protected by the market participant exception).

Had the Town of Hempstead used an ordinance rather than a contract to bind the Villages, would it have lost the case? The answer is maybe. *See, e.g., Huish Detergents, Inc. v. Warren County*, 214 F.3d 707 (6th Cir. 2000): "We agree . . . that the County could have achieved the same result, without implicating the Commerce Clause, by having [the hauler] as its exclusive waste hauler using public funds to pay for the service. But the County rejected that strategy, opting instead to use its regulatory leverage by forcing residents to do the purchasing for it." *Id.* at 717.

For a different take on the issues, *see, e.g., USA Recycling, Inc. v. Town of Babylon*, 66 F.3d 1272 (2d Cir. 1995), *cert. denied*, 517 U.S. 1135, 116 S. Ct. 1419 (1996). In *Babylon*, the Town hired one private company to pick up all commercial garbage and another to operate the incinerator where the garbage is burned. Costs for these services were payable out of property taxes and user fees for generators of garbage. Collections of commercial garbage by other companies was prohibited. The court characterized this arrangement as one that took over the market, and, therefore, was market regulation, not participation (participants do not have the power to eliminate the market in which they participate). Still, the court found no dormant Commerce Clause violation. First, there was no discrimination against interstate commerce, as the scheme did not favor in-state over out-of-state haulers. Second, there was no undue burden on interstate commerce: "[a]lthough the Town is now the lone provider of garbage collection services in the District, it does so as a local government providing services to those within its jurisdiction, not as a business selling to a captive consumer base." The court distinguished *Carbone* on the facts. In *Carbone*, local garbage haulers were required to buy processing or disposal services from a local facility. In *Babylon*, "local businesses [did] not buy services from anyone. Instead, the Town unilaterally provides garbage service to everyone in the District[.] In short, because Babylon is not selling anything, it cannot be considered to be a favored single local proprietor as in *Carbone*. . . ." *Id.* at 1283.

Should the Supreme Court have viewed the municipality in *Carbone* as a market participant?

The market participant doctrine has no application in state taxation cases. *New Energy Company of Indiana v. Limbach*, 486 U.S. 269, 108 S. Ct. 1803 (1988). Do you see why?

3. State taxation cases are treated less rigorously than police power cases under the undue burden prong of the dormant Commerce Clause. In *Commonwealth Edison Company v. Montana*, 453 U.S. 609, 101, S. Ct. 2946 (1981), the Court allowed a coal severance tax to stand even though the burden of the state's taxation fell disproportionately on out-of-state entities. The burden so fell because 90% of the coal mined in Montana was shipped for use outside Montana; thus, in real terms, the tax was paid by out-of-state consumers. The tax was the same for all coal mined in Montana, so there was no facial discrimination against interstate commerce.

The Court upheld the provision, applying a four-part test. Under this test, a tax will pass dormant Commerce Clause scrutiny if (a) it is "applied to an activity with a substantial nexus to the taxing state," (b) it is "fairly apportioned," (c) it "does not discriminate against interstate commerce," and (d) it is "fairly related to the services provided by the state." *Complete Auto Transit, Inc. v. Brady*, 430 U.S. 274, 279, 97 S. Ct. 1076, 1079 (1977). The Court subsequently made clear that proceeds from such taxes may ordinarily be used for any purpose, not merely those related to the taxable event. *Oklahoma Tax Comm'n v. Jefferson Lines, Inc.*, 514 U.S. 175, 115 S. Ct. 1331 (1995).

For a summary of cases applying the *Complete Auto Transit* test, see *Goldberg v. Sweet*, 488 U.S. 252, 260, n.12, 109 S. Ct. 582, 588, n.12 (1989).

4. For an interesting argument maintaining the absolute illegitimacy of the dormant Commerce Clause, see Redish and Nugent, *The Dormant Commerce Clause and the Constitutional Balance of Federalism*, 1987 Duke L.J. 569 (1987).

D. RIGHTS OF INDIVIDUALS

[1] EMINENT DOMAIN

Eminent domain is the power "to take private property for public use by the state, municipalities, and private persons authorized to exercise functions of public character." *Black's Law Dictionary* 523 (6th ed. 1990). The right is held by every "independent government," and since it is a matter of sovereignty, it need not be affirmed by constitutional declaration. *Boom Co. v. Patterson*, 98 U.S. 403 (1878). Constitutions, rather, serve only to limit the power. *Id.* The Takings Clause of the 5th Amendment to the U.S. Constitution, which provides that private property shall not "be taken for public use without just compensation," is the major constitutional limitation. The following case is the major United States Supreme Court statement on the meaning of the term "public use."

HAWAII HOUSING AUTHORITY v. MIDKIFF

467 U.S. 229, 104 S. Ct. 2321 (1984)

JUDGES: O'CONNOR, J., delivered the opinion of the Court, in which all other Members joined, except MARSHALL, J., who took no part in the consideration or decision of the cases.

The Fifth Amendment of the United States Constitution provides, in pertinent part, that "private property [shall not] be taken for public use, without just compensation." These cases present the question whether the Public Use Clause of that Amendment, made applicable to the States through the Fourteenth Amendment, prohibits the State of Hawaii from taking, with just compensation, title in real property from lessors and transferring it to lessees in order to reduce the concentration of ownership of fees simple in the State. We conclude that it does not.

I.

A

The Hawaiian Islands were originally settled by Polynesian immigrants from the western Pacific. These settlers developed an economy around a feudal land tenure system in which one island high chief, the ali'i nui, controlled the land and assigned it for development to certain subchiefs. The subchiefs would then reassign the land to other lower ranking chiefs, who would administer the land and govern the farmers and other tenants working it. All land was held at the will of the ali'i nui and eventually had to be returned to his trust. There was no private ownership of land. [citation omitted.]

Beginning in the early 1800's, Hawaiian leaders and American settlers repeatedly attempted to divide the lands of the kingdom among the crown, the chiefs, and the common people. These efforts proved largely unsuccessful, however, and the land remained in the hands of a few. In the mid-1960's, after extensive hearings, the Hawaii Legislature discovered that, while the State and Federal Governments owned almost 49% of the State's land, another 47% was in the hands of only 72 private landowners. . . . The legislature further found that 18 landholders, with tracts of 21,000 acres or more, owned more than 40% of this land and that on Oahu, the most urbanized of the islands, 22 landowners owned 72.5% of the fee simple titles. *Id.* at 32–33. The legislature concluded that concentrated land ownership was responsible for skewing the State's residential fee simple market, inflating land prices, and injuring the public tranquility and welfare.

To redress these problems, the legislature decided to compel the large landowners to break up their estates. The legislature considered requiring large landowners to sell lands which they were leasing to homeowners. However, the landowners strongly resisted this scheme, pointing out the significant federal tax liabilities they would incur. Indeed, the landowners claimed that the federal tax laws were the primary reason they previously had chosen to lease, and not sell, their lands. Therefore, to accommodate the needs of both lessors and lessees, the Hawaii Legislature enacted the Land Reform Act of 1967 (Act), Haw. Rev. Stat., ch. 516, which created a mechanism for condemning residential tracts and for transferring ownership of the condemned fees simple to existing lessees. By condemning the land in question, the Hawaii Legislature intended to make the land sales involuntary, thereby making the federal tax consequences less severe while still facilitating the redistribution of fees simple. [citation omitted.]

Under the Act's condemnation scheme, tenants living on single-family residential lots within developmental tracts at least five acres in size are entitled to ask the Hawaii Housing Authority (HHA) to condemn the property on which they live. Haw. Rev. Stat. §§ 516-1(2), (11), 516–22 (1977). When 25 eligible tenants, or tenants on half the lots in the tract, whichever is less, file appropriate applications, the Act authorizes HHA to hold a public hearing to determine whether acquisition by the State of all or part of the tract will "effectuate the public purposes" of the Act. § 516-22. If HHA finds that these public purposes will be served, it is authorized to designate some or all of the lots in the tract for acquisition. It then acquires, at prices set either by condemnation trial or by negotiation between lessors and lessees, the former fee owners' full "right, title, and interest" in the land. § 516-25.

After compensation has been set, HHA may sell the land titles to tenants who have applied for fee simple ownership. HHA is authorized to lend these tenants up to 90% of the purchase price, and it may condition final transfer on a right of first refusal for the first 10 years following sale. §§ 516-30, 516-34, 516-35. If HHA does not sell the lot to the tenant residing there, it may lease the lot or sell it to someone else, provided that public notice has been given. § 516-28. However, HHA may not sell to any one purchaser, or lease to any one tenant, more than one lot, and it may not operate for profit. §§ 516-28, 516-32. In practice, funds to satisfy the condemnation awards have been supplied entirely by lessees. . . . While the Act authorizes HHA to issue bonds and appropriate funds for acquisition, no bonds have issued and HHA has not supplied any funds for condemned lots. *See ibid.*

B

In April 1977, HHA held a public hearing concerning the proposed acquisition of some of appellees' lands. HHA made the statutorily required finding that acquisition of appellees' lands would effectuate the public purposes of the Act. Then, in October 1978, it directed appellees to negotiate with certain lessees concerning the sale of the designated properties. Those negotiations failed, and HHA subsequently ordered appellees to submit to compulsory arbitration.

Rather than comply with the compulsory arbitration order, appellees filed suit, in February 1979, in United States District Court, asking that the Act be declared unconstitutional and that its enforcement be enjoined. The District Court temporarily restrained the State from proceeding against appellees' estates. Three months later, while declaring the compulsory arbitration and compensation formulae provisions of the Act unconstitutional, the District Court refused preliminarily to enjoin appellants from conducting the statutory designation and condemnation proceedings. Finally, in December 1979, it granted partial summary judgment to appellants, holding the remaining portion of the Act constitutional under the Public Use Clause. *See* 483 F.Supp. 62 (Haw. 1979). The District Court found that the Act's goals were within the bounds of the State's police powers and that the means the legislature had chosen to serve those goals were not arbitrary, capricious, or selected in bad faith.

The Court of Appeals for the Ninth Circuit reversed. 702 F.2d 788 (1983). First, the Court of Appeals decided that the District Court had permissibly chosen not to abstain from the exercise of its jurisdiction. Then, the Court of Appeals determined that the Act could not pass the requisite judicial scrutiny of the Public Use Clause. It found that the transfers contemplated by the Act were unlike those of takings previously held to constitute "public uses" by this Court. The court further determined that the public purposes offered by the Hawaii Legislature were not deserving of judicial deference. The court concluded that the Act was simply "a naked attempt on the part of the state of Hawaii to take the private property of A and transfer it to B solely for B's private use and benefit." *Id.*, at 798. One judge dissented.

On applications of HHA and certain private appellants who had intervened below, this Court noted probable jurisdiction. 464 U.S. 932 (1983). We now reverse.

II

We begin with the question whether the District Court abused its discretion in not abstaining from the exercise of its jurisdiction. [This portion of the opinion is omitted].

III

The majority of the Court of Appeals next determined that the Act violates the "public use" requirement of the Fifth and Fourteenth Amendments. On this argument, however, we find ourselves in agreement with the dissenting judge in the Court of Appeals.

A

The starting point for our analysis of the Act's constitutionality is the Court's decision in *Berman v. Parker*, 348 U.S. 26 (1954). In *Berman*, the Court held constitutional the District of Columbia Redevelopment Act of 1945. That Act provided both for the comprehensive use of the eminent domain power to redevelop slum areas and for the possible sale or lease of the condemned lands to private interests. In discussing whether the takings authorized by that Act were for a "public use," *id.*, at 31, the Court stated:

> "We deal, in other words, with what traditionally has been known as the police power. An attempt to define its reach or trace its outer limits is fruitless, for each case must turn on its own facts. The definition is essentially the product of legislative determinations addressed to the purposes of government, purposes neither abstractly nor historically capable of complete definition. Subject to specific constitutional

limitations, when the legislature has spoken, the public interest has been declared in terms well-nigh conclusive. In such cases the legislature, not the judiciary, is the main guardian of the public needs to be served by social legislation, whether it be Congress legislating concerning the District of Columbia . . . or the States legislating concerning local affairs. . . . This principle admits of no exception merely because the power of eminent domain is involved. . . ." *Id.*, at 32 (citations omitted).

The Court explicitly recognized the breadth of the principle it was announcing, noting:

"Once the object is within the authority of Congress, the right to realize it through the exercise of eminent domain is clear. For the power of eminent domain is merely the means to the end. . . . Once the object is within the authority of Congress, the means by which it will be attained is also for Congress to determine. Here one of the means chosen is the use of private enterprise for redevelopment of the area. Appellants argue that this makes the project a taking from one businessman for the benefit of another businessman. But the means of executing the project are for Congress and Congress alone to determine, once the public purpose has been established." *Id.*, at 33.

The "public use" requirement is thus coterminous with the scope of a sovereign's police powers.

There is, of course, a role for courts to play in reviewing a legislature's judgment of what constitutes a public use, even when the eminent domain power is equated with the police power. But the Court in *Berman* made clear that it is "an extremely narrow" one. *Id.*, at 32. The Court in *Berman* cited with approval the Court's decision in *Old Dominion Co. v. United States*, 269 U.S. 55, 66 (1925), which held that deference to the legislature's "public use" determination is required "until it is shown to involve an impossibility." The *Berman* Court also cited to *United States ex rel. TVA v. Welch*, 327 U.S. 546, 552 (1946), which emphasized that "[any] departure from this judicial restraint would result in courts deciding on what is and is not a governmental function and in their invalidating legislation on the basis of their view on that question at the moment of decision, a practice which has proved impracticable in other fields." In short, the Court has made clear that it will not substitute its judgment for a legislature's judgment as to what constitutes a public use "unless the use be palpably without reasonable foundation." *United States v. Gettysburg Electric R. Co.*, 160 U.S. 668, 680 (1896).

To be sure, the Court's cases have repeatedly stated that "one person's property may not be taken for the benefit of another private person without a justifying public purpose, even though compensation be paid." *Thompson v. Consolidated Gas Corp.*, 300 U.S. 55, 80 (1937). *See, e.g., Cincinnati v. Vester*, 281 U.S. 439, 447 (1930); *Madisonville Traction Co. v. St. Bernard Mining Co.*, 196 U.S. 239, 251–252 (1905); *Fallbrook Irrigation District v. Bradley*, 164 U.S. 112, 159 (1896). Thus, in *Missouri Pacific R. Co. v. Nebraska*, 164 U.S. 403 (1896), where the "order in question was not, and was not claimed to be, . . . a taking of private property for a public use under the right of eminent domain," *id.* at 416, the Court invalidated a compensated taking of property for lack of a justifying public purpose. But where the exercise of the eminent domain power is rationally related to a conceivable public purpose, the Court has never held a compensated taking to be proscribed by the Public Use Clause. *See Berman v. Parker, supra; Rindge Co. v. Los Angeles*, 262 U.S. 700 (1923); *Block v. Hirsh*, 256 U.S. 135 (1921); *cf. Thompson v. Consolidated Gas Corp., supra* (invalidating an *uncompensated* taking).

On this basis, we have no trouble concluding that the Hawaii Act is constitutional. The people of Hawaii have attempted, much as the settlers of the original 13 Colonies did, to reduce the perceived social and economic evils of a land oligopoly traceable to their monarchs. The land oligopoly has, according to the Hawaii Legislature, created artificial deterrents to the normal functioning of the State's residential land market and forced thousands of individual homeowners to lease, rather than buy, the land underneath their homes. Regulating oligopoly and the evils associated with it is a classic exercise of a State's police powers. *See Exxon Corp. v. Governor of Maryland*, 437 U.S. 117 (1978); *Block v. Hirsh, supra; see also People of Puerto Rico v. Eastern Sugar Associates*, 156 F.2d 316 (CA1), *cert. denied*, 329 U.S. 772 (1946). We cannot disapprove of Hawaii's exercise of this power.

Nor can we condemn as irrational the Act's approach to correcting the land oligopoly problem. The Act presumes that when a sufficiently large number of persons declare that they are willing but unable to buy lots at fair prices the land market is malfunctioning. When such a malfunction is signalled, the Act authorizes HHA to condemn lots in the relevant tract. The Act limits the number of lots any one tenant can purchase and authorizes HHA to use public funds to ensure that the market dilution goals will be achieved. This is a comprehensive and rational approach to identifying and correcting market failure.

Of course, this Act, like any other, may not be successful in achieving its intended goals. But "whether *in fact* the provision will accomplish its objectives is not the question: the [constitutional requirement] is satisfied if . . . the . . . [state] Legislature *rationally could have believed* that the [Act] would promote its objective." *Western & Southern Life Ins. Co. v. State Bd. of Equalization*, 451 U.S. 648, 671–672 (1981); *see also Minnesota v. Clover Leaf Creamery Co.*, 449 U.S. 456, 466 (1981); *Vance v. Bradley*, 440 U.S. 93, 112 (1979). When the legislature's purpose is legitimate and its means are not irrational, our cases make clear that empirical debates over the wisdom of takings — no less than debates over the wisdom of other kinds of socioeconomic legislation — are not to be carried out in the federal courts. Redistribution of fees simple to correct deficiencies in the market determined by the state legislature to be attributable to land oligopoly is a rational exercise of the eminent domain power. Therefore, the Hawaii statute must pass the scrutiny of the Public Use Clause.

B

. . . .

The mere fact that property taken outright by eminent domain is transferred in the first instance to private beneficiaries does not condemn that taking as having only a private purpose. The Court long ago rejected any literal requirement that condemned property be put into use for the general public. "It is not essential that the entire community, nor even any considerable portion, . . . directly enjoy or participate in any improvement in order [for it] to constitute a public use." *Rindge Co. v. Los Angeles*, 262 U.S. at 707. "[What] in its immediate aspect [is] only a private transaction may . . . be raised by its class or character to a public affair." *Block v. Hirsh*, 256 U.S. at 155. As the unique way titles were held in Hawaii skewed the land market, exercise of the power of eminent domain was justified. The Act advances its purposes without the State's taking actual possession of the land. In such cases, government does not itself have to use property to legitimate the taking; it is only the taking's purpose, and not its mechanics, that must pass scrutiny under the Public Use Clause.

Similarly, the fact that a state legislature, and not the Congress, made the public use determination does not mean that judicial deference is less appropriate.[7] Judicial deference is required because, in our system of government, legislatures are better able to assess what public purposes should be advanced by an exercise of the taking power. State legislatures are as capable as Congress of making such determinations within their respective spheres of authority. *See Berman v. Parker*, 348 U.S. at 32. Thus, if a legislature, state or federal, determines there are substantial reasons for an exercise of the taking power, courts must defer to its determination that the taking will serve a public use.

The State of Hawaii has never denied that the Constitution forbids even a compensated taking of property when executed for no reason other than to confer a private benefit on a particular private party. A purely private taking could not withstand the scrutiny of the public use requirement; it would serve no legitimate purpose of government and would thus be void. But no purely private taking is involved in these cases. The Hawaii Legislature enacted its Land Reform Act not to benefit a particular class of identifiable individuals but to attack certain perceived evils of concentrated property ownership in Hawaii — a legitimate public purpose. Use of the condemnation power to achieve this purpose is not irrational. Since we assume for purposes of these appeals that the weighty demand of just compensation has been met, the requirements of the Fifth and Fourteenth Amendments have been satisfied. Accordingly, we reverse the judgment of the Court of Appeals, and remand these cases for further proceedings in conformity with this opinion.

It is so ordered.

JUSTICE MARSHALL took no part in the consideration or decision of these cases.

---

[7] It is worth noting that the Fourteenth Amendment does not itself contain an independent "public use" requirement. Rather, that requirement is made binding on the States only by incorporation of the Fifth Amendment's Eminent Domain Clause through the Fourteenth Amendment's Due Process Clause. *See Chicago, B. & Q. R. Co. v. Chicago*, 166 U.S. 226 (1897). It would be ironic to find that state legislation is subject to greater scrutiny under the incorporated "public use" requirement than is congressional legislation under the express mandate of the Fifth Amendment.

NOTES AND QUESTIONS

1. In *Midkiff*, the Court reduced the eminent domain power to the status of an alternate means to accomplish goals otherwise achievable by the police power. If an end may be sought by the police power, so also may it be sought by the eminent domain power. The case establishes as well that an alternative private use can qualify as a public use, and that courts will grant substantial deference on these questions to the decisions of governmental entities exercising the eminent domain power.

As a net result of all of this, challenges for failure to satisfy the public use requirement are prone to failure. Assume, for example, that a city with eminent domain authority is about to lose its National Football League franchise. Is it constitutional for the city to use eminent domain power to take title to the franchise in order to keep the football team in the city? *See City of Oakland v. Oakland Raiders*, 32 Cal. 3d 60, 646 P.2d 835 (1982) (yes).

2. Since it is extremely difficult to overturn an exercise of eminent domain authority on public use grounds, the bulk of litigation focuses on the issue of just compensation. The questions are (1) what harms qualify for compensation? and (2) how should "just compensation" be measured? As a general matter, courts have held that just compensation is fair market value (as distinct from replacement value) of the affected property. What is important is what the holder of property rights lost, not what the taker gained. *Boston Chamber of Commerce v. Boston*, 217 U.S. 189, 195, 30 S. Ct. 459 (1910).

[2] THE TAKINGS CLAUSE

As noted at the beginning of this section, the Takings Clause of the 5th Amendment to the federal Constitution provides that private property shall not "be taken for public use without just compensation. U.S. Constitution, Amendment V.

In its earliest deliberations, the United States Supreme Court held the Clause to be applicable in the classic circumstance, that is, when the federal government exercises eminent domain power. But the Court was soon called upon to consider whether the Clause applied as well to exercises of governmental authority other than eminent domain that caused the same kinds of harmful consequences to affected landowners. As soon as it had the opportunity to so hold, it did so. Thus, for example, in *Pumpelly v. Green Bay Co.*, 80 U.S. 166 (1871), the Court found the Takings Clause to apply when government flooded private land, stating that:

> . . . [i]t would be a very curious and unsatisfactory result . . . that if the government refrains from the absolute conversion of real property to the uses of the public it can destroy its value entirely, can inflict irreparable and permanent injury to any extent, can, in effect, subject it to total destruction without making any compensation, because, in the narrowest sense of that word, it is not taken for the public use.

Id. at 177–78.

The Court confirmed its ruling in *Pumpelly,* a state law case in which the Court was discussing the Wisconsin Constitution, in a subsequent flooding case entitled *United States v. Lynah*, 188 U.S. 445, 23 S. Ct. 349 (1903). It later extended the principle to cases where flooding involved only a portion of a parcel of land and even when the flooding was recurring rather than permanent. *United States v. Cress*, 243 U.S. 316, 328, 37 S. Ct. 380, 385 (1917) (taking a "partial" interest, a *de facto* easement interest over a portion of the land, meant only that less than a total divesting of property rights had occurred).

These matters settled, the Court moved to examine whether the Clause applied to government action that did not result in the physical dispossession of landowners. In *United States v. Causby*, 328 U.S. 256, 66 S. Ct. 1062 (1946), the complained-of transgression was the federal government's practice of persistently flying bombers, transports, and fighter planes at low altitudes over the plaintiff's land. The aircraft noise and vibration were sufficient to destroy the landowner's chicken business and make normal residential use of the property impossible. The federal government argued its aircraft operations, which were conducted in navigable airspace, caused "incidental" injuries only. *Id.* at 260, 66 S.Ct. at 1065. But the Court, finding these invasions of airspace to be "in the same category" as permanent occupations of land, ruled the practice to violate the Takings Clause. *Id.* at 265, 66 S. Ct. at 1068.

A critical question still unresolved at this time, and the most important question in the scheme of things, was whether a mere governmental regulatory action, involving neither a physical dispossession nor an invasion, could implicate the Takings Clause. The Court concluded in the affirmative in its landmark decision in *Pennsylvania Coal v. Mahon*, 260 U.S. 393, 43 S. Ct. 158 (1922), a case aptly called the "Everest" of takings decisions. Bruce A. Ackerman, Private Property and the Constitution 156 (1977). In *Pennyslvania Coal*, the Pennsylvania Coal Co. complained of the Commonwealth of Pennsylvania's Kohler Act, which forbade mining of anthracite coal (with some exceptions) in such a way as to cause land subsidence and destruction of or harm to residential structures. The Company argued it had both contract and property rights to mine the coal even if doing so caused subsidence. Justice Oliver Wendell Holmes, writing for the majority, began his analysis with one of the most quoted passages in the literature of the Supreme Court:

> Government hardly could go on if to some extent values incident to property could not be diminished without paying for every such change in the general law. As long recognized, some values are enjoyed under an implied limitation and must yield to the police power. But obviously the implied limitation must have its limits, or the contract and due process clauses are gone. One fact for consideration in determining such limits is the extent of the diminution. When it reaches a certain magnitude, in most if not in all cases there must be an exercise of eminent domain and compensation to sustain the act. So the question depends upon the particular facts. The greatest weight is given to the judgment of the legislature, but it always is open to interested parties to contend that the legislature has gone beyond its constitutional power.

Id. at 412, 43 S. Ct. at 159.

Justice Holmes then reasoned that the Kohler Act, as applied in the case at bar, violated the Takings Clause. He reached his conclusion by using a balancing test. He found, first, that while there was a public interest served by the statute — the protection of a "single private house" from destruction — this interest did not warrant "much of this kind of interference" with the mining company's rights. In fact, the statute could not be justified, said Justice Holmes, as a protection of personal safety; a provision requiring notice of intent to mine would have accomplished this. Having so concluded, he reasoned that the statute substantially interfered with Pennsylvania Coal's property and contract rights, abolishing its estate in land and voiding its contract. Thus, "[I]f we were called upon to deal with the plaintiffs' position alone, we should think it clear that the statute does not disclose a public interest sufficient to warrant so extensive a destruction of the defendant's constitutionally protected rights."

Id. at 414, 43 S. Ct.at 159.

On the matter of the general validity of the Kohler Act, he said:

> It is our opinion that the act cannot be sustained as an exercise of the police power, so far as it affects the mining of coal under streets or cities in places where the right to mine such coal has been reserved. As said in a Pennsylvania case, "For practical purposes, the right to coal consists in the right to mine it." [citation omitted] What makes the right to mine coal valuable is that it can be exercised with profit. To make it commercially impracticable to mine certain coal has very nearly the same effect for constitutional purposes as appropriating or destroying it. This we think that we are warranted in assuming that the statute does.
>
> . . . .
>
> The general rule at least is, that while property may be regulated to a certain extent, if regulation goes too far it will be recognized as a taking. It may be doubted how far exceptional cases, like the blowing up of a house to stop a conflagration, go — and if they go beyond the general rule, whether they do not stand as much upon tradition as upon principle. *Bowditch v. Boston,* 101 U.S. 16. In general it is not plain that a man's misfortunes or necessities will justify his shifting the damages to his neighbor's shoulders. *Spade v. Lynn & Boston R.R. Co.,* 172 Mass. 488, 489. We are in danger of forgetting that a strong public desire to improve the public condition is not enough to warrant achieving the desire by a shorter cut than the constitutional way of paying for the change. As we already have said, this is a question of degree — and therefore cannot be disposed of by general propositions. But we regard this as going beyond any of the cases decided by this Court.

Id. at 414-16, 43 S. Ct. at 159-60.

Justice Holmes's views were vigorously opposed by another giant of the court, Justice Louis Brandeis. In dissent, Justice Brandeis argued that the

Kohler Act was an appropriate regulation of personal behavior and should not be subject to Takings Clause invalidation. In his view, prohibiting one person from destroying the residence of another was fully within the reach of the police power:

> Coal in place is land; and the right of the owner to use his land is not absolute. He may not so use it as to create a public nuisance; and uses, once harmless, may, owing to changed conditions, seriously threaten the public welfare. Whenever they do, the legislature has power to prohibit such uses without paying compensation; and the power to prohibit extends alike to the manner, the character and the purpose of the use. . . .
>
> Every restriction upon the use of property imposed in the exercise of the police power deprives the owner of some right theretofore enjoyed, and is, in that sense, an abridgment by the State of rights in property without making compensation. But restriction imposed to protect the public health, safety or morals from dangers threatened is not a taking. The restriction here in question is merely the prohibition of a noxious use. The property so restricted remains in the possession of its owner. The State does not appropriate it or make any use of it. The State merely prevents the owner from making a use which interferes with paramount rights of the public. Whenever the use prohibited ceases to be noxious, — as it may because of further change in local or social conditions, — the restriction will have to be removed and the owner will again be free to enjoy his property as heretofore.

Id. at 417, 43 S. Ct. at 161.

Justice Brandeis went on to argue that, even if the Takings Clause applied, still the diminution of value was not so great as to qualify this plaintiff for protection. The value of the coal the statute locked up, he argued, was potentially "negligible" when compared to the value of the land as a whole or even to the coal that could still be extracted despite the statute. *Id.* at 419, 43 S. Ct. at 161. He was also unconcerned about the interference with contractual relationships. In his view, the presence of a contractual arrangement between individuals could not be read to preclude an exercise of public power. *Id.* at 393, 43 S. Ct. at 162.

That is where takings law stood for about fifty years, as the Supreme Court entered into a long period of inactivity on the issue. In the thirty years since it again took up the issue, the Court has changed takings doctrine in ways never envisioned by Justices Holmes and Brandeis. In many ways, the changes have created more confusion than they have shed light: as one commenter put it, even before the Court roiled the pot yet again, figuring out when a taking of private property has occurred was "the lawyer's equivalent of the physicist's hunt for the quark." Charles Haar, Land-Use Planning 766 (3d ed. 1976), *quoted in Williamson County Regional Planning Comm'n v. Hamilton Bank*, 473 U.S. 172, 199, n.17, 105 S.Ct. 3108, 3123, n.17 (1985). In words of another commenter, takings law in the current day is simply a "mess." Daniel A. Farber, *Public Choice and Just Compensation*, 9 Const. Commentary 279 (1992).

In this section, we are concerned with what is known as "regulatory takings," those takings caused, if at all, by government regulation restricting the use of land. As a general matter, regulatory takings doctrine is divided into two branches. One branch deals with so-called "total takings," the condition that exists when government regulation strips land of all use or value. The second branch deals with the much larger universe of cases in which regulations have diminished use rights in, or value of, land, but not entirely.

LUCAS v. SOUTH CAROLINA COASTAL COUNCIL

505 U.S. 1003, 112 S.Ct. 2886 (1992)

JUDGES: SCALIA, J., delivered the opinion of the Court, in which REHNQUIST, C.J., and WHITE, O'CONNOR, and THOMAS, JJ., joined. KENNEDY, J., filed an opinion concurring in the judgment. BLACKMUN, J., and STEVENS, J., filed dissenting opinions. SOUTER, J., filed a separate statement.

JUSTICE SCALIA delivered the opinion of the Court.

In 1986, petitioner David H. Lucas paid $ 975,000 for two residential lots on the Isle of Palms in Charleston County, South Carolina, on which he intended to build single-family homes. In 1988, however, the South Carolina Legislature enacted the Beachfront Management Act, S.C. Code § 48-39-250 *et seq.* (Supp. 1990) (Act), which had the direct effect of barring petitioner from erecting any permanent habitable structures on his two parcels. *See* § 48-39-290(A). A state trial court found that this prohibition rendered Lucas's parcels "valueless." Pet. for Cert. 37. This case requires us to decide whether the Act's dramatic effect on the economic value of Lucas's lots accomplished a taking of private property under the Fifth and Fourteenth Amendments requiring the payment of "just compensation." U.S. Const., Amdt. 5.

I

A

South Carolina's expressed interest in intensively managing development activities in the so-called "coastal zone" dates from 1977 when, in the aftermath of Congress's passage of the federal Coastal Zone Management Act of 1972, 86 Stat. 1280, as amended, 16 U.S.C. § 1451 *et seq.*, the legislature enacted a Coastal Zone Management Act of its own. *See* S.C. Code § 48-39-10 *et seq.* (1987). In its original form, the South Carolina Act required owners of coastal zone land that qualified as a "critical area" (defined in the legislation to include beaches and immediately adjacent sand dunes, § 48-39-10(J)) to obtain a permit from the newly created South Carolina Coastal Council (respondent here) prior to committing the land to a "use other than the use the critical area was devoted to on [September 28, 1977]." § 48-39-130(A).

In the late 1970's, Lucas and others began extensive residential development of the Isle of Palms, a barrier island situated eastward of the City of Charleston. Toward the close of the development cycle for one residential subdivision known as "Beachwood East," Lucas in 1986 purchased the two lots at issue in this litigation for his own account. No portion of the lots, which were located approximately 300 feet from the beach, qualified as a "critical area" under the 1977 Act; accordingly, at the time Lucas acquired these parcels, he was not legally obliged to obtain a permit from the Council in advance of any development activity. His intention with respect to the lots was to do what the owners of the immediately adjacent parcels had already done: erect single-family residences. He commissioned architectural drawings for this purpose.

The Beachfront Management Act brought Lucas's plans to an abrupt end. Under that 1988 legislation, the Council was directed to establish a "baseline" connecting the landward-most "points of erosion . . . during the past forty years" in the region of the Isle of Palms that includes Lucas's lots. § 48-39-280(A)(2) (Supp. 1988). In action not challenged here, the Council fixed this baseline landward of Lucas's parcels. That was significant, for under the Act construction of occupable improvements was flatly prohibited seaward of a line drawn 20 feet landward of, and parallel to, the baseline, § 48-39-290(A) (Supp. 1988). The Act provided no exceptions.

B

Lucas promptly filed suit in the South Carolina Court of Common Pleas, contending that the Beachfront Management Act's construction bar effected a taking of his property without just compensation. Lucas did not take issue with the validity of the Act as a lawful exercise of South Carolina's police power, but contended that the Act's complete extinguishment of his property's value entitled him to compensation regardless of whether the legislature had acted in furtherance of legitimate police power objectives. Following a bench trial, the court agreed. Among its factual determinations was the finding that "at the time Lucas purchased the two lots, both were zoned for single-family residential construction and . . . there were no restrictions imposed upon such use of the property by either the State of South Carolina, the County of Charleston, or the Town of the Isle of Palms." . . . The trial court further found that the Beachfront Management Act decreed a permanent ban on construction insofar as Lucas's lots were concerned, and that this prohibition "deprived Lucas of any reasonable economic use of the lots, . . . eliminated the unrestricted right of use, and rendered them valueless." *Id.* at 37. The court thus concluded that Lucas's properties had been "taken" by operation of the Act, and it ordered respondent to pay "just compensation" in the amount of $1,232,387.50. *Id.* at 40.

The Supreme Court of South Carolina reversed. It found dispositive what it described as Lucas's concession "that the Beachfront Management Act [was] properly and validly designed to preserve . . . South Carolina's beaches." 304 S.C. 376, 379, 404 S.E.2d 895, 896 (1991). Failing an attack on the validity of the statute as such, the court believed itself bound to accept the "uncontested . . . findings" of the South Carolina legislature that new construction in the coastal zone — such as petitioner intended — threatened this public resource. *Id.* at 383, 404 S.E.2d, at 898. The Court ruled that when a regulation respecting the use of property is designed "to prevent serious public harm," *id.* at 383, 404 S.E.2d, at 899 (citing, inter alia, *Mugler v. Kansas*, 123 U.S. 623 (1887)), no compensation is owing under the Takings Clause regardless of the regulation's effect on the property's value.

Two justices dissented. They acknowledged that our *Mugler* line of cases recognizes governmental power to prohibit "noxious" uses of property — *i.e.,* uses of property akin to "public nuisances" — without having to pay compensation. But they would not have characterized the Beachfront Management Act's "primary purpose [as] the prevention of a nuisance." 304 S. Ct. at 395 (Harwell, J., dissenting). To the dissenters, the chief purposes of the legislation, among them the promotion of tourism and the creation of a "habitat for indigenous flora and fauna," could not fairly be compared to nuisance abatement. *Id.* at 396, 404 S.E.2d, at 906. As a consequence, they would have affirmed the trial court's conclusion that the Act's obliteration of the value of petitioner's lots accomplished a taking.

We granted certiorari.

. . . .

III

A

Prior to Justice Holmes' exposition in *Pennsylvania Coal Co. v. Mahon*, 260 U.S. 393 (1922), it was generally thought that the Takings Clause reached only a "direct appropriation" of property, *Legal Tender Cases*, 12 Wall. 457, 551 (1871), or the functional equivalent of a "practical ouster of [the owner's] possession." *Transportation Co. v. Chicago*, 99 U.S. 635, 642 (1879). *See also Gibson v. United States*, 166 U.S. 269, 275–276 (1897). Justice Holmes recognized in *Mahon,* however, that if the protection against physical appropriations of private property was to be meaningfully enforced, the government's power to redefine the range of interests included in the ownership of property was necessarily constrained by constitutional limits. 260 U.S., at 414–415. If, instead, the uses of private property were subject to unbridled, uncompensated qualification under the police power, "the natural tendency of human nature [would be] to extend the qualification more and more until at last private property disappeared." *Id.* at 415. These considerations gave birth in that case to the oft-cited maxim that, "while property may be regulated to a certain extent, if regulation goes too far it will be recognized as a taking." *Ibid.*

Nevertheless, our decision in *Mahon* offered little insight into when, and under what circumstances, a given regulation would be seen as going "too far" for purposes of the Fifth Amendment. In 70-odd years of succeeding "regulatory takings" jurisprudence, we have generally eschewed any " 'set formula' " for determining how far is too far, preferring to "engage in . . . essentially ad hoc, factual inquiries," *Penn Central Transportation Co. v. New York City*, 438 U.S. 104, 124 (1978) (quoting *Goldblatt v. Hempstead*, 369 U.S. 590, 594 (1962)). *See* Epstein, *Takings: Descent and Resurrection,* 1987 Sup. Ct. Rev. 1, 4. We have, however, described at least two discrete categories of regulatory action as compensable without case-specific inquiry into the public interest advanced in support of the restraint. The first encompasses regulations that compel the property owner to suffer a physical "invasion" of his property. In general (at least with regard to permanent invasions), no matter how minute the intrusion, and no matter how weighty the public purpose behind it, we have required compensation. For example, in *Loretto v. Teleprompter Manhattan CATV Corp.*, 458 U.S. 419 (1982), we determined that New York's law requiring landlords to allow television cable companies to emplace cable facilities in their apartment buildings constituted a taking, *id.* at 435–440, even though the facilities occupied at most only 1 1/2 cubic feet of the landlords' property, *see id.* at 438, n. 16. *See also United States v. Causby*, 328 U.S. 256, 265, and n. 10 (1946) (physical invasions of airspace); cf. *Kaiser Aetna v. United States*, 444 U.S. 164 (1979) (imposition of navigational servitude upon private marina).

The second situation in which we have found categorical treatment appropriate is where regulation denies all economically beneficial or productive use of land. *See Agins*, 447 U.S., at 260; see also *Nollan v. California Coastal Comm'n*, 483 U.S. 825, 834 (1987); *Keystone Bituminous Coal Assn. v. DeBenedictis*, 480 U.S. 470, 495 (1987); *Hodel v. Virginia Surface Mining & Reclamation Assn., Inc.*, 452 U.S. 264, 295–296 (1981). As we have said on numerous occasions, the Fifth Amendment is violated when land-use regulation "does not substantially advance legitimate state interests or *denies an owner economically viable use of his land.*" *Agins, supra*, at 260 (citations omitted) (emphasis added).

We have never set forth the justification for this rule. Perhaps it is simply, as Justice Brennan suggested, that total deprivation of beneficial use is, from the landowner's point of view, the equivalent of a physical appropriation. See *San Diego Gas & Electric Co. v. San Diego*, 450 U.S., at 652 (Brennan, J., dissenting). "For what is the land but the profits thereof?" 1 E. Coke, Institutes ch. 1, § 1 (1st Am. ed. 1812). Surely, at least, in the extraordinary circumstance when no productive or economically beneficial use of land is permitted, it is less realistic to indulge our usual assumption that the legislature is simply "adjusting the benefits and burdens of economic life," *Penn Central Transportation Co.*, 438 U.S., at 124, in a manner that secures an "average reciprocity of advantage" to everyone concerned. *Pennsylvania Coal Co. v. Mahon*, 260 U.S., at 415. And the *functional* basis for permitting the government, by regulation, to affect property values without compensation — that "Government hardly could go on if to some extent values incident to property could not be diminished without paying for every such change in the general law," *id.* at 413 — does not apply to the relatively rare situations where the government has deprived a landowner of all economically beneficial uses.

On the other side of the balance, affirmatively supporting a compensation requirement, is the fact that regulations that leave the owner of land without economically beneficial or productive options for its use — typically, as here, by requiring land to be left substantially in its natural state — carry with them a heightened risk that private property is being pressed into some form of public service under the guise of mitigating serious public harm. *See, e.g., Annicelli v. South Kingstown*, 463 A.2d 133, 140–141 (R.I. 1983) (prohibition on construction adjacent to beach justified on twin grounds of safety and "conservation of open space"); *Morris County Land Improvement Co. v.*

Parsippany-Troy Hills Township, 40 N.J. 539, 552–553, 193 A.2d 232, 240 (1963) (prohibition on filling marshlands imposed in order to preserve region as water detention basin and create wildlife refuge). . . . We think, in short, that there are good reasons for our frequently expressed belief that when the owner of real property has been called upon to sacrifice *all* economically beneficial uses in the name of the common good, that is, to leave his property economically idle, he has suffered a taking.

B

The trial court found Lucas's two beachfront lots to have been rendered valueless by respondent's enforcement of the coastal-zone construction ban. Under Lucas's theory of the case, which rested upon our "no economically viable use" statements, that finding entitled him to compensation. Lucas believed it unnecessary to take issue with either the purposes behind the Beachfront Management Act, or the means chosen by the South Carolina Legislature to effectuate those purposes. The South Carolina Supreme Court, however, thought otherwise. In its view, the Beachfront Management Act was no ordinary enactment, but involved an exercise of South Carolina's "police powers" to mitigate the harm to the public interest that petitioner's use of his land might occasion. 304 S.C. at 384, 404 S.E.2d at 899. By neglecting to dispute the findings enumerated in the Act or otherwise to challenge the legislature's purposes, petitioner "conceded that the beach/dune area of South Carolina's shores is an extremely valuable public resource; that the erection of new construction, *inter alia*, contributes to the erosion and destruction of this public resource; and that discouraging new construction in close proximity to the beach/dune area is necessary to prevent a great public harm." *Id.* at 382–383, 404 S.E.2d at 898. In the court's view, these concessions brought petitioner's challenge within a long line of this Court's cases sustaining against Due Process and Takings Clause challenges the State's use of its "police powers" to enjoin a property owner from activities akin to public nuisances. *See Mugler v. Kansas*, 123 U.S. 623 (1887) (law prohibiting manufacture of alcoholic beverages); *Hadachek v. Sebastian*, 239 U.S. 394 (1915) (law barring operation of brick mill in residential area); *Miller v. Schoene*, 276 U.S. 272 (1928) (order to destroy diseased cedar trees to prevent infection of nearby orchards); *Goldblatt v. Hempstead*, 369 U.S. 590 (1962) (law effectively preventing continued operation of quarry in residential area).

It is correct that many of our prior opinions have suggested that "harmful or noxious uses" of property may be proscribed by government regulation without the requirement of compensation. For a number of reasons, however, we think the South Carolina Supreme Court was too quick to conclude that that principle decides the present case. The "harmful or noxious uses" principle was the Court's early attempt to describe in theoretical terms why government may, consistent with the Takings Clause, affect property values by regulation without incurring an obligation to compensate — a reality we nowadays acknowledge explicitly with respect to the full scope of the State's police power.

"Harmful or noxious use" analysis was . . . simply the progenitor of our more contemporary statements that "land-use regulation does not effect a

taking if it 'substantially advances legitimate state interests'. . . . *Nollan,
supra,* at 834 (quoting *Agins v. Tiburon,* 447 U.S., at 260); *see also Penn
Central Transportation Co., supra,* at 127; *Euclid v. Ambler Realty Co.,* 272
U.S. 365, 387–388 (1926).

The transition from our early focus on control of "noxious" uses to our
contemporary understanding of the broad realm within which government
may regulate without compensation was an easy one, since the distinction
between "harm-preventing" and "benefit-conferring" regulation is often in the
eye of the beholder. It is quite possible, for example, to describe in *either*
fashion the ecological, economic, and aesthetic concerns that inspired the
South Carolina legislature in the present case. One could say that imposing
a servitude on Lucas's land is necessary in order to prevent his use of it from
"harming" South Carolina's ecological resources; or, instead, in order to
achieve the "benefits" of an ecological preserve. . . . Whether one or the other
of the competing characterizations will come to one's lips in a particular case
depends primarily upon one's evaluation of the worth of competing uses of
real estate. . . . A given restraint will be seen as mitigating "harm" to the
adjacent parcels or securing a "benefit" for them, depending upon the observer's evaluation of the relative importance of the use that the restraint favors.
When it is understood that "prevention of harmful use" was merely our early
formulation of the police power justification necessary to sustain (without
compensation) any regulatory diminution in value; and that the distinction
between regulation that "prevents harmful use" and that which "confers
benefits" is difficult, if not impossible, to discern on an objective, value-free
basis; it becomes self-evident that noxious-use logic cannot serve as a touchstone to distinguish regulatory "takings" — which require compensation —
from regulatory deprivations that do not require compensation.

A fortiori the legislature's recitation of a noxious-use justification cannot
be the basis for departing from our categorical rule that total regulatory
takings must be compensated. If it were, departure would virtually always
be allowed. The South Carolina Supreme Court's approach would essentially
nullify *Mahon*'s affirmation of limits to the noncompensable exercise of the
police power. Our cases provide no support for this: None of them that
employed the logic of "harmful use" prevention to sustain a regulation involved
an allegation that the regulation wholly eliminated the value of the claimant's
land. . . .

Where the State seeks to sustain regulation that deprives land of all
economically beneficial use, we think it may resist compensation only if the
logically antecedent inquiry into the nature of the owner's estate shows that
the proscribed use interests were not part of his title to begin with. This
accords, we think, with our "takings" jurisprudence, which has traditionally
been guided by the understandings of our citizens regarding the content of,
and the State's power over, the "bundle of rights" that they acquire when they
obtain title to property. It seems to us that the property owner necessarily
expects the uses of his property to be restricted, from time to time, by various
measures newly enacted by the State in legitimate exercise of its police
powers; "as long recognized, some values are enjoyed under an implied
limitation and must yield to the police power." *Pennsylvania Coal Co. v.*

Mahon, 260 U.S., at 413. And in the case of personal property, by reason of the State's traditionally high degree of control over commercial dealings, he ought to be aware of the possibility that new regulation might even render his property economically worthless (at least if the property's only economically productive use is sale or manufacture for sale), *see Andrus v. Allard,* 444 U.S. 51, 66–67 (1979) (prohibition on sale of eagle feathers). In the case of land, however, we think the notion pressed by the Council that title is somehow held subject to the "implied limitation" that the State may subsequently eliminate all economically valuable use is inconsistent with the historical compact recorded in the Takings Clause that has become part of our constitutional culture.

Where "permanent physical occupation" of land is concerned, we have refused to allow the government to decree it anew (without compensation), no matter how weighty the asserted "public interests" involved, *Loretto v. Teleprompter Manhattan CATV Corp.,* 458 U.S., at 426 — though we assuredly *would* permit the government to assert a permanent easement that was a pre-existing limitation upon the landowner's title. *Compare Scranton v. Wheeler,* 179 U.S. 141, 163 (1900) (interests of "riparian owner in the submerged lands . . . bordering on a public navigable water" held subject to Government's navigational servitude), *with Kaiser Aetna v. United States,* 444 U.S., at 178–180 (imposition of navigational servitude on marina created and rendered navigable at private expense held to constitute a taking). We believe similar treatment must be accorded confiscatory regulations, *i. e.,* regulations that prohibit all economically beneficial use of land: Any limitation so severe cannot be newly legislated or decreed (without compensation), but must inhere in the title itself, in the restrictions that background principles of the State's law of property and nuisance already place upon land ownership. A law or decree with such an effect must, in other words, do no more than duplicate the result that could have been achieved in the courts — by adjacent landowners (or other uniquely affected persons) under the State's law of private nuisance, or by the State under its complementary power to abate nuisances that affect the public generally, or otherwise.

On this analysis, the owner of a lake bed, for example, would not be entitled to compensation when he is denied the requisite permit to engage in a landfilling operation that would have the effect of flooding others' land. Nor the corporate owner of a nuclear generating plant, when it is directed to remove all improvements from its land upon discovery that the plant sits astride an earthquake fault. Such regulatory action may well have the effect of eliminating the land's only economically productive use, but it does not proscribe a productive use that was previously permissible under relevant property and nuisance principles. The use of these properties for what are now expressly prohibited purposes was always unlawful, and (subject to other constitutional limitations) it was open to the State at any point to make the implication of those background principles of nuisance and property law explicit. *See* Michelman, *Property, Utility, and Fairness, Comments on the Ethical Foundations of "Just Compensation" Law,* 80 Harv. L. Rev. 1165, 1239–1241 (1967). In light of our traditional resort to "existing rules or understandings that stem from an independent source such as state law" to define the range of interests that qualify for protection as "property" under the Fifth (and Fourteenth) Amendments, *Board of Regents of State Colleges v. Roth*, 408 U.S. 564, 577 (1972); *see, e.g., Ruckelshaus v. Monsanto Co.*, 467 U.S. 986, 1011–1012 (1984); *Hughes v. Washington*, 389 U.S. 290, 295 (1967) (Stewart, J., concurring), this recognition that the Takings Clause does not require compensation when an owner is barred from putting land to a use that is proscribed by those "existing rules or understandings" is surely unexceptional. When, however, a regulation that declares "off-limits" all economically productive or beneficial uses of land goes beyond what the relevant background principles would dictate, compensation must be paid to sustain it.

The "total taking" inquiry we require today will ordinarily entail (as the application of state nuisance law ordinarily entails) analysis of, among other things, the degree of harm to public lands and resources, or adjacent private property, posed by the claimant's proposed activities, *see, e.g.*, Restatement (Second) of Torts §§ 826, 827, the social value of the claimant's activities and their suitability to the locality in question, *see, e.g., id.* §§ 828(a) and (b), 831, and the relative ease with which the alleged harm can be avoided through measures taken by the claimant and the government (or adjacent private landowners) alike, *see, e.g., id.* §§ 827(e), 828(c), 830. The fact that a particular use has long been engaged in by similarly situated owners ordinarily imports a lack of any common-law prohibition (though changed circumstances or new knowledge may make what was previously permissible no longer so, see Restatement (Second) of Torts, *supra*, § 827, comment G). So also does the fact that other landowners, similarly situated, are permitted to continue the use denied to the claimant.

It seems unlikely that common-law principles would have prevented the erection of any habitable or productive improvements on petitioner's land; they rarely support prohibition of the "essential use" of land, *Curtin v. Benson*, 222 U.S. 78, 86 (1911). The question, however, is one of state law to be dealt with on remand. We emphasize that to win its case South Carolina must do more than proffer the legislature's declaration that the uses Lucas desires are inconsistent with the public interest, or the conclusory assertion that they violate a common-law maxim such as sic utere tuo ut alienum non laedas. As we have said, a "State, by ipse dixit, may not transform private property into public property without compensation. . . ." *Webb's Fabulous Pharmacies, Inc. v. Beckwith*, 449 U.S. 155, 164 (1980). Instead, as it would be required to do if it sought to restrain Lucas in a common-law action for public nuisance, South Carolina must identify background principles of nuisance and property law that prohibit the uses he now intends in the circumstances in which the property is presently found. Only on this showing can the State fairly claim that, in proscribing all such beneficial uses, the Beachfront Management Act is taking nothing.

The judgment is reversed and the cause remanded for proceedings not inconsistent with this opinion.

So ordered.

[Additional opinions are omitted. In a separate statement, Justice Souter argued that the Court should not have taken this case because it later became apparent the effect of the statutory ban was less than a total deprivation of the plaintiff's property rights. Justice Kennedy concurred in the judgment, but argued that the common law of nuisance is "too narrow a confine for the exercise of regulatory power in a complex and interdependent society." Justice Blackmun's dissent relied on the presumption of constitutionality ("the State has the power to prevent any use of property it finds to be harmful to its citizens, and . . . a state statute is entitled to a presumption of constitutionality") and on the "noxious use" principle set forth in *Pennsylvania Coal*'s dissenting opinion. Justice Stevens objected to the formation of a categorical rule for takings law, and on the theory that the majority ruling essentially "freezes" state's abilities to revise land use law.]

NOTES AND QUESTIONS

1. After this decision, the state settled with Lucas for a reported $1.5 million. The Coastal Council then offered the lands for sale, saying that "with a house to either side and in between the lots, it is reasonable and prudent to allow houses to be built." *See* H. Jane Lehman, *Accord Ends Fight Over Use of Land,* Wash. Post., July 17, 1993, at E1.

2. Does the *Lucas* categorical takings rule apply if the denial of all economically beneficial use of property is temporary, not permanent? In *Tahoe-Sierra Preservation Council, Inc. v. Tahoe Regional Planning Agency*, 535 U.S. 302, 122 S. Ct. 1465 (2002), the question was whether moratoria on property development lasting for nineteen years, in place pending the adoption of a regional land use plan, caused an unconditional taking on its face. Refusing to find a *per se* taking, the Supreme Court held these should be decided on a case-by-case basis.

3. How does one know if a taking is total?

LOVELADIES HARBOR, INC. v. UNITED STATES

28 F.3d 1171 (D.C. Cir. 1994)

[This case presents the so-called "denominator" problem in takings law. The issue is how to determine the precise parcel, or portion thereof (i.e. the denominator), that is actually burdened by a governmental regulation. If the entirety of a parcel is burdened, the *Lucas* categorical rule should apply, much to a plaintiff's benefit. If less than the entirety of a parcel is burdened, however, the categorical rule should not apply. In *Loveladies*, plaintiffs sought a fill permit under § 404 of the Clean Water Act from the Army Corps of Engineers (Corps) to complete the final stage of an ongoing real estate development project. The permit was denied. Loveladies had started with a tract of about 250 acres, and had developed 199 of those acres when the permit denial took place.]

OPINION: PLAGER, Circuit Judge.

. . . .

On the facts of the case before us, the question of whether there has been a partial or total loss of economic use (in the latter case a "categorical" taking, *see Lucas*, 112 S. Ct. at 2893; *Florida Rock*, 18 F.3d at 1568), depends on what is the specific property that was affected by the permit denial. If the tract of land that is the measure of the economic value after the regulatory imposition is defined as only that land for which the use permit is denied, that provides the easiest case for those arguing that a categorical taking occurred. On the other hand, if the tract of land is defined as some larger piece, one with substantial residuary value independent of the wetlands regulation, then either a partial or no taking occurred, depending on the test as described in *Florida Rock*, 18 F.3d at 1567 et seq. This is the denominator problem.

In this case, the Government assumes that virtually all economic use must be taken (that is, destroyed by the regulatory imposition) in order to have a compensable regulatory taking. Under that assumption, the key question is, when comparing the value of the property before and after the imposition, what is the property whose value is compared. On the facts here, is the test the effect of the imposition on the value of just the 12.5 acres, or is it the effect of the imposition on the total value of, say, the original 250 acres, or on some other size unit.

The Government argues that the proper denominator is the original 250 acre parcel or, at the least, the total acreage remaining unsold in 1982, when the permit was denied. In 1982, as we have noted, Loveladies owned 51 undeveloped acres; the other 199 had been developed and all but 6.4 of those acres had been sold. Under their agreement with New Jersey in settlement of its lawsuit, Loveladies could develop only the 12.5 acres of the 51; the development rights in the remaining 38.5 acres were to be dedicated to the state in return for the NJDEP permit. Of the 12.5 acres, one acre was already filled; there remained 11.5 acres of wetlands for which Loveladies sought the § 404 permit. This array of possible denominators bears out the Lucas Court's observation that "the rhetorical force of [the] 'deprivation of all economically feasible use' rule is greater than its precision." *Lucas*, 112 S. Ct. at 2894.

Loveladies and the amici urge this court to adopt a bright-line rule that the denominator of the takings fraction is that parcel for which the owner seeks a permit. The Government, on the other hand, argues that such bright-line rules would encourage strategic behavior on the part of developers — "conveying away the non-wetlands portions of their parcels prior to applying to the Corps for a permit to fill the remaining wetlands."

Our precedent displays a flexible approach, designed to account for factual nuances. In *Deltona Corp. v. United States*, 228 Ct. Cl. 476, 657 F.2d 1184 (Ct. Cl. 1981), *cert. denied*, 455 U.S. 1017, 72 L. Ed. 2d 135, 102 S. Ct. 1712 (1982), the court was concerned with whether there remained substantial economically viable uses for plaintiff's property after the regulatory imposition. In determining this, the court took into account the facts that while plaintiffs were blocked from developing two of the three projects for which they sought permits, they were granted a permit for the third; and that within the two that were denied, they had 111 acres of uplands which could be developed, and whose value exceeded by twice the original price paid for the two tracts. There was no taking.

In *Whitney Benefits, Inc. v. United States*, 926 F.2d 1169 (Fed. Cir. 1991), *cert. denied*, 116 L. Ed. 2d 354, 112 S. Ct. 406 (1991), this court concluded that the regulatory enactment, the Surface Mining Control and Reclamation Act of 1977, had its intended effect, precluding the surface mining of plaintiff's coal field because of the overlying alluvial valley floor. This was based on extensive fact finding by the trial court regarding the purpose of the imposition, the nature of the property, its alternative uses, and the extent to which all or only a portion of plaintiff's property was so limited. "That finding [that the imposition deprived the plaintiff of all economically viable use of its property and destroyed its value] is not only correct and fully supported by the evidence, it is entitled to respect and may be upset only if it is shown to have been clearly erroneous." *Whitney Benefits*, 926 F.2d at 1172–73. The Claims Court judgment of compensable taking was affirmed.

These factual nuances include consideration of the timing of transfers in light of the developing regulatory environment. New Jersey apparently made no effort to impose restrictions on the development of this wetland area until after the initial project had been approved for development, and until 199 acres had been developed. This development occurred over a substantial period of years beginning in 1958, and involved many kinds of government permits. The trial court concluded that land developed or sold before the regulatory environment existed should not be included in the denominator. The Government has failed to convince us that the trial court clearly erred in this conclusion.

With regard to the land remaining after the regulatory fabric was in place, the trial court excluded from consideration the 38.5 acres which for all practical purposes had been promised to New Jersey in exchange for the NJDEP permit. This is only logical since whatever substantial value that land had now belongs to the state and not to Loveladies. It would seem ungrateful in the extreme to require Loveladies to convey to the public the rights in the 38.5 acres in exchange for the right to develop 12.5 acres, and then to include the value of the grant as a charge against the givers.

This leaves the conclusion that the relevant property for the takings analysis is the 12.5 acres, for which the trial court found the remaining value to be de minimis. This is not, then, a case of a partial taking, involving linedrawing between noncompensable 'mere diminution' and compensable partial taking. *See Florida Rock Industries, Inc. v. United States*, 18 F.3d 1560 (1994). Rather, this is a case in which the owner of the relevant parcel was deprived of all economically feasible use. The trial court's conclusion that the permit denial was effectively a total taking of the property owner's interest in these acres is fully supported in the record; there is no clear error in that conclusion. . . .

AFFIRMED.

[Remainder of opinion ommited.]

[b] LESS THAN TOTAL TAKINGS

PENN CENTRAL TRANSPORTATION CO. v. NEW YORK CITY

438 U.S. 104, 98 S. Ct. 1646 (1978)

[New York City enacted the Landmark Preservation Law, which precluded plaintiff from constructing office space above the Grand Central Terminal in Manhattan. Plaintiff argued this regulation worked a taking in violation of the federal Constitution. The lower court found for the City.]:

MR. JUSTICE BRENNAN delivered the opinion of the Court.

The question presented is whether a city may, as part of a comprehensive program to preserve historic landmarks and historic districts, place restrictions on the development of individual historic landmarks — in addition to those imposed by applicable zoning ordinances — without effecting a "taking" requiring the payment of "just compensation." Specifically, we must decide whether the application of New York City's Landmarks Preservation Law to the parcel of land occupied by Grand Central Terminal has "taken" its owners' property in violation of the Fifth and Fourteenth Amendments.

I

A

Over the past 50 years, all 50 States and over 500 municipalities have enacted laws to encourage or require the preservation of buildings and areas with historic or aesthetic importance. n1 These nationwide legislative efforts have been precipitated by two concerns. The first is recognition that, in recent years, large numbers of historic structures, landmarks, and areas have been destroyed without adequate consideration of either the values represented therein or the possibility of preserving the destroyed properties for use in economically productive ways. The second is a widely shared belief that structures with special historic, cultural, or architectural significance enhance the quality of life for all. Not only do these buildings and their workmanship represent the lessons of the past and embody precious features of our heritage, they serve as examples of quality for today. "[Historic] conservation is but one aspect of the much larger problem, basically an environmental one, of enhancing — or perhaps developing for the first time — the quality of life for people."

New York City, responding to similar concerns and acting pursuant to a New York State enabling Act, adopted its Landmarks Preservation Law in 1965. *See* N.Y.C. Admin. Code, ch. 8-A, § 205-1.0 *et seq.* (1976). The city acted from the conviction that "the standing of [New York City] as a world-wide tourist center and world capital of business, culture and government" would be threatened if legislation were not enacted to protect historic landmarks and neighborhoods from precipitate decisions to destroy or fundamentally alter their character. § 205-1.0(a). The city believed that comprehensive measures to safeguard desirable features of the existing urban fabric would benefit its citizens in a variety of ways: e.g., fostering "civic pride in the beauty and noble accomplishments of the past"; protecting and enhancing "the city's attractions to tourists and visitors"; "[supporting] and [stimulating] business and industry"; "[strengthening] the economy of the city"; and promoting "the use of historic districts, landmarks, interior landmarks and scenic landmarks for the education, pleasure and welfare of the people of the city." § 205-1.0(b).

The New York City law is typical of many urban landmark laws in that its primary method of achieving its goals is not by acquisitions of historic properties, but rather by involving public entities in land-use decisions affecting these properties and providing services, standards, controls, and incentives that will encourage preservation by private owners and users. While the law does place special restrictions on landmark properties as a necessary feature to the attainment of its larger objectives, the major theme of the law is to ensure the owners of any such properties both a "reasonable return" on their investments and maximum latitude to use their parcels for purposes not inconsistent with the preservation goals. . . .

Final designation as a landmark results in restrictions upon the property owner's options concerning use of the landmark site. First, the law imposes a duty upon the owner to keep the exterior features of the building "in good repair" to assure that the law's objectives not be defeated by the landmark's falling into a state of irremediable disrepair. See § 207-10.0(a). Second, the Commission must approve in advance any proposal to alter the exterior architectural features of the landmark or to construct any exterior improvement on the landmark site, thus ensuring that decisions concerning construction on the landmark site are made with due consideration of both the public interest in the maintenance of the structure and the landowner's interest in use of the property. See §§ 207-4.0 to 207-9.0. . . .

B

This case involves the application of New York City's Landmarks Preservation Law to Grand Central Terminal (Terminal). The Terminal, which is owned by the Penn Central Transportation Co. and its affiliates (Penn Central), is one of New York City's most famous buildings. Opened in 1913, it is regarded not only as providing an ingenious engineering solution to the problems presented by urban railroad stations, but also as a magnificent example of the French beaux-arts style.

The Terminal is located in midtown Manhattan. Its south facade faces 42d Street and that street's intersection with Park Avenue. At street level, the Terminal is bounded on the west by Vanderbilt Avenue, on the east by the Commodore Hotel, and on the north by the Pan-American Building. Although a 20-story office tower, to have been located above the Terminal, was part of the original design, the planned tower was never constructed. The Terminal itself is an eight-story structure which Penn Central uses as a railroad station and in which it rents space not needed for railroad purposes to a variety of commercial interests. The Terminal is one of a number of properties owned by appellant Penn Central in this area of midtown Manhattan. The others include the Barclay, Biltmore, Commodore, Roosevelt, and Waldorf-Astoria

Hotels, the Pan-American Building and other office buildings along Park Avenue, and the Yale Club. At least eight of these are eligible to be recipients of development rights afforded the Terminal by virtue of landmark designation. . . .

On January 22, 1968, appellant Penn Central, to increase its income, entered into a renewable 50-year lease and sublease agreement with appellant UGP Properties, Inc. (UGP), a wholly owned subsidiary of Union General Properties, Ltd., a United Kingdom corporation. Under the terms of the agreement, UGP was to construct a multistory office building above the Terminal. UGP promised to pay Penn Central $1 million annually during construction and at least $3 million annually thereafter. The rentals would be offset in part by a loss of some $700,000 to $1 million in net rentals presently received from concessionaires displaced by the new building. . . .

[Applicants were denied development rights.]

II

The issues presented by appellants are (1) whether the restrictions imposed by New York City's law upon appellants' exploitation of the Terminal site effect a "taking" of appellants' property for a public use within the meaning of the Fifth Amendment, which of course is made applicable to the States through the Fourteenth Amendment, see *Chicago, B. & Q. R. Co. v. Chicago*, 166 U.S. 226, 239 (1897), and, (2), if so, whether the transferable development rights afforded appellants constitute "just compensation" within the meaning of the Fifth Amendment. We need only address the question whether a "taking" has occurred. . . .

Before considering appellants' specific contentions, it will be useful to review the factors that have shaped the jurisprudence of the Fifth Amendment injunction "nor shall private property be taken for public use, without just compensation." The question of what constitutes a "taking" for purposes of the Fifth Amendment has proved to be a problem of considerable difficulty. While this Court has recognized that the "Fifth Amendment's guarantee . . . [is] designed to bar Government from forcing some people alone to bear public burdens which, in all fairness and justice, should be borne by the public as a whole," *Armstrong v. U.S.*, 354 U.S. 40, 49 (1960), this Court, quite simply, has been unable to develop any "set formula" for determining when "justice and fairness" require that economic injuries caused by public action be compensated by the government, rather than remain disproportionately concentrated on a few persons. *See Goldblatt v. Hempstead*, 369 U.S. 590, 594 (1962). Indeed, we have frequently observed that whether a particular restriction will be rendered invalid by the government's failure to pay for any losses proximately caused by it depends largely "upon the particular circumstances [in that] case." *United States v. Central Eureka Mining Co.*, 357 U.S. 155, 168 (1958); *see United States v. Caltex, Inc.*, 344 U.S. 149, 156 (1952).

In engaging in these essentially ad hoc, factual inquiries, the Court's decisions have identified several factors that have particular significance. The economic impact of the regulation on the claimant and, particularly, the extent to which the regulation has interfered with distinct investment-backed expectations are, of course, relevant considerations. *See Goldblatt v. Hempstead, supra,* at 594. So, too, is the character of the governmental action. A "taking" may more readily be found when the interference with property can be characterized as a physical invasion by government, *see, e.g., United States v. Causby,* 328 U.S. 256 (1946), than when interference arises from some public program adjusting the benefits and burdens of economic life to promote the common good.

"Government hardly could go on if to some extent values incident to property could not be diminished without paying for every such change in the general law," *Pennsylvania Coal Co. v. Mahon,* 260 U.S. 393, 413 (1922), and this Court has accordingly recognized, in a wide variety of contexts, that government may execute laws or programs that adversely affect recognized economic values. Exercises of the taxing power are one obvious example. A second are the decisions in which this Court has dismissed "taking" challenges on the ground that, while the challenged government action caused economic harm, it did not interfere with interests that were sufficiently bound up with the reasonable expectations of the claimant to constitute "property" for Fifth Amendment purposes. . . .

More importantly for the present case, in instances in which a state tribunal reasonably concluded that "the health, safety, morals, or general welfare" would be promoted by prohibiting particular contemplated uses of land, this Court has upheld land-use regulations that destroyed or adversely affected recognized real property interests. *See Nectow v. Cambridge,* 277 U.S. 183, 188 (1928). Zoning laws are, of course, the classic example, *see Euclid v. Ambler Realty Co.,* 272 U.S. 365 (1926) (prohibition of industrial use); *Gorieb v. Fox,* 274 U.S. 603, 608 (1927) (requirement that portions of parcels be left unbuilt); *Welch v. Swasey,* 214 U.S. 91 (1909) (height restriction). . . .

[The Court also addressed plaintiffs' argument that the Landmark Law abrogated the "air rights" above the Terminal]:

"Taking" jurisprudence does not divide a single parcel into discrete segments and attempt to determine whether rights in a particular segment have been entirely abrogated. In deciding whether a particular governmental action has effected a taking, this Court focuses rather both on the character of the action and on the nature and extent of the interference with rights in the parcel as a whole — here, the city tax block designated as the "landmark site."
. . .

[The Court found, in any event, that the New York law might well have permitted the construction of some smaller structure above the Terminal. Moreover, reasoned the Court] . . . to the extent appellants have been denied the right to build above the Terminal, it is not literally accurate to say that they have been denied *all* use of even those pre-existing air rights. Their ability to use these rights has not been abrogated; they are made transferable to at least eight parcels in the vicinity of the Terminal, one or two of which have been found suitable for the construction of new office buildings. Although appellants and others have argued that New York City's transferable development-rights program is far from ideal, the New York courts here supportably found that, at least in the case of the Terminal, the rights afforded are valuable. While these rights may well not have constituted "just compensation" if a "taking" had occurred, the rights nevertheless undoubtedly mitigate whatever financial burdens the law has imposed on appellants and, for that reason, are to be taken into account in considering the impact of regulation. . . . (emphasis in original).

Affirmed.

Justice Rehnquist, joined by Chief Justice Burger and Justice Stevens, dissented:

> . . . "Appellees are not prohibiting a nuisance. . . . Penn Central is . . . [denied rights] . . . because it did *too good* a job in designing and building [the Terminal]." (emphasis in original.)

NOTES AND QUESTIONS

1. While the test established in *Penn Central* remains the most widely used basis for deciding regulatory takings cases, it fails to produce predictable results, for several reasons. First, the decision characterizes takings cases as "essentially ad hoc inquiries . . .," an assertion drawn from *Goldblatt v. Town of Hempstead*, 369 U.S. 590, 82 S. Ct. 987 (1962), which stated that "[T]here is no set formula to determine where regulation ends and taking begins[.]" 369 U.S. 590, 594, 82 S. Ct. 987, 990 (1962). Declaring takings cases to be "ad hoc inquiries" is a virtual invitation to judges to resolve disputes by their own lights, rather than by honoring whatever Supreme Court precedents may be in place. Second, *Penn Central* elevates considerations of "justice and fairness" into a central position in takings analysis, giving judges even more leaway to fashion results to their liking. With respect to decisional mechanics, *Penn Central* offers no advice on how to strike a balance among the three designated factors, nor does the case explain what the factors mean. On this latter point, however, other cases have shed some light:

(A) *"Economic impact of the regulation:"* *Lucas* tells us that a total devaluation of property or a denial of all economically beneficial or productive use of land is *per se* a taking. *See supra.* But how far can legislation fall short of totally destroying the value and use of land and still survive constitutional scrutiny? The short answer is: very far. So long as a regulation does not leave land "economically idle" nor doom it to only token use, it is unlikely it will be disqualified on economic impact grounds. *See, e.g., Goldblatt v. Hempstead*, 369 U.S. 590, 594, 82 S. Ct. 987, 990 (1962) (holding that the deprivation of the most beneficial use of land is not an indication, without more, of a taking); *Hadachek v. Sebastian*, 239 U.S. 394, 36 S. Ct. 143 (1915) (an 87-1/2% diminution in value not a taking); *Palazzolo v. Rhode Island*, 533 U.S. 606, 121 S. Ct. 2448 (2001) (no taking when a regulation allows construction of a single dwelling only on an 18-acre parcel, thereby devaluing property from $3.2 million to $200,000); *Concrete Pipe and Products of California v. Construction Laborers Pension Trust for Southern California*, 508 U.S. 602, 645, 113 S.Ct. 2264, 2291 (1993) ("mere diminution in the value of property, however serious, is insufficient to demonstrate a taking"). *Concrete Pipe* was not a total takings case and, therefore, did not overrule *Lucas*.

See also Andrus v. Allard, 444 U.S. 51, 65–66, 100 S. Ct. 318, 327 (1979) ("[A]t least where an owner possesses a full 'bundle' of property rights, the destruction of one 'strand' of the bundle is not a taking, because the aggregate must be viewed in its entirety."). *But see Kaiser Aetna v. United States*, 444 U.S. 164, 178-79, 100 S. Ct. 383, 392-93 (1979) (holding, under the "logic" of *Pennsylvania Coal*, that a "fundamental element" of property, the right to exclude, "fall[s] within [the] category of interests that the government cannot take without compensation.")

Would a state's use of its police power to take title to all of a person's property at death run afoul of the Takings Clause? *See Hodel v. Irving*, 481 U.S. 704, 107 S. Ct. 2076 (1987) (yes). Whose property rights are taken in this instance? Those of the deceased? Of the recipients under the decedent's will or intestacy laws?

(B) *"Interference with investment-backed expectations" ("IBEs"):* As announced in *Penn Central*, this factor is a subunit of the "economic impact" factor. The origin of the IBE factor is said to be a law review article which maintained the validity of regulations that deprive only "desires or goals of property owners which are not 'distinctly crystalized.'" *See* Craig A. Peterson, *Land Use Regulatory "Takings" Revisited: The New Supreme Court Approaches,* 39 Hastings L.J. 335, 346 (1988) (indicating the concept came from Professor Frank Michelman, *Property, Utility, and Fairness: Comments on the Ethical Foundations of "Just Compensation" Law,* 80 Harv. L. Rev. 1165, 1230–34 (1967)).

The "investment-backed" part of this test brings to constitutional relevance the idea that property rights that have been made the subject of expenditures or other detrimental action by landowners warrant greater protection than what might be thought of as unattended property rights. The "expectations" part of IBEs promotes the idea that property rights can be burdened more significantly if the rightholder knew, or should have known, that regulation was in place or on its way. The Court made this latter point emphatically in *Concrete Pipe, supra*, when it held that a requirement for additional financial contributions by employers to employee pension plans did not upset investment-backed expectations of employers because employers, well aware of the longstanding federal regulation of pension plans, "could have had no reasonable expectation that [they] would not be faced with liability [. . . .]" *Id.* at 646, 113 S. Ct. at 2292. The *Lucas* decision voiced the same sentiment when it stated that "it seems to us that the property owner necessarily expects the uses of his property to be restricted, from time to time, by various measures newly enacted by the State in its legitimate exercise of its police powers. . . . And in the case of personal property, by reason of the State's traditionally high degree of control over commercial dealings, he ought to be aware of the possibility that new regulation might even render his property economically worthless [. . . .]" *Id.* at 1027, 112 S. Ct. at 2899.

A recent United States Supreme Court decision, however, was less accepting of the potentially disqualifying impact of the expectations component of IBEs. *Palazzolo v. Rhode Island*, 533 U.S. 606, 121 S. Ct. 2448 (2001), examined the plight of persons who acquire property rights after the enactment of a burdensome land use regulation. The issue was whether such persons are categorically excluded from relief because they knew of the regulation coming in. If so, the argument goes, the regulation could not have interfered with expectations, investment-backed or otherwise. The Supreme Court rejected this "coming to the taking" argument unequivocally. It refused to tolerate a rule that *de facto* absolves the state of takings liability regardless of any other considerations and, additionally, would strip landowners of the ability to transfer property in the future. In the Court's words, "[t]he State may not put so potent a Hobbesian stick into the Lockean bundle." *Id.* at 627, 121 S. Ct. at 2462. Unreasonable statutes "do not become less so through passage of time or title. Were we to accept the State's rule, the postenactment transfer of title would absolve the State of its obligation to defend any action restricting land use, no matter how extreme or unreasonable. A State would be allowed, in effect, to put an expiration date on the Takings Clause. This ought not to be the rule. Future generations, too, have a right to challenge unreasonable limitations on the use and value of land." *Id.* at 627, 121 S.Ct. at 2463.

(C) *"Character of the government action:"* This factor makes relevant for takings purposes the inherent worthiness of a government regulation. For an historical argument that this factor is appropriate, despite sparse constitutional history on the question, *see, e.g.,* Joseph L. Sax, *Takings and the Police Power,* 74 Yale L.J. 36 (1964). Under this "character factor," a regulation deemed worthwhile or necessary may impose a greater burden on property rights than one deemed to be less worthwhile or necessary. *See, e.g., Keystone Bituminous Coal Ass'n v. De Benedictus,* 480 U.S. 470, 107 S. Ct. 1232 (1987). *Keystone* involved a statutory restriction on coal mining much like the Kohler Act implicated in *Pennsylvania Coal.* The Supreme Court declined to find a taking in the case, in part because it viewed the statute to be a justifiable protection against land subsidence. In its words, "the character of the government action involved here leans heavily against a taking; the Commonwealth of Pennsylvania has acted to arrest what it perceives to be a significant threat to the common welfare." 480 U.S. at 485, 107 S. Ct. at 1242.

Note that, in a categorical basis, governmental regulations seem to be preferred for takings purposes over government direct actions. In *Penn Central,* Justice Brennan identified tax laws, zoning laws, and (curiously) laws interfering with interests insufficient to qualify as "property" as among the group of more worthy measures. 438 U.S. at 124–25, 98 S.Ct. at 2659. Governmental actions which "promote the health, safety, morals or general welfare" are in this group as well. *Id.* at 125, 98 S.Ct. at 2659.

On the other side of the scale, as *Lucas* affirms, a regulation that implements a permanent physical invasion on property must fail on character grounds. Such a measure is deemed to be so deficient that it causes a taking irrespective of other considerations. For this holding, *Lucas* drew upon *Loretto v. Teleprompter Manhattan CATV Corp.,* 458 U.S. 419, 102 S.Ct. 3164 (1982), which involved a regulation mandating property owners to submit to installation of cable television transmission lines on the exterior of buildings. In *Loretto,* the Court found a taking, even though the estimated damages to plaintiff were valued at one dollar. Another Supreme Court decision, *Agins v. Tiburon,* declares a taking if a regulation fails to "substantially advance legitimate state interests." *Kaiser Aetna v. United States,* 444 U.S. 164, 100

S.Ct. 383 (1979), which held that a statute depriving a landowner of a fundamental property right is a taking, also can be read as a judicial objection based on character grounds.

On these same grounds, the Court has objected to statutes that single out individuals. *See, e.g., Yee v. City of Escondido*, 503 U.S. 519, 522–23, 112 S.Ct. 1522, 1526 (1992) ("where the government merely regulates the use of property, compensation is required only if considerations such as the purpose of the regulation or the extent to which it deprives the owner of the economic use of the property suggest that the regulation has unfairly singled out the property owner to bear a burden that should be borne by the public"). *See also Pennell v. Tri-County Apartment House Owners Ass'n*, 485 U.S. 1, 108 S. Ct. 849 (1988). In *Pennell*, lessors of residential properties contested a law that limited the amount of rentals they could charge tenants whose incomes fell below a floor level. The lessors argued that such a provision placed a financial burden on a few (rent-controlled lessors) to help effect a remedy for a problem societal in scope (poverty) and thus a taking was accomplished. Although the majority, per Justice Rehnquist, found no taking under these circumstances, Justice Scalia, in dissent, argued the statute worked a "facial taking." *Id.* He wrote:

> [The poverty] is no more caused or exploited by landlords than it is by the grocers who sell needy renters their food, or the department stores that sell them their clothes, or the employers who pay them their wages, or the citizens of San Jose holding the higher-paying jobs from which they are excluded. . . . Here the City is not "regulating" rents in the relevant sense of preventing rents that are excessive; rather, it is using the occasion of rent regulation . . . to establish a welfare program privately funded by those landlords who happen to have "hardship" tenants.

Id. at 22, 108 S. Ct. at 863.

2. Recall the decision of *Weinhold v. Wolf*, in Chapter 2, *supra*, in which the defendant attempted (unsuccessfully) to invoke a statutory defense (the "right-to-farm" law) to secure an immunity from common law nuisance liability (in *Weinhold*, the dispute involved odors released from a hog operation). Suppose the defense had been available to the defendant in *Weinhold* and had precluded plaintiff's lawsuit. Could the plaintiff have argued that the right-to-farm law worked an unconstitutional taking of plaintiff's property rights? The Iowa Supreme Court decided this question in *Bormann v. Board of Supervisors in and for Kossuth County, Iowa*, 584 N.W.2d 309 (Iowa, 1998), *cert. denied*, 119 S. Ct. 1096 (1999) (held: a taking).

3. The "nexus" test: In *Nollan v. California Coastal Commission*, 483 U.S. 825, 107 S. Ct. 3141 (1987), a local governmental entity granted a permit to a landowner to allow her to replace a bungalow on oceanfront property with a larger house. It conditioned the permit, however, by requiring the plaintiff to grant to the public an easement across their private beach, which was situated between two public beaches. *Held*, per Justice Scalia, the condition caused a taking because it did not relate to the underlying purpose for which the permit itself was issued. If the condition were related, that is, if it somehow removed the adverse effects the construction of a larger house would produce,

it could be legitimate as an exercise of land use authority and not be a taking. But here the absence of any such nexus doomed the provision. If what a state really wants is access for members of the public across a private beach, it must use its eminent domain power, not its police power, to get it.

Any such nexus must manifest a "rough proportionality." *Dolan v. City of Tigard*, 512 U.S. 374, 114 S. Ct. 2309 (1994). In other words, the exaction demanded by a government entity must bear a "reasonable relationship" to the expected impact of the permission the entity intends to give. *Id.* The Supreme Court has restricted the use of the rough proportionality standard to takings cases involving exactions. *Del Monte Dunes v. City of Monterey*, 526 U.S. 687, 119 S. Ct. 1624 (1998).

4. A necessary prerequisite to a successful takings claim is a showing that a government regulation has actually deprived a person of property rights. In some cases, this can be a problem. Consider the following cases:

(A) *Mugler v. Kansas*, 123 U.S. 623, 8 S. Ct. 273 (1887): The State of Kansas had prohibited by statute the manufacture of intoxicants for other than medical, scientific, or mechanical purposes. *Id.* at 623, 8 S. Ct. at 295. The plaintiff, who brewed and sold beer before the statute was enacted, argued the measure, as applied to him, caused a taking. The Court disagreed:

> A prohibition simply upon the use of property for purposes that are declared, by valid legislation, to be injurious to the health, morals, or safety of the community, cannot, in any just sense, be deemed a taking or an appropriation of property for the public benefit. Such legislation does not disturb the owner in the control or use of his property for lawful purposes, nor restrict his right to dispose of it, but is only a declaration by the state that its use by any one, for certain forbidden purposes, is prejudicial to the public interests.

Id. at 668–69, 8 S. Ct. at 273.

For other cases announcing the same principle in different contexts, see *Powell v. Pennsylvania*, 127 U.S. 678, 8 S. Ct. 992 (1888) (regulating the manufacture of margarine not a taking); *Hadachek v. Sebastian*, 239 U.S. 394, 36 S. Ct. 143 (1915) (prohibiting the operation of a brickyard in a residential neighborhood not a taking); *Miller v. Schoene*, 276 U.S. 272, 48 S. Ct. 246 (1928) (requiring the destruction of disease-carrying cedar trees not a taking); and *Goldblatt v. Hempstead*, 369 U.S. 590, 82 S. Ct. 987 (1962) (prohibiting the operation of a gravel pit not a taking).

The idea here, first introduced in Justice Brandeis's discussion of noxious uses in his dissent in *Pennsylvania Coal* and elaborated by Justice Scalia in *Lucas*, is a straightforward one: since no-one has a property right to use land in a noxious way, that is, in a way that wrongly harms others, a government regulation that does no more than prohibit such behavior cannot implicate the Takings Clause. A regulation of this sort, *per force,* cannot be an interference with property rights. Thus, even if the regulation reduced property value to zero, there can be no cognizable takings claim.

The difficulty is determining which uses of land regulated by government implicate property rights and which do not. Is conventional underground mining that causes surface subsidence an activity finding its source in property rights? The Supreme Court was split on the question in *Pennsylvania Coal*. For a more current case, see *M & J Coal Co. v. United States*, 47 F.3d. 1148 (D.C. Cir. 1995) (requiring a coal mine operator to leave pillars of coal in an underground mine in order to reduce surface subsidence did not give rise to a takings claim because causing subsidence, a "nuisance-like activity," was never a property right to begin with).

In *Lucas*, the reader will recall, Justice Scalia went so far as to disparage courts' ability to even make these determinations ("[T]he distinction between 'harm-preventing' and 'benefit-confering' regulation is often in the eye of the beholder.") *See, supra. Lucas* also characterized the *Mugler* line of cases as "progenitor[s] of our more contemporary statements that 'land-use regulation' does not effect a taking if it 'substantially advance[s] legitimate state interests'") (citations omitted). *Id.* at 1023–24, 112 S. Ct. at 2897. The *Lucas* "nuisance exception" principle, moreover, could be read as an amendment of noxious use doctrine, not an affirmance. Any amendment of noxious use doctrine by *Lucas* would likely extend only to total takings cases.

(B) *Just v. Marinette County*, 56 Wis. 2d 7, 201 N.W.2d 761 (1972): *Just* dealt with an ordinance in place to protect shoreland areas from erosion and other pollution problems. The ordinance prohibited the placement of fill material too close to shorelines of lakes and rivers:

> This case causes us to re-examine the concepts of public benefit in contrast to public harm and the scope of an owner's right to use of his property. In the instant case, we have a restriction on the use of a citizens' property, not to secure a benefit for the public, but to prevent a harm from the change in the natural character of the citizens' property. We start with the premise that lakes and rivers in their natural state are unpolluted and the pollution which now exists is man made. The state of Wisconsin . . . has a duty to eradicate the present pollution and to prevent further pollution in its navigable waters. This is not, in a legal sense, a gain or a securing of a benefit by the maintaining of the natural status quo of the environment. What makes this case different from most condemnation or police power zoning cases is the interrelationship of the wetlands, the swamps and the natural environment of shorelands to the purity of the water and to such natural resources as navigation, fishing, and scenic beauty. Swamps and wetlands were once considered wasteland, undesirable, and not picturesque. But as the people became more sophisticated, an appreciation was acquired that swamps and wetlands serve a vital role in nature, are part of the balance of nature and are essential to the purity of the water in our lakes and streams. Swamps and wetlands are a necessary part of the ecological creation and now, even to the uninitiated, possess their own beauty in nature

> Is the ownership of a parcel of land so absolute that man can change its nature to suit any of his purposes? The great forests of our state were stripped on the theory man's ownership was unlimited. But in forestry, the land at least was used naturally, only the natural fruit of the land (the trees) were taken. The despoilage was in the failure to look to the future and provide for the reforestation of the land. An

owner of land has no absolute and unlimited right to change the essential natural character of his land so as to use it for a purpose for which it was unsuited in its natural state and which injures the rights of others. The exercise of the police power in zoning must be reasonable and we think it is not an unreasonable exercise of that power to prevent harm to public rights by limiting the use of private property to its natural uses.

Id. at 15-16, 201 N.W.2d at 767-68. *See, e.g.,* Richard Ausness, *Regulatory Taking & Wetland Protection in the Post-*Lucas *Era,* 30 Land & Water L. Rev. 349, 403–04 (1995) ("*Lucas* is inconsistent with the reasoning of *Just v. Marinette County* and other cases that concluded that property owners have no inherent right to change the 'natural' character of their land.").

(C) *Stevens v. City of Cannon Beach,* 317 Ore. 131, 854 P.2d 449 (1993), *cert. denied,* 510 U.S. 1207, 114 S.Ct. 1332 (1994): *Stevens* was a beachfront property case akin to *Lucas.* The Oregon court held plaintiffs "were on notice that exclusive use of the dry sand areas was not a part of the 'bundle of rights' that they acquired, because public use of the dry sand areas 'is so notorious that notice of the custom on the part of persons buying land along the shore must be presumed.'" *Id.* at 139, 854 P.2d at 454.

(D) *Broughton Lumber Co. v. United States,* 30 Fed. Cl. 239 (1994): A logging company with a state water right to transport logs down a stream wanted to convert its right for use in hydropower generation. It secured a preliminary permit from the Federal Energy Regulatory Commission to do so, but intervening legislation creating a national scenic area ended that possibility. The plaintiffs claimed a taking under these facts, but the court found the plaintiff's interest in the water for electricity generation purposes was too speculative. Apparently, only 7% of applications for such permits ever result in a completed project. "A compensable interest in property based on an expected future use must be grounded on much larger certainties than opinion testimony about the likelihood of gaining future regulatory approval." *Id.* at 243.

5. The mid-1990s saw a concerted push on Capitol Hill to strengthen private property rights against what was perceived as a too-lax judicial takings policy. One bill introduced in the Congress, H.R. 3875, which had 159 co-sponsors, would have: (1) provided for compensation for landowners who lost greater than 50% of the market or use value of land; (2) required federal compliance with state and tribal property rights laws; (3) prohibited federal agents from entering private property to secure information without prior consent of owners; and (4) set up an appeals process for persons adversely affected by decisions involving wetlands or the Endangered Species Act. Similar bills were introduced in the Senate. The bills provoked a strong response from 33 Attorneys General, who stated in a letter to Congress, that the bills, if enacted, would "severely constrain the government's ability to protect the environment and public health and safety." *Letter dated Sept. 26, 1994.* None of these bills was enacted.

Chapter 4

THE NATIONAL ENVIRONMENTAL POLICY ACT

I believe, Mr. President, when historians look back to the years 1969 and 1970, they will say those were watershed years in terms of the U.S. environmental movement. Congress, concerned that the environment needed greater protection, took the lead and enacted major environmental statutes. . . . Of all these and other significant actions that took place in those 2 years, few can rival in importance the creation of the National Environmental Policy Act. Signed into law on January 1, 1970, it is a short and simple law with dramatic purpose. To declare a national policy which will encourage productive and enjoyable harmony between man and his environment. . . . NEPA has been a tremendous success and has changed forever the way our Government makes decisions affecting the environment.

Statement of Sen. John Chafee, from TWENTY YEARS OF ENVIRONMENTAL PROGRESS, Senate proceedings, March 24, 1992, Cong. Rec. S4141.

A. INTRODUCTION

TWENTIETH ANNUAL REPORT OF THE COUNCIL OF ENVIRONMENTAL QUALITY, pp. 18–20 (1990)*

HISTORICAL PERSPECTIVE

In the early 1960's when several committees of Congress began seriously looking into pollution problems, the nature and extent of such problems were not fully understood. In hearings and seminars that spanned several Congresses, legislators learned that pollution was part of a multifaceted problem, having its roots in technologically induced change and "involving natural and social sciences, economics, and governmental and private institutions." Even

---

* Copyright 1990. Reprinted with permission.

more vexing was the revelation that no single environmental problem could be considered separately, "that apparently isolated changes interact in unanticipated ways and that the eventual restoration of environmental quality will depend upon the solution of a series of interrelated problems, none of which can be understood in isolation from its fellows." Indeed, the problem appeared so overwhelming that one observer, summarizing the views offered by several experts in the field during a joint committee hearing, was "left with a vaguely uneasy feeling that if we see the continuous complex here as one set of interconnecting realities that have to be understood as a total system, we may be broadening our interests so much that it is impossible to act on it all."

The complexities and interrelatedness of the "pollution problem" caused Congress to reevaluate its practice of passing laws in response to specific episodes of environmental degradation, a practice that had led to passage of the Federal Water Pollution Control Act of 1948 and the Air Pollution Control Act of 1955. The single-solution approach typified in those statutes was unworkable, and environmental laws in general were "floundering due to inadequate information, and misinterpretation of existing facts." Many in Congress began to see the need for a comprehensive approach to the environment, one that was capable of anticipating environmentally disruptive activities and avoiding them, rather than just reacting to episodes of pollution with abatement laws.

With a greater sense of purpose and perhaps some frustration, Congress began to look more closely at the federal establishment. The federal government in the 1960s was seen to be both a major cause of environmental degradation and a major source of regulatory authority. Consequently, the federal government itself became the principal focus of further efforts to fashion a comprehensive approach to the environment.

An area where improvements had long been thought necessary, and for which legislation had been introduced as far back as the early 1960s, was the organization of the federal government. In the 1960s environmental responsibilities were divided among 15 to 20 federal departments and agencies receiving direction and funding from two dozen different Congressional committees. Reorganization of the government on a large scale, however, was not desired; nor did it "seem practical to remedy the situation by any superimposed 'czar' of environmental quality. . . ." Existing institutions were thought to be up to the task, but there was no "coordinating group capable of systems analysis and broad management of federal projects." The concept of an advisory council that "would exert a preemptive coordinating role and strive to prevent, rather than correct environmental degradation," although not new, took firm hold in Congress in the late 1960s.

A Council on Environmental Quality was the centerpiece of H.R. 12549, introduced by Representative John Dingle of Michigan and others in February 1969. The purpose of the bill was to create "a council which can provide a consistent and expert source of review of national policies, environmental problems and trends, both long-term and short-term. Such a council would act entirely independently of the executive, mission-oriented agencies." The council envisioned in H.R., 12549 would have been composed of five members and located in the Executive Office of the President. With few changes, notably the number of members, the centerpiece of H.R. 12549 became a constituent element of NEPA.

Many in Congress believed that no amount of coordination would be able to overcome the tendency for agencies to pursue their primary missions, few of which at that time included environmental quality. Further, it was apparent that great potential existed for "conflicts when environmental quality is managed by different policies, originating in conservation, agriculture, esthetics, recreation, economic development, human health, and so forth." For this reason, federal agencies needed an overall policy for the environment . . . which integrates these purposes and objectives and which provides for choice when they are incompatible . . . [mindful that] [c]hoices are not always quantitative and trade-offs are not systematic."

Given the intricacies and interrelatedness of the human environment, a policy oriented toward very specific goals or objectives was seen as impractical. Thus, it was believed that "a comprehensive policy toward the environment cannot help but be philosophical rather than specific."

What was to become the national environmental policy was prepared at the direction of Senator Henry Jackson of Washington, who considered the policy a means of establishing priorities and giving expression to "our national goals and aspirations . . . [serving] a constitutional function in that people may refer to it for guidance in making decisions where environmental values are found to be in conflict with other values." According to Senator Jackson:

> A properly drafted Congressional statement of national environmental policy, along with a requirement for official statements of environmental findings in federal decisions and legislative proposals, will effectively make the quality of the environment everyone's responsibility. No agency will then be able to maintain that it has no mandate or no requirement to consider the environmental consequences of its actions.

The need for a comprehensive environmental policy was never seriously disputed. It was recognized, however, that the mere declaration of a national environmental policy would not assure pursuit of its objectives. Agencies could very well ignore a statement of policy if not compelled somehow to do otherwise. The concept of self-policing by federal agencies that pollute or license pollution was flatly rejected. A mechanism to implement the policy was needed, an " 'action-forcing' process that could be put into operation."

* * * * * *

NEPA would be that mechanism. The statute is divisible into two functional parts, one substantive and the other procedural. The substantive part, § 101, announces the nation's environmental policy: "it is the continuing policy of the Federal Government [in cooperation with other public and private entities] to use all practicable means and measures, including financial and technical assistance, in a manner calculated to foster and promote the general welfare, to create and maintain conditions under which man and nature can exist in productive harmony, and fulfill the social, economic, and other requirements of present and future generations of Americans." § 101(a), 42 U.S.C. § 4331(a). Section 101(b) specifies the government's responsibility to act in ways so that "the Nation may —

(1) fulfill the responsibilities of each generation as trustee of the environment for succeeding generations;

(2) assure for all Americans safe, healthful, productive, and esthetically and culturally pleasing surroundings;

(3) attain the widest range of beneficial uses of the environment without degradation, risk to health or safety, or other undesirable and unintended consequences;

(4) preserve important historic, cultural, and natural aspects of our national heritage, and maintain, wherever possible, an environment which supports diversity and variety of individual choice;

(5) achieve a balance between population and resource use which will permit high standards of living and a wide sharing of life's amenities; and

(6) enhance the quality of renewable resources and approach the maximum attainable recycling of depletable resources.

§ 101(b), 42 U.S.C. 4331(b).

The procedural part of NEPA is found in § 102. That provision identifies the steps to be taken to implement the substantive goals of § 101. First, it declares, "the policies, regulations and public laws of the United States shall be interpreted in accordance with the policies set forth in this chapter. . . ." § 102(1), 42 U.S.C. § 4332(1). Second, it requires federal agencies to undertake several responsibilities, *see* § 102(2), 42 U.S.C. 4332(2), the most important of which is to prepare environmental impact statements ("EISs") to accompany major initiatives.

Importantly, NEPA also created a governmental unit to orchestrate compliance with the statute. The Council on Environmental Quality ("CEQ"), located within the Executive Office of the President, has the job of coordinating the whole of the federal environmental effort to implement NEPA. Its assignment is to oversee agency implementation of the EIS process and to referee disagreements among agencies. CEQ also works to develop environmental policies and initiatives. The Chair of CEQ, appointed by the President with the advice and consent of the Senate, serves as the principal environmental policy adviser to the President. CEQ reports annually to the President on the state of the environment.

How NEPA should operate in the real world was the subject of the *Calvert Cliffs* decision of the D.C. Circuit. *Calvert Cliffs* was the first comprehensive interpretation of the new statute.

CALVERT CLIFFS' COORDINATING COMMITTEE, INC. v. U.S. ATOMIC ENERGY COMMISSION

449 F.2d 1109 (D.C. Cir. 1971)

J. SKELLY WRIGHT, Circuit Judge:

These cases are only the beginning of what promises to become a flood of new litigation — litigation seeking judicial assistance in protecting our natural environment. Several recently enacted statutes attest to the commitment of the Government to control, at long last, the destructive engine of material "progress." But it remains to be seen whether the promise of this legislation will become a reality. Therein lies the judicial role. In these cases, we must for the first time interpret the broadest and perhaps most important of the recent statutes: the National Environmental Policy Act of 1969 (NEPA). We must assess claims that one of the agencies charged with its administration has failed to live up to the congressional mandate. Our duty, in short, is to see that important legislative purposes, heralded in the halls of Congress, are not lost or misdirected in the vast hallways of the federal bureaucracy.

NEPA, like so much other reform legislation of the last 40 years, is cast in terms of a general mandate and broad delegation of authority to new and old administrative agencies. It takes the major step of requiring all federal agencies to consider values of environmental preservation in their spheres of activity, and it prescribes certain procedural measures to ensure that those values are in fact fully respected. Petitioners argue that rules recently adopted by the Atomic Energy Commission to govern consideration of environmental matters fail to satisfy the rigor demanded by NEPA. The Commission, on the other hand, contends that the vagueness of the NEPA mandate and delegation leaves much room for discretion and that the rules challenged by petitioners fall well within the broad scope of the Act. We find the policies embodied in NEPA to be a good deal clearer and more demanding than does the Commission. We conclude that the Commission's procedural rules do not comply with the congressional policy. Hence we remand these cases for further rule making.

I

We begin our analysis with an examination of NEPA's structure and approach and of the Atomic Energy Commission rules which are said to conflict with the requirements of the Act. The relevant portion of NEPA is Title I, consisting of five sections. Section 101 sets forth the Act's basic substantive policy: that the federal government "use all practicable means and measures" to protect environmental values. Congress did not establish environmental protection as an exclusive goal; rather, it desired a reordering of priorities, so that environmental costs and benefits will assume their proper place along with other considerations. In Section 101(b), imposing an explicit duty on federal officials, the Act provides that "it is the continuing responsibility of the Federal Government to use all practicable means, consistent with other essential considerations of national policy," to avoid environmental degradation, preserve "historic, cultural, and natural" resources, and promote "the widest range of beneficial uses of the environment without * * * undesirable and unintended consequences."

Thus the general substantive policy of the Act is a flexible one. It leaves room for a responsible exercise of discretion and may not require particular substantive results in particular problematic instances. However, the Act also contains very important "procedural" provisions — provisions which are designed to see that all federal agencies do in fact exercise the substantive discretion given them. These provisions are not highly flexible. Indeed, they establish a strict standard of compliance.

NEPA, first of all, makes environmental protection a part of the mandate of every federal agency and department. The Atomic Energy Commission, for example, had continually asserted, prior to NEPA, that it had no statutory authority to concern itself with the adverse environmental effects of its actions. Now, however, its hands are no longer tied. It is not only permitted, but compelled, to take environmental values into account. Perhaps the greatest importance of NEPA is to require the Atomic Energy Commission and other agencies to consider environmental issues just as they consider other matters within their mandates. This compulsion is most plainly stated in Section 102. There, "Congress authorizes and directs that, to the fullest extent possible: (1) the policies, regulations, and public laws of the United States shall be interpreted and administered in accordance with the policies set forth in this Act * * *." Congress also "authorizes and directs" that "(2) all agencies of the Federal Government shall" follow certain rigorous procedures in considering environmental values. Senator Jackson, NEPA's principal sponsor, stated that "no agency will [now] be able to maintain that it has no mandate or no requirement to consider the environmental consequences of its actions." He characterized the requirements of Section 102 as "action-forcing" and stated that "otherwise, these lofty declarations [in Section 101] are nothing more than that."

The sort of consideration of environmental values which NEPA compels is clarified in Section 102(2)(A) and (B). In general, all agencies must use a "systematic, interdisciplinary approach" to environmental planning and evaluation "in decisionmaking which may have an impact on man's environment." In order to include all possible environmental factors in the decisional equation, agencies must "identify and develop methods and procedures * * * which will insure that presently unquantified environmental amenities and values may be given appropriate consideration in decisionmaking along with economic and technical considerations." "Environmental amenities" will often be in conflict with "economic and technical considerations." To "consider" the former "along with" the latter must involve a balancing process. In some instances environmental costs may outweigh economic and technical benefits and in other instances they may not. But NEPA mandates a rather finely tuned and "systematic" balancing analysis in each instance.

To ensure that the balancing analysis is carried out and given full effect, Section 102(2)(C) requires that responsible officials of all agencies prepare a "detailed statement" covering the impact of particular actions on the environment, the environmental costs which might be avoided, and alternative measures which might alter the cost-benefit equation. The apparent purpose of the "detailed statement" is to aid in the agencies' own decision making process and to advise other interested agencies and the public of the environmental consequences of planned federal action. Beyond the "detailed statement," Section 102(2)(D) requires all agencies specifically to "study, develop, and describe appropriate alternatives to recommended courses of action in any proposal which involves unresolved conflicts concerning alternative uses of available resources." This requirement, like the "detailed statement" requirement, seeks to ensure that each agency decision maker has before him and takes into proper account all possible approaches to a particular project (including total abandonment of the project) which would alter the environmental impact and the cost-benefit balance. Only in that fashion is it likely that the most intelligent, optimally beneficial decision will ultimately be made. Moreover, by compelling a formal "detailed statement" and a description of alternatives, NEPA provides evidence that the mandated decision making process has in fact taken place and, most importantly, allows those removed from the initial process to evaluate and balance the factors on their own.

Of course, all of these Section 102 duties are qualified by the phrase "to the fullest extent possible." We must stress as forcefully as possible that this language does not provide an escape hatch for footdragging agencies; it does not make NEPA's procedural requirements somehow "discretionary." Congress did not intend the Act to be such a paper tiger. Indeed, the requirement of environmental consideration "to the fullest extent possible" sets a high standard for the agencies, a standard which must be rigorously enforced by the reviewing courts.

Unlike the substantive duties of Section 101(b), which require agencies to "use all practicable means consistent with other essential considerations," the procedural duties of Section 102 must be fulfilled to the "fullest extent possible." This contrast, in itself, is revealing. But the dispositive factor in our interpretation is the expressed views of the Senate and House conferees who wrote the "fullest extent possible" language into NEPA. They stated:

> "* * * The purpose of the new language is to make it clear that each agency of the Federal Government shall comply with the directives set out in * * * [Section 102(2)] unless the existing law applicable to such agency's operations expressly prohibits or makes full compliance with one of the directives impossible. * * * Thus, it is the intent of the conferees that the provision 'to the fullest extent possible' shall not be used by any Federal agency as a means of avoiding compliance with the directives set out in section 102. Rather, the language in section 102 is intended to assure that all agencies of the Federal Government shall comply with the directives set out in said section 'to the fullest extent possible' under their statutory authorizations and that no agency shall utilize an excessively narrow construction of its existing statutory authorizations to avoid compliance."

Thus the Section 102 duties are not inherently flexible. They must be complied with to the fullest extent, unless there is a clear conflict of statutory authority. Considerations of administrative difficulty, delay or economic cost will not suffice to strip the section of its fundamental importance.

We conclude, then, that Section 102 of NEPA mandates a particular sort of careful and informed decisionmaking process and creates judicially enforceable duties. The reviewing courts probably cannot reverse a substantive decision on its merits, under Section 101, unless it be shown that the actual balance of costs and benefits that was struck was arbitrary or clearly gave insufficient weight to environmental values. But if the decision was reached procedurally without individualized consideration and balancing of environmental factors — conducted fully and in good faith — it is the responsibility of the courts to reverse. As one District Court has said of Section 102 requirements: "It is hard to imagine a clearer or stronger mandate to the Courts."

In the cases before us now, we do not have to review a particular decision by the Atomic Energy Commission granting a construction permit or an operating license. Rather, we must review the Commission's recently promulgated rules which govern consideration of environmental values in all such individual decisions. The rules were devised strictly in order to comply with the NEPA procedural requirements — but petitioners argue that they fall far short of the congressional mandate.

The period of the rules' gestation does not indicate overenthusiasm on the Commission's part. NEPA went into effect on January 1, 1970. On April 2, 1970 — three months later — the Commission issued its first, short policy statement on implementation of the Act's procedural provisions. After another span of two months, the Commission published a notice of proposed rule making in the Federal Register. Petitioners submitted substantial comments critical of the proposed rules. Finally, on December 3, 1970, the Commission terminated its long rule making proceeding by issuing a formal amendment, labelled Appendix D, to its governing regulations. Appendix D is a somewhat revised version of the earlier proposal and, at last, commits the Commission to consider environmental impact in its decision making process.

The procedure for environmental study and consideration set up by the Appendix D rules is as follows: Each applicant for an initial construction permit must submit to the Commission his own "environmental report," presenting his assessment of the environmental impact of the planned facility and possible alternatives which would alter the impact. When construction is completed and the applicant applies for a license to operate the new facility, he must again submit an "environmental report" noting any factors which have changed since the original report. At each stage, the Commission's regulatory staff must take the applicant's report and prepare its own "detailed statement" of environmental costs, benefits and alternatives. The statement will then be circulated to other interested and responsible agencies and made available to the public. After comments are received from those sources, the staff must prepare a final "detailed statement" and make a final recommendation on the application for a construction permit or operating license.

Up to this point in the Appendix D rules petitioners have raised no challenge. However, they do attack four other, specific parts of the rules which, they say, violate the requirements of Section 102 of NEPA. Each of these parts in some way limits full consideration and individualized balancing of environmental values in the Commission's decision making process. (1) Although environmental factors must be considered by the agency's regulatory staff under the rules, such factors need not be considered by the hearing board conducting an independent review of staff recommendations, unless affirmatively raised by outside parties or staff members. (2) Another part of the procedural rules prohibits any such party from raising nonradiological environmental issues at any hearing if the notice for that hearing appeared in the Federal Register before March 4, 1971. (3) Moreover, the hearing board is prohibited from conducting an independent evaluation and balancing of certain environmental factors if other responsible agencies have already certified that their own environmental standards are satisfied by the proposed federal action. (4) Finally, the Commission's rules provide that when a construction permit for a facility has been issued before NEPA compliance was required and when an operating license has yet to be issued, the agency will not formally consider environmental factors or require modifications in the proposed facility until the time of the issuance of the operating license. Each of these parts of the Commission's rules will be described at greater length and evaluated under NEPA in the following sections of this opinion.

II

NEPA makes only one specific reference to consideration of environmental values in agency review processes. Section 102(2)(C) provides that copies of the staff's "detailed statement" and comments thereon "shall accompany the proposal through the existing agency review processes." The Atomic Energy Commission's rules may seem in technical compliance with the letter of that provision. They state:

> "12. If any party to a proceeding * * * raises any [environmental] issue * * * the Applicant's Environmental Report and the Detailed Statement will be offered in evidence. The atomic safety and licensing board will make findings of fact on, and resolve, the matters in controversy among the parties with regard to those issues. Depending on the resolution of those issues, the permit or license may be granted, denied, or appropriately conditioned to protect environmental values.

> "13. When no party to a proceeding * * * raises any [environmental] issue * * * such issues will not be considered by the atomic safety and licensing board. Under such circumstances, although the Applicant's Environmental Report, comments thereon, and the Detailed Statement will accompany the application through the Commission's review processes, they will not be received in evidence, and the Commission's responsibilities under the National Environmental Policy Act of 1969 will be carried out in toto outside the hearing process."

The question here is whether the Commission is correct in thinking that its NEPA responsibilities may "be carried out in toto outside the hearing process" — whether it is enough that environmental data and evaluations merely "accompany" an application through the review process, but receive no consideration whatever from the hearing board.

We believe that the Commission's crabbed interpretation of NEPA makes a mockery of the Act. What possible purpose could there be in the Section 102

(2)(C) requirement (that the "detailed statement" accompany proposals through agency review processes) if "accompany" means no more than physical proximity — mandating no more than the physical act of passing certain folders and papers, unopened, to reviewing officials along with other folders and papers? What possible purpose could there be in requiring the "detailed statement" to be before hearing boards, if the boards are free to ignore entirely the contents of the statement? NEPA was meant to do more than regulate the flow of papers in the federal bureaucracy. The word "accompany" in Section 102(2)(C) must not be read so narrowly as to make the Act ludicrous. It must, rather, be read to indicate a congressional intent that environmental factors, as compiled in the "detailed statement," be considered through agency review processes.

Beyond Section 102(2)(C), NEPA requires that agencies consider the environmental impact of their actions "to the fullest extent possible." The Act is addressed to agencies as a whole, not only to their professional staffs. Compliance to the "fullest" possible extent would seem to demand that environmental issues be considered at every important stage in the decision making process concerning a particular action — at every stage where an overall balancing of environmental and nonenvironmental factors is appropriate and where alterations might be made in the proposed action to minimize environmental costs. Of course, consideration which is entirely duplicative is not necessarily required. But independent review of staff proposals by hearing boards is hardly a duplicative function. A truly independent review provides a crucial check on the staff's recommendations. The Commission's hearing boards automatically consider nonenvironmental factors, even though they have been previously studied by the staff. Clearly, the review process is an appropriate stage at which to balance conflicting factors against one another. And, just as clearly, it provides an important opportunity to reject or significantly modify the staff's recommended action. Environmental factors, therefore, should not be singled out and excluded, at this stage, from the proper balance of values envisioned by NEPA.

The Commission's regulations provide that in an uncontested proceeding the hearing board shall on its own "determine whether the application and the record of the proceeding contain sufficient information, and the review of the application by the Commission's regulatory staff has been adequate, to support affirmative findings on" various nonenvironmental factors. NEPA requires at least as much automatic consideration of environmental factors. In uncontested hearings, the board need not necessarily go over the same ground covered in the "detailed statement." But it must at least examine the statement carefully to determine whether "the review * * * by the Commission's regulatory staff has been adequate." And it must independently consider the final balance among conflicting factors that is struck in the staff's recommendation.

The rationale of the Commission's limitation of environmental issues to hearings in which parties affirmatively raise those issues may have been one of economy. It may have been supposed that, whenever there are serious environmental costs overlooked or uncorrected by the staff, some party will intervene to bring those costs to the hearing board's attention. Of course, independent review of the "detailed statement" and independent balancing of factors in an uncontested hearing will take some time. If it is done properly, it will take a significant amount of time. But all of the NEPA procedures take time. Such administrative costs are not enough to undercut the Act's requirement that environmental protection be considered "to the fullest extent possible," * * * It is, moreover, unrealistic to assume that there will always be an intervenor with the information, energy and money required to challenge a staff recommendation which ignores environmental costs. NEPA establishes environmental protection as an integral part of the Atomic Energy Commission's basic mandate. The primary responsibility for fulfilling that mandate lies with the Commission. Its responsibility is not simply to sit back, like an umpire, and resolve adversary contentions at the hearing stage. Rather, it must itself take the initiative of considering environmental values at every distinctive and comprehensive stage of the process beyond the staff's evaluation and recommendation. * * *

The Honorable J. Skelly Wright
Photograph by Richard Avedon

IV

The sweep of NEPA is extraordinarily broad, compelling consideration of any and all types of environmental impact of federal action. However, the Atomic Energy Commission's rules specifically exclude from full consideration a wide variety of environmental issues. First, they provide that no party may raise and the Commission may not independently examine any problem of water quality — perhaps the most significant impact of nuclear power plants. Rather, the Commission indicates that it will defer totally to water quality standards devised and administered by state agencies and approved by the federal government under the Federal Water Pollution Control Act. Secondly, the rules provide for similar abdication of NEPA authority to the standards of other agencies:

> "With respect to those aspects of environmental quality for which environmental quality standards and requirements have been established by authorized Federal, State, and regional agencies, proof that the applicant is equipped to observe and agrees to observe such standards and requirements will be considered a satisfactory showing that there will not be a significant, adverse effect on the environment. Certification by the appropriate agency that there is reasonable assurance that the applicant for the permit or license will observe such standards and requirements will be considered dispositive for this purpose."

10 C.F.R. § 50, App. D, at 249.

The most the Commission will do is include a condition in all construction permits and operating licenses requiring compliance with the water quality or other standards set by such agencies. The upshot is that the NEPA procedures, viewed by the Commission as superfluous, will wither away in disuse, applied only to those environmental issues wholly unregulated by any other federal, state or regional body.

We believe the Commission's rule is in fundamental conflict with the basic purpose of the Act. NEPA mandates a case-by-case balancing judgment on the part of federal agencies. In each individual case, the particular economic and technical benefits of planned action must be assessed and then weighed against the environmental costs; alternatives must be considered which would affect the balance of values. * * * The magnitude of possible benefits and possible costs may lie anywhere on a broad spectrum. Much will depend on the particular magnitudes involved in particular cases. In some cases, the benefits will be great enough to justify a certain quantum of environmental costs; in other cases, they will not be so great and the proposed action may have to be abandoned or significantly altered so as to bring the benefits and costs into a proper balance. The point of the individualized balancing analysis is to ensure that, with possible alterations, the optimally beneficial action is finally taken.

Certification by another agency that its own environmental standards are satisfied involves an entirely different kind of judgment. Such agencies, without overall responsibility for the particular federal action in question, attend only to one aspect of the problem: the magnitude of certain environmental costs. They simply determine whether those costs exceed an allowable amount. Their certification does not mean that they found no environmental damage whatever. In fact, there may be significant environmental damage (e.g., water pollution), but not quite enough to violate applicable (e.g., water quality) standards. Certifying agencies do not attempt to weigh that damage against the opposing benefits. Thus the balancing analysis remains to be done.

It may be that the environmental costs, though passing prescribed standards, are nonetheless great enough to outweigh the particular economic and technical benefits involved in the planned action. The only agency in a position to make such a judgment is the agency with overall responsibility for the proposed federal action — the agency to which NEPA is specifically directed.

The Atomic Energy Commission, abdicating entirely to other agencies' certifications, neglects the mandated balancing analysis. Concerned members of the public are thereby precluded from raising a wide range of environmental issues in order to affect particular Commission decisions. And the special purpose of NEPA is subverted.

Arguing before this court, the Commission has made much of the special environmental expertise of the agencies which set environmental standards. NEPA did not overlook this consideration. Indeed, the Act is quite explicit in describing the attention which is to be given to the views and standards of other agencies. Section 102 (2)(C) provides:

> "Prior to making any detailed statement, the responsible Federal official shall consult with and obtain the comments of any Federal agency which has jurisdiction by law or special expertise with respect to any environmental impact involved. Copies of such statement and the comments and views of the appropriate Federal, State, and local agencies, which are authorized to develop and enforce environmental standards, shall be made available to the President, the Council on Environmental Quality and to the public * * *."

Thus the Congress was surely cognizant of federal, state and local agencies "authorized to develop and enforce environmental standards." But it provided, in Section 102(2)(C), only for full consultation. It most certainly did not authorize a total abdication to those agencies. Nor did it grant a license to disregard the main body of NEPA obligations.* * *

The Commission relies upon the flexible NEPA mandate to "use all practicable means consistent with other essential considerations of national policy." As we have previously pointed out, however, that mandate applies only to the substantive guidelines set forth in Section 101 of the Act. * * * The procedural duties, the duties to give full consideration to environmental protection, are subject to a much more strict standard of compliance. By now, the applicable principle should be absolutely clear. NEPA requires that an agency must — to the fullest extent possible under its other statutory obligations — consider alternatives to its actions which would reduce environmental damage. That principle establishes that consideration of environmental matters must be more than a pro forma ritual. Clearly, it is pointless to "consider" environmental costs without also seriously considering action to avoid them. Such a full exercise of substantive discretion is required at every important, appropriate and nonduplicative stage of an agency's proceedings. * * *

A full NEPA consideration of alterations in the original plans of a facility, then, is both important and appropriate well before the operating license proceedings. It is not duplicative if environmental issues were not considered in granting the construction permit. And it need not be duplicated, absent new information or new developments, at the operating license stage. In order that the pre-operating license review be as effective as possible, the Commission should consider very seriously the requirement of a temporary halt in construction pending its review and the "backfitting" of technological innovations. For no action which might minimize environmental damage may be dismissed out of hand. Of course, final operation of the facility may be delayed thereby. But some delay is inherent whenever the NEPA consideration is conducted — whether before or at the license proceedings. It is far more consistent with the purposes of the Act to delay operation at a stage where real environmental protection may come about than at a stage where corrective action may be so costly as to be impossible.

Thus we conclude that the Commission must go farther than it has in its present rules. It must consider action, as well as file reports and papers, at the pre-operating license stage. As the Commission candidly admits, such consideration does not amount to a retroactive application of NEPA. Although the projects in question may have been commenced and initially approved before January 1, 1970, the Act clearly applies to them since they must still pass muster before going into full operation. All we demand is that the environmental review be as full and fruitful as possible.

VI

We hold that, in the four respects detailed above, the Commission must revise its rules governing consideration of environmental issues. We do not impose a harsh burden on the Commission. For we require only an exercise of substantive discretion which will protect the environment "to the fullest extent possible." No less is required if the grand congressional purposes underlying NEPA are to become a reality.

Remanded for proceedings consistent with this opinion.

NOTES AND QUESTIONS

1. *Calvert Cliffs* is a landmark decision in environmental and natural resources law mainly because it held that the National Environmental Policy Act really means something. In particular, the case breathed life into § 102(2) of the statute, which was found to impose significant and enforceable obligations on federal agencies. The result has been the elevation of NEPA to prominent stature in environmental and natural resources law. An indicator of that stature is the frequency of judicial consideration of the measure. A LEXIS search in the federal courts library, using the search terms "National Environmental Policy Act," undertaken July 12, 2004, yielded more than 3000 citations. *See also* William H. Rodgers, Jr., *Environmental Law* § 9.1.C.3, at 817–18 (2d ed. West Pub. Co. 1994) (attesting to NEPA's production of "hundreds of injunctions, thousands of cases, tens of thousands of impact statements, hundreds of thousands of environmental assessments.").

Calvert Cliffs' reading of NEPA was by no means assured. NEPA, by its terms, only requires agencies to take the procedural steps of § 102 "to the fullest extent possible." Judge Wright eschewed the notion that this modifying phrase might serve as "an escape hatch for footdragging agencies . . .," but he easily could have found the phrase to be just that. Judicial reporters are replete with decisions that dilute the impact of legal obligations because the statute imposing the obligation required the task be done only to the extent "appropriate" or "reasonable," or "as much as possible."

Why did Judge Wright choose to give a full measure of rigor to the obligations of § 102? He offered two reasons. First, he noted the distinction between the phrasing of § 101, which requires compliance by use of "all practicable means consistent with other essential considerations . . ." with that of § 102, which requires compliance "to the fullest extent possible." Judge Wright found this contrast to be "revealing" although not dispositive.

What was dispositive for Judge Wright was NEPA's legislative history. In particular, he cited the report of Senate and House conferees which specified that the "fullest extent possible" language should not serve to excuse agency nonperformance. Thus was raised the longstanding issue of the role legislative history should play in the search for statutory meaning. Proponents of using legislative history assert it sheds important light on the meaning of often ambiguous legislative text. Associate Justice Stephen Breyer of the U.S. Supreme Court, an advocate for use of legislative history, has stated that "using legislative history to help interpret unclear statutory language seems natural. Legislative history helps a court understand the context and purpose of a statute." Stephen Breyer, *On the Uses of Legislative History in Interpreting Statutes*, 65 S. Cal. L. Rev. 845, 848 (1992).

Opponents maintain that legislative history is irrelevant to statutory meaning. Associate Justice Antonin Scalia of the U.S. Supreme Court, a leader in this camp, has commented that "it is simply incompatible with democratic government, or indeed, even with fair government, to have the meaning of a law determined by what the lawgiver meant, rather than by what the lawgiver promulgated. . . . It is the *law* that governs, not the intent of the lawgiver." Antonin Scalia, *A Matter of Interpretation: Federal Courts and the Law,* at 17 (Princeton Univ. Press 1997). Scalia and others maintain as well that legislative history is unreliable in any event. Lastly, they bemoan the ease with which legislative history can be manipulated by persons who prefer one interpretation of an ambiguous statute over another. As Judge Sentelle noted, reviewing legislative history is like "looking over a crowd and picking out your friends." *Citizens Coal Council v. Norton,* 330 F.2d 478, 484 (D.C. Cir. 2003).

If his opinion in *Calvert Cliffs* is a measure, Judge Skelly Wright obviously counted himself among those who view legislative history as a helpful analytical tool. Might there be other reasons he opted for such a strong pro-environment reading of NEPA? One possibility is a convergence of factors external to the case but possibly influential on the Judge. First, it is clear that Judge Wright did not seem to hold federal agencies in high regard: witness his fear, expressed in *Calvert Cliffs,* that "important legislative purposes" could be "lost or misdirected in the vast hallways of the federal bureaucracy." Second, because he presided over numerous environmental law cases, Judge Wright assuredly came to look upon himself as an expert on environmental law and regulation in his own right. Third, he viewed himself unabashedly as a judicial activist, and a liberal one at that. For an interesting analysis of Judge Wright in this regard, drawn from his own comments about himself and others on the D.C. Circuit, see Gary Lawson, *Federal Administrative Law* at 240, n.35 (West Pub. Co., 1998).[1]

2. Shortly after NEPA was enacted, President Richard Nixon issued Executive Order 11514, which directed the Council on Environmental Quality to issue guidelines on how NEPA should be implemented across the federal government. Despite these guidelines, agencies complained during the 1970s that NEPA imposed too heavy a work burden and caused too much delay. These concerns prompted President Jimmy Carter to issue Executive Order 11991, which instructed CEQ to issue regulations to make NEPA compliance less burdensome. These regulations, as amended, may be found at 40 C.F.R. Parts 1500–17.

NEPA AT 19: A PRIMER ON AN "OLD" LAW WITH SOLUTIONS TO "NEW" PROBLEMS, 19 Envt'l Law Rptr. 10060 (1989)[*]

. . . .

Regulatory Structure

The CEQ regulations implementing the procedural provisions of NEPA apply to all federal agencies of the government, excluding Congress and any of its institutions, the judiciary, and the President, including the performance of staff functions for the President. The CEQ regulations are generic in nature, and do not address the applicability of the various procedural requirements to specific agency actions. Instead, each federal department and agency is required to prepare its own NEPA procedures that address that agency's compliance in relation to its particular mission. CEQ reviews and approves all agency procedures and amendments to those procedures.

The agency procedures are required to establish specific criteria for and identification of three classes of actions: those that require preparation of an environmental impact statement; those that require preparation of an environmental assessment; and those that are categorically excluded from further NEPA review. Additionally, agencies are required to address NEPA compliance for actions initiated outside of the federal government that require federal approval, the introduction of supplemental EISs into the administrative record, the integration of NEPA analysis into the agency decisionmaking process, and to name a contact office for further information or documents prepared under NEPA.

---

[1] The United States Supreme Court later trimmed the activist wings of the D.C. Circuit, at least with respect to the judicial imposition of procedures on executive agencies, in *Vermont Yankee Nuclear Power Corp. v. Natural Resources Defense Council, Inc.*, 435 U.S. 519, 98 S. Ct. 1197 (1978).

Categorical Exclusions

"Categorical exclusions" refer to acts falling within a pre-designated category of actions that do not individually or cumulatively have a significant effect on the human environment. Thus, no documentation of environmental analysis is required. Agencies may list either very specific actions, or a broader class of actions with criteria and examples for guidance. However, federal officials must be alert to extraordinary circumstances in which a normally excluded action may have a significant environmental effect. A categorical exclusion is not an exemption from compliance with NEPA, but merely an administrative tool to avoid paperwork for those actions without significant environmental effects.

Environmental Assessments

An environmental assessment ("EA") is supposed to be a concise public document that may be prepared to achieve any of the following purposes: to provide sufficient evidence and analysis for determining whether to prepare an EIS; to aid an agency's compliance with NEPA when no EIS is necessary; and to facilitate preparation of an EIS if one is necessary. An EA should include a brief discussion of the need for the proposal, of alternatives as required by NEPA § 102(2)(E), and of the environmental impacts of the proposed action and alternatives. It should list agencies and persons consulted. An EA is followed by one of two conclusions: either a Finding of No Significant Impact ("FONSI") or a decision to prepare an EIS. A FONSI briefly presents the reasons why an action, not otherwise categorically excluded, will not have a significant effect on the human environment. It may include a summary of the EA, or simply be attached to the EA. Neither EAs nor FONSIs are filed in a central location (unlike EISs, which are filed with the Office of Federal Activities in the Environmental Protection Agency). However, they are public documents, and the agency responsible for their preparation must involve the public in an appropriate manner.

Agencies have discretion in selecting the appropriate level of public circulation of EAs and FONSIs, but there are two circumstances in which an agency is required to make a FONSI available for public review for thirty days. The first situation is when the proposed action is, or is closely similar to, an action which normally requires an EIS; the second case arises if the nature of the proposed action is without precedent in the agency's experience.

While the EA and FONSI process is a valuable and even essential tool, it has been subjected, far too often, to two types of abuse. On the one hand, some compliance has reduced the EA analysis to a one-page form that is so cursory that it is questionable whether the underlying decision about whether to prepare an EIS is sound. On the other hand, an EA all too frequently takes on the look, feel, and form of an EIS, complete with the same qualitative contents and volume and weight. There can be several reasons for this, but certainly one unfortunate rationale has been to avoid as much public involvement as an EIS would stimulate, while being prepared to turn the EA into an EIS rapidly if a court would so order. Agency officials thinking of that approach would be far better advised to simply proceed with circulation of the document as an EIS.

Environmental Impact Statements

The primary purpose of an EIS is to serve as an action-forcing device to ensure that the policies and goals defined in NEPA are infused into the ongoing programs and actions of the federal government. It must provide full and fair discussion of significant environmental impacts and shall inform decision-makers and the public of the reasonable alternatives that would avoid or minimize adverse impacts or enhance the quality of the human environment. In preparing EISs, agencies should focus on significant environmental issues and alternatives and reduce paperwork and the accumulation of extraneous background data. Texts should be concise, clear, and to the point, and should be supported by evidence that the agency has made the necessary environmental analyses. An EIS is more than a disclosure document; it should be used by federal officials to plan actions and make decisions. * * *

Two types of EISs that have received less attention than the typical project-specific EIS are the programmatic EIS and the legislative EIS. Programmatic EISs must be prepared prior to an agency's decision regarding a major program, plan, or policy with significant environmental impacts. It may be broad in scope, followed by site-specific EISs or EAs prepared at subsequent stages. The process of preparing a broad statement and subsequent, more narrowly focused NEPA documents is referred to as tiering. Legislative EISs meet the statutory requirement for a "detailed statement on proposals for legislation which would significantly affect the quality of the human environment." Although there are some modifications, the procedures for preparation of legislative EISs are similar to EISs prepared for proposals for executive branch action.

Once the decision is made to prepare an EIS of any type, the proponent federal agency publishes a Notice of Intent ("NOI") in the Federal Register. The NOI should describe the proposed action and possible alternatives, the agency's intent to prepare an EIS, the agency's proposed scoping process, and any planned scoping meetings, and the name and address of a contact person in the agency.

The agency must then engage in the "scoping process," a process to determine the scope of issues to be addressed in the EIS and for identifying the significant issues related to a proposed action. Scoping may or may not include meetings, but the process should involve interested parties at all levels of government, and all interested private citizens and organizations. Scoping is also the appropriate point to allocate responsibilities among lead and cooperating agencies, identify other environmental requirements that are applicable to the proposal, set any time and page limits, and, in general, structure the process in such a way that all identifiable participants are informed and involved at appropriate points. A well designed scoping process can have an extremely positive ripple effect throughout the rest of the NEPA process.

The next step is preparation of a draft EIS. The EIS may be prepared either by the lead agency, with assistance from any cooperating agencies, or by a contractor. However, if a contractor prepares the EIS, the contractor should be chosen by the agency and must execute a disclosure statement prepared by the lead agency, specifying that the contractor has no financial or other interest in the outcome of the project. The agency may accept information from any party, including the applicant, but it always has the duty to independently evaluate such information.

The content requirements of an EIS, from cover sheet to appendices, are set out in the CEQ regulations. The "heart" of the EIS is the alternatives analysis, which inevitably leads to the question of which alternatives must be analyzed. The answer to that, like the answer to the question of what is "significant," is addressed on a case-by-case basis, with the key judicial standard being that of reasonableness.

If the proposed action is the subject of a request for a federal permit or regulatory approval for a proposed action, the federal agency must consider both public and private purpose and need. Courts have stressed the need to consider the objectives of the permit applicant, but they have also emphasized the requirement for the agency to exercise independent judgment as to the appropriate articulation of objective purpose and need. Thus, NEPA requires the agency to consider both public and private purpose and need in formulating the alternatives to be examined in an EIS.

Once the draft EIS is prepared, it must be circulated for at least 45 days for public comment and review. Federal agencies with jurisdiction by law or special expertise with respect to any of the relevant environmental impacts are expected to comment, although this may take the form of a "no comment" letter. At the conclusion of the comment period, the agency must evaluate the comment letters and respond to the substantive comments in the final EIS. The final EIS is sent to all parties who commented on the draft EIS. No decision may be made concerning the proposed action until at least 30 days after the Notice of Availability of the final EIS or 90 days after the publication of the Notice of Availability of the draft EIS, whichever is later.

At the time of decision, the decisionmaker must sign a Record of Decision ("ROD"). The ROD states what the decision is, identifies which alternatives were considered by the agency in making the decision, specifies which alternatives were considered by the agency in making the decision, specifies which alternatives were considered to be environmentally preferable, and discusses factors that were balanced by the decisionmaker. Further, the ROD states whether all practical methods to avoid or minimize environmental harm are being adopted, and if not, why not. The ROD also includes a description of any applicable enforcement and monitoring programs.

B. EXCEPTIONS TO APPLICABILITY

The National Environmental Policy Act does not always apply according to its terms. In some circumstances it has been ruled to be inapplicable by courts, and in others by the Council on Environmental Quality, in its regulations at 40 C.F.R. Parts 1500–07. (Note that CEQ's regulations are binding on all federal agencies except where compliance with them would be "inconsistent with other statutory requirements." 40 C.F.R. § 1500.3). In the following circumstances, the statute, or at least the requirements of § 102(2) thereof, has been found not to apply:

(1) *Statutory conflicts*: The NEPA EIS requirement does not apply to government action where the statute authorizing the government action makes NEPA inapplicable. Sometimes a statute expressly makes NEPA inapplicable. *See, e.g.,* Clean Water Act, § 511(c)(1), 33 U.S.C.A. § 1371(c)(1). In other cases, a statute might impliedly make NEPA inapplicable. In this regard, *see, e.g., Alabama v. EPA*, 911 F.2d 499, 504 (11th Cir. 1990) (holding that NEPA does not apply to EPA's permit decisions under § 3005 of the federal Resource Conservation and Recovery Act because RCRA, enacted after NEPA and specifically directing the EPA permitting process, represents an implied exception to NEPA applicability).

(2) *Nondiscretionary actions:* NEPA does not apply to agency actions compelled by statute and regarding which the agency has no discretion. *Flint Ridge Development Co. v. Scenic Rivers Ass'n*, 426 U.S. 776, 96 S. Ct. 2430 (1976).

(3) *Functionally equivalent actions:* By judicial fiat, NEPA does not apply in limited circumstances when the action of the agency to which NEPA would normally apply is itself the "functional equivalent" of an EIS. *See, e.g., Environmental Defense Fund, Inc. v. United States Environmental Protection Agency*, 489 F.2d 1247 (D.C. Cir. 1973) (NEPA does not apply to the "environmentally protective regulatory activities of the Administrator conducted under the registration cancellation provision of the [Federal Insecticide, Fungicide, and Rodenticide Act].") While declining to endorse a broader exemption for EPA, the court stated: "we see little need in requiring a NEPA statement from an agency whose raison d'etre is the protection of the environment and whose decision on suspension is necessarily infused with the environmental considerations so pertinent to Congress in designing the statutory framework." *Id.* at 1256; *Portland Cement Ass'n v. Ruckelshaus*, 486 F.2d 375 (D.C. Cir. 1973) (EPA's promulgation of stationary source standards for cement plants under the Clean Air Act does not fall under NEPA as the Clean Air Act is the "functional equivalent" of an environmental impact statement). The idea is a logical one: if an agency decision by its very nature implicates a careful consideration of environmental issues, there is no need for an EIS:

> As long as the statutory and regulatory framework under [the statute] "provides for orderly consideration of diverse environmental factors and . . . [strikes] a workable balance between some of the advantages and disadvantages of full application of NEPA," the 'functional equivalent' doctrine applies. . . .

Alabamians for a Clean Env't v. Thomas, 26 ERC 2116, 2122 (D. Ala. 1987).

(4) *Emergencies*: Emergency actions may not be subject to NEPA. CEQ's regulations provide:

> Where emergency circumstances make it necessary to take an action with significant environmental impact without observing the provisions of these regulations, the Federal agency taking the action

should consult with the Council about alternative arrangements. Agencies and the Council will limit such arrangements to actions necessary to control the immediate impacts of the emergency. Other actions remain subject to NEPA review.

40 C.F.R. § 1506.11.

(5) *Categorical exclusions*: As noted in the preceding article, federal agencies, in accordance with rules established by the Council on Environmental Quality, may identify categories of actions which shall be exempt from NEPA. 40 C.F.R. 1501 et seq; *see, e.g., Jones v. Gordon*, 792 F.2d 821 (9th Cir. 1986). Under CEQ's regulations, however, each categorical exclusion must "provide for extraordinary circumstances in which a normally excluded action may have a significant environmental effect." 40 C.F.R. 1508.4. Some courts require agencies, if an extraordinary circumstance might exist, to engage in a particularized examination before making a decision regarding its presence, *see, e.g., Rhodes v. Johnson*, 153 F.3d 785 (7th Cir. 1998), while others tend to defer to agencies' interpretations of their own regulations when, for example, the agency identifies a particular action as falling within its categorical exclusions. *Southwest Center for Biological Diversity v. U.S. Forest Service*, 100 F.3d 1443 (9th Cir. 1996); *City of Alexandria, Va. v. Federal Highway Administration*, 756 F.2d 1014 (4th Cir. 1985).

(6) *Appropriation requests:* While section 102(2)(C) applies to "proposals for legislation," it does not apply to requests for Congressional appropriations. *Andrus v. Sierra Club*, 442 U.S. 347, 99 S. Ct. 2335 (1979) (since appropriations do not involve "planning and decisionmaking" such as that which accompanies the formation of underlying legislation, but rather serve only to implement authorized programs, the CEQ regulation which distinguishes requests for appropriations for purposes of NEPA applicability is valid).

(7) *Extraterritorial actions:* NEPA does not have international application. *Greenpeace USA v. Stone*, 748 F. Supp. 749 (D. Haw. 1990), *appeal dismissed as moot*, 924 F.2d 175 (9th Cir. 1991) (a federal statute should be construed as applying only within the territorial jurisdiction of the United States unless Congress has explicitly provided for extraterritorial application. NEPA contains no such explicit provision). *See also Environmental Defense Fund v. Massey*, 986 F.2d 528, 533 (1993) (". . . NEPA is designed to regulate conduct occurring within the territory of the United States, and imposes no substantive requirements which could be interpreted to govern conduct abroad . . .").

(8) *Moving targets*: No EIS is necessary for "moving targets." For example, the federal courts have held that the Office of the U.S. Trade Representative need not prepare an EIS on the North American Free Trade Agreement. *See Public Citizen v. U.S. Trade Representative*, 5 F.3d 549 (D.C. Cir. 1993). The reason is that NAFTA is not a "final agency action" unless and until the President submits the agreement to Congress for approval. In addition, the President could intervene and renegotiate provisions at his election. Would an EIS be required

at the time of presidential submission? No, because the President is not an agency.

NOTE

Even if NEPA is deemed to formally apply, a court may decline to issue an injunction in accordance with its terms if U.S. foreign policy interests "outweigh the benefits of the EIS requirement[.]" *Environmental Defense Fund v. Massey*, 986 F.2d 528, 535 (1993).

C. WHETHER TO PREPARE AN ENVIRONMENTAL IMPACT STATEMENT ("EIS")

Once it is clear that NEPA applies, the issue becomes how. Typically, attention shifts to § 102(2)(C), which, as noted above, requires agencies to prepare an EIS to accompany any agency recommendation or report on proposals for legislation as well as for any "major federal action significantly affecting the quality of the human environment."

Since most of the controversy involves the latter, the question, simply put, is "what is a major federal action significantly affecting the quality of the human environment." Answering that requires a parsing of terms:

"Federal": What makes an action "federal"? Actions taken by federal agencies qualify as federal. Thus, if the federal government builds a dam, issues a grant, runs a prison, or tests a nuclear explosive, it has taken a "federal" action. What if it takes a regulatory action, such as denying a permit? Certainly this action is "federal" as well. Would the provision of federal funding to support an otherwise private endeavor also qualify? *See, e.g., Friends of the Earth, Inc. v. Coleman*, 518 F.2d 323 (9th Cir. 1975) *Coleman* held that NEPA's EIS requirements apply to federally funded portions of an airport expansion project. The court, however, declined to apply the requirements of NEPA to locally funded portions of the same expansion project because those portions did not exhibit the requisite "functional interdependence" with the federally funded portions. *Id.* at 329. The locally funded portions, rather, were "distinct projects with separate functions and independent justifications." *Id.* at 328. Hence, they were not deemed to be "federal actions."

Is an action "federal" simply because there is a significant possibility at the outset of activities that federal funding will be available at some point later on? *See Atlanta Coalition on Transp. Crisis, Inc. v. Atlanta Regional Comm'n.*, 599 F.2d 1333 (5th Cir. 1979) (no).

Does a state project become "federal" for NEPA purposes because federal officials are involved? *See Almond Hill School v. United States Department of Agriculture*, 768 F.2d 1030 (9th Cir. 1985):

> There are no clear standards for defining the point at which federal participation transforms a state or local project into major federal action. The matter is simply one of degree. . . . "Marginal" federal action will not render otherwise local action federal. "Where federal funding is not present, this court has generally been unwilling to impose the NEPA requirement." . . . The employment of federal

officials in a state project, however, may be a factor in making the determination of whether the action is sufficiently federal to require an EIS when the officials are significantly involved in the state project.

Here, no federal funds have been sought by the state or spent on the state's . . . project. The appellants attempt to base their federal characterization of the project on the presence of three federal officials on the state's eight-member . . . advisory board. . . . [These officials, however] did not possess the authority to implement those aspects of the . . . program challenged here. This is primarily a state project that is neither controlled nor funded by the federal government to any significant degree.

Id. at 1031.

"Major" and *"significantly affecting the quality of the human environment"*: Here lies the more contentious issue. Every federal action that is "major" and that "significantly affects the quality of the human environment" must be accompanied by an EIS. What do these terms mean? CEQ has declared that "major" has "no meaning independent of 'significantly.'" 40 C.F.R. § 1508.18. Therefore, the search is for effects that are significant. What are effects? "Effects" and "impacts" are "synonymous" terms, 40 C.F.R. § 1508.8(b), and include "ecological (such as the effects on natural resources and on the components, structures and functioning of affected ecosystems), aesthetic, historic, cultural, economic, social, or health, whether direct, indirect, or cumulative." *Id.* Effects can be adverse or beneficial.

To prevail on a claim that a federal agency should have prepared an EIS, a claimant need not demonstrate that significant effects will occur. A "showing of substantial questions whether a project may have a significant effect on the environment is sufficient." *Anderson v. Evans*, 350 F.3d 815, 831 (9th Cir. 2003).

There are limits on what effects are important for NEPA purposes. First, effects that are essentially unrelated to the physical environment are not relevant. Thus, purely economic effects of a federal action do not trigger a requirement to prepare an EIS. *See, e.g. Central South Dakota Cooperative Grazing Dist. v. Dep't of Agriculture*, 266 F.3d 889 (8th Cir. 2001) (since the effects of the agency's decision to limit grazing on federal lands were economic only, no EIS is necessary); *Churchill Truck Lines, Inc. v. United States*, 533 F.2d 411, 416 (8th Cir. 1976) (economic interests are "clearly not within the zone of interests to be protected by [NEPA]"). Nor do certain psychological effects. *Metropolitan Edison Co. v. People Against Nuclear Energy*, 460 U.S. 766, 103 S. Ct. 2246 (1983), involved the licensing of a nuclear power plant at Three Mile Island in Pennsylvania. Residents maintained that bringing the plant back into operation, after its sister unit has suffered a serious accident, increased their levels of anxiety, tension, and fear. The Court found these psychological impacts to be too "remote" and too insufficiently causally related to a change in the physical environment to be reviewable in an EIS. The same is true of effects predominantly aesthetic. In *Olmstead Citizens for a Better Community v. United States*, 793 F.2d. 201 (8th Cir. 1986), plaintiffs feared the proposed conversion of part of a mental hospital campus into a federal prison hospital would cause a proliferation of drugs, weapons, and crime in the neighborhood. The court, however, declined to expand NEPA applicability beyond physical effects:

> While there is no "bright-line" between the "physical" and the "socio-economic" in the urban context, an impact statement generally should be necessary only when the federal action poses a threat to the physical resources of the area because of anticipated traffic, population-concentration, or water-supply problems or involves the irreversible alteration of a rare site. . . . [Here, the physical changes] . . . are the additions of harsh lighting, a double perimeter security fence with barbed wire, and a one-lane perimeter security road to be traversed by an armed mobile patrol. The main impact alleged from these changes, however, is apparently aesthetic, and the Seventh Circuit has suggested that aesthetic concerns alone should rarely be sufficient to compel preparation of an environmental impact statement. . . .

Id. at 205–06.

Even when effects do implicate the physical environment, "where an agency has no ability to prevent a certain effect due to its limited statutory authority over the relevant actions, the agency cannot be considered a legally relevant 'cause' of the effect." Hence, under NEPA and the implementing CEQ regulations, the agency need not consider these effects in its EA when determining whether its action is a major federal action. *Department of Transportation v. Public Citizen,* __ U.S. __, 124 S. Ct. 2204 (2004). Plaintiffs in *Public Citizen* were concerned with adverse effects on air quality that would accompany a decision to lift a trade moratorium on Mexican motor carriers. The decision to lift or not lift the moratorium, however, was not the agency's to make." Such matters aside, whether an effect is "significant" depends generally upon its context and intensity.

NATIONAL PARKS & CONSERVATION ASSOCIATION v. BABBITT

241 F.3d 722 (9th Cir. 2001)
cert. denied, 534 U.S. 1104, 122 S. Ct. 903 (2002)

REINHARDT, Circuit Judge:

Glacier Bay National Park and Preserve is a place of "unrivaled scenic and geological values associated with natural landscapes" and "wildlife species of inestimable value to the citizens." The Bay was proclaimed a national monument in 1925 and a national park in 1980. UNESCO designated Glacier Bay an international biosphere reserve in 1986 and a world heritage site in 1992.

Not surprisingly, many people wish to visit the park. As there are no roads to Glacier Bay, most tourists arrive by boat. To be more specific, most — approximately 80% of the park's visitors — arrive on large, thousand-passenger cruise ships. In 1996 the National Park Service (Parks Service) commenced implementation of a plan that increased the number of times cruise ships could enter Glacier Bay each summer season immediately by 30%

and overall by 72% if certain conditions were met. In its environmental assessments, the Parks Service acknowledged that this plan would expose the park's wildlife to increased multiple vessel encounters, noise pollution, air pollution, and an increased risk of vessel collisions and oil spills. The Parks Service also acknowledged that it did not know how serious these dangers to the environment were, or whether other dangers existed at all. Nevertheless, declaring that its plan would have "no significant impact" on the environment, the Parks Service put it into effect without preparing an environmental impact statement (EIS).

The plaintiff National Park and Conservation Association (NPCA), a non-profit citizen organization, alleges that the Parks Service's failure to prepare an EIS violated the National Environmental Policy Act (NEPA), 42 U.S.C. § 4321 et seq. It seeks an order requiring the Parks Service to prepare an EIS and enjoining implementation of the plan pending its completion. The district court ruled that an EIS was not required because the Parks Service had made its findings after adequately "canvassing the existing knowledge base." We reverse the district court's ruling and remand with instructions to enjoin the plan's increases in vessel traffic, including any portion already put into effect, until the Parks Service has completed an EIS.

Factual and Procedural History

There may be no place on Earth more spectacular than the Glacier Bay. Located in the Alaskan panhandle, surrounded by snow-capped mountain ranges, Glacier Bay extends sixty miles inland and encompasses ten deep fjords, four of which contain actively calving tidewater glaciers, and approximately 940 square miles of "pristine" marine waters. The air quality, though fragile, is still unspoiled and permits those fortunate enough to be visitors a crisp, clear view of the Bay with its glacier faces as well as the opportunity to breathe the fresh and invigorating air. The park is the habitat for an extraordinary array of wildlife. On the land, pioneer plant communities grow in areas recently exposed by receding glaciers. Moose, wolves, and black and brown bears roam the park's spruce and hemlock rain forest. Bald eagles, kittiwakes, murrelets, and other seabirds nest along the shore; sea otters, harbor seals, Steller sea lions, harbor and Dall's porpoises, minke, killer, and humpback whales reside in the bay.

The Steller sea lion and the humpback whale, two of the marine mammal species that inhabit Glacier Bay, are imperiled. The Steller sea lion was listed as a threatened species under the Endangered Species Act (ESA), 16 U.S.C. 1531 et seq., in 1990. The worldwide population of the species declined by as much as 48% in the thirty years prior to 1992. Glacier Bay has several "haul-out" sites where hundreds of Steller sea lions gather. The humpback whale, "the most gamesome and lighthearted of all the whales," Herman Melville, Moby Dick, 123 (Harrison Hayford & Hershel Parker, eds., W.W. Norton & Co. 1967) (1851), has been listed as an endangered species since the enactment of the ESA in 1973. Until a moratorium was instituted in 1965, commercial whaling decimated the worldwide population of humpback whales. Today only 10,000 to 12,000 remain. A subpopulation of humpbacks spends the summer feeding season in southeast Alaska, including the waters of Glacier Bay; other humpbacks remain there throughout the year.

Watercraft — cruise ships, tour boats, charter boats, and private boats — provide primary access to Glacier Bay's attractions. Approximately 80% of the park's visitors are cruise ship passengers. According to the Parks Service's environmental assessment, the "key attraction of the visit to Glacier Bay . . . [is] the glaciers at the head of the West Arm [of the Bay.] [They] are larger, more active, and considered by the [cruise-ship] companies to offer a more spectacular experience." The ships linger at the glaciers from between fifteen minutes to an hour and provide a large, high viewing platform from which to witness the crack and crash of the great ice masses as they cast off huge shards of floating ice. Although the ships' height permits an unobstructed view of the park's geologic features, it limits close views of the wildlife and vegetation that form such a significant feature of the park.

Between 1968 and 1978, vessel traffic in Glacier Bay increased dramatically. In 1978 the U.S. National Marine Fisheries Service (Fisheries Service) produced a "biological opinion" based on its studies of the humpback whale population in Glacier Bay. The biological opinion expressed concern over the "uncontrolled increase of vessel traffic" in the whales' departure from the Bay during 1978 and 1979, and cautioned that a continued increase in the amount of vessel traffic "would likely jeopardize the continued existence of the humpback whale population frequenting southeast Alaska." The Fisheries Service recommended that the Parks Service regulate the number of vessels entering Glacier Bay; restrict vessels from approaching and pursuing whales; and conduct studies on whale feeding behavior, the effect of vessels on whale behavior, and the acoustic environment.

The Parks Service soon thereafter promulgated regulations governing the entry and activity of cruise ships and other vessels in Glacier Bay. The regulations provided that only two cruise ships could enter the bay each day, with a maximum of 89 cruise ship entries between June 1 and August 31. Smaller boats, designated "private/pleasure craft," were limited to twenty-one entries per day with a seasonal maximum of 538 entries. Vessels were prohibited from intentionally positioning themselves within a quarter of a nautical mile of a whale or attempting to pursue a whale. Within "designated whale waters," vessels had to operate at a constant speed of ten knots or less and follow a mid-channel course.

In 1983 the Fisheries Service issued a second biological opinion, which concluded in part:

> If the existing restrictions on the operation of vessels within the Bay were removed, the associated disturbance would be likely to jeopardize the continued existence of the Southeast Alaska humpback whale stock. . . . Any increase in vessel traffic in Glacier Bay probably will add to the level of traffic encountered by humpback whales in southeast Alaska, and thereby add to cumulative impacts to the humpback whale.

Nevertheless, the Fisheries Service opinion stated that a slight increase in vessel traffic was tolerable, provided that the number of individual whales entering the bay did not fall below the 1982 level and that appropriate corrective measures were taken. Accordingly, in 1984 the Parks Service promulgated a Vessel Management Plan (VMP) and regulations that provided for a 20% increase, in increments, in the previously authorized vessel entry quotas. This overall increase — allowing for a total of 107 cruise ship entries per season — was fully realized in 1988.

In September 1992 the Parks Service completed an internal draft of a new VMP that proposed to increase the then current level of cruise ship entries in Glacier Bay by an additional 72%. On February 19, 1993, the Fisheries Service issued a third biological opinion expressing its concern "about the decline in humpback whale use of Glacier Bay," and stating that there were "no studies to show that this decline is not due to avoidance of vessel traffic." Although the Fisheries Service did not oppose the draft VMP, it urged the Parks Service "to take a conservative approach in all management actions that may affect humpback whales" and to implement particular research and monitoring programs. The Fisheries Service did not find that the Parks Service's proposed action was "likely to jeopardize the continued existence and recovery" of Steller sea lions.

As mandated by NEPA, the Parks Service investigated whether a substantial cruise-ship increase would significantly affect the environment in Glacier Bay. *See* 42 U.S.C. § 4332(2)(C); 40 C.F.R. § 1508.27. In May 1995 the Parks Service issued a combined proposed VMP and environmental assessment (EA). An EA is a document that, under NEPA, (1) provides "sufficient evidence and analysis for determining whether to prepare an environmental impact statement or a finding of no significant impact;" (2) aids an agency's compliance with NEPA when no EIS is necessary; and (3) facilitates preparation of an EIS when one is necessary. 40 C.F.R. § 1508.9(a). An EA is a "less formal and less rigorous" document than an EIS. *Conner v. Burford*, 848 F.2d 1441, 1446 (9th Cir. 1998).

The combined VMP/EA reported the existence of environmental questions that went far beyond the potential impact on the humpback whales. It also described and assessed six alternative approaches for managing vessels in Glacier Bay, ranging from Alternative Four's reduction in vessel traffic by between 14% and 22%, to Alternative One's maintenance of the status quo, to Alternative Five's increase of cruise ship entries by 72%. Notwithstanding the environmental problems it recognized, the Parks Service expressed its preference for Alternative Five. This alternative maintained the limit of two cruise ship entries per day, but increased the total number of seasonal entries from 107 to 184. It did not increase seasonal entries for other vessels.

The Parks Service conducted six public hearings on the VMP. The Parks Service received approximately 450 comments, approximately 85% of which opposed Alternative Five and favored Alternative Four. The Sierra Club, the Alaska Wildlife Alliance, and the plaintiff NPCA spoke out against Alternative Five at the hearings, and submitted expert opinion and evidence in opposition to the Parks Service's findings. On March 20, 1996, the Parks Service announced its decision to implement a modified version of Alternative Five as its new VMP. Under this modified plan, the seasonal entry quota for cruise ships would increase by 30% for 1996 and 1997, and by as much as 72% thereafter if certain conditions were met. Also, the entry quotas for charter boats and private/pleasure craft would increase by 8% and 15%, respectively. An accompanying revised EA, titled "Impacts of the Modified Alternative," discussed the effects of the new VMP on threatened and endangered marine mammals, other marine mammals, birds, and the human environment, including air quality.

The revised EA included the following observations:

— Steller sea lions using open water "would be subject to increased vessel traffic and its related disturbance. Little is known about the effects of the disturbance."

— The increased vessel traffic would expose the harbor seal, harbor porpoise, Dall's porpoise, humpback whale, killer whale, and minke whale to "increased levels of disturbance," causing the animals to expend energy reserves and possibly compromising "the survival and reproduction of individual animals." In addition, "the potential for daily and seasonal exposure of humpback whales to underwater noise would increase." "The effect of increased levels of disturbance" on these cetacean populations, it concluded, was "unknown."

— Marine mammals "using open-water habitats would be subject to increased vessel traffic and its related disturbance. However, little is known about the effects of the disturbance." The risk of vessels colliding with marine mammals would increase, although "the degree of increase is unknown." Similarly, there would be an increased risk of ship collisions, other accidents, and associated fuel spills. "The rate of actual spills could increase, but the degree of increase in unknown."

— "The degree to which disturbance and displacement would affect the humpback whale populations in Glacier Bay is unknown. Several mitigation measures implemented under this alternative would reduce the risk of whale/vessel interactions and the level of potential effects on individual whales. The implementation of oil-spill response plans by the cruise ship industry could reduce oil spill risks to individual whales."

— It was "unknown" whether populations of Marbled Murrelets and Kittlitz Murrelets would change under the VMP.

— "The overall effect on bald eagle populations is unknown."

— "It is unknown if waterfowl populations would change under this alternative."

Finally, the revised EA acknowledged that the increase in cruise ship entries would "result in more violations of state air quality standards," but stated that the "biological effects of these air pollutants from stack emissions are unknown."

At the same time it released its revised VMP and EA,[7] the Parks Service also released a proposed Finding of No Significant Impact (FONSI). As its title suggests, a FONSI states the reasons why an agency's proposed action will not have a significant effect on the environment and, therefore, it believes that the preparation of an EIS is unnecessary under NEPA. *See* 40 C.F.R. § 1508.13. The Parks Service's Glacier Bay FONSI stated, in relevant part:

---

[7] The revised VMP and EA will hereinafter be referred to simply as the VMP and EA.

> The [Parks Service] has determined that the modified alternative [Five] . . . can be implemented with no significant adverse effect to natural and cultural resources as documented by the environmental assessment. Key environmental issues associated with the modified alternative include effects on marine mammals and birds from vessel disturbance and air quality degradation from cruise ship stack emissions. Some disturbance to these resources would be expected. However, the mitigation strategies included in this action would significantly reduce environmental effects resulting from vessel entries.

The NPCA submitted objections to the VMP/EA and the proposed FONSI on April 19, 1996. The Parks Service adopted the VMP/EA and issued its FONSI and final regulations on the plan on May 30. *See* 61 Fed. Reg. 27,008, codified at 16 C.F.R. 13.65(b).

On May 2, 1997, the NPCA filed suit against Secretary Babbitt and Dennis J. Galvin, Acting Director of the Parks Service. The NPCA requested declaratory and injunctive relief requiring the Parks Service "to rescind the new VMP and prohibiting any activities to be conducted pursuant to these rules until such time as [the Parks Service has] complied with NEPA by preparing an adequate EIS for use in evaluating the new VMP before reimplementing it." Holland America Line Westours, Inc. ("Westours"), one of the two major cruise ship operators in Glacier Bay, intervened as a defendant pursuant to Federal Rule of Civil Procedure 24(a).

The NPCA [and] the Parks Service . . . each filed motions for summary judgment. On August 24, 1999, the district court issued an order denying NPCA's motion, [and] granting the Parks Service's motion. . . . The court observed that the EA made it "fairly clear that interactions between whales and vessels might be seriously disruptive to wildlife residing in the Park." It also acknowledged "that the effects cruise ship operations have on Glacier Bay National Park and the animals that live there are unknown, either before ship operations increased or since," and that the "Modified Alternative Description [EA] attached to the FONSI contains a long list of uncertainties about the potential effects of increased vessel traffic." While it proposed that further studies be conducted, it determined that the existence of the numerous uncertainties was not sufficient to require an EIS. "The EA in this case," the district court wrote, "thoroughly canvasses all existing information and recognizes that theoretical harms might occur, but concludes that there is no evidence suggesting that a significant risk exists that the harms will occur." It concluded:

> [A] modest increase in the number of visitors may be allowed while the studies are commissioned and the existing data base increased with care taken through ameliorization [sic] to recognize and eliminate problems as they arise.

The district court granted the Parks Service's cross-motion for summary judgment and dismissed the case. The NPCA appealed, and Westours cross-appealed.

Analysis

I. The Parks Service Violated NEPA

A. Standard of Review [discussion omitted]

. . . .

B. Environmental Assessment

NEPA requires that an Environmental Impact Statement (EIS) be prepared for all "major Federal actions significantly affecting the quality of the human environment." 42 U.S.C.A. § 4332(2)(C). However, if, as here, an agency's regulations do not categorically require the preparation of an EIS, then the agency must first prepare an Environmental Assessment (EA) to determine whether the action will have a significant effect on the environment. *See* 40 C.F.R. § 1501.4; *Salmon River Concerned Citizens v. Robertson*, 32 F.3d 1346, 1356 (9th Cir. 1994). If the EA establishes that the agency's action "may have a significant effect upon the . . . environment, an EIS must be prepared." *Foundation for N. Am. Wild Sheep v. United States Dep't of Agric.*, 681 F.2d 1172, 1178 (9th Cir. 1982); *see Blue Mountains*, 161 F.3d at 1212. If not, the agency must issue a Finding of No Significant Impact (FONSI), *see Blue Mountains*, 161 F.3d at 1212; 40 C.F.R. §§ 1501.4, 1508.9, accompanied by" 'a convincing statement of reasons' to explain why a project's impacts are insignificant." *Blue Mountains*, 161 F.3d at 1212 (quoting *Save the Yaak Comm. v. Block*, 840 F.2d 714, 717 (9th Cir. 1988).

Whether there may be a significant effect on the environment requires consideration of two broad factors: "context and intensity." *See* 40 C.F.R. § 1508.27; 42 U.S.C. § 4332(2)(C); *see also Sierra Club v. United States Forest Serv.*, 843 F.2d 1190, 1193 (9th Cir. 1988).[8]

---

[8] "Significantly" as used in NEPA requires considerations of both context and intensity:

(a) Context. This means that the significance of an action must be analyzed in several contexts such as society as a whole (human, national), the affected region, the affected interests, and the locality. Significance varies with the setting of the proposed action. For instance, in the case of a site-specific action, significance would usually depend upon the effects in the locale rather than in the world as a whole. Both short-and long-term effects are relevant.

(b) Intensity. This refers to the severity of impact. Responsible officials must bear in mind that more than one agency may make decisions about partial aspects of a major action. The following should be considered in evaluating intensity:

(1) Impacts that may be both beneficial and adverse. A significant effect may exist even if the Federal agency believes that on balance the effect will be beneficial.

(2) The degree to which the proposed action affects public health or safety.

(3) Unique characteristics of the geographic area such as proximity to historic or cultural resources, park lands, prime farmlands, wetlands, wild and scenic rivers, or ecologically critical areas.

(4) The degree to which the effects on the quality of the human environment are likely to be highly controversial.

(5) The degree to which the possible effects on the human environment are highly uncertain or involve unique or unknown risks.

(6) The degree to which the action may establish a precedent for future actions with significant effects or represents a decision in principle about a future consideration.

Context simply delimits the scope of the agency's action, including the interests affected. Intensity relates to the degree to which the agency action affects the locale and interests identified in the context part of the inquiry. Here, the context is Glacier Bay National Park, its natural setting, its variegated non-human inhabitants, and its pure but fragile air quality; intensity must be established in this case by using three of the standards enumerated in § 1508.27: (1) the unique characteristics of the geographic area; (2) the degree to which VMP Alternative Five's possible effects on the human environment are highly uncertain; and (3) the degree of controversy surrounding those possible effects. The unique characteristics of Glacier Bay are undisputed and of overwhelming importance. Accordingly, we next consider the agency's determination in light of the degree of uncertainty manifested, and the degree of controversy generated. Either of these factors may be sufficient to require preparation of an EIS in appropriate circumstances. *Sierra Club*, 843 F.2d at 1193, 1194; *Blue Mountains*, 161 F.3d at 1212–14. In the end, we conclude that the Parks Service clearly erred and that the high degree of uncertainty and the substantial controversy regarding the effects on the quality of the environment each necessitates preparation of an EIS.

C. Uncertainty

An agency must generally prepare an EIS if the environmental effects of a proposed agency action are highly uncertain. *See Blue Mountains*, 161 F.3d at 1213 ("significant environmental impact" mandating preparation of an EIS where "effects are 'highly uncertain or involve unique or unknown risks' "). Preparation of an EIS is mandated where uncertainty may be resolved by further collection of data, *see id.* at 1213–14 (lack of supporting data and cursory treatment of environmental effects in EA does not support refusal to produce EIS), or where the collection of such data may prevent "speculation on potential . . . effects. The purpose of an EIS is to obviate the need for speculation by insuring that available data are gathered and analyzed prior to the implementation of the proposed action." *Sierra Club*, 843 F.2d at 1195.

Here, scientific evidence presented in the Parks Service's own studies revealed very definite environmental effects. The uncertainty was over the

---

(7) Whether the action is related to other actions with individually insignificant but cumulatively significant impacts. Significance exists if it is reasonable to anticipate a cumulatively significant impact on the environment. Significance cannot be avoided by terming an action temporary or by breaking it down into small component parts.

(8) The degree to which the action may adversely affect districts, sites, highways, structures, or objects listed in or eligible for listing in the National Register of Historic Places or may cause loss or destruction of significant scientific, cultural, or historical resources.

(9) The degree to which the action may adversely affect an endangered or threatened species or its habitat that has been determined to be critical under the Endangered Species Act of 1973.

(10) Whether the action threatens a violation of Federal, State, or local law or requirements imposed for the protection of the environment.

40 C.F.R. § 1508.27.

intensity of those effects. The FONSI reported increased daily and seasonal exposure of humpback whales and other denizens of the Bay to underwater noise (and predicted a range of adverse behavioral responses), "traffic effects" (including increased risk of collision, affecting whales, harbor seals, sea otters, murrelets, and molting waterfowl), and increased risk of oil pollution for all animal life in the Park. An increase in cruise ships would also "result in more violations of state air quality standards for cruise ship stack emissions." Among the specific effects set forth in the VMP/EA upon which the FONSI was based were that increased vessel entry into the Bay would: subject steller sea lions to additional disturbance; increase the escape patterns of various types of whales; potentially increase mortality rates and change the social patterns of the harbor seal; preclude sea otters from colonizing the upper Bay; and increase disturbance of feeding murrelets, other seabird nesting colonies, and bald eagles.

The EA describes the intensity or practical consequences of these effects, individually and collectively, as "unknown." The uncertainty manifested through the EA stems from two sources: an absence of information about the practical effect of increased traffic on the Bay and its inhabitants; and a failure to present adequate proposals to offset environmental damage through mitigation measures. The lack of data regarding the practical effect of increased traffic, like the failure to investigate environmental impacts in *Blue Mountains*, 161 F.3d at 1213, undermines "the [Parks Service's] EA . . . [which] is where the [agency's] defense of its position must be found." *Id.* That document states that "little is known about the effects of the [cruise ship] disturbance" on steller sea lions; "the effect of increased levels of disturbance" on Glacier Bay's cetacean populations is "unknown"; and "the degree of increase [in oil spills as a result of increased traffic] is unknown." It also states that the effect of noise and air pollution on murrelets, bald eagles, and waterfowls remains "unknown" because unstudied. Moreover, the extent to which air pollution will diminish the beauty and quality of the natural environment is also unknown. The Parks Service's EA does, however, establish both that such information may be obtainable and that it would be of substantial assistance in the evaluation of the environmental impact of the planned vessel increase. The EA proposes a park research and monitoring program to "fill information needs, and understand the effects of vessel traffic on air quality, marine mammals [and] birds . . . to assist in the prediction, assessment, and management of potential effects on the human, marine, and coastal environments of Glacier Bay resulting from human use of the environment with particular emphasis on traffic." That is precisely the information and understanding that is required before a decision that may have a significant adverse impact on the environment is made, and precisely why an EIS must be prepared in this case.

The Parks Service proposes to increase the risk of harm to the environment and then perform its studies. It has in fact already implemented the first part of its VMP. This approach has the process exactly backwards. *See Sierra Club*, 843 F.2d at 1195. Before one brings about a potentially significant and irreversible change to the environment, an EIS must be prepared that sufficiently explores the intensity of the environmental effects it acknowledges. A part of the preparation process here could well be to conduct the studies that the Park Service recognizes are needed. That might be done here by performing the studies of the current vessel traffic and extrapolating or projecting the effects of the proposed increase. Ultimately, the Park Service may develop other means for obtaining the information it currently lacks. The point is, however, that the "hard look" must be taken before, not after, the environmentally-threatening actions are put into effect.

The Parks Service's lack of knowledge does not excuse the preparation of an EIS; rather it requires the Parks Service to do the necessary work to obtain it. In *Blue Mountains*, we found that general statements about possible environmental effects failed the "hard look" test required under NEPA. 161 F.3d at 1213. Here, the Parks Service's repeated generic statement that the effects are unknown does not constitute the requisite "hard look" mandated by the statute if preparation of an EIS is to be avoided. *See id.* (" 'general statements about "possible" effects and "some risk" do not constitute a "hard look" absent a justification regarding why more definitive information could not be provided' ") (citing *Neighbors of Cuddy Mountain v. United States Forest Serv.*, 137 F.3d 1372, 1380 (9th Cir. 1998)). The Park Service's statement of reasons does not provide a convincing explanation as to why the requisite information could not be obtained prior to placing the VMP into effect. *Id.* In short, the information currently provided by the Parks Service in its EA leaves us with the firm impression that, absent successful mitigation measures, there is a substantial possibility that the VMP will significantly affect Glacier Bay Park, including the air, the water, and the various species that inhabit the

The second source of uncertainty is the Parks Service's ability to offset the environmental impact of the increase in vessel traffic through its proposed mitigation measures. An agency's decision to forego issuing an EIS may be justified in some circumstances by the adoption of such measures. *Wetlands Action Network v. United States Army Corps of Eng'rs*, 222 F.3d 1105, 1121 (9th Cir. 2000); *Friends of Payette v. Horseshoe Bend Hydroelectric Co.*, 988 F.2d 989, 993 (9th Cir. 1993). "If significant measures are taken to 'mitigate the project's effects, they need not completely compensate for adverse environmental impacts.' " *Wetlands Action Network*, 222 F.3d at 1121 (quoting *Friends of Payette*, 988 F.2d at 993). While the agency is not required to develop a complete mitigation plan detailing the "precise nature of the mitigation measures," the proposed mitigation measures must be "developed to a reasonable degree." *Id.* A " 'perfunctory description,' " *Okanogan Highlands Alliance v. Williams*, 236 F.3d 468, 473 (9th Cir. 2000) (quoting *Neighbors of Cuddy Mountain*, 137 F.3d at 1380), or " 'mere listing' of mitigation measures, without supporting analytical data," is insufficient to support a finding of no significant impact. *Id.* (quoting *Idaho Sporting Congress v. Thomas*, 137 F.3d 1146, 1151 (9th Cir. 1998)). In evaluating the sufficiency of mitigation measures, we consider whether they constitute an adequate buffer against the negative impacts that may result from the authorized activity. Specifically, we examine whether the mitigation measures will render such impacts so minor as to not warrant an EIS. *See Greenpeace Action*, 14

There is a paucity of analytic data to support the Parks Service's conclusion that the mitigation measures would be adequate in light of the potential environmental harms. By contrast, in *Okanogan* the Forest Service conducted computer modeling to predict the quality and quantity of environmental effects, discussed the monitoring measures to be put in place, ranked the probable efficacy of the different measures, detailed steps to achieve compliance should the measures fail, and identified the environmental standards by which mitigation success could be measured. 236 F.3d at 473–75. Because the Forest Service "considered extensively the potential effects and mitigation processes," the court found that discussion of the mitigation measures was adequate to constitute the convincing statement of reasons to permit preparation of a FONSI. *Id.* at 477 (emphasis omitted). In this case, however, the Parks Service did not conduct a study of the anticipated effects of the mitigation measures nor did it provide criteria for an ongoing examination of them or for taking any needed corrective action (except for the plan to conduct "studies"). As with the rest of its proposal, it planned to act first and study later.

The Parks Service first described its proposed mitigation measures in the initial EA. That document reflects the uncertainty that exists as to whether the mitigation measures would work: moreover, it is unclear from that document whether the measures are sufficiently related to the effects they are designed to cure. The Parks Service simply noted, for example, that mitigation measures "could mitigate some potential effects to humpbacks in concentrated whale-use areas"; "could reduce whale/vessel collisions and reduce the noise emanating from the ships"; "special-use-area closures and restrictions implemented under . . . alternative [five] may off-set some of the expected disturbance." Air pollution measures "would be expected to contribute to a reduction in cruise ship stack emissions over time." Further, the service stated that it:

> intends to institute a comprehensive research and monitoring program to fill informational needs and quantity the effects of vessel traffic on air quality, marine mammals, birds and visitor-use enjoyment. The monitoring program, developed within one year of the record of decision, will stipulate research and protection actions [Parks Service] will undertake to ensure that environmental effects do not exceed acceptable levels. . . .

The final EA was similarly uncertain with respect to the proposed measures' effects. It recognized that a 10-knot speed restriction to offset the increased vessel traffic might disturb the creatures in the park, but that "very little is known about the effects of the disturbance." The EA also stated that the increase in seasonal entries "could reduce whale/vessel collisions and reduce the noise level emanating from the ships . . ., follow-up research and monitoring will be essential to define humpback whale use patterns in Glacier Bay resulting from this alternative"; and that "requiring cruise ships to implement oil-spill response plans could mitigate the effects of oil spills." As for air pollution, "the magnitude of increased violations would presumably be reduced over time." There is no indication, however, as to how long any such reduction might take or how great a reduction might ultimately be accomplished. In short, there is no evidence that the mitigation measures would significantly combat the mostly "unknown" or inadequately known effects of the increase in vessel traffic. The EA's speculative and conclusory statements are insufficient to demonstrate that the mitigation measures would render the environmental impact so minor as to not warrant an EIS. *See Greenpeace Action*, 14 F.3d at 1332.

It is instructive to contrast this case with *Wetlands Action Network*. In that case, the court made clear that, though the mitigation measures were underdeveloped, the imposition of special conditions, enforced through a permit, and reviewed by various other agencies ensured that the measures would be enforced in a manner that properly reduced negative environmental impact. *See Wetlands Action Network*, 222 F.3d at 1121. Here, there were no such special conditions applied to the Parks Service or the tour boat operators in connection with the measures designed to mitigate the effects of the proposed increase in cruise ships. In fact, whether the mitigation measures are fully enforced or not, the EA reflects significant uncertainty as to whether they could provide an adequate buffer against the harmful effects of the plan. This is understandable in light of the fact that the extent of those harmful effects is itself unknown, and that in such circumstance it is particularly difficult to estimate the effects of mitigation measures. That fact, however, does not help make the measures adequate for purposes of avoiding the preparation of an EIS — quite the contrary.

As with the question of the extent of the unremediated injury that might otherwise occur, the question of the impact of the proposed mitigation measures must be studied as part of the preparation of an EIS rather than after the injury has transpired. The fact that the agency plans to test the effect of its mitigation measures does not relieve it of the obligation to prepare an EIS prior to the time of the threatened environmental damage. Rather, the Parks Service's testing proposal shows that the information necessary to determine the impact of any mitigation measures, like the information relating to the extent of the injurious effects, may well be obtainable before any environmental injury occurs. The proposed mitigation studies thus argue in favor of preparing an EIS, not against it.

The district court found that the agency's decision not to prepare an EIS was justified because the uncertainty reflected the existing state of knowledge. The passage of cruise ships through Glacier Bay is not a new development, however. Both the vessels' sailings and the dispute over the potential environmental damage have existed for a substantial period of time. No new scientific developments are required in order to obtain the requisite information. The Parks Service itself proposes to conduct studies which it anticipates may provide the answers. We simply hold that, under these circumstances, where significant environmental damage may occur to a treasured natural resource, the studies must be conducted first, not afterwards.

D. Controversy

The district court also found that NPCA had not made a sufficient showing of controversy to require preparation of an EIS. Again, we disagree.

Agencies must prepare environmental impact statements whenever a federal action is "controversial," that is, when "substantial questions are raised as to whether a project . . . may cause significant degradation of some human environmental factor," *Northwest Envtl. Def. Ctr. v. Bonneville Power Admin.*, 117 F.3d 1520, 1539 (9th Cir. 1997) (quoting *LaFlamme v. FERC*, 852 F.2d 389, 397 (9th Cir. 1988)) (Reinhardt, J., concurring in part and dissenting in part), or there is "a substantial dispute [about] the size, nature, or effect of the major Federal action." *Blue Mountains*, 161 F.3d at 1212 (citing *Greenpeace Action*, 14 F.3d at 1335; *Sierra Club*, 843 F.2d at 1190). A substantial dispute exists when evidence, raised prior to the preparation of an EIS or FONSI, *see Greenpeace Action*, 14 F.3d at 1334 (holding that party may not establish controversy post hoc, when at the time of the agency's action no controversy existed), casts serious doubt upon the reasonableness of an agency's conclusions. *See Idaho Sporting Congress*, 137 F.3d at 1150; *Blue Mountains*, 161 F.3d at 1212. NEPA then places the burden on the agency to come forward with a "well-reasoned explanation" demonstrating why those responses disputing the EA's conclusions "do not suffice to create a public controversy based on potential environmental consequences." *LaFlamme*, 852 F.2d at 401 (citing *Jones v. Gordon*, 792 F.2d 821, 829 (1986)).[15] The term "well reasoned explanation" is simply a less direct way of saying that the explanation must be "convincing." *See Metcalf*, 214 F.3d at 1142.

After publication of the initial EA, and before publication of the EA and FONSI, the Parks Service received 450 comments on the VMP, approximately 85% of which opposed Alternative Five and favored Alternative Four. This volume of negative comment is more than sufficient to meet the "out-pouring of public protest" discussed in *Greenpeace Action*. *See* 14 F.3d at 1334. More important, to the extent the comments urged that the EA's analysis was incomplete, and the mitigation uncertain, they cast substantial doubt on the adequacy of the Parks Service's methodology and data. The dispute between NPCA and the Parks Service thus goes beyond a disagreement of qualified experts over the "reasoned conclusions" as to what the data reveal. *See Greenpeace Action*, 14 F.3d at 1335. Here, the agency's conclusions were not reached by reasoned extrapolation from the data, rather the data were simply insufficient. The Parks Service acknowledged that an increase in vessel traffic would have an environmental impact. The data, however, did not establish the intensity of that impact, nor the efficacy of the mitigation measures designed to offset that unquantified impact. NPCA asserted that the effects on the environment would likely be substantial. The Parks Service responded that the extent of the effects was unknown. Therein lay the controversy. In its response, the agency proposed to determine the extent of the effects by implementing the VMP and studying its consequences. As we have stated in Section I.C, the absence of currently available information does not excuse the Parks Service from preparing an EIS when there is a reasonable possibility that such information can be obtained in connection with the preparatory process. The agency's response is therefore not sufficient to resolve the

---

[15] Consensus among the parties over the proposed measures is ordinarily sufficient to satisfy the agency's burden. *See Greenpeace Action*, 14 F.3d at 1334 (holding that consensus among objecting parties before agency declined to prepare EIS sufficient to rebut showing of controversy); *Bonneville Power,* 117 F.3d at 1536 (holding that where agency cooperated with objecting parties, and alleviated most of those parties concerns, agency need not prepare EIS). No such consensus existed here.

controversy. . . . Here, preparation of an EIS is mandated by the "controversy," as well as by the "uncertainty," factor of the intensity provision. 40 C.F.R. § 1508.27(b).

II. Injunctive Relief

NPCA asks this court to "reverse the District Court and remand the case with instructions to enjoin further implementation of the 1996 Vessel Management Plan until a full Environmental Impact Statement is prepared." To determine whether injunctive relief is appropriate, "even in the context of environmental litigation," we apply "the traditional balance of harms analysis." *Forest Conservation Council v. United States Forest Serv.*, 66 F.3d 1489, 1496 (9th Cir. 1995) (citations omitted); *see also Amoco Prod. Co. v. Village of Gambell*, 480 U.S. 531, 541, 542, 94 L. Ed. 2d 542, 107 S. Ct. 1396 (1987) (holding that unless Congress directed otherwise, "a court must balance the competing claims of injury" in determining whether injunctive relief is appropriate). "Environmental injury, by its nature, can seldom be adequately remedied by money damages and is often permanent or at least of long duration, i.e., irreparable," *Amoco Prod. Co.*, 480 U.S. at 545. When the "proposed project may significantly degrade some human environmental factor," injunctive relief is appropriate. *Alaska Wilderness Recreation & Tourism Assoc. v. Morrison*, 67 F.3d 723, 732. *See also Sierra Club*, 843 F.2d at 1195; *Save the Yaak*, 840 F.2d at 722.

NPCA has made the requisite showing for injunctive relief. As we concluded in Section I, an EIS is required. We so held because of the significant adverse impact on the environment that might result from the implementation of the VMP. *See Blue Mountains*, 161 F.3d at 1216 (an EIS is required of an agency in order that it explore, more thoroughly than an EA, the environmental consequences of a proposed action whenever "substantial questions are raised as to whether a project may cause significant [environmental] degradation"). Where an EIS is required, allowing a potentially environmentally damaging project to proceed prior to its preparation runs contrary to the very purpose of the statutory requirement. Here, the Parks Service has already undertaken a 30% increase in cruise-ship traffic preliminary to a seventy-two percent increase. The potential effects of its action extend beyond the endangered marine mammal population to the rest of the wildlife at Glacier Bay, as well as the Park's air quality. Kittiwakes, murrelet, eagles, sea otters, seals, sea lions, porpoises, and killer and minke whales, as well as the better known humpbacks, are affected. Until an EIS is prepared and the effects of increased vessel traffic on the inhabitants and air quality of Glacier Bay are properly examined, there is a sufficient possibility of environmental harm that the VMP may not be implemented. * * *

We direct the district court to enjoin the further increases in vessel traffic, and to return traffic levels to their pre-1996 levels. We agree, however, with the Parks Service's contention that "the current vessel regulations are in important respects more environmentally protective than the 1984 regulations they replaced." The NPCA does not contend (and the record would not support a finding) that the 1996 VMP's establishment of protected "whale waters" in parts of Glacier Bay or implementation of oil-spill response plans pose an actual or potential threat to the environment. Accordingly, there is no basis for enjoining that part of Alternative Five. Our order is limited to the thirty to seventy-two percent increase in the seasonal entry quota for cruise ships, and the eight percent increase for charter boats and fifteen percent increase for "private/pleasure" craft. All entry quotas shall be returned to the levels preceding the introduction of Alternative Five. The other measures adopted by the Parks Service in its VMP shall remain in effect, and will not be subject to the injunction.

Notwithstanding the above, we recognize that the issuance of the mandate in this case may be delayed for some period of time as a result of the en banc procedures that this court follows, and that such delay may occur even if we ultimately decide not to grant a rehearing en banc. We do not believe, however, that a sufficient emergency exists to warrant our ordering that the injunction become effective prior to the completion of our customary process. Accordingly, we cannot know in advance how close to the opening of this year's cruising season the mandate will issue, or even whether issuance will be delayed until after the season has already begun. Nor can we determine how great may be the practical disruption that would occur were last minute cancellation of a significant number of voyages required. Accordingly, we leave it to the district court to decide upon the effective date of the injunction it is ordered to issue, and, specifically, to decide in its informed discretion, and on the basis of any evidence that may be presented, whether the injunction should take effect prior to the completion of this year's cruising season, sometime this September. * * *

REVERSED AND REMANDED WITH INSTRUCTIONS.

NOTES AND QUESTION

The D.C. Circuit established four criteria to assess the validity of an agency FONSI decision: (a) whether the agency accurately identified the critical environmental concerns; (b) whether it took a "hard look" at those environmental concerns; (c) whether it made a convincing case for its FONSI decision; and (d) if there are significant impacts, whether it found that changes in the action or project sufficiently reduced the impacts. *Sierra Club v. U.S. Dep't of Transportation*, 753 F.2d 120 (D.C. Cir. 1985).

As criterion (d), above, implies, and as discussed in the *NPCA* decision, EAs will often recommend specific actions that might be taken to mitigate environmental harms otherwise to be caused by a project. Is this a sensible procedure, or does this effectively transform the EA into an EIS? The D.C. Circuit says it is sensible, at least where adoption of the EA mitigation measures would completely remove adverse environmental impacts. In such a case, the threshold of "significant" effects would not be crossed. Requiring an EIS in this circumstance, commented the court, would trivialize NEPA and would "diminish its utility in providing useful environmental analysis for major federal actions that truly affect the environment." *Cabinet Mountains Wilderness / Scotchman's Peak Grizzly Bears v. Peterson*, 685 F.2d 687, 682 (D.C. Cir. 1982).

SIERRA CLUB v. UNITED STATES FOREST SERVICE

46 F.3d 835 (8th Cir. 1995)

OPINION: LAY, Senior Circuit Judge.

The Victoria Project Area (Victoria) is a 16,883 acre portion of the 1,235,780 acre Black Hills National Forest (Forest). Victoria includes 15,372 acres of National Forest System lands and 1,511 acres of private land. The Forest is located predominantly in western South Dakota, but extends into northeastern Wyoming. As required by the National Forest Management Act (NFMA), 16 U.S.C. §§ 1604–1614, a land management plan for the Black Hills Forest (Forest Plan) was approved in 1983. The Forest Plan covers ten years and, supplemented by the analysis of its effects contained within the Environmental Impact Statement (EIS), directs the Forest Service's management of the Forest. The plan "contains the overall management direction and describes the activities necessary to achieve the desired future condition of the Forest."

The National Environmental Policy Act (NEPA) requires an EIS be prepared for all "major Federal actions significantly affecting the quality of the human environment. . . ." 42 U.S.C. § 4332(2)(C). If these activities were not adequately analyzed in the Forest Plan EIS, and they constitute a "major Federal action," a project level EIS may be necessary in addition to the Forest Plan EIS. *See, e.g., Salmon River Concerned Citizens v. Robertson*, 32 F.3d 1346, 1356 (9th Cir. 1994). If an activity is contemplated that does not automatically require an EIS, an Environmental Assessment (EA) may be conducted to determine whether a project level EIS is necessary. 40 C.F.R. §§ 1501.3–1501.4. An EA analyzes and compares several alternative courses of action, including doing nothing, the "No Action" alternative. 40 C.F.R. § 1508.9(2)(b). The purpose of the document is to assist in determining whether any of the proposed actions will significantly affect the environment. 40 C.F.R. § 1508.9(a)(1).

In 1990, the Pactola Ranger District commenced planning projects to achieve the goals, or the desired future condition of the Forest, for the Victoria area. The Forest Plan has multiple goals. Timber harvesting is one, along with improving the quality and quantity of wood fiber. See 36 C.F.R. § 219.27(c); Forest Plan at II-16. Other goals are to increase the biological diversity of the Forest and maintain and improve appropriate habitats for existing wildlife species. *See* 36 C.F.R. § 219.27(g); *Forest Plan* at II-17. A 1990 survey of Victoria found an absence of vegetative diversity. Generally, the more diverse a habitat, the more species it will support. Forest Plan at II-17. The District considered timber sales as a way of meeting its timber production objectives while increasing the diversity of the habitat in Victoria by reducing the portion of the area occupied by closed-canopy and overmature timber stands.

To determine whether timber sales in Victoria would significantly affect the environment, the District undertook an EA which compared the effects of various alternative projects involving timber harvests to the effects of doing nothing, the No Action alternative. The Forest Supervisor considered the EA and issued notice of her decision. The notice indicated the Supervisor found no significant environmental impacts would result from the project selected. Thus, no EIS was required for the project.

The Sierra Club filed an administrative appeal within the agency, challenging the EA on the grounds that it was defective under NEPA because it analyzed an inadequate range of alternatives. As a result of that appeal, the Forest Service ordered a new EA to address the Sierra Club's concerns.

In January 1992, the Forest Service issued a second FONSI decision. The project selected called for two timber sales in the Victoria Area on 3,209 acres of land, for thinning timber stands on another 2,858 acres, for road work, and also included several measures to decrease the environmental impact of the timber sales.

The Sierra Club again appealed the decision within the agency. The Acting Regional Forester affirmed and the agency declined the Sierra Club's request for review at a higher agency level. In August 1992, the Sierra Club filed suit in district court claiming the second decision violated various provisions of NEPA.

The district court granted the Forest Service's motion for summary judgment, determining the Service did not act arbitrarily or capriciously in issuing a FONSI on the proposed timber sales. Contrary to the Sierra Club's claims, the district court found the Forest Service adequately considered the project's impacts. The court stated that NEPA did not require the Forest Service to consider the impacts of acts by private parties on private land in Victoria. The court rejected the argument that the Forest Service inappropriately relied on a computer model for assessing habitat capabilities. To the charge that the Forest Service should have prepared an additional EIS, the district court found the Sierra Club failed to prove the programmatic EIS inadequate.

On appeal, the Sierra Club claims the district court erred in affirming the FONSI and in failing to order a site specific EIS. It argues the court should not have upheld the Forest Service's EA with respect to its cumulative impact analysis as defined by 40 C.F.R. § 1508.7 and as required for EIS documents by 40 C.F.R. § 1508.25. It contends the Forest Service failed to: 1) consider impacts from activities on the 1,511 acres of private land in Victoria; 2) consider impacts from previous timber sales in the Area; 3) consider the effect of timber sales on habitat fragmentation, particularly with regard to species dependent on old growth forest; 4) consider the effect of changing the land designation for 1,504 acres; and 5) include an analysis of diversity unit PO7. In addition the Sierra Club charges the court also erred by interpreting the Sierra Club's request for a site specific, project level EIS as a request for a supplemental EIS and then upholding the Forest Service's decision not to prepare an EIS. We affirm.

Standard of Review [discussion omitted]

. . . .

Adequacy of the EA

The Sierra Club first attacks the EA on its failure to consider the cumulative impacts[7] from private acts on private lands within Victoria. 40 C.F.R.

---

[7] This section states:

"Cumulative impact is the impact on the environment which results from the incremental impact of the action when added to other past, present, and reasonably foreseeable

§ 1508.7 requires an EA to consider impacts resulting from the activities of Federal or non-Federal agencies or persons. The Ninth Circuit has interpreted this section, and we agree, to require analysis of the impacts activities on private land on the Forest. *Resources Ltd., Inc. v. Robertson*, 35 F.3d 1300, 1306 (9th Cir. 1993). The district court erred in concluding otherwise.

On our review of the record however, we find this error of little consequence because the EA's consideration of the impacts of activities on private land was not so deficient as to make the Forest Service's FONSI arbitrary and capricious. The EA included private land holdings in its maps and aerial photographs. The EA reasonably assumed current land uses would continue within Victoria and expected non-commercial thinning of timber to occur on private land. The watershed report and the road density portion of the wildlife report included private lands in Victoria. The EA also included private land in its fuel/fire risk and smoke assessments, and assumed private construction would continue to occur in the urban forest interface areas. The EA did not make elaborate findings but nothing in the record suggests a need for more extensive analysis. The Sierra Club asserts an EA must address the impacts from such events on private lands as the owners deciding to clear cut all 1,511 acres of their land, but we find no statutory or regulatory mandate that an EA do so. What is required is that the EA recognize the impacts of activities reasonably expected to occur on private lands and this the EA did. *See id.*

The Forest Service found no significant impacts involving the private lands. The Sierra Club suggests none. This observation does not alter the Forest Service's procedural burden to study these impacts, but finding none, after the obvious inclusions in the record pertaining to private land, maps, photos, road and watershed studies, etc., the Sierra Club cannot simply doubt the FONSI determination without pointing to more than speculative impacts.

Fragmentation/Biological Diversity

The Sierra Club's second and third criticisms of the EA are that it did not assess the impacts of previous timber sales or provide site-specific information about the effect of timber sales on habitat fragmentation and old growth dependent species. Past timber harvests in Victoria, according to an affidavit of a wildlife biologist, have resulted in decreasing the areas of closed-canopy forest and fragmenting the environment into open-forest stands.[8] This has the effect of decreasing the biological diversity within the project area and made the area less well suited for deer, elk, birds, and certain small mammals. The Forest Service contends the EA properly assessed the cumulative effects. The EA did incorporate the impacts of previous timber sales in Victoria because the timber clearing was completed when the existing conditions in Victoria were assessed.

---

future actions regardless of what agency (Federal or non-Federal) or person undertakes such other actions. Cumulative impacts can result from individually minor but collectively significant actions taking place over a period of time."

[8] Habitat fragmentation refers to "the creation of a complex mosaic of spatial and successional habitats from formerly contiguous habitat. Loss of habitat . . . threatens the viability of wildlife populations, the components of biotic diversity." John F. Lehmkuhl and Leonard F. Ruggiero, Forest Fragmentation in the Pacific Northwest and its Potential Effects on Wildlife, Appellant's Appendix at 240. Biodiversity refers to the number of different species present in a given habitat.

As to habitat fragmentation, the Forest Service points out that prior to European settlement the Black Hills Forest was fragmented to a greater degree than at present. The EA addressed the issue of wildlife and habitat diversity and considered measures to mitigate harmful impacts. The EA showed the alternatives considered would reduce open road density, maintain cover areas, and increase the areas be devoted to grass/forb, old growth, forest openings, and forage as called for in the Forest Plan. The alternatives were expected to have favorable impacts for species requiring more open habitats but unfavorable impacts for species requiring a maturer, closed-canopy forest, such as the ruby-crowned kinglet, goshawk, and three-toed woodpecker. Although the No Action alternative allowed for more potential old growth forest, the alternatives actually designated more land for old growth. Over time, the alternative projects would increase habitat diversity by reducing closed-canopy stands, increasing open-canopy stands, and increasing grass/forb areas. The action alternatives would also prevent encroachment by pine trees into aspen, birch, and oak stands, and increase the net growth and quality of timber by reducing overstocking and overmature stands. Fisheries and riparian communities would be little affected, given the proposed mitigation measures and the recommended techniques.

We note that an EA is supposed to be "a concise public document." 40 C.F.R. § 1508.9(a). It is supposed to "briefly provide sufficient evidence and analysis for determining whether to prepare an environmental impact statement or a finding of no significant impact." 40 C.F.R. § 1508.9(a)(1). An EA cannot be both concise and brief and provide detailed answers for every question. With regard to both the impacts of past timber sales and habitat fragmentation, we find the EA sufficient to prevent the FONSI from being arbitrary or capricious.

The fourth deficiency the Sierra Club found in the EA was its failure to assess the effects of changing of the land management designation of 1,504 acres in Victoria to permit commercial timber harvesting. The Forest Service claimed it made this change because the original designation was wrong and did not correspond to actual conditions. We do not believe an EA need consider impacts arising from an error in a Forest Plan. The purpose of an EA is to provide information for determining whether prospective projects may have significant environmental impacts.

Lastly, the Sierra Club contends the EA failed to include a complete analysis of the "diversity units" within Victoria. A "diversity unit" is an area of land quite distinct from project areas, designed for measuring the attainment of Forest Plan biological diversity goals over a large land area. Diversity unit PO6 and a small portion of unit PO7 lie within Victoria. That small portion of PO7, roughly ten percent of PO7's total area and constituting approximately ten percent of the Victoria area, was not analyzed in the community diversity section of the EA. We agree with the Forest Service that an analysis of PO7 would not have contributed much of value to the EA because so little of PO7 lies within Victoria.

Whether, as the Sierra Club claims, the district court misunderstood what kind of EIS it was seeking, and accordingly considered the issue under the wrong standard, is irrelevant. With a project-specific EIS such as the Sierra

Club claims to have sought, the standard is whether the Forest Service's FONSI was arbitrary and capricious. *See Marsh v. Oregon Natural Resources Council*, 490 U.S. 360, 376–78, 104 L. Ed. 2d 377, 109 S. Ct. 1851 (1989). Because we found the EA adequate, all we need consider is whether the Forest Service's FONSI was arbitrary or capricious. On our review, we find the Service thoughtfully reviewed the EA and reasonably concluded a FONSI was appropriate. We hold there was no requirement for the Forest Service to prepare a site specific EIS.

We affirm the order granting summary judgment to the Forest Service.

NOTE

Suppose that an agency determines an EIS is necessary because a proposed action is a major federal action significantly affecting the quality of the human environment. Does this mean that only one EIS needs to be done? The answer is usually yes — one EIS is plenty. Not infrequently, however, the issue arises whether a supplemental EIS ("SEIS") should be prepared. When might an agency be required to initiate the EIS process a second (or third) time?

NEPA does not comment on this matter, and one would think that at some juncture agency actions reach a point of no return. CEQ regulations, however, call for supplemental EISs two situations. First, an SEIS is required if "(i) [t]he agency makes substantial changes in the proposed action that are relevant to environmental concerns[.]" 40 C.F.R. § 1509(c)(1)(i). Requiring an SEIS under these cirumstances would seem to be axiomatic. Second, and more interestingly, the regulations call for an SEIS if "(ii) [t]here are significant circumstances or information relevant to environmental concerns and bearing on the proposed action or its impacts." 40 C.F.R. § 1509(c)(1)(ii). Does this regulation mean that every time significant new information comes along an SEIS must be prepared? The Supreme Court has made clear the answer is no.

As a general matter, the Court has taken a cautious view: "[a]n agency need not supplement an EIS every time new information comes to light after the EIS is finalized. To require otherwise would render agency decisionmaking intractable, always awaiting updated information only to find the new information outdated by the time a decision is made." *Marsh v. Oregon Natural Resources Council*, 490 U.S. 360, 373, 109 S.Ct. 1851, 1859 (1989) (footnotes omitted). Still, the Court noted, an agency may not blithely ignore significant new information. Rather, it must take a "hard look" at new information to determine whether to prepare an SEIS. *Id.* at 385, 109 S. Ct. at 1865. The *Marsh* Court cautioned that agency decisions whether to supplement EISs should not be overruled by the judiciary unless they are arbitrary or capricious. *Id.* There must be a "clear error of judgment" to justify a reversal. *See also Headwaters, Inc. v. Bureau of Land Management*, 914 F.2d 1174 (9th Cir. 1990).

More particularly, the Supreme Court has held that no SEIS is contemplated by NEPA unless there is some ongoing "major federal action" yet to occur. In *Norton v. Southwest Utah Wilderness Alliance*, __ U.S. __, 124 S. Ct. 2373 (2004), plaintiffs argued the federal Bureau of Land Management should prepare an SEIS because of a substantial increase in off-road vehicle use on federal lands that were being managed essentially as wilderness areas. The BLM was managing these lands under the auspices of a land use plan prepared in accordance with the Federal Land Policy and Management Act (*see* Chapter 5, *infra*). A unanimous Supreme Court denied the claim because the land use plan was already completed and had already been approved. As this was a *fait accompli*, there remained no ongoing major federal action and, *per force*, no legal basis for requiring an SEIS. Had the BLM taken some affirmative action, such as amending the plan, additional analysis under NEPA would have been necessary.

D. ENVIRONMENTAL IMPACT STATEMENTS

[1] THE ROLE OF EISs IN DECISIONMAKING

Assuming an EIS is required, what role should it play in framing or influencing an agency's final decision to go forward with a project as proposed, or as modified, or not at all?

The role of EISs in agency decisionmaking has been a matter of debate. Without doubt, Congress intended EISs to be informational documents. Their mere presence would make agencies aware of the environmental consequences of proposed actions. That awareness, in turn, would encourage agencies to be more solicitous of environmental protection and conservation. Given these facts, it seems obvious that EISs were intended by Congress to play some sort of substantive role in agency decisionmaking.

But how? Is the role of an EIS advisory only? Does it merely stand on the sidelines cajoling agencies into environmentally benign courses of action? If that were the case, agencies would be free to completely disregard an EIS's recommendations. Alternatively, does an EIS have some force and effect? Can it be read as amending an agency's organic law to require the implementation of more environmentally benign courses of action? The courts were split during the 1970's on this issue.

The United States Supreme Court addressed the matter in 1978 in its decision in *Vermont Yankee Nuclear Power Corp. v. Natural Resources Defense Council*, 435 U.S. 519, 98 S. Ct. 1197 (1978). In that case, it declared NEPA to have "altered slightly the statutory balance. . . ." *Id.* at 551, 98 S.Ct. at 1215. But the Court clarified that "NEPA does not set forth substantive goals for the Nation . . . its mandate to the agencies is essentially procedural. . . . It is to insure a fully informed and well-considered decision, not necessarily a decision the judges of the Court of Appeals or of this Court would have reached had they been members of the decisionmaking unit of the agency." *Id.* at 558, 98 S.Ct. at 1219. Two years later, the Court reiterated the point in *Strycker's Bay Neighborhood Council v. Karlan*, 444 U.S. 223, 100 S. Ct. 497 (1980): in "a decision subject to NEPA's procedural requirements, the only role for a court is to insure that the agency has considered the environmental consequences; it cannot 'interject itself within the area of discretion of the executive as to the choice of the action to be taken.'" *Id.* at 227–28, 100 S. Ct. at 500, *citing Kleppe v. Sierra Club*, 427 U.S. 390, 410, n.21 (1976).

A close reading of these comments reveals a lurking ambiguity. *Vermont Yankee,* by indicating that agency decisions must be "well-considered" and noting that NEPA had "altered slightly the statutory balance," intimated the possibility that § 102(2)(C) might impose some substantive obligations on agencies. And *Strycker's Bay* could be read as merely a judicial statement in favor of deferential review of agency decisions.

The ambiguity is now gone.

ROBERTSON v. METHOW VALLEY CITIZENS COUNCIL

490 U.S. 332, 109 S. Ct. 1835 (1989)

JUSTICE STEVENS delivered the opinion of the Court.

We granted certiorari to decide two questions of law. As framed by petitioners, they are:

> "1. Whether the National Environmental Policy Act requires federal agencies to include in each environmental impact statement: (a) a fully developed plan to mitigate environmental harm; and (b) a 'worst case' analysis of potential environmental harm if relevant information concerning significant environmental effects is unavailable or too costly to obtain."

> "2. Whether the Forest Service may issue a special use permit for recreational use of national forest land in the absence of a fully developed plan to mitigate environmental harm."

Concluding that the Court of Appeals for the Ninth Circuit misapplied the National Environmental Policy Act of 1969 (NEPA), 83 Stat. 852, 42 U.S.C. § 4321 et seq., and gave inadequate deference to the Forest Service's interpretation of its own regulations, we reverse and remand for further proceedings.

The Forest Service is authorized by statute to manage the national forests for "outdoor recreation, range, timber, watershed, and wildlife and fish purposes." 74 Stat. 215, 16 U.S.C. § 528. *See also* 90 Stat. 2949, 16 U.S.C. § 1600 et seq. Pursuant to that authorization, the Forest Service has issued "special use" permits for the operation of approximately 170 alpine and nordic ski areas on federal lands. *See* H. R. Rep. No. 99-709, pt. 1, p. 2 (1986).

The Forest Service permit process involves three separate stages. The Forest Service first examines the general environmental and financial feasibility of a proposed project and decides whether to issue a special use permit. *See* 36 C.F.R. § 251.54(f) (1988). Because that decision is a "major Federal action" within the meaning of NEPA, it must be preceded by the preparation of an Environmental Impact Statement (EIS). 42 U.S.C. § 4332. If the Service decides to issue a permit, it then proceeds to select a developer, formulate the basic terms of the arrangement with the selected party, and issue the permit. The special use permit does not, however, give the developer the right to begin construction. *See* 36 C.F.R. § 251.56(c) (1988). In a final stage of review, the Service evaluates the permittee's "master plan" for development, construction, and operation of the project. Construction may begin only after an additional environmental analysis (although it is not clear that a second EIS need always be prepared) and final approval of the developer's master plan. This case arises out of the Forest Service's decision to issue a special use permit authorizing the development of a major destination alpine ski resort at Sandy Butte in the North Cascades mountains.

Sandy Butte is a 6,000-foot mountain located in the Okanogan National Forest in Okanogan County, Washington. At present Sandy Butte, like the Methow Valley it overlooks, is an unspoiled, sparsely populated area that the district court characterized as "pristine." In 1968, Congress established the North Cascades National Park and directed the Secretaries of Interior and Agriculture to agree on the designation of areas within and adjacent to the park for public uses, including ski areas. 82 Stat. 926, 930, 16 U.S.C. §§ 90, 90d-3. A 1970 study conducted by the Forest Service pursuant to this congressional directive identified Sandy Butte as having the highest potential of any site in the State of Washington for development as a major downhill ski resort.

In 1978, Methow Recreation, Inc. (MRI) applied for a special use permit to develop and operate its proposed "Early Winters Ski Resort" on Sandy Butte and an 1,165 acre parcel of land it had acquired adjacent to the National Forest. The proposed development would make use of approximately 3,900 acres of Sandy Butte; would entice visitors to travel long distances to stay at the resort for several days at a time; and would stimulate extensive commercial and residential growth in the vicinity to accommodate both vacationers and staff.

In response to MRI's application, the Forest Service, in cooperation with state and county officials, prepared an EIS known as the Early Winters Alpine Winter Sports Study (Early Winters Study or Study). The stated purpose of the EIS was "to provide the information required to evaluate the potential for skiing at Early Winters" and "to assist in making a decision whether to issue a Special Use Permit for downhill skiing on all or a portion of approximately 3900 acres of National Forest System land." A draft of the Study was completed and circulated in 1982, but release of the final EIS was delayed as Congress considered including Sandy Butte in a proposed wilderness area. When the Washington State Wilderness Act of 1984 was passed, however, Sandy Butte was excluded from the wilderness designation, and the EIS was released.

The Early Winters Study is a printed document containing almost 150 pages of text and 12 appendices. It evaluated five alternative levels of development of Sandy Butte that might be authorized, the lowest being a "no action" alternative and the highest being development of a 16-lift ski area able to accommodate 10,500 skiers at one time. The Study considered the effect of each level of development on water resources, soil, wildlife, air quality, vegetation and visual quality, as well as land use and transportation in the Methow Valley, probable demographic shifts, the economic market for skiing and other summer and winter recreational activities in the Valley, and the energy requirements for the ski area and related developments. The Study's discussion of possible impacts was not limited to on-site effects, but also, as required by Council on Environmental Quality (CEQ) regulations, see 40 C.F.R.

§ 1502.16(b) (1987), addressed "off-site impacts that each alternative might have on community facilities, socio-economic and other environmental conditions in the Upper Methow Valley." As to off-site effects, the Study explained that "due to the uncertainty of where other public and private lands may become developed," it is difficult to evaluate off-site impacts, *id.*, at 76, and thus the document's analysis is necessarily "not site-specific," *id.*, at 1. Finally, the Study outlined certain steps that might be taken to mitigate adverse effects, both on Sandy Butte and in the neighboring Methow Valley, but indicated that these proposed steps are merely conceptual and "will be made more specific as part of the design and implementation stages of the planning process." *Id.*, at 14.

The effects of the proposed development on air quality and wildlife received particular attention in the Study. In the chapter on "Environmental Consequences," the first subject discussed is air quality. As is true of other subjects, the discussion included an analysis of cumulative impacts over several years resulting from actions on other lands as well as from the development of Sandy Butte itself. The Study concluded that although the construction, maintenance, and operation of the proposed ski area "will not have a measurable effect on existing or future air quality," the off-site development of private land under all five alternatives — including the "no action" alternative — "will have a significant effect on air quality during severe meteorological inversion periods." *Id.*, at 65. The burning of wood for space heat, the Study explained, would constitute the primary cause of diminished air quality and the damage would increase incrementally with each of the successive levels of proposed development. *Ibid.* The Study cautioned that without efforts to mitigate these effects, even under the "no action" alternative, the increase in automobile, fireplace, and wood stove use would reduce air quality below state standards, but added that "[t]he numerous mitigation measures discussed" in the Study "will greatly reduce the impacts presented by the model." *Id.*, at 67.

In its discussion of air quality mitigation measures, the EIS identified actions that could be taken by the county government to mitigate the adverse effects of development, as well as those the Forest Service itself could implement at the construction stage of the project. The Study suggested that Okanogan County develop an air quality management plan, requiring weatherization of new buildings, limiting the number of wood stoves and fireplaces, and adopting monitoring and enforcement measures. In addition, the Study suggested that the Forest Service require that the master plan include procedures to control dust and to comply with smoke management practices.

In its discussion of adverse effects on area wildlife, the EIS concluded that no endangered or threatened species would be affected by the proposed development and that the only impact on sensitive species was the probable loss of a pair of spotted owls and their progeny. *Id.*, at 75. With regard to other wildlife, the Study considered the impact on 75 different indigenous species and predicted that within a decade after development vegetational change and increased human activity would lead to a decrease in population for 31 species, while causing an increase in population for another 24 species on Sandy Butte. *Ibid.* Two species, the pine marten and nesting goshawk, would be eliminated altogether from the area of development. *Ibid.*

In a comment in response to the draft EIS, the Washington Department of Game voiced a special concern about potential losses to the State's largest migratory deer herd, which uses the Methow Valley as a critical winter range and as its migration route. The state agency estimated that the total population of mule deer in the area most likely to be affected was "better than 30,000 animals" and that "the ultimate impact on the Methow deer herd could exceed a 50 percent reduction in numbers." The agency asserted that "Okanogan County residents place of great deal of importance on the area's deer herd." In addition, it explained that hunters had "harvested" 3,247 deer in the Methow Valley area in 1981, and that in 1980 hunters on average spent $1,980 for each deer killed in Washington, they had contributed over $6 million to the State's economy. Because the deer harvest is apparently proportional to the size of the herd, the state agency predicted that "Washington business can expect to lose over $3 million annually from reduced recreational opportunity." The Forest Service's own analysis of the impact on the deer herd was more modest. It first concluded that the actual operation of the ski hill would have only a "minor" direct impact on the herd, but then recognized that the off-site effect of the development "would noticeably reduce numbers of deer in the Methow [Valley] with any alternative." *Id.*, at 76. Although its estimate indicated a possible 15 percent decrease in the size of the herd, it summarized the State's contrary view in the text of the EIS, and stressed that off-site effects are difficult to estimate due to uncertainty concerning private development.

As was true of its discussion of air quality, the EIS also described both on-site and off-site mitigation measures. Among possible on-site mitigation possibilities, the Study recommended locating runs, ski lifts, and roads so as to minimize interference with wildlife, restricting access to selected roads during fawning season, and further examination of the effect of the development on mule deer migration routes. Off-site options discussed in the Study included the use of zoning and tax incentives to limit development on deer winter range and migration routes, encouragement of conservation easements, and acquisition and management by local government of critical tracts of land. As with the measures suggested for mitigating the off-site effects on air quality, the proposed options were primarily directed to steps that might be taken by state and local government.

Ultimately, the Early Winters Study recommended the issuance of a permit for development at the second highest level considered — a 16-lift ski area able to accommodate 8,200 skiers at one time. On July 5, 1984, the Regional Forester decided to issue a special use permit as recommended by the Study. In his decision, the Regional Forester found that no major adverse effects would result directly from the federal action, but that secondary effects could include a degradation of existing air quality and a reduction of mule deer winter range. He therefore directed the supervisor of the Okanogan National Forest, both independently and in cooperation with local officials, to identify and implement certain mitigating measures.

Four organizations (respondents) opposing the decision to issue a permit appealed the Regional Forester's decision to the Chief of the Forest Service. After a hearing, he affirmed the Regional Forester's decision. Stressing that the decision, which simply approved the general concept of issuing a 30-year special use permit for development of Sandy Butte, did not authorize construction of a particular ski area and, in fact, did not even act on MRI's specific permit application, he concluded that the EIS's discussion of mitigation was "adequate for this stage in the review process."

Thereafter, respondents brought this action under the Administrative Procedure Act, 5 U.S.C. §§ 701–706, to obtain judicial review of the Forest Service's decision. Their principal claim was that the Early Winters Study did not satisfy the requirements of NEPA, 42 U.S.C. § 4332. With the consent of the parties, the case was assigned to a United States Magistrate. *See* 28 U.S.C. § 636(c). After a trial, the Magistrate filed a comprehensive written opinion and concluded that the EIS was adequate. Specifically, he found that the EIS had adequately disclosed the adverse impacts on the mule deer herd and on air quality and that there was no duty to prepare a "worst case analysis" because the relevant information essential to a reasoned decision was available. In concluding that the discussion of off-site, or secondary, impacts was adequate, the Magistrate stressed that courts apply a "rule of reason" in evaluating the adequacy of an EIS and "take the uncertainty and speculation involved with secondary impacts into account in passing on the adequacy of the discussion of secondary impacts." On the subject of mitigation, he explained that "[m]ere listing . . . is generally inadequate to satisfy the CEQ regulations," but found that "in this EIS there is more — not much more — but more than a mere listing of mitigation measures." Moreover, emphasizing the tiered nature of the Forest Service's decisional process, the Magistrate noted that additional mitigation strategies would be included in the master plan, that the Forest Service continues to develop mitigation plans as further information becomes available, and that the Regional Forester's decision conditioned issuance of the special use permit on execution of an agreement between the Forest Service, the State of Washington, and Okanogan County concerning mitigation.

Concluding that the Early Winters Study was inadequate as a matter of law, the Court of Appeals reversed. *Methow Valley Citizens Council v. Regional Forester*, 833 F.2d 810 (CA9 1987). The court held that the Forest Service could not rely on " 'the implementation of mitigation measures' " to support its conclusion that the impact on the mule deer would be minor "since not only has the effectiveness of these mitigation measures not yet been assessed, but the mitigation measures themselves have yet to be developed." It then added that if the agency had difficulty obtaining adequate information to make a reasoned assessment of the environmental impact on the herd, it had a duty to make a so-called "worst case analysis." Such an analysis is " 'formulated on the basis of available information, using reasonable projections of the worst possible consequences of a proposed action.' " *Save our Ecosystems*, 747 F.2d, at 1244–45 (quoting 46 Fed. Reg. 18032 (1981)

The court found a similar defect in the EIS's treatment of air quality. Since the EIS made it clear that commercial development in the Methow Valley will result in violations of state air quality standards unless effective mitigation measures are put in place by the local governments and the private developer, the Court of Appeals concluded that the Forest Service had an affirmative duty to "develop the necessary mitigation measures before the permit is granted." (emphasis in original) (footnote omitted). The court held that this duty was imposed by both the Forest Service's own regulations and § 102 of NEPA. *Ibid*. It read the statute as imposing a substantive requirement that "action be taken to mitigate the adverse effects of major federal actions." For this reason, it concluded that "an EIS must include a fair discussion of measures to mitigate the adverse environmental impacts of a proposed action." The Court of Appeals concluded by quoting this paragraph from an opinion it had just announced:

> " 'The importance of the mitigation plan cannot be overestimated. It is a determinative factor in evaluating the adequacy of an environmental impact statement. Without a complete mitigation plan, the decisionmaker is unable to make an informed judgment as to the environmental impact of the project — one of the main purposes of an environmental impact statement.' " (quoting *Oregon Natural Resources Council v. Marsh*, 832 F.2d 1489, 1493 (CA9 1987), *rev'd, post*, p. 360)).

II

* * *

The statutory requirement that a federal agency contemplating a major action prepare . . . an environmental impact statement serves NEPA's "action-forcing" purpose in two important respects. It ensures that the agency, in reaching its decision, will have available and will carefully consider detailed information concerning significant environmental impacts; it also guarantees that the relevant information will be made available to the larger audience that may also play a role in both the decisionmaking process and the implementation of that decision.

Simply by focusing the agency's attention on the environmental consequences of a proposed project, NEPA ensures that important effects will not be overlooked or underestimated only to be discovered after resources have been committed or the die otherwise cast. Moreover, the strong precatory language of § 101 of the Act and the requirement that agencies prepare detailed impact statements inevitably bring pressure to bear on agencies "to respond to the needs of environmental quality."

Publication of an EIS, both in draft and final form, also serves a larger informational role. It gives the public the assurance that the agency "has indeed considered environmental concerns in its decisionmaking process," and, perhaps more significantly, provides a springboard for public comment. Thus, in this case the final draft of the Early Winters Study reflects not only the work of the Forest Service itself, but also the critical views of the Washington State Department of Game, the Methow Valley Citizens Council, and Friends of the Earth, as well as many others, to whom copies of the draft Study were circulated. Moreover, with respect to a development such as Sandy Butte, where the adverse effects on air quality and the mule deer herd are primarily attributable to predicate off-site development that will be subject to regulation by other governmental bodies, the EIS serves the function of offering those bodies adequate notice of the expected consequences and the opportunity to plan and implement corrective measures in a timely manner.

The sweeping policy goals announced in § 101 of NEPA are thus realized through a set of "action-forcing" procedures that require that agencies take a " 'hard look' at environmental consequences," and that provide for broad dissemination of relevant environmental information. Although these procedures are almost certain to affect the agency's substantive decision, it is now well settled that NEPA itself does not mandate particular results, but simply prescribes the necessary process. *See Strycker's Bay Neighborhood Council, Inc. v. Karlen*, 444 U. S. 223, 227–228 (1980) (per curiam); *Vermont Yankee Nuclear Power Corp. v. Natural Resources Defense Council, Inc.*, 435 U. S. 519, 558 (1978). If the adverse environmental effects of the proposed action are adequately identified and evaluated, the agency is not constrained by NEPA from deciding that other values outweigh the environmental costs. In this case, for example, it would not have violated NEPA if the Forest Service, after complying with the Act's procedural prerequisites, had decided that the benefits to be derived from downhill skiing at Sandy Butte justified the issuance of a special use permit, notwithstanding the loss of 15 percent, 50 percent, or even 100 percent of the mule deer herd. Other statutes may impose substantive environmental obligations on federal agencies, but NEPA merely prohibits uninformed — rather than unwise — agency action.

To be sure, one important ingredient of an EIS is the discussion of steps that can be taken to mitigate adverse environmental consequences. The requirement that an EIS contain a detailed discussion of possible mitigation measures flows from both the language of the Act and, more expressly, from CEQ's implementing regulations. Implicit in NEPA's demand that an agency prepare a detailed statement on "any adverse environmental effects which cannot be avoided should the proposal be implemented," 42 U.S.C. § 4332(C)(ii), is an understanding that the EIS will discuss the extent to which adverse effects can be avoided. More generally, omission of a reasonably complete discussion of possible mitigation measures would undermine the "action-forcing" function of NEPA. Without such a discussion, neither the agency nor other interested groups and individuals can properly evaluate the severity of the adverse effects. An adverse effect that can be fully remedied by, for example, an inconsequential public expenditure is certainly not as serious as a similar effect that can only be modestly ameliorated through the commitment of vast public and private resources. Recognizing the importance of such a discussion in guaranteeing that the agency has taken a "hard look" at the environmental consequences of proposed federal action, CEQ regulations require that the agency discuss possible mitigation measures in defining the scope of the EIS, 40 C.F.R. § 1508.25(b) (1987), in discussing alternatives to the proposed action, § 1502.14(f), and consequences of that action, § 1502.16(h), and in explaining its ultimate decision, § 1505.2(c).

There is a fundamental distinction, however, between a requirement that mitigation be discussed in sufficient detail to ensure that environmental consequences have been fairly evaluated, on the one hand, and a substantive requirement that a complete mitigation plan be actually formulated and adopted, on the other. In this case, the off-site effects on air quality and on the mule deer herd cannot be mitigated unless nonfederal government agencies take appropriate action. Since it is those state and local governmental bodies that have jurisdiction over the area in which the adverse effects need be addressed and since they have the authority to mitigate them, it would be incongruous to conclude that the Forest Service has no power to act until the local agencies have reached a final conclusion on what mitigating measures they consider necessary. Even more significantly, it would be inconsistent with NEPA's reliance on procedural mechanisms — as opposed to substantive, result-based standards — to demand the presence of a fully developed plan that will mitigate environmental harm before an agency can act. *Cf. Baltimore Gas & Electric Co.*, 462 U.S., at 100 ("NEPA does not require agencies to adopt any particular internal decisionmaking structure").

Because NEPA imposes no substantive requirement that mitigations measures actually be taken, it should not be read to require agencies to obtain an assurance that third parties will implement particular measures.

We thus conclude that the Court of Appeals erred, first, in assuming that "NEPA requires that 'action be taken to mitigate the adverse effects of major federal actions,'" and, second, in finding that this substantive requirement entails the further duty to include in every EIS "a detailed explanation of specific measures which will be employed to mitigate the adverse impacts of a proposed action," 833 F.2d, at 819 (emphasis supplied).

III

The Court of Appeals also concluded that the Forest Service had an obligation to make a "worst case analysis" if it could not make a reasoned assessment of the impact of the Early Winters project on the mule deer herd. Such a "worst case analysis" was required at one time by CEQ regulations, but those regulations have since been amended. Moreover, although the prior regulations may well have expressed a permissible application of NEPA, the Act itself does not mandate that uncertainty in predicting environmental harms be addressed exclusively in this manner. Accordingly, we conclude that the Court of Appeals also erred in requiring the "worst case" study.

In 1977, President Carter directed the CEQ promulgate binding regulations implementing the procedural provisions of NEPA. Exec. Order No. 11991, 3 C.F.R. 123 (1977 Comp.). Pursuant to this presidential order, CEQ promulgated implementing regulations. Under § 1502.22 of these regulations — a provision which became known as the "worst case requirement" — CEQ provided that if certain information relevant to the agency's evaluation of the proposed action is either unavailable or too costly to obtain, the agency must include in the EIS a "worst case analysis and an indication of the probability or improbability of its occurrence." 40 C.F.R. § 1502.22 (1985). In 1986, however, CEQ replaced the "worst case" requirement with a requirement that federal agencies, in the face of unavailable information concerning a reasonably foreseeable significant environmental consequence, prepare "a summary of existing credible scientific evidence which is relevant to evaluating the . . . adverse impacts" and prepare an "evaluation of such impacts based upon theoretical approaches or research methods generally accepted in the scientific community." 40 C.F.R. § 1502.22(b) (1987). The amended regulation thus "retains the duty to describe the consequences of a remote, but potentially severe impact, but grounds the duty in evaluation of scientific opinion rather than in the framework of a conjectural 'worst case analysis.'" 50 Fed. Reg. 32237 (1985).

The Court of Appeals recognized that the "worst case analysis" regulation has been superseded, yet held that "[t]his rescission . . . does not nullify the requirement . . . since the regulations was merely a codification of prior NEPA case law." This conclusion, however, is erroneous in a number of respects. Most notably, review of NEPA case law reveals that the regulation, in fact, was not a codification of prior judicial decisions. The cases cited by the Court of Appeals ultimately rely on the Fifth Circuit's decision in *Sierra Club v. Sigler*, 695 F.2d 957 (1983). *Sigler*, however, simply recognized that the "worst case analysis" regulation codified the "judicially created principl[e]" that an EIS must "consider the probabilities of the occurrence of any environmental effects it discusses." *Id.*, at 970–971. As CEQ recognized at the time it superseded the regulation, case law prior to the adoption of the "worst case analysis" provision did require agencies to describe environmental impacts even in the face of substantial uncertainty, but did not require that this obligation necessarily be met through the mechanism of a "worst case analysis." *See* 51 Fed. Reg. 15625 (1986). CEQ's abandonment of the "worst case analysis" provision, therefore, is not inconsistent with any previously established judicial interpretation of the statute.

Nor are we convinced that the new CEQ regulation is not controlling simply because it was preceded by a rule that was in some respects more demanding. In *Andrus v. Sierra Club*, 442 U.S., at 358, we held that CEQ regulations are entitled to substantial deference. In that case we recognized that although less deference may be in order in some cases in which the "'administrative guidelines'" conflict "'with earlier pronouncements of the agency,'" *ibid.* (quoting *General Electric Co. v. Gilbert*, 429 U. S. 125, 143 (1976)), substantial deference is nonetheless appropriate if there appears to have been good reason for the change, 442 U.S., at 358. Here, the amendment only came after the prior regulation had been subjected to considerable criticism. Moreover, the amendment was designed to better serve the twin functions of an EIS—requiring agencies to take a "hard look" at the consequences of the proposed action and providing important information to other groups and individuals. CEQ explained that by requiring that an EIS focus on reasonably foreseeable impacts, the new regulation "will generate information and discussion on those consequences of greatest concern to the public and of greatest relevance to the agency's decision," 50 Fed. Reg. 32237 (1985), rather than distorting the decision making process by overemphasizing highly speculative harms, 51 Fed. Reg. 15624–15625 (1986); 50 Fed. Reg. 32236 (1985). In light of this well-considered basis for the change, the new regulation is entitled to substantial deference.

IV

The Court of Appeals also held that the Forest Service's failure to develop a complete mitigation plan violated the agency's own regulations. [The Court found no such violation of the Forest Service's regulations.]

V

In sum, we conclude that NEPA does not require a fully developed plan detailing what steps will be taken to mitigate adverse environmental impacts and does not require a "worst case analysis." In addition, we hold that the Forest Service has adopted a permissible interpretation of its own regulations. The judgment of the Court of Appeals is accordingly reversed and the case is remanded for further proceedings consistent with this opinion.

It is so ordered.

JUSTICE BRENNAN, concurring.

I write separately to highlight the Court's observation that "one important ingredient of an EIS is the discussion of steps that can be taken to mitigate adverse environmental consequences."

*   *   *   *   *   *

Thus, we see that, because NEPA is essentially procedural, it authorizes no cause of action to protest an agency's failure to adopt the recommendations of an EIS. NEPA requires preparation of an EIS, but not compliance with it. *See Methow Valley, supra; see also Noe v. MARTA,* 485 F. Supp. 501 (N.D. Ga. 1980), *aff'd* 644 F.2d 434 (5th Cir. 1981), *cert. denied,* 454 U.S. 1126, 102 S.Ct. 977 (1981). *Cf. Calvert Cliffs,* 449 F.2d at 1117: ("What possible purpose could there be in requiring the 'detailed statement' to be before hearing boards, if the boards are free to ignore entirely the contents of the statement? NEPA was meant to do more than regulate the flow of papers in the federal bureaucracy.")

Might there be a cause of action elsewhere? Theoretically, a cause of action could be framed under the Administrative Procedure Act ("APA"), 5 U.S.C. § 551 et seq. Section 706(2) of the APA authorizes courts, *inter alia,* to "hold unlawful and set aside agency action, findings and conclusions found to be . . . arbitrary, capricious, an abuse of discretion, or otherwise not in accordance with law." 5. U.S.C. § 706(2)(A). Agency decisions are deemed to violate this provision if they are not "based on relevant factors" or if they manifest a "clear error of judgment." *Citizens to Preserve Overton Park v. Volpe,* 401 U.S. 402, 91 S.Ct. 814 (1971). There seem to be no cases, however, where such a cause of action has succeeded. *See, e.g.,* William H. Rodgers, Jr., *Environmental Law,* at 861 (2d ed., West Pub. Co. 1994) ("[D]iligent researchers are still looking for the project that could not be built under NEPA because the environmental costs exceeded the economic benefits.").

If agencies are free to ignore the recommendations of EISs, has NEPA become the "paper tiger" Judge Wright wrote of in *Calvert Cliffs?* The CEQ certainly does not think so. In 1997, it issued a report detailing the performance of the Act in its first 25 years. Council on Environmental Quality, *The National Environmental Policy Act: A Study of Its Effectiveness After Twenty-five Years,* January, 1997. ("CEQ Report"). CEQ concluded that NEPA is a "success" because it made agencies take a hard look at the potential environmental consequences of their actions and brought the public into the decision-making arena. Still, CEQ observed, agencies are sometimes prone to engage in consultation only after their decisions, at least for all practical purposes, have been made. This leads the public to feel excluded from the decisionmaking process, which in turns produces unnecessary public opposition to what may well be worthy agency actions. CEQ also conceded that NEPA can present agencies with significant administrative burdens. *Id.* at iii. Beyond that, agencies sometimes think of EISs as an end in themselves, rather than as an aid to decisionmaking.

Perhaps most significantly, the CEQ Report bemoaned the practice of agencies to use NEPA on a "once and for all" basis. As characterized by CEQ, ". . . results from intensive research, modeling, and other computations or expert opinions are analyzed, the analysis of potential environmental impacts is prepared, mitigation measure are identified, and a document is released for public review. Unfortunately, most often the process ends there." *Id.* at 31. In CEQ's view, this practice of using NEPA on a "snapshot" basis is undesirable. NEPA, rather, should play a role not only at the outset of a project, but during construction and operation phases as well. The heart and soul of NEPA would no longer be "predict, mitigate, and implement;" it would become "predict, mitigate, implement, monitor, and adapt." *Id.* at 32.

CEQ's name for this pro-mid-course corrections approach is "adaptive environmental management." CEQ elaborates: "Instead of investing extensive resources into the initial analysis, the adaptive management approach would allow agencies to develop objective criteria for 'significant' environmental change in the status of the resource or ecosystem of concern (be it rangelands, wetlands, or forests). An agency can then analyze and approve a plan or project with an uncertain outcome, monitoring the status of the resource to make corrective changes to the project or mitigation plan to ensure that significant degradation does not occur. By incorporating adaptive management into their NEPA analyses, agencies can move beyond simple compliance and better target environmental improvement." *Id.* at 33. Projects could remain assuredly benign to the environment for the entirety of their useful lives.

[2] EIS CONTENT AND AVAILABILITY REQUIREMENTS

We have now seen that the role of an EIS in agency decisionmaking is procedural. This section discusses the procedural requirements of § 102(2)(C). Specifically, it assesses the who, what, when, and how of the provision. Note that CEQ's regulations play an important part in determining the mechanics of agency compliance with NEPA's requirements. Those regulations, however, require each federal agency to adopt its own procedures "as necessary" for NEPA compliance. 40 C.F.R. § 1507, 3(a).

(A) *Who?:* Who must prepare an EIS? The federal agency responsible for the action under review has the responsibility to prepare the EIS. That responsibility does not mean that the agency must, in every case, actually write the document. It does mean, however, that the agency is ultimately responsible for it. Accordingly, if an agency contracts with an outside entity to write the document, the agency must nonetheless adopt the EIS as its own and take on full legal responsibility for it.

In many instances, more than one agency is involved in a proposed action. In such a case, the common practice is to choose one of the group to act as lead agency; if they cannot agree, the determination is left to the CEQ. 40 C.F.R. § 1501.5. The lead agency can designate cooperating agencies, and conversely, non-lead agencies can request to be cooperating agencies. 40 C.F.R. § 1501.6. EISs should contain a list of the names and qualifications of the persons primarily responsible for document preparation. 40 C.F.R. § 1502.17.

(B) *What?:* The information an EIS should contain is specified by § 102(2)(C) itself. The section lists five matters that must be covered. They are:

(i) the environmental impact of the proposed action,

(ii) any adverse environmental effects which cannot be avoided should the proposal be implemented,

(iii) alternatives to the proposed action,

(iv) the relationship between local short-term uses of man's environment and the maintenance and enhancement of long-term productivity, and

(v) any irreversible and irretrievable commitments of resources which would be involved in the proposed action should it be implemented.

§ 102(2)(C), 42 U.S.C. § 4332(2)(C).

Of these five components, the most important are the first and the third. The first requirement, calling for review of environmental impacts, obligates agencies to examine direct, indirect, and cumulative effects of those proposed actions. "Direct" effects are those which are "caused by the action and occur at the same time and place." 40 C.F.R. § 1508.8(a). "Indirect" effects are also caused by the action but "are later in time or farther removed in distance, but are still reasonably foreseeable." 40 C.F.R. § 1508.8(b). To understand indirect effects, think of a proposal to build a new federal office building in a rural area. Indirect impacts of such a project would include construction of access roads to serve the soon-to-arrive workforce, increases in air pollution from additional automobiles, and other urbanization changes.

Finally, there are cumulative effects. Cumulative effects are impacts on the environment "which result[s] from the incremental impact of the action when added to other past, present, and reasonably foreseeable future actions regardless of what agency (Federal or non-Federal) or person undertakes such other actions. Cumulative impacts can result from individually minor but collectively significant actions taking place over a period of time." 40 C.F.R. § 1508.7. In other words, EISs must take into account the location at which a proposed action would take place. In addition, they must also examine *other* projects slated for construction in the same area. *Kleppe v. Sierra Club,* 427 U.S. 390, 410, 96 S. Ct. 2718 (1976) (stating that "when several proposals for actions that will have cumulative or synergistic environmental impact upon a region are pending concurrently before an agency, their environmental consequences must be considered together."). *See, also Earth Island Institute v. U.S. Forest Service,* 351 F.3d 1291, 1304 (9th Cir. 2003) ("[a] single NEPA review document is required for distinct projects when there is a single proposal governing the projects or when the projects are connected, cumulative, or similar actions under the regulations implementing NEPA." (quoting *Native Ecosystems Council v. Dombeck,* 304 F.3d 886, 893-94 (9th Cir. 2002)).

However, the courts have been unwilling to take this principle too far. Said the D.C. Circuit: ". . . an EIS need not delve into the possible effects of a hypothetical project, but need only focus on the impact of the particular proposal at issue and other pending or recently approved proposals that might be connected to or act cumulatively with the proposal at issue." *National Wildlife Federation v. Federal Energy Regulatory Comm'n*, 912 F.2d 1471, 1478 (D.C. Cir. 1990). And the Fourth Circuit has added: "[g]enerally, an administrative agency need consider the impact of other proposed projects when developing an EIS for a pending project only if the projects are so interdependent that it would be unwise or irrational to complete one without the others." *Webb v. Gorsuch*, 699 F.2d 157, 161 (4th Cir. 1983).

The third requirement of § 102(2)(C) of NEPA stipulates that EISs must examine alternatives to proposed courses of action. How broad is this requirement? The statute does not require consideration of alternatives "whose effect cannot be reasonably ascertained, and whose implementation is deemed remote and speculative." *Life of the Land v. Brinegar*, 485 F.2d 460, 472 (9th Cir. 1973), *cert. denied*, 416 U.S. 961, 94 S. Ct. 1979 (1974). Nor need an agency consider alternatives which are infeasible or ineffective. *California v. Block*, 690 F.2d at 753 (9th Cir. 1982); *see also Kilroy v. Ruckelshaus*, 738 F.2d 1448, 1454 (9th Cir. 1984) (agency need not examine alternatives that are "remote from reality"). Last, agencies do not have to undertake separate analyses of alternatives which are not significantly distinguishable from other alternatives already considered, or which have substantially similar consequences. *Northern Plains Resource Council v. Lujan*, 874 F.2d 661, (9th Cir. 1989). Thus, an agency's consideration of alternatives "is sufficient if it considers an appropriate range of alternatives, even if it does not consider every available alternative." *Headwaters, Inc. v. Bureau of Land Management*, 914 F.2d 1174, 1181 (9th Cir. 1990). "[C]ommon sense . . . teaches us that . . . [an EIS] . . . cannot be found wanting simply because the agency failed to include every alternative device and thought conceivable by the mind of man." *Vermont Yankee Nuclear Power Corp. v. Natural Resources Defense Council*, 435 U.S. 519, 551, 98 S. Ct. 1197, 1215 (1978).[2]

---

[2] The consideration of alternatives is so important that it must be done even when an agency is not preparing an EIS. Section 102(2)(E) of NEPA, 42 U.S.C. § 4332(2)(E), requires agencies to "study, develop, and describe appropriate alternatives to recommended courses of action in any proposal which involves unresolved conflicts concerning alternative uses of available resources." *See, e.g. Bob Marshall Alliance v. Hodel*, 852 F.2d 1223, 1228-29 (1988):

[C]onsideration of alternatives is critical to the goals of NEPA even where a proposed action does not trigger the EIS process. This is reflected in the structure of the statute: while an EIS must also include alternatives to the proposed action, 42 U.S.C. § 4332(2)(C)(iii) (1982), the consideration of alternatives requirement is contained in a separate subsection of the statute and therefore constitutes an independent requirement. *See id.* § 4332(2)(E). The language and effect of the two subsections also indicate that the consideration of alternatives requirement is of wider scope than the EIS requirement. The former applies whenever an action involves conflicts, while the latter does not come into play unless the action will have significant environmental effects. An EIS is required where there has been an irretrievable commitment of resources; but unresolved conflicts as to the proper use of available resources may exist well before that point. Thus the consideration of alternatives requirement is both independent of, and broader than, the EIS requirement. . . . [citations omitted] . . . In short, any proposed federal action involving unresolved conflicts as to the proper use of resources triggers NEPA's consideration of alternatives requirement, whether or not an EIS is also required.

Note, however, that NEPA's requirement for examination of alternatives requires agencies to consider how things might be if the agency abandoned its proposed action entirely. EISs, in other words, must address the "no-action" alternative.

(C) *When?*: If an EIS must be prepared, when must it be? *See Kleppe v. Sierra Club*, 427 U.S. 390, 405-06, 96 S.Ct. 2718, 2728 (1976):

> The statute clearly states when an impact statement is required[.] Under the first sentence of § 102(2)(C) the moment at which an agency must have a final statement ready 'is the time at which it makes a recommendation or report on a proposal for federal action. The procedural duty imposed upon agencies by this section is quite precise, and the role of the courts in enforcing that duty is similarly precise. A court has no authority to depart from the statutory language and, by a balancing of court-devised factors, determine a point during the germination process of a potential proposal at which an impact statement should be prepared. . . . The contemplation of a project and the accompanying study thereof do not necessarily result in a proposal for major federal action.

The EIS must be incorporated into the agency's decisional processes "at the earliest possible time." *Thomas v. Peterson*, 753 F.2d 754, 760 (9th Cir. 1985).

(D) *How?:* The governing standard regarding contents of an EIS is reasonableness. Courts have stated that evaluations in an EIS should be of a quality sufficient to enable decisionmakers to fairly weigh environmental considerations, and to enable the public to meaningfully comprehend those same considerations. *See, e.g., Town of Huntington v. Marsh*, 859 F.2d 1134 (2d Cir. 1988). EISs, moreover, must be well organized and clearly written. *Oregon Environmental Council v. Kunzman*, 817 F.2d 484 (D.D.C. 1983).

NOTES

1. There have been fourteen NEPA cases decided on the merits by the United States Supreme Court. In each of these cases, the Court reversed a court of appeals judgment that favored environmental plaintiffs. In reverse chronological order, the cases are:

Norton v. Southwest Utah Wilderness Alliance, __ U.S. __, 124 S. Ct. 2373 (2004) (supplementation of an EIS is necessary only if there remains some "major federal action" yet to occur).

Department of Transportation v. Public Citizen, __ U.S. __, 124 S. Ct. 2204 (2004) (an EA need not consider environmental effects which the agency is powerless to prevent).

Robertson v. Methow Valley Citizens Council, 490 U.S. 332, 109 S. Ct. 1835 (1989) (NEPA does not impose a substantive duty on agencies to mitigate adverse environmental effects or a duty to include a fully developed mitigation plan in an EIS; NEPA does not require "worst case" analysis);

Marsh v. Oregon Natural Resources Council, 490 U.S. 360, 109 S. Ct. 1851 (1989) (agency decision not to prepare supplemental EIS is reviewed under "arbitrary and capricious" standard of APA; courts must defer to informed discretion of agency on issues requiring high degree of technical expertise, but should independently review the record to assure that agency took the required "hard look");

Baltimore Gas & Electric Co. v. Natural Resources Defense Council, 462 U.S. 87, 103 S. Ct. 2246 (1983) (while an agency must allow all significant environmental risks to be factored into a decision whether to undertake a proposed action, it may determine in a generic proceeding that a particular risk is insufficient to affect any individual decision, so long as that determination is not arbitrary and capricious);

Metropolitan Edison Co. v. People Against Nuclear Energy, 460 U.S. 766, 103 S. Ct. 1556 (1983) (contentions of psychological health damage caused by risk of accident at nuclear reactor are not cognizable under NEPA — for an effect to be cognizable there must be a reasonably close causal relationship between the effect and a change in the physical environment);

Weinberger v. Catholic Action of Hawaii, 454 U.S. 139, 102 S. Ct. 197 (1981) (since information relating to the storage of nuclear weapons is exempt from disclosure under the Freedom of Information Act, courts cannot require EIS on the possible storage of nuclear weapons at a facility; Ninth Circuit's requirement of a "hypothetical EIS" in this situation is unsupported by the language of the statute);

Strycker's Bay Neighborhood Council v. Karlen, 444 U.S. 223, 100 S. Ct. 497 (1980) (per curiam) ("once an agency has made a decision subject to NEPA's procedural requirements, the only role for a court is to insure that the agency has considered the environmental consequences; it cannot interject itself with the area of discretion of the executive as to the choice of the action to be taken");

Andrus v. Sierra Club, 442 U.S. 347, 99 S. Ct. 2335 (1979) (no EIS required for agencies' appropriation requests, since they are not proposals for legislation or proposals for major federal actions; CEQ regulations are entitled to substantial deference);

Vermont Yankee Nuclear Power Corp. v. Natural Resources Defense Council, 435 U.S. 519, 98 S. Ct. 1197 (1978) (where agency addresses environmental issue in a rulemaking, NEPA cannot be used by reviewing court to impose procedures beyond those specified in the APA);

Consumers Power Co. v. Aeschliman, 435 U.S. 519, 98 S. Ct. 1197 (1978) (decided in conjunction with *Vermont Yankee*) (challengers must meaningfully alert the agency of their contentions; agency may require a threshold showing of materiality before having to respond to comments; duty to consider alternatives "must be bounded by some notion of feasibility");

Kleppe v. Sierra Club, 427 U.S. 390, 96 S. Ct. 2718 (1976) (agency need not prepare EIS on activities in entire region unless there has been an actual "proposal" for a regional plan of development; a comprehensive EIS may be required when several proposals for action will have cumulative or synergistic environmental impacts, but agency decision not to prepare such an EIS will be upheld unless arbitrary and capricious);

Flint Ridge Development Co. v. Scenic Rivers Ass'n, 426 U.S. 776, 96 S. Ct. 2430 (1976) (duty to prepare an EIS must yield before "a clear and unavoidable conflict in statutory authority");

Aberdeen & Rockfish R.R. v. SCRAP, 422 U.S. 289, 95 S. Ct. 2336 (1975) (EIS not required until the agency makes a recommendation or report on a proposal for action).

See David C. Shelton, *Is the Supreme Court Hostile to NEPA? Some Possible Explanations for a 12-0 Record, prepared for presentation at the conference on "NEPA at Twenty: The Past, Present, and Future of the National Environmental Policy Act,* Portland, Oregon, October 27, 1989.

2. At least sixteen states and the District of Columbia and Puerto Rico have enacted their own NEPA-like statutes. These statutes, commonly referred to as "SEPAs," vary. Some, unlike NEPA, directly govern the substance of agency decisionmaking. Most SEPAs, like NEPA, require consideration of environmental impacts if proposed state actions may produce significant environmental effects, although the threshold considerations triggering the state law-based EIS process may differ from those of the federal legislation. SEPAs typically apply to all categories of state actions, including government-undertaken projects, permitting, and subsidies.

"Where State laws or local ordinances have environmental impact statement requirements in addition to but not in conflict with those in NEPA, Federal agencies shall cooperate in fulfilling these requirements as well as those of Federal laws so that one document will comply with all applicable laws." 40 C.F.R. § 1506.2(c).

A NOTE ON ENVIRONMENTAL JUSTICE

Suppose that a manufacturing facility, Plant D, is scheduled for construction in Lowlands, a residential area that already serves as a home to Plants A, B, and C, which are polluters. Plant D needs a federal permit as a prerequisite to construction. The issue is whether the permitting of Plant D constitutes a "major federal action significantly affecting the quality of the human environment." As we have seen, this determination requires an assessment of direct, indirect, and cumulative effects. The EA, therefore, must examine the character of the proposed site, i.e., "the incremental impact of the [construction of Plant D] when added to other past, present, and reasonably foreseeable future actions[.]" 40 C.F.R. 1508.7.

In addition to these considerations, should the EA consider the state of affairs in other locales? Specifically, should it assess whether nearby locales are free, or relatively free, of polluting facilities, while Lowlands seems to be getting more than its share? And if that is the case, should that fact bear on the determination whether to proceed with an EIS? Expressed otherwise, should an EA contain a *comparative* impacts analysis? The text of NEPA announces no such obligation. Currently, however, a comparative analysis of this sort is necessary if Lowlands happens to be populated predominantly by persons of color or low income.

The reason is found in the Environmental Justice ("EJ") movement. Prompted in large part by a 1987 study prepared by the United Church of

Christ, entitled *Toxic Waste and Race in the United States: A National Report on the Racial and Socio-Economic Characteristics of Communities with Hazardous Waste Sites,* the EJ movement maintains that a disproportionate number of polluting facilities, especially hazardous waste disposal sites, have been constructed in areas populated predominantly by persons of color and low income. The movement asserts this proliferation is racist in origin. In response to this initiative, President Bill Clinton issued an Executive Order 12898 on February 11, 1994, which provides in relevant part:

> § 1-101. Agency Responsibilities. To the greatest extent practicable and permitted by law, and consistent with the principles set forth in the report on the National Performance Review, each Federal agency shall make achieving environmental justice part of its mission by identifying and addressing, as appropriate, disproportionately high and adverse human health or environmental effects of its programs, policies, and activities on minority populations and low-income populations in the United States and its territories and possessions, the District of Columbia, the Commonwealth of Puerto Rico, and the Commonwealth of the Mariana Islands.

For the full text of the Order, see 59 Fed. Reg. 7629 (Feb. 11, 1994).

This order has changed the way federal agencies comply with NEPA. The EPA, for example, released "draft guidance" on July 12, 1996, which proposed that its EIS evaluations should consider environmental justice factors such as demographics, economic conditions, human health and risk issues, and cultural differences. Accordingly, early in the NEPA process, the agency "should identify the presence of minority or low-income communities and whether such communities are likely to experience adverse environmental health effects as a result of proposed federal actions." The inclusion of such considerations, the draft commented, would allow for a "more focused analysis that identifies significant effects that might otherwise have been diluted by an examination of a larger population or area [.]" "[E]nvironmental justice concerns," it added, "should always trigger the serious evaluation of alternatives as mitigation options."

The EJ movement, it should be understood (and as the Executive Order indicates), is not confined to situations involving NEPA. Since the movement implicates core concepts of equality under the law, it has looked to both the Equal Protection Clauses of the federal Constitution and Title VI of the Civil Rights Act of 1964 for legal support. Indeed, these provisions can serve as substantive bases to contest an agency decision to locate a sewage treatment plant, a cement plant, a hazardous waste treatment or disposal plant or any other polluting facility. Title VI, for example, expressly provides that no person shall "on the grounds of race, color, or national origin, be denied the benefits of, or be subjected to discrimination under any program or activity" covered by that legislation. 42 U.S.C. § 2000d.

However, the Equal Protection Clauses and Title VI have proven to be of limited value to EJ plaintiffs because they prohibit only hard-to-prove *intentionally* discriminatory actions. *See, e.g., Regents of University of California v. Bakke,* 438 U.S. 265, 98 S. Ct. 2733 (1978); *Alexander v. Choate,* 469 U.S. 287, 83 L. Ed. 2d 661, 105 S. Ct. 712 (1985). Thus, if the motivation behind a siting decision is entirely for reasons of economics or politics, no cause of action lies regardless of whether the targeted locale is already overburdened with polluting facilities.

What EJ plaintiffs prefer is a disparate impact standard. For a *prima facie* case under this standard, plaintiffs need to demonstrate a statistically significant disproportionate and adverse impact on minorities, and beyond that, a causal connection between the agency action or policy and that disproportionate and adverse impact. *See, e.g., New York Environmental Justice Alliance v. Guiliani*, 214 F.3d 65 (2d Cir. 2000). This burden of proof presents its own level of difficulty: proving a causal connection can be difficult, especially when an agency policy, as distinct from an agency permit issuance, is at issue. Moreover, figuring out who is a member of a minority group, and which minorities are affected by which actions, can be difficult. This difficulty, if anything, was exacerbated by the 2000 census, which introduced a new classification system allowing persons to include themselves as members of more than one minority group. Still, with a disparate impact standard, plaintiffs at least do not need to prove the defendant's mental state, i.e., that defendant intended to discriminate.

Thanks to the United States Department of Justice ("DOJ"), plaintiffs have been using the disparate impact standard. This is because the DOJ promulgated rules that forbid recipients of federal funding, including state governments and private persons, to "utilize criteria or methods of administration which have the *effect* of subjecting individuals to discrimination because of their race, color, or national origin. . . ." 28 C.F.R. § 42.104(b)(2) (emphasis added). Thus did DOJ attempt to restore the disparate impact standard to Title VI cases.

The disparate impact standard, however, is no longer available for non-government EJ plaintiffs. In *Alexander v. Sandoval*, 532 U.S. 275, 121 S. Ct. 1511 (2001), a case involving the State of Alabama's practice of administering driving license examinations in the English language only, the Supreme Court, assuming the DOJ's regulations calling for a disparate impact standard were valid, concluded that no private right of action exists to enforce those regulations. (There remains a private right of action to enforce DOJ regulations prohibiting intentional discrimination.) The decision was 5-4, with Associate Justice Antonin Scalia writing for the majority. *Sandoval* means that agencies are still obligated to follow the DOJ regulations, but the public may not take action in the event an agency fails to meet its obligation.

Even though this was described as a devastating blow to EJ proponents, indeed as a "dagger in the middle of the forehead," *BNA Daily Environmental Report*, April 25, 2001, still, from the point of view of EJ plaintiffs, all may not be lost. While *Sandoval* rules out disparate impact causes of action under Title VI, there still remains a cause of action to enforce Title VI regulations under 42 U.S.C. § 1983. Justice Stevens, in his dissent in *Sandoval,* allowed for that possibility, and at least one subsequent decision has determined this alternative avenue is available. *South Camden Citizens in Action v. New Jersey Department of Environmental Protection*, 145 F. Supp. 2d 505 (2001). So the disparate impact standard lives.

The hotly debated question underlying all of this is whether it actually is a common practice to site plants for racist reasons. One view on the issue is well stated by Richard Samp, Chief Counsel of the Washington Legal Foundation: "I've never known a company to purposely choose a site that was more expensive than an alternative site simply because they wanted to stick it to some racial minority. They go to a particular site because they think it is the best one available to them at the cheapest cost." *All Things Considered* (National Public Radio, May 7, 2001). Unsurprisingly, residents of burdened localities often tend to view the matter differently. Empirical data one way or the other has been in short supply. But the data is coming in. Using recent census information, an environmental group, Environmental Defense, has assembled a database to shed light on the magnitude of the EJ problem. The group compared four environmental risks — toxic chemical releases, cancer risks from hazardous air pollutants, hazardous materials sites under the Comprehensive Environmental Response, Compensation and Liability Act (*see* Chapter 12, *infra*) and so-called "criteria" air pollutants (*see* Chapter 9, *infra*) — with seven demographic factors: race and ethnicity; income; poverty; childhood poverty; education; job classification; and home ownership. Environmental Defense concluded its data, while likely not the last take on the matter, failed to demonstrate any national trend with respect to environmental justice. Environmental Defense's information is available at *http://www.scorecard.org*.

A final note: in October, 2003, the U.S. Commission on Civil Rights issued a report entitled "Not In My Backyard." One hundred ninety-four pages in length, this report found that the Environmental Protection Agency, the Department of Housing and Urban Development, the Department of Transportation, and the Department of the Interior have failed to fully implement the 1994 Executive Order. *See http://www.usccr.gov/pubs/envjust/ej0104.pdf*. For a fifty-state survey of legislation, policies and initiatives relating to environmental justice, see *Environmental Justice For All*, a publication of the American Bar Association and Hastings College of the Law, 2004.

A NOTE ON NEPA § 102(1)

Section 102(1) of NEPA requires that "the policies, regulations and public laws of the United States shall be interpreted in accordance with the policies set forth in this chapter[.]" § 102(1), 42 U.S.C. § 4332(1). This duty is to be accomplished "to the fullest extent possible." § 102. Despite thousands of opportunities, this subsection has rarely been used and has never been determinative of the resolution of a disputed case. The Supreme Court, in fact, has never discussed § 102(1), and lower federal courts only rarely. Virtually all we know from the courts is that the provision does not authorize the disregard of a clear nondiscretionary duty established by organic law. *See, e.g., NRDC, Inc. v. Berklund*, 609 F.2d 553 (D.C. Cir. 1979) (holding NEPA did not authorize the U.S. Department of Interior to reject lease applications on independent NEPA grounds contrary to the governing organic statute, the Mineral Lands Leasing Act. In the Court's words: "the plain meaning of the [MLLA] as well as an undisturbed administrative practice for nearly 60 years leaves the Secretary no discretion to deny a . . . lease . . . to a qualified applicant.") *Id.* at 558. *Accord Cape May Greene, Inc. v. Warren,* 698 F.2d 179 (3rd Cir. 1982). *Cf. Environmental Defense Fund v. Matthews,* 410 F.Supp. 336, 338 (D.D.C. 1976) ("[W]e find that NEPA [§ 102(1)] provides [the Food and Drug Administration] with supplementary authority to base its substantive decisions on all environmental considerations including those not expressly identified in the [Food, Drug, and Cosmetic Act] and FDA's other statutes.").

Yet there are many instances in which § 102(1) could play a role. One such instance was *Calvert Cliffs.* The D.C. Circuit in that case, the reader will recall, examined the adequacy of the Atomic Energy Commission's interpretation of its regulations under the Atomic Energy Act. The *Calvert Cliffs* court could have held that the agency's diluted view of its statutory obligations, as expressed in its regulations, violated § 102(1) because it promoted NEPA's goals not at all, and certainly not "to the fullest extent possible."

Methow Valley was another opportunity. In that case (and, for that matter, in *Vermont Yankee* and *Strycker's Bay*), the Supreme Court could have used § 102(1) to read life into § 102(2), to justify a holding that a complete and unwarranted disregard of EIS recommendations is reversible error. The *Methow Valley* Court could have called upon § 102(1) to assess whether the Forest Service had violated its own regulations. Those regulations required that applications for special use permits include "measures and plans for the protection and rehabilitation of the environment during construction, operation, maintenance, and termination of the project," 36 C.F.R. § 251.54(e)(4) (1988), and that "[e]ach special use authorization . . . contain[s] . . . [t]erms and conditions which will . . . minimize damage to scenic and esthetic values and fish and wildlife habitat and otherwise protect the environment." 36 C.F.R. § 251.56(a)(1)(ii). The Court found "no basis for concluding that the Forest Service's own regulations must . . . be read in all cases to condition issuance of a special use permit on consideration (and implementation) of off-site mitigation measures." *Id.* at 357, 109 S. Ct. at 1849. Could not § 102(1) have served as a basis to find just such a general requirement, or to find one in this case? In an informal discussion, your author was told by a highly placed CEQ official that § 102(1) has no legal validity, that any attempt to use it to influence the exercise of agency discretion would be "a long shot." In this official's view, the Supreme Court's declaration that NEPA is procedural stripped § 102(1) of any vitality it might have had. This view, however, overlooks both the clear text of § 102(1) and the fact that the Supreme Court's NEPA decisions examine § 102(2), not § 102(1).

Chapter 5

FEDERAL LANDS

"[The public lands represent] in a sense, the breathing space of the nation."
Richard M. Nixon, February 8, 1971.

A. INTRODUCTION

The public lands of the United States extend from the northern reaches of Alaska to the most distant southeast points of Florida. They encompass frozen tundras, lush agricultural lands, breathtaking vistas, wildlife habitat, urban parks, deltas, forests, mineral lands, and just about every other natural setting you can imagine. They include Mount McKinley, North America's highest point, and Death Valley, its lowest. The public lands span about 740 million acres or about one-third of the nation's approximately 2.3 billion acre total land area. This acreage is titled in the United States in fee simple absolute. In addition to these properties, the federal government holds less-than-fee interests, such as waterfowl easements and reserved mineral interests, in over 60 million additional acres. Federal lands can be found in every state, but particularly in the eleven western states and in Alaska. Alaska itself, in fact, contains about one-half of all the public lands. Beyond these holdings, the federal government controls the resources of the outer continental shelf ("OCS"). The OCS is comprised of offshore submerged lands underlying the oceans extending out from the coastal states, measuring from a point 3 miles off the nation's dryland border seaward to the edge of the high seas, and comprising about 860,000 square miles. Finally, the federal government controls fishing rights out to 200 miles.

How the government manages federal lands significantly affects the environmental health of the nation, to say nothing of its economic welfare. In this chapter, we survey federal lands and their management. We begin our inquiry with an historical overview of the assembly of the public lands. An historical understanding is helpful to better appreciate current federal land management policies. After this review, coverage shifts to an examination of the constitutional and statutory authorities available to the Congress and the President to manage public lands. These authorities allow public lands to be dedicated to specific uses, to be distributed to individuals under several allocation schemes, and to be withdrawn as circumstances warrant. Last, the Chapter introduces the federal agencies responsible for federal land management and surveys the specific legal regimes governing the extraction of minerals, harvesting of timber, consumption of forage, and the recreational use of the public lands.

B. HISTORICAL BACKGROUND

[1] ACQUISITION OF THE PUBLIC LANDS

The story of federal lands begins with their assembly. Federal land acquisition can be said to have begun in 1781, the year in which the Articles of Confederation were ratified by the original states. The national government created by the Articles was weak, but it at least had enough power to begin the process of acquiring lands to expand the borders of the nation. The process would ultimately lead to the federal government assuming the rank of the nation's chief landowner and landlord.

How the federal government took on this status is a story of politics, graft, and opportunity. At the time the Articles of Confederation were adopted, seven states (Connecticut, Georgia, Massachusetts, New York, North Carolina, South Carolina, and Vermont) held claims to land between the Appalachian Mountains and the Mississippi River.[1] This became a matter of immediate concern to unlanded states. Led by Maryland, unlanded states maintained that territorial possessions ought to be held in common by all so that no states would be subordinate. The unlanded states wanted also to be able to reward their soldiers for Revolutionary War service in the same way that landed states could. To resolve the controversy, the landed states ceded their claims to the federal government during the 1780s. And so it happened that by 1790, the federal government, now reformed by the ratification of the United States Constitution in 1788, was already holding title to approximately 10% of the nation's land.

The next seventy-five years brought additional acquisitions. Foreign nations with claims to land on the North American continent, specifically England, Russia, Spain, and Mexico, one by one yielded their lands to the new nation. The single most significant land transfer during these years was the Louisiana Purchase of 1803, which in one fell swoop doubled the size of the United States, at the cost of three cents per acre. But there were many others as well:

- In 1818, by treaty with England, the United States secured the lands south of the 49th parallel from Lake Superior to the Rocky Mountains, lands that determine the modern border with Canada (no cost).

- In 1819, by treaty with Spain, the United States secured what is now Florida (no cost).

---

[1] Of the seven, New York based its claims on concessions from the Iroquois Indians, while the others traced their claims back to colonial charters from England.

• In 1846, the Oregon Compromise with England set the Canadian boundary at a single latitude west to the Pacific Ocean, adding 180 million acres to the federal storehouse (no cost).[2]

• In 1848, the Treaty of Guadaloupe Hidalgo with Spain brought into federal title what is now the nation's southwest, including California, from Mexico (cost: $15 million).

• In 1850, the United States purchased from Texas, itself annexed five years earlier, lands comprising what is now New Mexico, Colorado, and Oklahoma (cost: assumption of $10 million debt).

• In 1853, the Gadsen Purchase brought to the nation the southern strip of what is now New Mexico and Arizona to establish a southern transcontinental railroad service (cost: $10 million).

• In 1867, in what was popularly known as "Seward's Folly," named after the government official spearheading the acquisition, the federal government purchased Alaska from Russia. As a result, the federal government held title to almost 80% of the total land area of the United States by the middle of the 19th century. This 365 million acres would comprise the last addition to the public domain (cost: $7.2 million).

[2] PHASES OF FEDERAL LAND POLICY

Even during the period of acquisition of the public lands, the task of management of the rapidly growing storehouse of resources fell upon the federal government. At first, management took a back seat to disposition. It was settled wisdom that the best use of federal lands was to transfer ownership of them to individuals and business entities. This would both accelerate the human settlement of the lands and assure the development of natural resources, all to the betterment of the nation as a whole. Disposing of the lands, even at bargain prices, would provide a much-needed shot of revenues to boot. Not unexpectedly, the government was quite successful in its efforts to transfer its lands into private title: in the roughly two centuries from 1780 to the present, it depleted land holdings by more than one billion acres.

Unsurprisingly, this era in federal land management is known as the disposition phase. It was, in actuality, more a fervor than a phase, and, over time it gave rise to serious concerns that too much land was being lost. Why should the government give away natural resources, especially if it might be faced with the prospect of buying them back later? Under prevailing statutes, moreover, the dispositions were often accomplished by the unilateral actions of the acquiring parties, a process the government could not control. The growing apprehension signaled the beginning of a second phase of federal land policy, known as the withdrawal or retrenchment phase. This second phase was more a reassessment than a repudiation of the first.

---

[2] The national expansion into the Pacific Northwest was the origin of the famous election slogan, "Fifty four forty or fight." As American settlers migrated into the Pacific Northwest, and demands for annexation of the area from England grew, supporters of soon-to-be-elected President James Polk used the slogan in demanding land up to the parallel of 54 degrees and 40 minutes. After Polk's election, the compromise allowed for the United States to have land up to the 49th parallel. Marion Clawson, *Uncle Sam's Acres*, at 28–29 (Greenwood Press 1951).

In this second phase, the government slowed the pace of disposition and commensurately acted to protect much of the storehouse of federal land from private acquisition. To that end, national parks were created for the recreational use of the public at large. Similarly, natural resources on public "disposition lands" were made subject to leasing mechanisms that the government could control. And some disposition lands, ownership of which was about to be wrested from the government, were simply reclassified.

In the current day, federal policy has matured into a third phase, often referred to as the management or stewardship phase. An amalgam of its predecessors, this phase places the emphasis on land retention. Dispositions are still authorized, but only if doing so inures to the "maximum benefit for the general public." *See* 43 U.S. § 1391. Federal lands, moreover, are managed for long-term benefit. In some instances the lands serve a single dominant use; in others they are managed for several (often conflicting) uses.

It is impossible to declare with any certainty the beginning and end dates of these phases. If put to the task, however, one could select 1780, the date of the first land transfers away from the federal government, as the beginning of the disposition phase. The year 1872, at which time Yellowstone National Park was set aside for wilderness and recreational use, can suffice as the beginning of the withdrawal phase. Finally, 1960, the year of enactment of the federal Multiple Use-Sustained Yield Act, might be an appropriate starting point for the stewardship period. Note that the start of one phase did not signal the end of its predecessor. On the contrary, federal land policy has been more a matter of drift than sharp turns. For detailed reading on this saga of United States history, see P. Gates, *History of Public Land Law Development* (1967).

[a] ALIENATION OF THE PUBLIC LANDS

There are many mechanisms by which the federal government has transferred lands to the private sector:

(i) Grants to Settlers

A significant land disposal mechanism has been grants to settlers. These grants were preceded and facilitated by a good deal of federal groundwork. In accordance with the Land Ordinance of 1785, the government undertook the daunting task of surveying the vast west. The survey divided the west into square townships. Each township in turn was divided into 36 sections of 640 acres each. Survey in hand, the government was positioned to alienate lands on the grand scale. It proceeded to grant "patents" to land to thousands of persons, to reward military service, to make fertile the "Great American Desert," and for other purposes. The most significant legislative enactment to this end was the Homestead Act of 1862 (Act of May 20, 1862, 12 Stat. 392 (1862)). Under the terms of the Homestead Act, a settler could secure title to a parcel of land, not greater than a quarter-section in size, or 160 acres, if she or he agreed to live on the land and improve it with due diligence. About 287 million acres of federal land, mostly fertile lands in what is now the midwestern "breadbasket" of the nation, transferred into private hands under the terms of this legislation. In the more arid western states, where larger acreages were needed to entice settlers, the Desert Lands Act of 1877, 43 U.S.C. §§ 321-339, worked to the same end. The Desert Lands Act applied to the eleven western states, awarding settlers 640 acre parcels.

(ii) Grants to Railroads

With the vast reaches of the west and midwest becoming evermore populated, the government concluded there was a need for an intercontinental rail transportation system. Accordingly, it made lands available for this purpose as well. Land grants to railroads were made between 1862 and 1871. The first such grant was made by President Abraham Lincoln in a measure that also established the grantee, the Union Pacific Railroad. (Act of July 1, 1862, 12 Stat. 489). Railroad companies typically received not only rights of way, but also alternating sections of land on either side of each right of way. (In 1975, the Railroad Right of Way Act, 43 U.S.C. § 934 et seq. (1975), expanded these existing rights of way laterally to one hundred feet on either side of the central rail line, and extended rights to "take from the public lands adjacent to the line of said road, material, earth, stone, and timber necessary for the construction of said railroad." *Id.* at § 934). By these grant mechanisms, railroads secured title to over 130 million acres of public land. *See, e.g.,* Thomas E. Root, *Railroad Land Grants From Canals to Transcontinentals,* ABA, at 17-36 & Appendix C (1987). Interestingly, the amount of railroad trackage on federal land has decreased in this century. In 1920, railroads had 272,000 miles of track on federal land; by 1990, the trackage was reduced to 141,000 miles. Lawrence S. Lim, *Walking the Line: Rails to Trails Conversions and Presault v. Interstate Commerce Comm'n,* 53 Ohio St. L.J. 337 (1992).

(iii) Grants to States

(A) Charter grants: Lands were made available to states as well. Following the model state charter by which Ohio entered the Union in 1803, the government granted to incoming states, themselves carved out of federal lands, at least one section, specifically Section 16, in each township for educational purposes (after 1848, this allocation would double, and would double again with the admissions of Arizona, Utah, and New Mexico). These grants enabled the establishment of land grant universities and primary and secondary schools. Grants to states for these purposes transferred almost 80 million acres out of federal title, or an expanse roughly equivalent in size to New England, plus New York and New Jersey.

(B) Offshore submerged lands: The story of federal disposition of lands to states did not end with charter grants. There remained the matter of offshore submerged lands. By international law, the United States government holds title to submerged lands reaching out under the Atlantic and Pacific Oceans and the Gulf of Mexico to at least a distance of three miles.[3]

In the United States, however, the federal government no longer holds title to these often resource-rich submerged lands. It transferred these title interests to the coastal states in the Submerged Lands Act of 1953, 43 U.S.C. § 1301 et seq. This means that coastal states own the submerged lands for a seaward distance of three miles from their shores. From the three-mile

---

[3] The United States has declared its territorial sea to extend to twelve miles. *See* Proclamation No. 5928 of Dec. 27, 1988, 54 Fed. Reg. 777.

demarcation line seaward out to the edge of the continental shelf, the lands remain titled in the federal government. (No nation owns the high seas).

(C) Equal footing doctrine: Federal lands also have come into state title by means of the equal footing doctrine. Strongly associated with the sovereign status of states, this doctrine transfers title as a matter of constitutional law rather than by express federal legislative choice. *See, e.g., Montana v. United States*, 450 U.S. 544, 552 (1981). The doctrine traces back to 1842 when, in accordance with the common law of England, the United States Supreme Court declared that the original thirteen states held title to submerged lands underlying navigable streams. *Martin v. Waddell*, 41 U.S. (16 Pet.) 367 (1842). Streams were deemed navigable if they were navigable in fact, susceptible to navigation if modified, or affected by the ebb and flow of tides (in some instances, different segments of the same stream could be navigable and non-navigable). *See generally* Johnson & Austin, *Recreational Rights and Titles to Beds on Western Lakes and Streams*, 7 Nat. Res. J. 1, 7 (1967). When additional states were carved out of federal lands, the argument arose that they, like the original thirteen, should have title to submerged lands underlying navigable waters. The Supreme Court agreed. *Pollard's Lessee v. Hagan*, 44 U.S. (3 How.) 212 (1845). In the Court's view, because the federal constitution was premised on the notion that all states should be on an equal footing, title to submerged lands underlying navigable waterways transferred automatically to each new state upon its admission to the Union. *Id.* at 230. If two states happen to share a navigable waterway as a common border, whether the waterway be a minor navigable stream or a Great Lake, each is deemed to hold title to the middle thread, or thalweg, of that waterway.

The equal footing doctrine creates a strong presumption in favor of states when claims are made to lands in federal title at the time of a state's admission into the Union. "A court deciding a question of title to the bed of navigable water must . . . begin with a strong presumption against defeat of a State's title." *United States v. Alaska*, 521 U.S. 1, 34, 117 S. Ct. 1888, 1906 (1997). But the presumption is not irrebuttable. In a 2001 decision, the United States Supreme Court ruled, 5-4, that certain submerged lands underlying Lake Coeur d'Alene in Idaho remained in federal title, to be devoted to the use and benefit of the Coeur d'Alene Indian Tribe, and did not transfer to the State of Idaho at its admission into the Union, because Congress intended to reserve the title. *Idaho v. United States*, 533 U.S. 262, 121 S. Ct. 2135 (2001). Expressions of Congressional intent to defeat a State's title should be "definitely declared or otherwise made very plain." *Montana, supra,* at 552, 121 S.Ct. at 1906.

Notably, the equal footing doctrine has been limited in its geographical reach: it has not prevailed to secure to the states title to the whole of the federal public domain. *See, e.g., United States v. Clifford Gardner*, 107 F.3d 1314 (9th Cir. 1996).

(4) Land Sales

Another mechanism of disposition is land sales. Unlike the mechanisms previously discussed, this one retains viability. Land sales, at least for lands under the control of the Bureau of Land Management ("BLM") of the U.S. Department of Interior, are governed by § 203 of the Federal Land Policy and

Management Act ("FLPMA"), 43 U.S.C. § 1713. Under that section, the government must receive at least fair market value for any parcel it sells. § 203(d), 43 U.S.C. § 1713(d). FLPMA also calls for use of competitive bidding procedures to secure the best price. § 203(f), 43 U.S.C. § 1713(f). Sales may go forward only for tracts that are "difficult and uneconomic to manage" as part of the public lands; are not "suitable" for management by any other federal agency; no longer serve the purposes for which the lands were acquired; or if the disposal will "serve important public objectives." § 203(a), 43 U.S.C. § 1713(a). As a general matter, conveyances of land by the federal government, excepting land exchanges, *infra*, may not include transfer of mineral rights. § 209, 43 U.S.C. § 1719. Moneys paid by purchasers go to the federal treasury. Sales of parcels greater than 2,500 acres in size require Congressional approval. § 203(c), 43 U.S.C. § 1713(c).

(5) Land Exchanges

The federal government also can alienate title to public lands through land exchanges. The land exchange mechanism has been useful to satisfy outstanding charter-based claims of states to lands, to minimize patchwork patterns of land ownership, and to facilitate management of federal lands. It also helps to stop persons from using private land "inholdings" in ways deleterious to nearby or surrounding federal land. Entirely discretionary with the government, exchanges are governed by § 206 of the Federal Land Policy and Management Act, which provides that "[a] tract of public land or interests therein may be disposed of by exchange by the Secretary under this Act . . . where the Secretary . . . determines that the public interest will be well served by making that exchange." § 206, 43 U.S.C. § 1716. Regulations implementing this provision may be found at 43 C.F.R. Part 2200 (Bureau of Land Management) and 36 C.F.R. Part 254, Subpart A (Forest Service).

While the era of land grants is largely over, land exchanges still take place frequently. (A great many exchanges have taken place recently in Utah, for example, as a result of the Grand Staircase-Escalante national monument designation.) Exchanges can take years to complete. The government is most interested in a land exchange if the privately owned parcel is valuable for wildlife or recreation, or is contiguous to federal land, or if the acquisition would facilitate access to federal lands. Since exchanges are only permissible for parcels of approximately equal value, properties under consideration must be appraised for market value. Appraising value can be difficult, especially for lands that are diverse and undeveloped. Supervised by federal land agencies such as the Bureau of Land Management or the Forest Service, land exchanges often require accompanying environmental impact statements, prepared under the auspices of the National Environmental Policy Act (*see* Chapter 4, *supra*). *See, e.g., Muckleshoot Indian Tribe v. U.S. Forest Service*, 177 F.3d 800 (9th Cir. 1999). Interstate exchanges are impermissible, and in the case of the Forest Service, interforest exchanges are impermissible as well. For more complete information on land exchanges, including an explanation of the principles governing the process and a step-by-step flowchart on how the process works, see *http://www.blm.gov/nhp/what/lands/realty*.

The final result of all of this is that federal holdings have shrunk from over 1.8 billion acres to a bit more than 690 million acres today. Of these federal holdings, 92.7% are in the West (in fact, almost 54 percent of all the land in the West is federal land), 4% in the Midwest, 3% in the south, and a scant 0.03% in the East. About 56.6 million acres are tribal or Native-owned lands. To see the federal lands configuration in any particular state, visit the map site of the United States Geological Service at *http://www.nationalatlas.gov.* For percentages of federal land within specific states, see the following Figure entitled "Federally Owned Land."

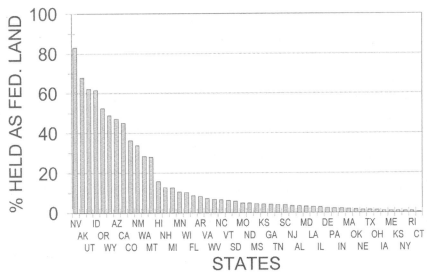

Federally Owned Land
As a % of Land Area per State

[b] RETENTION AND MANAGEMENT

As noted earlier, the federal government no longer freely yields title to public lands. Instead, it now keeps lands in federal title, preferring to manage them for maximum public long-term benefit. What this means in many cases is that lands are managed to serve a multitude of uses. The term "uses" is defined broadly, to include not just commercially valuable pursuits, but also recreation, conservation, and even preservation. The following article encapsulates the thinking behind this retention and management policy. (We will survey the particulars of federal land management in the current day in Part D of this Chapter, *infra*.)

MARION CLAWSON, UNCLE SAM'S ACRES (Greenwood Press, Westport, Connecticut, 1951 (reprint 1970))* 4

. . . .

WHY FEDERAL LAND OWNERSHIP?

What are the reasons why federal ownership of some classes of land is believed by some to be more satisfactory than private ownership? Very little farm land is federally owned. Federal lands are generally forested or covered with grasses and shrubs usable only for grazing. Federal ownership of such land owes much of its existence and strength to the following arguments:

1. Land management for multiple uses or benefits is more likely and is more satisfactory under federal than under private ownership. Much of the remaining federal land can be and is used at the same time for several purposes — timber production, recreation, grazing, mineral production, watersheds, and others. Within some limits, these uses do not compete seriously. But a private owner is more likely to be interested in but one of these uses or values, rather than in several or in all of them. Thus, if he is a lumberman, he is likely not to want to be bothered with grazing and almost surely won't want to give special consideration to recreation. A federal land administering agency is more likely to be able to balance one potential use against another, and to secure a substantial amount of each.

2. The development of land uses which produce nonmonetary benefits or satisfactions is particularly likely to be stressed and be more successful under public than under private land ownership. As our standard of living rises, as we have more leisure time, and as we become more mobile, our use of land for recreational, wildlife, and other non-monetary uses increases. A public agency can afford to encourage such uses, and perhaps make some investments for them, when a private landowner cannot.

3. The conservation of some land, particularly forest and watershed land, has in general been more successful under federal than under private ownership. We have not yet proven on a large scale that private land ownership can produce trees; it can cut them, but its record in growing them is still meager. The values created by good watershed management do not accrue to the landowner, in most cases, but to someone else further down the stream. While conceivably the landowner might sell watershed management to a down-stream landowner, in practice we have handled the problem by keeping and even putting much watershed land into public ownership.

4. Experience has shown that private ownership of some types of land is unsatisfactory, either because of damage to the land itself or because it is impossible to support an economic enterprise on it. While much of this land might be capable of private ownership under different uses, in practice it may

---

* Every effort has been made to find the holder of (the) original copyright, if any, to this article. Should anyone have information, please contact the author of this casebook.

4 Mr. Clawson was Director of the Bureau of Land Management, United States Department of Interior, at the time of preparation of the article.

be easier to deal with the problem by having the land in public ownership. * * *

. . . .

A mere recitation of the areas and uses of the federally owned lands minimize their importance to the communities in which they lie. The federally owned lands are not an empire separate and apart from the economy and life of the community; rather, they are an integral part of it.

Federally owned land has special significance for another reason. For nearly 100 years, the Federal Government and its leaders have sought to obtain better and more enduring use of land and its resources in this country. This effort, feeble at first, has become intensified in recent decades. With approximately one-fourth of the total area of the United States in its ownership and under its direct control, the Federal Government is in a position where its example as a landowner is probably far more important than its preaching. If it really seeks wise and enduring land use as a national policy, then let the Government practice it on its own lands. . . .

C. POWER OVER FEDERAL LAND

[1] CONSTITUTIONAL AUTHORITY

The federal government enjoys a paramount authority over federal lands by virtue of the federal Constitution. While there are several identifiable constitutional powers by which the federal government can exercise authority over federal lands, including the Commerce Clause and the General Welfare Clause, the most important constitutional provisions for these purposes are the following:

> *Article I, § 8, cl. 17 (the "Jurisdiction Clause")*: Congress shall have power to exercise exclusive Legislation in all Cases whatsoever over such District (not exceeding ten Miles square) as may, by Cession of particular States, and the Acceptance of Congress, become the Seat of the Government of the United States, and to exercise like Authority over all Places purchased by the Consent of the Legislature of the State in which the Same shall be, for the Erection of Forts, Magazines, Arsenals, dock-Yards, and other needful Buildings.

> *Article IV, § 3, cl. 2 (the "Property Clause")*: The Congress shall have Power to dispose of and make all needful Rules and Regulations respecting the Territory or other Property belonging to the United States. . . .

Lands subject to the Jurisdiction Clause (so-called because the phrase "exclusive Legislation" has been interpreted to mean "exclusive jurisdiction") are those which have been acquired (often reacquired) from private owners or from states. These lands are called "federal enclaves," and include the District of Columbia, some military bases, post offices and the like. Even some national parks fall within this category.

The governing legal structure for an enclave can take one of three forms:

— *exclusive*: the federal government possesses all authority of the state, except that the state can serve process in the area for activities that occur outside the area;

— *concurrent:* the federal government has powers, but the states have those same powers and can exercise them concurrently;

— *partial*: the federal government has powers normally possessed by the state, but the state has some other powers beyond rights to serve process.

Far more important than the Jurisdiction Clause is the Property Clause. The Property Clause applies to all non-enclave federal lands, i.e., the public domain lands, which make up the overwhelming percentage of federal land holdings. It is the Property Clause, therefore, that applies to all federal lands secured before states were carved out of those lands.

Federal power supplied by the Property Clause was described by the Public Land Law Review Commission as "proprietorial," expressing the notion of a limited managerial authority in the United States over these lands, with a significant residuum of authority vested in the respective states. This description is much too modest in the present day.

KLEPPE v. NEW MEXICO

426 U.S. 529, 96 S. Ct. 2285 (1976)

MR. JUSTICE MARSHALL delivered the opinion of the Court.

At issue in this case is whether Congress exceeded its powers under the Constitution in enacting the Wild Free-roaming Horses and Burros Act.

I

The Wild Free-roaming Horses and Burros Act, 85 Stat. 649, 16 U.S.C. §§ 1331-1340 (1970 ed., Supp. IV), was enacted in 1971 to protect "all unbranded and unclaimed horses and burros on public lands of the United States," § 2 (b) of the Act, 16 U.S.C. § 1332(b) (1970 ed., Supp. IV), from "capture, branding, harassment, or death." § 1, 16 U.S.C. § 1331 (1970 ed., Supp. IV). The Act provides that all such horses and burros on the public lands administered by the Secretary of the Interior through the Bureau of Land Management (BLM) or by the Secretary of Agriculture through the Forest Service are committed to the jurisdiction of the respective Secretaries, who are "directed to protect and manage [the animals] as components of the public lands . . . in a manner that is designed to achieve and maintain a thriving natural ecological balance on the public lands." § 3(a), 16 U.S.C. § 1333(a) (1970 ed., Supp. IV). If protected horses or burros "stray from public lands onto privately owned land, the owners of such land may inform the nearest federal marshal or agent of the Secretary, who shall arrange to have the animals removed." § 4, 16 U.S.C. § 1334 (1970 ed., Supp. IV).

Section 6, 16 U.S.C. § 1336 (1970 ed., Supp. IV), authorizes the Secretaries to promulgate regulations, *see* 36 C.F.R. § 231.11 (1975) (Agriculture); 43

C.F.R. pt. 4710 (1975) (Interior), and to enter into cooperative agreements with other landowners and with state and local governmental agencies in furtherance of the Act's purposes. On August 7, 1973, the Secretaries executed such an agreement with the New Mexico Livestock Board, the agency charged with enforcing the New Mexico Estray Law, N.M. Stat. Ann. § 47-14-1 et seq. (1966). The agreement acknowledged the authority of the Secretaries to manage and protect the wild free-roaming horses and burros on the public lands of the United States within the State and established a procedure for evaluating the claims of private parties to ownership of such animals.

The Livestock Board terminated the agreement three months later. Asserting that the Federal Government lacked power to control wild horses and burros on the public lands of the United States unless the animals were moving in interstate commerce or damaging the public lands and that neither of these bases of regulation was available here, the Board notified the Secretaries of its intent

> to exercise all regulatory, impoundment and sale powers which it derives from the New Mexico Estray Law, over all estray horses, mules or asses found running at large upon public or private lands within New Mexico. . . . This includes the right to go upon Federal or State lands to take possession of said horses or burros, should the Livestock Board so desire. App. 67, 72.

The differences between the Livestock Board and the Secretaries came to a head in February 1974. On February 1, 1974, a New Mexico rancher, Kelley Stephenson, was informed by the BLM that several unbranded burros had been seen near Taylor Well, where Stephenson watered his cattle. Taylor Well is on federal property, and Stephenson had access to it and some 8,000 surrounding acres only through a grazing permit issued pursuant to § 3 of the Taylor Grazing Act, 48 Stat. 1270, as amended, 43 U.S.C. § 315b. After the BLM made it clear to Stephenson that it would not remove the burros and after he personally inspected the Taylor Well area, Stephenson complained to the Livestock Board that the burros were interfering with his livestock operation by molesting his cattle and eating their feed.

Thereupon the Board rounded up and removed 19 unbranded and unclaimed burros pursuant to the New Mexico Estray Law. Each burro was seized on the public lands of the United States and, as the director of the Board conceded, each burro fit the definition of a wild free-roaming burro under § 2(b) of the Act. App. 43. On February 18, 1974, the Livestock Board, pursuant to its usual practice, sold the burros at a public auction. After the sale, the BLM asserted jurisdiction under the Act and demanded that the Board recover the animals and return them to the public lands.

On March 4, 1974, appellees filed a complaint in the United States District Court for the District of New Mexico seeking a declaratory judgment that the Wild Free-roaming Horses and Burros Act is unconstitutional and an injunction against its enforcement. A three-judge court was convened pursuant to 28 U.S.C. § 2282.

Following an evidentiary hearing, the District Court held the Act unconstitutional and permanently enjoined the Secretary of the Interior (Secretary) from enforcing its provisions. The court found that the Act "conflicts with . . . the traditional doctrines concerning wild animals," *New Mexico v. Morton*, 406 F. Supp. 1237, 1238 (1975), and is in excess of Congress' power under the Property Clause of the Constitution, Art. IV, § 3, cl. 2. That Clause, the court found, enables Congress to regulate wild animals found on the public land only for the "protection of the public lands from damage of some kind." 406 F. Supp., at 1239 (emphasis in original). Accordingly, this power was exceeded in this case because "[t]he statute is aimed at protecting the wild horses and burros, not at protecting the land they live on." *Ibid.* We noted probable jurisdiction, 423 U.S. 818 (1975), and we now reverse.

II

The Property Clause of the Constitution provides that "Congress shall have Power to dispose of and make all needful Rules and Regulations respecting the Territory or other Property belonging to the United States." U.S. Const., Art. IV, § 3, cl. 2. In passing the Wild Free-roaming Horses and Burros Act, Congress deemed the regulated animals "an integral part of the natural system of the public lands" of the United States, § 1, 16 U.S.C.§ 1331 (1970 ed., Supp. IV), and found that their management was necessary "for achievement of an ecological balance on the public lands." H.R. Conf. Rep. No. 92-681, p. 5 (1971). According to Congress, these animals, if preserved in their native habitats, "contribute to the diversity of life forms within the Nation and enrich the lives of the American people." § 1, 16 U.S.C. § 1331 (1970 ed., Supp. IV). *See* Hearing on Protection of Wild Horses and Burros on Public Lands before the Subcommittee on Public Lands of the Senate Committee on Interior and Insular Affairs, 92d Cong., 1st Sess., 69, 122, 128, 138, 169, 183 (1971). Indeed, Congress concluded, the wild free-roaming horses and burros "are living symbols of the historic and pioneer spirit of the West." § 1, 16 U.S.C. § 1331 (1970 ed., Supp. IV). Despite their importance, the Senate committee found:

> [These animals] have been cruelly captured and slain and their carcasses used in the production of pet food and fertilizer. They have been used for target practice and harassed for 'sport' and profit. In spite of public outrage, this bloody traffic continues unabated, and it is the firm belief of the committee that this senseless slaughter must be brought to an end. S. Rep. No. 92-242, pp. 1-2 (1971).

For these reasons, Congress determined to preserve and protect the wild free-roaming horses and burros on the public lands of the United States. The question under the Property Clause is whether this determination can be sustained as a "needful" regulation "respecting" the public lands. In answering this question, we must remain mindful that, while courts must eventually pass upon them, determinations under the Property Clause are entrusted primarily to the judgment of Congress. *United States v. San Francisco*, 310 U.S. 16, 29-30 (1940); *Light v. United States*, 220 U.S. 523, 537 (1911); *United States v. Gratiot*, 14 Pet. 526, 537–538 (1840).

Appellees argue that the Act cannot be supported by the Property Clause. They contend that the Clause grants Congress essentially two kinds of power: (1) the power to dispose of and make incidental rules regarding the use of federal property; and (2) the power to protect federal property. According to appellees, the first power is not broad enough to support legislation protecting wild animals that live on federal property; and the second power is not implicated since the Act is designed to protect the animals, which are not themselves federal property, and not the public lands. As an initial matter, it is far from clear that the Act was not passed in part to protect the public lands of the United States or that Congress cannot assert a property interest in the regulated horses and burros superior to that of the State. But we need not consider whether the Act can be upheld on either of these grounds, for we reject appellees' narrow reading of the Property Clause.

Appellees ground their argument on a number of cases that, upon analysis, provide no support for their position. . . .

In brief, . . . appellees have presented no support for their position that the Clause grants Congress only the power to dispose of, to make incidental rules regarding the use of, and to protect federal property. This failure is hardly surprising, for the Clause, in broad terms, gives Congress the power to determine what are "needful" rules "respecting" the public lands. *United States v. San Francisco*, 310 U.S., at 29-30; *Light v. United States*, 220 U.S., at 537; *United States v. Gratiot*, 14 Pet., at 537–538. And while the furthest reaches of the power granted by the Property Clause have not yet been definitively resolved, we have repeatedly observed that "[the] power over the public land thus entrusted to Congress is without limitations." *United States v. San Francisco, supra,* at 29. *See Ivanhoe Irrig. Dist. v. McCracken,* 357 U.S. 275, 294–295 (1958); *Alabama v. Texas,* 347 U.S. 272, 273 (1954); *FPC v. Idaho Power Co.,* 344 U.S. 17, 21 (1952); *United States v. California,* 332 U.S. 19, 27 (1947); *Gibson v. Chouteau,* 13 Wall. 92, 99 (1872); *United States v. Gratiot, supra,* at 537.

The decided cases have supported this expansive reading. It is the Property Clause, for instance, that provides the basis for governing the Territories of the United States. *Hooven & Allison Co. v. Evatt,* 324 U.S. 652, 673–674 (1945); *Balzac v. Porta Rico,* 258 U.S. 298, 305 (1922); *Dorr v. United States,* 195 U.S. 138, 149 (1904); *United States v. Gratiot, supra,* at 537; *Sere v. Pitot,* 6 Cranch 332, 336–337 (1810). *See also Vermilya-Brown Co. v. Connell,* 335 U.S. 377, 381 (1948). And even over public land within the States, "[t]he general Government doubtless has a power over its own property analogous to the police power of the several States, and the extent to which it may go in the exercise of such power is measured by the exigencies of the particular case." *Camfield v. United States, supra,* at 525. We have noted, for example, that the Property Clause gives Congress the power over the public lands "to control their occupancy and use, to protect them from trespass and injury and to prescribe the conditions upon which others may obtain rights in them. . . ." *Utah Power & Light Co. v. United States,* 243 U.S. 389, 405 (1917). And we have approved legislation respecting the public lands "[i]f it be found to be necessary for the protection of the public, or of intending settlers [on the public lands]." *Camfield v. United States, supra,* at 525. In short, Congress exercises the powers both of a proprietor and of a legislature over the public domain. *Alabama v. Texas, supra,* at 273; *Sinclair v. United States,* 279 U.S. 263, 297 (1929); *United States v. Midwest Oil Co.,* 236 U.S. 459, 474 (1915). Although the Property Clause does not authorize "an exercise of a general control over public policy in a State," it does permit "an exercise of the complete power which Congress has over particular public property entrusted to it." *United States v. San Francisco, supra,* at 30 (footnote omitted). In our view, the "complete power" that Congress has over public lands necessarily includes the power to regulate and protect the wildlife living there.

III

Appellees argue that if we approve the Wild Free-roaming Horses and Burros Act as a valid exercise of Congress' power under the Property Clause, then we have sanctioned an impermissible intrusion on the sovereignty, legislative authority, and police power of the State and have wrongly infringed upon the State's traditional trustee powers over wild animals. The argument appears to be that Congress could obtain exclusive legislative jurisdiction over the public lands in the State only by state consent, and that in the absence of such consent Congress lacks the power to act contrary to state law. This argument is without merit.

Appellees' claim confuses Congress' derivative legislative powers, which are not involved in this case, with its powers under the Property Clause. Congress may acquire derivative legislative power from a State pursuant to Art. I, § 8, cl. 17, of the Constitution by consensual acquisition of land, or by nonconsensual acquisition followed by the State's subsequent cession of legislative authority over the land. *Paul v. United States,* 371 U.S., at 264; *Fort Leavenworth R. Co. v. Lowe,* 114 U.S., at 541–542. In either case, the legislative jurisdiction acquired may range from exclusive federal jurisdiction with no residual state police power, *e.g., Pacific Coast Dairy v. Dept. of Agriculture of Cal.,* 318 U.S. 285 (1943), to concurrent, or partial, federal legislative jurisdiction, which may allow the State to exercise certain authority. *E.g., Paul v. United States, supra,* at 265; *Collins v. Yosemite Park Co.,* 304 U.S. 518, 528–530 (1938); *James v. Dravo Contracting Co.,* 302 U.S. 134, 147–149 (1937).

But while Congress can acquire exclusive or partial jurisdiction over lands within a State by the State's consent or cession, the presence or absence of such jurisdiction has nothing to do with Congress' powers under the Property Clause. Absent consent or cession a State undoubtedly retains jurisdiction over federal lands within its territory, but Congress equally surely retains the power to enact legislation respecting those lands pursuant to the Property Clause. *Mason Co. v. Tax Comm'n of Washington,* 302 U.S. 186, 197 (1937); *Utah Power & Light Co. v. United States,* 243 U.S., at 403–405; *Ohio v. Thomas,* 173 U.S. 276, 283 (1899). And when Congress so acts, the federal legislation necessarily overrides conflicting state laws under the Supremacy Clause. U.S. Const., Art. VI, cl. 2. *See Hunt v. United States,* 278 U.S., at 100; *McKelvey v. United States,* 260 U.S. 353, 359 (1922). As we said in *Camfield v. United States,* 167 U.S., at 526, in response to a somewhat different claim: "A different rule would place the public domain of the United States completely at the mercy of state legislation."

Thus, appellees' assertion that "[a]bsent state consent by complete cession of jurisdiction of lands to the United States, exclusive jurisdiction does not accrue to the federal landowner with regard to federal lands within the borders of the State," Brief for Appellees 24, is completely beside the point; and appellees' fear that the Secretary's position is that "the Property Clause totally exempts federal lands within state borders from state legislative powers, state police powers, and all rights and powers of local sovereignty and jurisdiction of the states," *id.*, at 16, is totally unfounded. The Federal Government does not assert exclusive jurisdiction over the public lands in New Mexico, and the State is free to enforce its criminal and civil laws on those lands. But where those state laws conflict with the Wild Free-roaming Horses and Burros Act, or with other legislation passed pursuant to the Property Clause, the law is clear. The state laws must recede. *McKelvey v. United States, supra,* at 359.

Again, none of the cases relied upon by appellees are to the contrary. . . .

Appellees' contention that the Act violates traditional state power over wild animals stands on no different footing. Unquestionably the States have broad trustee and police powers over wild animals within their jurisdictions. *Toomer v. Witsell,* 334 U.S. 385, 402 (1948); *Lacoste v. Department of Conservation,* 263 U.S. 545, 549 (1924); *Geer v. Connecticut,* 161 U.S. 519, 528 (1896). But, as *Geer v. Connecticut* cautions, those powers exist only "in so far as [their] exercise may be not incompatible with, or restrained by, the rights conveyed to the Federal government by the Constitution." *Ibid.* "No doubt it is true that as between a State and its inhabitants the State may regulate the killing and sale of [wildlife], but it does not follow that its authority is exclusive of paramount powers." *Missouri v. Holland,* 252 U.S. 416, 434 (1920). Thus, the Privileges and Immunities Clause, U.S. Const., Art. IV, § 2, cl. 1, precludes a State from imposing prohibitory licensing fees on nonresidents shrimping in its waters, *Toomer v. Witsell, supra;* the Treaty Clause, U.S. Const., Art. II, § 2, permits Congress to enter into and enforce a treaty to protect migratory birds despite state objections, *Missouri v. Holland, supra;* and the Property Clause gives Congress the power to thin overpopulated herds of deer on federal lands contrary to state law. *Hunt v. United States,* 278 U.S. 96 (1928). We hold today that the Property Clause also gives Congress the power to protect wildlife on the public lands, state law notwithstanding.

IV

In this case, the New Mexico Livestock Board entered upon the public lands of the United States and removed wild burros. These actions were contrary to the provisions of the Wild Free-roaming Horses and Burros Act. We find that, as applied to this case, the Act is a constitutional exercise of congressional power under the Property Clause. We need not, and do not, decide whether the Property Clause would sustain the Act in all of its conceivable applications.

Appellees are concerned that the Act's extension of protection to wild free-roaming horses and burros that stray from public land onto private land, § 4, 16 U.S.C. § 1334 (1970 ed., Supp. IV), will be read to provide federal jurisdiction over every wild horse or burro that at any time sets foot upon federal land. While it is clear that regulations under the Property Clause may have some effect on private lands not otherwise under federal control,

Camfield v. United States, 167 U.S. 518 (1897), we do not think it appropriate in this declaratory judgment proceeding to determine the extent, if any, to which the Property Clause empowers Congress to protect animals on private lands or the extent to which such regulation is attempted by the Act. We have often declined to decide important questions regarding "the scope and constitutionality of legislation in advance of its immediate adverse effect in the context of a concrete case," *Longshoremen v. Boyd,* 347 U.S. 222, 224 (1954), or in the absence of "an adequate and full-bodied record." *Public Affairs Press v. Rickover,* 369 U.S. 111, 113 (1962). *Cf. Eccles v. Peoples Bank,* 333 U.S. 426 (1948). We follow that course in this case and leave open the question of the permissible reach of the Act over private lands under the Property Clause.

For the reasons stated, the judgment of the District Court is reversed, and the case is remanded for further proceedings consistent with this opinion.

It is so ordered.

NOTES AND QUESTIONS

1. *Kleppe* states that the Property Clause gives the federal government a power over federal property "analogous to the police power of the several states," allowing the government to exercise "the powers both of a proprietor and of a legislature over the public domain." Would it make any difference if a federal regulation was an expression of proprietary authority rather than legislative authority? *See, e.g.,* Engdahl, *State and Federal Power over Federal Property,* 18 Ariz. L. Rev. 283 (1976) (arguing, *inter alia,* that proprietorial measures cannot preempt state law).

2. Do you think the Property Clause gives the federal government power to control activities on private land that are near to public lands? If so, when? *See, e.g., Camfield v. United States,* 167 U.S. 518, 17 S.Ct. 864 (1897). *See also* Sax, *Helpless Giants — The National Parks and the Regulation of Private Lands,* 75 Mich. L. Rev. 239 (1976).

3. By statute, the plenary authority of administration of public lands, including mineral lands, has been delegated to the Department of Interior, which has broad authority to issue rules and regulations for those purposes. *Best v. Humboldt Placer Mining Co.,* 371 U.S. 334, 83 S.Ct. 379 (1963). The Department has authority to:

(a) perform all duties relating to the sale of public lands, "or in anywise respecting such public lands, and also, such as relate to private claims of land, and the issuing of patents for all grants and of land under the authority of the Government." 43 U.S.C. § 2 (1994);

(b) enforce the provisions of Title 43 of the U.S. Code. 43 U.S.C. § 1201 (1994);

(c) supervise the public business relating to the Bureau of Land Management. 43 U.S.C. § 1457 (1994);

(d) administer the exploration and purchase of valuable mineral rights under the General Mining Law. 30 U.S.C. § 22 (1994); and

(e) prevent unnecessary or undue degradation of the public lands. 43 U.S.C. § 1732(b) (1994).

[2] POWER TO WITHDRAW AND RESERVE FEDERAL LANDS

During the disposition phase of federal land management, it became clear to many persons in government and elsewhere that the pendulum had swung too far, that the federal government's hellbent rush to dispose of lands was destructive to the public interest. The government was losing title to natural resources that would surely be needed in the future. When the time came, the government would be in the embarrassing and costly position of having to buy those resources back. The obvious remedy would have been to amend the disposition statutes. But, as students of government know, legislative relief can be hard to come by, especially when the relief involves terminating an entitlement. Perhaps for these reasons, Congress was conspicuously unresponsive as federal lands were transferring rapidly into private control. The executive branch, therefore, moved into the breach by denying access to public lands on its own. It did this by simply declaring select lands to be off limits from the operation of the disposition statutes. This practice of executive withdrawal and reservation became commonplace, and, predictably, encountered a major constitutional challenge.

UNITED STATES v. MIDWEST OIL CO.

236 U.S. 459, 35 S. Ct. 309 (1915)

MR. JUSTICE LAMAR delivered the opinion of the court.

All public lands containing petroleum or other mineral oils and chiefly valuable therefor, have been declared by Congress to be "free and open to occupation, exploration and purchase by citizens of the United States . . . under regulations prescribed by law." Act of February 11, 1897, c. 216, 29 Stat. 526; R. S. 2319, 2329.

As these regulations permitted exploration and location without the payment of any sum, and as title could be obtained for a merely nominal amount, many persons availed themselves of the provisions of the statute. Large areas in California were explored; and petroleum having been found, locations were made, not only by the discoverer but by others on adjoining land. And, as the flow through the well on one lot might exhaust the oil under the adjacent land, the interest of each operator was to extract the oil as soon as possible so as to share what would otherwise be taken by the owners of nearby wells.

The result was that oil was so rapidly extracted that on September 17, 1909, the Director of the Geological Survey made a report to the Secretary of the Interior which, with enclosures, called attention to the fact that, while there was a limited supply of coal on the Pacific coast and the value of oil as a fuel had been fully demonstrated, yet at the rate at which oil lands in California were being patented by private parties it would "be impossible for the people of the United States to continue ownership of oil lands for more than a few months. After that the Government will be obliged to repurchase the very oil that it has practically given away. . . ." "In view of the increasing use of fuel by the American Navy there would appear to be an immediate necessity for assuring the conservation of a proper supply of petroleum for the Government's own use . . ." and "pending the enactment of adequate legislation on this subject, the filing of claims to oil lands in the State of California should be suspended."

This recommendation was approved by the Secretary of the Interior. Shortly afterwards he brought the matter to the attention of the President who, on September 27, 1909, issued the following Proclamation:

"Temporary Petroleum Withdrawal No. 5.

"In aid of proposed legislation affecting the use and disposition of the petroleum deposits on the public domain, all public lands in the accompanying lists are hereby temporarily withdrawn from all forms of location, settlement, selection, filing, entry, or disposal under the mineral or nonmineral public-land laws. All locations or claims existing and valid on this date may proceed to entry in the usual manner after field investigation and examination."

The list attached described an area aggregating 3,041,000 acres in California and Wyoming — though, of course, the order only applied to the public lands therein, the acreage of which is not shown.

On March 27, 1910, six months after the publication of the Proclamation, William T. Henshaw and others entered upon a quarter section of this public land in Wyoming so withdrawn. They made explorations, bored a well, discovered oil and thereafter assigned their interest to the Appellees, who took possession and extracted large quantities of oil. On May 4, 1910, they filed a location certificate.

As the explorations by the original claimants, and the subsequent operation of the well, were both long after the date of the President's Proclamation, the Government filed, in the District Court of the United States for the District of Wyoming, a Bill in Equity against the Midwest Oil Company and the other Appellees, seeking to recover the land and to obtain an accounting for 50,000 barrels of oil alleged to have been illegally extracted. The court sustained the defendant's demurrer and dismissed the bill. Thereupon the Government took the case to the Circuit Court of Appeals of the Eighth Circuit which rendered no decision but certified certain questions to this court, where an order was subsequently passed directing the entire record to be sent up for consideration.

The case has twice been fully argued. Both parties, as well as other persons interested in oil lands similarly affected, have submitted lengthy and elaborate briefs on the single and controlling question as to the validity of the Withdrawal Order. On the part of the Government it is urged that the President, as Commander-in-Chief of the Army and Navy, had power to make the order for the purpose of retaining and preserving a source of supply of fuel for the Navy, instead of allowing the oil land to be taken up for a nominal sum, the Government being then obliged to purchase at a great cost what it had previously owned. It is argued that the President, charged with the care of the public domain, could, by virtue of the executive power vested in him by the Constitution (Art. 2, § 1), and also in conformity with the tacit consent of Congress, withdraw, in the public interest, any public land from entry or location by private parties.

The Appellees, on the other hand, insist that there is no dispensing power in the Executive and that he could not suspend a statute or withdraw from entry or location any land which Congress had affirmatively declared should be free and open to acquisition by citizens of the United States. They further insist that the withdrawal order is absolutely void since it appears on its face to be a mere attempt to suspend a statute — supposed to be unwise, — in order to allow Congress to pass another more in accordance with what the Executive thought to be in the public interest.

1. We need not consider whether, as an original question, the President could have withdrawn from private acquisition what Congress had made free and open to occupation and purchase. The case can be determined on other grounds and in the light of the legal consequences flowing from a long continued practice to make orders like the one here involved. For the President's proclamation of September 27, 1909, is by no means the first instance in which the Executive, by a special order, has withdrawn land which Congress, by general statute, had thrown open to acquisition by citizens. And while it is not known when the first of these orders was made, it is certain that "the practice dates from an early period in the history of the government." *Grisar v. McDowell*, 6 Wall. 381. Scores and hundreds of these orders have been made; and treating them as they must be (*Wolsey v. Chapman*, 101 U.S. 769), as the act of the President, an examination of official publications will show that (excluding those made by virtue of special congressional action, *Donnelly v. United States*, 228 U.S. 255) he has during the past 80 years, without express statutory authority — but under the claim of power so to do — made a multitude of Executive Orders which operated to withdraw public land that would otherwise have been open to private acquisition. They affected every kind of land — mineral and nonmineral. The size of the tracts varied from a few square rods to many square miles and the amount withdrawn has aggregated millions of acres. The number of such instances cannot, of course, be accurately given, but the extent of the practice can best be appreciated by a consideration of what is believed to be a correct enumeration of such Executive Orders mentioned in public documents.

They show that prior to the year 1910 there had been issued

> 99 Executive Orders establishing or enlarging Indian Reservations; 109 Executive Orders establishing or enlarging Military Reservations and setting apart land for water, timber, fuel, hay, signal stations, target ranges and rights of way for use in connection with Military Reservations; 44 Executive Orders establishing Bird Reserves.

In the sense that these lands may have been intended for public use, they were reserved for a public purpose. But they were not reserved in pursuance of law or by virtue of any general or special statutory authority. For, it is to be specially noted that there was no act of Congress providing for Bird Reserves or for these Indian Reservations. There was no law for the establishment of these Military Reservations or defining their size or location. There was no statute empowering the President to withdraw any of these lands from settlement or to reserve them for any of the purposes indicated.

But when it appeared that the public interest would be served by withdrawing or reserving parts of the public domain, nothing was more natural than to retain what the Government already owned. And in making such orders, which were thus useful to the public, no private interest was injured. For prior to the initiation of some right given by law the citizen had no enforceable interest in the public statute and no private right in land which was the property of the people. The President was in a position to know when the public interest required particular portions of the people's lands to be withdrawn from entry or location; his action inflicted no wrong upon any private citizen, and being subject to disaffirmance by Congress, could occasion no harm to the interest of the public at large. Congress did not repudiate the power claimed or the withdrawal orders made. On the contrary it uniformly and repeatedly acquiesced in the practice and, as shown by these records, there had been, prior to 1910, at least 252 Executive Orders making reservation for useful, though non-statutory purposes.

This right of the President to make reservations, — and thus withdraw land from private acquisition, — was expressly recognized in *Grisar v. McDowell*, 6 Wall. 364 (9), 381 (1867), where it was said that "from an early period in the history of the Government it has been the practice of the President to order, from time to time, as the exigencies of the public service required, parcels of land belonging to the United States to be reserved from sale and set apart for public uses." . . .

2. It may be argued that while these facts and rulings prove a usage they do not establish its validity. But government is a practical affair intended for practical men. Both officers, law-makers and citizens naturally adjust themselves to any long-continued action of the Executive Department — on the presumption that unauthorized acts would not have been allowed to be so often repeated as to crystallize into a regular practice. That presumption is not reasoning in a circle but the basis of a wise and quieting rule that in determining the meaning of a statute or the existence of a power, weight shall be given to the usage itself — even when the validity of the practice is the subject of investigation. . . .

3. These decisions do not, of course, mean that private rights could be created by an officer withdrawing for a Rail Road more than had been authorized by Congress in the land grant act. *Southern Pacific v. Bell*, 183 U.S. 685; *Brandon v. Ard*, 211 U.S. 21. Nor do these decisions mean that the Executive can by his course of action create a power. But they do clearly indicate that the long-continued practice, known to and acquiesced in by Congress, would raise a presumption that the withdrawals had been made in pursuance of its consent or of a recognized administrative power of the Executive in the management of the public lands. This is particularly true in view of the fact that the land is property of the United States and that the land laws are not of a legislative character in the highest sense of the term (Art. 4, § 3) "but savor somewhat of mere rules prescribed by an owner of property for its disposal." *Butte City Water Co. v. Baker*, 196 U.S. 126.

These rules or laws for the disposal of public land are necessarily general in their nature. Emergencies may occur, or conditions may so change as to require that the agent in charge should, in the public interest, withhold the land from sale; and while no such express authority has been granted, there is nothing in the nature of the power exercised which prevents Congress from granting it by implication just as could be done by any other owner of property under similar conditions. The power of the Executive, as agent in charge, to retain that property from sale need not necessarily be expressed in writing. *Lockhart v. Johnson*, 181 U.S. 520; *Bronson v. Chappell*, 12 Wall. 686; *Campbell v. City of Kenosha*, 5 Wall. 194.

For it must be borne in mind that Congress not only has a legislative power over the public domain, but it also exercises the powers of the proprietor therein. Congress "may deal with such lands precisely as a private individual may deal with his farming property. It may sell or withhold them from sale." *Camfield v. United States*, 167 U.S. 524; *Light v. United States*, 220 U.S. 536. Like any other owner it may provide when, how and to whom its land can be sold. It can permit it to be withdrawn from sale. Like any other owner, it can waive its strict rights, as it did when the valuable privilege of grazing cattle on this public land was held to be based upon an "implied license growing out of the custom of nearly a hundred years." *Buford v. Houtz*, 133 U.S. 326. So too, in the early days the "Government, by its silent acquiescence, assented to the general occupation of the public lands for mining." *Atchison v. Peterson*, 20 Wall. 512. If private persons could acquire a privilege in public land by virtue of an implied congressional consent, then for a much stronger reason, an implied grant of power to preserve the public interest would arise out of like congressional acquiescence.

The Executive, as agent, was in charge of the public domain; by a multitude of orders extending over a long period of time and affecting vast bodies of land, in many States and Territories, he withdrew large areas in the public interest. These orders were known to Congress, as principal, and in not a single instance was the act of the agent disapproved. Its acquiescence all the more readily operated as an implied grant of power in view of the fact that its exercise was not only useful to the public but did not interfere with any vested right of the citizen.

4. The appellees, however, argue that the practice thus approved, related to Reservations — to cases where the land had been reserved for military or other special public purposes — and they contend that even if the President could reserve land for a public purpose or for naval uses, it does not follow that he can withdraw land in aid of legislation.

When analyzed, this proposition, in effect, seeks to make a distinction between a Reservation and a Withdrawal — between a Reservation for a purpose, not provided for by existing legislation, and a Withdrawal made in aid of future legislation. It would mean that a Permanent Reservation for a purpose designated by the President, but not provided for by a statute, would be valid, while a merely Temporary Withdrawal to enable Congress to legislate in the public interest would be invalid. It is only necessary to point out that, as the greater includes the less, the power to make permanent reservations includes power to make temporary withdrawals. For there is no distinction in principle between the two. The character of the power exerted is the same in both cases. In both, the order is made to serve the public interest and in both the effect on the intending settler or miner is the same.

But the question need not be left solely to inference, since the validity of withdrawal orders, in aid of legislation, has been expressly recognized in a series of cases involving a number of such orders, made between 1850 and 1862. [citations omitted]

. . . .

But that the existence of this power was recognized and its exercise by the Executive assented to by Congress, is emphasized by the fact that the above-mentioned withdrawals were issued after the Report which the Secretary of the Interior made in 1902, in response to a resolution of the Senate calling for information "as to what, if any, of the public lands have been withdrawn from disposition under the settlement or other laws by order of the Commissioner of the General Land Office and *what, if any, authority of law exists for such order of withdrawal.*"

The answer to this specific inquiry was returned March 3, 1902, (Senate Doc. 232, 57th Cong., 1st Sess., Vol. 17). On that date the Secretary transmitted to the Senate the elaborate and detailed report of the Commissioner of the Land Office, who in response to the inquiry as to the authority by which withdrawals had been made, answered that

> the power of the Executive Department of the Government to make reservations of land for public use, and to temporarily withdraw lands from appropriation by individuals as exigencies might demand, to prevent fraud, to aid in proper administration and in aid of pending legislation is one that has been long recognized both in the acts of Congress and the decisions of the court; . . . that this power has been long exercised by the Commissioner of the General Land Office is shown by reference to the date of some of the withdrawals enumerated. . . . The attached list embraces only such lands as were withdrawn by this office, acting on its own motion, in cases where the emergencies appeared to demand such action in furtherance of public interest and does not include lands withdrawn under express statutes so directed.

The list, which is attached, refers to withdrawal orders about 100 in number, issued between 1870 and 1902. Many of them were in aid of the administration of the land laws to correct boundaries; to prevent fraud; to make a classification of the land, and like good — but non-statutory — reasons. Some were made to prevent settlements while the question was being considered as to whether the lands might not be included in a forest reservation to be thereafter established. One in 1889 (referred to also in 28 L. D. 358) was made in order to afford the State of Nebraska an opportunity to procure legislative relief, as in the *Iowa* cases above cited.

This report refers to *Withdrawals* and not to *Reservations*. It is most important in connection with the present inquiry as to whether Congress knew of the practice to make temporary withdrawals and knowingly assented thereto. It will be noted that the Resolution called on the Department to state the extent of such withdrawals and the authority by which they were made. The officer of the Land Department in his answer shows that there have been a large number of withdrawals made for good but for non-statutory reasons. He shows that these 92 orders had been made by virtue of a long-continued practice and under claim of a right to take such action in the public interest "as exigencies might demand. . . ." Congress with notice of this practice and of this claim of authority, received the Report. Neither at that session nor afterwards did it ever repudiate the action taken or the power claimed. Its silence was acquiescence. Its acquiescence was equivalent to consent to continue the practice until the power was revoked by some subsequent action by Congress.

Reversed.

MR. JUSTICE McREYNOLDS took no part in the decision of this case.

DISSENT: MR. JUSTICE DAY with whom concurred MR. JUSTICE McKENNA and MR. JUSTICE VAN DEVANTER, dissenting [omitted].

NOTES

1. A withdrawal can be accomplished by executive order, by statute, or by administrative order. It can be permanent or temporary in duration, in order to maintain the status quo until new legislation can be enacted, or for other purposes. It can be made in conjunction with other land management initiatives and it can be complete or partial in its injunctive effect.

A "reservation" of federal land also makes land unavailable to the public. A reservation is different from a withdrawal in that the former dedicates land for an affirmative purpose. For example, land can be "reserved" for use as a wildlife refuge or as a national park, for military use, or for any other designated purpose. Legally, there is little difference between a withdrawal and a reservation. There is no question that Congress has the constitutional authority to withdraw or reserve federal land. The Property Clause expressly grants the authority, and the Supreme Court in *Kleppe* embraced the substantial breadth of that power. Not unexpectedly, Congress has exercised this authority frequently. One major exercise was in the form of the Taylor Grazing Act of 1934, 43 U.S.C.A. § 315 et seq., which withdrew millions of acres from the operation of the homesteading laws. Similarly, the Alaska Native Claims Settlement Act of 1971, 43 U.S.C.A. §§ 1601 et seq., accomplished the withdrawal of much of Alaska.

Congress can delegate its withdrawal and reservation powers to the executive, and has done so on numerous occasions. Perhaps the most notable example of Congressional delegation was the Pickett Act of 1910, 43 U.S.C. § 141–2. The Act, noted in *Midwest Oil*, provided that "[t]he President may, at any time, in his discretion, temporarily withdraw from the United States, including Alaska, and reserve the same for water power sites, irrigation, classification of lands, or other public purposes to be specified in the orders of withdrawals, and such withdrawals or reservations shall remain in force by him or by an Act of Congress."

Every President, however, has steadfastly argued that, in addition to whatever powers the Congress might have delegated, the executive also has "inherent" authority under Article II of the Constitution to accomplish these ends. Presidents have withdrawn lands on this basis as well, especially for military purposes and for establishment of Indian reservations. What does *Midwest Oil* tell us of the President's inherent authorities to withdraw federal lands?

2. The Federal Land Policy and Management Act ("FLPMA"), 43 U.S.C. § 1701 et seq., expressly repealed the executive authority proffered by *Midwest Oil* in 1976:

> Effective on and after the date of approval of this Act, the implied authority of the President to make withdrawals and reservations resulting from the acquiescence of the Congress (*U.S. v. Midwest Oil Co.*, 236 U.S. 459) . . . [is] repealed.

§ 704(a), Pub. Law 94-576, 90 Stat. 2792.

FLPMA went on to specify new executive withdrawal authority. First, the statute redefined the term "withdrawal," giving it a meaning broad enough to encompass "reservations" as that term has been used:

> The term "withdrawal" means withholding an area of Federal land from settlement, sale, location, or entry, under some or all of the general land laws, for the purpose of limiting activities under those laws in order to maintain other public values in the area or reserving the area for a particular public purpose or program; or transferring jurisdiction over an area of Federal land, other than "property" governed by the Federal Property and Administrative Services Act, as amended (40 U.S.C. 472) from one department, bureau or agency to another department, bureau or agency.

FLPMA § 103(j), 43 U.S.C. § 1702(j).

In § 204, FLPMA reestablished the withdrawal power in the executive branch, "but only in accordance with the provisions and limitations of this section." § 204(a), 43 U.S.C. § 1714(a). The limitations imposed by the section are largely procedural. For withdrawals of lands comprising less than 5000 acres, the procedural burdens are relatively light. *See* § 204(d), 43 U.S.C. § 1714(d). For withdrawals of lands of 5000 or more acres, Congressional approval is required. § 204(c), 43 U.S.C. § 1714(c). Much of the procedural burden, therefore, is thrust upon Congress, rather than the executive branch. *Id.* The major substantive restriction on executive withdrawal authorities is a prohibition on modifying or revoking withdrawals made by Congress itself, and those made for national monuments or wildlife refuges. *See* § 204(j). Notably, some withdrawals, for example, the reservation of land for use as a national park, can only be made by Congress. Section 204(e) of the statute is directed specifically to emergency withdrawals, the type implicated in *Midwest Oil.* It gives the President an essentially unfettered authority.

3. The need to withdraw or reserve federal land to protect against private claims is less urgent in the current day. Only one law, the General Mining Law of 1872, presently allows individuals by their own initiative to secure title to federal lands. Other such disposition statutes, such as the Homestead Act of 1862, have been repealed. Moreover, Congress codified the national policy of retaining public lands in federal title in the Federal Land Policy and Management Act of 1976. 43 U.S.C. § 1701(a)(1). But Presidents still continue to withdraw lands, especially pursuant to the delegated authority of the American Antiquities Preservation Act, 34 Stat. 225, 16 U.S.C. § 431 ("Antiquities Act"). For more on the Antiquities Act, see the discussion of "national monuments," *infra.*

[3] FEDERAL RESERVED WATER RIGHTS

The power to withdraw and reserve federal lands and minerals has been extended to cases involving water rights. In this context, however, the legal issues can be somewhat more complex because state law generally controls water rights allocations among individuals. States control water rights because the federal government has acquiesced to this result. *See, e.g., California v. United States,* 438 U.S. 645, 98 S. Ct. 2985 (1978):

> The history of the relationship between the Federal Government and the States in the reclamation of the arid lands of the Western States is both long and involved, but through it runs the consistent thread of purposeful and continued deference to state water law by Congress.

Id. at 653, 98 S. Ct. at 2990. *See also,* Chapter 8, *infra.* Accordingly, it is states, not the federal government, which determine to whom water is allocated. The effect of allocation is to create property rights in water in individuals. *Id.*

Any attempt by the federal government to withdraw or reserve water already appropriated to individuals under state law would run afoul of the Takings Clause of the 5th Amendment of the federal Constitution. Thus, if the federal government wants property rights to appropriated water, it must secure those rights by purchase, eminent domain, or some other transfer mechanism. But what of waters that are unappropriated under state law? May the federal government secure rights to these waters, free of obligations to pay compensation, by the same withdrawal or reservation mechanisms used to curtail public access to public lands? The answer to that question is yes: the federal government may do so, and it has. *See, e.g.,* The Wild and Scenic Rivers Act, 16 U.S.C. §§ 1271, 1284(c) (in which Congress expressly reserved the amount of water "necessary to fulfill the purposes of the Act."). The next question is whether federal withdrawals and reservations of water rights can occur in the absence of an express statutory declaration.

CAPPAERT v. UNITED STATES

426 U.S. 128, 96 S. Ct. 2062 (1976)

MR. CHIEF JUSTICE BURGER delivered the opinion of the Court.

The question presented in this litigation is whether the reservation of Devil's Hole as a national monument reserved federal water rights in unappropriated water.

Devil's Hole is a deep limestone cavern in Nevada. Approximately 50 feet below the opening of the cavern is a pool 65 feet long, 10 feet wide, and at least 200 feet deep, although its actual depth is unknown. The pool is a remnant of the prehistoric Death Valley Lake System and is situated on land owned by the United States since the Treaty of Guadalupe Hidalgo in 1848, 9 Stat. 922. By the Proclamation of January 17, 1952, President Truman withdrew from the public domain a 40-acre tract of land surrounding Devil's

Hole, making it a detached component of the Death Valley National Monument. Proclamation No. 2961, 3 C.F.R. 147 (1949-1953 Comp.). The Proclamation was issued under the American Antiquities Preservation Act, 34 Stat. 225, 16 U.S.C. § 431, which authorizes the President to declare as national monuments "objects of historic or scientific interest that are situated upon the lands owned or controlled by the Government of the United States. . . ."

The 1952 Proclamation notes that Death Valley was set aside as a national monument "for the preservation of the unusual features of scenic, scientific, and educational interest therein contained." The Proclamation also notes that Devil's Hole is near Death Valley and contains a "remarkable underground pool." Additional preambulary statements in the Proclamation explain why Devil's Hole was being added to the Death Valley National Monument:

> "Whereas the said pool is a unique subsurface remnant of the prehistoric chain of lakes which in Pleistocene times formed the Death Valley Lake System, and is unusual among caverns in that it is a solution area in distinctly striated limestone, while also owing its formation in part to fault action; and

> "Whereas the geologic evidence that this subterranean pool is an integral part of the hydrographic history of the Death Valley region is further confirmed by the presence in this pool of a peculiar race of desert fish, and zoologists have demonstrated that this race of fish, which is found nowhere else in the world, evolved only after the gradual drying up of the Death Valley Lake System isolated this fish population from the original ancestral stock that in Pleistocene times was common to the entire region; and

> "Whereas the said pool is of such outstanding scientific importance that it should be given special protection, and such protection can be best afforded by making the said forty-acre tract containing the pool a part of the said monument. . . ."

The Proclamation provides that Devil's Hole should be supervised, managed, and directed by the National Park Service, Department of the Interior. Devil's Hole is fenced off, and only limited access is allowed by the Park Service.

The Cappaert petitioners own a 12,000-acre ranch near Devil's Hole, 4,000 acres of which are used for growing Bermuda grass, alfalfa, wheat, and barley; 1,700 to 1,800 head of cattle are grazed. The ranch represents an investment of more than $7 million; it employs more than 80 people with an annual payroll of more than $340,000.

In 1968 the Cappaerts began pumping groundwater on their ranch on land 2 1/2 miles from Devil's Hole; they were the first to appropriate groundwater. The groundwater comes from an underground basin or aquifer which is also the source of the water in Devil's Hole. After the Cappaerts began pumping from the wells near Devil's Hole, which they do from March to October, the summer water level of the pool in Devil's Hole began to decrease. Since 1962 the level of water in Devil's Hole has been measured with reference to a copper washer installed on one of the walls of the hole by the United States Geological Survey. Until 1968, the water level, with seasonable variations, had been stable at 1.2 feet below the copper marker. In 1969 the water level in Devil's

Hole was 2.3 feet below the copper washer; in 1970, 3.17 feet; in 1971, 3.48 feet; and, in 1972, 3.93 feet.

When the water is at the lowest levels, a large portion of a rock shelf in Devil's Hole is above water. However, when the water level is at 3.0 feet below the marker or higher, most of the rock shelf is below water, enabling algae to grow on it. This in turn enables the desert fish (cyprinodon diabolis, commonly known as Devil's Hole pupfish), referred to in President Truman's Proclamation, to spawn in the spring. As the rock shelf becomes exposed, the spawning area is decreased, reducing the ability of the fish to spawn in sufficient quantities to prevent extinction.

In April 1970 the Cappaerts, pursuant to Nevada law, Nev. Rev. Stat. § 533.325 (1973), applied to the State Engineer, Roland D. Westergard, for permits to change the use of water from several of their wells. Although the United States was not a party to that proceeding and was never served, employees of the National Park Service learned of the Cappaerts' application through a public notice published pursuant to Nevada law. § 533.360. An official of the National Park Service filed a protest as did a private firm. Nevada law permits interested persons to protest an application for a permit; the protest may be considered by the State Engineer at a hearing. § 533.365. A hearing was conducted on December 16, 1970, and a field solicitor of the Department of the Interior appeared on behalf of the National Park Service. He presented documentary and testimonial evidence, informing the State Engineer that because of the declining water level of Devil's Hole the United States had commissioned a study to determine whether the wells on the Cappaerts' land were hydrologically connected to Devil's Hole and, if so, which of those wells could be pumped safely and which should be limited to prevent lowering of the water level in Devil's Hole. The Park Service field solicitor requested either that the Cappaerts' application be denied or that decision on the application be postponed until the studies were completed.

The State Engineer declined to postpone decision. At the conclusion of the hearing he stated that there was no recorded federal water right with respect to Devil's Hole, that the testimony indicated that the Cappaerts' pumping would not unreasonably lower the water table or adversely affect existing water rights, and that the permit would be granted since further economic development of the Cappaerts' land would be in the public interest. In his oral ruling the State Engineer stated in part that "the protest to the applications that are the subject of this hearing are overruled and the applications will be issued subject to existing rights." The National Park Service did not appeal. *See* Nev. Rev. Stat. § 533.450 (1973).

In August 1971 the United States, invoking 28 U.S.C. § 1345, sought an injunction in the United States District Court for the District of Nevada to limit, except for domestic purposes, the Cappaerts' pumping from six specific wells and from specific locations near Devil's Hole. The complaint alleged that the United States, in establishing Devil's Hole as part of Death Valley National Monument, reserved the unappropriated waters appurtenant to the land to the extent necessary for the requirements and purposes of the reservation. The complaint further alleged that the Cappaerts had no perfected water rights as of the date of the reservation. The United States asserted that pumping from certain of the Cappaerts' wells had lowered the water level in Devil's Hole, that the lower water level was threatening the survival of a unique species of fish, and that irreparable harm would follow if the pumping were not enjoined. On June 2, 1972, the United States filed an amended complaint, adding two other specified wells to the list of those to be enjoined.

The Cappaerts answered, admitting that their wells draw water from the same underlying sources supplying Devil's Hole, but denying that the reservation of Devil's Hole reserved any water rights for the United States. The Cappaerts alleged that the United States was estopped from enjoining use of water under land which it had exchanged with the Cappaerts. The State of Nevada intervened on behalf of the State Engineer as a party defendant but raised no affirmative defenses.

On June 5, 1973, the District Court, by Chief Judge Roger D. Foley, entered a preliminary injunction limiting pumping from designated wells so as to return the level of Devil's Hole to not more than 3.0 feet below the marker. Detailed findings of fact were made and the District Judge then appointed a Special Master to establish specific pumping limits for the wells and to monitor the level of the water at Devil's Hole. The District Court found that the water from certain of the wells was hydrologically connected to Devil's Hole, that the Cappaerts were pumping heavily from those wells, and that pumping had lowered the water level in Devil's Hole. The court also found that the pumping could be regulated to stabilize the water level at Devil's Hole and that neither establishing an artificial shelf nor transplanting the fish was a feasible alternative that would preserve the species. The District Court further found that if the injunction did not issue "there is grave danger that the Devil's Hole pupfish may be destroyed, resulting in irreparable injury to the United States." 375 F. Supp. 456, 460 (1974).

The District Court then held that in establishing Devil's Hole as a national monument, the President reserved appurtenant, unappropriated waters necessary to the purpose of the reservation; the purpose included preservation of the pool and the pupfish in it. The District Court also held that the federal water rights antedated those of the Cappaerts, that the United States was not estopped, and that the public interest required granting the injunction. On April 9, 1974, the District Court entered its findings of fact and conclusions of law substantially unchanged in a final decree permanently enjoining pumping that lowers the level of the water below the 3.0-foot level. 375 F. Supp. 456 (1974).

The Court of Appeals for the Ninth Circuit affirmed, 508 F.2d 313 (1974), in a thorough opinion by Senior District Judge Gus J. Solomon, sitting by designation, holding that the implied-reservation-of-water doctrine applied to groundwater as well as to surface water. The Court of Appeals held that "[t]he fundamental purpose of the reservation of the Devil's Hole pool was to assure that the pool would not suffer changes from its condition at the time the Proclamation was issued in 1952. . . ." *Id.*, at 318. The Court of Appeals further held that neither the Cappaerts nor their successors in interest had any water rights in 1952, nor was the United States estopped from asserting its water rights by exchanging land with the Cappaerts. In answer to contentions raised by the intervenor Nevada, the Court of Appeals held that "the United States is not bound by state water laws when it reserves land from the public domain," *id.,* at 320, and does not need to take steps to perfect its rights with the State; that the District Court had concurrent jurisdiction with the state courts to resolve this claim; and, that the state administrative procedures granting the Cappaerts' permit did not bar resolution of the United States' suit in Federal District Court.

We granted certiorari to consider the scope of the implied-reservation-of-water-rights doctrine. 422 U.S. 1041 (1975). We affirm.

I

Reserved-Water-Rights Doctrine

This Court has long held that when the Federal Government withdraws its land from the public domain and reserves it for a federal purpose, the Government, by implication, reserves appurtenant water then unappropriated to the extent needed to accomplish the purpose of the reservation. In so doing the United States acquires a reserved right in unappropriated water which vests on the date of the reservation and is superior to the rights of future appropriators. Reservation of water rights is empowered by the Commerce Clause, Art. I, § 8, which permits federal regulation of navigable streams, and the Property Clause, Art. IV, § 3, which permits federal regulation of federal lands. The doctrine applies to Indian reservations and other federal enclaves, encompassing water rights in navigable and nonnavigable streams. *Colorado River Water Cons. Dist. v. United States,* 424 U.S. 800, 805 (1976); *United States v. District Court for Eagle County,* 401 U.S. 520, 522–523 (1971); *Arizona v. California,* 373 U.S. 546, 601 (1963); *FPC v. Oregon,* 349 U.S. 435 (1955); *United States v. Powers,* 305 U.S. 527 (1939); *Winters v. United States,* 207 U.S. 564 (1908).

Nevada argues that the cases establishing the doctrine of federally reserved water rights articulate an equitable doctrine calling for a balancing of competing interests. However, an examination of those cases shows they do not analyze the doctrine in terms of a balancing test. For example, in *Winters v. United States, supra,* the Court did not mention the use made of the water by the upstream landowners in sustaining an injunction barring their diversions of the water. The "Statement of the Case" in *Winters* notes that the upstream users were homesteaders who had invested heavily in dams to divert the water to irrigate their land, not an unimportant interest. The Court held that when the Federal Government reserves land, by implication it reserves water rights sufficient to accomplish the purposes of the reservation.

In determining whether there is a federally reserved water right implicit in a federal reservation of public land, the issue is whether the Government intended to reserve unappropriated and thus available water. Intent is inferred if the previously unappropriated waters are necessary to accomplish the purposes for which the reservation was created. . . . Both the District Court and the Court of Appeals held that the 1952 Proclamation expressed an intention to reserve unappropriated water, and we agree. The Proclamation discussed the pool in Devil's Hole in four of the five preambles and recited that the "pool . . . should be given special protection." Since a pool is a body of water, the protection contemplated is meaningful only if the water remains; the water right reserved by the 1952 Proclamation was thus explicit, not implied.

Also explicit in the 1952 Proclamation is the authority of the Director of the Park Service to manage the lands of Devil's Hole Monument "as provided in the act of Congress entitled 'An Act to establish a National Park Service, and for other purposes,' approved August 25, 1916 (39 Stat. 535; 16 U.S.C. 1-3). . . ." The National Park Service Act provides that the "fundamental purpose of the said parks, monuments, and reservations" is "to conserve the scenery and the natural and historic objects and the wild life therein and to provide for the enjoyment of the same in such manner and by such means as will leave them unimpaired for the enjoyment of future generations." 39 Stat. 535, 16 U.S.C. § 1.

The implied-reservation-of-water-doctrine, however, reserves only that amount of water necessary to fulfill the purpose of the reservation, no more. *Arizona v. California, supra,* at 600–601. Here the purpose of reserving Devil's Hole Monument is preservation of the pool. Devil's Hole was reserved "for the preservation of the unusual features of scenic, scientific, and educational interest." The Proclamation notes that the pool contains "a peculiar race of desert fish . . . which is found nowhere else in the world" and that the "pool is of . . . outstanding scientific importance. . . ." The pool need only be preserved, consistent with the intention expressed in the Proclamation, to the extent necessary to preserve its scientific interest. The fish are one of the features of scientific interest. The preamble noting the scientific interest of the pool follows the preamble describing the fish as unique; the Proclamation must be read in its entirety. Thus, as the District Court has correctly determined, the level of the pool may be permitted to drop to the extent that the drop does not impair the scientific value of the pool as the natural habitat of the species sought to be preserved. The District Court thus tailored its injunction, very appropriately, to minimal need, curtailing pumping only to the extent necessary to preserve an adequate water level at Devil's Hole, thus implementing the stated objectives of the Proclamation.

Petitioners in both cases argue that even if the intent of the 1952 Proclamation were to maintain the pool, the American Antiquities Preservation Act did not give the President authority to reserve a pool. Under that Act, according to the Cappaert petitioners, the President may reserve federal lands only to protect archaeologic sites. However, the language of the Act which authorizes the President to proclaim as national monuments "historic landmarks, historic and prehistoric structures, and other objects of historic or scientific interest that are situated upon the lands owned or controlled by the Government" is not so limited. The pool in Devil's Hole and its rare inhabitants are "objects of historic or scientific interest." *See generally Cameron v. United States,* 252 U.S. 450, 451–456 (1920).

II
Groundwater

No cases of this Court have applied the doctrine of implied reservation of water rights to groundwater. Nevada argues that the implied-reservation doctrine is limited to surface water. Here, however, the water in the pool is surface water. The federal water rights were being depleted because, as the evidence showed, the "[g]roundwater and surface water are physically interrelated as integral parts of the hydrologic cycle." Here the Cappaerts are causing the water level in Devil's Hole to drop by their heavy pumping. It appears that Nevada itself may recognize the potential interrelationship between surface and groundwater since Nevada applies the law of prior appropriation to both. Nev. Rev. Stat. §§ 533.010 et seq., 534.020, 534.080, 534.090 (1973). Thus, since the implied-reservation-of-water-rights doctrine is based on the necessity of water for the purpose of the federal reservation, we hold that the United States can protect its water from subsequent diversion, whether the diversion is of surface or groundwater.

III

State Law

Petitioners in both cases argue that the Federal Government must perfect its implied water rights according to state law. They contend that the Desert Land Act of 1877, 19 Stat. 377, 43 U.S.C. § 321, and its predecessors severed nonnavigable water from public land, subjecting it to state law. That Act, however, provides that patentees of public land acquire only title to land through the patent and must acquire water rights in nonnavigable water in accordance with state law. This Court held in *FPC v. Oregon,* 349 U.S. 435, 448 (1955), that the Desert Land Act does not apply to water rights on federally reserved land. . . .

The Cappaert petitioners argue that *FPC v. Oregon, supra,* must be overruled since, inter alia, the Court was unaware at the time that case was decided that there was no longer any public land available for homesteading. However, whether or not there was public land available for homesteading in 1955 is irrelevant to the meaning of the 1877 Act. The Desert Land Act still provides that the water rights of those who received their land from federal patents are to be governed by state law. That there may be no more federal land available for homesteading does not mean the Desert Land Act now applies to all federal land. Since the Act is inapplicable, determination of reserved water rights is not governed by state law but derives from the federal purpose of the reservation; the fact that the water rights here reserved apply to nonnavigable rather than navigable waters is thus irrelevant.

Since *FPC v. Oregon, supra,* was decided, several bills have been introduced in Congress to subject at least some federal water uses to state appropriation doctrines, but none has been enacted into law. * * *

Federal water rights are not dependent upon state law or state procedures and they need not be adjudicated only in state courts; federal courts have jurisdiction under 28 U.S.C. § 1345 to adjudicate the water rights claims of the United States. . . . The McCarran Amendment, 66 Stat. 560, 43 U.S.C. § 666, did not repeal § 1345 jurisdiction as applied to water rights. 424 U.S., at 808–809. Nor, as Nevada suggests, is the McCarran Amendment a substantive statute, requiring the United States to "perfect its water rights in the state forum like all other land owners." The McCarran Amendment waives

United States sovereign immunity should the United States be joined as a party in a state-court general water rights' adjudication, and the policy evinced by the Amendment may, in the appropriate case, require the United States to adjudicate its water rights in state forums.

[The portion of the opinion dealing with res judicata and collateral estoppel is omitted.]

We hold, therefore, that as of 1952 when the United States reserved Devil's Hole, it acquired by reservation water rights in unappropriated appurtenant water sufficient to maintain the level of the pool to preserve its scientific value and thereby implement Proclamation No. 2961. Accordingly, the judgment of the Court of Appeals is

Affirmed.

NOTES

1. Devil's Hole was left behind when lakes during the Pleistocene Age receded 50,000 to 500,000 years ago. Other than the tiny pupfish, the only creatures residing in its 90-100 degree waters are snails and flatworms. The pupfish are about 250-500 in number, and live near the ten-foot mouth of the pool down to a depth of about ninety feet. The pupfish have been in residence at this location for over 20,000 years. Below the mouth of the pool is a dark network of caverns so vast that it has never been fully explored. At the mouth of the pool stands a monument which reads, "In the small pool at the bottom of this limestone cavern lives the entire population of Cyprinodon diabolis, one type of desert pupfish. These fish live in what is probably the most restricted environment of any animal in the world." Devil's Hole was made part of the Death Valley National Monument in 1952.

Monitoring the rapidly fluctuating water levels of the pool had been a continuing challenge. Because the entrance to the pool is located about forty miles from the main part of Death Valley National Monument, National Park Service rangers had to drive to and from Devil's Hole to check water levels several times daily. In later times, however, a wireless remote monitoring system, using satellite technology, was installed.

While the *Caeppart* decision saved the pupfish, Devil's Hole is not yet free of jeopardy. Nearby Las Vegas, the fastest growing metropolitan area in the nation, is competing for the pool's waters.

2. Once federal water rights are reserved, state law cannot extinguish them. Supremacy Clause, U.S. Constitution, Art. VI, cl. 2.

3. *Cappaert* tells us that the legal test for federal withdrawal or reservation of water rights is Congressional intent. Can the mere passage of a statute effect an implied withdrawal or reservation? Notably, a district court has held that the enactment of the Wilderness Act of 1964 effected a reservation of federal water rights on the twenty-four wilderness areas administered by the Forest Service. *Sierra Club v. Lyng*, 661 F. Supp. 1490 (D. Colo. 1987). On review, the Tenth Circuit declined to examine the issue on ripeness grounds. *Sierra Club v. Yeutter*, 911 F.2d. 1405 (10th Cir. 1990).

In *United States v. New Mexico*, 438 U.S. 696, 98 S. Ct. 3012 (1978), the Supreme Court decided the same issue with respect to the Multiple-Use Sustained-Yield Act of 1960, the legislation that empowers the U.S. Forest Service, part of the Department of Agriculture, to administer national forest lands. This statute expanded the permissible purposes for which lands in the national forest system are to be managed to include, in addition to timber production, recreation, grazing, watershed management, and fish and wildlife promotion. Did this legislation accomplish an implied reservation of water rights for these newly designated forest uses? In a 5-4 opinion, the Court said no: "Congress did not intend . . . [by its enactment of the Act] . . . to expand the reserved rights of the United States." *Accord United States v. Denver*, 656 P.2d 1, 26 (Colo. 1982) ("When Congress passed the [Multiple Use Sustained Yield Act], it was aware of the reserved rights doctrine. [citations omitted]. Congress, however, chose not to reserve additional water explicitly. In the face of its silence, we must assume that Congress intended the federal government to proceed like any other appropriator and to apply for or purchase water rights when there was a need for water."); *In re Snake River Adjudication*, 133 Idaho 525, 532, 988 P.2d 1199, 1206 (Idaho, 1999) ("[The Multiple-Use Sustained-Yield Act] was intended to broaden the purposes for which the national forests had been administered, but did not create a reservation of land and moreover, did not establish an express or implied reservation of water because the expanded purposes created . . . are merely supplemental and secondary.").

In dissent, Justice Powell, joined by Justices Brennan, White, and Marshall, disagreed:

> I do not agree . . . that the forests which Congress intended to "improve and protect" are the still, lifeless places envisioned by the Court. In my view, the forests consist of the birds, animals, and fish — the wildlife — that inhabit them, as well as the trees, flowers, shrubs and grasses. I therefore would hold that the United States is entitled to so much water as is necessary to sustain the wildlife of the forests, as well as the plants. . . .

Id. at 719, 98 S.Ct. at 3023-24.

New Mexico is the most recent decision from the United States Supreme Court on these matters.

4. *Indian Reserved Water Rights:* In the landmark case of *Winters v. United States*, 207 U.S. 564, 28 S. Ct. 207 (1908), the question arose whether the federal government impliedly reserves water rights for American Indians when it expressly reserves land for their occupancy. In *Winters,* a tribe of Indians living on the Ft. Belknap Reservation in Montana and using the waters of the Milk River, objected when upstream defendants diverted the river's streamflow for their own purposes. Defendants claimed a right to divert the water under state law; the tribe claimed a prior right by virtue of an implied water rights reservation made on the tribe's behalf by the federal government when it set aside Ft. Belknap in 1888 for the tribe's use. To resolve the dispute, the Supreme Court examined the agreement that resulted in the creation of Ft. Belknap, and ruled for the tribe, largely on the theory that

ambiguities in agreements and treaties with Indians should be resolved in their favor.

5. Federal reserved rights questions make it to federal courts less frequently in the current day due to the McCarran Amendment, which consents to joinder of the United States in state court proceedings in "any suit (1) for the adjudication of rights to the use of water of a river system or other source or (2) for the administration of such rights, where it appears the United States is the owner of or is in the process of acquiring water rights by appropriation under state law, by purchase, and the United States is a necessary party thereto." 43 U.S.C. § 666(a).

6. *"Nonreserved water rights:"* We have seen that the federal government can expressly or impliedly withdraw federal lands, minerals and water. A final question is whether the federal government can hold property rights in water in the absence of any express or implied withdrawal or reservation, or indeed, without taking any action whatsoever.

The argument that it cannot centers on the notion that the United States has acceded to states the power to control water rights, even with respect to waters that cross federal lands. *See, supra.* A 1979 Opinion of the Solicitor of the United States Department of Interior, however, reached the opposite conclusion with respect to waters that course across federal land. 86 I.D. 553 (1979). The Opinion concluded the federal government, not the states, holds property rights to such water unless (1) the federal government has expressly yielded to state law and (2) the state has exercised its power by actually appropriating water in accordance with state law. These "nonreserved water rights" lay in the federal government, the Opinion contended, because that entity owns the underlying land. The theory found its source in *Kleppe.*

The Opinion created a great controversy, and was overruled by the Department of Interior in the next Administration. 88 I.D. 1055 (1981). The reassessment confirmed the earlier view that unreserved water fell under state control, and found additional authority for the assertion in FLPMA, enacted only six years earlier. FLPMA, the new Opinion noted, mandated the maintenance of the *status quo ante*, that is, state control arising by virtue of a consistent pattern of federal acquiescence to state law. The result: the federal government claims no nonreserved water rights.

[4] THE WILDERNESS ACT OF 1964

At the turn of the twentieth century, it became apparent to people like Theodore Roosevelt, Gifford Pinchot, and John Muir, that certain of the federal lands should be reserved for the recreational use of members of the public. This recognition was the genesis of a new "conservation ethic" which eventually culminated in the establishment of national parks, monuments, and other recreational lands. But the new ethic did not stop there. Fifty years later, this heightened respect for nature qua nature produced the wilderness movement. The idea behind wilderness is definitely not recreation. The idea behind wilderness, rather, is the simple — some would say elegant — notion that the best use of some lands is to use them not at all, that to render land commercially worthless is to secure its highest value. That the wilderness movement could take root in a nation dedicated to productivity and individuality is one of the truly remarkable political stories of our national history.

The culmination of this far-reaching movement is the Wilderness Act of 1964, 16 U.S.C. §§ 1131-1136. The Act is the legal tool by which federal lands can be *pre*served, as distinct from *con*served. The Act has a tone and feel rarely found in legislative products:

> A wilderness, in contrast with those areas where man and his own works dominate the landscape, is hereby recognized as an area where the earth and its community of life are untrammeled by man, where man himself is a visitor who does not remain. An area of wilderness is further defined to mean in this chapter an area of undeveloped Federal land retaining its primeval character and influence, without permanent improvements or human habitation, which is protected and managed so as to preserve its natural conditions and which (1) generally appears to have been affected primarily by the forces of nature, with the imprint of man's work substantially unnoticeable; (2) has outstanding opportunities for solitude or a primitive and unconfined type of recreation; (3) has at least five thousand acres of land or is of sufficient size as to make practicable its preservation and use in an unimpaired condition; and (4) may also contain ecological, geological, or other features of scientific, educational, scenic, or historical value.

16 U.S.C. § 1131(c).

What is the story of the Wilderness Act? Prior to 1960, the authority of federal agencies (as distinct from the President) to withdraw lands was somewhat in doubt. That ambiguity had not deterred the Secretary of Agriculture, however, from engaging in the practice of withdrawing forest lands for wilderness purposes. Predictably, the legality of these "administrative wilderness areas" was tested in the courts. The litigation produced a victory for the Secretary. *McMichael v. United States*, 355 F.2d 283 (9th Cir. 1965). For devotees of wilderness, though, administrative wilderness areas were not good enough. For one thing, they lacked permanence: they could be undesignated as easily as they were designated. Beyond that, there were no assurances federal land management agencies would be pro-wilderness in any event, namely because public lands can be commercially valuable. Administrative wilderness areas, moreover, could be made subject to a variety of restrictions that would dilute the impact of wilderness designation.

As such, wilderness proponents wanted *statutory* wilderness protection. The first inroad in this direction came in the form of the Multiple-Use Sustained Yield Act of 1960, 16 U.S.C.A. § 528 et seq., which ratified the Secretary of Agriculture's administrative wilderness areas. The zenith would come four years later, with passage of the Wilderness Act.

The Wilderness Act began by making previously designated wilderness areas, 54 in number and 9.1 million acres in area, the first components of what is called the National Wilderness Preservation System. At the same time, it reserved the power to designate new wilderness areas exclusively for Congress. 16 U.S.C. § 1131(a). The statute went on to require the Forest Service to study another 5.4 million acres to see if those lands warranted inclusion in the System. It required the Department of Interior to undertake similar studies respecting park and refuge lands under its control. Reports on the suitability of these "wilderness study areas" were to be sent to the President 10 years thereafter.[5]

Under the terms of the Act, any federal lands can be designated as wilderness. Once designated, wilderness lands continue to be managed by the same agency with management responsibility before designation. 16 U.S.C. § 1131(b). But management of wilderness lands is decidedly in pursuit of much different goals. The goal is preservation. Section 1133(c) of the Act makes the point unambiguously: ". . . there shall be no commercial enterprise and no permanent road within any wilderness area designated by this chapter and, except as necessary to meet minimum requirements for the administration of the area for the purpose of this chapter (including measures required in emergencies involving the health and safety of persons within the area), there shall be no temporary road, no use of motor vehicles, motorized equipment or motorboats, no landing of aircraft, no other form of mechanical transport, and no structure or installation within any such area."[6] The Act grandfathers in any uses in place at the time of designation. 16 U.S.C. § 1133(d).

Lands are added to the wilderness system in either of two ways. Sometimes Congress simply adds the new addition to the list of sites directly governed by the Wilderness Act. The list may be found at 16 U.S.C.A. § 1132 and the "Note" that follows it. On many occasions, Congress creates new wilderness areas by separate federal legislation. These separate bills may refer to the Wilderness Act but may add differing requirements to govern the new addition.

There are relatively few judicial decisions on this subject, mainly because flat prohibitions leave little room for litigation. But cases come along still, especially when wilderness management conflicts with recreational or other uses on contiguous or nearby non-wilderness land.

---

[5] Resource lands controlled by the Bureau of Land Management were not included, perhaps because these lands are thought to be the least valuable of the federal holdings. Notably, the Boundary Waters Canoe Area of Superior National Forest in Minnesota was excepted from coverage as well. The BWCA was left to be managed by administrative regulations "in accordance with the general purpose of maintaining, without unnecessary restrictions on other uses, including that of timber, the primitive character of the area . . ." § 1133(d)(5). Motorboat usage in the BWCA was expressly ratified. *Id.* In short, the Act maintained the tradition of multiple use in the BWCA. *Minnesota Public Interest Research Group v. Butz*, 541 F.2d 1292 (8th Cir. 1976). A separate Boundary Waters Canoe Area Wilderness Act was passed in 1978, repealing former Section 1133(d)(5) and terminating timber contracts one year after enactment.

[6] Not that humans are entirely banned. The Act also provided that "[n]othing in this chapter shall prevent within national forest wilderness areas any activity, including prospecting, for the purpose of gathering information about mineral or other resources, if such activity is carried on in a manner compatible with the preservation of the wilderness environment." 16 U.S.C. § 1133(d)(2). The Act also authorized continued mining on forest lands designated as wilderness until midnight, December 31, 1983. 16 U.S.C. § 1133(d)(3). Finally, the protective provisions of the Act were made "subject to existing private rights. . . ." 16 U.S.C. § 1133(c).

STUPAK-THRALL v. UNITED STATES

70 F.3d. 881 (6th Cir. 1995)

[The United States Forest Service of the Department of Agriculture imposed surface use restrictions for Crooked Lake, located in Michigan's Upper Peninsula near the Wisconsin border. The vast majority of the Lake's shoreline, about 95%, lies within the Sylvania Wilderness Area. The Forest Service adopted "Amendment No. 1" which prohibited, among other things, the use of "sail-powered watercraft," "watercraft designed for or used as floating living quarters," and "nonburnable disposable food and beverage containers."]

KAREN NELSON MOORE, Circuit Judge:

Plaintiffs own a small piece of land abutting the lake's northern shore, and, therefore, like the federal government itself, are riparian to the lake. They argue that, in their capacity as riparians, they have rights to use the surface of the Lake in the ways prohibited by the Forest Service. Specifically, they argue that the Forest Service's actions, taken under authority of the federal Wilderness Act, cannot stand, because the Wilderness Act itself requires the protection of valid existing rights:

> Except as specifically provided for in this chapter, and *subject to existing private rights*, there shall be no commercial enterprise and no permanent road within any wilderness area designated by this chapter and, except as necessary to meet minimum requirements for the administration of the area for purposes of this chapter, . . . there shall be no temporary road, no use of motor vehicles, motorized equipment or motorboats, no landing of aircraft, no other form of mechanical transport, and no structure or installation within any such area.

Wilderness Act, Sec. 1133(c) (emphasis added).

Plaintiffs argue as well that the federal act which specifically created the wilderness area, the Michigan Wilderness Act, contains the same kind of provision, its terms being made "subject to valid existing rights." Pub. Law 100-184, Sec. 5; 101 Stat. 1274, 1275–76 (1987). As their riparian rights include the right to boating and other recreational uses of riparian waters, plaintiffs contend the regulatory restrictions must fail.

There can be little question that Congress has the power to regulate Crooked Lake in the manner described by Amendment No. 1's management prescriptions. The Property Clause gives Congress broad authority to decide what are "needful" regulations "respecting" federal property. *Kleppe* instructs: "We must remain mindful that, while courts must eventually pass upon them, determinations under the Property Clause are entrusted primarily to the judgment of Congress." 426 U.S. at 536. In this case, the management prescriptions at issue are clearly tailored toward protecting federal property. The avowed purpose of the prohibition against sailboats, houseboats, and "nonburnable" food containers is "to protect and perpetuate wilderness character and values." Wilderness Management Amendment No. 1, IV 5.1-1. There is no doubt that the restrictions assist in protecting the wilderness character of the area. The Wilderness Act itself states that "wilderness" is defined as "an area where the earth and its community of life are untrammeled by man . . . retaining its primeval character and influence, without permanent improvements or human habitation." 16 U.S.C. Sec. 1131(c). Certainly, Congress could rationally conclude that certain forms of mechanical transport, including sailboats and houseboats, should be excluded from the Sylvania Wilderness in order to preserve the "wilderness character" of the property. The protection of wilderness character is a valid objective under the Property Clause to the same extent that Congress's objectives in enacting the Wild Free-Roaming Horses and Burros Act in *Kleppe,* "for achievement of an ecological balance on the public lands," were valid. 426 U.S. at 535. Just as Congress's authority may sometimes extend to purely private property in order to provide adequate protection of public property, so in this instance may federal regulations encompass shared property rights between the United States and private owners, at least to the extent that the regulations are designed to govern the portion of the water surface contained completely within the borders of government-owned land. This at a minimum is what the Property Clause allows — regulation to protect not only the government's own riparian interest in the lake, but also its interest in the surrounding national wilderness.

. . . .

III [omitted]

. . . .

IV

What distinguishes this case from others applying the Property Clause is that the statutory scheme for the federal wilderness areas appears to make explicit room for state law.Therefore, although the Forest Service might otherwise have the delegated authority to regulate in line with the Property Clause, Congress in the Wilderness Act and MWA expressly made such regulation "subject to existing private rights" or "subject to valid existing rights." In order to determine how much of a limitation this might be on the Forest Service, we must examine the scope of such "existing" rights under state law.

As indicated earlier, riparian rights are not absolute. [The court at this point discounted the idea that federal power might be found in the common law riparian "reasonable use" doctrine, which allows riparian owners certain recreational rights. In the court's language, "the 'reasonable use' doctrine itself only makes sense when one riparian owner challenges another's use as unreasonable and the court makes a subsequent determination of reasonableness. It is inapplicable when one riparian proprietor unilaterally decides to ban certain uses of others, whether or not the uses themselves are unreasonable, and whether or not the banning proprietor actually has the power to do so. Indeed, the federal government's ability to impose restrictions does not stem from its status as a fellow riparian proprietor; it stems from its status as a sovereign."] * * *

Instead, we find that Amendment No. 1's management prescriptions are permissible because they constitute a legitimate exercise of the sovereign's police power. The Michigan Supreme Court has explicitly held that local governments may regulate their citizens' riparian rights pursuant to their inherent police powers. In *Miller v. Fabius Township Board*, 366 Mich. 250, 114 N.W.2d 205 (Mich. 1962), the court allowed time restrictions on waterskiing. In *Square Lake Hills Condo. Assn. v. Bloomfield Township*, 437 Mich. 310, 471 N.W.2d 321 (Mich. 1991), the court allowed regulation of boat docking and launching. In *Square Lake Hills*, especially, the court made it clear that plaintiffs' recreational riparian rights were subject to regulation for the protection of "health, safety, and welfare" of the general public. *Id.* at 322. The federal government's actions here are similar to those of the townships in *Miller* and *Square Lake Hills*, except that the "general public" in this case is the nation at large instead of the local community, and the power now comes from a highly particularized source, the Property Clause, rather than from the state's inherent powers. *Kleppe* in fact makes the comparison explicit: "The general Government doubtless has a power over its own property analogous to the police power of the several States, and the extent to which it may go in the exercise of such power is measured by the exigencies of the particular case." 426 U.S. at 540, *citing Camfield*, 167 U.S. at 525. *Kleppe* continues by stating that "Congress exercises the powers both of a proprietor and of a legislature over the public domain." 426 U.S. at 540.

Thus, the Forest Service possesses a power delegated to it by Congress that is "analogous to the police power," and its exercise of this federal power does not violate Congress's express limitation deferring to "existing" state law rights in the wilderness acts, so long as it does not exceed the bounds of permissible police power regulation under state law. The management prescriptions of Amendment No. 1 are clearly valid restrictions within the state law police power. According to *Square Lake Hills*, validity depends upon reasonableness, which in turn "depends upon the particular facts of each case." 471 N.W.2d at 324. "The test for determining whether an ordinance is reasonable requires us to assess the existence of a rational relationship between the exercise of police power and the public health, safety, morals, or general welfare in a particular manner in a given case." *Id.* (citations omitted). *See also People v. McKendrick*, 188 Mich. App. 128, 468 N.W.2d 903, 908 (Mich.Ct.App. 1991). As has already been noted, Amendment No. 1's purpose of preserving wilderness character is undoubtedly a proper aim under the Property Clause's police power and under Congress's delegation to the Forest Service, and the prohibition of certain forms of mechanical transport and certain types of food containers on Crooked Lake is certainly rationally related to achieving this goal. The prohibitions are also a reasonable means of doing so. They do not affect plaintiffs' rights to "natural" riparian uses, only plaintiffs' "artificial" uses — in this case (as in *Miller* and *Square Lake Hills*), for "commercial profit and recreation." *Thompson*, 154 N.W.2d at 484. Plaintiffs do not argue that they need to use sailboats or houseboats in order to subsist, or even that they need them for transportation. In fact, as the district court found, "there is no evidence that sailboats or houseboats, which are now banned, have ever been used on the lake." 843 F. Supp. at 334. Moreover, the determination that regulations should only apply to the area of the lake lying within the wilderness shoreline provides another reasonable limit on the scope of Amendment No.1's prescriptions. Given the "minimal impact on plaintiffs' riparian uses of Crooked Lake," 843 F. Supp. at 334, we conclude that the Forest Service's restrictions here are a valid exercise of the police power under state law, and they are therefore a valid exercise of the police power conferred on the Forest Service by the Property Clause and limited by Congress's express reservation for state law rights in the wilderness acts. We reiterate that we do not refer to state law for the sake of determining the scope of Congress's regulatory power under the Property Clause. State law only affects the Forest Service's authority here, and it does so only because Congress has placed a specific constraint on the Forest Service's regulatory authority, requiring that it be exercised "subject to" plaintiffs' "existing" state law property rights.

If sailboats and houseboats have indeed never been used on Crooked Lake, one could justifiably ask why this action was even brought in the first place. The answer, it appears, is that plaintiffs are going after a bigger fish — Amendment No. 5, which regulates motorboat use on wilderness lakes. The Forest Service had not issued Amendment No. 5 when this case was originally filed, and the amendment does not go into effect until April 1996. Nevertheless, at various points in their brief, plaintiffs intertwine the Amendment No. 5 issue with their discussion of Amendment No. 1, and they use a significant amount of space to attack the merits of the motorboat restrictions. We decline plaintiffs' invitation to decide the motorboat issue, as it has not been properly presented in this court. Plaintiffs cannot short-circuit the administrative process by challenging Forest Service regulations here, before they have been decided upon in the appropriate agency proceedings. *See Lavapies v. Bowen,* 883 F.2d 465, 468 (6th Cir. 1989) (citing *Weinberger v. Salfi,* 422 U.S. 749, 45 L. Ed. 2d 522, 95 S. Ct. 2457 (1975)). The Secretary of Agriculture has set forth specific appeals procedures for land and resource management plans in 36 C.F.R. Sec. 217, and plaintiffs' appeal of Amendment No. 5 is currently making its way through this administrative pipeline. As plaintiffs have failed to exhaust their administrative remedies, we will not address their arguments regarding the motorboat restrictions.

[Remainder of opinion omitted]

NOTES

1. According to the National Wilderness Preservation System Database, as of 2004, the National Wilderness Preservation System contained 662 units comprising more than 105 million acres. *See http://www.wilderness.net/ swps/db/default.cfm.* About 4.67% of federal land is wilderness. The largest single wilderness designation, a 56 million acre set-aside in Alaska, was made in the Alaska National Interest Lands Conservation Act ("ANILCA") of 1980. About 54% of all wilderness is in Alaska.

A significant addition to the ranks of federal wilderness, accomplished by use of independent legislation, occurred on Oct. 31, 1994, when President Bill Clinton signed the California Desert Protection Act. The Act designated as wilderness about 7.7 million acres of BLM-and FS-managed federal land in that state. It also added about 3 million acres to the national park system, including the new Death Valley and Joshua Tree National Parks and the Mojave National Preserve. In its specific provisions, the Act permits hunting and grazing on the wilderness lands. Then-Secretary of Interior Bruce Babbitt called the legislation "America's most significant environmental victory in more than a decade."

2. A federal statute analogous to the Wilderness Act, in that it operates to insulate public lands from human intrusion, is the Archeological Resources Protection Act of 1979, 16 U.S.C. §§ 470aa–470ll. The statute prohibits unauthorized "removal, damage, alteration, or defacement" of archeological resources on public lands. 16 U.S.C. § 470ee(a). Archeological resources include pottery, basketry, bottles, tools, graves, rock paintings, human skeletal remains, and other items of interest. 16 U.S.C. § 470bb(1). The Act provides that "no person may sell, purchase, exchange, transport, receive, or offer to sell, purchase or exchange" any such artifact. 16 U.S.C. § 470ee(b). Violators may face criminal fines in amounts not exceeding $10,000, or incarceration for not more than one year, or both, 16 U.S.C. § 470ee(d), as well as civil penalties. 16 U.S.C. § 470ff. Interestingly, ignorance of the law can be a defense in a criminal prosecution under the statute. *See, e.g.,United States v. Lynch*, 233 F.3d 1139, 1142 (9th Cir. 2000) (quoting Representative Udall: "Certainly, no sponsor of this legislation and probably no reasonable person would want some overzealous bureaucrat to arrest a Boy Scout who finds an arrowhead along a trail or a purple bottle out in the desert. . . . The thrust of this act is not to harass the casual visitor who happens to find some exposed artifact, but to stop the needless, careless, and intentional destruction of archeological sites and organized and intentional theft of the valuable remains of previous civilizations.").

D. FEDERAL LAND MANAGEMENT

Our review thus far has surveyed the source of federal power over public lands and the exercise of those powers both to dispose of federal lands and, in a reactive mode, to arrest that disposition. Let us now take a look at federal land management in the current day. At present, federal lands are pledged to a variety of uses. In some cases, such as with national parks, a single use (recreation) is all that is allowed by law. (In the case of wilderness, no permanent use is allowed at all). But for the vast majority of federal lands, the management regime is not "dominant use;" it is "multiple use." As the name suggests, the idea is to allow lands to serve the variety of uses for which they are suited, and on a sustained basis. This idea may sound good in theory, but it can be exceedingly difficult to pull off in practice. Recreation and mining, for example, do not easily mix.

In this final part of Chapter 5, we look to the management regimes that govern the public lands. This review entails, first, an introduction to the four federal agencies with land management responsibilities, and second, a review of the legal principles that govern: (a) mineral lands, managed chiefly by the Bureau of Land Management of the Department of Interior; (b) forest lands, managed chiefly by the Forest Service of the Department of Agriculture; (c) grazing lands, managed chiefly by the Bureau of Land Management; and (d) recreation and wildlife lands, managed by the National Park Service and the Fish and Wildlife Service of the Department of Interior.

[1] MANAGING AGENCIES

The federal agencies with significant management authority over the public lands are four in number:

1. The Forest Service of the U.S. Department of Agriculture.

2. The Bureau of Land Management (BLM) of the U.S. Department of the Interior.

3. The Fish and Wildlife Service of the U.S. Department of the Interior.

4. The National Park Service of the U.S. Department of the Interior.

1. The Forest Service

As its name indicates, the Forest Service is the executive entity with management authority over the national forests, which comprise approximately one-fourth of all public lands. National forest land is located in overwhelming proportion in the western states, and especially Alaska.

The Forest Service operates under the authority of three major statutory enactments. They are the Organic Act of 1897, 16 U.S.C. § 475 et seq., which was the agency's first organic authority, the Multiple Use-Sustained Yield Act of 1960, 16 U.S.C. § 528 et seq., and Forest and Rangeland Renewable Resources Planning Act of 1974, 16 U.S.C. § 1600 et seq., better known in its expanded form as the National Forest Management Act. Under the Organic Act, national forests were managed largely for purposes of timber production. The Multiple Use-Sustained Yield Act enlarged the universe of uses of national forests to include outdoor recreation, range use, watershed management, and fish and wildlife maintenance. The 1960 legislation also declared a "sustained yield" management regime which was described as "the achievement and maintenance in perpetuity of a high-level annual or regular periodic output of the various renewable resources of the national forests without impairment of the productivity of the land." Overall, the MUSYA called for management of all "the various renewable surface resources of the national forests" to best serve the needs of the American people. § 4(b), 16 U.S.C. § 531(b).

The Multiple Use-Sustained Yield Act also required the Forest Service to prepare a multiple use plan for each forest. Completed plans serve as a guide for future agency management decisions. The National Forest Management Act enlarged the Forest Service's planning responsibility by requiring more long-term planning. Under the NFMA, the Forest Service is obligated to prepare detailed plans spanning a decade in length. *See infra.*

2. The Bureau of Land Management

The BLM manages approximately 60 percent of onshore federal lands, or about 470 million acres. Almost two-thirds of the BLM lands are located in Alaska, and virtually the entirety of the remainder is found in the eleven western states. A good deal of this land is open for public use and resource exploitation, including grazing. The BLM also takes a dominant role in managing oil resources, mainly oil reserves, in offshore federal lands.

The BLM does not have cohesive organic legislation governing its management operations. Thus, for varying purposes at varying locations, the BLM will take action as authorized by the Stock Raising Homestead Act, Act of Dec. 29, 1916, 39 Stat. 862 (1916), the General Mining Law of 1872, 30 U.S.C. § 22 et seq., the Mineral Leasing Act of 1920, 30 U.S.C. § 181 et seq., the Taylor Grazing Act of 1934, Act of June 28, 1934, 43 U.S.C. § 315 et seq., and other measures. A single enactment that best qualifies for the status of organic authority, however, is the Federal Land Policy and Management Act, 43 U.S.C. §§ 1701-1782. Enacted in 1976, FLPMA represents a Congressional attempt to bring some consistency and coherence to BLM public lands management. Like the NFMA, FLPMA is premised on management of federal lands for multiple uses. *See infra.*

3. The Fish and Wildlife Service

A subunit of the Department of Interior, the Fish and Wildlife Service is in charge of the National Wildlife Refuge System, an array of refuges totaling more than 30 million acres. As their name indicates, wildlife refuges are land areas set aside for the protection and conservation of fish and wildlife. Since its inception, the FWS has managed wildlife refuges under authority of the National Wildlife Refuge System Administration Act of 1966, 16 U.S.C. § 668dd et seq. Since 1997, however, its major organic authority has been the National Wildlife Refuge System Improvement Act ("NWRSIA"). The NWRSIA was enacted to resolve controversies regarding conflicting multiple uses of refuges. *See, infra.*

4. The National Park Service

The National Park Service administers the National Park System, which spans more than 23 million acres of land. Park lands are in place for recreational purposes. The NPS manages national parks under authority of the National Park Service Act of 1916, 16 U.S.C. § 1 et seq., which stipulated the governing purposes as follows:

> To conserve the scenery and the natural and historic objects and the wildlife therein and to provide for the enjoyment of the same in such manner and by such means as will leave them unimpaired for the enjoyment of future generations.

16 U.S.C. § 1.

The pieces that make up the national park system include natural, historic and recreational areas. The natural areas are the national parks and monuments. National monuments are designated for their scientific significance under authority of a 1906 statute, the American Antiquities Preservation Act, 16 U.S.C. § 431. Historic areas are diverse lands having historical or archaeological significance. And recreation areas encompass an array of lands, including national seashores, lakeshores, scenic parkways, wild and scenic rivers, and other such parcels. *See infra.*

[2] MANAGEMENT REGIMES

[a] MINERAL LANDS

Early legislation allowed for miners, by their own independent action, to secure rights to minerals on the public lands. The major statute creating this self-initiation method of mineral rights acquisition was the General Mining Act of 1872, 30 U.S.C. §§ 22-39, commonly referred to as the "General Mining Law" or "GML." In the next section, we will examine how this statute operates. Note that "operates" is in the present tense: the GML is still good law. But, as we shall see, the GML no longer has the reach and force it once did. Its scope has been limited in succeeding years, and regulations now affect the extractive activities themselves. In other instances, the GML has given way to new legislation.

[i] THE GENERAL MINING ACT OF 1872

The General Mining Act of 1872 remains the major statutory provision governing the rights of individuals to secure so-called hard rock minerals from the public lands. To be sure, subsequent statutes have come along, such as the Surface Resources Act, 30 U.S.. § 611 et seq. (1955), the Multiple Mineral Development Act, 30 U.S.C. § 521 et seq. (1954), and the Mining and Mineral Policy Act, 30 U.S.C. § 21a (1970). And while these later statutes alter the legal landscape, chiefly by withdrawing minerals from coverage under the General Mining Law, none of them has changed the overall scheme by which persons can secure hard rock mineral rights under that legislation.

The GML provides that, with some exceptions, "all valuable mineral deposits in lands belonging to the United States shall be free and open to exploration and purchase, and the lands in which the minerals are found shall be open to occupation and purchase, by U.S. citizens." 30 U.S.C. § 22. This provision allows for mineral extraction on federal lands "held for disposal under the land laws." Not all federal lands fall into this category. Lands withdrawn by Congress from the operation of the GML and other resource disposal statutes, for example, are off limits. Other lands, such as national parks (and the grounds of the U.S. Capitol Building — *see, e.g., Oklahoma v. Texas*, 258 U.S. 574, 42 S.Ct. 406 (1922)) are off limits as well. As the Supreme Court stated, "it is a familiar principle of public land law that statutes providing generally for disposal of the public domain are inapplicable to lands which are not unqualifiedly subject to sale and disposition because they have been appropriated to some other purpose." *Federal Power Comm'n v. Oregon*, 349 U.S. 435, 448, 75 S. Ct. 832, 840 (1955), *quoting United States v. O'Donnell*, 303 U.S. 501, 510, 58 S. Ct. 708, 714 (1938).

Beyond that, not all "minerals" are subject to the GML. What are minerals? Neither the Act nor the BLM tells us. The term, moreover, is maddeningly imprecise: the Oxford dictionary defines it, first, as "any substance which is obtained by mining," and second, as "any natural substance that is neither animal or vegetable." The Shorter Oxford English Dictionary, Oxford University Press, 1973, at 1327. *See also,* Braunstein, *All That Glitters: Discovering the Meaning of Mineral in the Mining Law of 1872*, XXI Land & Water L. Rev. 293 (1986). What is a mineral for purposes of the GML remains a question even to this day. In one relatively recent case, the United States Supreme Court decided that *water* is not a mineral for purposes of the GML, not because water could not be, but because Congress did not intend to include water under the statute. *Andrus v. Charlestone Stone Products Co.*, 436 U.S. 604, 98 S. Ct. 2002 (1978) (Congress intended to protect the pre-existing water rights regime; to conclude otherwise would "def[y] common sense. . . .") *Id.* at 614, 98 S. Ct at 2008. For more on water rights, see Chapter 8.

Such matters aside, at its enactment the GML applied to all "minerals" except for coal, which was already the subject of disposition under the Coal Lands Act of 1864, 13 Stat. 205, as amended by the Coal Lands Act of 1873, 17 Stat. 607. In succeeding years, Congress by legislative decree has withdrawn other minerals from the ambit of the statute. (For a snapshot on these legislative enactments and the current arrangement of statutory law governing the extraction of minerals from federal land, see the chart entitled "Mineral Rights Allocations on Federal Lands.") Minerals that remain under the governance of the GML are the "hardrock" minerals, including gold, silver, platinum, uranium, molybdenum, and some others.

MINERAL RIGHTS ALLOCATIONS ON FEDERAL LANDS
(Does not include Native American Lands. Bold italics print indicates current allocation authority.)

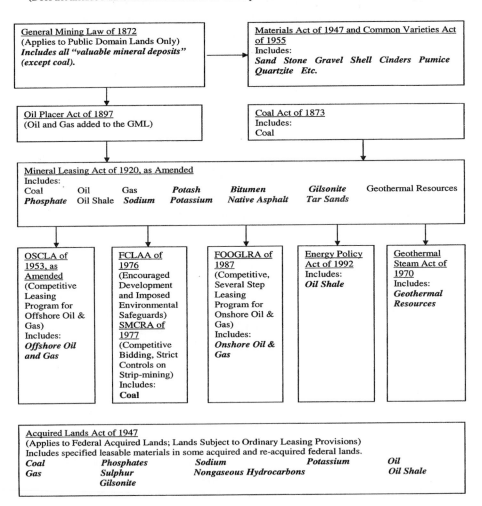

How does one go about securing property rights to minerals on federal land under the GML? The first step is to "locate" a claim. To do this, miners physically enter federal land in search of minerals and stake out the find. They need not identify the minerals they seek at this time; identification is required, however, at a later stage. Location must be made in accordance with rules of the applicable mining district, which rules govern "the location, manner of recording, [and the] amount of work necessary to hold possession of a mining claim. . . ." 30 U.S.C. § 28. Each location must be distinctly marked. *Id.*

The GML gives protection to miners engaged in prospecting by the doctrine of *pedis possessio,* which stipulates that the party making the first good faith entrance onto federal land for purposes of making a discovery shall be given priority over those arriving subsequently. When a "junior locator" contests the right of a "senior locator" to prospect, the latter can prevail by showing either a first-in-time right to possession or by demonstrating the junior locator's entry was not undertaken in good faith. Good faith has been described as "honesty of purpose and absence of intent to defraud." *Goldfield Mines, Inc. v. Hand,* 147 Ariz. 498, 505, 711 P.2d 637, 644 (1985). It has been held that good faith is lacking where a junior seeks possession solely on the basis of defects in a senior's claims. *See, e.g., Columbia Standard Corp. v. Ranchers Exploration & Dev't., Inc.,* 468 F.2d 547 (10th Cir. 1972). To successfully invoke the protections of the doctrine of pedis possessio, the senior must be in actual occupancy of the land. *Id.* The senior must be working toward a discovery of "valuable mineral deposits" as well. 30 U.S.C. § 22. A relaxation in occupancy opens the door for a peaceful entry by another. *Goldfield Mines, supra.* Rights secured by this mechanism have been held to be transferrable. *United Western Minerals Co. v. Hannsen,* 147 Colo. 272, 363 P.2d 677 (1961).

Minerals, once discovered, may only be secured under the GML if they are "valuable."

UNITED STATES v. COLEMAN

390 U.S. 599 (1968)

MR. JUSTICE BLACK delivered the opinion of the Court.

In 1956 respondent Coleman applied to the Department of the Interior for a patent to certain public lands based on his entry onto and exploration of these lands and his discovery there of a variety of stone called quartzite, one of the most common of all solid materials. It was, and still is, respondent Coleman's contention that the quartzite deposits qualify as "valuable mineral deposits" under 30 U.S.C. § 22 and make the land "chiefly valuable for building stone" under 30 U.S.C. § 161. The Secretary of the Interior held that to qualify as "valuable mineral deposits" under 30 U.S.C. § 22 it must be shown that the mineral can be "extracted, removed and marketed at a profit" — the so-called "marketability test." Based on the largely undisputed evidence in the record, the Secretary concluded that the deposits claimed by respondent Coleman did not meet that criterion. As to the alternative "chiefly valuable for building stone" claim, the Secretary held that respondent Coleman's quartzite deposits were a "common [variety]" of stone within the meaning of 30 U.S.C. § 611, and thus they could not serve as the basis for a valid mining claim under the mining laws. The Secretary denied the patent application, but respondent Coleman remained on the land, forcing the Government to bring this present action in ejectment in the District Court against respondent Coleman and his lessee, respondent McClennan. The respondents filed a counterclaim seeking to have the District Court direct the Secretary to issue a patent to them. The District Court, agreeing with the Secretary, rendered summary judgment for the Government. On appeal the Court of Appeals for the Ninth Circuit reversed, holding specifically that the test of profitable marketability was not a proper standard for determining whether a discovery of "valuable mineral deposits" under 30 U.S.C. § 22 had been made and that building stone could not be deemed a "common [variety]" of stone under 30 U.S.C. § 611. We granted the Government's petition for certiorari because of the importance of the decision to the utilization of the public lands. 389 U.S. 970.

We cannot agree with the Court of Appeals and believe that the rulings of the Secretary of the Interior were proper. The Secretary's determination that the quartzite deposits did not qualify as valuable mineral deposits because the stone could not be marketed at a profit does no violence to the statute. Indeed, the marketability test is an admirable effort to identify with greater precision and objectivity the factors relevant to a determination that a mineral deposit is "valuable." It is a logical complement to the "prudent-man test" which the Secretary has been using to interpret the mining laws since 1894. Under this "prudent-man test" in order to qualify as "valuable mineral deposits," the discovered deposits must be of such a character that "a person of ordinary prudence would be justified in the further expenditure of his labor and means, with a reasonable prospect of success, in developing a valuable mine. . . ." *Castle v. Womble*, 19 L.D. 455, 457 (1894). This Court has approved the prudent-man formulation and interpretation on numerous occasions. See, for example, *Chrisman v. Miller*, 197 U.S. 313, 322; *Cameron v. United States*, 252 U.S. 450, 459; *Best v. Humboldt Placer Mining Co.*, 371 U.S. 334, 335-336. Under the mining laws Congress has made public lands available to people for the purpose of mining valuable mineral deposits and not for other purposes. The obvious intent was to reward and encourage the discovery of minerals that are valuable in an economic sense. Minerals which no prudent man will extract because there is no demand for them at a price higher than the cost of extraction and transportation are hardly economically valuable. Thus, profitability is an important consideration in applying the prudent-man test, and the marketability test which the Secretary has used here merely recognizes this fact.

The marketability test also has the advantage of throwing light on a claimant's intention, a matter which is inextricably bound together with valuableness. For evidence that a mineral deposit is not of economic value and cannot in all likelihood be operated at a profit may well suggest that a claimant seeks the land for other purposes. Indeed, as the Government points out, the facts of this case — the thousands of dollars and hours spent building a home on 720 acres in a highly scenic national forest located two hours from Los Angeles, the lack of an economically feasible market for the stone, and the immense quantities of identical stone found in the area outside the claims — might well be thought to raise a substantial question as to respondent Coleman's real intention.

Finally, we think that the Court of Appeals' objection to the marketability test on the ground that it involves the imposition of a different and more onerous standard on claims for minerals of widespread occurrence than for rarer minerals which have generally been dealt with under the prudent-man test is unwarranted. As we have pointed out above, the prudent-man test and the marketability test are not distinct standards, but are complementary in that the latter is a refinement of the former. While it is true that the marketability test is usually the critical factor in cases involving nonmetallic minerals of widespread occurrence, this is accounted for by the perfectly natural reason that precious metals which are in small supply and for which there is a great demand, sell at a price so high as to leave little room for doubt that they can be extracted and marketed at a profit.

We believe that the Secretary of the Interior was also correct in ruling that "[in] view of the immense quantities of identical stone found in the area outside the claims, the stone must be considered a 'common variety'" and thus must fall within the exclusionary language of § 3 of the 1955 Act, 69 Stat. 368, 30 U.S.C. § 611, which declares that "[a] deposit of common varieties of . . . stone . . . shall not be deemed a valuable mineral deposit within the meaning of the mining laws. . . ." Respondents rely on the earlier 1892 Act, 30 U.S.C. § 161, which makes the mining laws applicable to "lands that are chiefly valuable for building stone" and contend that the 1955 Act has no application to building stone, since, according to respondents, "[stone] which is chiefly valuable as building stone is, by that very fact, not a common variety of stone." This was also the reasoning of the Court of Appeals. But this argument completely fails to take into account the reason why Congress felt compelled to pass the 1955 Act with its modification of the mining laws. The legislative history makes clear that this Act (30 U.S.C. § 611) was intended to remove common types of sand, gravel, and stone from the coverage of the mining laws, under which they served as a basis for claims to land patents, and to place the disposition of such materials under the Materials Act of 1947, 61 Stat. 681, 30 U.S.C. § 601, which provides for the sale of such materials without disposing of the land on which they are found. * * *

For these reasons we hold that the United States is entitled to eject respondents from the land and that respondents' counterclaim for a patent must fail. The case is reversed and remanded to the Court of Appeals for the Ninth Circuit for further proceedings to carry out this decision.

It is so ordered.

MR. JUSTICE MARSHALL took no part in the consideration or decision of this case.

NOTES

Under the Clinton Administration, there was some thought that what constitutes a "valuable" claim under the GML is best determined by comparing the value of mining with other potentially foregone or impaired land uses. While not deciding the matter, then-Secretary of the Interior Bruce Babbitt commented in 1998 that there may be a need to consider the term "'valuable' relative to other quantifiable and non-quantifiable land use values." He noted that such an interpretation "would be consistent with contemporary land use needs. . . ." *United States v. United Mining Corporation*, 142 ILBA 339 (1998).

It has also been suggested that the test for establishing a "valuable" discovery should be more stringent when minerals are sought from national forest lands. *See, e.g. Converse v. Udall*, 399 F.2d 616, 622 (9th Cir. 1968) ("The prudent man test has long been strictly applied against one who asserts discovery on national forest lands, when the contest is between him and the government."). There seems to be no legal basis for this suggestion.

* * * * * *

Upon making a valuable discovery, locators must demarcate the boundaries of the claimed area, post a notice at the site, and file a mining claim at the proper government office. The filing must contain the name of the locator, the date of the location, and a description of the claim. Locators must invest at least $100 per year in labor or improvements on each claim. 30 U.S.C. §26.

Once a claim is recorded, the claimant has an "unpatented mining right." Having an unpatented mining right means the miner has exclusive possession of (a) surface rights, (b) intraliminal rights (veins and lodes lying inside of the surface lines as those lines extend downward vertically, and (c) extra-lateral rights (rights to follow a vein or lode downward even as it extends beyond the subterranean dimensions of the overlying parcel). *See, e.g., The Wilderness Society v. Dombeck*, 168 F.3d 367 (9th Cir. 1999). The right is "property" in a real sense, and accordingly, may be sold, mortgaged, taxed, inherited, and otherwise used by the holder of the interest. It also enjoys the protections of the Takings Clause. *See, e.g., United States v. Shumway*, 199 F.3d 1093, 1103 (9th Cir. 1999) ("The owner of a mining claim owns property, and is not a mere social guest of the Department of the Interior to be shooed out the door when the Department chooses.") There are no requirements for payment of royalties to the government for hardrock minerals produced from the land. There are no requirements in the GML for the reclaiming of sites when mining activity is completed.

But the unpatented mining right is not unlimited. The holder of the mining right possesses the land only for mining-related purposes: the "right of enjoyment which Congress intended to grant extends only to mining uses." *United States v. Rizzinelli*, 182 Fed. 675 (D.C. Idaho, 1910). Beyond that, the right of possession does not include the right to exclude the public from pursuit of normal recreational activities. *See. e.g., United States v. Curtis-Nevada Mines, Inc.*, 611 F.2d. 1277 (9th Cir. 1980).

Miners need not stop with the unpatented mining right. While not required, and not necessary in many cases, locators may obtain patents to located lands. 30 U.S.C. § 29. Once a patent application is received, the right to a patent accrues, so long as the application itself comports with all applicable legal requirements and is accompanied by the appropriate fee. *See, e.g., United States v. Shumway*, 199 F.3d 1093 (9th Cir. 1999). The patent review process involves two stages. First is the mineral examination stage, during which the applicant's compliance with the mining laws is verified. The second stage is "secretarial review." Instituted in 1993, this stage assures that patent issuances come personally from the Secretary of the Interior. The Department has a duty under the "rule of reason" to issue patents without undue delay. In this regard "reasonable means expeditious." *Independence Mining Co. v. Babbitt*, 885 F. Supp. 1356, 1361 (D. Nev. 1995). Yet, even a five year wait may not be sufficient to compel issuance of the "truly extraordinary measure of a writ of mandamus." *Id.* at 1364. Once a patent is received, the recipient must file annually and show evidence of assessment work or at least of intention to hold the claim. Issuance of a patent typically creates in the patentholder a fee simple absolute interest in the parcel for which the patent is issued. Because of that, some patented sites are no longer used for mining, having been transformed into ski resorts or other recreational facilities. Patented lands are subject to state taxation, land use controls, and other such restrictions, to the same extent as other interests in property.

NOTES AND QUESTIONS

1. Does the issuance of a patent under the GML require the preparation of an EIS under NEPA? *See, e.g., State of South Dakota v. Andrus*, 614 F.2d 1190, *cert. denied*, 449 U.S. 822 (1980) (no EIS is necessary, since the issuance of a patent is a nondiscretionary act).

2. Despite the restrictions on mining, it is widely agreed that the General Mining Law has been, and remains, a boon for miners. Any private citizen or corporation can patent land for bargain basement prices, historically not more than $5 an acre. A particularly illustrative example: on March 16, 1994, under the provisions of the GML, then-Secretary of Interior Bruce Babbitt signed over 1,793 acres of federal land in Nevada, estimated to contain $10 billion in gold, to a domestic subsidiary of a foreign company. The government expected to receive less than $10,000 in fees from the recipient company. Babbitt called the transaction "the biggest ripoff since the Yankees stole Babe Ruth from the Red Sox for pocket change." The Director of the Office of Management and Budget lamented the loss of such valuable public resources "for less money than they charge NBA players for fighting during a game."

Still, as a general matter, the mining of hardrock minerals on federal land is in decline. There has been a serious downturn in production due to market forces, most prominently a persistent slump in world gold prices. A precipitous decline occurred in 1992 as well, when an annual fee of $100 per claim was legislated. Pub. L. No. 102-381, 106 Stat. 374, 1378-79 (1992). By operation of law, over 400,000 claims were voided after the fees were imposed. Since that time, the number of mining claims in force has remained at about 300,000. On average, the Bureau of Land Management collects less than $30 million from these claims.

The 103rd Congress, which concluded business in December, 1994, seriously considered the first widespread revisions of the General Mining Law in many years. Both the Senate and House passed legislation (S. 775; HR 332) but the bills differed sharply. The Senate bill was more favorable for the mineral industry, while the House bill would have required royalty payments set at 8% (the Senate bill provided for royalties at a 2% rate), tougher reclamation after conclusion of mining activity, and provisions for environmental protection. After months of wrangling, the Conference Committee assembled to merge the bills gave up. The Secretary of Interior blamed industry stonewalling for the death of the legislation. The GML remains unmodified.

3. Mining rights are subject to independent government regulation, like any other property interest. Accordingly, the government can regulate mining activity to protect the environment and for other legitimate purposes. Is regulation of mining on public land needed? Note that federal lands are strewn with abandoned mining sites which have never been cleaned up: by one estimate, there are more than 557,000 of these. These sites cause significant contamination of surface and ground water: mining activity releases vast amounts of toxic chemicals, including mercury, hydrogen, cyanide gas, heavy metals and arsenic. The cost of cleaning these sites has been estimated to range between $32 billion and $71 billion. A recent study, moreover, identified mining, along with grazing, as the most destructive federally subsidized use of federal land. *See Taking from the Taxpayer: Public Subsidies for Natural Resource Development,* House Natural Resources Committee, Aug. 8, 1994.

The BLM acted to regulate mining for environmental purposes in 1980. 43 C.F.R. Part 3809 ("surface management regulations" or "3809 regulations"). Its primary authority for the 3809 regulations was the Federal Land Policy and Management Act of 1976, 43 U.S.C. § 1701 et seq. FLPMA obligates the Secretary of Interior to "take any action necessary to prevent unnecessary or undue degradation of the [public] lands." § 302(b), 43 U.S.C. § 1732(b). (The BLM also relied on the General Mining Law itself, which provides that the process of securing rights to minerals shall be done "under regulations prescribed by law." 30 U.S.C. § 22.)

These regulations have proven to be contentious. The dispute has centered on the meaning of "unnecessary or undue degradation" ("UUD"). In the 1980 regulations, BLM viewed this phrase to mean essentially any degradation more severe than would be expected if a mining site were operated prudently, in accordance with generally applicable environmental protection statutes, assuming mitigation of harms caused. 45 Fed. Reg. 78,910 (Nov. 26, 1980). In the 1990s, however, the BLM commenced a rulemaking to review and amend the 1980 regulations. It undertook the review in part to address a new mining technique known as "heap-leach" mining, which involves the use of cyanide to treat massive amounts of low-grade ores to extract trace amounts of minerals. The BLM's efforts culminated in a new rulemaking. 65 Fed. Reg. 69997, November 21, 2000. (The regulations were designated to take effect on January 10, 2001, during the final hours of the Clinton Administration). The 2000 regulations tossed aside the so-called "prudent man" standard of the 1980 regulations in favor of a "substantial irreparable harm" ("SIH") standard. The SIH standard was significantly tougher than its predecessor. Under the SIH standard, BLM would be empowered to deny a mining permit if the proposed mining site was environmentally sensitive or culturally significant. *Id.* at 70,016. In other words, it could stop a mining activity in its tracks based on environmental considerations.

The Bush Administration amended the 2000 regulations. 66 Fed. Reg. 54,834 (October 30, 2001). The new regulations eliminated the SIH standard for reasons of unworkability, expense, and a projected 10–30% decline in mineral production the 2000 regulations would supposedly have caused. In the 2001 regulations, BLM concluded that FLPMA's reference to "unnecessary or undue degradation" precluded BLM from disapproving any activity "necessary to mining" — regardless of the environmental harm that activity might cause.

The 2001 regulations were challenged in *Mineral Policy Center v. Norton*, 292 F. Supp. 2d 30 (D.C. Civ. 2003). The District Court in that case flatly rejected the BLM's legal interpretation: "FLPMA, by its plain terms, vests the Secretary of the Interior with the authority — and indeed the obligation — to disapprove of an otherwise permissible mining operation because the operation, though necessary for mining, would unduly harm or degrade the public land." *Id.* Still, the court found no indication the 2001 regulations were inadequate as written to prevent UUD as required by FLPMA. The court remanded the regulations on other grounds.

Note that FLPMA § 302(b), in addition to the much-debated UUD requirement, contains the following language, which went undiscussed in the *Mineral Policy Center* decision: "no provision of this Act shall in any way amend the Mining Law of 1872 or impair the rights of any locators or claims under that Act. . . ."

4. *FLPMA*: Enacted largely due to the efforts of Senator Henry (Scoop) Jackson of Washington, the Federal Land Policy and Management Act, 43 U.S.C. §§ 1701-1785 (1976), is surely the most important public land management statute of the 20th century. While it serves as the organic law for the Bureau of Land Management, it also does much more. First, FLPMA cleaned up unweildy records regarding claims to mineral rights on public lands. It did this by requiring that all claimants file with BLM within three years, or forfeit the claim. § 314, 43 U.S.C. § 1744. It followed this up with an ongoing requirement for an inventory of public lands, lest the problem arise again. § 201(a), 43 U.S.C. § 1711(a). Second, FLPMA established generally applicable land management principles, for example, by placing new constraints on land exchanges, § 206, 43 U.S.C. § 1716, and sales, § 203, 43 U.S.C. § 1713, and by specifying the Executive's extra-Constitutional withdrawal authority, § 204, 43 U.S.C. § 1714. *See supra.* Last, it modified predecessor legislation with respect to BLM lands, and to a lesser extent, to lands managed by the Forest Service, by imposing a multiple use regime on those lands as well as by calling for the preparation and use of plans to coordinate management efforts. § 102(8), 43 U.S.C. § 1701(8); § 202, 43 U.S.C. § 1712.

[ii] THE MINERAL LEASING ACT OF 1920

Dissatisfaction with the self-initiation system of the General Mining Law prompted Congress at the turn of the century to look at different ways of allocating mineral resources to the public.

In 1920, it took a major step in this regard by enacting the Mineral Leasing Act ("MLA") of 1920, 30 U.S.C.A. § 181 et seq. The MLA withdrew numerous minerals from the ambit of the GML and applied to them a new allocation system, leasing. The MLA allows for leasing by U.S. citizens, corporations, states, territories, and (for certain minerals) municipalities.

The minerals withdrawn by the MLA include fossil fuels such as oil, gas, oil shale, native asphalt, and bitumen, and chemical minerals such as phosphate, potash, and sodium. Recall, however, that post-MLA legislation has resulted in the withdrawal of minerals from its — the MLA's — reach. *See* chart, *supra.* For example, the Outer Continental Shelf Lands Act of 1953, 43 U.S.C. § 1331 et seq., withdrew offshore oil and gas,[9] and the Geothermal Steam Act of 1970, 30 U.S.C. § 1001 et seq.,withdrew geothermal resources. The Common Varieties Act, 30 U.S.C. § 611, withdrew sand, gravel, cinders, and other common minerals unless of "distinct and special value." *Id.* at § 601. The Federal Coal Leasing Amendments of 1975, 30 U.S.C. § 201 et seq., did the same for coal, and Federal Onshore Oil and Gas Leasing Reform Act of 1987, 30 U.S.C. § 226 et seq., for onshore oil and gas. In the main, these statutes establish leasing mechanisms that depend upon competitive bidding. Under competitive bidding procedures, a party requests the Bureau of Land Management to offer certain lands for leasing, or alternatively, the BLM can decide to do so on its own. Once the offer is publicized, eligible persons submit bids in line with very particularized and exhaustive requirements. The United States may reject all bids if it chooses, and indeed it should do so if all bids are inadequate.

As exemplified by the MLA, the generic differences between these leasing mechanisms and the self-initiation system of the GML are the following:

(1)   leasing systems grant no right of self-initiation to individuals;

(2)   leasing systems secure to the United States royalties, rents, or other payments for leased resources;

(3)   leases contain provisions designed to protect other public resources, and to comply with requirements for environmental protection. Accordingly, lessees must submit operation and reclamation plans and have them approved by the BLM before beginning extraction activities;

(4)   the United States has discretion in choosing the lessee;

(5)   the United States can force lessees to diligently develop the leased resource; and

(6)   the United States has greater authority under leasing mechanisms to manage extraction activities for environmental, land use or other purposes.

Leases vary in duration. Coal leases typically have an initial term of 20 years; competitive oil and gas leases generally have terms of 10 years (up from 5), and noncompetitive leases usually have terms of 10 years as well. In most cases, leases can be extended if the leasehold is producing minerals in commercial quantities. Leases can be cancelled for violations.

Acreage limitations also vary. Oil and gas leases, and geothermal leases, are typically limited to 2560 acres. Oil shale leases may cover up to 5120 acres. No person may secure coal leases so to aggregate a "logical mining unit" greater than 25,000 acres.

---

[9] The OCSLA also withdrew offshore hardrock minerals from the GML, although for understandable reasons these are unimportant players offshore.

Bids normally offer royalties for the federal government, in the range of 12-1/2% to 25% for oil and gas, and perhaps 10% for geothermal steam. Lease bids typically also offer some bonus; it is this bonus that makes for a winning accepted bid, for the royalty percentage is usually fixed in advance of the bidding itself.

While competitive bidding is required at all times under some statutes, the Mineral Leasing Act established a different procedure when minerals to be leased are (if at all) in an area not known to contain such resources. In such cases, a prospecting permit would be issued to the first qualified applicant, who was required to pay a minimal filing fee and the first year's rental (25 cents per acre but not less than $20). The holder of a prospecting permit had to diligently explore for minerals, for the permit was set to expire two years after its issuance (although it could be extended in some circumstances). Moreover, failure to explore constituted grounds for cancellation of the permit. A valuable discovery, however, entitled the permit holder to a "preference-right" on a non-competitive basis, as a reward for the expense and time consumed in the discovery process. These noncompetitive leases returned royalties to the United States at rates established in advance of issuance of the leases, and no bonuses were received from lessees. The noncompetitive leasing system was so rapt with fraud that it was suspended in 1980. The system is no longer available for oil, gas, and coal.

Unlike the case with hardrock minerals, the extraction of fossil fuels on federal lands has climbed in recent years. In 1991, federal coal production stood at 285 million tons; in 1998, it was at 371 million tons. Production of oil and gas on federal lands has increased also, largely due to offshore leasing.

[iii] THE OUTER CONTINENTAL SHELF LANDS ACT

The federal law that controls allocation of minerals on offshore federal land is the Outer Continental Shelf Lands Act of 1953 ("OCSLA"), as amended in 1978, 43 U.S.C.A. § 1331 et seq. There has been fervent interest in securing rights to oil under OCSLA because offshore oil reserves, especially in the Gulf of Mexico and off southern California, are substantial. It has been estimated that about 20 percent of United States production of domestic oil and gas comes from federal lands comprising the Outer Continental Shelf.

Managed by the Mineral Management Service of the U.S. Department of Interior, rights are secured by leasing, and leases are awarded by a process of competitive bidding. OCSLA, however, allows the Secretary of the Interior to try other bidding systems. See Watt v. Energy Action Education Foundation, 454 U.S. 151, 102 S. Ct. 205 (1981).

Securing a lease for offshore oil and gas involves several stages. First, the DOI prepares a five-year leasing plan, which is submitted to Congress and the President for review. Once the plan is in place, DOI holds a lease sale, for which bids are solicited. Affected states may submit recommendations at this stage, and the DOI is constrained to accept them if they strike a reasonable balance between the national interest and the well-being of the state. 43 U.S.C. § 1345(a) (1976 ed., Supp. V) (Local governments are also permitted to submit recommendations, and the Secretary "may" accept these.

43 U.S.C. §§ 1345(a), (c) (1976 ed., Supp. V)). Securing a lease allows the purchaser a right to conduct "preliminary" activities, such as exploration activities that do not cause significant environmental harms. 30 C.F.R. § 250.34-1.

Working in conjunction with OCSLA is the Coastal Zone Management Act ("CZMA") of 1972, 16 U.S.C. § 1451 et seq. An attempt at cooperative federalism, the CZMA incorporates states into the federal decisionmaking process of OCSLA. Under the CZMA, states, helped by federal funding, may fashion management plans for their coastal areas. These plans are then submitted for federal approval to two agencies. The federal Department of Commerce is directed to approve any plan that sufficiently takes into account the national interest in the siting and operation of energy facilities, and the Department of Interior, in its so-called "consistency review" function, must approve state plans if they are compatible with federal land management.

Potential lessees under OCSLA must submit exploration plans to the DOI and have them approved before large-scale exploration is warranted. Exploration plans must certify that proposed extraction activities comport with state management programs prepared under the CZMA. The DOI will disapprove plans that are inconsistent or that would likely result in serious harm to the environment unless the Secretary of Commerce determines to the contrary or finds the exploration plan to be in the interest of national security. 43 U.S.C. § 1340(c)(1)-(2) (1976 ed., Supp. V).

Only after all of this may development and production begin. At this stage yet another plan, and the additional review by affected states and localities that comes with it, is necessary. 43 U.S.C. §§ 1345(a), 1351(a)(3) (1976 ed., Supp. V). *See generally Secretary of the Interior v. California*, 464 U.S. 312, 104 S. Ct. 656 (1983); 43 U.S.C. § 1345(c) (1976 ed., Supp. V).

NOTES

1. Revenues to the federal government for oil extracted from federal lands are based on the value of the oil. Regulations governing valuation of crude oil produced from onshore and offshore federal leases were amended in 2004. 69 Fed. Reg. 24,959 (May 5, 2004).

The Department of Interior conducted 18 oil and gas lease sales for leases in the Gulf of Mexico and offshore of Alaska between 1993 and 1999, resulting in the issuance of more than six thousand leases covering about 35 million acres. For these leases, the government received nearly $5 billion in bonus bids.

As a general matter, mineral leasing revenues are substantial: for fiscal years 1991-2000, they totaled almost $50 billion. In accordance with federal statutes, the federal government shares these revenues. Accordingly, in fiscal year 2000 states received over $840 million out of a total revenue of almost $8 billion, American Indian tribes and allottees received about $235 million, and special funds, including the Historic Preservation Fund and the Land and Water Conservation Fund, received almost $1.6 billion.

2. OCS leases on federal lands within Alaska must comply with the Alaska National Interest Lands Conservation Act ("ANILCA") to protect native

subsistence rights. Under this statute, the government must show that any restriction on subsistence uses is necessary and that reasonable steps are being taken to minimize adverse impacts. Courts have been instructed to balance competing interests in reaching these decisions; the public interest in preserving subsistence resources is one factor in the decisionmaking mix. *See Amoco Production Co. v. Village of Gambell*, 480 U.S. 531, 107 S. Ct. 1396 (1987).

3. There are other federal statutes which affect oceanic resource acquisition and protection. The first is the so-called "Ocean Dumping Act," formally known as the Marine Protection, Research and Sanctuaries Act of 1972 ("MPRSA"). It controls routine dumping of materials into the ocean (as distinct from accidental spills) by means of a permit system administered by the United States Environmental Protection Agency. Second, § 311 of the Clean Water Act penalizes and requires clean-up of accidental or intentional spills. Third is the Oil Pollution Act of 1990, enacted after the Exxon Valdez spill in Alaskan waters.

Federal statutes that protect living species will be covered later in these materials.

4. The predominant legal authority used to challenge federal mineral leasing is the National Environmental Policy Act. *See* Chapter 4, *supra*. (As sarcastically stated by some persons in the energy business, NEPA stands for "no energy project anywhere").

[b] TIMBER LANDS

The national forests comprise approximately one-fourth of all public lands or about 187 million acres. The overwhelming percentage of this land, about 85% or 160 million acres, is found in the western states, including Alaska. Overall, there are 155 national forests in 40 states. The vast majority of federal forest lands are managed by the Forest Service, established in the Department of Agriculture in 1905. (Some of the federal forest lands, particularly in the Pacific Northwest, are managed by the Bureau of Land Management under authority of Federal Land Management and Policy Act of 1976).

In its early years, the Service managed forest lands under the authority of the 1897 Forest Service Organic Act, 16 U.S.C. § 471 et seq., which expressed a threefold purpose for forest management: timber, water, and forest protection. In the first half of the twentieth century, timbering on the public lands was a minor enterprise — most lumber came from private lands.

The years following World War II, however, saw a surge in consumer demand for timber, due in large part to housing needs of returning troops and the post-war baby boom.[11] This demand brought pressure to bear on the national forests unlike anything before. Whereas annual timber production from the national forests in the 1920s was less than one billion board feet, by the 1960s it had spiked to more than twelve times that amount. Bureau

---

[11] For an interesting account of the transformation of America in the middle of the 20th century, including a discussion on the proliferation of tract housing, as typified by "Levittown," a 17,000 cookie-cutter house construction project in Hempstead, Long Island, New York, see David Halberstam, *The Fifties*, at Ch. 9 (Ballantine Books 1993).

of Census, *Historical Statistics of the United States*, Series L 15-23, p. 534 (1970). Subject to this pressure, the Forest Service became a timber production agency. This transformation, in turn, brought on a cascade of objection from the then-forming environmental movement.

A focal point of the national debate was the logging practice known as "even-aged management." Even-aged management involves any of three harvesting methods. The first is clearcutting. Clearcutting is the removal of virtually all trees in a target area, followed by the planting of a replacement stand. It is, in other words, a "clean sweep" method of timber production. The second type, seedtree cutting, is a diluted version of clearcutting. By this method, about ten trees are left in place on each acre of land to produce seeds to regenerate the new stand. Last is shelterwood cutting, which calls for leaving about 20 trees per acre, both for reseeding purposes and to give some protection to new growth. Because even-aged management involves neither the process of selecting each tree to be harvested, nor any significant expertise in the logger, it is remarkably less expensive than traditional "uneven-aged" or "selection" management.

The controversy over even-aged management centers on the environmental consequences of the practice. The pro-conservation community objects strenuously to all forms of even-aged management, and especially clearcutting, in large part for aesthetic reasons — these practices can leave a scarred and torn landscape — but also for classic environmental reasons: even-aged management reduces habitat for certain wildlife species, diminishes soil quality, adds to erosion and sediment pollution, especially when severe slopes are cut, and can lead to uniform replacement forests, made up of trees identical in type and age. The forest industry holds a kinder view of even-aged management. It argues the practice helps much wildlife, including deer, ruffed grouse, bobwhite, and songbirds, by increasing the amount of open space these species need. Beyond that, the industry contends, these practices can rid a forest of infected stands of trees and can help shade-intolerant plants, such as Douglas fir trees, pine trees, aspen, and others. Finally, it asserts, when natural seeding is combined with artificial reforestation, a replacement forest can be diverse, and even genetically superior, to its predecessor. *See, e.g., Clearcutting — The Position of the Society of American Foresters,* available at *http://www/safnet.org/. See also* G. Tyler Miller, Jr., *Living in the Environment* 641 10th ed. (Wadsworth Pub. Co. 1998).[12]

The pitched battle over even-aged management, coupled with the heightened demand for forest products, unavoidably found its way to the halls of Congress. A result was the 1960 Multiple Use — Sustained Yield Act ("MUSYA"), 16 U.S.C. §§ 528-531. While not repealing the Organic Act, the MUSYA established new goals for forest management. The Act designated forests for the multiple uses of recreation, range, timber, watershed, and fish and

---

[12] Some additional websites with clearcutting information: http://www.fs.fed.us (website of the Forest Service of the Department of Agriculture); http://www.nofc.forestry.ca/ (website of Canada Forest Management); and http://www.wvu.edu/~agexten/forestry/clrcut.htm (website of forest industry consultants).

wildlife.[13] The Act stipulated further that forests should be managed for the long term, that is, on a sustained yield basis.[14]

However, announcing multiple use goals and realizing them are two different things, and eliminating even-aged management is another matter entirely. In the view of many observers, the MUSYA did not change forest management in any appreciable way. Even in a multiple use era, the Forest Service was able to designate timber production as the single most important use for the great majority of forest lands.

As it turned out, it was neither MUSYA, nor NEPA, nor the Endangered Species Act (*see* Chapter 7, *infra*) that produced the environmentalists' ringing victory over even-aged management. Instead, it was the original Organic Act. In *West Virginia Div. of Izaak Walton League of America, Inc. v. Butz*, 522 F.2d 945 (4th Cir. 1975), the so-called "Monongahela case" (named after the forest in West Virginia implicated in the facts), plaintiffs charged that clearcutting violated the Organic Act because that legislation called for the culling of "dead, matured, and large growth" trees, as distinct from all trees in a forest, and required, furthermore, that trees be "marked and designated" before cutting. 16 U.S.C. § 476. The Forest Service conceded it was not enforcing these requirements, but argued essentially that the requirements should be ignored as inappropriate and unworkable. The court rejected the contention:

> Economic exigencies . . . do not grant the courts a license to rewrite a statute no matter how desirable the purpose or result might be. "If the words of the statute are clear, the court should not add to or alter them to accomplish a purpose that does not appear on the face of the statute or from its legislative history." [Citation omitted]

> We are not insensitive to the fact that our reading of the Organic Act will have serious and far-reaching consequences, and it may well be that this legislation enacted over seventy-five years ago is an anachronism which no longer serves the public interest. However, the appropriate forum to resolve this complex and controversial issue is not the courts but the Congress. The controlling principle was stated in *United States v. City and County of San Francisco*, 310 U.S. 16, 29-30, 84 L. Ed. 1050, 60 S. Ct. 749 (1940):

---

[13] The Act defined "multiple use" as "the management of all the various renewable surface resources of the national forests so that they are utilized in the combination that will best meet the needs of the American people; making the most judicious use of the land for some or all of these resources or related services over areas large enough to provide sufficient latitude for periodic adjustments in use to conform to changing needs and conditions; that some land will be used for less than all of the resources; and harmonious and coordinated management of the various resources, each with the other, without impairment of the productivity of the land, with consideration being given to the relative value of the various resources, and not necessarily the combination of uses that will give the greatest dollar return or the greatest unit output." MUSYA § 4(a), 16 U.S.C. § 531 (a).

[14] The Act defined "sustained yield of the several products and services" as "the achievement and maintenance in perpetuity of a high-level annual or regular periodic output of the various renewable resources of the national forests without impairment of the productivity of the land." MUSYA § 4(b), 16 U.S.C. § 531(b).

Article 4, § 3, Cl. 2 of the Constitution provides that "The Congress shall have Power to dispose of and make all needful Rules and Regulations respecting the Territory and other Property belonging to the United States." The power over the public land thus entrusted to Congress is without limitations. "And it is not for the courts to say how that trust shall be administered. That is for Congress."(footnotes omitted).

Id. at 954–55.

The Forest Service chose not to appeal the decision to the Supreme Court.

In 1976, Congress repealed the Organic Act and replaced it with the National Forest Management Act of 1976, 16 U.S.C. § 1604 et seq. The NFMA imposed a tighter management regime on the Forest Service, but it still authorized a limited use of even-aged management practices. No longer may even-aged management be undertaken in disregard of habitat requirements of fish and widlife. *See, e.g., Sierra Club v. Peterson,* 185 F.3d 349 (5th Cir. 1999).

The NFMA was part of a triple whammy imposed on the timber industry in the early 1970s. In 1970, Congress had passed the National Environmental Policy Act. NEPA required federal agencies, including the Forest Service, to examine and explain proposed actions in environmental impact statements, and provided an independent ground for challenging Forest Service decisions. *See* Chapter 4, *supra.* In 1976, Congress enacted the Endangered Species Act ("ESA"), the substantive requirements of which have independently restricted and, in many circumstances, eliminated logging operations in order to protect species of animals or plants falling under its umbrella of protection. *See* Chapter 7, *infra.* Together, and with the assistance of the Wilderness Act of 1964, these statutory tools have reduced timber production on federal lands enormously. Whereas in the 1980s timber production on federal lands approximated 10-12 billion board feet per year, the yield as of 2000 was 3-4 billion board feet.

The most significant political development involving national forests involves the designation of much of it for wilderness uses. Recall the preceding discussion of the requirement imposed on the Forest Service by the Wilderness Act to determine which forest areas, if any, should be included in the National Wilderness Preservation System. The Service undertook the task by examining "roadless areas" within the forests, specifically those larger than 5000 acres in size or adjacent to areas already designated as wilderness. Roadless areas were selected for this purpose because, at least on a categorical basis, they offer the greatest potential for future membership in the wilderness system. As described by the Forest Service, roadless areas:

provide clean drinking water and function as biological strongholds for populations of threatened and endangered species. They provide large, relatively undisturbed landscapes that are important to biological diversity and the long-term survival of many at-risk species. Inventoried roadless areas provide opportunities for dispersed outdoor recreation, opportunities that diminish as open space and natural settings are developed elsewhere. They also serve as bulwarks against the spread of non-native invasive plant species and provide reference areas for study and research.

66 Fed. Reg. 3445 (Jan. 12, 2001).

The Service's efforts in this regard, known as "RARE II" ("roadless area review and evaluation"), produced significant results. Whereas the Wilderness Act itself declared 9.1 million acres of forest land to be wilderness effective upon enactment, the RARE II process resulted in the addition of about 26 million more acres, so that as of 2000 about 18% of the national forest system is wilderness. *Remarks of Prof. Joseph Feller,* ALI-ABA Conference on Environmental Law, Bethesda, Md. (Feb. 8, 2001.)

Thus, the breakdown is fundamentally as follows: 51% of inventoried forest lands is designated as roaded areas (roughly 93 million acres); 18% is wilderness (roughly 35 million acres); and the remaining 31% is roadless non-wilderness (roughly 58.5 million acres). *Id.*

This last 31% has been the focus of controversy. Industry wants a "hard release" of these areas to make them available for timbering. Environmentalists, on the other hand, want additional wilderness designations. After considerable wrangling, the Forest Service took its stand on the controversy in what is known as the Roadless Area Conservation Rule. 33 C.F.R. Part 294 (2001). The Rule imposes a general prohibition on both road building and timber production on the entirety of the inventoried roadless non-wilderness lands. Thus, it applies to over 49 million acres in the Pacific Northwest and another 9.3 million acres in the Tongass National Forest in Alaska.* The Rule provides for narrow exceptions to the road construction ban: (a) to protect health and safety in cases of imminent threat by flood, fire, or other catastrophic event; (b) to facilitate environmental clean-up efforts; (c) in recognition of independent rights arising by statute or treaty; (d) to prevent resource damage by an existing road; (e) to rectify existing hazardous road conditions for roads that either are part of a Federal Aid Highway project or are needed in connection with a mineral lease. There are narrow exceptions as well to the timber ban: trees may be removed: (a) if small diameter, to maintain or improve forest characteristics and to improve species habitat or the ecosystem composition; (b) if incidental to a management activity otherwise not prohibited; (c) for personal or administrative use; or (d) where roadless characteristics of the removal area were substantially altered before the publication date of the rule.

The future status of the Rule is in doubt. A district court in the Tenth Circuit struck it down, although the Court of Appeals for the 9th Circuit upheld it. More significantly, in July, 2004, the Bush Administration formally proposed scuttling the Rule. 69 Fed. Reg. 42636 (July 16, 2004). The Bush proposal aims to increase the participation of states in wilderness decisions. Under the terms of the proposal, a governor may petition the Forest Service to expand or reduce roadless area protection or to keep it as is. State petitions would be evaluated and, if approved, the Forest Service would initiate subsequent state-specific

---

* Senator Frank Murkowski of Alaska called the inclusion of the Tongass National Forest under this ban an "outrageous affront." "This administration wants to revise the Tongass plan as often as the Vice President wants to count ballots in Florida," he complained.

rulemaking to address the petition. While the Secretary would make any final decision on the rulemaking, the entire process would undertaken in coordination with the affected state. *Id.* The Bush Administration characterized this proposed rule as entirely procedural in nature, but environmentalists have criticized it as a not-so-veiled attempt to facilitate more logging.

[c] GRAZING LANDS

Approximately three-fourths of federal land has been used for grazing. Often inadequately monitored, grazing has resulted in a good deal of environmental degradation, in the form of erosion, ecosystem destruction, and water pollution.

An accusation commonly made is that the formula used to compute grazing fees systematically keeps those fees at below market value and, thereby, encourages overgrazing. (Note that the Federal Land Policy and Management Act stipulates the government should receive fair market value for lands and resources it disposes to the public. 43 U.S.C. § 1701(a)(9)). The House Government Operations Committee asserted in 1992 that the government had lost about $118 billion in revenues by pricing its grazing fees below market value. Efforts of the Clinton administration to increase grazing fees were no match for the opposition of Senators from the western states.

Do artificially low fees encourage overgrazing? As the chart below demonstrates, grazing on public lands, as measured in "animal unit months" ("AUMs"), has been in decline for many years:

ACTUAL GRAZING USE IN AUMs
USDI-BLM Lands, 1953 to 1998

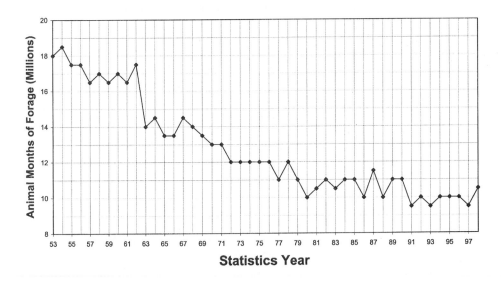

Grazing on federal land was a customary practice long before the enactment of federal legislation specifically regulating it. In *Buford v. Houtz*, 133 U.S. 320, 10 S. Ct. 305 (1890), the Supreme Court ratified the practice:

We are of opinion that there is an implied license, growing out of the custom of nearly a hundred years, that the public lands of the United States, especially those in which the native grasses are adapted to the growth and fattening of domestic animals, shall be free to the people who seek to use them where they are left open and unenclosed, and no act of government forbids this use. * * * The government of the United States, in all its branches, has known of this use, has never forbidden it, nor taken any steps to arrest it. No doubt it may be safely stated that this has been done with the consent of all branches of the government, and, as we shall attempt to show, with its direct encouragement.

The whole system of the control of the public lands of the United States as it had been conducted by the government, under acts of Congress, shows a liberality in regard to their use which has been uniform and remarkable. They have always been open to sale at very cheap prices. Laws have been enacted authorizing persons to settle upon them, and to cultivate them, before they acquire any title to them. While in the incipiency of the settlement of these lands, by persons entering upon them, the permission to do so was a tacit one, the exercise of this permission became so important that Congress, by a system of laws, called the preemption laws, recognized this right so far as to confer a priority of the right of purchase on the persons who settled upon and cultivated any part of this public domain. During the time that the settler was perfecting his title, by making the improvements which that statute required and paying, by installments or otherwise, the money necessary to purchase it, both he and all other persons who desired to do so had full liberty to graze their stock upon the grasses of the prairies and upon other untritious [sic] substances found upon the soil.

The value of this privilege grew as the population increased, and it became a custom for persons to make a business or pursuit of gathering herds of cattle or sheep, and raising them and fattening them for market upon these unenclosed lands of the government of the United States. Of course the instances became numerous in which persons purchasing land from the United States put only a small part of it in cultivation, and permitted the balance to remain unenclosed and in no way separated from the lands owned by the United States. All the neighbors who had settled near one of these prairies or on it, and all the people who had cattle that they wished to graze upon the public lands, permitted them to run at large over the whole region, fattening upon the public lands of the United States, and upon the unenclosed lands of the private individual, without let or hindrance. The owner of a piece of land, who had built a house or enclosed twenty or forty acres of it, had the benefit of this universal custom, as well as the party who owned no land. Everybody used the open unenclosed country, which produced nutritious grasses, as a public common on which their horses, cattle, hogs and sheep could run and graze.

Id. at 326-28, 10 S. Ct. at 307-08.

Federal regulation of grazing on public lands did not come in any overarching form until enactment of the Taylor Grazing Act ("TGA") of 1934, 43 U.S.C. § 315 et seq. Characterized as an act "to stop injury to the public grazing lands by preventing overgrazing and soil deterioration, to provide for their orderly use, improvement and development, to stabilize the livestock industry dependent upon the public range, and for other purposes," the Act was by design a multiple-use statute. 48 Stat. 1269.

The TGA was enacted in large part to curtail the deteriorization of range conditions, but in the view of many, the BLM has implemented it much more for ranchers than for environmental quality.

The TGA remains the governing legislation to this day. The Act calls for the establishment of grazing districts and gives preference rights for grazing on districted lands to landowners, settlers, and water rights holders on or near the districts themselves. Grazing permits last for a maximum of ten years, but notably, in contrast with the mineral laws, "the issuance of a permit . . . shall not create any right, title, interest, or estate in or to the lands." § 3, 48 Stat. 1271.

Grazing is now subject to latter-enacted statutes as well. The National Environmental Policy Act (see Chapter 4, supra), of course, is one. In addition, certain provisions of the Federal Land Policy and Management Act of 1976 apply to grazing. FLPMA, however, is respectful of grazing rights secured pursuant to the TGA. Section 1752(h) of FLPMA provides that "[n]othing in this Act shall be construed as modifying in any way law existing on [FLPMA's enactment date] with respect to the creation of right, title, interest, or estate in or to the public lands or lands in National Forests by issuance of grazing permits and leases." If anything, FLPMA enhances grazing rights by allowing compensation for ranchers who have installed "permanent improvements" on the public land when their grazing rights are cancelled. Id. at § 43 U.S.C. § 1752(g).

For an interesting review of the history of grazing and of some current issues, see Public Lands Council v. Babbitt, 529 U.S. 728, 120 S. Ct. 1815 (2000). Public Lands Council is the first federal lands/grazing decision from the United States Supreme Court in more than twenty-five years.

See also, Joseph M. Feller, Back to the Present: The Supreme Court Refuses to Move Public Range Law Backward, but Will the BLM Move Public Range Management Forward?, 31 Envt'l L. Rep. 10021 (2001). In December, 2003, the Department of the Interior proposed new regulations to govern grazing on public lands. 68 Fed. Reg. 68,452 (Dec. 8, 2003). For a negative review of the proposed regulations, see Joseph M. Feller, The BLM's Proposed New Grazing Regulations: Serving the Most Special Interest, 24 Journal of Land, Resources, and Envt'l Law 241 (2004).

* * * * * *

In addition to forage, livestock need water. There was considerable concern in early years that a relatively few stockraisers might secure rights to water under state law, and thereby de facto secure for themselves the exclusive benefit of public lands. Recognizing this possibility, the government acted to keep water available to all stockraisers. In § 10 of the Stock Raising Homestead Act, Congress provided:

> That lands containing water holes or other bodies of water needed or used by the public for watering purposes shall not be designated under this Act [for entry] but may be reserved under the provisions of the [Pickett] Act . . ., and such land heretofore or hereafter reserved shall, while so reserved, be kept and held open to the public use for such purposes under such general rules and regulations as the Secretary of the Interior may prescribe.

Pub. L. No. 64-290, § 10, 30 Stat. 862, 865 (1917).

Ten years later, President Calvin Coolidge issued an executive order accomplishing the withdrawal:

> Under and pursuant to the provisions of the [Pickett] Act . . . it is hereby ordered that every smallest legal subdivision of the public-land surveys which is vacant unappropriated unreserved public land and contains a spring or water hole, and all land within one quarter of a mile of every spring or water hole located on unsurveyed public land be, and the same is hereby, withdrawn from settlement, location, sale, or entry, and reserved for public use in accordance with the provisions of Section 10 of [the Stock Raising Homestead Act], and in aid of pending legislation.

Selections, 51 Land Dec. at 457 (quoting Exec. Or. Pub. Water Reserve No. 107 (April 17, 1926)). *See generally* James Muhn, *Public Water Reserves: The Metamorphosis of a Public Land Policy*, 21 J. Land, Resources & Envtl. L. 67 (2001).

[d] RECREATION AND WILDLIFE LANDS

The last category of federal lands we examine are recreation and wildlife lands. The recreation lands of the United States are the national parks and monuments (and sundry other parcels — *see infra*). The wildlife lands are the national wildlife refuges. Note that multiple use lands, such as mineral and timber lands, can serve recreation and wildlife interests. Multiple use lands, however, are not limited to those uses.

[i] NATIONAL PARK SYSTEM

By recent tally, there are 384 national park units comprising more than 80 million acres. The National Park System has been assembled by Congressional action and by use of revenues from the Land and Water Conservation Fund, 16 U.S.C. §§ 460l-4 to 4601-11, established in 1965 and itself funded largely by royalties from offshore oil and gas leasing.

[a] NATIONAL PARKS

The national parks are often referred to as the jewels of the federal lands. The first national park, Yellowstone Park in northwest Wyoming, is stunning for its geysers and thermal pools. Glacier National Park of Montana offers breathtaking views of the untamed Rocky Mountains. Yosemite National Park represents the best California has to offer. The largest national park is the Wrangell–St. Elias National Park and Preserve in Alaska. Encompassing more than 13,200,000 acres, this single park accounts for more than 16% of the entire National Park System.

The national parks are managed by the National Park Service of the U.S. Department of Interior under its organic legislation, the National Park Service Organic Act, 16 U.S.C. § 1 et seq. The Act calls for management of the parks, as well as of national monuments, *see infra,* and other recreation lands, "to conserve the scenery and the natural and historic objects and the wild life therein and to provide for the enjoyment of the same in such manner and by such means as will leave them unimpaired for the enjoyment of future generations." *Id.* The Act characterizes the parks as "distinct in character" but still forming one system of public lands "as cumulative expressions of a single national heritage. . . ." 16 U.S.C. § 1a-1. The Act prohibits hunting as a general matter, but allows fishing, with the proviso that fish be released back into the waters. 16 U.S.C. § 3201; 36 C.F.R. §§ 2.2, 2.3. Mining is prohibited in the parks, although mining rights that predate park designations are honored. 36 C.F.R. Part 9. While the Organic Act is the organizing principle for the parks, still each park is subject to its own set of particularized directives.[16] The NPS regulations governing the parks are located at 36 C.F.R. § 1.1 et seq.

The Park Service has managed its lands by using general management plans. The plans must include, but not be limited to:

(1) measures for the preservation of the area's resources;

(2) indications of the types and general intensities of development (including visitor circulation and transportation patterns, systems and modes) associated with public enjoyment and use of the area, including general locations, timing of implementation, and anticipated costs;

(3) identification of and implementation commitments for visitor carrying capacities for all areas of the unit; and

(4) indications of potential modifications to the external boundaries of the unit, and the reasons therefor.

16 U.S.C. § 1a-7(b).

Managing the parks can be difficult, largely because the Organic Act obligates the NPS to pursue contradictory ends. The Service must simultaneously protect the parks from impairment and facilitate what has become an intense level of public use. The consensus is that parks and other federal recreational lands have suffered impairment in recent years. As part of the effort to reverse this slide, a demonstration project was established to allow the NPS to retain visitor fees collected at various units of the park system, rather than lose those revenues to the federal treasury. Under the program, 80% of collected fees were made available to improve the site at which the fees were collected. This new revenue stream resulted in access and infrastructure improvements without markedly affecting the numbers of visitors.

---

[16] The index to the Organic Act, which gives citations to these specific authorities for the many subunits of the park system, runs almost 60 pages.

[b] NATIONAL MONUMENTS

National monuments are *de facto* national parks. They are created by action of the President in accordance with the American Antiquities Preservation Act, 34 Stat. 225, 16 U.S.C. § 431 ("Antiquities Act"). Enacted in 1906, this statute proclaims that:

> The President of the United States is authorized, in his discretion, to declare by public proclamation historic landmarks, historic and prehistoric structures, and other objects of historic or scientific interest that are situated upon the lands owned or controlled by the Government of the United States to be national monuments, and may reserve as a part thereof parcels of land, the limits of which in all cases shall be confined to the smallest area compatible with the proper care and management of the objects to be protected.

16 U.S.C. § 431.

Various Presidents have used this authority to establish, in the aggregate, more than 100 monuments in 24 states and the Virgin Islands, covering some 70 million acres or about 10% of all federal lands. National monuments can be on a small scale — President Bill Clinton, for example, designated Abraham Lincoln's summer retreat as a monument. They can be large as well: the Grand Canyon started out as a national monument. Also designated under the Act: Death Valley and Muir Woods in California; Glacier Bay, Misty Fjords, and Admiralty Island in Alaska; the Grand Tetons in Wyoming; portions of Washington's Olympic Peninsula; and Utah's Bryce and Zion canyons. Like the Grand Canyon, some of these have since been designated as national parks. In 1978, President Jimmy Carter used the Antiquities Act to set aside more than 50 million acres of federal land in Alaska, lands which later received statutory protection by virtue of the Alaska National Interest Lands Conservation Act. Presidents Ronald Reagan and George H. Bush were the only Presidents in the history of the statute *not* to create a national monument.[17]

President Bill Clinton was singularly active in using the Antiquities Act. He designated more land as national monuments in the lower 48 states than any president preceding him. His most significant reservation occurred on September 18, 1996, when he used the Antiquities Act to reserve the Grand Staircase–Escalante National Monument, an expanse of 1.7 million acres of federal lands in southern Utah, second only in size in the lower 48 states to Death Valley. The reservation was particularly controversial, not only because it came during the heat of a presidential election campaign, but also because it was done without consultation with state officials or the public.

Several legal questions remain almost 100 years after the enactment of the Antiquities Act. First is whether the statute was repealed with the enactment of FLPMA in 1976. There has been no judicial ruling to this effect, and with designations continuing apace since 1976, there is little indication that

---

[17] An interesting side note: since 1950, because of the flap caused by President Franklin Roosevelt's reservation of the Grand Tetons, no additional monuments can be created in Wyoming under the Antiquities Act without Congressional authorization. 16 U.S.C. § 431a. This provision is the only amendment to the Act in its history.

Congress finds merit with the idea. Second is the question of the size of designated parcels. The Antiquities Act stipulates that monument boundaries "shall be confined to the smallest area compatible with the proper care and management of the objects to be protected." 16 U.S.C. § 431. Yet, as we have seen, national monuments on numerous occasions are anything but confined. A third question goes to management. The National Park Service Organic Act, 16 U.S.C. § 1 et seq., designates the National Park Service as the managing agency for national monuments, yet several Clinton directives have purported to leave management authority with the BLM or FS, the agencies in charge before designation. A last issue is revocability. May a monument established by Presidential proclamation be de-designated by subsequent proclamation? This issue has received a good bit of play since the advent of the new Bush Administration. *See, e.g.,* BNA Daily Environment Report, Jan. 5, 2001. The judiciary has never ruled on the question, although an early opinion of the U.S. Department of Justice indicated the President lacks revocation authority. *Proposed Abolishment of Castle Pinckney National Monument*, 39 U.S. Opp. Atty. Gen. 185 (1938) ("[T]he Executive can no more destroy his own authorized work, without some other legislative sanction, than any other person can. To assert such a principle is to claim for the Executive the power to repeal or alter an act of Congress at will.").

Cf. Midwest Oil, supra.

[c] OTHER FEDERAL LANDS

Lands in the National Park System are not limited to parks and monuments. The System includes other lands as well, lands that go by a variety of names and are difficult to categorize. Diverse in character and size (the smallest unit of these is the Thaddeus Kosciuszko National Memorial in Pennsylvania, comprising about 1/50 of an acre), these lands may fall, at least in a formal sense, under one of the land categories we have already encountered.

The following material, largely taken from the website of the Department of Interior, lists these diverse areas and gives a short explanation of each:

ALTERNATIVE LAND DESIGNATIONS IN THE NATIONAL PARK SYSTEM

National Preserve: National preserves are areas having characteristics associated with national parks, but in which Congress has permitted continued public hunting, trapping, oil/gas exploration and extraction. Many existing national preserves, without sport hunting, would qualify for national park designation.

National Historic Site: Usually, a national historic site contains a single historical feature that was directly associated with its subject. Derived from the Historic Sites Act of 1935, a number of historic sites were established by secretaries of the Interior, but most have been authorized by acts of Congress.

National Historical Park: This designation generally applies to historic parks that extend beyond single properties or buildings.

National Memorial: A national memorial is commemorative of an historic person or episode; it need not occupy a site historically connected with its subject.

National Battlefield: This general title includes national battlefield, national battlefield park, national battlefield site, and national military park. In 1958, an NPS committee recommended "national battlefield" as the single title for all such park lands.

National Cemetery: There are presently 14 national cemeteries in the National Park System, all of which are administered in conjunction with an associated unit and are not accounted for separately.

National Recreation Area: Twelve NRAs in the system are centered on large reservoirs and emphasize water-based recreation. Five other NRAs are located near major population centers. Such urban parks combine scarce open spaces with the preservation of significant historic resources and important natural areas in location that can provide outdoor recreation for large numbers of people.

National Seashore: Ten national seashores have been established on the Atlantic, Gulf and Pacific coasts; some are developed and some are relatively primitive. Hunting is allowed at many of these sites.

National Lakeshore: National lakeshores, all on the Great Lakes, closely parallel the seashores in character and use.

National River: There are several variations to this category: national river and recreation area, national scenic river, wild river, etc. The first was authorized in 1964 and others were established following passage of the Wild and Scenic Rivers Act of 1968, 16 U.S.C. § 1271 et seq.

National Parkway: The title parkway refers to a roadway and the parkland paralleling the roadway. All were intended for scenic motoring along a protected corridor and often connect cultural sites.

National Trail: National scenic trails and national historic trails are the titles given to these linear parklands (over 3,600 miles) authorized under the National Trails System Act of 1968.

National Fish Hatcheries: There are 66 of these. They produce 160 million fish valued at $5 billion.

Affiliated Areas: In an Act of August 18, 1970, the National Park System was defined in law as, "any area of land and water now or hereafter administered by the Secretary of the Interior through the National Park Service for park, monument, historic, parkway, recreational or other purposes." The Affiliated Areas comprise a variety of locations in the United States and Canada that preserve significant properties outside the National Park System. Some of these have been recognized by Acts of Congress, others have been designated national historic sites by the Secretary of the Interior under authority of the Historic Sites Act of 1935. All draw on technical or financial aid from the National Park Service.

[ii] NATIONAL WILDLIFE REFUGES

The National Wildlife Refuge System is a collection of federal lands designated as havens for wildlife. President Theodore Roosevelt established the first refuge in 1903 on Pelican Island in Florida. Congress approved the President's action, and Roosevelt went on to designate fifty more refuges. The refuge system grew again in the 1930s as hunters became increasingly concerned about waterfowl losses caused by wetlands reductions and drought. As of 2000, there were 509 wildlife refuges comprising approximately 92 million acres in all fifty states and territories of the nation. Some refuges are tiny; the largest is the Arctic National Wildlife Refuge, which covers 19.6 million acres of northeast Alaska. Hunting is allowed in 283 refuges and fishing in 276. About 29 million people visit refuges each year. Refuges are managed by the United States Fish and Wildlife Service of the Department of Interior. It was not until the enactment of the National Wildlife Refuge System Administration Act of 1966 that the refuges were consolidated into a system, with a somewhat uniform management regime. The NWRSAA directs the Fish and Wildlife Service to "administer a national network of lands and waters for the conservation, management, and where appropriate, restoration of the fish, wildlife, and plant resources and their habitats within the United States." § 4(a)(2), 16 U.S.C. § 668dd(a)(2).

The major difficulty for refuge managers is determining which uses to allow. The NWRSAA expressly permits hunting, fishing, and other recreational uses on refuge lands but only if they are "compatible with" the overarching conservation purpose. § 4(d)(1), 16 U.S.C. § 688dd(d)(1). The issue is what uses are compatible. In fact, the agency's compatibility determinations have come under fire. One legal challenge brought by the National Audubon Society resulted in a settlement requiring an end to all secondary refuge uses unless and until a determination was made, in writing, that the uses were, in fact, compatible. Settlement in hand, the Service proceeded to inventory over 500 refuges and over 50 uses, and found a wide array of permitted secondary pursuits: walking, hiking, and backpacking were allowed on more than 130 refuges; hunting was allowed on more than 220; wildlife observation, photography, environmental education, and interpretation were undertaken on more than 300 refuges; and power boating, jetskiing, horseback riding, and camping were allowed on more than 100. *See* 1997 U.S. Code and Administrative News 1798-7 to 1798-8.

This litigation and the resultant inventory prompted the Congress to enact the National Wildlife Refuge System Improvement Act ("NWRSIA") of 1997. Thus did the Fish and Wildlife Service finally receive an "organic law" to call its own, joining the ranks of the Forest Service and the National Park Service, *inter alia*. The NWRSIA attempts to impose some uniformity into refuge management by shoring up defects of the 1966 legislation. The NWRSIA begins by reemphasizing conservation of wildlife and plants as the primary use for all refuges, and in that regard calls for refuge-by-refuge comprehensive conservation plans. The Act addresses the matter of compatible uses as well. It defines "compatible use" as "a wildlife-dependent recreational use or any other use of a refuge that, in the sound professional judgment of the Director, will not materially interfere with or detract from the fulfillment of the mission of the System or the purposes of the refuge." § 5(1), 16 U.S.C. § 668ee(1). A "wildlife-dependent recreational use" is, in turn, defined as "use of a refuge involving hunting, fishing, wildlife observation and photography, or environmental education and preservation." § 5(2), 16 U.S.C. § 688ee(2). Among compatible uses, wildlife-dependent uses are slated to receive priority over all other compatible uses. § 4(a)(3)(C), 16 U.S.C. § 688dd(a)(3)(C). Thus, to the extent that mineral or timber production, grazing, power boating, horse-back riding, and other pursuits might be compatible at all, they are relatively disfavored. Rights to undertake compatible uses on wildlife refuges are secured by permit. The Fish and Wildlife Service's regulations implementing the NWRSIA are located at 50 C.F.R. Part 25.

The refuges are financially supported by revenues from sale of Duck Stamps and by user fees.

Chapter 6

THE PUBLIC TRUST DOCTRINE

———

"There is a limit to the number of lands of shorelines on the lakes; there is a limit to the number of lakes in existence; there is a limit to the mountainous area of the world, and . . . there are portions of natural scenic beauty . . . which of a right should be the property of all people." — *Arthur Carhart*

A. INTRODUCTION

In its classic form, the public trust doctrine is a restraint on government power both narrow in scope and dramatic in effect. It provides that title in lands submerged by navigable waters may not be alienated to private ownership if doing so would frustrate public use of the lands and, more importantly, of the waters that overlie them. *See Illinois Central Railroad v. Illinois*, 146 U.S. 387, 13 S. Ct. 110 (1892) (*infra*). Any such purported transfer is revocable if not invalid *ab initio*.

The public trust doctrine derives its historical roots from ancient Roman law, which categorized natural resources by function. Roman property law divided real property into categories which in turn determined the rights of individuals and the public at large to use the lands. *See, e.g.*, Richard Ausness, *Water Rights, The Public Trust Doctrine, and the Protection of Instream Uses*, 1986 U. Ill. L. Rev. 407, 407–9. In Rome, property other than conventional private property (held by persons in their individual capacities), fell into three major classifications. Some properties were *res nullius*, viewed as belonging to no-one. Other properties were *res publicae*, belonging to the state. Still other property was *res communes*, belonging to everyone. *See, e.g.*, Frank J. Trelease, *Government Ownership and Trusteeship of Water*, 45 Calif. L. Rev. 638, 640 (1957). The so-called *res communes* lands were so highly valued in the Roman system that individual members of the public, despite the lack of formal title, could bring legal proceedings to protect them from destructive private action. Jan S. Stevens, *The Public Trust: A Sovereign's Ancient Prerogative Becomes the People's Environmental Right*, 14 U.C. Davis L. Rev. 195, n.3 (1980).[1]

---

[1] Additional minor classifications existed also. Some property was *res universitatis*, belonging to a corporate body rather than to any one individual. *See* T. Sandars, *The Institutes of Justinian*

These principles of Roman law migrated to England. In England, *res communes* resources could include land, seas, seashores, air, and running water. Title to these resources (excepting, perhaps, air), however, lay in the powerful royalty, which had secured these property interests during feudalism. Thus was created a problem: royalty could royally squander these resources. To avert such indiscretions, an arrangement was finally worked out, by which ascendants to the throne were compelled to manage these especially valued resources in trust for the public. Thus was the protection of public resources molded into a "trust" form, a form which substantially circumscribed, in this specific context, the common law-based land use and disposal powers normally enjoyed by holders of fee interests in property. To the extent that private property rights were limited, public rights were enhanced.

With the passage of time, the public trust doctrine waned in England. Nonetheless, it traveled quietly to America with the early settlers. The doctrine's presence on these shores became known when state courts invoked it to adjudicate private disputes over riverbeds. The first decision announcing a common law-based public trust doctrine was *Arnold v. Mundy*, 6 N.J.L. 1 (1821), a New Jersey Supreme Court decision involving claims to oysters planted in a riverbed. The plaintiff in *Arnold* claimed property rights to the streambed and to the oysters he had planted there based on an unbroken chain of title running from the time of creation of the state. The court, however, held that title to the streambed, and hence to the oysters, lay in the state because the public trust doctrine nullified the initial transfer upon which plaintiff's chain of title depended. *Id.* at 14. As the court termed it, a transfer of property rights away from the state "would be contrary to the great principles of our constitution, and never could be borne by a free people." *Id.* at 13. (The New Jersey courts later overruled *Arnold,* in *Gough v. Bell*, 22 N.J.L. 441, *aff'd* 23 N.J.L. 624 (1852)).

B. *ILLINOIS CENTRAL*

The public trust doctrine received its greatest boost, when the United States Supreme Court weighed in.

ILLINOIS CENTRAL RAILROAD v. ILLINOIS

146 U.S. 387, 13 S. Ct. 110 (1892)

MR. JUSTICE FIELD delivered the opinion of the court.

This suit was commenced on the 1st of March, 1883, in a Circuit Court of Illinois, by an information or bill in equity, filed by the Attorney General of

160 (1876). *See also* Coquillette, *Mosses from an Old Manse: Another Look at Some Historic Property Cases About the Environment,* 12 Land Use and Environment L. Rev. 67 (1981). Other properties in Roman law were *res sacrae* or *res religiosae,* properties devoted to service of God, and *res sanctae,* properties such as city gates and walls which needed special protection. *Id.* at 82. *See also* Richard J. Lazarus, *Changing Conceptions of Property and Sovereignty in Natural Resources: Questioning the Public Trust Doctrine,* 71 Iowa L. Rev. 631, 633–5 (1986).

the State, in the name of its people against the Illinois Central Railroad Company, a corporation created under its laws, and against the city of Chicago. The United States were also named as a party defendant, but they never appeared in the suit, and it was impossible to bring them in as a party without their consent. The alleged grievances arose solely from the acts and claims of the railroad company, but the city of Chicago was made a defendant because of its interest in the subject of the litigation.

The object of the suit is to obtain a judicial determination of the title of certain lands on the east or lake front of the city of Chicago, situated between the Chicago River and Sixteenth street, which have been reclaimed from the waters of the lake, and are occupied by the tracks, depots, warehouses, piers and other structures used by the railroad company in its business; and also of the title claimed by the company to the submerged lands, constituting the bed of the lake, lying east of its tracks, within the corporate limits of the city, for the distance of a mile, and between the south line of the south pier near Chicago River extended eastwardly, and a line extended, in the same direction, from the south line of lot 21 near the company's round-house and machine shops. The determination of the title of the company will involve a consideration of its right to construct, for its own business, as well as for public convenience, wharves, piers and docks in the harbor.

We agree with the court below that, to a clear understanding of the numerous questions presented in this case, it was necessary to trace the history of the title to the several parcels of land claimed by the company. And the court, in its elaborate opinion, (33 Fed. Rep. 730) for that purpose referred to the legislation of the United States and of the State, and to ordinances of the city and proceedings thereunder, and stated, with great minuteness of detail, every material provision of law and every step taken. We have with great care gone over the history detailed and are satisfied with its entire accuracy. It would, therefore, serve no useful purpose to repeat what is, in our opinion, clearly and fully narrated. In what we may say of the rights of the railroad company, of the State, and of the city, remaining after the legislation and proceedings taken, we shall assume the correctness of that history.

The State of Illinois was admitted into the Union in 1818 on an equal footing with the original States in all respects. Such was one of the conditions of the cession from Virginia of the territory northwest of the Ohio River, out of which the State was formed. But the equality prescribed would have existed if it had not been thus stipulated. There can be no distinction between the several States of the Union in the character of the jurisdiction, sovereignty and dominion which they may possess and exercise over persons and subjects within their respective limits. The boundaries of the State were prescribed by Congress and accepted by the State in its original Constitution. They are given in the bill. It is sufficient for our purpose to observe that they include within their eastern line all that portion of Lake Michigan lying east of the main land of the State and the middle of the lake south of latitude forty-two degrees and thirty minutes. . . .

. . . .

The case proceeds upon the theory and allegation that the defendant, the Illinois Central Railroad Company, has, without lawful authority, encroached, and continues to encroach, upon the domain of the State, and its original ownership and control of the waters of the harbor and of the lands thereunder, upon a claim of rights acquired under a grant from the State and ordinance of the city to enter the city and appropriate land and water two hundred feet wide in order to construct a track for a railway, and to erect thereon warehouses, piers and other structures in front of the city, and upon a claim of riparian rights acquired by virtue of ownership of lands originally bordering on the lake in front of the city. It also proceeds against the claim asserted by the railroad company of a grant by the State, in 1869, of its right and title to the submerged lands, constituting the bed of Lake Michigan lying east of the tracks and breakwater of the company, for the distance of one mile, and between the south line of the south pier extended eastwardly and a line extended in the same direction from the south line of lot twenty-one south of and near the machine shops and round-house of the company; and of a right thereby to construct at its pleasure, in the harbor, wharves, piers and other works for its use.

The State prays a decree establishing and confirming its title to the bed of Lake Michigan and exclusive right to develop and improve the harbor of Chicago by the construction of docks, wharves, piers and other improvements, against the claim of the railroad company, that it has an absolute title to such submerged lands by the act of 1869, and the right, subject only to the paramount authority of the United States in the regulation of commerce, to fill all the bed of the lake within the limits above stated, for the purpose of its business; and the right, by the construction and maintenance of wharves, docks and piers, to improve the shore of the lake for the promotion generally of commerce and navigation. And the State, insisting that the company has, without right, erected and proposes to continue to erect wharves and piers upon its domain, asks that such alleged unlawful structures may be ordered to be removed, and the company be enjoined from erecting further structures of any kind.

. . . .

We do not deem it material, for the determination of any questions presented in this case, to describe in detail the extensive works of the railroad company under the permission given to locate its road within the city by the ordinance. It is sufficient to say that when this suit was commenced it had reclaimed from the waters of the lake a tract, two hundred feet in width, for the whole distance allowed for its entry within the city, and constructed thereon the tracks needed for its railway, with all the guards against danger in its approach and crossings as specified in the ordinance, and erected the designated breakwater beyond its tracks on the east, and the necessary works for the protection of the shore on the west. Its works in no respect interfered with any useful freedom in the use of the waters of the lake for commerce, foreign, interstate or domestic. They were constructed under the authority of the law by the requirement of the city as a condition of its consent that the company might locate its road within its limits, and cannot be regarded as such an encroachment upon the domain of the State as to require the interposition of the court for their removal or for any restraint in their use.

. . . .

We proceed to consider the claim of the railroad company to the ownership of submerged lands in the harbor, and the right to construct such wharves, piers, docks and other works therein as it may deem proper for its interest and business. The claim is founded upon the third section of the act of the legislature of the State passed on the 16th of April, 1869, the material part of which is as follows:

> "SEC. 3. The right of the Illinois Central Railroad Company under the grant from the State in its charter, which said grant constitutes a part of the consideration for which the said company pays to the State at least seven per cent of its gross earnings, . . . is hereby confirmed; and all the right and title of the State of Illinois in and to the submerged lands constituting the bed of Lake Michigan, and lying east of the tracks and breakwater of the Illinois Central Railroad Company, for the distance of one mile, . . . are hereby granted in fee to the said Illinois Central Railroad Company, its successors and assigns: provided, however, that the fee to said lands shall be held by said company in perpetuity, and that the said company shall not have power to grant, sell or convey the fee to the same; and that all gross receipts from use, profits, leases or otherwise of said lands, or the improvements thereon, or that may hereafter be made thereon, shall form a part of the gross proceeds, receipts and income of the said Illinois Central Railroad Company, . . . and provided also, that nothing herein contained shall authorize obstructions to the Chicago harbor, or impair the public right of navigation. . . .

The act, of which this section is a part, was accepted by a resolution of the board of directors of the company. . . . On the 15th of April, 1873, the legislature of Illinois repealed the act. The questions presented relate to the validity of the section cited of the act and the effect of the repeal upon its operation.

The section in question has two objects in view: one was to confirm certain alleged rights of the railroad company under the grant from the State in its charter and under and "by virtue of its appropriation, occupancy, use and control, and the riparian ownership incident" thereto, in and to the lands submerged or otherwise lying east of a line parallel with and four hundred feet east of the west line of Michigan Avenue, in fractional sections ten and fifteen. The other object was to grant to the railroad company submerged lands in the harbor.

. . . .

This clause is treated by the counsel of the company as an absolute conveyance to it of title to the submerged lands. . . .

. . . .

The question, therefore, to be considered is whether the legislature was competent to thus deprive the State of its ownership of the submerged lands in the harbor of Chicago, and of the consequent control of its waters; or, in other words, whether the railroad corporation can hold the lands and control the waters by the grant, against any future exercise of power over them by the State.

That the State holds the title to the lands under the navigable waters of Lake Michigan, within its limits, in the same manner that the State holds title to soils under tide water, by the common law, we have already shown, and that title necessarily carries with it control over the waters above them whenever the lands are subjected to use. But it is a title different in character from that which the State holds in lands intended for sale. It is different from the title which the United States hold in the public lands which are open to preemption and sale. It is a title held in trust for the people of the State that they may enjoy the navigation of the waters, carry on commerce over them, and have liberty of fishing therein freed from the obstruction or interference of private parties. The interest of the people in the navigation of the waters and in commerce over them may be improved in many instances by the erection of wharves, docks and piers therein, for which purpose the State may grant parcels of the submerged lands; and, so long as their disposition is made for such purpose, no valid objections can be made to the grants. It is grants of parcels of lands under navigable waters, that may afford foundation for wharves, piers, docks and other structures in aid of commerce, and grants of parcels which, being occupied, do not substantially impair the public interest in the lands and waters remaining, that are chiefly considered and sustained in the adjudged cases as a valid exercise of legislative power consistently with the trust to the public upon which such lands are held by the State. But that is a very different doctrine from the one which would sanction the abdication of the general control of the State over lands under the navigable waters of an entire harbor or bay, or of a sea or lake. Such abdication is not consistent with the exercise of that trust which requires the government of the State to preserve such waters for the use of the public. The trust devolving upon the State for the public, and which can only be discharged by the management and control of property in which the public has an interest, cannot be relinquished by a transfer of the property. The control of the State for the purposes of the trust can never be lost, except as to such parcels as are used in promoting the interests of the public therein, or can be disposed of without any substantial impairment of the public interest in the lands and waters remaining. It is only by observing the distinction between a grant of such parcels for the improvement of the public interest, or which when occupied do not substantially impair the public interest in the lands and waters remaining, and a grant of the whole property in which the public is interested, that the language of the adjudged cases can be reconciled. General language sometimes found in opinions of the courts, expressive of absolute ownership and control by the State of lands under navigable waters, irrespective of any trust as to their use and disposition, must be read and construed with reference to the special facts of the particular cases. A grant of all the lands under the navigable waters of a State has never been adjudged to be within the legislative power; and any attempted grant of the kind would be held, if not absolutely void on its face, as subject to revocation. The State can no more abdicate its trust over property in which the whole people are interested, like navigable waters and soils under them, so as to leave them entirely under the use and control of private parties, except in the instance of parcels mentioned for the improvement of the navigation and use of the waters, or when parcels can be disposed of without impairment of the public interest in what remains, than it can abdicate its police powers in the administration of government and the preservation of the peace. In the administration of government the use of such powers may for a limited period be delegated to a municipality or other body, but there always remains with the State the right to revoke those powers and exercise them in a more direct manner, and one more conformable to its wishes. So with trusts connected with public property, or property of a special character, like lands under navigable waters, they cannot be placed entirely beyond the direction and control of the State.

The harbor of Chicago is of immense value to the people of the State of Illinois in the facilities it affords to its vast and constantly increasing commerce; and the idea that its legislature can deprive the State of control over its bed and waters and place the same in the hands of a private corporation created for a different purpose, one limited to transportation of passengers and freight between distant points and the city, is a proposition that cannot be defended.

The area of the submerged lands proposed to be ceded by the act in question to the railroad company embraces something more than a thousand acres, being, as stated by counsel, more than three times the area of the outer harbor, and not only including all of that harbor but embracing adjoining submerged lands which will, in all probability, be hereafter included in the harbor. It is as large as that embraced by all the merchandise docks along the Thames at London; is much larger than that included in the famous docks and basins at Liverpool; is twice that of the port of Marseilles, and nearly if not quite equal to the pier area along the water front of the city of New York. And the arrivals and clearings of vessels at the port exceed in number those of New York, and are equal to those of New York and Boston combined. Chicago has nearly twenty-five per cent of the lake carrying trade as compared with the arrivals and clearings of all the leading ports of our great inland seas. In the year ending June 30, 1886, the joint arrivals and clearances of vessels at that port amounted to twenty-two thousand and ninety-six, with a tonnage of over seven millions; and in 1890 the tonnage of the vessels reached nearly nine millions. As stated by counsel, since the passage of the Lake Front Act, in 1869, the population of the city has increased nearly a million souls, and the increase of commerce has kept pace with it. It is hardly conceivable that the legislature can divest the State of the control and management of this harbor and vest it absolutely in a private corporation. Surely an act of the legislature transferring the title to its submerged lands and the power claimed by the railroad company, to a foreign State or nation would be repudiated, without hesitation, as a gross perversion of the trust over the property under which it is held. So would a similar transfer to a corporation of another State. It would not be listened to that the control and management of the harbor of that great city — a subject of concern to the whole people of the State — should thus be placed elsewhere than in the State itself. All the objections which can be urged to such attempted transfer may be urged to a transfer to a private corporation like the railroad company in this case. Any grant of the kind is necessarily revocable, and the exercise of the trust by which the property was held by the State can be resumed at any time. Undoubtedly there may be expenses incurred in improvements made under such a grant which the State ought to pay; but, be that as it may, the power to resume the trust whenever the State judges best is, we think, incontrovertible. The position advanced by the railroad company in support of its claim to the ownership of the submerged lands and the right to the erection of wharves, piers and docks at its pleasure, or for its business in the harbor of Chicago, would place every harbor in the country at the mercy of a majority of the legislature of the State in which the harbor is situated.

We cannot, it is true, cite any authority where a grant of this kind has been held invalid, for we believe that no instance exists where the harbor of a great city and its commerce have been allowed to pass into the control of any private corporation. But the decisions are numerous which declare that such property is held by the State, by virtue of its sovereignty, in trust for the public. The ownership of the navigable waters of the harbor and of the lands under them is a subject of public concern to the whole people of the State. The trust with which they are held, therefore, is governmental and cannot be alienated, except in those instances mentioned of parcels used in the improvement of the interest thus held, or when parcels can be disposed of without detriment to the public interest in the lands and waters remaining.

This follows necessarily from the public character of the property, being held by the whole people for purposes in which the whole people are interested.

. . . .

. . . We hold, therefore, that any attempted cession of the ownership and control of the State in and over the submerged lands in Lake Michigan, by the act of April 16, 1869, was inoperative to affect, modify or in any respect to control the sovereignty and dominion of the State over the lands, or its ownership thereof, and that any such attempted operation of the act was annulled by the repealing act of April 15, 1873, which to that extent was valid and effective. There can be no irrepealable contract in a conveyance of property by a grantor in disregard of a public trust, under which he was bound to hold and manage it.

DISSENT: MR. JUSTICE SHIRAS, with whom concurred MR. JUSTICE GRAY and MR. JUSTICE BROWN, dissenting.

That the ownership of a State in the lands underlying its navigable waters is as complete, and its power to make them the subject of conveyance and grant is as full, as such ownership and power to grant in the case of the other public lands of the State, I have supposed to be well settled.

. . . .

The opinion of the majority, if I rightly apprehend it, . . . concedes that a State does possess the power to grant the rights of property and possession in such lands to private parties, but the power is stated to be, in some way restricted to "small parcels, or where such parcels can be disposed of without detriment to the public interests in the lands and waters remaining." But it is difficult to see how the validity of the exercise of the power, if the power exists, can depend upon the size of the parcel granted. . . .

. . . .

Doubtless there are limitations, both expressed and implied, on the title to and control over these lands by the company. As we have seen, the company is expressly forbidden to obstruct Chicago harbor, or to impair the public right of navigation. So, from the nature of the railroad corporation and of its relation to the State and the public, the improvements put upon these lands by the company must be consistent with their duties as common carriers, and must be calculated to promote the efficiency of the railroad in the receipt and shipment of freight from and by the lake. But these are incidents of the grant and do not operate to defeat it.

. . . .

Should the State of Illinois see, in the great and unforeseen growth of the city of Chicago and of the[lake commerce, reason to doubt the prudence of her legislature in entering into the contract created by the passage and acceptance of the act of 1869, she can take the rights and property of the railroad company in these lands by a constitutional condemnation of them. . . .

NOTES AND QUESTIONS

1. *Illinois Central* remains the major judicial decision in support of the public trust doctrine. It has been cited repeatedly by state courts as a source of authority for the doctrine and is a staple in casebooks on natural resources law. In large part because of it, all states now have public trust doctrines. But what is the case's legal foundation? Unfortunately, *Illinois Central* is silent on this seminal question. One commentater has suggested the doctrine to be a corollary to the navigational servitude, *see infra* Chapter 8, and having its roots in the Commerce Clause. Wilkinson, *The Headwaters of the Public Trust: Some Thoughts on the Source and Scope of the Traditional Doctrine,* 19 Envt'l L. 425, 458–59 (1989). Professor Wilkinson argues states may expand the doctrine but may not abrogate it. *Id.* at 461–62.

Could *Illinois Central* be justified as an expression of federal common law? *See, e.g., Oregon ex. rel. State Land Board v. Corvallis Sand and Gravel Company,* 429 U.S. 363, 379–80, 97 S. Ct. 582, 591 (1977):

> [U]nder our federal system, property ownership is not governed by a general federal law, but rather by the laws of the several States. "The great body of law in this country which controls acquisition, transmission, and transfer of property, and defines the rights of its owners in relation to the state or to private parties, is found in the statutes and decisions of the state." *Davies Warehouse Co. v. Bowles,* 321 U.S. 144, 155, 64 S.Ct. 474, 480, 88 L.Ed. 635 (1944). This is particularly true with respect to real property, for even when federal common law was in its heyday under the teachings of *Swift v. Tyson,* 16 Pet. 1, 10 L.Ed. 865 (1842), an exception was carved out for the local law of real property. *Id.,* at 18.

See also Board of Regents of State Colleges v. Roth, 408 U.S. 564, 577, 92 S. Ct. 2701, 2709 (1972) ("[P]roperty interests . . . are not created by the Constitution. Rather, they are created and their dimensions are defined by existing rules or understandings that stem from an independent source such as state law — rules or understandings that secure certain benefits and that support claims of entitlement to those benefits.").

Alternatively, is the doctrine merely a manifestation of traditional property theory? Consider: (a) under English law, title in important public resources was burdened by trust obligations; (b) English law was imported into state law; (c) thus, title to public resources held by states carries the same trust obligations. Good reasoning?

2. The Supreme Court has never specifically affirmed *Illinois Central* and may currently disfavor it. *See, e.g., Montana v. United States*, 450 U.S. 544, 551, 101 S. Ct. 1245, 1251 (1984) ("[a] state's power over the beds of navigable waters remains subject to only one limitation: the paramount power of the United States to ensure that such waters remain free to interstate and foreign commerce . . ."); *Phillips Petroleum Co. v. Mississippi*, 484 U.S. 469, 483, 108 S. Ct. 791, 799 (1988) (a state's management of lands underlying navigable waters should accord with each state's views "of justice and policy."); *United States v. Oregon*, 295 U.S. 1, 14, 55 S. Ct. 610, 615 (1934) ("upon the admission of a State to the Union, the title of the United States to lands underlying navigable waters within the States passes to it, as incident to the transfer to the State of local sovereignty, and is subject only to the paramount power of the United States to control such waters for purposes of navigation in interstate and foreign commerce."). *See also Appleby v. City of New York*, 271 U.S. 364 (1926), in which the Supreme Court declared that the conclusion in *Illinois Central* "was necessarily a statement of Illinois law." *Id.* at 395. *See generally* Pearson, Illinois Central *and the Public Trust Doctrine in State Law*, 15 Va. Envt'l L. J. 713 (1996).

3. The academic community has welcomed the public trust doctrine with open arms. The major article that revived the doctrine in the current day is Sax, *The Public Trust Doctrine in Natural Resources Law: Effective Judicial Intervention*, 68 Mich. L. Rev. 471 (1970). Professor Sax's support for the doctrine was rooted in his healthy disgust for government squandering of valuable natural resources. *Id.* at 474. In his view, the doctrine has a singular ability to work into the law a logical and necessary ethic of environmental protection as well as a respect for "certain interests . . . so intrinsically important to every citizen that their free availability tends to mark the society as one of citizens rather than of serfs." *Id.* Professor Sax followed up on these themes ten years later in *Liberating the Public Trust Doctrine from its Historical Shackles*, 14 U. Cal. Davis L. Rev. 185 (1980). Other articles praising the doctrine include: Dunning, *The Public Trust: A Fundamental Doctrine of American Property Law*, 19 Envt'l L. 515 (1989), and Wilkinson, *The Public Trust Doctrine in Public Land Law*, 14 U. Cal. Davis L. Rev. 269 (1980).

However, the doctrine is not universally applauded. In the view of some commentaters, it is counter-majoritarian, at least when it originates by judicial fiat. By this view, when courts invoke the public trust doctrine to reverse a decision of a legislature, they usurp the legislature's policymaking function. *See, e.g.,* Huffman, *Trusting the Public Interest to Judges: A Comment on the Public Trust Writings of Professor Sax, Wilkinson, Dunning and Johnson*, 63 Denver L. Rev. 565 (1986); Jawetz, *The Public Trust Totem in*

Public Land Law: Ineffective — And Undesirable — Judicial Intervention, 14 U. Cal. Davis L. Rev. 455 (1982).

C. THE PUBLIC TRUST DOCTRINE IN STATE LAW

The public trust doctrine varies from state to state. It can vary by origin. As we have seen, the doctrine can arise from judicial decision, but it also can arise by constitution or statute. Pennsylvania, for one, has announced a trust principle in its constitution, while Nebraska has stipulated by statute that waters of the state shall be administered in trust for the public. The doctrine can vary in physical dimension. When applicable to submerged lands, its landward limit may be the low water mark, the ordinary low water mark, the winter tide, the neap tide, the highest tide, the vegetation line, or the mean high water mark. The doctrine can also vary in scope. Originally reaching only submerged lands, the doctrine has since been held to apply to resources such as marine life, wildlife, sand and gravel, rural park lands, battlefields, archeological remains, and a downtown area. *See* Richard J. Lazarus, *Changing Conceptions of Property and Sovereignty in Natural Resources: Questioning the Public Trust Doctrine*, 71 Iowa L. Rev. 631, 649, n.1 (1986). And it can vary in function. The doctrine has served to promote public pursuits such as hunting, fishing, boating, swimming, ecological preservation, and scientific study, *see, e.g., Marks v. Whitney*, 491 P.2d 374, 380 (Cal. 1971), and public rights to use navigable and nonnavigable waterways, *see, e.g., Montana Coalition for Stream Access v. Curran*, 682 P.2d 163, 171 (Mont. 1984). The doctrine has forced government agencies to plan for long-term conservation and development of natural resources as a prerequisite to issuing water rights permits. *United Plainsmen's Association v. North Dakota State Water Conservation Commission*, 247 N.W.2d 457 (N.D. 1976). The public trust doctrine has even been used as an interpretive device, which in one case converted "the rocks" of a private entity's arguments into "no more than shifting sands." *State ex rel Rohere v. Credle*, 369 S.E.2d 825, 832 (N.C. 1988).

NATIONAL AUDUBON SOCIETY v. SUPERIOR COURT OF ALPINE COUNTY

33 Cal. 3d 419, 189 Cal. Rptr. 346, 658 P.2d 709 (1983)

OPINION: BROUSSARD, J.

Mono Lake, the second largest lake in California, sits at the base of the Sierra Nevada escarpment near the eastern entrance to Yosemite National Park. The lake is saline; it contains no fish but supports a large population of brine shrimp which feed vast numbers of nesting and migratory birds. Islands in the lake protect a large breeding colony of California gulls, and the lake itself serves as a haven on the migration route for thousands of Northern Phalarope, Wilson's Phalarope, and Eared Grebe. Towers and spires of tufa on the north and south shores are matters of geological interest and a tourist attraction.

Although Mono Lake receives some water from rain and snow on the lake surface, historically most of its supply came from snowmelt in the Sierra

Nevada. Five freshwater streams — Mill, Lee Vining, Walker, Parker and Rush Creeks — arise near the crest of the range and carry the annual runoff to the west shore of the lake. In 1940, however, the Division of Water Resources, the predecessor to the present California Water Resources Board, granted the Department of Water and Power of the City of Los Angeles (hereafter DWP) a permit to appropriate virtually the entire flow of four of the five streams flowing into the lake. DWP promptly constructed facilities to divert about half the flow of these streams into DWP's Owens Valley aqueduct. In 1970 DWP completed a second diversion tunnel, and since that time has taken virtually the entire flow of these streams.

Mono Lake
Photograph courtesy of the Mono Lake Committee

As a result of these diversions, the level of the lake has dropped; the surface area has diminished by one-third; one of the two principal islands in the lake has become a peninsula, exposing the gull rookery there to coyotes and other predators and causing the gulls to abandon the former island. The ultimate effect of continued diversions is a matter of intense dispute, but there seems little doubt that both the scenic beauty and the ecological values of Mono Lake are imperiled.

Plaintiffs filed suit in superior court to enjoin the DWP diversions on the theory that the shores, bed and waters of Mono Lake are protected by a public trust. Plaintiffs' suit was transferred to the federal district court, which requested that the state courts determine the relationship between the public trust doctrine and the water rights system, and decide whether plaintiffs must exhaust administrative remedies before the Water Board prior to filing suit. The superior court then entered summary judgments against plaintiffs on both matters, ruling that the public trust doctrine offered no independent basis for challenging the DWP diversions, and that plaintiffs had failed to exhaust administrative remedies. Plaintiffs petitioned us directly for writ of mandate to review that decision; in view of the importance of the issues presented, we issued an alternative writ.

This case brings together for the first time two systems of legal thought: the appropriative water rights system which since the days of the gold rush has dominated California water law, and the public trust doctrine which, after evolving as a shield for the protection of tidelands, now extends its protective scope to navigable lakes. Ever since we first recognized that the public trust protects environmental and recreational values (Marks v. Whitney (1971) 6 Cal.3d 251 [98 Cal.Rptr. 790, 491 P.2d 374]), the two systems of legal thought have been on a collision course. They meet in a unique and dramatic setting which highlights the clash of values. Mono Lake is a scenic and ecological treasure of national significance, imperiled by continued diversions of water; yet, the need of Los Angeles for water is apparent, its reliance on rights granted by the board evident, the cost of curtailing diversions substantial.

Attempting to integrate the teachings and values of both the public trust and the appropriative water rights system, we have arrived at certain conclusions which we briefly summarize here. In our opinion, the core of the public trust doctrine is the state's authority as sovereign to exercise a continuous supervision and control over the navigable waters of the state and the lands underlying those waters. This authority applies to the waters tributary to Mono Lake and bars DWP or any other party from claiming a vested right to divert waters once it becomes clear that such diversions harm the interests protected by the public trust. The corollary rule which evolved in tideland and lakeshore cases barring conveyance of rights free of the trust except to serve trust purposes cannot, however, apply without modification to flowing waters. The prosperity and habitability of most of this state requires the diversion of great quantities of water from its streams for purposes unconnected to any navigation, commerce, fishing, recreation, or ecological use relating to the source stream. The state must have the power to grant non-vested usufructuary rights to appropriate water even if diversions harm public trust uses. Approval of such diversion without considering public trust values, however, may result in needless destruction of those values. Accordingly, we believe that before state courts and agencies approve water diversions they should consider the effect of such diversions upon interests protected by the public trust, and attempt, so far as feasible, to avoid or minimize any harm to those interests.

The water rights enjoyed by DWP were granted, the diversion was commenced, and has continued to the present without any consideration of the impact upon the public trust. An objective study and reconsideration of the water rights in the Mono Basin is long overdue. The water law of California — which we conceive to be an integration including both the public trust doctrine and the board-administered appropriative rights system — permits such a reconsideration; the values underlying that integration require it.

With regard to the secondary issue of exhaustion of administrative remedies, the powers, experience, and expertise of the Water Board all argue in favor of granting that agency primary jurisdiction. Long-established precedent, however, declares that courts have concurrent jurisdiction in water right controversies. The Legislature, instead of overturning that precedent, has implicitly acknowledged its vitality by providing a procedure under which the courts can refer water rights disputes to the water board as referee. We therefore conclude that the courts may continue to exercise concurrent jurisdiction, but note that in cases where the board's experience or expert knowledge may be useful the courts should not hesitate to seek such aid.

. . . .

DWP expects that its future diversions of about 100,000 acre-feet per year will lower the lake's surface level another 43 feet and reduce its surface area by about 22 square miles over the next 80 to 100 years, at which point the lake will gradually approach environmental equilibrium (the point at which inflow from precipitation, groundwater and nondiverted tributaries equals outflow by evaporation and other means). At this point, according to DWP, the lake will stabilize at a level 6,330 feet above the sea's, with a surface area of approximately 38 square miles. Thus, by DWP's own estimates, unabated diversions will ultimately produce a lake that is about 56 percent smaller on the surface and 42 percent shallower than its natural size.

Plaintiffs consider these projections unrealistically optimistic. They allege that, 50 years hence, the lake will be at least 50 feet shallower than it now is, and hold less than 20 percent of its natural volume. Further, plaintiffs fear that "the lake will not stabilize at this level," but "may continue to reduce in size until it is dried up." Moreover, unlike DWP, plaintiffs believe that the lake's gradual recession indirectly causes a host of adverse environmental impacts. Many of these alleged impacts are related to an increase in the lake's salinity, caused by the decrease in its water volume.

As noted above, Mono Lake has no outlets. The lake loses water only by evaporation and seepage. Natural salts do not evaporate with water, but are left behind. Prior to commencement of the DWP diversions, this naturally rising salinity was balanced by a constant and substantial supply of fresh water from the tributaries. Now, however, DWP diverts most of the fresh water inflow. The resultant imbalance between inflow and outflow not only diminishes the lake's size, but also drastically increases its salinity.

Plaintiffs predict that the lake's steadily increasing salinity, if unchecked, will wreck havoc throughout the local food chain. They contend that the lake's algae, and the brine shrimp and brine flies that feed on it, cannot survive the projected salinity increase. To support this assertion, plaintiffs point to a 50 percent reduction in the shrimp hatch for the spring of 1980 and a startling 95 percent reduction for the spring of 1981. These reductions affirm experimental evidence indicating that brine shrimp populations diminish as the salinity of the water surrounding them increases. (See Task Force Report at pp. 20–21.) DWP admits these substantial reductions, but blames them on factors other than salinity.

[The court then discusses other potential environmental problems, such as danger to wildlife, and then disposes of preliminary issues.]

2. The Public Trust Doctrine in California.

"By the law of nature these things are common to mankind — the air, running water, the sea and consequently the shores of the sea." (Institutes of Justinian 2.1.1.) From this origin in Roman law, the English common law evolved the concept of the public trust, under which the sovereign owns "all of its navigable waterways and the lands lying beneath them 'as trustee of a public trust for the benefit of the people.' " (*Colberg, Inc. v. State of California ex rel. Dept. Pub. Wks.* (1967) 67 Cal.2d 408, 416 [62 Cal.Rptr. 401, 432 P.2d 3].) The State of California acquired title as trustee to such lands and waterways upon its admission to the union; from the earliest days its judicial decisions have recognized and enforced the trust obligation.

Three aspects of the public trust doctrine require consideration in this opinion: the purpose of the trust; the scope of the trust, particularly as it applies to the nonnavigable tributaries of a navigable lake; and the powers and duties of the state as trustee of the public trust. We discuss these questions in the order listed.

(a) The purpose of the public trust.

The objective of the public trust has evolved in tandem with the changing public perception of the values and uses of waterways. As we observed in *Marks v. Whitney, supra,* 6 Cal.3d 251, "[p]ublic trust easements [were] traditionally defined in terms of navigation, commerce and fisheries. They have been held to include the right to fish, hunt, bathe, swim, to use for boating and general recreation purposes the navigable waters of the state, and to use the bottom of the navigable waters for anchoring, standing, or other purposes." (P. 259.) We went on, however, to hold that the traditional triad of uses — navigation, commerce and fishing — did not limit the public interest in the trust res. In language of special importance to the present setting, we stated that "[t]he public use to which tidelands are subject are sufficiently flexible to encompass changing public needs. In administering the trust the state is not burdened with an outmoded classification favoring one mode of utilization over another. [Citation.] There is a growing public recognition that one of the most important public uses of the tidelands — a use encompassed within the tidelands trust — is the preservation of those lands in their natural state, so that they may serve as ecological units for scientific study, as open space, and as environments which provide food and habitat for birds and marine life, and which favorably affect the scenery and climate of the area." (Pp. 259–260.)

Mono Lake is a navigable waterway. (*City of Los Angeles v. Aitken, supra,* 10 Cal.App.2d 460, 466.) It supports a small local industry which harvests brine shrimp for sale as fish food, which endeavor probably qualifies the lake as a "fishery" under the traditional public trust cases. The principal values plaintiffs seek to protect, however, are recreational and ecological — the scenic views of the lake and its shore, the purity of the air, and the use of the lake for nesting and feeding by birds. Under *Marks v. Whitney, supra,* 6 Cal.3d 251, it is clear that protection of these values is among the purposes of the public trust.

(b) The scope of the public trust.

. . . .

It is, however, well settled in the United States generally and in California that the public trust is not limited by the reach of the tides, but encompasses all navigable lakes and streams.

. . . .

Mono Lake is, as we have said, a navigable waterway. The beds, shores and waters of the lake are without question protected by the public trust. The streams diverted by DWP, however, are not themselves navigable. Accordingly, we must address in this case a question not discussed in any recent public trust case — whether the public trust limits conduct affecting nonnavigable tributaries to navigable waterways.

. . . .

We conclude that the public trust doctrine, as recognized and developed in California decisions, protects navigable waters from harm caused by diversion of nonnavigable tributaries.

(c) Duties and powers of the state as trustee.

In the following review of the authority and obligations of the state as administrator of the public trust, the dominant theme is the state's sovereign power and duty to exercise continued supervision over the trust. One consequence, of importance to this and many other cases, is that parties acquiring rights in trust property generally hold those rights subject to the trust, and can assert no vested right to use those rights in a manner harmful to the trust.

As we noted recently in *City of Berkeley v. Superior Court, supra,* 26 Cal.3d 515, the decision of the United States Supreme Court in *Illinois Central Railroad Company v. Illinois, supra,* 146 U.S. 387, "remains the primary authority even today, almost nine decades after it was decided." . . .

. . . .

In *State of California v. Superior Court (Fogerty), supra,* 29 Cal.3d 240, 249, we stated that owners of shoreline property in Lake Tahoe would be entitled to compensation if enforcement of the public trust required them to remove improvements. By implication, however, the determination that the property was subject to the trust, despite its implication as to future uses and improvements, was not considered a taking requiring compensation.

In summary, the foregoing cases amply demonstrate the continuing power of the state as administrator of the public trust, a power which extends to the revocation of previously granted rights or to the enforcement of the trust against lands long thought free of the trust.

Except for those rare instances in which a grantee may acquire a right to use former trust property free of trust restrictions, the grantee holds subject to the trust, and while he may assert a vested right to the servient estate (the right of use subject to the trust) and to any improvements he erects, he can claim no vested right to bar recognition of the trust or state action to carry out its purposes.

Since the public trust doctrine does not prevent the state from choosing between trust uses, . . . [case citations omitted] . . . the Attorney General of California, seeking to maximize state power under the trust, argues for a broad concept of trust uses. In his view, "trust uses" encompass all public uses, so that in practical effect the doctrine would impose no restrictions on the state's ability to allocate trust property. We know of no authority which supports this view of the public trust. . . .

. . . .

3. The California Water Rights System.

. . . .

4. The relationship between the Public Trust Doctrine and the California Water Rights System.

. . . .

. . . In our opinion, both the public trust doctrine and the water rights system embody important precepts which make the law more responsive to the diverse needs and interests involved in the planning and allocation of water resources. To embrace one system of thought and reject the other would lead to an unbalanced structure, one which would either decry as a breach of trust appropriations essential to the economic development of this state, or deny any duty to protect or even consider the values promoted by the public trust. Therefore, seeking an accommodation which will make use of the pertinent principles of both the public trust doctrine and the appropriative water rights system, and drawing upon the history of the public trust and the water rights system, the body of judicial precedent, and the views of expert commentators, we reach the following conclusions:

a. The state as sovereign retains continuing supervisory control over its navigable waters and the lands beneath those waters. This principle, fundamental to the concept of the public trust, applies to rights in flowing waters as well as to rights in tidelands and lakeshores; it prevents any party from acquiring a vested right to appropriate water in a manner harmful to the interests protected by the public trust.

b. As a matter of current and historical necessity, the Legislature, acting directly or through an authorized agency such as the Water Board, has the power to grant usufructuary licenses that will permit an appropriator to take water from flowing streams and use that water in a distant part of the state, even though this taking does not promote, and may unavoidably harm, the trust uses at the source stream. The population and economy of this state depend upon the appropriation of vast quantities of water for uses unrelated to in-stream trust values. California's Constitution (*see* art. X, § 2), its statutes (*see* Wat. Code, §§ 100, 104), decisions (*see, e.g., Waterford I. Dist. v. Turlock I. Dist.* (1920) 50 Cal.App. 213, 220 [194 P. 757]), and commentators (e.g., Hutchins, *The Cal. Law of Water Rights, op. cit. supra,* p. 11) all emphasize the need to make efficient use of California's limited water resources: all recognize, at least implicitly, that efficient use requires diverting water from in-stream uses. Now that the economy and population centers of this state have developed in reliance upon appropriated water, it would be disingenuous to hold that such appropriations are and have always been improper to the extent that they harm public trust uses, and can be justified only upon theories of reliance or estoppel.

c. The state has an affirmative duty to take the public trust into account in the planning and allocation of water resources, and to protect public trust uses whenever feasible. Just as the history of this state shows that appropriation may be necessary for efficient use of water despite unavoidable harm to public trust values, it demonstrates that an appropriative water rights system administered without consideration of the public trust may cause unnecessary and unjustified harm to trust interests. As a matter of practical necessity the state may have to approve appropriations despite foreseeable harm to public trust uses. In so doing, however, the state must bear in mind its duty as trustee to consider the effect of the taking on the public trust, and to preserve, so far as consistent with the public interest, the uses protected by the trust.

. . . .

Once the state has approved an appropriation, the public trust imposes a duty of continuing supervision over the taking and use of the appropriated water. In exercising its sovereign power to allocate water resources in the public interest, the state is not confined by past allocation decisions which may be incorrect in light of current knowledge or inconsistent with current needs.

The state accordingly has the power to reconsider allocation decisions even though those decisions were made after due consideration of their effect on the public trust. The case for reconsidering a particular decision, however, is even stronger when that decision failed to weigh and consider public trust uses. In the case before us, the salient fact is that no responsible body has ever determined the impact of diverting the entire flow of the Mono Lake tributaries into the Los Angeles Aqueduct. This is not a case in which the Legislature, the Water Board, or any judicial body has determined that the needs of Los Angeles outweigh the needs of the Mono Basin, that the benefit gained is worth the price. Neither has any responsible body determined whether some lesser taking would better balance the diverse interests. Instead, DWP acquired rights to the entire flow in 1940 from a water board which believed it lacked both the power and the duty to protect the Mono Lake environment, and continues to exercise those rights in apparent disregard for the resulting damage to the scenery, ecology, and human uses of Mono Lake.

It is clear that some responsible body ought to reconsider the allocation of the waters of the Mono Basin. No vested rights bar such reconsideration.

. . . .

6. Conclusion

. . . .

This opinion is but one step in the eventual resolution of the Mono Lake controversy. We do not dictate any particular allocation of water. Our objective is to resolve a legal conundrum in which two competing systems of thought — the public trust doctrine and the appropriative water rights system — existed independently of each other, espousing principles which seemingly suggested opposite results. We hope by integrating these two doctrines to clear away the legal barriers which have so far prevented either the Water Board or the courts from taking a new and objective look at the water resources of the Mono Basin. The human and environmental uses of Mono Lake — uses protected by the public trust doctrine — deserve to be taken into account. Such uses should not be destroyed because the state mistakenly thought itself powerless to protect them.

[Concurring opinion and dissenting opinion omitted]

NOTES AND QUESTIONS

1. In settlement of the *Audubon* litigation, the parties signed an agreement requiring Los Angeles to reduce lake levels to no lower than 6,391 feet above sea level. At this level, most of the "spires of tufa" would again be submerged. Los Angeles is replacing Mono Lake water with water from the Colorado River and other sources. Los Angeles has also undertaken water conservation initiatives.

2. Is the public trust doctrine value-neutral? Could it be used, for example, to require resource development on public lands? Or is it restricted to promoting "pro-environment" or "pro-conservation" ends?

After *Audubon*, does the public trust doctrine still find its moorings in concepts of property law? If not, how does this bear on its relationship with takings principles?

3. Because of its historical origins, one could speculate the public trust doctrine might reside in federal law as well as in state law. Just as the doctrine cabins the exercise of the police power at the state level, so also could it cabin the exercise of, say, the Property Clause power at the federal level. In fact, the United States Supreme Court has found the public trust doctrine to exist in federal law, but in that context it seems to expand government power, not limit it. In *Light v. United States*, 220 U.S. 523 31 S. Ct. 485 (1911), for example, a defendant, who had pastured cattle on federal land in violation of federal regulations, argued that the government could not withdraw large bodies of public land from public access. The Supreme Court's opinion had none of the ring of *Illinois Central* about it:

> [I]t is not for the courts to say how th[e public] trust shall be administered. That is for Congress to determine. The courts cannot compel it to set aside the lands for settlement; or to suffer them to be used for agricultural or grazing purposes, nor interfere when, in the exercise of its discretion, Congress establishes a forest reserve for what it decides to be national and public purposes. In the same way and in the exercise of the same trust it may disestablish a reserve, and devote the property to some other national and public purpose. These are rights incident to proprietorship, to say nothing of the power of the United States as a sovereign over the property belonging to it.

Id. at 537, 31 S. Ct. at 488. *See also United States v. Trinidad Coal Co.*, 137 U.S. 160, 11 S. Ct. 57 (1890) (public trust doctrine found to justify a land disposal statute); *United States v. San Francisco*, 310 U.S. 16, 60 S. Ct. 749 (1940) (decisions under the Property Clause are primarily for Congress); Pearson, *The Public Trust Doctrine in Federal Law*, 24 Journal of Land, Resources and Envt'l Law 173 (2004).

Do you think the federal public trust doctrine should have been applied in *Midwest Oil*?

Chapter 7

ENDANGERED SPECIES ACT

"The first rule of intelligent tinkering is to save all the pieces." Aldo Leopold

A. INTRODUCTION

The Nature Conservancy has calculated that one-third of all U.S. plants and animals are at risk of extinction. Moreover, since the European discovery of North America, 110 "irreplaceable" flora and fauna have disappeared, and another 416 are "missing." Approximately 7,000 U.S. species are threatened, and, according to an estimate of the U.S. Public Interest Research Group, 50,000 plants and animals become extinct worldwide each year. One quarter of the world's species might be gone within 50 years. At risk among the "charismatic megafauna" are the Giant Panda, the Asian Tiger, the Kemp's Ridley Sea Turtle, the Black-Footed Ferret, the Karner Blue Butterfly, the Northern Right Whale, the Orangutan, the Roseate Tern, the Florida Panther, and the Black Rhinoceros. *See, e.g.,* Jim Motavalli and Jennifer Bogo, *The Last of Their Kind,* E/The Environmental Magazine, May-June, 1999.

The extinction of species is international in concern. A massive and persistent demand for wildlife products, especially in the United States, the Far East, and western Europe, is threatening "thousands of species of flora and fauna," according to a report prepared for a November, 1994 meeting of the United Nations Convention on International Trade in Endangered Species of Wild Fauna and Flora ("CITES"). CITES has 124 member nations and controls trade in about 34,000 species of animals and plants. The report estimates global trade in illegal wildlife at $5 billion. Rhinos (about 10,000 left by common estimate), tigers (about 500 remaining), and Asian bears are at particular risk. Illustrative of the problem, an estimated 100,000 wild birds are smuggled into the United States from Mexico each year. Illegal trade is not the sole reason for species jeopardy. Habitat loss, toxic chemicals and other such factors are significant contributors as well. Beyond that, it is not abnormal for species to meet with extinction. It has been estimated that 99% of all species ever in existence have already passed on. Gregg Easterbrook, *A Moment on the Earth, The Coming Age of Environmental Optimism* at 552 (Viking, 1991).

In this Chapter, we will review the legal framework in place to protect these non-human living creatures of the earth. We begin with a brief historical recitation.

KAREN P. SHELDON, OVERVIEW OF WILDLIFE LAW, in ENVIRONMENTAL LAW — FROM RESOURCES TO RECOVERY § 6.1(B)(2), pp. 203-09 (West Publishing Co., 1993)*

. . . .

Milestones in the History of Wildlife

The critical milestones for wildlife in the United States relate to its terrible decline in the early years of the Republic, to the efforts to secure its continued existence and protection, and to increases in understanding about the effects of human actions on populations and habitat. Because much of the understanding of wildlife and effort to protect it are expressed in law, these milestones are guides to the discussion of the evolution of wildlife law.

(a) The Era of Free Taking — 1600s-1850s

The early history of European exploration and occupation of North America is one of virtually unrestrained slaughter of animals — for food, for fashion, and later to aid the settlement of the West by subduing Indians through the extermination of the buffalo.[1] Wildlife species that today exist only in remnant populations on federal lands in the West once covered the continent. Wolves were so prevalent in Massachusetts in the early 1700s that local citizens seriously considered building a fence across Cape Cod to protect livestock from predation.[2] Bison ranged through New York and Pennsylvania and as far south as Georgia. The last bison east of the Mississippi River was killed in 1801.[3] Woodland caribou and other large and small mammals and hundreds of species of birds and fish existed in the forests and waters of the East Coast.

From the 1700s to the 1850s, many of these species, particularly those that could be eaten, were subjected to hunting pressures no population could withstand. Most of this hunting was carried out by market or "pot" hunters who sold venison, wild fowl, fish, and shellfish to a public with limited domestic sources of meat. Passenger pigeons, once the largest number of birds of one species ever known on one continent, were clubbed, netted, shot, and trapped for food and sport. So were the heath hen, wild turkey, ruffed grouse,

---

* Reprinted from Campbell-Mohn, Breen, Futrell, ENVIRONMENTAL LAW — FROM RESOURCES TO RECOVERY, Copyright © 1993, with permission of Thomson West.

[1] *See generally,* P. Mathiessen, *Wildlife in America* (1987).

[2] *Id.* at 57–58.

[3] *Id.* at 63.

and quail. In 200 years, the immense wealth of wildlife all but disappeared from the East.[4]

Expansion westward in the 1800s was accompanied by wildlife losses as well. In 1806, the demand for beaver hats sent mountain men into the Oregon Territory and the Rocky Mountains, where they virtually trapped out the beaver in less than 40 years. When the market for beaver fell in the late 1830s, it was replaced by the demand for buffalo skins and meat. In 1840, one fur company alone sent 67,000 buffalo skins down the Missouri River to St. Louis.[5]

Once the Great Plains fell to the plow and the advance of the railroads in the 1860s and 1870s, the buffalo and the Indian culture that depended on it were doomed. By 1900, nearly 60 million buffalo had been destroyed to make way for settlers and agriculture.[6]

(b) Gestures of Regret — 1850s-1900

By the second half of the 19th century, the decimation of wildlife had taken its toll. Americans began to realize that the vast natural resources of their nation were not inexhaustible. The conservation of wildlife was acknowledged as an important goal, one that required public involvement. Private citizens created organizations dedicated to the welfare of wildlife. Among the earliest of these were groups of recreational hunters who believed in the "sport" of taking wildlife according to rules designed to avoid waste and prevent extinction.[7] These groups supported enactment of state laws to protect wildlife and to restrain its exploitation. In the 1850s, many states passed game laws setting seasons and bag limits to stem the terrible decline of wildlife. Unfortunately, these laws were "largely gestures of regret," too late to save what had existed and without effective means of enforcement.[8]

(c) The Rise of Conservation — 1900-20

By the 1880s, it was clear that the states were unable to enforce their wildlife laws and that the alarming drop in wildlife populations was a national problem requiring federal action.[9] In 1884, George Grinnell, a prominent sportsman and editor of *Forest and Stream*, began to advocate the establishment of interest groups to lobby Congress on behalf of wildlife. Grinnell founded the National Audubon Society (1886) and the Boone and Crockett Club (1888),[10] both of which were instrumental in achieving passage of the Lacey Act of 1900,[11] the first federal wildlife statute.

---

[4] *Id.* at 62–71.

[5] H. Borland, *The History of Wildlife in America* 84 (1975).

[6] Mathiessen, *supra,* note 2, at 148–52.

[7] W. Harrington, i 213 (K. Frederick & R. Sedjo, eds. (1991)) (Resources for the Future, Washington, D.C.).

[8] Mathiessen, *supra,* note 2, at 157.

[9] Borland, *supra,* note 6, at 122.

[10] Harrington, *supra,* note 8, at 213.

[11] Ch. 553, 31 Stat. 187. The Lacey Act was amended substantially in 1981. The current version appears at 16 U.S.C.A. §§ 701, 3371–3378 and 18 U.S.C.A. § 42 (1985).

The Lacey Act, which prohibits the interstate shipment of wildlife taken in violation of state law, is one of the most important pieces of wildlife legislation ever passed. It not only put the market hunters out of business and prohibited the importation of foreign wildlife, except by permit, it gave real authority to the U.S. Biological Survey, predecessor to the U.S. Fish and Wildlife Service. The Survey, founded in 1885 to carry out a national biological survey and various bird studies, was charged with the administration and implementation of the Lacey Act. This signaled the beginning of active federal involvement in wildlife management and protection.[12]

In the years following the enactment of the Lacey Act, Congress vested increasing authority over wildlife in federal agencies, thereby fostering the development of effective federal institutions for wildlife management and protection. Between 1900 and 1913, for example, Congress concluded the Fur Seal Treaty[13] regulating the harvest of the Northern fur seal; enacted the Federal Tariff Act, which prohibited the importation of feathers and other parts of certain birds used in millinery; and enacted the Migratory Bird Act of 1913,[14] which gave control over migratory birds to the federal government.[15]

The federal statutes expressed a new theme in wildlife law: conservation. The recognition of the importance of conserving wildlife corresponded to the growing federal interest in the retention and conservation of other resources of the federal lands.[16] In the late 1800s and early 1900s, the active disposition of federal lands into private hands pursuant to statutes like the Mining Law of 1872 and the Homestead Act was arrested by the recognition of the importance of retaining lands with special values in the public domain. Yellowstone Park was set aside in 1872 to protect its stunning natural resources, including its wildlife, and other park designations followed. Forest lands were reserved, initially by Presidents McKinley and Theodore Roosevelt, and then by Congress under the Forest Reserve Act of 1891 and other statutes. A few years later, in 1911, Congress enacted the Weeks Act, which called for the reacquisition of private lands to provide for federal forests in the East. Although these forests were not reserved explicitly for wildlife conservation, the protection of habitat that was accomplished was beneficial.[17]

The conservation movement of the early 1900s reflected two strands of thought about conserving wildlife and other natural resources: a utilitarian view and a preservation view.[18] The utilitarian view, represented by people like Gifford Pinchot, the creator of the Forest Service and head of Roosevelt's National Conservation Committee, regarded conservation as "the use of natural resources for the greatest good of the greatest number for the longest time."[19] Implicit in this outlook is the idea that natural resources should be managed in a sustainable way to assure continued human use.

---

[12] Borland, *supra,* note 6, at 122.

[13] *See,* note 171, *infra.*

[14] *See,* note 68, *infra.*

[15] Mathiessen, *supra,* note 2, at 191.

[16] *See,* § 1.2(A)(1) of Chapter 1, *supra.*

[17] Harrington, *supra,* note 8, at 218.

[18] *Id.* at 215. *See, also* § 1.2(C)(2) of Chapter 1, *supra.*

[19] G. Pinchot, *Breaking New Ground* 326 (1947).

The preservation view was not utilitarian. Taking its antecedents from H.D. Thoreau, and listening hard to the words of John Muir, it called for a realization of the intrinsic value of wildlife and wild places not measured by human use. [20]

Neither the utilitarian nor the preservation view, however, regarded conservation of predators, "pests," and "vermin" with the same benevolent attitude extended to other wildlife. These species were systematically and ruthlessly attacked. [21]

(d) Lessons of Failure — 1920-40

Early conservation efforts focused on reintroduction of species and the elimination of predators. These efforts, along with controls on hunting and trapping, were thought to be appropriate to recover diminished wildlife populations. While the restrictions on hunting and trapping did halt the precipitous decline of target species, reintroduction and predator control were spectacularly unsuccessful wildlife management tools. [22]

Efforts to introduce or reintroduce wildlife began in colonial times, but reached a fever pitch in the early 1900s. Hundreds of attempts were made to restore or stock species in areas where wildlife was diminished or extirpated. European variants of American species were released across the United States. Game farms were established to raise animals for transfer to the wild. Animals were transported from one part of the country to another, regardless of whether the new area was appropriate range or habitat. [23]

Most of these efforts failed. Where they succeeded, the results were often harmful or fatal to native species. Rarely did the introduced species function as intended in its new ecosystem. The English sparrow, for example, which was imported to eat cankerworms, turned out to be a voracious eater of agricultural seeds. The carp, brought in as a food source after the Civil War, so muddies a stream in its foraging for food that the waters are uninhabitable by other fish. [24]

One of the most disastrous wildlife management efforts, and one that has been repeated across the West, was the elimination of the natural predators of the mule deer on the Kaibab Plateau in the 1920s. Following destruction of the wolves, bobcats, cougars, and coyotes that had kept the herd in balance, the Kaibab deer population exploded. Thousands died of starvation after overgrazing ruined the habitat. [25]

By the 1920s it was apparent that other wildlife management techniques were required. The failures of reintroduction and predator controlled to the development of the science of wildlife management and to an expanded role

[20] Harrington, *supra,* note 8, at 215.

[21] Mathiessen, *supra,* note 2, at 192.

[22] Harrington, *supra,* note 8, at 220; Mathiessen, *supra,* note 2, at 186.

[23] Harrington, *supra,* note 8, at 220.

[24] Mathiessen, *supra,* note 2, at 187.

[25] Borland, *supra,* note 6, at 138.

for the federal government in all aspects of wildlife regulation and protection.[26]

Aldo Leopold, whose field experience later included the Kaibab deer situation, was the first person to work out the fundamental principles of wildlife management. In 1920, he began a study of the relationships among animal and plant species that altered the previously held assumptions about how wild animal populations function. Leopold articulated the principle of carrying capacity-the idea that an ecosystem can support only a certain number of a single species-which is now a central premise of wildlife biology.[27] Leopold's book, *Game Management,* published in 1929, remains a basic text in the field.[28]

Leopold's new approach to wildlife management fostered much scientific research and the recognition of wildlife management as a profession. In 1935, the Biological Survey established a network of wildlife research units at land grant universities. This Cooperative Wildlife Research Unit Program began training thousands of wildlife professionals.[29] In 1936, the first North American Wildlife Conference was held, assembling biologists, agency administrators, hunters, and other persons interested in wildlife to discuss wildlife issues.[30] In 1940, the Biological Survey and the Bureau of Fisheries were merged into the Fish and Wildlife Service and located in the Department of the Interior (DOI).[31] It was an encouraging time for wildlife.

(e) A Corner Is Turned — 1940-70

By 1940, a corner had been turned for many significant wildlife species. There was no longer danger of widespread extinctions of once common animals like the passenger pigeon. Game species, particularly elk and deer, were increasing in numbers and distribution.[32] Waterfowl habitat was being set aside in federal wildlife refuges, although the low numbers of waterfowl were still a concern. Other wildlife habitat became available, serendipitously, as Americans left the farm and moved to the city. In the late 1930s the rate of conversion of forest land to agriculture slowed and then reversed.[33] In addition, the federal government was funding wildlife projects across the country through the Federal Aid to Wildlife Restoration Act.[34]

This good news masked the plight of species dependent on water as development continued to encroach on wetlands and polluted habitat. It also masked the plight of species of no value to hunters and fishers, and those that continued to be the target of predator and pest control programs.[35]

---

[26] Harrington, *supra,* note 8, at 222.

[27] Borland, *supra,* note 6, at 144.

[28] Harrington, *supra,* note 8, at 222.

[29] Borland, *supra,* note 6, at 148.

[30] Mathiessen, *supra,* note 2, at 220.

[31] Borland, *supra,* note 6, at 148.

[32] Harrington, *supra,* note 8, at 223.

[33] *Id.* at 217.

[34] 16 U.S.C.A. §§ 669–669i (1985); Borland, *supra,* note 6, at 148.

[35] Harrington, *supra,* note 8, at 224.

Perhaps the most significant factor in achieving wildlife protection during this period was the change in public attitude. By World War II, wildlife was used less for commercial production of furs and food than for consumptive and nonconsumptive recreation. The utilitarian view of wildlife that had prevailed through most of U.S. history, even during the conservation movement, gave way further to the idea that wildlife should be preserved for its own intrinsic value. The regard for wildlife extended to all species, with the exception of predators and pests, not just to those that could be hunted, trapped, and hooked. [36]

The attitude change is seen most clearly in the efforts to protect species in danger of extinction. [37] In North America, more than 500 species are known to have become extinct since 1600. In 1945, the Smithsonian Institute published the first endangered species list of 40 animals, including several that are recognizable today: the black footed ferret, the California condor, and the whooping crane. The list was part of the Smithsonian's program to identify and aid species in trouble. [38]

Until 1966, endangered species' protection, such as it was, was carried out in state and federal wildlife programs geared to other purposes, principally game management. The first federal law designed to protect endangered species was the Endangered Species Act (ESA) of 1966, [39] which directed the Secretary of the Interior to conduct a program of endangered species protection and authorized the expenditure of $15 million from the Land and Water Conservation Fund[40] for acquisition of endangered species habitat. The act did not prohibit or limit the taking of endangered species, and, therefore, was regarded as weak. [41]

The 1966 ESA was superseded by the Endangered Species Act of 1973, [42] which made a significant change in the federal approach to endangered species protection. The 1973 ESA declared it unlawful to take any member of an endangered species, regardless of where the species was found. Thus, the killing of endangered species was prohibited on private and state, as well as federal, lands. Critical habitat protection and a process for intergovernmental consultation to prevent federal actions from jeopardizing the continued existence of endangered species were also added. [43]

(f) Awake After Silent Spring — 1970-present

Concern for endangered species carried forward to the 1970s, joining with the flowering of the environmental movement. [44] Wildlife benefitted from the

---

[36] *Id.*

[37] *Id.* at 234.

[38] *Id.*

[39] Pub.L. No. 89-669, §§ 1–3, 80 Stat. 926 (repealed 1973).

[40] 16 U.S.C.A. §§ 460*l*-4 to 460*l*-11 (1976 & Supp. V. 1981); See § 5.2(A)(2)(c) of Chapter 5, *supra.*

[41] *Id.* at 235.

[42] *See,* note 110, *infra.*

[43] *Id.*

[44] *See,* § 1.2(H) of Chapter 1, *supra.*

host of statutes passed during the beginning of the decade: the Clean Air Act, the Clean Water Act, the National Environmental Policy Act, the Marine Mammal Protection Act, the National Forest Management Act, the Federal Land Policy and Management Act, and so on. These laws reflect a new understanding of the impact of human activities on the environment and direct significant federal resources to environmental clean up and to a change in industrial practices that cause pollution.

For wildlife, the single most important event of the period may well be the publication in 1962 of Rachel Carson's *Silent Spring*, which described the terrible threat posed by DDT (dichloro-diphenyl-trichloro-ethane) and other pesticides to the osprey, brown pelican, peregrine falcon, and other birds, animals, and fish.[45] Once again, common animals were at the brink of disappearing. Although it took 10 years from publication of the book, the Environmental Protection Agency (EPA) banned the use of DDT and related pesticides in 1972. In the years since then, the affected bird species, particularly the brown pelican, have made a remarkable comeback.

At the present time, the future for many species of American wildlife is uncertain. Understanding of wildlife needs has grown tremendously, but so has the human impact on wildlife habitat and water resources. More is known about the causes of species decline and extinction, but a corresponding understanding of how to solve these problems is lacking. Wildlife law will continue to be an important vehicle for grappling with these issues.

* * *

The preceding historical piece demonstrates that, while conservation of wildlife became a national goal early in the last century, efforts to accomplish the goal lagged seriously behind. Hampering pro-conservation efforts were a severely deficient understanding of the operation of natural ecosystems and a propensity to favor some species while ignoring, if not affirmatively demolishing, others. The result was a virtual parade of species-specific federal statutes,[1] which in the aggregate failed to sustain wildlife populations. What was sought, therefore, was a statute that would protect the whole of threatened wildlife rather than designated subgroups, and would do so by mandatory, not voluntary, controls. The first statute to do that was the Endangered Species Act of 1973, 16 U.S.C. §§ 1531–1543 ("ESA").[2]

---

[45] *See*, § 1.2(F) of Chapter 1, *supra*.

[1] In addition to the Lacey Act, 16 U.S.C. § 701 and 18 U.S.C. §§ 42–44, and the other measures noted in the Sheldon piece, other federal enactments specifically aimed at protecting wildlife include: the Migratory Bird Treaty Act of 1918, 16 U.S.C. § 703 et seq.; the Black Bass Act of 1926, 44 Stat. 576, as amended, 16 U. S. C. § 851 et seq. (1976 ed.); the Migratory Bird Conservation Act of 1929, 16 U.S.C. § 715 et seq.; the Fish and Wildlife Coordination Act of 1934, 16 U.S.C. § 661 et seq.; the Bald Eagle Protection Act of 1940, 16 U.S.C. § 668 et seq.; the Wild Free-Roaming Horses and Burros Act of 1971, 16 U.S.C. §§ 1331–1340; the Marine Mammal Protection Act of 1972, 16 U.S.C. § 1361 et seq.; and the Magnuson Fishery Conservation and Management Act of 1976, 16 U.S.C. § 1801 et seq.

[2] As noted in the Sheldon excerpt, *see, supra*, the Endangered Species Act of 1966 was "weak," largely because compliance with its provisions was voluntary. In 1969, Congress followed it up with the Endangered Species Conservation Act, 83 Stat. 275, repealed, 87 Stat. 903, which limited the import and sale of species in danger of "worldwide extinction." Neither of these statutes decelerated the increasingly rapid rate of species extinction.

The ESA simply towers over all other wildlife protection measures. The United States Supreme Court described it as "the most comprehensive legislation for the preservation of endangered species ever enacted by any nation." *Tennessee Valley Authority v. Hill*, 437 U.S. 153, 180, 98 S. Ct. 2279, 2294 (1978); *see infra*. Former Secretary of Interior Bruce Babbitt characterized the statute as "undeniably the most innovative, wide-reaching, and successful environmental law which has been enacted in the last quarter century." Bruce Babbitt, *The Endangered Species Act and "Takings": A Call for Innovation Within the Terms of the Act*, 24 Envt'l L. 355, 356 (1994).

One would speculate that a far-reaching legislative initiative of this sort would have generated a great deal of controversy in the Congress, but, as a political matter, enacting the ESA turned out to be easy. For one thing, Congress was distracted by more compelling problems, namely the Middle East oil embargo, and the looming prospect of a Presidential impeachment. For another, the Congress was suffering from a serious lack of appreciation for what it was doing. The conventional wisdom was that there would be perhaps 100 species that might warrant protection. Congress did not foresee the legislation it was about to enact would go far beyond protecting the grand statements of natural evolution, like the bald eagle, wolf, and grizzly, all the way to furbish louseworts, kangaroo rats, mollusks, and a wide array of plants. As one Congressman put it, "The fact is that if Congress knew in 1974 how the Act would have turned out, it never would have passed the legislation in the first place — at least not in this form." Congressman Bill Thomas, *Externalization of Federal Public Policy Costs: The Endangered Species Act*, 8 Fordham Envt'l L.J. 171, 175 (1996).

But Congress did not know. Its debate on the bill was cursory, focusing on the arguably insignificant issue whether the federal government should supplant traditional state wildlife regulation. In the end, the Senate enacted the statute 92-0, and the House followed suit by 355-4. President Jimmy Carter signed the bill into law on December 28, 1973.

In the nearly thirty years since its enactment, the ESA has become precisely what Congress did not envision. It is broadly protective of hundreds of species of plants and animals. Protection comes at a significant cost — the Act has upset the plans and expectations of thousands of people at a cost in the many millions of dollars.

In the remainder of Chapter, we examine this prodigious statute. Our coverage will center on the ESA's major regulatory provisions, §§ 4, 7, and 9. Section 4, 16 U.S.C. § 1533, is the ESA's triggering mechanism. It establishes the process by which species are listed as endangered or threatened, and thereby come under the protective shield of the statute. Section 4 also calls for designations of "critical habitat" for each protected species. Once the trigger is pulled, § 7, 16 U.S.C. § 1536, and § 9, 16 U.S.C. § 1538, bring the force of the statute into play. Section 7 is a broad prohibition on any action by the federal government that might jeopardize an endangered or threatened species or destroy or adversely modify its critical habitat. Section 9, applicable to all persons, including the federal government, prohibits a variety of independent actions that could injure, directly or indirectly, those same species. The Chapter concludes with a look at initiatives designed to work flexibility into the regulatory system.

B. SECTION 4

[1] THE LISTING PROCESS

According to the ESA, a "species" is defined to include "any subspecies of fish or wildlife or plants, and any distinct population segment of any species of vertebrate fish or wildlife which interbreeds when mature." § 3(16), 16 U.S.C. § 1532(16). If a species is "listed" as endangered or threatened, the provisions of the ESA apply. A species, other than a member of the Class Insecta found to be a pest, qualifies as "endangered" if it is determined that the species is "in danger of extinction throughout all or a significant portion of its range[.]" § 3(6), 16 U.S.C. § 1532(6). A species qualifies as "threatened" if it is determined that the species "is likely to become an endangered species within the foreseeable future throughout all or a significant portion of its range." § 3(20), 16 U.S.C. § 1532(20).

The Secretary[1] is directed to determine the identity of species that are endangered or threatened and to list all of the species so qualifying. § 4(a), 16 U.S.C. § 1533(a). The process of listing can begin by a unilateral decision of the appropriate Secretary to engage in what is known as the candidate assessment process. Or the process can begin by the filing of a petition by an interested third party in accordance with § 4(e) of the Administrative Procedure Act, 5 U.S.C. § 553(e), § 4(b)(3)(A), 16 U.S.C. §1533(b)(3)(A).[2]

If a listing is found to be warranted, the Secretary is directed to publish in the Federal Register "a general notice and the complete text of a proposed regulation to implement [the listing decision]," § 4(b)(3)(B)(ii),16 U.S.C. § 1533(b)(3)(B)(ii), providing at least 90 days for comment. § 4(b)(5)(A), 16 U.S.C. § 1533(b)(5)(A). Within one year after publication of the proposed rule, the Secretary must make a final decision whether to place the species on the endangered or threatened species list. § 4(b)(6)(A), 16 U.S.C. § 1533(b)(6)(A). The one-year period runs from the date of publication of the proposed rule. *Oregon Natural Resources Council v. Kantor*, 99 F.3d 334, 339 (9th Cir 1996). The Secretary can extend the period by six months if "there is substantial

---

[1] If terrestrial species are involved, the appropriate Secretary is the Secretary of the Interior. The Secretary of the Interior has delegated listing authority to the United States Fish and Wildlife Service ("FWS"), a subunit of the Department of Interior. If ocean species or anadromous fish are involved, the appropriate Secretary is the Secretary of Commerce. The Secretary of Commerce has delegated listing authority to the National Marine Fisheries Service ("NMFS"), a subunit of the Department of Commerce.

[2] In this event, "[t]o the maximum extent practicable," the Secretary must make a finding within 90 days of receiving the petition "as to whether the petition presents substantial scientific or commercial information indicating that the petitioned action may be warranted." *Id.;* § 7(b)(1), 16 U.S.C. § 1536(b)(1). (The ninety-day requirement was added to the ESA in 1982, in response to complaints that the process was too slow — in the immediately preceding year, for example, only two species had made it through the listing process). If the Secretary finds the petitioned action may be warranted, he shall "promptly commence a review of the status of the species concerned." *Id.* Within 12 months of receiving the petition, the Secretary must make one of three findings: (1) the listing is warranted, (2) the listing is not warranted, or (3) at the present time the listing is warranted but precluded, primarily by "pending proposals to determine whether any species is an endangered species or a threatened species." § 4(b)(3)(B), 16 U.S.C. § 1533(b)(3)(B).

Note that the same process applies with respect to petitions to delist a species.

disagreement regarding the sufficiency or accuracy of the available data relevant to the determination . . . concerned." § 4(b)(6)(B)(1), 16 U.S.C. § 1533(b)(6)(B)(i). The Act calls for consultations with states during this process. § 4(b)(5)(A)(2), 16 U.S.C. § 1533(b)(5)(A)(ii).

ALSEA VALLEY ALLIANCE v. EVANS

161 F. Supp. 2d 1154 (D.Ore. 2001)

MICHAEL R. HOGAN, UNITED STATES DISTRICT JUDGE.

ORDER

Plaintiffs bring this action challenging the validity of the listing decision. Currently before the court are plaintiffs' motion (# 74 for suumary judgement and defendants' cross motion (# 81) for summary judgement.

I. Background

In 1973, Congress enacted the ESA "to provide a program for the conservation of . . . endangered and threatened species." 16 U.S.C. § 1531(b). The purposes of the ESA are "to provide a means whereby the ecosystems upon which endangered species and threatened species depend may be conserved, to provide a program for the conservation of such endangered species and threatened species, and to take such steps as may be appropriate to achieve [these] purposes . . . ." *Id.* § 2(b). The ESA also recognizes that conservation of listed species may be facilitated by artificial means. Specifically, the ESA defined the term "conservation" as:

> . . . the use of all methods and procedures which are necessary to bring any endangered species or threatened species to the point at which the measures provided pursuant to [the ESA] are no longer necessary. Such methods and procedures include, but are not limited to, all activities associated with scientific resources management such as research, census, law enforcement, habitat acquisition and maintenance, propagation, live trapping, and transplantation. . . .

16 U.S.C. § 1532(3) . . . .

Section 4(a) of the ESA commits to the Secretary of Commerce ("Secretary") the responsibility of determining whether certain species are "endangered" or "threatened." The Secretary has delegated this authority to the NMFS. . . .

The ESA defines "species" to include "any subspecies of fish or wildlife or plants, and any distinct population segment of any species of vertebrate fish or wildlife which interbreeds when mature." 16 U.S.C. § 1532(16) (emphasis added). Congress did not define the term "distinct population segment" ("DPS") and the ESA does not set forth any restrictive criteria for defining a DPS. *See Southwest Center for Biological Diversity v. Babbitt,* 980 F. Supp. 1080, 1083 (D. Ariz. 1997).

Beginning in 1991, NMFS issued various policies that interpreted the ESA and its DPS provision, relevant to the Pacific salmon. NMFS eventually applied these policies to the coho salmon in its August 10, 1998, listing decision.

On November 20, 1991, NMFS issued its "Policy on Applying the Definition of Species Under the Endangered Species Act to Pacific Salmon" (hereinafter the "ESU Policy"). 56 Fed. Reg. 58,612 (1991). In the ESU Policy, NMFS introduced the term "evolutionary significant unit" ("ESU") to interpret the ESA's meaning of "distinct population segment." 56 Fed. Reg. at 58,613 (Nov. 20, 1991). NMFS explained:

> a stock of Pacific salmon will be considered a distinct population, and hence a "species" under the ESA, if it represents an Evolutionary significant unit (ESU) of the biological species. A stock must satisfy two criteria to be considered an ESU:
>
> (1) It must be substantially reproductively isolated from other conspecific population units; and
>
> (2) It must represent an important component in the evolutionary legacy of the species.

56 Fed. Reg. at 58,618.

NMFS states that the first criterion can be measured "by movements of tagged fish, recolonization rates of other populations, measurements of genetic differences between populations, and evaluations of the efficacy of natural barriers." *Id.*

The second criterion is concerned with the "ecological/genetic diversity" of the species as a whole. *Id.* NMFS states that the following questions are relevant in determining whether this criterion is met 1) is the population genetically distinct from other conspecific populations, 2) does the population occupy unusual or distinctive habitat, 3) does the population show evidence of unusual or distinctive adaptation to its environment. *Id.*

On April 5, 1993, the NMFS published its policy entitled "Interim Policy on Artificial Propagation of Pacific Salmon Under the Endangered Species Act" (the "Hatchery Policy"). 58 Fed. Reg. 17,573 (1993). The Hatchery Policy describes how the NMFS considers hatchery populations when making listing decisions about the Pacific salmon. The Hatchery Policy interprets the ESA as requiring NMFS to focus its recovery efforts on "natural populations." The Hatchery Policy builds upon this cornerstone interpretation with the position that "artificial propagation may represent a potential method to conserve listed salmon species when the artificially propagated fish are determined similar to the listed natural population in genetic, phenotypic, and life-history traits, and in habitat use characteristics." 58 Fed. Reg. at 17,573-74 (April 5, 1993) (emphasis added). Although hatchery populations may be included as part of a listed species, NMFS policy is that it should be done sparingly because artificial propagation could pose risks to natural populations. Id. at 17,575. Thus, the Hatchery Policy states:

> If available information indicates that existing hatchery fish can be considered part of the biological ESU, a decision must be made whether to include them as part of the listed species. In general, such fish will not be included as part of the listed species. An exception may be made for existing hatchery fish if they are considered to be essential for recovery.

Id. at 17,575 (emphasis added).

NMFS excludes hatchery populations from its listing decision unless the hatchery population can be considered part of the ESU and the NMFS considers the hatchery population "essential to recovery." *Id.* at 17,575.[2] at 42,587-88. One of the ESU's proposed as "threatened" by NMFS was the "Oregon Coast ESU." NMFS subsequently revoked this decision based partly on conservation measures in the Oregon Coastal Salmon Restoration Initiative and a Memorandum of Agreement between the NMFS and the State of Oregon that assured state protection of this species. 62 Fed. Reg. 24,588 (May 6, 1997). However, a lawsuit was filed in this district that challenged NMFS' decision not to list Oregon Coast coho as threatened. *See Oregon Natural Resources Council v. Daley,* 6 F. Supp. 2d 1139 (D. Or. 1998) (Stewart, J.) The court ultimately found that NMFS should not have considered the conservation measures in the state restoration initiative and the memorandum agreement with the state of Oregon and remanded to the agency to reconsider its decision. *Id.* at 1161.

Pursuant to court order, on August 10, 1998, NMFS issued a final rule listing the Oregon Coast coho ESU as threatened. 63 Fed. Reg. 42,587 (Aug. 10, 1998). However, within this ESU, NMFS only listed all "naturally spawned" coho inhabiting streams between Cape Blanco and the Columbia River. *Id.* In reaching this listing decision, NMFS applied its April 5, 1993 Hatchery Policy to the coho salmon. 63 Fed. Reg. 42,589. NMFS concluded that nine Oregon hatchery populations were part of the same Oregon Coast ESU as the natural populations. However, the hatchery populations were not included in the listing decision because the hatchery populations were not "deemed 'essential' to recovery." *Id.* Although excluded from the listing decision, NMFS stated that it might consider using these hatchery populations for future recovery but that "in this context, an 'essential' hatchery population is one that is vital for full incorporation into recovery efforts." *Id.*

Plaintiffs seek to invalidate the August 10, 1998 listing decision. Plaintiffs central argument is that NMFS' distinction between "naturally spawned" and "hatchery spawned" coho salmon is arbitrary and capricious and thus unlawful under the Administrative Procedures Act ("APA") 5 U.S.C. § 706.

II. Standards (discussion of standard of review omitted)

III. Discussion

Both parties move for summary judgment on plaintiffs' claims. Defendants further move for summary judgment on statute of limitations grounds.

---

[2] NMFS Policy states that a hatchery population will not be considered part of the ESU if the available information indicates that:

   1) the hatchery population in question is of a different genetic lineage than the listed natural populations,

   2) artificial propagation has produced appreciable changes in the hatchery population in characteristics that are believed to have a genetic basis, or

   3) there is substantial uncertainty about the relationship between existing hatchery fish and the natural population.

58 Fed. Reg. 17,575.

A. Statute Of Limitations

Defendants correctly note that the ESA contains no express statute of limitations. Therefore, the applicable statute of limitations is found at 28 U.S.C. § 2401(a), the general statute of limitations for civil actions against the federal government. (citations omitted).

28 U.S.C. § 2401(a) provides that "every civil action commenced against the United States shall be barred unless the complaint is filed within six years after the right of action first accrues." Under section 2401(a), a cause of action first accrues when the "person challenging the action can institute and maintain a suit in court." *Trafalgar Capital Assoc. v. Cuomo*, 159 F.3d 21, 34 (1st Cir. 1998).

. . . It was appropriate for plaintiffs to await defendants' final listing decision of August 10, 1998, before bringing suit. This presents a justiciable issue for the court and does not run afoul of the statute of limitations. Defendants' motion for summary judgment on statute of limitations grounds is denied.

B. The ESA Challenge

Plaintiffs argue that the distinction between hatchery spawned and naturally spawned coho is untenable under the ESA because the ESA does not allow the Secretary to make listing distinctions below that of species, subspecies or a distinct population segment of a species. Essentially, plaintiffs argue that the Secretary, in this instance, must include or exclude all members of a distinct population segment, as opposed to only some members of a distinct population segment. Defendants argue that the distinction between hatchery coho and natural coho is valid because the NMFS interpretation of the ESA, and in particular its interpretation of a "distinct population segment," should be afforded great deference by this court.

After reviewing the administrative record and the relevant statutes and legislative history, the court finds that the NMFS August 10, 1998 listing decision is arbitrary and capricious and therefore invalid because it relied on factors upon which Congress did not intend the NMFS to rely. The NMFS decision defines the ESU and thus [sic] DSP, but then takes an additional step, beyond its definition of an ESU, to eliminate hatchery coho from its listing decision.

NMFS defined a "distinct population segment" by making it the equivalent of a term (it created) called an "evolutionary significant unit" ("ESU"). A species is considered an ESU, and hence a DPS, if it is "substantially reproductively isolated from other conspecific population units" and "represent[s] an important component in the evolutionary legacy of the species." 56 Fed. Reg. at 58,618.

The NMFS interpretation of what constitutes a "distinct population segment" is a permissible agency construction of the ESA. *See Panamsat Corp. v. Federal Communications Comm'n*, 339 U.S. App. D.C. 143, 198 F.3d 890, 894 (D.C. Cir. 1999) (citing *Chevron U.S.A., Inc. v. NRDC*, 467 U.S. 837, 842-43, 81 L. Ed. 2d 694, 104 S. Ct. 2778 (1983) (court must defer to a permissible agency construction of a statute). Specifically, the NMFS creation of an

ESU and the factors used to define it, geography and genetics, are within permissible limits under the ESA.

The central problem with the NMFS listing decision of August 10, 1998, is that it makes improper distinctions, below that of a DPS, by excluding hatchery coho populations from listing protection even though they are determined to be part of the same DPS as natural coho populations.

The ESA "specifically states in the definition of 'species' that a 'species' may include any subspecies . . . and any distinct population segment (DPS) of any species . . . which interbreeds when mature." 16 U.S.C. § 1532(16); *Southwest Center for Biological Diversity v. Babbitt,* 980 F. Supp. 1080, 1085 (D. Ariz. 1997). Listing distinctions below that of subspecies or a DPS of a species are not allowed under the ESA. *Southwest Center,* 980 F. Supp. at 1085. Yet, this is precisely what the NMFS did in its final listing decision of August 10, 1998. NMFS concluded that nine hatchery stocks were part of the same Oregon Coast ESU/DPS as the "natural" populations but none of the hatchery stocks were included in the listing decision because NMFS did not consider them "essential for recovery." 63 Fed. Reg. 42,589.

The distinction between members of the same ESU/DPS is arbitrary and capricious because NMFS may consider listing only an entire species, subspecies or distinct population segment ("DPS") of any species. 16 U.S.C. § 1532(16). Once NMFS determined that hatchery spawned coho and naturally spawned coho were part of the same DPS/ESU, the listing decision should have been made without further distinctions between members of the same DPS/ESU.

The NMFS listing decision could arguably be proper under the ESA if the NMFS had defined "hatchery spawned" coho as a separate DPS, but it does not appear that this is possible. To classify hatchery spawned coho as a DPS under NMFS's own standard, hatchery spawned coho would have to be 1) "substantially reproductively isolated from other conspecific population units," and 2) "represent an important component in the evolutionary legacy of the species." 56 Fed. Reg. at 58,618. Here, hatchery spawned coho are likely not "substantially reproductively isolated" from naturally spawned coho because, once released from the hatchery, it is undisputed that "hatchery spawned" coho and "naturally spawned" coho within the Oregon Coast ESU share the same rivers, habitat and seasonal runs. (Plts.' Stmt. of Mat. Facts at ¶2; Dfts.' Resp. to Plts.' Stmt. of Mat. Facts at ¶2.) It is undisputed that "hatchery spawned" coho may account for as much as 87% of the naturally spawning coho in the Oregon coast ESU. (AR Ex. 12 at 120.) In addition, hatchery spawned and natural coho are the same species (Dfts.' Resp. to Plts.' Stmt. of Mat. Facts at ¶1.), and interbreed when mature (*Id.* at ¶4). Finally, the NMFS considers progeny of hatchery fish that are born in the wild as "naturally spawned" coho that deserve listing protection.

Despite these facts, NMFS decided that hatchery coho, that are part of the same DPS/ESU as natural coho, should not be listed because they were not "essential" to recovery. Thus, the NMFS listing decision creates the unusual circumstance of two genetically identical coho salmon swimming side-by-side in the same stream, but only one receives ESA protection while the other does not. The distinction is arbitrary.

Finally, NMFS argues that its listing decision does not contradict the terms of the ESA because the listing decision, and relevant polices, are in accordance with ESA goals that prioritize "natural" salmon populations and "genetic diversity" within those populations. Although I agree with the general concept that "genetic diversity" is one factor in the long term success of a threatened species, and thus is one of many underlying goals of the ESA, genetics cannot, by itself, justify a listing distinction that runs contrary to the definition of a DPS.

The term "distinct population segment" was amended in the ESA in 1978 so that it "would exclude taxonomic [biological] categories below subspecies [smaller taxa] from the definition." H.R. Conf. Rep. No. 95-1804, at 17 (1978), reprinted in 1978 U.S.C.C.A.N. 9485, 14855.

Congress adopted the DPS language stating:

> The committee agrees that there may be instances in which [the Fish and Wildlife Service] should provide for different levels of protection for populations of the same species. For instance, the U.S. population of an animal should not necessarily be permitted to become extinct simply because the animal is more abundant elsewhere in the world. Similarly, listing populations may be necessary when the preponderance of evidence indicates that a species faces a widespread threat, but conclusive data is available with regard to only certain populations.

S. Rep. No. 96-151.

Thus, Congress expressly limited the Secretary's ability to make listing distinctions among species below that of subspecies or a DPS of a species. Here, the NMFS listing decision was based on distinctions below that of subspecies or distinct population segment of a species.

Therefore, the NMFS's listing decision is arbitrary and capricious, because the Oregon Coast ESU includes both "hatchery spawned" and "naturally spawned" coho salmon, but the agency's listing decision arbitrarily excludes "hatchery spawned" coho. Consequently, the listing decision is unlawful. 5 U.S.C. § 706(2)(A).

IV. Conclusion

For the foregoing reasons, plaintiffs' motion (#74) for summary judgment is granted. Defendants' cross-motion (#81) for summary judgment is denied. The August 10, 1998 NMFS listing decision, contained at 63 Fed. Reg. 42,587, declared unlawful and set aside as arbitrary and capricious. The matter is remanded to the NMFS for further consideration consistent with this opinion. The agency is further directed to consider the best available scientific information, including the most recent data, in any further listing decision concerning the Oregon coast coho salmon.

IT IS SO ORDERED.

SOUTHWEST CENTER FOR BIOLOGICAL DIVERSITY v. BABBITT

215 F.3d 58 (D.C. Cir. 2000)

JUDGES: Before: EDWARDS, Chief Judge, RANDOLPH and ROGERS, Circuit Judges.

EDWARDS, Chief Judge: The only issue raised on appeal in this case is whether the Endangered Species Act ("Act") requires the Fish and Wildlife Service to conduct an on-site population count of birds when the currently available data are sparse and calculations of a bird species population must of necessity be based on estimates. The Act provides that the Secretary of the Interior must make decisions whether to list a species as endangered or threatened "solely on the basis of the best scientific and commercial data available to him. " 16 U.S.C. § 1533(b)(1)(A) (1994). Appellees, the Southwest Center for Biological Diversity, et al., ("Center"), argued below that the best available evidence demonstrates that the Fish and Wildlife Service should list the Queen Charlotte goshawk as a threatened or endangered species under 16 U.S.C. § 1533. Appellants, Bruce Babbitt, et al., ("Government") countered that the data did not compel such a listing. The principal dispute between the parties before the District Court was over what to make of the best available data, not whether such data existed. The District Court, however, sidestepped the parties' real dispute and concluded instead that the best available data simply was not good enough.

Indeed, instead of resolving the parties' dispute on the basis of the best available data in the record, the District Court issued an order remanding the case back to the Fish and Wildlife Service with instructions to count the goshawk population. *See Southwest Ctr. for Biological Diversity v. Babbitt,* Civ. No. 98-934, Order (D.D.C. July 20, 1999) ("Order"), reprinted in Joint Appendix ("J.A.") 1973. Appellants now challenge this order, claiming that the District Court's decision is completely at odds with the statute. We agree. The statute provides that the Secretary's decision must be made "solely on the basis of the best scientific and commercial data available to him." Therefore, on the record at hand, the District Court was without authority to order the Secretary to conduct an independent population count of the birds. Accordingly, we reverse the District Court's order, and we remand the case to the District Court for proper consideration of the parties' positions in light of the Act and an assessment of the available evidence.

I. Facts

On May 9, 1994, the Southwest Center for Biological Diversity filed a petition requesting that the Queen Charlotte goshawks, which are a "large, but rarely-seen" subspecies of hawks, be listed as threatened or endangered under the Act. *Southwest Ctr. for Biological Diversity v. Babbitt,* 939 F. Supp. 49, 50 (D.D.C. 1996); *see* 16 U.S.C. § 1533(b)(3)(A) (1994).* On May 19, 1995,

---

* [Ed. note: the listing petition was granted in August, 1994, triggering the 12-month period within which the agency was to decide whether a listing was warranted. *Southwest Center for Biological Diversity v. Babbitt,* 939 F. Supp. 49, 50–51 (1996).]

the Fish and Wildlife Service found that, based on the best available scientific and commercial evidence, no listing was warranted. *See Babbitt,* 939 F. Supp. at 51. This initial decision was based on the Fish and Wildlife Service's conclusion that the Forest Service would address land management options to ensure goshawk habitat conservation. The Center challenged this decision, and, on September 25, 1996, the District Court granted a summary judgment in favor of the Center, finding that the Secretary could not rely on the Forest Service's possible future actions "as an excuse for not making a determination based on the existing record." *Id.* at 52.

On remand, the Fish and Wildlife Service once again declined to list the Queen Charlotte goshawk as a threatened or endangered species, and the Center once again challenged the agency's determination. In a July 9, 1999 hearing before the District Court, the Government argued that its sole obligation under the Endangered Species Act is to consider and act on the best available data, which the Government claimed it had done. The District Court persisted, however, in suggesting that a population count was necessary. *See, e.g.,* Trial Tr. at 2–3, reprinted in J.A. 1913–14. The trial judge could not be moved from this position, not even by plaintiffs' acknowledgment that the District Court was required to assess the parties' positions in light of the best available evidence, not a population count. Following argument by the parties, the District Court issued an opinion on July 20, 1999, remanding the case to the Fish and Wildlife Service "for a more reliable determination of the Queen Charlotte goshawk population. . . ." Order at 3, reprinted in J.A. 1975. This appeal followed.

II. Analysis

On the record before us, it is clear that the District Court exceeded its authority in ordering the Government to conduct a population count of the goshawk species. 16 U.S.C. § 1533(a)(1) instructs the Secretary to

determine whether any species is an endangered species or a threatened species because of any of the following factors:

(A)   the present or threatened destruction, modification, or curtailment of its habitat or range;

(B)   overutilization for commercial, recreational, scientific or educational purposes;

(C)   disease or predation;

(D)   the inadequacy of existing regulatory mechanisms; or

(E)   other natural or manmade factors affecting its continued existence.

16 U.S.C. § 1533(a)(1) (1994). The Secretary is to make such a determination "solely on the basis of the best scientific and commercial data available to him. . . ." 16 U.S.C. § 1533(b)(1)(A). Read together, the two statutory provisions require the Secretary to list a species as endangered or threatened if, based solely on the best available data, any of § 1533(a)(1)'s five factors are sufficiently implicated. The "best available data" requirement makes it clear that the Secretary has no obligation to conduct independent studies. As we noted in *City of Las Vegas v. Lujan,* 282 U.S. App. D.C. 57, 891 F.2d 927, 933

(D.C. Cir. 1989), in the context of emergency listings under 16 U.S.C. § 1533(b)(7), 16 U.S.C. § 1533(b)(1)(A) "merely prohibits the Secretary from disregarding available scientific evidence that is in some way better than the evidence he relies on. Even if the available scientific and commercial data were quite inconclusive, he may — indeed must — still rely on it at that stage."

Appellees do not claim — for good reason, we think — that the statute's reference to "best scientific data available" requires the Secretary to find and consider any information that is arguably susceptible to discovery. In other words, appellees never have contended in this case that the Government is obliged to conduct an on-site population count of the goshawk. And appellees never have contended that the Secretary acted on the basis of no data. Rather, appellees have argued that the best available scientific data in this record demonstrate that the goshawk is already on the verge of extinction due to low population estimates and "some 'natural or manmade factors affecting its continued existence.'" Appellees Br. at 20 (quoting 16 U.S.C. § 1533(a)(1)(E)). This is the issue that properly was before the District Court, and this is the issue that should have been decided below.

The trial judge, however, ignored the statute, disregarded the parties' arguments, and determined instead that, because he found the available evidence inconclusive, the Secretary was obligated to find better data. The Government forthrightly concedes that "the district court's view has a superficial appeal — certainly the [Fish and Wildlife Service] would like to know how many [Queen Charlotte] goshawks there are. . . ." Reply Br. at 3. But, as the Government contends (with no real contest from appellees), this superficial appeal cannot circumvent the statute's clear wording: The Secretary must make his decision as to whether to list a species as threatened or endangered "solely on the basis of the best scientific and commercial data available to him. . . ." 16 U.S.C. § 1533(b)(1)(A); Reply Br. at 3 ("The court's view is at odds with both the practical realities of endangered species work and the governing legal regime."). The Secretary argued below that the best available evidence supports the Government's decision not to list the goshawk, while the Center argued that the available evidence supports the opposite view. The District Court's responsibility was to assess the evidence and resolve the parties' dispute. The court's decision to sidestep this responsibility by imposing an obligation upon the Secretary to find better data was error.

III. Conclusion

For the foregoing reasons, we reverse the District Court's decision to remand the case to the Fish and Wildlife Service, and we remand the case to the District Court for consideration of the parties' positions in light of the Endangered Species Act and an assessment of the available evidence.

NOTES AND QUESTIONS

1. *Southwest Center* stands for the proposition that only "available" data needs to be considered in a listing decision, and, of that, only the "best scientific and commercial" data. What constitutes "available" information is largely unrevealed. However, the opinion sheds some light on the matter:

"available" information is not the universe of information "arguably susceptible to discovery." But would "available" encompass information *reasonably*
susceptible to discovery? One would think, for example, that the Secretary
should have a legal obligation to review current scientific literature. For what
purpose is 12 months allotted for species status review if not at least for that?
The question then becomes, if current scientific literature is "available," why
is information not collectable by an on-site population count not also "available"? Instead of grappling with these matters, *Southwest Center* merely cites
City of Las Vegas v. Lujan, 891 F.2d 927 (D.C. Cir. 1989), to support its ruling.
But *City of Las Vegas* assumed the availability of information. *City of Las
Vegas*, moreover, involved an *emergency* listing of a species, which, is an
entirely different matter than the "routine" listing considered in *Southwest
Center*. § 4(b)(7), 16 U.S.C. § 1533(b)(7).

For more on the quality of information necessary for species listing, *see, e.g.,
Blue Water Fisherman's Ass'n. v. National Marine Fisheries Service*, 226 F.
Supp. 330, 338 (D. Mass. 2002) ("The agency's conclusion need not be airtight
and indisputable. When an agency relies on the analysis and opinion of experts
and employs the best evidence available, the fact that the evidence is 'weak,'
and thus not dispositive, does not render the agency's decision 'arbitrary and
capricious.'") (citing *Greenpeace Action v. Franklin*, 14 F.3d 1324, 1336 (9th
Cir. 1992).

An unanswered question is whether weak information should ever produce
an affirmative decision to list a species. Note that § 4(b)(3) of the ESA, 16
U.S.C. § 1533(b)(3), requires petitioners for listing to present "substantial . . .
information indicating that the petitioned action may be warranted" and calls
for listing only where the "listing is warranted." In addition, the Administrative Procedure Act expressly places the burden of proof on the "proponent"
of a rule, at least when formal proceedings are called for. APA, § 556(d), 5
U.S.C. § 556(d).

2. How should the presence of conservation efforts by other governmental
entities bear on a listing decision? The answer may depend on the status of
the effort. There would seem to be three possibilities: (a) an effort not yet in
place but projected; (b) one "newly implemented" but not yet "operational";
and (c) one both implemented and in operation. Clearly, conservation efforts
that fall into category (c) should be considered in listing decisions. *See, e.g.,
Defenders of Wildlife v. Babbitt*, 1999 U.S. Dist. LEXIS 10366 (S.D. Cal., June
14, 1999). But, as the *Defenders* court notes, there is disagreement among
federal courts with respect to categories (a) and (b). Your view? Note that ESA
§ 4(a)(1)(D) directs decisionmakers to examine the "inadequacy of existing
regulatory mechanisms." (emphasis added).

3. Is the Endangered Species Act a constitutional exercise of the Congress'
affirmative Commerce Clause authorities, even when it is applied to protect
a subspecies of no known economic value and located solely on a discrete
intrastate parcel of land? *See, e.g., Gibbs v. Babbitt*, 214 F.3d. 483, *cert. denied,*
531 U.S. 1145, 121 S. Ct. 1081 (2001). *See also* Chapter 3, *supra.*

4. In 1980, seven years after enactment of the ESA, the number of listed
species totaled 281–36 of which were mammals and 59 of which were plants.
As of July, 2004, there were 746 species of plants and 519 species of animals

listed as endangered or threatened in the United States. These numbers demonstrate a doubling in the number of protected mammals and a more than twelvefold increase in the number of plants. Only about one percent of listed species have been delisted. As of that same date, one hundred thirty seven species of animals and 143 species of plants were designated as candidate species.

The list of endangered and threatened species may be found at 50 C.F.R. Part 17. *See also* http://ecos.fws.gov/tess_public/TESSBoxscore. Regulatory provisions to be followed when species are proposed for listing may be found at 50 C.F.R. Part 424. The FWS publishes its list of candidate species in the Federal Register on an annual basis, and the NMFS does the same periodically.

[2] DESIGNATION OF CRITICAL HABITAT

In addition to listing endangered and threatened species, the ESA requires the appropriate Secretary to designate a "critical habitat" for all listed species. § 4(a)(3), 16 U.S.C. § 1533(a)(3); *Bennett v. Spear*, 520 U.S. 154, 117 S. Ct. 1154 (1997). The ESA contemplates designation of both "occupied" and "unoccupied" critical habitat. Occupied critical habitat is defined as "the specific areas within the geographic area occupied by the species, at the time it is listed . . . on which are found those physical or biological features (I) essential to the conservation of the species and (II) which may require special management considerations or protection." § 3(5)(A)(i), 16 U.S.C. § 1532(5)(A)(i). Unoccupied critical habitat consists of "specific areas outside the geographical area occupied by the species at the time it is listed . . . upon a determination by the Secretary that such areas are essential for the conservation of the species." § 3(5)(A)(ii), 16 U.S.C. § 1532(5)(A)(ii). Except in special circumstances determined by the Secretary, critical habitat "shall not include the entire geographic area which can be occupied" by the species. § 3(5)(C), 16 U.S.C. § 1532(5)(C).

The ESA requires a designation of critical habitat concurrent with the listing of a species "to the maximum extent prudent or determinable." § 4(a)(3), 16 U.S.C. § 1533(a)(3). The designation should be made "on the basis of the best scientific data available and after taking into consideration the economic impact, and any other relevant impact, of specifying any particular area as critical habitat." § 4(b)(2), 16 U.S.C. § 1533(b)(2). Congress speculated that a "not prudent" finding would be rare. H.R. Conf. Rep. No. 97-835, at 24 (1982), *reprinted in* 1982 U.S. Cong. Code and Admin. News 2860, 2865; H.R. Rep. No. 95-1625, at 16–17 (1978), *reprinted in* 1978 U.S. Cong. Code and Admin. News 9453, 9466-67; *see also Enos v. Marsh*, 769 F.2d 1363, 1371 (9th Cir. 1985) (the FWS "may only fail to designate a critical habitat under rare circumstances").

NATURAL RESOURCES DEFENSE COUNCIL v. UNITED STATES DEPARTMENT OF INTERIOR

113 F.3d 1121 (9th Cir. 1997)

JUDGES: Before: HARRY PREGERSON, DOROTHY W. NELSON, and DIARMUID F. O'SCANNLAIN, Circuit Judges.

PREGERSON, Circuit Judge:

This case presents the question whether the defendants violated the Endangered Species Act by failing to designate critical habitat for the coastal California gnatcatcher. Upon cross-motions for summary judgment, the district court denied the plaintiffs' motion and granted summary judgment for the defendants. We have jurisdiction pursuant to 28 U.S.C. § 1291. We reverse.

Facts

The coastal California gnatcatcher is a songbird unique to coastal southern California and northern Baja California. The gnatcatcher's survival depends upon certain subassociations of coastal sage scrub, a type of habitat that has been severely depleted by agricultural and urban development. Approximately 2500 pairs of gnatcatchers survive in southern California today.

On March 30, 1993, the U.S. Fish and Wildlife Service (the "Service") listed the gnatcatcher under the Endangered Species Act (the "Act") as a "threatened species." 58 Fed. Reg. 16742 (1993). Under section 4 of the Act, the listing of a threatened species must be accompanied by the concurrent designation of critical habitat for that species "to the maximum extent prudent and determinable." 16 U.S.C. § 1533(a)(3). The designation of critical habitat in turn triggers the protections of section 7 of the Act. Section 7 requires that federal agencies consult with the Secretary of the Interior (the "Secretary") to ensure that actions authorized, funded, or carried out by federal agencies do not harm critical habitat. *Id.* § 1536(a)(2).

At the time of the gnatcatcher's listing as a threatened species, the Service found that coastal sage scrub habitat loss posed "a significant threat to the continued existence of the coastal California gnatcatcher." 58 Fed. Reg. at 16748. Nevertheless, the Service concluded that critical habitat designation would not be "prudent" within the meaning of section 4 for two reasons. *Id.* at 16756. First, the Service claimed that the public identification of critical habitat would increase the risk that landowners might deliberately destroy gnatcatcher habitat. Second, the Service claimed that critical habitat designation "would not appreciably benefit" the gnatcatcher because most gnatcatcher habitat is found on private lands to which section 7's consultation requirement does not apply.

The Natural Resources Defense Council, the National Audubon Society, and biologist Elisabeth Brown (collectively, the "plaintiffs") challenged the Service's failure to designate critical habitat in this suit against the Service, various Service officials, the Secretary, and the U.S. Department of the

Interior (collectively, the "defendants"). Each side moved for summary judgment. The district court denied the plaintiffs' motion and granted summary judgment to the defendants.

On this appeal, the plaintiffs contend that the district court erred in granting summary judgment to the defendants rather than the plaintiffs. In response, the defendants contend that the case is moot and must therefore be dismissed for lack of jurisdiction; or, in the alternative, that the district court's grant of summary judgment for the defendants should be affirmed.* * *

[Discussion of standard of review and justiciability omitted]

II. The Service's Failure to Designate Critical Habitat

Section 4 of the Act requires that the gnatcatcher's listing as a threatened species be accompanied by concurrent designation of critical habitat "to the maximum extent prudent and determinable":

The Secretary, by regulation promulgated in accordance with subsection (b) of this section and to the maximum extent prudent and determinable —

(A) shall, concurrently with making a determination under paragraph (1) that a species is an endangered species or a threatened species, designate any habitat of such species which is then considered to be critical habitat; and

(B) may, from time-to-time thereafter as appropriate, revise such designation.

16 U.S.C. § 1533(a)(3) (emphasis added).

The Act itself does not define the term "prudent." The Service has defined what would not be prudent, however, in the regulations promulgated under the Act. According to the regulations, critical habitat designation is not prudent "when one or both of the following situations exist":

(i) The species is threatened by taking or other human activity, and identification of critical habitat can be expected to increase the degree of such threat to the species, or

(ii) Such designation of critical habitat would not be beneficial to the species.

50 C.F.R. § 424.12(a)(1)(i)-(ii) (1996) (emphasis added).

When the Service published the gnatcatcher's final listing as a threatened species, the Service stated that critical habitat designation would not be prudent under either prong of the regulatory definition. 58 Fed. Reg. at 16756. The final listing fails to show, however, that the Service adequately "considered the relevant factors and articulated a rational connection between the facts found and the choice made" as required under *Resources Ltd.,* 35 F.3d at 1304 (quoting *Pyramid Lake Paiute Tribe,* 898 F.2d at 1414).

A. Increased Threat to the Species

The Service's first reason for declining to designate critical habitat was that designation would increase the degree of threat to the gnatcatcher. 58 Fed.

Reg. at 16756. The final listing referred to eleven cases in which landowners or developers had destroyed gnatcatcher sites; in two of these cases, habitat was destroyed after the Service notified local authorities that gnatcatchers were present at a proposed development site. *Id.* at 16753, 16756. On the basis of this history, the Service concluded that because the publication of critical habitat descriptions and maps would enable more landowners to identify gnatcatcher sites, designating critical habitat "would likely make the species more vulnerable to [prohibited takings] activities." *Id.* at 16756.

This "increased threat" rationale fails to balance the pros and cons of designation as Congress expressly required under section 4 of the Act. Section 4(b)(2) states that the Secretary may only exclude portions of habitat from critical habitat designation "if he determines that the benefits of such exclusion outweigh the benefits of specifying such area as part of the critical habitat." 16 U.S.C. § 1533(b)(2) (emphasis added). In addition, the Service itself has said that it will forgo habitat designation as a matter of prudence only "in those cases in which the possible adverse consequences would outweigh the benefits of designation." 49 Fed. Reg. 38900, 38903 (1984) (emphasis added).

In this case, the Service never weighed the benefits of designation against the risks of designation. The final listing decision cited only eleven cases of habitat destruction, out of 400,000 acres of gnatcatcher habitat. The listing did not explain how such evidence shows that designation would cause more landowners to destroy, rather than protect, gnatcatcher sites. The absence of such an explanation is particularly troubling given that the record shows these areas had already been surveyed extensively in other gnatcatcher or coastal sage scrub studies published prior to the date of final listing.

By failing to balance the relative threat of coastal sage scrub takings both with and without critical habitat designation, the Service failed to consider all relevant factors as required under *Resources Ltd.,* 35 F.3d at 1304. The Service's reliance on the "increased threat" exception to section 4 designation was therefore improper.

B. No Benefit to the Species

The Service's second reason for declining to designate habitat was that designation "would not appreciably benefit the species." 58 Fed. Reg. at 16756. According to the Service's final listing decision, most populations of gnatcatchers are found on private lands to which section 7's consultation requirement would not apply. *Id.* The final listing decision suggests that designation may only be deemed "beneficial to the species" and therefore "prudent" if it would result in the application of section 7 to "the majority of land-use activities occurring within critical habitat." *Id.* (emphasis added).

By rewriting its "beneficial to the species" test for prudence into a "beneficial to most of the species" requirement, the Service expands the narrow statutory exception for imprudent designations into a broad exemption for imperfect designations. This expansive construction of the "no benefit" prong to the imprudence exception is inconsistent with clear congressional intent.

The fact that Congress intended the imprudence exception to be a narrow one is clear from the legislative history, which reads in part:

> The committee intends that in most situations the Secretary will . . . designate critical habitat at the same time that a species is listed as either endangered or threatened. It is only in rare circumstances where the specification of critical habitat concurrently with the listing would not be beneficial to the species.

H.R. Rep. No. 95-1625 at 17 (1978), reprinted in 1978 U.S.C.C.A.N. 9453, 9467 (emphasis added). *See also Enos v. Marsh,* 769 F.2d 1363, 1371 (9th Cir. 1985) (holding that the Secretary "may only fail to designate a critical habitat under rare circumstances") (emphasis added); *Northern Spotted Owl v. Lujan,* 758 F. Supp. 621, 626 (W.D. Wash. 1991) ("This legislative history leaves little room for doubt regarding the intent of Congress: The designation of critical habitat is to coincide with the final listing decision absent extraordinary circumstances.") (emphasis added).

By expanding the imprudence exception to encompass all cases in which designation would fail to control "the majority of land-use activities occurring within critical habitat," 58 Fed. Reg. at 16756 (emphasis added), the Service contravenes the clear congressional intent that the imprudence exception be a rare exception. Since "the court, as well as the agency, must give effect to the unambiguously expressed intent of Congress," *Chevron,* 467 U.S. at 842–43, we reject the Service's suggestion that designation is only necessary where it would protect the majority of species habitat.

In the present case, the Service found that of approximately 400,000 acres of gnatcatcher habitat, over 80,000 acres were publicly-owned and therefore subject to section 7 requirements. 58 Fed. Reg. at 16743. Other privately-owned lands would also be subject to section 7 requirements if their use involved any form of federal agency authorization or action. *See* 16 U.S.C. § 1536(a)(2).

The Service does not explain why a designation that would benefit such a large portion of critical habitat is not "beneficial to the species" within the plain meaning of the regulations and "prudent" within the clear meaning of the statute. Accordingly, we conclude that the Service's "no benefit" argument fails to "articulate[] a rational connection between the facts found and the choice made" as required under *Resources Ltd.,* 35 F.3d at 1304. The Service's reliance on the "no benefit" exception to section 4 designation was therefore improper.

C. Less Benefit to the Species

In addition to the above two rationales which were stated in the final listing, the defendants now offer a third argument in defense of the Service's failure to designate critical habitat. The defendants contend that a "far superior" means of protecting gnatcatcher habitat is provided by the state-run "comprehensive habitat management program" created under California's Natural Communities Conservation Program ("NCCP"). The Service has endorsed the NCCP as a "special rule" for gnatcatcher protection under section 4(d) of the Act, 16 U.S.C. § 1533(d).

Regulations under the Act provide that "the reasons for not designating critical habitat will be stated in the publication of proposed and final rules listing a species." 50 C.F.R. § 424.12(a). The NCCP alternative was not identified in the Service's proposed or final listings as a reason not to designate critical habitat. Therefore, this argument is not properly before us for consideration. *See Olin Corp. v. FTC,* 986 F.2d 1295, 1305 n.9 (9th Cir.1993) (declining to review potential justification for FTC ruling because "the Commission did not explicitly consider this argument in its opinion").

Even if we were to consider the NCCP alternative, however, the existence of such an alternative would not justify the Service's failure to designate critical habitat. The Act provides that designation of critical habitat is necessary except when designation would not be "prudent" or "determinable." 16 U.S.C. § 1533(a)(3). The Service's regulations define "not prudent" as "increasing the degree of [takings] threat to the species" or "not . . . beneficial to the species." 50 C.F.R. § 424.12(a)(1)(i)–(ii) (emphasis added). Neither the Act nor the implementing regulations sanctions nondesignation of habitat when designation would be merely less beneficial to the species than another type of protection.

In any event, the NCCP alternative cannot be viewed as a functional substitute for critical habitat designation. Critical habitat designation triggers mandatory consultation requirements for federal agency actions involving critical habitat. The NCCP alternative, in contrast, is a purely voluntary program that applies only to non-federal land-use activities. The Service itself recognized at the time of its final listing decision that "no substantive protection of the coastal California gnatcatcher is currently provided by city/county enrollments [in the NCCP]." 58 Fed. Reg. at 16754. Accordingly, we reject the defendants' post hoc invocation of the NCCP to justify the Service's failure to designate critical habitat.

Conclusion

The Service failed to discharge its statutory obligation to designate critical habitat when it listed the gnatcatcher as a threatened species, or to articulate a rational basis for invoking the rare imprudence exception. We therefore reverse the district court's finding that the Service's actions were not "arbitrary, capricious, an abuse of discretion or otherwise not in accordance with law."

Accordingly, we reverse the district court's grant of summary judgment to the defendants; reverse the denial of summary judgment to the plaintiffs; and remand to the district court with directions to remand to the Service so that the Service may issue a new decision consistent with this opinion.

REVERSED and REMANDED

DISSENT: O'SCANNLAIN, Circuit Judge, dissenting:

[The dissent argued first, that determinations of prudence need not include a weighing of benefits and risks of designation (all that is required is a "rational decision-making process"). Still, the dissent noted, the Service did conduct a balancing test, and the conclusion it reached based on that balancing effort was both "rational" and "defensible."

Second, the dissent argued that "the majority takes too narrow a view of the phrase 'beneficial to the species.' The question should not be whether any member of the species would be better off by a slender margin, but whether the species as a whole would benefit from the designation. Even though the gnatcatchers in most of the habitat would not benefit, reasons the majority, some of the gnatcatchers would benefit, and hence designation would be beneficial for the species. The problem with this argument is that it overlooks the Service's expert opinion, to which we are required to defer, that designation may harm the gnatcatchers when landowners intentionally destroy the habitat. Even though individual pockets of gnatcatchers may benefit, the species as a whole may not."]

NOTE

The FWS has often declined to designate critical habitat contemporaneous with its decisions to list endangered and threatened species. As of February, 2001, despite having listed 736 plants and 511 animals, the agency had designated critical habitat on only 142 occasions. The *NRDC* decision represents the first time a federal court of appeals reversed a FWS decision not to designate critical habitat. There have since been others: *See, e.g., Conservation Council for Hawaii v. Babbitt*, 2 F. Supp. 2d 1280 (1998) (concluding that FWS's failure to designated critical habitat when listing as endangered 245 plants in Hawaii was arbitrary and capricious). A more recent case discusses FWS methodology for declining to designate critical habitat:

NEW MEXICO CATTLE GROWERS v. UNITED STATES FISH AND WILDLIFE SERVICE

248 F.3d 1277 (10th Cir. 2001)

JUDGES: Before TACHA, Chief Judge, KELLY, Circuit Judge, and LUNG-STRUM,[1] District Judge.

TACHA, Chief Circuit Judge.

The New Mexico Cattle Growers Association, New Mexico Farm & Livestock Bureau, New Mexico Wool Growers, Inc., New Mexico Wheat Growers Association, New Mexico Public Lands Council, Albuquerque Production Credit Association, Coalition of Arizona/New Mexico Counties for Stable Economic Growth, and Hidalgo County Cattle Growers Association (collectively "Appellants") all represent, in some fashion, elements of New Mexico's agricultural industry. Appellants appeal an order of the district court dismissing their suit against Appellee U.S. Fish & Wildlife Service ("FWS"). We exercise jurisdiction pursuant to the Administration Procedures Act ("APA"), 28 U.S.C. §§ 701–06, and reverse.

---

[1] Honorable John W. Lungstrum, Chief District Judge for the District of Kansas, sitting by designation.

I.

The Southwestern Willow Flycatcher ("flycatcher"), empidonax traillii extimus, is one of four sub-species of the willow flycatcher, a small bird that nests in riparian areas along river beds. On July 23, 1993, the FWS published its "Proposed Rule to List the Southwestern Willow Flycatcher as Endangered With Critical Habitat." 58 Fed. Reg. 39495. On February 27, 1995, the FWS issued its "Final Rule Determining Endangered Status for the Southwestern Willow Flycatcher." 60 Fed. Reg. 10694. The Final Rule listed the flycatcher as endangered, but deferred the critical habitat designation ("CHD") in order to gather more information. However, the FWS did not, on its own initiative, move forward with the CHD for the flycatcher.

On March 20, 1997, the U.S. District Court for the District of Arizona, in the case *Southwest Ctr. for Biological Diversity v. Babbitt,* Civ. No. 96-1874-PHX-RGS (D. Ariz. March 20, 1997), ordered the FWS to complete the CHD for the flycatcher within 120 days. Pursuant to the court order, the FWS issued its CHD for the flycatcher on July 22, 1997. At that time, the known population of the flycatcher was between 300 and 500 nesting pairs spread across seven states and parts of Mexico. The CHD designated eighteen critical habitat units, including four in New Mexico, totaling 599 miles of stream and river beds.

The Endangered Species Act ("ESA"), which controls CHDs, requires the FWS to perform an economic analysis of the effects of the CHD before making a final designation. 16 U.S.C. § 1533(b)(2). In order to determine what the "economic impact" of a CHD will be, the FWS has adopted an incremental baseline approach (the "baseline approach"). The baseline approach utilized by the FWS is premised on the idea that the listing of the species (which will occur prior to or simultaneously with the CHD) will have economic impacts that are not to be considered. The primary statutory rationale for this position comes from 16 U.S.C. § 1533(b)(1)(A), which states that listing determinations be made "solely on the basis of the best scientific and commercial data available." Thus, the baseline approach moves any economic impact that can be attributed to listing below the baseline and, when making the CHD, takes into account only those economic impacts rising above the baseline. Using the baseline approach, the FWS determined that the flycatcher CHD resulted in no economic impact, stating that "critical habitat designation will . . . result in no additional protection for the flycatcher nor have any additional economic effects beyond those that may have been caused by listing and by other statutes." Division of Economics, U.S. Fish and Wildlife Service, Economic Analysis of Critical Habitat Designation for the Southwestern Flycatcher, S3 (1997).

The appellants filed suit in district court in March 1998, challenging the flycatcher designation and alleging that the FWS had violated various provisions of both the ESA and the National Environmental Protection Act ("NEPA"). * * *

Specifically, the appellants make the following arguments on appeal: (1) that the FWS's adoption of the baseline approach to measuring the economic impact of the flycatcher CHD is an erroneous construction and, thus, a violation of the ESA; (2) that the district court erred in ruling the declaration and its attachments admissible; (3) that the FWS misapplied the critical habitat definition set forth in the ESA; (4) that the FWS violated NEPA by applying the baseline approach to the environmental impact analysis undertaken in the EA; (5) that the FWS failed to address adequate alternatives to the CHD pursuant to NEPA; and (6) that the FWS, in making the flycatcher CHD, failed to properly cooperate with state and local agencies as required by NEPA. Because we rule in favor of the appellants on the first issue raised by holding that the baseline approach to economic impact analysis is not permitted by the ESA, thus setting aside the flycatcher CHD, we need not address any of the other issues raised.

II.

[In this section, the court determines to review the decision of the FWS without deference because the agency's determinations were made informally, rather than by rule in accordance with procedures of the APA. The FWS conceded that no deference was due].

III.

Our primary task in construing statutes is to "determine congressional intent, using 'traditional tools of statutory interpretation.'" *NLRB v. United Food & Commercial Workers Union,* 484 U.S. 112, 123, 98 L. Ed. 2d 429, 108 S. Ct. 413 (1987) (quoting *INS v. Cardoza-Fonseca,* 480 U.S. 421, 446, 94 L. Ed. 2d 434, 107 S. Ct. 1207 (1987)). "As in all cases requiring statutory construction, 'we begin with the plain language of the law.'" *St. Charles Inv. Co. v. CIR,* 232 F.3d 773, 776 (10th Cir. 2000) (quoting *United States v. Morgan,* 922 F.2d 1495, 1496 (10th Cir. 1991)). "In so doing, we will assume that Congress's intent is expressed correctly in the ordinary meaning of the words it employs. . . . Where the language of the statute is plain, it is improper for this Court to consult legislative history in determining congressional intent." *Id.* However, "if the statutory language is ambiguous, a court can then resort to legislative history as an aid to interpretation." *United States v. Simmonds,* 111 F.3d 737, 742 (10th Cir. 1997).

Enacted in 1973, the ESA, 16 U.S.C. § 1531 et seq., was the congressional response to increasing concern about the extent to which "various species of fish, wildlife, and plants in the United States have been rendered extinct as a consequence of economic growth and development untempered by adequate concern and conservation." 16 U.S.C. § 1531(a)(1). The stated purpose of the ESA is, in part, "to provide a means whereby the ecosystems upon which endangered species and threatened species depend may be conserved, [and] to provide a program for the conservation of such endangered species and threatened species." *Id.* § 1531(b).

The process set forth in the ESA for the protection of endangered and threatened species and the conservation of their ecosystem begins by granting the Secretary of the Interior, through the FWS, authority to list species in need of protection as either endangered or threatened. *Id.* § 1533(a). The ESA enumerates the factors to be considered by the agency when making a listing decision, including "the present or threatened destruction, modification, or curtailment of its habitat or range." *Id.* § 1533(a)(1). Further, the ESA specifically requires that the listing determination be based "solely on the basis of the best scientific and commercial data available." *Id.* § 1533(b)(1)(A). Thus, economic analysis is not a factor in the listing determination. Once a species is listed, all federal agencies are required to consult with the FWS to "insure that any action authorized, funded, or carried out by such agency . . . is not likely to jeopardize the continued existence of any endangered species or threatened species." *Id.* § 1536(a)(2).

In addition to the protections afforded listed species by the ESA, the Act requires the agency to designate "critical habitat" for all listed species, to the extent determinable. *Id.* § 1533(a)(3). Critical habitat is defined as:

> (i) the specific areas within the geographic area occupied by the species, at the time it is listed . . . on which are found those physical or biological features (I) essential to the conservation of the species and (II) which may require special management considerations or protection; and (ii) specific areas outside the geographic area occupied by the species at the time it is listed . . . upon a determination by the Secretary that such areas are essential for the conservation of the species.

Id. § 1532(5)(A). Thus, the CHD may include specific areas found both inside of and outside of the geographic area occupied by the species.

The CHD is required to be based on "the best scientific data available" considering "the economic impact, and any other relevant impact, of specifying any particular area as critical habitat." *Id.* § 1533(b)(2). The agency "may exclude" a particular area from the CHD if the agency determines that "the benefits of such exclusion outweigh the benefits of specifying such area as part of the critical habitat, unless . . . the failure to designate such area . . . will result in the extinction of the species concerned." *Id.* § 1533(b)(2). Once critical habitat is designated, federal agencies must consult with the FWS to "insure that any action authorized, funded, or carried out by such agency . . . is not likely to . . . result in the destruction or adverse modification of [designated critical] habitat." *Id.* § 1536(a)(2). Thus, agency action that is prohibited is both (1) action that is likely to jeopardize the existence of a listed species and (2) action that is likely to result in the adverse modification of any area within a CHD.

The crux of the statutory dispute is in determining the meaning of "economic impact" in 16 U.S.C. § 1533(b)(2). The baseline approach adopted by the FWS utilizes a "but for" method for determining what economic impacts flow from the CHD. Thus, unless an economic impact would not result but for the CHD, that impact is attributable to a different cause (typically listing) and is not an "economic impact . . . of specifying any particular area as critical habitat." Conversely, the approach advocated by the appellants would take into account all of the economic impact of the CHD, regardless of whether those impacts are caused co-extensively by any other agency action (such as listing) and even if those impacts would remain in the absence of the CHD. The issue presented is a question of first impression in this circuit and, to our knowledge, has not been decided by any of our sister circuits.

The root of the problem lies in the FWS's long held policy position that CHDs are unhelpful, duplicative, and unnecessary. Between April 1996 and July 1999, more than 250 species had been listed pursuant to the ESA, yet CHDs had been made for only two. S. Rep. No. 106-126, at 2 (1999). Further, while we have held that making a CHD is mandatory once a species is listed, *Forest Guardians v. Babbitt,* 174 F.3d 1178, 1186 (10th Cir. 1999), the FWS has typically put off doing so until forced to do so by court order. S. Rep. No. 106-126, at 2 (1999).

In turn, the policy position of the FWS finds its root in the regulations promulgated by the FWS in 1986 defining the meaning of both the "jeopardy standard" (applied in the context of listing) and the "adverse modification standard" (applied in the context of designated critical habitat). Action violating the jeopardy standard is action reasonably expected "to reduce appreciably the likelihood of both the survival and recovery of a listed species." 50 C.F.R. 402.02. Action violating the adverse modification standard is action "that appreciably diminishes the value of critical habitat for both the survival and recovery of a listed species." *Id.* Thus, the standards are defined as virtually identical, or, if not identical, one (adverse modification) is subsumed by the other (jeopardy). *See Am. Rivers v. Nat'l Marine Fisheries Serv.,* 1999 U.S. App. LEXIS 3860 (9th Cir. Jan. 11, 1999) (agreeing with the agency that "'jeopardy' and 'critical habitat' . . . are 'closely related,' and [thus] the jeopardy discussion properly 'encompasses' the critical habitat analysis"). While these regulatory definitions are not before us today, they have been the cause of much confusion in that they inform the FWS's interpretation of the ESA's economic impact language.

Consistent with its long standing position, the FWS argues in the instant case that the impacts of the flycatcher listing and the flycatcher CHD are co-extensive. The FWS stated in its economic analysis that, because all actions "that result in adverse modification of critical habitat will also result in a jeopardy decision, designation of critical habitat for the flycatcher is not expected to result in any incremental restrictions on agency activities." Division of Economics, U.S. Fish and Wildlife Service, Economic Analysis of Critical Habitat Designation for the Southwestern Flycatcher, S3 (1997). The CHD itself states that "common to both [the jeopardy standard and the adverse modification standard] is an appreciable detrimental effect on both survival and recovery of a listed species," and thus "actions satisfying the standard for adverse modification are nearly always found to also jeopardize the species concerned, and the existence of a critical habitat designation does not materially affect the outcome of consultation." 60 Fed. Reg. 39,131 (July 22, 1997). Moreover, the FWS continues to assert that agency action that is "likely to adversely modify critical habitat but not to jeopardize the species for which it is designated are extremely rare historically, and none have been issued in recent years." Appellee's Brief at 31.

However, as we have previously said, the fact that the FWS says that no real impact flows from the CHD does not make it so. *Catron County Bd. of Comm'rs v. United States Fish & Wildlife Serv.,* 75 F.3d 1429, 1436 (10th Cir. 1996) ("We disagree with the [Ninth Circuit] that no actual impact flows from the critical habitat designation. Merely because the Secretary says it does not make it so. The record in this case suggests that the impact will be immediate and the consequences could be disastrous."). Because *Catron County* dealt with whether an environmental impact statement had to be prepared pursuant to NEPA when the FWS made a CHD, the court was dealing specifically with the environmental impacts of the CHD rather than its economic impacts. However, our holding in that case casts doubt on the FWS's position in this case.

In fact, the district court in this case, by granting the appellants standing to challenge the CHD, implicitly acknowledged that they have been impacted by the flycatcher CHD. *N.M. Cattle Growers Ass'n v. United States Fish & Wildlife Serv.*, 81 F. Supp. 2d 1141, 1153 (D.N.M. 1999) (holding that the appellants had alleged an injury in fact flowing from the flycatcher CHD). If none of the impacts of the CHD are actually attributable to the CHD, the district court's standing decision is rendered incoherent. If the injury alleged is attributable wholly to listing, then the appellants suffer no injury from the CHD, and cannot establish standing to challenge it. The district court's standing determination further points to the inconsistency between the policy position of the FWS and the language of the ESA itself. But the question of whether the impacts of listing and a CHD are co-extensive is not the precise question before us. Rather, the question is whether the FWS must analyze all of the economic impacts of critical habitat designation (regardless of whether the impacts are co-extensive with other causes), or only those impacts that are a "but for" result of the CHD.

It is true that the ESA clearly bars economic considerations from having a seat at the table when the listing determination is being made. "The addition of the word 'solely' is intended to remove from the process of the listing or delisting of species any factor not related to the biological status of the species. . . . Economic considerations have no relevance to determinations regarding the status of species." H.R. Rep. No. 97-567, pt. 1, at 29 (1982), reprinted in 1982 U.S.C.C.A.N. 2807. However, Congress clearly intended that economic factors were to be considered in connection with the CHD. 16 U.S.C. § 1533(b)(2).

The statutory language is plain in requiring some kind of consideration of economic impact in the CHD phase. Although 50 C.F.R. 402.02 is not at issue here, the regulation's definition of the jeopardy standard as fully encompassing the adverse modification standard renders any purported economic analysis done utilizing the baseline approach virtually meaningless. We are compelled by the canons of statutory interpretation to give some effect to the congressional directive that economic impacts be considered at the time of critical habitat designation. *Bridger Coal Co. / Pac. Minerals, Inc. v. Dir., Office of Workers' Compensation Programs*, 927 F.2d 1150, 1153 (10th Cir. 1991) ("We will not construe a statute in a way that renders words or phrases meaningless, redundant, or superfluous."). Because economic analysis done using the FWS's baseline model is rendered essentially without meaning by 50 C.F.R. § 402.02, we conclude Congress intended that the FWS conduct a full analysis of all of the economic impacts of a critical habitat designation, regardless of whether those impacts are attributable co-extensively to other causes. Thus, we hold the baseline approach to economic analysis is not in accord with the language or intent of the ESA.

The FWS contends that should they be forced to abandon the baseline approach and consider all of the economic impact of a CHD, even if that impact is attributable co-extensively to another cause, they will be injecting economic analysis improperly into the listing process. The only two federal courts to consider this question come to essentially the same conclusion. *N. M. Cattle Growers Ass'n*, 81 F. Supp. 2d at 1158; *Trinity County Concerned Citizens v. Babbitt*, 1993 WL 650393 (D.D.C. Sept. 20, 1993) (holding that absent the baseline approach, "the Secretary would be required to include . . . certain costs that might have already been incurred as a result of the listing of the species, for example, through the ESA's jeopardy and take provisions," even though "the Secretary is expressly forbidden from considering such economic costs in making the decision to list species"). We cannot agree.

Requiring that the FWS comply with the intent of the legislative body by considering economic impacts at a point subsequent to listing does not inject economic considerations into the listing process, but rather, situates those considerations in precisely the spot intended by Congress. Moreover, should this ruling result in certain areas being excluded from future CHDs, it will not undermine congressional intent that economic factors be excluded from the listing decision. The listing of the species will remain in effect and the significant protections afforded a species by listing will not be undermined. Indeed, if the FWS's position that the protections afforded by a CHD are subsumed by the protections of listing is accepted, this ruling will result in no decreased protection for endangered species or their habitat.

IV.

As set forth above, the baseline approach to economic analysis pursuant the 16 U.S.C. § 1533(b)(2) is expressly rejected. The flycatcher CHD is thus set aside and the FWS is instructed to issue a new flycatcher CHD in compliance with this opinion as required by the ESA. Accordingly, the decision of the district court is REVERSED and the case is REMANDED to the district court for proceedings not inconsistent with this decision.

NOTES

1. As of March, 2001, the agency faced such a backlog of habitat designations that it stopped listing any new species until it caught up. The FWS now is designating critical habitat with far greater regularity. *See generally* Thomas F. Darin, Comment, *Designating Critical Habitat Under the Endangered Species Act: Habitat Protection Versus Agency Discretion*, 24 Harv. Envt'l L. Rev. 209 (2000); Pamela Baldwin, *The Role of Designation of Critical Habitat under the Endangered Species Act*, CRS Report for Congress (1999).

2. The NEPA process does not apply to species listing decisions, *Pacific Legal Foundation v. Andrus*, 657 F.2d 829 (6th Cir. 1981), but there is a split of authority regarding NEPA's applicability to designations of critical habitat of those listed species. The Ninth Circuit has held that NEPA is inapplicable to such decisions, *Douglas County v. Babbitt*, 48 F.3d. 1495, *cert. denied*, 116 S. Ct. 1296 (1996) (holding that listing has "displaced" the provisions of NEPA), but the Tenth Circuit has held the opposite. *Catron County Board*

of Comm'rs., New Mexico v. United States Fish and Wildlife Serv., 735 F.3d 1429 (10th Cir. 1996). In the latter case, consistent with *Cattle Growers*, the court disagreed that no impacts flow from the habitat designation decision. It stipulated as well that ESA procedures did not supplant those of NEPA, and argued that compliance with NEPA would further the goals of the ESA, not the opposite, as suggested by the *Douglas* court. At this writing, the United States Supreme Court has not resolved this split in the circuits and no decision is pending. For a discussion of the applicability of NEPA to agency implementation of the Endangered Species Act, see Lori Hackleman Patterson, *NEPA's Stronghold: A Noose for the Endangered Species Act?*, 27 Cumb. L. Rev. 753 (1996-97) (arguing in favor of exemption).

C. SECTION 7

The listing of a species triggers the applicability of the major regulatory provisions of the ESA, §§ 7 and 9 respectively. We begin with a look at §7. Euphemistically entitled "Inter-agency Cooperation," the section provides in salient part:

> Each federal agency shall, in consultation with and with the assistance of the Secretary, insure that any action authorized, funded, or carried out by such agency . . . is not likely to jeopardize the continued existence of any endangered species or threatened species or result in the destruction or adverse modification of habitat of such species which is determined by the Secretary . . .to be critical . . .

§ 7(a)(2), 16 U.S.C. § 1536(a)(2) (1976 ed.)

Compliance with this directive is accomplished via a three-step process. First, a federal agency proposing to take an action must inquire of the FWS or the NMFS whether any threatened or endangered species "may be present" in the area of the proposed action. § 7(c)(1), 16 U.S.C. § 1536(c)(1). Second, if such a species may be present, the agency must prepare a "biological assessment" examining whether the species "is likely to be affected" by the proposed action. *Id.* The biological assessment may be prepared in conjunction with and be a part of an environmental impact statement or environmental assessment under the National Environmental Policy Act. *Id.* Failure to prepare a biological assessment is a significant procedural violation of the ESA and constitutes grounds for issuance of an injunction halting the federal action. *Thomas v. Peterson*, 753 F.2d 754 (9th Cir. 1985). Third, if the assessment concludes the species is "likely to be affected," the agency must formally "consult" with the FWS or NMFS. § 7(a)(3), 16 U.S.C. § 1536(a)(3) ("jeopardy consultation"). Consultation is also required if an agency action might result in destruction of any designated critical habitat. § 7(a)(2), 16 U.S.C. § 1536(a)(2) ("habitat consultation"). *See, e.g., Pacific Coast Federation of Fisherman's Assn's v. U.S. Bureau of Reclamation*, 138 F. Supp. 2d 1228 (N.D. Cal. 2001). The formal consultation process results in a "biological opinion" ("BiOp" (often referred to as a "B.O.")) issued by the FWS or NMFS. § 7(b), 16 U.S.C.§ 1536(b). The BiOp is the vehicle used to determine whether the proposed federal action would jeopardize the species or destroy or adversely modify its critical habitat.

The first matter is figuring what § 7(a)(2) means.

TENNESSEE VALLEY AUTHORITY v. HILL

437 U.S. 153, 98 S. Ct. 2279 (1978)

MR. CHIEF JUSTICE BURGER delivered the opinion of the Court.

The questions presented in this case are (a) whether the Endangered Species Act of 1973 requires a court to enjoin the operation of a virtually completed federal dam — which had been authorized prior to 1973 — when, pursuant to authority vested in him by Congress, the Secretary of the Interior has determined that operation of the dam would eradicate an endangered species; and (b) whether continued congressional appropriations for the dam after 1973 constituted an implied repeal of the Endangered Species Act, at least as to the particular dam.

I

The Little Tennessee River originates in the mountains of northern Georgia and flows through the national forest lands of North Carolina into Tennessee, where it converges with the Big Tennessee River near Knoxville. The lower 33 miles of the Little Tennessee takes the river's clear, free-flowing waters through an area of great natural beauty. Among other environmental amenities, this stretch of river is said to contain abundant trout. Considerable historical importance attaches to the areas immediately adjacent to this portion of the Little Tennessee's banks. To the south of the river's edge lies Fort Loudon, established in 1756 as England's southwestern outpost in the French and Indian War. Nearby are also the ancient sites of several native American villages, the archeological stores of which are to a large extent unexplored. These include the Cherokee towns of Echota and Tennase, the former being the sacred capital of the Cherokee Nation as early as the 16th century and the latter providing the linguistic basis from which the State of Tennessee derives its name.

In this area of the Little Tennessee River the Tennessee Valley Authority, a wholly owned public corporation of the United States, began constructing the Tellico Dam and Reservoir Project in 1967, shortly after Congress appropriated initial funds for its development. Tellico is a multipurpose regional development project designed principally to stimulate shoreline development, generate sufficient electric current to heat 20,000 homes, and provide flat-water recreation and flood control, as well as improve economic conditions in "an area characterized by underutilization of human resources and outmigration of young people." Hearings on Public Works for Power and Energy Research Appropriation Bill, 1977, before a Subcommittee of the House Committee on Appropriations, 94th Cong., 2d Sess., pt. 5, p. 261 (1976). Of particular relevance to this case is one aspect of the project, a dam which TVA determined to place on the Little Tennessee, a short distance from where the river's waters meet with the Big Tennessee. When fully operational, the dam would impound water covering some 16,500 acres — much of which represents valuable and productive farmland — thereby converting the river's shallow, fast-flowing waters into a deep reservoir over 30 miles in length.

The Tellico Dam has never opened, however, despite the fact that construction has been virtually completed and the dam is essentially ready for operation. Although Congress has appropriated monies for Tellico every year since 1967, progress was delayed, and ultimately stopped, by a tangle of lawsuits and administrative proceedings. After unsuccessfully urging TVA to consider alternatives to damming the Little Tennessee, local citizens and national conservation groups brought suit in the District Court, claiming that the project did not conform to the requirements of the National Environmental Policy Act of 1969 (NEPA), 83 Stat. 852, 42 U.S.C. § 4321 *et seq.* After finding TVA to be in violation of NEPA, the District Court enjoined the dam's completion pending the filing of an appropriate environmental impact statement. *Environmental Defense Fund v. TVA*, 339 F.Supp. 806 (ED Tenn.), *aff'd*, 468 F.2d 1164 (CA6 1972). The injunction remained in effect until late 1973, when the District Court concluded that TVA's final environmental impact statement for Tellico was in compliance with the law. *Environmental Defense Fund v. TVA*, 371 F.Supp. 1004 (ED Tenn. 1973), *aff'd*, 492 F.2d 466 (CA6 1974).

Snail Darter

Percina tanisi, breeding male

A few months prior to the District Court's decision dissolving the NEPA injunction, a discovery was made in the waters of the Little Tennessee which would profoundly affect the Tellico Project. Exploring the area around Coytee Springs, which is about seven miles from the mouth of the river, a University of Tennessee ichthyologist, Dr. David A. Etnier, found a previously unknown species of perch, the snail darter, or *Percina (Imostoma) tanasi.** This three-inch, tannish-colored fish, whose numbers are estimated to be in the range of 10,000 to 15,000, would soon engage the attention of environmentalists, the TVA, the Department of the Interior, the Congress of the United States, and ultimately the federal courts, as a new and additional basis to halt construction of the dam.

Until recently the finding of a new species of animal life would hardly generate a cause celebre. This is particularly so in the case of darters, of which

---

* [Ed. note: this representation of a snail darter is not part of the Supreme Court's opinion.]

there are approximately 130 known species, 8 to 10 of these having been identified only in the last five years.[7] The moving force behind the snail darter's sudden fame came some four months after its discovery, when the Congress passed the Endangered Species Act of 1973 (Act), 87 Stat. 884, 16 U.S.C. § 1531 *et seq.* (1976 ed.). This legislation, among other things, authorizes the Secretary of the Interior to declare species of animal life "endangered" and to identify the "critical habitat" of these creatures. When a species or its habitat is so listed, the following portion of the Act — relevant here — becomes effective:

> "The Secretary [of the Interior] shall review other programs administered by him and utilize such programs in furtherance of the purposes of this chapter. All other Federal departments and agencies shall, in consultation with and with the assistance of the Secretary, utilize their authorities in furtherance of the purposes of this chapter by carrying out programs for the conservation of endangered species and threatened species listed pursuant to section 1533 of this title and *by taking such action necessary to insure that actions authorized, funded, or carried out by them do not jeopardize the continued existence of such endangered species and threatened species* or result in the destruction or modification of habitat of such species which is determined by the Secretary, after consultation as appropriate with the affected States, to be critical." 16 U.S.C. § 1536 (1976 ed.) (emphasis added).

In January 1975, the respondents in this case and others petitioned the Secretary of the Interior to list the snail darter as an endangered species. After receiving comments from various interested parties, including TVA and the State of Tennessee, the Secretary formally listed the snail darter as an endangered species on October 8, 1975. 40 Fed. Reg. 47505-47506; *see* 50 C.F.R. § 17.11(i) (1976). In so acting, it was noted that "the snail darter is a living entity which is genetically distinct and reproductively isolated from other fishes." 40 Fed. Reg. 47505. More important for the purposes of this case, the Secretary determined that the snail darter apparently lives only in that portion of the Little Tennessee River which would be completely inundated by the reservoir created as a consequence of the Tellico Dam's completion. *Id.*, at 47506.[12] The Secretary went on to explain the significance of the dam to the habitat of the snail darter:

---

[7] In Tennessee alone there are 85 to 90 species of darters, *id.*, at 131, of which upward to 45 live in the Tennessee River system. *Id.*, at 130. New species of darters are being constantly discovered and classified — at the rate of about one per year. *Id.*, at 131. This is a difficult task for even trained ichthyologists since species of darters are often hard to differentiate from one another. *Ibid.*

[12] Searches by TVA in more than 60 watercourses have failed to find other populations of snail darters. App. 36, 410–412. The Secretary has noted that "more than 1,000 collections in recent years and additional earlier collections from central and east Tennessee have not revealed the presence of the snail darter outside the Little Tennessee River." 40 Fed. Reg. 47505 (1975). It is estimated, however, that the snail darter's range once extended throughout the upper main Tennessee River and the lower portions of its major tributaries above Chattanooga — all of which are now the sites of dam impoundments. *See* Hearings on Public Works for Water and Power Development and Energy Research Appropriation Bill, 1978, before a Subcommittee of the House Committee on Appropriations, 95th Cong., 1st Sess., pt. 4, pp. 240–241 (1977) (statement of witness for TVA); Hearings on Endangered Species Act Oversight, before the Subcommittee on Resource Protection of the Senate Committee on Environment and Public Works, 95th Cong., 1st Sess., 291 (1977); App. 139.

"[The] snail darter occurs only in the swifter portions of shoals over clean gravel substrate in cool, low-turbidity water. Food of the snail darter is almost exclusively snails which require a clean gravel substrate for their survival. *The proposed impoundment of water behind the proposed Tellico Dam would result in total destruction of the snail darter's habitat." Ibid.* (emphasis added).

Subsequent to this determination, the Secretary declared the area of the Little Tennessee which would be affected by the Tellico Dam to be the "critical habitat" of the snail darter. 41 Fed. Reg. 13926-13928 (1976) (to be codified as 50 C.F.R. § 17.81). Using these determinations as a predicate, and notwithstanding the near completion of the dam, the Secretary declared that pursuant to § 7 of the Act, "all Federal agencies must take such action as is necessary to insure that actions authorized, funded, or carried out by them do not result in the destruction or modification of this critical habitat area." 41 Fed. Reg. 13928 (1976) (to be codified as 50 C.F.R. § 17.81 (b)). This notice, of course, was pointedly directed at TVA and clearly aimed at halting completion or operation of the dam.

During the pendency of these administrative actions, other developments of relevance to the snail darter issue were transpiring. Communication was occurring between the Department of the Interior's Fish and Wildlife Service and TVA with a view toward settling the issue informally. These negotiations were to no avail, however, since TVA consistently took the position that the only available alternative was to attempt relocating the snail darter population to another suitable location. To this end, TVA conducted a search of alternative sites which might sustain the fish, culminating in the experimental transplantation of a number of snail darters to the nearby Hiwassee River. However, the Secretary of the Interior was not satisfied with the results of these efforts, finding that TVA had presented "little evidence that they have carefully studied the Hiwassee to determine whether or not" there were "biological and other factors in this river that [would] negate a successful transplant."[13] 40 Fed. Reg. 47506 (1975).

Meanwhile, Congress had also become involved in the fate of the snail darter. Appearing before a Subcommittee of the House Committee on Appropriations in April 1975 — some seven months before the snail darter was listed as endangered — TVA representatives described the discovery of the fish and the relevance of the Endangered Species Act to the Tellico Project. Hearings on Public Works for Water and Power Development and Energy Research Appropriation Bill, 1976, before a Subcommittee of the House Committee on Appropriations, 94th Cong., 1st Sess., pt. 7, pp. 466-467 (1975); Hearings on H.R. 8122, Public Works for Water and Power Development and Energy Research Appropriations for Fiscal Year 1976, before a Subcommittee of the

---

[13] The Fish and Wildlife Service and Dr. Etnier have stated that it may take from 5 to 15 years for scientists to determine whether the snail darter can successfully survive and reproduce in this new environment. *See* General Accounting Office, The Tennessee Valley Authority's Tellico Dam Project — Costs, Alternatives, and Benefits 4 (Oct. 14, 1977). In expressing doubt over the long-term future of the Hiwassee transplant, the Secretary noted: "That the snail darter does not already inhabit the Hiwassee River, despite the fact that the fish has had access to it in the past, is a strong indication that there may be biological and other factors in this river that negate a successful transplant." 40 Fed. Reg. 47506 (1975).

Senate Committee on Appropriations, 94th Cong., 1st Sess., pt. 4, pp. 3775-3777 (1975). At that time TVA presented a position which it would advance in successive forums thereafter, namely, that the Act did not prohibit the completion of a project authorized, funded, and substantially constructed before the Act was passed. TVA also described its efforts to transplant the snail darter, but contended that the dam should be finished regardless of the experiment's success. Thereafter, the House Committee on Appropriations, in its June 20, 1975, Report, stated the following in the course of recommending that an additional $29 million be appropriated for Tellico:

> "The *Committee* directs that the project, for which an environmental impact statement has been completed and provided the Committee, should be completed as promptly as possible. . . ." H.R. Rep. No. 94-319, p. 76 (1975). (Emphasis added.)

Congress then approved the TVA general budget, which contained funds for continued construction of the Tellico Project. In December 1975, one month after the snail darter was declared an endangered species, the President signed the bill into law. Public Works for Water and Power Development and Energy Research Appropriation Act, 1976, 89 Stat. 1035, 1047.

In February 1976, pursuant to § 11 (g) of the Endangered Species Act, 87 Stat. 900, 16 U.S.C. § 1540(g) (1976 ed.), respondents filed the case now under review, seeking to enjoin completion of the dam and impoundment of the reservoir on the ground that those actions would violate the Act by directly causing the extinction of the species *Percina (Imostoma) tanasi*. The District Court denied respondents' request for a preliminary injunction and set the matter for trial. Shortly thereafter the House and Senate held appropriations hearings which would include discussions of the Tellico budget.

At these hearings, TVA Chairman Wagner reiterated the agency's position that the Act did not apply to a project which was over 50% finished by the time the Act became effective and some 70% to 80% complete when the snail darter was officially listed as endangered. It also notified the Committees of the recently filed lawsuit's status and reported that TVA's efforts to transplant the snail darter had "been very encouraging." Hearings on Public Works for Water and Power Development and Energy Research Appropriation Bill, 1977, before a Subcommittee of the House Committee on Appropriations, 94th Cong., 2d Sess., pt. 5, pp. 261-262 (1976); Hearings on Public Works for Water and Power Development and Energy Research Appropriations for Fiscal Year 1977, before a Subcommittee of the Senate Committee on Appropriations, 94th Cong., 2d Sess., pt. 4, pp. 3096-3099 (1976).

Trial was held in the District Court on April 29 and 30, 1976, and on May 25, 1976, the court entered its memorandum opinion and order denying respondents their requested relief and dismissing the complaint. The District Court found that closure of the dam and the consequent impoundment of the reservoir would "result in the adverse modification, if not complete destruction, of the snail darter's critical habitat," making it "highly probable" that "the continued existence of the snail darter" would be "[jeopardized]." 419 F.Supp. 753, 757 (ED Tenn.). Despite these findings, the District Court declined to embrace the plaintiffs' position on the merits: that once a federal project was shown to jeopardize an endangered species, a court of equity is compelled to issue an injunction restraining violation of the Endangered Species Act.

In reaching this result, the District Court stressed that the entire project was then about 80% complete and, based on available evidence, "there [were] no alternatives to impoundment of the reservoir, short of scrapping the entire project." *Id.*, at 758. The District Court also found that if the Tellico Project was permanently enjoined, "some $53 million would be lost in nonrecoverable obligations," *id.*, at 759, meaning that a large portion of the $78 million already expended would be wasted. The court also noted that the Endangered Species Act of 1973 was passed some seven years after construction on the dam commenced and that Congress had continued appropriations for Tellico, with full awareness of the snail darter problem. Assessing these various factors, the District Court concluded:

> "At some point in time a federal project becomes so near completion and so incapable of modification that a court of equity should not apply a statute enacted long after inception of the project to produce an unreasonable result. . . . Where there has been an irreversible and irretrievable commitment of resources by Congress to a project over a span of almost a decade, the Court should proceed with a great deal of circumspection."

Id., at 760. To accept the plaintiffs' position, the District Court argued, would inexorably lead to what it characterized as the absurd result of requiring "a court to halt impoundment of water behind a fully completed dam if an endangered species were discovered in the river on the day before such impoundment was scheduled to take place. We cannot conceive that Congress intended such a result." *Id.*, at 763.

Less than a month after the District Court decision, the Senate and House Appropriations Committees recommended the full budget request of $9 million for continued work on Tellico. *See* S. Rep. No. 94-960, p. 96 (1976); H.R. Rep. No. 94-1223, p. 83 (1976). In its Report accompanying the appropriations bill, the Senate Committee stated:

> "During subcommittee hearings, TVA was questioned about the relationship between the Tellico project's completion and the November 1975 listing of the snail darter (a small 3-inch fish which was discovered in 1973) as an endangered species under the Endangered Species Act. TVA informed the Committee that it was continuing its efforts to preserve the darter, while working towards the scheduled 1977 completion date. TVA repeated its view that the Endangered Species Act did not prevent the completion of the Tellico project, which has been under construction for nearly a decade. The subcommittee brought this matter, as well as the recent U.S. District Court's decision upholding TVA's decision to complete the project, to the attention of the full Committee. *The Committee does not view* the Endangered Species Act as prohibiting the completion of the Tellico project at its advanced stage and directs that this project be completed as promptly as possible in the public interest." S. Rep. No. 94-960, *supra,* at 96. (Emphasis added.)

On June 29, 1976, both Houses of Congress passed TVA's general budget, which included funds for Tellico; the President signed the bill on July 12, 1976. Public Works for Water and Power Development and Energy Research Appropriation Act, 1977, 90 Stat. 889, 899.

Thereafter, in the Court of Appeals, respondents argued that the District Court had abused its discretion by not issuing an injunction in the face of "a blatant statutory violation." 549 F.2d 1064, 1069 (CA6 1977). The Court of Appeals agreed, and on January 31, 1977, it reversed, remanding "with instructions that a permanent injunction issue halting all activities incident to the Tellico Project which may destroy or modify the critical habitat of the snail darter." *Id.*, at 1075. The Court of Appeals directed that the injunction "remain in effect until Congress, by appropriate legislation, exempts Tellico from compliance with the Act or the snail darter has been deleted from the list of endangered species or its critical habitat materially redefined." *Ibid.*

The Court of Appeals accepted the District Court's finding that closure of the dam would result in the known population of snail darters being "significantly reduced if not completely extirpated." *Id.*, at 1069. TVA, in fact, had conceded as much in the Court of Appeals, but argued that "closure of the Tellico Dam, as the last stage of a ten-year project, falls outside the legitimate purview of the Act if it is rationally construed." *Id.*, at 1070. Disagreeing, the Court of Appeals held that the record revealed a prima facie violation of § 7 of the Act, namely that TVA had failed to take "such action . . . necessary to insure" that its "actions" did not jeopardize the snail darter or its critical habitat.

The reviewing court thus rejected TVA's contention that the word "actions" in § 7 of the Act was not intended by Congress to encompass the terminal phases of ongoing projects. Not only could the court find no "positive reinforcement" for TVA's argument in the Act's legislative history, but also such an interpretation was seen as being "inimical to . . . its objectives." 549 F.2d, at 1070. By way of illustration, that court pointed out that "the detrimental impact of a project upon an endangered species may not always be clearly perceived before construction is well underway." *Id.*, at 1071. Given such a likelihood, the Court of Appeals was of the opinion that TVA's position would require the District Court, sitting as a chancellor, to balance the worth of an endangered species against the value of an ongoing public works measure, a result which the appellate court was not willing to accept. Emphasizing the limits on judicial power in this setting, the court stated:

> "Current project status cannot be translated into a workable standard of judicial review. Whether a dam is 50% or 90% completed is irrelevant in calculating the social and scientific costs attributable to the disappearance of a unique form of life. Courts are ill-equipped to calculate how many dollars must be invested before the value of a dam exceeds that of the endangered species. Our responsibility under § 1540(g)(1)(A) is merely to preserve the status quo where endangered species are threatened, thereby guaranteeing the legislative or executive branches sufficient opportunity to grapple with the alternatives." *Ibid.*

As far as the Court of Appeals was concerned, it made no difference that Congress had repeatedly approved appropriations for Tellico, referring to such legislative approval as an "advisory [opinion]" concerning the proper application of an existing statute. In that court's view, the only relevant legislation was the Act itself, "[the] meaning and spirit" of which was "clear on its face." *Id.*, at 1072.

Turning to the question of an appropriate remedy, the Court of Appeals ruled that the District Court had erred by not issuing an injunction. While recognizing the irretrievable loss of millions of dollars of public funds which would accompany injunctive relief, the court nonetheless decided that the Act explicitly commanded precisely that result:

> "It is conceivable that the welfare of an endangered species may weigh more heavily upon the public conscience, as expressed by the final will of Congress, than the writeoff of those millions of dollars already expended for Tellico in excess of its present salvageable value." *Id.*, at 1074.

Following the issuance of the permanent injunction, members of TVA's Board of Directors appeared before Subcommittees of the House and Senate Appropriations Committees to testify in support of continued appropriations for Tellico. The Subcommittees were apprised of all aspects of Tellico's status, including the Court of Appeals' decision. TVA reported that the dam stood "ready for the gates to be closed and the reservoir filled," Hearings on Public Works for Water and Power Development and Energy Research Appropriation Bill, 1978, before a Subcommittee of the House Committee on Appropriations, 95th Cong., 1st Sess., pt. 4, p. 234 (1977), and requested funds for completion of certain ancillary parts of the project, such as public use areas, roads, and bridges. As to the snail darter itself, TVA commented optimistically on its transplantation efforts, expressing the opinion that the relocated fish were "doing well and [had] reproduced." *Id.*, at 235, 261-262.

Both Appropriations Committees subsequently recommended the full amount requested for completion of the Tellico Project. In its June 2, 1977, Report, the House Appropriations Committee stated:

> "It is *the Committee's view* that the Endangered Species Act was not intended to halt projects such as these in their advanced stage of completion, and [the Committee] strongly recommends that these projects not be stopped because of misuse of the Act." H.R. Rep. No. 95-379, p. 104. (Emphasis added).

As a solution to the problem, the House Committee advised that TVA should cooperate with the Department of the Interior "to relocate the endangered species to another suitable habitat so as to permit the project to proceed as rapidly as possible." *Id.*, at 11. Toward this end, the Committee recommended a special appropriation of $2 million to facilitate relocation of the snail darter and other endangered species which threatened to delay or stop TVA projects. Much the same occurred on the Senate side, with its Appropriations Committee recommending both the amount requested to complete Tellico and the special appropriation for transplantation of endangered species. Reporting to the Senate on these measures, the Appropriations Committee took a particularly strong stand on the snail darter issue:

"This committee has not viewed the Endangered Species Act as preventing the completion and use of these projects which were well under way at the time the affected species were listed as endangered. If the act has such an effect, which is contrary to *the Committee's understanding* of the intent of Congress in enacting the Endangered Species Act, funds should be appropriated to allow these projects to be completed and their benefits realized in the public interest, the Endangered Species Act notwithstanding." S. Rep. No. 95-301, p. 99 (1977). (Emphasis added).

TVA's budget, including funds for completion of Tellico and relocation of the snail darter, passed both Houses of Congress and was signed into law on August 7, 1977. Public Works for Water and Power Development and Energy Research Appropriation Act, 1978, 91 Stat. 797.

We granted certiorari, 434 U.S. 954 (1977), to review the judgment of the Court of Appeals.

II

We begin with the premise that operation of the Tellico Dam will either eradicate the known population of snail darters or destroy their critical habitat. Petitioner does not now seriously dispute this fact. In any event, under § 4(a)(1) of the Act, 87 Stat. 886, 16 U.S.C. § 1533(a)(1) (1976 ed.), the Secretary of the Interior is vested with exclusive authority to determine whether a species such as the snail darter is "endangered" or "threatened" and to ascertain the factors which have led to such a precarious existence. By § 4(d) Congress has authorized — indeed commanded — the Secretary to "issue such regulations as he deems necessary and advisable to provide for the conservation of such species." 16 U.S.C. § 1533(d) (1976 ed.). As we have seen, the Secretary promulgated regulations which declared the snail darter an endangered species whose critical habitat would be destroyed by creation of the Tellico Reservoir. Doubtless petitioner would prefer not to have these regulations on the books, but there is no suggestion that the Secretary exceeded his authority or abused his discretion in issuing the regulations. Indeed, no judicial review of the Secretary's determinations has ever been sought and hence the validity of his actions are not open to review in this Court.

Starting from the above premise, two questions are presented: (a) would TVA be in violation of the Act if it completed and operated the Tellico Dam as planned? (b) if TVA's actions would offend the Act, is an injunction the appropriate remedy for the violation? For the reasons stated hereinafter, we hold that both questions must be answered in the affirmative.

(A)

It may seem curious to some that the survival of a relatively small number of three-inch fish among all the countless millions of species extant would require the permanent halting of a virtually completed dam for which Congress has expended more than $100 million. The paradox is not minimized by the fact that Congress continued to appropriate large sums of public money for the project, even after congressional Appropriations Committees were apprised of its apparent impact upon the survival of the snail darter. We conclude, however, that the explicit provisions of the Endangered Species Act require precisely that result.

One would be hard pressed to find a statutory provision whose terms were any plainer than those in § 7 of the Endangered Species Act. Its very words affirmatively command all federal agencies "to *insure* that actions *authorized, funded,* or *carried out* by them do not *jeopardize* the continued existence" of an endangered species or "*result* in the destruction or modification of habitat of such species. . . ." 16 U.S.C. § 1536 (1976 ed.). (Emphasis added.) This language admits of no exception. Nonetheless, petitioner urges, as do the dissenters, that the Act cannot reasonably be interpreted as applying to a federal project which was well under way when Congress passed the Endangered Species Act of 1973. To sustain that position, however, we would be forced to ignore the ordinary meaning of plain language. It has not been shown, for example, how TVA can close the gates of the Tellico Dam without "carrying out" an action that has been "authorized" and "funded" by a federal agency. Nor can we understand how such action will "*insure*" that the snail darter's habitat is not disrupted.[18] Accepting the Secretary's determinations, as we must, it is clear that TVA's proposed operation of the dam will have precisely the opposite effect, namely the *eradication* of an endangered species.

Concededly, this view of the Act will produce results requiring the sacrifice of the anticipated benefits of the project and of many millions of dollars in public funds. But examination of the language, history, and structure of the legislation under review here indicates beyond doubt that Congress intended endangered species to be afforded the highest of priorities. * * *

[The Court then discussed legislation preceding the ESA and factual findings underlying the enactment of the ESA]

As it was finally passed, the Endangered Species Act of 1973 represented the most comprehensive legislation for the preservation of endangered species ever enacted by any nation. Its stated purposes were "to provide a means whereby the ecosystems upon which endangered species and threatened species depend may be conserved," and "to provide a program for the conservation of such . . . species. . . ." 16 U.S.C. § 1531(b) (1976 ed.). In furtherance of these goals, Congress expressly stated in § 2 (c) that "all Federal departments and agencies *shall seek to conserve endangered species* and threatened species. . . ." 16 U.S.C. § 1531(c) (1976 ed.). (Emphasis added.) Lest there be any ambiguity as to the meaning of this statutory directive, the Act specifically defined "conserve" as meaning "to use and the use of *all methods and procedures which are necessary* to bring *any endangered species* or

---

[18] In dissent, MR. JUSTICE POWELL argues that the meaning of "actions" in § 7 is "far from 'plain,'" and that "it seems evident that the 'actions' referred to are not all actions that an agency can ever take, but rather actions that the agency is deciding whether to authorize, to fund, or to carry out." Aside from this bare assertion, however, no explanation is given to support the proffered interpretation. This recalls Lewis Carroll's classic advice on the construction of language:

"'When *I* use a word,' Humpty Dumpty said, in rather a scornful tone, 'it means just what *I* choose it to mean — neither more nor less.'" Through the Looking Glass, in The Complete Works of Lewis Carroll 196 (1939).

threatened species to the point at which the measures provided pursuant to this chapter are no longer necessary." § 1532(2). (Emphasis added.) Aside from § 7, other provisions indicated the seriousness with which Congress viewed this issue: Virtually all dealings with endangered species, including taking, possession, transportation, and sale, were prohibited, 16 U.S.C. § 1538 (1976 ed.), except in extremely narrow circumstances, see § 1539(b). The Secretary was also given extensive power to develop regulations and programs for the preservation of endangered and threatened species. § 1533(d). Citizen involvement was encouraged by the Act, with provisions allowing interested persons to petition the Secretary to list a species as endangered or threatened, § 1533(c)(2) . . . and bring civil suits in United States district courts to force compliance with any provision of the Act, §§ 1540(c) and (g). * * *

[The Court next discussed the path of the ESA through Congress and quotes statements of significant legislators during the Congressional consideration of the measure.]

It is against this legislative background[29] that we must measure TVA's claim that the Act was not intended to stop operation of a project which, like Tellico Dam, was near completion when an endangered species was discovered in its path. While there is no discussion in the legislative history of precisely this problem, the totality of congressional action makes it abundantly clear that the result we reach today is wholly in accord with both the words of the statute and the intent of Congress. The plain intent of Congress in enacting this statute was to halt and reverse the trend toward species extinction, whatever the cost. This is reflected not only in the stated policies of the Act, but in literally every section of the statute. All persons, including federal agencies, are specifically instructed not to "take" endangered species, meaning that no one is "to harass, harm, pursue, hunt, shoot, wound, kill, trap, capture, or collect" such life forms. 16 U.S.C. §§ 1532(14), 1538(a)(1)(B) (1976 ed.). Agencies in particular are directed by §§ 2 (c) and 3 (2) of the Act to "use . . . *all methods* and procedures which are necessary" to preserve endangered species. 16 U.S.C. §§ 1531(c), 1532(2) (1976 ed.) (emphasis added). In addition, the legislative history undergirding § 7 reveals an explicit congressional decision to require agencies to afford first priority to the declared national policy of saving endangered species. The pointed omission of the type of qualifying language previously included in endangered species legislation reveals a conscious decision by Congress to give endangered species priority over the "primary missions" of federal agencies.

It is not for us to speculate, much less act, on whether Congress would have altered its stance had the specific events of this case been anticipated. In any event, we discern no hint in the deliberations of Congress relating to the 1973 Act that would compel a different result than we reach here. Indeed, the repeated expressions of congressional concern over what it saw as the potentially enormous danger presented by the eradication of *any* endangered

---

[29] When confronted with a statute which is plain and unambiguous on its face, we ordinarily do not look to legislative history as a guide to its meaning. *Ex parte Collett,* 337 U.S. 55, 61 (1949), and cases cited therein. Here it is not necessary to look beyond the words of the statute. We have undertaken such an analysis only to meet MR. JUSTICE POWELL's suggestion that the "absurd" result reached in this case, is not in accord with congressional intent.

species suggest how the balance would have been struck had the issue been presented to Congress in 1973. * * *

. . .[N]either the Endangered Species Act nor Art. III of the Constitution provides federal courts with authority to make such fine utilitarian calculations. On the contrary, the plain language of the Act, buttressed by its legislative history, shows clearly that Congress viewed the value of endangered species as "incalculable." Quite obviously, it would be difficult for a court to balance the loss of a sum certain — even $100 million — against a congressionally declared "incalculable" value, even assuming we had the power to engage in such a weighing process, which we emphatically do not.

In passing the Endangered Species Act of 1973, Congress was also aware of certain instances in which exceptions to the statute's broad sweep would be necessary. Thus, § 10, 16 U.S.C. § 1539 (1976 ed.), creates a number of limited "hardship exemptions," none of which would even remotely apply to the Tellico Project. In fact, there are no exemptions in the Endangered Species Act for federal agencies, meaning that under the maxim *expressio unius est exclusio alterius*, we must presume that these were the only "hardship cases" Congress intended to exempt. *Cf. National Railroad Passenger Corp. v. National Assn. of Railroad Passengers*, 414 U.S. 453, 458 (1974).

Notwithstanding Congress' expression of intent in 1973, we are urged to find that the continuing appropriations for Tellico Dam constitute an implied repeal of the 1973 Act, at least insofar as it applies to the Tellico Project. * * *

There is nothing in the appropriations measures, as passed, which states that the Tellico Project was to be completed irrespective of the requirements of the Endangered Species Act. These appropriations, in fact, represented relatively minor components of the lump-sum amounts for the *entire* TVA budget. To find a repeal of the Endangered Species Act under these circumstances would surely do violence to the "'cardinal rule . . . that repeals by implication are not favored.'" *Morton v. Mancari*, 417 U.S. 535, 549 (1974), quoting *Posadas v. National City Bank*, 296 U.S. 497, 503 (1936). In *Posadas* this Court held, in no uncertain terms, that "the intention of the legislature to repeal must be clear and manifest." *Ibid. See Georgia v. Pennsylvania R. Co.*, 324 U.S. 439, 456-457 (1945) ("Only a clear repugnancy between the old . . . and the new [law] results in the former giving way . . ."); *United States v. Borden Co.*, 308 U.S. 188, 198-199 (1939) ("[Intention] of the legislature to repeal 'must be clear and manifest.' . . . '[A] positive repugnancy [between the old and the new laws]'"); *Wood v. United States*, 16 Pet. 342, 363 (1842), must be a positive repugnancy . . ."). In practical terms, this "cardinal rule" means that "[in] the absence of some affirmative showing of an intention to repeal, the only permissible justification for a repeal by implication is when the earlier and later statutes are irreconcilable." *Mancari, supra*, at 550.

The doctrine disfavoring repeals by implication "applies with full vigor when . . . the subsequent legislation is an appropriations measure." *Committee for Nuclear Responsibility v. Seaborg*, 149 U.S. App. D.C. 380, 382, 463 F.2d 783, 785 (1971) (emphasis added); *Environmental Defense Fund v. Froehlke*, 473 F.2d 346, 355 (CA8 1972). This is perhaps an understatement since it would be more accurate to say that the policy applies with even *greater* force when the claimed repeal rests solely on an Appropriations Act. We recognize that both substantive enactments and appropriations measures are "Acts of Congress," but the latter have the limited and specific purpose of providing funds for authorized programs. When voting on appropriations measures, legislators are entitled to operate under the assumption that the funds will be devoted to purposes which are lawful and not for any purpose forbidden. Without such an assurance, every appropriations measure would be pregnant with prospects of altering substantive legislation, repealing by implication any prior statute which might prohibit the expenditure. * * *

(B)

Having determined that there is an irreconcilable conflict between operation of the Tellico Dam and the explicit provisions of § 7 of the Endangered Species Act, we must now consider what remedy, if any, is appropriate. It is correct, of course, that a federal judge sitting as a chancellor is not mechanically obligated to grant an injunction for every violation of law. This Court made plain in *Hecht Co. v. Bowles*, 321 U.S. 321, 329 (1944), that "[a] grant of *jurisdiction* to issue compliance orders hardly suggests an absolute duty to do so under any and all circumstances." As a general matter it may be said that "[since] all or almost all equitable remedies are discretionary, the balancing of equities and hardships is appropriate in almost any case as a guide to the chancellor's discretion." D. Dobbs, Remedies 52 (1973). Thus, in *Hecht Co.* the Court refused to grant an injunction when it appeared from the District Court findings that "the issuance of an injunction would have 'no effect by way of insuring better compliance in the future' and would [have been] 'unjust' to [the] petitioner and not 'in the public interest.'" 321 U.S., at 326.

But these principles take a court only so far. Our system of government is, after all, a tripartite one, with each branch having certain defined functions delegated to it by the Constitution. While "[it] is emphatically the province and duty of the judicial department to say what the law is," *Marbury v. Madison,* 1 Cranch 137, 177 (1803), it is equally — and emphatically — the exclusive province of the Congress not only to formulate legislative policies and mandate programs and projects, but also to establish their relative priority for the Nation. Once Congress, exercising its delegated powers, has decided the order of priorities in a given area, it is for the Executive to administer the laws and for the courts to enforce them when enforcement is sought.

Here we are urged to view the Endangered Species Act "reasonably," and hence shape a remedy "that accords with some modicum of common sense and the public weal." But is that our function? We have no expert knowledge on the subject of endangered species, much less do we have a mandate from the people to strike a balance of equities on the side of the Tellico Dam. Congress has spoken in the plainest of words, making it abundantly clear that the balance has been struck in favor of affording endangered species the highest of priorities, thereby adopting a policy which it described as "institutionalized caution."

Our individual appraisal of the wisdom or unwisdom of a particular course consciously selected by the Congress is to be put aside in the process of interpreting a statute. Once the meaning of an enactment is discerned and its constitutionality determined, the judicial process comes to an end. We do not sit as a committee of review, nor are we vested with the power of veto. The lines ascribed to Sir Thomas More by Robert Bolt are not without relevance here:

> "The law, Roper, the law. I know what's legal, not what's right. And I'll stick to what's legal. . . . I'm *not* God. The currents and eddies of right and wrong, which you find such plain-sailing, I can't navigate, I'm no voyager. But in the thickets of the law, oh there I'm a forester. . . . What would you do? Cut a great road through the law to get after the Devil? . . . And when the last law was down, and the Devil turned round on you — where would you hide, Roper, the laws all being flat? . . . This country's planted thick with laws from coast to coast — Man's laws, not God's — and if you cut them down . . . d'you really think you could stand upright in the winds that would blow then? . . . Yes, I'd give the Devil benefit of law, for my own safety's sake." R. Bolt, A Man for All Seasons, Act I, p. 147 (Three Plays, Heinemann ed. 1967).

We agree with the Court of Appeals that in our constitutional system the commitment to the separation of powers is too fundamental for us to pre-empt congressional action by judicially decreeing what accords with "common sense and the public weal." Our Constitution vests such responsibilities in the political branches.

Affirmed.

MR. JUSTICE POWELL, with whom MR. JUSTICE BLACKMUN joins, dissenting.

[The dissent argued the ESA and its legislative history need not be read to apply to all "actions." Specifically, it should not apply to projects either completed or substantially completed. Instead of offering up "an extreme example of a literalist construction, not required by the language of the Act and adopted without regard to its manifest purpose[,]", argued Powell, the Court should "adopt a permissible construction that accords with some modicum of common sense and the public weal."]

> "[Frequently] words of general meaning are used in a statute, words broad enough to include an act in question, and yet a consideration of the whole legislation, or of the circumstances surrounding its enactment, or of the absurd results which follow from giving such broad meaning to the words, makes it unreasonable to believe that the legislator intended to include the particular act." *Church of the Holy Trinity v. United States*, 143 U.S. 457, 459 (1892). The result that will follow in this case by virtue of the Court's reading of § 7 makes it unreasonable to believe that Congress intended that reading. Moreover, § 7 may be construed in a way that avoids an "absurd result" without doing violence to its language. * * *

[Justice Powell concluded the statute should apply to prospective actions only, i.e. "actions with respect to which the agency has reasonable decision-making alternatives still available, actions not yet carried out."]

MR. JUSTICE REHNQUIST, dissenting.

[Chief Justice Rehnquist contended the ESA does not compel the issuance of an injunction, and the refusal of the District Court to issue one in this case was not abusive.]

NOTES AND QUESTION

1. *Tennessee Valley Authority v. Hill* is to the ESA what *Calvert Cliffs* (*see* Chapter 4, *supra*) was to NEPA except for the significant distinction that *TVA v. Hill* could not be overruled by a higher court. The decision alerted the world that the ESA would be understood according to its text. "[I]nsure no jeopardy" would mean *make absolutely certain not even a little bit of jeopardy* takes place. And more: it has been held subsequently that the Secretary must "do far more than merely avoid elimination of the protected species; he must bring such species back from the brink so that they may be removed from the protected class, and he must use all necessary methods to do so." *Carson-Truckee Water Conservancy Dist. v. Watt*, 549 F. Supp 704 (D. Nev. 1982), *aff'd*, 741 F.2d 257 (9th Cir. 1984). Do you read § 7 as requiring the Secretary to undertake affirmative restoration efforts?

2. Does a BiOp have the same influence on an agency's decision as an EIS? *See, e.g., Bennett v. Spear*, 520 U.S. 154, 169-70, 157 S. Ct. 1154, 1164-65 (1997):

> By the Government's own account, while the Service's Biological Opinion theoretically serves an "advisory function," 51 Fed. Reg. 19928 (1986), in reality it has a powerful coercive effect on the action agency:
>
>> The statutory scheme . . . presupposes that the biological opinion will play a central role in the action agency's decisionmaking process, and that it will typically be based on an administrative record that is fully adequate for the action agency's decision insofar as ESA issues are concerned. . . . [A] federal agency that chooses to deviate from the recommendations contained in a biological opinion bears the burden of 'articulating in its administrative record its reasons for disagreeing with the conclusions of a biological opinion,' 51 Fed. Reg. 19,956 (1986). In the government's experience, action agencies very rarely choose to engage in conduct that the Service has concluded is likely to jeopardize the continued existence of a listed species." Brief for Respondents 20-21.
>
> What this concession omits to say, moreover, is that the action agency must not only articulate its reasons for disagreement (which ordinarily requires species and habitat investigations that are not within the action agency's expertise), but that it runs a substantial risk if its (inexpert) reasons turn out to be wrong. A Biological Opinion of the sort rendered here alters the legal regime to which the action agency is subject. . . . The action agency is technically free to disregard the Biological Opinion and proceed with its proposed action, but it does so at its own peril (and that of its employees), for "any person" who knowingly "takes" an endangered or threatened species is subject to substantial civil and criminal penalties, including imprisonment. See §§ 1540(a) and (b) (authorizing civil fines of

up to $ 25,000 per violation and criminal penalties of up to $ 50,000 and imprisonment for one year) . . .

3. The Supreme Court's decision in *TVA v. Hill,* handed down on June 15, 1978, was less than warmly received in high places. Particularly troubled by the decision was then-Republican Minority Leader of the United States Senate, Senator Howard H. Baker of Tellico's home state of Tennessee. A devotee of the water project, Senator Baker took on the completion of the Tellico project as his personal mission.

As a first volley, Senator Baker engineered an important amendment to the ESA. At his behest, on November 10, 1978, less than five months after the decision in *TVA v. Hill,* the Congress created the Endangered Species Committee ("ESC"). *See* § 7(e), 16 U.S.C. § 1536(e). One of the bluest of blue-ribbon panels, the Committee has seven designated members: the Secretaries of Agriculture, Army, and Interior, the Chairman of the Council of Economic Advisors, the Administrators of the Environmental Protection Agency and the National Oceanic and Atmospheric Administration, and one individual from the affected state. § 7(e)(3), 16 U.S.C. § 1536(e)(3). Aptly nicknamed the "God Squad," the Committee is authorized to issue wholesale exemptions from the provisions of § 7. Senator Baker provided in the legislation that Tellico would be the ESC's first order of business.

The ESC promptly took up the matter, but, on January 23, 1979, voted against exempting Tellico. Notably, all six federal members of the panel voted to deny. The major motivation for the negative vote, however, was not the snail darter, but Tellico itself. As the Chairman of the Council of Economic Advisors, Charles Schultze, put it, "[The project] does not pay. The costs clearly outweigh the benefits. It would have cost $35 million to complete it and we would be inundating $40 million worth of land. You would lose important Indian archeological sites, scenic values and the river in its natural state." Margot Hornblower, *Panel Junks TVA Dam; Cites Cost, Not Snail Darter,* The Wash. Post, Jan. 24, 1979, p. A12.

At this point, Senator Baker settled on a more blunt approach, to simply have Congress authorize the project. Working with Rep. John J. Duncan, a Tennessee colleague in the House of Representatives, amendments were offered to that effect. The authorization passed the House in the summer of 1979. The story is that the amendment was hidden in a larger bill and that the House had no idea it was voting to construct the Tellico Dam. The Senate followed suit on September 19, 1979, after a good bit of blatant arm-twisting by the Minority Leader. The measure arrived at President Jimmy Carter's desk as part of a $10.8 billion energy and water resources spending bill. Despite his on-the-record opposition to Tellico, President Carter signed the measure into law, reportedly to avoid Congressional reprisals on other important pending legislation. On November 29, 1979, the dam was completed and waters impounded. The result was Lake Tellico, a 15,860-acre lake with miles of shoreline. Dotting the shores are an estimated 2000 residential homes known as Tellico Village.

In 1980, additional snail darters were discovered 80 miles south of the damsite, and more were found later in Alabama and Georgia. Dr. Etnier, who made the original discovery that triggered the *TVA v. Hill* saga, explained the other colonies of snail darters were not found sooner because scientists misunderstood the species' tolerance for pollution. Apparently, snail darters can withstand a great deal more contamination than was earlier believed. On July 5, 1984, nine years after it was listed as endangered, the snail darter was downgraded to "threatened." 49 Fed Reg. 27510, 27514.

4. A longstanding ESA controversy involves the northern spotted owl, which populates timberlands in the Pacific Northwest. In 1987, litigation had begun to protect the spotted owl on timberlands managed by BLM, which comprise the bulk of the owl habitat. The theory was that logging operations were threatening the continued existence of the species. At this time, though, the spotted owl had not been designated under the ESA, so plaintiffs were relying on NEPA arguments to effect an end to logging activities. The case resulted in the entry of an injunction against the loggers.

Congress became involved in the controversy as well. It enacted § 318 of the Interior and Related Agencies Appropriations Act for FY 1990, Pub. L. No. 101-121, 103 Stat. 701, 745-50 (1990), which expressly allowed resumption of timber operations in these old growth forests in Oregon and Washington in FY 1992.

But, thereafter, the Ninth Circuit ruled § 318 to be unconstitutional as violating separation of powers principles because it interfered with ongoing litigation. As the court termed it, § 318 was an instruction to the court "to reach a particular result in pending cases identified by caption and case number." *Seattle Audubon Society et al. v. Robertson*, 914 F.2d 1311, 1314 (9th Cir. 1990).

At about this same time, the Fish and Wildlife Service of DOI designated the spotted owl as "threatened" throughout its entire range. *See* 55 Fed. Reg. 26114 (June 26, 1990). After designation, the Bureau of Land Management, which manages federally-owned owl habitat lands, took steps to stop timber harvesting in the range until further notice.

On June 6, 1994, the court-ordered injunction was lifted on the theory that the Forest Service's new forest management plan made the ban unnecessary.

For more information about the spotted owl controversy, see Hungerford, *Changing the Management of Public Forest Lands: The Role of the Spotted Owl Injunctions*, 24 Envt'l L. 1396 (1994); Victor M. Sher, *Travels with Strix: The Spotted Owl's Journey Through the Federal Courts*, 14 Pub. Land L. Rev. (1993).

5. In *Sierra Club v. U.S. Fish and Wildlife Service*, 245 F.3d 434 (5th Cir. 2001), a regulation implementing § 7 was found to violate the ESA. Section 7, the reader will recall, requires "habitat consultation" (as distinct from "jeopardy consultation") whenever an agency action might "result in the destruction or adverse modification of [designated] habitat." § 7(a)(2), 16 U.S.C. § 1536(a)(2). The regulation defined "destruction or adverse modification" as "a direct or indirect alteration that appreciably diminishes the value of critical habitat for *both the survival and recovery* of a listed species." 50 C.F.R. § 402.02 (emphasis added). The court found this regulation to violate the ESA because it does not require habitat consultation where an agency action affects survival alone. The gravamen of the court's reasoning was that critical habitat

is "essential to conservation" and conservation speaks to recovery, not just survival. Thus, there should be habitat consultation on both counts.

D. SECTION 9

BABBITT v. SWEET HOME CHAPTER OF COMMUNITIES FOR A GREAT OREGON

515 U.S. 684, 115 S. Ct. 2407 (1995)

JUDGES: STEVENS, J., delivered the opinion of the Court, in which O'CONNOR, KENNEDY, SOUTER, GINSBURG, and BREYER, JJ., joined. O'CONNOR, J., filed a concurring opinion. SCALIA, J., filed a dissenting opinion, in which REHNQUIST, C. J., and THOMAS, J., joined.

The Endangered Species Act of 1973, 87 Stat. 884, 16 U.S.C. § 1531 (1988 ed. and Supp. V) (ESA or Act), contains a variety of protections designed to save from extinction species that the Secretary of the Interior designates as endangered or threatened. Section 9 of the Act makes it unlawful for any person to "take" any endangered or threatened species. The Secretary has promulgated a regulation that defines the statute's prohibition on takings to include "significant habitat modification or degradation where it actually kills or injures wildlife." This case presents the question whether the Secretary exceeded his authority under the Act by promulgating that regulation.

I

Section 9(a)(1) of the Endangered Species Act provides the following protection for endangered species:

> "Except as provided in sections 1535(g)(2) and 1539 of this title, with respect to any endangered species of fish or wildlife listed pursuant to section 1533 of this title it is unlawful for any person subject to the jurisdiction of the United States to — . . . .
>
> "(B) take any such species within the United States or the territorial sea of the United States[.]" 16 U.S.C. § 1538(a)(1).

Section 3(19) of the Act defines the statutory term "take":

> "The term 'take' means to harass, harm, pursue, hunt, shoot, wound, kill, trap, capture, or collect, or to attempt to engage in any such conduct." 16 U.S.C. § 1532(19).

The Act does not further define the terms it uses to define "take." The Interior Department regulations that implement the statute, however, define the statutory term "harm":

> "*Harm* in the definition of 'take' in the Act means an act which actually kills or injures wildlife. Such act may include significant habitat modification or degradation where it actually kills or injures wildlife by significantly impairing essential behavioral patterns, including breeding, feeding, or sheltering." 50 C.F.R. § 17.3 (1994).

This regulation has been in place since 1975.

A limitation on the § 9 "take" prohibition appears in § 10(a)(1)(B) of the Act, which Congress added by amendment in 1982. That section authorizes the Secretary to grant a permit for any taking otherwise prohibited by § 9(a)(1)(B) "if such taking is incidental to, and not the purpose of, the carrying out of an otherwise lawful activity." 16 U.S.C. § 1539(a)(1)(B).

In addition to the prohibition on takings, the Act provides several other protections for endangered species. Section 4, 16 U.S.C. § 1533, commands the Secretary to identify species of fish or wildlife that are in danger of extinction and to publish from time to time lists of all species he determines to be endangered or threatened. Section 5, 16 U.S.C. § 1534, authorizes the Secretary, in cooperation with the States, see 16 U.S.C. § 1535, to acquire land to aid in preserving such species. Section 7 requires federal agencies to ensure that none of their activities, including the granting of licenses and permits, will jeopardize the continued existence of endangered species "or result in the destruction or adverse modification of habitat of such species which is determined by the Secretary . . . to be critical." 16 U.S.C. § 1536(a)(2).

Respondents in this action are small landowners, logging companies, and families dependent on the forest products industries in the Pacific Northwest and in the Southeast, and organizations that represent their interests. They brought this declaratory judgment action against petitioners, the Secretary of the Interior and the Director of the Fish and Wildlife Service, in the United States District Court for the District of Columbia to challenge the statutory validity of the Secretary's regulation defining "harm," particularly the inclusion of habitat modification and degradation in the definition. Respondents challenged the regulation on its face. Their complaint alleged that application of the "harm" regulation to the red-cockaded woodpecker, an endangered species, and the northern spotted owl, a threatened species, had injured them economically. App. 17-23.

Respondents advanced three arguments to support their submission that Congress did not intend the word "take" in § 9 to include habitat modification, as the Secretary's "harm" regulation provides. First, they correctly noted that language in the Senate's original version of the ESA would have defined "take" to include "destruction, modification, or curtailment of [the] habitat or range" of fish or wildlife, but the Senate deleted that language from the bill before enacting it. Second, respondents argued that Congress intended the Act's express authorization for the Federal Government to buy private land in order to prevent habitat degradation in § 5 to be the exclusive check against habitat modification on private property. Third, because the Senate added the term "harm" to the definition of "take" in a floor amendment without debate, respondents argued that the court should not interpret the term so expansively as to include habitat modification. . . .

[The Court then reviewed the decisions in the instant case at the District and Court of Appeals levels.]

II

Because this case was decided on motions for summary judgment, we may appropriately make certain factual assumptions in order to frame the legal issue. First, we assume respondents have no desire to harm either the red-cockaded woodpecker or the spotted owl; they merely wish to continue logging activities that would be entirely proper if not prohibited by the ESA. On the other hand, we must assume *arguendo* that those activities will have the effect, even though unintended, of detrimentally changing the natural habitat of both listed species and that, as a consequence, members of those species will be killed or injured. Under respondents' view of the law, the Secretary's only means of forestalling that grave result — even when the actor knows it is certain to occur — is to use his § 5 authority to purchase the lands on which the survival of the species depends. The Secretary, on the other hand, submits that the § 9 prohibition on takings, which Congress defined to include "harm," places on respondents a duty to avoid harm that habitat alteration will cause the birds unless respondents first obtain a permit pursuant to § 10.

The text of the Act provides three reasons for concluding that the Secretary's interpretation is reasonable. First, an ordinary understanding of the word "harm" supports it. The dictionary definition of the verb form of "harm" is "to cause hurt or damage to: injure." Webster's Third New International Dictionary 1034 (1966). In the context of the ESA, that definition naturally encompasses habitat modification that results in actual injury or death to members of an endangered or threatened species.

Respondents argue that the Secretary should have limited the purview of "harm" to direct applications of force against protected species, but the dictionary definition does not include the word "directly" or suggest in any way that only direct or willful action that leads to injury constitutes "harm." Moreover, unless the statutory term "harm" encompasses indirect as well as direct injuries, the word has no meaning that does not duplicate the meaning of other words that § 3 uses to define "take." A reluctance to treat statutory terms as surplusage supports the reasonableness of the Secretary's interpretation. [citation omitted.]

Second, the broad purpose of the ESA supports the Secretary's decision to extend protection against activities that cause the precise harms Congress enacted the statute to avoid. In *TVA v. Hill,* 437 U.S. 153, 98 S. Ct. 2279, 57 L. Ed. 2d 117 (1978), we described the Act as "the most comprehensive legislation for the preservation of endangered species ever enacted by any nation." *Id.,* at 180. Whereas predecessor statutes enacted in 1966 and 1969 had not contained any sweeping prohibition against the taking of endangered species except on federal lands, *see id.,* at 175, the 1973 Act applied to all land in the United States and to the Nation's territorial seas. As stated in § 2 of the Act, among its central purposes is "to provide a means whereby the ecosystems upon which endangered species and threatened species depend may be conserved. . . ." 16 U.S.C. § 1531(b).

In *Hill,* we construed § 7 as precluding the completion of the Tellico Dam because of its predicted impact on the survival of the snail darter. *See* 437 U.S. at 193. Both our holding and the language in our opinion stressed the importance of the statutory policy. "The plain intent of Congress in enacting this statute," we recognized, "was to halt and reverse the trend toward species extinction, whatever the cost. This is reflected not only in the stated policies of the Act, but in literally every section of the statute." *Id.,* at 184. Although the § 9 "take" prohibition was not at issue in *Hill*, we took note of that prohibition, placing particular emphasis on the Secretary's inclusion of habitat modification in his definition of "harm." In light of that provision for habitat protection, we could "not understand how TVA intends to operate Tellico Dam without 'harming' the snail darter." *Id.*, at 184, n. 30. Congress' intent to provide comprehensive protection for endangered and threatened species supports the permissibility of the Secretary's "harm" regulation.

Respondents advance strong arguments that activities that cause minimal or unforeseeable harm will not violate the Act as construed in the "harm" regulation. Respondents, however, present a facial challenge to the regulation. *Cf. Anderson v. Edwards*, 514 U.S. 143, 155-153, n. 6 (1995) . . . ; *INS v. National Center for Immigrants' Rights, Inc.*, 502 U.S. 183, 188, 116 L. Ed. 2d 546, 112 S. Ct. 551 (1991). Thus, they ask us to invalidate the Secretary's understanding of "harm" in every circumstance, even when an actor knows that an activity, such as draining a pond, would actually result in the extinction of a listed species by destroying its habitat. Given Congress' clear expression of the ESA's broad purpose to protect endangered and threatened wildlife, the Secretary's definition of "harm" is reasonable.

Third, the fact that Congress in 1982 authorized the Secretary to issue permits for takings that § 9(a)(1)(B) would otherwise prohibit, "if such taking is incidental to, and not the purpose of, the carrying out of an otherwise lawful activity," 16 U.S.C. § 1539(a)(1)(B), strongly suggests that Congress understood § 9(a)(1)(B) to prohibit indirect as well as deliberate takings. *Cf. NLRB v. Bell Aerospace Co. of Textron, Inc.*, 416 U.S. 267, 274–275, 40 L. Ed. 2d 134, 94 S. Ct. 1757 (1974). The permit process requires the applicant to prepare a "conservation plan" that specifies how he intends to "minimize and mitigate" the "impact" of his activity on endangered and threatened species, 16 U.S.C. § 1539(a)(2)(A), making clear that Congress had in mind foreseeable rather than merely accidental effects on listed species. No one could seriously request an "incidental" take permit to avert § 9 liability for direct, deliberate action against a member of an endangered or threatened species, but respondents would read "harm" so narrowly that the permit procedure would have little more than that absurd purpose. "When Congress acts to amend a statute, we presume it intends its amendment to have real and substantial effect." *Stone v. INS*, 514 U.S. 386, 397, 131 L. Ed. 2d 465, 115 S. Ct. 1537 (1995). . . . Congress' addition of the § 10 permit provision supports the Secretary's conclusion that activities not intended to harm an endangered species, such as habitat modification, may constitute unlawful takings under the ESA unless the Secretary permits them.

The Court of Appeals made three errors in asserting that "harm" must refer to a direct application of force because the words around it do. First, the court's premise was flawed. Several of the words that accompany "harm" in the § 3 definition of "take," especially "harass," "pursue," "wound," and "kill," refer to actions or effects that do not require direct applications of force. Second, to the extent the court read a requirement of intent or purpose into the words used to define "take," it ignored § 9's express provision that a "knowing" action is enough to violate the Act. Third, the court employed *noscitur a sociis* to give "harm" essentially the same function as other words in the definition, thereby denying it independent meaning. The canon, to the contrary, counsels that a word "gathers meaning from the words around it." *Jarecki v. G. D. Searle & Co.*, 367 U.S. 303, 307, 6 L. Ed. 2d 859, 81 S. Ct. 1579 (1961). The statutory context of "harm" suggests that Congress meant that term to serve a particular function in the ESA, consistent with but distinct from the functions of the other verbs used to define "take." The Secretary's interpretation of "harm" to include indirectly injuring endangered animals through habitat modification permissibly interprets "harm" to have "a character of its own not to be submerged by its association." *Russell Motor Car Co. v. United States*, 261 U.S. 514, 519, 67 L. Ed. 778, 43 S. Ct. 428 (1923).

Nor does the Act's inclusion of the § 5 land acquisition authority and the § 7 directive to federal agencies to avoid destruction or adverse modification of critical habitat alter our conclusion. . . .

We need not decide whether the statutory definition of "take" compels the Secretary's interpretation of "harm," because our conclusions that Congress did not unambiguously manifest its intent to adopt respondents' view and that the Secretary's interpretation is reasonable suffice to decide this case. *See generally Chevron U.S.A. Inc. v. Natural Resources Defense Council, Inc.*, 467 U.S. 837, 81 L. Ed. 2d 694, 104 S. Ct. 2778 (1984). The latitude the ESA gives the Secretary in enforcing the statute, together with the degree of regulatory expertise necessary to its enforcement, establishes that we owe some degree of deference to the Secretary's reasonable interpretation. *See* Breyer, *Judicial Review of Questions of Law and Policy*, 38 Admin. L. Rev. 363, 373 (1986).

III

[Herein a discussion of the legislative history of the Endangered Species Act.]

IV

When it enacted the ESA, Congress delegated broad administrative and interpretive power to the Secretary. *See* 16 U.S.C. §§ 1533, 1540(f). The task of defining and listing endangered and threatened species requires an expertise and attention to detail that exceeds the normal province of Congress. Fashioning appropriate standards for issuing permits under § 10 for takings that would otherwise violate § 9 necessarily requires the exercise of broad discretion. The proper interpretation of a term such as "harm" involves a complex policy choice. When Congress has entrusted the Secretary with broad discretion, we are especially reluctant to substitute our views of wise policy for his. *See Chevron*, 467 U.S. at 865–866. In this case, that reluctance accords with our conclusion, based on the text, structure, and legislative history of the ESA, that the Secretary reasonably construed the intent of Congress when he defined "harm" to include "significant habitat modification or degradation that actually kills or injures wildlife."

In the elaboration and enforcement of the ESA, the Secretary and all persons who must comply with the law will confront difficult questions of proximity and degree; for, as all recognize, the Act encompasses a vast range of economic and social enterprises and endeavors. These questions must be addressed in the usual course of the law, through case-by-case resolution and adjudication.

The judgment of the Court of Appeals is reversed.

It is so ordered.

CONCUR: JUSTICE O'CONNOR, concurring.

My agreement with the Court is founded on two understandings. First, the challenged regulation is limited to significant habitat modification that causes actual, as opposed to hypothetical or speculative, death or injury to identifiable protected animals. Second, even setting aside difficult questions of scienter, the regulation's application is limited by ordinary principles of proximate causation, which introduce notions of foreseeability. . . .

In my view, the regulation is limited by its terms to actions that actually kill or injure individual animals. JUSTICE SCALIA disagrees, arguing that the harm regulation "encompasses injury inflicted, not only upon individual animals, but upon populations of the protected species." At one level, I could not reasonably quarrel with this observation; death to an individual animal always reduces the size of the population in which it lives, and in that sense, "injures" that population. But by its insight, the dissent means something else. Building upon the regulation's use of the word "breeding," JUSTICE SCALIA suggests that the regulation facially bars significant habitat modification that actually kills or injures *hypothetical* animals (or, perhaps more aptly, causes potential additions to the population not to come into being). Because "impairment of breeding does not 'injure' living creatures," JUSTICE SCALIA reasons, the regulation *must* contemplate application to "a population of animals which would otherwise have maintained or increased its numbers."

I disagree. As an initial matter, I do not find it as easy as JUSTICE SCALIA does to dismiss the notion that significant impairment of breeding injures living creatures. To raze the last remaining ground on which the piping plover currently breeds, thereby making it impossible for any piping plovers to reproduce, would obviously injure the population (causing the species' extinction in a generation). But by completely preventing breeding, it would also injure the individual living bird, in the same way that sterilizing the creature injures the individual living bird. To "injure" is, among other things, "to impair." Webster's Ninth New Collegiate Dictionary 623 (1983). One need not subscribe to theories of "psychic harm," to recognize that to make it impossible for an animal to reproduce is to impair its most essential physical functions and to render that animal, and its genetic material, biologically obsolete. This, in my view, is actual injury.

In any event, even if impairing an animal's ability to breed were not, *in and of itself,* an injury to that animal, interference with breeding can cause an animal to suffer other, perhaps more obvious, kinds of injury. The regulation has clear application, for example, to significant habitat modification that kills or physically injures animals which, because they are in a vulnerable breeding state, do not or cannot flee or defend themselves, or to environmental pollutants that cause an animal to suffer physical complications during gestation. Breeding, feeding, and sheltering are what animals do. If significant habitat modification, by interfering with these essential behaviors, actually kills or injures an animal protected by the Act, it causes "harm" within the meaning of the regulation. In contrast to JUSTICE SCALIA, I do not read the regulation's "breeding" reference to vitiate or somehow to qualify the clear actual death or injury requirement, or to suggest that the regulation contemplates extension to nonexistent animals. . . .

By the dissent's reckoning, the regulation at issue here, in conjunction with 16 U.S.C. § 1540(1), imposes liability for any habitat-modifying conduct that ultimately results in the death of a protected animal, "regardless of whether that result is intended or even foreseeable, and no matter how long the chain of causality between modification and injury." Even if § 1540(1) does create a strict liability regime (a question we need not decide at this juncture), I see no indication that Congress, in enacting that section, intended to dispense with ordinary principles of proximate causation. Strict liability means liability without regard to fault; it does not normally mean liability for every consequence, however remote, of one's conduct. . . . I would not lightly assume that Congress, in enacting a strict liability statute that is silent on the causation question, has dispensed with this well-entrenched principle. In the absence of congressional abrogation of traditional principles of causation, then, private parties should be held liable under § 1540(1) only if their habitat-modifying actions proximately cause death or injury to protected animals. . . .

DISSENT: JUSTICE SCALIA, with whom THE CHIEF JUSTICE and JUSTICE THOMAS join, dissenting.

I think it unmistakably clear that the legislation at issue here (1) forbade the hunting and killing of endangered animals, and (2) provided federal lands and federal funds *for the acquisition of private lands*, to preserve the habitat of endangered animals. The Court's holding that the hunting and killing prohibition incidentally preserves habitat on private lands imposes unfairness to the point of financial ruin — not just upon the rich, but upon the simplest farmer who finds his land conscripted to national zoological use. I respectfully dissent. * * *

I

The regulation has three features which, for reasons I shall discuss at length below, do not comport with the statute. First, it interprets the statute to prohibit habitat modification that is no more than the cause-in-fact of death or injury to wildlife. *Any* "significant habitat modification" that in fact produces that result by "impairing essential behavioral patterns" is made unlawful, regardless of whether that result is intended or even foreseeable, and no matter how long the chain of causality between modification and injury. *See, e.g., Palila v. Hawaii Dept. of Land and Natural Resources*, 852 F.2d 1106, 1108-1109 (CA9 1988) (*Palila II*) (sheep grazing constituted "taking" of palila birds, since although sheep do not destroy full-grown mamane trees, they do destroy mamane seedlings, which will not grow to full-grown trees, on which the palila feeds and nests). *See also* Davison, *Alteration of Wildlife Habitat as a Prohibited Taking under the Endangered Species Act*, 10 J. Land Use & Envtl. L. 155, 190 (1995) (regulation requires only causation-in-fact).

Second, the regulation does not require an "act": the Secretary's officially stated position is that an *omission* will do. The previous version of the regulation made this explicit. *See* 40 Fed. Reg. 44412, 44416 (1975) ("'Harm' in the definition of 'take' in the Act means an act or omission which actually kills or injures wildlife . . ."). When the regulation was modified in 1981 the phrase "or omission" was taken out, but only because (as the final publication of the rule advised) "the [Fish and Wildlife] Service feels that 'act' is inclusive of either commissions or omissions which would be prohibited by section [1538(a)(1)(B)]." 46 Fed. Reg. 54748, 54750 (1981). In its brief here the Government agrees that the regulation covers omissions, see Brief for Petitioners 47 (although it argues that "an 'omission' constitutes an 'act' . . . only if there is a legal duty to act"), *ibid.*

The third and most important unlawful feature of the regulation is that it encompasses injury inflicted, not only upon individual animals, but upon populations of the protected species. "Injury" in the regulation includes "significantly impairing essential behavioral patterns, including *breeding*," 50 C.F.R. § 17.3 (1994) (emphasis added). Impairment of breeding does not "injure" living creatures; it prevents them from propagating, thus "injuring" *a population* of animals which would otherwise have maintained or increased its numbers. What the face of the regulation shows, the Secretary's official pronouncements confirm. The Final Redefinition of "Harm" accompanying publication of the regulation said that "harm" is not limited to "direct physical injury to an individual member of the wildlife species," 46 Fed. Reg. 54748 (1981), and refers to "injury to *a population*," *id.*, at 54749 (emphasis added). *See also Palila II, supra*, at 1108; *Davison, supra*, at 190, and n. 177, 195; M. Bean, *The Evolution of National Wildlife Law* 344 (1983).

[Justice Scalia then undertook a lengthy dissent which made many points including these: to "take" a wild animal means "to reduce the animal, by killing or capturing, to human control." Accordingly, the proper definition of the term is not as the majority opinion would indicate. Indeed, one must rely not only on the statute's definition of "take" but also on its placement as a functional piece of an entire statutory design, and to the legislative intent behind the statute; the regulation is unreasonably broad; whatever furthers a statute's primary objective does not necessarily control the interpretation of particular terms in the statute; and legislative history shows the opposite of what the majority says it does; the regulation considers impairment of breeding as a means of harming individual members of a species, but this impairment does not harm individuals. It only harms the population by disturbing normal propagation.]

Fourth and lastly, the Court seeks to avoid the evident shortcomings of the regulation on the ground that the respondents are challenging it on its face rather than as applied. [internal citations omitted] (O'CONNOR, J., concurring). The Court seems to say that even if the regulation dispenses with the foreseeability of harm that it acknowledges the statute to require, that does not matter because this is a facial challenge: So long as habitat modification that *would* foreseeably cause harm is prohibited by the statute, the regulation must be sustained. Presumably it would apply the same reasoning to all the other defects of the regulation: The regulation's failure to require injury to particular animals survives the present challenge, because at least *some* environmental modifications kill particular animals. This evisceration of the facial challenge is unprecedented. It is one thing to say that a facial challenge to a regulation that omits statutory element *x* must be rejected if there is any set of facts on which the statute *does not require x*. It is something quite different — and unlike any doctrine of "facial challenge" I have ever encountered — to say that the challenge must be rejected if the regulation could be applied to a state of facts in which element *x happens to be present*. On this analysis, the only regulation susceptible to facial attack is one that not only is invalid in all its applications, but also does not sweep up *any* person who *could have been* held liable under a proper application of the statute. That is not the law. Suppose a statute that prohibits "premeditated killing of a human being," and an implementing regulation that prohibits "killing a human being." A facial challenge to the regulation would not be rejected on the ground that, after all, it could be applied to a killing that happened to be premeditated. It *could not* be applied to such a killing, because it does not require the factfinder to find premeditation, as the statute requires. In other words, to simplify its task the Court today confuses lawful application of the challenged regulation with lawful application of a *different regulation, i.e.,* one requiring the various elements of liability that this regulation omits. . . .

The Endangered Species Act is a carefully considered piece of legislation that forbids all persons to hunt or harm endangered animals, but places upon the public at large, rather than upon fortuitously accountable individual landowners, the cost of preserving the habitat of endangered species. There is neither textual support for, nor even evidence of congressional consideration of, the radically different disposition contained in the regulation that the Court sustains. For these reasons, I respectfully dissent.

NOTES AND QUESTIONS

1. Thus, the ESA elevates a subset of wildlife and plant-life to a virtual state of invulnerability, at least insofar as the human threat is concerned. Should there be any limits on the principle? Should one be entitled to kill a protected animal if one paid for it and owns it? Before answering the question, consider whether one can "own" such an animal. Under state law, one surely can. *See, e.g., Pierson v. Post*, 3 Cai. R. 175, 2 Am. Dec. 264 (N.Y., 1805). Cannot one kill what one owns? If not, is this a taking? Assume that a person owns an animal before its species is listed. If the animal were old and suffering, might the owner "put it to sleep"? Would that act violate § 9? Alternatively, might a person kill a protected animal in self-defense? *See* § 11(a)(3), 16 U.S.C. § 1540(a)(3) (providing that civil penalties not be imposed if the actor was motivated by "a good faith belief that he was acting to protect himself or herself, a member of his or her family or any other individual from bodily harm . . ."). *See also Christy v. Hodel*, 857 F.2d. 1324 (9th Cir. 1988), *cert. denied*, 490 U.S. 1114 (1989). In *Christy*, a rancher killed one of a group of marauding grizzly bears that was attacking the rancher's herd of sheep. For this action, he was assessed a civil penalty of $3000 for violating the ESA and its regulations. The court upheld the penalty, finding no statutory right to kill the grizzly in defense of property. The court declined to imply such a right

as a matter of constitutional law: "In light of the Supreme Court's admonition that we exercise restraint in creating new definitions of substantive due process, we decline plaintiffs' invitation to construe the fifth amendment as guaranteeing the right to kill federally protected wildlife in defense of property." *Id.* at 1330.

2. The government is legally able to transfer land that serves as habitat for endangered species, because the transfer of land, without more, does not *per se* jeopardize a listed species. But both §§ 7 and 9 play a role. Section 7 applies to the act of negotiating and executing a contract for sale; accordingly, a proposed sale would trigger a reinitiation of consultation with the FWS. If the land were ultimately transferred to private control, § 9 would come into play, prohibiting the private owner from harming the species.

The problem with such a transaction is finding a purchaser. One way to do that is by changing the legal framework governing the sale. *See, e.g., Tinoqui-Chalola Council v. Department of Interior*, 232 F.3d 1300 (9th Cir. 2000). In that case, the Department of Energy needed to sell an oil field south of Bakersfield, California. The seventh largest oil field in the United States at 47,000 acres, the parcel was home to several endangered species. The DOE needed to sell the field because the National Defense Authorization Act of 1996, Pub. L. No. 104-106, § 3412(a), 110 Stat. 631, 631–32 (1997), instructed it to do so within two years of the statute's effective date. The court held under these facts that the DOE did not need to reinitiate consultation with F&W: "By passing the DAA, Congress waived the DOE's duty to reinitiate consultation under section 7 as to the . . . sale." *Id.* at 1309. The Act, actually, did more than that. It also made the incidental take statement governing the government's activities on the oil field transferrable to the purchaser. *See* § E, *infra*. So long as the purchaser's activities on the parcel remain identical to the activities evaluated in the biological opinion, no new incidental take permit was necessary. *Id.* at 1309.

E. STATUTORY FLEXIBILITY INITIATIVES

As interpreted in both *TVA v. Hill* and *Sweet Home,* the ESA epitomizes inflexibility. The statute applies according to its terms, regardless of the press of competing considerations. This uncompromising rigor engendered a flood of objection over the course of many years. The call for reform was so incessant that amending the Act became necessary if only to avoid an outright statutory repeal. Thus were both Congress and the Executive moved to make significant changes.[5]

The first significant change of this sort was the creation of the Endangered Species Committee ("ESC"). *See* notes following *TVA v. Hill*. The ESC, by a vote of five of the seven designated Committee members, can exempt a project from the strictures of § 7. § 7(h)(1), 16 U.S.C. § 1536(h)(1). To warrant an

---

[5] Many attempts to amend the legislation have not been successful. In 1998, for example, one bill offered tax incentives to landowners for voluntary habitat preservation, and another bill proposed both a heightened evidentiary showing before a species might be listed and an increase in requirements for recovery plans for species. Both bills failed. In the preceding year, another failed bill promoted an increase in use of cost-benefit analysis and comparative risk assessment in environmental regulation, a proposal that would have affected the ESA.

exemption, there must be "no reasonable and prudent alternatives" to the agency action, the benefits of the action must "clearly outweigh" the benefits of alternative actions that are more "consistent" with wildlife protection, the action must be of "regional or national significance," and there must be no "irreversible or irretrievable commitment of resources" that would foreclose alternative actions. In addition, exempted actions must be accompanied by reasonable mitigation measures. § 7(h)(1)(A)–(B), 16 U.S.C. § 1536(h)(1)(A)–(B).

The ESC has convened only rarely. Contemporaneous with the exemption denial in the Tellico Dam case, the ESC granted an exemption to the Grayrocks water project on the Laramie River in Wyoming. This project was at issue because the Laramie feeds the North Platte River, which in turn feeds the Platte River, which serves as habitat for endangered whooping cranes during their biannual migrations to Nebraska. Grayrocks prevailed before the ESC because project sponsors agreed to manage water releases to avoid harming the cranes and to establish and fund a crane protection organization, the Platte River Whooping Crane Habitat Maintenance Trust. Headquartered in Grand Island, Nebraska, the Trust is still in place working to preserve habitat for whoopers. The only other time the ESC has been called into action was in 1992, when it exempted 13 BLM timber sales, thereby allowing injury to northern spotted owls. Endangered Species Committee Notice of Decision, 57 Fed. Reg. 23,405 (1992).

Exemption decisions are themselves exempt from the requirements of NEPA. § 7(k), 16 U.S.C. § 1536(k).

Much more important than the ESC in the scheme of things are the amendatory provisions regarding incidental takings. In the first decade after enactment of the ESA, the complaint was made that even if a government agency fully complied with § 7, it might still cause an incidental or unintentional injury to a member of a protected species and thereby be exposed to liability. A private actor acting on private land, moreover, could do the same and face § 9 liability. To remedy the potential for inflexible application of the ESA, in 1982 the Congress amended §§ 7 and 9 by creating a mechanism to exempt from the prohibitions of the ESA takings of species that were merely incidental to actions otherwise allowable. "Incidental takes" are "takings that result from, but are not the purpose of, carrying out an otherwise lawful activity conducted by the Federal agency or applicant." 50 C.F.R. § 402.02 (1996).

(a) *Incidental take statements ("ITSs")*: Section 7 was amended to incorporate "incidental take statements." As now constructed, § 7 instructs the Secretary to include in each BiOp "those reasonable and prudent alternatives which he believes would not violate [§ 7(a)(2)] and can be taken by the Federal agency or applicant in implementing the agency action." § 7(b)(3)(A), 16 U.S.C. § 1536(b)(3)(A). "Reasonable and prudent alternatives" ("RPAs") are defined as:

> alternative actions identified during formal consultation that can be implemented in a manner consistent with the intended purpose of the action, that can be implemented consistent with the scope of the Federal agency's authority and jurisdiction, that is economically and technologically feasible, and that the [Service] believes will avoid the

likelihood of jeopardizing the continued existence of listed species.
. . .

50 C.F.R. § 2.02 (1996). Where the Service concludes that a federal action or the implementation of any RPA and the resultant incidental take of a listed species will not violate § 7(a)(2), the Secretary must provide an ITS with the biological opinion. § 7(b)(4), 16 U.S.C. § 1536(b)(4); 50 C.F.R. § 402.14(i) (1996). An ITS must specify the impact of the incidental taking on the species, specify the "reasonable and prudent measures that the Secretary considers necessary or appropriate to minimize such impact," and set forth "terms and conditions" that must be complied with by the federal agency to implement the reasonable and prudent measures. *Id.* Thereafter, so long as there is compliance with the terms and conditions of the statement, any incidental takings are exempted from liability. § 7(o), 16 U.S.C. § 1536(o).

This process has been somewhat troublesome from the point of view of environmentalists. As it turns out, action agencies frequently fail to implement the conditions of an ITS in timely fashion. To compound the problem, the FWS often has simply adjusted the time line to allow the failure, a practice that belies the overarching message of *TVA v. Hill.*

The day for breezily extending deadlines may have come to an end, however. In *Southwest Center for Biological Diversity v. Babbitt*, 2000 U.S. Dist. LEXIS 17177 (D. Ariz. 2000), the court held that, since the original deadlines in the BiOp were mandatory, revisions of them were only justified upon a scientific determination that the extension would not jeopardize the species.

(b) *Incidental take permits ("ITPs")*: Section 9 was amended, *de facto*, by the addition of § 10. Section 10(a)(1)(B) of the ESA now authorizes the Secretary to permit "any taking otherwise prohibited by [§ 9] if such taking is incidental to, and not the purpose of, the carrying out of an otherwise lawful activity." § 10(a)(1)(B), 16 U.S.C. § 1538(a)(1)(B). If the Secretary finds that any such taking would be incidental, would be mitigated appropriately, and would not "appreciably reduce the likelihood of the survival and recovery of the species in the wild," he or she is instructed to issue the permit. § 10(a)(2)(B), 16 U.S.C. § 1538(a)(2)(B). No ITP, however, may be issued unless the applicant has submitted to the Secretary a conservation plan, typically known as a "habitat conservation plan" or an "HCP." HCPs are legally binding agreements in which a landowner adopts conservation measures in exchange for permission from the federal government to develop property. HCPs must be adequately funded. They often are designed to be in force for more than fifty years.

In the almost twenty years since § 10 came into being, there have been several hundred incidental take permits issued. Only a relative few of these have been challenged in the courts. For a recent case finding an HCP to be insufficient, see *National Wildlife Federation v. Babbitt*, 128 F. Supp. 2d 1274 (E.D. Cal. 2000) (holding the HCP failed to meet the substantive standards of the ESA and lacked an EIS under NEPA). For some information on ITPs, see *Volusia County, infra,* and the notes that follow.

LOGGERHEAD TURTLE v. COUNTY COUNCIL OF VOLUSIA COUNTY, FLORIDA

148 F.3d 1231 (11th Cir. 1998)*

JUDGES: Before HATCHETT, Chief Judge, and RONEY and CLARK, Senior Circuit Judges. RONEY, Senior Circuit Judge, dissenting.

OPINION: HATCHETT, Chief Judge:

[The loggerhead sea turtle and the green sea turtle ("turtles") were designated as threatened and endangered respectively in 1978. 50 C.F.R. § 1711. These species of turtles, which live in the Gulf of Mexico and in the South Atlantic, are known to come ashore on to the beaches of Volusia County, which sports about forty miles of Atlantic Ocean coastline in northeast Florida. The turtles come ashore from May to October, during their nesting season, to lay eggs. After laying their eggs, mother turtles return to the sea.

After an incubation period of about two months, turtle hatchlings break out of their shells and emerge from the sand. Emerging at nighttime when sands are cooling, they instinctively attempt to reach the sea. In normal circumstances, they can do so in a matter of minutes. Because of risks of dehydration, predators, and exhaustion, it is essential that they do so. The hatchlings are guided in this trek to safety by the light of the night sky reflecting on the waters of the sea.

Turtles on the beaches of Volusia County, however, have faced two significant barriers to this age-old natural process. First is "urban glow." The inland ambient light caused by the proliferation of private residences near the beaches has been shown to confuse turtles. Instead of making their way to the sea, hatchlings have been observed moving inland toward city lights. The mistake spells certain doom. The second problem is vehicular traffic. Vehicles driven on the beaches: can crush eggs or recently emerged hatchlings; cause ruts in the sand, which trap turtles and cause them to migrate not to the sea but in the rut itself; disorient turtles with their headlights; compact sand, reducing the supply of oxygen to underlying eggs and thereby interfering with incubation; and shift sand off incubating eggs, making them vulnerable to predators and weather.

In 1994, the U.S. Fish and Wildlife Service ("FWS"), the agency with jurisdiction over nesting turtles (the National Marine Fisheries Service has jurisdiction over turtles in the sea), warned the County of the problem of vehicular access. The County set to work to develop a conservation plan. As developed, the plan attempted to restrict vehicular beach access, create a conservation zone, assure beach raking to remove ruts, and enforce a "turtle-friendly" lighting ordinance. The County also hired an environmental consultant and pledged to work with a volunteer "turtle patrol." It applied on July 17, 1995, to the FWS for an "incidental take permit" ("ITP") under § 10 of the Endangered Species Act.

However, on June 8, 1995, a month before it applied for an ITP, Volusia County was sued in federal court under the Endangered Species Act's citizen

---

* [Ed. Note: Certiorari denied April 19, 1999.]

suit provision, 16 U.S.C. § 1540(g)(1)(A), to enjoin all beach vehicular access to the beach during the turtles' nesting season, and to require the County to enforce a "Model Lighting Ordinance for Sea Turtle Protection."

On August 1, 1995, the District Court for the Middle District of Florida denied the requested injunctive relief on the beach lighting issue because it was unable to conclude that specific lights for which the County was responsible was disorienting turtles. 896 F. Supp 1181. Moreover, the court viewed itself as lacking authority to require enactment of any particular piece of legislation. *Id.* at 1181. On the beach access issue, the court found Volusia County responsible for ensuring the well-being of protected turtles because of its regulatory authority. It determined also that the County's practice of permitting nighttime vehicular use of the beaches was causing a "taking" of listed turtles. Consequently, it enjoined the nighttime use. *Id.* at 1192.

On November 21, 1996, the FWS issued an ITP to the County. "As part of the permit process, Volusia County agreed to adopt extensive mitigatory measures, including the development of a 'Beach Lighting Management Plan'" under which the County was required, inter alia, to survey every lighting sources, study their impacts and implement methods to correct light sources that misorient sea turtles." *Loggerhead Turtles v. Babbitt,* 92 F. Supp. 1296, 1299–1300. The District Court then dismissed the cause of action before it as to all issues. *Id.*

Plaintiffs appealed at this point to the 11th Circuit Court of Appeals, where the issue was the legal effect of the ITP.]

. . . .

The loggerhead sea turtle (*Caretta caretta*) and green sea turtle (*Chelonia mydas*) with appellants Shirley Reynolds and Rita Alexander (collectively the Turtles) challenge the district court's dismissal of their case brought pursuant to the Endangered Species Act (ESA), 16 U.S.C. §§ 1531–1544 (1994). They present: (1) an issue of first impression, whether the incidental take permit exception to the ESA's "take" prohibition applies to an activity performed as a purely mitigatory measure upon which the issuing agency conditions the permit; (2) an issue of standing, whether a governmental entity's regulatory control of minimum wildlife protection standards can cause redressable injury to protected wildlife in locations where non-party governmental entities possess supplemental authority to regulate and/or exclusively control enforcement; and (3) an issue of pleading amendment, whether another federally protected sea turtle should have been allowed to join the Turtles as a party. We reverse on all issues and remand for further proceedings.

[The following text will cover only the first of these issues.]

. . . .

II. Issues

We address . . . : (1) whether the district court erred in concluding that Volusia County's incidental take permit excepted it from liability for taking protected sea turtles through artificial beachfront lighting[.]

III. Contentions

As to the first issue, the Turtles contend that Volusia County's incidental take permit authorizes only incidental takes of sea turtles from beach driving, not from artificial beachfront lighting. The Turtles argue that to fall within the incidental take permit exception to the "take" prohibition, the Service's permission must be express and activity-specific. The Turtles also assert that the district court could not infer such permission from the Service's conditioning the permit on lighting-related mitigatory measures.

Volusia County responds that under the permit, it must survey every light source, study their impacts and implement methods to correct light sources that misorient sea turtles. Volusia County argues that given those extensive mitigatory requirements, the Service clearly contemplated that it be excepted from liability for any incidental takes that artificial beachfront lighting causes during the life of the permit. * * *

IV. Discussion

Under the ESA, it is unlawful to "take" endangered or threatened wildlife unless a statutory exception applies. 16 U.S.C. § 1538(a)(1)(B) (1994) (the "take" prohibition); see 50 C.F.R. § 17.31(a) (1997) (the "take" prohibition applies to threatened as well as endangered wildlife). Defined broadly, "take" means "to harass, harm, pursue, hunt, shoot, wound, kill, trap, capture, or collect[.]" 16 U.S.C. § 1532(19); see Babbitt v. Sweet Home Chapter of Communities for a Great Or., 515 U.S. 687, 115 S. Ct. 2407, 2416, 132 L. Ed. 2d 597 (1995) ("Congress intended 'take' to apply broadly to cover indirect as well as purposeful actions."). It is equally unlawful "to attempt to commit, solicit another to commit, or cause to be committed" a "take." 16 U.S.C. § 1538(g).

"Harass" and "harm," within the meaning of "take," are defined through regulation. The Secretary of the Interior, through the Service, has construed "harass" as "an intentional or negligent act or omission which creates the likelihood of injury to wildlife by annoying it to such an extent as to significantly disrupt normal behavioral patterns which include, but are not limited to, breeding, feeding or sheltering." 50 C.F.R. § 17.3; see 16 U.S.C. § 1533(d) (delegating regulatory authority to the "Secretary"); Sweet Home, 515 U.S. 687, 115 S. Ct. at 2410 & n. 2 (noting that the Secretary of the Interior, through the Director of the Service, promulgated 50 C.F.R. § 17.3).

The crux of the Turtles' artificial beachfront lighting allegations centered on "harm," "an act which actually kills or injures wildlife" that may include "significant habitat modification or degradation where it actually kills or injures wildlife by significantly impairing essential behavioral patterns, including breeding, feeding or sheltering." 50 C.F.R. § 17.3 (the "harm" regulation). At the preliminary injunction stage, the district court found "overwhelming" evidence that artificial beachfront lighting "harms" sea turtles on Volusia County's beaches. 896 F. Supp. at 1180-81. Similarly, at the summary judgment stage, the district court found a genuine factual dispute "as to whether the artificial beachfront lighting controlled by Volusia County is responsible for "taking' sea turtles."

A.

The incidental take permit exception to the "take" prohibition and its regulatory constructions, including the "harm" regulation, can be found in 16 U.S.C. § 1539(a). As relevant to this case, the Service "may permit, under such terms and conditions as [it] shall prescribe . . . any taking otherwise prohibited by section 1538(a)(1)(B) of [the ESA] if such taking is incidental to, and not the purpose of, the carrying out of an otherwise lawful activity." 16 U.S.C. § 1539(a)(1)(B). As a prerequisite to receiving an incidental take permit, the applicant must submit a habitat conservation plan that specifies: "(i) the impact which will likely result from such taking; (ii) what steps the applicant will take to minimize and mitigate such impacts, and the funding that will be available to implement such steps; (iii) what alternative actions to such taking the applicant considered and the reasons why such alternatives are not being utilized; and (iv) such other measures that the [issuing agency] may require as being necessary or appropriate for purposes of the plan." 16 U.S.C. § 1539(a)(2)(A). Service regulations further instruct the applicant to include a "complete description of the activity sought to be authorized" and "the common and scientific names of the species sought to be covered by the permit, as well as the number, age, and sex of such species, if known[.]" 50 C.F.R. § 17.22(b)(1)(i)–(ii) (endangered wildlife); 50 C.F.R. § 17.32(b)(1)(iii)(A)–(B) (threatened wildlife).

We turn first to the Turtles' contention that Volusia County's incidental take permit does not expressly authorize takings through artificial beachfront lighting. Such express authority, if it exists, can be found only within the four corners of the permit. *See generally* 16 U.S.C. § 1539(a) (issuing official must "prescribe" the permit's "terms and conditions"). In its introductory headline, Volusia County's incidental take permit states that the Service "authorizes incidental take within the Defined Area or County Beaches, associated with the activities described in Condition F below, of [appellant loggerhead sea turtle, appellant green sea turtle, leatherback sea turtle, hawksbill sea turtle (*Eretmochelys imbricata*) and Kemp's ridley sea turtle (*Lepidochelys kempii*)] conditioned upon implementation of the terms and conditions of this Permit." Condition F, in turn, lists eleven "authorized" types of incidental take: * * *

Indisputably, these eleven types of incidental take relate only to vehicular access on Volusia County's beaches. None of the eleven authorized activities listed in Condition F concerns artificial beachfront lighting. The only form of lighting mentioned in Condition F is vehicular headlights.

Although the majority of its conditions concern beach driving, the incidental take permit does address artificial beachfront lighting [in] Condition G of the permit, entitled "Mitigation/Minimization Measures" * * *

The mitigation measures relative to artificial beachfront lighting occupy less than two out of twenty-five pages of Volusia County's incidental take permit: * * *

In light of the foregoing, it is readily apparent that the incidental take permit exhaustively lists all authorized activities within Condition F and all mitigation measures within Condition G. Activities relative to driving on the beach are mentioned in both conditions. Activities relative to artificial beachfront lighting, however, are mentioned only in Condition G. Given the permit's structure, the express authority to take sea turtles through artificial beachfront lighting — if the Service had so intended — would be memorialized in Condition F. This absence is dispositive. Accordingly, Volusia County lacks the Service's express permission to take sea turtles incidentally through artificial beachfront lighting.

Volusia County argues that even if it lacks the Service's express permission, it has the Service's implied permission to take sea turtles incidentally through artificial beachfront lighting because the Service expressly conditioned the permit on Volusia County's implementation of detailed lighting-related mitigatory measures. This argument presents an issue of first impression in this and other circuits, whether the incidental take permit exception (16 U.S.C. § 1539(a)) to the "take" prohibition (16 U.S.C. § 1538(a)(1)(B)) applies to, and thus excepts from liability, an activity performed as a purely mitigatory measure upon which the Service conditions the permit. We hold that it does not.

The ESA's text and the Service's regulations provide every indication that incidental take permission must be express and activity-specific. To be excepted from liability, the ESA mandates that the "take" be "incidental to . . . the carrying out of an . . . *activity*." 16 U.S.C. § 1539(a)(1)(B) (emphasis added). Moreover, in addressing the requirements of the habitat conservation plan, the ESA semantically separates the "action[]" at issue from the applicant's intentions to "mitigate" the taking. *Compare* 16 U.S.C. § 1539(a)(2)(A)(iii) ("what alternative *actions* to such taking the applicant considered") (emphasis added) *with* 16 U.S.C. § 1539(a)(2)(A)(ii) ("what steps the applicant will take to minimize and mitigate such impacts") (emphasis added). *See generally Friends of Endangered Species, Inc. v. Jantzen*, 760 F.2d 976, 984 (9th Cir.1985) (separating semantically the activity for which the applicants sought an incidental take permit — a development "project" — from the mitigatory measures — "restrictions" on the development). Furthermore, before the Service issues an incidental take permit, the fact-finding official must resolve at least two statutorily distinct questions: (1) whether the *activity* will be free of purposeful takes; and (2) whether the applicant will *mitigate* the authorized takes' effect. *Compare* 16 U.S.C. § 1539(a)(2)(B)(i) ("the *taking* will be incidental") (emphasis added) *with* 16 U.S.C. § 1539(a)(2)(B)(ii) ("the applicant will . . . minimize and *mitigate* the impacts of such taking") (emphasis added).

The statutory dividing line between activities sought to be permitted and mitigatory measures is further reinforced in the Service's regulations. The Service requires applicants to describe completely "the *activity* sought to be authorized." 50 C.F.R. §§ 17.22(b)(1)(i), 17.32(b)(1)(iii)(A) (emphasis added); *see also* 50 C.F.R. § 222.22(b)(4) (incidental take permit applications to the National Marine Fisheries Service must include a "detailed description of the proposed *activity*") (emphasis added). The incidental take permit, in turn, "may authorize a single transaction, a series of transactions, or a number *of activities*[.]" 50 C.F.R. §§ 17.22, 17.32 (emphasis added). Finally, the Service emphasizes that the "authorizations on the face of a permit which set forth specific . . . *methods of taking* . . . are to be strictly construed and shall not be interpreted to permit similar or related matters outside the scope of strict construction." 50 C.F.R. § 13.42 (emphasis added); *see also* 50 C.F.R. § 222.22(d) (incidental take permits that the National Marine Fisheries Service issues must "contain such terms and conditions as the Assistant Administrator deems necessary and appropriate, including . . . the authorized *method of taking*") (emphasis added).

Even the Service's informal publication advises applicants to describe specifically "all *actions* . . . that . . . are likely to result in incidental take" so that the permit holder "can determine the applicability of the incidental take authorization to the *activities* they undertake." United States Fish & Wildlife Serv., Dep't of the Interior; Nat'l Marine Fisheries Serv., Dep't of Commerce, Habitat Conservation Planning Handbook (Nov.1996), at 3-12 to 3-13 (emphasis added). Otherwise, the Service warns, "broadly defined types of *activities* . . . generally would not be authorized." Habitat Handbook, at 3-13 (emphasis added).

The content of Volusia County's application and correspondence with the Service reflects the statutory and regulatory dividing line between authorized activities and mitigatory measures. In its initial application to the Service, Volusia County "completely described . . . the activity sought to be authorized" as "vehicular access to Volusia County beaches[.]" (Citing 50 C.F.R. §§ 17.22(b)(1)(i).) A follow-up letter from a Service official acknowledging receipt of the application summarized that Volusia County sought "a permit to cover any incidental take of sea turtles that may occur on Volusia County beaches . . . as a result of *vehicular access* to county beaches." (Emphasis added.) Another follow-up letter from the Service pointedly expressed that

> it is important to state for the record that the County of Volusia is not seeking incidental take authority for marine sea turtles resulting from lights owned or operated by the County. The purpose of any such discussion in the habitat conservation plan . . . is to provide mitigation for impacts to marine sea turtles resulting from *permitted activities*. The [incidental take permit] application you submitted requests incidental take authority for sea turtle species from *beach-driving* and associated activities only.

(Emphasis added.) Finally, in a responsive letter to the Service, an assistant county attorney reiterated that "Volusia County is seeking an Incidental Take Permit for vehicles [sic] access to the beaches. However, Volusia County has addressed lighting throughout its permit application as a mitigating factor." (Emphasis added.)

Contrary to Volusia County's position, no published case law even purports to suggest that purely mitigatory measures fall within the scope of the incidental take permit exception, 16 U.S.C. § 1539(a). . . .

Volusia County argues that the Service "clearly anticipated" takes resulting from artificial beachfront lighting in the incidental take permit. . . . We are not convinced. . . .

In any event, the law governing incidental take statements issued under 16 U.S.C. § 1536(b), . . . differs from the law governing incidental take permits issued under 16 U.S.C. § 1539(a), the statutory source in this case. *See generally Ramsey [v. Kantor]*, 96 F.3d [434], at 439 [(9th Cir. 1996)]. First, the issuing agency's prerequisite findings are not the same. To permit an incidental taking under 16 U.S.C. § 1536(b), the issuing agency must conclude, in pertinent part, that:

> [1] the agency action will not [likely jeopardize the continued existence of any protected species or result in the destruction or adverse modification of its critical habitat ("likely jeopardize protected species")], or [the agency] offers reasonable and prudent alternatives which the Secretary believes would not [jeopardize protected species]; [and]

> [2] the taking of an endangered species or a threatened species incidental to the agency action will not [likely jeopardize protected species][.]

16 U.S.C. § 1536(b)(4) (incorporating by reference 16 U.S.C. § 1536(a)(2)). To permit an incidental taking under 16 U.S.C. § 1539(a), however, the issuing agency must find, in pertinent part, that:

> [1] the taking will be incidental;

> [2] the applicant will . . . minimize and mitigate the impacts of such taking;

> [3] the applicant will ensure that adequate funding for the [habitat conservation] plan will be provided;

> [4] the taking will not appreciably reduce the likelihood of the survival and recovery of the species in the wild; and

> [5] the [other measures that the issuing agency may require] will be met[.]

16 U.S.C. § 1539(a)(2)(B) (incorporating by reference 16 U.S.C. § 1539(a)(2)(A)(iv)). Both, of course, require a finding that the take sought to be authorized will be "incidental." Both also focus on the ultimate effect of the incidental take on the species. *See* 16 U.S.C. § 1539(a)(2)(B)(iv) ("the taking will not appreciably reduce the likelihood of the survival and recovery of the species in the wild"); 50 C.F.R. § 402.02 (proposed action "jeopardizes" the species at issue if it can "reasonably . . . be expected, directly or indirectly, to reduce appreciably the likelihood of both the survival and recovery of a listed species in the wild by reducing the reproduction, numbers, or distribution of that species"). Only 16 U.S.C. § 1539, however, expressly requires a finding of future mitigation. . . .

A second important difference between an incidental take statement (16 U.S.C. § 1536(b)) and an incidental take permit (16 U.S.C. § 1539(a)) lies in the broad language of 16 U.S.C. § 1536(o), which applies only to holders or beneficiaries of the former. Under section 1536(o), "*any* taking that is in compliance with the terms and conditions specified in [an incidental take statement issued under 16 U.S.C. § 1536(b)] shall not be considered to be a prohibited taking of the species concerned." 16 U.S.C. § 1536(o)(2). No similar provision applies to "any" taking in compliance with an incidental take permit's terms and conditions, including mitigatory measures. The closest analogous provision in section 1539 appears only in the converse: the issuing official "shall revoke [an incidental take permit] if he finds that the permittee is not complying with the terms and conditions of the permit." 16 U.S.C. § 1539(a)(2)(C).

Finally, the prohibitions that underlie the incidental take exceptions are unique. The prohibition that underlies the incidental take statement exception applies only to federal agencies, and imposes upon them a duty to consult with the statement-issuing agency and ensure that their proposed action will not likely "jeopardize the continued existence of any endangered species or threatened species or result in the destruction or adverse modification of [critical] habitat[.]" 16 U.S.C. § 1536(a)(2) (the "jeopardy" clause). The prohibition that underlies the incidental take permit exception applies to federal, state, local and private actors, and creates no similar duty to consult. *See* 16 U.S.C. §§ 1532(13), 1538(a)(1)(B) (the "take" prohibition). Additionally, the "jeopardy" clause applies to protected fish, wildlife and plants, whereas the "take" prohibition applies only to protected fish and wildlife. *See* 16 U.S.C. §§ 1532(16), 1536(a)(2), 1538(a)(1). Consequently, some activities — especially those relating to land use — are more likely to result in "jeopardy" than a "take." *See Sweet Home,* 115 S. Ct. at 2415 ("Section 7 [16 U.S.C. § 1536] imposes a broad, affirmative duty to avoid adverse habitat modifications that § 9 [16 U.S.C. § 1539] does not replicate, and § 7 does not limit its admonition to habitat modification that actually kills or injures wildlife.") (internal quotation marks and citations omitted); Andrew J. Doyle, Note, *Sharing Home Sweet Home with Federally Protected Wildlife,* 25 Stetson L.Rev. 889, 911 n. 174 (1996) ("It is easier to 'jeopardize' than it is to 'harm.' "). These differences further militate against broadening the scope of the incidental take permit exception (16 U.S.C. § 1539(a)) even if some courts have suggested that section 1536(o) serves to broaden the scope of the incidental take statement exception (16 U.S.C. § 1536(b)). *See Ramsey,* 96 F.3d at 441 ("Any taking . . . that complies with the conditions set forth in the incidental take statement is permitted."). *See generally Mount Graham Red Squirrel v. Espy,* 986 F.2d 1568, 1580 (9th Cir.1993) ("Under [16 U.S.C. § 1536], . . . limited takings may be permitted if they are incorporated into the 'terms and conditions' of a Reasonable and Prudent Alternative drawn up in connection with the issuance of a Biological Opinion.").

The fact remains that no court has been presented with the issue facing us today. To be sure, protecting troubled wildlife is serious business. *See Tennessee Valley Auth. v. Hill,* 437 U.S. 153, 174, 98 S. Ct. 2279, 57 L. Ed. 2d 117 (1978) ("The language, history, and structure of the [Endangered Species Act] indicates beyond doubt that Congress intended endangered species to be afforded the highest of priorities."); *Strahan v. Linnon,* 967 F. Supp. 581, 618 (D.Mass.1997) ("The Endangered Species Act is a powerful and substantially unequivocal statute."). Consequently, permits that purport to excuse takes of wildlife must be clear on their face. *See* 50 C.F.R. § 13.42 ("The authorizations on the face of a permit which . . . permit a specifically limited matter[] are to be strictly construed[.]"); *see also* 50 C.F.R. § 220.42. In this case, "the Secretary . . . permitted" only takes of sea turtles incidental to driving on the beach. 16 U.S.C. § 1539(a)(1). Accordingly, the district court erred in dismissing the Turtles' claim that artificial beachfront lighting takes sea turtles.

[Remainder of opinion omitted.]

REVERSED and REMANDED.

DISSENT: RONEY, Senior Circuit Judge, dissenting:

[Dissent omitted].

NOTES AND QUESTIONS

1. Does this opinion strike you as odd? Is there any real question whether the FWS intended to allow incidental takes caused by beach lighting? Concededly, the Service did place all mitigatory measures in a separate section of the ITP, but do you suppose it meant, thereby, to exclude lighting-caused incidental takes from the protective scope of the permit?

2. With a moment's reflection, it becomes obvious why plaintiffs found Volusia County to be an attractive defendant. It is far more efficient from a plaintiff's point of view to sue a single defendant who can mandate an array of species-protective actions than it is to locate, serve, and proceed in court against an undefined and numerous group of occasional beach users and residents. The County, for its part, did not view itself as an appropriate defendant. On remand, the District Court considered the question:

> Congress imposed upon federal agencies the responsibility for implementing and enforcing the Act. The Act authorizes the Secretary of the Interior to enter into management and cooperation agreements with the States, whose participation in conservation programs the Act encourages. The Act requires no affirmative conservation action by states or local governments. The Act neither compels nor precludes local regulation; it preempts that which is in conflict. Volusia County cannot be made to assume liability for the act of its private citizens merely because it has chosen to adopt regulations to ameliorate sea turtle takings. Such an anomalous result would frustrate the intent and purpose of the Act's cooperative agreement provisions. Accordingly, the Court finds that Volusia County has not violated the Endangered Species Act by enacting and enforcing its Minimum Standards for Sea Turtle Protection.

Loggerhead Turtle v. County Council of Volusia County, 92 F. Supp. 2d 1296, 1308 (2000). The court noted that a possible remedy would be the adoption of federal beach lighting regulations.

So, after all the wrangling, Volusia County was found to be free of liability! Do you think the District Court is correct in finding no liability? For another view, see *Strahan v. Coxe*, 127 F.3d 155 (1st Cir. 1997). *Strahan* held the ESA "not only prohibits the acts of those parties that directly exact the taking, but also bans those acts of a third party that bring about the acts exacting a taking." *Id.* at 163. In *Strahan*, plaintiffs contended the State of Massachusetts was liable for the taking of endangered whales by fishing vessels because it had licensed the fishing activity:

> The defendants argue that the statute was not intended to prohibit state licensure activity because such activity cannot be a "proximate cause" of the taking. The defendants direct our attention to long-standing principles of common law tort in arguing that the district

court improperly found that its regulatory scheme "indirectly causes" these takings. Specifically, the defendants contend that to construe the proper meaning of "cause" under the ESA, this court should look to common law principles of causation and further contend that proximate cause is lacking here. The defendants are correct that when interpreting a term in a statute which is, like "cause" here, well-known to the common law, the court is to presume that Congress intended the meaning to be interpreted as in the common law. . . . We do not believe, however, that an interpretation of "cause" that includes the "indirect causation" of a taking by the Commonwealth through its licensing scheme falls without the normal boundaries.

. . . [W]hereas it is possible for a person licensed by Massachusetts to use a car in a manner that does not risk the violations of federal law suggested by the defendants, it is not possible for a licensed commercial fishing operation to use its gillnets or lobster pots in the manner permitted by the Commonwealth without risk of violating the ESA by exacting a taking. Thus, the state's licensure of gillnet and lobster pot fishing does not involve the intervening independent actor that is a necessary component of . . . other licensure schemes. . . . Where the state has licensed an automobile driver to use that automobile and her license in a manner consistent with both state and federal law, the violation of federal [law] is caused only by the actor's conscious and independent decision to disregard or go beyond the licensed purposes of her automobile use and instead to violate federal, and possibly state, law.

Id. at 163-64.

Do you view *Volusia County* and *Strahan* as inconsistent with each other, or merely distinguishable on the facts? What would your advice be to a municipality about to enact a zoning ordinance permitting the residential development of land occupied by members of an endangered species? What advice would you have for the EPA which, in its administration of the Federal Insecticide, Fungicide and Rodenticide Act ("FIFRA," 7 U.S.C. §§ 136–136y), is proposing to approve "registration" of a pesticide known to kill both target and non-target species? (Registration of a pesticide under FIFRA constitutes approval for its sale and distribution. FIFRA allows the registration of any pesticide which will "perform its intended function without unreasonable adverse effects on the environment.")

3. As mentioned in the notes preceding *Volusia*, HCPs are voluntary binding agreements between the government and the permittee. Since Volusia County has been determined not to be liable under the ESA, is it free to disregard its HCP? Or, having entered into the agreement, is the County bound to honor it, despite the erroneous premise? There is relatively little case law to answer questions involving HCPs. There were only about 20 HCPs in existence before 1994. By 1997, due to a push by the Clinton Administration, there were approximately 200 in place.

4. When either the FWS or the NMFS issues an ITP, must it comply with § 7 of the ESA? If so, with whom must it consult? Do you suppose ITP decisions fall under § 102(2)(C) of NEPA?

F. ADMINISTRATIVE FLEXIBILITY INITIATIVES

Unlike the Congress, the FWS and the NMFS do not have an entirely free hand when it comes to revising the mandates of the ESA. Agencies are not empowered, obviously, to revise statutes; they are constrained, rather, to operate within the parameters of statutes they administer. Still, the FWS and the NMFS have done what they can to make the ESA, as written, apply with somewhat less rigor. Following are the flexibility initiatives they have established:

(a) *Candidate Conservation Agreements*: CCAs are formal agreements between the FWS and independent parties, primarily other federal agencies, state and local agencies, and conservation organizations, designed to make listing unnecessary by meeting the conservation needs of candidate or proposed species. Signatories agree to implement specific actions to stabilize or restore species.

(b) *Candidate Conservation Agreements with Assurances*: CCAAs are FWS agreements with private landowners who face land use restrictions if a species is listed. Under a CCAA, a landowner agrees to manage private land in a way that protects and restores populations of species or their habitats on that land. In return, the FWS agrees to issue to the landowner an ITP under § 10(a)(1)(A) of the statute, authorizing any "takes" that might accompany habitat modification or other CCAA-authorized actions. Moreover, so long as the landowner abides by the CCAA, should a species covered by the CCAA be listed subsequently, the landowner is free from the otherwise applicable new land use restrictions.

(c) *Safe Harbor Agreements*: SHAs afford to listed species essentially the same protections that CCAAs afford to candidate and proposed species. SHAs allow landowners who voluntarily take steps to attract endangered species onto private land or attempt to increase the numbers or distribution of such species to avoid prosecution for takings.

(d) *Exemptions from prosecution for incidental takes of threatened species*: In 1994, the FWS and NMFS announced an exemption policy for certain incidental takes of threatened species. Under the policy, certain persons, specifically occupiers of single residential households, persons involved in one-time activities affecting five or fewer acres of contiguous property acquired before an affected species was listed, and persons undertaking "negligible" activities, are exempt from prosecution. (The policy extends solely to threatened species on the belief that exemptions for endangered species could only be granted if the ESA itself were rewritten).

(e) *The "No Surprises" Policy*. The No Surprises Policy guarantees landowners who develop HCPs and receive incidental take permits that they will not be required to spend more money or conduct additional mitigation measures to meet future ESA requirements for species covered by their HCPs. In a press release on the policy, Secretary of Interior Bruce Babbitt stated that "[T]he new policy assures that landowners participating in a single-or multi-species [habitat conservation plan] will not be subject to additional restrictions or costs at a later time, even if unlisted species adequately covered under the terms of an HCP are subsequently listed as endangered or threatened. If extraordinary circumstances subsequently indicate the need for additional action to protect such species, the new policy states that the obligation for additional action shall not rest with an HCP permittee."

NOTES

1. How would you modify the Endangered Species Act if given the opportunity? One approach under consideration is "ecosystem management." The idea is to change the statutory focus from protecting discrete species, and only some of them at that, to protecting entire ecosystems. Ecosystem management would allow for earlier intervention, without the legal necessity of awaiting a species' near-extinction, and would reach beyond a select organism or two to protecting all plants and animals in a habitat. By necessity, it would call for a combined effort by federal and state governmental agencies, and presumably would be multidisciplinary in approach. Some efforts of this sort are underway at present. Do you think this approach holds promise?

2. Many states have their own state-law endangered species acts. *See, e.g.,* The Nebraska Endangered Species and Conservation Act ("NESCA"), Neb. Rev. Stat. §§ 37-430 to -438 (Reissue 1984). Modeled after the federal ESA, the NESCA varies from the ESA in several important particulars. For example, while the federal ESA requires federal agencies to insure their actions are "not likely to jeopardize" endangered species, the Nebraska counterpart demands that agencies "do not jeopardize" endangered species. *Id.* at § 37–435(3).

A NOTE ON THE ANIMAL WELFARE AND ANIMAL RIGHTS MOVEMENTS

Well before the federal government moved to protect endangered species by statute, individual efforts to do so were underway. In the nineteenth century, with the creation of the American Society for the Prevention of Cruelty to Animals ("ASPCA"), the Animal Welfare Movement rose to prominence. Utilitarian in philosophy, Welfarists have sought greater protection and care for animals essentially by balancing their interests with those of humans. By one approach, the human interest should receive some greater weight in the balancing; other Welfarists would weigh human and animal interests equally. Accordingly, Welfarists may disagree on the propriety of animal experimentation. But, however the balance is struck, the idea is to maximize the interests of both communities. Significantly, Animal Welfarists operate within the current legal system. They accept the traditional view of animals as property. They do not propose formal legal rights for non-humans.

Relatively more recent in origin, the Animal Rights Movement does not accept the current legal regime as justified. On the contrary, Animal Rights adherents maintain that all living things have legal and political rights. Phrased in another way, animals are not mere property, subject to the free will of humans. Because they are living, they have rights co-equal with those of humans. Rightists insist, moreover, that these rights are non-negotiable, and, *per force,* should be honored in the human legal system. Given this approach, it is not surprising that Rightists strenuously object to animal experimentation for the same reasons they would discourage a policy of human experimentation. In the opinion of an adherent of this view, the law should be modified in the short term to recognize highly cognitive animals, and, in the long term, to include other animals. Steven Wise, *Rattling the Cage: Toward Legal Rights for Animals* xvi, 362 (Perseus Books 2000). *See also* Robert Verchick, *A New Species of Rights Rattling the Cage: Toward Legal Rights for Animals*, 89 Cal. L. Rev 207 (2001).

There are a number of organizations involved in these matters. A non-exhaustive list includes the American Society for the Prevention of Cruelty to Animals (*see http://www.aspca.org*); the Animal Legal Defense Fund (*see http://www.aldf.org*); the Humane Society of the United States (*see http://www.hsus.org*); and People for the Ethical Treatment of Animals (*see http:www.peta.org*.

Chapter 8

WATER RIGHTS

———————

"Water is the lifeblood of peoples and economies. Water entitlements establish and sustain a social order." *Public Land Review*, Spring, 1990.

"We'll never know the worth of water 'till the well goes dry." — *Scottish Proverb*

A. INTRODUCTION

An increasingly important area of natural resource law involves rights to water. As population increases and water distribution systems deteriorate, the contest for water among competing interests has intensified, and the stakes have grown. The concern about future water availability extends to entire regions of the nation, to municipalities, and down to the family farmer as well.

In this section, we take a brief look at the law governing water rights. Our goal is not to teach a three-credit course in the span of a single chapter, but rather to learn the outline and structure of the legal system of water rights allocation. The Chapter first reviews how state law allocates rights to water, and then examines the effect of federal law on that legal condition.

With that goal in mind, it should be understood at the outset that legal systems controlling water are usually divided into two distinct and often independent parts. One controls allocation of rights to surface water, namely, running streams, lakes, ponds, and the like. The other part controls allocation of rights to groundwater. Groundwater is found in formations called aquifers, which are saturated soils, not free-flowing bodies of subsurface water. Groundwater can migrate through soils, but they do so quite slowly.

It is hydrologic nonsense to allocate legal rights in surface water and groundwater independently in all circumstances, because groundwater can become surface water, and vice-versa. In many cases, for example, extracting groundwater can lower flow levels of surface streams; similarly, diverting surface waters can lower the "water table" — the upper level of groundwater. These two hydrologic regimes, however, have been treated independently by law, as if they never interrelate. The reason is timing — the law developed before there was a fuller understanding of hydrology.

The law allocates water, as one would expect, for uses. Uses can be categorized as either "consumptive" or "non-consumptive." A consumptive use is one that removes the water from its source and precludes its return; a nonconsumptive use is one which does not result in permanent loss of the water from the source. Many uses are both consumptive and nonconsumptive. Irrigation is one. Much irrigation water is consumed by plants or expired into the atmosphere. To that extent, irrigation is a consumptive use. Some irrigation water, however, can make its way back to its original source *i.e.* its "stream of origin" (when dealing with surface waters), in the form of "irrigation return flows." To this extent, the use is non-consumptive.

When water taken from one waterway is transported to another, the use is deemed to be consumptive insofar as the stream of origin is concerned. An example on the grand scale, known as an "interbasin transfer," would be the removal of water from the Missouri River "basin" or "watershed" (the land area which drains into the Missouri River) and its transport into the Ohio River basin. (On this notion of "basin" or "watershed," you might note that both the Missouri River and the Ohio River, for example, are "subbasins" of the Mississippi. Thus, the above-noted transfer would not be consumptive insofar as the main stem of the Mississippi is concerned.) Likewise, a transfer of water from the Platte River basin in Nebraska to the Little Blue River basin in Nebraska would be a consumptive use insofar as the Platte River is concerned. Uses can also be categorized by location. Some are "out-of-stream" uses (water diverted from a source for use on land near or far from the source) and others are "instream" uses (water serving a use while remaining in its natural location). Irrigation is an example of an out-of-stream use while hydropower generation is an example of instream use.

Uses of water by type include domestic use, irrigation (the most massive use by quantity), industrial or manufacturing use (which can be consumptive or nonconsumptive), waste disposal, recreation, aesthetics, wildlife and aquatic life maintenance, hydropower generation, and aquifer recharge.

In these materials, we begin by looking at state legal systems that allocate surface water rights among individuals. There are two such systems. The first is riparianism, the water rights allocation system used in most eastern states, where water is relatively abundant. The second is the prior appropriation system, which is found in most western states, where water is relatively scarce. (The 100th longitudinal meridian is considered to be the divider between eastern and western states; that median runs from North Dakota south to Texas.) As you read these materials, give some thought on why riparianism is found in states with abundant water, and why prior appropriation is in place in arid states.

You might also give some thought as to the overall role legal constraints should play in the matter of water allocation. Why should the law get involved at all (other than to provide a market, that is)? Should not the market system, that (sometimes) great unregulated barter-and-sale mechanism that allocates resources and commodities generally, be allowed to allocate water as well? Under a market system, persons who most highly value water presumably would get it, because they would be willing to pay the highest price for it. Under this scenario, water would be used for its most highly valued purposes. If this is an appropriate national goal for a water rights allocation system, why intervene with law? Why not let market forces allocate the water?

One of the great water law scholars, the late Frank Trelease, has commented on this question: "Water law should provide for maximum benefits from the use of the resource, and this end should be reached by means of granting private property rights in water, secure enough to encourage development and flexible enough for economic forces to change them to better uses, and subject to public regulation only when private economic action does not protect the public interests." Frank Trelease, *Policies for Water Law: Property, Economic Forces, and Public Regulation* (1965).

B. SURFACE WATERS

[1] RIPARIANISM

The riparian system of water law arrived in this nation from England. England is a country with abundant water supplies. Under English law, persons who own land that abuts a waterway enjoy rights to take water for personal use. These persons are known as "riparians" and the abutting land they own is "riparian land." A parcel of land can be riparian to one stream and "nonriparian" to another.

Thus, under the riparian system, one who owns a defined parcel of land bordering a stream, or through which a stream runs, is a riparian and has rights to water in the stream. Water can be taken out of the stream for use on the riparian land. The right to the water is secured by virtue of land ownership, and is lost upon transfer of the title interest to the riparian land (at which time the new landowner gets that right).

This system has its virtues. First, by limiting water rights to landowners, the demand on the water resource (i.e. the potential for a "tragedy of the commons") is reduced. Second, the system obviates any need for a system of recording or otherwise certifying water rights. Third, water rights have a decent measure of security — they cannot be taken away easily. This allows water rights holders to plan and rely on the continued availability of the right. And (a virtue to some) the system inures to the benefit of the landed set.

Critics of riparianism stipulate that it prevents maximum use of water, and therefore, from an economic perspective, is anti-growth.

The basic features of the riparian water rights system are:

- the system applies only to flowing surface waters. This includes rivers, lakes, some ponds;

- the right to water depends on land ownership. It makes no difference how much land fronts the waterway to which the land is riparian. Nonuse of the right does not result in loss of it; loss occurs upon land transfer. If a stream shifts out of its channel, land once riparian may become nonriparian, and the water right may be lost;

- water must be used (in most jurisdictions) on the riparian land itself, or not at all. Additionally, water must be used within the watershed of the stream of origin;

- there are no gallonage limitations on the right. Rather, water must be dedicated to a "reasonable use." If the use is reasonable, all the water necessary for that use may be taken as a matter of right;

- in times of shortage, riparians must share the burden of reducing water use. In this way, riparian rights are "correlative."

NOTES

1. This outline of riparian law describes the so-called "reasonable use" theory of riparianism. In olden times, in England especially, the so-called "natural flow doctrine" governed riparianism. Under this form of riparianism, one could not justify use of water based on considerations of reasonableness. Rather, a use was justified only if it in no way impaired the natural flow of a stream. As stated traditionally, under the natural flow doctrine, "[e]very proprietor of lands on the banks of a river has naturally an equal right to the use of the water which flows in the stream adjacent to his lands, as it was wont to run (currere solebat) without diminution or alteration." (*Chancellor Kent*). This doctrine has fallen into disuse because it effectively prohibits out-of-stream water uses, a condition unworkable in an industrialized society. (This system did make an exception — water used for domestic purposes could be removed from the stream.)

2. The determination of what land is "riparian" depends on the legal configuration of title. The entirety of a contiguous parcel of riparian land is riparian. If, however, that parcel is divided into two or more subparcels, one of which does not abut the waterway, the new non-abutting subparcel, no longer riparian, may lose its water right. If these subparcels are later reunited, the water right may or may not be regained, depending on the jurisdiction.

3. In "reasonable use" jurisdictions (and all jurisdictions are of this type these days), nonriparian uses typically have been entirely prohibited as *per se* unreasonable. Over time, some states have lifted this restriction either partially (allowing some nonriparian uses) or entirely (treating nonriparian uses on the same par as riparian uses).

4. Water rights are use rights, unlike rights in land. Downstream riparians have a great interest in how upstream riparians use water, especially regarding the consumptive nature of upstream use. Thus water rights do not supply the water right holder with exclusive possession; the right holder has exclusive right to use but must return the unused portion to the stream.

Because of this condition, the doctrine of adverse possession is inapplicable to water rights. In its place, however, is the doctrine of adverse use, which operates on essentially the same principles as the doctrine of adverse possession. One with such rights is called an "adverse user;" once the adverse use right has matured, the holder is said to have "prescriptive rights" in the water.

Give some thought on how the adverse use doctrine would, or should, operate in the field of riparian water law.

[2] PRIOR APPROPRIATION

In the eastern United States, where precipitation usually exceeds evaporation, there is relatively little need for irrigation. And when irrigation is necessary, there is usually a stream nearby from which to take water. That, however, is not the case in the expansive western United States. In these vast reaches, evaporation exceeds precipitation. In the west, irrigation is the rule, not the exception. To irrigate, moreover, water must be transported over long distances. The Supreme Court commented on this phenomenon in the major decision of *California v. United States*, 438 U.S. 645, 648–49, 98 S. Ct. 2985, 2987–88 (1978):

> Those who first set foot in North America from ships sailing the tidal estuaries of Virginia did not confront the same problems as those who sailed flat boats down the Ohio River in search of new sites to farm. Those who cleared the forests in the old Northwest Territory faced totally different physiographic problems from those who built sod huts on the Great Plains. The final expansion of our Nation in the 19th century into the arid lands beyond the hundredth meridian of longitude, which had been shown on early maps as the "Great American Desert," brought the participants in that expansion face to face with the necessity for irrigation in a way that no previous territorial expansion had.

> . . . .

> "[The] afternoon of July 23, 1847, was the true date of the beginning of modern irrigation. It was on that afternoon that the first band of Mormon pioneers built a small dam across City Creek near the present site of the Mormon Temple and diverted sufficient water to saturate some 5 acres of exceedingly dry land. Before the day was over they had planted potatoes to preserve the seed." During the subsequent half century, irrigation expanded throughout the arid States of the West, supported usually by private enterprise or the local community.

For reasons that became apparent upon reflection, settlers in the west found the riparian rights system unsuitable. Accordingly, a different system of water rights developed. The prior appropriation system was either engrafted on to the riparian system (in so-called "California doctrine" states) or it arose as the initial water rights allocation system (in so-called "Colorado doctrine" states).

The following case is regarded as the one that "created" the prior appropriation system.

IRWIN v. PHILLIPS

5 Cal. 140 (1855)

HEYDENFELDT, J., delivered the opinion of the Court. MURRAY, C.J., concurred.

The several assignments of error will not be separately considered, because the whole merits of the case depend really on a single question, and upon that question the case must be decided. The proposition to be settled is whether the owner of a canal in the mineral region of this State, constructed for the purpose of supplying water to miners, has the right to divert the water of a stream from its natural channel, as against the claims of those who, subsequent to the diversion, take up lands along the banks of the stream, for the purpose of mining. It must be premised that it is admitted on all sides that the mining claims in controversy, and the lands through which the stream runs and through which the canal passes, are a part of the public domain, to which there is no claim of private proprietorship; and that the miners have the right to dig for gold on the public lands was settled by this Court in the case of *Hicks et al. v. Bell et al.,* 3 Cal. 219.

It is insisted by the appellants that in this case the common law doctrine must be invoked, which prescribes that a water course must be allowed to flow in its natural channel. But upon an examination of the authorities which support that doctrine, it will be found to rest upon the fact of the individual rights of landed proprietors upon the stream, the principle being both at the civil and common law that the owner of lands on the banks of a water course owns to the middle of the stream, and has the right in virtue of his proprietorship to the use of the water in its pure and natural condition. In this case the lands are the property either of the State or of the United States, and it is not necessary to decide to which they belong for the purposes of this case. It is certain that at the common law the diversion of water courses could only be complained of by riparian owners, who were deprived of the use, or those claiming directly under them. Can the appellants assert their present claim as tenants at will? To solve this question it must be kept in mind that their tenancy is of their own creation, their tenements of their own selection, and subsequent, in point of time, to the diversion of the stream. They had the right to mine where they pleased throughout an extensive region, and they selected the bank of a stream from which the water had been already turned, for the purpose of supplying the mines at another point.

Courts are bound to take notice of the political and social condition of the country which they judicially rule. In this State the larger part of the territory consists of mineral lands, nearly the whole of which are the property of the public. No right or intent of disposition of these lands has been shown either by the United States or the State governments, and with the exception of certain State regulations, very limited in their character, a system has been permitted to grow up by the voluntary action and assent of the population, whose free and unrestrained occupation of the mineral region has been tacitly assented to by the one government, and heartily encouraged by the expressed legislative policy of the other. If there are, as must be admitted, many things connected with this system, which are crude and undigested, and subject to fluctuation and dispute, there are still some which a universal sense of necessity and property have so firmly fixed as that they have come to be looked upon as having the force and effect of res judicata. Among these the most important are the rights of miners to be protected in the possession of their selected localities, and the rights of those who, by prior appropriation, have taken the waters from their natural beds, and by costly artificial works have conducted them for miles over mountains and ravines, to supply the necessities of gold diggers, and without which the most important interests of the mineral region would remain without development. So fully recognized have become these rights, that without any specific legislation conferring or confirming them, they are alluded to and spoken of in various acts of the Legislature in the same manner as if they were rights which had been vested by the most distinct expression of the will of the law makers; as for instance, in the Revenue Act "canals and water races" are declared to be property subject to taxation, and this when there was none other in the State than such as were devoted to the use of mining. Section 2 of Article IX. of the same Act, providing for the assessment of the property of companies and associations, among others mentions "dam or dams, canal or canals, or other works for mining purposes." This simply goes to prove what is the purpose of the argument, that however much the policy of the State, as indicated by her legislation, has conferred the privilege to work the mines, it has equally conferred the right to divert the streams from their natural channels, and as these two rights stand upon an equal footing, when they conflict, they must be decided by the fact of priority, upon the maxim of equity, qui prior est in tempore, potier est in jure. The miner who selects a piece of ground to work, must take it as he finds it, subject to prior rights, which have an equal equity, on account of an equal recognition from the sovereign power. If it is upon a stream, the waters of which have not been taken from their bed, they cannot be taken to his prejudice; but if they have been already diverted, and for as high and legitimate a purpose as the one he seeks to accomplish, he has no right to complain, no right to interfere with the prior occupation of his neighbor, and must abide the disadvantages of his own selection.

It follows from this opinion that the judgement of the Court below was substantially correct, upon the merits of the case presented by the evidence, and it is therefore affirmed.

*   *   *   *   *   *

The prior appropriation system is far different from the riparian system. The operative features of the prior appropriation system are:

- the right to water inures upon the act of taking water (and applying it to a beneficial use). Land ownership is irrelevant to water right acquisition, and the water may be used on other than riparian land. Usually, taking water means diverting it out of its stream of origin. The requirement of a diversion as an element in securing a prior appropriation right has been dropped in some states, however, so as to allow "instream" rights to water;

- a right to water is superior (i.e. "senior") or inferior (i.e. "junior") to another's right based on the time at which the right is secured. The operative principle is "first in time, first in right." Senior rights are said to have "priority" over juniors;

- rights to water are quantified;

- cessation of use (i.e. abandonment) extinguishes the right. Rights can also be forfeited for violations of governing statutes or regulations;

- the use to which water is applied must be "beneficial";

- in times of shortage, the rights are clearly not correlative. Juniors must yield to seniors in such times. In other words, a junior appropriator may have to cease diverting water entirely so that enough water will remain in the stream to satisfy the entirety of the right of the senior appropriator;

- unlike the riparian system, which is largely common law-based, the prior appropriation system is managed by state regulatory agencies and its requirements are specified by statute and agency regulation.

NOTES AND QUESTIONS

1. Water taken for use on land is transported typically by ditches or pipes. When ditches, especially earthen ditches, serve as water conduits, water can be lost both to ground infiltration and to evaporation. Losses can be great in arid regions. Do you think an inordinantly wasteful use of water should be viewed as non-beneficial so as to strip one of a prior appropriation water right? Or should these "efficiency" considerations be irrelevant?

On a related note, since prior appropriation rights are quantified, at what location should the amount of water diverted from a stream be measured? At the point of diversion? At the point of application to its ultimate use?

2. In the current day, an appropriator must comply with administrative rules and regulations to secure a water right. For example, instead of physically diverting water, the appropriator must apply for a permit to do so. Issuance of a permit constitutes award of the right. Compliance with permit terms is necessary to retain the right. For their part, agencies keep track of available stream flows. Still, agencies may grant water rights to persons even when all of the water in a stream is already appropriated. Why would an agency "overappropriate" a stream?

3. As noted above, uses must be "beneficial"? Should persons be allowed to switch from one use to another freely? Or should a switch in use be deemed a request for a new prior appropriation right (with a new, and later, priority date)?

4. A prior appropriation right is a property right. Assume that a government agency passed a regulation indicating that all ditches had to be lined to reduce water loss. Could that regulation cause an unconstitutional taking? What if the agency took measures to reduce the quantity or change the priority date of a water right to the detriment of the right holder. Taking?

5. Persons sometimes effectively add to the available water in a stream. They can do so, for example, by eliminating foliage that itself removes water and transpires it into the atmosphere. This foliage, collectively known as "phreatophytes," can take away a surprisingly large amount of water otherwise available for beneficial use. Should an appropriator be given "credit" for such "salvaged" waters? In the parlance of water lawyers, should such water be "free from the call of the river"?

Another way to increase flow in a stream is by "importing" water from another watershed. Should an appropriator be given credit for imported waters?

6. Should the doctrine of adverse use have more or less applicability to the prior appropriation system than to the riparian system? Why?

7. Regarding interstate transfers of water, see *Sporhase v. Nebraska,* Chapter 3, *supra,* of these materials.

A NOTE ON DIFFUSE WATERS

The riparian and prior appropriation systems of water allocation deal with rights to water found in discrete channels. These systems do not control rights to water found in a diffuse state, that is, water which is not in a channel or other discrete "conveyance" but which instead is washing over the land.

For diffuse waters, a separate rights regime exists. Normally, one who captures diffuse water owns it, in a complete sense (akin to ownership of land). Capture and containment give rise to the right.

Controversy over diffuse waters often arises is a different context, however. Persons often do not want the diffuse water on their land. So they push it off on to nearby land titled in another. May a person do that? As a general matter, the answer is yes. Disputes of this sort frequently are decided by use of the "common enemy rule." As the name indicates, this common law doctrine stipulates that diffuse water is the common enemy of all and therefore may be removed by any person from her land, without liability. *Jorgenson v. Stephens,* 10 N.W.2d 337 (Neb. 1971). *See also Bulldog Battery Corp. v. Pica Investments, Inc.,* 736 N.E.2d 333 (Ind. App. 2000). An exception to the common enemy rule, in place in some jurisdictions, requires that diffuse waters be removed in some reasonable fashion. *Currens v. Sleek,* 983 P.2d 626 (Wash. 1999); *Hall v. Wood,* 443 So. 2d 834 (Miss. 1983). Removal should not cause unnecessary damage or injury to the land of another. *Snyder v. Platte Valley Public Power and Irrigation District,* 13 N.W.2d 160 (Neb. 1944); *Zollinger v. Carter,* 837 S.W.2d 613 (Tenn. App. 1992). The mere fact of damage to another's property, however, is not *per se* proof of unreasonableness or negligence. *See, e.g., Erickson v. Tyler,* 186 N.W.2d 123 (Neb. 1971); *Sheehan v. Flynn,* 61 N.W. 462 (Minn. 1894); *Ambrosio v. Perl-Mack Const. Co.,* 351 P.2d 803 (Colo. 1960).

C. GROUNDWATER

Groundwater is water which "occurs or moves, seeps, filters, or percolates through the ground under the surface of the land." *Metropolitan Utilities District v. Merritt Beach Co.,* 140 N.W.2d 626 (Neb. 1966).

In some states, the right to use groundwater arises by virtue of land ownership: the owner of overlying land has rights to extract water for use on that overlying land. In many "overlying rights" jurisdictions, water use is permissible only on the overlying land itself; transfer of water for use on other parcels is prohibited. Other jurisdictions may allow use on non-overlying land.

While there are no specific quantitative limitations in place in overlying rights jurisdictions, use of more than a reasonable amount, however determined, is disallowed. But this requirement of reasonableness is not an injunction against harming other users. A water user may extract water, for example, in such large quantities that little or none is left for others to extract, and still qualify as reasonable. The mere fact of harm to another, standing alone, is insufficient to demonstrate unreasonableness.

Overlying rights to groundwater are essentially correlative. Consequently, in times of shortage, all users must reduce their amounts of use for the benefit of all other users.

In other states, groundwater rights are not determined by title to overlying land. In these jurisdictions, allocations of groundwater may be accomplished by use of a prior appropriation system, the features of which are essentially identical to those of the surface water prior appropriation system. In prior appropriation jurisdictions, groundwater rights are separate from interests in land, are quantified, are subject to a beneficial use requirement, and so on.

D. FEDERAL WATER RIGHTS

[1] FEDERAL LEGISLATION AND WATER PROJECTS

We have already observed the prominence of state law in the legal world of water rights allocations. State law controls by default — the federal government has acquiesced to the operation of state law in this arena. The federal government has ample constitutional authority to take over the field. These authorities include the General Welfare Clause, Art. I, §§ 8 and 9; the Treaties Clause, Art. II, § 2, which can authorize projects on international waters; the Property Clause, Art. IV, § 3; the Common Defense Clause, Art. I, §§ 8 and 9, and, of course, the staple of federal constitutional power, the Commerce Clause, Art. I, § 8. But, excepting the creation of federal reserved water rights, see Chapter 5, supra, the federal government has chosen not to use its authorities to supplant the states.

When the federal government has acted in this area, it has not been to reorder water rights allocations, but to enable the construction of water projects. We now look briefly to federal actions to effect the construction or regulation of water projects, for irrigation, electricity production, flood control, or other purposes. What impact have these enactments had on the state water rights allocation schemes? The following case explores the impact of state law.

CALIFORNIA v. FEDERAL ENERGY REGULATORY COMMISSION*

495 U.S. 490, 110 S. Ct. 2024 (1990)

O'CONNOR, J.

This case concerns overlapping federal and state regulation of a hydroelectric project located near a California stream. California seeks to ensure that the project's operators maintain water flowing in the stream sufficient, in the State's judgment, to protect the stream's fish. The Federal Government claims the exclusive authority to set the minimum stream flows that the federally licensed power plant must maintain. Each side argues that its position is consistent with the Federal Power Act, 16 U.S.C. § 791a et seq. (1982 ed.), and, in particular, with § 27 of that Act. We granted certiorari to resolve these competing claims.

I

The Rock Creek hydroelectric project lies near the confluence of the South Fork American River and one of the river's tributaries, Rock Creek. Rock Creek runs through federally managed land located within California. The project draws water from Rock Creek to drive its generators and then releases the water near the confluence of the stream and river, slightly less than one mile from where it is drawn. The state and federal requirements at issue govern the "minimum flow rate" of water that must remain in the bypassed section of the stream and that thus remains unavailable to drive the generators.

In 1983, pursuant to the Federal Power Act (FPA), the Federal Energy Regulatory Commission (FERC) issued a license authorizing the operation of the Rock Creek project. Section 4(e) of the FPA empowers FERC to issue licenses for projects "necessary or convenient . . . for the development, transmission, and utilization of power across, along, from, or in any of the streams . . . over which Congress has jurisdiction." 16 U.S.C. § 797(e) (1982 ed.). Section 10(a) of the Act also authorizes FERC to issue licenses subject to the conditions that FERC deems best suited for power development and other public uses of the waters. 16 U.S.C. § 802(b) (1982 ed.). Congress' subsequent amendments to those provisions expressly direct that FERC consider a project's effect on fish and wildlife as well as "power and development purposes." Electric Consumers Projection Act of 1986, Pub. L. 99-495, 100 Stat. 1243, 16 U.S.C. §§ 797(e), 803(a). FERC issued the 1983 license and set minimum flow rates after considering the project's economic feasibility and environmental consequences. In part to protect trout in the stream, the license required that the project maintain interim minimum flow rates of 11 cubic feet per second (cfs) during May through September and 15 cfs during the remainder of the year. The license also required the licensee to submit studies recommending a permanent minimum flow rate, after consulting with federal and state fish and wildlife protection agencies. The licensee submitted a report

---

* [Ed. note: This case is also referred to as *Rock Creek*.]

recommending that FERC adopt the interim flow rates as permanent rates. The California Department of Fish and Game (CDFG) recommended that FERC require significantly higher minimum flow rates.

The licensee had also applied for state water permits, and in 1984 the State Water Resources Control Board (WRCB) issued a permit that conformed to FERC's interim minimum flow requirements but reserved the right to set different permanent minimum flow rates. When the WRCB in 1987 considered a draft order requiring permanent minimum flow rates of 60 cfs from March through June and 30 cfs during the remainder of the year, the licensee petitioned FERC for a declaration that FERC possessed exclusive jurisdiction to determine the project's minimum flow requirements. The licensee, by then respondent Rock Creek Limited Partnership, also claimed that the higher minimum flow rates sought by the WRCB would render the project economically infeasible.

In March 1987, FERC issued an order directing the licensee to comply with the minimum flow requirements of the federal permit. In that order, FERC concluded that the task of setting minimum flows rested within its exclusive jurisdiction. The Commission reasoned that setting minimum flow requirements was integral to its planning and licensing process under FPA § 10(a); giving effect to competing state requirements "would interfere with the Commission's balancing of competing considerations in licensing" and would vest in States a veto power over federal projects inconsistent with the FPA, as interpreted in *First Iowa Hydro-Electric Cooperative v. FPC*, 328 U.S. 152 (1946). FERC also directed an administrative law judge to hold a hearing to determine the appropriate permanent minimum flow rates for the project. After considering proposals and arguments of the licensee, the CDFG, and FERC staff, the administrative law judge set the minimum flow rate for the project at 20 cfs during the entire year. Four days after FERC's declaratory order, the WRCB issued an order directing the licensee to comply with the higher minimum flow requirements contained in its draft order. . . . [The Court of Appeals for the Ninth Circuit affirmed. . . .]

We granted certiorari and we now affirm.

II

In the Federal Power Act of 1935, 49 Stat. 863, Congress clearly intended a broad federal rule in the development and licensing of hydroelectric power. That broad delegation of power to the predecessor of FERC, however, hardly determines the extent to which Congress intended to have the Federal Government exercise exclusive powers, or intended to pre-empt concurrent state regulation of matters affecting federally licensed hydroelectric projects. The parties' dispute regarding the latter issue turns principally on the meaning of § 27 of the FPA, which provides the clearest indication of how Congress intended to allocate the regulatory authority of the States and the Federal Government. That section provides:

> "Nothing contained in this chapter shall be construed as affecting or intending to affect or in any way to interfere with the laws of the respective States relating to the control, appropriation, use, or

distribution of water used in irrigation or for municipal or other uses, or any vested right acquired therein." 16 U.S.C. § 821 (1982 ed.).

Were this a case of first impression, petitioner's argument based on the statute's language could be said to present a close question. As petitioner argues, California's minimum stream flow requirement might plausibly be thought to "relat[e] to the control, appropriation, use, or distribution of water used . . . for . . . other uses," namely the generation of power or the protection of fish. This interpretation would accord with the "presumption against finding preemption of state law in areas traditionally regulated by the States" and " 'with the assumption that the historic police powers of the States were not to be superseded by the Federal Act unless that was the clear and manifest purpose of Congress.' " *California v. ARC America Corp.,* 490 U.S. (1989) (slip op., at 5), *quoting Rice v. Santa Fe Elevator Corp.,* 331 U.S. 218, 230 (1947); *see California v. United States,* 438 U.S. 645, 653–663 (1978) (tracing States' traditional powers over exploitation of water). Just as courts may not find state measures pre-empted in the absence of clear evidence that Congress so intended, so must they give full effect to evidence that Congress considered and sought to preserve the States' coordinate regulatory role in our federal scheme.

But the meaning of § 27 and the pre-emptive effect of the FPA are not matters of first impression. Forty-four years ago, this Court in First Iowa construed the section and provided the understanding of the FPA that has since guided the allocation of state and federal regulatory authority over hydroelectric projects. The Court interpreted § 27 as follows:

> "The effect of § 27, in protecting state laws from supersedure, is limited to laws as to the control, appropriation, use or distribution of water in irrigation or for municipal or other uses of the same nature. It therefore has primary, if not exclusive, reference to such proprietary rights. The phrase 'any vested right acquired therein' further emphasizes the application of the section to property rights. There is nothing in the paragraph to suggest a broader scope unless it be the words 'other uses.' Those words, however, are confined to rights of the same nature as those relating to the use of water in irrigation or for municipal purposes." *First Iowa,* 328 U.S., at 175–176 (emphasis added).

The Court interpreted § 27's reservation of limited powers to the States as part of the congressional scheme to divide state from federal jurisdiction over hydroelectric projects and, "in those fields where rights are not thus 'saved' to the States . . . to let the supersedure of the state laws by federal legislation take its natural course." *Id.,* at 176.

We decline at this late date to revisit and disturb the understanding of § 27 set forth in *First Iowa.* * * *

Petitioner asks this Court fundamentally to restructure a highly complex and long-enduring regulatory regime, implicating considerable reliance interests of licensees and other participants in the regulatory process. That departure would be inconsistent with the measured and considered change that marks appropriate adjudication of such statutory issues. * * *

Adhering to *First Iowa*'s interpretation of § 27, we conclude that the California requirements for minimum instream flows cannot be given effect and allowed to supplement the federal flow requirements. A state measure is "pre-empted to the extent it actually conflicts with federal law, that is, when it is impossible to comply with both state and federal law, or where the state law stands as an obstacle to the accomplishment of the full purposes and objectives of Congress." *Silkwood v. Kerr-McGee Corp.*, 464 U.S. 238, 248 (1984) (citations omitted). As Congress directed in FPA § 10(a), FERC set the conditions of the license, including the minimum stream flow, after considering which requirements would best protect wildlife and ensure that the project would be economically feasible, and thus further power development. Allowing California to impose significantly higher minimum stream flow requirements would disturb and conflict with the balance embodied in that considered federal agency determination. FERC has indicated that the California requirements interfere with its comprehensive planning authority, and we agree that allowing California to impose the challenged requirements would be contrary to congressional intent regarding the Commission's licensing authority and would "constitute a veto of the project that was approved and licensed by FERC."

For the foregoing reasons, the decision of the Court of Appeals for the Ninth Circuit is Affirmed.

NOTES

1. Because many hydropower projects are governed by the Federal Power Act, this determination of the statute's preemptive effect is significant. Another important federal statute is the Reclamation Act of 1902, as amended, 43 U.S.C. § 371 *et seq*. This statute is applicable to many irrigation projects. The section of the Reclamation Act which establishes its preemptive effect is § 8, 43 U.S.C. § 383, which provides in part:

> [N]othing in this Act shall be construed as affecting or intended to affect or in any way interfere with the laws of any State or Territory relating to the control, appropriation, use, or distribution of water used in irrigation, or any vested right acquired thereunder, and the Secretary of the Interior, in carrying out the provisions of this Act, shall proceed in conformity with such laws, and nothing herein shall in any way affect any right of any State or of the Federal Government or of any landowner, appropriator, or user of water in, to, or from any interstate stream or the waters thereof. . . .

Rock Creek, in a portion of the opinion not provided above, discussed the preemptive effect of § 8 of the Reclamation Act and distinguished it from § 27 of the Federal Power Act:

> [T]he FPA envisioned a considerably broader and more active federal oversight role in hydropower development than did the Reclamation Act. Section 8, after referring to State water laws relating to water used in irrigation and preserved by the Act, contains an explicit direction that "the Secretary of the Interior, in carrying out the provisions of this Act, shall proceed in conformity with such [state] laws."

This language has no counterpart in § 27 and was crucial to the Court's interpretation of § 8. *See California v. United States*, 438 U.S., at 650, 664–665, 674–675. . . . The Secretary in executing a particular reclamation project is in a position analogous to a licensee under the FPA, and need not comply with state laws conflicting with congressional directives respecting particular reclamation projects; similarly, a federal licensee under the FPA need not comply with state requirements that conflict with the federal license provisions established pursuant to the FPA's directives. An additional textual difference is that § 8 refers only to "water used in irrigation" and contains no counterpart to § 27's reference to "other uses." . . . Laws controlling water used in irrigation relate to proprietary rights . . . and § 8 does not indicate the appropriate treatment of laws relating to other water uses that do not implicate proprietary rights. . . .

2. As you can see, while these federal statutes have preemptive effect, they have not been enacted to accomplish a complete preemption. Accordingly, when the federal government seeks to construct an irrigation project under the Reclamation Act, it must endeavor to secure water rights under state law. Once it has done so, it can enter into contractual or other arrangements with irrigators for the provision of water from the stored accumulation. The federal government cannot by legal fiat secure rights to waters already appropriated under state law without contravening constitutional takings principles.

3. Federal involvement has been central to virtually the entirety of large-scale water resource development in the United States, and the major federal actor for these purposes has been the Bureau of Reclamation. The Bureau has been described as the largest purveyor of water in the West. Indeed, the agency diverts between 40 percent and 85 percent of the annual flow of major western river systems such as the Colorado, Rio Grande, Snake, Sacramento, and San Joaquin.

Still, the era of big government water projects is all but over — economic and environmental considerations, and especially the dearth of feasible sites, have seen to that. Consequently, the role of the Bureau, which was originally to develop water supplies to facilitate settlement of the arid West, is changing. The Bureau has become less a water resources development agency and more a water resources management and protection agency. In addition to irrigation, the Bureau's responsibilities now include water conservation, hydroelectric power generation, municipal and industrial water supplies, flood control, outdoor recreation, enhancement of fish and wildlife habitats, and research.

In the current day, if more water is required for urban areas, endangered species preservation, or for other purposes, it must come from some other use. The prime target is agriculture. *See generally, Water Use Conflicts in the West: Implications of Reforming the Bureau of Reclamation's Water Supply Policies*, August, 1997, § 3.

[2] THE NAVIGATIONAL SERVITUDE

The United States Supreme Court has found a "navigational servitude" to exist in situations where the federal government exercises Commerce Clause authority to regulate navigation on a stream or other waterway. This servitude interest is distinctly different from the powers secured to the federal government through the constitution's enumerated powers.

UNITED STATES v. CHEROKEE NATION OF OKLAHOMA

480 U.S. 700, 107 S. Ct. 1487 (1987)

CHIEF JUSTICE REHNQUIST delivered the opinion of the Court.

In *Choctaw Nation v. Oklahoma*, 397 U.S. 620 (1970), the Court determined that certain treaties between the Cherokee, Chickasaw, and Choctaw Tribes and the United States granted to the Tribes fee simple title to the riverbed underlying specified portions of the Arkansas River in Oklahoma. The Court found the circumstances sufficient to overcome the "strong presumption against conveyance by the United States" of title to the bed of a navigable water. *Montana v. United States*, 450 U.S. 544, 552 (1981). *See United States v. Holt State Bank*, 270 U.S. 49 (1926). The question presented in this case is whether the United States must pay the Cherokee Nation compensation for damage to these riverbed interests caused by navigational improvements which it has made on the Arkansas River. The damage to sand and gravel deposits resulted from the McClellan-Kerr Project, approved by Congress in 1946, Act of July 24, 1946, ch. 595, 60 Stat. 634, 635–636, and designed to improve navigation by construction of a channel in the Arkansas River from its mouth at the Mississippi to Catoosa, Oklahoma. The project was completed in 1971.

After our decision in *Choctaw Nation*, the Cherokee Nation sought compensation from the Government. Congress refused to fund the claim after the Department of the Interior and the Army Corps of Engineers concluded that the United States' navigational servitude rendered it meritless. *See* Department of the Interior and Related Agencies Appropriations for 1980: Hearings Before a Subcommittee of the House Committee on Appropriations, 96th Cong., 1st Sess., pt. 7, pp. 379–392 (1979). Congress did, however, provide respondent with the opportunity to seek judicial relief, conferring jurisdiction on the United States District Court for the Eastern District of Oklahoma to determine "any claim which the Cherokee Nation of Oklahoma may have against the United States for any and all damages to Cherokee tribal assets related to and arising from the construction of the [McClellan-Kerr Project]." H. R. 2329, 97th Cong., 1st Sess. (1981).

The Cherokee Nation filed a complaint contending that the construction of the McClellan-Kerr Project resulted in a taking under the Fifth Amendment of the Tribe's riverbed interests without just compensation. The United States in response claimed that its navigational servitude precluded liability for the alleged taking. The District Court granted the Tribe's motion for summary judgment, finding that the decision in *Choctaw Nation* created a "unique situation by which a portion of the navigable Arkansas River is, essentially, a private waterway belonging exclusively to the Cherokee Nation." App. to Pet. for Cert. 26a. Because the United States did not reserve its navigational servitude in the relevant treaties, the court held, it owed the Tribe just compensation.

A divided panel of the Court of Appeals for the Tenth Circuit affirmed, adopting a different analysis. 782 F.2d 871 (1986). The court rejected the District Court's conclusion that the United States' failure to reserve its navigational servitude defeated that interest. It found it "certain [that] the United States retained a navigational servitude in the Arkansas River." *Id.*, at 876. Nevertheless, the court held that the servitude was insufficient to protect the United States from liability. Finding that "the assertion of a navigational servitude on particular waters acknowledges *only* that the property owner's right to *use* these waters is shared with the public at large," *id.*, at 877, the court believed that the effect of the navigational servitude varied with the owner's intended use: "When the exercise of that public power affects private ownership rights not connected to a navigational use, the court must balance the public and private interests to decide whether just compensation is due." *Ibid.* Applying this test, the court concluded that though the Cherokee Nation could not interfere with the United States' exercise of the navigational servitude, it had a right to compensation for any consequent loss of property or diminution in value.

We think the Court of Appeals erred in formulating a balancing test to evaluate this assertion of the navigational servitude. No such "balancing" is required where, as here, the interference with in-stream interests results from an exercise of the Government's power to regulate navigational uses of "the deep streams which penetrate our country in every direction." *Gibbons v. Ogden*, 9 Wheat. 1, 195 (1824). Though "this Court has never held that the navigational servitude creates a blanket exception to the Takings Clause whenever Congress exercises its Commerce Clause authority to promote navigation," *Kaiser Aetna v. United States*, 444 U.S. 164, 172 (1979), there can be no doubt that "[the] Commerce Clause confers a unique position upon the Government in connection with navigable waters." *United States v. Rands*, 389 U.S. 121, 122 (1967). It gives to the Federal Government "a 'dominant servitude,' *FPC v. Niagara Mohawk Power Corp.*, 347 U.S. 239, 249 (1954), which extends to the entire stream and the stream bed below ordinary high-water mark. The proper exercise of this power is not an invasion of any private property rights in the stream or the lands underlying it, for the damage sustained does not result from taking property from riparian owners within the meaning of the Fifth Amendment but from the lawful exercise of a power to which the interests of riparian owners have always been subject." *Rands, supra*, at 123.[3] *See also United States v. Kansas City Life Ins. Co.*, 339 U.S. 799, 808 (1950); *Scranton v. Wheeler*, 179 U.S. 141, 163 (1900).

The application of these principles to interference with streambed interests has not depended on balancing this valid public purpose in light of the

---

[3] Though *Rands* spoke in terms of riparian owners, rather than those holding fee simple title to riverbed interests, our cases make clear that the navigational servitude is dominant to riverbed interests no matter how acquired. *See, e.g., United States v. Chicago, M., St. P. & P. R. Co.*, 312 U.S. 592, 596 (1941) ("Whether, under local law, the title to the bed of the stream is retained by the State or the title of the riparian owner extends to the thread of the stream, or . . . to low-water mark, the rights of the title holder are subject to the dominant power of the federal Government in respect of navigation") (footnotes omitted).

intended use of those interests by the owner. Thus, in *Lewis Blue Point Oyster Cultivation Co. v. Briggs*, 229 U.S. 82 (1913), the Court held that no taking occurred where dredging carried out under the direction of the United States destroyed oysters that had been cultivated on privately held lands under the waters of the Great South Bay in New York. The decision rested on the view that the dominant right of navigation "must include the right to use the bed of the water for every purpose which is in aid of navigation." *Id.*, at 87. The Court did not rely on the particular use to which the private owners put the bed, but rather observed that their very title to the submerged lands "is acquired and held subject to the power of Congress to deepen the water over such lands or to use them for any structure which the interest of navigation, in its judgment, may require." *Id.*, at 88. See also *United States v. Commodore Park*, 324 U.S. 386, 390 (1945); *United States v. Chicago, M., St. P. & P. R. Co.*, 312 U.S. 592, 596–597 (1941).

These well-established principles concerning the exercise of the United States' dominant servitude would, in the usual case, dictate that we reject respondent's "takings" claim. We do not understand respondent to argue otherwise. [citations omitted]. Instead, the Cherokee Nation asserts that its title to the Arkansas River bed is unique in scope and that interference with that interest requires just compensation. Respondent does not rely explicitly on any language of the relevant treaties, but rather on its reading of *Choctaw Nation v. Oklahoma*, 397 U.S. 620 (1970). We have noted that *Choctaw Nation* involved "very peculiar circumstances," *Montana v. United States*, 450 U.S., at 555, n. 5, in that "the Indians were promised virtually complete sovereignty over their new lands." *Choctaw Nation, supra*, at 635. These circumstances allowed the claimants to overcome the strong presumption against conveyance of riverbed interests by the United States, designed to protect the interests of the States under the equal-footing doctrine. *See Montana v. United States, supra*, at 551–553; *Shively v. Bowlby*, 152 U.S. 1, 48–50 (1894). Respondent urges that these circumstances further indicate that the United States abandoned its navigational servitude in the area. Thus, in respondent's view, the treaties by which it gained fee simple title to the bed of the Arkansas River were such as to make the Arkansas River a "private stream," Brief for Respondent 28, "not intended as a public highway or artery of commerce." *Id.*, at 23.

We think that the decision in *Choctaw Nation* was quite generous to respondent, and we refuse to give a still more expansive and novel reading of respondent's property interests. There is certainly nothing in *Choctaw Nation* itself that suggests such a broad reading of the conveyance. To the contrary, the Court expressly noted that the United States had no interest in retaining title to the submerged lands because "it had all it was concerned with in its *navigational easement* via the constitutional power over commerce." *Choctaw Nation, supra*, at 635 (emphasis added). The parties, including respondent here, clearly understood that the navigational servitude was dominant no matter how the question of riverbed ownership was resolved. *See, e. g.*, Brief for Petitioner in *Cherokee Nation v. Oklahoma*, O.T. 1969, No. 59, p. 19 ("[There] is nothing in the conveyance of title to the land beneath the navigable waters which conflicts with the power of the Government to hold such lands for navigation").

Any other conclusion would be wholly extraordinary, for we have repeatedly held that the navigational servitude applies to *all* holders of riparian and riverbed interests. *See Montana v. United States, supra,* at 555; *United States v. Grand River Dam Authority,* 363 U.S. 229, 233 (1960); *United States v. Chandler-Dunbar Water Power Co.,* 229 U.S. 53, 63 (1913), citing *Gibson v. United States,* 166 U.S. 269, 271 (1897). Indeed, even when the sovereign States gain "the absolute right to all their navigable waters and the soils under them for their own common use" by operation of the equal-footing doctrine, *Martin v. Waddell,* 16 Pet. 367, 410 (1842), this "absolute right" is unquestionably subject to "the paramount power of the United States to ensure that such waters remain free to interstate and foreign commerce." *Montana v. United States, supra,* at 551. If the States themselves are subject to this servitude, we cannot conclude that respondent — though granted a degree of sovereignty over tribal lands — gained an exemption from the servitude simply because it received title to the riverbed interests. Such a waiver of sovereign authority will not be implied, but instead must be " 'surrendered in unmistakable terms.' " *Bowen v. Public Agencies Opposed to Social Security Entrapment,* 477 U.S. 41, 52 (1986), quoting *Merrion v. Jicarilla Apache Tribe,* 455 U.S. 130, 148 (1982). Respondent can point to no such terms.

We also reject respondent's suggestion that the fiduciary obligations of the United States elevate the Government's actions into a taking. It is, of course, well established that the Government in its dealings with Indian tribal property acts in a fiduciary capacity. *See Seminole Nation v. United States,* 316 U.S. 286, 296–297 (1942). When it holds lands in trust on behalf of the tribes, the United States may not "give the tribal lands to others, or . . . appropriate them to its own purposes, without rendering, or assuming an obligation to render, just compensation for them." *United States v. Creek Nation,* 295 U.S. 103, 110 (1935). These principles, however, do little to aid respondent's cause, for they do not create property rights where none would otherwise exist but rather presuppose that the United States has interfered with existing tribal property interests. As we have explained, the tribal interests at issue here simply do not include the right to be free from the navigational servitude, for exercise of the servitude is "not an invasion of any private property rights in the stream or the lands underlying it. . . ." *United States v. Rands,* 389 U.S. at 123.

The judgment of the Court of Appeals is reversed, and the case is remanded for further proceedings consistent with this opinion.

It is so ordered.

NOTES AND QUESTIONS

1. *United States v. Rands,* 389 U.S. 121, 88 S. Ct. 265 (1967), cited in the main text, is a major statement on the navigational servitude:

> The Commerce Clause confers a unique position upon the Government in connection with navigable waters. 'The power to regulate commerce comprehends the control for that purpose, and to the extent necessary, of all the navigable waters of the United States. . . . For this purpose, they are the public property of the nation, and subject

to all the requisite legislation by Congress . . . This power to regulate navigation confers upon the United States a "dominant servitude" . . . which extends to the entire stream and the stream bed below ordinary high-water mark. The proper exercise of this power is not an invasion of any private property rights in the stream or the lands underlying it, for the damage sustained does not result from taking property from riparian owners within the meaning of the Fifth Amendment but from the lawful exercise of a power to which the interests of riparian owners have always been subject. . . . Thus, without being constitutionally obligated to pay compensation, the United States may change the course of a navigable stream . . . or otherwise impair or destroy a riparian owner's access to navigable waters, . . . even though the market value of the riparian owner's land is substantially diminished.

The navigational servitude of the United States does not extend beyond the high-water mark. Consequently, when fast lands are taken by the Government, just compensation must be paid. But "just as the navigational privilege permits the Government to reduce the value of riparian lands by denying the riparian owner access to the stream without compensation for his loss . . . it also permits the Government to disregard the value arising from this same fact of riparian location in compensating the owner when fast lands are appropriated."

Id. at 123-24

The constitutional principle established in the last-supplied sentence of *Rands* evoked sufficient controversy to prompt its statutory reversal in § 111 of the Rivers and Harbors and Flood Control Act of 1970. Congress can waive the servitude if it wishes and elect to pay compensation.

2. What is the source of the navigational servitude? *Cherokee Nation* states it is a property right finding its source in the affirmative Commerce Clause. Since when does an enumerated power in the federal government create a property right in it? Perhaps the navigational servitude finds its source elsewhere. Justice Blackmun has given one view: "what is at issue is a matter of power, not of property. The servitude, in order to safeguard the Federal Government's paramount control over waters used in interstate commerce, limits the power of the States to create conflicting interests based on local law. That control does not depend on the form of the water body or the manner in which it was created, but on the fact of navigability and the corresponding commercial significance the waterway attains. . . ." *Kaiser Aetna v. United States*, 100 S. Ct. 383, 396-97 (1979) (Blackmun, J., dissenting).

Why is there not a "dominant servitude" created when the government exercises Commerce Clause authorities in contexts other than navigation on waterways? Why does the Takings Clause not operate here but continue to operate with respect to other Commerce Clause applications? You might compare the federal navigational servitude to the public trust doctrine, at least as it was invoked by California in the *Mono Lake* case.

3. *Submerged Lands Act,* 43 U.S.C. § 1314(a): "The United States retains all its navigational servitude and rights in and powers of regulation and control of said lands and navigable waters for the constitutional purposes of

commerce, navigation, national defense, and international affairs, all of which shall be paramount to, but shall not be deemed to include, proprietary rights of ownership, or the rights of management, administration, leasing, use, and development of the lands and natural resources which are specifically recognized, confirmed, established, and vested in and assigned to the respective States and others by section 3 of this Act." *See also United States v. Alaska,* 503 U.S. 569, 586, 112 S. Ct. 1606, 1616 (1992); Chapter 5, *supra.*

4. Some states now have their own navigational servitudes, based on state law and presumably tied to *intra*-state commerce regulation.

A NOTE ON INTERSTATE ALLOCATION

Interstate allocation of water among states is accomplished in three ways. The first is equitable apportionment. In *Kansas v. Colorado,* 206 U.S. 46, 27 S. Ct. 655 (1907), the Court held that all states were equal and it (the Court) could use equitable principles in allocating the waters of an interstate, flowing stream among such equal states. This rationale for allocating water is perhaps most appropriately used when competing states have different intrastate allocation systems (i.e. one uses riparian principles and the other prior appropriation). When both states are prior appropriation jurisdictions, the Court may simply allow the existing intrastate vested rights to remain, and thereby *de facto* determine the interstate allocation. However, this is not always the case. In *Colorado v. New Mexico,* 459 U.S. 176, 103 S. Ct. 539 (1982), the Court did not simply rely on existing intrastate appropriations to undergird the equitable apportionment, as to do so would have sanctioned waste and inefficient use of water.

The second allocation method is "interstate compact." As the name indicates, interstate compacts are state agreements on the allocation of waters in an interstate stream. Such compacts are permitted by the U.S. Constitution (Art. I, § 10, cl. 3) only if ratified by Congress. Interstate compacts are binding on water users within states, regardless of their participation, or lack thereof, in proceedings producing the compact.

The third method is federal legislation. Congress has the power to allocate water among states, and on some occasions has done so (one example: The Boulder Canyon Project Act of 1928). It can do so even if the allocation would contravene an interstate compact already in place.

Chapter 9

THE CLEAN AIR ACT

". . . There is no choice but to breathe the air, whether it is clean or polluted. Air is inhaled regardless of its quality. This is a national resource that should be protected as our parks and national monuments are protected." *Senate Report No. 101-228, accompanying the 1990 Amendments to the Clean Air Act, P.L. 101-549 (Nov. 15, 1990), U.S. Code Congressional and Administrative News, 101st Cong., 2d Sess. (1990), at 3389.*

A. INTRODUCTION

The American Lung Association, in a study conducted at the University of California School of Medicine, reported that lung function among persons living in chronically polluted areas can decline to a degree comparable to that of persons who smoke more than a pack of cigarettes a day. American Journal of Respiratory and Critical Care Medicine, May, 1994. The study was done in and near Los Angeles, considered at the time to be the most polluted air basin in the United States (Houston later earned the honor, not because it surpassed Los Angeles in absolute terms, but because it reduced its pollution levels more slowly than did the City of Angels).

This and a legion of comparable other studies have demonstrated the serious adverse health effects of unclean air. Since people breathe about 300 gallons of air a day, the concern was sure to find its way into the federal legislative arena, and it did so, as early as 1955. In that year, Congress authorized a limited federal involvement, merely instructing the Surgeon General of the United States to study the problem. 69 Stat. 322. But, despite its modesty, this legislative intervention was at least a federal foot in the door. It opened the way for future federal action. In 1960, Congress acted again, this time authorizing the Surgeon General to study health risks from emissions from motor vehicles. 74 Stat. 162. In 1963 and 1967, it expanded federal research efforts. 77 Stat. 392; Air Quality Act of 1967, 81 Stat. 485.

These early initiatives reflected the prevailing view of the time that pollution control should be the purview of states. However, as the 1970s neared, it became appallingly clear that relying on states to clean the nation's air was a failed strategy. For one thing, air pollution had become a problem of national proportions, beyond the capacity of states, acting singly, to solve. If a state cleaned up, it might still be polluted by its upwind neighbors. State regulatory efforts were hampered also by political realities. Major polluting industries often exerted substantial political sway in halls of state legislatures. In many cases, industries were able to entirely frustrate state air pollution regulatory initiatives by bandying the prospect of massive worker layoffs. Since the public had come to view pollution as an unavoidable cost of economic prosperity, it was tough, if not impossible, to assemble the political will to clamp down on large industrial sources of air pollution.

Given this political impasse, and bolstered by the staunch leadership of a true champion of environmental protection, Senator Edmund Muskie of Maine, among others, Congress finally took decisive action. Abandoning its earlier respectful deference, this time it "took a stick to the States." The result was the Clean Air Act ("CAA") Amendments of 1970, Pub. L. 91-604. The CAA did not remove states from the game, to be sure, but it unambiguously supplanted them: in the new federal-state partnership to regulate air pollution, the senior partner would be Uncle Sam.

Senator Edmund Muskie of Maine.
Used by permission. Copyright Stephen O. Muskie
www.outtakes.com

The Clean Air Act of 1970, as amended, 42 U.S.C. § 7401 et seq., remains the central statute regulating air pollution in this nation. In this Chapter, we will take an historical approach in our examination of it. Our inquiry begins with a review of the statute's original design, for upon that all else is built. The original Act relied on three major initiatives. First, it attempted to limit emissions of the most common pollutants ("criteria pollutants") by a regulatory system involving states. Under the plan, the federal government determines how clean the air should be, using "national ambient air quality standards" ("NAAQSs") for that purpose, and states then endeavor to accomplish the actual cleaning, typically by using "source emission limitations" or "source standards." Second, the CAA instituted a separate set of standards for so-called "new sources." The idea behind "new source performance standards" is that industrial facilitites not yet constructed should be designed and built to operate in as clean a manner as possible. Last, the Act made specific provision for hazardous pollutants, sometimes known as "air toxics."

After a review of the original statute, we will examine the amendments to the statute enacted in 1977. These amendments were borne of Congressional frustration at the uneven success achieved by the original enactment. The 1977 amendments imposed new restrictions on emissions of air pollutants in both "dirty air" and "clean air" areas.

We complete our survey of the Clean Air Act with a review of the Clean Air Act Amendments of 1990, Congress's most recent and comprehensive revision to the statute. The 1990 amendments added several entirely new regulatory provisions, including an innovative market-based regulatory approach to reduce acid deposition.

The Clean Air Act is divisible into two halves. The half upon which we will focus is regulation of so-called "stationary sources" of air pollution, including factories, incinerators, and other such facilities. The other half is regulation of "mobile sources" of air pollution; we do not cover mobile source regulation in these materials.

B. THE 1970 ACT

[1] REGULATION OF CRITERIA POLLUTANTS

[a] NATIONAL AMBIENT AIR QUALITY STANDARDS

The primary concern of the drafters of the Clean Air Act of 1970 was to rid the air of the most commonly found air pollutants. "Air pollutant" is defined by the Act as:

> any air pollution agent or combination of such agents, including any physical, chemical, biological, radioactive (including source material, special nuclear material, and byproduct material) substance or matter which is emitted into or otherwise enters the ambient air. Such term includes any precursors to the formation of any air pollutant, to the extent the Administrator has identified such precursor or precursors for the particular purpose for which the term "air pollutant" is used.

§ 302(g), 42 U.S.C. § 7602(g).

Commonly found air pollutants include:

- *Carbon Monoxide* (CO): this colorless and odorless gas enters the atmosphere primarily from tailpipes of gasoline-powered vehicles. Inhallation adversely affects the body's capacity to carry oxygen in the bloodstream, which in turn can cause various cardiovascular and other problems.

- *Hydrocarbons* (HC): emitted into the air when fuels are incompletely combusted, these pollutants can combine with nitrogen oxides to form photochemical oxidants, or smog, a complicated and hazy mixture of gases, including ozone. Hydrocarbons can irritate eyes and lungs, harm vegetation, and produce odors.

- *Lead* (Pb): ingestion of this heavy metal is shown to cause brain damage, especially in children. For more information, see the text accompanying the *Lead Industries* case, *infra*.

- *Nitrogen Dioxide* (NO_2): produced by combustion of fossil fuels, these pollutants react in the atmosphere with volatile organic compounds (VOCs) to form ozone. They contribute to lung damage and respiration problems.

- *Ozone* (O_3): commonly known as smog, ozone is found in the stratosphere, where it works to shield the earth from ultraviolet radiation, and in the troposphere, where it is a component of photochemical smog. In that latter capacity, ozone adversely affects respiration, damages the lungs, and contributes to asthma, nasal congestion, and the like. Ninety percent of ozone inhaled into the lungs is never exhaled. Instead, ozone reacts rapidly with cells and tissues that line the respiratory tract.

- *Particulate Matter* (PM_{10} and $PM_{2.5}$): this pollutant includes materials which are normally liquid or solid in form but have become airborne. Fine particulates, those of 10 microns or less in diameter ("PM_{10}"), can invade the body, causing a variety of health problems. Very fine particulates, those 2.5 microns in diameter or less, have also been linked to cardiovascular problems among the elderly.

- *Sulfur Dioxide* (SO2): emitted largely by combustion of fossil fuel, this pollutant contributes to acid deposition, aggravates respiratory activity and contributes to lung disability.

The Clean Air Act first envisioned dividing the nation into "air quality control regions." § 107, 42 U.S.C. § 7407. AQCRs are the geographic units within which pollution controls apply. There have been 247 AQCRs designated under the Act.

To bring about a reduction in emissions of air pollutants, the Act directed EPA to establish NAAQSs for commonly found air pollutants, and set time frames within which they should be attained in each AQCR. NAAQSs are minimal standards for cleanliness of air, set on a pollutant-by-pollutant basis. Pollutants for which NAAQSs are in place are known as "criteria" air pollutants, for reasons that will be clear upon your reading of the case which follows. The Clean Air Act calls for primary and secondary NAAQSs. § 109, 42 U.S.C. § 7409. Primary NAAQSs are to be set at levels that are "requisite to protect the public health, while 'allowing an adequate margin of safety.'" § 109(b)(1), 42 U.S.C. 7409(b)(1). Secondary NAAQSs are to be set at levels "requisite to protect the public welfare from any known or anticipated adverse effects associated with the presence of such air pollutant in the ambient air." § 109(b)(2), 42 U.S.C. § 7409(b)(2).

Even though the term, "public," is undefined in the statute, the *Lead Industries* case, *infra*, makes clear that the term includes discrete subunits of the general population. This means that EPA is not limited to creating ambient standards designed to protect the healthy adult only. On the contrary, it is legally authorized to fashion more stringent NAAQSs to protect more vulnerable population subgroups such as children and the elderly. *See, e.g.* Senate Report No. 91-1196, at 10 (specifying that "sensitive citizens" — children, for example, or people with asthma, emphysema, or other respiratory conditions rendering them particularly vulnerable to air pollution — "should be protected").[1]

The EPA has promulgated NAAQSs for each of the above-listed pollutants (the NAAQS for hydrocarbons was repealed in 1983). These standards are set forth in the chart that immediately follows.

---

[1] General considerations do not always control specific cases. In one instance, EPA declined to revise the NAAQS for sulfur dioxide to protect one population subgroup, asthmatics, from "high level short-term SO_2 bursts," that is, temporary severe exposures to sulfur dioxide, on the theory that there was no *public* health problem. In EPA's view, these so-called bursts were "localized," "site-specific," and "infrequent," and not the type of "ubiquitous" health problem for which an NAAQS was appropriate. *American Lung Ass'n v. U.S. Environmental Protection Agency,* 134 F.3d 388, 391-92 (D.C. Cir. 1998), *cert. denied,* 528 U.S. 818, 120 S. Ct. 58 (1999). Reviewing the agency refusal, the D.C. Circuit Court of Appeals conceded that EPA might be right to decide that excessive exposures to sulfur dioxide to be suffered by 41,500 asthmatics do not rise to the level of "a public health problem warranting national protective regulation, or that three or six or twelve annual exposures present no cause for annual concern[.]" The court nonetheless remanded the case because EPA failed to plausibly explain why the "local" nature of this pollution precluded regulation. *Id.* at 392.

From all of this, one may rightly conclude the Clean Air Act is in reality more a public health and welfare measure than a classic "environmental law" in place to improve environmental quality for its own sake.

NATIONAL AMBIENT AIR QUALITY STANDARDS				
Pollutant	Primary		Secondary	
	Standard	Measurement Period	Standard	Measurement Period
Carbon Monoxide	9 ppm (10 mg/m³)	8-hour	None	
	35 ppm (40 mg/m³)	1-hour		
Lead	1.5 mg/m³	Quarterly (averaged)	Same as primary standard	
Nitrogen Dioxide	.053 ppm (100 μ/m³)	Annual (mean)	Same as primary standard	
Ozone	0.12 ppm (235 μ/m³)	Daily (1-hour average)	Same as primary standard	
	0.08 ppm*	Daily (8-hour average)	Same as primary standard	
Particulate Matter$_{10}$	50 μg/m³	Annual (mean)	Same as primary standard	
	150 μg/m³	24-hour	Same as primary standard	
Particulate Matter$_{2.5}$	15 μg/m³	Annual (mean)	Same as primary standard	
	65 μg/m³	24-hour	Same as primary standard	
Sulfur Dioxide	0.03 ppm (80 μg/m³)	Annual (mean)	0.50 ppm (1,300 μg/m³)	3-hour
	0.14 ppm (365 μg/m³)	24-hour		

The PM$_{10}$ standard was vacated by the D.C. Circuit Court of Appeals in *American Trucking Assn's v. EPA*, 175 F.3d. 1027 (D.C. Cir. 1999), *modified on other grounds*, *Whitman v. American Trucking Assn's*, 531 U.S. 457, 121 S. Ct. 903 (2001) (*see, infra*), and withdrawn from the Code of Federal Regulations in July, 2004. 69 Fed. Reg. 45592 (July 30, 2004). [2]

At this point, you should read §§ 107-109 of the Clean Air Act and the *Lead Industries* case, which follows. *Lead Industries* examines the validity of national ambient air quality standards established for the pollutant, lead. Air pollution from lead is not a new problem. The ambient air in the ancient Roman Empire was apparently heavily contaminated with lead from open-air furnaces, so much so that the entire northern hemisphere was fouled for centuries. Airborne lead particles made it as far north as the Arctic as early as 500 B.C. to 300 B.C. A major cause was the introduction of silver coinage. Silver was extracted from lead in smelters, a process that apparently resulted in enormous pollutant loadings. *See, e.g.*, Curt Suplee, *Environment: Roman Air was Full of Lead*, Wash. Post, Sept. 26, 1994, at A2.

---

[2] Source: 40 C.F.R. §§ 50.4-50.12. Current as of July, 2000. Methodology of measurement can vary dramatically among the pollutants. No converted standard expressed in μ/m³ supplied in regulation. 40 C.F.R. § 50.10.

In the current day, lead remains a problem. While lead exposure levels have declined dramatically in the last twenty years, in large part because of reduced use of lead in gasoline, soldered cans and housepaint, the public is still exposed to this material from house dust, soils, and water delivery pipes. More than 900,000 children younger than six years of age, largely those of low-income families living in older homes, have elevated levels of lead in their bloodstreams. Elevated lead levels can cause cognitive defects in math, reading, memory function, and visual construction skills, and general declines in intelligence. *See, e.g.,* M.J. Friedrich, *Poor Children Subject to "Environmental Injustice"*, 283 JAMA 23 (June 21, 2000); Thomas D. Matte, *Reducing Blood Lead Levels: Benefits and Strategies*, 281 JAMA 24 (June 1999).

LEAD INDUSTRIES ASS'N, INC. v. U.S. ENVIRONMENTAL PROTECTION AGENCY

647 F.2d 1130 (D.C. Cir. 1980)

WRIGHT, Chief Judge:

This is the third occasion on which this court has been asked to review Environmental Protection Agency (EPA or Agency) regulations promulgated under authority of the Clean Air Act, as amended, 42 U.S.C. § 7401 et seq. (Supp. I 1977) (the Act), and specifically designed to deal with the health problems associated with lead in the ambient air. . . .

II. The Statutory Scheme

The first step toward establishing national ambient air quality standards for a particular pollutant is its addition to a list, compiled by EPA's Administrator, of pollutants that cause of contribute to air pollution "which may reasonably be anticipated to endanger public health or [welfare.]" Section 108(a)(1), 42 U.S.C. § 7408(a)(1). Within twelve months of the listing of a pollutant under Section 108(a) the Administrator must issue "air quality criteria" for the pollutant. Section 108 makes it clear that the term "air quality criteria" means something different from the conventional meaning of "criterion"; such "criteria" do not constitute "standards" or "guidelines," but rather refer to a document to be prepared by EPA which is to provide the scientific basis for promulgation of air quality standards for the pollutant. This criteria document must "accurately reflect the latest scientific knowledge useful in indicating the kind and extent of all identifiable effects on public health or welfare which may be expected from the presence of such pollutant in the ambient air, in varying quantities." Section 108(a)(2), 42 U.S.C. § 7408(a)(2).

At the same time as he issues air quality criteria for a pollutant, the Administrator must also publish proposed national primary and secondary air quality standards for the pollutant. Section 109(a)(2), 42 U.S.C. § 7409(a)(2). National primary ambient air quality standards are standards "the attainment and maintenance of which in the judgment of the Administrator, based on such criteria and allowing an adequate margin of safety, are requisite to protect the public health." Section 109(b)(1), 42 U.S.C.

§ 7409(b)(1). Secondary air quality standards "specify a level of air quality the attainment and maintenance of which in the judgment of the Administrator, based on such criteria, is requisite to protect the public welfare from any known or anticipated adverse effects associated with the presence of such air pollutant in the ambient air." Section 109(b)(2), 42 U.S.C. § 7409(b)(2). Effects on "the public welfare" include "effects on soils, water, crops, vegetation, manmade materials, animals, wildlife, weather, visibility, and climate, damage to and deterioration of property, and hazards to transportation, as well as effects on economic values and on personal comfort and well-being." Section 302(h), 42 U.S.C. § 7602(h). The Administrator is required to submit the proposed air quality standards for public comment in a rulemaking proceeding, the procedure for which is prescribed by Section 307(d) of the Act, 42 U.S.C. § 7607(d).

Within six months of publication of the proposed standards the Administrator must promulgate final primary and secondary ambient air quality standards for the pollutant. Section 307(d)(10), 42 U.S.C. § 7607(d)(10). Once EPA has promulgated national ambient air quality standards, responsibility under the Act shifts from the federal government to the states. Within nine months of promulgation of the standards each state must prepare and submit to EPA for approval a state implementation plan. Section 110(a)(1), 42 U.S.C. § 7410(a)(1). These state implementation plans must contain emission limitations and all other measures necessary to attain the primary standards "as expeditiously as practicable," but no later than three years after EPA approval of the plan, and to attain the secondary standards within a reasonable period of time. Section 110(a)(2)(A) & (B), 42 U.S.C. § 7410(a)(2)(A) & (B). The Administrator is authorized to extend the deadline for attainment of the primary air quality standards by two years, but thereafter it must be met. Section 110(e), 42 U.S.C. § 7410(e). . . .

[The court then discusses at length the rulemaking proceedings leading up to the establishment of the primary ambient air quality standard for lead, the criteria document used by the agency, and the scope of review to be used by the court. Thereafter, it discusses the arguments put forth in the case]:

V. Statutory Authority

The petitioners' first claim is that the Administrator exceeded his authority under the statute by promulgating a primary air quality standard for lead which is more stringent than is necessary to protect the public health because it is designed to protect the public against "subclinical" effects which are not harmful to health. According to petitioners, Congress only authorized the Administrator to set primary air quality standards that are aimed at protecting the public against health effects which are known to be clearly harmful. They argue that Congress so limited the Administrator's authority because it was concerned that excessively stringent air quality standards could cause massive economic dislocation. . . .

This argument is totally without merit. [Plaintiff] is unable to point to anything in either the language of the Act or its legislative history that offers any support for its claim that Congress, by specifying that the Administrator is to allow an "adequate margin of safety" in setting primary air quality standards, thereby required the Administrator to consider economic or technological feasibility. . . .

The legislative history of the Act [also] shows the Administrator may not consider economic and technological feasibility in setting air quality standards; the absence of any provision requiring consideration of these factors was no accident; it was the result of a deliberate decision by Congress to subordinate such concerns to the achievement of health goals. Exasperated by the lack of significant progress toward dealing with the problem of air pollution under the Air Quality Act of 1967, 81 STAT. 485, and prior legislation, Congress abandoned the approach of offering suggestions and setting goals in favor of "taking a stick to the States in the form of the Clean Air Amendments of 1970 * * *." *Train v. Natural Resources Defense Council, Inc., supra,* 421 U.S. at 64; *see Union Electric Co. v. EPA,* 427 U.S. 246, 256–257 (1976). Congress was well aware that, together with Sections 108 and 110, Section 109 imposes requirements of a "technology-forcing" character. . . .

It may well be that underlying St. Joe's argument is its feeling that Congress could not or should not have intended this result, and that this court should supply relief by grafting a requirement of economic or technological feasibility onto the statute. The Supreme Court confronted a similar suggestion in the Tellico Dam case. *TVA v. Hill,* 437 U.S. 153 (1978). There TVA argued that the Endangered Species Act should not be construed to prevent operation of the dam since it had already been completed at a cost of approximately $100 million, Congress had appropriated funds for the dam even after the Act was passed, and the species at risk — the snail darter — was relatively unimportant and ways might ultimately be found to save it. The Court rejected the invitation to "view the * * * Act' reasonably,' and hence shape a remedy that'accords with some modicum of common sense and the public weal.' " *Id.* at 194. . . .

[The court then discussed LIA's arguments that the Clean Air Act only allows regulation to remove health threats that are clearly determined]:

LIA's argument appears to touch on two issues. The first concerns the type of health effects on which the Administrator may base air quality standards, i.e., the point at which the Administrator's regulatory authority may be exercised. This issue, as LIA suggests, does concern the limits that the Act, and its legislative history, may place on the Administrator's authority. The second issue appears to be more in the nature of an evidentiary question: whether or not the evidence in the record substantiates the Administrator's claim that the health effects on which the standards were based do in fact satisfy the requirements of the Act. Although these two issues are closely related, they are conceptually distinct, and they are best examined separately.

Section 109(b) does not specify precisely what Congress had in mind when it directed the Administrator to prescribe air quality standards that are "requisite to protect the public health." The legislative history of the Act does, however, provide some guidance. The Senate Report explains that the goal of the air quality standards must be to ensure that the public is protected from "adverse health effects." S. Rep. No. 91-1196, *supra,* at 10. And the report is particularly careful to note that especially sensitive persons such as asthmatics and emphysematics are included within the group that must be protected. . . .

The Administrator begins by pointing out that the Act's stated goal is "to protect and enhance the quality of the Nation's air resources so as to promote the public health and welfare and the productive capacity of its [population.]" Section 101(b)(1), 42 U.S.C. § 7401(b)(1). This goal was reaffirmed in the 1977 Amendments. . . .

We agree that LIA's interpretation of the statute is at odds with Congress' directives to the Administrator. . . . It may be that it reflects LIA's view that the Administrator must show that there is a "medical consensus that [the effects on which the standards were based] are harmful * * *." If so, LIA is seriously mistaken. This court has previously noted that some uncertainty about the health effects of air pollution is inevitable. And we pointed out that "[awaiting] certainty will often allow for only reactive, not preventive [regulatory action]." *Ethyl Corp. v. EPA, supra,* 541 F.2d at 25. Congress apparently shares this view; it specifically directed the Administrator to allow an adequate margin of safety to protect against effects which have not yet been uncovered by research and effects whose medical significance is a matter of disagreement. . . .

Questions involving the environment are particularly prone to uncertainty. Technological man has altered his world in ways never before experienced or anticipated. The health effects of such alterations are often unknown, sometimes unknowable. While a concerned Congress has passed legislation providing for protection of the public health against gross environmental modifications, the regulators entrusted with the enforcement of such laws have not thereby been endowed with a prescience that removes all doubt from their decisionmaking. Rather, speculation, conflicts in evidence, and theoretical extrapolation typify their every action. How else can they act, given a mandate to protect the public health but only a slight or non-existent data base from which to draw? * * * Sometimes, of course, relatively certain proof of danger or harm from such modifications can readily be found. But, more commonly, "reasonable medical concerns" and theory long precede certainty. Yet the statutes — and common sense — demand regulatory action to prevent harm, even if the regulator is less than certain that harm is otherwise inevitable.

Undoubtedly, certainty is the scientific ideal — to the extent that even science can be certain of its truth. But certainty in the complexities of environmental medicine may be achievable only after the fact, when scientists have the opportunity for leisurely and isolated scrutiny of an entire mechanism. . . .

[The court then undertakes an extensive examination of the EPA's decisionmaking on this particular standard, both substantively and procedurally, and dismisses the contentions of petitioners.]

We have accorded these cases the most careful consideration, combining as we must careful scrutiny of the evidence in the record with deference to the Administrator's judgments. We conclude that in this rulemaking proceeding the Administrator complied with the substantive and procedural requirements of the Act, and that his decisions are both adequately explained and amply supported by evidence in the record. Accordingly, we reject petitioners' claims of error. The regulations under review herein are

Affirmed.

NOTES AND QUESTIONS

1. As we will see in the upcoming section, NAAQSs drive the stringency of emissions controls. Thus, as a general matter, (but subject to exceptions: *see, infra*), if the ambient air is loaded with, say, sulfur dioxide, polluters will have to cut back SO_2 emissions so that the ambient air will exhibit the mandated level of cleanliness. If the ambient air is relatively free of SO_2, on the other hand, polluters enjoy a free, or freer, ride.

2. *Lead Industries* comments that NAAQSs are "technology-forcing." What does this mean? Assume you are a member of a regulated industry in a SO_2-polluted AQCR and are under orders to reduce your emissions of sulfur dioxide by 85% from present levels. The vexing problem for you is plain: it can't be done. There is no pollution control technology in existence on the planet that can reduce emissions of SO_2 from your plant by the requisite percentage. The Clean Air Act, in short, is requiring you to do what is technologically impossible. Of course, it is not actually *impossible*; you could always just shut down. And, in fact, if you fail to clean up your emissions by the requisite 85% in the three or however many years you are granted, you will have to do just that. So, if you want to stay in business, you had better get about the task of inventing a pollution control technology. *That* is what technology-forcing means. Why did Congress do such a thing? The answer is twofold: in the view of Congress, the job had to be done, and industry would be able to advance the state of technology to get the job done. After all, the nation had just placed a man on the moon, so cleaning up air emissions should be a piece of cake.

Right?

Still, is there a constitutional question here? Are there grounds on which to challenge this scheme? If a plant actually had to shut down, would this be a taking?

3. The holding in *Lead Industries* that NAAQSs should be fashioned without regard to considerations of costs of implementation remained a matter of lingering dispute for over thirty years. It is no longer.

WHITMAN v. AMERICAN TRUCKING ASSN'S

531 U.S. 457, 121 S. Ct. 903 (2001)

JUSTICE SCALIA delivered the opinion of the Court.

. . . .

Section 109(b)(1) [of the Clean Air Act] instructs the EPA to set primary ambient air quality standards "the attainment and maintenance of which . . . are requisite to protect the public health" with "an adequate margin of safety."

42 U.S.C. § 7409(b)(1). Were it not for the hundreds of pages of briefing respondents have submitted on the issue, one would have thought it fairly clear that this text does not permit the EPA to consider costs in setting the standards. The language, as one scholar has noted, "is absolute." D. Currie, Air Pollution: Federal Law and Analysis 4-15 (1981). The EPA, "based on" the information about health effects contained in the technical "criteria" documents compiled under § 108(a)(2), 42 U.S.C. § 7408(a)(2), is to identify the maximum airborne concentration of a pollutant that the public health can tolerate, decrease the concentration to provide an "adequate" margin of safety, and set the standard at that level. Nowhere are the costs of achieving such a standard made part of that initial calculation.

Against this most natural of readings, respondents make a lengthy, spirited, but ultimately unsuccessful attack. They begin with the object of § 109(b)(1)'s focus, the "public health." When the term first appeared in federal clean air legislation — in the Act of July 14, 1955 (1955 Act), 69 Stat. 322, which expressed "recognition of the dangers to the public health" from air pollution — its ordinary meaning was "the health of the community." Webster's New International Dictionary 2005 (2d ed. 1950). Respondents argue, however, that § 109(b)(1), as added by the Clean Air Amendments of 1970 (1970 Act), 84 Stat. 1676, meant to use the term's secondary meaning: "the ways and means of conserving the health of the members of a community, as by preventive medicine, organized care of the sick, etc." *Ibid.* Words that can have more than one meaning are given content, however, by their surroundings, *FDA v. Brown & Williamson Tobacco Corp.*, 529 U.S. 120, 132–133, 146 L. Ed. 2d 121, 120 S. Ct. 1291 (2000); *Jones v. United States*, 527 U.S. 373, 389, 144 L. Ed. 2d 370, 119 S. Ct. 2090 (1999), and in the context of § 109(b)(1) this second definition makes no sense. Congress could not have meant to instruct the Administrator to set NAAQS at a level "requisite to protect" "the art and science dealing with the protection and improvement of community health." Webster's Third New International Dictionary 1836 (1981). We therefore revert to the primary definition of the term: the health of the public.

Even so, respondents argue, many more factors than air pollution affect public health. In particular, the economic cost of implementing a very stringent standard might produce health losses sufficient to offset the health gains achieved in cleaning the air — for example, by closing down whole industries and thereby impoverishing the workers and consumers dependent upon those industries. That is unquestionably true, and Congress was unquestionably aware of it. Thus, Congress had commissioned in the Air Quality Act of 1967 (1967 Act) "a detailed estimate of the cost of carrying out the provisions of this Act; a comprehensive study of the cost of program implementation by affected units of government; and a comprehensive study of the economic impact of air quality standards on the Nation's industries, communities, and other contributing sources of pollution." § 2, 81 Stat. 505. The 1970 Congress, armed with the results of this study, *see* The Cost of Clean Air, S. Doc. No. 91-40 (1969) (publishing the results of the study), not only anticipated that compliance costs could injure the public health, but provided for that precise exigency. . . . [The Court then proceeded to discuss CAA provisions which take economic considerations into account.] . . . We have therefore refused to find implicit in ambiguous sections of the CAA an authorization to consider costs that has elsewhere, and so often, been expressly granted. *See Union Elec. Co. v. EPA*, 427 U.S. 246, 257, 49 L. Ed. 2d 474, 96 S. Ct. 2518, and n. 5 (1976). *Cf. General Motors Corp. v. United States*, 496 U.S. 530, 538, 541, 110 L. Ed. 2d 480, 110 S. Ct. 2528 (1990) (refusing to infer in certain provisions of the CAA deadlines and enforcement limitations that had been expressly imposed elsewhere).

Accordingly, to prevail in their present challenge, respondents must show a textual commitment of authority to the EPA to consider costs in setting NAAQS under § 109(b)(1). And because § 109(b)(1) and the NAAQS for which it provides are the engine that drives nearly all of Title I of the CAA, 42 U.S.C. §§ 7401–7515, that textual commitment must be a clear one. Congress, we have held, does not alter the fundamental details of a regulatory scheme in vague terms or ancillary provisions — it does not, one might say, hide elephants in mouseholes. *See MCI Telecommunications Corp. v. American Telephone & Telegraph Co.*, 512 U.S. 218, 231, 129 L. Ed. 2d 182, 114 S. Ct. 2223 (1994); *FDA v. Brown & Williamson Tobacco Corp., supra*, at 159–160. Respondents' textual arguments ultimately founder upon this principle.

Their first claim is that § 109(b)(1)'s terms "adequate margin" and "requisite" leave room to pad health effects with cost concerns. Just as we found it "highly unlikely that Congress would leave the determination of whether an industry will be entirely, or even substantially, rate-regulated to agency discretion — and even more unlikely that it would achieve that through such a subtle device as permission to 'modify' rate-filing requirements," *MCI Telecommunications Corp. v. American Telephone & Telegraph Co., supra*, at 231, so also we find it implausible that Congress would give to the EPA through these modest words the power to determine whether implementation costs should moderate national air quality standards. . . .

The same defect inheres in respondents' next two arguments: that while the Administrator's judgment about what is requisite to protect the public health must be "based on [the] criteria" documents developed under § 108(a)(2), *see* § 109(b)(1), it need not be based *solely* on those criteria; and that those criteria themselves, while they must include "effects on public health or welfare which may be expected from the presence of such pollutant in the ambient air," are not necessarily *limited* to those effects. Even if we were to concede those premises, we still would not conclude that one of the unenumerated factors that the agency can consider in developing and applying the criteria is cost of implementation. That factor is *both* so indirectly related to public health *and* so full of potential for canceling the conclusions drawn from direct health effects that it would surely have been expressly mentioned in §§ 108 and 109 had Congress meant it to be considered. Yet while those provisions describe in detail how the health effects of pollutants in the ambient air are to be calculated and given effect, *see* § 108(a)(2), they say not a word about costs.

Respondents point, finally, to a number of provisions in the CAA that *do* require attainment cost data to be generated. Section 108(b)(1), for example, instructs the Administrator to "issue to the States," simultaneously with the criteria documents, "information on air pollution control techniques, which information shall include data relating to the cost of installation and operation." 42 U.S.C. § 7408(b)(1). And § 109(d)(2)(C)(iv) requires the Clean Air

Scientific Advisory Committee to "advise the Administrator of any adverse public health, welfare, social, economic, or energy effects which may result from various strategies for attainment and maintenance" of NAAQS. 42 U.S.C. § 7409(d)(2)(C)(iv). Respondents argue that these provisions make no sense unless costs are to be considered in setting the NAAQS. That is not so. These provisions enable the Administrator to assist the States in carrying out their statutory role as primary *implementers* of the NAAQS. It is to the States that the Act assigns initial and primary responsibility for deciding what emissions reductions will be required from which sources. *See* 42 U.S.C. §§ 7407(a), 7410 (giving States the duty of developing implementation plans). It would be impossible to perform that task intelligently without considering which abatement technologies are most efficient, and most economically feasible — which is why we have said that "the most important forum for consideration of claims of economic and technological infeasibility is before the state agency formulating the implementation plan," *Union Elec. Co. v. EPA*, 427 U.S. at 266. Thus, federal clean air legislation has, from the very beginning, directed federal agencies to develop and transmit implementation data, including cost data, to the States. *See* 1955 Act, § 2(b), 69 Stat. 322; Clean Air Act of 1963, amending §§ 3(a), (b) of the CAA, 77 Stat. 394; 1967 Act, §§ 103(a)–(d), 104, 107(c), 81 Stat. 486–488. That Congress chose to carry forward this research program to assist States in choosing the means through which they would implement the standards is perfectly sensible, and has no bearing upon whether cost considerations are to be taken into account in formulating the standards.

[Remainder of opinion omitted.]

NOTES

1. The holding of *American Trucking* applies to secondary NAAQSs as well as to primary NAAQSs. *Id.* at n3 (not reproduced in this text). *American Trucking* is significant as well for its resolution of a major separation of powers issue, whether the CAA's delegation of authority to EPA to set NAAQSs violates the nondelegation doctrine. The Court found no violation. *American Trucking* also resolved another issue involving implementation of the revised ozone NAAQS.

2. Ambient air quality standards are effective and enforceable upon promulgation. They may be challenged in court by filing a petition with the Circuit Court of Appeals of the District of Columbia. *See* § 307(b)(1), 42 U.S.C. § 7607(b)(1). As a factual matter, all promulgations of NAAQSs are challenged. Once an NAAQS has been judicially reviewed, if it has survived the review unscathed, it is, as a general matter, no longer available for challenge in later judicial proceedings for enforcement, even on grounds unraised in the review proceeding. *See* § 307(b)(2), 42 U.S.C. § 7607(b)(2).

3. Is the promulgation of an NAAQS a "major federal action significantly affecting the quality of the human environment" for purposes of the National Environmental Policy Act? *See* 15 U.S.C. § 793(c)(1) ("No action taken under the Clean Air Act shall be deemed a major Federal action significantly affecting the quality of the human environment within the meaning of the [NEPA]").

4. *Lead Industries* gives some indication of the daunting complexity of setting health-based standards: EPA must examine the adverse effects imposed on various groups of persons who come into contact with a variety of pollutants at differing exposure levels over varying periods of time. To do this, the agency must assemble a massive amount of scientific information, much of which will likely be internally conflicting. This is the risk assessment phase of standard-setting. Then, being careful to factor in a margin of safety, the agency must translate the data into a single numerical standard that supposedly represents an optimal condition of environmental quality for public health and welfare. This is the risk management phase of standard-setting. How well the agency undertakes both phases is, in reality, the grist of every lawsuit challenging an NAAQS. The following article, written by a two-time, former Administrator of the EPA, sheds some light on these considerations, and demonstrates as well why environmental lawyers, to be effective advocates, need to make themselves conversant with the science underlying environmental regulations.

WILLIAM D. RUCKELSHAUS, RISK, SCIENCE AND DEMOCRACY, Issues in Science and Technology 1(3) at 19–38 (Spring 1985)*

"Risk" is the key concept here. It was hardly mentioned in the early years of EPA, and it does not have an important place in the Clean Air or Clean Water Acts passed in that period. Of the events that contributed to this change, the most important were the focus of public attention on PCBs and asbestos (two substances that are ubiquitous in the American environment and that are capable of causing cancer) and the realization that exposure to a very large number of unfamiliar and largely untested chemicals is universal. The discovery by cancer epidemiologists that cancer rates vary with environment suggested that pollution might play a role in causing this disease. And finally, the cancer risk was pushed to the forefront by the emergence of abandoned dumps of toxic chemicals as a consuming public issue. As a direct result of this shift in attention, the relation of EPA to its science base was altered; the problem of uncertainty was moved from the periphery to the center.

This shift occurred because the risks of effects from typical environmental exposures to toxic substances — unlike the touchable, visible, and malodorous pollution that stimulated the initial environmental revolution — are largely constructs or projections based on scientific findings. We would know nothing at all about chronic risk attributable to most toxic substances if scientists had not detected and evaluated them. Our response to such risks, therefore, must be based on a set of scientific findings. Science, however, is hardly ever unambiguous or unanimous, especially when the data on which definitive science must be founded scarcely exist. The toxic effects on health of many of the chemicals EPA considers for regulation fall into this class.

"Risk assessment" is the device that government agencies such as EPA have adopted to deal with this quandary. It is the attempt to quantify the degree of hazard that might result from human activities — for example, the risks to human health and the environment from industrial chemicals. Essentially, it is a kind of pretense; to avoid the paralysis of protective action that would result from waiting for "definitive" data, we assume that we have greater knowledge than scientists actually possess and make decisions based on those assumptions.

Of course, not all risk assessment is on the controversial outer edge of science. We have been looking at the phenomenon of toxic risk from environmental levels of chemicals for a number of years, and as evidence has accumulated for certain chemicals, controversy has diminished and consensus among scientists has become easier to obtain. For other substances — and these are the ones that naturally figure most prominently in public debate — the data remain ambiguous.

In such cases, risk assessment is something of an intellectual orphan. Scientists are uncomfortable with it when the method must use scientific information in a way that is outside the normal constraints of science. They are encroaching on political judgments and they know it. As Alvin Weinberg has written:

> Attempts to deal with social problems through the procedures of science hang on the answers to questions that can be asked of science and yet which cannot be answered by science. I propose the term *trans-scientific* for these questions. . . . Scientists have no monopoly on wisdom where this kind of trans-science is involved; they shall have to accommodate the will of the public and its representatives.

However, the representatives of the public, in this instance policy officials in protective agencies, have their problems with risk assessment as well. The very act of quantifying risk tends to reify dreaded outcomes in the public mind and may make it more difficult to gain public acceptance for policy decisions or push those decisions in unwise directions. It is hard to describe, say, one cancer case in 70 years among a population of a million as an "acceptable risk" when such a description may too easily summon up for any individual the image of some close relative on his deathbed. Also, the use of risk assessment as a policy basis inevitably provokes endless arguments about the validity of the estimates, which can seriously disrupt the regulatory timetables such officials must live by.

Despite this uneasiness, there appears to be no substitute for risk assessment, in that some sort of risk finding is what tells us that there is any basis for regulatory action in the first place. The alternative to not performing risk assessment is to adopt a policy of either reducing all *potentially* toxic emissions to the greatest degree technology allows (of which more later) or banning all substances for which there is any evidence of harmful effect, a policy that no technological society could long survive. Beyond that, risk assessment is an irreplaceable tool for setting priorities among the tens of thousands of substances that could be subjects of control actions — substances that vary enormously in their apparent potential for causing disease. In my view, therefore, we must use and improve risk assessment with full recognition of its current shortcomings.

This accommodation would be much easier from a public policy viewpoint were it possible to establish for all pollutants the environmental levels that present zero risk. This is prevented, however, by an important limitation of the current technique; the difficulty of establishing definitive no-effect levels for exposure to most carcinogens. Consequently, whenever there is any exposure to such substances, there is a calculable risk of disease. The environmentalist ethos, which is reflected in many of our environmental laws, and which requires that zero-risk levels of pollutant exposure be established, is thus shown to be an impossible goal for an industrial society, as long as we retain the no-threshold model for carcinogenesis. . . .

This situation has given rise to two conflicting viewpoints on protection. The first, usually proffered by the regulated community, argues that regulation ought not to be based on a set of unprovable assumptions but only on connections between pollutants and health effects that can be demonstrated under the canons of science in the strict sense. It points out that for the vast majority of chemical species, we have no evidence at all that suggests effects on human health from exposures at environmental levels. Because many important risk assessments are based on assumptions that are scientifically untestable, the method is too susceptible to manipulation for political ends and, the regulated community contends, it has been so manipulated by environmentalists.

The second viewpoint, which has been adopted by some environmentalists, counters that waiting for firm evidence of human health effects amounts to using the nation's people as guinea pigs, and that is morally unacceptable. It proposes that far from overestimating the risks from toxic substances, conventional risk assessments underestimate them, for there may be effects from chemicals in combination that are greater than would be expected from the sum effects of all chemicals acting independently. While approving of risk assessment as a priority-setting tool, this viewpoint rejects the idea that we can use risk assessment to distinguish between "significant" and "insignificant" risks. Any identifiable risk ought to be eliminated up to the capacity of available technology to do so.

It is impossible to evaluate the merits of these positions without first drawing a distinction between the assessment of risk and the process of deciding what to do about it, which is "risk management." The arguments in the form sketched here are really directed at both these processes, a common confusion that has long stood in the way of sensible policymaking.

Risk assessment is an exercise that combines available data on a substance's potency in causing adverse health effects with information about likely human exposure, and through the use of plausible assumptions, it generates an estimate of human health risk. Risk management is the process by which a protective agency decides what action to take in the face of such estimates. Ideally the action is based on such factors as the goals of public health and environmental protection, relevant legislation, legal precedent, and application of social, economic, and political values. *Risk Assessment in the Federal Government*, a National Research Council (NRC) document, recommends that regulatory agencies establish a strict distinction between the two processes, to allay any confusion between them. In my view Congress should do the same in all statutes seeking to deal with risk.

Returning now to the opposing viewpoints we see that both reflect the fear that risk assessment may be imbued with values repugnant to one or more of the parties involved. That is, some people in the regulated community believe that the structure of risk assessment inherently exaggerates risk, while many environmentalists believe that it will not capture all the risk that may actually exist. As we have seen, this disagreement is not resolvable in the short run through recourse to science. Risk assessment is necessarily dependent on choices made among a host of assumptions, and these choices will inevitably be affected by the values of the choosers, whether they be scientists, civil servants, or politicians.

The NRC report suggests that this problem can be substantially alleviated by the establishment of formal public rules guiding the necessary inferences and assumptions. These rules should be based on the best available information concerning the underlying scientific mechanisms. Adoption of such guidelines reduces the possibility that an EPA administrator may manipulate the findings of some risk assessment so as to avoid making the difficult, and perhaps politically unpopular, choices involved in a risk-management decision. Both industry and environmentalists fear this manipulation — from different brands of administrator, needless to say. Although we cannot remove values from risk assessment, we can and should keep those values from shifting arbitrarily with the political winds.

The explicit and open codification suggested by the NRC will also ensure that the assumptions used in risk assessment will at least be uniform among all agencies that adopt them, will be plausible scientifically, and will reflect a predictable and relatively constant policy amid this complex and chaotic hybrid discipline. It also offers the possibility that one day all the protective agencies of the government will speak with one voice when they address risks, so that estimates of risk will be comparable among agencies and the public at last will be able to make a fair comparison of the individual risk-management decisions of separate agencies.

The remaining points of both positions are really about risk management and on this issue both are flawed. At its extreme, the first position — that regulation should be based solely on scientifically provable connections between pollutants and health effects — would allow the release of unlimited quantities of substances that cause cancer in animals, on the assumption that there will be no analogous effect on people and that there must be thresholds for carcinogenesis. I expect that most Americans would reject that assumption as imprudent, given our current knowledge about carcinogenesis (for example, the similarity of cancer causing genes across species). At some level we have to regard the possibility that we are controlling somewhat in excess of the true risk as a kind of insurance, with the cost of control as its premium. The effort to reduce apprehension, even so-called unreasonable apprehension, about the future results of current practices is a valid social function. Risk-management agencies such as EPA could be chartered to do precisely that. If so, we had better make clear what we are doing, and establish rules for doing it.

The weakness of the second viewpoint, that any identifiable risk ought to be eliminated up to the capacity of available technology to do so, lies in the concept of a best available technology that must invariably be applied where risk is discovered. "Best" and "available" are terms as infinitely debatable as the assumptions of risk assessment. There is always a technology conceivable that is an improvement on a previous one, and as the last increments of pollution are removed, the cost of each successive fix goes up very steeply. Because, according to the no-threshold assumption, even minute quantities of carcinogens can be projected out to cause cases of disease, arguments about technology reduce in the end to arguments about risk and cost: technology A allows a residual risk of 10^{-5} and costs $1 million; technology B allows a residual risk of 10^{-6} and costs $10 million, and so on ad infinitum. It is specious to pretend that costs do not matter, because it is always possible to show that a certain level of removal, costs in fact do matter: technology Z allows residual risks of 10^{-15} and costs $1 trillion.

Once this is admitted, as it almost always is when we come down to debating actual regulations, the position is reduced to arguments about affordability. This too is treacherous ground. Firms vary in their ability to pay, and what is affordable for one may bankrupt another. If requirements are adjusted so as not to cripple the poorest firms, the policy amounts to an environmental subsidy to the less efficient players in our economy. . . .

My point is that in confronting any risk there is no way to escape the question "Is controlling it worth it?" We must ask this question not only in terms of the relationship of the risk reduced and the cost to the economy but also as it applies to the resources of the agency involved. Policy attention is the most precious commodity in government, and a regulation that marginally protects only 20 people may take up as much attention as a regulation that surely protects a million.

"Is it worth it?" That this question must be asked and asked carefully is a token of how the main force of the environmental idea has been modified by the recent focus on toxic risk to human health. In truth this question should always have been asked, but because the early goals of environmentalism were so obviously good, the requirement to ask, "Is it worth it?" was not firmly built into all our environmental laws. Who would dare to question the worth of saving Lake Erie? Environmentalism at its inception was a grand vision, one that nearly all Americans willingly shared. Somehow that vision of the essential unity of nature and of the need for bringing industrial society into harmony with it has been lost among the parts per billion, and with it we have lost the capacity to reach social consensus on environmental policy.

[b] EMISSIONS LIMITATIONS

Once generally applicable ambient standards are in place under §§ 108-109 of the Clean Air Act, the task becomes to affix specific emissions limits on pollution sources. Compliance with these "source standards," in turn, should result in improvement of overall air quality to levels stipulated by the NAAQSs.

In an arrangement known as "cooperative federalism," the Clean Air Act allocates to states the task of fashioning emissions limitations and requiring compliance with them, subject to EPA's approval. Section 110 of the Act explains how this is accomplished. The section calls for states to prepare plans for meeting the NAAQSs, which plans are known as state implementation plans, or "SIPs." SIPs are submitted to EPA. Upon receipt of a SIP, EPA must ultimately approve or disapprove it, in whole or in part. § 110(a)(3); 42 U.S.C. § 7410(a)(3); § 110(k) 42 U.S.C. § 7410(k); 40 C.F.R. Part 52. Once approved, a SIP becomes the framework for achieving the NAAQS for which it was prepared. SIPs have elaborate content requirements. *See* § 110(a)(2) 42 U.S.C. § 7410(a)(2); 40 C.F.R. Part 51.

The United States Supreme Court declared early on that states enjoy substantial discretion in fashioning source standards within their SIPs:

> The Agency is plainly charged by the Act with the responsibility for setting the national ambient air standards. Just as plainly, however, it is relegated by the Act to a secondary role in the process of determining and enforcing the specific, source-by-source emission limitations which are necessary if the national standards it has set are to be met. Under § 110(a)(2), the Agency is required to approve a state plan which provides for the timely attainment and subsequent maintenance of ambient air standards, and which also satisfies that section's other general requirements. The Act gives the Agency no authority to question the wisdom of a State's choices of emission limitations if they are part of a plan which satisfies the standards of § 110(a)(2), and the Agency may devise and promulgate a specific plan of its own only if a State fails to submit an implementation plan which satisfies those standards. § 110(c). Thus, so long as the ultimate effect of a State's choice of emission limitations is compliance with the national standards for ambient air, the State is at liberty to adopt whatever mix of emission limitations it deems best suited to its particular situation.

Train v. Natural Resources Defense Council, Inc., 421 U.S. 60, 78, 95 S. Ct. 1470, 1481 (1975).

Not only are states authorized to choose the most suitable "mix of emission limitations," but the EPA is constrained to approve SIPs even if it believes the selected emission limitations are economically or technologically infeasible. *See Union Electric Co. v. EPA*, 427 U.S. 246, 256, 96 S. Ct. 2518, 2525 (1976) ("Congress intended claims of economic and technological infeasibility to be wholly foreign to the Administrator's consideration of a state implementation plan."). The same broad discretion afforded to states with respect to initial SIP preparations extends to SIP revisions as well. States may revise SIPs as they wish. EPA must approve SIP revisions for them to be effective. So long as a proposed revision will not interfere with the attainment of the relevant NAAQS, EPA is constrained to do so.

On some occasions, SIP revisions are prompted by individual polluters seeking variances or exceptions from the state. When a polluter seeks a variance, it does so on its own time:

> [A] polluter is subject to existing requirements [in a SIP] until such time as he obtains a variance, and variances are not available under

the revision authority until they have been approved by both the State and the Environmental Protection Agency. Should either entity determine that granting the variance would prevent attainment or maintenance of national air standards, the polluter is presumably within his rights in seeking judicial review. This litigation, however, is carried out on the polluter's time, not the public's, for during its pendency the original regulations remain in effect, and the polluter's failure to comply may subject him to a variety of enforcement procedures.

Train v. NRDC, 421 U.S. 60, 92, 95 S. Ct. 1470, 1488 (1975).

On other occasions, however, it is EPA that wants SIPs to be revised. Typically, EPA requires SIP revisions when the NAAQS for which a SIP is in place has itself been revised. In such instances, EPA will issue what is known as a "SIP call," in effect telling states that changes in their SIPs are necessary. *See, e.g., Michigan v. EPA*, 213 F.3d 663 (D.C. Cir. 1999) (evaluating an EPA SIP Call to 22 northeastern states to reduce NOx emissions). Sometimes EPA will issue a SIP call to upwind states because their air emissions are contributing to air quality problems in downwind states, a condition known as "transboundary air pollution." The EPA has express authority to do this under § 110(a)(2)(D)(i)(I), 42 U.S.C. § 7410(a)(2)(D)(i)(I). When it exercises this authority, states are bound to make the necessary changes in their SIPs for the benefit of downwind states.

In addition to the SIP call mechanism, downwind states may petition EPA to *directly* regulate stationary sources to stop transboundary air pollution. § 126, 42 U.S.C. § 7426. After granting a § 126 petition, EPA will promulgate a rule to provide the requisite relief for downwind states. *See, e.g., Appalachian Power Co. v. U.S. Environmental Protection Agency*, 249 F.3d 1032 (D.C. Cir. 2001) (upholding an EPA rule setting limits on NOx emissions for nearly 400 electric power plants in twelve midwestern and southern states and the District of Columbia for the benefit of eight downwind states).

Failure to comply with SIP requirements exposes sources to potentially serious state-law-based penalties and injunctive actions. Industry remains unhappy with this latter fact. It has long maintained that perfect compliance with emission limitations is impossible because of numerous variables, human and technological, that inevitably bear on the industrial process. Even the best run plants, industry asserts, will experience malfunctions on occasion, especially during start-up and shutdown operations. Since these are unavoidable, the argument continues, the regulatory regime should accommodate by forgiving penalties otherwise to be assessed. And the accommodation should be in the form of a formal exoneration from prosecution.

EPA disagrees with these contentions. First, it claims a lack of legal authority to approve any SIP that features a formal exemption from liability because doing so might interfere with attainment of NAAQSs. Beyond that, as a general matter at least, EPA views industrial malfunction events as foreseeable. As such, malfunctions "may be addressed in the underlying standards themselves through narrowly-tailored SIP revisions that take into account the potential impacts on ambient air quality caused by the inclusion of these allowances." Better yet, in EPA's view, leave the matter to prudent exercise of enforcement discretion. *See* Memorandum of U.S. Environmental

Protection Agency, *State Implementation Plans (SIPs): Policy Regarding Excess Emission During Malfunctions, Startup, and Shutdown* (undated).

Despite these views, EPA has agreed that states may place in SIPs a provision affording industry an affirmative defense in limited circumstances. The restrictions are three: first, no affirmative defense can undermine attainment (thus, there can be no defense made available to an industry that can single-handedly cause a NAAQS exceedance. This is often the case with lead and SO_2 emitters); second, no affirmative defense can preclude injunctive relief; and third, no affirmative defense can impede either EPA or citizen enforcement (as distinct from state enforcement). *Id.*

What recourse exists if a state refuses to prepare a SIP? As a matter of federal constitutional law, is the federal government empowered to compel states to prepare an acceptable SIP? *See, e.g., New York v. United States*, in Chapter 3, *supra*. If the federal government cannot compel states to comply, what can it do? *See* CAA § 110(c), 42 U.S.C. § 7410(c) (welcome to the world of "FIPs"). Does EPA have any role to play if a person violates a state SIP, or if a state refuses to enforce its own SIP provisions? *See* CAA § 113(a)(1)-(2) 42 U.S.C. § 7413(a)(1)-(2).

Are states the only entities with responsibilities under § 110? What of Indian tribes? (Welcome to the world of "TIPs.") Section 301(d) of the Act, 42 U.S.C. § 7601(d), authorizes the EPA to treat Indian tribes as states. Section 110(o), 42 U.S.C. § 7410(o), in turn, allows for the submission of tribal implementation plans, which upon EPA approval apply to all areas "located within the exterior boundaries of the reservation. . . ." EPA regulations allow for these plans to govern emission limitations on tribal reservations, including fee interests held by nonmembers of the governing tribe. The regulations also allow Indian regulation beyond the boundaries of reservation lands, to include Indian trust lands and pueblos. *See* 63 Fed. Reg. 7254 (1998), *codified at* 40 C.F.R. Parts 9, 35, 49, 50, and 81 (Tribal Authority Rule). The regulations produced this latter result by defining "reservation" to include "trust lands that have been validly set apart for the use of a tribe even though the land has not been formally designated as a reservation." 63 Fed. Reg. at 7258. EPA's regulations were upheld on judicial review. *Arizona Public Service Co. v. Environmental Protection Agency*, 211 F.3d 1280 (D.C. Cir. 2000).

NOTES AND QUESTIONS

One way to clean the ambient air is to disperse air pollutants over a greater area. Dispersal of this sort can be accomplished by building extremely tall smokestacks. Pollutants released at higher elevations typically spread out and travel farther before settling to the ground and, therefore, tend to contribute less heavily to local pollution loadings. Is dilution the solution to pollution? *See* CAA § 123, 42 U.S.C. § 7423.

Another way to clean ambient air is by using intermittent controls. Intermittent controls reduce air pollution concentrations by restricting emissions during times when pollution levels are high, and allowing more loading during times when air quality is better. Such intermittent controls are most easily accomplished by switching to less polluting fuels during bad times, and to other fuels in good times. Are these methods of pollution control consonant with the Clean Air Act? *See, e.g., Kennecott Copper v. Train*, 526 F.2d 1149 (9th Cir. 1975). *See also* § 123, 42 U.S.C. § 7423.

Using SIPs, can states regulate air emissions from federally owned and operated facilities? *See* CAA § 118, 42 U.S.C. § 7418.

[2] NEW SOURCE PERFORMANCE STANDARDS

[a] APPLICABILITY

We have now reviewed the regulatory centerpiece of the Clean Air Act, the control of criteria pollutants by health-based NAAQSs, themselves primarily implemented through the vehicle of SIPs. We now turn to the second pollution control mechanism established in the 1970 Clean Air Act Amendments. Entitled "New Source Performance Standards" and found at § 111, 42 U.S.C. § 7411, the provision (as revised in some particulars in 1990) establishes performance requirements primarily for "new" sources. To understand how § 111 does this, it is best to begin by looking at the statutory text. As you do so, there are numerous questions you should resolve. Among them are: (a) to which entities and facilities does § 111 apply? (b) what are "new sources"? and (c) does § 111 also apply to existing as well as new sources, and if so, how?

POTOMAC ELECTRIC POWER CO. v. U.S. ENVIRONMENTAL PROTECTION AGENCY

650 F.2d 509 (4th Cir. 1981)

PHILLIPS, Circuit Judge:

The Potomac Electric Power Company (PEPCO) has petitioned this court, pursuant to § 307(b)(1) of the Clean Air Act, 42 U.S.C. § 7607(b)(1), for review of a decision of the Environmental Protection Agency (EPA), through one of its regional administrators, finding that the boiler at PEPCO's Chalk Point Unit #4 electric generating station is subject to the new source performance standard (NSPS), *see* 40 C.F.R. § 60.40 et seq., promulgated by the EPA for fossil fuel-fired steam generating units under the Clean Air Act, 42 U.S.C. § 7401 et seq. The regional administrator's decision was based on his determination that PEPCO had not "commenced construction" of the Chalk Point Unit #4 boiler prior to EPA's publication of the relevant NSPS on August 17, 1971.

Two questions are presented by PEPCO's petition for review of the regional administrator's decision. First, is the EPA's interpretation of the regulations it has promulgated for determining whether an NSPS is to be applied to a particular facility "plainly erroneous"? Second, was the regional administrator's decision, on application of the EPA's regulations and interpretation of those regulations to the facts of this case, arbitrary, capricious or an abuse of discretion? Answering both questions in the negative, we affirm the decision of the regional administrator that PEPCO's Chalk Point Unit #4 must comply with the NSPS promulgated for fossil fuel-fired steam generators. . . .

[The court began by denying PEPCO's request for an injunction. PEPCO argued EPA had wrongfully withheld action in denying PEPCO's NSPS exemption request. The court found PEPCO lacked clean hands]:

. . . [E]ven if this court were to recognize PEPCO's potential right to relief, we believe PEPCO would be estopped from asserting any prejudice resulting from the EPA's delay in acting on its request for an NSPS exemption by its own lengthy delay in requesting that exemption. Although PEPCO began construction on its Chalk Point Unit #4 facility in late 1971, it did not ask for a ruling on the applicability of the NSPS to that facility, which PEPCO admittedly had the burden of requesting, 40 C.F.R. § 60.5(a), until 1977. PEPCO suggests that it only discovered the possibility of the NSPS' applicability to this facility two months prior to its request for a ruling. In view of the fact that several other utilities had long before requested rulings in this precise matter, we think that this major utility must be charged with at least constructive notice at a much earlier time, saving any question of actual notice.

I

Because the decision of the EPA concerning the applicability of an NSPS to a particular facility turns largely upon the facts of each case, a brief review of the facts underlying PEPCO's present petition for review is essential for an understanding of our disposition of this appeal. Chalk Point Units #3 and #4 are two of the four electric generating facilities that collectively comprise PEPCO's Chalk Point Generating Station south of Aguasco, Maryland. At the core of each unit is an oil-fired boiler designed to generate steam to power a turbine that produces electricity. The two units share several ancillary facilities, including a common water treatment system, fuel oil tank farm and control room, and a single building houses the boilers and turbines for both units. Units #3 and #4 were planned in the late 1960s as a single procurement and were to be placed in service "back to back" in 1974 and 1975. A sudden and unprecedented decline in electricity use following the Arab Oil Embargo of 1973, however, caused construction of both units to be slowed after their commencement. Unit #3 was placed in service in 1975; Unit #4 is scheduled to go into operation in the fall of 1981.

The information that PEPCO later submitted to the EPA indicates that negotiations for the construction of Unit #4 were commenced in 1970 and that PEPCO was dealing primarily with General Electric (GE), United Engineers & Constructors (UE&C) and Combustion Engineering (CE). PEPCO's negotiations with GE were for the main turbine-generator and boiler feed pump turbines. On March 12, 1971, PEPCO awarded the order to GE subject to the final approval of PEPCO's board of directors and mutually agreeable contract terms. On March 25, 1971, GE confirmed the order but stipulated that PEPCO could cancel the order without charge up to the earlier of the 30-month period prior to shipment or the release of the units for engineering and manufacturing. On June 30, 1971, PEPCO notified GE of approval of the order by its board of directors. On August 2, 1971, the units were released by GE for design and manufacture. A formal contract for the units, however, was not signed until April 23, 1973.

PEPCO's negotiations with UE&C were for engineering and construction services at the Chalk Point site. The contract for these services was signed on November 12, 1974 but had an "effective date" of April 12, 1971. This contract covered services for both Units #3 and #4. Prior to August 17, 1971, UE&C had developed drawings that indicated the planned construction of Unit #4. Site preparation for Unit #4, however, did not begin until late 1971.

PEPCO's negotiations with CE were for fabrication of the boiler to be used in Unit #4. On August 17, 1970, PEPCO received a price quotation from CE on a boiler unit for an undetermined facility; that boiler was eventually used in Unit #4. A CE "Parts Shipment Forecast" dated February 18, 1971 listed this unit for initial parts shipment during the first quarter of 1973. The unit was listed as a "Forecast Unit" that was identified by an internal control number as contrasted to listing as a "Booked Unit" identified by a domestic contract number.

On March 11, 1971, CE stated in a letter to PEPCO that it had committed space in its production schedule for the Unit #4 boiler pending a final decision by PEPCO. Also included in the letter were a price quotation and a projected delivery date. On July 12, 1971, PEPCO sent a letter to CE stating that "we are now considering a design for proposed Chalk Point No. 4." This letter concluded with the statement that, "[s]ubject to a mutually satisfactory contract, it is our intent to award the No. 4 boiler unit to you." This letter also referred to a meeting between PEPCO and CE to be held on August 3, 1971 to review a design proposal for Unit #4.

Although a CE engineering and production team began to design the Unit #4 boiler after CE's August 3 meeting with PEPCO, no subcontracts were let or materials acquired prior to August 17, 1971. On October 26, 1971, CE prepared a "Contract Abstract" for Unit #4 that included descriptions of the major boiler components, the total price, shipping and payment conditions, and an "award date" of July 12, 1971.

A formal contract for the Unit #4 boiler was not executed until April 18, 1973, at which time fabrication of the boiler was 75% complete. Affidavits later sworn to by PEPCO's Vice President for Nuclear Engineering and Environmental Affairs and CE's principal representative in the boiler negotiations, however, indicate that the parties felt that they had a binding agreement based on PEPCO's letter of July 12, 1971.

Construction of Chalk Point Unit #4, although slowed or "deferred" as a result of the 1973 oil embargo, has continued substantially uninterrupted to the present day. It was not until May 20, 1977, however, that PEPCO, pursuant to 40 C.F.R. § 60.5(a), requested a ruling from the EPA on whether Unit #4 would be subject to the NSPS for fossil fuel-fired steam generating units published by the EPA on August 17, 1971. Appended to this request were 156 pages of pertinent documents.

Fifteen months after receiving PEPCO's request, EPA communicated its first response to PEPCO — a request for further information. This request, dated August 17, 1978, stated that the EPA had "preliminarily determined" that Unit #4 was subject to the 1971 NSPS for steam electric plants but requested additional information to determine the "exact status" of the unit.

The reasons given for the EPA's preliminary determination were that construction of Unit #4 had been neither continuous nor of reasonable length, as required by 40 C.F.R. § 60.2(i). PEPCO supplied the requested information and urged that the EPA make its decision "just as quickly as possible."

At a meeting requested by PEPCO that took place on July 3, 1979, the EPA informed PEPCO for the first time that its ruling would turn on the question whether a "contractual obligation" to construct the Unit #4 boiler existed before August 17, 1971. Following PEPCO's compliance with two more EPA requests for information, the EPA staff briefed the regional administrator in October 1979 and again in March 1980. His final ruling on PEPCO's Chalk Point Unit #4 request was published on March 27, 1980. 45 Fed. Reg. 20,155 (1980). In this ruling the regional administrator determined that, because PEPCO had not entered into a "contractual obligation" on the Unit #4 boiler — the "affected facility" in the present case — PEPCO had not "commenced construction" at its Chalk Point Unit #4 prior to the EPA's publication of the NSPS for steam electric plants on August 17, 1971. He therefore concluded that the NSPS for steam electric plants was applicable to Unit #4.

II

Before addressing the specific issues raised by this appeal, a brief discussion of the regulatory scheme out of which they arise is essential. Section 111 of the Clean Air Act, 42 U.S.C. § 7411, requires that the EPA promulgate new source performance standards (NSPS), reflecting the best demonstrated pollution control technology, for application to any new stationary source, "the construction or modification of which is commenced after the publication of [the NSPS] applicable to such source." The only statutory guidance that the EPA is given in promulgating the NSPS, however, is the definition of "stationary source" in § 111(a)(3) of the Clean Air Act, 42 U.S.C. § 7411(a)(3), as "any building, structure, facility, or installation which emits or may emit any air pollutant."

Based on this loosely defined statutory authorization, the EPA has promulgated a detailed regulatory scheme establishing and implementing the NSPS. See 40 C.F.R. Part 60. Included in this regulatory scheme is a subpart dealing with the procedural applications of the NSPS that are established in other subparts, see id. Subpart A, which is applicable "to the owner or operator of any stationary source which contains an affected facility, the construction or modification of which is commenced after the date of publication in this part of any standard applicable to that facility." Id. § 60.1. The term "affected facility" is defined as "any apparatus to which a standard is applicable." Id. § 60.2(e). The word "construction" is defined as the "fabrication, erection, or installation of an affected facility." Id. § 60.2(g). The word "commenced" is defined to require a showing "that an owner or operator has entered into a contractual obligation to undertake and complete, within a reasonable time, a continuous program of construction or modification." Id. § 60.2(i).*

---

* [Ed. note: The full definition of "commenced" in EPA's regulations is "that an owner or operator has undertaken a continuous program of construction or modification or that an owner or operator has entered into a contractual obligation to undertake and complete, within a reasonable time, a continuous program of construction or modification." 40 C.F.R. § 60.2.]

Based on its interpretation of the regulations it has promulgated pursuant to the authorization of § 111 of the Clean Air Act, 42 U.S.C. § 7411, the EPA has contended that PEPCO's Chalk Point Unit #4 is subject to the NSPS for steam electric plants because PEPCO was unable to establish that, prior to the EPA's publication of the applicable NSPS on August 17, 1971, it had entered into a "contractual obligation" for "construction" of its Unit #4 boiler — which the EPA contends is the "affected facility" — so that PEPCO could not cancel that obligation without incurring "significant liability," either because an agreed upon cancellation fee had come into operation or because the manufacturer of the facility had made expenditures in reliance upon an agreement for construction of the facility. PEPCO, on the other hand, has contended that, under well-settled principles of contract law, it had entered into a "contractual obligation" for the construction of Chalk Point Unit #4 generating station, based either on its contract with UE&C to construct the entire Unit #4 generating station — which PEPCO contends is the "affected facility" — or on its contract with CE to construct the boiler that is to be used in that generating station.

We note at the outset that some of PEPCO's contentions may be read as challenging not only the EPA's interpretation of its regulations but also the regulations themselves. To the extent that the regulations themselves are challenged, the challenge is untimely and in the wrong court; section 307(b) of the Clean Air Act, 42 U.S.C. § 7607(b), requires that challenges to EPA regulations of nationwide applicability be brought within 60 days of promulgation in the United States Court of Appeals for the District of Columbia Circuit. Since the procedural regulations governing application of the NSPS that are now under consideration were promulgated by the EPA on December 23, 1971, see 36 Fed. Reg. 24,876 (1971), any challenge to those regulations could only have been brought in the District of Columbia Circuit on or before February 23, 1972. This court therefore has jurisdiction to review only the EPA's interpretation of those regulations, and the scope of that review is limited to whether the EPA's interpretation is plainly erroneous. See Udall v. Tallman, 380 U.S. 1, 16–17 (1965); Talley v. Mathews, 550 F.2d 911, 919 (4th Cir. 1977).

A.

With respect to whether a "contractual obligation" was entered into for Unit #4 prior to publication of the applicable NSPS, PEPCO has argued persuasively that it had entered binding contracts with UE&C and CE prior to August 17, 1971 or, at the very least, it was liable to those companies on a theory of promissory estoppel. However, while principles of contract law undoubtedly would have been reasonable standards by which to determine the existence of a "contractual obligation" for purposes of 40 C.F.R. § 60.2(i), the fact remains that contract law principles are not the standards that were chosen by the EPA for that purpose. Therefore, we must restrict our analysis in the present case to whether the "significant liability" test contended for by EPA is a plainly erroneous interpretation of "contractual obligation."

The EPA has presented two cogent policy reasons for the use of its "significant liability" standard. The first policy argument is based on the congressional goal in § 111 of the Clean Air Act, 42 U.S.C. § 7401, of ensuring the best demonstrated system of pollution control in new sources of air pollution without requiring costly retrofitting of existing sources of pollution. *See* H.R. Rep. No. 95-294, 95th Cong., 1st Sess. 184–86 (1977). The EPA interpretation of "contractual obligation" effectuates this goal by requiring a commitment to construction of a polluting facility that cannot be entered into simply for purposes of avoiding the NSPS requirements while leaving the polluting company the option of cancelling or postponing the commitment with the incursion of little or no liability. Stated another way, the EPA's interpretation effectively requires the incorporation of new pollution control technology by all those who can do so without incurring "significant liability" as a result of the cancellation of a previous commitment.

The second policy reason asserted by EPA is essentially one of administrative convenience. The requirement of significant liability, based on either a cancellation fee or expenditures made in reliance on a construction contract by the contractor for a polluting facility, provides bright-line documentation by which the EPA may quickly and easily determine whether an applicant for exemption from NSPS has incurred a "contractual obligation" meriting that exemption.This interpretation thus avoids the often convoluted application of contract principles to masses of business correspondence that would be the result under PEPCO's interpretation.

Support for this argument is amply supplied by PEPCO's contention in the present case that it is "common practice" in the utility industry for a utility to use a "letter of intent" to signify the award of a "binding contract" to a contractor for the construction of an electric generating facility and that PEPCO's "award letter" of July 12, 1971 to CE was such a letter of intent. For the EPA to find a "contractual obligation" on the basis of this contention, however, would require the EPA to gather evidence of the purported usage of trade in the utility industry and to then determine whether the "award letter" of July 12, 1971, or possibly some other piece of documentation submitted by PEPCO, comported with this "common practice." When this type of inquiry is multiplied by the number of different industries in which the NSPS regulations must be applied, the EPA's argument of administrative convenience is transformed into one bordering on administrative necessity.

PEPCO has argued that these policy considerations should be rejected as post hoc reasoning. This argument, however, is undercut by the EPA's consistent determination in three earlier decisions that utilities that fail to meet the requirements of the "significant liability" test will not be exempted from NSPS. . . .

Judicial support for the EPA's present interpretation can be found in *United States v. City of Painesville*, 431 F. Supp. 496 (N.D. Ohio 1977), *aff'd*, No. 78-3551 (6th Cir., March 26, 1981), in which the court upheld an NSPS applicability ruling by the EPA that is consistent with the "significant liability" standard. In Painesville a municipal utility had executed a letter of intent with one boiler manufacturer in 1970, but it changed the design of the boiler to be fabricated and, on July 28, 1972, executed a contract with a second boiler manufacturer for construction of the redesigned boiler. *Id.* at 498. The EPA argued that the commencement of construction of the "affected facility" dated from either the execution of a formal contract with the boiler manufacturer or the progression of construction at the building site to the point that a change in design would have required the facility already erected to be modified in order to comply with the relevant NSPS. Id. at 500. Adopting EPA's definition of "commencement" as a reasonable interpretation of the NSPS applicability regulations that was in keeping with the intent of Congress in enacting § 111 of the Clean Air Act, the district court found that "construction" of the new power plant had not "commenced" prior to August 17, 1971 because neither of the specified events had occurred prior to that time. Id. at 500–01. While the *Painesville* court admittedly did not construe the phrase "contractual obligation," it must be remembered that that phrase is found in the definition of "commenced" in 40 C.F.R.§ 60.2(i) and that a finding of a "contractual obligation" must therefore be thought of as nothing more than a means of making the ultimate determination of whether "construction" has "commenced."

Based on the persuasive policy justifications presented by the EPA and that agency's consistent application of the "significant liability" standard, which has been upheld by other courts, we conclude that the EPA's requirement of "significant liability" to demonstrate a "contractual obligation" sufficient to exempt a pollution source from compliance with the relevant NSPS is not a plainly erroneous interpretation of 40 C.F.R. § 60.2(i).

B.

A similar analysis can be applied to the EPA's conclusion that a power plant's boiler is the "affected facility" for which a "contractual obligation" had to exist for exemption in the present case. PEPCO contends that this interpretation is unreasonable and that the only reasonable interpretation is that "affected facility" refers to an entire electric generating facility and not just its boiler. The EPA's interpretation, however, is supported by a number of considerations.

First, EPA's interpretation comports with a tracing of the relevant regulations. "Affected facility" is equated in 40 C.F.R. § 60.2(e) with "any apparatus to which a standard is applicable." With respect to a steam electric plant, the "affected facility" to which the NSPS is applicable is "each fossil fuel-fired steam electric generating unit." Id. § 60.40(a)(1). "Fossil fuel-fired steam generating unit" is in turn defined as a "furnace or boiler." Id. § 60.41(a). Thus, the definition of "affected facility" as a "boiler" seems compelled by a reading of the pertinent regulations. . . .

. . . [P]erhaps most persuasively, the EPA's requirement for exemption of a "contractual obligation" for construction of the "boiler" as the "affected facility" is supported by common sense. PEPCO contends that the EPA can base its exemption determination only on construction of a "functional entity" and that, therefore, the EPA should find an exemption if there was a "contractual obligation" for any portion of PEPCO's Chalk Point Unit #4, including its turbine generator and the equipment and buildings it shares with Unit #3, that is essential to its ultimate operation as a power plant. Such a construction, however, would create a means of avoidance of the NSPS that we do not believe Congress possibly could have intended. Through the simple expedient of planning generating units in tandem and providing for their use of some common equipment or facilities — a practice that utility companies seem to follow often — a utility could obtain exemption of both units from the NSPS even though it actually "commenced construction" of only one unit prior to publication of the relevant NSPS and the best demonstrated technology could be incorporated into the second unit at little or no retrofitting cost. Such a two-for-one exemption is obviously absurd, but it is the logical result of PEPCO's interpretation of the unit for which a "contractual obligation" must be incurred in order to qualify for an exemption.

We therefore conclude that it is not plainly erroneous for the EPA, in making its exemption determination, to focus on a power plant's boiler as the "affected facility" for which a "contractual obligation" had to exist prior to publication of the relevant NSPS.

C.

[In this section of the opinion, the court commented on the relevance of § 111 to "construction" of equipment in place to support an "affected facility." The court held that construction of support facilities essential to the erection and installation of the affected facility is "construction" for purposes of the section. The opinion concluded with a discussion of whether the EPA's refusal to exempt PEPCO from § 111 applicability was arbitrary, capricious, or an abuse of discretion. The court upheld EPA's action.]

AFFIRMED AS MODIFIED.

NOTE

Observe that the standards of § 111 apply to sources that have been modified. *See* § 111(a)(2), 42 U.S.C. § 7411(a)(2) (defining "new source" to include "any stationary source, the construction or *modification* of which is commenced after the publication of regulations . . ." (emphasis added)); *see also*, § 111(a)(4), 42 U.S.C. § 7411(a)(4) (defining "modification"). As you would expect, there has been substantial litigation about what changes in a source constitute "modification" so to bring the source under § 111. Our discussion of this critical issue is postponed until coverage of the PSD program, *infra*.

[b] OPERATION

Once issues of applicability are resolved, issues of operation arise. How does the provision affect new sources? In particular, who must fashion emission standards under this section and upon what basis? How does this process compare with that of §§ 107–110 of the Act?

LIGNITE ENERGY COUNCIL v. U.S. ENVIRONMENTAL PROTECTION AGENCY

198 F.3d 930 (D.C. Cir. 1999)

JUDGES: Before: EDWARDS, Chief Judge, SILBERMAN and HENDERSON, Circuit Judges.

OPINION: Per Curiam:

Petitioners challenge EPA's new source performance standards for nitrogen oxides emissions from utility and industrial boilers. We conclude that EPA did not exceed its discretion under section 111 of the Clean Air Act in promulgating these standards, and therefore deny the petitions.

Fossil-fuel fired steam generating units ("boilers") emit nitrogen oxides (NOx), air pollutants that can cause deleterious health effects and contribute to the formation of acid rain. Section 111 of the Clean Air Act requires EPA to establish performance standards for the emission of NOx from newly constructed boilers; these "new source performance standards" are to be set at a level that reflects the degree of emission limitation achievable through the application of the best system of emission reduction which (taking into account the cost of achieving such reduction and any nonair quality health and environmental impact and energy requirements) the Administrator determines has been adequately demonstrated. 42 U.S.C. § 7411(a)(1). In its 1990 Clean Air Act Amendments Congress specifically directed EPA to exercise its section 111 authority and establish new NOx standards that incorporate "improvements in methods for the reduction of emissions of oxides of nitrogen." 42 U.S.C. § 7651f(c)(1).

In response to these statutory mandates, EPA promulgated a rule lowering its NOx new source performance standards to .15 lb/MMBtu (pounds of NOx emitted per million BTU burned) for utility boilers and .20 lb/MMBtu for industrial boilers. See 63 Fed. Reg. 49,442, 49,443 (1998) (to be codified at 40 C.F.R. pt. 60). These standards reflect the level of NOx emissions achievable by what EPA considers to be the "best demonstrated system" of emissions reduction: the use of selective catalytic reduction (SCR) in combination with combustion control technologies. Petitioners' central claim is that EPA selected SCR as the basis for its NOx standards without properly balancing the factors that section 111 requires it to "take into account." Because section 111 does not set forth the weight that be should assigned to each of these factors, we have granted the agency a great degree of discretion in balancing them, see, e.g., New York v. Reilly, 297 U.S. App. D.C. 147, 969 F.2d 1147, 1150 (D.C. Cir. 1992); EPA's choice will be sustained unless the environmental or economic costs of using the technology are exorbitant. See National Asphalt Pavement Ass'n v. Train, 176 U.S. App. D.C. 296, 539 F.2d 775, 786 (D.C. Cir. 1976).

Petitioners argue that SCR is not the "best demonstrated system" under section 111 because the incremental cost of reducing NOx emissions is considerably higher with SCR than with combustion controls. Recent improvements in combustion controls will enable many boilers to attain emissions levels close to EPA's SCR-based standards; accordingly, petitioners assert that EPA should have based its standards on these less expensive technologies. However, in light of EPA's unchallenged findings showing that the new standards will only modestly increase the cost of producing electricity in newly constructed boilers, *see* 62 Fed. Reg. 36,948, 36,958 (1997) (proposed NOx revisions), we do not think that EPA exceeded its considerable discretion under section 111. Moreover, petitioners' argument stressing the comparable environmental merits of advanced combustion controls is to a certain extent self-defeating, since the new source performance standards set by EPA are not technology-forcing, and continuing advances in combustion control technologies will reduce the amount of NOx reduction that must be captured by the more expensive SCR technology.

It was also within EPA's discretion to issue uniform standards for all utility boilers, rather than adhering to its past practice of setting a range of standards based on boiler and fuel type. *See, e.g.,* 44 Fed. Reg. 33,580 (1979) (establishing varying NOx emissions standards for utility boilers). Petitioners recognize that EPA is not required by law to subcategorize — section 111 merely states that "the Administrator may distinguish among classes, types, and sizes within categories of new sources," 42 U.S.C. § 7411(b)(2) (emphasis added) — but argue that it was arbitrary and capricious for EPA to decline to do so. EPA explains that its change to uniform standards is justified by SCR's performance characteristics: Unlike the technologies on which past new source performance standards were based, flue gas treatment technologies like SCR limit NOx emissions after combustion, and the effectiveness of SCR is thus far less dependent upon boiler design or fuel type. Petitioners respond that there are reasons to expect SCR to perform less adequately on boilers burning high-sulfur coals, but EPA collected continuous emissions monitoring data on two high-sulfur coal-fired utility boilers that showed that the .15 lb/ MMBtu standard was achievable, and supplemented this study with similar evidence from foreign utility boilers. EPA also considered petitioners' concerns about the impact of alkaline metals on the performance of the catalyst used in the SCR process, and concluded that such "catalyst poisoning" is not a significant problem in coal-fired boilers. *See* 63 Fed. Reg. at 49,445. Mindful of the high degree of deference we must show to EPA's scientific judgment, *see, e.g., Appalachian Power Co. v. EPA,* 328 U.S. App. D.C. 379, 135 F.3d 791, 801–02 (D.C. Cir. 1998), we accept these determinations and sustain EPA's uniform standard for utility boilers.

Petitioners offer a broader challenge to EPA's .20 lb/ MMBtu standard for industrial boilers, claiming that SCR is not "adequately demonstrated" for any coal-fired industrial boilers. EPA was unable to collect emissions data for the application of SCR to these boilers, but this absence of data is not surprising for a new technology like SCR, nor does it in and of itself defeat EPA's standard. Because it applies only to new sources, we have recognized that section 111 "looks toward what may fairly be projected for the regulated future, rather than the state of the art at present." *Portland Cement Ass'n v. Ruckelshaus,* 158 U.S. App. D.C. 308, 486 F.2d 375, 391 (D.C. Cir. 1973). Of course, where data are unavailable, EPA may not base its determination that a technology is adequately demonstrated or that a standard is achievable on mere speculation or conjecture, *see, e.g., National Asphalt Pavement Ass'n,* 539 F.2d at 787, but EPA may compensate for a shortage of data through the use of other qualitative methods, including the reasonable extrapolation of a technology's performance in other industries. *See, e.g., Weyerhaeuser Co. v. Costle,* 191 U.S. App. D.C. 309, 590 F.2d 1011, 1054 n.70 (D.C. Cir. 1978).

EPA has done precisely that here, concluding from its study of utility boilers that SCR is "adequately demonstrated" and the .20 lb/MMBtu standard is "achievable" for coal-fired industrial boilers as well. Utility and industrial boilers are similar in design and both categories of boilers can attain similar levels of NOx emissions reduction through combustion controls, which means that SCR will be required to capture comparable quantities of NOx for both boiler types. While petitioners argue that SCR is less likely to be effective on industrial boilers because they have widely fluctuating load cycles, EPA has shown that SCR can be successfully applied to coal-fired utility boilers under a "wide range of operating conditions" including those analogous to the load cycles of industrial boilers. 63 Fed. Reg. at 49,444. We think that it was reasonable for EPA to extrapolate from its studies of utility boilers in setting an SCR-based new source performance standard for coal-fired industrial boilers.

We also sustain EPA's application of the .20 lb/MMBtu standard to combination boilers, which simultaneously combust a mixture of fuels. The preexisting NOx emissions standards established a range of values for combustion boilers that varied by fuel type: while combination boilers burning natural gas with non-coal solid fuels (e.g., wood) were subject to a .30 lb/MMBtu standard, the performance standards for combination boilers combusting coal with oil or natural gas were determined based upon the proportion of the boiler's total heat input provided by each fuel. *See* 51 Fed. Reg. 42,768, 42,790 (1986). It is difficult to understand petitioners' objection to the application of the industrial boiler standard to boilers burning natural gas and wood. A reduction of that standard from .30 to .20 lb/MMBtu is perfectly reasonable in light of the significant advances in NOx emissions technology since 1986; indeed, EPA studies show that wood-fired boilers can reach emissions levels far lower than .20 lb/MMBtu through the application of flue gas treatment technologies. And our conclusion that the .20 lb/MMBtu standard is achievable for boilers burning only coal necessarily defeats petitioners' objection that the industrial boiler standard is unreasonable as applied to combination boilers burning coal simultaneously with other fuels with lower NOx emissions characteristics.

Petitioners' final objection is to EPA's valuation of steam energy produced by "cogeneration facilities." EPA's adoption of an output-based standard for utility boilers raised the question of how to calculate the energy produced by these units, which generate thermal steam energy in addition to electrical energy. Steam energy produced by cogeneration facilities is exported for several different industrial uses; however, because of inefficiencies in transporting and converting steam, only a fraction of steam energy produced by cogeneration facilities is actually used in the industrial process. EPA resolved this problem by assigning a 50% credit for steam energy when determining a cogeneration unit's output. *See* 63 Fed. Reg. at 49,447. Petitioners describe this credit as an arbitrary and capricious "discounting" of steam energy's value, but it just as easily could be called a subsidy: The maximum efficiency for the conversion of steam to electrical energy is only 38%, and EPA's final rule justifies the 50% credit on the ground that it will encourage cogeneration. Id. In light of the difficulties that would attend calculating the useful energy of steam heat produced by cogeneration facilities on a unit-by-unit basis, we conclude that EPA's resolution of this issue was acceptable.

The petitions for review are denied.

So ordered.

NOTES AND QUESTIONS

1. Section 111 stipulates that new sources shall meet emission limitations reflecting "the degree of emission reduction achievable through the application of the best system of continuous emission reduction which (taking into consideration the cost of achieving such emissions reduction, any nonair quality health and environmental impact and energy requirements) the Administrator determines has been adequately demonstrated [for the category of sources subject to the limitation]." § 111(a)(1), 42 U.S.C. § 7411(a)(1). For short, this standard has been referred as the "best demonstrated technology" or "BDT" standard, *New York v. Reilly*, 969 F.2d 1147 (D.C. Cir. 1992). BDT, it should be clear, is not a health-based standard like those governing establishment of NAAQSs. It is, rather, technology-based. You might give some thought to the use of "tech-based" standards generically. A raft of questions arises. Are tech-based standards a better approach to pollution control than health-based standards? What are their advantages and disadvantages? If you were administering a pollution control program, would you prefer a tech-based or a health-based regulatory system?

2. In the view of some observers, the NSPS program is proof of the adage, attributed to Fred Emery, that "regulation is the substitution of error for chance." The obvious goal underlying § 111 was to insure that plants coming on line be state-of-the-art when it comes to pollution controls. It was thought § 111 would usher in a shiny new generation of efficient and clean industrial facilities. But in significant measure, that has not happened. Instead, many industrial entities, in order to avoid the high costs of compliance with § 111 (and with other CAA programs such as nonattainment and PSD; *see, infra*), have chosen to string out the operating lives of their old, leaky plants.

[3] HAZARDOUS AIR POLLUTANTS

Commonly referred to as air toxics or toxic air pollutants, hazardous air pollutants are substances known or suspected to cause cancer or other serious adverse effects. Air toxics are emitted from thousands of sources, including major stationary sources, mobile sources, and smaller "area sources," such as dry cleaners. Major stationary sources are responsible for approximately 61% of total air toxics emissions, mobile sources for 21%, and area sources for 18%. *http://www.epa.gov/oar*. Section 112 of the Clean Air Act, 42 U.S.C. § 7412, addresses hazardous air pollutants. As originally enacted in 1970, its purpose was to provide emission standards for pollutants "which in trace quantities in the ambient air contribute to a high risk of serious irreversible or incapacitating effects on health." Continuing Senate Debate on S. 4358, 93rd Cong.

(1970) (statement of Senator Jennings Randolph, Chairman, Committee on Public Works). The provision defined a hazardous pollutant as any "air pollutant to which no ambient air quality standard is applicable and which in the judgment of the Administrator causes, or contributes to, air pollution which may be reasonably be anticipated to result in an increase in mortality or an increase in serious irreversible, or incapacitating reversible, illness." § 112(a)(1), 42 U.S.C. § 7412(a)(1) (1982). It called upon EPA to designate a list of pollutants meeting the statutory definition, and to develop "national emission standards for hazardous air pollutants" ("NESHAPS") on a pollutant-by-pollutant basis. Congress directed that each such standard be set at a level assuring "an ample margin of safety to protect the public health." § 112(b)(1)(B), 42 U.S.C. § 7412(b)(1)(B) (1982).

For two decades following § 112's enactment, EPA dragged its feet in implementing the provision. The reasons were several. One was EPA's belief that much of the hazardous air pollution problem would be solved by the new source performance standards of § 111. Another, more important, reason was § 112 itself. For one thing, Congress gave EPA little guidance on the meaning of "ample margin of safety." Thus the agency was forced to face the vexing problem of so-called "nonthreshold" pollutants. As distinguished from "threshold" pollutants, nonthreshold pollutants are those for which science has determined no safe minimal level of exposure. EPA reasoned that only a zero emissions standard for nonthreshold pollutants would satisfy § 112.[3] Congress contemplated this severe standard because it thought the number of hazardous pollutants would be small. (By latest count, the number of hazardous pollutants designated for purposes of § 112 is 188. *See infra.*) Understandably, EPA was extremely hesitant to set air toxics standards certain to cause catastrophic effects in major sectors of the domestic economy. Simply put, it wanted to take costs into account.[4] Industry agreed with that sentiment: one industry trade group, the Chemical Manufacturers Association, for example, characterized zero-emission standards as arbitrary, unenforceable, and inequitable, as well as impossible to meet or measure.

In any event, by 1990, EPA had designated as hazardous air pollutants only eight substances. These were asbestos, benzene, beryllium, coke oven emissions, inorganic arsenic, mercury, radionuclides, and vinyl chloride. 40 C.F.R. § 61.01(a). (It had, however, considered others for potential listing. *See* 40 C.F.R. § 61.01(b)).

---

[3] There was some legislative history supporting this result. Senator Edmund Muskie, for example, had characterized the health-based standard of § 112 as meaning "that a plant would be required to close because of the absence of control techniques. It could include emission standards which allowed for no measurable emissions." Summary of Conference Report presented to the U.S. Senate, *reprinted in* A Legislative History of the Clean Air Act of 1970, Ser. No. 93-18, 93d Cong. 2d. Sess., at 133 (1974).

[4] On some occasions it did precisely that. For the nonthreshold hazardous pollutant, asbestos, for example, EPA refused to establish a zero emissions standard, because, in its view, such a standard "would result in the prohibition of many activities which are extremely important; moreover, the available evidence relating the health hazards of asbestos does not suggest that such prohibition is necessary to protect public health." 38 Fed. Reg. 8820 (4/6/73). In the case of vinyl chloride, the agency hit the issue head-on, stating it did not believe Congress wanted the agency to close major industries. Accordingly, the agency set a NESHAP for vinyl chloride based on best available control technology, unless costs would be "grossly disproportionate" to benefits derived therefrom. 40 Fed. Reg. 59534 (12/24/75).

Due to § 112's unworkability and EPA's poor record of implementation, Congress rewrote the provision in the 1990 Clean Air Act Amendments. The new legislation was designed to lighten the agency's burdens, in part by setting aside the health-based regulatory approach in favor of a rigorous technology-based approach. We take up § 112 in its current form later in the Chapter.

C. THE 1977 AMENDMENTS

Congress understood as it engaged the enterprise of air pollution regulation that it was embarking on a grand experiment. It was obvious the Clean Air Act would work revolutionary changes in the way industry does business, would transform the way the public viewed the environment, and, most importantly, would demand an extensive national commitment by government, the scientific community, the regulated community, and the public at large. Therefore, Congress committed itself to review its handiwork five years hence, to see what had gone right or wrong. When the time came to do so, the august body was displeased with what it saw. In many places, especially in urban areas, air quality still remained unhealthful, and in some areas had even worsened. In addition, in another manifestation of the law of unintended consequences, the Act was having a deleterious effect on historically clean air basins. Some of these areas were being degraded down to the level of the ambient standards because industries, acting in their economic self-interest, were moving operations out of dirty air areas into clean air areas. In not insignificant measure, pollution was being spread around rather than being removed, a phenomenon referred to as the "greying of America."

Congress, still imbued with a sense of mission but mindful of weakness in the domestic economy at the time, moved to correct these problems. After a couple of years of wrangling and debate, the result was the 1977 Amendments. The 1977 Amendments added two major parts to the statute. Part D, entitled "Nonattainment," was installed for the purpose of cleaning "nonattainment areas," those air basins not in compliance with NAAQSs. Part C, entitled "Prevention of Significant Deterioration" ("PSD"), was installed for the purpose of arresting the deterioration of air basins having air quality already in compliance with, or better than, the NAAQSs. These new Parts, as we shall see, have changed the structure and reality of air quality regulation, most significantly by affixing rigorous emissions controls on major new sources. For that reason, regulatory efforts under both Parts C and D are referred to collectively as "new source review" ("NSR"). NSR has been the major regulatory focus under the Clean Air Act since its inception, and there is every indication it will remain EPA's main emphasis. We look at each of these statutory subparts in the next sections.

[1] NONATTAINMENT

Sections 171-179B, 42 U.S.C. §§ 7501-09B, of the Act are the major operative provisions governing the nonattainment program. A very careful reading of these provisions is in order, for it is the only way to appreciate the complexity and the mechanics of this program. As you examine the new provisions, you will come to understand how significant the new legislation really was.

The Amendments largely recast the focus of the federal air pollution control effort. First, with NSR, the regulatory emphasis shifted to new, "major" polluters. The brunt of air pollution control was made to fall on these entities because of Congress's belief that large polluters cause the most damage to air resources and are financially best able to clean up emissions. Second, the Amendments represented a significant movement toward tech-based controls.

The Amendments also altered the relationship between the federal government and the states. Since the Amendments became law, states have enjoyed less of a free hand in determining the contents of their SIPs. If the 1970 Act "took a stick to the states," the 1977 Amendments took a two-by-four.

The first task under Part D is to determine which areas are nonattainment for a criteria pollutant. Assuming an area is designated as a nonattainment area, the second question is to determine its appropriate classification within the nonattainment regulatory regime (a determination made necessary by the 1990 Amendments; *see* Part D, [1], *infra*). After that, the states must submit SIPs demonstrating how the host of new emission restrictions that come with designation will be implemented.

SIERRA CLUB v. ENVIRONMENTAL PROTECTION AGENCY

356 F.3d 296 (D.C. Cir. 2004)

JUDGES: Before: SENTELLE, HENDERSON, and GARLAND, Circuit Judges.

GARLAND, Circuit Judge:

In these consolidated cases, Sierra Club challenges two final actions of the Environmental Protection Agency (EPA) regarding ozone control plans for the Washington, D.C. area. Those plans were designed to bring the area into compliance with ozone standards prescribed by the Clean Air Act and EPA regulations. Sierra Club contends that EPA violated the Act by giving conditional approval to the plans notwithstanding that they lacked required statutory elements. Sierra Club also challenges the substance of two elements that were included in the plans, as well as EPA's extension of the deadlines by which revised plans must be submitted for final approval.

We agree with Sierra Club's principal contention that EPA was not authorized to grant conditional approval to plans that did nothing more than promise to do tomorrow what the Act requires today. We therefore vacate the conditional approval and remand the matter to EPA for further action consistent with this opinion. In other respects we deny the petions for review.

I.

The Clean Air Act (CAA), 42 U.S.C. § 7401 et seq., directs EPA to establish National Ambient Air Quality Standards (NAAQS) that set maximum permissible concentration levels for air pollutants that endanger the public health and welfare. 42 U.S.C. §§ 7408, 7409. Pursuant to that direction, the agency has adopted NAAQS for ozone. 40 C.F.R. § 50.9. Under the Act, EPA designates areas of the country as "attainment" or "nonattainment" (or as "unclassifiable") based on whether they comply with the ozone NAAQS. 42 U.S.C. § 7407(d). Nonattainment areas are further classified as "marginal," "moderate," "serious," "severe," or "extreme," depending upon the severity and duration of their noncompliance. *Id.* § 7511(a). The Act establishes air quality planning and control requirements that increase in stringency as the classification increases in severity. *See id.* § 7511a. It also establishes deadlines for attainment of the NAAQS depending upon an area's nonattainment classification. *Id.* §§ 7410, 7502, 7511 (a). If an area fails to attain the NAAQS by the applicable deadline, EPA must reclassify it to a higher classification. *Id.* § 7511 (b)(2). Generally, reclassification grants the area a later attainment deadline, but requires it to comply with the more stringent pollution control measures applicable to the higher classification. *Id.* § 7511(a)(1), (b)(2); *id.* § 7511a.

The Act also prescribes the process by which areas must arrive at and maintain compliance with the NAAQS. Each state must adopt and submit for approval to EPA a state implementation plan (SIP) that provides for "implementation, maintenance, and enforcement" of applicable NAAQS in each air quality region (or portion thereof) within the state. *Id.* § 7410(a)(1). In addition to the general SIP requirements, states in ozone nonattainment areas must submit SIPs meeting additional requirements that depend upon the severity of the ozone problem. *Id.* §§ 7502, 7511a. Each SIP must contain an "attainment demonstration" that shows that the area will achieve the NAAQS by the area's statutory attainment deadline. *Id.* § 7511a(c)(2)(A); 40 C.F.R. § 51.112. The attainment demonstration is based on the state's control strategy for ozone-precursor emissions, which must "include" enforceable emissions limitations, and such other control measures . . . as may be necessary or appropriate to provide for attainment of such standard in such area by the applicable attainment date. 42 U.S.C. § 7502(c)(6).

Particularly relevant for this case, SIPs from states in nonattainment areas must also: (1) provide for "the implementation of all reasonably available control measures [RACM] as expeditiously as practicable," id. § 7502(c)(1); and, for serious and severe areas; (2) contain a rate of progress (ROP) plan that demonstrates an average reduction of baseline emissions of 3% per year for each consecutive three-year period commencing in 1996 until the attainment deadline for the classification area, *id.* § 7511a(c)(2)(B), (d); and (3) "provide for the implementation of specific [contingency] measures to be undertaken if the area fails" to meet any ROP milestone or to attain the NAAQS by the statutory deadline, *id.* §§ 7502(c)(9), 7511a(c)(9) & (d).

The Washington D.C. Metropolitan Area ("D.C.") is made up of the District of Columbia and several Maryland and Virginia counties. Pursuant to the Clean Air Act, EPA classified the D.C. area as a "serious" nonattainment area for ozone in 1991. Designation of Areas for Air Quality Planning Purposes, Final Rule, 56 Fed. Reg. 56,694, 56,738, 56,772, 56,841 (Nov. 6, 1991). The statutory deadline for ozone attainment by serious areas was November 15, 1999, and revised SIPs including the attainment demonstration and ROP plans were due by November 15, 1994. 42 U.S.C. §§ 7511(a)(1), 7511a(c)(2).

Maryland, Virginia, and the District of Columbia ("the States") did not submit their attainment demonstration and other plan provisions for the D.C.

area until 1997-1998; they amended and supplemented those submissions during 1998-2000. *See* Approval and Promulgation of Air Quality Implementation Plans, Final Rule, 66 Fed. Reg. 586 (Jan. 3, 2001). Those SIPs lacked the three statutory elements noted above: (1) the RACM analysis; (2) ROP plans for post-1999 emissions reductions; and (3) contingency measures. *Id.* at 603, 608, 615. Moreover, the SIPs did not demonstrate that the area would reach attainment by the statutory deadline of November 15, 1999. *Id.* at 630-31. Instead, the States asked EPA to extend the attainment deadline by six years to November 15, 2005, without reclassifying the area as "severe" as the Act would otherwise have required. *Id.* at 586. On January 3, 2001, EPA fully approved the SIPs and granted the States' requests to extend the attainment deadline without reclassifying the D.C. area. *Id.* at 603, 608, 605, 630-31.

Sierra Club petitioned this court for review, contending (inter alia) that EPA could not approve the SIPs without the missing statutory elements, and that it had no authority to extend the statutory attainment deadline without reclassifying the area as severe. We agreed, vacated EPA's approval of the SIPs, and remanded the matter to the agency. *Sierra Club v. EPA*, 352 U.S. App. D.C. 357, 294 F.3d 155, 160-65 (D.C. Cir. 2002) [*Sierra Club I*]. On November 13, 2002, Sierra Club filed a new action in the U.S. District Court for the District of Columbia, seeking an injunction to compel EPA to reclassify the D.C. area as severe and to take final action either approving or disapproving the previously submitted SIPs. The district court granted those requests and ordered EPA: (1) by January 27, 2003, to determine whether the D.C. area had attained the NAAQS for ozone by the applicable attainment date of November 15, 1999, and, if not, to reclassify the area; and (2) by April 17, 2003, to approve or disapprove the SIP submittals that had been remanded in *Sierra Club I*. *Sierra Club v. Whitman*, No. 02-2235 (D.D.C. Dec. 18, 2002).

On January 24, 2003, in a decision known as the "bump-up" action, EPA determined that the D.C. area had not attained the NAAQS for serious ozone nonattainment areas by the statutory deadline and therefore reclassified the area as severe. Determination of Nonattainment as of November 15, 1999 and Reclassification of the Metropolitan Washington, D.C. Ozone Nonattainment Area, Final Rule, 68 Fed. Reg. 3410 (Jan. 24, 2003) [herein *Reclassification*]. A statutory consequence of the reclassification was the extension of the ozone attainment deadline to "as expeditiously as possible but no later than" November 15, 2005. 42 U.S.C. § 7511(a)(1). At the same time, EPA extended until March 1, 2004 the deadline for submitting revised SIPs to comply with the requirements for severe nonattainment areas. *Reclassification*, 68 Fed. Reg. at 3410.

In a second decision issued on April 17, 2003, the so-called "conditional approval" action, EPA granted conditional approval to the existing SIPs, notwithstanding the absence of the three elements that *Sierra Club I* had identified as precluding final approval. Approval and Promulgation of Air Quality Implementation Plans, Final Rule, 68 Fed. Reg. 19,106, 19,107 (Apr. 17, 2003) [hereinafter Conditional Approval]. The agency based its conditional approval on letters submitted by the States that committed to cure those deficiencies and to comply with the additional requirements of the severe area classification by April 17, 2004. *Id.* at 19,131-33. The agency also made determinations regarding, inter alia, two elements that were contained in the existing SIPs: it concluded that the attainment demonstration showed that implementation of already adopted control measures would result in attainment of the ozone NAAQS by the statutory deadline, and it conditionally approved the States' ROP plans for 1996-1999.

Sierra Club now petitions for review of both actions pursuant to the jurisdictional grant of 42 U.S.C. § 7607(b)(1). . . .

II.

We begin with Sierra Club's primary challenge: its contention that EPA violated the Clean Air Act by conditionally approving the concededly deficient D.C. area SIPs on the basis of the States' commitment letters. EPA's response is that conditional approval was authorized by CAA § 110(k)(4), which provides:

> (4) Conditional approval
>
> The administrator may approve a plan revision based on a *commitment of the State to adopt specific enforceable measures* by a date certain, but not later than 1 year after the date of approval of the plan revision. Any such conditional approval shall be treated as a disapproval if the State fails to comply with such commitment.

42 U.S.C. § 7410(k)(4) (emphasis added). . . . We conclude that EPA's construction of the conditional approval provision is contrary to Congress' unambiguous intent, and we therefore reject it.

EPA acknowledges that the SIPs did not contain a number of the elements required for full approval. Indeed, it concedes that the SIPs were missing the same three features that led this court to vacate EPA's full approval in *Sierra Club I*: . . . As the agency further concedes, the plans were also missing the additional elements required for severe nonattainment areas, including specific enforceable measures to offset growth in vehicle emissions and reasonably available control technology for additional major sources. Conditional Approval, 68 Fed. Reg. at 19, 106-07; *see* 42 U.S.C. § 7511a(d).

Notwithstanding these deficiencies, EPA argues that the SIPs qualified for conditional approval — rather than disapproval — because they contained other required elements (including the attainment demonstration and control strategy), and because the States submitted letters committing to remedy the deficiencies within one year, by April 17, 2004. But while the States did file commitment letters, those letters identified no "specific enforceable measures" of any kind. Maryland's commitment regarding contingency measures and RACM is typical of the States' submissions, and reads in full:

> *We also commit to submit to EPA, not later than April 17, 2004, adopted contingency measures* to be implemented if the D.C. area does not attain the one-hour ozone NAAQS by November 15, 2005. *Additionally, by April 17, 2004, we commit to submitting* to EPA an appropriate RACM analysis for the D.C. Area, along with any revisions to the attainment demonstration SIP necessitated by such analysis, including *adopted measures* to demonstrate timely attainment and *to meet RACM requirements, should there be any.*

Letter from Md. Dep't of Env't to EPA 2 (Apr. 7, 2003) (J.A. at 784) (emphasis added); *see also* Letter from D.C. Dep't of Health to EPA 2 (Apr. 7, 2003) (J.A. at 791); Letter from Va. Dep't of Env't Quality to EPA 2 (Apr. 8, 2003) (J.A. at 798).

EPA does not dispute that the States' letters failed to identify specific measures that the States committed to adopt. Indeed, EPA argues that the States do not yet know what those measures will be because they have not yet completed the necessary analyses. . . . EPA's contention is that all that the States need do to qualify for conditional approval is to *commit to adopt* specific enforceable measures by a date certain; they do not need to tell EPA what those measures are — or even know what they are. Oral Arg. Tr. at 35. . . .

EPA's interpretation cannot be squared with the unambiguous statutory language. The statute requires that the States commit to adopt *specific* enforceable measures. Here, the agency has accepted as sufficient a commitment to adopt what it concedes are *unspecified* measures — with the specifics to be named later. Moreover, the statute requires a commitment to *adopt* specific enforceable measures by a date certain. Here, not only are the measures unspecified, but the States have committed to adopt them only "*if* such measures are determined to be needed based on further analysis." Conditional Approval, 68 Fed. Reg. at 19,109 (emphasis added); *see id.* ("The States have clarified in [their] letters their intent to submit specific measures in support of the demonstrations, *if appropriate*.") (emphasis added). Section 110(k)(4), however, contains no such qualifier.

This is not the first time that EPA has defended a construction of § 110(k)(4) that we have found plainly inconsistent with the statute. . . .

. . . EPA's conditional approval purports to grant the States an additional year to adopt such measures — without specifying what they will be. In short, as EPA conceded at oral argument, the agency's position is that it may grant conditional approval on nothing more than the States' promise to do next year what the Clean Air Act requires them to have already done. Oral Arg. Tr. at 34-35. And that amounts to nothing more than the use of § 110(k)(4) "to postpone SIP deadlines," a power that the section does not confer. *NRDC*, 22 F.3d at 1135.

III.

In the previous Part, we considered Sierra Club's attack on EPA's conditional approval action insofar as it was based on mere promises to adopt SIP elements in the future. In this Part, we consider petitioner's attacks on the substance of two elements that the States did submit as part of their SIPs.

A

The Clean Air Act requires that each SIP contain an attainment demonstration showing that the area will achieve the ozone NAAQS by the statutory deadline. 42 U.S.C. § 7511a(c). After reclassification as a severe nonattainment area, the D.C. area's outside attainment deadline became November 15, 2005. *Id.* § 7511(a)(1). In the conditional approval action, EPA determined that the States had demonstrated that the D.C. area would in fact meet the

NAAQS by that date. Sierra Club contends that EPA should not have approved the States' attainment demonstration, because it was inconsistent with statutory requirements.

Under CAA § 182(c)(2)(A), each state in a serious or severe nonattainment area must submit a SIP that includes:

> A demonstration that the plan, as revised, will provide for attainment of the ozone national ambient air quality standard by the applicable attainment date. This attainment demonstration *must be based on photochemical grid modeling* or any other analytical method determined by the Administrator, in the Administrator's discretion, to be at least as effective.

42 U.S.C. § 7511a(c)(2)(A) (emphasis added). Sierra Club argues that, in this case, the States' attainment demonstration was insufficient because it was neither "based on photochemical grid modeling," nor based on "any other analytical method that the Administrator had determined . . . to be at least as effective." EPA defends solely on the first ground: that the attainment demonstration was in fact "based on" photochemical grid modeling.

A photochemical grid model is a mathematical model that predicts ozone levels on the attainment date based on monitoring data, meteorology, planned emission reductions, the area's projected growth, and other factors. *BCCA Appeal Group v. EPA,* 348 F.3d 93, 106 n.12 (5th Cir. 2003). Both parties agree that the States' demonstration began with a photochemical grid model known as the Urban Airshed Model (UAM). The model was used to predict ozone levels in 2005 by assuming implementation of the control strategy adopted in the SIPs and extrapolating from data collected on three high-ozone summer days in 1991: July 16, 19, and 20. Both parties also agree that use of the model alone showed peak ozone concentrations exceeding the NAAQS on those three days in 2005; the model indicated that on those days the area's SIPs would result in daily one-hour maximum ozone levels of 139, 150, and 178 parts per billion (ppb) — all in excess of the 120 ppb NAAQS for ozone. EPA, First Amendment to Technical Support Document for Approval and Promulgation of Air Quality Implementation Plans 5 (Table IV G-1) (Apr. 10, 2003) (J.A. at 808) [hereinafter Amendment to Technical Support Document].

EPA did not, however, conclude its analysis with these exceedances. Rather, it adjusted the model's extrapolations in light of the agency's concerns about the model's reliability and uncertainty. In particular, the agency noted that, when it applied the model to the three days in the base year (1991) and compared the model's results to the actual monitored results for those days, the model over-predicted known ozone concentrations by an average of 19%. *Id.* at 10-11 (J.A. at 813-14). It therefore adjusted the model's calculations, using a variety of supplemental statistical techniques, to correct "average modeled peak over-prediction" and "day-specific over-prediction." *Id.* Those adjustments resulted in demonstrated attainment for two out of the three modeled days. *Id.* Although the adjustments still did not indicate attainment for July 20, 2005, EPA determined that the base-year data used to model that day was too anomalous to demonstrate nonattainment. July 20, 1991, the agency found, had been the 13th most severe ozone-producing day in 44 years. *Id.* at 12-13 (J.A. at 815-16). EPA reasoned that "this type of day is not likely to occur often enough to be a major causative factor for nonattainment because the [NAAQS] allows up to three monitored exceedances in any three year period." Conditional Approval, 68 Fed. Reg. at 19,114. It therefore concluded "that attainment of the 1-hour ozone standard has been successfully demonstrated for the Washington area by no later than 2005." Amendment to Technical Support Document at 13 (J.A. at 816).

Sierra Club insists that once the model showed exceedances on three days, that should have been the end of the matter. In petitioner's view, because the SIPs did not demonstrate attainment without EPA's adjustments, the demonstration was not "based on" photochemical grid modeling within the meaning of § 182(c)(2)(A). According to Sierra Club, the Clean Air Act "uses 'based on' to identify the *sole* basis for a decision." Reply Br. at 13.

We disagree. Under *Chevron*, "when the statute 'is silent or ambiguous' we must defer to a reasonable construction by the agency charged with its implementation." [Citation omitted.] There is no question that the phrase "based on" is ambiguous. As EPA points out, it does not necessarily require that attainment demonstrations rest *solely on* grid modeling. . . . On the other hand, as the agency also properly concedes, the phrase would not permit an attainment demonstration that wholly abandoned the results of a model by using a supplemental analysis that effectively supplanted the model's calculations. Oral Arg. Tr. at 26-27.

Because the statute is ambiguous, the question is whether the results obtained by adjusting the model can still reasonably be described as "based on" that model. We agree with EPA that in this case they can, because here "photochemical modeling is the primary basis for the attainment demonstration," while the supplementary analysis "is merely an adjunct for assessing the photochemical grid modeling." Conditional Approval, 68 Fed. Reg. at 19,113. As explained above, that analysis was employed to ensure that the model achieved its statutory purpose: determining whether the SIPs actually "provide for attainment of the ozone national ambient air quality standard by the applicable attainment date." 42 U.S.C. § 7511a(c)(2)(A). And the adjustments appear well suited to that end, as they do no more than correct for the model's over-prediction of ozone levels as compared to actual observations, and for its reliance on a base day that appears to be a statistical outlier.

Sierra Club further contends that, even if supplemental adjustments of the model are not statutorily barred, the agency was nonetheless arbitrary and capricious in applying them in this case. *See* 5 U.S.C. § 706(2)(A) But to withstand such an attack, the agency need only demonstrate that it "examined the relevant data and articulated a satisfactory explanation for its action including a rational connection between the facts found and the choice made." *Motor Vehicle Mfg. Ass'n v. State Farm Mut. Auto. Ins. Co.*, 463 U.S. 29, 43, 77 L. Ed. 2d 443, 103 S. Ct. 2856 (1983) (internal quotation marks omitted). The agency has done so.

The relevant data here are the agency's findings that the model "systematically over-predicted ozone concentration" in comparison to actual observed results, and that it overweighted conditions on a single day that were "not likely to occur often enough to be a major causative factor for nonattainment." Conditional Approval, 68 Fed. Reg. at 19,114-15. Sierra Club offers no evidence to dispute either finding. The rational connection between these data and the agency's choice is that which we have just described: the adjustments were necessary to ensure consistency with real-world observations and thus to ensure reliable prognostications about the future. Making adjustments in such circumstances is hardly arbitrary; indeed, the failure to make such adjustments may itself incur such a charge. *Cf. Columbia Falls Aluminum Co. v. EPA*, 329 U.S. App. D.C. 221, 139 F.3d 914, 923 (D.C. Cir. 1998) ("An agency's use of a model is arbitrary if that model bears no rational relationship to the reality it purports to represent") (internal quotation marks omitted); *Chemical Mfrs. Ass'n v. EPA*, 307 U.S. App. D.C. 392, 28 F.3d 1259, 1265 (D.C. Cir. 1994) (noting that "we must reverse the agency's application of [a] model as arbitrary and capricious if there is simply no rational relationship between the model and the known behavior of the hazardous air pollutant to which it is applied"). Accordingly, "[to] reject the EPA's conclusion under these circumstances would be to substitute our judgment concerning mathematical modeling techniques for that of the Agency . . . This we cannot do." *Connecticut v. EPA*, 696 F.2d 147, 159 (2d Cir. 1982).

Finally, we note that our conclusion, that EPA was reasonable in interpreting § 182(c)(2)(A) to permit the supplementation of the photochemical grid model, is in accord with that reached by the other circuits that have considered the issue. [citations omitted]. Our conclusion certainly does not mean that EPA has unlimited authority to adjust the calculations of a photochemical grid model. Neither the government nor this court disputes Sierra Club's contention that EPA is not free to apply any "adjustment" that it wishes and still claim that the results are "based on" the model. In this case, however, the agency has offered both substantial (and uncontradicted) evidence and a reasonable explanation for the alterations that it has made. Nothing more is required.

B

Sierra Club also takes issue with another component of the States' SIPs that EPA conditionally approved in its order of April 17, 2003: the rate-of-progress (ROP) plans for 1996-1999. Petitioner contends that the agency's approval of those plans was arbitrary and capricious because the plans relied on an outdated emissions model.

As we have discussed, the Clean Air Act requires that SIPs for serious and severe nonattainment areas include ROP plans that demonstrate an average reduction of baseline emissions of 3% per year for each consecutive three-year period from 1996 to the attainment deadline. 42 U.S.C. § 7511a(c)(2)(B), (d). To facilitate compliance with the Act, EPA makes available computer programs that determine baseline emissions and predict future emissions from motor vehicles. At issue here is the computer model on which the States' ROP plans for 1996-1999 were based: the so-called MOBILE5 model. Sierra Club contends that the ROP plans were inaccurate because they were not based on the updated MOBILE6 model.

EPA explained that it accepted the States' use of MOBILE5 because it was the most recent model available at the time the plans were prepared. Conditional Approval, 68 Fed. Reg. at 19,121. The States originally submitted their

ROP plans in 1999, and then resubmitted them as part of the D.C. area SIPs in February 2002. EPA did not make MOBILE6 available until January 29, 2002 — just one month before the States submitted their SIPs and long after the modeling had been completed and the ROP plans prepared.

Sierra Club argues that the States should nonetheless have revised the D.C. ROP plans to incorporate the advances of MOBILE6, for two reasons. First, MOBILE6 was available, albeit for only one month, before the States submitted their plans. Second, EPA did not approve the plans until April 17, 2003, over a year after MOBILE6's release. EPA responds that, although it requires that states use the latest model available at the time a plan is developed, *see* 42 U.S.C. § 7502(c)(3); 40 C.F.R. § 51.112(a)(1), its policy was not to "require states that have already submitted SIPs or will submit SIPs shortly after MOBILE6's release to revise these SIPs simply because a new motor vehicle emissions model is now available." Conditional Approval, 68 Fed. Reg. at 19,121; *see also* Memorandum from EPA Office of Air Quality Planning & Standards 2 (Jan. 18, 2002) (J.A. at 530) (same). As the agency explains, "emissions factors, as well as inventory calculation methodologies, are continually being improved." 68 Fed. Reg. at 19,120. Indeed, as its name suggests, MOBILE5 is the fifth generation of this particular model; MOBILE6 is the sixth. To require states to revise completed plans every time a new model is announced would lead to significant costs and potentially endless delays in the approval processes. EPA's decision to reject that course, and to accept the use of MOBILE5 in this case, was neither arbitrary nor capricious. [remainder of opinion omitted].

V

For the foregoing reasons, we vacate and remand EPA's conditional approval action insofar as it granted conditional approval based on the States' commitment letters.

In all other respects, we deny the petition for review of that action, as well as the petition to review the bump-up action.

NOTES AND QUESTIONS

1. EPA tracks air quality by using monitors. Monitors are getting better, but they do not tell a perfect story. For example, one monitor might be in a particularly dusty, urban location, while another might be placed in a spot relatively unaffected by dust. If monitors record inaccurate data about ambient air concentrations, the whole regulatory system gets skewed.

Well aware of this problem, EPA has engaged in new methods of calibrating monitoring data. One method is "spatial monitoring." By this approach, the agency averages the results from air quality monitors across a given region. Critics argue that spatial monitoring can result in the agency ignoring pollution "hot spots," thereby shortchanging persons most in need of air quality improvement. Another approach is to give greater weight to results from monitors located in areas of higher population density. Such "population-weighted monitoring" is often criticized for making health protection dependent upon how many neighbors one has.

2. Nonattainment SIPs are designed to allow new sources to come on line while contemporaneously reducing overall emissions within the AQCR. § 172, 42 U.S.C. § 7502. They reserve their most stringent restrictions for "new and modified major stationary sources." These sources must: secure permits, § 172(c)(5), 42 U.S.C. § 7502(c)(5); meet stringent "offset" requirements, § 173(a)(1)(A), 42 U.S.C. § 7503(a)(1)(A); and reduce emissions to levels representing the "lowest achievable emission rate" ("*LAER*"), § 173(a)(2), 42 U.S.C. § 7503(a)(2). "Major stationary source" is defined at § 302(j), 42 U.S.C. § 7602(j); "new" and "modified" take on the same meaning they have in § 111 (new source performance standards); *LAER* is defined at § 171(3), 42 U.S.C. § 7501(3).

3. By one calculation, the nation has spent $22 billion per year from 1970-1990 on air pollution control and, in return, received about $200 billion per year in benefits. According to EPA, the percentage reductions in air quality concentrations of criteria pollutants between 1977 and 1996 were as follows: carbon monoxide: -61%; lead: -97%; nitrogen oxides: -27%; ozone: -30%; PM_{10}: (data not available); and sulfur dioxide: -58%. The emissions percentage reductions of these same pollutants over the same time frame were: carbon monoxide: -31%; lead: -98%; nitrogen oxides: -increased 8%; ozone: -38%; PM_{10}: -73%; and sulfur dioxide: -39%. For more detailed emissions information, *see http://www.epa.gov/ttn/chief/trends/trends98/chapter3.pdf.*

For information on which areas of the country still suffer from unhealthy air contamination, see the map below.

Nonattainment Areas of the United States

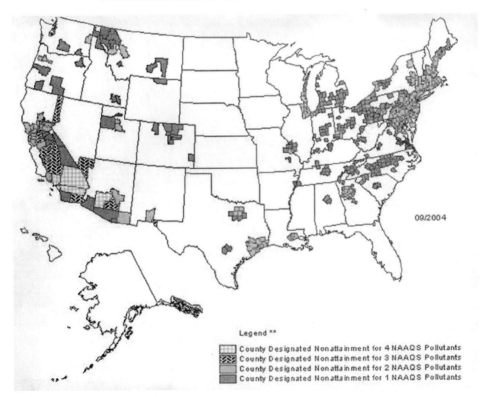

09/2004

Legend **

County Designated Nonattainment for 4 NAAQS Pollutants
County Designated Nonattainment for 3 NAAQS Pollutants
County Designated Nonattainment for 2 NAAQS Pollutants
County Designated Nonattainment for 1 NAAQS Pollutants

[2] PREVENTION OF SIGNIFICANT DETERIORATION

Since the 1970 Clean Air Act contained no explicit provision designed to protect air resources that were cleaner than required by the NAAQSs, the EPA thought it had no authority to enact regulations to this end. It believed it could act to clean up the "dirty air areas," but could not maintain the "clean air areas." These, it believed, could be degraded down to the level of the ambient standards. Manufacturers, faced with costly SIP obligations, could simply relocate to areas with clean skies and easy SIPs. Environmentalists, however, thought the 1970 CAA authorized EPA to prevent the "significant deterioration" of air quality in parts of the country where ambient standards were being met. To test the theory, the Sierra Club filed a lawsuit against EPA in 1972, and surprisingly, they won. *Sierra Club v. Ruckelshaus*, 344 F. Supp. 253 (D.D.C. 1972), *aff'd*, 2 Envt'l L. Rep. 20656 (D.C. Cir. 1972, *aff'd, sub nom. Fri v. Environmental Protection Agency*, 412 U.S. 541, 93 S.Ct. 2770 (1973). According to the District Court for the District of Columbia, EPA's authority to protect clean air areas lay in the "purposes" clause of the Act, § 101(b), 42 U.S.C. § 7401(b). In that section, Congress had declared a purpose of the Act to be "to *protect and enhance* the quality of the Nation's air resources so as to promote the public health and welfare and the productive capacity of its population." § 101(b)(1), 42 U.S.C. § 7401(b)(1) (emphasis added). This language, coupled with legislative history and past administrative interpretations of the statute, convinced the court that EPA could move in this direction.

Armed with new-found authority, EPA in 1974 enacted regulations to maintain clean air areas. When Congress amended the CAA in 1977, it incorporated much of the EPA regulations in new Part C. Congress's concerns were both environmental and economic. On the one hand, it wanted clean air areas to stay that way, at least as much as possible. On the other, it wanted to forestall any single industry from consuming the entire "increment" of clean air in an AQCR (that is, polluting it all the way down to the NAAQS), thus foreclosing future industrial growth. *See, e.g.,* Senate Debate on S. 252, 95th Cong. (1977) (statement of Edmund Muskie, Committee on Environment and Public Works). The following case is the major judicial statement on the PSD program.

ALABAMA POWER COMPANY v. COSTLE

636 F.2d 323 (D.C. Cir. 1979)

[This case resolved challenges by industry and environmentalists to the regulations promulgated by EPA to implement Part C of the Clean Air Act. The case was exceedingly complex and relatively urgent, prompting the court to hear oral argument in lengthy and informal fashion, to issue a per curiam preliminary opinion announcing its resolution of the multitudinous issues, and finally issuing this decision. This decision was written in part by all three of the judges on the panel, and was preceded by a table of contents for the convenience of the reader.]

LEVENTHAL, CIRCUIT JUDGE:

I. Background of PSD Program and Regulations Under Review

. . . .

C. Clean Air Act Amendments of 1977

The 1977 Amendments maintain the basic structure of regulation of stationary sources through state plans, but made substantial changes in the requirements governing those plans. The Amendments provide for additional controls on existing sources to ensure protection of the ambient standards and visibility. Further, they establish strict requirements for major new sources to be located in areas where the national standards have not yet been attained ("non-attainment areas").

The central focus of this case is Part C of title I (sections 160-169) added to the Clean Air Act by the 1977 Amendments. Section 161 of the Act now provides an express directive that state plans include measures to prevent the significant deterioration of air quality in areas designated by the states under section 107(d)(1)(D) & (E) of the Act as having ambient air quality better than the applicable national primary or secondary ambient air quality standard, or for which there is insufficient data to make a determination of the air quality.[5] An area so designated has commonly been referred to in the legislative history and in the literature that has developed as a "clean air area," a description often contrasted with the term "non-attainment area," which is defined by section 171(2) of the Act as an area that has been demonstrated to exceed an NAAQS for a given pollutant. We wish to alert the reader that the phrase "clean air areas" is a generalization that may be confusing when employed in technical usages. A so-called clean air area for a given air pollutant may include an area that for the same pollutant would be classified as a non-attainment area if sufficient data existed. Further, since classification of areas is pollutant-specific, the same area may be a clean air area due to the air quality with respect to one pollutant, yet be a non-attainment area with respect to another pollutant. Finally, the areas of the country subject to regulation under the PSD provisions of the Act include areas other than those commonly referred to as clean air areas. With these caveats, . . . we will continue to use the term "clean air areas" as a shorthand expression where we do not feel the context calls for a more technical usage.

. . . .

D. PSD Regulations Under the 1977 Amendments

Following several notices of proposed rulemaking, comment periods, and public hearings, EPA promulgated two sets of final PSD regulations on June

---

[5] Ed. note: An attainment area is one in which the air "meets the national primary or secondary ambient air quality standard for [a regulated pollutant]." § 107(d)(1)(A)(ii), 42 U.S.C. § 7407(d)(1)(A)(ii). Air in an unclassifiable area "cannot be classified on the basis of available information as meeting or not meeting the national primary or secondary ambient air quality standard for the pollutant." § 107(d)(1)(A)(iii), 42 U.S.C. § 7407(d)(1)(A)(iii).

19, 1978. One set amended 40 C.F.R. Part 51 to provide guidance to the states on the development of revised state implementation plans. The other set amended 40 C.F.R. Part 52 to incorporate the immediately effective changes required by the 1977 Amendments.

The regulations require that each major stationary source and each modification covered by the regulations undergo a detailed preconstruction review and obtain a permit prior to the commencement of construction. * * *

II. Potential to Emit

At the heart of the PSD provisions lies a definition that is jurisdictional in nature. We refer to the section 169(1) definition of "major emitting facility," which identifies sources of air pollution that are subject to the preconstruction review and permit requirements of section 165. The definition is not pollutant-specific, but rather identifies sources that emit more than a threshold quantity of any air pollutant. Once a source has been so identified, it may become subject to section 165's substantial administrative burdens and stringent technological control requirements for each pollutant regulated under the Act, even though the air pollutant, emissions of which caused the source to be classified as a "major emitting facility," may not be a pollutant for which NAAQS have been promulgated or even one that is otherwise regulated under the Act. As will become apparent from consideration of the ramifications of this definition, Congress's intention was to identify facilities which, due to their size, are financially able to bear the substantial regulatory costs imposed by the PSD provisions and which, as a group, are primarily responsible for emission of the deleterious pollutants that befoul our nation's air. Such facilities are defined in section 169(1) as those stationary sources of air pollutants from among 28 listed categories which "emit, or have the potential to emit" 100 tons per year or more of any air pollutant plus any other stationary source with the "potential to emit" 250 tons per year or more of any air pollutant.* * *

EPA has interpreted the phrase "potential to emit" as referring to the measure of a source's "uncontrolled emissions" — i.e., the projected emissions of a source when operating at full capacity, with the projection increased by hypothesizing the absence of air pollution control equipment designed into the source. Yet, the language and comprehensive scheme of the statute reveal that an emitting facility is "major" within the meaning of section 169(1), only if it either (1) actually emits the specified annual tonnage of any air pollutant, or (2) has the potential, when operating at full design capacity, to emit the statutory amount. The purpose of Congress was to require preconstruction review and a permit before major amounts of emissions were released into the air. When determining a facility's potential to emit air pollutants, EPA must look to the facility's "design capacity" — a concept which not only includes a facility's maximum productive capacity (a criterion employed by EPA) but also takes into account the anticipated functioning of the air pollution control equipment designed into the facility. * * *

The coverage of the 100 ton-per-annum threshold of the first sentence of section 169(1) extends to 28 categories of facilities. A look at these categories, and a further look at the legislative history reveal that Congress was concerned with large industrial enterprises — major actual emitters of air pollution. The draftsmen were of the view that certain small industrial facilities within these categories might actually and potentially emit less than the threshold amount. But the submissions of the parties establish that no operational industrial facility that could be described as within the listed categories would have the "potential to emit" less than the threshold amount if the operation of cleansing control equipment is totally discounted.

EPA recognized that its definition placed an intolerable burden on both the agency and minor sources of pollution and sought to cope with it by creating a broad exemption for smaller sources . . . the Act does not give the agency a free hand authority to grant broad exemptions. Though the costs of compliance with section 165 requirements are substantial, they can reasonably be borne by facilities that actually emit, or would actually emit when operating at full capacity, the large tonnage thresholds specified in section 169(1).

. . . .

IV. Protection of the Increments

The regulations provide that once it is determined that a state implementation plan "is substantially inadequate to prevent significant deterioration or that an applicable increment is being violated," then the SIP must "be revised to correct the inadequacy or the violation." We rule that EPA has authority under the statute to prevent or to correct a violation of the increments, but the agency is without authority to dictate to the States their policy for management of the consumption of allowable increments. * * *

V. Sources Located in Non-Attainment Areas

Section 165 (a) provides that a PSD permit is required before a major emitting facility "may be constructed in any area to which this part applies." Industry petitioners contend that this language limits the application of the PSD review requirements to sources constructed in certain locations, and that those locations are the statutorily defined "clean air areas." On this premise, industry petitioners argue that section 165 does not apply to sources located in the so-called "non-attainment" areas. EPA, on the other hand, takes the position that the identification of "clean air" and "non-attainment" areas in section 107(d) of the Act are only a starting point for the planning process that will lead to revised state implementation plans, that these identifications do not shape the "area" to which the PSD review requirements apply, and that preconstruction review must precede the construction anywhere of a major emitting facility which will adversely affect the air quality of an area to which this part applies. EPA's regulations extend the permit requirements of section 165 to all sources, wherever located, if the emissions from the source have an impact on any clean air area. The issue, then, is whether a source becomes subject to the PSD review process because of its location within an area to which this part applies, or because of its impact upon the air quality of one.* * *

After careful consideration of the statute and the legislative history, we must accept the contention of the industry petitioners that the phrase "constructed in any area to which this part applies" limits the application of Section 165 to major emitting facilities to be constructed in certain locations. But, we reject the proposition that the only statutory means available to fulfill the purposes of Part C are the permit provisions of § 165.

The plain meaning of the inclusion in section 165 of the words "any area to which this part applies" is that Congress intended location to be the key determinant of the applicability of the PSD review requirements. That this is the correct interpretation is underscored by the inclusion of the same words in section 165(a)(3)(A), and by the precise language employed by Congress in those provisions where its concern was more source (rather than area) specific.

The legislative history supports our interpretation. . . . Therefore, we conclude, as noted above, that the phrase "constructed in any area to which this part applies" limits the application of section 165 to major emitting facilities to be constructed in certain locations. * * *

. . . We have now held that section 165 does not, by its own terms, apply to sources located outside of clean air areas. In this light, and in view of the legislative desire to prevent interstate impacts, the authority granted to the EPA by the plain language of section 161 — "each [SIP] shall contain emission limitations and such other measures as may be necessary, as determined under regulations promulgated under this part, to prevent significant deterioration of air quality [in clean air areas]" — grants to the Administrator the power to promulgate rules requiring that SIPs adequately address the problem. We hold that the Administrator may promulgate rules to require the inclusion of such provisions in the SIP of the state whose clean air area is affected, of the state which is the source of the adverse impact, or of both. * * *

[Opinions of Robinson, Circuit Judge, and Wilkey, Circuit Judge, are omitted.]

NOTES

1. Currently, sources with a "potential to emit" which fall below the statutory minima are not subject to the onerous regulatory requirements of § 165. EPA by rule dictated that a source's "potential to emit" shall be determined by assessing its "maximum capacity . . . to emit a pollutant under its physical and operational design." 40 CFR 51.165(a)(1)(iii). The rule also provides that "[a]ny physical or operational limitation on the capacity of the stationary source to emit a pollutant, including air pollution control equipment and restrictions on hours of operation or on the type or amount or material combusted, stored, or processed, shall be treated as part of its design if the limitation or the effect it would have on emissions is federally enforceable." *Id.* "Federally enforceable" includes all limitations and conditions which are enforceable by the Administrator and requirements within any applicable State implementation plan. *Id.* at 51.165(a)(1)(xiv).

2. Once an AQCR is designated as a PSD area, strict pollution control requirements come into play. Chief among these is the requirement for new or modified stationary sources to reduce emissions to a level reflecting "best

available control technology." ("BACT"). The following case is the United States Supreme Court's statement on who decides what BACT is.

ALASKA DEPARTMENT OF ENVIRONMENTAL CONSERVATION v. ENVIRONMENTAL PROTECTION AGENCY

__ U.S.__, 124 S.Ct. 983 (2004)

JUDGES: GINSBURG, J., delivered the opinion of the Court, in which STEVENS, O'CONNOR, SOUTER, and BREYER, JJ., joined. KENNEDY, J., filed a dissenting opinion, in which REHNQUIST, C.J., and SCALIA and THOMAS, JJ., joined.

JUSTICE GINSBURG delivered the opinion of the Court.

This case concerns the authority of the Environmental Protection Agency (EPA or Agency) to enforce the provisions of the Clean Air Act's (CAA or Act) Prevention of Significant Deterioration (PSD) program. Under that program, no major air pollutant emitting facility may be constructed unless the facility is equipped with "the best available control technology" (BACT). As added by § 165, 91 Stat 735, and amended, 42 U.S.C. § 7475(a)(4), BACT, as defined in the CAA, means, for any major air pollutant emitting facility, "an emission limitation based on the maximum degree of [pollutant] reduction . . . which the permitting authority, on a case-by-case basis, taking into account energy, environmental, and economic impacts and other costs, determines is achievable for [the] facility. . . ." § 7479(3). Regarding EPA oversight, the Act includes a general instruction and one geared specifically to the PSD program. The general prescription, § 113(a)(5) of the Act, authorizes EPA, when it finds that a State is not complying with a CAA requirement governing construction of a pollutant source, to issue an order prohibiting construction, to prescribe an administrative penalty, or to commence a civil action for injunctive relief. 42 U.S.C. § 7413(a). Directed specifically to the PSD program, CAA § 167 instructs EPA to "take such measures, including issuance of an order, or seeking injunctive relief, as necessary to prevent the construction" of a major pollutant emitting facility that does not conform to the PSD requirements of the Act. 42 U.S.C. § 7477.

In the case before us, "the permitting authority" under § 7479(3) is the State of Alaska, acting through Alaska's Department of Environmental Conservation (ADEC). The question presented is what role EPA has with respect to ADEC's BACT determinations. Specifically, may EPA act to block construction of a new major pollutant emitting facility permitted by ADEC when EPA finds ADEC's BACT determination unreasonable in light of the guides § 7479(3) prescribes? We hold that the Act confers that checking authority on EPA.

I

A

. . . The PSD requirements, enacted as part of 1977 amendments to the Act, Title I, § 160 et seq., 91 Stat 731, "are designed to ensure that the air quality in attainment areas or areas that are already 'clean' will not degrade," Belden, *supra*, p. 43. *See* 42 U.S.C. § 7470(1) (purpose of PSD program is to "protect public health and welfare from any actual or potential adverse effect which in [EPA's] judgment may reasonably be anticipate[d] to occur from air pollution . . . notwithstanding attainment and maintenance of all national ambient air quality standards").

The PSD program imposes on States a regime governing areas "designated . . . as attainment or unclassifiable." § 7471. . . . Northwest Alaska, the region this case concerns, is classified as an attainment or unclassifiable area for nitrogen dioxide, 40 CFR § 51.302 (2002), therefore, the PSD program applies to emissions of that pollutant in the region. In 2002, the Agency reported that "[a]ll areas of the country that once violated the NAAQS for [nitrogen dioxide] now meet that standard." EPA, Latest Findings on National Air Quality 7 (Aug. 2003).

Section 165 of the Act, 42 USC § 7475, installs a permitting requirement for any "major emitting facility," defined to include any source emitting more than 250 tons of nitrogen oxides per year, § 7479(1). No such facility may be constructed or modified unless a permit prescribing emission limitations has been issued for the facility. § 7475(a)(1); *see* § 7479(2)(C) (defining "construction" to the include "modification"). Alaska's SIP imposes an analogous requirement. 18 Alaska Admin. Code § 50.300(c)(1) (2003). Modifications to major emitting facilities that increase nitrogen oxide emissions in excess of 40 tons per year require a PSD permit. 40 CFR § 51.166(b)(23)(i) (2002); 18 Alaska Admin. Code § 50.300(h)(3)(B)(ii) (2003). The Act sets out preconditions for the issuance of PSD permits. *Inter alia*, no PSD permit may issue unless "the proposed facility is subject to the best available control technology for each pollutant subject to [CAA] regulation . . . emitted from . . . [the] facility." 42 U.S.C. 7475(a)(4). As described in the Act's definitional provisions, "best available control technology" (BACT) means:

> "[A]n emission limitation based on the maximum degree of reduction of each pollutant subject to regulation under this chapter emitted from or which results from any major emitting facility, which the permitting authority, on a case-by-case basis, taking into account energy, environmental, and economic impacts and other costs, determines is achievable for such facility through application of production processes and available methods, systems, and techniques. . . . In no event shall application of 'best available control technology' result in emissions of any pollutants which will exceed the emissions allowed by any applicable standard established pursuant to section 7411 or 7412 of this title [emission standards for new and existing stationary sources]." § 7479(3).

40 CFR § 51.166(b)(12) (2002) (repeating statutory definition). Alaska's SIP contains provisions that track the statutory BACT requirement and definition. 18 Alaska Admin. Code §§ 50.310(d)(3) and 50.990(13) (2003). The State with slightly variant terminology, defines BACT as "the emission limitation that represents the maximum reduction achievable for each regulated air containment, taking into account energy, environmental and economic impacts, and other costs." *Ibid*. Under the federal Act, limited class of sources must gain

advance EPA approval for the BACT prescribed in the permit. 42 U.S.C. § 7475(a)(8).

CAA also provides that a PSD permit may issue only if a source "will not cause, or contribute to, air pollution in excess of any . . . maximum allowable increase or maximum allowable concentration for any pollutant" or any NAAQS. § 7475(a)(3). Congress left to the Agency the determination of most maximum allowable increases, or "increments," in pollutants. EPA regulations have defined increments for nitrogen oxides. 40 CFR § 51.166(c) (2002). Typically, to demonstrate that increments will not be exceeded, applicants use mathematical models of pollutant plumes, their behavior, and their dispersion. Westbrook, *Air Dispersion Models: Tools to Assess Impacts from Pollution Sources,* 13 Natural Resources & Env. 546, 547-548 (1999).

Among measures EPA may take to ensure compliance with the PSD program, two have special relevance here. The first prescription, § 113(a)(5) of the Act, provides that "[w]henever, on the basis of any available information, [EPA] finds that a State is not acting in compliance with any requirement or prohibition of the chapter relating to the construction of new sources or the modification of existing sources," EPA may "issue an order prohibiting the construction or modification of any major stationary source in any area to which such requirement applies." 42 U.S.C. § 7413(a)(5)(A). The second measure, § 167 of the Act, trains on enforcement of the PSD program; it requires EPA to "take such measures, including issuance of an order, or seeking injunctive relief, as necessary to prevent the construction or modification of a major emitting facility which does not conform to the [PSD] requirements." § 7477.

B

Teck Cominco Alaska, Inc. Cominco), operates a zinc concentrate mine, the Red Dog Mine, in northwest Alaska approximately 100 miles north of the Arctic Circle and close to the native Alaskan villages of Kivalina and Noatak. App. to Pet. for Cert. 3a; Brief for Petitioner 8; Brief for Respondents 4. The mine is the region's largest private employer. Brief for Petitioner 9. It supplies a quarter of the area's wage base. *Ibid.* Cominco leases the land from the NANA Regional Corporation, an Alaskan corporation formed pursuant to the Alaska Native Claims Settlement Act, 85 Stat 688, as amended, 43 U.S.C. 1601 et seq. Brief for NANA Regional Corporation, Inc., as *Amicus Curiae* 1-2, 4.

In 1988, Cominco obtained authorization to operate the mine, a "major emitting facility" under the Act and Alaska's SIP. App. 106. The mine's PSD permit authorized five 5,000 kilowatt Wartsila diesel electric generators, MG-1 through MG-5, subject to operating restrictions; two of the five generators were permitted to operate only in standby status. *Ibid.* Petitioner Alaska Department of Environmental Conservation (ADEC) issued a second PSD permit in 1994 allowing addition of a sixth full-time generator (MG-6), removing standby status from MG-2, and imposing a new operational cap that allowed all but one generator to run full time. *Ibid.*

In 1996, Cominco initiated a project, with funding from the State, to expand zinc production by 40%. Brief for Petitioner 5; Reply Brief for Petitioner 11, n 9. Anticipating that the project would increase nitrogen oxide emissions by more than 40 tons per year, *see supra*, at ___, *157 L. Ed. 2d, at 986*, Cominco applied to ADEC for a PSD permit to allow, *inter alia*, increased electricity generation by its standby generator, MG-5. App. 107-108; App. Pet. for Cert. 33a. On March 3, 1999, ADEC preliminarily proposed as BACT for MG-5 the emission control technology known as selective catalytic reduction (SCR), which reduces nitrogen oxide emissions by 90%. App. 72, 108. In response, Cominco amended its application to add a seventh generator, MG-17, and to propose as BACT an alternative control technology — Low NOx — that achieves a 30% reduction in nitrogen oxide pollutants. Brief for Respondents 5, and n.1; App. 84.

On May 4, 1999, ADEC, in conjunction with Cominco's representative, issued a first draft PSD permit and preliminary technical analysis report that concluded Low NOx was BACT for MG-5 and MG-17. *Id.*, at 55-95. To determine BACT, ADEC employed EPA's recommended top-down methodology, *id.*, at 61:

> "In brief, the top-down process provides that all available control technologies be ranked in descending order of control effectiveness. The PSD applicant first examines the most stringent — or 'top' — alternative. That alternative is established as BACT unless the applicant demonstrates, and the permitting authority in its informed judgment agrees, that technical considerations, or energy, environmental, or economic impacts justify a conclusion that the most stringent technology is not 'achievable' in that case. If the most stringent technology is eliminated in this fashion, then the next most stringent alternative is considered, and so on." EPA, New Source Review Workshop Manual B2 (Draft Oct. Cf1990) (hereinafter New Source Review Manual); App. 61-62.

No hing in the Act or its implementing regulations mandates top-down analysis. *See* 42 U.S.C. § 7479(3); 40 CFR § 52.21(j) (2002). EPA represents that permitting authorities "commonly" use top-down methodology. Brief for Respondents 3. Applying top-down methodology, ADEC first homed in on SCR as BACT for MG-5, and the new generator, MG-17. "[W]ith an estimated reduction of 90%," ADEC stated, SCR "is the most stringent" technology. *Id.*, at 79. Finding SCR "technically and economically feasible," *id.*, at 65, ADEC characterized as "overstated" Cominco's cost estimate of $5,643 per ton of nitrogen oxide removed by SCR. *Id.*, at 113. Using Cominco's data, ADEC reached a cost estimate running between $1,586 and $2,279 per ton. *Id.*, at 83. Costs in that range, ADEC observed, "are well within what ADEC and EPA conside[r] economically feasible." *Id.*, at 84. Responding to Cominco's comments on the preliminary permit, engineering staff in ADEC's Air Permits Program pointed out that, according to information Cominco provided to ADEC, "SCR has been installed on similar diesel-fired engines throughout the world." *Id.*, at 102.

Despite its staff's clear view "that SCR (most effective individual technology) [was] technologically, environmentally, and economically feasible for the Red Dog power plant engines," *id.*, at 103-104, ADEC endorsed the alternative proffered by Cominco. To achieve nitrogen oxide emission reductions commensurate with SCR's 90% impact, Cominco proposed fitting the new generator MG-17 and the six existing generators with Low NOx. *Ibid.* Cominco asserted that it could lower net emissions by 396 tons per year if it fitted all seven generators with Low NOx rather than fitting two (MG-5 and MG-17) with SCR and choosing one of them as the standby unit. *Id.*, at 87. Cominco's proposal hinged on the"assumption . . . that under typical operating conditions one or more engines will not be running due to maintenance of .standby-generation capacity." *Ibid.* If all seven generators ran continuously, however, Cominco's alternative would increase emissions by 79 tons per year. *Ibid.* Accepting Cominco's submission, ADEC stated that Cominco's Low NOx solution "achieve[d] a similar maximum NOx reduction as the most stringent controls; [could] potentially result in a greater NOx reduction; and is logistically and economically less onerous to Cominco." *Id.*, at 87-88.

On the final day of the public comment period, July 2, 1999, the United States Department of the Interior, National Parks Service (NPS), submitted comments to ADEC. App. to Pet. for Cert. 33a; App. 97, 108. NPS objected to the projected offset of new emissions from MG-5 and MG-17 against emissions from other existing generators that were not subject to BACT. Letter from John Notar, NPS Air Resources Division, to Jim Baumgartner, ADEC (June 2, 1999). Such an offset, NPS commented, "is neither allowed by BACT, nor achieves the degree of reduction that would result if all the generators that are subject to BACT were equipped with SCR." *Id.*, at 3. NPS further observed that the proposed production-increase project would remove operating restrictions that the 1994 PSD permit had placed on four of the existing generators — MG-1, MG-3, MG-4, and MG-5. App. to Pet. for Cert. 34a. Due to that alteration, NPS urged, those generators, too, became part of the production-expansion project and would be subject to the BACT requirement. *Ibid.*

Following NPS' lead, EPA wrote to ADEC on July 29, 1999, commenting: "Although ADEC states in its analysis that [SCR], the most stringent level of control, is economically and technologically feasible, ADEC did not propose to require SCR . . . [O]nce it is determined that an emission unit is subject to BACT, the PSD program does not allow the imposition of a limit that is less stringent than BACT." App. 96-97. A permitting authority, EPA agreed with NPS, could not offset new emissions "by imposing new controls on other emission units" that were not subject to BACT. *Id.*, at 97. New emissions could be offset only against reduced emissions from sources covered by the same BACT authorization. *Id.*, at 285-286. EPA further agreed with NPS that, based on the existing information, BACT would be required for MG-1, MG-3, MG-4, and MG-5. *Id.*, at 97.

After receiving EPA comments, ADEC issued a second draft PSD permit and technical analysis report on September 1, 1999, again finding Low NOx to be BACT for MG-17. *Id.*, at 105-117. Abandoning the emissions-offsetting justification advanced in the May 4 draft permit, ADEC agreed with NPS and EPA that "emission reductions from sources that were not part of the permit action," here MG-1, MG-2, MG-3, MG-4, MG-5, and MG-6, could not be considered in determining BACT for MG-17. *Id.*, at 111; *id.*, at 199 (same).

ADEC conceded that, lacking data from Cominco, it had made "no judgment . . . as to the impact of . . . [SCR] on the operation, profitability, and competitiveness of the Red Dog Mine." *Id.*, at 116. Contradicting its May 1999 conclusion that SCR was "technically and economically feasible," *see supra*, at ___, 157 L Ed 2d, at 989, ADEC found in September 1999 that SCR imposed "a disproportionate cost" on the mine. App. 116. ADEC concluded, on a "cursory review," that requiring SCR for a rural Alaska utility would lead to a 20% price increase, and that in comparison with other BACT technologies, SCR came at a "significantly higher" cost. *Ibid.* No economic basis for a comparison between the mine and a rural utility appeared in ADEC's technical analysis.

EPA protested the revised permit. In a September 15, 1999, letter, the Agency stated: "Cominco has not adequately demonstrated any site-specific factors to support their claim that the installation of [SCR] is economically infeasible at the Red Dog Mine. Therefore, elimination of SCR as BACT based on cost-effectiveness grounds is not supported by the record and is clearly erroneous." *Id.*, at 127; *see id.*, at 138 (ADEC's record does not support the departure from ADEC's initial view that the costs for SCR were economically feasible).

To justify the September 1, 1999, permit, EPA suggested, ADEC could "include an analysis of whether requiring Cominco to install and operate [SCR] would have any adverse economic impacts upon Cominco specifically." *Id.*, at 127. Stating that such an inquiry was unnecessary and expressing "concerns related to confidentiality," Cominco declined to submit financial data. *Id.*, at 134. In this regard, Cominco simply asserted, without detail, that the company's "overall debt remains quite high" despite continuing profits. *Id.*, at 134-135. Cominco also invoked the need for "[i]ndustrial development in rural Alaska." *Id.*, at 135.

On December 10, 1999, ADEC issued the final permit and technical analysis report. Once again, ADEC approved Low NOx as BACT for MG-17 "[t]o support Cominco's Red Dog Mine Production Rate Increase Project, and its contributions to the region." *Id.*, at 208. ADEC did not include the economic analysis EPA had suggested. *Id.*, at 152-246. Indeed, ADEC conceded again that it had made "no judgment . . . as to the impact of . . . [SCR's] cost on the operation, profitability, and competitiveness of the Red Dog Mine." *Id.*, at 207. Nonetheless, ADEC advanced, as cause for its decision, SCR's adverse effect on the mine's "unique and continuing impact on the economic diversity of th[e] region" and on the venture's "world competitiveness." *Id.*, at 208. ADEC did not explain how its inferences of adverse effects on the region's economy or the mine's "world competitiveness" could be made without financial information showing SCR's impact on the "operation, profitability, and competitiveness" of the mine. *Id.*, at 207, 299. Instead, ADEC reiterated its rural Alaska utility analogy, and again compared SCR's cost to the costs of other, less stringent, control technologies. *Id.*, at 205-207.

The same day, December 10, 1999, EPA issued an order to ADEC, under §§ 113(a)(5) and 167 of the Act, 42 U.S.C. §§ 7413(a)(5) and 7477, prohibiting ADEC from issuing a PSD permit to Cominco "unless ADEC satisfactorily documents why SCR is not BACT for the Wartsila diesel generator [MG-17]."

App. to Pet. for Cert. 36a. In the letter accompanying the order, the Agency stated that "ADEC's own analysis supports the determination that BACT is [SCR], and that ADEC's decision in the proposed permit therefore is both arbitrary and erroneous." App. 149.

On February 8, 2000, EPA, again invoking its authority under §§ 113(a)(5) and 167 of the Act, issued a second order, this time prohibiting Cominco from beginning "construction or modification activities at the Red Dog mine." App. to Pet. for Cert. 49a. A third order, issued on March 7, 2000, superseding and vacating the February 8 order, generally prohibited Cominco from acting on ADEC's December 10 PSD permit but allowed limited summer construction. *Id.*, at 62a-64a. On April 25, 2000, EPA withdrew its December 10 order. App. 300; App. to Pet. for Cert. 6a. Once ADEC issued the permit, EPA explained, that order lacked utility. On July 16, 2003, ADEC granted Cominco a PSD permit to construct MG-17 with SCR as BACT. Letter from Theodore B. Olson, Solicitor General, to William K. Suter, Clerk of the Court (Aug. 21, 2003). Under the July 16, 2003, permit, SCR ceases to be BACT "if and when the case currently pending before the Supreme Court of the United States of America is decided in favor of the State of Alaska." ADEC, Air Quality Construction Permit, Final Technical Analysis Report, Permit No. 9932-AC005, Revision 2, p.7.

The day EPA issued its first order against Cominco, February 8, 2000, ADEC and Cominco petitioned the Court of Appeals for the Ninth Circuit for review of EPA's orders. . . .

The Court of Appeals resolved the merits in a judgment released July 30, 2002. 298 F.3d 814 (CA9). It held that EPA had authority under §§ 113(a)(5) and 167 to issue the contested orders, and that the Agency had properly exercised its discretion in doing so. *Id.*, at 820-823. Concerning EPA's authority under §§ 113(a)(5) and 167, the Court of Appeals observed first that "the question presented is what requirements the *state* must meet" under the Act to issue a PSD permit, not what the correct BACT might be. *Id.*, at 821 (emphasis in original). Concluding that EPA had "authority to determine the reasonableness or adequacy of the state's justification for its decision," the Court of Appeals emphasized that the "provision of a reasoned justification" by a permitting authority is undeniably a "requirement" of the Act. *Ibid.* EPA had properly exercised its discretion in issuing the three orders, the Ninth Circuit ultimately determined, because (1) Cominco failed to "demonstrat[e] that SCR was economically infeasible," and (2) "ADEC failed to provide a reasoned justification for its elimination of SCR as a control option." *Id.*, at 823. We granted certiorari, 537 U.S. 1186, 154 L. Ed. 2d 1017, 123 S. Ct. 1253 (2003), to resolve an important question of federal law, *i.e.*, the scope of EPA's authority under §§ 113(a)(5) and 167, and now affirm the Ninth Circuit's judgment. . . .

II

[The Court's discussion of administrative issues is omitted.]

III

A

Centrally at issue in this case is the question whether EPA's oversight role, described by Congress in CAA §§ 113(a)(5) and 167, *see supra*, at ___, 157 L. Ed. 2d, at 987, extends to ensuring that a state permitting authority's BACT determination is reasonable in light of the statutory guides. Sections 113(a)(5) and 167 lodge in the Agency encompassing supervisory responsibility over the construction and modification of pollutant emitting facilities in areas covered by the PSD program. 42 U.S.C. §§ 7413(a)(5) and 7477. In notably capacious terms, Congress armed EPA with authority to issue orders stopping construction when "a State is not acting in compliance with any [CAA] requirement or prohibition . . . relating to the construction of new sources or the modification of existing sources," § 7413(a)(5), or when "construction or modification of a major emitting facility . . . does not conform to the requirements of [the PSD program]," § 7477.

The federal Act enumerates several "[p]reconstruction requirements" for the PSD program. § 7475. Absent these, "[n]o major emitting facility . . . may be constructed." *Ibid.* One express preconstruction requirement is inclusion of a BACT determination in a facility's PSD permit. §§ 7475(a)(1) and (4). As earlier set out, see *supra*, at ___ -___, 157 L. Ed. 2d, at 986-987, the Act defines BACT as "an emission limitation based on the maximum degree of reduction of [a] pollutant . . . which the permitting authority, on a case-by-case basis, taking into account energy, environmental, and economic impacts and other costs, determines is achievable for [a] facility." § 7479(3). Under this formulation, the permitting authority, ADEC here, exercises primary or initial responsibility for identifying BACT in line with the Act's definition of that term.

All parties agree that one of the "many requirements in the PSD provisions that the EPA may enforce" is "that a [PSD] permit contain a BACT limitation." Brief for Petitioner 34; *see id.*, at 22, 25 (same). *See also* Brief for Respondents 23. It is therefore undisputed that the Agency may issue an order to stop a facility's construction if a PSD permit contains no BACT designation.

EPA reads the Act's definition of BACT, together with CAA's explicit listing of BACT as a "[p]reconstruction requiremen[t]," to mandate not simply a BACT designation, but a determination of BACT faithful to the statute's definition. In keeping with the broad oversight role §§ 113(a)(5) and 167 vest in EPA, the Agency maintains, it may review permits to ensure that a State's BACT determination is reasonably moored to the Act's provisions. *See id.*, at 24. We hold, as elaborated below, that the Agency has rationally construed the Act's text and that EPA's construction warrants our respect and approbation.

BACT's statutory definition requires selection of an emission control technology that results in the "maximum" reduction of a pollutant "achievable for [a] facility" in view of "energy, environmental, and economic impacts, and other costs." 42 U.S.C. § 7479(3). This instruction, EPA submits, cabins state permitting authorities' discretion by granting only "authority to make *reasonable* BACT determinations," Brief for Respondents 27 (emphasis in original), *i.e.*, decisions made with fidelity to the Act's purpose "to insure that economic growth will occur in a manner consistent with the preservation of existing clean air resources," 42 U.S.C. § 7470(3). Noting that state permitting authorities' statutory discretion is constrained by CAA's strong, normative terms "maximum" and "achievable," § 7479(3), EPA reads §§ 113(a)(5) and 167 to empower the federal Agency to check a state agency's unreasonably lax BACT designation. *See* Brief for Respondents 27.

EPA stresses Congress' reason for enacting the PSD program — to prevent significant deterioration of air quality in clean-air areas within a State and in neighboring States. §§ 7470(3), (4); *see id.*, at 33. That aim, EPA urges, is unlikely to be realized absent an EPA surveillance role that extends to BACT determinations. The Agency notes in this regard a House Report observation:

> "Without national guidelines for the prevention of significant deteri-oration a State deciding to protect its clean air resources will face a double threat. The prospect is very real that such a State would lose existing industrial plants to more permissive States. But additionally the State will likely become the target of 'economic-environmental blackmail' from new industrial plants that will play one State off against another with threats to locate in whichever State adopts the most permissive pollution controls." H. R. Rep. No. 95-294, p 134 (1977).

The House Report further observed that "a community that sets and enforces strict standards may still find its air polluted from sources in another community or another State." *Id.*, at 135 (quoting 116 Cong. Rec. 32909 (1970)). Federal agency surveillance of a State's BACT designation is needed, EPA asserts, to restrain the interjurisdictional pressures to which Congress was alert. *See* Brief for Respondents 33-34, 43; Brief for Vermont et al. as Amici Curiae 12 ("If EPA has authority to ensure a reasonable level of consistency among BACT determinations nationwide, then every State can feel more confident about maintaining stringent standards without fear of losing its current industry or alienating prospective industry.").

The House Report further observed that "a community that sets and enforces strict standards may still find its air polluted from sources in another community or another State." *Id.*, at 135 (quoting 116 Cong. Rec. 32909 (1970)). Federal agency surveillance of a State's BACT designation is needed, EPA asserts, to restrain the interjurisdictional pressures to which Congress was alert. See Brief for Respondents 33-34, 43; Brief for Vermont et al. as *Amici Curiae* 12 ("If EPA has authority to ensure a reasonable level of consistency among BACT determinations nationwide, then every State can feel more confident about maintaining stringent standards without fear of losing its current industry or alienating prospective industry.").

The CAA construction EPA advances in this litigation is reflected in interpretive guides the Agency has several times published. . . .

We have previously accorded dispositive effect to EPA's interpretation of an ambiguous CAA provision. See *Chevron U.S.A. Inc. v. Natural Resources Defense Council, Inc.*, 467 U.S. 837, 865-866, 81 L. Ed. 2d 694, 104 S. Ct. 2778

(1984); *Union Elec.*, 427 U.S. 246, at 256, 49 L. Ed. 2d 474, 96 S. Ct. 2518. The Agency's interpretation in this case, presented in internal guidance memoranda, however, does not qualify for the dispositive force described in *Chevron. See Christensen v. Harris County*, 529 U.S. 576, 587, 146 L. Ed. 2d 621, 120 S. Ct. 1655 (2000) ("Interpretations such as those in . . . policy statements, agency manuals, and enforcement guidelines, all of which lack the force of law — do not warrant *Chevron*-style deference."); *accord, United States v. Mead Corp.*, 533 U.S. 218, 234, 150 L. Ed. 2d 292, 121 S. Ct. 2164 (2001). Cogent "administrative interpretations . . . not [the] products of formal rulemaking . . . nevertheless warrant respect." *Wash. State Dep't of Soc. & Health Servs. v. Guardianship Estate of Keffeler*, 537 U.S. 371, 385, 154 L. Ed. 2d 972, 123 S. Ct. 1017 (2003). We accord EPA's reading of the relevant statutory provisions, §§ 7413(a)(5), 7470(3), 7470(4), 7475(a)(4), 7477, and 7479(3), that measure of respect. . . .

[The Court then rejected ADEC's arguments with respect to the meaning of the CAA and determined EPA's exercise of its discretionary authority was nonarbitrary.]

. . . In sum, we conclude that EPA has supervisory authority over the reasonableness of state permitting authorities' BACT determinations and may issue a stop construction order, under §§ 113(a)(5) and 167, if a BACT selection is not reasonable. We further conclude that, in exercising that authority, the Agency did not act arbitrarily or capriciously in finding that ADEC's BACT decision in this instance lacked evidentiary support. EPA's orders, therefore, were neither arbitrary nor capricious. The judgment of the Court of Appeals is accordingly affirmed.

JUSTICE KENNEDY, with whom the CHIEF JUSTICE, JUSTICE SCALIA, and JUSTICE THOMAS join, dissenting.

. . . The BACT definition presumes that the permitting authority will exercise discretion. It presumes, in addition, that the BACT decision will accord full consideration to the statutory factors and other relevant and necessary criteria. Contrary to the majority's holding, the statute does not direct the State to find as BACT the technology that results in the "maximum reduction of a pollutant achievable for [a] facility" in the abstract. Indeed, for a State to do so without regard to the other mandatory criteria would be to ignore the words of the statute. The Act requires a more comprehensive judgment. It provides that the permitting authority must "tak[e] into account" a set of contextual considerations — "energy, environmental, and economic impacts and other costs" — to identify the best control technology "on a case-by-case basis." 42 U.S.C. § 7479(3). The majority reaches its narrow view of the scope of the State's discretion only by wresting two adjectives, "maximum" and "achievable," out of context. In doing so, it ignores "the cardinal rule that a statute is to be read as a whole." *King v. St. Vincent's Hospital*, 502 U.S. 215, 221, 116 L. Ed. 2d 578, 112 S.Ct. 570 (1991).

To be sure, §§ 113(a)(5) and 167 authorize EPA to enforce requirements of the Act. These provisions, however, do not limit the States' latitude and responsibility to balance all the statutory factors in making their discretionary judgments. If a State has complied with the Act's requirements, §§ 113(a)(5) and 167 are not implicated and can supply no separate basis for EPA to exercise a supervisory role over a State's discretionary decision. . . .

If cooperative federalism . . . is to achieve Congress' goal of allowing state governments to be accountable to the democratic process in implementing environmental policies, federal agencies cannot consign States to the ministerial tasks of information gathering and making initial recommendations, while reserving to themselves the authority to make final judgments under the guise of surveillance and oversight. For these reasons, and with all respect, I dissent from the opinion and the judgment of the Court.

A NOTE ON "MODIFICATION"

For many individuals and corporations, the best way to avoid the cost and hassle of NSR is by making sure existing major sources do not undergo a "modification." This is because the most burdensome NSR requirements fall on new or "modified" major sources. Avoiding modification can be tricky, though, since all plants require alteration and equipment replacement during their useful lives. And each of these activities can easily qualify as a "modification." Section 111 of the CAA defines "modification" as follows: "any physical change [in], or change in the method of operation of, a stationary source which increases the amount of any air pollutant emitted by such source or which results in the emission of any air pollutant not previously emitted." § 111(a)(4), 42 U.S.C. § 7411(a)(4).

Given this fact, it might be surprising to learn that EPA issues only 140–175 PSD permits each year to major sources, and most of these are for new, as distinct from modified, sources. Why so few? It would seem two phenomena are occurring. First, a good number of manufacturers are declining to alter their plants, perhaps for this exact reason: they do not wish to incur the not insignificant financial burdens of NSR. A knowledgeable former EPA official argues the incentive to avoid plant upgrading has given the nation in the current day a fleet of large, leaky facilities forced into service long beyond their expected useful lives. Comments of Bruce C. Buckheit, Director, Air Enforcement Division, U.S. Environmental Protection Agency, at the ALI-ABA Conference on Environmental Law (Bethesda, MD, Feb.8, 2001).

A second reason for the relative paucity of modifications can be traced to EPA itself. EPA opened the door to allow industrial entities to alter plants without taking on the dreaded "modified" status. It did so by promulgating a regulatory subdefinition of "modification" that excepted from the term actions qualifying as "maintenance, repair, and replacement which the Administrator determines to be routine. . . ." 40 C.F.R. § 60.14(e); 40 C.F.R. § 52.21(b)(2)(iii).

The issue has become what is "routine maintenance, repair, and replacement" ("RMRR"). EPA did not define this phrase in its regulations, opting instead to decide these questions on a case-by-case, "common sense," basis, taking into account the nature, scope, extent, and cost of each alleged RMRR project. But, predictably, EPA and the regulated community vigorously disagree on what RMRR is. EPA has argued for years that substantial changes to plants nearing the end of their useful lives are about as close to RMRR as a heart transplant is to a flu shot. Industry has countered that even significant plant alterations can fall short of "modification." In its view, for example, even the replacement of primary and essential components of a manufacturing facility is "routine." This ongoing dispute has provoked a good deal of litigation. The leading case, which failed to definitively resolve the question, is *Wisconsin Electric Power Company v. Reilly*, 893 F.2d 901 (7th Cir. 1990) (*"WEPCO"*). For a case siding with EPA's position, see *United States v. Ohio Edison Co.*, 276 F. Supp. 2d 829 (S.D. Ohio, 2003); for one siding with industry, see *United States v. Duke Energy Corp.*, 278 F. Supp. 2d 619 (M.D.N.C. 2003).

The controversy shows no sign of abating and, in fact, has heated up with EPA's seeming change of heart, as evidenced by a new rule it promulgated after the change of administrations. 68 Fed. Reg. 61247 (Oct. 27, 2003) ("2003 NSR rule"). The 2003 NSR rule primarily addresses the matter of equipment replacement projects ("ERPs"). It declares that ERPs qualify as RMRR if (a) the new equipment is identical or functionally equivalent to the replaced equipment; (b) the cost of the ERP does not exceed 20% of the replacement value of the process unit of which the replaced equipment is a part; and (c) the replacement does not change the process unit's basic design parameters. *Id.* The rule was immediately contested. On December 24, 2003, two days before the rule would have come into effect, the D.C. Circuit Court of Appeals issued an order to stay it pending review. *State of New York v. EPA*, No. 02-1387 (D.C. Cir. Dec. 24, 2003). Environmentalists view the 2003 NSR rule as a complete cave-in by the Administration. In particular, they maintain the 20% cost factor is a gaping hole that would allow polluters to avoid a "modification" designation with virtual impunity. In other words, the rule as they see it essentially guts NSR. Industry, which reportedly suggested the 20% cost factor to the Administration and never expected to get it, has pooh-poohed the whole affair as much ado about very little. As one industry lawyer (a former EPA general counsel) put it: "NSR benefits health only incidentally and indirectly in the way that anything that reduces pollution may also have ancillary health benefits, but that is not the program's purpose or focus." E. Donald Elliott, *NSR, An Industry Lawyer's Perspective on the Ongoing Battle Over Who Speaks for EPA*, EM, pp 27-29 (January, 2004). This argument, at bottom, asserts it is NAAQS system that protects the public health, not NSR. EPA, for its part, maintains these regulatory changes inure to environmental quality by encouraging upgrades at plants that otherwise remain unimproved. The rule, contends the agency, should encourage a more efficient and clean fleet of manufacturing facilities.

Stay tuned.

A NOTE ON EMISSIONS TRADING

The regulations we have seen thus far are known as "command-and-control" regulations. Regulations of this type operate as the name indicates: they require a set of responses, leaving few or no options available to the regulated community. Command-and-control regulations have been criticized for sweeping too broadly and inflexibly across industry. When not attuned to peculiarities of industrial operations, such regulations can be costly, inefficient, and unduly burdensome.

There are several alternatives to command-and-control regulations. One is taxation to encourage environment-friendly behavior. Another, more of which we shall see shortly, is market-based regulation. These alternatives allow the regulated community more flexibility in choosing how to most cost-effectively meet regulatory goals.

Since the early 1980s, the EPA has been trying to work more flexibility into its regulatory structure, and nowhere more concertedly than in its regulation of air quality. Notably, EPA does not have an entirely free hand in doing so: it is constrained to follow the directives of the legislation it administers. The following piece is the summary portion of a major regulatory policy statement established by EPA for these purposes.

EPA EMISSIONS TRADING POLICY STATEMENT
51 Fed. Reg. 43, 814, 43,830 et seq. (1986)

. . . .

A. What is Emissions Trading?

Emissions trading consists of bubbles, netting, emission offsets, and emission reduction banking. These steps involve creation of surplus emission reductions at certain stacks, vents or similar sources of emissions and use of these emission reductions to meet or redefine pollution control requirements applicable to other emission sources. Such emissions trades can provide more flexibility to meet environmental requirements, and may therefore be used to reduce control costs and encourage faster compliance. Moreover, by developing "generic" trading rules (see Section III below) states[6] may be able to expedite bubble approvals by eliminating the need for case-by-case SIP revisions[7] and by providing more predictable approval criteria.

B. The Bubble

EPA's bubble lets existing plants (or groups of plants) increase emissions at one or more emission sources in exchange for compensating extra decreases in emissions at other emission sources. Approved bubbles give plant managers the ability to implement less costly ways of meeting air quality requirements. To be approvable, each bubble must produce results which are equivalent to or better than the baseline emission levels in terms of ambient impact and enforceability. Thus, bubbles should jeopardize neither ambient standards nor applicable PSD increments and visibility requirements. Under EPA's bubble, emission reductions from existing sources can not be used to meet technology-based requirements applicable to new or modified stationary sources.

This Policy Statement . . . tightens general bubble principles as well as requirements for bubbles in primary nonattainment areas which require but

---

[6] "States" includes any entity properly delegated authority to administer relevant parts of a State Implementation Plan (SIP) under the Clean Air Act.

[7] "Case-by-case SIP revision" means case-by-case approval by EPA as a SIP revision. This is the traditional mechanism by which bubbles and other SIP changes have been approved by EPA.

lack demonstrations of attainment, and requires bubbles in these areas to produce progress towards attainment, beyond equivalence to stringent emission limits. * * *

C. Netting

Netting may exempt "modifications" of existing major sources from certain preconstruction permit requirements under New Source Review (NSR), so long as there is no net emissions increase within the major source or any such increase falls below significance levels. By "netting out," the modification is not considered "major" and is therefore not subject to associated preconstruction permit requirements for major modifications under 40 CFR 51.18, 51.24, 52.21, 52.24, 52.27, or 52.28. The modification must nevertheless meet applicable new source performance standards (NSPS), national emissions standards for hazardous air pollutants (NESHAPs), preconstruction applicability review requirements under 40 CFR 51.18(a)–(h) and (l), and SIP requirements. * * *

Netting's scope is determined by the definition of "source" for review of major modifications. In general, PSD areas use a single, plantwide definition, allowing actual emission reductions anywhere in a contiguous plant to compensate for potential emission increases at individual emitting units within the plant. Nonattainment areas can choose either this single, plantwide definition or a dual definition, so long as the definition selected does not interfere with attainment and maintenance of NAAQS and is consistent with progress towards attainment. Under the plantwide definition, significant net actual increases at the plant as a whole will trigger new source review. Under the dual definition, significant increases at either the plant as a whole or individual emitting units will trigger new source review.

In addition to these federal definitions for major new sources and modifications, state preconstruction permits for major or minor new sources and modifications may be required under 40 CFR 51.18(a), and some states preclude netting.

D. Emission Offsets

In nonattainment areas, major new stationary sources and major modifications are subject to a presconstruction permit requirement that they secure sufficient surplus emission reductions to more than "offset" their emissions. This requirement is designed to allow industrial growth in nonattainment areas without interfering with attainment and maintenance of ambient air quality standards. It is currently implemented through SIP regulations adopted by states to meet the requirements of 40 CFR 51.18(j).

In attainment areas, some new sources and modifications might not otherwise be able to be constructed because their emissions would result in an exceedance of the applicable PSD increment or ambient air quality standard, would significantly contribute to a violation of an ambient air quality standard in a designated primary nonattainment area, or would significantly contribute to visibility impairment in a Federal Class I area. These sources may use emissions offsets to allow desired growth while protecting that increment, standard, or visibility.

E. Emission Reduction Banking

Firms may store qualified emission reduction credits (ERCs) in EPA-approvable banks for later use in bubble, offset or netting transactions. Depending on the bank's rules, banked ERCs may also be sold or transferred to other firms which seek to meet certain regulatory requirements by use of emissions trades.

EPA's revised Offset Ruling (40 CFR Part 51, Appendix S) allows states to establish banking rules as part of their SIPs. . . . While many areas also allow banking of emission reductions for various purposes through various formal or informal banking mechanisms, banks which do not meet today's criteria (e.g., by not making banked emission reductions enforceable by the state by the time the reductions are actually banked, or by not assuring that deposits are taken explicitly into account for SIP planning purposes) cannot qualify emission reductions as ERCs, and may offer substantially less protection in the event of future SIP corrections or changes in ambient attainment status. * * *

G. Effect of This Policy Statement

Emissions trading is largely voluntary: no source is required to trade, and no state is required by EPA to approve a particular trade or to adopt a generic rule. Trading merely offers states and stationary sources alternative ways to meet regulatory requirements. For example, states are free to adopt generic rules or continue to implement trades as individual SIP revisions. They may adopt rules which incorporate all or any combination of the above trading approaches.[8] * * *

This notice reflects the current Clean Air Act and existing EPA regulations. A policy statement cannot legally alter such requirements. However, this notice establishes EPA policy in areas not governed by applicable regulations and sets out general principles which may help states and industry apply those regulations in individual cases. Federal or state rulemaking in response to, e.g., future litigation or changes in ambient standards, attainment status, or SIP validity, may affect states or firms that plan to engage or have engaged in emissions trading activities. * * *

EPA intends to apply changes made by today's policy prospectively (e.g., not to actions which have already been approved as case-by-case SIP revisions or under generic rules). If, however, ambient violations are discovered in an area where EPA has approved a trade, or if other violations of Clean Air Act

---

[8] Some requirements underlying emissions trading are not voluntary. For example, construction of a major new source or major modification in a nonattainment area requires sufficient existing-source reductions to constitute "reasonable progress toward attainment" despite the new emissions. 40 CFR 51.18(j); Part 51, Appendix S. However, where the area has an established a "growth margin" of extra reductions in a SIP which is currently approved by EPA, the state may provide the offsets from that growth margin rather than require them from the source, so long as it reduces the margin accordingly. *See* CAA § 173(1)(A) and (B), 42 U.S.C. § 7503(1)(A) and (B).

requirements are discovered in that area, sources involved in the trade should be aware that they are potentially subject to requirements for additional emission reductions, just as are all other sources in the area. * * *

NOTES AND QUESTION

1. Market-based regulatory approaches include items such as marketable permits, emission fees, fees on sale of items the use of which contribute to pollution, incentives to reduce automobile emissions or automobile use, and many others. The EPA has required market-based regulatory options in areas deemed in extreme nonattainment for ozone (at this writing, only the Los Angeles, California, air basin falls in this category). It has required as well economic incentive programs for serious carbon monoxide nonattainment areas failing to reach emission reduction milestones.

Industry favors these alternative regulatory approaches, at least as a general matter. In fact, it would like to see trading go beyond intersource, all the way to interstate.

2. EPA has implemented the bubble concept at every opportunity, with varying success. Its initial attempt to treat a combination of facilities as a single "source" for purposes of § 111 was found to be invalid. *ASARCO v. EPA*, 578 F.2d 319 (D.C. Cir. 1978). EPA has since reinstated the bubble in the new source program in certain circumstances. *See* 52 Fed. Reg. 28,946 (1987). EPA was successful in instituting a bubble in the nonattainment program, *Chevron v. Natural Resources Defense Council*, 467 U.S. 837, 104 S. Ct. 2778 (1984), and in the PSD program. *Alabama Power, supra,* 636 F.2d at 402.

For an analysis on the extent of emissions trading before the 1990 Amendments to the Clean Air Act, see Robert Hahn and Gorden Hester, *Where Did All the Markets Go? An Analysis of EPA's Emission Trading Program,* 6 Yale J. Reg. 109 (1989).

Some states have initiated emissions trading programs of their own.

D. THE 1990 AMENDMENTS

We complete our review of stationary source regulation under the Clean Air Act with a survey of the modifications brought into the Act in 1990. The Amendments were divided into eight titles. Of these, we will decline review of three.[9] The five we will review, albeit briefly, are:

- Title I: Provisions for Attainment and Maintenance of National Ambient Air Standards,
- Title III: Hazardous Air Pollutants,
- Title IV: Acid Deposition Control,
- Title V: Permits, and

---

[9] Title II, dealing with regulation of mobile sources of air pollution, is beyond the scope of our course. Title VII, relating to enforcement, is better investigated in a course in Environmental Litigation. And Title VIII, containing miscellaneous provisions, is not essential to our survey.

- Title VI: Stratospheric Ozone Protection.

[1] NATIONAL AMBIENT AIR QUALITY STANDARDS

As we have seen, the 1970 CAA called for attainment of primary ambient air quality standards by 1975. When that goal fell by the wayside, the Act was amended. The 1977 Clean Air Act Amendments posited a ten year compliance framework, but, as the 1990s approached, the goal remained unmet. Despite impressive gains in many quarters, still more than half of the nation's population was breathing unhealthful air. The chief offenders were carbon monoxide, ozone, and particulate matter. These pollutants remained abundantly present in the ambient air for several reasons, including the propensity of states to understate emissions in inventories submitted to the EPA, the use of erroneous models to project air quality gains, the failure to adequately enforce existing regulatory standards, design flaws in the standards themselves, and the inertia of agencies in the face of circumstances calling for change.

Accordingly, in Title I of the 1990 Amendments, Congress retooled the non-attainment provisions, mainly by subcategorizing nonattainment areas. The Amendments called for classifying nonattainment area for CO, O_3 and PM as one of five types: *marginal, moderate, serious, severe, or extreme*. The idea was to build into the Act a scheme for incremental progress in meeting the NAAQSs for these pollutants. Different requirements were established for each subcategorized area — the more polluted the area, the stiffer the requirements (for extreme areas, for example, construction moratoria may be in order). The Act went on to mandate remedial actions when areas fail to improve air quality over time, and added the additional deterrence of authorizing restrictions on the availability of federal highway funds. The Amendment called for attainment over five years, although EPA was authorized to extend the date by another five years.

Other features of Title I include a mandatory enlargement of ozone nonattainment areas, to better reflect this pollutant's pattern of travel over hundreds of miles after emission; new requirements for monitoring; additional funding to assist emissions inventory efforts; shifting of federal transportation expenditures in nonattainment areas to discourage single occupancy vehicle use; and payments of fees to EPA of no less than $15 per ton of VOC, NOx, CO, and PM_{10} emitted.

[2] HAZARDOUS AIR POLLUTANTS

Hazardous air pollutants are governed by § 112 of the Clean Air Act. *See supra*. As discussed earlier in this Chapter, § 112 as originally enacted was unwieldy. Identifying which pollutants qualified as hazardous was a first administrative obstacle and fashioning health-based emissions standards furnishing an "ample" margin of safety was another. Frustrated, EPA found itself devoting its energies to other pursuits.

Observing the inertia of the program, Congress finally got to the task of revising § 112 in 1990. The result was a major rewrite, a reworking of § 112 from the ground up. Congress began by relieving EPA of its first burden, identifying which pollutants are hazardous. The new § 112 begins by listing the hazardous air pollutants subject to the provision. The rewritten provision specifies 188 pollutants or chemical groups to be regulated. § 112(b)(1), 42 U.S.C. § 7412(b)(1). Notably, EPA is empowered to revise and modify the list. § 112(b)(2), 42 U.S.C. § 7412(b)(2). Included in Congress's list are substances such as benzene, dioxin, mercury, chromium, and methyl isocyanate, the pollutant that killed more than 2,000 people in the 1984 disaster at Bhopal, India. Commensurate with this change, "hazardous air pollutant" is now defined as "any air pollutant listed pursuant to subsection (b) of this section." § 112(a)(6), 42 U.S.C. § 7412(a)(6).

That done, Congress required new emissions standards for hazardous air pollutant emissions based on "maximum achievable control technology" ("MACT") and "generally achievable control technology" ("GACT"). The MACT standard, applicable to categories and subcategories of "new," see § 112(a)(1), 42 U.S.C. § 7412(a)(1), or existing "major," see § 112(a)(4), 42 U.S.C. § 7412(a)(4), sources, requires "the maximum degree of reduction in emissions of the hazardous air pollutants subject to this section (including a prohibition on such emissions, where achievable) that the Administrator, taking into consideration the cost of achieving such emission reduction, and any non-air quality health and environmental impacts and energy requirements, determines is achievable for new or existing sources. . . ." § 112(d)(2), 42 U.S.C. § 7412(d)(2). What constitutes MACT may vary depending upon whether a source is "new" or "existing." § 112(d)(3), 42 U.S.C. § 7412(d)(3). The GACT standard, less stringent than MACT but undefined in the legislation, is applicable to new or existing "area" sources. See § 112(a)(2), 42 U.S.C. § 7412(a)(2); see also § 112(d)(5), 42 U.S.C. § 7412(d)(5). EPA is directed to list only those area sources that present "a threat of adverse effects to human health or the environment." § 112(c)(3), 42 U.S.C. § 7412(c)(3). If the Administrator finds an emission limitation to be infeasible in a particular case, she may promulgate in its place a "design, equipment, work practice, or operational standard." § 112(h)(1), 42 U.S.C. § 7412(h)(1).

In enacting this new regulatory scheme, Congress projected a 75% decrease in air toxics emissions. However, in the event the new controls failed to clean the air to healthful levels, it supplied EPA with authority to implement more stringent health-based standards to solve the problem. Thus did the Congress relegate the previously required "ample margin of safety" health-based standard to a backup role. § 112(f), 42 U.S.C. § 7412(f).

The legislation also provided that no person may modify, construct, or reconstruct a major source of air toxics without implementing MACT. Where no applicable emissions limitations are in place, EPA can make a case-by-case determination. § 112(g)(2)(A)–(B), 42 U.S.C. § 7412(g)(2)(A)–(B). "Modification" is defined in terms of increased emissions of any hazardous air pollutant, § 112(a)(5), 42 U.S.C. § 7412(a)(5), but modifications are made expressly subject to a statutory offset policy. § 112(g)(1)(A), 42 U.S.C. § 7412(g)(1)(A).

In July 1992, pursuant to § 112(c)(1), EPA published an initial list of categories of sources that emit hazardous air pollutants. 57 Fed. Reg. 31,576 (1992). About seventeen months later, it published a schedule for promulgation of emission standards for these listed source categories, as required by

§ 112(e). 58 Fed. Reg. 63,941 (1993). In March, 1994, it promulgated final rules to implement the section. 59 Fed. Reg. 12,408 (1994).

How does EPA determine MACT? For "new" sources, those for which construction begins after EPA publishes emission standards, § 111(a)(2), 42 U.S.C. § 7411(a)(2), MACT requires a degree of reduction of emissions not "less stringent than the emission control that is achieved in practice by the best controlled similar source. . . ." § 112(d)(3), 42 U.S.C. § 7412(d)(3). For existing sources, the degree of reduction of emissions "shall not be less stringent than the average emission limitation achieved by the best performing 12 percent of the existing sources (for which the Administrator has emissions information). . . ." *Id.* EPA uses a two-step process to implement these requirements. First the Agency establishes minimum stringency requirements known as "emission floors," which "apply without regard to either costs or the other factors and methods listed in section 7412(d)(2)." *National Lime Ass'n v. EPA*, 233 F.3d 625, 629 (D.C. Cir. 2000) ("*National Lime II*"). Then, for each pollutant and source category, it determines whether stricter standards, known as "beyond-the-floor" limits, are achievable in light of the factors listed in section § 112(d)(2), 42 U.S.C. § 7412(d)(2). *National Lime II*, 233 F.3d at 629. *See generally, Cement Kiln Recycling Coalition v. U.S. Environmental Protection Agency*, 255 F.3d 855 (D.C. Cir. 2001).

NOTE

Emissions of hazardous air pollutants remain at significant levels at the present time. *See* below.

Figure 5-3. HAP Emissions by state, based on 1993 NTI.

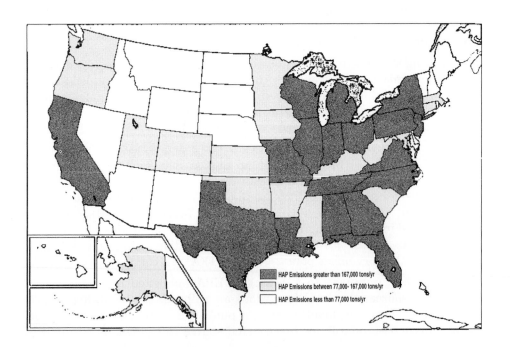

Nonetheless, EPA has predicted in its 1997 National Air Quality and Emissions Trends Report that these emissions will decline by 1.5 million tons in each of the following ten years. *Second Report to Congress on the Status of the Hazardous Air Pollutant Program under the CAA*, Draft EPA-453, R-96-015 (October, 1997). Since there exists no national monitoring network for hazardous air pollutants, complete information about the concentrations of these pollutants in the ambient air is unavailable.

[3] ACID DEPOSITION CONTROL

Sulfur and nitrogen oxides, emitted into the ambient air largely from combustion of fossil fuels, react in the upper atmosphere to form compounds. After transport over potentially long distances, these compounds fall to ground level in the form of pollutants such as particulate matter (sulfates and nitrates), SO_2, NO_2, nitric acid and, when reacting with volatile organic compounds (VOCs), ozone. This process is known as acid deposition. Acid deposition takes both dry and wet forms (hence, the familiar term, "acid rain"). Dry deposits account for somewhere between 20–60% of total acid deposition. *See http://www.epa.gov/oar/aqtrnd97/chapter7.pdf.*

The national problem with acid deposition was explained by the Senate in its Report accompanying the enactment of Title IV:

SENATE REPORT NO. 101-228,

101st Cong. 2d Sess., U.S. Code Congressional and Administrative News, at pp. 3645–47

Sources and acid rain. Acid rain is created when oxides of sulfur and nitrogen are emitted most often from electric utilities B and then transformed in the atmosphere or on surfaces into sulfuric and nitric acids. The process is relatively straightforward.

Sulfur (S) is contained in almost all fossil fuels, but especially coal. When burned, the sulfur combines with the oxygen in the air to create sulfur dioxide (SO_2).

Sulfur dioxide (SO_2) is a colorless gas, so it cannot be seen with the naked eye. It is, nevertheless, a powerful lung irritant which can cause lung seizures in asthmatics and other sensitive groups. When SO_2 is transformed into sulfate, a process which begins almost immediately, it escapes regulation under the Clean Air Act. SO_2 emitted by powerplants and other industrial sources combines with oxygen in the atmosphere to form sulfate (SO_4).

Sulfate (SO_4) is an extremely fine particle, capable of reaching the deepest recesses of the lung. Coincidentally, the sulfate particle is also perfectly sized for reducing visibility. This is one reason that airport visibility measurements are sometimes used as a surrogate for sulfate concentrations. When sulfate settles out of the air onto leaves, buildings or other surfaces it attracts water, which converts it into sulfuric acid (H_2SO_4). If inhaled, the lung's own moisture supports the conversion. And, if the SO_4 is washed out [of] the air by fog, clouds, mist or rain, it has become "acid" rain, as it is popularly called.

Sulfuric acid (H_2SO_4) is powerfully corrosive and can therefore directly damage tissues and materials. But it can also start a chemical reaction of its own, with effects that ripple through an ecosystem. When common dirt is washed in acid, heavy metals that were tightly bound to the soil particles — aluminum, lead, and mercury are three examples — are dissolved, entering the water runoff in massive quantities. Aluminum, for example, increases 1000 percent for every 100 percent increase in rainfall acidity. Thus if the acidity of rain increases 10-fold — which almost all agree is a fair definition of how "acid" today's acid rain is — the aluminum content of rainwater runoff increases 10,000 percent.

Exactly what damages can be fairly attributed to aluminum and other heavy metals freed by acid rain has not been sorted out completely. It is well established that the aluminum is extremely toxic to fish if it reaches lakes and streams. Many scientist believe that it is aluminum which is primarily responsible for the losses of lakes throughout Scandanavia, Canada and New England, rather than the sulfuric acid itself. It is equally clear that some of the other heavy metals — especially lead, cadmium and mercury — can pose a serious threat to human health as drinking water contaminants. Whether they are reaching these dangerous levels because of acid rain and, if so, in how many cases, is unclear.

Nitric acid (HNO_3). Nitrogen undergoes a fairly similar process of conversion: nitrogen (N_2) combines with oxygen (O_2) to form several different oxides (N_2O_2, N_2O, NO_2, etc.). These, in turn, form nitrates which, when exposed to water convert to nitric acid. There are, however, some important differences.

Oxides of nitrogen (N_2O_2, N_2O, NO_2) can be created because nitrogen is found both in fuels and in the air. Roughly 80 percent of the air is nitrogen, and almost all fuels other than natural gas also contain it. But the oxides are not formed until the heat and pressure of the combustion process are brought to bear. The combustion may take place in the cylinder of a car or the furnace of a giant coal-fired powerplant. But in either case, the combustion temperature and pressure are determinants of how much nitrogen is converted to oxides of nitrogen.

These oxides, like SO_2, are irritants which are regulated under the Clean Air Act. And, again like SO_2, they escape its coverage when they combine with oxygen to form nitrates (NO_3).

Nitrates (NO_3), like sulfates, are fine particles which can reach the cellular levels of the lung. Unlike sulfates, nitrates and other nitrogen-based compounds are considered beneficial to vegetation because they are plant nutrients. For this reason, some scientists and policy makers have tended to minimize the role which oxides of nitrogen, nitrates and nitric acid have played in the damage caused by acid rain and plans for its control.

Within the past several years, however, as scientists have searched for plausible explanations for the forest damages found throughout much of Europe and Eastern North America, they have begun to question whether one answer might be an "over fertilizing" effect of nitrogen compounds. There have also been suggestions that nitric acid could free heavy metals before being taken up by vegetation.

Nitric acid (HNO_3) thus may or may not be the equal of sulfuric acid in terms of the damages caused by acid rain. But the bill, including this title, imposes additional controls on nitrogen for reasons in addition to concerns over acid rain; namely, the role which it plays in the formation of ozone.

Ozone (O_3), better known as an ingredient in "smog", is the indicator for a variety of chemicals which are formed when the combination of nitrogen and organic chemicals (e.g. gasoline) are exposed to sunlight. Ozone is a powerful bleach, so effective at destroying organic matter that it is used by some cities to disinfect their drinking water supplies.

Although the chain of chemical reactions which leads to the formation of ozone and other oxidants is not completely understood, there is no disagreement that there are three essential ingredients. Without all three, ozone is not formed in substantial quantities. These are hydrocarbons, oxides of nitrogen, and sunlight. Historically, the Federal government has relied on a strategy of controlling ozone by controlling hydrocarbons emissions. This has achieved mixed results, leading some States to begin implementing a strategy based on controlling oxides of nitrogen. California has been the leading advocate of this approach and, according to State officials, has enjoyed considerable success.

Both ozone and acid aerosols pervade the atmosphere of eastern North America. Any one of them may pose a potent threat standing alone. But in combination, their impacts are multiplicative. This has been established in laboratory studies, but the extent to which these experiments represent the real environment [is] unclear. Nitrogen and its compounds, however, play a substantial role whether the specific problem being examined is acid rain, ozone, or the synergistic effects of the two.

*   *   *   *   *   *

New Title IV of the 1990 Amendments added an entirely new program to control acid deposition. 42 U.S.C. §§ 7651-7651o. With respect to nitrogen oxide emissions, the Act sought a two million ton reduction from emissions levels of the year 2000. To do this, the Act employed a conventional regulatory approach, establishing emission limitations for some sources and directing EPA to fashion others based on "the degree of reduction achievable through the retrofit application of the best system of continuous emission reduction, taking into account available technology, costs and energy and environmental impacts. . . ." § 407(b)(1)-(2), 42 U.S.C. § 7651f(b)(1)-(2).

However, Title IV is more interesting for its market-based regulation of sulfur dioxide (SO_2) emissions. Rather than opt for traditional command-and-control, the Act established for these emissions an innovative cap-and-trade regulatory system. As described in President George H. Bush's signing statement, the idea was to "set tough standards, allow freedom of choice in how to meet them, and let the power of markets help us in allocating the costs most efficiently." *Statement by President George Bush upon Signing S. 1630*, 26 Weekly Compilation of Presidential Documents 1824, November 19, 1990, *reprinted at* U.S. Code Congressional and Administrative News, 101st Cong., 2d Sess., at 3887.

The SO_2 control provisions exemplified the approach. For SO_2 emissions, the legislation first imposed a national cap of 8.95 million tons of SO_2 emissions per year on electric utilities, an amount representing a ten million ton reduction from 1980 emission levels, § 403(a)(1), 42 U.S.C. § 7651b(a)(1); § 405(a)(3), 42 U.S.C. § 7651d(a)(3). (Note: the text of the Act reads "8.90 million tons." § 403(a)(1), 42 U.S.C. § 7651b(a)(1).) The Act contemplated reaching this goal over two phases. Phase I represented an interim step toward the goal. In Phase I, effective from 1995-2000, 110 designated utilities with major coal-fired generating units were required to reduce emissions to 2.50 pounds of SO_2 per million British thermal units of fuel consumed, as measured against benchmark years 1985 -1987. § 404, 42 U.S.C. § 7651c. To start the game, each of these utility units was allocated, free of charge, a predetermined number of pollution allowances on an annual basis; each allowance authorized the emission of one ton of sulfur dioxide for one year. Beginning in 1995, the Act prohibited polluters from emitting SO_2 in excess of their total number of Phase I allowances.

Beginning in 2000, Phase II of the program kicked in. Phase II brought under regulation all fossil fuel-fired power plants and further restricted aggregate allowances to a number assuring attainment of the 8.95 million ton national goal. § 405(3), 42 U.S.C. § 7651d(3). Beginning in 2000, polluters must have reduced SO_2 emissions to no more than authorized by their Phase II allowances.[10]

Thus, to comply with the law, a utility has two options, to be taken singly or in concert. First, the utility can reduce emissions by changing the fuel it uses, or by installing pollution control equipment (typically, "scrubbers"), or both. In addition, and here is the innovative part of the system, the utility can engage in allowance trading. With this option, a regulated utility can keep high its emissions and still solve its legal problem by securing a sufficient number of allowances to make up the difference. Entities may do this because the Act declares allowances to be fully marketable — they can be bought, sold, traded, or banked for future use or sale. § 402, 42 U.S.C. § 7651. These transactions may occur independently among contracting parties or at an EPA-sponsored auction. Auctions are held in March of each year at the Chicago Board of Trade.

It is up to each utility how best to meet its legal obligation. One utility might decide to rely fully on emissions reductions, while another might aggressively enter the marketplace to buy allowances. A utility that can reduce emissions cheaply might pull back more than is required and sell the difference, or carry those "credits" over for use in subsequent years. Another utility might both reduce emissions and purchase allowances. And so it goes.

By all accounts, the cap-and-trade program has been a huge success. Beneficial results were immediate. EPA reported that sulfate precipitation

---

[10] In addition to these annual allocations, in accordance with the legislation, EPA established three reserves. The first two reserves supply additional pollution rights for persons who (a) install high performance technologies ("qualifying Phase I technologies") (§ 404(d), 42 U.S.C. § 7651c(d)), or (b) implement customer-oriented conservation measures or renewable energy generation. The third reserve supplies additional allowances to persons who buy them at EPA-sponsored auctions (more of which later).

after 1995 fell to levels 10-25% below what would have been otherwise expected, with major gains in regions that need it most, such as the Ohio Valley. EPA attributed this improvement directly to Phase I emission reductions. (Comparatively, nitrate concentrations did not change appreciably.) EPA, *National Air Quality and Emissions Trends Report (1977), http/ / :www.epa.gov / ora / aqtrnd97 / chapter7.pdf.* In meeting the 1995 levels, utilities used 5,302,081 allowances, or 61% of the total issued by EPA for that year; those not used were carried over for later use. By one estimate, total emissions reductions exceeded statutory goals by 39%. Emissions, moreover, declined in every state having a regulated utility unit. Not a single utility failed to meet its Phase I-required SO_2 emissions reductions obligation, according to an EPA report dated August 8, 1996. In 2002, SO_2 emissions from power plants fell to 10.2 million tons, a level nine percent lower than the year 2000 and 41 percent lower than 1980. *http:/ / www.epa.gov / air / acidrain / index.html* (visited September, 2004). There has been no need for enforcement.

The program accomplished these positive environmental results at exceedingly low cost. When the 1990 Amendments were under consideration by Congress, skeptical utilities warned that cleaning the air of SO_2 would cost as much as $1500 a ton. EPA itself countered with a $600 per ton cost estimate. Yet, in the first auction, held in 1994, allowances traded in the $150 range. In the following year, prices dipped to about $125-130. In 1999, allowances sold in the "spot auction" went for an average of $200 and 7-year-advance allowances traded at approximately $165. Some utilities purchased tens of thousands of allowances; others were sellers. And it is not only emitters who participate. Organizations as diverse as the Creighton University Environmental Law Society, the Clean Air Conservancy, and even elementary school classes, have submitted bids in the auctions. Non-commercial entities typically "retire" the allowances they purchase.

[4] PERMITS

Another significant alteration of the 1990 Amendments is its installation of a comprehensive permit system to streamline stationary source regulation. The idea of using permits had been gaining credence for twenty years. For one thing, permits have proven to be facile regulatory tools under the Clean Water Act (*see* Chapter 10, *infra*), in large part because they assemble in one easily found location the universe of requirements imposed on a regulated entity. As such, permits assist sources wanting to comply, and they effectively rob those who would not comply of excuses based on mistake. SIPs, moreover, were increasingly seen as unwieldy and as better suited for planning than for enforcement and program implementation. *See, e.g.,* Stephen E. Roady, *Permitting and Enforcement Under the Clean Air Act Amendments of 1990,* 21 Envt'l L. Rev. 10,178 (News & Analysis) (April 1991).

Congress imposed its new permit requirements in what is now Subchapter V of the Act. As a general matter, the new provisions prohibit sources from operating without a permit, and declare unlawful activities that contravene the terms of a permit. "Major" sources, "affected sources" under the acid deposition program, new sources under § 111, sources of hazardous pollutants subject to § 112, and sources already subject to permitting under Parts C

(PSD) and D (Nonattainment) fall under the requirements. § 502(a), 42 U.S.C. § 7661a(a).

Permits serve as a convenient location for a compendium of requirements and conditions. First and foremost, they announce the emission limitations applicable to permitted sources. In addition, they stipulate each source's schedule of compliance, its monitoring requirements, "and other such conditions as are necessary to assure compliance with applicable requirements of this chapter, including the requirements of the applicable implementation plan." § 504(a), 42 U.S.C. § 7661c(a). As a general matter, compliance with a permit is deemed to be compliance with the Act. This latter principle is known as the "permit shield." § 504(f), 42 U.S.C. § 7661c(f).

[5] STRATOSPHERIC OZONE PROTECTION

Finally, Title VI imposes controls for the purpose of protecting stratospheric ozone. These controls are in addition to those in place under the Clean Air Act's Section 108-110 SIP process, which are aimed primarily at reducing concentrations of ozone at ground level. (At ground level, ozone is a threat to life; at high levels, it saves lives.) Congress enacted Title VI for two independent reasons. First is global warming. Ozone-depleting substances in the atmosphere are seen as contributors to this perceived calamity in the making, although, as discussed in the Note that follows, the science is in conflict on this issue. The second, and more important reason, has to do with the penetration of harmful ultraviolet rays from the sun through the Earth's atmosphere. Too much ultraviolet radiation can cause skin cancer, cataracts, and genetic aberrations in humans. Ozone in the upper atmosphere performs the helpful function of blocking ultraviolet rays.

The call for stratospheric ozone protection arose in 1974, when two scientists from the University of California published a paper demonstrating that clorofluorocarbons, or "CFCs," destroy ozone. CFCs have been used primarily for refrigeration and as aerosols. CFCs and other ozone-depleting substances (for a list, see CAA § 602 et seq., 42 U.S.C. § 7671a et seq.) have been floating high into the atmosphere for many years. At high altitudes, they come into contact with the stratospheric ozone layer, and work to destroy it.

For reasons not entirely clear, the greatest destruction of upper-level ozone has taken place in skies over the Antarctic, where a "hole" in the ozone layer has appeared each September through December since the 1970s. The hole is characterized by reduced levels of ozone: ozone concentrations outside the hole are generally in the 7-7.5 ppm range, but inside the hole the concentrations fall to about 4 ppm. In September, 1994, for example, the hole measured 2400 kilometers in diameter, encompassing literally *millions* of square miles. The volume of ozone was found to be 40% less than it was in the 1970s, and the lowest since measurements began in 1961. Because of past use of ozone-diminishing materials, the hole has continued to grow. For example, between July and September, 1996, levels were 10 to 15% less than the average levels of the mid-1980s.

The international community has taken steps to address the ozone depletion problem. In the United States, use of ozone-depleting materials was more than halved in the 1990s, in part because of a federal tax increasing the cost of such materials from about fifty cents a pound to five dollars. Under the Montreal Protocol on Substances that Deplete the Ozone Layer, the European Union and the United States agreed to stop CFC production and importation. (The phaseout in developing countries is projected for 2010.)

Title VI constitutes the Congress's response to the "environmental crisis" of ozone depletion. Senate Report No. 101-228, accompanying the Clean Air Act Amendments of 1990, U.S. Code Congressional and Administrative News, 101st Cong. 2d Sess., at 3768. It calls for elimination of production of CFCs "as expeditiously as possible." Production of so-called "Class I substances," mostly CFCs, was made illegal as of January 1, 2000. § 604(b), 42 U.S.C. § 7671c(b). Production of "Class II substances," mostly hydroflourochlorocarbons, or HCFCs (which are ozone-unfriendly, but not as much as CFCs), must begin phasing out in 2015 and cease as of January 1, 2030. § 605, 42 U.S.C. § 7671d. Title VI also calls for recycling and emissions reductions in the interim. § 608, 42 U.S.C. § 7671g.

A NOTE ON GLOBAL WARMING

The temperature of air near the surface of the Earth has increased by 0.5 to 1.0 degree F. since the late 19th century and the warming trend seems to be accelerating. Records show the years 1985-2000 are home to the ten warmest years of the 20th century. The year 1995, during which an iceberg the size of Rhode Island broke off Antarctica, was at one time ranked as the warmest year of the century, but 1998 later overtook it and, at this writing, holds the title. EPA, *Global Warming Site: Impacts http://www.epa.gov/globalwarming/climate/index.html* (visited September, 2004.

An awakened scientific interest in climate change and a highly attentive media have brought this geological trend into prominence as a political issue. The public at large, not just in this nation but around the world, fears a warming pattern that could produce an array of harrowing consequences, both short and long term. In the short term, those consequences could include flooding of low-lying regions, disruption of agriculture, and the wholesale disturbance, if not destruction, of natural ecosystems. In the long term, nothing less than human survival could be at risk. *See, e.g.*, Daniel Botkin, *Global Warming: What It Is, What Is Controversial About It, and What We Might Do in Response to It*, 9 UCLA J. Envtl. L. & Pol'y 119 (1991). While this abiding concern has not yet found formal expression in the body of environmental or natural resources law, its high profile earns it mention here.

Why is the planet warm at all? The Earth basks in a blanket of warmth because of the good services of the planet's atmosphere. Heat energy from the Sun, without which the Earth would be a giant iceball, enters the atmosphere in the form of light. After solar light has penetrated, it comes into contact with the surface of the planet, which reflects a good portion of it back into outer space. If all of solar heat managed to reflect back, the Earth would remain an iceball. But, and here is the key to global warming, not all of the heat that makes its way in escapes out again. Much is trapped by the atmosphere.

The reason for solar heat's poor escape record has to do with wavelengths. When light from the Sun arrives at its planetary target, it has a relatively short wavelength (the one observable to the human eye). The wavelength, in turn, is a product of the measure of heat: the more heat content, the shorter the wavelength. Solar light is able to penetrate to the Earth's surface because the gases in the atmosphere are transparent to visible light. Upon contact with the relatively cool surface of the planet, however, the light is changed to infrared radiation, which has a longer wavelength. Infrared radiation cannot exit the planet as readily as the light entered it because the same atmospheric gases that are transparent to visible light are opaque to infrared radiation. Accordingly, upon exit, the atmosphere absorbs reflected infrared radiation. Some of this absorbed radiation ultimately radiates out into space, but a good deal of it re-radiates back to the planetary surface. Because this phenomenon resembles the function of a greenhouse, it has been called the "greenhouse effect." Atmospheric gases that provide this important heat-trapping service are known as "greenhouse gases."

The greenhouse effect, by overall standards, is obviously a good thing. The worry is not that the globe is warm, but that it might be getting too warm. In short, maybe we are getting too much of a good thing.

The purported cause of global warming is the increasing accumulation of greenhouse gases in the atmosphere. The most prominent greenhouse gases are five. They are carbon dioxide (CO_2), methane (CH_4), nitrous oxide (NO_2), water vapor (H_2O), and chloroflourocarbons (CFCs). These gases make their way into the stratosphere from a variety of sources, human and non-human. CO_2 is a product of natural processes such as respiration and photosynthesis, but also comes from combustion of waste materials and carbon-containing fossil fuels. It is estimated that levels of CO_2 in the atmosphere have increased by almost 30% since the industrial revolution. By some projections, by 2100, if nothing is done, concentrations will be yet again 30-150% higher. Methane finds its way to the atmosphere from landfills, natural gas and petroleum operations, agriculture and mining. While not as prevalent in the atmosphere as CO_2, methane reputedly is 20-50 times more efficient in trapping heat than CO_2. Nitrous oxide, released from fertilizers and fuel combustion, is found in even lesser amounts than methane, but is about three hundred times more effective in trapping heat than CO_2. Atmospheric concentrations of nitrous oxides are purported to have risen 13% over the past two centuries. Water vapor is virtually omnipresent, and may or may not be in the form of clouds. Finally, CFCs, also blamed for thinning the ozone layer, *see supra*, find their way into the atmosphere largely from spray cans and refrigeration.

EPA asserts that humans account for 98% of U.S. CO_2 emissions, 24% of methane emissions, and 18% of NO_2 emissions. As of 1997, moreover, the United States was said to be responsible for about one-fifth of total global greenhouse gas emissions. Subsequent data shows that the nation's greenhouse gas emissions increased in 1999 by nearly one percent over 1998 emission levels. Theoretically, as atmospheric greenhouse gases increase in quantity, more trapping of heat will occur, and temperatures will rise. The theory is plausible, but questions persist whether it is true.

First, there are questions of the reliability of scientific data and the capacity of scientists to interpret it. Data accumulation on the amount of ongoing warming has been imprecise in many instances, and collection methods non-uniform. This is of great concern because even slight errors in information can seriously skew the final results. In addition, the amount of data that must be analyzed is simply monumental. It has been said that a computer would have to track and evaluate over five million data parameters to reach a scientifically viable analytical result, and overlay that analysis with an independent assessment of the interactions among them.

Second, the data currently in place, even if it were unassailable on credibility grounds, may not demonstrate an unprecedented warming trend. Based on ice core data and other indirect indicators, current earth temperatures are currently at about the planet's 3000 year average. Atmospheric temperatures, moreover, as distinct from surface air temperatures, have not risen over the last two decades; they did warm, apparently, during the 1970's. Planetary temperatures, in any event, have been anything but constant. From 800-1200 A.D., the "Medieval Warm Period," the northern hemisphere was so hot that Vikings cultivated Greenland and Newfoundland. By 1300, the "Little Ice Age" had begun. This cooling trend persisted until the early 20th century. However, as the chart below illustrates, from the 1890s to the 1940s, surface temperatures inched up again. But temperatures fell again from the 1940s to the 1970s. For reasons not understood, tropospheric air temperatures warmed more during the 1970s than did surface air temperatures. In the last thirty-five years, stratospheric air temperatures have cooled. In short, the current warming trend may not be out of the ordinary. If it is happening at all, it may be well within geologic deviations.

Surface Data Source: National Climatic Data Center, 2001.
Satellite Data Source: John R. Christy, University of Alabama in Huntsville, and
Roy Spencer, National Aeronautics and Space Administration.

Third is the vexing problem of causation. Assuming the planet is warming dangerously, is human behavior the cause? Warming trends seem to correlate with solar activity. Heat emanations from the sun can vary significantly over decades and centuries, and records going back a couple of centuries show a strong correlation between increases in temperature in the northern hemisphere and this variable energy output (apparently, there is no similar data available for the southern hemisphere). Another variable is volcanic activity. For example, when Mount Pinatubo in the Phillippines erupted in 1991, global temperatures actually declined for a time. In addition, humans account for only 7 billion metric tons of CO_2 emissions each year, of total annual emissions of 160 billion metric tons. Additionally, if CO_2 emissions by humans were a major cause of global warming, one might have expected the bulk of current warming to have taken place in the wake of the Industrial Revolution, when the human CO_2 contributions dramatically increased. But most of the warming took place in the three centuries preceding the Industrial Revolution. Another uncertainty: when fossil fuel combustion releases CO_2, it also releases sulfate aerosols. In the atmosphere, these latter substances reflect away solar radiation, producing a cooling effect. How much? Who knows? (A side question comes to mind: has the nation's success in reducing SO_2 emissions actually contributed to global warming?) In the same vein, increased evaporation resulting from warmer temperatures could cause increased cloud production and a concomitant blockage of solar radiation.

In an attempt to bring some consensus to the debate, the White House requested the National Academy of Sciences to conduct a study to identify areas of certainty and uncertainty in the scientific data amassed on climate change. On June 6, 2001, the NAS issued its report, entitled "Climate Change Science: An Analysis of Some Key Questions" (*"NAS Report"* or *"Report"*). The *NAS Report* concluded that temperatures are rising. On the core question of whether greenhouse gases are the cause, the Report was more cautious:

> The . . . conclusion that most of the observed warming of the last 50 years is likely to have been due to the increase in greenhouse gas concentrations accurately reflects the current thinking of the scientific community on this issue. The stated degree of confidence in [this] assessment is higher today than it was ten, or even five years ago, but uncertainty remains because of (1) the level of natural variability inherent in the climate system on time scales of decades to centuries, (2) the questionable ability of models to accurately simulate natural variability on those long time scales, and (3) the degree of confidence that can be placed on reconstructions of global mean temperatures over the past millennium based on proxy evidence. Despite the uncertainties, there is general agreement that the observed warming is real and particularly strong within the past twenty years. Whether it is consistent with the change that would be expected in response to human activities is dependent upon what assumptions one makes about the time history of atmospheric concentrations of the various forcing agents, particularly aerosols.

NAS Report, Summary, at 5.

The body of the *NAS Report* reiterated this uncertainty, flatly stating that the linkage between the increase of greenhouse gases and the observed changes in climate is not proven. *NAS Report,* § 5, at 2. Beyond that, the document proclaimed that "current estimates of the magnitude of future warming should be regarded as tentative and subject to future adjustments (either upward or downward)." *NAS Report,* Summary, at 1. Overall, the *NAS Report* used the words "uncertainty" and "uncertain" 43 times over its 28 pages. The *Report* refrained from offering any policy suggestions to address the matter.

The federal government, of course, cannot so neatly sidestep issues of policy. Should the government do something to reduce greenhouse gases? Doing so would bring with it high costs. Are those costs worth assuming in light of uncertain scientific proofs? Should the government go forward with costly restrictions on industrial activity because the risk of not doing so might be cataclysmic? Thus far, the current Administration has taken a cautious approach. On the one hand, the White House announced support for reductions in greenhouse gas emissions, primarily by implementing clean energy technologies and through conservation. It also increased scientific inquiry into the causes of global warming, pledged a joint venture with other nations to monitor climate change, and promoted international cooperative efforts on the issue. Significantly, however, the current White House declined to endorse the Kyoto Protocol, the major international treaty directed at the problem. Under the terms of the Protocol, as a general matter, nations are to reduce their greenhouse gas emissions to about five percent below 1990 emissions levels by the year 2012. The Clinton Administration, however, agreed in the Protocol for the United States to reduce its emissions by 7 percent. Japan and Canada agreed to 6 percent reductions, and Australia signed on for 8 percent.

Calling the treaty "fatally flawed," President Bush objected to it on several grounds. First, of course, was the matter of scientific uncertainty. Beyond that, the treaty exempts from its terms major emitting nations such as China (the second largest greenhouse gas emitter behind the United States) and India. In the President's view, the global effort must be shared by all nations; the burden should not fall in disproportionate measure on the United States, which produces 20 percent of global emissions. While not stating so directly, surely the President was mindful of cost considerations as well. Compliance with the treaty, according to the Department of Energy under President Clinton, would cost the United States millions of jobs, and somewhere in the range of $300 billion to $400 billion, or about 3–4% of the gross domestic product, per year.

The treaty took effect on February 16, 2005, following ratification of it by Russia in October, 2004. Russia's ratification brought the number of ratifying nations to 125, but, more significantly, brought into the fold nations responsible for at least 55% of total global CO_2 emissions. By its terms, the treaty could not take effect until that latter benchmark was reached.

Russia's decision to ratify was substantially eased by economic realities. Because of a general economic downturn, Russia's emissions at this writing stand at approximately 25% *below* 1990 levels. This means that, under the terms of the treaty, Russia can sell its excess emissions for profits potentially in the "billions" of dollars. For that reason, and because Russia lacks the capacity to monitor emissions, it will be years before any curtailments of emissions become necessary, if ever. Last, Russia is the beneficiary of ecoonomic concessions from Europe, supplied to encourage the nation's ratification. Morning Edition, *National Public Radio,* October 22, 2004.

For its part, the United States Senate voted 95-0 in July, 1997, to not ratify unless and until all nations were included under the terms of the treaty and only if the treaty would not seriously harm the domestic economy. Four months thereafter, despite that unanimous Senate vote, former Vice President Al Gore signed the treaty on behalf of the United States. His signature did not bind the nation to the terms of the Protocal.

Since that time, proposals to modify the Protocol have circulated, among them one that would allow the use of "carbon sinks" as a means to meet CO_2 limits. "Carbon sinks" is a fancy term for plant life that takes in CO_2 and gives off oxygen. Under the proposal, a nation could make progress toward meeting treaty obligations by planting forests.

Could EPA reduce greenhouse gas emissions by regulating CO_2 as a criteria pollutant under the Clean Air Act?

Chapter 10

THE CLEAN WATER ACT

"Water is the most critical resource issue of our lifetime and our children's lifetime. The health of our waters is the principal measure of how we live on the land." *Statement of Luna Leopold, quoted in "Clean Water Action Plan: Restoring and Protecting America's Waters," U.S. EPA and U.S. DOA (1998), at 1.*

A. INTRODUCTION

Just as the nation's air resources have been in need of a good cleaning, so also have the nation's waters. Before the onset of federal regulation, water pollution problems were addressed at the state and local level by resort to the common law of nuisance and negligence, and by attempts to balance competing water uses. Only after World War II did the federal government take a seat at the table. Wanting states to maintain the lead, it chose a decidedly subordinate role. Consequently, the announced policy of the Water Pollution Control Act of 1948 was not to clean the water, but was, rather, "to recognize, preserve, and protect the primary responsibilities of the States in controlling water pollution[.]" Water Pollution Control Act of 1948, § 1, 62 Stat. 1155. The federal government intended to assist states by funding their water pollution control efforts and by coordinating interstate pollution abatement efforts.[1] The Federal Water Pollution Control Act of 1956 built on this structure by instructing the Surgeon General to prepare "comprehensive programs for eliminating or reducing" pollution. FWPCA, § 2, 70 Stat. 498.

These cautious federal interventions produced little improvement in water quality. In 1965, Congress acted again, this time requiring states to establish

---

[1] The legislation did propound a diluted brand of federal enforcement. If the Surgeon General found an unhealthful condition, he could give notice to the polluter. If nothing resulted from this, he could give notice to the polluter and the state. If still nothing happened, the Federal Security Administrator was authorized to hold a hearing. If the hearing produced no progress, he could then request the U.S. Attorney General to file a lawsuit. If a lawsuit was filed, the federal court was authorized to render "such judgment . . . as the public interest and the equities of the case may require." WQA of 1948, § 2(d), 62 Stat. 1156–57.

water quality standards for streams and to fashion implementation plans. (Sound familiar?) This legislation did not work either, in part because water quality standards were written to accomplish a multiplicity of stream uses, some of which, such as recreation, protection of aquatic life, and drinking water protection, required cleaner water, while others, such as agricultural and industrial use, depended on reduced water quality. States compounded this problem of ambivalence with ineffectual enforcement. State implementation plans were sometimes left unfinished, and other times made to rely on education initiatives and cajolery as their enforcement methodology. The result was slow progress to protect water quality, and even less water quality improvement.

Repeated tinkering by the Congress notwithstanding, effective federal intervention did not take place until eye-openers such as the combustion of urban rivers[2] elevated the issue to national prominence. The Federal Water Pollution Control Act of 1972 (later renamed the Clean Water Act) was the result. Opposed by states, industry, and President Nixon (it was enacted over his veto), the legislation came into being primarily because of strong Senate leadership. Despite several amendments in succeeding years, the 1972 Act remains to this day the core of the federal water pollution control program.

As you read through these materials, you will recognize concepts similar to those already seen in Chapter 9's coverage of the Clean Air Act. Terminology varies, however. Instead of emission limitations or standards, here we see *effluent limitations* or *standards*. Instead of criteria pollutants, we see *conventional pollutants*. Hazardous pollutants are *toxic pollutants* or, simply, *toxics*. National ambient air quality standards (NAAQSs) give way to *water quality standards ("WQSs")*. Water pollutants are not emitted; they are *discharged*. No FIPs or SIPs here, either. Look instead for *National Pollutant Discharge Elimination System ("NPDES")* permits as the vehicle to implement regulatory standards. In both the Clean Air and Clean Water Acts you will find new source performance standards, citizen suit provisions, saving clauses, provisions for judicial review, definitional sections, regulation of federal facilities, and a host of other like provisions.

But the Clean Water Act ("CWA") is far from a retooled Clean Air Act ("CAA") applied to water. On the contrary, the CWA adopts an approach to pollution control fundamentally distinct from that of its counterpart (at least as the CAA was originally designed). On a basic level, the CWA has a hard-edged resolve about it noticeably missing in the 1970 CAA. A comparison of the goal statements of the two statutes is illustrative. The 1970 Clean Air Act called for "protect[ing] and enhanc[ing] the quality of the Nation's air resources so to promote the public health and welfare and the productive capacity of its population." CAA § 101(b)(1), 42 U.S.C. § 7401(b)(1). The 1972 CWA, however, while calling for a restoration of the integrity of the nation's waters, § 101(a), 33 U.S.C. § 1251(a), went on to pronounce as its specific goal,

---

[2] A major event in national environmental history was the spontaneous combustion of the Cuyahoga River in Cleveland, Ohio, on June 29, 1969. A small amount of oil-and chemical-soaked floating debris caught fire, drifted downstream and in turn ignited two wooden railroad trestles. The fire was extinguished in a scant 25 minutes, and received only sparse local media coverage, but the event took on national significance as a symbol of the nation's water pollution crisis. Randy Newman even wrote a song about it (representative lyrics: "Burn on, big river, burn on").

inter alia, the *zero* discharge of pollutants by 1985, and, as an interim measure, the attainment of "fishable and swimmable" waters by 1983.[3] The CWA, in short, abhors the concept of "good enough."

The statutes are divergent in regulatory approach as well. Signaling a decisive rejection of the regulatory philosophy embraced only two years earlier, the 1972 CWA declined to construct for water the health-based standards/implementation plan regulatory model used in the CAA. Instead, the CWA's frontline soldier is technology-based standards. Effluent limitations imposed on dischargers, accordingly, spring in the main from considerations of technological feasibility, not from calculations of how clean receiving waters should be. *See generally* § 301, 33 U.S.C. § 1311. The CWA moves health-based effluent standards to a backup position. *See* §§ 302 & 303, 33 U.S.C. §§ 1312 & 1313.

The Senate Report accompanying the 1972 Act explained the reasoning behind this significant change:

> Under the 1965 Act, water quality standards were to be set as the control mechanism. States were to decide the uses of water to be protected, the kinds and amounts of pollutants to be permitted, the degree of pollution abatement to be required, the time to be allowed a polluter for abatement.
>
> The water quality standards program is limited in its success. After five years, many States do not have approved standards. Officials are still working to establish relationships between pollutants and water uses. Time schedules for abatement are slipping away because of failure to enforce, lack of effluent controls, and disputes over Federal-State standards.
>
> The Committee adopted this substantial change because of the great difficulty associated with establishing reliable and enforceable precise effluent limitations on the basis of a given stream quality. Water quality standards, in addition to their deficiencies in relying on the assimilative capacity of receiving waters, often cannot be translated

---

[3] The complete text of the 1972 Clean Water Act's goal statements is as follows:

(1) it is the national goal that the discharge of pollutants into the navigable waters be eliminated by 1985;

(2) it is the national goal that wherever attainable, an interim goal of water quality which provides for the protection and propagation of fish, shellfish, and wildlife and provides for recreation in and on the water be achieved by July 1, 1983;

(3) it is the national policy that the discharge of toxic pollutants in toxic amounts be prohibited;

(4) it is the national policy that Federal financial assistance be provided to construct publicly owned waste treatment works;

(5) it is the national policy that areawide waste treatment management planning processes be developed and implemented to assure adequate control of sources of pollutants in each State; and

(6) it is the national policy that a major research and demonstration effort be made to develop technology necessary to eliminate the discharge of pollutants into the navigable waters, waters of the contiguous zone, and the oceans.

§ 101(a)(1)–(6).

into effluent limitations — defendable in court tests, because of the imprecision of models for water quality and the effects of effluents in most waters.

Under this Act the basis of pollution prevention and elimination will be the application of effluent limitations. Water quality will be a measure of program effectiveness and performance, not a means of elimination and enforcement.

The Committee recommends the change to effluent limits as the best available mechanism to control water pollution. With effluent limits, the Administrator can require the best control technology; he need not search for a precise link between pollution and water quality.

Senate Report No.92-414, U.S. Code Congressional and Administrative News, 92d Cong. 2d Sess. at 3675.

The water pollution world, as structured by the Clean Water Act, is divided into two halves. Instead of stationary and mobile sources (*see* Chapter 9, *supra*) here we have point and nonpoint sources. Point sources, we will see, are governed chiefly by the aforementioned technology-based effluent standards. As designed in 1972, the CWA dealt primarily with point sources, an emphasis consistent with the prevailing understanding that industry was the major cause of water pollution. The legislation dealt less so with nonpoint sources. Point sources, generally speaking, discharge pollution via pipes, outfalls or other confined channels. Since 1972, however, it has become apparent that nonpoint source pollution, particularly runoff from agricultural, ranch, and forest lands, dwarfs point source pollution (note, for example, that a single cow gives off as much waste as 14.5 human beings). One dramatic indicator of the severity of nonpoint source pollution is the 8,000 square mile hypoxic "dead zone" in the Gulf of Mexico at the mouth of the Mississippi River. Hypoxia refers to depleted levels of oxygen in a water body. The hypoxic condition of these waters is caused by excessive amounts of nutrients — primarily nitrogen and phosphorus — that have leached into the Mississippi River from upstream agricultural operations and then made their way to the Gulf. (In July, 2000, in an attempt to reduce the problem, EPA issued a draft "Action Plan for Reducing, Mitigating, and Controlling Hypoxia in the Northern Gulf of Mexico." The plan calls for reduction in point source discharges of nutrients, increased assistance to landowners to create wetlands and other buffers of water pollution, and aid to farmers to implement best management practices to cut runoff.) In 1987, Congress added § 319 to help address nonpoint pollution. In the last decade, a new initiative to use the CWA to control nonpoint pollution has taken root. We will look at this development later in this Chapter.

The CWA was amended in 1977 and again in 1987. Because these amendments more refined the legislation than revised it in the way the 1977 amendments to the CAA did, this Chapter is organized differently than Chapter 9. Here, we consider point and nonpoint source regulation in distinct sections, and review changes in legislation internally within those sections.

The particulars of the Clean Water Act can be found by reviewing the legislation itself, which is in your statutory supplement. Please take notice of the various subchapters of the enactment, but pay most attention to Subchapters III, IV, and V.

After reviewing the overall organization of the Act, the best place to start a particularized inquiry is § 301(a). This section is the statute's triggering mechanism, for it largely determines the subject matter reach of the legislation. This section is considered by some knowledgeable people to be the most important single statutory provision in the entirety of pollution control law. Can you see why?

It is important to understand what the specific terms within § 301(a) mean. In this regard, *see* § 502, 33 U.S.C. § 1362.

B. ISSUES OF APPLICABILITY

SOUTH FLORIDA WATER MANAGEMENT DISTRICT v. MICCOSUKEE TRIBE OF INDIANS

124 S. Ct. 1537 (2004)

JUSTICE O'CONNOR delivered the opinion of the Court.

Petitioner South Florida Water Management District operates a pumping facility that transfers water from a canal into a reservoir a short distance away. Respondents Miccosukee Tribe of Indians and the Friends of the Everglades brought a citizen suit under the Clean Water Act contending that the pumping facility is required to obtain a discharge permit under the National Pollutant Discharge Elimination System. The District Court agreed and granted summary judgment to respondents. A panel of the United States Court of Appeals for the Eleventh Circuit affirmed. Both the District Court and the Eleventh Circuit rested their holdings on the predicate determination that the canal and reservoir are two distinct water bodies. For the reasons explained below, we vacate and remand for further development of the factual record as to the accuracy of that determination.

I

A

The Central and South Florida Flood Control Project (Project) consists of a vast array of levees, canals, pumps, and water impoundment areas in the land between south Florida's coastal hills and the Everglades. Historically, that land was itself part of the Everglades, and its surface and groundwater flowed south in a uniform and unchanneled sheet. Starting in the early 1900's, however, the State began to build canals to drain the wetlands and make them suitable for cultivation. These canals proved to be a source of trouble; they lowered the water table, allowing salt water to intrude upon coastal wells, and they proved incapable of controlling flooding. Congress established the Project in 1948 to address these problems. It gave the United States Army Corps of Engineers the task of constructing a comprehensive network of levees, water storage areas, pumps, and canal improvements that would serve several simultaneous purposes, including flood protection, water conservation, and drainage. These improvements fundamentally altered the hydrology of the Everglades, changing the natural sheet flow of ground and surface water. The local sponsor and day-to-day operator of the Project is the South Florida Water Management District (District).

Five discrete elements of the Project are at issue in this case. One is a canal called "C-11." C-11 collects groundwater and rainwater from a 104 square-mile area in south central Broward County. App. 110. The area drained by C-11 includes urban, agricultural, and residential development, and is home to 136,000 people. At the western terminus of C-11 is the second Project element at issue here: a large pump station known as "S-9." When the water level in C-11 rises above a set level, S-9 begins operating and pumps water out of the canal. The water does not travel far. Sixty feet away, the pump station empties the water into a large undeveloped wetland area called "WCA-3," the third element of the Project we consider here. WCA-3 is the largest of several "water conservation areas" that are remnants of the original South Florida Everglades. The District impounds water in these areas to conserve fresh water that might otherwise flow directly to the ocean, and to preserve wetlands habitat. *Id.*, at 112.

Using pump stations like S-9, the District maintains the water table in WCA-3 at a level significantly higher than that in the developed lands drained by the C-11 canal to the east. Absent human intervention, that water would simply flow back east, where it would rejoin the waters of the canal and flood the populated areas of the C-11 basin. That return flow is prevented, or, more accurately, slowed, by levees that hold back the surface waters of WCA-3. Two of those levees, L-33 and L-37, are the final two elements of the Project at issue here. The combined effect of L-33 and L-37, C-11, and S-9 is artificially to separate the C-11 basin from WCA-3; left to nature, the two areas would be a single wetland covered in an undifferentiated body of surface and ground water flowing slowly southward.

B

As the above description illustrates, the Project has wrought large-scale hydrologic and environmental change in South Florida, some deliberate and some accidental. Its most obvious environmental impact has been the conversion of what were once wetlands into areas suitable for human use. But the Project also has affected those areas that remain wetland ecosystems.

Rain on the western side of the L-33 and L-37 levees falls into the wetland ecosystem of WCA-3. Rain on the eastern side of the levees, on the other hand, falls on agricultural, urban, and residential land. Before it enters the C-11 canal, whether directly as surface runoff or indirectly as groundwater, that rainwater absorbs contaminants produced by human activities. The water in C-11 therefore differs chemically from that in WCA-3. Of particular interest here, C-11 water contains elevated levels of phosphorous, which is found in fertilizers used by farmers in the C-11 basin. When water from C-11 is pumped across the levees, the phosphorous it contains alters the balance of WCA-3's ecosystem (which is naturally low in phosphorous) and stimulates the growth of algae and plants foreign to the Everglades ecosystem.

The phosphorous-related impacts of the Project are well known and have received a great deal of attention from state and federal authorities for more than 20 years. A number of initiatives are currently under way to reduce these impacts and thereby restore the ecological integrity of the Everglades. Respondents Miccosukee Tribe of Indians and the Friends of the Everglades (hereinafter simply Tribe), impatient with the pace of this progress, brought this Clean Water Act suit in the United States District Court for the Southern District of Florida. They sought, among other things, to enjoin the operation of S-9 and, in turn, the conveyance of water from C-11 into WCA-3.

C

Congress enacted the Clean Water Act (Act) in 1972. Its stated objective was "to restore and maintain the chemical, physical, and biological integrity of the Nation's waters." 86 Stat 816, 33 U.S.C. § 1251. To serve those ends, the Act prohibits "the discharge of any pollutant by any person" unless done in compliance with some provision of the Act. § 1311(a). The provision relevant to this case, § 1342, establishes the National Pollutant Discharge Elimination System, or "NPDES." Generally speaking, the NPDES requires dischargers to obtain permits that place limits on the type and quantity of pollutants that can be released into the Nation's waters. The Act defines the phrase "'discharge of a pollutant'" to mean "any addition of any pollutant to navigable waters from any point source." § 1362(12). A "'point source,'" in turn, is defined as "any discernible, confined and discrete conveyance," such as a pipe, ditch, channel, or tunnel, "from which pollutants are or may be discharged." § 1362(14).

According to the Tribe, the District cannot operate S-9 without an NPDES permit because the pump station moves phosphorous-laden water from C-11 into WCA-3. The District does not dispute that phosphorous is a pollutant, or that C-11 and WCA-3 are "navigable waters" within the meaning of the Act. The question, it contends, is whether the operation of the S-9 pump constitutes the "discharge of [a] pollutant" within the meaning of the Act. . . .

II

The District and the Federal Government, as *amicus*, advance three separate arguments, any of which would, if accepted, lead to the conclusion that the S-9 pump station does not require a point source discharge permit under the NPDES program. Two of these arguments involve the application of disputed contentions of law to agreed-upon facts, while the third involves the application of agreed-upon law to disputed facts. For reasons explained below, we decline at this time to resolve all of the parties' legal disagreements, and instead remand for further proceedings regarding their factual dispute.

A

In its opening brief on the merits, the District argued that the NPDES program applies to a point source "only when a pollutant originates from the point source," and not when pollutants originating elsewhere merely pass through the point source. Brief for Petitioner 20. This argument mirrors the question presented in the District's petition for: "Whether the pumping of water by a state water management agency that adds nothing to the water being pumped constitutes an 'addition' of a pollutant 'from' a point source triggering the need for a National Pollutant Discharge Elimination System permit under the Clean Water Act." Pet. for Cert. i. Although the Government rejects the District's legal position, Brief for United States as *Amicus Curiae* 21, it and the Tribe agree with the factual proposition that S-9 does not itself add any pollutants to the water it conveys into WCA-3.

This initial argument is untenable, and even the District appears to have abandoned it in its reply brief. Reply Brief for Petitioner 2. A point source is, by definition, a "discernible, confined, and discrete *conveyance*." § 1362(14) (emphasis added). That definition makes plain that a point source need not be the original source of the pollutant; it need only convey the pollutant to "navigable waters," which are, in turn, defined as "the waters of the United States." § 1362(7). Tellingly, the examples of "point sources" listed by the Act include pipes, ditches, tunnels, and conduits, objects that do not themselves generate pollutants but merely transport them. § 1362(14). In addition, one of the Act's primary goals was to impose NPDES permitting requirements on municipal wastewater treatment plants. *See, e.g.,* § 1311(b)(1)(B) (establishing a compliance schedule for publicly owned treatment works). But under the District's interpretation of the Act, the NPDES program would not cover such plants, because they treat and discharge pollutants added to water by others. We therefore reject the District's proposed reading of the definition of "'discharge of a pollutant'" contained in § 1362(12). That definition includes within its reach point sources that do not themselves generate pollutants.

B

Having answered the precise question on which we granted certiorari, we turn to a second argument, advanced primarily by the Government as *amicus curiae* in merits briefing and at oral argument. For purposes of determining whether there has been "any addition of any pollutant to navigable waters from any point source," *ibid.,* the Government contends that all the water bodies that fall within the Act's definition of "'navigable waters'" (that is, all "the waters of the United States, including the territorial seas," § 1362(7)) should be viewed unitarily for purposes of NPDES permitting requirements. Because the Act requires NPDES permits only when there is an addition of a pollutant "to navigable waters," the Government's approach would lead to the conclusion that such permits are *not* required when water from one navigable water body is discharged, unaltered, into another navigable water body. That would be true even if one water body were polluted and the other pristine, and the two would not otherwise mix. *See Catskill Mountains Chapter of Trout Unlimited, Inc. v. New York,* 273 F.3d 481, 492 (2nd Cir. 2001); *Dubois v. United States Dep't of Agric.,* 102 F.3d 1273 (1st Cir. 1996). Under this "unitary waters" approach, the S-9 pump station would not need an NPDES permit.

1

The "unitary waters" argument focuses on the Act's definition of a pollutant discharge as "any addition of any pollutant to navigable waters from any point source." § 1362(12). The Government contends that the absence of the word "any" prior to the phrase "navigable waters" in § 1362(12) signals Congress' understanding that NPDES permits would not be required for pollution caused by the engineered transfer of one "navigable water" into another. It argues that Congress intended that such pollution instead would be addressed through local nonpoint source pollution programs. Section 1314(f)(2)(F), which concerns nonpoint sources, directs the Environmental Protection Agency (EPA) to give States information on the evaluation and control of "pollution resulting from . . . changes in the movement, flow, or circulation of any navigable waters or ground waters, including changes caused by the construction of dams, levees, channels, causeways, or flow diversion facilities."

We note, however, that § 1314(f)(2)(F) does not explicitly exempt nonpoint pollution sources from the NPDES program if they *also* fall within the "point source" definition. And several NPDES provisions might be read to suggest a view contrary to the unitary waters approach. For example, under the Act, a State may set individualized ambient water quality standards by taking into consideration "the designated uses of the navigable waters involved." 33 U.S.C. § 1313(c)(2)(A). Those water quality standards, in turn, directly affect local NPDES permits; if standard permit conditions fail to achieve the water quality goals for a given water body, the State must determine the total pollutant load that the water body can sustain and then allocate that load among the permit-holders who discharge to the water body. § 1313(d). This approach suggests that the Act protects individual water bodies as well as the waters of the United States as a whole.

The Government also suggests that we adopt the "unitary waters" approach out of deference to a longstanding EPA view that the process of "transporting, impounding, and releasing navigable waters" cannot constitute an "'addition'" of pollutants to "'the waters of the United States.'" Brief for United States as *Amicus Curiae* 16. But the Government does not identify any administrative documents in which EPA has espoused that position. Indeed, an *amicus* brief filed by several former EPA officials argues that the agency once reached the opposite conclusion. *See* Brief for Former Administrator Carol M. Browner et al. as *Amici Curiae* 17 (citing *In re Riverside Irrigation Dist., 1975 WL 23864* (Off. Gen. Couns., June 27, 1975) (irrigation ditches that discharge to navigable waters require NPDES permits even if they themselves qualify as navigable waters)). The "unitary waters" approach could also conflict with current NPDES regulations. For example, 40 CFR § 122.45(g)(4) (2003) allows an industrial water user to obtain "intake credit" for pollutants present in water that it withdraws from navigable waters. When the permit holder discharges the water after use, it does not have to remove pollutants that were in the water before it was withdrawn. There is a caveat, however: EPA extends such credit "only if the discharger demonstrates that the intake water is drawn from the same body of water into which the discharge is made." The NPDES program thus appears to address the movement of pollutants among water bodies, at least at times.

Finally, the Government and numerous *amici* warn that affirming the Court of Appeals in this case would have significant practical consequences. If we read the Clean Water Act to require an NPDES permit for every engineered diversion of one navigable water into another, thousands of new permits might have to be issued, particularly by western States, whose water supply networks often rely on engineered transfers among various natural water bodies. *See* Brief for Colorado et al. as *Amici Curiae* 2-4. Many of those diversions might also require expensive treatment to meet water quality criteria. It may be that construing the NPDES program to cover such transfers would therefore raise the costs of water distribution prohibitively, and violate Congress' specific instruction that "the authority of each State to allocate quantities of water within its jurisdiction shall not be superseded, abrogated or otherwise impaired" by the Act. § 1251(g). On the other hand, it may be that such permitting authority is necessary to protect water quality, and that the States or EPA could control regulatory costs by issuing general permits to point sources associated with water distribution programs. *See* 40 CFR §§ 122.28, 123.25 (2003). * Indeed, that is the position of the one State that has interpreted the Act to cover interbasin water transfers. *See* Brief for Pennsylvania Department of Environmental Protection as *Amicus Curiae* 11-18. = "*"

2

Because WCA-3 and C-11 are both "navigable waters," adopting the "unitary waters" approach would lead to the conclusion that the District may operate S-9 without an NPDES permit. But despite its relevance here, neither the District nor the Government raised the unitary waters approach before the Court of Appeals or in their briefs respecting the petition for certiorari. (The District adopted the position as its own in its reply brief on the merits.) Indeed, we are not aware of any reported case that examines the unitary waters argument in precisely the form that the Government now presents it. As a result, we decline to resolve it here. Because we find it necessary to vacate the judgment of the Court of Appeals with respect to a third argument presented by the District, the unitary waters argument will be open to the parties on remand.

C

In the courts below, as here, the District contended that the C-11 canal and WCA-3 impoundment area are not distinct water bodies at all, but instead are two hydrologically indistinguishable parts of a single water body. The Government agrees with the District on this point, claiming that because the C-11 canal and WCA-3 "share a unique, intimately related, hydrological association," they "can appropriately be viewed, for purposes of Section 402 of the Clean Water Act, as parts of a single body of water." Brief for United States in Opposition 13. The Tribe does not dispute that if C-11 and WCA-3 are simply two parts of the same water body, pumping water from one into the other cannot constitute an "addition" of pollutants. As the Second Circuit put it in *Trout Unlimited*, "[i]f one takes a ladle of soup from a pot, lifts it above the pot, and pours it back into the pot, one has not 'added' soup or anything else to the pot." 273 F.3d at 492. What the Tribe disputes is the accuracy of the District's factual premise; according to the Tribe, C-11 and WCA-3 are two pots of soup, not one.

The record does contain information supporting the District's view of the facts. Although C-11 and WCA-3 are divided from one another by the L-33 and L-37 levees, that line appears to be an uncertain one. Because Everglades soil is extremely porous, water flows easily between ground and surface waters, so much so that "[g]round and surface waters are essentially the same thing." App. 111, 117. C-11 and WCA-3, of course, share a common underlying aquifer. Tr. of Oral Arg. 42. Moreover, the L-33 and L-37 levees continually leak, allowing water to escape from WCA-3. This means not only that any boundary between C-11 and WCA-3 is indistinct, but also that there is some significant mingling of the two waters; the record reveals that even without use of the S-9 pump station, water travels as both seepage and groundwater flow between the water conservation area and the C-11 basin. App. 172, *see also id.*, at 37 (describing flow between C-11 and WCA-3 as "cyclical").

The parties also disagree about how the relationship between S-9 and WCA-3 should be assessed. At oral argument, counsel for the Tribe focused on the differing "biological or ecosystem characteristics" of the respective waters, Tr. of Oral Arg. 43; *see also* Brief for Respondent Miccosukee Tribe of Indians of Florida 6-7; Brief for Respondent Friends of the Everglades 18-22, while counsel for the District emphasizes the close hydrological connections between the two. *See, e.g.*, Brief for Petitioner 47. Despite these disputes, the District Court granted summary judgment to the Tribe. It applied a test that neither party defends; it determined that C-11 and WCA-3 are distinct "because the transfer of water or its contents from C-11 into the Everglades would not occur naturally." App. to Pet. for Cert. 28a. The Court of Appeals for the Eleventh Circuit endorsed this test. 280 F.3d at 1368.

We do not decide here whether the District Court's test is adequate for determining whether C-11 and WCA-3 are distinct. Instead, we hold only that the District Court applied its test prematurely. Summary judgment is appropriate only where there is no genuine issue of material fact. *See Celotex Corp. v. Catrett*, 477 U.S. 317, 91 L. Ed. 2d 265, 106 S. Ct. 2548 (1986). The record before us leads us to believe that some factual issues remain unresolved. The District Court certainly was correct to characterize the flow through the S-9 pump station as a non-natural one, propelled as it is by diesel-fired motors against the pull of gravity. And it also appears true that if S-9 were shut down, the water in the C-11 canal might for a brief time flow east, rather than west, as it now does. But the effects of shutting down the pump might extend beyond that. The limited record before us suggests that if S-9 were shut down, the area drained by C-11 would flood quite quickly. *See* 280 F.3d at 1366 ("Without the operation of the S-9 pump station, the populated western portion of Broward County would flood within days"). That flooding might mean that C-11 would no longer be a "distinct body of navigable water," *id.*, at 1368, but part of a larger water body extending over WCA-3 and the C-11 basin. It also might call into question the Eleventh Circuit's conclusion that S-9 is the cause in fact of phosphorous addition to WCA-3. Nothing in the record suggests that the District Court considered these issues when it granted summary judgment. Indeed, in ordering later emergency relief from its own injunction against the operation of the S-9 pump station, the court admitted that it had not previously understood that shutting down S-9 would "literally ope[n] the flood gates." *Id.*, at 1371.

We find that further development of the record is necessary to resolve the dispute over the validity of the distinction between C-11 and WCA-3. After reviewing the full record, it is possible that the District Court will conclude that C-11 and WCA-3 are not meaningfully distinct water bodies. If it does so, then the S-9 pump station will not need an NPDES permit. In addition, the Government's broader "unitary waters" argument is open to the District on remand. Accordingly, the judgment of the United States Court of Appeals for the Eleventh Circuit is vacated, and the case is remanded for further proceedings consistent with this opinion.

It is so ordered.

[JUSTICE SCALIA's partial concurrence and dissent is omitted.]

* * * * *

WASHINGTON WILDERNESS COALITION v. HECLA MINING CO.

870 F. Supp. 983 (E.D. Wash. 1994)

[This case involved a placer mine for gold and silver situated in the State of Washington. In a placer mining operation, raw materials containing gold and silver are immersed in a liquid solution of cyanide and other chemical agents. This extraction process generates a significant amount of wastewater. Hecla Mining Company ("Hecla"), in accordance with a waste discharge permit, pumped wastewater into a 38 acre tailings impoundment known as Aspen Pond. The complaint in the case contended that chemicals and heavy metals were seeping out of the pond and into the waters of the United States, in violation of the Clean Water Act.]

JUDGES: FRED VAN SICKLE, United States District Judge

. . . .

2. Failure to State a claim.

The CWA makes it unlawful for any person or entity to "discharge any pollutant" without an NPDES permit. 33 U.S.C. § 1311(a) & § 1342(a). "Discharge of any pollutant" is defined as "any addition of any pollutant to navigable waters from a point source." 33 U.S.C. § 1362(12)(a) (emphasis added). Hecla argues that plaintiffs have not stated a claim under the CWA, because the mining runoff at issue does not flow from a "point source," and does not enter "navigable waters."

(a) "point source."

Section 1362(14) defines "point source" as:

> any discernible, confined and discrete conveyance, including but not limited to any pipe, ditch, channel, tunnel, conduit, well, discrete fissure, container, rolling stock, concentrated animal feeding operation, or vessel or other floating craft, from which pollutants are or may be discharged.

A nonpoint source is anything else. *Idaho v. Hanna Mining Co.*, 699 F. Supp. 827, 832 (D.Id. 1987), *aff'd*, 882 F.2d 392 (1988).

Hecla argues that its tailings ponds are not point sources, but merely "areas of low topography into which mine tailings from mineral processing activities have been deposited and through which water may percolate." (Defendant's memo at 13). Noting that a point source is usually a pipe or a ditch, Hecla points out that here we are dealing here with a 38 acre man-made pond.

Initially, it is clear that the size of the pond is not relevant to determining whether or not it is a point source. As plaintiffs explain, it would be irrational to conclude that the bigger the source of pollution, the less likely it is to be a "source" under the CWA. Cases cited by defendants support the conclusion that man-made ponds, designed to receive tailings, are "conveyances" or "containers" under the definitions in the Clean Water Act. *See United States v. Earth Sciences, Inc.*, 599 F.2d 368, 370 (10th Cir. 1979) (system of sump pumps, ditches, and hoses is "point source"); *Appalachian Power Co. v. Train*, 545 F.2d 1351, 1352, 1373 (4th Cir. 1976) (distinguishing point sources from "unchanneled and uncollected surface waters"); *Consolidation Coal Co. v. Costle*, 604 F.2d 239, 249 (4th Cir. 1979) (point sources include slurry ponds, drainage ponds, and coal refuse piles); *Trustees for Alaska v. E.P.A.*, 749 F.2d 549, 557–58 (9th Cir. 1984) (adopting *Earth Sciences* interpretation of point source to apply to placer mine). To similar effect is *Abston Constr.*, where the Fifth Circuit noted: "gravity flow (from rain or runoff water) . . . may be part of a point source discharge if the miner at least initially collected or channeled the water and other materials"). *Sierra Club v. Abston Const. Co.*, 620 F.2d 41 (5th Cir. 1980); *see also, Committee to Save Mokelumne River v. East Bay Util.*, 13 F.3d 305, 308 (9th Cir. 1993) (holding that an NPDES permit is required for "surface runoff that is collected or channelled" into a Mine Run Dam Reservoir).

These cases make clear that the touchstone for finding a point source is the ability to identify a discrete facility from which pollutants have escaped. Particularly persuasive is the reasoning of the *Earth Sciences* court, adopted by the Ninth Circuit in *Trustees for Alaska*. 599 F.2d at 370. There, the court noted that "point source" must be interpreted broadly to effectuate the remedial purposes of the CWA. 599 F.2d at 373. The non-point source designation is limited to uncollected runoff water from, for example, oil and gasoline on a highway, which is difficult to ascribe to a single polluter. *Trustees for Alaska*, 749 F.2d at 558. Discharges from a pond or refuse pile can easily be traced to their source. Thus, even though runoff may be caused by rainfall or snow melt percolating through a pond or refuse pile, the discharge is from a point source because the pond or pile acts to collect and channel contaminated water. 599 F.2d at 374.

It appears that EPA agrees with the *Earth Sciences* analysis. The preamble to EPA's NPDES Permit Application Regulations for Storm Water Discharges, 55 Fed. Reg. 47990 (Nov. 16, 1990), states that the agency "intends to embrace the broadest possible definition of point source consistent with the legislative intent of the CWA." (*See* Plaintiff's opposition memo, appendix A at 3). Accordingly, the federal regulations define "discharge of a pollutant" to include "surface runoff which is collected or channeled by man." 40 C.F.R. 122.2. In a letter from EPA region VIII, "point source" is defined to include "any seeps coming from identifiable sources of pollution (i.e., mine workings, land application sites, ponds, pits, etc.). Defendants correctly note that the EPA statements from Region VIII are not authoritative. *See Village of Oconomowoc Lake v. Dayton Hudson Corp.*, 24 F.3d 962, 1994 WL 192793 (1994). Nonetheless, they are persuasive, as they reflect a view which was endorsed by the Ninth Circuit in *Trustees for Alaska.*

Even if it is not certain that the ponds in this case are similar enough to those in other cases to constitute a point source under the CWA, dismissal would be premature. Several courts note that the question whether a discharge occurred from a point source is fact-laden; the court must consider evidence of the "precise nature" of the Defendant's facility. *See Abston Const. Co.*, 620 F.2d at 47; *Hanna Mining*, 699 F. Supp. at 832; *Concerned Area Residents v. Southview Farm*, 834 F. Supp. 1410, 1417 (W.D.N.Y. 1993). Thus, at this stage in the proceedings, plaintiffs' allegations are sufficient to establish that Hecla's tailings ponds are point sources within the meaning of the CWA.

(b) "Navigable Waters"

Hecla next argues that Plaintiffs merely allege discharge to groundwater, which is not part of the "navigable waters" of the United States. In fact, the complaint does allege that polluted wastewater from the Hecla mine enters surface waters, including Eureka creek and Mud Lake.[1] (Complaint at 7). The connection to groundwater is Plaintiffs' acknowledgment that a large volume of discharge "seeps and leaks" from the ponds into the soil and groundwater, and thereafter into the surface waters. Given this indirect path of discharge, the court must decide whether the Clean Water Act's prohibition of the discharge of any pollutant into "navigable waters" encompasses discharges which migrate through groundwater.

The Clean Water Act generously defines "navigable waters" as "waters of the United States." 33 U.S.C. § 1362(7). Given the Act's purpose to regulate as fully as possible all sources of water pollution, the Supreme Court recognized that "the term navigable is of little import." *United States v. Riverside Bayview Homes, Inc.*, 474 U.S. 121, 133, 88 L. Ed. 2d 419, 106 S. Ct. 455 (1985). To the extent permitted under the Constitution, Congress intended "navigable waters" to embrace virtually "every creek, stream, river or body of water that in any way may affect interstate commerce." *Quivira Min. Co. v. E.P.A.*, 765 F.2d 126, 129 (10th Cir. 1985); *accord Leslie Salt Co. v. Froehlke*, 578 F.2d 742, 755 (9th Cir. 1978).

Nonetheless, Congress did not intend to include isolated groundwater as part of the "navigable waters." The language and structure of the Act make this clear. First, the CWA consistently refers to "navigable waters and ground waters" in those portions of the Act dealing with EPA program development as well as the study of water pollution. *E.g.* 33 U.S.C. § 1252(a), § 1254(a)(5),

---

[1] In a side-note, Plaintiffs also suggest that the tailings ponds themselves constitute "navigable waters." (Plaintiff's brief at 11). This is wrong. The EPA definition of navigable waters includes only "natural" ponds, as opposed to manmade collection systems. Besides, it is illogical for plaintiffs to maintain that the tailings ponds can be both a "point source" of discharge and "navigable water." *See Oconomowac Lake*, 24 F.2d at 963.

& § 1256(e)(1). In the provisions for water quality standards and discharge permitting, on the other hand, only the phrase "navigable waters" is used. *E.g.* 33 U.S.C. § 1312(a), § 1342(a)(4). If the terms were synonymous, it would not be necessary for Congress to make distinct references to groundwater and navigable water.

More importantly, the legislative history of the CWA demonstrates that Congress did not intend that discharges to isolated groundwater be subject to permit requirements. The Report of the Senate Committee on Public Works that accompanied the bill stated:

> Because the jurisdiction regarding groundwaters is so complex and varied from State to State, the Committee did not adopt this recommendation [to approve groundwater standards]. The Committee recognizes the essential link between ground and surface waters and the artificial nature of any distinction.

S.Rep.No. 414, 92d Cong., 1st Sess. 73 (1971), U.S. Code Cong. & Admin. News 1972, pp. 3668, 3739, reprinted in 2 Congressional Research Service of the Library of Congress, A Legislative History of the Water Pollution Control Act Amendments of 1972, 93d Cong., 1st Sess., at 1491 (Comm. Print 1973) (hereinafter "Leg.Hist."). Congress rejected an amendment offered by Senator Aspin to "bring groundwater into the subject of the bill." 118 Cong. Rec. 10,669 (1972), 1 Leg. Hist. 597. (*See* Remarks of Sen. Aspin). Congress's main concern was expressed by Representative Harsha: "We do not have the knowledge or the technology to devise water-quality standards for ground water; we do not as yet know how to do that." 1 Leg.Hist. 594 (remarks of Rep. Harsha).

Guided by the legislative history, courts that have considered the issue agree that "waters of the United States" do not include "isolated/nontributary groundwater." *See, Exxon Corp. v. Train,* 554 F.2d 1310 (5th Cir. 1977); *United States v. GAF Corp.,* 389 F. Supp. 1379 (S.D. Tx. 1975). They are split, however, on the present question of whether tributary groundwater, which is naturally connected to surface water, is subject to CWA regulation.

On the one hand are published decisions which hold that Congress intended regulation of "discharges of pollutants that could affect surface waters of the United States." *McClellan (MESS),* 707 F. Supp. at 1196 (E.D. Cal. 1196); *Sierra Club v. Colorado Refining Co.,* 838 F. Supp. 1428 (D.Colo. 1993) ("discharge of any pollutant into 'navigable waters' includes such discharge which reaches 'navigable waters' through groundwater"). On the other hand are those courts which conclude that the possibility of a hydrological connection between ground and surface waters is insufficient to justify CWA regulation. *Oconomowoc Lake,* 24 F.3d 962 (7th Cir. 1994); *Kelley v. United States,* 618 F. Supp. 1103 (W.D.Mich. 1985). One court, rather than sorting through the conflicting authorities, deferred to an agency interpretation excluding groundwater from coverage under the CWA. *Town of Norfolk v. Corps of Engineers,* 968 F.2d 1438, 1450 (1st Cir. 1992).

After reviewing the authorities, this court comes down on the side of *MESS* and *Colorado Refining.* The logic of these cases is compelling: since the goal of the CWA is to protect the quality of surface waters, any pollutant which enters such waters, whether directly or through groundwater, is subject to regulation by NPDES permit. Applying effluent limitations to tributary groundwater does not change nature of CWA monitoring. As *MESS* explains,

> Plaintiffs must still demonstrate that pollutants from a point source affect surface waters of the United States. 707 F. Supp. at 1196. It is not sufficient to allege groundwater pollution, and then to assert a general hydrological connection between all waters. Rather, pollutants must be traced from their source to surface waters, in order to come within the purview of the CWA. *Id.*

This approach to groundwater pollution has been favorably acknowledged by EPA on at least one occasion. Preamble, NPDES Permit Regulations for Storm Water Discharges, 55 Fed. Reg. 47990, 47997 (Nov. 16, 1990). Citing to *MESS* and *Exxon,* EPA stated that rulemaking in 40 C.F.R. parts 122, 123, and 124, does not apply to groundwater, "unless there is a hydrological connection between the ground water and a nearby surface water body." *Id.* The court in *Oconomowac Lake* dismissed the EPA statements as a "collateral reference to a problem." 24 F.2d at 966. It appears to this court, however, that the preamble explains EPA's policy to require NPDES permits for discharges which may enter surface water via groundwater, as well as those that enter directly.

Plaintiffs' complaint alleges a hydrological connection between seepage into groundwater and the nearby surface waters of Eureka creek and Mud lake. Taking the allegation as true, the complaint is thus sufficient to support a claim under the CWA.

Conclusion

Hecla's Motion to Dismiss must be denied. The Court has subject matter jurisdiction over citizens suits to require issuance of a NPDES permit through state CWA administration. The tailings ponds are "point sources," since they collect and channel contaminated water into a discrete conveyance. Plaintiffs allege discharge into "navigable waters," by describing pollution which migrates from ground waters beneath the tailings ponds into surface waters of the United States.

IT IS SO ORDERED.

NOTES

1. Groundwater is a stressed resource. One report cites overdrafts of aquifers of at least 160 billion cubic meters each year, leaks in 100,000 underground petroleum storage tanks at gas stations and factories across the United States, and pesticide and nitrate runoffs that percolate into groundwater in both wealthy and poor nations, threatening the availability of fresh water. *See Vital Signs 2000: The Environmental Trends That Are Shaping Our Future,* Worldwatch Institute (May 27, 2000).

EPA believes the CWA allows it to regulate discharges to groundwaters that are hydrologically connected to surface water — even if groundwaters are not themselves "waters of the United States" — because "such discharges are effectively discharges to the directly connected surface waters." *See, e.g.* 56 Fed. Reg. 64876. EPA thus has adopted a "purposive" reading of the statute, using the CWA's underlying purpose of restoring and maintaining the nation's water quality and integrity as its interpretive guidepost.

The federal courts remain split on the question. As noted in *Hecla*, the Seventh Circuit has ruled the CWA does not apply in this situation. *Village of Oconomowoc Lake v. Dayton Hudson Corp.*, 24 F.3d 962 (7th Cir. 1994). Likewise, the First and Fifth Circuits have also held the CWA to be inapplicable. *Town of Norfolk v. U.S. Army Corps of Engineers*, 968 F.2d 1438 (1st Cir. 1992) (deferring to the Army Corps' definition of "groundwaters" as not "waters of the United States" under the CWA); *Rice v. Harken Exploration Company*, 250 F.3d 264 (5th Cir. 2001) (holding that the possibility that groundwater might contaminate surface waters was insufficient to establish liability).

The Tenth Circuit, however, has taken the contrary view. In *Quivira Mining Co. v. E.P.A.*, 765 F.2d 126, 129 (10th Cir. 1985), the court ruled the CWA to be applicable when polluted water "soak[ed] into the earth's surface, became part of the underground aquifers, and after a lengthy period, perhaps centuries, the underground water moves toward eventual discharge" in surface waters. *See also Friends of Santa Fe County v. LAC Minerals*, 892 F. Supp. 1333, 1358 (D.N.M. 1995) (the Tenth Circuit's construction of the CWA's jurisdictional reach forecloses "any argument that the CWA does not protect groundwater with some connection to surface waters"); *Sierra Club v. Colorado Refining Co.*, 838 F. Supp. 1428, 1434 (D. Colo. 1993) ("discharge of any pollutant into 'navigable waters' includes such discharge which reaches 'navigable waters' through groundwater").

There is also disagreement on the issue within circuits. In the Ninth Circuit, for example, compare *Idaho Rural Council v. Bosma*, 143 F. Supp. 2d 1169 (D. Idaho 2001) (the "CWA extends to hydrologically connected groundwater) *Umatilla Waterquality Protective Association, Inc. v. Smith Frozen Foods, Inc.*, 962 F. Supp. 1312 (D. Or. 1997) (the CWA does not extend to hydrologically connected groundwater). In the Eighth Circuit, compare *Williams Pipeline Co. v. Bayer Corp.*, 964 F. Supp. 1300 (S.D. Iowa 1997) ("the unpermitted discharges of pollution through spills, leaks, and other releases into the groundwater and into [a] wetland area . . . violated the CWA") with *Patterson Farm, Inc. v. City of Britton*, 22 F. Supp. 1085 (D.S.D. 1998) (under the *Hecla* rationale, the court lacks subject matter jurisdiction even if the plaintiff alleged that discharges into groundwater were migrating to surface water).

2. Can a human being be a "point source" under the Clean Water Act? In *United States v. Plaza Health Laboratories*, 3 F.3d 643 (2d Cir. 1992), *cert. denied*, 114 S. Ct. 2764 (1994), an individual appealed his criminal conviction under §§ 301 and 309(c)(2) for knowingly discharging pollution "from a point source" into the Hudson River. He had on at least two occasions emptied vials of human blood into the river. The District Court had ruled that a human could be a point source for purposes of the statute.

The Court of Appeals reversed, holding that the statutory term is used "invariably" in the context of pollution from municipal and industrial discharges. *Id.* at 646. The Court also found the Act would be unintelligible if read this way:

. . . we assume that congress did not intend the awkward meaning that would result if we were to read "human being" into the definition of "point source." Section 1362(12)(A) defines "discharge of a pollutant" as "any addition of any pollutant to navigable waters from any point source." Enhanced by this definition, § 1311(a) reads in effect "the addition of any pollutant to navigable waters *from any point source by any person* shall be unlawful" (emphasis added). But were a human being to be included within the definition of "point source," the prohibition would then read: "the addition of any pollutant to navigable waters from any person by any person shall be unlawful," and this simply makes no sense. As the statute stands today, the term "point source" is comprehensible only if it is held to the context of industrial and municipal discharges.

Id. at 647.

4. What is a "pollutant"? The CWA broadly defines the term at § 502(6), 33 U.S.C. § 1362(6), as "dredged spoil, solid waste, incinerator residue, sewage, garbage, sewage sludge, munitions, chemical wastes, biological materials, radioactive materials, heat, wrecked or discarded equipment, rock, sand, cellar dirt and industrial, municipal, and agricultural waste discharged into water." There are some exceptions to the term — your attention is called to § 502(6), 33 U.S.C. § 1362(6), for those. *See also Waste Action Project v. Dawn Mining Corp.*, 137 F.3d 1426 (9th Cir. 1998) ("[A]lthough the CWA defines 'pollutant' to include radioactive materials, the CWA's legislative history makes clear that Congress did not intend for the CWA to regulate any materials that the [Atomic Energy Commission (now the Nuclear Regulatory Commission)] was already regulating under the [Atomic Energy Act]").

C. POINT SOURCE REGULATION

[1] EFFLUENT LIMITATIONS

In the 1972 Act, the Congress established a system of effluent limitations to control discharges of pollutants from point sources into navigable waters:

(A) *Effluent limitations based on "best practicable control technology currently available" ("BPT" or "BPCTCA"): § 301(b)(1)(A), 33 U.S.C. § 1311(b)(1)(A).* These are interim standards for point sources.

(B) *Effluent limitations based on "best available technology economically achievable" ("BAT" or BATEA"): § 301(b)(2)(A), 33 U.S.C. § 1311(b)(2)(A).* These are more stringent, permanent standards to be implemented after BPT.

(C) *Effluent limitations for new sources: (National Standards of Performance ("NSP" or "NSPS")) § 306, 33 U.S.C. § 1316.* These are the CWA's analog to the new source performance standards of § 111 of the CAA.

(D) *Effluent limitations based on secondary treatment: §§ 301(b)(1)(B), 304(d), 33 U.S.C. §§ 1311(b)(1)(B), 1314(d).* These are standards for treatment of municipal wastewaters from sewage treatment plants. Primary treatment is a physical sedimentation process for removal of "settleable solids" from a waste stream. Secondary treatment refers to a physical/biological process for removing solids and pollutants characterized by biological oxygen demand ("BOD") and pH. It relies largely on chlorination of wastewater. Tertiary treatment is more elaborate pollution removal involving elimination of additional pollutants such as non-biodegradable toxics.

(E) *Effluent limitations for pretreatment: § 307(b), 33 U.S.C. § 1317(b).* In the water pollution world, in addition to direct dischargers — those who deposit pollutants directly into "navigable waters" — there are also indirect dischargers. These entities discharge pollutants into sewer systems that then convey the materials into navigable waters. To bring these entities under the regulatory umbrella, Congress took two steps. First, it declared discharges into sewer systems to be the legal equivalent of direct discharges into navigable waters. Second, it established pretreatment standards. These technology-based effluent limitations are designed to insure that indirect dischargers neither upset sewage treatment plants nor cause those plants to exceed their own secondary treatment effluent limitations.

This group of standards remains in place to the present. In 1977, however, Congress amended the CWA to refine them, and in the process created an additional standard. Why it did so warrants some attention. As EPA assumed its massive regulatory obligations under the original legislation, it took what appears to be the path of least resistance. It concentrated its BAT regulation development efforts to limit discharges of "conventional" pollutants, such as BOD, total suspended solids, oil and grease, fecal coliform, and pH. Conversely, it did not focus its efforts on restraining discharges of toxic pollutants. Why? Like criteria pollutants governed by the NAAQSs of the Clean Air Act, the commonly found conventional pollutants were easier to regulate because they were made regulable under the above-recited technology-based standards. Toxic pollutants, on the other hand, fell under a more cumbersome health-based regulatory system. § 307(a), 33 U.S.C. § 1317(a). Under § 307(a), the agency had to undertake a process not unlike the one imposed for hazardous air pollutants under § 112 of the pre-1990 CAA. *See* Chapter 9, *supra*. First, it had to identify toxic pollutants within ninety days of enactment of the statute, taking into account each substance's toxicity, persistence, degradability, presence in water, and effects it caused on important organisms, and thereafter establish for each an effluent standard deemed sufficient to protect human health and the environment, with an "ample margin of safety." § 307(a)(1), (4), 86 Stat. at 856, 857. Faced with the prospect of unsure science, inadequate administrative resources and funding, and too much other work to do, this task was one EPA preferred to avoid.

Predictably, the environmental community, objected, filing a wave of lawsuits. One such case, filed by the Natural Resources Defense Council in the District Court for the District of Columbia, resulted in the now-famous (in narrow circles) "Flannery Decree," a consent decree named for Judge Thomas A. Flannery, who approved the decree. The decree contained a list of 65 classes of toxic pollutants, a grouping later refined to designate 129 "priority" pollutants from 34 industrial categories. In the decree, EPA agreed to refocus its regulatory efforts on these pollutants. The list became EPA's game plan governing virtually all of its BAT work for a ten year period.[5]

These developments prompted Congress to enter the affray. Like the environmental community, Congress also wanted EPA to focus on toxic pollutants. Accordingly, it amended § 301(b)(2)(C) in 1977 to make BAT applicable to a broad list of toxic substances and to command EPA to regulate those substances on an expedited basis. Congress derived its list from the Flannery Decree. (Because of continuing problems with toxic water pollutants, the Congress revisited the problem again in 1987, when it added § 304(m), 33 U.S.C. § 1314(m), to force development of regulations in the BAT toxic and nonconventional pollutants programs. As of February, 2004, EPA had designated about 65 toxic pollutants. 40 C.F.R. § 401.15. For the conventional pollutants, Congress devised a new technology-based standard, best conventional pollution control technology ("BCT"), a tech-based standard less stringent than BAT but more stringent than BPT. § 301(b)(2)(E), 33 U.S.C. § 1311(b)(2)(E). The list of designated conventional pollutants may be found at 40 C.F.R. § 401.16 (1987). Thus, the post-1977 lineup remained essentially the same, except that BCT substituted for BAT with respect to conventional pollutants. BAT, was, accordingly, reserved for toxic pollutants. § 301(b)(2)(A) & (C), 33 U.S.C. § 1311(b)(2)(A) & (C). For the remaining universe of pollutants, the "non-conventional non-toxics," BAT is the standard. § 301(b)(2)(F), 33 U.S.C. § 1311(b)(2)(F).

When EPA engages in CWA regulation, it prefers to do so in an administratively expedient way. Accordingly, it often will regulate an entire category of industry in one fell swoop by establishing numerical effluent limitations representing BPT, BAT, BCT, and pretreatment in a single rulemaking. Whether the CWA authorized EPA to manage its workload in these efficient ways was the subject of early, and crucial, litigation. One early landmark Supreme Court decision, *E.I. DuPont de Nemours & Co. v. Train,* 430 U.S. 112, 97 S. Ct. 965 (1977), resolved the major question whether EPA could regulate point sources on an industry-wide basis, establishing effluent limitations for classes of plants at one time (which EPA preferred) or, alternatively, whether it could only regulate dischargers on a case-by-case basis (which industry preferred). The dispute involved the interplay of § 301, 33 U.S.C. § 1311, which identifies the standards to be used, and § 304, 33 U.S.C. § 1314, which describes how the agency should determine effluent limitations in specific cases. The *DuPont* decision saved the EPA from an administrative nightmare:

> The broad outlines of the parties' respective theories may be stated briefly. EPA contends that § 301(b) authorizes it to issue regulations establishing effluent limitations for classes of plants. The permits granted under § 402, in EPA's view, simply incorporate these across-the-board limitations, except for the limited variances allowed by the

---

[5] The decree was upheld by a divided panel of the District of Columbia Circuit. *Citizens for a Better Environment v. Gorsuch,* 718 F.2d 1117 (D.C. Cir. 1983). In 1992, because of EPA's violations of the aforementioned consent decree, the NRDC and EPA entered into another consent decree. This later decree required EPA to promulgate about eighteen new or revised standards for several industrial categories.

regulations themselves and by § 301(c). The § 304(b) guidelines, according to EPA, were intended to guide it in later establishing § 301 effluent-limitation regulations. Because the process proved more time consuming than Congress assumed when it established this two-stage process, EPA condensed the two stages into a single regulation.

In contrast, petitioners contend that § 301 is not an independent source of authority for setting effluent limitations by regulation. Instead, § 301 is seen as merely a description of the effluent limitations which are set for each plant on an individual basis during the permit-issuance process. Under the industry view, the § 304 guidelines serve the function of guiding the permit issuer in setting the effluent limitations.

The jurisdictional issue is subsidiary to the critical question whether EPA has the power to issue effluent limitations by regulation. Section 509(b)(1), 86 Stat. 892, 33 U.S.C. 1369(b)(1), provides that "[r]eview of the Administrator's action . . . (E) in approving or promulgating any effluent limitation . . . under section 301" may be had in the courts of appeals. On the other hand, the Act does not provide for judicial review of § 304 guidelines. If EPA is correct that its regulations are "effluent limitation[s] under section 301," the regulations are directly reviewable in the Court of Appeals. If industry is correct that the regulations can only be considered § 304 guidelines, suit to review the regulations could probably be brought only in the District Court, if anywhere. Thus, the issue of jurisdiction to review the regulations is intertwined with the issue of EPA's power to issue the regulations.

The statutory language concerning the 1983 limitations, in particular, leaves no doubt that these limitations are to be set by regulation. Subsection (b)(2)(A) of § 301 states that by 1983 "effluent limitations for categories and classes of point sources" are to be achieved which will require "application of the best available technology economically achievable for such category or class[.]" These effluent limitations are to require elimination of all discharges if "such elimination is technologically and economically achievable for a category or class of point sources[.]" This is "language difficult to reconcile with the view that individual effluent limitations are to be set when each permit is issued." *American Meat Institute v. EPA*, 526 F.2d 442, 450 (CA7 1975). The statute thus focuses expressly on the characteristics of the "category or class" rather than the characteristics of individual point sources. Normally, such class wide determinations would be made by regulation, not in the course of issuing a permit to one member of the class.

Thus, we find that § 301 unambiguously provides for the use of regulations to establish the 1983 effluent limitations. Different language is used in § 301 with respect to the 1977 limitations. Here, the statute speaks of "effluent limitations for point sources," rather than "effluent limitations for categories and classes of point sources." Nothing elsewhere in the Act, however, suggests any radical difference in the mechanism used to impose limitations for the 1977 and 1983 deadlines. *See American Iron & Steel Institute v. EPA*, 526 F. 2d 1027, 1042 n. 32 (CA3 1975). For instance, there is no indication in either § 301 or § 304 that the § 304 guidelines play a different role in setting 1977 limitations. Moreover, it would be highly anomalous if the 1983 regulations and the new-source standards were directly reviewable in the Court of Appeals, while the 1977 regulations based on the same administrative record were reviewable only in the District Court. The magnitude and highly technical character of the administrative record involved with these regulations makes it almost inconceivable that Congress would have required duplicate review in the first instance by different courts. We conclude that the statute authorizes the 1977 limitations as well as the 1983 limitations to be set by regulation, so long as some allowance is made for variations in individual plants, as EPA has done by including a variance clause in its 1977 limitations.

The question of the form of § 301 limitations is tied to the question whether the Act requires the Administrator or the permit issuer to establish the limitations. Section 301 does not itself answer this question, for it speaks only in the passive voice of the achievement and establishment of the limitations. But other parts of the statute leave little doubt on this score. Section 304(b) states that "[f]or the purpose of adopting or revising effluent limitations . . . the Administrator shall" issue guideline regulations; while the judicial-review section, § 509(b)(1), speaks of "the Administrator's action . . . in approving or promulgating any effluent limitation or other limitation under section 301. . . ." And § 101(d) requires us to resolve any ambiguity on this score in favor of the Administrator. It provides that "[e]xcept as otherwise expressly provided in this Act, the Administrator of the Environmental Protection Agency . . . shall administer this Act[.]" In sum, the language of the statute supports the view that § 301 limitations are to be adopted by the Administrator, that they are to be based primarily on classes and categories, and that they are to take the form of regulations.

Id. at 124–28, 97 S. Ct. at 973–75.

Twenty years later, EPA was challenged for establishing secondary treatment effluent limitations for wastewater treatment plants on a case-by-case basis. The Tenth Circuit Court of Appeals, deferring to EPA's reading of the statute, upheld the practice. *Maier v. U.S. Environmental Protection Agency*, 114 F.3d 1032 (10th Cir. 1997).

Another issue noted in *Du Pont*, and resolved at the Circuit Court level, was whether effluent limitations could be expressed as a single number. The Fourth Circuit had ruled that single number limitations were permitted by the statute:

The regulations impose limitations in terms of single numbers rather than in a range of numbers. Industry attacks this method saying in effect that EPA promulgated guidelines and that guidelines are not absolutes. Nothing in the Act prohibits the Administrator from using single numbers in establishing effluent limitations. The use of a single number limitation for discharge, permits any discharge from zero up to the allowed amount, subject always to the principle of presumptive validity which we have stated.

We are aware that the Third Circuit, *American Iron and Steel Institute v. EPA, supra,* has held that the regulations there considered are invalid because "they failed to provide meaningful ranges or guidance in considering individual factors." 526 F.2d [1027] at 1046 [(1975)]. On the facts presented to us, we cannot accept that conclusion. The EPA has promulgated zero discharge limitations with regard to many of the discharge sources which are before us. If a range is required, a zero discharge provision violates the Act. An objective of the Act is the elimination of all pollutant discharges by 1985. § 101(a)(1). The expertise of the Administrator is persuasive as to whether the limitations be fixed in single numbers or ranges. A claim of arbitrary action in this regard may be considered in court review under § 509(b)(1)(E) of the issuance or denial of a permit. Then specific facts may be presented and the problem will be actual rather than hypothetical. It may be that with some categories ranges are desirable and with others single numbers are appropriate. We are dealing with the general problem and decline to make advisory statements covering specific applicability. For the purposes of the suit before us relating to "inorganic chemicals manufacturing," we accept the Administrator's use of single numbers.

E. I. DuPont de Nemours & Company v. Train, 541 F.2d 1018, 1029–30 (4th Cir. 1976).

Given the holding of the United States Supreme Court in *DuPont* in favor of mandatory effluent limitations that could be installed into permits, the Third Circuit Court of Appeals abandoned its position on the "single-number v. range" issue, bringing itself into line with the other federal circuits. *American Iron and Steel Institute v. EPA,* 568 F.2d 284, 296 (3d Cir. 1977).

* * * * *

The process of preparing regulations is a laborious one. Before proposing new effluent limitations, EPA must engage in a good deal of data gathering. To this end, the agency will survey scientific studies, published literature, and information from trade associations and manufacturers. It also will hold meetings with industry representatives and will send them data collection portfolios and questionnaires to secure operations information. EPA is interested particularly in information on the chemical composition of industries' influent and effluent. To this end, it often conducts its own waste stream sampling. All collected samples are subjected to rigorous laboratory analysis.

Simultaneous with this data collection effort, the agency also surveys the available pollution control technologies that might be useful in reducing the pollutant loadings of discharges (*see infra*). The end result is the proposal of effluent limitations representing BPT, BAT, BCT, pretreatment, and secondary treatment, as applicable. When subsequently promulgated, these standards take on the force and effect of law.

Note that EPA need not establish an effluent limitation for every pollutant found in an industry's waste stream. On many occasions, only one or several may be regulated. The agency knows that installing pollution control equipment to remove a regulated pollutant will result in the removal of other pollutants as well.

In the next sections, we examine how EPA establishes BPT, BAT, and BCT effluent limitations.

[a] BEST PRACTICABLE TECHNOLOGY (BPT)

WEYERHAEUSER CO. v. COSTLE

590 F.2d 1011 (D.C. Cir. 1978)

McGOWAN, Circuit Judge:

Under the aegis of the Federal Water Pollution Control Act Amendments of 1972 (the Act), the Environmental Protection Agency has embarked upon a step-by-step process of issuing effluent limitations for each industry that discharges pollutants into the waters of the United States. By these consolidated petitions, members of one such industry, American pulp and paper makers, challenge the validity of EPA regulations limiting the 1977-83 effluent discharges of many pulp, paper, and paperboard mills. *See* 42 Fed. Reg. 1398–426 (1977). We are satisfied that EPA properly construed and rationally exercised the authority delegated to it by Congress, and that, with one exception, it did so according to the appropriate procedures. Accordingly, we uphold the resulting effluent limitations in all but one instance. * * *

EPA's consideration of the factors bearing on "the best practicable technology currently available" (BPCTCA) has inspired several challenges from petitioners. Some of these challenges concern the Agency's refusal to consider receiving water quality, while others concern EPA's manner of assessing the factors that all agree must be considered: cost and nonwater environmental impacts. We uphold the Agency's interpretation and application of the statute against both sets of challenges.

1.

Some of the paper mills that must meet the effluent limitations under review discharge their effluent into the Pacific Ocean. Petitioners contend that the ocean can dilute or naturally treat effluent, and that EPA must take this capacity of the ocean ("receiving water capacity") into account in a variety of ways. They urge what they term "common sense," i.e., that because the amounts of pollutant involved are small in comparison to bodies of water as vast as Puget Sound or the Pacific Ocean, they should not have to spend heavily on treatment equipment, or to increase their energy requirements and sludge levels, in order to treat wastes that the ocean could dilute or absorb. * * *

EPA's secondary response to this claim was that pollution is far from harmless, even when disposed of in the largest bodies of water. As congressional testimony indicated, the Great Lakes, Puget Sound, and even areas of the Atlantic Ocean have been seriously injured by water pollution. Even if the ocean can handle ordinary wastes, ocean life may be vulnerable to toxic compounds that typically accompany those wastes. In the main, however, EPA simply asserted that the issue of receiving water capacity could not be raised in setting effluent limitations because Congress had ruled it out. We have examined the previous legislation in this area, and the 1972 Act's wording, legislative history, and policies, as underscored by its 1977 amendments. These sources, which were thoroughly analyzed in a recent opinion of the administrator of the Agency, fully support EPA's construction of the Act. They make clear that based on long experience, and aware of the limits of technological knowledge and administrative flexibility, Congress made the deliberate decision to rule out arguments based on receiving water capacity. * * *

The earliest version of the Federal Water Pollution Control Act was passed in 1948 and amended five times before 1972. Throughout that 24 year period, Congress attempted to use receiving water quality as a basis for setting pollution standards. W. Rodgers, *Environmental Law* 355–57 (1977). At the end of that period, Congress realized not only that its water pollution efforts until then had failed, but also that reliance on receiving water capacity as a crucial test for permissible pollution levels had contributed greatly to that failure. *EPA v. State Water Resources Control Board,* 426 U.S. 200, 202 (1976). * * *

Based on this experience, Congress adopted a new approach in 1972. Under the Act, "a discharger's performance is . . . measured against strict technology-based effluent limitations — specified levels of treatment — to which it must conform, rather than against limitations derived from water quality standards to which it and other polluters must collectively conform." *Id.* at 204–05 (footnotes omitted). *See Save the Bay, Inc. v. EPA,* 556 F.2d 1282, 1284 (5th Cir. 1977); *American Frozen Foods Inst., supra,* 539 F.2d at 115. * * *

Moreover, by eliminating the issue of the capacity of particular bodies of receiving water, Congress made nationwide uniformity in effluent regulation possible. Congress considered uniformity vital to free the states from the temptation of relaxing local limitations in order to woo or keep industrial facilities. In addition, national uniformity made pollution clean-up possible without engaging in the divisive task of favoring some regions of the country over others. * * *

More fundamentally, the new approach implemented changing views as to the relative rights of the public and of industrial polluters. Hitherto, the right of the polluter was pre-eminent, unless the damage caused by pollution could be proven. Henceforth, the right of the public to a clean environment would be pre-eminent, unless pollution treatment was impractical or unachievable. The Senate Committee declared that "[the] use of any river, lake, stream or ocean as a waste treatment system is unacceptable" regardless of the measurable impact of the waste on the body of water in question. Legislative History at 1425 (Senate Report). The Conference Report stated that the Act "specifically bans pollution dilution as an alternative to waste treatment." *Id.* at 284. This new view of relative rights was based in part on the hard-nosed assessment of our scientific ignorance: "we know so little about the ultimate consequences of injection of new matter into water that [the Act requires] a presumption of pollution. . . ." *Id.* at 1332 (remarks of Sen. Buckley). It also was based on the widely shared conviction that the nation's quality of life depended on its natural bounty, and that it was worth incurring heavy cost to preserve that bounty for future generations. * * *

2.

Petitioners also challenge EPA's manner of assessing two factors that all parties agree must be considered: cost and non-water quality environmental impacts. They contend that the Agency should have more carefully balanced costs versus the effluent reduction benefits of the regulations, and that it should have also balanced those benefits against the non-water quality environmental impacts to arrive at a "net" environmental benefit conclusion. * * *

In order to discuss petitioners' challenges, we must first identify the relevant statutory standard. Section 304(b)(1)(B) of the Act, 33 U.S.C. § 1314(b)(1)(B), identifies the factors bearing on BPCTCA in two groups. First, the factors shall

> include consideration of the total cost of application of technology in relation to the effluent reduction benefits to be achieved from such application, and second, they shall also take into account the age of equipment and facilities involved, the process employed, the engineering aspects of the application of various types of control techniques, process changes, non-water quality environmental impact (including energy requirements), and such other factors as the Administrator deems [appropriate.]

The first group consists of two factors that EPA must compare: total cost versus effluent reduction benefits. We shall call these the "comparison factors." The other group is a list of many factors that EPA must "take into account:" age, process, engineering aspects, process changes, environmental impacts (including energy), and any others EPA deems appropriate. We shall call these the "consideration factors." Notably, section 304(b)(2)(B) of the Act, 33 U.S.C. § 1314(b)(2)(B), which delineates the factors relevant to setting 1983 BATEA limitations, tracks the 1977 BPCTCA provision before us except in one regard: in the 1983 section, all factors, including costs and benefits, are consideration factors, and no factors are separated out for comparison.

Based on our examination of the statutory language and the legislative history, we conclude that Congress mandated a particular structure and weight for the 1977 comparison factors, that is to say, a "limited" balancing test. In contrast, Congress did not mandate any particular structure or weight for the many consideration factors. Rather, it left EPA with discretion to decide how to account for the consideration factors, and how much weight to give each factor. In response to these divergent congressional approaches, we conclude that, on the one hand, we should examine EPA's treatment of cost and benefit under the 1977 standard to assure that the Agency complied with Congress' "limited" balancing directive. On the other hand, our scrutiny of the Agency's treatment of the several consideration factors seeks to assure that the Agency informed itself as to their magnitude, and reached its own express and considered conclusion about their bearing. More particularly, we do not believe that EPA is required to use any specific structure such as a balancing test in assessing the consideration factors, nor do we believe that EPA is required to give each consideration factor any specific weight. * * *

[The court then discussed the meaning of a "limited" balancing test for comparison factors. It began by noting the legislative history of the CWA. That history stipulates that "the balancing test between total cost and effluent reduction benefits is intended to limit the application of technology only where the additional degree of effluent reduction is wholly out of proportion to the costs of achieving such marginal level of reduction for any class or category of sources." A Legislative History of the Water Pollution Control Act Amendments of 1972, at 170 (statement of Senator Muskie), *Weyerhauser* at 1045, n52. With that in mind, the court considered plaintiffs' arguments that EPA was required to do an overall cost-benefit analysis as well as another cost-benefit analysis for each "additional increment of waste treatment control, from bare minimum to complete pollution removal."

[Held the Court: EPA must perform a cost-benefit analysis but it has "some" discretion on how to do it. Costs need not be balanced against benefits]:

> . . . with pinpoint precision. A requirement that EPA perform the elaborate task of calculating incremental balances would bog the Agency down in burdensome proceedings on a relatively subsidiary task. Hence, the Agency need not on its own undertake more than a net cost-benefit balancing to fulfill its obligation under Section 304.

However, when an incremental analysis has been performed by industry and submitted to EPA, it is worthy of scrutiny by the Agency, for it may "avoid the risk of hidden imbalances between cost and benefit." . . . If such a "hidden imbalance" were revealed here, and if the Agency had ignored it, we might remand for further consideration. But in this case the incremental analysis proferred by industry showed that the last and most expensive increment of BOD treated in sulfite mills cost less than $.15 per pount of BOD removed, which is below the average cost of treatment in most of the industry's subcategories. . . . We would be reluctant to find that EPA ignored a "hidden imbalance" when the most unfavorable incremental cost-benefit balance that is challenged falls well within the range of averages for the industry as a whole.

NOTE

Section 301(c) of the 1972 CWA expressly provided for variances from BAT standards, but no provision of the Act did so for BPT. Undeterred, EPA created a variance for BPT by regulation. Unsurprisingly, EPA's regulation was challenged, but surprisingly, the regulation was upheld. *See E.I. du Pont de Nemours v. Train*, 430 U.S. 112, 97 S. Ct. 965 (1977) (variances from BPT standards are appropriate as necessary to the regulatory scheme despite the lack of any language to that effect in the Clean Water Act). *See also Chemical Manufacturers Association v. Natural Resources Defense Council*, 470 U.S. 116 (1985). In *EPA v. National Crushed Stone Association*, 449 U.S. 64, 101 S. Ct. 295 (1980), the Court held that, to secure a BPT variance, the discharger must demonstrate that the "factors relating to the equipment or facilities involved, the process applied, or other such factors relating to such discharger are fundamentally different from the factors considered in the establishment of the guidelines." *Id.* BPT variances, however, are not available to a discharger upon a showing of financial hardship. "FDF" variances are now made available in § 301(n) of the Act. To better understand what is "fundamental," see *Georgia-Pacific Co. v. U.S. Environmental Protection Agency*, 671 F.2d 1235 (9th Cir. 1982).

For more information on variances, see the notes following *American Paper Institute, infra.*

[b] BEST AVAILABLE TECHNOLOGY (BAT)

KENNECOTT v. U.S. ENVIRONMENTAL PROTECTION AGENCY

780 F.2d 445 (4th Cir. 1985)

WILKINSON, Circuit Judge:

Petitioners challenge the effluent limitations set by the Environmental Protection Agency for the non-ferrous metals manufacturing industry. EPA established the limitations in a rulemaking pursuant to the Clean Water Act of 1977, 33 U.S.C. §§ 1251–1376 (1982). Congress passed the Clean Water Act as an amendment to the Federal Water Pollution Control Act of 1972. The amendment preserves the fundamental purpose of the 1972 Act: "to restore and maintain the chemical, physical, and biological integrity of the Nation's waters." 33 U.S.C. § 1251. In setting effluent limitations for the nonferrous metals industry, EPA acted to implement this congressional mandate to clean up the nations' navigable waterways. We have reviewed with care petitioners' challenges to these regulations. We conclude, however, the EPA has properly discharged the task it is required by Congress to perform.

I.

The instant action reflects the tensions recurrent in every case of environmental regulation. The first group of petitioners here produce substantial amounts of the country's primary copper, lead, and zinc. Others recycle discarded lead batteries for a variety of uses, and still another produces columbium-tantalum, of importance to the aerospace, energy, and transportation industries. The industries contend that the effluent limitations adopted by EPA in the name of the Act are unachievable and will impose widespread costs upon the industries themselves and upon those who depend for their economic livelihood upon non-ferrous metals use.

EPA in turn states that petitioners discharge massive amounts of pollutants, over 3 million pounds annually, including "some of the most toxic metals found in industrial waste streams . . . lead, cadmium, arsenic, antimony, and zinc." It contends these pollutants create "a variety of serious adverse health and environmental effects, including cancer, brain damage, and kidney failure." The effluent limits are, in EPA's view, based upon achievable technologies and must be met promptly to fulfill the basic purposes of the Clean Water Act.

The record in this case is voluminous. The rulemaking itself is highly technical. Petitioners have challenged EPA's choice of data, its statistical methods, and its economic analysis. It is something of an understatement to say that the expertise of the parties with regard to the non-ferrous metals industry exceeds that of this court. Without suspending our critical faculties, we nonetheless believe that the benefit of the doubt in the battle of the data belongs to the agency in which Congress has reposed responsibility for administration of the Act, *see* 33 U.S.C. § 1251(d). In addition, this court is bound by the general rules of deference that run throughout administrative law. We may not overturn the agency's judgment simply because we might have drafted different regulations; remand is limited to those cases in which the agency has acted without reasonable basis. *American Meat Inst. v. EPA*, 526 F.2d 442, 450 (7th Cir. 1975).

We begin with the philosophy of the Clean Water Act. . . .

For the purposes of this case, the non-ferrous metals industry was generally subject to BAT requirements. Defining Best Available Technology requires substantial technical expertise in evaluating both the efficiency of advanced technologies and the adaptability of those technologies to the production processes of the companies in this case. Our review of the EPA rulemaking is appropriately cautious. As this court has previously noted, "The scope of our review is further colored by the policy of the Clean Water Act and the sophisticated data evaluations mandated by that lengthy and complicated statute. . . . Further, technological and scientific issues, such as those presented in this case, are by their very nature difficult to resolve by traditional principles of judicial decisionmaking." *Reynolds Metals Co. v. EPA*, 760 F.2d 549, 558–59 (4th Cir. 1985).

We proceed, however, on the understanding that Best Available Technology was the means chosen by Congress to achieve "the national goal that the discharge of pollutants into the navigable waters be eliminated by 1985," 33 U.S.C. § 1251(a)(1), a goal that implies some urgency to the environmental task that Congress set. While Congress was careful to require agency consideration of such factors as the cost to industry of achieving appropriate effluent reductions, it left EPA some latitude in defining BAT, permitting in addition to enumerated criteria, the consideration of "such other factors as the Administrator deems appropriate." *See* 33 U.S.C. § 1314(b)(2)(B).

To achieve a reasoned result in a dispute over technologies, EPA is bound to consider industry data, but it is not bound to accept it. Any other resolution would undermine the integrity of agency decision-making. For obvious reasons, this court should be loathe to compel an agency to accept data submitted by a regulated industry. That does not imply we are blind to the capacities of agencies to enthrone their own agendas and dismiss contending views. In considering petitioners' challenges to the non-ferrous metals rulemaking, we ask whether EPA's technical judgments find support in the record and whether they reflect the rule of reason, not the imposition of fiat.

The deference to the technical expertise of the Administrator supplements the deference generally required of courts reviewing administrative actions.

[At this juncture, the court discusses the appropriate judicial scope of review standards applicable to administrative decisionmaking].* * *

EPA did not approach casually the task of non-ferrous metals rulemaking. In 1977, the agency began gathering data for the proposed rules which it published on February 17, 1983. 48 Fed. Reg. 7032–7126. Data was obtained from plant visits, plant samplings, studies of scientific journals, and consultations with industry. Three hundred and nineteen firms, operating 416 facilities, received questionnaires from EPA asking for information on flow rates, production rates, wastewater treatment, and cost. *Id.* at 7044. Each plant visited by EPA also received an opportunity to comment on the trip report prepared by the agency. Various of the petitioners met with EPA both before and after publication of the proposed rules.

The resulting record ran 24,000 pages. EPA solicited public comment on all aspects of the regulations, highlighting points on which the agency wanted additional information. *Id.* at 7073. The initial comment period lasted eleven weeks. EPA reopened the comment period twice and accepted late-filed comments from one of the petitioners. 48 Fed. Reg. 50906 (Nov. 4, 1983); 48 Fed. Reg. 52604 (Nov. 21, 1983).

The agency considered the comments and contacted each petitioner with follow-up inquiries. The comments led EPA to re-examine its selections of model technologies and data bases. EPA likewise considered additional data on the treatment of lead and ammonia, as well as continuing to request and evaluate data from plants that had not previously submitted data. The long process of gathering data and the ongoing dialogue with the industry culminated in the final rule promulgated March 8, 1984.

We do not imply, in detailing this lengthy consideration, that a matter of the magnitude and complexity of non-ferrous metals rulemaking deserved anything less. We note only that an appellate court cannot be oblivious to the expenditure of effort that preceded its consideration and that, if the process has been a fair one, a time does come when rulemaking may cease and compliance must commence.

II.

For the purposes of this appeal, petitioners have been grouped according to industry. The first group of petitioners are Kennecott, American Mining Congress, AMAX, Inc., ASARCO Incorporated, St. Joe Minerals corporation, and GTE Products Corporation (hereinafter "Kennecott"). Together these companies are responsible for much of the United States production of primary copper, primary lead and primary zinc. * * *

Kennecott objects to the non-ferrous metals rulemaking, arguing that the agency's data base was flawed, that petitioners were not given the opportunity to comment on part of the model technology, sulfide precipitation, and that EPA incorrectly calculated flow allowances. After carefully considering petitioners' numerous and specific objections, we have concluded that EPA acted within the bounds of its discretion when it set effluent limits for the primary metals industry.

A.

When it set effluent limits for the primary metals industry, EPA used as its model technology a waste treatment process called lime, settle and filtration (L,S&F). Briefly, this treatment technique works in the following way: adding lime to wastewater increased the pH; it makes the wastewater more alkaline. At different pHs, different metals precipitate, that is, emerge from solution and become suspended as solids in the wastewater. Eventually, most solids settle at the bottom of the tank. The precipitate can then be disposed of separately from the wastewater. The wastewater is often subsequently filtered through coal or sand in order to remove additional suspended solids.

A number of industries use lime and settle. Beginning in the late 1970's EPA collected data from six such industries (aluminum forming, battery manufacturing, secondary lead, coil coating, copper forming, and porcelain enameling). After deleting unreliable data, EPA compiled the Combined Metals Data Base (CMDB). The agency then used the CMDB to calculate achievable effluent limitations for several related industries, including the primary base metals industry.

Kennecott objects to EPA's use of the CMDB. It argues that the CMDB data was limited, that the wastewaters of CMDB plants differed significantly from those of the primary metals plants, and that EPA should not have rejected data submitted by the primary metals industry.

Kennecott's basic objection is that EPA used data from the waste treatment systems of other industries (the CMDB) rather than using data submitted by the primary metals industry. Specifically, Kennecott makes the following argument: EPA's data base was limited, containing only 300 raw and treated data points from nineteen plants. EPA did not obtain samples from any given plants over a long term; therefore, the data cannot accurately reflect long-term performance. Kennecott contends that long-term data is necessary because fluctuations in pollutant concentrations occur even in properly operated treatment facilities due to "seasonal changes in temperature and precipitation, production surges or slow downs" and other variables. Because EPA did not collect enough samples, over a long enough period of time, Kennecott contends that the data does not accurately reflect achievable concentrations. Therefore, Kennecott says, petitioners will not be able to meet the effluent limitations.

In response, EPA notes that courts customarily defer to an agency's choice of data, and that in any case, EPA could use the CMDB to predict long-term performance accurately. On the first point, the agency is indisputably correct. This court has consistently given EPA a reasonable leeway in its selection of data and statistical methods. *FMC Corp. v. Train*, 539 F.2d 973, 986 (4th Cir. 1976). "[W]e note that an agency's data selection and choice of statistical methods are entitled to great deference . . . and its conclusions with respect to data and analysis need only fall within a 'zone of reasonableness'." *Reynolds Metals*, 760 F.2d at 559 (citations omitted). The question is thus whether EPA acted reasonably in basing effluent limitations for the primary base metals industry on the CMDB.

EPA contends that it does not necessarily need long-term data to predict long-term performance. It notes that the data base at issue here has been used in regulations in a number of other metals industries. By using well-established statistical methods, EPA could factor in the variability one would expect in an optimally operating plant. It is true that prediction of long-term performance would not account for fluctuations resulting from operational failures. However, the agency argues that plants with operating problems do not represent the Act's goal of Best Available Technology. *FMC Corp. v. Train,* 539 F.2d at 986. ("The purpose of these variability factors is to account for the routine fluctuations that occur in plant operation, not to allow for poor performances.") Moreover, the agency contends that the addition of second-step sulfide precipitation to the model technology further reduces the variability of lime and settle treatment. *See* subsection IIB, *infra.* Courts have traditionally respected the agency's selection of a data base in the fact of challenges that the data failed to account for variable pollution loads, Ass'n of Pac. *Fisheries v. EPA,* 615 F.2d 694, 812–13 (9th Cir. 1980); *American Petroleum Inst. v. EPA,* 540 F.2d 1023, 1035–36 (10th Cir. 1976). The number of data points here is not insignificant, and there must exist some reasonable termination point in the process of data collection.

Kennecott responds that even if EPA collected a sufficient number of data points, the CMDB remains flawed. It argues that the CMDB wastewater is so different from the wastewater in the primary metals industries that EPA cannot use the CMDB to set effluent limits that would apply to Kennecott. Without quantifying its claim, Kennecott says that the base metals industry has "huge amounts of wastewater," "tremendously high concentrations of metals," and a "very large variety of different metals" in the wastewater. EPA's similarly unquantified response is that the wastewaters in the CMDB industries and those of the primary base metals industry are indeed comparable. The agency agrees that the differences in concentration of metals may be statistically significant. However, there is evidence to show that the treatability of wastewater depends on the solubility of the pollutants, not on their concentrations. A difference in concentration of influents would thus not affect the concentration of effluents. *See* Proposed Rules, 48 Fed. Reg. 7050 (Feb. 17, 1983). This judgment constitutes a reasonable basis for EPA's belief that the wastewaters are comparable. We cannot say that EPA has acted arbitrarily or capriciously in using the CMDB to set effluent limitations for the primary metals industries.

Finally, we do not believe that EPA acted arbitrarily in rejecting the data submitted by the industry. EPA examined the data from petitioners' plants and concluded that six of the plants were not operating properly, and the seventh was unrepresentative. EPA determined that three plants were improperly operating one or more steps of the lime and settle process; they had ineffective pH adjustment, inadequate wastewater settling time, or lacked wastewater equalization. Plants use equalization to send more uniform loads of pollutants to the treatment system, ensuring that the system is not overloaded. In three other plants, patterns of extreme variability in treated effluents suggested to EPA that the plants were not equalizing their wastewaters properly. Finally, EPA considered that the seventh plant was unrepresentative because nearly all of its wastewater came from sources not related to the manufacturing processes covered by these regulations. We cannot say, therefore, that EPA abused its discretion by rejecting the industry data.

B.

EPA had originally proposed lime, settle and filtration as the BAT for treating wastewater in the primary base metals industry. Commentators objected that they would not be able to meet the proposed effluent limitations. In the Final Rules, EPA responded that any plant unable to meet the effluent limitations by using the model lime, settle and filtration technology could add an additional step: sulfide precipitation. While the APA requires the opportunity for public participation in rulemaking, "there is no question that an agency may promulgate a final rule that differs in some particulars from its proposal." *Chocolate Manufacturers,* 755 F.2d at 1103–04. * * *

[In the next portion of this section of the opinion, the court finds that EPA complied with the requisite rulemaking procedural requirements.] * * *

There remains the question of whether EPA acted arbitrarily in selecting sulfide precipitation as part of the Best Available Technology. Kennecott argues that sulfide precipitation will not reduce effluent concentrations to the required levels. Specifically, Kennecott charges that data from the model plants which currently use sulfide precipitation (Ashio, Japan; Boliden, Sweden; AMAX Ft. Madison) cannot be used to predict achievable concentrations at Kennecott's plants, because conditions at the two groups of plants are so different. Kennecott notes that the plant in Ashio, Japan, for example, uses sulfide precipitation to produce arsenic trioxide as an end-product, rather than to treat wastewater. EPA replies that the ultimate disposition of the solid precipitate is irrelevant, as long as the concentration levels of pollutants in the wastewater are acceptable.

The model technology may exist at a plant not within the primary base metals industry. Congress contemplated that EPA might use technology from other industries to establish the Best Available Technology. *Reynolds Metals,* 760 F.2d at 562. Progress would be slowed if EPA were invariably limited to treatment schemes already in force at the plants which are the subject of the rulemaking. Congress envisioned the scanning of broader horizons and asked EPA to survey related industries and current research to find technologies which might be used to decrease the discharge of pollutants. Leg. Hist. at 170.

To determine that technology from one industry can be applied to another, the agency must:

(1) show that the transfer technology is available outside the industry;

(2) determine that the technology is transferable to the industry;

(3) make a reasonable prediction that the technology if used in the industry will be capable of removing the increment required by the effluent standards.

[citations omitted]

EPA has demonstrated that sulfide precipitation — a process it terms "familiar" and "well established" — is available outside the primary base metals industry and that the technology is transferable to that industry. The agency notes that "the low solubility of metal sulfides" has made sulfide precipitation a more effective treatment than the conventional lime and settle process. We do not think it disqualifying that the Ashio plant, for example, uses sulfide precipitation to produce an end-product rather than to clean its wastewater, so long as the process adequately reduces pollutant concentrations in wastewater. Again, granting the agency a proper measure of deference in technical judgments, it was not arbitrary for EPA to decide that sulfide precipitation would remove pollutants to the degree required by the effluent limitations.

Kennecott discusses two other differences between the sulfide precipitation process at the model plants and the process at the primary base metals plants. Kennecott points out that the Ashio plant treats wastewater in batches, while the primary base metals plants treat wastewater continuously. EPA answers that the choice of the batch or continuous processes affects only cost, not effectiveness, and that study demonstrates the installation and operation of sulfide precipitation is economically achievable.

Kennecott also notes that all three model plants use sulfide pretreatment, rather than sulfide polishing. Again, EPA believes that the difference is irrelevant; whether sulfide precipitation is the step before or after L,S&F will not affect the achievability of the desire effluent limitations. The critical matter, in the agency's judgment, is the application of the proper amount of precipitant and the maintenance of proper levels of pH, factors entirely independent of the timing of wastewater treatment.

We hold that EPA had a reasonable basis for deciding that the sulfide precipitation technology is transferable. We are unable to conclude the agency acted arbitrarily or capriciously in selecting sulfide precipitation as part of the Best Available Technology for the primary base metals industry.

C.

EPA expresses its effluent limitations as "mass limits." EPA derives the mass limit by multiplying the maximum concentration level of a pollutant times water flow. The agency sets flow allowances as well as concentration limits in order to prevent plants from avoiding "the regulatory impact by diluting their effluent." *Weyerhaeuser Co. v. Costle*, 590 F.2d 1011, 1059 (D.C. Cir. 1978). In setting flow allowances, the agency uses a "building block approach." That is, EPA sets a flow allowance for each individual process step; the state or regional permit writer then calculates the total flow allowance for each individual plant by summing the allowances for each process step used at that plant.

Kennecott contends that EPA improperly denied a flow allowance for a step on the process of manufacturing primary lead called blast furnace slag granulation. In the final rules, the BAT standard for blast furnace slag granulation is zero discharge. The New Source Performance Standard (NSPS), which governs new plants, is also zero discharge. Because Congress thought that new plants have the opportunity to install the best and most efficient production processes, NSPS is normally at least as stringent as, if not more stringent than, BAT. *American Iron and Steel Inst. v. EPA*, 526 F.2d 1027, 1058–59 (3d Cir. 1975). Obviously, nothing can be more stringent than zero discharge.

The blast furnace slag granulation step can be either a wet or a dry process. Kennecott contends that dry slag is not an option because it produces uncontrollable dust. Therefore, plants use wet slag, which produces wastewater. Kennecott requests a flow allowance for this wastewater. EPA responds that zero discharge for blast furnace slag granulation is appropriate because three of four existing plants recycle 100 percent of their wastewater and thus achieve zero discharge for reasons which are not site-specific. The agency did not abuse its discretion in concluding that no flow allowance need be set for the blast furnace slag granulation process step.

With regard to the NSPS, Kennecott lodges one additional objection. It says that the NSPS is based on pyrometallurgical plants, but that new primary lead smelters are likely to be hydrometallurgical. Kennecott admits that no hydrometallurgical plant is in the process of being built or even contemplated. When such a plant is built, it can be designed according to EPA specifications. if zero discharge is indeed impossible for a hydrometallurgical plant, EPA has said that at that time, it will receive a petition for a new rulemaking. 48 Fed. Reg. 8764 (Mar. 8, 1984).

D.

On occasion, EPA sets catastrophic storm allowances. These allowances permit a plant to discharge additional wastewater under emergency circumstances. Some plants hold liquid waste in "surface impoundments," which are simply natural or man-made depressions. A catastrophic storm allowance permits a plant to discharge untreated wastewater when a storm of a certain size strikes and causes the surface impoundment to overflow. EPA has set no catastrophic storm allowances for primary lead and zinc plants. Copper smelters are permitted to discharge untreated wastewater if a "twenty-five year storm" occurs. A twenty-five year storm is a storm of such magnitude that it is likely to occur only once per quarter century.

Kennecott can no longer challenge the catastrophic storm allowances for zinc and copper. EPA denied the catastrophic storm allowance for zinc and copper. EPA denied the catastrophic storm allowance for zinc in a 1975 rulemaking; the BAT and BPT allowances for copper were set in 1975 and 1980. See 40 Fed. Reg. 8528 (Feb. 27, 1975); 40 Fed. Reg. 8524 (Feb. 27, 1975); 45 Fed. Reg. 44929 (July 2, 1980). Petitioners failed to raise their objections within the ninety days specified by the Clean Water Act. 33 U.S.C. § 1369(b)(1).

Kennecott is free to challenge the denial of a storm allowance for the primary lead industry, but we do not find its arguments persuasive. EPA did not set a catastrophic storm allowance for primary lead plants because surface impoundments are not part of the model technology. 48 F.2d Reg. 7048–49 (Feb. 17, 1983). EPA made a conscious decision to discourage impoundments because of associated problems: the risk of groundwater contamination and the danger that heavy pollutants will be discharged all at once. Given EPA's reservations about impoundments and the fact that impoundments are not part of the model technology, EPA did not act arbitrarily in refusing to grant an allowance for catastrophic storms.

EPA also did not set allowances for non-scope flows, that is, wastewater which is not generated by the manufacturing process but comes from other sources like employee showers or handwashing. The preamble to the Final Rules asks permit writers to consider non-scope flows when they write permits for individual plants. 47 Fed. Reg. 8778 (March 8, 1984). Kennecott is concerned that because EPA does not specifically authorize allowances for non-scope flows in the body of the regulations, permit writers will erroneously deny allowances. However, EPA did not set allowances for non-scope flows because these flows are so idiosyncratic. We do not believe that EPA was required to list site-specific sources as a separate subpart of the final regulations. Individual plants will, of course, be able to challenge the flow allowances set by permit writers.

[The remainder of the opinion deals with procedural issues and the legal arguments of the other industry group, the secondary lead industry, regarding the EPA standards promulgation. It is omitted on the assumption that the foregoing gives you a sense of the game.]

NOTES AND QUESTIONS

1. What does *Kennecott* tell us about the potential stringency of effluent limitations based on BAT? About the source of data upon which to base such effluent limitations?

In this regard, note that EPA has authority to establish discharge limitations for toxic pollutants which might be discharged "associated with or ancillary to" industrial processes otherwise regulated by BAT standards. Such ancillary discharges are "plant site runoff, spillage or leaks, sludge or waste disposal, and drainage from raw material storage" which "may contribute significant amounts of such pollutants to navigable waters." Requirements to control these discharges are to be based upon "best management practices" or "BMPs." *See* § 304(e), 33 U.S.C. § 1314.

2. Section 304 (b)(2)(B) of the CWA, 33 U.S.C. § 1314(b)(2)(B), provides that factors such as costs of achieving effluent reduction shall be "take[n] into account" by the agency in fashioning BAT standards. *See also Natural Resources Defense Council v. EPA*, 863 F.2d 1420 (9th Cir. 1988):

> Technology-based limitations under BAT must be both technologically available and economically achievable. *See* 33 U.S.C. § 1314(b)(2)(B). To be technologically available, it is sufficient that the best operating facilities are able achieve the limitation. *Association of Pac. Fisheries v. EPA*, 615 F.2d 794, 816–17 (9th Cir. 1980). To demonstrate economic achievability, no formal balancing of costs and benefits is required. *See id.* at 817–18. *Reynolds Metals Co. v. EPA*, 760 F.2d. 549, 565 (4th Cir. 1985); BAT should represent "a commitment of the maximum resources economically possible to the ultimate goal of eliminating all pollutant discharges." *See EPA v. National Crushed Stone Assn.*, 449 U.S. 64, 74, 101 S.Ct. 295, 302, 66 L.Ed. 2d 268 (1980). EPA has considerable discretion in weighing the costs of BAT. *American Iron and Steel. Inst. v. EPA*, 526 F.2d 589 (3d Cir. 1977). *Id.* at 1426.

What this means is that BAT standards cannot be less stringent than BPT, and in many instances should be more stringent. The differences between the two standards are basically three: (a) BAT is based on the best performer in an industry; BPT is based on the average of exemplary performers; (b) BAT is based on end-of-pipe technologies and in-process changes, or both, and EPA may look beyond the regulated industry itself to find BAT; BPT is based primarily (but not exclusively) on end-of-pipe technologies from the regulated industry itself; and (c) BAT standards may only be established upon a consideration of the costs the chosen technology would impose; BPT standards may be established only upon a comparison of costs and benefits. *See supra.*

[c] BEST CONVENTIONAL TECHNOLOGY (BCT)

AMERICAN PAPER INSTITUTE v. ENVIRONMENTAL PROTECTION AGENCY

660 F.2d 954 (4th Cir. 1981)

ERVIN, Circuit Judge:

The petitioners in these consolidated cases seek judicial review of the actions of the Administrator of the Environmental Protection Agency (EPA) in issuing regulations pursuant to section 304(b)(4)(B) of the Clean Water Act ("the Act") promulgating effluent water limitations controlling conventional pollutants from private industrial sources in accordance with section 301(b)(2)(E) of the Act. This court is vested with the responsibility and authority for making a pre-enforcement examination of the EPA guidelines by section 509(b)(1)(e) of the Act.

Although the petitioners challenge the best conventional technology (BCT) regulations issued pursuant to section 304(b)(4)(B), their primary objection is to the methodology used by the Administrator in promulgating the regulations. In particular, the petitioners contend that Congress in section 304(b)(4)(B) mandated that EPA incorporate two main factors in its methodology for determining BCT: an industry cost-effectiveness test and a test that compares the cost for private industry to reduce its effluent levels with that incurred by publicly owned treatment works (POTWs) for a similar purpose. The petitioners assert that EPA considered only the latter factor and that EPA's benchmark for this latter factor was arbitrary and capricious. Some of the other challenges that the petitioners raise are that EPA used statistically unreliable and internally inconsistent data, and that deprived petitioners of their right to comment. We hold that all the regulations promulgated pursuant to section 301(b)(2)(E) must be invalidated on the ground that EPA did not consider all the factors mandated by section 304(b)(4)(B). The only other contention that has merit is that the data on which EPA relied in formulating its POTW benchmark are statistically unreliable.

I. BACKGROUND

In 1972, Congress amended the Federal Water Pollution Control Act to establish a timetable for achieving certain water pollution control objectives.

Congress declared as its policy that the discharge of pollutants in our nation's navigable waters be eliminated by 1985. 33 U.S.C. § 1251(a)(1). With respect to private industrial sources, such as these petitioners, this achievement was to be accomplished in two stages: an interim level of control effective in 1977, and a final level effective in 1983. The 1977 standard was designated "best practicable technology" (BPT) and the more stringent 1983 standard was "best available technology" (BAT).

Five years later Congress undertook to re-examine these standards. Ultimately, the Federal Water Pollution Control Act was amended again, and the Act as amended became known as the Clean Water Act. Under the Clean Water Act, the 1977 requirements (BPT) were left intact, but changes were made in the 1983 requirements (BAT). As part of these changes, Congress established various standards and schedules for three classifications of pollutants: (1) conventional pollutants; (2) toxic substances; and (3) non-conventional non-toxic pollutants not otherwise classified. 33 U.S.C. § 1311. The strict BAT standards were retained for toxic pollutants known to be dangerous and for non-conventional non-toxic pollutants, the effects of which are uncertain, but the effective date for both categories was delayed.

While the parties disagree over precisely what Congress intended to do when it enacted the 1977 amendments to the Act and draw markedly different conclusions from the language of the amendments and the legislative history, it is clear that Congress felt that the results produced by the BPT had provided a high degree of water quality improvement, and that in some instances, BAT for conventional pollutants about which much was known might require treatment not deemed necessary to meet the 1983 water quality goals of the Act. Concern was expressed about requiring "treatment for treatment's sake," and there was much discussion about comparing the cost of treatment with the benefits obtained from the reductions achieved.

Out of this came the development of a new standard, best conventional pollutant control technology (BCT). The new requirement was described by one Senate-House conferee as "the equivalent of best practical technology or something a little bit better, even as far as best available technology in some circumstances."

In directing EPA to promulgate regulations concerning BCT standards, Congress passed section 304(b)(4)(B) of the Act, which provides in part:

> Factors relating to the assessment of best conventional pollutant control technology (including measures and practices) shall include consideration of the reasonableness of the relationship between the costs of attaining a reduction in effluents and the effluent reduction benefits derived, and the comparison of the cost and level of reduction of such pollutants from the discharge from publicly owned treatment works to the cost and level of reduction of such pollutants from a class or category of industrial sources, and shall take into account the age of equipment and facilities involved, the process employed, the engineering aspects of the application of various types of control techniques, process changes, non-water quality environment impact (including energy requirements), and such other factors as the Administrator deems appropriate.

33 U.S.C. § 1314(b)(4)(B).

. . . .

Pursuant to this Congressional directive, EPA proceeded to carry out its duties. On August 23, 1978, proposed rules were published relating to 13 secondary industry categories. These rules also contained a methodology for determining the reasonableness of any proposed effluent limitation under the BCT criteria. Critical comments were received, and on April 2, 1979, a notice was published indicating that the use of two additional documents was being considered for the data contained therein and that such data might be used in the future for computing the costs and levels of pollutants from POTWs. EPA published its final BCT determinations on August 29, 1979, and the petitioners filed these petitions on May 9, 1980, thus presenting these final regulations for our review. . . .

II. ANALYSIS

A. COST EFFECTIVENESS TEST

EPA's position is that Congress did not require it to utilize an industry cost-effectiveness test, but instead only mandated a POTW cost comparison standard in arriving at BCT regulations for industry. In interpreting section 304(b)(4)(B), EPA concludes that the proposed effluent guidelines are not required to pass two reasonableness tests. In support of its position, EPA reads the seemingly dual requirements of section 304(b)(4)(B) as one, commanding only a consideration of reasonableness. It contends that the second clause in the relevant portion of section 304(b)(4)(B) sets forth the benchmark of reasonableness — a comparison of the proposed BCT cost and level of effluent reduction for industry to the cost and level of reduction from the discharge of POTWs.

We are unable to accept this suggested statutory interpretation. When faced with such a question, our starting point for discerning congressional intent is the words of the statute itself. *See American Textile Manufacturers Institute, Inc. v. Donovan,* 49 U.S.L.W. 4720, 4725 (U.S. June 16, 1981); *State Water Control Board v. Train,* 559 F.2d 921, 924-25 n.20 (4th Cir. 1977). The law which empowers EPA to act directs that EPA's effluent regulations "shall . . . specify factors to be taken into account in determining the best conventional pollutant control technology measures and practices to comply with section 1311(b)(2)(E) of this title to be applicable to any point source (other than publicly owned treatment works) within such categories or classes." 33 U.S.C. § 1314(b)(4)(B). Congress did not leave EPA free to select these factors. The statute continues:

> Factors relating to the assessment of best conventional pollutant control technology . . . shall include consideration of the reasonableness of the relationship between the costs of attaining a reduction in effluents and the effluent reduction benefits derived, and the comparison of the cost and level of reduction of such pollutants from the discharge from publicly owned treatment works to the cost and level of reduction of such pollutants from a class or category of industrial sources. *Id.* (emphasis added).

We find the language of this statute to be clear and straight-forward. We thus find no reason to resort to additional rules of statutory construction or to rely on the legislative history, which has minimum probative value because of the numerous conflicts contained therein.

EPA's construction of section 304(b)(4)(B) is contrary to the plain meaning of the words contained therein. EPA ignores the mandatory language of the law ("shall"), disregards the conjunctive ("and"), and completely eliminates the first factor. By its own admission, the agency made no effort to determine what it would cost an affected industry to remove a pound of pollutant past the BPT level nor did it compare the cost of such removal with the benefits derived from the removal, as specifically required by statute. *See American Textile Manufacturers Institute, Inc. v. Donovan,* 49 U.S.L.W. 4720, 4725 & n.30 (U.S. June 16, 1981).

This court has made it clear that EPA must be held to a standard of at least literal compliance with the language of a statute which it is authorized to implement. *Appalachian Power Co. v. Train,* 545 F.2d 1351, 1357 (4th Cir. 1976). Where, as here, the language of the Act is unambiguous and EPA has failed to comply with its directives, we must grant the petitions to set aside the regulations involved and remand the regulations to EPA for reconsideration. On remand EPA is to develop an industry cost-effectiveness test in accordance with the provisions of section 304(b)(4)(B), employ that test in a manner consistent with the statute, and re-examine all existing BCT regulations to ensure that they are not inconsistent with the proper employment or this industry cost-effectiveness test.

B. POTW COMPARISON TEST

The petitioners also challenge the action of EPA in the formation and application of the POTW comparison test. They argue that EPA erred in using an incremental approach, i.e., one going beyond the cost of normal secondary treatment for POTWs, in arriving at a POTW benchmark. They also contend that even if EPA were permitted to use an incremental POTW comparison, it acted arbitrarily and capriciously because the increment was too large to comply with congressional intent. The petitioners also object to the POTW cost data as being inadequate and statistically unreliable. We reject each of these challenges, except the one directed to the errors in the cost data. . . .

1.

The petitioners specifically argue that EPA erred in concluding that it was appropriate to consider the cost of upgrading POTWs beyond secondary treatment. The petitioners object to the POTW benchmark for several reasons because: (1) secondary treatment is the only specifically defined treatment level that POTWs are required by law to meet; (2) advanced secondary treatment (AST), the increment which EPA chose, was not in existence when Congress enacted section 304 of the Act; and (3) the legislative history indicates that the POTW benchmark should be based on the average cost of normal secondary treatment.

We reject the petitioners' contentions. Section 304(b)(4)(B) explicitly authorizes EPA in establishing BCT limitations to compare "the cost and level of reduction of such pollutants from, the discharge from publicly owned treatment works to the cost and level of reduction of such pollutants from a class or category of industrial sources." This controlling statute unequivocally directs EPA to employ a POTW comparison test. Contrary to the suggestions, we find nothing on the face of the statute or in the legislative history to suggest that Congress intended for EPA to use a specific POTW benchmark. Although Congress specifically directed the use of this comparison test, it did not issue any instructions as to how EPA was to structure or administer the test.

EPA considered a number of ways in which a POTW test could be formulated. 43 Fed. Reg. 37,572 (1978). One of the suggestions was that the POTW benchmark be based on the average pollutant removal costs for secondary treatment at POTWs, i.e., the increment from no treatment to secondary treatment. 43 Fed. Reg. 37,572 (1978). In addition to looking at average POTW costs for secondary treatment, EPA considered various incremental approaches below secondary treatment. EPA rejected these proposals primarily because it felt that a proper POTW benchmark should be one roughly paralleling that with which it is to be compared — the industrial increment from BPT to BAT. Whereas industry was required to be at a BPT level in 1977, POTWs were required to have met effluent limitations based upon secondary treatment by 1977. EPA believed that a relevant basis of comparison for POTWs would be at an incremental level beyond secondary treatment since BCT would be at a level at least equal to BPT and in many cases beyond BPT. EPA considered several such increments. After a careful consideration of various alternatives, EPA adopted a test employing a comparison of the cost of upgrading POTWs from secondary treatment levels. The selection of this upgrade comparison does not do violence to the language of the statute, and we do not find it to be arbitrary or capricious.

Not only do the petitioners object to an incremental POTW benchmark, but they also object specifically to the use of the increment from secondary to AST as being too costly. In essence, the petitioners contend that even if EPA were permitted to use an incremental POTW benchmark, it should have used a narrower increment, one that more closely straddles the marginal cost of secondary treatment.

We reject this contention. We cannot substitute our judgment for that of EPA and condemn EPA for not choosing what we may consider to be the best increment. *See Ethyl Corp. v. EPA*, 541 F.2d 1, 36 (D.C. Cir.), *cert. denied*, 426 U.S. 941 (1976). While we are obligated to scrutinize the record, particularly in a complex technical case such as this one, "we must look at the [agency's] decision not as the chemist, biologist or statistician that we are qualified neither by training nor experience to be, but as a reviewing court exercising our narrowly defined duty of holding agencies to certain minimal standards of rationality." *Id.*

EPA based its proposal on separate and distinct technologies for small and large POTWs and arrived at POTW cost-effectiveness ratios at an increment progressing from normal secondary treatment at 30 mg/l each of BOD and TSS to better secondary treatment defined as 12 mg/l each of BOD and TSS. 43 Fed. Reg. 37,571-72 (1978).

. . . [T]here may be any number of increments based on slightly different technology or slightly different sizes of a given technology that EPA could have used. . . . Instead of using POTW cost reasonableness figures based on specific separate and distinct technologies employed by small and large POTWs, as it had proposed initially, in its final rules, EPA used a single POTW cost reasonableness figure based on the average of all cost-effective technologies used by POTWs operating beyond secondary treatment, but employing basic secondary treatment technology.

We cannot conclude that EPA acted arbitrarily and capriciously in choosing AST as the increment beyond secondary treatment for the POTW benchmark. While EPA sought to use an increment that narrowly straddled secondary treatment, i.e., one that closely approximated marginal cost, and although it admitted its failure to find the narrowest increment that would have more closely approximated marginal cost, there is no statutory mandate requiring EPA to use an increment that equals marginal cost.

EPA has rationally justified its use of the AST increment. AST is the "knee-of-the-curve" point, the maximum cost-effective level of control for POTWs. The increment from secondary treatment to AST for POTWs was also determined by EPA to be roughly analogous to the industrial increment from BPT to BAT. While comments received by EPA have suggested that there may have been a narrower increment that EPA could have used, the suggestions by the commentors imply that EPA would have had to limit itself to a specific POTW technology to arrive at a smaller increment.

We are unwilling to place a straitjacket on EPA to so limit its decision making process. We find that EPA made its decision on its POTW comparison after it fully considered various alternatives, and that its decision is rationally based. We thus conclude that EPA's choice of an increment for POTWs from secondary treatment to AST was neither arbitrary nor capricious.

3.

The petitioners also challenge the POTW benchmark on the grounds that the POTW cost data upon which it was based are inadequate, statistically unreliable, and internally inconsistent. Recently, we have been apprised that EPA confesses error in the data in the two documents on which it relied in formulating its POTW benchmark. EPA has moved this court for a voluntary remand, and the petitioners do not contest the propriety of a remand solely to allow EPA to correct its data errors. Under these circumstances, therefore, we find it proper to remand this aspect of the case to EPA, but only for the purpose of allowing it to correct its data errors and to revise its BCT figures accordingly.

III. CONCLUSION

We find no merit to the petitioners other challenges. Accordingly, we vacate the regulations promulgated pursuant to section 304 of the Act. We remand this action to the agency with instructions to devise a cost-effectiveness test in accordance with the guidelines of this opinion and to correct its data errors.

AFFIRMED IN PART, REVERSED IN PART AND REMANDED.

DISSENT: PHILLIPS, Circuit Judge, concurring and dissenting: [omitted]

NOTES

1. *Variances*: In some cases, point sources might be spared, at least temporarily, the burden of meeting effluent limitations based on regulations establishing effluent limitations for BAT, BCT, BPT, or secondary treatment. They can be spared if they qualify for a variance. A variance protects a point source from failure to meet otherwise governing effluent limitations. Instead, the point source receives a less stringent limitation or is given a greater time within which to meet the governing standards, or both. On some occasions, variances may be granted because a plant is fundamentally different from those which formed the basis of the effluent limitations for that industrial category or subcategory (these are "FDF" or "fundamentally different factors" variances). Sometimes a variance may be granted if a point source will install a particularly innovative technology for its pollution control. In limited circumstances, variances are available based on receiving water quality or economic hardship.

Following is a list of variances allowed under the Clean Water Act.

BPT	FDF variance (nonstatutory)
BAT Toxics	§ 301(c): economic hardship (*but see,* § 301(1))
	§ 301(k): innovative technology
	§ 301(n): FDF
BAT Nonconventionals	§ 301(c): economic hardship
	§ 301(g): water quality variance for certain pollutants
	§ 301(n): FDF
BCT Conventionals	§ 301(k): innovative technology
	§ 301(n): FDF (no variances)
NSPS	
POTWs	§ 301(h): water quality variance (for discharges into marine waters)

2. The total number of point sources required meet tech-based standards, and consequently to have NPDES permits, is about 400,000. There is some consensus that technology-based controls are the best mechanisms to control pollution yet devised. Since the Clean Water Act was enacted in 1970, industrial discharges have declined precipitously. From 1987 to 1990 alone, the time during which "Phase II" BAT standards for toxic discharges came on line, industrial discharges of toxics fell from 412 million to 197 million pounds per year. Whereas thirty years ago, two-thirds of the nation's waters were considered to be "unhealthy," at present the percentage is one-third.

This is true despite the fact that much of industry remains free of BAT regulation. In a 1989 report to Congress (the last time EPA apparently has made such a report), EPA indicated that fully four-fifths of the approximately 75,000 facilities discharging toxic or nonconventional pollutants were not subject to federal BAT standards. EPA, *Report to Congress: Water Quality*

Improvement Study 17 (1989). Moreover, many of the BAT standards that are in place are aging and no longer reflect what is currently the "best available technology."

Municipal discharges are deemed to have declined since 1972, from about 7 million to 4.3 million tons per day, while populations served by municipal facilities have increased from 90 million to 160 million people. This progress is largely due to the expenditure of $66 billion in federal funds for public treatment facilities.

[2] WATER QUALITY STANDARDS

Water quality standards (WQSs) are the CWA's analog to the national ambient air quality standards of the Clean Air Act, in that they are measurements of the healthfulness of water. Before 1972, the task of setting water quality standards was for states. Congress had not taken it on, fearing that assumption of this authority would be akin to federal zoning. H. Rep. 215, 89th Cong., 1st Sess., *reprinted in* U.S.C.C.A.N. 3313, 3320–23 (1965). In those days, state standards were submitted to the federal administrator, who reviewed them for consistency with federal requirements. If a state did not adopt standards consistent with federal requirements, the administrator promulgated water quality uses and criteria. This arrangement, while awkward and fraught with administrative and enforcement problems, S. Rep. 92-414, 92d Cong., 2d Sess., *reprinted in* U.S.C.C.A.N., pp. 3668, 3669-77 (1972), remains in place by virtue of § 303 of the CWA. Under § 303, a state is required to promulgate a WQS and submit it to EPA for approval. Upon EPA approval, the state standard takes on force and effect. § 303(c)(3), 33 U.S.C. § 1313(c)(3). EPA can establish a new standard if it finds the state did not adopt a WQS consistent with the Act or if it determines that another standard "is necessary to meet the requirements of [the Act]." § 303(c)(4), 33 U.S.C. § 1313(c)(4).

NATURAL RESOURCES DEFENSE COUNCIL v. UNITED STATES ENVIRONMENTAL PROTECTION AGENCY

16 F.3d 1395 (4th Cir. 1993)

BRITT, District Judge:

I. Facts

[The Maryland Department of the Environment ("MDE") and the Virginia State Water Control Board ("VSWQB") revised their water quality standards for dioxin, a "highly probable" potent carcinogen that originates primarily as a by-product of chlorine bleaching of pulp by the paper manufacturing industry, for a body of water used as a source of drinking water and edible fish. These water quality standards were intended to reduce risks of exposures that cause harm to humans.

The MDE and VSWQB revised their standard to 1.2 parts per quadrillion ("ppq"), a concentration less stringent than EPA's guidance criterion of .0013 ppq. EPA had reached its guidance criterion of .0013 ppq by reference to its "1984 dioxin criteria document," a publication in which the agency summarized specific scientific information regarding dioxin toxicity. The criteria document's recommended 0013 ppq level represented EPA's judgment of the level of dioxin sufficient to present an excess risk of cancer to one out of every ten million persons.[1] The state's 1.2 ppq standard, on the other hand, was thought to present that same risk to one out of every ten thousand persons. The MDE (and presumably the VSWQB) chose the less stringent standard based on information from the U.S. Food and Drug Administration, which viewed dioxin as a less potent carcinogen.

EPA conceded to the court that its view of dioxin's cancer potency was among the most conservative in the world. All parties conceded that the choice of a risk level is essentially a matter of policy preference. EPA approved the states' 1.2 ppq water quality standard for dioxin, prompting the lawsuit.]

II. Statutory Scheme

The main purpose of the CWA is to "restore and maintain the chemical, physical, and biological integrity of the Nation's waters" by reducing, and eventually eliminating, the discharge of pollutants into these waters. 33 U.S.C. § 1251(a) (Supp. 1993). While the states and EPA share duties in achieving this goal, primary responsibility for establishing appropriate water quality standards is left to the states. *See id.* §§ 1251(b) (1982); [citations omitted]. EPA sits in a reviewing capacity of the state-implemented standards, with approval and rejection powers only. 33 U.S.C. § 1313(c) (1982 & Supp. 1993). Water quality standards are a critical component of the CWA regulatory scheme because such standards serve as a guideline for setting applicable limitations in individual discharge permits.

In an effort to meet the CWA's primary goal, section 402 of the Act (33 U.S.C. § 1342) establishes the National Pollutant Discharge Elimination System ("NPDES") permit program. Under this program, permits are issued by either the EPA or by states that have been allocated NPDES permitting authority. *Id.* § 1342 (1982 & Supp. 1993). However, a state's exercise of NPDES permitting authority is subject to EPA approval. *Id.* §§ 1342(c), (d) (1982 & Supp. 1993). All NPDES permits must take into account technology-based effluent limitations that reflect the pollution reduction achievable based on specific equipment or process changes, without reference to the effect on the receiving water, and, where necessary, more stringent limitations representing the level of control necessary to ensure that the receiving waters attain and maintain state water quality standards. *Id.* §§ 1311(b) (1982), 1313(c) (1982 & Supp. 1993).

Additionally, the CWA requires each state to adopt water quality standards for all waters of that state and to review them at least every three years. *Id.*

---

[1] EPA considered six factors in choosing numeric dioxin criteria: (1) cancer potency; (2) risk level; (3) fish consumption (the projected consumption levels of persons in the general population); (4) bioconcentration ("BC Factor" or "BCF"), which is a prediction of how concentrated a pollutant such as dioxin will be in the tissues of living organisms, such as fish, as compared to the concentration of that pollutant in the ambient water in which the fish lives. EPA calculated the dioxin BCF as 5000; (5) water intake; and (6) body weight. The first four of these factors were at issue in this case. *See, infra.*

§§ 1313(a), (b), (c)(1) (1982 & Supp. 1993). To adopt these standards, states must first classify the uses for which the water is to be protected, such as fishing and swimming, and then each state must determine the level of water quality necessary to protect those uses. Thus, the following three factors are considered when adopting or evaluating a water quality standard: (1) one or more designated uses of the state waters involved; (2) certain water quality criteria, expressed as numeric pollutant concentration levels or narrative statements representing a quality of water that supports a particular designated use; and (3) an antidegradation policy to protect existing uses and high quality waters. *Id.* § 1313(c)(2)(A) (Supp. 1993); 40 C.F.R. § 131.

States are directed to adopt numerical water quality criteria for specific toxic pollutants, such as dioxin, for which EPA has published numerical criteria guidance under 33 U.S.C. § 1314(a), if that pollutant can reasonably be expected to interfere with the designated uses of the states' waters. *Id.* § 1313(c)(2)(B) (Supp. 1993). As mentioned previously, states must submit their new or revised water quality standards to EPA for review. *Id.* § 1313(c)(2)(A) (Supp. 1993). On review, each submission must contain at least six elements: (1) use designations consistent with the CWA; (2) a description of methods used and analyses conducted to support revisions of water quality standards; (3) water quality criteria sufficient to protect the designated uses; (4) an antidegradation policy; (5) certification of compliance with state law; and (6) general information to assist EPA in determining the adequacy of the scientific basis for standards that do not include the "fishable/swimmable" uses as set forth in 33 U.S.C. § 1251(a)(2). 40 C.F.R. § 131.6.

EPA regulations also provide that states should develop numerical criteria based on EPA's criteria guidance under § 304(a) of the CWA, EPA's criteria guidance modified to reflect site-specific conditions, or other scientifically defensible methods. 40 C.F.R. § 131.11(b)(1). Alternatively, states should establish narrative criteria or criteria based on biomonitoring methods if numerical criteria cannot be ascertained, or to supplement numerical criteria. *Id.* § 131.11(b)(2).

III. Discussion

* * *

C. The District Court's Affirmance of EPA's Approval of the Maryland and Virginia Dioxin Standards

Appellants argue that the district court's affirmance of EPA's approval of the Maryland and Virginia water standards should be reversed primarily for two reasons. First, they assert that EPA's approval was arbitrary and capricious because it was not based on all relevant factors, ignored key aspects of the record before it, and failed to show a rational connection between the facts found and the choices made. Second, they maintain that EPA's action was contrary to law because it did not ensure, as required by § 303(c) of the CWA (33 U.S.C. § 1313(c)), that state standards were consistent with the CWA; that is, that the standard protected all designated water uses.

Specifically, NRDC attacks EPA's assessment of the Maryland and Virginia standards regarding the first four factors used in the numeric dioxin criteria determination, namely: (1) cancer potency, (2) risk level, (3) fish consumption, and (4) bioconcentration factor ("BCF"). Of these four, NRDC emphasizes its challenge with respect to the latter two factors, fish consumption and BCF. NRDC contends that these two factors, when considered together, are important because they determine the ultimate "exposure" of an individual to dioxin, while the remaining factors only involve choices about risk or toxicity.

1. Fish Consumption

EPA estimates, on a national average, that an individual eats 6.5 grams of fish per day. Maryland and Virginia used this estimate, inter alia, in calculating the 1.2 ppq water quality standard. Appellants argue that by affirming EPA's approval of the states' use of this estimate, the district court failed to require EPA to protect subpopulations with higher than average fish consumption, particularly recreational and subsistence fishers. Specifically, appellants contend that EPA's 6.5 grams per day fish consumption factor underestimates the actual fish consumption of subpopulations in Maryland and Virginia, and therefore is not protective of a designated use. Appellants further contend that EPA's use of the 6.5 grams per day fish consumption factor is unsupported by the record and violates EPA's own policy and regulations. They emphasize that Maryland and Virginia are coastal states and, as such, are entitled — according to EPA recommendations — to higher than average values for fish consumption.

Appellants argue that the risk is especially high for the Mattaponi and Native American peoples who live near a major paper mill in Virginia and who, it is argued, consume higher-than-average amounts of fish. EPA counters that the fish consumption of these subpopulations is speculative at best, that it is based on anecdotal evidence, and that there is no evidence that the fish that actually are consumed are maximum residue fish. In fact, EPA argues that the Native Americans fish in the streams primarily for shad and herring, both of which are anadromous fish that spend a large part of their lives in the oceans and migrate to the rivers only at certain stages during their lives.

The District Court concluded that the EPA, in exercising its judgment, "relied on scientifically defensible means to reach reasoned judgments regarding fish consumption levels." *NRDC II,* at 1276. We agree.

2. Bioconcentration Factor (BCF)

Based on EPA laboratory studies, dioxin is more soluble in fat tissues than it is in water. As a result, it tends to accumulate in fish fat tissues at concentrations higher than those present in the water. By averaging the fat content of fish likely to be eaten by an exposed population, a generic BCF can be calculated that reflects dioxin's presence in fish as some multiple of its concentration in ambient water. In its 1984 dioxin criteria document, EPA calculates a dioxin BCF of 5000 for fish of average (3%) lipid content. Maryland and Virginia used this BCF figure, inter alia, to derive their numeric water quality criteria.

Appellants challenge EPA's use and approval of a 5000 BCF. They essentially contend that the 5000 BCF figure is outdated because the latest scientific research suggests that a higher BCF should be used. Citing the administrative record, appellants emphasize that: (1) EPA admits that scientific literature and research has changed significantly since preparation of the 1984 dioxin criteria document; (2) EPA further admits that BCF factors now range from 26,000 to 150,000, depending on test species; (3) Virginia conducted a state-specific study which revealed a BCF calculation of 22,000; and (4) Maryland refused to conduct such a study. Appellants contend that, taking all of these factors into account, EPA ignored all the current scientific data and simply "defaulted" to its old BCF assumption. Appellants argue that EPA acted arbitrarily and improperly in not requiring a higher BCF, especially when Virginia and Maryland chose less stringent factors for cancer potency and risk. We disagree.

Once again, we are confronted with an area dominated by complex scientific inquiry and judgment. Although EPA is aware that some recent BCF studies suggested a higher BCF than 5000, EPA maintains that such results are inconclusive and that no compelling scientific evidence indicates that a 5000 BCF is no longer within the range of scientific defensibility. We simply are not in a position to secondguess this technical decision by administrative experts. A review of the record does indicate that several more recent BCF studies have been conducted and that some have suggested a higher BCF; however, the court concludes that the best course of action is to leave this debate to the world of science to ultimately be resolved by those with specialized training in this field. Upon a careful review of the administrative record, we find no clear evidence showing that the 5000 BCF figure is not supported by sound scientific rationale. Accordingly, we hold that EPA did not act arbitrarily in approving the BCF figure used by Maryland and Virginia, and that EPA has made a rational connection between the facts found in the administrative record and its choice to approve the BCF figure. EPA's approval of the 5000 BCF will not be disturbed.

3. Protection of All Stream Uses

Appellants next contend that the district court ratified EPA's approval of the state dioxin standards without ensuring protection of all stream uses. Appellants suggest that when EPA adopted the 1.2 ppq standard, it was required to demonstrate that other stream uses were protected. They maintain that EPA ignored record evidence revealing that the 1.2 ppq standard could cause serious, direct, toxic effects to aquatic life and other wildlife that consume fish tainted with dioxin. Appellants thus argue that EPA did not follow the CWA, its regulations, or its own guidelines by asserting that the water quality criteria were intended to address only one of the minimum statutory uses, human health protection. Essentially, appellants claim that states must adopt a single criterion for dioxin that protects against all identifiable effects on human health, aquatic life, and wildlife. We disagree.

Section 303(c)(2)(A) of the CWA (33 U.S.C. § 1313(c)(2)(A) (Supp. 1993)) requires that new or revised water quality standards "consist of designated uses of the navigable waters involved and the water quality criteria for such waters based upon such uses." That section also provides:

Such standards shall be such as to protect the public health or welfare, enhance the quality of water and serve the purposes of this chapter. Such standards shall be established taking into consideration their use and value for public water supplies, propagation of fish and wildlife, recreational purposes, and agricultural, industrial, and other purposes, and also taking into consideration their use and value for navigation.

Id.

Reference to the regulations also is instructive: "A water quality standard . . . defines the water quality goals of a water body, or portion thereof, by designating the use or uses to be made of the water and by setting criteria necessary to protect the uses." 40 C.F.R. §§ 130.3, 131.2. The regulations define "criteria" as "elements of State water quality standards, expressed as constituent concentrations, levels, or narrative statements, representing a quality of water that supports a particular use. When criteria are met, water quality will generally protect the designated use." *Id.* § 131.3(b). Section 131.11(a) further provides that "states must adopt those water quality criteria that protect the designated use. Such criteria must be based on sound scientific rationale and must contain sufficient parameters or constituents to protect the designated use. For waters with multiple use designations, the criteria shall support the most sensitive use." *Id.* § 131.11(a).

As previously indicated, states should develop either numerical criteria based upon CWA guidance (or other scientific methods), or narrative criteria, if numerical criteria cannot be established. Narrative criteria might also be developed to supplement numerical criteria. *Id.* § 131.11(b). Clearly, the form of a particular state's water criteria may be either numeric or narrative, depending upon the designated use, as the district court correctly recognized. NRDC II, 806 F.2d at 1277.

In view of the above, we find that use of the term "criteria" in CWA § 303(c)(2)(A) and the regulations means that states may adopt multiple criteria for the same pollutant. Thus, where multiple uses are designated for a body of water, there may be multiple criteria applicable to it, as long as the criteria support the most sensitive use of that particular body of water. States have exclusive responsibility to designate water uses. *See* 40 C.F.R. § 131.10. However, in determining these use designations, states must take into account whether the body of water serves as a public water supply, its role in the protection and propagation of fish, shellfish and wildlife, recreation in and on the water, and agricultural, industrial, and other uses, including navigation. *Id.*

EPA avers that its review of the Maryland and Virginia standards was limited exclusively to protection of human health against any potential adverse effects (both cancerous and non-cancerous) caused by dioxin. The TSDs reflect this position. In reviewing the Virginia water quality standard, EPA stated:

The Virginia criterion for [dioxin] is designed to protect human health. Accordingly, EPA has limited its review to assessing the adequacy of the numeric criterion for that purpose. Virginia did not submit a criterion for [dioxin] for the protection of aquatic life. Depending on the circumstances, greater protection than is afforded by Virginia's 1.2 ppq criterion may be required for this purpose. In the absence of a numeric criterion for [dioxin] to protect aquatic life, Virginia's narrative criterion must, consistent with 40 C.F.R. § 122.44(d), be interpreted in individual permitting actions to prevent harm to aquatic life.

J.A. at 280–81 (footnote omitted). EPA's comments in the Maryland TSD are similar:

The Maryland criterion for [dioxin] is designed to protect human health. Accordingly, EPA's review is limited to assessing the adequacy of the numeric criterion for that purpose. In the absence of a numeric criterion for dioxin to protect aquatic life, Maryland's narrative criteria must be interpreted in individual permitting actions to prevent harm to aquatic life. *See* COMAR § 26.10.01.03.B(5)(b). Depending on the circumstances, greater protection than is afforded by Maryland's 1.2 ppq criterion may be required for this purpose.

Id. at 314 (footnote omitted). Thus, EPA duly acknowledged that dioxin may have adverse effects on aquatic life. However, EPA also noted that application of existing, separate narrative criteria protecting such aquatic life and wildlife could require more stringent controls in some cases than would be required through use of the human health criteria alone.

EPA conducted an extensive review of the adequacy of the states' criteria to protect human health, aquatic life and wildlife. Appellants have failed to cite any convincing authority showing that states have an obligation under the CWA or its accompanying regulations to adopt a single numeric criterion for dioxin that protects against all identifiable effects to human health, aquatic life, and wildlife.

D. Summary

We find that EPA's review of the Maryland and Virginia water quality standards was neither arbitrary nor capricious. Each review conducted by EPA was supported by lengthy, highly scientific, technical support documents explaining in detail EPA's rationale in approving the 1.2 ppq standards. EPA has satisfied this court that substantial evidence exists in the administrative record to support its decision, and that it acted rationally and in accordance with the CWA and its regulations. We therefore refuse to upset either EPA's decision to approve Maryland's and Virginia's adoption of the 1.2 ppq standard or the district court decision affirming the same.

[Remainder of opinion omitted]

For the foregoing reasons, the judgment of the district court is

AFFIRMED.

AMERICAN WILDLANDS v. BROWNER

260 F.3d 1192 (10th Cir. 2001)

JUDGES: Before TACHA, Chief Judge, REAVLEY* , and LUCERO, Circuit Judges.

TACHA, Chief Circuit Judge.

This appeal presents a challenge by Appellant American Wildlands to the Environmental Protection Agency's ("the EPA") approval pursuant to the Clean Water Act of certain of Montana's water quality standards. Specifically, two questions are presented to this court for review: (1) whether the EPA properly approved Montana's statutory exemption from antidegradation review of nonpoint sources of pollution; and (2) whether the EPA properly approved Montana's mixing zone policies and procedures. The district court held in favor of the EPA. We exercise jurisdiction pursuant to 28 U.S.C. § 1291 and affirm.

I. Statutory and Regulatory Scheme

1. Point and Nonpoint Source Discharges

The Clean Water Act ("the Act") was adopted "to restore and maintain the chemical, physical, and biological integrity of the Nation's waters." 33 U.S.C. § 1251(a). To achieve this goal, Congress prohibited the discharge from a point source of any pollutant into the waters of the United States unless that discharge met specific requirements set forth in the Act. 33 U.S.C. § 1311(a). . . .

In order for point source discharges to be in compliance with the Act, such discharges must adhere to the terms of a National Pollutant Discharge Elimination System ("NPDES") permit issued pursuant to the Act. 33 U.S.C. § 1342. NPDES permits are issued by the EPA or, in certain jurisdictions, by state agencies authorized to do so by the EPA. 33 U.S.C. § 1342(a)-(d). Unlike point source discharges, nonpoint source discharges are not defined by the Act. One court has described nonpoint source pollution as "nothing more that [sic] a [water] pollution problem not involving a discharge from a point source." *Nat'l Wildlife Found. v. Gorsuch,* 224 U.S. App. D.C. 41, 693 F.2d 156, 166 n.28 (D.C. Cir. 1982) (internal quotation marks omitted).

Rather than vest the EPA with authority to control nonpoint source discharges through a permitting process, Congress required states to develop water quality standards for intrastate waters. 33 U.S.C. § 1313. Water quality standards consist of three elements: first, each water body must be given a "designated use," such as recreation or the protection of aquatic life; second, the standards must specify for each body of water the amounts of various pollutants or pollutant parameters that may be present without impairing the designated use; and finally, each state must adopt an antidegradation review

---

* Honorable Thomas M. Reavley, Senior Circuit Judge, United States Court of Appeals for the Fifth Circuit, sitting by designation.

policy which will allow the state to assess activities that may lower the water quality of the water body. 33 U.S.C. § 1313(c)(2)(A); 40 C.F.R. §§ 130.3, 130.10(d)(4), 131.6, 131.10, 131.11. Further, each state is required to identify all of the waters within its borders not meeting water quality standards and establish "total maximum daily loads" ("TMDL") for those waters. 33 U.S.C. § 1313(d). A TMDL defines the specified maximum amount of a pollutant which can be discharged into a body of water from all sources combined. *Dioxin / Organochlorine Ctr. v. Clarke,* 57 F.3d 1517, 1520 (9th Cir. 1995). . . .

3. Antidegradation

The antidegradation review policies adopted by the states as a part of their water quality standards must be consistent with the federal antidegradation policy. 40 C.F.R. § 131.12. The EPA's regulations establish three levels of water quality protection: Tier I, Tier II, and Tier III. Tier I protection establishes the minimum water quality standard for all waters and requires that "existing instream water uses and the level of water quality necessary to protect the existing uses shall be maintained and protected." 40 C.F.R. § 131.12(a)(1). Tier II protection provides that, where the water quality of a water body exceeds that necessary to support aquatic life and recreation, that level of water quality shall be maintained unless the state determines that "allowing lower water quality is necessary to accommodate important economic or social development in the area in which the waters are located." 40 C.F.R. § 131.12(a)(2). Tier III protection provides that, where a water body "constitutes an outstanding National resource, such as waters of National and State parks and wildlife refuges and waters of exceptional recreational or ecological significance, that water quality shall be maintained and protected." 40 C.F.R. § 131.12(a)(3).

4. Mixing Zones

Pursuant to the EPA's regulations, a state may, at its discretion, include within its water quality standards "policies generally affecting . . . mixing zones." 40 C.F.R. § 131.13. Mixing zones are "areas where an effluent discharge undergoes initial dilution and are extended to cover the secondary mixing in the ambient water body. A mixing zone is an allocated impact zone where acute and chronic water quality criteria can be exceeded as long as a number of protections are maintained." Environmental Protection Agency, Water Quality Standards Handbook § 5.1.1, at 5-5 (2d ed.1994) (hereinafter Handbook). The protections that must be maintained include the absence of "toxic conditions to aquatic life," "objectionable deposits," "floating debris," "objectionable color, odor, taste, or turbidity," and substances resulting in "a dominance of nuisance species." *Id.* at 5-5 to 5-6. Mixing zones are allowable as a practical necessity because "it is not always necessary to meet all water quality criteria within the discharge pipe to protect the integrity of the water body as a whole. Sometimes it is appropriate to allow for ambient concentrations above the criteria in small areas near outfalls." *Id.* § 5.1, at 5-1. Should a state decide to include "policies generally affecting . . . mixing zones" within their water quality standards, those policies are subject to review and approval by the EPA. 40 C.F.R. § 131.13.

5. Montana's Policies

1. Montana's Exemption of Nonpoint Source Pollution from Antidegradation Review

In drafting its water quality standards, the Montana legislature exempted "existing activities that are nonpoint sources of pollution as of April 29, 1993" from antidegradation review with respect to Tier II waters. Mont. Code Ann. § 75-5-317(2)(a). Further, nonpoint sources initiated after April 29, 1993 are exempted from antidegradation review with respect to Tier II waters "when reasonable land, soil, and water conservation practices are applied and existing and anticipated beneficial uses will be fully protected." Mont. Code Ann. § 75-5-317(2)(b).

2. Montana's Mixing Zone Policies and Procedures

Montana's antidegradation rules provide that, where degradation to a water body at the edge of a mixing zone is not significant, no antidegradation review of the mixing zone itself is required. Mont. Admin. R. § 17.30.715(1)(c), 17.30.505(1)(b). Montana does, however, impose a number of other requirements on mixing zones designed to limit their impact on the receiving water body. Montana requires that mixing zones have "(a) the smallest practicable size, (b) a minimum practicable effect on water uses, and (c) definable boundaries." Mont. Code Ann. § 75-5-301(4). A mixing zone may not "threaten or impair existing beneficial uses." Mont. Admin. R. § 17.30.506(1). A discharge permit may not be renewed if "there is evidence that the previously allowed mixing zone will impair existing or anticipated uses." Mont. Admin. R. § 17.30.505(1)(c). The Montana Department of Environmental Quality is required to consider various factors in deciding whether or not to grant a mixing zone, such as the toxicity and persistence of the substance being discharged and the cumulative effects of multiple mixing zones. Mont. Admin. R. § 17.30.506(2). Finally, the water quality within the mixing zone itself is regulated to prohibit discharge from blocking passage of aquatic organisms or from causing the death of organisms passing through the mixing zone. Mont. Admin. R. § 17.30.602(14).

II. Proceedings Below

American Wildlands filed this lawsuit in 1998, alleging that the EPA had failed to take timely action under section 303(c) of the Act to approve or disapprove Montana's new and revised water quality standards. The original complaint alleged that the EPA violated the Act by: (1) failing to approve or disapprove Montana's new and revised water quality standards; and (2) by failing to promptly prepare and promulgate replacement standards for those Montana standards that failed to meet the requirements of the Act. In October 1998, American Wildlands moved for summary judgment. The parties stayed briefing of that motion, however, when the EPA stipulated that it would complete its review of Montana's water quality standards by January 15, 1999.

On December 24, 1998, the EPA disapproved some of Montana's revised standards and approved others. The EPA addressed the remaining standards on January 26, 1999, again disapproving some and approving others. On March 31, 1999, American Wildlands amended its complaint to challenge the EPA's approval of several of Montana's standards. The district court affirmed each of the EPA's actions. *Am. Wildlands v. Browner*, 94 F. Supp. 2d 1150 (D. Colo. 2000). This appeal followed. Specifically, American Wildlands appeals the district court's conclusion that: (1) the EPA properly approved Montana water quality standards that exempt nonpoint source pollution from antidegradation review; and (2) the EPA properly approved Montana mixing zone policies and procedures exempting the areas within the mixing zone from antidegradation review. . . .

IV. The EPA's Approval of Montana's Water Quality Standards

1. Montana's Standard Exempting Nonpoint Source Pollution from Antidegradation Review

It is the position of American Wildlands in this case that Montana's Tier II antidegradation policy, which does not consider nonpoint source pollution, is not consistent with the Act and must be disapproved by the EPA. The EPA maintains that the Act does not grant it authority to regulate nonpoint sources of pollution, and therefore, it is powerless to disapprove state antidegradation review policies on the basis of how those policies deal with nonpoint source pollution.

The district court, ruling in favor of the EPA, held that "nothing in the CWA demands that a state adopt a regulatory system for nonpoint sources." *Am. Wildlands*, 94 F. Supp. 2d at 1161. We agree. In the Act, Congress has chosen not to give the EPA the authority to regulate nonpoint source pollution. *See Kennecott Copper Corp. v. EPA*, 612 F.2d 1232, 1243 (10th Cir. 1979) (holding that the EPA lacks authority to regulate nonpoint sources of pollution); *Appalachian Power Co. v. Train*, 545 F.2d 1351, 1373 (4th Cir. 1976) ("Congress consciously distinguished between point source and nonpoint source discharges, giving EPA authority under the [Clean Water] Act to regulate only the former.").

Because the Act nowhere gives the EPA the authority to regulate nonpoint source discharges, the EPA's determination — that Montana's water quality standards exempting nonpoint source discharges from antidegradation review are consistent with the Act — is a permissible construction of the Act. It is true that states are required to "assure that there shall be achieved . . . cost-effective and reasonable best management practices for nonpoint source control." 40 C.F.R. § 131.12(a)(2). It is also true that the standard-setting process in 33 U.S.C. § 313 applies generally to waters polluted by both point source and nonpoint source pollution. 33 U.S.C. § 1313 (making no distinction between pollution from point and nonpoint sources). However, this does not mean, as American Wildlands argues, that states are required to regulate nonpoint sources at the antidegradation stage. Rather, the effect of nonpoint source discharges on water bodies will be diminished by state adoption of TMDLs for water bodies not meeting state water quality standards. Consequently, we find that the EPA did not act arbitrarily or misinterpret the Act when it approved Montana's antidegradation review rules.

B. *Montana's Mixing Zone Policies and Procedures*

American Wildlands argues that Montana's mixing zone policy allowing point source discharges to degrade water quality within the mixing zone so long as the discharge does not degrade the water quality outside the zone is inconsistent with the Act because it allows point source pollution to escape antidegradation review within certain areas of Montana's water bodies. The EPA maintains that the Act's antidegradation requirements apply to the waterbody as a whole, not specifically to the mixing zone. We find the EPA's interpretation of the Act to be permissible.

The use of mixing zones is widespread. Indeed, the water quality regulations specifically allow for their use. 40 C.F.R. § 131.13. "Practically every state and Puerto Rico have adopted mixing zone criteria. . . ." *P.R. Sun Oil Co. v. EPA,* 8 F.3d 73, 75 (1st Cir. 1993). As noted above, mixing zones are allowable as a practical necessity because "it is not always necessary to meet all water quality criteria within the discharge pipe to protect the integrity of the water body as a whole. Sometimes it is appropriate to allow for ambient concentrations above the criteria in small areas near outfalls." Handbook § 5.1, at 5-1. While "the entire extent of the water body is not required to be given full existing use protection," all effects "on the existing use must be limited to the area of the regulatory mixing zone." *Id.* § 4.4.4, at 4-6.

Moreover, courts have previously recognized that the reality of mixing zones makes measuring water quality standards at the edge of the zone a necessity. *P.R. Sun Oil Co.,* 8 F.3d at 75 ("Measuring pollutants at the edge of the mixing zone is widespread in the application of the Clean Water Act."); *Marathon Oil Co. v. EPA,* 830 F.2d 1346, 1349 (5th Cir. 1987) ("By definition, the effluent itself [within the mixing zone] does not meet water quality standards. . . . It necessarily follows, then, that the edge or outer circumference of the mixing zone is defined as the boundary at which water quality standards are first met."). Finally, as mentioned above, Montana has provided a number of safeguards to ensure that mixing zones do not damage the water quality of the entire water body. Consequently, we find that the EPA did not act arbitrarily or misinterpret the Act when it approved Montana's mixing zone policies.

V. Conclusion

In sum, we hold that the EPA's approval of Montana's water quality standards was not done arbitrarily or capriciously. Furthermore, the EPA's interpretation of the Clean Water Act implicit in its decision to approve those standards is permissible. Therefore, we AFFIRM.

NOTE

According to the 2000 Clean Water Act § 305 analysis of the nation's waterways, 39% of assessed rivers and streams, 51% of estuarine square miles, and 46% of assessed lake, pond, and reservoir acres (not including the Great Lakes) fail to meet all applicable water quality standards.

* * * * *

We have now surveyed the regime of standards governing water pollution control. Next, we look to the two mechanisms by which those standards are affixed to persons. The first is the broadly applicable certification program of § 401, 33 U.S.C. § 1341. The certification provision bars the issuance of any federal license or permit to authorize an activity that may result in a discharge, unless the applicant for that permit or license has secured from the appropriate state a certification that the activity will not violate state laws relating to water quality. § 401(a)(1), 33 U.S.C. § 1341(a)(1).

The second implementation mechanism is the National Pollutant Discharge Elimination System, established in § 402 of the CWA, 33 U.S.C. § 1342. The NPDES is the CWA's permit system. Unlike the CAA, the CWA has always relied on permits as its implementation vehicle. Under § 402, no person may discharge pollutants into navigable waters except in accordance with an NPDES permit.

[3] SECTION 401: CERTIFICATION

AMERICAN RIVERS, INC. v. FEDERAL ENERGY REGULATORY COMM'N

129 F.3d 99 (2d Cir. 1997)

[The Federal Energy Regulatory Commission ("FERC") issued hydropower licenses under the Federal Power Act to several projects, refusing to incorporate several conditions imposed by the State of Vermont pursuant to its authority under § 401 of the Clean Water Act. According to FERC, the rejected conditions were beyond the scope of the State's authority under § 401. Petitioners contend FERC must incorporate all state-imposed certification conditions; challenges to such conditions, it contends, may only be brought in court proceedings by licensees. The Court discussed that issue as well as the interrelationship of the certification requirement with the FPA.]

WALKER, Circuit Judge:

. . . .

II. Discussion

The principal dispute between petitioners and the Commission in this case surrounds the relative scope of authority of the states and the Commission under the CWA and the [Federal Power Act]. Petitioners' contention is straightforward, resting on statutory language. In their view, the plain language of § 401(d) indicates that FERC has no authority to review and reject the substance of a state certification or the conditions contained therein and must incorporate into its licenses the conditions as they appear in state certifications. FERC disagrees, arguing that the language of § 401(d) is not as clear as petitioners would have it. Rather, FERC contends, it is bound to accede only to those conditions that are within a state's authority under § 401, that is, conditions that are reasonably related to water quality and that otherwise conform to the dictates of § 401. *See Tunbridge Mill,* 68 Fed. Energy Reg. Comm'n Rep. (CCH) ¶61,078 at 61,387. The Commission also argues that without the authority to reject state-imposed § 401 conditions its Congressionally mandated role under the FPA of ensuring comprehensive planning and development of hydropower would be undermined.

A. The Clean Water Act

Before considering the Commission's contentions regarding the CWA, we note that FERC's interpretation of § 401, or any other provision of the CWA, receives no judicial deference under the doctrine of *Chevron USA, Inc. v. Natural Resources Defense Council,* 467 U.S. 837, 81 L. Ed. 2d 694, 104 S. Ct. 2778 (1984), because the Commission is not Congressionally authorized to administer the CWA. *See* 33 U.S.C. § 1251(d) ("Except as otherwise expressly provided in this chapter, the Administrator of the Environmental Protection Agency . . . shall administer this chapter."); *see also West v. Bowen,* 879 F.2d 1122, 1137 (3d Cir. 1989) (holding that "no deference is owed an agency's interpretation of another agency's statute"); *Oregon Natural Desert Assoc. v. Thomas,* 940 F. Supp. 1534, 1540 (D. Or. 1996) (holding that United States Forest Service's interpretation of § 401 of the CWA is not entitled to deference because Congress delegated administration of the CWA to the EPA alone). Thus, we review de novo the Commission's construction of the CWA.

We begin, as we must, with the statute itself. In this case, the statutory language is clear. Section 401(a), which is directed both to prospective licensees and to the federal licensing agency (in this case, the Commission), provides, in relevant part:

> Any applicant for a Federal license or permit to conduct any activity . . . which may result in any discharge into the navigable waters, shall provide the licensing or permitting agency a certification from the State in which the discharge originates or will originate. . . . No license or permit shall be granted until the certification required by this section has been obtained or has been waived . . . . No license or permit shall be granted if certification has been denied by the State. . . .

33 U.S.C. § 1341(a). More important, § 401(d), reads, in pertinent part:

> Any certification provided under this section . . . shall become a condition on any Federal license or permit subject to the provisions of this section.

33 U.S.C. § 1341(d) (emphasis added). This language is unequivocal, leaving little room for FERC to argue that it has authority to reject state conditions it finds to be ultra vires. Rather, in this case, to the extent that the Commission contends that Congress intended to vest it with authority to reject "unlawful" state conditions, the Commission faces a difficult task since it is generally assumed — absent a clearly expressed legislative intention to the contrary — "that Congress expresses its purposes through the ordinary

meaning of the words it uses. . . ." *Escondido Mut. Water Co. v. La Jolla Band of Mission Indians,* 466 U.S. 765, 772, 80 L. Ed. 2d 753, 104 S. Ct. 2105 (1984).

The Commission argues that, notwithstanding the mandatory language of the provision, § 401(d) itself restricts the substantive authority of states to impose conditions: "Section 401 authorizes states to impose only conditions that relate to water quality." Tunbridge Mill, 68 Fed. Energy Reg. Comm'n (CCH) ¶61,078 at 61,387. This is plainly true. Section 401(d), reasonably read in light of its purpose, restricts conditions that states can impose to those affecting water quality in one manner or another. *See* P.U.D. No. 1 of Jefferson County, 114 S. Ct. at 1909 (holding that a state's authority to impose conditions under § 401(d) "is not unbounded"). However, this is not tantamount to a delegation to FERC of the authority to decide which conditions are within the confines of § 401(d) and which are not. And this is the crux of the dispute in this case.

In addition to § 401(d), the Commission relies on several other provisions of the CWA in arguing that it has the authority to review and reject state-imposed conditions that are deemed by the Commission to exceed a state's power under § 401 of the CWA. In particular, the Commission invokes § 401(a)(3) and § 401(a)(5) of the CWA.

Section 401(a)(3) establishes a presumption that a state's § 401 certification obtained in order to procure a federal construction permit — for instance, a dredge-and-fill permit issued by the Army Corps of Engineers pursuant to § 404 of the CWA, 33 U.S.C. § 1344(a) — will fulfill the requirements for a subsequent federal permit governing the operation of the facility constructed pursuant to that certification. The presumption, however, may be overcome if certain conditions arise and the state then takes the procedural steps set forth by § 401(a)(3). However, even assuming the applicability of § 401(a)(3) to the facts of this case (a matter that is far from certain), the Commission has not established that it has been vested by Congress with the authority to determine whether state-imposed conditions are consistent with this provision. Nor has the Commission done so with respect to § 401(a)(5) of the CWA, 33 U.S.C. § 1341(a)(5), which provides the licensing agency (in this case FERC) with authority to enforce the terms of a license — which pursuant to § 401(d) include a state's § 401 certification conditions — once such a federal license has issued. Thus, the Commission's arguments relying on these provisions suffer from the same infirmity as does its argument relying on § 401(d). The Commission assumes the very question to be decided: whether FERC — and not a court of appropriate jurisdiction on appeal by an applicant — has the authority to review the legality of state-imposed § 401 conditions in the first instance. * * *

. . . While the Commission may determine whether the proper state has issued the certification or whether a state has issued a certification within the prescribed period, the Commission does not possess a roving mandate to decide that substantive aspects of state-imposed conditions are inconsistent with the terms of § 401.

B. The Federal Power Act

Independent of FERC's concerns that Vermont's § 401 conditions violate the terms of the CWA, the Commission contends that the § 401 conditions run afoul of the FPA. The Commission primarily fears that "to accept the conditions proposed would give the state the kind of governance and enforcement authority that is critical and exclusive to the Commission's responsibility to administer a license under the Federal Power Act, a power the Courts have repeatedly concluded belongs exclusively to the Commission." Brief of the Fed. Energy Regulatory Comm'n at 16. In particular, FERC argues (1) that the conditions that impose deadlines on construction conflict with § 13 of the FPA, 16 U.S.C. § 806, which places construction deadlines largely within the discretion of the Commission and generally contemplates that construction will be commenced within two years of the date of the license, *see First Iowa Hydro-Elec. Coop. v. Federal Power Comm'n,* 328 U.S. 152, 168 n.13, 90 L. Ed. 1143, 66 S. Ct. 906 (1946); (2) that the reopener conditions and pre-approval conditions violate § 6 of the FPA, 16 U.S.C. § 799, which provides that a license, once issued, "may be revoked only for the reasons and in the manner prescribed under the provisions of this chapter, and may be altered or surrendered only upon mutual agreement between the licensee and the Commission," as well as other provisions of the FPA, *see* 16 U.S.C. §§ 803(b), 820, 823b; and, (3) more generally, that the conditions "eviscerate the carefully balanced approach" to environmental concerns expressed in the Electric Consumers Protection Act ("ECPA"), Pub.L. No. 99-495, 100 Stat. 1243 (1986), amending the FPA, *see, e.g.,* 16 U.S.C. §§ 797(e), 803(a), 803(j).

We have no quarrel with the Commission's assertion that the FPA represents a congressional intention to establish "a broad federal role in the development and licensing of hydroelectric power." *California v. Federal Energy Regulatory Comm'n,* 495 U.S. 490, 496, 109 L. Ed. 2d 474, 110 S. Ct. 2024 (1990). Nor do we dispute that the FPA has a wide preemptive reach. *Id.* The CWA, however, has diminished this preemptive reach by expressly requiring the Commission to incorporate into its licenses state-imposed water-quality conditions. *See* 33 U.S.C. § 1341(a)(1). Although we are sympathetic to the Commission's suggestion that without the authority to reject states' conditions that are beyond the scope of § 401, the preemptive reach of the FPA may be narrowed at the will of the states, *see, e.g.,* Brief of Amici Curiae Edison Elec. Inst. at 14, the Commission's concerns are overblown.

The Commission fails to acknowledge appropriately its ability to protect its mandate from incursion by exercising the authority to refuse to issue a hydropower license altogether if the Commission concludes that a license, as conditioned, sufficiently impairs its authority under the FPA. *See, e.g., Escondido,* 466 U.S. at 778 n.20. If the Commission is concerned that the conditions imposed by a state "intrude upon the Commission's exclusive authority under the FPA," Brief of the Fed. Energy Regulatory Comm'n at 44, nothing in the CWA prevents it from protecting its field of authority by simply refusing to issue the license as so conditioned.

The Commission, however, has chosen to forgo this route, arguing that refusing to issue a license is not a "practical option" in relicensing cases, such as CVPS. *Id.* at 20 n.10. Although we understand that refusing to relicense a hydroelectric project would result in the disassembly of the project, presenting "serious practical and economic problems" and affecting all manner of local interests, *id.,* the Commission's dissatisfaction with the remedy of license denial is not reason enough to turn a blind eye to FERC's assumption of authority to review and reject a state's § 401 conditions. Rather, the Commission must establish that the authority it proposes is rooted in a Congressional mandate. And this they have failed to do.

Finally, with respect to the ECPA amendments to the FPA, the Commission is mistaken. Under these provisions, the Commission must "give equal consideration to . . . the protection, mitigation of damage to, and enhancement of, fish and wildlife . . . and the preservation of other aspects of environmental quality," 16 U.S.C. § 797(e), and must impose conditions, based on recommendations of relevant federal agencies and affected states, to "protect, mitigate damages to, and enhance, fish and wildlife . . . affected by the development, operation, and management of the project . . .," 16 U.S.C. § 803(j)(1). *See United States Dep't of Interior v. Federal Energy Regulatory Comm'n,* 952 F.2d 538, 543 (D.C. Cir. 1992) (describing environmental aspects of the ECPA amendments). The Commission argues that absent the authority to reject state-imposed conditions beyond the scope of § 401 of the CWA, the carefully balanced approach of the ECPA amendments, in general, and § 10(j), 16 U.S.C. § 803(j), in particular, would be "eviscerated . . . through the simple expedient of [states'] labeling . . . recommendations 'conditions' to the Section 401 certification." Brief of the Fed. Energy Regulatory Comm'n at 39. In short, the Commission is concerned that it would be "held hostage" to every state imposed condition, compromising its role under the ECPA amendments of reconciling competing interests. *Id.* Such a result, the Commission contends, is impermissible under § 511(a) of the CWA, 33 U.S.C. § 1371(a), which provides, in part, that the Act "shall not be construed as . . . limiting the authority or functions of any officer or agency of the United States under any other law or regulation not inconsistent with this chapter. . . ."

The Commission's claim that the CWA — as we construe it — and the ECPA amendments are incompatible must be rejected. The Commission's concern that states will hold the Commission hostage through the § 401 process is misplaced because states' authority under § 401 is circumscribed in notable respects. First, applicants for state certification may challenge in courts of appropriate jurisdiction any state-imposed condition that exceeds a state's authority under § 401. In so doing, licensees will surely protect themselves against state-imposed ultra vires conditions. Second, even assuming that certification applicants will not always challenge ultra vires state conditions, the Commission may protect its mandate by refusing to issue a license which, as conditioned, conflicts with the FPA. In so doing, the Commission will not only protect its mandate but also signal to states and licensees the limits of its tolerance. Third, and most important, to the extent that the existence of states' authority to impose § 401 conditions may otherwise conflict with the ECPA amendments, the ECPA is inconsistent with the terms of the CWA, thus, making inapplicable § 511(a) of the CWA. *See* 33 U.S.C. 1371(a) (the Act "shall not be construed as . . . limiting the authority or functions of any officer or agency of the United States under any other law or regulation not inconsistent with this chapter . . .").

III. Conclusion

We have considered the Commission's remaining arguments and find them to be without merit. For the foregoing reasons, we grant the petition for review, vacate the orders of the Commission, and remand for proceedings consistent with this opinion.

NOTE

EPA has promulgated regulations to govern the certification process. 40 C.F.R. Part 121. Under the rules, every certification must include a statement "that there is a reasonable assurance that the activity will be conducted in a manner which will not violate applicable water quality standards" and a statement of conditions deemed "necessary or desirable with respect to the discharge of the activity." 40 C.F.R. §§ 121.2(3), 121.2(4). It is EPA's role to determine whether a certified discharge will affect other states' water quality standards. 40 C.F.R. § 121.13. If a state is potentially affected, the information is forwarded to it for a hearing.

PUD NO. 1 OF JEFFERSON COUNTY AND CITY OF TACOMA v. WASHINGTON DEPARTMENT OF ECOLOGY

511 U.S. 700, 114 S. Ct. 1900 (1994)

JUDGES: O'CONNOR, J., delivered the opinion of the Court, in which REHNQUIST, C.J., and BLACKMUN, STEVENS, KENNEDY, SOUTER, and GINSBURG, JJ., joined. STEVENS, J., filed a concurring opinion. THOMAS, J., filed a dissenting opinion, in which SCALIA, J., joined.

Petitioners, a city and a local utility district, want to build a hydroelectric project on the Dosewallips River in Washington State. We must decide whether respondent, the state environmental agency, properly conditioned a permit for the project on the maintenance of specific minimum stream flows to protect salmon and steelhead runs.

I

This case involves the complex statutory and regulatory scheme that governs our Nation's waters, a scheme which implicates both federal and state administrative responsibilities. The Federal Water Pollution Control Act, commonly known as the Clean Water Act, 86 Stat. 816, as amended, 33 U.S.C. § 1251 et seq., is a comprehensive water quality statute designed to "restore and maintain the chemical, physical, and biological integrity of the Nation's waters." § 1251(a). The Act also seeks to attain "water quality which provides for the protection and propagation of fish, shellfish, and wildlife." § 1251(a)(2).

To achieve these ambitious goals, the Clean Water Act establishes distinct roles for the Federal and State Governments. Under the Act, the Administrator of the Environmental Protection Agency is required, among other things, to establish and enforce technology-based limitations on individual discharges into the country's navigable waters from point sources. *See* §§ 1311, 1314. Section 303 of the Act also requires each State, subject to federal approval, to institute comprehensive water quality standards establishing water quality goals for all intrastate waters. §§ 1311(b)(1)(C), 1313. These state water quality standards provide "a supplementary basis . . . so that numerous point sources, despite individual compliance with effluent limitations, may be further regulated to prevent water quality from falling below acceptable levels." *EPA v. California ex rel. State Water Resources Control Bd.*, 426 U.S. 200, 205, n. 12, 48 L. Ed. 2d 578, 96 S. Ct. 2022 (1976).

A state water quality standard "shall consist of the designated uses of the navigable waters involved and the water quality criteria for such waters based upon such uses." 33 U.S.C. § 1313(c)(2)(A). In setting standards, the State must comply with the following broad requirements:

> "Such standards shall be such as to protect the public health or welfare, enhance the quality of water and serve the purposes of this chapter. Such standards shall be established taking into consideration their use and value for public water supplies, propagation of fish and wildlife, recreational [and other purposes.]" *Ibid.*

See also § 1251(a)(2).

A 1987 amendment to the Clean Water Act makes clear that § 303 also contains an "antidegradation policy" — that is, a policy requiring that state standards be sufficient to maintain existing beneficial uses of navigable waters, preventing their further degradation. Specifically, the Act permits the revision of certain effluent limitations or water quality standards "only if such revision is subject to and consistent with the antidegradation policy established under this section." § 1313(d)(4)(B). Accordingly, EPA's regulations implementing the Act require that state water quality standards include "a statewide antidegradation policy" to ensure that "existing instream water uses and the level of water quality necessary to protect the existing uses shall be maintained and protected." 40 C.F.R. § 131.12 (1992). At a minimum, state water quality standards must satisfy these conditions. The Act also allows States to impose more stringent water quality controls. *See* 33 U.S.C. §§ 1311(b)(1)(C), 1370. *See also* 40 C.F.R. 131.4(a) ("As recognized by section 510 of the Clean Water Act [33 U.S.C. § 1370], States may develop water quality standards more stringent than required by this regulation").

The State of Washington has adopted comprehensive water quality standards intended to regulate all of the State's navigable waters. *See* Washington Administrative Code (WAC) 173-201-010 to 173-201-120 (1990). The State created an inventory of all the State's waters, and divided the waters into five classes. 173-201-045. Each individual fresh surface water of the State is placed into one of these classes. 173-201-080. The Dosewallips River is classified AA, extraordinary. 173-201-080(32). The water quality standard for Class AA waters is set forth at 173-201-045(1). The standard identifies the designated uses of Class AA waters as well as the criteria applicable to such waters.[1]

---

[1] WAC 173-201-045(1) provides in pertinent part:

(1) Class AA (extraordinary).

(a) General characteristic. Water quality of this class shall markedly and uniformly exceed the requirements for all or substantially all uses.

In addition to these specific standards applicable to Class AA waters, the State has adopted a statewide antidegradation policy. That policy provides:

"(a) Existing beneficial uses shall be maintained and protected and no further degradation which would interfere with or become injurious to existing beneficial uses will be allowed.

"(b) No degradation will be allowed of waters lying in national parks, national recreation areas, national wildlife refuges, national scenic rivers, and other areas of national ecological importance.

. . . .

"(f) In no case, will any degradation of water quality be allowed if this degradation interferes with or becomes injurious to existing water uses and causes long-term and irreparable harm to the environment." 173-201-035(8).

As required by the Act, EPA reviewed and approved the State's water quality standards. *See* 33 U.S.C. § 1313(c)(3); 42 Fed. Reg. 56792 (1977). Upon approval by EPA, the state standard became "the water quality standard for the applicable waters of that State." 33 U.S.C. § 1313(c)(3).

States are responsible for enforcing water quality standards on intrastate waters. 33 U.S.C. § 1319(a). In addition to these primary enforcement responsibilities, § 401 of the Act requires States to provide a water quality certification before a federal license or permit can be issued for activities that

---

(b) Characteristic uses. Characteristic uses shall include, but not be limited to, the following:

    (i) Water supply (domestic, industrial, agricultural).

    (ii) Stock watering.

    (iii) Fish and shellfish: Salmonid migration, rearing, spawning, and harvesting. . . . Other fish migration, rearing, spawning, and harvesting. . . .

    (iv) Wildlife habitat.

    (v) Recreation (primary contact recreation, sport fishing, boating, and aesthetic enjoyment).

    (vi) Commerce and navigation.

(c) Water quality criteria

    (i) Fecal coliform organisms.

        (A) Freshwater — fecal coliform organisms shall not exceed a geometric mean value of 50 organisms/100 mL, with not more than 10 percent of samples exceeding 100 organisms/100 mL.

        (B) Marine water — fecal coliform organisms shall not exceed a geometric mean value of 14 organisms/100 mL, with not more than 10 percent of samples exceeding 43 organisms/100 mL.

    (ii) Dissolved oxygen [shall exceed specific amounts].

    (iii) Total dissolved gas shall not exceed 110 percent of saturation at any point of sample collection.

    (iv) Temperature shall not exceed [certain levels].

    (v) pH shall be within [a specified range].

    (vi) Turbidity shall not exceed [specific levels].

    (vii) Toxic, radioactive, or deleterious material concentrations shall be less than those which may affect public health, the natural aquatic environment, or the desirability of the water for any use.

    (viii) Aesthetic values shall not be impaired by the presence of materials or their effects, excluding those of natural origin, which offend the senses of sight, smell, touch, or taste.

may result in any discharge into intrastate navigable waters. 33 U.S.C. § 1341. Specifically, § 401 requires an applicant for a federal license or permit to conduct any activity "which may result in any discharge into the navigable waters" to obtain from the state a certification "that any such discharge will comply with the applicable provisions of sections 1311, 1312, 1313, 1316, and 1317 of this title." 33 U.S.C. § 1341(a). Section 401(d) further provides that "any certification . . . shall set forth any effluent limitations and other limitations, and monitoring requirements necessary to assure that any applicant . . . will comply with any applicable effluent limitations and other limitations, under section 1311 or 1312 of this title . . . and with any other appropriate requirement of State law set forth in such certification." 33 U.S.C. § 1341(d). The limitations included in the certification become a condition on any Federal license. *Ibid.*

II

Petitioners propose to build the Elkhorn Hydroelectric Project on the Dosewallips River. If constructed as presently planned, the facility would be located just outside the Olympic National Park on federally owned land within the Olympic National Forest. The project would divert water from a 1.2-mile reach of the River (the bypass reach), run the water through turbines to generate electricity and then return the water to the River below the bypass reach. Under the Federal Power Act (FPA), 41 Stat. 1063, as amended, 16 U.S.C. § 791 *et seq.*, the Federal Energy Regulatory Commission has authority to license new hydroelectric facilities. As a result, the petitioners must get a FERC license to build or operate the Elkhorn Project. Because a federal license is required, and because the project may result in discharges into the Dosewallips River, petitioners are also required to obtain State certification of the project pursuant to § 401 of the Clean Water Act, 33 U.S.C. § 1341.

The water flow in the bypass reach, which is currently undiminished by appropriation, ranges seasonally between 149 and 738 cubic feet per second (cfs). The Dosewallips supports two species of salmon, Coho and Chinook, as well as Steelhead trout. As originally proposed, the project was to include a diversion dam which would completely block the river and channel approximately 75% of the River's water into a tunnel alongside the streambed. About 25% of the water would remain in the bypass reach, but would be returned to the original riverbed through sluice gates or a fish ladder. Depending on the season, this would leave a residual minimum flow of between 65 and 155 cfs in the River. Respondent undertook a study to determine the minimum stream flows necessary to protect the salmon and steelhead fisheries in the bypass reach. On June 11, 1986, respondent issued a § 401 water quality certification imposing a variety of conditions on the project, including a minimum stream-flow requirement of between 100 and 200 cfs depending on the season.

A state administrative appeals board determined that the minimum flow requirement was intended to enhance, not merely maintain, the fishery, and that the certification condition therefore exceeded respondent's authority under state law. App. to Pet. for Cert. 55a–57a. On appeal, the state Superior Court concluded that respondent could require compliance with the minimum flow conditions. *Id.*, at 29a–45a. The Superior Court also found that respondent had imposed the minimum flow requirement to protect and preserve the fishery, not to improve it, and that this requirement was authorized by state law. *Id.*, at 34a.

The Washington Supreme Court held that the antidegradation provisions of the State's water quality standards require the imposition of minimum stream flows. 121 Wash. 2d 179, 186–187, 849 P.2d 646, 650 (1993). The court also found that § 401(d), which allows States to impose conditions based upon several enumerated sections of the Clean Water Act and "any other appropriate requirement of State law," 33 U.S.C. § 1341(d), authorized the stream flow condition. Relying on this language and the broad purposes of the Clean Water Act, the court concluded that § 401(d) confers on States power to "consider all state action related to water quality in imposing conditions on section 401 certificates." 121 Wash. 2d, at 192, 849 P.2d, at 652. We granted certiorari, 510 U.S. 810 (1993), to resolve a conflict among the state courts of last resort [citation omitted]. We now affirm.

III

The principal dispute in this case concerns whether the minimum stream flow requirement that the State imposed on the Elkhorn project is a permissible condition of a § 401 certification under the Clean Water Act. To resolve this dispute we must first determine the scope of the State's authority under § 401. We must then determine whether the limitation at issue here, the requirement that petitioners maintain minimum stream flows, falls within the scope of that authority.

A

There is no dispute that petitioners were required to obtain a certification from the State pursuant to § 401. Petitioners concede that, at a minimum, the project will result in two possible discharges — the release of dredged and fill material during the construction of the project, and the discharge of water at the end of the tailrace after the water has been used to generate electricity. Brief for Petitioners 27–28. Petitioners contend, however, that the minimum stream flow requirement imposed by the State was unrelated to these specific discharges, and that as a consequence, the State lacked the authority under § 401 to condition its certification on maintenance of stream flows sufficient to protect the Dosewallips fishery.

If § 401 consisted solely of subsection (a), which refers to a state certification that a "discharge" will comply with certain provisions of the Act, petitioners' assessment of the scope of the State's certification authority would have considerable force. Section 401, however, also contains subsection (d), which expands the State's authority to impose conditions on the certification of a project. Section 401(d) provides that any certification shall set forth "any effluent limitations and other limitations . . . necessary to assure that any *applicant*" will comply with various provisions of the Act and appropriate state law requirements. 33 U.S.C. § 1341(d) (emphasis added). The language of this subsection contradicts petitioners' claim that the State may only impose water quality limitations specifically tied to a "discharge." The text refers to the compliance of the applicant, not the discharge. Section 401(d) thus allows the State to impose "other limitations" on the project in general to assure compliance with various provisions of the Clean Water Act and with "any other appropriate requirement of State law." Although the dissent asserts that this interpretation of § 401(d) renders § 401(a)(1) superfluous . . . we see no such anomaly. Section 401(a)(1) identifies the category of activities subject to certification — namely those with discharges. And § 401(d) is most reasonably read as authorizing additional conditions and limitations on the activity as a whole once the threshold condition, the existence of a discharge, is satisfied.

Our view of the statute is consistent with EPA's regulations implementing § 401. The regulations expressly interpret § 401 as requiring the State to find that "there is a reasonable assurance that the *activity* will be conducted in a manner which will not violate applicable water quality standards." 40 C.F.R. § 121.2(a)(3) (1992) (emphasis added). *See also* EPA, Wetlands and 401 Certification 23 (Apr. 1989) ("In 401(d), the Congress has given the States the authority to place any conditions on a water quality certification that are necessary to assure that the applicant will comply with effluent limitations, water quality standards, . . . and with 'any other appropriate requirement of State law.' "). EPA's conclusion that *activities* — not merely discharges — must comply with state water quality standards is a reasonable interpretation of § 401, and is entitled to deference. [citations omitted]

Although § 401(d) authorizes the State to place restrictions on the activity as a whole, that authority is not unbounded. The State can only ensure that the project complies with "any applicable effluent limitations and other limitations, under [33 U.S.C. §§ 1311, 1312]" or certain other provisions of the Act, "and with any other appropriate requirement of State law." 33 U.S.C. § 1341(d). The State asserts that the minimum stream flow requirement was imposed to ensure compliance with the state water quality standards adopted pursuant to § 303 of the Clean Water Act, 33 U.S.C. § 1313.

We agree with the State that ensuring compliance with § 303 is a proper function of the § 401 certification. Although § 303 is not one of the statutory provisions listed in § 401(d), the statute allows states to impose limitations to ensure compliance with § 301 of the Act, 33 U.S.C. § 1311. Section 301 in turn incorporates § 303 by reference. *See* 33 U.S.C. § 1311(b)(1)(C); *see also* H. R. Conf. Rep. No. 95-830, p. 96 (1977) ("Section 303 is always included by reference where section 301 is listed"). As a consequence, state water quality standards adopted pursuant to § 303 are among the "other limitations" with which a State may ensure compliance through the § 401 certification process. This interpretation is consistent with EPA's view of the statute. *See* 40 C.F.R. § 121.2(a)(3) (1992); EPA, Wetlands and 401 Certification, *supra*. Moreover, limitations to assure compliance with state water quality standards are also permitted by § 401(d)'s reference to "any other appropriate requirement of State law." We do not speculate on what additional state laws, if any, might be incorporated by this language. But at a minimum, limitations imposed pursuant to state water quality standards adopted pursuant to § 303 are "appropriate" requirements of state law. Indeed, petitioners appear to agree that the State's authority under § 401 includes limitations designed to ensure compliance with state water quality standards. Brief for Petitioners 9, 21.

B

Having concluded that, pursuant to § 401, States may condition certification upon any limitations necessary to ensure compliance with state water quality standards or any other "appropriate requirement of State law," we consider whether the minimum flow condition is such a limitation. Under § 303, state water quality standards must "consist of the designated uses of the navigable waters involved and the water quality criteria for such waters based upon such uses." 33 U.S.C. § 1313(c)(2)(A). In imposing the minimum stream flow requirement, the State determined that construction and operation of the project as planned would be inconsistent with one of the designated uses of Class AA water, namely "salmonid [and other fish] migration, rearing, spawning, and harvesting." App. to Pet. for Cert. 83a–84a. The designated use of the River as a fish habitat directly reflects the Clean Water Act's goal of maintaining the "chemical, physical, and biological integrity of the Nation's waters." 33 U.S.C. § 1251(a). Indeed, the Act defines pollution as "the manmade or man induced alteration of the chemical, physical, biological, and radiological integrity of water." § 1362(19). Moreover, the Act expressly requires that, in adopting water quality standards, the State must take into consideration the use of waters for "propagation of fish and wildlife." 33 U.S.C. § 1313(c)(2)(A).

Petitioners assert, however, that § 303 requires the State to protect designated uses solely through implementation of specific "criteria." According to petitioners, the State may not require them to operate their dam in a manner consistent with a designated "use"; instead, say petitioners, under § 303 the State may only require that the project comply with specific numerical "criteria."

We disagree with petitioners' interpretation of the language of § 303(c)(2)(A). Under the statute, a water quality standard must "consist of the designated uses of the navigable waters involved *and* the water quality criteria for such waters based upon such uses." 33 U.S.C. § 1313(c)(2)(A) (emphasis added). The text makes it plain that water quality standards contain two components. We think the language of § 303 is most naturally read to require that a project be consistent with *both* components, namely the designated use *and* the water quality criteria. Accordingly, under the literal terms of the statute, a project that does not comply with a designated use of the water does not comply with the applicable water quality standards.

Consequently, pursuant to § 401(d) the State may require that a permit applicant comply with both the designated uses and the water quality criteria of the state standards. In granting certification pursuant to § 401(d), the State "shall set forth any . . . limitations . . . necessary to assure that [the applicant] will comply with any . . . limitations under [§ 303] . . . and with any other appropriate requirement of State law." A certification requirement that an applicant operate the project consistently with state water quality standards — i.e., consistently with the designated uses of the water body and the water quality criteria — is both a "limitation" to assure "compliance with . . . limitations" imposed under § 303, and an "appropriate" requirement of State law.* * *

The State also justified its minimum stream flow as necessary to implement the "antidegradation policy" of § 303, 33 U.S.C. § 1313(d)(4)(B). When the Clean Water Act was enacted in 1972, the water quality standards of all 50 States had antidegradation provisions. These provisions were required by federal law. *See* U.S. Dept. of Interior, Federal Water Pollution Control Administration, Compendium of Department of Interior Statements on Non-degradation of Interstate Waters 1–2 (Aug. 1968); *see also* Hines, *A Decade of Nondegradation Policy in Congress and the Courts: The Erratic Pursuit of Clean Air and Clean Water,* 62 Iowa L. Rev. 643, 658–660 (1977). By providing in 1972 that existing state water quality standards would remain in force until revised, the Clean Water Act ensured that the States would continue their antidegradation programs. *See* 33 U.S.C. § 1313(a). EPA has consistently required that revised state standards incorporate an antidegradation policy. And, in 1987, Congress explicitly recognized the existence of an "antidegradation policy established under [§ 303]." § 1313(d)(4)(B).

EPA has promulgated regulations implementing § 303's antidegradation policy, a phrase that is not defined elsewhere in the Act. These regulations require States to "develop and adopt a statewide antidegradation policy and identify the methods for implementing such policy." 40 C.F.R. § 131.12 (1992). . . . The Solicitor General, representing EPA, asserts, . . . and we agree, that the State's minimum stream flow condition is a proper application of the state and federal antidegradation regulations, as it ensures that an "existing instream water use" will be "maintained and protected." 40 C.F.R. § 131.12(a)(1) (1993).

Petitioners also assert more generally that the Clean Water Act is only concerned with water "quality," and does not allow the regulation of water "quantity." This is an artificial distinction. In many cases, water quantity is closely related to water quality; a sufficient lowering of the water quantity in a body of water could destroy all of its designated uses, be it for drinking water, recreation, navigation or, as here, as a fishery. In any event, there is recognition in the Clean Water Act itself that reduced stream flow, *i.e.,* diminishment of water quantity, can constitute water pollution. First, the Act's definition of pollution as "the man-made or man induced alteration of the chemical, physical, biological, and radiological integrity of water" encompasses the effects of reduced water quantity. 33 U.S.C. § 1362(19). This broad conception of pollution — one which expressly evinces Congress' concern with the physical and biological integrity of water — refutes petitioners' assertion that the Act draws a sharp distinction between the regulation of water "quantity" and water "quality." Moreover, § 304 of the Act expressly recognizes that water "pollution" may result from "changes in the movement, flow, or circulation of any navigable waters . . . including changes caused by the construction of dams." 33 U.S.C. § 1314(f). This concern with the flowage effects of dams and other diversions is also embodied in the EPA regulations, which expressly require existing dams to be operated to attain designated uses. 40 C.F.R. § 131.10(g)(4) (1992).

Petitioners assert that two other provisions of the Clean Water Act, §§ 101(g) and 510(2), 33 U.S.C. §§ 1251(g) and 1370(2), exclude the regulation of water quantity from the coverage of the Act. Section 101(g) provides "that the authority of each State to allocate quantities of water within its jurisdiction shall not be superseded, abrogated or otherwise impaired by this chapter." 33 U.S.C. § 1251(g). Similarly, § 510(2) provides that nothing in the Act shall "be construed as impairing or in any manner affecting any right or jurisdiction of the States with respect to the waters . . . of such States." 33 U.S.C. § 1370. In petitioners' view, these provisions exclude "water quantity issues from direct regulation under the federally controlled water quality standards authorized in § 303." Brief for Petitioners 39 (emphasis omitted).

This language gives the States authority to allocate water rights; we therefore find it peculiar that petitioners argue that it prevents the State from regulating stream flow. In any event, we read these provisions more narrowly than petitioners. Sections 101(g) and 510(2) preserve the authority of each State to allocate water quantity as between users; they do not limit the scope of water pollution controls that may be imposed on users who have obtained, pursuant to state law, a water allocation. . . .

IV

[This portion of the opinion, concluding that this regulation of streamflow does not interfere with regulatory efforts of the Federal Energy Regulatory Commission, is omitted].

In summary, we hold that the State may include minimum stream flow requirements in a certification issued pursuant to § 401 of the Clean Water Act insofar as necessary to enforce a designated use contained in a state water quality standard. The judgment of the Supreme Court of Washington, accordingly, is affirmed.

So ordered.

[Concurring opinion by Stevens, J., omitted.]

[Dissenting opinion by Thomas, J. omitted.]

NOTE

The *Jefferson* case is the most important case in years on the subject of certification under the Clean Water Act. (Do you see why?) Its underlying message has not been lost on the environmental community. Environmentalists have sought, for example, to apply the § 401 certification process to federal grazing permits. The argument was that grazing livestock destroy banks of streams and their vegetative cover, thereby causing rises in water temperature which can in turn be deadly to coldwater salmon, trout, and other fish. Grazing activities also can increase stream sedimentation and fecal coliform and fecal streptococci levels. However, in a test case before the Ninth Circuit, the argument that federal grazing permits may only be issued if accompanied by a CWA certification was rejected on the ground that the certification requirement was meant to apply only to point source releases. *Oregon Natural Desert Ass'n v. Dombeck,* 172 F.3d 1092 (9th Cir. 1998), *cert. denied,* 528 U.S. 964, 120 S. Ct. 397 (1999).

[4] THE NATIONAL POLLUTANT DISCHARGE ELIMINATION SYSTEM

Section 402 of the Clean Water Act, 33 U.S.C. § 1342, establishes the primary regulatory tool by which effluent limitations are made applicable to specific point sources. That tool is the permit: persons may discharge pollutants into waters of the United States only if they meet applicable effluent limitations and have a permit in hand confirming that right.

ATLANTIC STATES LEGAL FOUNDATION v. EASTMAN KODAK CO.

12 F.3d 353 (2d Cir. 1993)

WINTER, Circuit Judge:

This appeal raises the issue of whether private groups may bring a citizen suit pursuant to Section 505 of the Federal Water Pollution Control Act (commonly known as the Clean Water Act), 33 U.S.C. § 1365, to stop the discharge of pollutants not listed in a valid permit issued pursuant to the Clean Water Act ("CWA" or "the Act"), 33 U.S.C. § 1342 (1988). We hold that the discharge of unlisted pollutants is not unlawful under the CWA. We also hold that private groups may not bring such a suit to enforce New York State environmental regulations.

Background

Appellee Eastman Kodak Company ("Kodak") operates an industrial facility in Rochester, New York that discharges wastewater into the Genesee River and Paddy Hill Creek under a State Pollutant Discharge Elimination System ("SPDES") permit issued pursuant to 33 U.S.C. § 1342. Appellant Atlantic States Legal Foundation, Inc. ("Atlantic States") is a not-for-profit environmental group based in Syracuse, New York.

Kodak operates a wastewater treatment plant at its Rochester facility to purify waste produced in the manufacture of photographic supplies and other laboratory chemicals. The purification plant employs a variety of technical processes to filter harmful pollutants before discharge into the Genesee River at the King's Landing discharge point (designated Outfall 001) pursuant to its SPDES permit.

Kodak first received a federal permit in 1975. At that time, the pertinent regulatory scheme was the National Pollutant Discharge Elimination System ("NPDES") that was administered directly by the federal Environmental Protection Agency ("EPA"). Subsequently, 33 U.S.C. § 1342(b), (c) delegated authority to the states to establish their own programs in place of the EPA's. As a result, Kodak applied in July 1979 to renew its permit to the New York State Department of Environmental Conservation ("DEC"). The DEC declined to act on Kodak's renewal application, and Kodak's NPDES permit remained in effect. As part of the pending application for a SPDES permit, in April 1982 Kodak provided the DEC with a Form 2C describing estimated discharges of

164 substances from each of its outfalls. Kodak also submitted an Industrial Chemical Survey ("ICS") disclosing the amounts of certain chemicals used in Kodak's facility and whether they might appear in the plant's wastewater. Although the ICS originally requested information on 144 substances, including some broad classes such as "unspecified metals," the DEC restricted the inquiry to chemicals used in excess of specified minimum levels.

On the basis of these disclosures, DEC issued Kodak a SPDES permit, number 000-1643, effective November 1, 1984, establishing specific effluent limitations for approximately 25 pollutants. The permit also included "action levels" for five other pollutants as well as for three of the pollutants for which it had established effluent limits. DEC further required Kodak to conduct a semi-annual scan of "EPA Volatile, Acid and Base/Neutral Fractions and PCB's priority pollutants on a 24-hr. composite sample." In May 1989, Kodak applied to renew the SPDES permit submitting a new Form 2C and ICS, but the 1984 permit will continue to remain in effect until DEC issues a final determination.

Kodak's SPDES permit contains both "general provisions" and "special reporting requirements" pursuant to EPA policy directives devised to implement the Clean Water Act and to DEC policy directives devised to implement both the Clean Water Act and New York law, N.Y. Envtl. Conserv. Law § 17-0815 (McKinney 1984).

The present action arises out of an ongoing dispute between Atlantic States and Kodak during which Atlantic States has claimed that Kodak both exceeded the effluent limits imposed by its SPDES permit and discharged pollutants for which Kodak had no discharge authorization. The procedural history of this dispute is set out in full in our previous decision, *Atlantic States Legal Found., Inc. v. Eastman Kodak Co.*, 933 F.2d 124 (2d Cir. 1991) ("*Atlantic States I*"). * * *

Atlantic States brought the present action under the citizen suit provision of Section 505, which permits private suits to enforce a CWA "effluent standard or limitation." 33 U.S.C. § 1365(a)(1)(A). Section 505 defines such an enforceable standard or limitation as, inter alia, "an unlawful act under . . . section 1311," and "a permit or condition thereof issued under section 1342 of this title, which is in effect under this chapter." 33 U.S.C. § 1365(f)(1), (6). The question then is whether Atlantic States' action seeks to enforce an "effluent standard or limitation" imposed by the Act or by Kodak's SPDES permit issued by the DEC.

A. "Standards and Limitations" of the Clean Water Act

Atlantic States argues first that the plain language of Section 301 of the CWA, 33 U.S.C. § 1311, prohibits the discharge of any pollutants not expressly permitted. With regard to this claim, therefore, Atlantic States' standing to bring this action turns on the merits of the action itself.

Section 301(a) reads: "Except as in compliance with this section and sections 1312, 1316, 1317, 1328, 1342, and 1344 of this title, the discharge of any pollutant by any person shall be unlawful." This prohibition is tempered, however, by a self-referential host of exceptions that allow the discharge of many pollutants once a polluter has complied with the regulatory program of the CWA. The exception relevant to the instant matter is contained in Section 402, which outlines the NPDES, 33 U.S.C. § 1342(a), and specifies the requirements for suspending the national system with the submission of an approved state program, 33 U.S.C. § 1342(b), (c). Section 402(k) contains the so-called "shield provision," 33 U.S.C. § 1342(k), which defines compliance with a NPDES or SPDES permit as compliance with Section 301 for the purposes of the CWA's enforcement provisions. The Supreme Court has noted that "The purpose of [Section 402(k)] seems to be . . . to relieve [permit holders] of having to litigate in an enforcement action the question whether their permits are sufficiently strict." *E.I. du Pont de Nemours & Co. v. Train,* 430 U.S. 112, 138 n.28, 51 L. Ed. 2d 204, 97 S. Ct. 965 (1977).

Atlantic States' view of the regulatory framework stands that scheme on its head. Atlantic States treats permits as establishing limited permission for the discharge of identified pollutants and a prohibition on the discharge of unidentified pollutants. Viewing the regulatory scheme as a whole, however, it is clear that the permit is intended to identify and limit the most harmful pollutants while leaving the control of the vast number of other pollutants to disclosure requirements. Once within the NPDES or SPDES scheme, therefore, polluters may discharge pollutants not specifically listed in their permits so long as they comply with the appropriate reporting requirements and abide by any new limitations when imposed on such pollutants.

The EPA lists tens of thousands of different chemical substances in the Toxic Substances Control Act Chemical Substance Inventory pursuant to 15 U.S.C. § 2607(b) (1988). However, the EPA does not demand even information regarding each of the many thousand chemical substances potentially present in a manufacturer's wastewater because "it is impossible to identify and rationally limit every chemical or compound present in a discharge of pollutants." Memorandum from EPA Deputy Assistant Administrator for Water Enforcement Jeffrey G. Miller to Regional Enforcement Director, Region V, at 2 (Apr. 28, 1976). "Compliance with such a permit would be impossible and anybody seeking to harass a permittee need only analyze that permittee's discharge until determining the presence of a substance not identified in the permit." *Id.* Indeed, Atlantic States conceded at oral argument that even plain water might be considered a "pollutant" under its view of the Act.

The EPA has never acted in any way to suggest that Atlantic States' absolutist and wholly impractical view of the legal effect of a permit is valid. In fact, the EPA's actions and policy statements have frequently contemplated discharges of pollutants not listed under a NPDES or SPDES permit. It has addressed such discharges by amending the permit to list and limit a pollutant when necessary to safeguard the environment without considering pre-amendment discharges to be violations calling for enforcement under the CWA. 33 U.S.C. §§ 1319, 1365. The EPA thus stated in its comments on proposed 40 C.F.R. § 122.68(a), which applied the "application-based" limits approach to implementation of the CWA reporting scheme,

> There is still some possibility . . . that a [NPDES or SPDES] permittee may discharge a large amount of a pollutant not limited in its permit, and EPA will not be able to take enforcement action against the

permittee as long as the permittee complies with the notification requirements [pursuant to the CWA].

45 Fed. Reg. 33516, 33523 (1980). The EPA's statement went on to note that this possibility constituted a "regulatory gap," and that, "the final regulations control discharges only of the pollutants listed in the [NPDES or SPDES] permit application, which consist primarily of the listed toxic pollutants and designated hazardous substances." *Id.* * * *

The EPA is the federal agency entrusted with administration and enforcement of the CWA. 33 U.S.C. § 1251(d). As such, EPA's reasonable interpretations of the Act are due deferential treatment in the courts. . . . Because the EPA's implementation of the CWA is entirely reasonable, we defer to it.

B. New York Environmental "Standards and Limitations"

Atlantic States argues alternatively that the permit itself provides grounds for enforcement of New York State's regulations. States may enact stricter standards for wastewater effluents than mandated by the CWA and federal EPA regulations. 33 U.S.C. § 1342(b). These states' standards may be enforced under the CWA by the states or the EPA, 33 U.S.C. § 1342(h), but private citizens have no standing to do so. New York chose to implement its own environmental policies through its DEC's issuance of SPDES permits pursuant to N.Y. Envtl. Conserv. Law § 17-0815 (McKinney 1984).

However, state regulations, including the provisions of SPDES permits, which mandate "a greater scope of coverage than that required" by the federal CWA and its implementing regulations are not enforceable through a citizen suit under 33 U.S.C. § 1365. 40 C.F.R. § 123.1(i)(2). *Cf. United States Dep't of Energy v. Ohio,* 118 L. Ed. 2d 255, 112 S. Ct. 1627, 1638 (1992) (holding that "penalties prescribed by state statutes approved by EPA and supplanting the CWA" did not "arise under federal law" and thus could not be enforced under 33 U.S.C. § 1319). * * *

. . . [E]ven if Atlantic States is right about New York law, the action would fail because New York would be implementing a regulatory scheme broader than the CWA, . . . and such broader state schemes are unenforceable through Section 505 citizen suits. A citizen's suit under Section 505 is thus barred either because Section 17-0815(3) and the final clause of General Provision 1(b) implement a program with broader scope than that promulgated under the CWA and EPA regulations or because the permit more narrowly interpreted shields Kodak from such an action.

Conclusion

For the reasons stated above, we affirm the order of the district court granting summary judgment to Kodak.

NOTES

1. To secure an NPDES permit, applicants must submit effluent characteristics to EPA. Doing so may require collection of discharge samples. "Grab

samples" are permissible for specified pollutants, including pH, temperature, cyanide, total phenols, residual chlorine, oil and grease, fecal coliform, and fecal streptococcus. For others, a 24-hour composite sample is required. Samples must be analyzed in accordance with specified testing methods. These sampling and analysis requirements do not apply if the pollutant is solely the result of intake. 40 C.F.R. § 122.21(g)(7)(i).

Except for toxic effluent standards and prohibitions in place under §§ 307 and 405 (relating to sewage sludge use or disposal), EPA's regulations implementing the NPDES program provide that compliance with a permit constitutes compliance with the CWA itself. "However, a permit may be modified, revoked and reissued, or terminated during its term for cause[.]" 40 C.F.R. § 122.5(a)(1). Permits are not property rights in respective permittees. 40 C.F.R. § 122.5(b). All permits expressly require applicants, *inter alia*, to comply with permit terms, to reapply for a new permit when necessary, to mitigate any discharges causing adverse effects to human health or the environment, to properly operate and maintain equipment, to monitor discharges and keep records, and to report a wide variety of information to the regulating agency. 40 C.F.R. § 122.41.

In the absence of established effluent limitations for a point source, EPA can set its performance standards in its NPDES permit on a case-by-case basis. CWA § 402(a)(1), 33 U.S.C. § 1342(a)(1). In some cases, the standard might be framed in terms of "best management practices." 40 C.F.R. § 122.2. EPA does not have authority to exempt point sources entirely from the NPDES program. *Natural Resources Defense Council v. Costle*, 568 F.2d 1369 (D.C. Cir. 1977).

2. *Bypasses, upsets, and excursions.* Permits may contain provisions addressing bypasses and upsets. A bypass occurs when a waste stream is diverted away from pollution control equipment. The resulting "raw" discharge is permissible if it does not cause an exceedance of effluent limitations, "but only if it also is for essential maintenance to assure efficient operation." 40 C.F.R. § 122.41(m). Bypasses are otherwise prohibited unless they are "unavoidable to prevent loss of life, personal injury, or severe property damage," there are "no feasible alternatives," and regulatory authorities are notified. 40 C.F.R. § 122.41(m)(4). An upset is defined as "an exceptional incident in which there is unintentional and temporary noncompliance with technology-based effluent limitations because of factors beyond the reasonable control of permittee. An upset does not include noncompliance to the extent caused by operational error, improperly designed treatment facilities, inadequate treatment facilities, lack of preventative maintenance, or careless or improper operation." 40 C.F.R. § 122.41(n)(1). EPA's regulations allow the occurrence of an upset to serve as an affirmative defense to a cause of action for violation of the CWA. *Id.* at 122.41(n)(2). The burden of proof is on the permittee. *Id.* at 122.41(n)(2)–(3).

An excursion is an excedance of an effluent limitation not because of any act or omission on the part of a point source, but because pollution control equipment, for reasons unrelated to fault, simply failed to remove as much of a regulated pollutant as it should have. EPA's regulations do not address "excursions."

3. As of 2004, 46 states and one territory had authority to issue SPDES permits. The states without delegated authority were Idaho, Arizona, New Mexico, and Alaska. The territory with authority was the U.S. Virgin Islands.

4. *Antibacksliding*: In 1987, the Congress added current section 402(o), 33 U.S.C. § 1342(o), the "antibacksliding" provision. Subject to exceptions listed in § 402(o)(2), the provision prohibits any renewal, reissuance, or modification of an existing permit so as "to contain effluent limitations which are less stringent than the comparable effluent limitations in the previous permit." § 402(o)(1), 33 U.S.C. § 1342(o)(1). If effluent limitations have become more stringent during the effective period of a permit, the renewed, reissued, or modified permit must reflect the new, more stringent effluent limitation. § 402(o)(3), 33 U.S.C. § 1342(o)(3).

5. *General Permits*: In addition to individual permits, the EPA can issue "general permits." Such permits typically cover all similar facilities in a given area. The EPA can issue a general permit if point sources in the covered area discharge the same types of wastes, require the same effluent limitations and operating restrictions, and require the same or similar monitoring. Use of general permits can vastly reduce EPA's administrative workload and that of permittees as well. One such example: in December, 1994, the EPA issued a notice in the Federal Register to the effect that more than one thousand waste water treatment facilities in Maine, Massachusetts, and New Hampshire were eligible for inclusion under one of three general discharge permits.

AMERICAN FOREST AND PAPER ASSOCIATION v. U.S. ENVIRONMENTAL PROTECTION AGENCY

137 F.3d 291 (5th Cir. 1998)

JUDGES: Before JONES and SMITH, Circuit Judges, and FITZWATER,[*] District Judge.

OPINION: JERRY E. SMITH, Circuit Judge:

Pursuant to the Clean Water Act ("CWA"), 33 U.S.C. § 1251 et seq., the Environmental Protection Agency ("EPA") delegated to Louisiana the responsibility for administering the Louisiana Pollutant Discharge Elimination System ("LPDES"). In exchange for its approval, EPA required Louisiana to consult with the Fish and Wildlife Service ("FWS") and the National Marine Fisheries Service ("NMFS") before issuing permits. If FWS or NMFS determines that the proposed permit threatens endangered species — and if Louisiana refuses to modify the permit — EPA will veto the permit under its continuing oversight authority. American Forest and Paper Association ("AFPA") challenges this rule as exceeding EPA's authority under the CWA. Because we agree that EPA lacked statutory authority, we grant the petition for review and vacate and remand the portion of the rule that imposes the consultation requirement and declares that EPA will veto any permit to which FWS or NMFS objects.

---

[*] District Judge of the Northern District of Texas, sitting by designation.

I.

Under the CWA, one needs a permit to discharge a pollutant. At least as an initial matter, permitting authority is vested in EPA through the National Pollutant Discharge Elimination System ("NPDES"). EPA may, however, delegate permitting authority to a state if the state demonstrates that it will comply with a list of enumerated requirements and that it will monitor and enforce the terms of the permits. *See* CWA § 402(b)(1)–(9), 33 U.S.C. § 1342(b)(1)–(9). EPA does not enjoy wide latitude in deciding whether to approve or reject a state's proposed permit program. "Unless the Administrator of EPA determines that the proposed state program does not meet [the specified] requirements, he must approve the proposal." *Save the Bay, Inc. v. EPA,* 556 F.2d 1282, 1285 (5th Cir. 1977).

EPA retains oversight authority even when it delegates permitting authority to a state. Should the agency determine that a state is not complying with the CWA, it may withdraw its approval of the state program. EPA also retains oversight authority over individual permits issued under approved state programs. States are required to submit permit applications and proposed permits to EPA; the agency may veto a proposed permit if it concludes that the permit violates the CWA. *See* CWA § 402(d), 33 U.S.C. § 1342(d).

Until recently, EPA administered the permitting program in Louisiana through the NPDES. Before issuing a permit, EPA chose to consult with FWS and NMFS to ensure that endangered species would not be threatened by the discharges contemplated in the permit. When EPA announced plans to delegate the permitting program to Louisiana, environmental groups cried foul, pointing out that because the Endangered Species Act ("ESA") does not apply to the states, nothing would prevent the issuance of permits that might harm endangered species.

EPA then devised the following scheme: In exchange for approving Louisiana's program, EPA directed the Louisiana Department of Environmental Quality ("LDEQ") to submit proposed permits to FWS and NMFS for review. If the federal agencies agree that the proposed permit does not threaten endangered species, the permit may be issued. But if the federal agencies conclude that the permit does threaten endangered species — and if LDEQ refuses to modify the permit to the agencies' satisfaction — EPA will exercise its veto power and formally object to the permit. Louisiana consented to this arrangement, and EPA issued its final rule. *See* Approval of Application by Louisiana To Administer the National Pollutant Discharge Elimination System Program, 61 Fed. Reg. 47,932 (1996).

EPA invoked CWA § 304(i), 33 U.S.C. § 1314(i), as authority for attaching this condition to its approval of Louisiana's program. That section allows EPA to promulgate guidelines "establishing the minimum procedural and other elements" for state permitting programs. The agency also pointed to ESA § 7(a)(2) as justifying its action. That section provides:

> Each Federal agency shall, in consultation with and with the assistance of the Secretary [of the Interior, Commerce, or Agriculture], insure that any action authorized, funded, or carried out by such agency

. . . is not likely to jeopardize the continued existence of any endangered species or threatened species or result in the destruction or adverse modification of habitat of such species. . . .

16 U.S.C. § 1536(a)(2). The spirit of this general mandate is echoed in the statement of congressional purpose underlying the ESA, 16 U.S.C. § 1531(c)(1), which declares it "the policy of Congress that all Federal departments and agencies shall seek to conserve endangered species and threatened species and shall utilize their authorities in furtherance of the purposes of this chapter." * * *

[The following portions of the opinion, dealing with availability of review and issues of standing, are omitted.]

V.

EPA contends that its rule is authorized by CWA § 304(i), 33 U.S.C. § 1314(i), which directs EPA to promulgate guidelines governing state permitting programs under CWA § 402(b), 33 U.S.C. § 1342(b). EPA also suggests that its decision is not only authorized but compelled by ESA § 7(a)(2), 16 U.S.C. § 1536(a)(2). That section directs federal agencies to consult with FWS and NMFS before undertaking any "agency action," to ensure that the action will not threaten an endangered species. * * *

B.

Specifically, CWA § 402(b), 33 U.S.C. § 1342(b), provides that the EPA Administrator "shall approve" proposed state permitting programs that meet nine specified requirements. The key question is whether EPA may deny a state's proposed program based on a criterion — the protection of endangered species — that is not enumerated in § 402(b).

EPA calls our attention to CWA § 304(i), 33 U.S.C. § 1314(i), construing that section as authorizing the agency to regard the nine requirements § 402(b) as minimum, not exhaustive, criteria. EPA further contends that because nothing in § 402(b) prohibits EPA from adding additional criteria, its interpretation of the statute is reasonable and worthy of deference. . . .

We cannot agree. The language of § 402(b) is firm: It provides that EPA "shall" approve submitted programs unless they fail to meet one of the nine listed requirements. We interpreted this language as non-discretionary in *Save the Bay, Inc. v. EPA,* 556 F.2d 1282 (5th Cir. 1977), noting that "the Amendments [to the CWA] set out the full list of requirements a state program must meet. . . . Unless the Administrator of EPA determines that the proposed state program does not meet these requirements, he must approve the proposal." *Id.* at 1285 & n.3. *See also Natural Resources Defense Council v. EPA,* 859 F.2d 156, 174 (D.C. Cir. 1988); *Citizens for a Better Env't v. EPA,* 596 F.2d 720, 722 (7th Cir. 1979).

EPA's claim is further weakened by CWA § 402(b)(6), 33 U.S.C. § 1342(b)(6), which grants EPA veto power over a proposed permit if the Secretary of the Army concludes that the discharges contemplated by the permit would substantially impair anchorage and navigation. Congress could have, but did not, grant EPA an analogous veto power to protect endangered species.

Nothing in § 304(i) undermines this conclusion. That subsection simply directs EPA to issue regulations governing the approval process for state programs. There is no hint that Congress intended to grant EPA authority to erect additional hurdles to the permitting process beyond those expressly noted in § 402(b). Moreover, neither section even mentions endangered species or the ESA. The statute's plain language directs EPA to approve proposed state programs that meet the enumerated criteria; particularly in light of the command "shall approve," § 304(i) cannot be construed to allow EPA to expand the list of permitting requirements. Applying *Chevron,* we conclude that Congress has spoken directly to the precise question at issue: EPA's discretion lies not in modifying the list of enumerated criteria, but simply in ensuring that those criteria are met.

C.

In *American Iron & Steel Inst. v. EPA,* 325 U.S. App. D.C. 76, 115 F.3d 979 (D.C. Cir. 1997) ("*AISI*"), the court concluded that EPA may require states to include provisions in certain permitting programs to ensure the protection of endangered species. EPA argues that *AISI*'s logic is applicable to the instant case.

AISI is distinguishable, however, in that the case arose under a different provision of the CWA — § 118(c)(2), 33 U.S.C. § 1268(c)(2). That section directs EPA to promulgate "water quality guidance" for the Great Lakes. But § 118(c)(2) is structured quite differently from § 402: The former grants EPA authority to specify pollutant limits for the Great Lakes and develop "guidances" to which state programs must conform; the section does not direct the agency to approve state programs that meet certain requirements.

In addition to this far broader grant of authority, § 118(c)(2) specifically mentions that EPA's development of pollutant limits should aim to protect aquatic life and wildlife in the Great Lakes. The *AISI* court relied on this language in concluding that EPA did not exceed its statutory authority under § 118(c):

> We uphold this portion of the Guidance, but not because of the ESA. Section 118(c)(2) provides that the Guidance "shall specify numerical limits on pollutants in ambient Great Lakes waters to protect human health, aquatic life, and wildlife, and shall provide guidance to the Great Lakes States on minimum water quality standards. . . ." (emphasis added) This is all the authority the EPA needed to promulgate regulations designed to protect endangered, threatened and other species in the Great Lakes System.

115 F.3d at 1003. *AISI*'s reasoning, insofar as it concerns a section of the CWA that materially differs in language and purpose, is inapplicable here.

D.

Finally, EPA argues that ESA § 7(a)(2), when construed alongside the Court's broad reading of the statute in *Tennessee Valley Auth. v. Hill,* 437 U.S.

153, 173, 57 L. Ed. 2d 117, 98 S. Ct. 2279 (1978), compels EPA to do everything reasonably within its power to protect endangered species. The flaw in this argument is that if EPA lacks the power to add additional criteria to CWA § 402(b), nothing in the ESA grants the agency the authority to do so. Section 7 of the ESA merely requires EPA to consult with FWS or NMFS before undertaking agency action; it confers no substantive powers.

The District of Columbia Circuit construed ESA § 7(a)(2) in *Platte River Whooping Crane Critical Habitat Maintenance Trust v. FERC,* 295 U.S. App. D.C. 218, 962 F.2d 27 (D.C. Cir. 1992), holding that the statute "does not expand the powers conferred on an agency by its enabling act," but rather directs the agencies to "utilize" their existing powers to protect endangered species. 962 F.2d at 34. In that case, the petitioner, Whooping Crane Trust, pressed virtually the same argument EPA advances here. The court observed:

> The Trust reads section 7 essentially to oblige the [Federal Energy Regulatory Commission] to do "whatever it takes" to protect the threatened and endangered species that inhabit the Platte River basin; any limitations on FERC's authority contained in the [Federal Power Act] are implicitly superseded by this general command. . . . We think the Trust's interpretation of the ESA is far-fetched.

Id. We agree that the ESA serves not as a font of new authority, but as something far more modest: a directive to agencies to channel their existing authority in a particular direction. The upshot is that EPA cannot invoke the ESA as a means of creating and imposing requirements that are not authorized by the CWA.

Accordingly, we GRANT the petition for review and VACATE the portion of the rule that imposes the consultation requirement and declares that EPA will reject any proposed permit to which FWS or NMFS objects. This matter is REMANDED to the EPA for further appropriate proceedings.

D. NONPOINT SOURCE REGULATION

As we have seen, the EPA has dedicated its best efforts to the abatement of pollution from point sources. And with good reason. Point sources were viewed by the Congress in 1972 as the major cause of water pollution, and, with the CWA riveting its attention upon them, EPA had good cause to make the valiant effort. This emphasis has yielded substantial benefits in the form of healthier and more aesthetically pleasing waterways. In recent times, however, the continued, virtually exclusive focus on point sources has come under attack. It has become clear that many waterways, despite the regulation of point sources discharging into them, remain foul. The National Water Quality Inventory Report to Congress for 1998, for example, indicated that of the 23% of streams actually assessed, more than one-third failed to meet water quality standards. Lakes and estuaries were similarly stressed.

A major reason is nonpoint source pollution. As noted earlier, nonpoint sources are the universe of sources not point sources. By negative implication, they are, therefore, sources that discharge pollutants to waters of the United

States other than through conduits, pipes, and other discrete conveyance mechanisms. Nonpoint pollution is a serious problem in many watersheds.[7]

While it can occur naturally, it often results from activities such as ranching, forestry, and agriculture. Farms are a particularly significant source. In fact, agriculture is the *leading* source of water pollution. (In second place is hydro-modification, which reduces stream flows, and third is urban runoff.) Polluted runoff from agricultural lands harms surface and groundwater on a nationally significant scale. Unchecked soil erosion, furthermore, increases sedimentation of rivers and lakes, causing severe reductions in the quantity of nutrients available for aquatic life. (Farms also overtake wildlife habitat, but that is another matter.)

The CWA did not address in any effective way the significant pollution contribution from agriculture, in large part because Congress wrote farms out of a good deal of the Clean Water Act.[8] However, this is not to say that the 1972 CWA overlooked nonpoint source pollution entirely. Actually, the Act went to some length to address the problem. Sections 102 and 104 of the 1972 legislation, for example, called for EPA and state cooperation in comprehensive planning to protect fish and wildlife. 33 U.S.C. §§ 1252, 1254. Section 201, 33 U.S.C. § 1281, authorized grants for "waste treatment management" on an "areawide" basis to "provide control or treatment of all point and nonpoint sources of pollution. . . ." § 201(c), 33 U.S.C. § 1281(c). And § 208 called for "areawide waste treatment management" planning by the states, expressly including plans for "nonpoint source" pollution. The legislation called on states to identify these areas, § 208(a)(2), 33 U.S.C. § 1281(a)(2), and thereafter "have in operation a continuing areawide waste treatment management planning process." § 208(b)(1), 33 U.S.C. § 1281(b)(1). Section 208 plans were to include a variety of measures, the most germane of which were explicitly directed at "nonpoint source" pollution.

But these statutory provisions produced no meaningful results. States blithely ignored them and EPA, busy with point sources, did, too. Looking around for some way to force EPA's hand, the environmental community decided to make its stand by relying on a provision we have already seen, § 303, 33 U.S.C. § 1313, the water quality standards provision of the original legislation. *See supra.* Specifically, it turned its attention to § 303(d), 33 U.S.C. § 1313(d).

Section 303(d) begins by calling on states to identify their "impaired waters," those water bodies or segments thereof in need of more cleaning even after BAT has done its work, and then to rank them, "taking into account the

---

[7] For current information on the "environmental profile" of a watershed near you, see *http://www.epa.gov/surf.*

[8] As we have seen, while the CWA prohibits the "discharge of any pollutant by any person," § 301(a), 33 U.S.C. § 1311(a), it focuses regulation on discharges from "point sources" and then excludes from the definition of "point source" "return flows from irrigated agriculture." § 502(14), 33 U.S.C. § 1362(14). The CWA describes return flows as "nonpoint sources of pollution." § 208(b)(2)(F), 33 U.S.C. § 1288(b)(2)(F). In 1987, in the CWA amendments addressing pollution by stormwater, Congress moved again to exempt agriculture, redefining "point source" to exclude "agricultural stormwater discharges." § 502(14), 33 U.S.C. § 1362(14). And the § 404 wetlands program, *see infra,* was also written to exempt discharges from typical farming activities such as plowing, seeding, and cultivating. § 404(f)(A), 33 U.S.C. § 1344(f)(A).

severity of the pollution and the uses to be made of such waters."
§ 303(d)(1)(A), 33 U.S.C. § 1313(d)(1)(A). Having done that, states must
determine the amounts of contamination, on a pollutant by pollutant basis,
that can be added to the stream on a daily basis without causing a WQS
exceedance. § 303(d)(1)(C), 33 U.S.C. § 1313(d)(1)(C). (It is up to EPA to
identify the pollutants that are "suitable for such calculation." *Id.*) These
specific amounts that may be added are known as "total maximum daily
loads," or "TMDLs." Section 303(d)(2), 33 U.S.C. § 1313(d)(2), then directs
states to submit their lists of impaired waters (or their "water quality-limited
segments," or "WQLSs,") and the TMDLs established for them, to EPA for
approval or disapproval. If EPA approves a state's submission, the state must
then "incorporate" the lists and TMDLs into the "continuing planning process"
required by § 303(e), 33 U.S.C. § 1313(e). If EPA disapproves a state's submission, however, EPA itself must do the work of identifying impaired waters
in the affected state and establishing the requisite TMDLs. § 303(d)(2), 33
U.S.C. § 1313(d)(2). Once the system is in place, limits on pollutant contributions from specific nonpoint sources should be quantified and regulated.

All of this would seem to have given the teeth to nonpoint source control
back in 1972, but, as noted above, history has proven otherwise. EPA believed
that BAT standards on point sources, coupled with "basin planning" under
§§ 208 and 303(e) (without TMDLs), would clean streams fully and promptly,
so it was not about to devote precious time and resources to what it viewed
as an unnecessary safety net. Beyond that, the agency found the business of
nonpoint regulation to be vexing: it can be extraordinarily difficult, for
example, to calculate the precise pollutant loading traceable to each nonpoint
source on a waterway. Consequently, EPA never did get around to designating
the pollutants for which TMDLs were suitable, and, without such designations
in place, the TMDL ball never started rolling. That was only one roadblock.
Even after pollutants were finally designated (EPA now says all pollutants
are suitable for TMDL development), EPA claimed its statutory authority
authorized it to do no more than approve or disapprove submissions sent in
by the states. Under this reading, if a state failed to submit anything, there
being nothing to approve or disapprove, EPA's hands were tied.

After a time, the environmental community took severe exception to this
willing impotence. A wave of judicial challenges ensued, and the environmentalists won. In *Scott v. City of Hammond*, 741 F.2d 992 (4th Cir. 1984), and
in several other judicial challenges, environmentalists convinced the court
that EPA had a good deal more power than it was letting on. In *Scott*, the
court held that a state's failure to make a submission under § 303(d) should
be viewed by EPA as a constructive and insufficient submission, which in turn
sparks EPA's duty to act. (For a vivid recount of this history of the TMDL
program, see Oliver A. Houck, *The Clean Water Act TMDL Program: Law,
Policy and Implementation*, Environmental Law Institute (1999).)

In August, 1999, EPA finally took up the TMDL banner on its own, albeit
grudgingly, by proposing regulations for a national TMDL program. 64 Fed.
Reg. 46012 (1999). Things have not gone smoothly since then. Congress, it
turned out, was quite unhappy with EPA's regulatory initiative, so, in June,
2000, it added a rider to a military construction appropriation bill which

prohibited the expenditure of any monies to effect a promulgation of the TMDL rule. This placed former President Clinton in an obvious bind. He solved the problem by having the EPA rush the TMDL proposal to promulgation while he delayed signing the appropriation bill. EPA promulgated the TMDL rule on July 13, 2000. 65 Fed. Reg. 43586 (2000).

The rule remained controversial, in large part because of considerations of cost: on August 3, 2001, EPA projected the rule's national cost at somewhere between $900 million and $4.3 billion annually. As expected, the regulations were challenged by several lawsuits filed in the federal Court of Appeals for the District of Columbia. Upon taking office in January, 2001, the Bush Administration asked the court to stay the litigation. It also delayed the effective date of the regulations pending additional administrative review. On December 27, 2002, EPA proposed to withdraw the rule entirely, and it did so on March 19, 2003.

Accordingly, more than 30 years after the enactment of § 303(d), at this writing there still remains relatively little in the way of nonpoint source regulation. With some states having done TMDL work, the program limps along, but vigorous it is not. For an update on the program, see *http://www.epa.gov/owow/tmdl*.

Since the withdrawal of the TMDL rule, attention has shifted to what EPA calls "watershed-based NPDES permitting," an approach favored by agriculture, some industries, states, and municipalities, as well as the United States Department of Agriculture, because it would return the focus to point source regulation, and, relatively speaking, take the heat off nonpoint sources. As EPA described it, watershed-based NPDES permitting is "an approach that produces NPDES permits that are issued to point sources on geographic or watershed bases to meet watershed goals." *See* EPA's *Watershed-Based NPDES Permitting Policy Statement*, Jan. 7, 2003, at *www.epa.gov/npdes/pubs/watershed-permitting-policy.pdf* (specifying, *inter alia*, EPA's suggested six step process for watershed permitting). The idea is to issue permits to point sources affecting a single watershed instead of regulating each source in isolation. Such permits would contain performance standards that reflect the needs of the basin and the presence of other point sources within the basin rather than merely the technological capacities of the individual permittee. Determining the needs of a basin would require a "detailed, integrative, and inclusive watershed planning process." That process, in turn, would embody "monitoring and assessment activities that generate the data necessary for clear watershed goals to be established and permits to be designed to specifically address the goals." *Id*. EPA intends to do what it can in this regard on a case-by-case basis within the legal constraints of the CWA and NPDES regulations. As of the date of this writing, there has been no promulgation of a watershed rule or of a replacement TMDL rule.

A larger issue raised by all of this is whether watershed permitting, and TMDL development for that matter, would represent a step forward or backward in water pollution control. EPA views these approaches as innovative and cost-effective, but critics argue that environmental quality-based regulation has already been shown to be foolhardy.

NOTE

In large part because of the success of the air emissions trading program, *see* Chapter 9, *supra*, EPA has endeavored to institute a cap-and-trade program for point and nonpoint source control. Its efforts culminated in EPA's "Water Quality Trading Policy" in January, 2003 (*"Policy"*). As the *Policy* put it, "[M]arket-based approaches can . . . create economic incentives for innovation, emerging technology, voluntary pollution reductions and greater efficiency in improving the quality of the nation's waters." *Policy* at 2. Trading, moreover, "capitalizes on economies of scale and the control cost differentials among and between sources." *Policy* at 1.

As the agency views it, water trading would allow sources to meet regulatory obligations by using pollutant reductions created by other sources that can accomplish those reductions less expensively. Trading would be voluntary, subject to EPA approval on a case-by-case basis, and could not be done in lieu of mandatory CWA or regulatory requirements.

EPA envisions the establishment of trading areas, typically within a single watershed, and actively supports trading of specific pollutants, especially nutrients and sediments, both of which are nonpoint pollutants. In this regard, the *Policy* would allow for trading of nutrients and sediments pre-TMDL, to meet an established TMDL, or to maintain unimpaired waters. Not all trading could be "pound for pound." A ten pound reduction of a pollutant, for example, might be weighted for trading purposes as something less than ten because only a lesser amount would find its way into the watershed area to be protected.

The regulatory authority, be it EPA or a state, would need to be mindful of the major potential pitfall of "hot spots," areas of high pollutant concentration. To avoid causing hot spots, might be necessary to limit trading at stressed locations.

EPA has implemented a trading mechanism for the western Long Island Sound. That water body, like the Gulf of Mexico, experiences a "dead zone" in summers, the result of excessive nutrient loadings. To eliminate this hypoxic condition, the Connecticut TMDL called for a 64% reduction of nitrogen discharges by 79 Connecticut POTWs by the year 2014. The trading solution for this problem included the establishment of a Nitrogen Exchange that gave each POTW several options. Each POTW may reduce nitrogen to the required regulatory level, or keep nitrogen discharges higher and buy offsetting nitrogen reductions from the Exchange, or reduce nitrogen discharges beyond the required regulatory level and sell the difference. As an administrative vehicle, in January, 2002, EPA issued a single permit to all 79 POTWs. The permit established an aggregate cap for nitrogen discharges that declines every two years until 2014 as well as individual water quality standards-based nitrogen discharge limits for the respective POTWs.

As of September, 2003, 39 municipalities had purchased credits at a cost of $1,317,223, 39 had sold credits for a total value of $2,757,323, and the State of Connecticut had purchased all the excess credits at a cost of $1,440,100. EPA, which as part of this effort has helped POTWs fund upgrades in facilities, expects the 64% reduction goal will be reached five to six years early. For more information, *see dep.state.ct.us\wtr/lis/nitrocntr/nitoindex.htm.*

E. WETLANDS PROTECTION

A century ago, the Congress enacted a statute called the Rivers and Harbors Act of 1899, commonly known as the "Refuse Act." Brandishing civil and criminal penalties, the measure prohibited the discharge of any "refuse" unless authorized by a permit issued by the Secretary of the Army. The statute was promptly ignored. Not until 1971, after the emergence of the environmental movement, did the Refuse Act stir from its long sleep, when, pursuant to an Executive Order, the U.S. Army Corps of Engineers promulgated regulations to implement it.

Contemporaneous with this development, Congress was considering the soon-to-be-enacted 1972 CWA. The Refuse Act having been discovered, Congress endeavored to fold it into the new legislation. Early on, it was included in § 402 (NPDES permits), but by the time the bill was ready for enactment, Congress had determined to enshrine the provisions of the Refuse Act in an independent location, the new CWA § 404, 33 U.S.C. § 1344.

Some alterations of the original legislation were in order, however, in large part because the newly created EPA was poised to become the central federal player in all things environmental. Thus, Congress needed to accommodate both the Corps and the new environmental agency. The Senate chose to give all regulatory responsibility to EPA, but the House proposed to continue authority in the Corps. The Conference substitute, as it turned out, split the difference. As enacted, § 404 keeps permitting authority in the Corps, (although states can take over this permitting function, *see* § 404(g), 33 U.S.C. § 1344(g)) but gives the EPA a veto power whenever it finds that a permitted § 404 discharge "will have an unacceptable adverse effect on municipal water supplies, shellfish beds and fishery areas (including spawning and breeding areas), wildlife, or recreational areas." §404(c), 33 U.S.C. § 1344(c). (As of this writing, EPA has used its veto provision only eleven times, despite more than 150,000 applications having been submitted for § 404 permits. The only time the veto has been used since 1989 was in March, 1994, when EPA used it to stop a $180 million highway project outside Nashua, New Hampshire. According to EPA, construction of the highway would have caused severe adverse effects on wetlands and wildlife in the Merrimack River ecosystem. This represents the only use of the veto to stop highway construction).

Section 404, in conjunction with § 301, prohibits disposal of "dredged and fill" materials into the navigable waters of the United States except in accordance with a permit. § 404(a), 33 U.S.C. § 1344(a). Dredged material is "material dredged or excavated from the waters of the United States." 40 C.F.R. § 232.2. (EPA definition); 33 C.F.R. § 323.2(c) (Corps definition). The term does not include trash or garbage. Fill material is any material placed into the waters of the United States which replaces portions of those waters with dry land or changes the bottom elevation of a water body. 40 C.F.R. § 232.2 (EPA definition); 33 C.F.R. § 323(e)(1) (Corps definition). Section 404 exempts from its reach "normal farming, silviculture, and ranching activities such as plowing, seeding, cultivating, minor drainage, harvesting for the production of food, fiber and forest products, or upland soil and water conservation practices." § 404(f), 33 U.S.C. § 1344(f); 40 C.F.R. § 232.3 (EPA regulation); 33 C.F.R. § 323.4 (Corps regulation).

To the extent § 404 prohibits deposits of dredged and fill materials into lakes, rivers, and ponds, it serves as a natural companion to the NPDES permit system of § 402. But § 404 rose in controversy and significance after a crucial administrative decision on an issue of regulatory scope: the Secretary interpreted § 404 as prohibiting disposal of dredged and fill materials into (or onto) "wetlands." Wetlands, commonly held in either public and private title, are, as their name indicates, *lands*. That activities involving lands could fall under the constraints of a statute in place to protect *waters of the United States* was nothing short of an epiphany to many people. The debate became a battle for the future of the program, and its resolution awaited review by the highest court of the land.

UNITED STATES v. RIVERSIDE BAYVIEW HOMES, INC.

474 U.S. 121, 106 S. Ct. 455 (1985)

JUSTICE WHITE delivered the opinion of the Court.

This case presents the question whether the Clean Water Act (CWA), 33 U.S.C. § 1251 *et seq.*, together with certain regulations promulgated under its authority by the Army Corps of Engineers, authorizes the Corps to require landowners to obtain permits from the Corps before discharging fill material into wetlands adjacent to navigable bodies of water and their tributaries.

I

The relevant provisions of the Clean Water Act originated in the Federal Water Pollution Control Act Amendments of 1972, 86 Stat. 816, and have remained essentially unchanged since that time. Under §§ 301 and 502 of the Act, 33 U.S.C. §§ 1311 and 1362, any discharge of dredged or fill materials into "navigable waters" — defined as the "waters of the United States" — is forbidden unless authorized by a permit issued by the Corps of Engineers pursuant to § 404, 33 U.S.C. § 1344. After initially construing the Act to cover only waters navigable in fact, in 1975 the Corps issued interim final regulations redefining "the waters of the United States" to include not only actually navigable waters but also tributaries of such waters, interstate waters and their tributaries, and nonnavigable intrastate waters whose use or misuse could affect interstate commerce. 40 Fed. Reg. 31320 (1975). More importantly for present purposes, the Corps construed the Act to cover all "freshwater wetlands" that were adjacent to other covered waters. A "freshwater wetland" was defined as an area that is "periodically inundated" and is "normally characterized by the prevalence of vegetation that requires saturated soil conditions for growth and reproduction." 33 C.F.R. § 209.120(d)(2)(h) (1976). In 1977, the Corps refined its definition of wetlands by eliminating the reference to periodic inundation and making other minor changes. The 1977 definition reads as follows:

"The term 'wetlands' means those areas that are inundated or saturated by surface or ground water at a frequency and duration sufficient to support, and that under normal circumstances do support, a prevalence of vegetation typically adapted for life in saturated soil conditions. Wetlands generally include swamps, marshes, bogs and similar areas."

33 C.F.R. § 323.2(c) (1978).*

In 1982, the 1977 regulations were replaced by substantively identical regulations that remain in force today. *See* 33 C.F.R. § 323.2 (1985).

Respondent Riverside Bayview Homes, Inc. (hereafter respondent), owns 80 acres of low-lying, marshy land near the shores of Lake St. Clair in Macomb County, Michigan. In 1976, respondent began to place fill materials on its property as part of its preparations for construction of a housing development. The Corps of Engineers, believing that the property was an "adjacent wetland" under the 1975 regulation defining "waters of the United States," filed suit in the United States District Court for the Eastern District of Michigan, seeking to enjoin respondent from filling the property without the permission of the Corps.

The District Court held that the portion of respondent's property lying below 575.5 feet above sea level was a covered wetland and enjoined respondent from filling it without a permit. Civ. No. 77-70041 (Feb. 24, 1977) (App. to Pet. for Cert. 22a); Civ. No. 77-70041 (June 21, 1979) (App. to Pet. for Cert. 32a). Respondent appealed, and the Court of Appeals remanded for consideration of the effect of the intervening 1977 amendments to the regulation. 615 F.2d 1363 (1980). On remand, the District Court again held the property to be a wetland subject to the Corps' permit authority. Civ. No. 77-70041 (May 10, 1981) (App. to Pet. for Cert. 42a).

Respondent again appealed, and the Sixth Circuit reversed. 729 F.2d 391 (1984). The court construed the Corps' regulation to exclude from the category of adjacent wetlands — and hence from that of "waters of the United States" — wetlands that were not subject to flooding by adjacent navigable waters at a frequency sufficient to support the growth of aquatic vegetation. The court adopted this construction of the regulation because, in its view, a broader definition of wetlands might result in the taking of private property without just compensation. The court also expressed its doubt that Congress, in granting the Corps jurisdiction to regulate the filling of "navigable waters," intended to allow regulation of wetlands that were not the result of flooding by navigable waters. Under the court's reading of the regulation, respondent's property was not within the Corps' jurisdiction, because its semiaquatic characteristics were not the result of frequent flooding by the nearby navigable waters. Respondent was therefore free to fill the property without obtaining a permit.

We granted certiorari to consider the proper interpretation of the Corps' regulation defining "waters of the United States" and the scope of the Corps'

---

* [Ed. note: this definition, which is the same as that of the EPA (*see* 40 C.F.R. § 232.2) remains in place at this writing.]

jurisdiction under the Clean Water Act, both of which were called into question by the Sixth Circuit's ruling. 469 U.S. 1206 (1985). We now reverse.

II

The question whether the Corps of Engineers may demand that respondent obtain a permit before placing fill material on its property is primarily one of regulatory and statutory interpretation: we must determine whether respondent's property is an "adjacent wetland" within the meaning of the applicable regulation, and, if so, whether the Corps' jurisdiction over "navigable waters" gives it statutory authority to regulate discharges of fill material into such a wetland. In this connection, we first consider the Court of Appeals' position that the Corps' regulatory authority under the statute and its implementing regulations must be narrowly construed to avoid a taking without just compensation in violation of the Fifth Amendment.

We have frequently suggested that governmental land-use regulation may under extreme circumstances amount to a "taking" of the affected property. *See, e.g., Williamson County Regional Planning Comm'n v. Hamilton Bank,* 473 U.S. 172 (1985); *Penn Central Transportation Co. v. New York City,* 438 U.S. 104 (1978). We have never precisely defined those circumstances, *see id.,* at 123–128; but our general approach was summed up in *Agins v. Tiburon,* 447 U.S. 255, 260 (1980), where we stated that the application of land-use regulations to a particular piece of property is a taking only "if the ordinance does not substantially advance legitimate state interests . . . or denies an owner economically viable use of his land." Moreover, we have made it quite clear that the mere assertion of regulatory jurisdiction by a governmental body does not constitute a regulatory taking. *See Hodel v. Virginia Surface Mining & Reclamation Assn.,* 452 U.S. 264, 293–297 (1981). The reasons are obvious. A requirement that a person obtain a permit before engaging in a certain use of his or her property does not itself "take" the property in any sense: after all, the very existence of a permit system implies that permission may be granted, leaving the landowner free to use the property as desired. Moreover, even if the permit is denied, there may be other viable uses available to the owner. Only when a permit is denied and the effect of the denial is to prevent "economically viable" use of the land in question can it be said that a taking has occurred.

If neither the imposition of the permit requirement itself nor the denial of a permit necessarily constitutes a taking, it follows that the Court of Appeals erred in concluding that a narrow reading of the Corps' regulatory jurisdiction over wetlands was "necessary" to avoid "a serious taking problem." 729 F.2d, at 398. We have held that, in general, "[equitable] relief is not available to enjoin an alleged taking of private property for a public use, duly authorized by law, when a suit for compensation can be brought against the sovereign subsequent to a taking." *Ruckelshaus v. Monsanto Co.,* 467 U.S. 986, 1016 (1984) (footnote omitted). This maxim rests on the principle that so long as compensation is available for those whose property is in fact taken, the governmental action is not unconstitutional. *Williamson County, supra,* at 194–195. For precisely the same reason, the possibility that the application of a regulatory program may in some instances result in the taking of individual pieces of property is no justification for the use of narrowing constructions to curtail the program if compensation will in any event be available in those cases where a taking has occurred. Under such circumstances, adoption of a narrowing construction does not constitute avoidance of a constitutional difficulty, *cf. Ashwander v. TVA*, 297 U.S. 288, 341–356 (1936) (Brandeis, J., concurring); it merely frustrates permissible applications of a statute or regulation. Because the Tucker Act, 28 U.S.C. § 1491, which presumptively supplies a means of obtaining compensation for any taking that may occur through the operation of a federal statute, *see Ruckelshaus v. Monsanto Co., supra*, at 1017, is available to provide compensation for takings that may result from the Corps' exercise of jurisdiction over wetlands, the Court of Appeals' fears that application of the Corps' permit program might result in a taking did not justify the court in adopting a more limited view of the Corps' authority than the terms of the relevant regulation might otherwise support.

III

Purged of its spurious constitutional overtones, the question whether the regulation at issue requires respondent to obtain a permit before filling its property is an easy one. The regulation extends the Corps' authority under § 404 to all wetlands adjacent to navigable or interstate waters and their tributaries. Wetlands, in turn, are defined as lands that are "inundated or saturated by surface or ground water at a frequency and duration sufficient to support, and that under normal circumstances do support, a prevalence of vegetation typically adapted for life in saturated soil conditions." 33 C.F.R. § 323.2(c) (1985) (emphasis added). The plain language of the regulation refutes the Court of Appeals' conclusion that inundation or "frequent flooding" by the adjacent body of water is a sine qua non of a wetland under the regulation. Indeed, the regulation could hardly state more clearly that saturation by either surface or ground water is sufficient to bring an area within the category of wetlands, provided that the saturation is sufficient to and does support wetland vegetation.

The history of the regulation underscores the absence of any requirement of inundation. The interim final regulation that the current regulation replaced explicitly included a requirement of "[periodic] inundation." 33 C.F.R. § 209.120(d)(2)(h) (1976). In deleting the reference to "periodic inundation" from the regulation as finally promulgated, the Corps explained that it was repudiating the interpretation of that language "as requiring inundation over a record period of years." 42 Fed. Reg. 37128 (1977). In fashioning its own requirement of "frequent flooding" the Court of Appeals improperly reintroduced into the regulation precisely what the Corps had excised.

Without the nonexistent requirement of frequent flooding, the regulatory definition of adjacent wetlands covers the property here. * * *

IV

A

An agency's construction of a statute it is charged with enforcing is entitled to deference if it is reasonable and not in conflict with the expressed intent of Congress. *Chemical Manufacturers Assn. v. Natural Resources Defense Council, Inc.*, 470 U.S. 116, 125 (1985); *Chevron U. S. A. Inc. v. Natural Resources Defense Council, Inc.*, 467 U.S. 837, 842–845 (1984). Accordingly, our review is limited to the question whether it is reasonable, in light of the language, policies, and legislative history of the Act for the Corps to exercise jurisdiction over wetlands adjacent to but not regularly flooded by rivers, streams, and other hydrographic features more conventionally identifiable as "waters."

On a purely linguistic level, it may appear unreasonable to classify "lands," wet or otherwise, as "waters." Such a simplistic response, however, does justice neither to the problem faced by the Corps in defining the scope of its authority under § 404(a) nor to the realities of the problem of water pollution that the Clean Water Act was intended to combat. In determining the limits of its power to regulate discharges under the Act, the Corps must necessarily choose some point at which water ends and land begins. Our common experience tells us that this is often no easy task: the transition from water to solid ground is not necessarily or even typically an abrupt one. Rather, between open waters and dry land may lie shallows, marshes, mudflats, swamps, bogs — in short, a huge array of areas that are not wholly aquatic but nevertheless fall far short of being dry land. Where on this continuum to find the limit of "waters" is far from obvious.

Faced with such a problem of defining the bounds of its regulatory authority, an agency may appropriately look to the legislative history and underlying policies of its statutory grants of authority. Neither of these sources provides unambiguous guidance for the Corps in this case, but together they do support the reasonableness of the Corps' approach of defining adjacent wetlands as "waters" within the meaning of § 404(a). Section 404 originated as part of the Federal Water Pollution Control Act Amendments of 1972, which constituted a comprehensive legislative attempt "to restore and maintain the chemical, physical, and biological integrity of the Nation's waters." CWA § 101, 33 U.S.C. § 1251. This objective incorporated a broad, systemic view of the goal of maintaining and improving water quality: as the House Report on the legislation put it, "the word 'integrity' . . . refers to a condition in which the natural structure and function of ecosystems [are] maintained." H. R. Rep. No. 92-911, p. 76 (1972). Protection of aquatic ecosystems, Congress recognized, demanded broad federal authority to control pollution, for "[water] moves in hydrologic cycles and it is essential that discharge of pollutants be controlled at the source." S. Rep. No. 92-414, p. 77 (1972).

In keeping with these views, Congress chose to define the waters covered by the Act broadly. Although the Act prohibits discharges into "navigable waters," *see* CWA §§ 301(a), 404(a), 502(12), 33 U.S.C. §§ 1311(a), 1344(a), 1362(12), the Act's definition of "navigable waters" as "the waters of the United States" makes it clear that the term "navigable" as used in the Act is of limited import. In adopting this definition of "navigable waters," Congress evidently intended to repudiate limits that had been placed on federal regulation by earlier water pollution control statutes and to exercise its powers under the Commerce Clause to regulate at least some waters that would not be deemed "navigable" under the classical understanding of that term. *See* S. Conf. Rep.

No. 92-1236, p. 144 (1972); 118 Cong. Rec. 33756–33757 (1972) (statement of Rep. Dingell).

Of course, it is one thing to recognize that Congress intended to allow regulation of waters that might not satisfy traditional tests of navigability; it is another to assert that Congress intended to abandon traditional notions of "waters" and include in that term "wetlands" as well. Nonetheless, the evident breadth of congressional concern for protection of water quality and aquatic ecosystems suggests that it is reasonable for the Corps to interpret the term "waters" to encompass wetlands adjacent to waters as more conventionally defined. Following the lead of the Environmental Protection Agency, *see* 38 Fed. Reg. 10834 (1973), the Corps has determined that wetlands adjacent to navigable waters do as a general matter play a key role in protecting and enhancing water quality:

> "The regulation of activities that cause water pollution cannot rely on . . . artificial lines . . . but must focus on all waters that together form the entire aquatic system. Water moves in hydrologic cycles, and the pollution of this part of the aquatic system, regardless of whether it is above or below an ordinary high water mark, or mean high tide line, will affect the water quality of the other waters within that aquatic system.

> "For this reason, the landward limit of Federal jurisdiction under Section 404 must include any adjacent wetlands that form the border of or are in reasonable proximity to other waters of the United States, as these wetlands are part of this aquatic system." 42 Fed. Reg. 37128 (1977).

We cannot say that the Corps' conclusion that adjacent wetlands are inseparably bound up with the "waters" of the United States — based as it is on the Corps' and EPA's technical expertise — is unreasonable. In view of the breadth of federal regulatory authority contemplated by the Act itself and the inherent difficulties of defining precise bounds to regulable waters, the Corps' ecological judgment about the relationship between waters and their adjacent wetlands provides an adequate basis for a legal judgment that adjacent wetlands may be defined as waters under the Act.

This holds true even for wetlands that are not the result of flooding or permeation by water having its source in adjacent bodies of open water. The Corps has concluded that wetlands may affect the water quality of adjacent lakes, rivers, and streams even when the waters of those bodies do not actually inundate the wetlands. For example, wetlands that are not flooded by adjacent waters may still tend to drain into those waters. In such circumstances, the Corps has concluded that wetlands may serve to filter and purify water draining into adjacent bodies of water, *see* 33 C.F.R. § 320.4(b)(2)(vii) (1985), and to slow the flow of surface runoff into lakes, rivers, and streams and thus prevent flooding and erosion, *see* §§ 320.4(b)(2)(iv) and (v). In addition, adjacent wetlands may "serve significant natural biological functions, including food chain production, general habitat, and nesting, spawning, rearing and resting sites for aquatic . . . species." § 320.4(b)(2)(i). In short, the Corps has concluded that wetlands adjacent to lakes, rivers, streams, and other bodies of water may function as integral parts of the aquatic environment even when the moisture creating the wetlands does not find its source in the adjacent bodies of water. Again, we cannot say that the Corps' judgment on these matters is unreasonable, and we therefore conclude that a definition of "waters of the United States" encompassing all wetlands adjacent to other bodies of water over which the Corps has jurisdiction is a permissible interpretation of the Act. Because respondent's property is part of a wetland that actually abuts on a navigable waterway, respondent was required to have a permit in this case.

B

Following promulgation of the Corps' interim final regulations in 1975, the Corps' assertion of authority under § 404 over waters not actually navigable engendered some congressional opposition. The controversy came to a head during Congress' consideration of the Clean Water Act of 1977, a major piece of legislation aimed at achieving "interim improvements within the existing framework" of the Clean Water Act. H. R. Rep. No. 95-139, pp. 1–2 (1977). In the end, however, as we shall explain, Congress acquiesced in the administrative construction.

Critics of the Corps' permit program attempted to insert limitations on the Corps' § 404 jurisdiction into the 1977 legislation: the House bill as reported out of committee proposed a redefinition of "navigable waters" that would have limited the Corps' authority under § 404 to waters navigable in fact and their adjacent wetlands (defined as wetlands periodically inundated by contiguous navigable waters). H. R. 3199, 95th Cong., 1st Sess., § 16 (1977). The bill reported by the Senate Committee on Environment and Public Works, by contrast, contained no redefinition of the scope of the "navigable waters" covered by § 404, and dealt with the perceived problem of overregulation by the Corps by exempting certain activities (primarily agricultural) from the permit requirement and by providing for assumption of some of the Corps' regulatory duties by federally approved state programs. S. 1952, 95th Cong., 1st Sess., § 49(b) (1977). On the floor of the Senate, however, an amendment was proposed limiting the scope of "navigable waters" along the lines set forth in the House bill. 123 Cong. Rec. 26710–26711 (1977).

In both Chambers, debate on the proposals to narrow the definition of navigable waters centered largely on the issue of wetlands preservation. *See id.,* at 10426–10432 (House debate); *id.,* at 26710–26729 (Senate debate). Proponents of a more limited § 404 jurisdiction contended that the Corps' assertion of jurisdiction over wetlands and other nonnavigable "waters" had far exceeded what Congress had intended in enacting § 404. Opponents of the proposed changes argued that a narrower definition of "navigable waters" for purposes of § 404 would exclude vast stretches of crucial wetlands from the Corps' jurisdiction, with detrimental effects on wetlands ecosystems, water quality, and the aquatic environment generally. The debate, particularly in the Senate, was lengthy. In the House, the debate ended with the adoption of a narrowed definition of "waters"; but in the Senate the limiting amendment was defeated and the old definition retained. The Conference Committee adopted the Senate's approach: efforts to narrow the definition of "waters" were abandoned; the legislation as ultimately passed, in the words of Senator

Baker, "[retained] the comprehensive jurisdiction over the Nation's waters exercised in the 1972 Federal Water Pollution Control Act."

The significance of Congress' treatment of the Corps' § 404 jurisdiction in its consideration of the Clean Water Act of 1977 is twofold. First, the scope of the Corps' asserted jurisdiction over wetlands was specifically brought to Congress' attention, and Congress rejected measures designed to curb the Corps' jurisdiction in large part because of its concern that protection of wetlands would be unduly hampered by a narrowed definition of "navigable waters." Although we are chary of attributing significance to Congress' failure to act, a refusal by Congress to overrule an agency's construction of legislation is at least some evidence of the reasonableness of that construction, particularly where the administrative construction has been brought to Congress' attention through legislation specifically designed to supplant it. *See Bob Jones University v. United States*, 461 U.S. 574, 599–601 (1983); *United States v. Rutherford*, 442 U.S. 544, 554, and n. 10 (1979).

Second, it is notable that even those who would have restricted the reach of the Corps' jurisdiction would have done so not by removing wetlands altogether from the definition of "waters of the United States," but only by restricting the scope of "navigable waters" under § 404 to waters navigable in fact and their adjacent wetlands. In amending the definition of "navigable waters" for purposes of § 404 only, the backers of the House bill would have left intact the existing definition of "navigable waters" for purposes of § 301 of the Act, which generally prohibits discharges of pollutants into navigable waters. As the House Report explained: "'Navigable waters' as used in section 301 includes all of the waters of the United States including their adjacent wetlands." H. R. Rep. No. 95-139, p. 24 (1977). Thus, even those who thought that the Corps' existing authority under § 404 was too broad recognized (1) that the definition of "navigable waters" then in force for both § 301 and § 404 was reasonably interpreted to include adjacent wetlands, (2) that the water quality concerns of the Clean Water Act demanded regulation of at least some discharges into wetlands, and (3) that whatever jurisdiction the Corps would retain over discharges of fill material after passage of the 1977 legislation should extend to discharges into wetlands adjacent to any waters over which the Corps retained jurisdiction. These views provide additional support for a conclusion that Congress in 1977 acquiesced in the Corps' definition of waters as including adjacent wetlands.

Two features actually included in the legislation that Congress enacted in 1977 also support the view that the Act authorizes the Corps to regulate discharges into wetlands. First, in amending § 404 to allow federally approved state permit programs to supplant regulation by the Corps of certain discharges of fill material, Congress provided that the States would not be permitted to supersede the Corps' jurisdiction to regulate discharges into actually navigable waters and waters subject to the ebb and flow of the tide, "including wetlands adjacent thereto." CWA § 404(g)(1), 33 U.S.C. § 1344(g)(1). Here, then, Congress expressly stated that the term "waters" included adjacent wetlands. Second, the 1977 Act authorized an appropriation of $6 million for completion by the Department of Interior of a "National Wetlands Inventory" to assist the States "in the development and operation of programs under this Act." CWA § 208(i)(2), 33 U.S.C. § 1288(i)(2). The enactment of this provision reflects congressional recognition that wetlands are a concern of the Clean Water Act and supports the conclusion that in defining the waters covered by the Act to include wetlands, the Corps is "implementing congressional policy rather than embarking on a frolic of its own." *Red Lion Broadcasting Co. v. FCC*, 395 U.S. 367, 375 (1969).

C

We are thus persuaded that the language, policies, and history of the Clean Water Act compel a finding that the Corps has acted reasonably in interpreting the Act to require permits for the discharge of fill material into wetlands adjacent to the "waters of the United States." The regulation in which the Corps has embodied this interpretation by its terms includes the wetlands on respondent's property within the class of waters that may not be filled without a permit; and, as we have seen, there is no reason to interpret the regulation more narrowly than its terms would indicate. Accordingly, the judgment of the Court of Appeals is

Reversed.

NOTE

Why regulate discharges into wetlands? EPA has given its views:

The discharge of dredged or fill material in wetlands is likely to damage or destroy habitat and adversely affect the biological productivity of wetlands ecosystems by smothering, by dewatering, by permanently flooding, or by altering substrate elevation or periodicity of water movement. The addition of dredged or fill material may destroy wetland vegetation or result in advancement of succession to dry land species. It may reduce or eliminate nutrient exchange by a reduction of the system's productivity, or by altering current patterns and velocities. Disruption or elimination of the wetland system can degrade water quality by obstructing circulation patterns that flush large expanses of wetland systems, by interfering with the filtration function of wetlands, or by changing the aquifer recharge capability of a wetland. Discharges can also change the wetland habitat value for fish and wildlife. . . . When disruptions in flow and circulation patterns occur, apparently minor loss of wetland acreage may result in major losses through secondary impacts. Discharging fill material in wetlands as part of municipal, industrial or recreational development may modify the capacity of wetlands to retain and store floodwaters and to serve as a buffer zone shielding upland areas from wave actions, storm damage and erosion.

40 C.F.R. § 230.41(b).

SOLID WASTE AGENCY v. U.S. ARMY CORPS OF ENGINEERS

531 U.S. 159, 121 S. Ct. 675 (2001)

JUDGES: REHNQUIST, C.J., delivered the opinion of the Court, in which O'CONNOR, SCALIA, KENNEDY, and THOMAS, JJ., joined. STEVENS, J., filed a dissenting opinion, in which SOUTER, GINSBURG, and BREYER, JJ., joined.

CHIEF JUSTICE REHNQUIST delivered the opinion of the Court.

Section 404(a) of the Clean Water Act (CWA or Act), 86 Stat. 884, as amended, 33 U.S.C. § 1344(a), regulates the discharge of dredged or fill material into "navigable waters." The United States Army Corps of Engineers (Corps), has interpreted § 404(a) to confer federal authority over an abandoned sand and gravel pit in northern Illinois which provides habitat for migratory birds. We are asked to decide whether the provisions of § 404(a) may be fairly extended to these waters, and, if so, whether Congress could exercise such authority consistent with the Commerce Clause, U.S. Const., Art. I, § 8, cl. 3. We answer the first question in the negative and therefore do not reach the second.

Petitioner, the Solid Waste Agency of Northern Cook County ("SWANCC"), is a consortium of 23 suburban Chicago cities and villages that united in an effort to locate and develop a disposal site for baled nonhazardous solid waste. The Chicago Gravel Company informed the municipalities of the availability of a 533-acre parcel, bestriding the Illinois counties Cook and Kane, which had been the site of a sand and gravel pit mining operation for three decades up until about 1960. Long since abandoned, the old mining site eventually gave way to a successional stage forest, with its remnant excavation trenches evolving into a scattering of permanent and seasonal ponds of varying size (from under one-tenth of an acre to several acres) and depth (from several inches to several feet).

The municipalities decided to purchase the site for disposal of their baled nonhazardous solid waste. By law, SWANCC was required to file for various permits from Cook County and the State of Illinois before it could begin operation of its balefill project. In addition, because the operation called for the filling of some of the permanent and seasonal ponds, SWANCC contacted federal respondents (hereinafter respondents), including the Corps, to determine if a federal landfill permit was required under § 404(a) of the CWA, 33 U.S.C. § 1344(a).

Section 404(a) grants the Corps authority to issue permits "for the discharge of dredged or fill material into the navigable waters at specified disposal sites." *Ibid.* The term "navigable waters" is defined under the Act as "the waters of the United States, including the territorial seas." § 1362(7). The Corps has issued regulations defining the term "waters of the United States" to include

"waters such as intrastate lakes, rivers, streams (including intermittent streams), mudflats, sandflats, wetlands, sloughs, prairie potholes, wet meadows, playa lakes, or natural ponds, the use, degradation or destruction of which could affect interstate or foreign commerce. . . ."

33 C.F.R. § 328.3(a)(3) (1999).

In 1986, in an attempt to "clarify" the reach of its jurisdiction, the Corps stated that § 404(a) extends to intrastate waters:

"a. Which are or would be used as habitat by birds protected by Migratory Bird Treaties; or

"b. Which are or would be used as habitat by other migratory birds which cross state lines; or

"c. Which are or would be used as habitat for endangered species; or

"d. Used to irrigate crops sold in interstate commerce."

51 Fed. Reg. 41217.

This last promulgation has been dubbed the "Migratory Bird Rule."

The Corps initially concluded that it had no jurisdiction over the site because it contained no "wetlands," or areas which support "vegetation typically adapted for life in saturated soil conditions," 33 C.F.R. § 328.3(b) (1999). However, after the Illinois Nature Preserves Commission informed the Corps that a number of migratory bird species had been observed at the site, the Corps reconsidered and ultimately asserted jurisdiction over the balefill site pursuant to subpart (b) of the "Migratory Bird Rule." The Corps found that approximately 121 bird species had been observed at the site, including several known to depend upon aquatic environments for a significant portion of their life requirements. Thus, on November 16, 1987, the Corps formally "determined that the seasonally ponded, abandoned gravel mining depressions located on the project site, while not wetlands, did qualify as 'waters of the United States' . . . based upon the following criteria: (1) the proposed site had been abandoned as a gravel mining operation; (2) the water areas and spoil piles had developed a natural character; and (3) the water areas are used as habitat by migratory bird [sic] which cross state lines." U.S. Army Corps of Engineers, Chicago District, Dept. of Army Permit Evaluation and Decision Document, Lodging of Petitioner, Tab No. 1, p. 6. * * *

The Court of Appeals . . . [held] . . . that Congress has the authority to regulate such waters based upon "the cumulative impact doctrine, under which a single activity that itself has no discernible effect on interstate commerce may still be regulated if the aggregate effect of that class of activity has a substantial impact on interstate commerce." 191 F.3d 845, 850 (CA7 1999). The aggregate effect of the "destruction of the natural habitat of migratory birds" on interstate commerce, the court held, was substantial because each year millions of Americans cross state lines and spend over a billion dollars to hunt and observe migratory birds. *Ibid.* The Court of Appeals then turned to the regulatory question. The court held that the CWA reaches as many waters as the Commerce Clause allows and, given its earlier Commerce Clause ruling, it therefore followed that respondents' "Migratory Bird Rule" was a reasonable interpretation of the Act. *See* 191 F.3d at 851–852.

We granted certiorari, 529 U.S. 1129 (2000), and now reverse.

Congress passed the CWA for the stated purpose of "restoring and maintaining the chemical, physical, and biological integrity of the Nation's waters." 33 U.S.C. § 1251(a). In so doing, Congress chose to "recognize, preserve, and protect the primary responsibilities and rights of States to prevent, reduce, and eliminate pollution, to plan the development and use (including restoration, preservation, and enhancement) of land and water resources, and to consult with the Administrator in the exercise of his authority under this chapter." § 1251(b). Relevant here, § 404(a) authorizes respondents to regulate the discharge of fill material into "navigable waters," 33 U.S.C. § 1344(a), which the statute defines as "the waters of the United States, including the territorial seas," § 1362(7). Respondents have interpreted these words to cover the abandoned gravel pit at issue here because it is used as habitat for migratory birds. We conclude that the "Migratory Bird Rule" is not fairly supported by the CWA.

This is not the first time we have been called upon to evaluate the meaning of § 404(a). In *United States v. Riverside Bayview Homes, Inc.*, 474 U.S. 121, 88 L. Ed. 2d 419, 106 S. Ct. 455 (1985), we held that the Corps had § 404(a) jurisdiction over wetlands that actually abutted on a navigable waterway. In so doing, we noted that the term "navigable" is of "limited import" and that Congress evidenced its intent to "regulate at least some waters that would not be deemed 'navigable' under the classical understanding of that term." *Id.* at 133. But our holding was based in large measure upon Congress' unequivocal acquiescence to, and approval of, the Corps' regulations interpreting the CWA to cover wetlands adjacent to navigable waters. *See* 474 U.S. at 135–139. We found that Congress' concern for the protection of water quality and aquatic ecosystems indicated its intent to regulate wetlands "inseparably bound up with the 'waters' of the United States." 474 U.S. at 134.

It was the significant nexus between the wetlands and "navigable waters" that informed our reading of the CWA in *Riverside Bayview Homes*. Indeed, we did not "express any opinion" on the "question of the authority of the Corps to regulate discharges of fill material into wetlands that are not adjacent to bodies of open water. . . ." 474 U.S. at 131–132, n. 8. In order to rule for respondents here, we would have to hold that the jurisdiction of the Corps extends to ponds that are not adjacent to open water. But we conclude that the text of the statute will not allow this.

Indeed, the Corps' original interpretation of the CWA, promulgated two years after its enactment, is inconsistent with that which it espouses here. Its 1974 regulations defined § 404(a)'s "navigable waters" to mean "those waters of the United States which are subject to the ebb and flow of the tide, and/or are presently, or have been in the past, or may be in the future susceptible for use for purposes of interstate or foreign commerce." 33 C.F.R. § 209.120(d)(1). The Corps emphasized that "it is the water body's capability of use by the public for purposes of transportation or commerce which is the determinative factor." § 209.260(e)(1). Respondents put forward no persuasive evidence that the Corps mistook Congress' intent in 1974.

Respondents next contend that whatever its original aim in 1972, Congress charted a new course five years later when it approved the more expansive definition of "navigable waters" found in the Corps' 1977 regulations. In July 1977, the Corps formally adopted 33 C.F.R. § 323.2(a)(5) (1978), which defined "waters of the United States" to include "isolated wetlands and lakes, intermittent streams, prairie potholes, and other waters that are not part of a tributary system to interstate waters or to navigable waters of the United States, the degradation or destruction of which could affect interstate commerce." Respondents argue that Congress was aware of this more expansive interpretation during its 1977 amendments to the CWA. Specifically, respondents point to a failed House bill, H. R. 3199, that would have defined "navigable waters" as "all waters which are presently used, or are susceptible to use in their natural condition or by reasonable improvement as a means to transport interstate or foreign commerce." 123 Cong. Rec. 10420, 10434 (1977). They also point to the passage in § 404(g)(1) that authorizes a State to apply to the Environmental Protection Agency for permission "to administer its own individual and general permit program for the discharge of dredged or fill material into the navigable waters (other than those waters which are presently used, or are susceptible to use in their natural condition or by reasonable improvement as a means to transport interstate or foreign commerce . . . including wetlands adjacent thereto) within its jurisdiction . . . ." 33 U.S.C. § 1344(g)(1). The failure to pass legislation that would have overturned the Corps' 1977 regulations and the extension of jurisdiction in § 404(g) to waters "other than" traditional "navigable waters," respondents submit, indicate that Congress recognized and accepted a broad definition of "navigable waters" that includes nonnavigable, isolated, intrastate waters.

Although we have recognized congressional acquiescence to administrative interpretations of a statute in some situations, we have done so with extreme care. "Failed legislative proposals are 'a particularly dangerous ground on which to rest an interpretation of a prior statute.'" *Central Bank of Denver, N. A. v. First Interstate Bank of Denver, N. A.,* 511 U.S. 164, 187, 128 L. Ed. 2d 119, 114 S. Ct. 1439 (1994) (quoting *Pension Benefit Guaranty Corporation v. LTV Corp.,* 496 U.S. 633, 650, 110 L. Ed. 2d 579, 110 S. Ct. 2668 (1990)). A bill can be proposed for any number of reasons, and it can be rejected for just as many others. The relationship between the actions and inactions of the 95th Congress and the intent of the 92d Congress in passing § 404(a) is also considerably attenuated. Because "subsequent history is less illuminating than the contemporaneous evidence," *Hagen v. Utah,* 510 U.S. 399, 420, 127 L. Ed. 2d 252, 114 S. Ct. 958 (1994), respondents face a difficult task in overcoming the plain text and import of § 404(a).

We conclude that respondents have failed to make the necessary showing that the failure of the 1977 House bill demonstrates Congress' acquiescence to the Corps' regulations or the "Migratory Bird Rule," which, of course, did not first appear until 1986. Although respondents cite some legislative history showing Congress' recognition of the Corps' assertion of jurisdiction over "isolated waters," as we explained in *Riverside Bayview Homes,* "in both Chambers, debate on the proposals to narrow the definition of navigable waters centered largely on the issue of wetlands preservation." 474 U.S. at 136. Beyond Congress' desire to regulate wetlands adjacent to "navigable waters," respondents point us to no persuasive evidence that the House bill was proposed in response to the Corps' claim of jurisdiction over nonnavigable, isolated, intrastate waters or that its failure indicated congressional acquiescence to such jurisdiction.

Section 404(g) is equally unenlightening. In *Riverside Bayview Homes* we recognized that Congress intended the phrase "navigable waters" to include "at least some waters that would not be deemed 'navigable' under the classical understanding of that term." 474 U.S. at 133. But § 404(g) gives no intimation of what those waters might be; it simply refers to them as "other . . . waters." Respondents conjecture that "other . . . waters" must incorporate the Corps' 1977 regulations, but it is also plausible, as petitioner contends, that Congress simply wanted to include all waters adjacent to "navigable waters," such as nonnavigable tributaries and streams. The exact meaning of § 404(g) is not before us and we express no opinion on it, but for present purposes it is sufficient to say, as we did in *Riverside Bayview Homes,* that "§ 404(g)(1) does not conclusively determine the construction to be placed on the use of the term 'waters' elsewhere in the Act (particularly in § 502(7), which contains the relevant definition of 'navigable waters'). . . ." 474 U.S. at 138, n. 11.

We thus decline respondents' invitation to take what they see as the next ineluctable step after *Riverside Bayview Homes*: holding that isolated ponds, some only seasonal, wholly located within two Illinois counties, fall under § 404(a)'s definition of "navigable waters" because they serve as habitat for migratory birds. As counsel for respondents conceded at oral argument, such a ruling would assume that "the use of the word navigable in the statute . . . does not have any independent significance." Tr. of Oral Arg. 28. We cannot agree that Congress' separate definitional use of the phrase "waters of the United States" constitutes a basis for reading the term "navigable waters" out of the statute. We said in *Riverside Bayview Homes* that the word "navigable" in the statute was of "limited effect" and went on to hold that § 404(a) extended to nonnavigable wetlands adjacent to open waters. But it is one thing to give a word limited effect and quite another to give it no effect whatever. The term "navigable" has at least the import of showing us what Congress had in mind as its authority for enacting the CWA: its traditional jurisdiction over waters that were or had been navigable in fact or which could reasonably be so made. *See, e.g., United States v. Appalachian Elec. Power Co.,* 311 U.S. 377, 407–408, 85 L. Ed. 243, 61 S. Ct. 291 (1940).

[The Court next explained why it declined to defer to the agency decision, under the rule of *Chevron U.S.A. Inc. v. Natural Resources Defense Council, Inc.,* 467 U.S. 837, 104 S. Ct. 2778 (1984)]:

Where an administrative interpretation of a statute invokes the outer limits of Congress' power, we expect a clear indication that Congress intended that result. *See Edward J. DeBartolo Corp. v. Florida Gulf Coast Building & Constr. Trades Council,* 485 U.S. 568, 575, 99 L. Ed. 2d 645, 108 S. Ct. 1392 (1988). This requirement stems from our prudential desire not to needlessly reach constitutional issues and our assumption that Congress does not casually authorize administrative agencies to interpret a statute to push the limit of congressional authority. *See ibid.* This concern is heightened where the administrative interpretation alters the federal-state framework by permitting federal encroachment upon a traditional state power. *See United States v. Bass,* 404 U.S. 336, 349, 30 L. Ed. 2d 488, 92 S. Ct. 515 (1971)

("Unless Congress conveys its purpose clearly, it will not be deemed to have significantly changed the federal-state balance"). Thus, "where an otherwise acceptable construction of a statute would raise serious constitutional problems, the Court will construe the statute to avoid such problems unless such construction is plainly contrary to the intent of Congress." *DeBartolo,* 485 U.S. at 575.

These are significant constitutional questions raised by respondents' application of their regulations, and yet we find nothing approaching a clear statement from Congress that it intended § 404(a) to reach an abandoned sand and gravel pit such as we have here. Permitting respondents to claim federal jurisdiction over ponds and mudflats falling within the "Migratory Bird Rule" would result in a significant impingement of the States' traditional and primary power over land and water use. *See, e.g., Hess v. Port Authority Trans-Hudson Corporation,* 513 U.S. 30, 44, 130 L. Ed. 2d 245, 115 S. Ct. 394 (1994) ("Regulation of land use [is] a function traditionally performed by local governments"). Rather than expressing a desire to readjust the federal-state balance in this manner, Congress chose to "recognize, preserve, and protect the primary responsibilities and rights of States . . . to plan the development and use . . . of land and water resources. . . ." 33 U.S.C. § 1251(b). We thus read the statute as written to avoid the significant constitutional and federalism questions raised by respondents' interpretation, and therefore reject the request for administrative deference.

We hold that 33 C.F.R. § 328.3(a)(3) (1999), as clarified and applied to petitioner's balefill site pursuant to the "Migratory Bird Rule," 51 Fed. Reg. 41217 (1986), exceeds the authority granted to respondents under § 404(a) of the CWA. The judgment of the Court of Appeals for the Seventh Circuit is therefore

Reversed.

DISSENT: JUSTICE STEVENS, with whom JUSTICE SOUTER, JUSTICE GINSBURG, and JUSTICE BREYER join, dissenting.

. . . .

In its decision today, the Court draws a new jurisdictional line, one that invalidates the 1986 migratory bird regulation as well as the Corps' assertion of jurisdiction over all waters except for actually navigable waters, their tributaries, and wetlands adjacent to each. Its holding rests on two equally untenable premises: (1) that when Congress passed the 1972 CWA, it did not intend "to exert anything more than its commerce power over navigation," *ante,* at 7, n. 3; and (2) that in 1972 Congress drew the boundary defining the Corps' jurisdiction at the odd line on which the Court today settles. * * *

[The dissent then undertook an historical review of the development of the Rivers and Harbors Act ("RHA") and the subsequent CWA.] . . . Because of the [CWA's] ambitious and comprehensive goals, it was, of course, necessary to expand its jurisdictional scope. Thus, although Congress opted to carry over the traditional jurisdictional term "navigable waters" from the RHA and prior versions of the FWPCA, it broadened the definition of that term to encompass all "waters of the United States." § 1362(7). Indeed, the 1972 conferees arrived at the final formulation by specifically deleting the word "navigable" from the definition that had originally appeared in the House version of the Act. The majority today undoes that deletion.

The Conference Report explained that the definition in § 502(7) was intended to "be given the broadest possible constitutional interpretation." S. Conf. Rep. No. 92-1236, p. 144 (1972), reprinted in 1 Leg. Hist. 327. . . . The majority accuses respondents of reading the term "navigable" out of the statute. But that was accomplished by Congress when it deleted the word from the § 502(7) definition. After all, it is the definition that is the appropriate focus of our attention. *Babbitt v. Sweet Home Chapter, Communities for Great Ore.,* 515 U.S. 687, 697–698, n. 10, 132 L. Ed. 2d 597, 115 S. Ct. 2407 (1995) (refusing to be guided by the common-law definition of the term "take" when construing that term within the Endangered Species Act of 1973 and looking instead to the meaning of the terms contained in the definition of "take" supplied by the statute). Moreover, a proper understanding of the history of federal water pollution regulation makes clear that — even on respondents' broad reading — the presence of the word "navigable" in the statute is not inexplicable. The term was initially used in the various Rivers and Harbors Acts because (1) at the time those statutes were first enacted, Congress' power over the Nation's waters was viewed as extending only to "water bodies that were deemed 'navigable' and therefore suitable for moving goods to or from markets," Power 513; and (2) those statutes had the primary purpose of protecting navigation. Congress' choice to employ the term "navigable waters" in the 1972 Clean Water Act simply continued nearly a century of usage. Viewed in light of the history of federal water regulation, the broad § 502(7) definition, and Congress' unambiguous instructions in the Conference Report, it is clear that the term "navigable waters" operates in the statute as a shorthand for "waters over which federal authority may properly be asserted."

[In the remainder of the dissent, Justice Stevens made three arguments: (1) that the Court had previously ruled in *Riverside Bayview* that Congress had acquiesced to the Corps' expansive definition of "waters of the United States" and should not disregard that determination in this case; (2) that the Corps' definition should receive *Chevron* deference; and (3) that the Commerce Clause is not offended by the Corps' expansive definition.]

NOTES

1. *SWANCC* put to rest a conflict between the Fourth Circuit Court of Appeals and EPA. In *United States v. Wilson,* 133 F.3d 251, 257 (4th Cir. 1997), the Fourth Circuit had found the migratory bird rule to be invalid, but EPA had refused to honor the Circuit's declaration outside Fourth Circuit states (Maryland, Virginia, West Virginia, North Carolina, and South Carolina). *See* U.S. Environmental Protection Agency and U.S. Department of Defense (Army), *Guidance for Corps and EPA Field Offices Regarding Clean Water Act § 404 Jurisdiction over Isolated Waters in light of U.S. v. James J. Wilson.*

After *SWANCC,* the regulatory definition of "wetlands" was changed to remove isolated, solely intrastate water bodies. 69 U.S.L.W. 2561, March 20, 2001.

2. In the wake of *SWANCC*, courts have continued to find CWA § 404 jurisdiction over wetlands that are adjacent to or have some "significant nexus" to navigable waters. *See, e.g., United States v. Deaton*, 332 F.3d 698 (4th Cir. 2003), *cert. denied*, 124 S. Ct. 1874 (2004) (upholding federal jurisdiction over wetlands adjacent to a roadside ditch that linked to the Chesapeake Bay by a winding, thirty-two-mile path); *United States v. Hummel*, 2003 U.S. Dist. LEXIS 5656, (N.D. Ill., 2003) (finding jurisidiction over a wetland that was adjacent to a stream that flowed into a creek which flowed into another wetland which flowed into the Illinois River). *But see, e.g., In the Matter of Needham*, 354 F.3d. 340, 345 (5th Cir. 2003) ("the CWA and O[il] P[ollution] A[ct] are not so broad as to permit the federal government to impose regulations over 'tributaries' that are neither themselves navigable nor truly adjacent to navigable waters. Consequently, in this circuit the United States may not simply impose regulations over puddles, sewers, roadside ditches and the like; under *SWANCC* 'a body of water is subject to regulation . . . if the body of water is actually navigable or adjacent to an open body of navigable water.' "); *United States v. RGM Corp.*, 222 F. Supp. 2d 780, 785 (E.D. Va. 2002) (" . . . the unilateral expansion of Corps jurisdiction [can] not be allowed to continue in a limitless fashion.").

3. By one estimate, *SWANCC* eliminated CWA protection for 30 to 79% of the nation's wetlands. John Kusler, Attorney, Memorandum, *The SWANCC Decision and State Regulation of Wetlands*, Association of State Wetland Managers (Feb. 8, 2001).

Next we take a look at § 404 in action.

UNITED STATES v. BRACE

41 F.3d 117 (3d Cir. 1994)

JUDGES: Before: BECKER and COWEN, Circuit Judges and POLLAK[*], District Judge

COWEN, Circuit Judge.

The United States brought this action in the United States District Court for the Western District of Pennsylvania against Robert Brace, individually, and Robert Brace Farms, Inc., a Pennsylvania corporation (collectively, "Brace" or "defendants"), alleging violations of the requirement in Section 404 of the Clean Water Act ("CWA"), 33 U.S.C. § 1344, that a permit be obtained for the discharge of dredged or fill material into waters of the United States. The United States sought restoration of the site, a permanent injunction and civil penalties pursuant to 33 U.S.C. § 1319(d).

The district court bifurcated the action: a trial on liability issues and a trial on remedy issues. Shortly before the liability trial, Brace stipulated that at the time of the discharges, "the approximately thirty-acre site that is the subject of this lawsuit was wetlands as defined at 33 C.F.R. § 328.3(b) and

---

[*] Honorable Louis H. Pollak, United States District Judge for the Eastern District of Pennsylvania, sitting by designation.

40 C.F.R. § 232.2(r)." Pre-Trial Stipulation (Dec. 16, 1993); Appendix ("App.") at 40.

The United States, either by stipulation or at trial, established the five elements of a prima facie case for violations of Section 404 of the CWA: (1) defendants admitted that they are "persons" within the meaning of the CWA; (2) defendants admitted that the activities at the site were conducted without a permit; (3) defendants stipulated that the site was a wetland at the time of the discharges; (4) the district court held that the site constituted waters of the United States at the time of defendants' activities; and (5) the district court held that defendant's clearing, mulching, churning, and levelling of the formerly wooded and vegetated site constituted a discharge of pollutants into the waters of the United States and that defendants paid for excavation and installation of drainage tubing in an effort to drain the site.

Brace asserted, and the district court held, that the discharges were exempt from the permit requirement under Section 404(f)(1). The court concluded that: (1) Brace's activities on the wetland constituted "normal farming activities" exempt under Section 404(f)(1)(A); and (2) Brace's activities constituted "upland soil and water conservation practices" also exempt under that same provision of the CWA. *United States v. Brace*, C.A. No. 90-229 (W.D. Pa. Dec. 16, 1993), slip op. at 22–23. In addition, the court found that Brace's conduct in "preserving and regularly cleaning the existing drainage system on the site" was exempt from the permit requirement as "maintenance of the drainage system" under Section 404(f)(1)(C). *Id.* at 23. The court also held that the recapture provision of Section 404(f)(2) does not apply to this case because "the land is not being converted to a use to which it was not previously subject, nor has significant impairment to the reach or flow of waters been proven." *Id.* at 22.

The district court entered judgment in defendants' favor. We hold that the district court incorrectly applied the requirements of the CWA permit exemption provisions. We will reverse the order of the district court and remand the case to determine the appropriate remedy.

I.

Brace is a farmer who owns approximately 600 acres of real property in Erie County, Pennsylvania, including the subject thirty-acre wetland site ("the site"). Brace Farms, Inc. is a Pennsylvania corporation engaged principally in the farming business. Brace's parents and other family members have always earned their principal livelihood from farming activities. Brace purchased a parcel of farm property from his father in 1975. A portion of that property contains the site. The property has been in the Brace family since the 1930's when Brace's grandfather farmed the land. Prior to 1975, Brace's father used the site for pasturing of cows and horses, and Brace's brother used the site for pasturing cows until 1976.

Brace purchased the property from his father with the intent of continuing and improving his father's established farming operation. It was Brace's intention to integrate the various portions of the property into an overall operation for an effective and productive farming business. At the time Brace purchased the property containing the site from his father, the site was vegetated with areas of scrub brush, including red brush and briars.

In 1977, Brace sought the advice and assistance of the Agricultural Stabilization and Conservation Service ("ASCS") as part of his plan to develop an integrated farming operation on the property that includes the site. The ASCS is "an agency of the United States Department of Agriculture which is generally responsible for administering commodity production adjustment and certain conservation programs of the Department." 7 C.F.R. § 12.2(a)(2) (1994). Brace's father had previously worked with the ASCS to prepare a drainage plan relating to the site for the purpose of farming the entire property. At the time he purchased the property from his father, Brace obtained and utilized the soil and conservation plans that had been prepared for his father by the ASCS. The drainage system impacts the ability to produce crops on all parts of Brace's property.

The existing drainage system was in poor condition and not yet complete at the time of Brace's acquisition. Brace began cleaning the system in 1976 in order to improve upon the existing system and make it effective for agricultural development. In the following years, Brace maintained and improved the drainage system pursuant to the plan recommended by the ASCS. From 1977 to 1985 the ASCS periodically visited the site and provided technical assistance and cost-sharing arrangements to Brace.

As of 1977, the essential portions of Brace's improvements to the existing drainage system were intact and operating. Brace's work in improving upon the interconnected drainage system progressed continuously from 1977 to 1987, as time, funds and equipment were available. If the necessary funds had been available to him in 1977, Brace would have expedited his farming plans and completed the project at that time. As a result of Brace's efforts, by the end of 1979 the site was dry, with the exception of times of excessive rainfall.

Brace cleared, mulched, churned, levelled, and drained the formerly wooded and vegetated site from 1985 through 1987. In 1986 and 1987, Brace paid for excavation in the site and the burying of plastic tubing or "drainage tile" in an effort to drain the site. Throughout the 1980's, Brace used appropriate equipment to remove unconsolidated soil, pebbles, silt, and growth which were impeding water flow. Farmers in the area typically engaged in such practices.

As a result of Brace's levelling, spreading, and tiling, Brace began to grow crops on the site in 1986 and 1987. Brace did not have a permit issued pursuant to Section 404 of the CWA authorizing his activities.

The United States became aware of Brace's activities in 1987. During 1987 and 1988, the United States issued three orders to Brace, directing him, inter alia, to refrain from further disturbing the site, so that it could naturally revegetate with indigenous plant species. After the issuance of these orders, Brace continued to mow vegetation on the site. . . .

In the summer of 1988, Brace approached the ASCS in order to gain the status of "commenced conversion from wetlands" prior to December 23, 1985 with respect to the site. The ASCS was authorized to make such a determination under the Food Security Act of 1985, 16 U.S.C. §§ 3801, et seq. This Act contains a provision, referred to as the "Swampbuster," which denies certain Department of Agriculture benefits to farmers who produce an "agricultural commodity on converted wetland," unless such conversion commenced before December 23, 1985. 16 U.S.C. §§ 3821, 3822 (1988 & Supp. V 1993).

The ASCS granted the status to the site, finding that Brace's on-going farming activities had commenced prior to December of 1985, which would enable Brace to complete conversion and produce an agricultural commodity without losing USDA benefits. Letter from Erie County ASCS Office to Robert Brace (9/21/88); App. at 172. However, the ASCS expressly noted that "the granting of a commencement . . . request does not remove other legal requirements that may be required under State or Federal water laws." USDA Form; App. at 173.

In April 1990, as a cautionary measure, Brace approached the Army Corps of Engineers ("COE") in an effort to obtain an after-the-fact permit to conduct his farming activities on the site, despite his belief that the activities were exempt from the permit requirements of the CWA. The United States Environmental Protection Agency ("EPA") requested that the COE not review an application from Brace for an after-the-fact permit. Brace was advised that because the matter was then in litigation, the government would not act on his request for a permit. Since the time of the cease and desist orders Brace has terminated farming activity on the site except for routinely mowing the vegetation.

II.

The district court exercised its jurisdiction pursuant to 33 U.S.C. § 1319(b) (1988) and 28 U.S.C. §§ 1331, 1345, 1355 (1988 & Supp. V 1993). Our jurisdiction rests on 28 U.S.C. § 1291 (1988).

Presently, there are three issues before us. The first issue is whether the district court erred in determining that Brace's discharges of dredged and fill material into the wetland were exempt from the permit requirement pursuant to Section 404(f)(1) of the CWA, 33 U.S.C. § 1344(f)(1). The second issue is whether the district court erred in determining that Brace's discharges were not "recaptured" by the permit requirement under Section 404(f)(2) of the CWA, 33 U.S.C. § 1344(f)(2). . . .

The third issue is whether the district court erred in determining that Brace was not subject to liability for violations of administrative orders. Our review of questions of law such as this is plenary. *Moody,* 971 F.2d at 1063; *Manor Care,* 950 F.2d at 124.

III.

. . . .

Section 404 of the CWA authorizes the Secretary of the Army, through the COE, to issue permits "for the discharge of dredged or fill material into the navigable waters at specified disposal sites." 33 U.S.C. § 1344(a) (1988). *See also* 33 C.F.R. § 323.1 (1993). The permit program, as we recognized in [*United States v.*] *Pozsgai* [, 999 F.2d 719 (3d Cir. 1993), *cert. denied* 510 U.S.

1110, 44 S. Ct. 1052 (1994)], "is the central enforcement tool of the Clean Water Act . . . . Unpermitted discharge is the archetypical Clean Water Act violation, and subjects the discharger to strict liability." 999 F.2d at 724–25.

The COE and EPA have issued regulations defining the term "waters of the United States" to include "wetlands," among other bodies of water: . . .

. . . The parties have stipulated that the site constituted wetlands at the time of Brace's activities.

Exemptions to the general requirement for a Section 404 permit are contained in Section 404(f) of the CWA. Under Section 404(f)(1), a permit is not required for: (1) the discharge of dredged or fill material "from normal farming, silviculture, and ranching activities such a plowing, seeding, cultivating, minor drainage, harvesting for the production of food, fiber, and forest products, or upland soil and water conservation practices," 33 U.S.C. § 1344(f)(1)(A); and (2) the discharge of dredged or fill material "for the purpose of . . . the maintenance of drainage ditches." 33 U.S.C. § 1344(f)(1)(C).

The COE and EPA have promulgated regulations which provide that the "normal farming activities" exemption is available only to discharge activities that are "part of an established (i.e., on-going) farming . . . operation," and expressly stipulate that the exemption is not available either: (1) for "activities which bring an area into farming . . . use"; or (2) where "modifications to the hydrological regime are necessary to resume operations." 33 C.F.R. § 323.4(a)(1)(ii) (1993); 40 C.F.R. § 232.3(c)(1)(ii)(A), (B) (1993). . . .

Even where Section 404(f)(1) exempts a discharge from the permit requirement, the discharge may be "recaptured" by the permit requirement under Section 404(f)(2):

> Any discharge of dredged or fill material into the navigable waters incidental to any activity having as its purpose bringing an area of the navigable waters into a use to which it was not previously subject, where the flow or circulation of navigable waters may be impaired or the reach of such waters be reduced, shall be required to have a permit under this section.

33 U.S.C. § 1344(f)(2). The regulation governing the "recapture" provision stipulates in part that "[a] conversion of a section 404 wetland to a nonwetland is a change in use of an area of waters of the United States," 33 C.F.R. § 323.4(c), and states as an example, that "a permit will be required for the conversion of a cypress swamp to some other use . . . when there is a discharge of dredged or fill material into waters of the United Stated in conjunction with construction of . . . structures used to effect such conversion." *Id.*

. . . .

IV.

The district court held that Brace's activities on the thirty-acre wetland site were exempt from Section 404's permit requirement "because they constitute: (a) normal farming activities; (b) upland soil and water conservation practices; and (c) maintenance of drainage ditches." *Brace,* slip op. at 22. We find that the district court's determination is erroneous as a matter of law. . . .

The applicable regulation provides that, to constitute "normal farming activity" within the meaning of the statute, the activity:

> must be part of an established (i.e., on-going) farming . . . operation and must be in accordance with the definitions in § 323.4(a)(1)(iii) . . . . Activities which bring an area into farming . . . use are not part of an established operation. An operation ceases to be established when the area on which it was conducted has been converted to another use or has lain idle so long that modifications to the hydrological regime are necessary to resume operations.

33 C.F.R. § 323.4(a)(1)(ii). Brace's activities between 1985 and 1987 meet neither prong of this provision: they were neither part of an "established (i.e., on-going) farming operation," nor were they conducted "in accordance with the definitions in § 323.4(a)(1)(iii)."

A.

Brace points out that in determining whether farming activities are established and continuing, the conduct must be analyzed by a contextual review of the total activities. *Cumberland Farms,* 647 F. Supp. at 1175. He argues that the district court correctly undertook a contextual analysis in its determination that the site was an integral part of an established and on-going farm operation, and Brace's activities between 1985 and 1987 did not bring a new area into the operation. *Brace,* slip op. at 12. The district court based its conclusion on: (1) its determination that the site is an integral part of the drainage system previously installed in adjoining crop producing fields; (2) its finding that the installation of a drainage system at the site "is normal farming activity in order to make land suitable for farming," because "extensive underground drainage systems are typical and necessary aspects of farming in Erie County," *id.* at 3; and (3) the ASCS determination that Brace had "commenced conversion" of the site from wetland to cropland prior to December 23, 1985.

The district court's reasoning and conclusion are improper. The district court misinterpreted the meaning of the "established farming operation" requirement. The district court believed it was appropriate to examine the relationship of the site in question to the rest of the land owned by the same property-owner in determining whether land was being brought into farming use. Brace maintains that it is arbitrary to delineate artificially a portion of the farm and without rational justification sever it from his overall operations. We cannot agree with this interpretation of the statute's requirement.

The regulations provide that, "activities which bring an area into farming . . . use are not part of an established operation." 33 C.F.R. § 323.4(a)(1)(ii); 40 C.F.R. § 232.3(c)(1)(ii)(B) (emphasis added). The regulations do not specify the precise area to which we should look in determining whether there is an established farming operation. There are no minimum limits placed on the "area" being brought into farming use. Thus, we read the regulations to provide that an exemption is available only to activities that are part of an "established farming operation" at the site. A proper "contextual review of its total activities" only requires us to analyze whether such activities are "established and continuing" on the thirty-acre wetland site itself. . . . Our reading of the regulation recognizes the statute's legislative history and is in accord with the strict construction of the permit exemptions afforded by other Courts of Appeals. *See, e.g., Akers,* 785 F.2d at 819, 823; *United States v. Huebner,* 752 F.2d 1235, 1240–41 (7th Cir.), *cert. denied,* 474 U.S. 817, 106 S. Ct. 62, 88 L. Ed. 2d 50 (1985); *Marsh,* 715 F.2d at 925 n.44.

Brace himself testified that: (1) for the nine-year period prior to the discharges onto the site, from 1977 to 1986, his activities at the site included no pasturing or growing of any crops, but consisted entirely of efforts to drain the wetland; (2) the site was fully covered in 1983 with indigenous plants, but that all plants had been stripped from the site in 1987, subsequent to the discharge activities; and (3) the purpose of his 1985-1987 discharges was to drain the wetland and make it suitable for row cropping. The district court found that "as a result of Defendants' levelling, spreading and tiling, Defendants began to grow crops on the site in 1986 and 1987." *Brace,* slip op. at 9 (emphasis added). These facts do not justify the district court's determination that Brace's activities on the site were exempt from the permit requirements as "normal farming activities." Indeed, the factual findings of the district court can only lead to the opposite conclusion. Brace converted a thirty-acre site that was not suitable for farming into a site that is suitable for farming, and thus "brought an area into farming use."

Even if Brace's father's pre-1975 use of the site for pasturing could be considered to have been a prior, "established farming operation" on the site, Brace's drainage activities demonstrate that the court erred as a matter of law in finding the exemption from the permit requirement available for his subsequent activities. Under the regulations, a farming operation is not "ongoing" where "modifications to the hydrological regime are necessary to resume operations." 33 C.F.R. § 323.4(a)(1)(ii); 40 C.F.R. § 232.3(c)(1)(ii)(B). Here, Brace admitted that "modifications to the hydrological regime," i.e., drainage of the site through excavating and burying four miles of plastic tubing for drainage, were necessary to grow crops on the site. * * *

. . . Section 404 of the CWA requires a permit for "activities which bring an area into farming . . . use," as opposed to activities that are part of an "established farming operation." Brace did not have an "established farming operation" on the site prior to his discharges, and brought the site into farming use by discharging pollutants into waters of the United States. . . .

B.

As we explained above, the regulation governing the "normal farming activities" exemption has a second prong, under which drainage activities, in addition to being a part of an "established farming operation" as defined by the regulation, must be "in accordance with definitions in § 323.4(a)(1)(iii)." 33 C.F.R. § 323.4(a)(1)(ii). Brace's activities failed to meet the requirements of this second prong in addition to not being a part of an ongoing, established farming operation. Brace's undisputed activities: (1) excavating soil and discharging in connection with burying approximately four miles of plastic tubing for drainage; (2) levelling and clearing the formerly wooded and vegetated site; and (3) spreading dredged material, are all excluded from the activities allowed under 33 C.F.R. § 323.4(a)(1)(iii).

Brace's installation of four miles of tubing which drains the site is barred by the provision's express prohibition of both: (1) "the construction of any . . . structure which drains or otherwise significantly modifies . . . a wetland or aquatic area constituting waters of the United States"; and (2) "drainage associated with the immediate or gradual conversion of a wetland to a non-wetland . . ., or conversion from one wetland use to another." 33 C.F.R. § 323.4(a)(1)(iii)(C)(2). *See also* 40 C.F.R. § 232.3(d)(3)(D)(ii). Brace's clearing of all vegetation from the wetland site, and his spreading of dredged materials onto the site, are barred by the provision's express prohibition of both: (1) "the redistribution of soil, rock, sand, or other surficial materials in a manner which changes any area of the waters of the United States to dryland"; and (2) "the redistribution of surface materials by blading, grading, or other means to fill in wetland areas." 33 C.F.R. § 323.4(a)(1)(iii)(D). *See also* 40 C.F.R. § 232.3(d)(4). Accordingly, by definition, Brace's discharge activities cannot constitute "normal farming activities" under the applicable regulation. . . .

V.

As we discussed above, Brace has the burden of proving both that he qualifies under Section 404(f)(1) for the normal farming activities exemption, and that the permit requirement was not "recaptured" under Section 404(f)(2) of the CWA, 33 U.S.C. § 1344 (f)(2). The "recapture" provision stipulates that:

> Any discharge of dredged or fill material into the navigable waters incidental to any activity having as its purpose bringing an area of the navigable waters into a use to which it was not previously subject, where the flow or circulation of navigable waters may be impaired or the reach of such waters be reduced, shall be required to have a permit under this section. * * *

Since we have held that Brace's drainage activities on the thirty-acre wetland site are not exempt from the CWA permit requirement under the "normal farming activities" or maintenance of drainage ditches exemptions, we need not reach the application of the recapture provision. . . .

VII. Conclusion

For the foregoing reasons, the order entered December 17, 1993, granting judgment in favor of the defendants, Robert Brace and Robert Brace Farms, Inc., will be reversed. This matter will be remanded to the district court to enter judgment in favor of the United States and to assess upon further proceedings appropriate penalties for defendants' violations of the permit requirements, and to assess what, if any, penalties are appropriate for violations of the EPA administrative orders.

NOTES

1. Wetlands permitting requirements call for minimizing adverse effects to aquatic ecosystems. If adverse impacts are foreseeable, permits typically

require mitigation. Mitigation can take the form of restoration, enhancement of an existing wetland or even creation of a new one. It can also mean payment of a fee to an environmental group or other third party to accomplish the same ends.

There are efforts in place to make the trek toward wetlands protection less onerous and unfriendly to landowners. In a great many cases, persons need not secure individual permits under § 404. The Corps of Engineers reported in 1996, for example, that 83% of its § 404 permits were approved under a general permit. The Corps has also issued "nationwide" permits to authorize and regulate activities affecting particularly small wetlands.

2. By separate legislation, the federal government funds "water bank" programs and "wetland reserve" programs to encourage farmers to preserve, restore, and improve high priority wetlands. Landowners who agree to do this receive compensation from the Department of Agriculture.

NATIONAL MINING ASSOCIATION v. U.S. ARMY CORPS OF ENGINEERS

145 F.3d 1399 (D.C. Cir. 1998)

WILLIAMS, Circuit Judge:

Section 404 of the Clean Water Act (the "Act") authorizes the United States Army Corps of Engineers (the "Corps") to issue permits "for the discharge of dredged or fill material into the navigable waters at specified disposal sites." 33 U.S.C. § 1344. Section 301(a) of the Act provides that the "discharge of any pollutant by any person" is unlawful unless in compliance with Act's permit requirements, including those of § 404. *Id.* § 1311(a). "Discharge," in turn, is defined as "any addition of any pollutant to navigable waters from any point source." *Id.* § 1362(12).

In 1986 the Corps issued a regulation defining the term "discharge of dredged material," as used in § 404, to mean "any addition of dredged material into the waters of the United States," but expressly excluding "de minimis, incidental soil movement occurring during normal dredging operations." 51 Fed. Reg. 41,206, 41,232 (Nov. 13, 1986). In 1993, responding to litigation, the Corps issued a new rule removing the de minimis exception and expanding the definition of discharge to cover "any addition of dredged material into, including any redeposit of dredged material within, the waters of the United States." 33 C.F.R. § 323.2(d)(1) (emphasis added). Redeposit occurs when material removed from the water is returned to it; when redeposit takes place in substantially the same spot as the initial removal, the parties refer to it as "fallback." In effect the new rule subjects to federal regulation virtually all excavation and dredging performed in wetlands.

The plaintiffs, various trade associations whose members engage in dredging and excavation, mounted a facial challenge to the 1993 regulation, claiming that it exceeded the scope of the Corps's regulatory authority under the Act by regulating fallback. The district court agreed and granted summary judgment for the plaintiffs. *American Mining Congress v. United States Army*

Corps of Engineers, 951 F. Supp. 267 (D.D.C. 1997). The district court also entered an injunction prohibiting the Corps and the Environmental Protection Agency, who jointly administer § 404, from enforcing the regulation anywhere in the United States. *Id.* at 278. We affirm. * * *

In 1977 the Corps promulgated regulations that generally tracked the statutory language, defining "discharge of dredged material" as "any addition of dredged material into the waters of the United States," with a few limited exceptions. 42 Fed. Reg. 37,145 (July 19, 1977). A new regulation issued in 1986 exempted from the permit requirement "de minimis, incidental soil movement occurring during normal dredging operations." 51 Fed. Reg. at 41,232. Although this regulation did not define "normal dredging operations," its preamble gave some guidance as to the exemption's coverage:

Section 404 clearly directs the Corps to regulate the discharge of dredged material, not the dredging itself.

Dredging operations cannot be performed without some fallback. However, if we were to define this fallback as a "discharge of dredged material," we would, in effect, be adding the regulation of dredging to section 404 which we do not believe was the intent of Congress. *Id.* at 41,210. The parties agree that the 1986 rule did, however, regulate "sidecasting," which involves placing removed soil in a wetland but at some distance from the point of removal (e.g., by the side of an excavated ditch). *See* 58 Fed. Reg. 45,008, 45,013/3 (Aug. 25, 1993) (noting that sidecasting has "always been regulated under Section 404.").

The 1993 rulemaking under challenge here was prompted by a lawsuit, *North Carolina Wildlife Federation v. Tulloch,* Civ. No. C90-713-CIV-5-BO (E.D. N.C. 1992), concerning a developer who sought to drain and clear 700 acres of wetlands in North Carolina. *See* 58 Fed. Reg. at 45,016. Because the developer's efforts involved only minimal incidental releases of soil and other dredged material, the Corps's field office personnel determined that, under the terms of the 1986 regulation, § 404's permit requirements did not apply. Environmental groups, concerned by what they viewed as the adverse effects of the developer's activities on the wetland, filed an action seeking enforcement of the § 404 permit requirement. As part of the settlement of the *Tulloch* case (a settlement to which the developer was not a party), the two administering agencies agreed to propose stiffer rules governing the permit requirements for landclearing and excavation activities. The result — the regulation at issue here — has come to be called the "Tulloch Rule."

As mentioned above, the Tulloch Rule alters the preexisting regulatory framework primarily by removing the de minimis exception and by adding coverage of incidental fallback. Specifically, the rule defines "discharge of dredged material" to include "any addition, including any redeposit, of dredged material, including excavated material, into waters of the United States which is incidental to any activity, including mechanized landclearing, ditching, channelization, or other excavation." 33 C.F.R. § 323.2(d)(1)(iii) (emphasis added).

The Tulloch Rule does have its own de minimis exception, but it is framed in terms of the Act's overall goals. A permit is not required for "any incidental addition, including redeposit, of dredged material associated with any activity that does not have or would not have the effect of destroying or degrading an area of waters of the United States." 33 C.F.R. § 323.2(d)(3)(i). Persons engaging in "mechanized landclearing, ditching, channelization and other excavation activity," however, bear the burden of proving to the Corps that their activities would not have destructive or degrading effects. *Id.* Degradation is defined as any effect on the waters of the United States that is more than de minimis or inconsequential. *Id.* § 323.2(d)(5). Thus, whereas the 1986 rule exempted de minimis soil movement, the Tulloch Rule covers all discharges, however minuscule, unless the Corps is convinced that the activities with which they are associated have only minimal adverse effects. In promulgating the new rule the Corps "emphasized that the threshold of adverse effects for the de minimis exception is a very low one." 56 Fed. Reg. at 45,020.

It is undisputed that by requiring a permit for "any redeposit," 33 C.F.R. § 323.2(d)(1)(iii) (emphasis added), the Tulloch Rule covers incidental fallback. According to the agencies, incidental fallback occurs, for example, during dredging, "when a bucket used to excavate material from the bottom of a river, stream, or wetland is raised and soils or sediments fall from the bucket back into the water." Agencies' Br. at 13. (There is no indication that the rule would not also reach soils or sediments falling out of the bucket even before it emerged from the water.) Fallback and other redeposits also occur during mechanized landclearing, when bulldozers and loaders scrape or displace wetland soil, *see* 58 Fed. Reg. 45,017–18, as well as during ditching and channelization, when draglines or backhoes are dragged through soils and sediments. *See id.* at 45,018. Indeed, fallback is a practically inescapable by-product of all these activities. In the preamble to the Tulloch Rule the Corps noted that "it is virtually impossible to conduct mechanized landclearing, ditching, channelization or excavation in waters of the United States without causing incidental redeposition of dredged material (however small or temporary) in the process." *Id.* at 45,017. As a result, the Tulloch Rule effectively requires a permit for all those activities, subject to a limited exception for ones that the Corps in its discretion deems to produce no adverse effects on waters of the United States. * * *

The plaintiffs claim that the Tulloch Rule exceeds the Corps's statutory jurisdiction under § 404, which, as we have noted, extends only to "discharge," defined as the "addition of any pollutant to navigable waters." 33 U.S.C. §§ 1344, 1362(12). It argues that fallback, which returns dredged material virtually to the spot from which it came, cannot be said to constitute an addition of anything. Therefore, the plaintiffs contend, the Tulloch Rule conflicts with the statute's unambiguous terms and cannot survive even the deferential scrutiny called for by *Chevron U.S.A., Inc. v. NRDC,* 467 U.S. 837, 81 L. Ed. 2d 694, 104 S. Ct. 2778 (1984). The "jurisdictional" character of the issue has no effect on the level of deference, *Oklahoma Natural Gas Co. v. FERC,* 307 U.S. App. D.C. 414, 28 F.3d 1281, 1283–84 (D.C. Cir. 1994), as the plaintiffs seem to acknowledge by their silence on the subject.

The agencies argue that the terms of the Act in fact demonstrate that fallback may be classified as a discharge. The Act defines a discharge as the addition of any pollutant to navigable waters, 33 U.S.C. § 1362(12), and defines "pollutant" to include "dredged spoil," as well as "rock," "sand," and "cellar dirt." *Id.* § 1362(6). The Corps in turn defines "dredged material" as "material that is excavated or dredged from waters of the United States," 33 C.F.R. § 323.2(c), a definition that is not challenged here. Thus, according to the agencies, wetland soil, sediment, debris or other material in the waters of the United States undergoes a legal metamorphosis during the dredging process, becoming a "pollutant" for purposes of the Act. If a portion of the material being dredged then falls back into the water, there has been an addition of a pollutant to the waters of the United States. Indeed, according to appellants National Wildlife Federation et al. ("NWF"), who intervened as defendants below, this reasoning demonstrates that regulation of redeposit is actually required by the Act.

We agree with the plaintiffs, and with the district court, that the straightforward statutory term "addition" cannot reasonably be said to encompass the situation in which material is removed from the waters of the United States and a small portion of it happens to fall back. Because incidental fallback represents a net withdrawal, not an addition, of material, it cannot be a discharge. As we concluded recently in a related context, "the nearest evidence we have of definitional intent by Congress reflects, as might be expected, that the word 'discharge' contemplates the addition, not the withdrawal, of a substance or substances." *North Carolina v. FERC*, 324 U.S. App. D.C. 209, 112 F.3d 1175, 1187 (D.C. Cir. 1997). The agencies' primary counterargument — that fallback constitutes an "addition of any pollutant" because material becomes a pollutant only upon being dredged — is ingenious but unconvincing. Regardless of any legal metamorphosis that may occur at the moment of dredging, we fail to see how there can be an addition of dredged material when there is no addition of material. Although the Act includes "dredged spoil" in its list of pollutants, 33 U.S.C. § 1362(6), Congress could not have contemplated that the attempted removal of 100 tons of that substance could constitute an addition simply because only 99 tons of it were actually taken away.[5] In fact the removal of material from the waters of the United States, as opposed to the discharge of material into those waters, is governed by a completely independent statutory scheme. Section 10 of the Rivers and Harbors Act of 1899, 33 U.S.C. § 403, makes it illegal "to excavate or fill" in the navigable waters of the United States without the Corps's approval. As the general counsel of the Army noted in a law review article published a few years after the passage of the Clean Water Act, Congress enacted "two separate statutory frameworks. Section 10 of the 1899 Act covers the act of dredging, while Section 404 [of the Clean Water Act] covers the disposal of the dredged material." Charles D. Ablard and Brian B. O'Neill, *Wetland*

---

[5] The unreasonableness of the agencies' statutory interpretation was illustrated by some of the hypotheticals posed at oral argument. For instance, counsel for the agencies admitted that under their interpretation of the term "discharge" in § 301(a), it "might very well" be permissible to require any landowner in the United States wishing to cut down a tree in a wetland to obtain a § 402 permit, since 33 U.S.C. § 1362(6) defines "pollutant" to include "biological material." Oral Arg. Tr. at 22. Similarly, counsel agreed that the Corps could require a permit to ride a bicycle across a wetland under its interpretation of § 404, although bicycle-riding seems — for now — to be exempted under the Tulloch Rule as an activity that does not generally destroy or degrade waters of the United States. Oral Arg. Tr. at 25; see 58 Fed. Reg. at 45,023 (indicating that "walking, grazing, vehicular traffic, and boating" would not generally be regulated).

Protection and Section 404 of the Federal Water Pollution Control Act Amendments of 1972: A Corps of Engineers Renaissance, 1 Vt. L. Rev. 51, 93 (1976).

The agencies, though acknowledging that the Tulloch Rule effectively requires a permit for all mechanized landclearing, ditching, channelization or excavation in waters of the United States, see 58 Fed. Reg. at 45,017, locate their permitting requirement under § 404, not under the Rivers and Harbors Act's explicit coverage of "excavation." The explanation for this choice is apparently that the scope of the Corps's geographic jurisdiction is narrower under the Rivers and Harbors Act than under the Clean Water Act, extending only to waters subject to the ebb and flow of the tide, or waters that are used, have been used, or may be susceptible for use to transport interstate or foreign commerce. 33 C.F.R. § 329.4; *see also id.* § 328.1 (noting difference between geographic jurisdiction under the two statutes).

There may be an incongruity in Congress's assignment of extraction activities to a statute (the Rivers and Harbors Act) with a narrower jurisdictional sweep than that of the statute covering discharges (the Clean Water Act). This incongruity, of course, could be cured either by narrowing the jurisdictional reach of the Clean Water Act or broadening that of the Rivers and Harbors Act. But we do not think the agencies can do it simply by declaring that incomplete removal constitutes addition.

The agencies also point to some specific exemptions set forth in § 404(f) of the Act in support of their view that fallback can reasonably be said to constitute discharge. Congress added the subsection in 1977, apparently in response to the broad construction of "discharge" in the 1977 regulations. It provides that "the discharge of dredged or fill material . . . is not prohibited . . . or otherwise subject to regulation" under the Act's permitting requirements when the discharge results from any of a number of specifically exempted activities, including "normal farming, silviculture, and ranching activities such as plowing, seeding, cultivating, [or] minor drainage," 33 U.S.C. § 1344(f)(1)(A), and "maintenance of drainage ditches," *id.* § 1344(f)(1)(C). After listing these exemptions, § 404(f) provides that a permit shall nonetheless be required for any activity "having as its purpose bringing an area of the navigable waters into a use to which it was not previously subject, where the flow or circulation of navigable waters may be impaired or the reach of such waters be reduced." *Id.* § 1344(f)(2).

The agencies claim these exemptions show that as a general matter Congress considered fallback to be covered by § 404. They especially note that § 404(f)(1) uses the term "discharge of dredged or fill material" to describe the consequences of the protected activities, supposedly reflecting a congressional belief that fallback is a form of discharge.

We find the exemptions far less telling. Some of the named activities— plowing, ditch maintenance, and the like-may produce fallback, but they may also produce actual discharges, i.e., additions of pollutants, so that § 404(f) accomplishes a useful purpose simply by exempting them insofar as they produce the latter. Some others, such as seeding, seem to us just as unlikely to produce fallback as actual discharge, so we are reluctant to draw any inference other than that Congress emphatically did not want the law to impede these bucolic pursuits.

NWF complains that our understanding of "addition" reads the regulation of dredged material out of the statute. They correctly note that since dredged material comes from the waters of the United States, 33 C.F.R. § 323.2(c), any discharge of such material into those waters could technically be described as a "redeposit," at least on a broad construction of that term. The Fifth Circuit made a similar observation fifteen years ago: " 'Dredged' material is by definition material that comes from the water itself. A requirement that all pollutants must come from outside sources would effectively remove the dredge-and-fill provision from the statute." *Avoyelles Sportsmen's League v. Marsh,* 715 F.2d 897, 924 n.43 (5th Cir. 1983). But we do not hold that the Corps may not legally regulate some forms of redeposit under its § 404 permitting authority. We hold only that by asserting jurisdiction over "any redeposit,"including incidental fallback, the Tulloch Rule outruns the Corps's statutory authority. Since the Act sets out no bright line between incidental fallback on the one hand and regulable redeposits on the other, a reasoned attempt by the agencies to draw such a line would merit considerable deference. *Cf. Dubois v. U.S. Dep't of Agriculture,* 102 F.3d 1273, 1296–99 (1st Cir. 1996) (although movement of pollutants within the same body of water might not constitute an "addition" for purposes of NPDES permit requirement, movement from one body of water to a separate one with different water quality is an addition). But the Tulloch Rule makes no effort to draw such a line, and indeed its overriding purpose appears to be to expand the Corps's permitting authority to encompass incidental fallback and, as a result, a wide range of activities that cannot remotely be said to "add" anything to the waters of the United States.

The agencies cite opinions from several other circuits in support of the proposition that redeposit may be regulated under § 404. Because all of these decisions predated the Tulloch Rule, however, none addressed the fallback issue directly. Indeed, none of them contains any language suggesting that regulation of fallback would be proper.

There remains only the question of remedy. The agencies challenge the district court's issuance of a nationwide injunction ordering "that the so-called Tulloch rule is declared invalid and set aside, and henceforth is not to be applied or enforced by the Corps of Engineers or the Environmental Protection Agency." 951 F. Supp. 267 at 278. The agencies make two arguments: first, that the plaintiffs are not entitled to an injunction because they presented no record evidence, and the district court made no explicit findings, as to the elements necessary for injunctive relief; and second, that even if the plaintiffs were entitled to an injunction the district court erred by granting nationwide relief to plaintiffs and non-parties alike.

As for the first argument, we note at the outset that district courts enjoy broad discretion in awarding injunctive relief. *See, e.g., Wagner v. Taylor,* 266 U.S. App. D.C. 402, 836 F.2d 566, 575 (D.C. Cir. 1987). The district court was well within its discretion in finding that the complaint placed the agencies on notice that appellees sought both declaratory and injunctive relief. See First Amended Complaint For Declaratory and Injunctive Relief (filed Sept. 20, 1993), at 25–26. Although the court made no express findings as to the elements necessary for a permanent injunction (the most salient of which is the inadequacy of legal remedies), we do not think it was required to do so. Even now the agencies identify no legal remedy as adequate. Money damages were never sought in this action, and even if the government were somehow found to have waived its sovereign immunity against damage actions, it is hard to see the relevance of such remedies in the context of a pre-enforcement challenge to agency regulations. The plaintiffs did seek (and obtain) a declaration of the Tulloch Rule's invalidity, but this brand of relief is itself more equitable than legal in nature. *See In re United States Brass Corp.,* 110 F.3d 1261, 1267 (7th Cir. 1997); *Penthouse International, Ltd. v. Meese,* 291 U.S. App. D.C. 183, 939 F.2d 1011, 1019–20 (D.C. Cir. 1991). Moreover, in their summary judgment motion the agencies failed to argue that a declaratory judgment would be adequate, or to contest any of the elements necessary for an injunction. And once the court reached the conclusion that the rule was indeed illegal (i.e., not merely that the plaintiffs had a reasonable probability of success on the merits, as would be necessary for a preliminary injunction), there was no separate need to show irreparable injury, as that is merely one possible "basis for showing the inadequacy of the legal remedy." 11A Wright & Miller, *Federal Practice and Procedure* § 2944, at 94 (2d ed. 1995). In sum we do not think the district court was required to make explicit findings as to these elements before issuing its injunction.

The agencies' argument about the breadth of the injunction fares no better. We have made clear that "when a reviewing court determines that agency regulations are unlawful, the ordinary result is that the rules are vacated — not that their application to the individual petitioners is proscribed." *Harmon v. Thornburgh,* 278 U.S. App. D.C. 382, 878 F.2d 484, 495 n.21 (D.C. Cir. 1989). Justice Blackmun made a similar observation in *Lujan v. National Wildlife Federation,* 497 U.S. 871, 111 L. Ed. 2d 695, 110 S. Ct. 3177 (1990), writing in dissent but apparently expressing the view of all nine Justices on this question:

> The Administrative Procedure Act permits suit to be brought by any person "adversely affected or aggrieved by agency action." In some cases the "agency action" will consist of a rule of broad applicability; and if the plaintiff prevails, the result is that the rule is invalidated, not simply that the court forbids its application to a particular individual. Under these circumstances a single plaintiff, so long as he is injured by the rule, may obtain "programmatic" relief that affects the rights of parties not before the court. On the other hand, if a generally lawful policy is applied in an illegal manner on a particular occasion, one who is injured is not thereby entitled to challenge other applications of the rule.

Id. at 913 (Blackmun, J., dissenting) (citation omitted). *See also id.* at 890 n.2 (majority opinion) (noting that under APA, successful challenge by aggrieved individual can affect entire agency program).* * *

Moreover, if persons adversely affected by an agency rule can seek review in the district court for the District of Columbia, as they often may, *see* 28 U.S.C. § 1391(e), our refusal to sustain a broad injunction is likely merely to generate a flood of duplicative litigation. Even though our jurisdiction is not exclusive, an injunction issued here only as to the plaintiff organizations and their members would cause all others affected by the Tulloch Rule (or at least all those with enough at stake and with astute enough lawyers) to file separate actions for declaratory relief in this circuit. Issuance of a broad injunction obviates such repetitious filings. It does so, to be sure, at the cost of somewhat diminishing the scope of the "non-acquiescence" doctrine, under which the government may normally relitigate issues in multiple circuits. *See United States v. Mendoza,* 464 U.S. 154, 78 L. Ed. 2d 379, 104 S. Ct. 568 (1984). By contrast, agency defeats in other circuits cannot produce as severe an effect, because, although other courts can also issue nationwide injunctions, they need not fear a flood of relitigation since venue restrictions would exclude many would-be plaintiffs from access to the invalidating court. The resulting gap in the effective scope of the non-acquiescence doctrine appears to be no more than an inevitable consequence of the venue rules in combination with the APA's command that rules "found to be . . . in excess of statutory jurisdiction" shall be not only "held unlawful" but "set aside." 5 U.S.C. § 706(2)(C). * * *

In a press release accompanying the adoption of the Tulloch Rule, the White House announced: "Congress should amend the Clean Water Act to make it consistent with the agencies' rulemaking." White House Office on Environmental Policy, Protecting America's Wetlands: A Fair, Flexible, and Effective Approach 23 (Aug. 24, 1993). While remarkable in its candor, the announcement contained a kernel of truth. If the agencies and NWF believe that the Clean Water Act inadequately protects wetlands and other natural resources by insisting upon the presence of an "addition" to trigger permit requirements, the appropriate body to turn to is Congress. Without such an amendment, the Act simply will not accommodate the Tulloch Rule. The judgment of the district court is

Affirmed.

[Concurring opinion by Judge Silberman is omitted].

NOTES

1. Because of *National Mining,* the EPA and the Corps promulgated regulations that declare a presumption that all land-clearing, ditching, draining and other earth-moving activities in navigable waters result in regulable fallback discharges. 40 C.F.R. § 232.2(2)(i). The presumption was made rebuttable by a showing that the fallback is indeed incidental. *Id.* Incidental fallback is defined in the rule as "small volumes" of dredged material that fall back into "substantially the same place." 40 C.F.R. § 232.2(2)(ii) (EPA regulation); 33 U.S.C. § 323.2(2)(ii) (Corps definition). The National Association of Homebuilders filed an action to challenge the rule the following month, declaring the rule "essentially brings *Tulloch* back to life." The challenge was dismissed on ripeness grounds. *National Ass'n of Home Builders v. U.S. Army Corps of Engineers,* 311 F. Supp. 2d 91 (D.C.D.C. 2004).

2. For a contrary view on this question of statutory interpretation, see *United States v. Deaton,* 209 F.3d 331, 335 (4th Cir. 2000):

. . . the statute does not prohibit the addition of material; it prohibits "the addition of any pollutant." The idea that there could be an addition of a pollutant without an addition of material seems to us entirely unremark-able, at least when an activity transforms some material from a nonpollu-tant into a pollutant, as occurred here. In the course of digging a ditch across the [defendant's] property, the contractor removed earth and vegetable matter from the wetland. Once it was removed, that material became "dredged spoil," a statutory pollutant and a type of material that up until then was not present on the [defendant's] property. It is of no consequence that what is now dredged spoil was previously present on the same property in the less threatening form of dirt and vegetation in an undisturbed state. What is important is that once the material was excavated from the wetland, its redeposit in that same wetland added a pollutant where none had been before. *See* 33 U.S.C. § 1362(6), (12). Thus, even under the defini-tion of "addition" (that is, "something added") . . . sidecasting adds a pollutant that was not present before.

3. According to a study based on aerial photography taken primarily in the 1980s and announced by the Fish and Wildlife Service in September, 1997, there remain about 100.9 million acres of wetlands in the United States, down from 221 million acres in the 1700s. Forty-eight percent of these wetlands are forested lands. The amount of wetlands continues to decrease, but the rate of decrease is declining. According to the study, the average annual loss of wetlands in the United States between 1985 and 1995 was 117,000 acres, down from 290,000 acres each year between 1970 and 1980. A total of 1.2 million acres of wetlands were lost between 1985 and 1995, about one percent of the total. About 80% of these wetlands losses are traceable to agriculture, another 6% to urban development, and the remainder to other activity, such as infrastructure construction. Losses are greatest in the southeastern United States. The report indicates the drop in wetlands losses is due to the Clean Water Act and to provisions in farm bills enacted during the 1990s. One entity, however, the Competitive Enterprise Institute, has debunked the study as based on stale data. The Institute argues there has been a net gain in wetlands since 1995.

On Earth Day, 2004, the Bush Administration announced a policy to restore, improve and protect at least three million additional acres of wetlands over the next five years. The President's 2005 budget proposed to increase EPA funding by $5 million for grants to help states address gaps in wetlands protection.

Chapter 11

THE RESOURCE CONSERVATION AND RECOVERY ACT

"The most alarming of all man's assaults upon the environment is the contamination of air, earth, rivers, and sea with dangerous and even lethal materials. This pollution is for the most part irrecoverable; the chain of evil it initiates not only in the world that must support life but in living tissues is for the most part irreversible." *Rachel Carson, 1962*

A. INTRODUCTION

It became clear after the enactments of the Clean Air Act in 1970 and the Clean Water Act in 1972 that land was becoming a comparatively attractive choice as a medium for waste disposal. Not only was land largely unprotected by federal law, but with air and surface water off-limits, it was a logical default choice as a practical matter. Accordingly, the Resource Conservation and Recovery Act, or "RCRA" (usually pronounced "Ricra"), was enacted in 1976 as the last of the big three pollution control statutes. RCRA's purpose was to "close the loop," to protect land, in both its surface and its subterranean reaches, from pollution.

Congress's primary concern in enacting RCRA was to insure that wastes would be managed safely. H.R. Rep. No. 1491, 94th Cong., 2d Sess. 3 (1976). As expressed in its statutory findings, Congress had come to the understanding that:

> the economic and population growth of our Nation, and the improvements in the standard of living enjoyed by our population, have required increased industrial production to meet our needs, and have made necessary the demolition of old buildings, the construction of new buildings, and the provision of highways and other avenues of transportation, which, together with related industrial, commercial, and agricultural operations, have resulted in a rising tide of scrap, discarded, and waste materials.

§ 1002(a), 42 U.S.C. § 6901(a). Thus, Congress wanted "to reduce the amount of waste and unsalvageable materials and to provide for proper and economical solid waste disposal practices," § 1002(a)(4), 42 U.S.C. § 6901(a)(4),

587

thereby to insure the protection of human health and the environment. § 1003, 42 U.S.C. § 6902.

RCRA is divided into numerous subtitles, two of which establish major regulatory regimes. Subchapter IV deals with regulation of disposal of "solid waste." Section 1004(27) of the statute, 42 U.S.C. § 9603(27), gives the primary definition of "solid waste" and should be scrutinized. The definition, you will observe, contains exclusions; these exclusions play a large role in determining the reach of the statute. Subchapter III, which will receive the majority of our attention, regulates disposal of "hazardous waste." Note that hazardous wastes *are* solid wastes; they are merely solid wastes of a particular kind.

Since a "solid" or "hazardous waste" must first be a "waste," we begin there.

AMERICAN MINING CONGRESS v. U.S. ENVIRONMENTAL PROTECTION AGENCY ("AMC I")

824 F.2d 1177 (D.C. Cir. 1987)

STARR, Circuit Judge:

These consolidated cases arise out of EPA's regulation of hazardous wastes under the Resource Conservation and Recovery Act of 1976 ("RCRA"), as amended, 42 U.S.C. §§ 6901–6933 (1982 & Supp. III 1985). Petitioners, trade associations representing mining and oil refining interests, challenge regulations promulgated by EPA that amend the definition of "solid waste" to establish and define the agency's authority to regulate secondary materials reused within an industry's ongoing production process. In plain English, petitioners maintain that EPA has exceeded its regulatory authority in seeking to bring materials that are not discarded or otherwise disposed of within the compass of "waste."

RCRA is a comprehensive environmental statute under which EPA is granted authority to regulate solid and hazardous wastes. RCRA was enacted in 1976, and amended in 1978, 1980, and 1984. See The Quiet Communities Act of 1978, Pub. L. No. 95-609, 92 Stat. 3081; The Solid Waste Disposal Act Amendments of 1980, Pub. L. No. 96-482, 94 Stat. 2334; Hazardous and Solid Waste Amendments of 1984, Pub. L. No. 98-616, 98 Stat. 3221. . . .

RCRA includes two major parts: one deals with non-hazardous solid waste management and the other with hazardous waste management. Under the latter, EPA is directed to promulgate regulations establishing a comprehensive management system. *Id.* § 6921. EPA's authority, however, extends only to the regulation of "hazardous waste." Because "hazardous waste" is defined as a subset of "solid waste," *id* § 6903(5), the scope of EPA's jurisdiction is limited to those materials that constitute "solid waste." That pivotal term is defined by RCRA as

> any garbage, refuse, sludge from a waste treatment plant, water supply treatment plant, or air pollution control facility and other discarded material, including solid, liquid, semisolid or contained

gaseous material, resulting from industrial, commercial, mining, and agricultural operations, and from community activities. . . .

42 U.S.C. § 6903(27) (emphasis added). As will become evident, this case turns on the meaning of the phrase, "and other discarded material," contained in the statute's definitional provisions.

EPA's interpretation of "solid waste" has evolved over time. . . .

After receiving extensive comments, EPA issued its final rule on January 4, 1985. 50 Fed. Reg. 614 (1985). Under the final rule, materials are considered "solid waste" if they are abandoned by being disposed of, burned, or incinerated; or stored, treated, or accumulated before or in lieu of those activities. In addition, certain recycling activities fall within EPA's definition. EPA determines whether a material is a RCRA solid waste when it is recycled by examining both the material or substance itself and the recycling of "secondary materials" (spent materials, sludges, by-products, commercial chemical products, and scrap metal). These "secondary materials" constitute "solid waste" when they are disposed of; burned for energy recovery or used to produce a fuel; reclaimed; or accumulated speculatively. *Id.* at 618–19, 664. Under the final rule, if a material constitutes "solid waste," it is subject to RCRA regulation unless it is directly reused as an ingredient or as an effective substitute for a commercial product, or is returned as a raw material substitute to its original manufacturing process. In the jargon of the trade, the latter category is known as the "closed-loop" exception. In either case, the material must not first be "reclaimed" (processed to recover a usable product or regenerated). EPA exempts these activities "because they are like ordinary usage of commercial products." *Id.* at 619. . . .

II

Petitioners, American Mining Congress ("AMC") and American Petroleum Institute ("API"), challenge the scope of EPA's final rule. Relying upon the statutory definition of "solid waste," petitioners contend that EPA's authority under RCRA is limited to controlling materials that are discarded or intended for discard. They argue that EPA's reuse and recycle rules, as applied to in-process secondary materials, regulate materials that have not been discarded, and therefore exceed EPA's jurisdiction. * * *

III

We observe at the outset of our inquiry that EPA's interpretation of the scope of its authority under RCRA has been unclear and unsteady. As previously recounted, EPA has shifted from its vague "sometimes discarded" approach of 1980 to a proposed exclusion from regulation of all materials used or reused as effective substitutes for raw materials in 1983, and finally, to a very narrow exclusion of essentially only materials processed within the meaning of the "closed-loop" exception under the final rule. We emphasize, therefore, that we are confronted with neither a consistent nor a long-standing agency interpretation. Under settled doctrine, "[a]n agency interpretation of a relevant provision which conflicts with the agency's earlier interpretation is'entitled to considerably less deference' than a consistently held agency view." [citations omitted]. . . .

B

Guided by these principles, we turn to the statutory provision at issue here. Congress, it will be recalled, granted EPA power to regulate "solid waste." Congress specifically defined "solid waste" as "discarded material." EPA then defined "discarded material" to include materials destined for reuse in an industry's ongoing production processes. The challenge to EPA's jurisdictional reach is founded, again, on the proposition that in-process secondary materials are outside the bounds of EPA's lawful authority. Nothing has been discarded, the argument goes, and thus RCRA jurisdiction remains untriggered.

1

The first step in statutory interpretation is, of course, an analysis of the language itself. . . . Here, Congress defined "solid waste" as "discarded material." The ordinary, plain-English meaning of the word "discarded" is "disposed of," "thrown away" or "abandoned." Encompassing materials retained for immediate reuse within the scope of "discarded material" strains, to say the least, the everyday usage of that term. . . .

Although the "ordinary and obvious meaning of the [statutory] phrase is not to be lightly discounted," . . . [citation omitted] . . ., we are hesitant to attribute decisive significance to the ordinary meaning of statutory language. To be sure, our inquiry might well and wisely stop with the plain language of the statute, since it is the statute itself that Congress enacts and the President signs into law. But as the Supreme Court recently observed, the "more natural interpretation" (or plain meaning) is not necessarily determinative. . . . And it is not infrequently said, odd as it may seem in a society governed by codified and thus knowable rules, that a matter may be within the letter of a statute but not within its spirit. . . .

In short, a complete analysis of the statutory term "discarded" calls for more than resort to the ordinary, everyday meaning of the specific language at hand. For, "the sense in which [a term] is used in a statute must be determined by reference to the purpose of the particular legislation." . . . .

As we previously recounted, the broad objectives of RCRA are "to promote the protection of health and the environment and to conserve valuable material and energy resources. . . ." 42 U.S.C. § 6902. But that goal is of majestic breadth, and it is difficult . . . to pour meaning into a highly specific term by resort to grand purposes. Somewhat more specifically, we have seen that RCRA was enacted in response to Congressional findings that the "rising tide of scrap, discarded, and waste materials" generated by consumers and increased industrial production has presented heavily populated urban communities with "serious financial, management, intergovernmental, and technical problems in the disposal of solid wastes." *Id.* § 6901(a). In light of this problem, Congress determined that "federal action through financial and technical assistance and leadership in the development, demonstration, and application of new and improved methods and processes to reduce the amount of waste and unsalvageable materials and to provide for proper and economical solid waste disposal practices was necessary." *Id.* Also animating Congress were its findings that "disposal of solid and hazardous waste" without careful planning and management presents a danger to human health and the environment; that methods to "separate usable materials from solid waste" should be employed; and that usable energy can be produced from solid waste. *Id.* § 6901(b), (c), (d).

The question we face, then, is whether, in light of the National Legislature's expressly stated objectives and the underlying problems that motivated it to enact RCRA in the first instance, Congress was using the term "discarded" in its ordinary sense — "disposed of" or "abandoned" — or whether Congress was using it in a much more open-ended way, so as to encompass materials no longer useful in their original capacity though destined for immediate reuse in another phase of the industry's ongoing production process.

For the following reasons, we believe the former to be the case. RCRA was enacted, as the Congressional objectives and findings make clear, in an effort to help States deal with the ever-increasing problem of solid waste disposal by encouraging the search for and use of alternatives to existing methods of disposal (including recycling) and protecting health and the environment by regulating hazardous wastes. To fulfill these purposes, it seems clear that EPA need not regulate "spent" materials that are recycled and reused in an ongoing manufacturing or industrial process. These materials have not yet become part of the waste disposal problem; rather, they are destined for beneficial reuse or recycling in a continuous process by the generating industry itself. . . .

In sum, our analysis of the statute reveals clear Congressional intent to extend EPA's authority only to materials that are truly discarded, disposed of, thrown away, or abandoned. . . .

IV

We are constrained to conclude that, in light of the language and structure of RCRA, the problems animating Congress to enact it, and the relevant portions of the legislative history, Congress clearly and unambiguously expressed its intent that "solid waste" (and therefore EPA's regulatory authority) be limited to materials that are "discarded" by virtue of being disposed of, abandoned, or thrown away. While we do not lightly overturn an agency's reading of its own statute, we are persuaded that by regulating in-process secondary materials, EPA has acted in contravention of Congress' intent. Accordingly, the petition for review is

Granted.

[Dissent by Mikva, Circuit Judge, omitted.]

NOTES

1. *Accord Association of Battery Recyclers, Inc. v. U.S. Environmental Protection Agency*, 208 F.3d 1047 (D.C. Cir. 2001) (secondary materials stored and intended for reuse in another phase of an industrial process are not "discarded" for purposes of RCRA).

2. *Compare*:

(a) *Owen Electric Steel Co. v. Browner*, 37 F.3d 146, 149–50 (4th Cir. 1994): [In *Owen*, the issue was whether so-called "KO61" slag, left untouched for six months before sale to other entities, was a "waste" for purposes of RCRA]. "Were *AMC I* the final case offering interpretation of the phrase 'discarded material,' Owen might be victorious here: because Owen's slag is eventually recycled, it cannot be said to have been discarded. Subsequent cases, however, have read *AMC I* narrowly. First, in *American Petroleum Institute v. United States EPA*, 285 U.S. App. D.C. 35, 906 F.2d 729 (D.C. Cir. 1990), the EPA asserted that the District of Columbia Circuit's holding in *AMC I* precluded it from regulating as waste hazardous slag that was delivered to a plant for metal reclamation. The court of appeals held otherwise, explaining:

> . . . The issue in *AMC [I]* was whether the EPA could, under the RCRA, treat as "solid wastes" "materials that are recycled and reused in an ongoing manufacturing or industrial process." [*AMC I*, 824 F.2d at 1186.] We held that it could not because these materials have not yet become part of the waste disposal problem; rather, they are destined for beneficial reuse or recycling in a continuous process by the generating industry itself. *Id*. Materials subject to such a process were not "discarded" because they were never "disposed of, abandoned, or thrown away." *Id*. at 1193.
>
> *AMC [I]* is by no means dispositive of EPA's authority to regulate K061 slag. Unlike the materials in question in *AMC [I]*, K061 is indisputably "discarded" before being subject to metals reclamation. Consequently, it has "become part of the waste disposal problem . . ."

[W]e glean that the fundamental inquiry in determining whether a byproduct has been "discarded" is whether the byproduct is immediately recycled for use in the same industry; if not, then the byproduct is justifiably seen as "part of the waste disposal problem," *AMC I*, 824 F.2d at 1186, and therefore as a "solid waste."

(b) *American Mining Congress v. United States EPA*, 907 F.2d 1179 (D.C. Cir. 1990) ("*AMC II*"):

[In *AMC II*, petitioners, relying on *AMC I*, claimed that three hazardous substances were not wastes on the basis that "sludges [containing the substances] from wastewater that are stored in surface impoundments and that may at some time in the future be reclaimed are not 'discarded.'" *AMC II*, 907 F.2d at 1186. The court of appeals rejected petitioners' reading of *AMC I*, stating]:

> Petitioners read *AMC [I]* too broadly. *AMC [I]*'s holding concerned only materials that are "destined for immediate reuse in another phase of the industry's ongoing production process," *Id*. at 1185 (emphasis added), and that "have not yet become part of the waste disposal problem," *Id*. at 1186. Nothing in *AMC [I]* prevents the agency from treating as "discarded" the wastes at issue in this case, which are managed in land disposal units that are part of wastewater treatment

systems, which have therefore become "part of the waste disposal problem," and which are not part of the ongoing industrial processes.

Id. at 1186 (emphasis omitted).

(c) *United States v. ILCO, Inc.*, 996 F.2d 1126 (11th Cir. 1993):

[ILCO, Inc. ("ILCO") purchased spent batteries from various sources, subsequently recycling them. It contended the activity of recycling was inconsistent with discarding, and since the materials were not discarded, they were not solid waste. The Eleventh Circuit disagreed]:

> ILCO argues that it has never "discarded" the plates and groups [of the batteries] and, therefore, the material it recycles is not "solid waste" as defined in [section] 6903(27). The lead plates and groups are, no doubt, valuable feedstock for a smelting process. Nevertheless, EPA, with congressional authority, promulgated regulations that classify these materials as "discarded solid waste." Somebody has discarded the battery in which these components are found. This fact does not change just because a reclaimer has purchased or finds value in the components.

Id. at 1131.

3. Even if it is a solid waste, is it? *See, e.g., Connecticut Coastal Fishermen's Ass'n. v. Remington Arms Co.*, 989 F.2d 1305 (2d Cir. 1993):

> The RCRA regulations create a dichotomy in the definition of solid waste. The EPA distinguishes between RCRA's regulatory and remedial purposes and offers a different definition of solid waste depending upon the statutory context in which the term appears. In its amicus brief, the EPA tells us that the regulatory definition of solid waste — found at 40 C.F.R. § 261.2(a) — is narrower than its statutory counterpart. The regulations define solid waste as "any discarded material" and further define discarded material as that which is "abandoned." 40 C.F.R. § 261.2(a). Materials that are abandoned have been "disposed of." 40 C.F.R. § 261.2(b). According to RCRA regulations, this definition of solid waste "applies only to wastes that also are hazardous for purposes of the regulations implementing Subtitle C of RCRA." 40 C.F.R. § 261.1(b)(1). As previously noted, Subtitle C [Subchapter III] contains more stringent handling standards for hazardous waste, and hazardous waste is a subset of solid waste.

Id. at 1314.

The opinion then discusses EPA's regulatory decision to apply the broader definition with respect to both "imminent hazard" lawsuits brought under § 2003, 42 U.S.C. § 6973, and citizen suits, brought under § 7002, 42 U.S.C. § 6972.]

> We recognize the anomaly of using different definitions for the term "solid waste" and that such view further complicates an already complex statute. Yet, we believe on balance that the EPA regulations reasonably interpret the statutory language. Hence, we defer to them. Dual definitions of solid waste are suggested by the structure and language of RCRA. Congress in Subchapter III isolated hazardous

wastes for more stringent regulatory treatment. Recognizing the serious responsibility that such regulations impose, Congress required that hazardous waste — a subset of solid waste as defined in the RCRA regulations — be clearly identified. The statute directs the EPA to develop specific "criteria" for the identification of hazardous wastes as well as to publish a list of particular hazardous wastes. 42 U.S.C. § 6921(a) & (b). By way of contrast, Subchapter IV that empowers the EPA to publish "guidelines" for the identification of problem solid waste pollution areas, does not require explanation beyond RCRA's statutory definition of what constitutes solid waste. *Id.* § 6942(a). Hence, the words of the statute contemplate that the EPA would refine and narrow the definition of solid waste for the sole purpose of Subchapter III regulation and enforcement.

Id. at 1315.

4. EPA continues to tinker with the regulatory definition of "solid waste." At this writing, the regulation follows the lead of the above-discussed cases, characterizing as "discarded" materials which are "abandoned," "recycled," or "considered inherently waste-like." "Abandoned" materials are those disposed of, burned or incinerated, or accumulated, stored or treated before, or in lieu of, being abandoned. "Recycled" materials are those used in a manner constituting disposal, burned for energy recovery, reclaimed, or accumulated speculatively. Materials "inherently waste-like" are those so specified and determined by the Administrator as meeting a list of criteria. *See* 40 C.F.R. § 261.2. EPA has also specified a lengthy list of materials which shall not be considered as solid waste for purposes of RCRA. 40 C.F.R. § 261.4(a). On October 28, 2003, EPA proposed a new rule stipulating that any material which is generated and reclaimed in a continuous process within the same industry is not "discarded" for purposes of Subtitle C, provided that the recycling process is "legitimate." 61 Fed. Reg. 61,558 (Oct. 28, 2003). Whether a particular recycling practice qualifies as "legitimate" would depend on satisfaction of four specific criteria. *Id.* As of August, 2004, there was no further action or decision regarding promulgation.

B.   SUBCHAPTER IV — SOLID WASTE REGULATION

Solid wastes are routinely disposed in municipal solid waste landfills. Estimates are that over 220 million tons of solid waste materials were disposed in the year 2000 alone. RCRA-regulated solid waste landfills are discrete areas of land that receive household waste, and in some instances, commercial and industrial non-hazardous waste. They can be publicly or privately owned. Legally, they are distinguishable from other waste disposal units, such as land application units, surface impoundments, injection wells and waste piles, which are regulated under the Clean Water Act and the Safe Drinking Water Act.

Solid waste disposal in landfills is regulated under Subchapter IV of RCRA. The Subchapter prohibits "open dumps" and requires the regulation of "sanitary landfills" by states or tribes, subject to EPA approval. §§ 4002–03, 42 U.S.C. §§ 6942–43. The EPA has established a set of requirements for construction and operation of these sanitary landfills. *See* 40 C.F.R. § 256.01 et seq. In the main, sanitary landfills must be operated in a manner designed to reduce or eliminate the formation of leachate and the release of leachate materials into groundwater.

EPA's regulations control sanitary landfills in six particulars:

• *location*: as a general matter, landfills must not be located near airports, floodplains, wetlands, fault areas, seismic impact zones, or unstable areas;

• *operation*: operators of municipal landfills may not receive hazardous waste and must set up a system, including inspections, record keeping, and personnel training, to detect hazardous wastes that might be mixed in with a drop-off load. To reduce or eliminate leachate, operators must cover disposed wastes with at least six inches of earthen material at the end of each working day. For the same reason, they must also prevent storm waters from running on to active parts of the landfill. Waters that do run off the landfill must be managed in compliance with the Clean Water Act. Operators must also control vectors, check for potentially explosive methane gas emissions, reduce air pollution from open burning, and restrict access by illegal dumpers and the public at large.

• *design*: new landfills (those that did not receive wastes before October 9, 1993) must be built to meet EPA's "Maximum Contaminant Levels" ("MCLs") (federal drinking water standards established under the Safe Drinking Water Act) at a "relevant point of compliance." This is a performance-based requirement that means that a landfill may not contaminate groundwater beyond a certain amount (the MCL) as measured at a predetermined point, one no farther than 150 meters from the landfill's outer boundary and on the landfill property. Meeting this standard requires different actions at different sites. Meeting the standard gets expensive, for example, if soils are permeable and the climate is wet. In such circumstances, the landfill will likely need a composite liner, typically a flexible sheet of synthetic material set over a two-foot base of impermeable soil, and a leachate collection system to reduce amounts of leachate collecting over the liner to less than 30 centimeters.

• *groundwater monitoring and corrective action:* monitoring systems allow for the sampling and analysis of groundwater in the immediate vicinity of the landfill to assess whether any leachate is making its way out of the impoundment. How extensive the system must be depends on geographic and climatic considerations, and the requirement can even be waived in some cases. If it is determined that groundwater has been contaminated by the landfill in violation of applicable standards, clean-up is required, by whatever appropriate methods.

• *closure and post-closure*: after disposal activity ceases, landfills must be "closed." A major closure requirement is the emplacement of an impermeable "final cover" of at least 18 inches of earthen material and an additional erosion-control layer of at least another 6 inches of earth capable of supporting foliage. Additionally, owners and operators must insure the integrity of the landfill for 30 years thereafter. Deeds used to transfer title to the property in the future must note the land's prior use and must restrict future use appropriately.

- *financial assurance:* owners and operators must demonstrate sufficient financial strength to meet all of the construction, operation, closure, and post-closure requirements.

Small landfills, which comprise approximately 50% of all municipal landfills, may secure a partial exemption from these requirements for reasons of cost. Defined as landfills that dispose of less than 20 tons of municipal solid waste per day, averaged yearly, these facilities typically serve communities of fewer than 10,000 people. Owners and operators of small landfills may be exempted from design, monitoring, and corrective action requirements if there is no evidence of groundwater contamination, no practical waste management alternative, and the landfill is located in an area that receives less than 25 inches of precipitation per year, *or* if there is no evidence of groundwater contamination and the community endures an annual surface transportation interruption lasting at least three consecutive months (this latter exemption applies mainly to communities in difficult weather areas, such as in less developed reaches of Alaska).

Whether landfilling or recycling solid waste is preferable is a subject of debate. Some persons, maintaining that landfills are inherently not protective of human health, argue that recycling should be the national policy. Others argue that landfills are safe, are more economical than recycling, and can serve the nation's needs easily for at least the next one thousand years. For an interesting article making the latter case, see John Tierney, *Recycling is Garbage*, New York Times Magazine, June 30, 1996.

While many municipalities have established voluntary recycling programs, some have gone beyond recycling wastes to a strategy of reducing the volume of such wastes. These municipalities would revolutionize the current system of solid waste disposal by using "unit-based pricing" systems, also known as "pay as you throw" programs. Unit-based pricing programs charge households by the bag, or by weight, or by container, for their wastes, thus creating an economic disincentive to waste generation. With such a system, individual payment amounts are better tailored to the landfill services each customer uses. Some concerns about unit-based pricing involve how to charge multi-family housing areas for trash removal, and how to allay increased financial burdens on large families (which generate relatively more waste) and poor families (which have less ability to pay for landfilling services).

C. SUBCHAPTER III* — HAZARDOUS WASTE REGULATION

[1] APPLICABILITY

MOBIL OIL CORP. v. U.S. ENVIRONMENTAL PROTECTION AGENCY

35 F.3d 579 (D.C. Cir. 1994)

JUDGES: Before EDWARDS, BUCKLEY, and RANDOLPH, Circuit Judges.

BUCKLEY, Circuit Judge:

Petitioners raise numerous challenges to the "mixture" and "derived-from" rules promulgated by the Environmental Protection Agency under authority of Subtitle C of the Resource Conservation and Recovery Act of 1976 ("RCRA"), 42 U.S.C. §§ 6901–92k (1988 & Supp. IV 1992). We do not address these challenges, however, because we conclude that subsequent congressional action has rendered the dispute moot. Petitioners American Mining Congress and The Fertilizer Institute also challenge the so-called "Bevill mixture rule," promulgated under the same authority, which we vacate in part.

I. Background

RCRA provides a comprehensive scheme for handling solid wastes. As part of this regime, Subchapter III, 42 U.S.C. §§ 6921–6939b (1988 & Supp. IV 1992) ("Subtitle C"), subjects hazardous wastes to stringent cradle-to-grave regulation. The statute defines "hazardous waste" as a solid waste, or combination of solid wastes, which because of its quantity, concentration, or physical, chemical, or infectious characteristics may —

(A) cause, or significantly contribute to an increase in mortality or an increase in serious irreversible, or incapacitating reversible, illness; or

(B) pose a substantial present or potential hazard to human health or the environment when improperly treated, stored, transported, or disposed of, or otherwise managed.

42 U.S.C. § 6903(5) (1988). Subtitle C also established a two-step process for the identification of hazardous wastes: The EPA would first promulgate criteria for identifying the "characteristics" of hazardous waste, "taking into account toxicity, persistence, and degradability in nature, potential for accumulation in tissue, and other related factors such as flammability, corrosiveness, and other hazardous characteristics." *Id.* § 6921(a) (1988). Then, on the basis of those criteria, the EPA would "promulgate regulations identifying the characteristics of hazardous waste, and listing particular hazardous wastes (within the meaning of section 6903(5) of this title), which shall be subject to the provisions of [Subtitle C]." *Id.* § 6921(b)(1).

---

* Subchapter III is often referred to as "Subtitle C."

Pursuant to this mandate, the EPA issued proposed rules in 1978. 43 Fed. Reg. 58,946 (1978). In that proposal, the EPA stated that it would identify hazardous wastes on the basis of the following characteristics: ignitability, corrosivity, reactivity and toxicity. 43 Fed. Reg. at 58,950, 58,955–57. Wastes displaying any of these characteristics were to be listed, as were wastes that independently satisfied the statutory definition of "hazardous waste" contained in 42 U.S.C. § 6903(5). 43 Fed. Reg. at 58,955, col. 2. A listed waste would remain subject to Subtitle C regulation until it was certified to the EPA that the waste was "non-hazardous according to the results of each characteristic or property tested." 43 Fed. Reg. at 58,953, col. 3.

The EPA issued its final rule on May 19, 1980, in which it published a list of some 400 hazardous wastes. 45 Fed. Reg. 33,084, 33,122–27 (1980). The final rule also promulgated the "mixture" and "derived-from" rules. The mixture rule provided that a solid waste would be treated as hazardous if "it is a mixture of solid waste and one or more [listed] hazardous wastes. . . ." *Id.* at 33,119, col.3. The derived-from rule provided that

> any solid waste generated from the treatment, storage, or disposal of a hazardous waste, including any sludge, spill residue, ash, emission control dust or leachate (but not including precipitation run-off) is a hazardous waste.

45 Fed. Reg. at 33,120, col. 1. Thus a substance that was mixed with a listed hazardous waste or derived from a hazardous waste was to be regulated as a hazardous waste regardless of whether the mixture or derivative actually "pose[d] a substantial present or potential hazard to human health or the environment. . . ." 42 U.S.C. § 6903(5). Any mixture or derived-from waste, however, could escape Subtitle C regulation through a "delisting" process. *See* 45 Fed. Reg. at 33,116, col. 3 (waste may be delisted if demonstrated that it is non-hazardous "based on the results of specific tests for each of the hazardous properties for which the waste was listed").

The initial promulgation of the mixture and derived-from rules was challenged on both substantive and procedural grounds. On December 6, 1991, we vacated both rules because the EPA had "entirely failed to comply with [the Administrative Procedure Act's ("APA")] notice-and-comment requirements. . . ." *Shell Oil Co. v. EPA,* 292 U.S. App. D.C. 332, 950 F.2d 741, 752 (D.C. Cir. 1991). As we disposed of the case on procedural grounds, we did not determine whether the EPA had exceeded its authority under RCRA in issuing the rules.

On March 3, 1992, the EPA issued an "interim final rule," reinstating the vacated mixture and derived-from rules under authority of the APA's "good cause" exception, 5 U.S.C. § 553(b)(3)(B), which permits the issuance of a rule without notice and prior opportunity for comment on a finding that such are "impractical, unnecessary, or contrary to the public interest." 57 Fed. Reg. 7,628, 7,628–29 (1992). In doing so, the EPA sought to obtain "the time to sort through more fully the implications of alternative regulatory approaches and understand the scope and effect of current Subtitle C rules." 57 Fed. Reg. at 7,630, col. 3. The EPA promised to publish options for modifying or replacing the rules by April 28, 1992; and it included a provision terminating the interim final rules on April 28, 1993 ("sunset provision"). *Id.*

The promised revisions were issued on May 20, 1992. These included a "Hazardous Waste Identification Rule" ("HWIR") that would effect "modifications to the RCRA regulatory framework which will address over-regulatory situations created by the 'mixture' and 'derived-from' rules." 57 Fed. Reg. 21,450, 21,452, col. 1 (1992). In the HWIR, the EPA conceded that the mixture and derived-from rules were overinclusive, resulting in a regime where "millions of tons of mixtures and derived-from residuals that must be managed as hazardous waste [under Subtitle C] because of their history (i.e., what they were mixed with or derived-from) may actually pose quite low hazards." *Id.* at 21,451, col. 3.

Five months later, on October 6, 1992, Congress adopted an amendment to an EPA appropriations bill that reads as follows:

EPA shall promulgate revisions to paragraphs (a)(2)(iv) [the mixture rule] and (c)(2)(i) [the derived-from rule] of 40 C.F.R. 261.3, as reissued on March 3, 1992, by October 1, 1993, but any revision to such paragraphs shall not be promulgated or become effective prior to October 1, 1994. Notwithstanding paragraph (e) of 40 C.F.R. 261.3 [the "sunset provision"], as reissued on March 3, 1992, paragraphs (a)(2)(iv) and (c)(2)(i) of such regulations shall not be terminated or withdrawn until revisions are promulgated and become effective in accordance with the preceding sentence. The deadline of October 1, 1994 shall be enforceable under section 7002 of the Solid Waste Disposal Act.

Pub. L. No. 102-389, 106 Stat. 1571, 1602 (Oct. 6, 1992) ("Chafee Amendment"). The EPA contends that this amendment codifies the mixture and derived-from rules, mooting petitioners' challenges thereto.

Three weeks later, the EPA issued notices announcing its withdrawal of the HWIR proposal and rescission of the sunset provision. 57 Fed. Reg. 49,280, 49,280, col. 1 (1992) (withdrawing HWIR proposal); 57 Fed. Reg. 49,278, 49,278, col. 1 (withdrawing the sunset provision). In both notices, the EPA announced its intent to promulgate revisions to the mixture and derived-from rules within 12 to 24 months. 57 Fed. Reg. at 49,278, col. 2; 57 Fed. Reg. at 49,280, col. 3.

We are also asked to review the EPA's treatment of wastes consisting of a mixture of a "Bevill waste" and one or more hazardous wastes. Bevill wastes are derived from the extraction, beneficiation, and processing of ores and minerals and are exempted from Subtitle C regulation by virtue of the Bevill Amendment to RCRA, 42 U.S.C. § 6921(b)(3)(A)(ii) (1988). *See generally Horsehead Resource Dev. Co. v. Browner,* 305 U.S. App. D.C. 35, 16 F.3d 1246 (D.C. Cir. 1994). In 1989, the EPA promulgated regulations determining which mineral processing wastes qualified as Bevill wastes. At the same time, the agency issued what petitioners refer to as the "Bevill mixture rule." The "Bevill mixture rule" had two distinct provisions that are relevant here. One provision described how mixtures of Bevill wastes and characteristic wastes were to be treated, while the other declared that mixtures of Bevill wastes and listed wastes were governed by the Subtitle C mixture rule. 54 Fed. Reg. 36,592, 36,622–23, 36,641 (1989). The Bevill mixture rule was contested in *Solite Corp. v. EPA,* 952 F.2d 473, 293 U.S. App. D.C. 117 (D.C. Cir. 1991), where we concluded that, because the EPA had assumed the validity of the Subtitle

C mixture rule in "extending it to the Bevill content," our decision in *Shell Oil* vacating and remanding the Subtitle C mixture rule required us to vacate and remand the Bevill mixture rule as well. *Id.* at 493–94. In the interim final rule, the EPA repromulgated the characteristic waste provision of the Bevill mixture rule as well as the Subtitle C mixture and derived-from rules. 57 Fed. Reg. 7,628–32. Petitioners American Mining Congress and The Fertilizer Institute ("Bevill petitioners") challenge that action. . . .

III. Conclusion

We hold that petitioners' challenges to the Subtitle C mixture and derived-from rules, including the EPA's interpretation of the former to apply to mixtures of Bevill and listed wastes, are moot because the Chafee Amendment has enacted those rules as so interpreted into law. We vacate the provision of the Bevill mixture rule concerning Bevill/characteristic waste mixtures because the provision was reissued without compliance with the rulemaking requirements of the APA.

So ordered.

NOTES

1. The regulatory definition of "hazardous waste" may be found at 40 C.F.R. § 261.3. In addition to promulgating a regulatory definition, EPA has specified certain solid wastes which shall not be regulated as hazardous. 40 C.F.R. § 261.4(b). It has also exempted certain narrow subsets of hazardous wastes from regulation under the Act. 40 C.F.R. § 261.4(c).

2. With *Shell* invalidating the mixture rule on administrative law grounds, what about the efficacy of the rule prior to the effective date of the Chafee Amendment? *See United States v. Goodner Brothers Aircraft, Inc.*, 966 F.2d 380 (8th Cir. 1992) (indicating that *Shell* stands for the principle that the mixture rule was void *ab initio* and accordingly was not in effect until established by the Chafee Amendment); *United States v. Bethlehem Steel Co.*, 38 F.3d 862 (7th Cir. 1994) ("we must reject the notion that the policy behind the mixture rule is 'embodied' as a general principle within the definition [of 'hazardous waste'] and that such a principle may operate to reach wastes that would have been covered by the mixture rule, but for its invalidation.").

3. Not to be lost in this discussion is EPA's "Contained-in Policy," found in an EPA memorandum dated November 13, 1986. This policy represents EPA's interpretation of the mixture and derived-from rules. The policy stipulates that any combination of a listed hazardous waste and a non-solid waste (*e.g.* soil or groundwater) is a hazardous waste for purposes of regulation under Subchapter III of RCRA so long as it contains the listed hazardous waste.

[2] REGULATORY STRUCTURE

Subchapter III of RCRA divides the regulated community into three groups: generators (§ 3002, 42 U.S.C. § 6922); transporters (§ 3003, 42 U.S.C. § 6823); and owners and operators of hazardous waste treatment, storage, or disposal facilities ("TSDs" or "TSDFs") (§§ 3004-05, 42 U.S.C. §§ 6824-25). The terms "generator," "transporter," and "owner and operator" are undefined in the statute. All of these entities are regulated with the overall purpose of tracking hazardous waste from "cradle to grave." This means that wastes are controlled from initial generation, through transport from the generation site, up to and including final treatment or other disposition. The regulatory structure is summarized in the following paragraphs.

● *Generators:* As set forth in § 3002 and implementing regulations, generators have the responsibility of identifying wastes and caring for them while onsite. (Generators may accumulate hazardous waste on site for ninety days without taking on the status of a hazardous waste storage facility regulable under § 3004.) When the time comes to remove wastes, generators must prepare a "manifest," *see* § 1004(12), 42 U.S.C. § 6903(12) designate the facility to which the wastes shall be transported, and package and mark the wastes in accordance with the particularized standards of regulations of EPA and the Department of Transportation ("DOT"). Generators must also prepare biennial reports for EPA on their activities and their compliance with the regulatory requirements. The regulations carve out exceptions for farmers who use pesticides: there is no need to comply with § 3002 standards so long as the farmer triple-rinses pesticide containers and disposes of residues on the farm consistent with pesticide package labels. *See* 40 C.F.R. Part 262.

● *Transporters:* Transporters (other than generators and TSD operators transporting wastes onsite) must meet regulatory requirements under § 3003 and implementing regulations. In important part, their major responsibility is to transport all wastes they receive to their ultimate resting place. To insure this end, transporters must comply with the manifest system: they may not accept wastes for transport in the absence of a manifest, they must sign and date the manifest to indicate acceptance of wastes, and upon delivery they must secure the signature of the receiving party. Should an accidental discharge occur, transporters must take immediate action to protect the public health, must clean up the mess, and must notify the appropriate regulatory authorities. *See* 40 C.F.R. Part 263.

● *Owners and Operators of TSDFs:* The most detailed and intrusive standards are reserved for owners and operators of TSDFs. Authorized by § 3004 and accompanying regulations, these standards are implemented through the permit system established by § 3005. The § 3004 regulations require owners and operators of TSDFs, *inter alia*, to:

● locate facilities in earthquake-safe areas, away from floodplains or other geologically risky areas;

● construct TSDFs in accordance with rigid standards, including use of foundations and dikes as necessary, low permeability double-liners to avoid loss of materials to groundwater, provision for leachate collection and removal systems, and groundwater monitoring;

● secure the TSDF to limit human and livestock intrusion by fence or barrier and, if necessary, by 24-hour surveillance;

● prepare an emergency plan and supply such communication and other equipment as necessary to implement the plan should the need arise;

- prepare and have ready corrective action plans for use in the event of discharges of hazardous materials to the environment;

- inform generators in advance of willingness to accept wastes from that generator;

- insure that wastes actually received are precisely those shipped by the generator;

- train workers in the proper handling of hazardous wastes;

- separate characteristic wastes as necessary, especially ignitable ones;

- treat, store and dispose of hazardous wastes in accordance with rigorous standards;

- follow specific requirements for container use and maintenance, surface impoundments, waste piles, land treatment units, landfills, incinerators, drip pads, and miscellaneous units;

- conduct regular facility inspections to insure smooth operation;

- provide for liability coverage in case of a major accident;

- provide for proper closure after receipt of wastes ceases;

- prepare and implement a post-closure plan designed to insure no loss of hazardous materials for at least 30 years after closure; and

- provide assurance of financial capacity to correct any problems that might occur over the 30 year post-closure period.

See 40 C.F.R. Part 264.

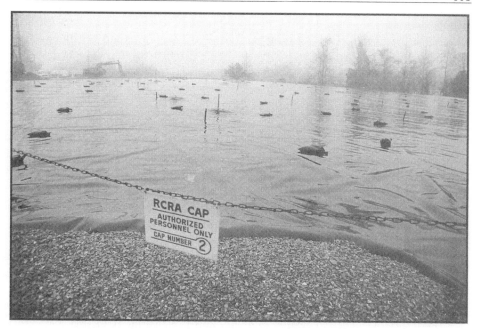

Ten acres of black plastic covering a radioactive waste landfill at Oak Ridge, TN. The cap prevents gases from escaping and keeps precipitation from entering.
U.S. Dept. of Energy Photograph, 1994.

A variety of treaters, storers, and disposers, especially those who fall under other regulatory regimes or those who do not resemble the classic TSDF, are exempted from these requirements.

NOTE

Akin to the CAA and CWA, RCRA provides for states to participate in regulatory efforts. State programs can operate in lieu of the federal program upon approval by EPA. To warrant approval, state programs must be "equivalent" to the federal program, "consistent" with federal or state programs applicable in other states, and provide for adequate enforcement. § 3006(b), 42 U.S.C. § 6926(b).

Once a state program is approved, EPA moves into standby mode. The state does the heavy lifting. But EPA need not sit by idly. Even if a state program is operating satisfactorily, the federal agency still can intercede in specific instances by filing civil or criminal enforcement actions. *See* § 3008, 42 U.S.C. § 6928. EPA is apt to do this when it believes a state has failed to enforce its laws against a specific polluter. As a legal matter, stepping in under these circumstances is uncontroversial.

What is more controversial is EPA's penchant to intercede even when a state is enforcing or has already enforced its laws against a specific polluter. This practice, known as "overfiling," results in two causes of action for the same allegedly illegal behavior, one in federal court (brought by EPA) and the other in state court (brought by the state enforcement agency). Until recently, courts rejected the notion that enforcement by one entity barred enforcement by the other. *See, e.g., Wyckoff v. U.S. Environmental Protection Agency*, 796 F.2d 1197 (9th Cir. 1986). But a controversial 1999 decision ruled to the contrary. In *Harmon Industries, Inc. v. Browner*, 191 F.3d 894 (8th Cir. 1999), EPA had filed against a polluter in Missouri, a state with "primacy" (authority to run the federal program under auspices of state law). The state filed its own enforcement action eighteen months later. The issue in *Harmon* was whether the state's cause of action operated to terminate the ongoing federal suit. The court found that it did, on the theory that the state program operates "in lieu of" the federal program, and, therefore, duplicate enforcement actions are impermissible. EPA was extremely aggravated by the *Harmon* decision, for reasons of potential abuse: with the *Harmon* rule in place, a state could arrange a sweetheart deal with a polluter precisely to frustrate a vigorous federal enforcement effort.

Harmon, it turns out, was not the last word on this important enforcement question. Other cases are already weighing in, some of which outright disagree with *Harmon*, *see, e.g. United States v. Power Eng'g Co.*, 303 F.3d 1232 (10th Cir. 2002) (opining that the "in lieu of" principle may extend to permitting functions, but not to enforcement), and others which choose to read *Harmon* narrowly. *See, e.g. United States v. Elias*, 269 F.3d 1003, 1011 (9th Cir. 2001) ("'The position of the Eighth Circuit in [*Harmon*] is not that the federal government loses its civil enforcement power after a state program is authorized. The Eighth Circuit concludes only that the federal government loses its primary role in enforcing hazardous waste regulations.' [*quoting United States v. Flanagan*, 126 F. Supp. 2d 1284, 1289 (C.D. Cal. 2000)]. Thus understood, [*Harmon*] does not support Elias's contention that federal law is supplanted or that the United States lacks power to try him.").

[3] HAZARDOUS AND SOLID WASTE AMENDMENTS OF 1984

In 1984, Congress amended RCRA. The Hazardous and Solid Waste Amendments ("HSWA") of 1984 attempted to plug gaps in the regulatory structure of the 1976 RCRA as implemented by EPA. Some of the changes were in the nature of regulatory refinements. For one, the HSWA brought previously unregulated "small quantity generators," those which produce less than 1000 kilograms per month of hazardous waste, into the system. Now, small quantity generators down to those which produce as little as 100 kilograms per month of hazardous waste are regulated. The HSWA also imposed more rigorous design and operation standards for TSDFs and incinerators (these standards have already been incorporated in the discussion immediately above). The new legislation also conditioned permit receipt on satisfactory performance at all "solid waste management units" ("SWMUs"). These have been defined as "any discernable unit at which solid wastes have been placed at any time, irrespective of whether the unit was intended for the management of solid or hazardous waste. Such units include any area at a facility at which solid wastes have been routinely and systematically released." 55 Fed. Reg. at 30,874 (proposed 40 C.F.R. § 264.501). And the HSWA broadened criminal penalties.

More important for our purposes, the 1984 legislation made several programmatic changes of enduring significance. First, it shifted the focus of hazardous waste regulation from disposal to treatment. Second, it introduced a "corrective action" program to clean up leaks at TSDFs. And, third, it began a federal effort to rein in pollution from underground storage tanks, previously unregulated at the federal level. In the remainder of this section, we will discuss each of these three statutory innovations.

[a] LAND DISPOSAL RESTRICTIONS

Perhaps the most significant change worked by the HSWA is its renewed emphasis on treatment of hazardous wastes as contrasted with disposal. Before the HSWA, the preferred compliance method was land disposal: persons buried their hazardous wastes. Congress found this widespread practice to be unacceptable, declaring in the 1984 amendments that:

> [Certain] classes of land disposal facilities are not capable of assuring long-term containment of certain hazardous wastes, and to avoid substantial risk to human health and the environment, reliance on land disposal should be minimized or eliminated. . . . [Land] disposal . . . should be the least favored method for managing hazardous wastes.

§ 1002(b)(7), 42 U.S.C. § 6901(b)(7). Accordingly, Congress amended § 3004 to provide as follows:

> [T]he Administrator shall, after notice and opportunity for hearings . . . , promulgate regulations specifying those levels or methods of treatment, if any, which substantially diminish the toxicity of the waste or substantially reduce the likelihood of migration of hazardous constituents from the waste so that short-term and long-term threats to human health and the environment are minimized.

§ 3004(m)(1), 42 U.S.C. § 6924(m)(1).

Congress directed EPA to set waste treatment standards in accord with a strict timetable. Congress divided hazardous wastes into three groups (the first third, second third, and third third), identified others wastes as well, and specified the time frame for standard setting for each. Most significantly, it provided that, should EPA fail to enact treatment standards for any of the designated wastes as required by the Act, land disposal of those wastes must cease. These so-called "hammer" provisions come in two forms. A "soft hammer" drops if EPA fails to promulgate treatment standards by a specified date certain. In such a case, land disposal of the affected subclass of wastes is prohibited unless the disposal site complies with minimum technological design standards and the generator certifies the absence of practical waste treatment alternatives. See, e.g., § 3004(g)(6)(A), 42 U.S.C. § 6924(g)(6)(A) (specifying the soft hammer for first-third wastes). A "hard hammer," banning waste disposal for all purposes, drops if regulations remain unpromulgated by an even later date. See, e.g., § 3004(g)(6)(C), 42 U.S.C. § 6924(g)(6)(C) (specifying the hard hammer for most hazardous wastes). The amended statute required EPA to enact regulations in accordance with the following dates:

Spent solvent and dioxin-containing wastes	November 8, 1986
California list wastes	July 8, 1987
First Third Wastes	August 8, 1988
Spent solvent, dioxin-containing, and California list soil and debris from CERCLA/RCRA Corrective Actions	November 8, 1988
Second Third Wastes	June 8, 1989
Third Third Wastes	May 8, 1990
Newly Identified Wastes	Within 6 months of identification as a hazardous waste

EPA moved on its mission with alacrity. As of May, 1991, hard hammer deadlines had fallen only for California list cyanides and metals. The agency promulgated regulations requiring hazardous wastes to be treated to levels that are achievable by use of the "best demonstrated available technology" ("BDAT") or be treated by methods that constitute BDAT. *See* 40 C.F.R. Part 268, Subpart D. EPA decided not to engage in comparative risk assessment in determining BDAT, and was upheld in that determination. *American Petroleum Inst. v. EPA*, 906 F.2d 729 (D.C. Cir. 1990). EPA's preferred treatment method for most hazardous wastes is incineration.

Notably, these "land ban" provisions offer some flexibility. If the EPA determines, "to a reasonable degree of certainty, that there will be no migration of hazardous constituents from the disposal unit or injection zone for as long as the wastes remain hazardous," the prohibition on land disposal may be lifted. § 3004(d), (e), (g), (m), 42 U.S.C. § 6924(d), (e), (g), (m). Additionally, once a waste has been treated to meet standards established by EPA pursuant to § 3004(m), 42 U.S.C. § 6924(m), it may be disposed of in land. EPA is authorized to grant exemptions upon a showing by an individual that a prohibition on land disposal is "not required in order to protect human health and the environment for as long as the waste remains hazardous. . . ." § 3004(d)(1), 42 U.S.C. § 6924(d)(1).

CHEMICAL WASTE MANAGEMENT, INC. v. U.S. ENVIRONMENTAL PROTECTION AGENCY

976 F.2d 2 (D.C.Cir. 1992)

JUDGES: Before EDWARDS, BUCKLEY, and HENDERSON, Circuit Judges.

Opinion Per Curiam:

[This litigation involved a variety of challenges to EPA's "third-third" rule, in place to regulate land disposal of certain wastes deemed to be hazardous because of their defined characteristics. EPA's rule was challenged as allegedly going beyond the authority of the agency, for being arbitrary and capricious, and for improperly modifying regulations previously in place under the Clean Water Act and the Safe Drinking Water Act. These challenges are discussed in the body of the opinion, which follows]:

. . . .

II. Treatment Standards for Characteristic Wastes

A. Proposed Rule

. . . [A]t the outset of the RCRA program, the EPA identified four characteristics as hazardous: ignitability, corrosivity, reactivity, and EP toxicity. In its proposed rules, and in the final regulations, the Agency divided characteristic wastes into subcategories, suggesting treatment standards or levels for each subcategory. For some of these, the EPA proposed treatment to reduce the presence of the characteristic below the level at which the waste was defined as hazardous. For example, a waste is considered corrosive, and therefore hazardous, if it is aqueous and has a pH of less than two or greater than 12.5. The proposed rule required treatment that would result in a pH between six and nine. *See* 54 Fed. Reg. 48,372, 48,422 (1989). For other subcategories, however, the EPA suggested treatment to the characteristic level and no further. *See id.* at 48,420–26 (setting treatment levels and standards).

The Agency stated that it possessed the authority to compel treatment below characteristic levels. *See* 54 Fed. Reg. at 48,419. It took note of the argument that the characteristic levels represent the limit of subtitle C authority — that the Agency had no power to regulate a waste where the characteristic had been brought below the level deemed hazardous. *Id.* at 48,490. The Agency believed, however, that section 3004(m) extended its authority beyond that point. "Once wastes become subject to section 3004(m), they remain subject to the requirements of that section until the section 3004(m) standard is satisfied." *Id.* The EPA concluded that it was directed by the statute to require a waste that is hazardous at the point of generation and is destined for land disposal to "be treated by methods which substantially reduce toxicity and minimize threats to human health and the environment." *Id.*

As to methods of treatment, the proposed rule largely followed the judgment made by the EPA in previous land-ban program rulemakings. In those earlier rules, the EPA determined that treatment would be accomplished through the use of "best demonstrated available technologies." *See, e.g.,* 51 Fed. Reg. 40,572, 40,578 (1986) (solvents and dioxins); 53 Fed. Reg. 31,138, 31,142 (1988) (first-third wastes). The proposed rule specified the particular technology to be used in the treatment of most ICR wastes.* *See* 54 Fed. Reg. at 48,420–26. For a handful of others, the Agency offered a measure of flexibility by creating a "deactivation" category of treatment. According to the proposal, the EPA had "determined that within [several ICR subcategories] there appear to be a further variety of different waste groups, each with a certain degree of uniqueness with respect to hazard and handling requirements." *Id.* at 48,419. Therefore, while the Agency recommended a number of methods, it proposed to allow generators or treaters of those wastes to select the appropriate method of treatment. *Id.* at 48,419–20.

---

* [Ed. note: "ICR" wastes are those hazardous due to ignitability, corrosivity, or reactivity.]

In implementing the land-ban program for solvents and wastes containing dioxins, the EPA barred dilution as an alternative for "adequate treatment." *See* 51 Fed. Reg. at 40,639. [codified at 40 C.F.R. § 268.3].* * *

At several points in the proposed third-third rule, the EPA reaffirmed its decision that a generator or treater might not dilute wastes to escape the dictates of the land disposal program. In its discussion of ignitable wastes, the Agency stated that "a prohibited form of dilution that is used to remove a characteristic from a prohibited hazardous waste would be a violation of the dilution prohibition in [40 C.F.R.] section 268.3." 54 Fed. Reg. at 48,422. Among the EPA's concerns was the possibility that dilution of ignitable wastes would lead to dangerous emissions of volatile organic compounds, a problem that could be avoided by using other treatment methods. *Id.* "Accordingly, the Agency believes that dilution should not be a legitimate method for treating ignitable wastes." *Id.*

The EPA proposed a similar bar with regard to reactive wastes: "Dilution of reactive wastes should not automatically be considered to be a legitimate form of treatment." *Id.* at 48,426. It proposed that reactive cyanides and sulfides be treated like any toxic waste; "with respect to other reactive wastes, most cannot be diluted without violent reaction so that dilution is not a viable management alternative[.]" *Id.*

Finally, the EPA suggested that corrosives be treated by neutralization, not dilution, to alter their pH. *Id.* at 48,422–23. According to the Agency, dilution would require the use of large amounts of water and would create a greater volume of waste; moreover, dilution "does not treat or remove hazardous constituents in the wastes." *Id.* at 48,423. * * *

B. Final Rule

In the final rule, the EPA revised many of its proposed treatment standards for ICR and toxic characteristic wastes. The EPA, however, did not back away from its basic position that it could require treatment below characteristic levels. Because "Congress has given apparently conflicting guidance on how the Agency should address land disposal prohibitions for characteristic wastes," the EPA "believes it has authority to reconcile these potential conflicts and to harmonize statutory provisions to forge a coherent regulatory system." 55 Fed. Reg. at 22,651. The EPA agreed with many participants in the comment period that "one permissible construction of the language in section 3004(g)" (which requires the promulgation of regulations "prohibiting . . . methods of land disposal of the [listed] hazardous wastes") is that subtitle C rules applied only to hazardous wastes, and therefore the applicability of the land disposal regulations must be judged at the moment of disposal. 55 Fed. Reg. at 22,652. Ultimately, the EPA concluded that Congress did not state when the status of the waste should be evaluated for purposes of the ban on land disposal; therefore, the EPA could choose to regulate the waste "at the point of generation or at the point of disposal (and possibly at some other point or combination of the two)." *Id.*

While viewing its authority broadly, the EPA decided to exercise it sparingly:

Today's rule reflects a decision to take limited, but nonetheless significant, steps within the point of generation framework. As a general matter, the Agency believes that the goals of [the program] may require application of standards which go beyond the characteristic level . . . in some future cases.

Id. at 22,654. The final regulations call for treatment below characteristic levels for only a handful of wastes. Among ICR wastes, ignitable liquids with high total organic carbons (a subset of the subcategory of ignitable liquids for which the proposed rule required treatment to below characteristic levels by technology), *see id.* at 22,543–44, and reactive cyanides, *see id.* at 22,550c-51, would be subject to enhanced treatment. The Agency backed away from its original plan to mandate enhanced treatment for corrosive characteristic wastes.

The EPA determined that for most ICR wastes, treatment to characteristic levels would be sufficient. The Agency found upon review that

the environmental concerns from the properties of ignitability, corrosivity, and reactivity are different from the environmental concern from EP toxic wastes. Toxic constituents can pose a cumulative impact on land disposal even where waste is below the characteristic level. Where wastes pose an ascertainable toxicity concern . . . the Agency has developed treatment standards that address the toxicity concern and (in effect) require treatment below the characteristic level. . . . Otherwise, treatment that removes the properties of ignitability, corrosivity, and reactivity, fully addresses the environmental concern from the properties themselves.

Id. at 22,655.

The EPA also retreated from its emphasis on technology-based treatment in the final regulations, altering its position on the use of dilution as a method of treatment:

In all cases, the Agency has determined that for non-toxic hazardous characteristic wastes, it should not matter how the characteristic property is removed so long as it is removed. Thus, dilution is an acceptable treatment method for such wastes.

Id. at 22,532. The Agency included dilution within the ambit of the "deactivation" treatment standard. The final rule defined the standard as "deactivation to remove the hazardous characteristics of a waste due to its ignitability, corrosivity, and/or reactivity." *Id.* at 22,693. As long as these characteristics are removed, any method can be employed under the final regulations. The EPA allowed full discretion among specified technological methods of treatment (such as neutralization or incineration) as well as dilution with water or other wastes. For toxic wastes, the prohibition on dilution remained. *See id.* at 22,656.

The Agency admitted that it

believes the mixing of waste streams to eliminate certain characteristics is appropriate treatment for most wastes which are purely corrosive, or in some cases, reactive or ignitable. As a general matter, these are properties which can effectively be removed by mixing.

Id. (emphasis added). It further conceded that

this approach does not fully address the potential problem of toxic constituents that may be present in such wastes, nor encourages minimization or recovery of non-toxic characteristic hazardous wastes. EPA has determined that these potential problems should be addressed, if at all, in other rulemakings . . . and are too difficult to resolve in this proceeding, given the extraordinary pressures and limited review time imposed by the May 8 [1990] statutory deadline.

Id. at 22,665–66. Only in three subcategories of ICR wastes did the EPA mandate the use of technological treatment: reactive sulfides, 57 Fed. Reg. 8,086, 8,089 (1992) (technical correction to third-third rule); reactive cyanides, 55 Fed. Reg. at 22,551; and ignitable liquid nonwastewater wastes containing more than ten percent total organic compounds, *id.* at 22,544. For all corrosive wastes, other ignitable liquid wastes (nonwastewaters with low total organic compounds and ignitable wastewaters), ignitable compressed gases, ignitable reactive wastes, explosive wastes, water reactives, and other reactives dilution would be acceptable. *Id.* at 22,543–53. . . .

D. Industry Petitioners' Challenge to the Treatment Standards

Industry petitioners contend that RCRA does not provide authority for the EPA to mandate treatment of characteristic wastes after their ignitability, corrosiveness, reactivity, or EP toxicity has been addressed. They make a straightforward argument: Subtitle C regulations attach to a waste only when it is hazardous. The moment a waste ceases to meet the regulatory definition of a hazardous waste, the EPA loses its authority to regulate further. Thus, in industry petitioners' view, RCRA's cradle-to-grave system covers waste only if it remains hazardous throughout its life and at the moment of its burial.

Industry petitioners point to a welter of provisions in RCRA where the words "hazardous waste" are used as proof that the statute applies only to waste defined as hazardous. Subtitle C, they explain, is entitled "Hazardous Waste Management," and the entire subtitle addresses that problem — the management of hazardous waste. They add that some statements by the EPA have suggested the same reading of the statute. *See, e.g.,* 54 Fed. Reg. 1,056, 1,093 (1989) (a waste that no longer exhibits a hazardous characteristic "is no longer subject to the requirements of Subtitle C of RCRA").

In their view, the 1984 Amendments did not change this boundary. They point out that land disposal is defined in part as "any placement of such hazardous waste in a landfill, [or] surface impoundment," RCRA § 3004(k), 42 U.S.C. § 6924(k); that section 3004(g) similarly "prohibits one or more methods of land disposal of [] hazardous wastes," *id.* § 6924(g)(5); and, finally, that section 3004(m) authorizes land disposal of hazardous waste that has been treated, suggesting to industry petitioners that the provision specifically authorizes only the disposal of wastes that remain hazardous after treatment. Thus, they conclude, the disposal restrictions can apply only to wastes that are hazardous at the moment of disposal. . . .

. . . The Agency reasons that the subtitle C program can attach at the point of generation, and the broad language of section 3004(m)(1) allows additional treatment to remove risks posed by wastes beyond those inherent in the characteristic. * * *

. . . In *API [v. EPA,* 906 F.2d 729 (D.C. Cir. 1990)], we explained that "once a waste is listed or identified as hazardous, its subsequent management is regulated." *API,* 906 F.2d at 733. After the 1984 Amendments, we added, regulation of the waste included the prohibitions of section 3004. *Id.* In *Shell Oil,* we noted that the power to manage waste is created "at [the] point" a waste is defined as hazardous and discarded. *Shell Oil,* 950 F.2d at 754. Once in the system, we found that the power to manage hazardous waste provided by RCRA gave the EPA the authority to regulate waste until "it ceases to pose a hazard to the public." *Id.; see also* RCRA § 1004(7), 42 U.S.C. § 6903(7) (defining "hazardous waste management"). . . .

The 1984 Amendments also provide the EPA with the authority to mandate treatment past the point at which a characteristic is removed. Section 3004(g)(5) requires the Administrator to promulgate regulations prohibiting land disposal of hazardous wastes "except with respect to a hazardous waste which has complied with the pretreatment regulations promulgated under subsection (m) of this section." 42 U.S.C. § 6924(g)(5). Subsection (m)(1), in turn, calls on the Administrator to

> specify[ ] those levels or methods of treatment, if any, which substantially diminish the toxicity of the waste or substantially reduce the likelihood of migration of hazardous constituents from the waste so that short-term and long-term threats to human health and the environment are minimized.

RCRA § 3004(m)(1), 42 U.S.C. § 6924(m)(1). The requirement that treatment "substantially diminish the toxicity" or substantially reduce the likelihood of migration of hazardous constituents suggests concerns that go beyond the characteristics identified in 40 C.F.R. Part 261, subpart C. Similarly, in concluding that the EPA had the authority to require technologies that go beyond the elimination of hazardous characteristics, we have noted that "minimize" offers a broad mandate: "To 'minimize' something is, to quote the Oxford English Dictionary, to 'reduce [it] to the smallest possible amount, extent, or degree.'" *HWTC III,* 886 F.2d at 361. * * *

E. NRDC Petitioners' Challenge to Deactivation Treatment Standard

NRDC petitioners ask this court to vacate the deactivation treatment standard as applied to ICR wastes because it authorizes the dilution of these wastes to eliminate their ignitability, corrosiveness, or reactivity rather than mandating use of technological treatment. . . .

. . . In their view, the removal of these characteristics through dilution only affects the short-term risk that the waste will manifest that property; it does not address the threats posed by the hazardous organic and inorganic constituents of those wastes. * * *

We believe that dilution can, in principle, constitute an acceptable form of treatment for ICR wastes. We do not read the 1984 Amendments as mandating the use of the best demonstrated available technologies ("BDAT") in all situations. . . .

We agree that [Section 3004(m)(1)] imposes an exacting standard: It requires that treatment prior to land disposal "substantially diminish the toxicity of the waste or substantially reduce the likelihood of migration of hazardous constituents from the waste so that short-term and long-term threats to human health and the environment are minimized." RCRA 3004(m)(1), 42 U.S.C. § 6924(m)(1). But this provision does not bar dilution as a means of treating ICR wastes; instead, it defines the purposes that a method of treatment must achieve. Any treatment that meets those objectives is permissible. When read against RCRA's broad definition of treatment, we cannot say Congress clearly barred dilution as an acceptable methodology. . . .

[In applying this test, the court affirmed generally the agency's use of dilution as a treatment method for corrosive wastes, but objected to its use as treatment for ignitable or reactive waste.

[Later in the opinion, the court addressed the impact, if any, of the RCRA third third rule on surface impoundments usually regulated under the Clean Water Act. These impoundments can accept characteristic wastes as part of their waste stream. Because surface impoundments constitute "land disposal" for RCRA purposes, the issue arose whether surface impoundments accepting such wastes should be subject to RCRA requirements, CWA requirements, or both. Held the court]:

We already have held that RCRA section 3004(m)(1) requires treatment both to remove the characteristic and to substantially reduce the toxicity of all hazardous constituents present in the characteristic waste. The treatment standards are the core of RCRA's hazardous waste management scheme, and nothing in RCRA or the CWA permits the EPA to establish different treatment standards when wastewaters are treated in CWA systems instead of facilities operated solely to RCRA standards. Nevertheless, Congress, when enacting RCRA, was cognizant of the substantial development of CWA systems, and, thus, permitted regulatory "accommodation" of RCRA and CWA systems. Thus, we agree with the EPA that, under RCRA, diluted formerly characteristic wastes may be placed in subtitle D surface impoundments which are part of an integrated CWA treatment train. However, in order for true "accommodation" to be accomplished, we find that RCRA treatment requirements cannot be ignored merely because CWA is implicated; that is, the CWA does not override RCRA. Thus, we hold that, whenever wastes are put in CWA surface impoundments before they have been treated pursuant to RCRA to reduce the toxicity of all hazardous constituents, these wastes must be so treated before exiting the CWA treatment facilities. In other words, CWA facilities handling characteristic wastes must remove the characteristic and decrease the toxicity of the waste's hazardous constituents to the same degree that treatment outside a CWA system would. * * *

. . . Congress, when enacting RCRA, recognized that prior environmental statutes, such as the Clean Water Act, would need to be accommodated.

The Administrator shall integrate all provisions of this chapter for purposes of administration and enforcement and shall avoid duplication, to the maximum extent practicable, with the appropriate provisions of the . . . Federal Water Pollution Control Act [and] the Safe Drinking Water Act . . ., and such other Acts of Congress as grant regulatory authority to the Administrator. Such integration shall be effected only to the extent that it can be done in a manner consistent with the goals and policies expressed in this chapter and in the other acts referred to in this subsection.

RCRA § 1006(b)(1), 42 U.S.C. § 6905(b)(1) (1988); see 55 Fed. Reg. at 22,654, 22,657. The EPA's decision to permit "decharacterized" hazardous wastes to be deposited in surface impoundments as part of continuing treatment is a reasonable accommodation.

We wish to make explicit the impact of our holding because we find merit in significant parts of both parties' positions. First, where dilution to remove the characteristic meets the definition of treatment under section 3004(m)(1), nothing more is required. Second, where dilution removes the characteristic but does not "treat" the waste by reducing the toxicity of hazardous constituents, then the decharacterized waste may be placed in a surface impoundment if and only if the resulting CWA treatment fully complies with RCRA § 3004(m)(1). In other words, the material that comes out of CWA treatment facilities that employ surface impoundments must remove the hazardous constituents to the same extent that any other treatment facility that complies with RCRA does.[5]

. . . [T]his case differs from *API*, 906 F.2d 729. In that case, which considered aspects of the first-third rule, several industry representatives challenged the EPA's decision not to consider land treatment as a form of treatment for hazardous wastes under section 3004(m)(1). The court affirmed the EPA's action, ruling that land treatment was a form of land disposal and that "RCRA clearly specifies . . . that hazardous wastes must be treated before being land disposed." *Id.* at 735. The *API* court also noted that "pursuant to 42 U.S.C. § 6925(j)(11), Congress allowed surface impoundments (a type of land disposal unit under § 6924(k)) to receive, on an interim basis, hazardous wastes that have not been treated to meet § 6924(m) standards" only so long as the impoundments met certain minimum technological standards. *Id.* at 736; see RCRA § 3004(o)(1), 42 U.S.C. § 6924(o)(1) (1988) (requiring double-lining, leachate collection and groundwater monitoring). Here, however, the liquids, at the time they are placed in the surface impoundments, are not technically "hazardous wastes," although they are fully subject to RCRA's strictures because they were hazardous and have not yet met the treatment requirements. Additionally, the liquids here are only placed in the surface impoundments temporarily; in API, the "land treatment" represented the final resting place of the hazardous wastes. . . .

---

[5] To illustrate RCRA's focus on treatment of the hazardous constituents in a waste, consider a waste stream hazardous by characteristic for cadmium. Both the characteristic and treatment levels for the hazardous waste are 1.0 mg/l. Assume that a stream of 3.0 mg/l daily deposits 1000 liters into a treatment facility. A RCRA treatment facility would remove at least 2000 mg of cadmium from the waste stream. A CWA treatment facility must do the same — although to do so it will have to process at least three times as much water (because dilution of 1000 liters of 3.0 mg/l to just below the characteristic level will yield just over 3000 liters). Allowing dilution alone would decharacterize the waste, but it would not reduce the total amount of cadmium entering the environment. One thousand liters of 3.0 mg/l cadmium yields the same amount of hazardous constituent as 3000 liters of 1.0 mg/l cadmium.

B. Deep Injection Wells Regulated Under the Safe Drinking Water Act

1. Generally

. . . Consistent with our resolution of the Clean Water Act systems issue, we hold that dilution followed by injection into a deep well is permissible only where dilution itself fully meets section 3004(m)(1) standards or where the waste will subsequently meet section 3004(m)(1) standards. Because is permanent land disposal, our holding in effect permits diluted decharacterized wastes to be deep well injected only when dilution meets the section 3004(m)(1) standard or where the deep well secures a no-migration variance. . . .

[Portions of the opinion dealing with issues of administrative law are omitted].

3. Should Rule 268.3(b) Include Listed Wastes for which the EPA has Developed Concentration-Based Treatment Standards?

[In discussing this question, the court held the rule to be adequate, in major part because of the difference between listed and characteristic wastes. Said the court: "listed wastes generally contain a certain substance that is per se harmful (such as arsenic). Dilution does nothing to remove that element from the waste stream and prevent it from entering the environment where it may reaccumulate. By contrast, some characteristic wastes may be altered permanently by dilution and, hence, it is reasonable to permit aggregation. In these cases, dilution and treatment are one and the same[.]"

[The remainder of the opinion is omitted].

NOTES

1. On March 26, 1996, President Clinton signed into law the so-called "rifle shot bill," which revised RCRA by relaxing Subtitle C treatment standards for decharacterized hazardous wastes headed for disposal in facilities regulated under the Clean Water Act and the Safe Drinking Water Act. The law, a bipartisan effort, was an attempt to address regulatory problems that arise when more than one regulatory regime applies to a single set of circumstances (in a given case, for example, a single activity might be regulable as a point source under the CWA, as an injection well under the Safe Drinking Water Act (*see* Note 2, *infra*, and *Chemical Waste Management, supra*) and as a TSDF under RCRA). Certain holdings of *Chemical Waste Management* (not reproduced here) were overturned by Congress in that measure. The Act, formally titled the Land Disposal Program Flexibility Act of 1996, was codified as part of RCRA itself. The amendatory provisions regarding land disposal are found at RCRA § 3004((g)(7)–(11).

2. *Safe Drinking Water Act*: The Safe Drinking Water Act ("SDWA"), 42 U.S.C. § 300f *et seq.*, is a federal statute that moves in the same circles as RCRA. The SDWA is divided into two parts. The first deals with public water supplies, the entities that deliver drinking water to your faucet (Part B). The

second, of relevance to RCRA, deals with "underground injection" of "contaminants" which "endanger[s]" 'underground sources of drinking water' (Part C). Part C of the SDWA has traditionally been the legal control on injection into "wells" (at least where an "underground source of drinking water" is implicated)." For that reason, RCRA has often taken a back seat when well injection is involved, even though it could be used: as you know, RCRA addresses all "disposal" of "solid wastes," even if by the mechanism of "injection." *See* § 1004(3), 42 U.S.C. § 6903(3) (defining "disposal" as including "injection").

In 1984, however, Congress added § 3004(f), 42 U.S.C. § 6924(f), to RCRA to deal with disposal of hazardous wastes into deep injection wells, and § 3020, 42 U.S.C. § 6939b, to deal with interim control of hazardous waste injection. These new provisions are broader in scope than the companion provisions in the SDWA, in that they protect from well injection groundwater resources not designated as underground sources of drinking water. The provisions in RCRA, as interpreted by EPA, prohibit all "migration of hazardous constituents from the disposal unit or injection zone for as long as the wastes remain hazardous." EPA determined that "wastes" means wastes that migrate outside the injection zone, that "migration" encompasses not only fluid migration, but also migration by molecular diffusion, and that an injector must demonstrate compliance with the no-migration standard for as long as the wastes remain hazardous, or for 10,000 years, whichever is shorter. These regulatory provisions were upheld on review. *Natural Resources Defense Council v. U.S. Environmental Protection Agency*, 907 F.2d 1146 (D.C. Cir. 1990).

3. Since RCRA's enactment in 1976, the EPA has regulated hazardous waste disposal closely but has been less attentive to solid waste regulation. This is purportedly because hazardous waste poses a greater risk to public health. Given that hypothesis, it is notable that EPA commented, in an October 9, 1991, Federal Register notice, that available data "do not provide strong support for distinguishing the health and environmental threats" presented by solid waste disposal as compared to hazardous waste disposal.

[b] CORRECTIVE ACTION

As Congress considered its 1984 Amendments to RCRA, it learned that the problem with hazardous waste facilities was not just about operation and maintenance. It was also about past performance. About 5700 active RCRA-regulated hazardous waste facilities had already contaminated soils and groundwater, and a great deal of that contamination needed rectification. Indeed, the clean-up task was ominous: the cost of restoring privately owned RCRA Subtitle C sites alone had been projected at nearly $42 billion, and contamination from federal facilities likely would add millions to that figure.

The original RCRA, however, did not contain any provisions requiring clean-up at regulated TSDFs. Congress took care of that problem in the HSWA by creating a new program known as Corrective Action ("CA"). The major CA provisions are found in two short subsections, §§ 3004(u) and (v), 42 U.S.C. §§ 6924(u) and (v). Section 3004(u), the more significant of the two provisions, specifies that all RCRA permits issued after November 8, 1984, must contain requirements for "corrective action for all releases of hazardous wastes or hazardous constituents from any solid waste management unit" located at the permitted facility "regardless of the time at which waste was placed in the unit." Section 3004(v) expressly extends the corrective action requirement to pollution that has made its way beyond the boundaries of the affected facility.

These provisions are complemented by others. Section 3013, 42 U.S.C. § 6934, adopted originally in 1980, authorizes EPA to require owners and operators of TSDFs to monitor, test, and take other action to determine if environmental damage has occurred. If the required information is either not forthcoming or is unsatisfactory, EPA can do the investigation itself and seek cost reimbursement. § 3013(d)(1), 42 U.S.C. § 6934(d)(1). *But see* § 3013(d)(2), 42 U.S.C. § 6934(d)(2). In addition, Section 3008(h), 42 U.S.C. § 6928(h), empowers EPA to issue corrective action orders for interim status facilities, and § 7003, 42 U.S.C. § 6973, part of the original 1976 statutory enactment but amended a couple of times thereafter, allows EPA to bring enforcement actions in cases presenting "imminent and substantial endangerment to health or the environment."

Under the terms of § 3004(u), all *releases* of *hazardous wastes or constituents* from *any solid waste management unit* at a TSD *facility seeking a permit* are now subject to corrective action requirements. Elaborating these requirements has been a daunting task for EPA: it took the agency six years to simply issue proposed rules to implement the section, and still only small portions of the overall program are under promulgated regulations. Even though the July 27, 1990, regulation remains a proposal only, EPA uses it as guidance for its corrective action decisions.

In understanding this section, the relevant questions are: (1) which are the TSD facilities "seeking a permit;" (2) what is a "facility;" (3) what is a "solid waste management unit;" (4) what are "hazardous wastes or constituents;" and (5) what are "releases." Note that the meanings of these terms for CA purposes may differ from their meanings for other statutory purposes.

(1) *"Seeking a permit"*: Under RCRA § 3005, all owners and operators of an "existing facility or planning to construct a new facility for the treatment, storage, or disposal of hazardous waste . . . [must secure] . . . a permit. . . ." Clearly, then, when one submits a permit application, that TSDF becomes subject to the CA program. What do you project would be the result if a person violated § 3005 by receiving hazardous wastes without benefit of a permit? Would that person be free of CA requirements? *See* 40 C.F.R. 264.101 (no).

Note in this regard that not all TSD facilities need a permit. Those that never fell within RCRA's regulatory reach are exempt. These are the sites where all treatment, storage, and disposal of hazardous wastes took place before November 19, 1980, the date EPA's initial Subtitle C regulations took effect. Sites which were regulated under RCRA but which obtained a "closure" certificate by January 26, 1983, are also exempt from CA requirements.

(2) *"Facility"*: Corrective action requirements apply to facilities, which have been defined by EPA in the July 27 Rulemaking as including "all contiguous property" under the control of a single owner or operator. *See* 55 Fed. Reg. 30808 (July 27, 1990).

(3) *"Solid Waste Management Unit"* or *"SWMU"*: EPA defined this term as:

Any discernible unit at which solid wastes have been placed at any time, irrespective of whether the unit was intended for the management of solid or hazardous waste. Such units include any area at a facility at which solid wastes have been routinely and systematically released.

55 Fed. Reg. 30,808 (July 27, 1990).

What is a "discernible unit"? EPA explains the term as including units "typically" under RCRA, such as landfills and land treatment units, impoundments, waste piles, tanks, containers, container storage areas, wells, incinerators, waste recycle operations, and the like.

As the definition indicates, SWMUs are also areas "at which solid wastes have been routinely and systematically released." EPA includes in this category loading areas, where spillage can commonly occur, solvent washing areas, and even "kickback drippage" areas, which are storage places for pressure-treated wood and where substances applied to the wood might leak into soils.

Would a facility roadway traveled by trucks carrying hazardous wastes be such an area? What if a truck had an accident that resulted in a release? How about a sewer or a ditch which conveys wastes?

(4) *"Hazardous wastes or constituents"*: As we have seen in this Chapter, hazardous wastes under RCRA are those listed specifically as hazardous or having hazardous characteristics. *See* § 3001, 42 U.S.C. § 6921. Also hazardous for RCRA CA purposes are wastes identified under the "derived-from" rule, the "mixture" rule, and the "contained-in" interpretation. *See supra.*

Materials subject to CA, however, also include solid wastes with hazardous constituents. This language means that a subset of solid wastes, those with hazardous constituents, fall under the CA program, even if those wastes do not rise to the level of hazardous wastes.

(5) *"Release"*: There must be a "release" to trigger CA responsibility. We will discuss "releases" in Chapter 12, *infra.*

[c] UNDERGROUND STORAGE TANKS

In contrast to the relatively few hazardous waste facilities, there currently exist two million underground storage tanks ("USTs") at more than 75,000 sites. Ziegele and Evans, *Regulating Underground Storage Tank Systems*, 27 Trial 34 (Sept. 1991). The vast majority of USTs are made of bare steel and contain petroleum, and at least one hundred thousand of them are leaking. *Id.* USTs leak because of corrosion, improper installation, overfilling, mechanical compromises caused by pressurization, and for other reasons. Upon escape, leaking materials can contaminate groundwater. Since groundwater provides over 50% of the nation's drinking water, and 95% in rural areas, and since a single drop of gasoline can ruin a gallon of water, leaks can occasion serious consequences.

To address this problem, Congress in the Hazardous and Solid Waste Amendments of 1984 added Subchapter IX to RCRA. The Subchapter applies to "underground storage tanks" containing "regulated substances." "Underground storage tanks" are defined as:

any one or combination of tanks (including underground pipes connected thereto) which is used to contain an accumulation of regulated substances, and the volume of which (including the volume of the underground pipes connected thereto) is 10 per centum or more beneath the surface of the ground, but does not include any —

(A) farm or residential tank of 1,100 gallons or less capacity used for storing motor fuel for non-commercial purposes,

(B) tank used for storing heating oil for consumptive use on the premises where stored,

(C) septic tank,

(D) pipeline facility (including gathering lines) . . .,

(E) surface impoundment, pit, pond, or lagoon,

(F) storm water or waste water collection system,

(G) flow-through process tank,

(H) liquid trap or associated gathering lines directly related to oil and gas production and gathering operations, or

(I) storage tank situated in an underground area (such as a basement, cellar, mineworking, drift, shaft, or tunnel) if the storage tank is situated upon or above the surface of the floor.

§ 9001(1), 42 U.S.C. § 6991(1).

"Regulated substances" include petroleum and hazardous substances (as defined in CERCLA), but not hazardous wastes regulated under Subchapter III. § 9001(2), 42 U.S.C. § 6991(2). Of the regulated tanks, 49% are owned by gas stations and 47% are owned by other industries that store petroleum for their own purposes. Less than 5% of regulated tanks contain hazardous materials.

Subchapter IX is specifically directed to "owners and operators" of USTs. In a major sense, these terms are undefined: the statute characterizes owners as persons "who own" and operators as persons involved in daily "operation." §§ 9001(3)–(4), 42 U.S.C. §§ 6991(3)–(4). But the statute does draw some limits on the definitions. First, the definition of "owner" is divided into two parts. If the UST was in use on the effective date of the HSWA, or November 8, 1984, or brought into use thereafter, the "owner" subject to regulation is the current owner, that is, the person holding title at the time the lawsuit is brought. § 9001(3), 42 U.S.C. § 6991(3). If the UST, however, was out of service before November 8, 1984, the "owner" is "any person who owned such tank immediately before the discontinuation of its use." § 9001(4), 42 U.S.C. § 6991(4). While this definition allows for current and past owners to be liable, for the most part, the number of liable owners in any given case is limited to one. The definition of "operator" is not similarly bifurcated. An "operator" is "any person in control of, or having responsibility for, the daily operation of the underground storage tank." § 9001(4), 42 U.S.C. § 6991(4). It is uncertain whether this definition contemplates liability for past operators. As with "owners," it seems that liability is largely limited to one operator per UST. Outside of several cases in the 7th Circuit, there is little judicial discussion of the meaning of this provision or the meaning of these statutory terms. *See, e.g., Singer v. Bulk Petroleum Corp.*, 9 F. Supp. 2d 916 (N.D. Ill. 1998).

Subchapter IX establishes a comprehensive regulatory regime. First, section 9001a(a)(1), 42 U.S.C. § 6991a(a)(1), requires owners to notify state or local environmental agencies of their tanks, as well as information about "age, size, type, location and uses. . . ." *Id.* Those agencies in turn are instructed to compile inventories of tanks and to supply that information to the EPA. § 9001a(c), 42 U.S.C. § 6991a(c). EPA's obligation is to promulgate "release detection, prevention and correction regulations applicable to all owners and operators of underground storage tanks, as may be necessary to protect human health and the environment." § 9003(a), 42 U.S.C. § 6991b(a). EPA's regulations, found at 40 C.F.R. § 280.60 *et seq.*, impose automatic clean-up responsibility for leaks. 40 C.F.R. § 280.64(a). The regulations also establish requirements for spill and overfill control, corrosion protection, and release detection; procedural requirements for reporting, investigating, confirming and recording release incidents; abatement measures, free product removal, and corrective action standards; standards for closure; and, added in 1989, financial requirements for owners and operators.

Should a leak be discovered, owners and operators must take immediate action to report the release, to prevent its continuation, and to mitigate fire, explosion, and vapor hazards. 40 C.F.R. § 280.61. Initial abatement actions include removal of the regulated substance from the UST, prevention of further migration of the materials into soils and waters, and monitoring. 40 C.F.R. § 280.62. Depending on circumstances, permanent clean-up may need to accord with a corrective action plan. 40 C.F.R. § 280.66. Subject to limitations, the EPA is authorized to undertake clean-up of petroleum releases on its own if the action is necessary to protect human health and the environment. § 9003(h)(2), 42 U.S.C. § 6991b(h)(2). *See generally* Gauthier, *The Enforcement of Federal Underground Storage Tank Regulations*, 20 Envtl. L. 261 (1990); Day-Wilson, *Federal Environmental Issues In Commercial Leasing Transactions: A Practitioner's Guide*, 2 Envtl. L. 597 (1996).

Just as RCRA calls for state participation in the overall regulatory effort *(see, supra), so also does it call for state participation in the UST program. § 9004, 42 U.S.C. § 6991c.*

Since RCRA does not allow for private parties to recover damages or clean-up costs, private parties seeking such relief typically must rely on common law. *See generally,* Chapter 2, *supra.* In early leaking underground storage tank ("LUST") litigation, strict liability proved to be a useful tool on the theory that UST operation is abnormally dangerous activity. Acknowledging that USTs are very common and are valuable in comparison to the dangers they pose in the current day, courts hesitate to employ strict liability theories liberally. *See* Basile, *Still No Remedy After All These Years: Plugging the Hole in the Law of Leaking Underground Storage Tanks*, 73 Ind. L.J. 675 (1998). Still, the case can be made upon a showing that a tank is poorly situated, as, for example, if it is located near a well, *see, e.g., (Yommer v. McKenzie*, 257 A.2d 138 (Md. 1969), or by a showing that the tank's size is uncommon or inappropriate, *see, e.g., City of Northglenn v. Chevron, Inc.*, 519 F. Supp. 515

(D. Colo. 1981). *See also* Hayward, *Common Law Remedies and the UST Regulations,* 21 B.C. Envt'l Aff. L. Rev. 619 (1994). In the absence of strict liability, plaintiffs must typically rely on conventional negligence, nuisance, and trespass theories, or on contract theories. For a more detailed discussion of common law actions in both tort and contract, see Maher, *Lesson in L.U.S.T: The Complete Story of Liability for Leaking Underground Storage Tanks,* 16 N. Ill. U. L. Rev. 581 (1996). On some occasions, state statutes may operate to preempt rights of plaintiffs to sue under common law theories. *See generally,* Chapter 2 *supra.*

Recently controversial is the matter of methyl tertiary butyl ether ("MTBE") leakage from USTs. MTBE is a gasoline additive that increases octane in premium-grade fuel and helps improve air quality by reducing the concentration of ozone-forming compounds in tailpipe emissions. MTBE, however, is also an animal carcinogen that can, even in extremely small quantities, make water unfit for consumption. *See* Hinck, *Testing the Waters in MTBE Litigation,* 37 JUL Trial 44 (2001). MTBE, moreover, is hydrophilic, or water-seeking; thus, upon escaping an UST, it travels quickly through soil and into groundwater. When this happens, lawsuits are sure to follow. For example, numerous MTBE suits have been filed in the states of California, Connecticut, Florida, New Jersey, and New York, alleging claims ranging from negligence and trespass to illegal and unfair business practices to even infliction of emotional distress and fear of future injury. *See, eg.* Hinck, *supra;* Faulk, Berlanga, et. al., *Salem Revisited: Updating the MTBE Controversy,* SF97 ALI-ABA 949 (2001).

An ancillary dispute involves the question whether groundwater contamination lawsuits can be brought as class actions. Courts are split on the question. *See, e.g., Sterling v. Veliscol Chemical Corp.,* 855 F.2d 1188 (6th Cir. 1988) (class action allowed); *Millett v. Atlantic Richfield Co.,* 760 A.2d 250 (Me. 2000) (class action not allowed).

Chapter 12

THE COMPREHENSIVE ENVIRONMENTAL RESPONSE, COMPENSATION AND LIABILITY ACT ("CERCLA")

It's an ill bird that fouls his own nest. — *Latin Proverb*

A. INTRODUCTION

As we have seen in the preceding three Chapters, the goal of federal environmental law has been the elimination or curtailment of pollution. This approach is premised on the idea that once the persistent burden of additional pollution is lifted, the receiving "media" (*e.g.* the ambient air or water) can get about the task of cleaning themselves by natural processes. In major measure, this approach has worked: ambient air is much cleaner nationally than it once was, and many stream segments are supporting aquatic life once again.

This convenient self-cleaning feature, however, has worked less well in the third medium of pollutant disposal — land. Rather than cleanse itself, land tends to hold pollution in place, often for many years. This unhappy geologic fact burst into public consciousness with the episode at Love Canal in 1978. The Hooker Chemical Company, it was learned at that time, had buried about 28,500 tons of hazardous chemicals in a 16-acre site in the Niagara Falls, New York, area from 1942 to 1953. Using a deed which both disclosed the dumping activity and disclaimed future responsibility for it, the company sold the contaminated land to the local school board for a single dollar. As time passed, populations moved in and the site evolved into a residential community known as Love Canal.

In 1978, after a spate of heavy rains, Hooker's chemical mix leached into the yards and homes of many of Love Canal's residents. Spurred by the image of schoolchildren playing in toxic substances, these families were hastily evacuated, and what was an active neighborhood quickly became an eerie ghost town. Allegations of birth defects, miscarriages, skin irritations, and respiratory ailments soon followed, as did revelations of "other Love Canals," such as the infamous "Valley of the Drums" in Kentucky, and Meadowlands in New Jersey. [1]

The nation was horrified at all of this, and Congress reacted swiftly. In 1980, it enacted the Comprehensive Environmental Response, Compensation, and Liability Act ("CERCLA"), better known as "Superfund." CERCLA was to be the vehicle by which thousands of abandoned hazardous waste dumps would be cleaned. (CERCLA would be joined in 1984 by the Solid and Hazardous Waste Amendments to the Resource Conservation and Recovery Act, which established the corrective action program (*see* Chapter 11, *supra*) and in 1990 by the Oil Pollution Act ("OPA"), 33 U.S.C. § 2701 *et seq.*, Congress's response to the Exxon Valdez oil spill in Alaskan waters. The OPA is aimed at the clean-up of contaminated waterways.

CERCLA is the touchstone of this new era in environmental law. Unlike the CAA, CWA, and RCRA, CERCLA's purpose is not behavior modification. It does not protect environmental quality by telling persons how to alter their pollution-causing activities. Its mission, rather, is the repair of environmental harms already done. CERCLA looks to restore damaged sites to pre-contamination, less unhealthful, condition.

The Love Canal-prompted interest in giving the land a good scrubbing produced a statute dramatically different in design than the pollution control measures that preceded it. CERCLA (a) looks backward, not forward; (b) directly addresses both environmental quality and public health protection; and (c) creates liability in the absence of conventional considerations of fault. It thereby gathers under its regulatory umbrella entire classes of persons

---

[1] Hooker was later found to be negligent in the Love Canal case for failing to notify the board that chemicals were buried, often in shallow graves, in the central part of the school site; for failing to respond adequately when it learned that children were actually playing with and being harmed by the dumped material; and for failing to work harder to keep residents off the property. *See* BNA Daily Environment Report, Item 3 (March 18, 1994).

In succeeding years, the case remained active. In 1994, a federal court determined punitive damages were not called for in the case. *See U.S. v. Hooker Chemicals and Plastics Corp.*, 850 F. Supp. 993 (W.D.N.Y. 1994): "Although Hooker's activities after the transfer [to the school board] were clearly unacceptable by present standards and at times violative of common sense, in general, given the state of scientific knowledge and the legal principles of that time, they did not exhibit the degree of recklessness which would warrant a punitive damages award." *Id.* at 1068. The court noted that while information about the quantity and composition of chemicals was never revealed to the school board, still there was no effort to deliberately withhold that information. *Id.*

On June 21, 1994, the parties agreed to a settlement for an announced $120 million. *U.S. v. Occidental Chemical Corp.*, No. 79-990C (W.D.N.Y. 1994). Under the settlement, the company agreed to pay New York $98 million over three years and undertake responsibility for operating and maintaining a remedial facility at Love Canal, at an estimated cost of $ 25 million over 30 years. It would also drop any claims it had made against the state. The state in return agreed to abandon all outstanding claims against Occidental, the successor in interest to Hooker, and agreed not to appeal the punitive damages decision mentioned above.

That left the claims of the United States and the City of Niagara Falls to be resolved. The United States settled its claims with Occidental in March, 1996. Occidental agreed to pay for federal remediation of the contaminated site and the United States dropped its lawsuit. The liability issues between the City of Niagara Falls and Occidental were resolved by judicial decision in May, 1997. The decree found both parties to be liable under CERCLA for remediation costs at the site. *United States v. Occidental Chemical Corp.*, 965 F. Supp. 408 (W.D.N.Y. 1997). The court did not decide the issue of damages.

previously unconcerned with and largely unaffected by "environmental law." It was truly a "sea change" in federal policy (some might say a "rude awakening") and it took legal form despite a dearth of legislative debate and an almost complete unappreciation of the enormity of the problem. (Sound familiar?)

CERCLA was first enacted in 1980 and was amended in 1986 by the Superfund Amendments and Reauthorization Act ("SARA"). The statute was amended a second time by The Small Business Liability Relief and Brownfields Revitalization Act, Pub. L. No. 107-118 (2002).[2]

CERCLA is best understood as having four operative parts:

(1) First, CERCLA enables the federal government to compile information on the enormity and character of the abandoned dump site problem. It requires owners of sites to tell EPA of their sites' existences and to inform the agency of the materials buried at those sites.

(2) Second, CERCLA designates the Hazardous Substances Superfund, found in the Internal Revenue Code at 26 U.S.C. § 9507, as a funding mechanism to pay for site remediations. § 111, 42 U.S.C. § 9611. The Superfund draws monies from general revenues, from violators of CERCLA, and in accordance with the Superfund Revenue Act of 1986 (SARA § 113).

(3) Third, CERCLA empowers the federal government to clean sites as well as to take other action should a hazardous waste emergency occur. Section 104, 42 U.S.C. § 9604, authorizes the President to use Superfund money to respond to any threatened or actual release of any hazardous substance that may pose an imminent and substantial public health threat.[3] The EPA decides which sites to clean up by reference to the "National Priorities List," the agency's tally of the most polluted sites in the nation. The List is compiled by use of a Hazard Ranking System, and includes more than 1000 sites. *See* 40 C.F.R. Part 300, Appendices A and B. When the EPA cleans a site, it must do so in accordance with the National Contingency Plan ("NCP"), 40 C.F.R. Part 300, promulgated by EPA in accordance with CERCLA § 105, 42 U.S.C. § 9605. The NCP sets forth "procedures and standards for responding to releases of hazardous substances, pollutants, and contaminants. . . ." *Id.*

Section 107 of CERCLA, 42 U.S.C. § 9607, allows for recovery of governmental "response" costs from all persons liable for releases of hazardous substances at the location. The Agency prefers to see private money used to clean sites, and accordingly spends a good deal of time trying to identify potentially responsible parties ("PRPs") to do the work.

(4) Lastly, the Act identifies an array of persons potentially liable for the costs of environmental repair. *See infra.*

The following pages demonstrate the mechanics of CERCLA in graphic form:

---

[2] In these materials, the acronym "CERCLA" will be used for the statute as currently configured, unless otherwise specified.

[3] The President has delegated much of his authorities under CERCLA to the Administrator of the EPA. *See* Executive Order No. 12,580, 52 Fed. Reg. 2923 (Jan. 23, 1987), *reprinted in*, 42 U.S.C. § 9615 App. at 168–72 (West Supp. 1989).

SITE DISCOVERY AND STUDY: FINDING THE MOST SERIOUS SITES

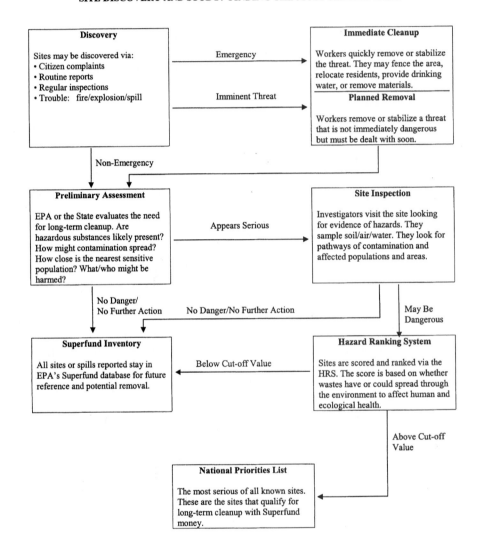

LONG-TERM CLEANUP: FIXING THE MOST SERIOUS SITES

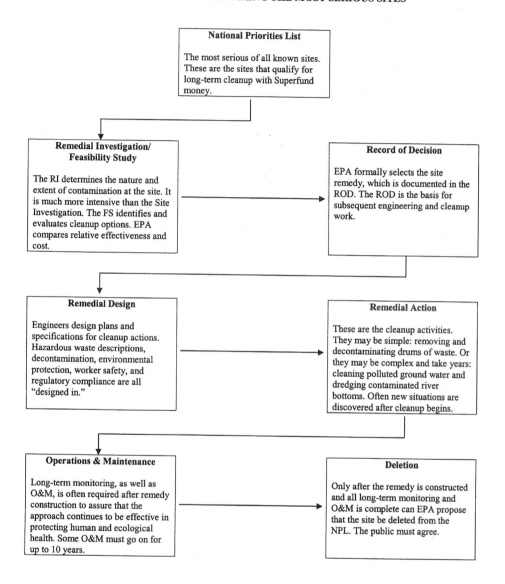

National Priorities List

The most serious of all known sites. These are the sites that qualify for long-term cleanup with Superfund money.

Remedial Investigation/ Feasibility Study

The RI determines the nature and extent of contamination at the site. It is much more intensive than the Site Investigation. The FS identifies and evaluates cleanup options. EPA compares relative effectiveness and cost.

Record of Decision

EPA formally selects the site remedy, which is documented in the ROD. The ROD is the basis for subsequent engineering and cleanup work.

Remedial Design

Engineers design plans and specifications for cleanup actions. Hazardous waste descriptions, decontamination, environmental protection, worker safety, and regulatory compliance are all "designed in."

Remedial Action

These are the cleanup activities. They may be simple: removing and decontaminating drums of waste. Or they may be complex and take years: cleaning polluted ground water and dredging contaminated river bottoms. Often new situations are discovered after cleanup begins.

Operations & Maintenance

Long-term monitoring, as well as O&M, is often required after remedy construction to assure that the approach continues to be effective in protecting human and ecological health. Some O&M must go on for up to 10 years.

Deletion

Only after the remedy is constructed and all long-term monitoring and O&M is complete can EPA propose that the site be deleted from the NPL. The public must agree.

Both emergency and long-term cleanup work can be led either by EPA or by an individual State, or under their supervision, by parties responsible for the contamination. The public is afforded opportunities to participate throughout the process.

EPA has explained these mechanics in greater detail in the following Federal Register notice, which accompanied a revision of the National Priorities List.

ENVIRONMENTAL PROTECTION AGENCY, NATIONAL PRIORITIES LIST FOR UNCONTROLLED HAZARDOUS WASTE SITES, 40 C.F.R. Part 300, 64 F.R. 56966

DATE: Friday, October 22, 1999

ACTION: Final rule.

SUMMARY: The Comprehensive Environmental Response, Compensation, and Liability Act of 1980 ("CERCLA" or "the Act"), as amended, requires that the National Oil and Hazardous Substances Pollution Contingency Plan ("NCP") include a list of national priorities among the known releases or threatened releases of hazardous substances, pollutants, or contaminants throughout the United States. The National Priorities List ("NPL") constitutes this list. The NPL is intended primarily to guide the Environmental Protection Agency ("EPA" or "the Agency") in determining which sites warrant further investigation to assess the nature and extent of public health and environmental risks associated with the site and to determine what CERCLA-financed remedial action(s), if any, may be appropriate. This rule adds 10 new sites to the NPL: 9 sites to the General Superfund Section of the NPL and one site to the Federal Facilities Section of the NPL.

EFFECTIVE DATE: The effective date for this amendment to the NCP shall be November 22, 1999.

. . . .

I. Background

A. What Are CERCLA and SARA?

In 1980, Congress enacted the Comprehensive Environmental Response, Compensation, and Liability Act, 42 U.S.C. 9601–9675 ("CERCLA" or "the Act"), in response to the dangers of uncontrolled releases of hazardous substances. CERCLA was amended on October 17, 1986, by the Superfund Amendments and Reauthorization Act ("SARA"), Public Law 99-499, 100 Stat. 1613 et seq.

B. What Is the NCP?

To implement CERCLA, EPA promulgated the revised National Oil and Hazardous Substances Pollution Contingency Plan ("NCP"), 40 C.F.R. part 300, on July 16, 1982 (47 FR 31180), pursuant to CERCLA section 105 and Executive Order 12316 (46 FR 42237, August 20, 1981). The NCP sets guidelines and procedures for responding to releases and threatened releases of hazardous substances, pollutants, or contaminants under CERCLA. EPA has revised the NCP on several occasions. The most recent comprehensive revision was on March 8, 1990 (55 FR 8666).

As required under section 105(a)(8)(A) of CERCLA, the NCP also includes "criteria for determining priorities among releases or threatened releases throughout the United States for the purpose of taking remedial action and, to the extent practicable, taking into account the potential urgency of such action for the purpose of taking removal action." ("Removal" actions are defined broadly and include a wide range of actions taken to study, clean up, prevent or otherwise address releases and threatened releases 42 U.S.C. 9601(23).)

C. What Is the National Priorities List (NPL)?

The NPL is a list of national priorities among the known or threatened releases of hazardous substances, pollutants, or contaminants throughout the United States. The list, which is appendix B of the NCP (40 C.F.R. part 300), was required under section 105(a)(8)(B) of CERCLA, as amended by SARA. Section 105(a)(8)(B) defines the NPL as a list of "releases" and the highest priority "facilities" and requires that the NPL be revised at least annually. The NPL is intended primarily to guide EPA in determining which sites warrant further investigation to assess the nature and extent of public health and environmental risks associated with a release of hazardous substances. The NPL is only of limited significance, however, as it does not assign liability to any party or to the owner of any specific property. Neither does placing a site on the NPL mean that any remedial or removal action necessarily need be taken.

For purposes of listing, the NPL includes two sections, one of sites that are generally evaluated and cleaned up by EPA (the "General Superfund Section"), and one of sites that are owned or operated by other Federal agencies (the "Federal Facilities Section"). With respect to sites in the Federal Facilities Section, these sites are generally being addressed by other Federal agencies. Under Executive Order 12580 (52 FR 2923, January 29, 1987) and CERCLA section 120, each Federal agency is responsible for carrying out most response actions at facilities under its own jurisdiction, custody, or control, although EPA is responsible for preparing an HRS score and determining whether the facility is placed on the NPL. EPA generally is not the lead agency at Federal Facilities Section sites, and its role at such sites is accordingly less extensive than at other sites.

D. How Are Sites Listed on the NPL?

There are three mechanisms for placing sites on the NPL for possible remedial action (see 40 C.F.R. 300.425(c) of the NCP): (1) A site may be included on the NPL if it scores sufficiently high on the Hazard Ranking System ("HRS"), which EPA promulgated as appendix A of the NCP (40 C.F.R. part 300). The HRS serves as a screening device to evaluate the relative potential of uncontrolled hazardous substances to pose a threat to human health or the environment. On December 14, 1990 (55 FR 51532), EPA promulgated revisions to the HRS partly in response to CERCLA section 105(c), added by SARA. The revised HRS evaluates four pathways: ground water, surface water, soil exposure, and air. As a matter of Agency policy, those sites that score 28.50 or greater on the HRS are eligible for the NPL; (2) Each State may designate a single site as its top priority to be listed on the NPL, regardless of the HRS score. This mechanism, provided by the NCP at 40 C.F.R. 300.425(c)(2) requires that, to the extent practicable, the NPL include within the 100 highest priorities, one facility designated by each State representing the greatest danger to public health, welfare, or the environment among known facilities in the State (see 42 U.S.C. 9605(a)(8)(B)); (3) The third mechanism for listing, included in the NCP at 40 C.F.R. 300.425(c)(3), allows certain sites to be listed regardless of their HRS score, if all of the following conditions are met:

— The Agency for Toxic Substances and Disease Registry (ATSDR) of the U.S. Public Health Service has issued a health advisory that recommends dissociation of individuals from the release.

— EPA determines that the release poses a significant threat to public health.

— EPA anticipates that it will be more cost-effective to use its remedial authority than to use its removal authority to respond to the release.

EPA promulgated an original NPL of 406 sites on September 8, 1983 (48 FR 40658). The NPL has been expanded since then, most recently on September 17, 1999 (64 FR 50459).

E. What Happens to Sites on the NPL?

A site may undergo remedial action financed by the Trust Fund established under CERCLA (commonly referred to as the "Superfund") only after it is placed on the NPL, as provided in the NCP at 40 C.F.R. 300.425(b)(1). ("Remedial actions" are those "consistent with permanent remedy, taken instead of or in addition to removal actions * * *." 42 U.S.C. 9601(24).) However, under 40 C.F.R. 300.425(b)(2) placing a site on the NPL "does not imply that monies will be expended." EPA may pursue other appropriate authorities to respond to the releases, including enforcement action under CERCLA and other laws.

F. How Are Site Boundaries Defined?

The NPL does not describe releases in precise geographical terms; it would be neither feasible nor consistent with the limited purpose of the NPL (to identify releases that are priorities for further evaluation), for it to do so.

Although a CERCLA "facility" is broadly defined to include any area where a hazardous substance release has "come to be located" (CERCLA section 101(9)), the listing process itself is not intended to define or reflect the boundaries of such facilities or releases. Of course, HRS data (if the HRS is used to list a site) upon which the NPL placement was based will, to some extent, describe the release(s) at issue. That is, the NPL site would include all releases evaluated as part of that HRS analysis.

When a site is listed, the approach generally used to describe the relevant release(s) is to delineate a geographical area (usually the area within an installation or plant boundaries) and identify the site by reference to that area. As a legal matter, the site is not coextensive with that area, and the boundaries of the installation or plant are not the "boundaries" of the site. Rather, the site consists of all contaminated areas within the area used to identify the site, as well as any other location to which that contamination has come to be located, or from which that contamination came.

In other words, while geographic terms are often used to designate the site (e.g., the "Jones Co. plant site") in terms of the property owned by a particular party, the site properly understood is not limited to that property (e.g., it may extend beyond the property due to contaminant migration), and conversely may not occupy the full extent of the property (e.g., where there are uncontaminated parts of the identified property, they may not be, strictly speaking, part of the "site"). The "site" is thus neither equal to nor confined by the boundaries of any specific property that may give the site its name, and the name itself should not be read to imply that this site is coextensive with the entire area within the property boundary of the installation or plant. The precise nature and extent of the site are typically not known at the time of listing. Also, the site name is merely used to help identify the geographic location of the contamination. For example, the name "Jones Co. plant site," does not imply that the Jones company is responsible for the contamination located on the plant site.

EPA regulations provide that the "nature and extent of the problem presented by the release" will be determined by a remedial investigation/feasibility study (RI/FS) as more information is developed on site contamination (40 C.F.R. 300.5). During the RI/FS process, the release may be found to be larger or smaller than was originally thought, as more is learned about the source(s) and the migration of the contamination. However, this inquiry focuses on an evaluation of the threat posed; the boundaries of the release need not be exactly defined. Moreover, it generally is impossible to discover the full extent of where the contamination "has come to be located" before all necessary studies and remedial work are completed at a site. Indeed, the known boundaries of the contamination can be expected to change over time. Thus, in most cases, it may be impossible to describe the boundaries of a release with absolute certainty.

Further, as noted above, NPL listing does not assign liability to any party or to the owner of any specific property. Thus, if a party does not believe it is liable for releases on discrete parcels of property, supporting information can be submitted to the Agency at any time after a party receives notice it is a potentially responsible party.

For these reasons, the NPL need not be amended as further research reveals more information about the location of the contamination or release.

G. How Are Sites Removed From the NPL?

EPA may delete sites from the NPL where no further response is appropriate under Superfund, as explained in the NCP at 40 C.F.R. 300.425(e). This section also provides that EPA shall consult with states on proposed deletions and shall consider whether any of the following criteria have been met:

(i) Responsible parties or other persons have implemented all appropriate response actions required;

(ii) All appropriate Superfund-financed response has been implemented and no further response action is required; or

(iii) The remedial investigation has shown the release poses no significant threat to public health or the environment, and taking of remedial measures is not appropriate.

As of October 12, 1999, the Agency has deleted 201 sites from the NPL.

H. Can Portions of Sites be Deleted From the NPL as They Are Cleaned Up?

In November 1995, EPA initiated a new policy to delete portions of NPL sites where cleanup is complete (60 FR 55465, November 1, 1995). Total site cleanup may take many years, while portions of the site may have been cleaned up and available for productive use. As of October 12, 1999, EPA has deleted portions of 16 sites.

I. What Is the Construction Completion List (CCL)?

EPA also has developed an NPL construction completion list ("CCL") to simplify its system of categorizing sites and to better communicate the successful completion of cleanup activities (58 FR 12142, March 2, 1993). Inclusion of a site on the CCL has no legal significance.

Sites qualify for the CCL when: (1) Any necessary physical construction is complete, whether or not final cleanup levels or other requirements have been achieved; (2) EPA has determined that the response action should be limited to measures that do not involve construction (e.g., institutional controls); or (3) the site qualifies for deletion from the NPL.

Of the 201 sites that have been deleted from the NPL, 192 sites were deleted because they have been cleaned up (the other 9 sites were deleted based on deferral to other authorities and are not considered cleaned up). As of October 12, 1999, there are a total of 670 sites on the CCL. This total includes the 192 deleted sites. For the most up-to-date information on the CCL, see EPA's Internet site at www.epa.gov/superfund.

. . . .

B. Status of NPL

With the 10 new sites added to the NPL in today's final rule; the NPL now contains 1,221 final sites; 1,062 in the General Superfund Section and 159 in the Federal Facilities Section. With a separate rule (published elsewhere in today's Federal Register) proposing to add 9 new sites to the NPL, there are now 57 sites proposed and awaiting final agency action, 52 in the General Superfund Section and 5 in the Federal Facilities Section. Final and proposed sites now total 1,278. (These numbers reflect the status of sites as of October 12, 1999. Sites deletions may affect these numbers at time of publication in the Federal Register.)

. . . .

*   *   *   *   *

The basic proofs necessary to establish liability in a CERCLA case are as follows:

- The site involved in the dispute must be a "facility" or "vessel."
  § 107(a), 42 U.S.C. § 9607(a). The term "facility" is defined broadly

(*see* § 101(9), 42 U.S.C. § 9601(9)), but the definition expressly excludes "vessels" (defined at § 101(28), 42 U.S.C. § 9601(28)). EPA gives "facility" an even broader interpretation. For example, in *In re Port Authority of New York and New Jersey*, EPA EAB, No. 96-5 (5/30/01), the Environmental Appeals Board of the Agency ruled the ocean floor to be a facility because substances released from a vessel came to rest at a discrete place. Thus, a facility was created post-release. Had the dumped wastes dispersed over a large area, no new facility would have been created and the "vessel exclusion" would have controlled.

• A "release" or "threatened release" of a "hazardous substance" from that facility or vessel must have occurred. § 107(a)(4), 42 U.S.C. § 9607(a)(4). "Release" is defined extremely broadly in the statute (*see* § 101(22), 42 U.S.C. § 9601(22)), as is the term "hazardous substance." § 101(14), 42 U.S.C. § 9601(14). Note that abandonment of hazardous substances may qualify as a "release" under CERCLA. *See* § 101(22), 42 U.S.C. § 9601(22). EPA may declare an abandonment "when hazardous waste presents a serious, immediate threat and the waste's owner is not present to take control[.]" *A&W Smelter & Refiners, Inc. v. Clinton*, 146 F.3d 1102, 1112 (1998). "Federally permitted releases" (defined at § 101(10), 42 U.S.C. § 9601(10)) are free of CERCLA regulation.

• The "release" or "threatened release" must have caused the plaintiff to incur "response costs." The term, "response," includes both removal and remedial actions. § 101(25), 42 U.S.C. § 9601(25). Removal actions are immediate or interim responses, and remedial actions are more permanent responses. Response costs must be "necessary." In order to show that response costs were necessary under CERCLA, plaintiffs must show they were responding to a real, as distinct from a theoretical, threat to public health or the environment, and that the costs were necessary to meet the threat. *Carson Harbor Village v. Unocal Corp.*, 227 F.3d 1196, (9th Cir. 2000). In addition, response costs must be "not inconsistent with the national contingency plan." § 107(a)(4)(A), 42 U.S.C. § 9607(a)(4)(A). (In a private cost recovery action, response costs must be "consistent with the national contingency plan." § 107(a)(4)(B), 42 U.S.C. § 9607(a)(4)(B).

• The defendant is a member of at least one of four classes of persons subject to liability. § 107(a), 42 U.S.C. § 9607(a). The classes are (a) current owners and operators; (b) certain past owners and operators; (c) arrangers (often, the generators of hazardous wastes); and (d) transporters.

The first three of these essential proofs goes to the nature of statutory liability, while the fourth is the mechanism by which liability may be affixed to an individual. The *Alcan* case that follows directs itself to the former issues; we will review issues of personal liability in Part B of this Chapter.

UNITED STATES v. ALCAN ALUMINUM CORP.

964 F.2d 252 (3d Cir. 1992)

JUDGES: BEFORE: GREENBERG and SCIRICA, Circuit Judges, and DE-BEVOISE, District Judge*

GREENBERG, Circuit Judge.

[This case was on appeal from a summary judgment entered against Alcan, the only party among 20 defendants in the case which did not settle with the EPA. The release of hazardous substances for which EPA sought reimbursement of response costs under CERCLA was one into the Susquehanna River via a system of underground tunnels, caverns, pools and waterways near Pittston, Pennsylvania. Wastes were deposited into the underground tunnel network through an entry point designated the "Borehole."]

Alcan did not respond to EPA's early settlement overtures. At trial, it maintained that the toxicity of its wastes was ". . . orders of magnitude below ambient or naturally occurring background levels. Moreover, the trace quantities of metal compounds in the emulsion [were] immobile. . . ." The government did not contest these assertions, arguing instead their irrelevance to the question of CERCLA liability.

On May 8, 1991, the district court entered judgment against Alcan in the amount of $473,790.18, which was the difference between the full response costs the Government had incurred in cleaning the Susquehanna River and the amount the Government had recovered from the defendants which settled with it. This court agreed with the reasoning of the district court, but vacated and remanded the district court judgment for further factual development on the scope of Alcan's liability.

. . . .

II. Discussion

A. CERCLA Framework:

. . . .

Reimbursement for response costs can be obtained in a variety of ways. For example, the Government can clean the sites itself using monies in the Hazardous Substance Response Trust Fund established by section 221 of CER-CLA, 42 U.S.C. § 9631 and now the Hazardous Substance Superfund or "Superfund" (see 26 U.S.C. § 9507); EPA can then seek reimbursement from responsible parties, as it has done in this case. In addition, section 106(a) permits EPA to request the Attorney General to "secure such relief as may be necessary to abate such danger or threat" by filing a civil action in federal district court. That section also permits EPA to issue administrative orders "as may be necessary to protect public health and welfare and the environment." . . .

---

* Honorable Dickinson R. Debevoise, United States District Judge for the District of New Jersey, sitting by designation.

Finally, and of great significance in this case, CERCLA imposes strict liability on responsible parties. 42 U.S.C. § 9601(32).

. . . .

B. CERCLA Contains No Quantitative Requirement in its Definition of "Hazardous Substance":

Alcan argues that it should not be held liable for response costs incurred by the Government in cleaning the Susquehanna River because the level of hazardous substances in its emulsion was below that which naturally occurs and thus could not have contributed to the environmental injury. It asserts that we must read a threshold concentration requirement into the definition of "hazardous substances" for the term "hazardous" to have any meaning. The United States Chamber of Commerce (the "Chamber") as amicus curiae agrees, observing that "Congress took pains to define 'hazardous substance'. . . . Congress clearly never intended to abandon altogether the requirement that the substance at issue be hazardous." Chamber Br. at 20–21 (footnote omitted). The Chamber further states that "the uncontested facts show that Alcan's waste contained less of these [hazardous] elements than can be found in clean dirt." Chamber Br. at 18. For these reasons it too claims that Alcan should not be held liable for any environmental injury to the Susquehanna River.

The Government responds that under a plain reading of the statute, there is no quantitative requirement in the definition of "hazardous substance." . . .

. . . [T]he district court in this case agreed with the Government. Quoting *Amoco Oil Co. v. Borden, Inc.,* 889 F.2d 664, 669 (5th Cir. 1989), the district court in Alcan New York observed, "'the plain statutory language fails to impose any quantitative requirement on the term hazardous substance,'" 755 F. Supp. at 537, and concluded that "there is no principled basis upon which to deviate from the . . . rule that the mere listing of a substance by EPA renders that substance hazardous." *Id.* at 537–38. In response to Alcan's argument that virtually everything in the universe would constitute a hazardous substance under this reading of the statute, the court held:

> The corporate generator, a non-natural person, has added to what nature has already seen fit to provide for the continued existence of various life forms on this planet; that Congress has enacted laws to limit, and perhaps limit quite severely, additions to nature for the sake of the environment and of life on this planet seems eminently reasonable.

Id. at 538.

For the reasons that follow, we are satisfied that the court was correct in that conclusion. [The court then discusses the plain meaning of the statute, the legislative history (which in this case was unhelpful), and the wealth of jurisprudence indicating that liability does not depend on threshhold quantities of hazardous substances.]

. . . .

It may be that Congress did not intend such an all-encompassing definition of "hazardous substances," but this argument is best directed at Congress itself. If Congress had intended to impose a threshold requirement, it could easily have so indicated. We should not rewrite the statute simply because the definition of one of its terms is broad in scope.

. . . .

4. Environmental Policy:

In Alcan's view, the district court's construction of the statute is at odds with environmental policy because it imposes liability on generators of allegedly "hazardous" substances although the substances pose no real threat to the environment. Alcan's argument, though superficially appealing, is flawed. First, as noted above, the Government responds to "releases" that threaten environmental safety. Thus, it is the release alone that must justify the response costs, not the particular waste generated by one given defendant. Here, there is no question but that a release occurred. Second, the fact that a single generator's waste would not in itself justify a response is irrelevant in the multi-generator context, as this would permit a generator to escape liability where the amount of harm it engendered to the environment was minimal, though it was significant when added to other generators' waste. Accordingly, we find that the district court's construction of the statute furthers important environmental goals. . . .

D. Causation:

Alcan maintains that, if we decline to construe the determination of "hazardous substance" to encompass a concentration threshold, we must at least require the Government to prove that Alcan's emulsion caused or contributed to the release or the Government's incurrence of response costs. The Government contends . . . that the statute imposes no such causation requirement, but rather requires that the plaintiff in a CERCLA proceeding establish that the release or threatened release caused the incurrence of response costs; it underscores the difficulty CERCLA plaintiffs would face in the multi-generator context if required to trace the cause of the response costs to each responsible party.

1. Plain Meaning:

The plain meaning of the statute supports the Government's position. As noted above, section 107 imposes liability upon a generator of hazardous substances who contracts with another party to dispose of the hazardous substances at a facility "from which there is a release, or threatened release which causes the incurrence of response costs." 42 U.S.C. § 9607 (emphasis supplied). The statute does not, on its face, require the plaintiff to prove that the generator's hazardous substances themselves caused the release or caused the incurrence of response costs; rather, it requires the plaintiff to prove that the release or threatened release caused the incurrence of response costs, and that the defendant is a generator of hazardous substances at the facility.

2. Legislative History:

The legislative history also supports the Government's position that CER-CLA does not require the plaintiff to establish a specific causal relationship between a generator's waste and the release or the plaintiff's incurrence of response costs. It appears that the early House of Representatives' version of CERCLA imposed liability upon those persons who "caused or contributed to the release or threatened release." H.R. 7020, 96th Cong., 2d Sess. § 3071(a)(D), 126 Cong. Rec. 26,779. However, the version ultimately passed by Congress deleted the causation requirement and instead imposed liability upon a class of responsible persons without regard to whether the person specifically caused or contributed to the release and the resultant response costs. *See* 126 Cong. Rec. 31,981–82. Moreover, Congress added three limited defenses to liability based on causation which are contained in 42 U.S.C. § 9607(b): acts of God, acts of war, and acts or omissions of a contractually unrelated third party when the defendant exercised due care and took appropriate responses. Imputing a specific causation requirement would render these defenses superfluous.

In sum, the legislative history indicates that Congress considered and rejected a requirement that the plaintiff establish that the defendant's waste caused or contributed to the release or the incurrence of response costs.

3. Jurisprudence:

Further, virtually every court that has considered this question has held that a CERCLA plaintiff need not establish a direct causal connection between the defendant's hazardous substances and the release or the plaintiff's incurrence of response costs. . . . [citations omitted] . . . [*See, e.g.,*] *United States v. Wade,* 577 F. Supp. at 1333 ("the release which results in the incurrence of response costs and liability need only be of 'a' hazardous substance and not necessarily one contained in the defendant's waste. The only required nexus between the defendant and the site is that the defendant have dumped his waste there and that the hazardous substances found in the defendant's waste are also found at the site."). . . .

. . . Accordingly, we reject Alcan's argument that the Government must prove that Alcan's emulsion deposited in the Borehole caused the release or caused the Government to incur response costs. Rather, the Government must simply prove that the defendant's hazardous substances were deposited at the site from which there was a release and that the release caused the incurrence of response costs.

[The court then rejects Alcan's argument that its wastes fall within the "petroleum exclusion" of CERCLA section 101(14), 42 U.S.C. section 9601(14). The last portion of the case, dealing with joint and several liability, is omitted. The court remanded on this issue for a hearing on the divisibility of harm.]

NOTES

1. The *Alcan* case makes mention of the express exemption of petroleum from the definition of hazardous substances. Congress implemented the

petroleum exclusion because it was considering, contemporaneous with its hasty deliberations on CERCLA, a companion statute going by the name of the "Oil Pollution Liability and Compensation Act" or "OPLCA." H.R. 85. The OPLCA passed the House but failed in the Senate. When CERCLA was enacted, the petroleum exclusion nonetheless remained in place.

2. In the words of one highly placed EPA official, liability under CERCLA is joint, several, strict, retroactive, and perpetual. We will study the joint and several aspects of liability later in this Chapter. "Perpetual" is self-explanatory. What about the others?

(A) *Strict*: *Alcan* removes the element of causation from the universe of necessary proofs for a plaintiff to prevail. The point was made as early as 1983, in *United States v. Wade*, 577 F. Supp. 1326, 1333 (E.D. Pa. 1983) (cited in *Alcan*):

> The government's experts have admitted that scientific technique has not advanced to a point that the identity of the generator of a specific quantity of waste can be stated with certainty. All that can be said is that a site contains the same kind of hazardous substances as are found in a generator's waste. Thus, to require a plaintiff under CERCLA to "fingerprint" wastes is to eviscerate the statute. Given two possible constructions of a statute, one which renders it useless should be rejected. Generators are adequately protected by requiring a plaintiff to prove that a defendant's waste was disposed of at a site and that the substances that make the defendant's waste hazardous are also present at the site.

(B) *Retroactive:* That CERCLA liability is retroactive means that persons may be liable even though they never violated an in-place legal standard. Are there constitutional problems with retroactive liability? *See, e.g., United States of America v. Northeastern Pharmaceutical & Chemical Co.*, 810 F.2d 726 (8th Cir. 1986) (justifying the liability scheme because of the remedial nature of the statute).

Even if retroactive application of statutes is constitutional, under what circumstances should a court conclude a statute in fact applies to pre-enactment behavior? Note that *Alcan* was decided before the decision in *Landgraf v. USI Film Products*, 511 U.S. 244, 114 S. Ct. 1483 (1994). In *Landgraf*, the Supreme Court found a presumption against retroactive application of statutes. *See also Eastern Enterprises v. Apfel*, 524 U.S. 498, 118 S.Ct. 2131 (1998). Following the *Landgraf* lead, a district court refused to find CERCLA liability where the releases of hazardous materials into the environment predated the 1980 enactment of CERCLA itself. *United States v. Olin Corp.*, 927 F. Supp. 1502 (S.D. Ala. 1996). The *Olin* court concluded CERCLA's failure to mention retroactive liability meant that the statute failed to overcome the *Landgraf* presumption.

The Eleventh Circuit promptly overruled the district court:

> Although the *Landgraf* Court reaffirmed the presumption against retroactive application of statutes, it emphasized that courts must effectuate congressional intent regarding retroactivity. *See Landgraf*, 511 U.S. at 272–74, 114 S. Ct. at 1501 (stating that "constitutional

impediments to retroactive civil legislation are now modest"). The Court ruled that its approach simply was designed to "assure[] that Congress itself has affirmatively considered the potential unfairness of retroactive application and determined that it is an acceptable price to pay for the countervailing benefits." *Id.* As a result, we conclude that even absent explicit statutory language mandating retroactivity, laws may be applied retroactively if courts are able to discern "clear congressional intent favoring such a result."

United States v. Olin, 107 F.3d 1506, 1512 (11th Cir. 1997). The Circuit Court found the requisite Congressional intent readily demonstrated by the statute's designation of former owners and operators as liable persons.

B. PERSONAL LIABILITY

The critical legal question under CERCLA is upon whom does liability fall. Section 107(a), 42 U.S.C. § 9607(a), provides the answer by establishing the elements of *prima facie* liability. Section 107(b), 42 U.S.C. § 9607(b), sets forth defenses to such liability. We will consider these matters in order.

[1] PRIMA FACIE LIABILITY

[a] OWNERS AND OPERATORS

Section 107(a)(1), 42 U.S.C. § 9607(a)(1), assesses liability on current owners and operators of a vessel or facility; § 107(a)(2), 42 U.S.C. § 9607(a)(2), assesses liability on owners and operators at the time of disposal ("past" owners and operators). The statutory definitions of these terms, contained in § 101(20)(A), 42 U.S.C. § 9601(20)(A), are not helpful. Predictably, because of the enormous financial consequences, the meaning of these terms has been, and continues to be, vigorously debated. Let us look to "owners" first. Who, or what, is an "owner" for purposes of CERCLA? Surely a person holding fee simple absolute title to real property would qualify. But would a holder in fee simple defeasible be an "owner"? A life tenant? A lessee for a term of years? Would it make any difference if a lessee for a term of years held a ninety-nine year lease as compared to a three month one?

COMMANDER OIL CORP. v. BARLO EQUIPMENT CORP.

215 F.3d 321 (2d Cir. 2000)*

JUDGES: Before: WALKER, CABRANES, and KATZMANN, Circuit Judges.

JOHN M. WALKER, Jr., Circuit Judge:

[The issue in the case was whether a lessee of a 75 × 250′ parcel of land in Uniondale, New York, may be held liable as an "owner" for purposes of CERCLA § 107. Commander Oil had taken title to two lots, designated 7A

---

* Petition for writ of certiorari to the U.S. Court of Appeals for the Second Circuit denied. *See* 531 U.S. 979, 121 S. Ct. 427 (2000).

and 7B, in 1963. Lot 7A contained office and warehouse space. Lot 7B, at issue in this case, was the site of twelve above-ground petroleum storage tanks. In 1964, Commander Oil leased Lot 7A to Barlo. In 1969, it leased Lot 7B to Pasley Solvent and Chemicals, Inc. Under this latter lease, Commander Oil retained use of three oil storage tanks on Lot 7B. In 1972, Commander Oil consolidated its leases. The result was that both lots were leased to Barlo, and Barlo in turn subleased Lot 7B to Pasley.

[In the litigation, Barlo characterized its role as merely a rent conduit with respect to Lot 7B, arguing that Pasley treated Commander Oil as its lessor and that it undertook the legal arrangement at Commander Oil's behest and merely for bookkeeping purposes. Commander Oil, however, argued that Barlo was involved with Pasley's activities on the subleased parcel, and derived a profit, albeit a small one, from the sublease arrangement.

[In 1981, the state Nassau County Department of Health discovered contamination on Lot 7B. Six years later, the EPA order Commander Oil to conduct an investigation and feasibility study. In 1988, EPA moved to secure response costs for its expenses in remediating the site. This led in turn to a consent decree, agreed to, inter alia, by Commander Oil and Barlo. Commander Oil agreed to design and implement the response action, and received contribution in the amount of $1,849,127.91.

[In 1990, Commander Oil filed this action for contribution and indemnification for additional costs from Barlo and Pasley. Commander Oil's complaint seeks, inter alia, indemnification or contribution under CERCLA, contractual indemnification, and damages for various state-law claims including trespass, negligence, nuisance, and waste. The contested issue in the case was whether Barlo was an owner for purposes of § 107 of CERCLA. The district court held that Barlo was, on the theory that a lessee who "has control over and responsibility for the use of the property is the owner of the property."]

Discussion

We are called upon in this case to resolve yet another ambiguity within CERCLA's miasmatic provisions. CERCLA creates a regime of broad-ranging liability, permitting the government to recover its remediation expenses directly from parties responsible for pollution, *see* 42 U.S.C. § 9607(a)(4)(A), and authorizing private parties to pursue contribution or indemnification from potentially responsible parties for expenses incurred responding to environmental threats, *see* 42 U.S.C. § 9607(a)(4)(B). CERCLA creates various categories of potentially responsible parties, one of which is pertinent to this case: owners and operators of facilities. *See* 42 U.S.C. § 9607(a)(1); *B.F. Goodrich Co. v. Murtha,* 958 F.2d 1192, 1198 (2d Cir. 1992) (delineating potentially responsible parties as: "past and present owners or operators of facilities, transporters of hazardous substances, and those . . . who generate or arrange for the disposal or treatment of hazardous substances"). Absent a showing that one of CERCLA's affirmative defenses applies, liability for owners and operators is strict. *See B.F. Goodrich,* 958 F.2d at 1198.

Commander Oil's suit against Barlo seeks either contribution or indemnification for the costs it has and will continue to incur under its consent decree with the EPA. The district court granted partial summary judgment to

Commander Oil for contribution on the theory that Barlo, as a lessee/ sublessor, was an "owner" of lot 7B and was therefore strictly liable. Other courts to have considered whether lessees/sublessors are owners for purposes of CERCLA's strict owner liability provisions have reached the same conclusion on similar facts. *See, e.g., Delaney v. Town of Carmel,* 55 F. Supp. 2d 237, 258–59 (S.D.N.Y. 1999) ("The owner of a leasehold of a CERCLA facility may be liable as an owner of that facility."); *United States v. A & N Cleaners & Launderers, Inc.,* 788 F. Supp. 1317, 1332–34 (S.D.N.Y. 1992); *United States v. South Carolina Recycling & Disposal, Inc.,* 653 F. Supp. 984, 1002–03 (D.S.C. 1984), *aff'd in part, vacated in part sub nom. United States v. Monsanto Co.,* 858 F.2d 160 (4th Cir. 1988). Essentially, these courts have interpreted the term "owner" to extend beyond the fee or record owner to anyone possessing the requisite degree of control over the property. Whether, and under what circumstances, a lessee/sublessor may be held liable as an owner for CERCLA purposes is a question of first impression in this circuit and we review the district court's legal conclusions de novo. *See Maguire v. Citicorp Retail Servs., Inc.,* 147 F.3d 232, 235 (2d Cir. 1998).

I.

CERCLA's text offers no helpful guidance for interpreting the extent of owner liability. According to the statute: "The term 'owner or operator' means . . . any person owning or operating [a] facility." 42 U.S.C. § 9601(20)(A). We are thus required to give content to a statutory tautology, a position to which we have become increasingly accustomed in the environmental context. Nor are we the first court to have recognized that CERCLA is hardly a model of legislative clarity. *See, e.g., Exxon Corp. v. Hunt,* 475 U.S. 355, 363, 89 L. Ed. 2d 364, 106 S. Ct. 1103 (1986); *Artesian Water Co. v. New Castle County,* 851 F.2d 643, 648 (3d Cir. 1988) ("CERCLA is not a paradigm of clarity or precision. It has been criticized frequently for inartful drafting and numerous ambiguities attributable to its precipitous passage.").

A.

Our statutory interpretation is guided by CERCLA's few well-established principles. "Because it is a remedial statute, CERCLA must be construed liberally to effectuate its two primary goals: (1) enabling the EPA to respond efficiently and expeditiously to toxic spills, and (2) holding those parties [potentially] responsible for the releases liable for the costs of the cleanup." *B.F. Goodrich,* 958 F.2d at 1198. The scheme envisioned by Congress protects taxpayers generally from bearing the costs of nationwide cleanup. *See id.* Instead, potentially responsible parties must shoulder the frequently heavy burden of liability. Potentially responsible parties are not limited to parties who were the cause in fact of the contamination, *see New York v. Shore Realty Corp.,* 759 F.2d 1032, 1044 (2d Cir. 1985) ("Section 9607(a)(1) unequivocally imposes strict liability on the current owner of a facility from which there is a release or threat of release, without regard to causation."), but neither does CERCLA automatically assign liability to every party with any connection to a contaminated facility. * * *

We therefore begin our analysis of the term "owner" in § 9607(a) by doing "the best we can to give the term its ordinary or natural meaning." [*United States v.*] *Bestfoods,* 524 U.S. [51,] at 66, [118 S. Ct. 1876 (1998)] (internal quotation marks omitted). But unlike "operator," the term "owner" has no natural meaning that can resolve the present dispute. Barlo urges that CERCLA's owner liability is restricted to record owners. Commander Oil argues for a more expansive definition that relies primarily on the right to control property, whether the right is possessory or is a recorded property interest. Neither position is obviously implausible. According to Webster's dictionary, an owner is "One that has the legal or rightful title whether the possessor or not." Webster's Third New International Dictionary of the English Language Unabridged 1612 (1981). Black's Law Dictionary, however, equivocates between titular and possessory owner, defining an owner variously as "one who has the right to possess, use, and convey something," and as "one who has the primary or residuary title to property." Black's Law Dictionary 1130 (7th ed. 1999). This definition's ambiguity comes as no surprise. Long-standing scholarship has informed us that ownership — and its attendant concept "property" — has limited inherent content. *See, e.g.,* Wesley Newcomb Hohfeld, *Some Fundamental Legal Conceptions as Applied in Judicial Reasoning and Other Legal Essays* 96 (Walter Wheeler Cook ed., 1923) (stating that property "consists of a complex aggregate of rights (or claims), privileges, powers, and immunities").

Courts and commentators have supplied no consistent guidance as to which rights in the proverbial property bundle define ownership. *Compare, e.g., Hodel v. Irving,* 481 U.S. 704, 716, 95 L. Ed. 2d 668, 107 S. Ct. 2076 (1987) (stating that "the right to pass on property — to one's family in particular" constitutes a protected property right under the Fifth Amendment), *with Andrus v. Allard,* 444 U.S. 51, 65–66, 62 L. Ed. 2d 210, 100 S. Ct. 318 (1979) (holding that abrogating the right to sell endangered eagles' feathers did not implicate the Fifth Amendment); *see also* William A. Fischel, *Introduction: Utilitarian Balancing and Formalism in Takings,* 88 Colum. L. Rev. 1581, 1590–94 (1988) (reviewing various commentators' disagreements over the content of protectable property interests). Our task today is less theoretical yet is still grounded in the same basic controversy over defining ownership. Its manifestation in this case is whether, and under what circumstances, the rights possessed by a lessee are sufficient to rise to the level of "ownership" for CERCLA purposes.

Most of the district courts that have considered this question have held that site control is a sufficient indicator of ownership to impose liability on lessees or sublessors. *See, e.g., Castlerock Estates, Inc. v. Estate of Markham,* 871 F. Supp. 360, 367 (N.D. Cal. 1994); *Burlington N. R.R. Co. v. Wood Indus., Inc.,* 815 F. Supp. 1384, 1391–92 (E.D. Wash. 1993); *Pape v. Great Lakes Chem. Co.,* 1993 U.S. Dist. LEXIS 14674, No. 93 C 1585, 1993 WL 424249, at *3 (N.D. Ill. Oct. 19, 1993); *see also, e.g., Delaney,* 55 F. Supp. 2d at 258–59 ("The owner of a leasehold interest in a CERCLA facility may be liable as an owner of that facility, as long as the lessee exercised sufficient site control to place it in the shoes of owners.") (internal quotation marks omitted); *A & N Cleaners & Launderers, Inc.,* 788 F. Supp. at 1333 ("The undisputed facts establish that [the sublessor] exercised a degree of site control over the Property, that . . .

confers ownership status upon it for purposes of CERCLA . . . ."); *South Carolina Recycling & Disposal, Inc.*, 653 F. Supp. at 1003 ("[The lessee] maintained control over and responsibility for the use of the property and, essentially, stood in the shoes of the property owners."). The reasoning of these district courts is not without its appeal; if the lessee is the active user and polluter of the property, imposition of CERCLA liability seems particularly appropriate. But, while the imposition of liability in such a situation is surely correct, imposing owner liability instead of operator liability threatens to conflate two statutorily distinct categories of potentially responsible parties.

It is settled in this circuit that owner and operator liability should be treated separately. *See, e.g., Schiavone v. Pearce*, 79 F.3d 248, 254 (2d Cir. 1996) ("Observing that 'owner' liability and 'operator' liability denote two separate concepts, courts stress the disjunctive character of CERCLA liability." (internal quotation marks omitted)); *cf. Bestfoods*, 524 U.S. at 64 ("If the act rested liability entirely on ownership of a polluting facility, this opinion might end here; but CERCLA liability may turn on operation as well as ownership . . . ."). Even a cursory examination of the basis for operator liability reveals that it would be almost entirely subsumed by owner liability that relied on site control analysis. As the Supreme Court recently explained, "an operator must manage, direct, or conduct operations specifically related to pollution, that is, operations having to do with the leakage or disposal of hazardous waste, or decisions about compliance with environmental regulations." *Bestfoods*, 524 U.S. at 66–67. If control over a facility could establish ownership then operator liability in these circumstances would be just a subset of owner liability. Imposing owner liability on the basis of site control threatens to make owners of all operators and surplusage of most of operator liability. *See Castlerock*, 871 F. Supp. at 367 ("The test for 'ownership' liability under CERCLA . . . has become similar to [the] test for 'operator' liability under CERCLA."). Because we strive to avoid redundancy in our interpretation of statutes, *see, e.g., Exxon Corp.*, 475 U.S. at 369–70, we believe that site control alone is an improper basis for the imposition of owner liability. Lessees may frequently be liable as operators but most lessees are not owners within the meaning of § 9607(a).

B.

While the typical lessee should not be held liable as an owner, there may be circumstances when owner liability for a lessee would be appropriate. Some district courts, for example, have treated lessees as owners for CERCLA purposes when they sublet the premises to other entities. *See, e.g., South Carolina Recycling & Disposal, Inc.*, 653 F. Supp. at 1003 ("The fact that during part of its leasehold [the lessee] sublet a portion of the site does not diminish its responsibility. If anything, it strengthens the case [against the lessee]."). These courts have reasoned that a sublessor, by virtue of its relationship to the sublessee, will often be in the best position — or at least in a better position than the record owner — to prevent pollution at a facility. However, this reasoning improperly emphasizes the relationship between the lessee/sublessor and the sublessee, instead of the relationship between the owner and the lessee/sublessor.

Ownership has consistently defied easy definition across a variety of legal contexts, but we know at least that it is relational. *See* Restatement (First) of Property ch. 1 intro. note (1936) ("[Property comprises] legal relations between persons with respect to a thing."). Ownership exists vis-a-vis someone else; it represents a priority of rights and claims and not a concrete status. Lessees/sublessors necessarily have relationships with both the original lessor — often the record owner — and the sublessee. A lessee/sublessor has many of the rights and obligations of ownership in relation to the sublessee; he usually retains, inter alia, the power to lease, to exclude, and to govern the terms of property's use. But lessees/sublessors are simply lessees in relation to the original owner/lessor, incapable of granting to a sublessee more than they originally acquired from their lessor. Since a typical lessee is not liable as an owner, then logically a sublessor should not be liable either, unless its status with regard to the sublessee operates somehow to confer owner liability. However, we find no basis in CERCLA for supposing that the relationship between the sublessor and sublessee is the critical relationship for identifying owner liability and therefore no principled basis for assuming that a lessee/sublessor's relationship with a sublessee automatically transforms the lessee/sublessor into an owner under § 9607(a). In fact, there are good reasons why this relationship cannot be dispositive for purposes of establishing strict owner liability.

Strict liability is a narrowly tailored tool, capturing a specific kind of responsibility. CERCLA's admittedly disjointed legislative history offers some useful insights into the congressional purposes motivating strict owner liability. *Cf. Shore Realty Corp.*, 759 F.2d at 1039 (stating that "CERCLA's history reveals as much about the nature of the legislative process as about the nature of the legislation," but nevertheless finding important guidance from the Act's history). The report of the Senate Committee on Environment and Public Works justified CERCLA's imposition of strict liability in part by referring to the English case of *Rylands v. Fletcher*, L.R. 3 H.L. 330 (1868). *See, e.g.,* S. Rep. No. 96-848, at 33 (1980), *reprinted in* 1 Legislative History of the Comprehensive Response, Compensation, and Liability Act of 1980 (Superfund), Public Law 96-510, at 305, 340 (1983) [hereinafter "CERCLA Legislative History"]. The reference is instructive. The principle enunciated in *Rylands v. Fletcher* has been succinctly stated by this court in *United States v. FMC Corp.*, 572 F.2d 902, 907 (2d Cir. 1978): "When one enters into a business or activity for his own benefit, and that benefit results in harm to others, the party should bear the responsibility for that harm." Central to the *Rylands v. Fletcher* theory of strict liability is the underlying fairness of imposing on the beneficiaries of an ultra-hazardous activity the ultimate costs of that activity. The Senate Committee wrote: "To establish provisions of liability any less than strict, joint, and several liability would be to condone a system in which innocent victims bear the actual burden of releases, while those who conduct commerce in hazardous substances which cause such damage benefit with relative impunity." 1 CERCLA Legislative History, *supra* at 320. CERCLA's strict owner liability, therefore, can be justified in part on the grounds that owners — even as lessors — derive benefit from the activities conducted on their property.

The same justification for strict liability does not necessarily or automatically apply to lessees/sublessors, as the facts of the present case make clear. The arrangement that led to Pasley's contamination of the site was between Commander Oil and Pasley, not between Pasley and Barlo. The terms of the original lease between Pasley and Commander Oil were set before Barlo was interposed as a sublessor. Commander was a sophisticated lessor and fully capable of including in the price of the lease the risk of Pasley contaminating the site. As we explain in part II of this opinion, infra, owner liability might attach to a sophisticated lessee/sublessor who exploits unanticipated risks on the property of an unsophisticated owner. But here, and in the normal course of events, such liability will not attach to lessees/sublessors.

There is an additional policy reason supporting our conclusion that owner liability should not automatically apply to lessees/sublessors. When buyers are considering purchasing property they will usually conduct an environmental assessment prior to closing. CERCLA has raised the costs of owning polluted land, and owners and potential owners are on notice of their liability and are wise to ensure that a potential acquisition is not encumbered by massive environmental liability. So far as we are able to discern, the same is not true of lessees/sublessors. A lessee/sublessor's concern about environmental hazards on a site will usually be limited to ensuring "that the property is adequate for the tenant's purposes and that there are no on-site environmental conditions or features which would impair the tenant's ability to operate." Richard D. Jones & Ivan S. DeVoren, *Managing Environmental Risks in Commercial Real Estate Leases,* SA81 ALI-ABA 121, 126 (1996). We are reluctant to surprise Barlo with new and unexpected liability, and to undermine the security of lessees/sublessors throughout the circuit who have entered into subleases before this decision.

II.

We do not foreclose the possibility that in some circumstances lessees/sublessors may be liable as owners under CERCLA. Certain lessees may have the requisite indicia of ownership vis-a-vis the record owner to be de facto owners and therefore strictly liable. Such would probably be true of a lessee with the proverbial 99-year lease. While we need not define with specificity those factors that might transform a lessee into an owner, we note several that we think could be important, specifically: (1) whether the lease is for an extensive term and admits of no rights in the owner/lessor to determine how the property is used; (2) whether the lease cannot be terminated by the owner before it expires by its terms; (3) whether the lessee has the right to sublet all or some of the property without notifying the owner; (4) whether the lessee is responsible for payment of all taxes, assessments, insurance, and operation and maintenance costs; and (5) whether the lessee is responsible for making all structural and other repairs. This non-exclusive list is meant to reinforce the point that the critical question is whether the lessee's status is that of a de facto owner and not whether it exercises control over the facility. *Cf. Bedford Affiliates v. Sills,* 156 F.3d 416, 425 (2d Cir. 1998) (noting that the innocent owner exception to liability is premised on an entity's status and not on its participation in activities relating to contamination). Moreover, the critical relationship is that between the lessee/sublessor and the owner/lessor, not that between the lessee/sublessor and the sublessee.

For example, sale-leaseback arrangements may not serve to insulate the former-owner/lessee from owner liability if the lessee actually retains most rights of ownership with respect to the new record owner. *See* 2 Powell on Real Property § 17A, at 3 (1997) ("The tenant's position as to use and occupancy and responsibility for operating expenses does not differ, from a practical standpoint, from the position that the tenant occupied as owner prior to sale."). Likewise, extremely long-term leases may create owner liability in the lessee if, according to the terms of the lease, the lessee retains so many of the indicia of ownership that he is the de facto owner. And owner liability might also lie where a lessee/sublessor has impermissibly exploited — by use himself or through a sublease — more rights than he originally leased, effectively expropriating from the owner the right to benefit from activity on the property.

Applying these principles to the case at hand, we conclude that the district court erred in holding Barlo strictly liable as an owner pursuant to 42 U.S.C. § 9607(a)(1). Whether or not Barlo was simply a rent conduit between Commander Oil and Pasley — as Barlo claims — it did not possess sufficient attributes of ownership over lot 7B. By the terms of the lease between Barlo and Commander Oil, Barlo was, inter alia, (1) limited to using lot 7A, and only "for that business presently conducted by tenant on a portion of the same premises leased hereunder"; (2) required to obtain written consent from Commander Oil before making "any additions, alterations or improvements" on the land, which alterations would become Commander Oil's property in any event; (3) required to obtain written approval from Commander Oil to sublet the property, and prohibited from subletting to any entity that had "any connection with the fuel, fuel oil or oil business"; (4) required to obtain written permission from Commander Oil to display any "sign, advertisement, notice or other lettering" on the building; (5) required to keep the property "clean and in order to the satisfaction of" Commander Oil, and responsible for any damage Barlo itself caused to the premises or to the "systems or equipment or any installation therein"; and (6) prohibited from doing anything that would "in any way increase the rate of fire insurance" on the property, and from bringing or keeping upon the premises "any inflammable, combustible or explosive fluid, chemical or substance." In addition, the lease was limited to a five-year term with one option for renewal.

Moreover, Commander Oil retained many of the rights and obligations of ownership. Among other things, the fuel company: (1) reserved a right to enter onto the lot for various purposes; (2) reserved for its own use three oil storage tanks on lot 7B; (3) reserved an "option" to use, on written notice to Barlo, "certain office space" within lot 7A; (4) reserved the right to maintain "its aerial or a comparable aerial" on the roof of the building; and (6) assumed responsibility to make structural repairs.

To be sure, Barlo possessed some attributes of ownership with respect to lot 7B. For instance, Barlo was obligated to secure insurance for the property, was liable to Commander Oil for all assessments on the property and anyincreases (but only increases) in taxes, and assumed responsibility for all nonstructural repairs, including "all repairs to heating, plumbing and lighting fixtures and equipment; cesspool maintenance, repair and replacement; snow removal; driveway, parking area and pavement repairs, etc." Notwithstanding these attributes, however, Barlo lacked most of the bundle of rights that comes with ownership of property. Accordingly, it may not be held liable under CERCLA as an owner, and the judgment of the district court is reversed to the extent that it imposed liability against Barlo for the contamination on lot 7B. * * *

[Remainder of opinion omitted.]

Conclusion

For the reasons stated above, the judgment of the district court is RE-VERSED to the extent that it imposes CERCLA liability against Barlo. * * *

NOTES AND QUESTIONS

1. Is a trustee an "owner" under CERCLA? *See, e.g., City of Phoenix v. Garbage Services Co.*, 827 F. Supp. 600, 605, n.5 (D. Ariz. 1993):

> This court disagrees with the holding in [other] cases that these trustees are not "owners" of the trust property. "From the traditional point of view it would seem that the trustee is the legal owner of the trust property and is subject to the duties and responsibilities of an owner as far as the outer world is concerned." 2A Scott on Trusts § 265.4 (4th ed. 1988). However, a trustee's CERCLA liability in these situations is necessarily limited to the extent the trust is sufficient to indemnify him; under no circumstances could the trustee's personal assets be reached.

2. *Passive Migration:* Assume Person A is the owner of Blackacre at the time hazardous substances are dumped into a permeable lagoon on the property. A transfers title to B; during B's time of ownership, no hazardous substances are dumped. B transfers title to C. C is the "owner" at the time a lawsuit is brought under CERCLA. Who is *prima facie* liable under these facts? Certainly A and C are. What about B? B may be liable if the court subscribes to the theory of passive migration. The theory is that if wastes already in place migrated into the environment during B's tenure as owner (i.e. "passive migration"), then B is an owner "at the time of disposal" and is, therefore, liable under § 107(a)(2), 42 U.S.C. § 9607(a)(2).

The theory remains a matter of vigourous dispute among the circuit courts, some finding liability for "interim owners," others refusing to do so. *Compare Nurad, Inc. v. William Hooper & Sons Co.*, 966 F.2d 837, 844–46 (4th Cir. 1992) ("disposal" includes passive migration); *with United States v. 150 Acres of Land*, 204 F.3d 698, 705–06 (6th Cir. 2000) ("disposal" requires active human conduct); *ABB Indus. Sys. Inc. v. Prime Technology, Inc.*, 120 F.3d 351, 357–59 (2d Cir. 1997) (same); *United States v. CDMG Realty Co.*, 96 F.3d 706, 713–18 (3d Cir. 1996) (same). The debate centers on the meaning of "disposal." CERCLA declares the term shall have the meaning provided in RCRA. § 101(29), 42 U.S.C. § 9691(29). RCRA, in turn, defines "disposal" as "the discharge, deposit, injection, dumping, spilling, leaking, or placing of any solid waste or hazardous waste into or on any land or water so that such solid waste or hazardous waste or any constituent thereof may enter the environment or be emitted into the air or discharged into any waters, including ground waters." § 1004(3), 42 U.S.C. § 6903(3).

Those who conclude this definition contemplates passive migration focus on the defining terms "discharge," "spill," or "leak," all of which can occur without human participation. They contend as well that a broad reading of "disposal" is warranted by the remedial nature of CERCLA and the statute's strict liability design. In that regard, they maintain an "active migration" reading would exempt from liability interim owners who knew of ongoing contamination and chose to do nothing about it.

Proponents of the active migration reading have arguments of their own. They contend the broad reading of these defining terms is unjustified because other modifiers in the same definition envision human participation. Moreover, in their view, the broad reading makes "disposal" synonymous with "release," even though the definition of "release" includes "disposing" as well as other terms such as "leaching" and "escaping." § 101 (22), 42 U.S.C. § 9601 (22). Third, they argue Congress could have created liability for all owners "after introduction of wastes" into a facility had it wanted to do so; it would not have chosen the phrase "at time of disposal" if that were its intent. Last, they assert the passive migration reading effectively eviscerates the so-called "innocent landowner" defense. *See, infra.*

As of this writing, and to the amazement of many, the Supreme Court has not decided the question. Congress, however, has addressed the matter at least tangentially. In the Brownfields Revitalization and Environmental Restoration Act, (P.L. 107-118, January, 2002), Congress added a new provision to CERCLA, designated as § 107(q), 42 U.S.C. § 9607(q). The provision states that persons who own or operate "real property that is contiguous to or otherwise similarly situated with respect to, and that is or may be contaminated by a release or threatened release of a hazardous substance from real property that is not owned by that person shall not be considered to be an owner or operator" for purposes of CERCLA liability. To fall under this exclusion, persons must not have contributed to the release or threatened release of hazardous substances, and must otherwise be free of liability and have complied with applicable legal requirements.

UNITED STATES v. GURLEY

43 F.3d 1188 (8th Cir. 1994)

JUDGES: Before HANSEN, Circuit Judge, FLOYD R. GIBSON, Senior Circuit Judge, and KOPF, District Judge.*

HANSEN, Circuit Judge.

---

* The HONORABLE RICHARD G. KOPF, United States District Judge for the District of Nebraska, sitting by designation.

The Environmental Protection Agency (EPA), on behalf of the United States, brought this action to recover the costs of cleaning up a hazardous waste site near Edmondson, Arkansas. The district court entered judgment for the EPA, imposing liability for past costs ($1,786,502.92) and future costs (estimated at $6,000,000) on defendants Gurley Refining Company, Inc.; its principal shareholder and president, William Gurley; and an employee, Larry Gurley.

These defendants appeal, raising several issues, the most significant of which are the argument that the present action is precluded by a prior action brought against the Gurley Refining Company, Inc., in 1983 and the argument that Larry Gurley's role in the company's disposal of hazardous waste was too tenuous to make him liable as an "operator" of a hazardous waste facility. We affirm in part and reverse in part.

I.

The facts of this case are well stated in the district court's memorandum order, *see United States v. Gurley Refining Co.*, 788 F. Supp. 1473, 1476–78 (E.D. Ark. 1992), and we will merely summarize them here. From 1970 to 1975, the Gurley Refining Company (GRC) rerefined used motor oil. GRC treated the used motor oil with sulfuric acid, mixed it with clay to absorb impurities, filtered out the clay, and sold the resulting rerefined oil. GRC then disposed of an acidic sludge and the spent clay in a borrow pit[3] it had leased from R. A. Caldwell pursuant to a permit issued for that purpose by the Arkansas Department of Pollution Control and Ecology (ADPCE). *Id.* The wastes of the rerefining process contained hazardous materials such as barium, lead, zinc, PCBs, and sulfuric acid. (Appellee's Br. at 4.)

In October 1975, GRC discontinued its rerefining processes and stopped disposing of wastes at the pit. In 1978, the United States Fish and Wildlife Service discovered that contaminated water from the pit had spilled over and damaged nearby fish and waterfowl habitats. The Service reported this to the EPA, which performed some work on the pit to prevent future spillovers.

But in the spring of 1979, after heavy rains, the pit overflowed again, releasing about a half million gallons of oily water into the surrounding area. The EPA could not persuade Caldwell or GRC to clean up the pit, so later that year it again performed work on the site to contain and treat wastes. In 1983, the EPA brought an action against Caldwell and GRC under the Federal Water Pollution Control Act, also known as the Clean Water Act (CWA), 33 U.S.C. §§ 1251–1376, to recover the costs it had incurred in 1979. In 1985, the district court entered judgment in favor of the EPA and against Caldwell and GRC in the amount of $76,758.60. *See United States v. Caldwell*, J-C-83-399, slip op. at 9 (E.D. Ark. Oct. 30, 1985), *reprinted in* Appellant GRC's & William Gurley's Br. at A37–A45. GRC did not appeal.

Meanwhile, in 1983, the pit was listed on the EPA's National Priorities List. In 1985, an investigation conducted on behalf of the EPA revealed that the site was still contaminated. In 1986, a feasibility study proposed four alternative courses of remedial action. The EPA chose the third alternative, which

---

[3] A "borrow pit" is "an excavated area where material (as earth) has been borrowed to be used as fill at another location." Webster's Third New Int'l Dictionary 257 (1986).

called for stabilization of the soil and contaminates, disposal of the soil and contaminates in an on-site landfill, backfilling of the excavated area, construction of flood protection, on-site treatment of contaminated water, and annual groundwater monitoring. *Gurley Refining Co.,* 788 F. Supp. at 1477.

Then in 1987, the EPA brought this action to recover the costs, both past and future, of the remedial action it had adopted after the 1986 study. Before trial, defendant Betty Gurley was dismissed from the case, and defendant R. A. Caldwell settled with the EPA. *Id.* at 1476 n.2. The matter was tried to the court for eight days in June and September of 1990. The district court entered judgment for the EPA on March 27, 1992, concluding that GRC, William Gurley, and Larry Gurley should be jointly and severally liable for cleanup costs, with prejudgment interest from September 10, 1990. The district court also entered a declaratory judgment that those three defendants shall be liable for the costs of all remedial action taken by the EPA in the future. The three defendants appeal.

II.

In 1980, Congress passed the Comprehensive Environmental Response, Compensation, and Liability Act (CERCLA), 42 U.S.C. §§ 9601–9675. Under the Act, persons who are responsible for the release of hazardous substances may be liable for the costs of removing or remedying the contamination, the costs associated with damage to natural resources, and the costs to human health. *See id.* § 9607(a); *see also Dravo Corp. v. Zuber,* 13 F.3d 1222, 1225 (8th Cir. 1994). The EPA may initiate a civil action to recover these costs. See 42 U.S.C. §§ 9607(a), 9613(h).

A.

Larry Gurley argues that he should not be held liable because, in short, he was merely an employee of GRC. He argues in the alternative that imposing liability on him for conduct that preceded CERCLA's enactment would violate the Due Process Clause.

1.

Liability for the release of hazardous substances may be imposed on "any person who at the time of disposal of any hazardous substance owned or operated any facility at which such hazardous substances were disposed of." 42 U.S.C. § 9607(a)(2) (emphasis added). The EPA does not contend that Larry Gurley had an ownership interest in either GRC or the site of the facility. Thus, he can be held liable only if he is an "operator." Larry Gurley argues specifically that the term "operator" should be limited to those individuals who had the "authority, responsibility, and capacity to control the corporate conduct in question." He contends that he did not have the authority to determine whether or how to dispose of hazardous wastes because he was not an officer, director, or shareholder in GRC and because his father, William Gurley, possessed nearly exclusive authority over GRC's operations.

CERCLA defines "owner or operator" simply as, "in the case of an onshore facility or an offshore facility, any person owning or operating such facility."

Id. § 9601(20)(A)(ii). It is clear that the term "person" may include individuals, *see id.* § 9601(21), but it is not clear when an individual should be deemed to have "operated" a hazardous waste disposal facility. In *United States v. Northeastern Pharm. & Chem. Co.,* 810 F.2d 726 (8th Cir. 1986) (NEPACCO), *cert. denied,* 484 U.S. 848, 98 L. Ed. 2d 102, 108 S. Ct. 146 (1987), we held that an individual could be held liable for the release of hazardous substances under a different subsection, which imposes liability on a person who "arranged for disposal or treatment . . . of hazardous substances owned or possessed by such person," *see* 42 U.S.C. § 9607(a)(3). We found that the individual defendant "possessed" the hazardous substances because he "had actual 'control' over the NEPACCO plant's hazardous substances." *NEPACCO,* 810 F.2d at 743. We also stated, "It is the authority to control the handling and disposal of hazardous substances that is critical under the statutory scheme." *Id.* Thus, we affirmed a finding that the individual had "possessed" hazardous substances on two closely related but distinct grounds: that the individual had "actual control" of the hazardous substances and that he had "authority to control" their disposal.

Federal courts have struggled with these two concepts when addressing the question of whether an individual may be found liable as an "operator" under § 9607(a)(2). In some circuits, a plaintiff must prove that an individual defendant had actual responsibility for, involvement in, or control over the disposal of hazardous waste at a facility. *See Sidney S. Arst Co. v. Pipefitters Welfare Educ. Fund,* 25 F.3d 417, 421 (7th Cir. 1994) (holding that plaintiff must allege that individual defendant "directly and personally engaged in conduct that led to the specific environmental damage at issue"); *Riverside Market Devel. Corp. v. International Bldg. Prods., Inc.,* 931 F.2d 327, 330 (5th Cir.) (holding that proper focus is "the extent of [individual] defendant's personal participation in the alleged wrongful conduct"), *cert. denied,* 112 S. Ct. 636 (1991); *New York v. Shore Realty Corp.,* 759 F.2d 1032, 1052 (1st Cir. 1985) (holding that individual defendant was "operator" because he was "in charge of the operation of the facility"); *see also Levin Metals Corp. v. Parr–Richmond Terminal Co.,* 781 F. Supp. 1454, 1457 (N.D. Cal. 1991) ("an individual cannot be liable as an 'operator' under CERCLA Section 107(a)(2) [42 U.S.C. § 9607(a)(2)] unless that individual actually participates in the operation of the facility at which hazardous substances are disposed of, exercised control over the company immediately responsible for the operation of that facility, or is otherwise intimately involved in that company's operations").

On the other hand, in one circuit, a plaintiff can succeed by proving less than that; an individual defendant "'need not have exercised actual control in order to qualify as [an] operator under § 9607(a)(2), so long as the authority to control the facility was present.'" *United States v. Carolina Transformer Co.,* 978 F.2d 832, 836–37 (4th Cir. 1992) (emphasis added) (quoting *Nurad, Inc. v. Hooper & Sons Co.,* 966 F.2d 837, 842 (4th Cir.), *cert. denied,* 113 S. Ct. 377 (1992)); *see also Northwestern Mut. Life Ins. Co. v. Atlantic Research Corp.,* 847 F. Supp. 389, 397 (E.D. Va. 1994) (holding that individual defendant may be liable if he has "the 'authority to control' activities on the facility"); *Robertshaw Controls Co. v. Watts Regulator Co.,* 807 F. Supp. 144, 152–53 (D. Me. 1992) (holding that liability is proper if individual defendant had authority such that he "could have prevented the hazardous waste discharge"); *cf. Kelley v. Thomas Solvent Co.*, 727 F. Supp. 1532, 1543–44 (W.D. Mich. 1989) (stating that court should "weigh the factors of the corporate individual's degree of authority" but also should consider "evidence of responsibility undertaken and neglected").

An individual defendant who has actual control over the operation of a facility presumably also has authority to control the operation of the facility, with the possible exception of an individual acting ultra vires, a situation not present in this case or in the cases cited above. Thus, in reality, the two approaches differ in that one requires a plaintiff to prove that the defendant both had the authority to control the operation of the facility and actually exercised that authority, while the other requires a plaintiff to prove only that a defendant had the authority to control the operation of the facility.

We believe that the latter approach is inconsistent with the term "operator," whose common meaning is "one that produces a physical effect or engages himself in the mechanical aspect of any process or activity." Webster's Third New Int'l Dictionary 1581 (1986). Likewise, the verb "to operate" means "to perform a work or labor," to "exert power or influence," to "produce an effect," "to cause to occur," or to "bring about by or as if by the exertion of positive effort or influence." *Id.* at 1580–81. These definitions connote some type of action or affirmative conduct, an element not required by those courts that ask only whether a defendant had the authority to control the operation of the facility. We prefer not to interpret the statute in a manner that would produce the anomalous result of imposing CERCLA liability on an "operator" who in fact never "operated" a facility. Thus, we hold that an individual may not be held liable as an "operator" under § 9607(a)(2) unless he or she (1) had authority to determine whether hazardous wastes would be disposed of and to determine the method of disposal and (2) actually exercised that authority, either by personally performing the tasks necessary to dispose of the hazardous wastes or by directing others to perform those tasks. We believe that this rule is the wiser of the two choices reflected in the existing case law and is faithful to our closely analogous decision in *NEPACCO*.

The district court made oral findings that Larry Gurley "personally participated in the disposal of the hazardous substances in question in the pit that is involved in this litigation" and that he "had extensive authority in an effort to implement the policies and practices of the corporate entity, which included the disposal of these hazardous substances." (Trial Tr. at 210–11.) In fact, the district court found those facts to be "crystal clear." *Id.* These findings address both prongs of the standard we have set out above. We review the district court's findings for clear error. *See* Fed. R. Civ. P. 52(a).

The record reveals that GRC had approximately six employees from 1970 to 1975 and that William Gurley, who was the principal shareholder, had ultimate responsibility for the business and took an active role in its management. In particular, William Gurley negotiated the lease with R. A. Caldwell for the property that later contained the pit, oversaw construction of the disposal facility, and directed employees to dispose of rerefining wastes there. The record also reveals that Larry Gurley began working in the rerefining plant in 1969 after his graduation from college. In that role, he helped load the trucks that hauled hazardous wastes to the pit. In 1972, he moved into the administrative offices, where he served as GRC's purchasing agent.

But several parts of the record also reveal that Larry Gurley's duties were broader than just purchasing. First, Larry Gurley testified in 1983 in *Caldwell v. Gurley Refining Co.,* No. J-C-79-101 (E.D. Ark.), *aff'd,* 755 F.2d 645 (8th Cir. 1985), that he eventually became "director of operations," a job which "basically put me in control of the day to day operations of the plant and anything that pertains to that." (Appellee's App. at 41.) He testified that his father tended to other businesses while he took care of GRC. (*Id.*) Second, when the ADPCE contacted GRC in 1973 to express its concern about the pit, Larry Gurley personally responded in a letter that said, "I received your letter concerning the pit where we dump our waste material. I made a visual inspection of the pit area today." (*Id.* at 1.) Third, Larry Gurley testified in 1983 that he "would have to take responsibility for" installing a pump and hose in the pit in 1974 that caused ADPCE to complain. (*Id.* at 45–46.) Fourth, in 1974, Larry Gurley personally responded to a letter from the West Memphis, Arkansas, City Attorney concerning the discharge of oil from the pit into the surrounding area. (*Id.* at 2–3.) Fifth and finally, Larry Gurley's responsibility for waste disposal is evidenced by the role he played in closing down the pit and filing reports with the ADPCE. He personally sent at least one letter to the ADPCE, (*id.* at 9), and he wrote and signed a report concerning the closure of the pit. He testified that the report reflected an engineer's recommendations and GRC's agreement with the ADPCE, which he apparently had negotiated. (*Id.* at 49–50).

Although Larry Gurley argues that he acted as a mere "wordsmith" for his father, (Appellant Larry Gurley's Reply Br. at 9), we are not convinced. The letters were sent under Larry Gurley's name. In fact, William Gurley testified in 1983 that Larry Gurley bore responsibility for the report filed with the ADPCE because "he was operational manager; he had the latitude to make decisions of this kind." (*Id.* at 39.) Although Larry Gurley testified at the trial of this case that he simply followed William Gurley's directions on these matters, it is apparent that he had substantial responsibilities of his own between 1972 and 1975. The district court, which read the transcripts of the 1983 trial and heard the testimony of Larry Gurley and William Gurley at the trial of this action, reasonably concluded that Larry Gurley "personally participated in the disposal of the hazardous substances" and "had extensive authority" over GRC's disposal of hazardous wastes.

We think Larry Gurley's argument places too much emphasis on his status within GRC and not enough emphasis on his actual activities. Although he was not an officer, director, or shareholder, he nonetheless had substantial responsibilities for GRC's waste disposal. Perhaps persons who are officers, directors, or shareholders are more likely to cause a company to dispose of hazardous wastes, but we decline to confer immunity on all persons who do not hold such positions. An individual defendant's responsibility for the disposal of hazardous waste should be judged on a case-by-case basis. In this case, the evidence clearly and strongly supports the district court's findings that Larry Gurley had authority to determine GRC's hazardous waste disposal activities and that he actually exercised that authority.

For these reasons, the district court did not err when it found that Larry Gurley was liable as an "operator." *See* 42 U.S.C. § 9607(a)(2).

2.

Larry Gurley's second argument, that the imposition of liability for conduct that preceded CERCLA's effective date violates due process, is squarely foreclosed by *NEPACCO,* where we held that CERCLA was intended to apply retroactively and that such retroactive application does not violate the Due Process Clause. 810 F.2d at 732–34. For due process purposes, Larry Gurley's circumstances are no different from the circumstances of the defendants in *NEPACCO.*

[Remainder of opinion omitted.]

UNITED STATES v. BESTFOODS

524 U.S. 51, 118 S. Ct. 1876 (1998)

JUSTICE SOUTER delivered the opinion of the Court.

The United States brought this action for the costs of cleaning up industrial waste generated by a chemical plant. The issue before us, under the Comprehensive Environmental Response, Compensation, and Liability Act of 1980 (CERCLA), 94 Stat. 2767, as amended, 42 U.S.C. § 9601 *et seq.*, is whether a parent corporation that actively participated in, and exercised control over, the operations of a subsidiary may, without more, be held liable as an operator of a polluting facility owned or operated by the subsidiary. We answer no, unless the corporate veil may be pierced. But a corporate parent that actively participated in, and exercised control over, the operations of the facility itself may be held directly liable in its own right as an operator of the facility.

I

In 1980, CERCLA was enacted in response to the serious environmental and health risks posed by industrial pollution. *See Exxon Corp. v. Hunt,* 475 U.S. 355, 358–359, 89 L. Ed. 2d 364, 106 S. Ct. 1103 (1986). "As its name implies, CERCLA is a comprehensive statute that grants the President broad power to command government agencies and private parties to clean up hazardous waste sites." *Key Tronic Corp. v. United States,* 511 U.S. 809, 814, 128 L. Ed. 2d 797, 114 S. Ct. 1960 (1994). If it satisfies certain statutory conditions, the United States may, for instance, use the "Hazardous Substance Superfund" to finance cleanup efforts, *see* 42 U.S.C. §§ 9601(11), 9604; 26 U.S.C. § 9507, which it may then replenish by suits brought under § 107 of the Act against, among others, "any person who at the time of disposal of any hazardous substance owned or operated any facility." 42 U.S.C. § 9607(a)(2). So, those actually "responsible for any damage, environmental harm, or injury from chemical poisons [may be tagged with] the cost of their actions," S. Rep. No. 96-848, p. 13 (1980). The term "person" is defined in CERCLA to include corporations and other business organizations, *see* 42 U.S.C. § 9601(21), and the term "facility" enjoys a broad and detailed definition as well, *see* § 9601(9).

The phrase "owner or operator" is defined only by tautology, however, as "any person owning or operating" a facility, § 9601(20)(A)(ii), and it is this bit of circularity that prompts our review. *Cf. Exxon Corp. v. Hunt, supra,* at 363 (CERCLA, "unfortunately, is not a model of legislative draftsmanship").

II

In 1957, Ott Chemical Co. (Ott I) began manufacturing chemicals at a plant near Muskegon, Michigan, and its intentional and unintentional dumping of hazardous substances significantly polluted the soil and ground water at the site. In 1965, respondent CPC International Inc.[3] incorporated a wholly owned subsidiary to buy Ott I's assets in exchange for CPC stock. The new company, also dubbed Ott Chemical Co. (Ott II), continued chemical manufacturing at the site, and continued to pollute its surroundings. CPC kept the managers of Ott I, including its founder, president, and principal shareholder, Arnold Ott, on board as officers of Ott II. Arnold Ott and several other Ott II officers and directors were also given positions at CPC, and they performed duties for both corporations.

In 1972, CPC sold Ott II to Story Chemical Company, which operated the Muskegon plant until its bankruptcy in 1977. Shortly thereafter, when respondent Michigan Department of Natural Resources (MDNR) examined the site for environmental damage, it found the land littered with thousands of leaking and even exploding drums of waste, and the soil and water saturated with noxious chemicals. MDNR sought a buyer for the property who would be willing to contribute toward its cleanup, and after extensive negotiations, respondent Aerojet-General Corp. arranged for transfer of the site from the Story bankruptcy trustee in 1977. Aerojet created a wholly owned California subsidiary, Cordova Chemical Company (Cordova/California), to purchase the property, and Cordova/California in turn created a wholly owned Michigan subsidiary, Cordova Chemical Company of Michigan (Cordova/Michigan), which manufactured chemicals at the site until 1986.

By 1981, the federal Environmental Protection Agency had undertaken to see the site cleaned up, and its long-term remedial plan called for expenditures well into the tens of millions of dollars. To recover some of that money, the United States filed this action under § 107 in 1989, naming five defendants as responsible parties: CPC, Aerojet, Cordova/California, Cordova/Michigan, and Arnold Ott. (By that time, Ott I and Ott II were defunct.) After the parties (and MDNR) had launched a flurry of contribution claims, counterclaims, and cross-claims, the District Court consolidated the cases for trial in three phases: liability, remedy, and insurance coverage. So far, only the first phase has been completed; in 1991, the District Court held a 15-day bench trial on the issue of liability. Because the parties stipulated that the Muskegon plant was a "facility" within the meaning of 42 U.S.C. § 9601(9), that hazardous substances had been released at the facility, and that the United States had incurred reimbursable response costs to clean up the site, the trial focused on the issues of whether CPC and Aerojet, as the parent corporations of Ott II and the Cordova companies, had "owned or operated" the facility within the meaning of § 107(a)(2).

---

[3] CPC has [since] changed its name to Bestfoods . . . we use the name CPC herein.

The District Court said that operator liability may attach to a parent corporation both directly, when the parent itself operates the facility, and indirectly, when the corporate veil can be pierced under state law. *See CPC Int'l, Inc. v. Aerojet-General Corp.*, 777 F. Supp. 549, 572 (WD Mich. 1991). The court explained that, while CERCLA imposes direct liability in situations in which the corporate veil cannot be pierced under traditional concepts of corporate law, "the statute and its legislative history do not suggest that CERCLA rejects entirely the crucial limits to liability that are inherent to corporate law." *Id.*, at 573. As the District Court put it,

> "a parent corporation is directly liable under section 107(a)(2) as an operator only when it has exerted power or influence over its subsidiary by actively participating in and exercising control over the subsidiary's business during a period of disposal of hazardous waste. A parent's actual participation in and control over a subsidiary's functions and decision-making creates 'operator' liability under CERCLA; a parent's mere oversight of a subsidiary's business in a manner appropriate and consistent with the investment relationship between a parent and its wholly owned subsidiary does not." *Ibid.*

Applying that test to the facts of this case, the District Court held both CPC and Aerojet liable under § 107(a)(2) as operators. As to CPC, the court found it particularly telling that CPC selected Ott II's board of directors and populated its executive ranks with CPC officials, and that a CPC official, G.R.D. Williams, played a significant role in shaping Ott II's environmental compliance policy.

After a divided panel of the Court of Appeals for the Sixth Circuit reversed in part, *United States v. Cordova/Michigan*, 59 F.3d 584, that court granted rehearing en banc and vacated the panel decision, 67 F.3d 586 (1995). This time, 7 judges to 6, the court again reversed the District Court in part. 113 F.3d 572 (1997). The majority remarked on the possibility that a parent company might be held directly liable as an operator of a facility owned by its subsidiary: "At least conceivably, a parent might independently operate the facility in the stead of its subsidiary; or, as a sort of joint venturer, actually operate the facility alongside its subsidiary." *Id.*, at 579. But the court refused to go any further and rejected the District Court's analysis with the explanation.

> "that where a parent corporation is sought to be held liable as an operator pursuant to 42 U.S.C. § 9607(a)(2) based upon the extent of its control of its subsidiary which owns the facility, the parent will be liable only when the requirements necessary to pierce the corporate veil [under state law] are met. In other words, . . . whether the parent will be liable as an operator depends upon whether the degree to which it controls its subsidiary and the extent and manner of its involvement with the facility, amount to the abuse of the corporate form that will warrant piercing the corporate veil and disregarding the separate corporate entities of the parent and subsidiary." *Id.*, at 580.

Applying Michigan veil-piercing law, the Court of Appeals decided that neither CPC nor Aerojet was liable for controlling the actions of its subsidiaries, since the parent and subsidiary corporations maintained separate personalities and the parents did not utilize the subsidiary corporate form to perpetrate fraud or subvert justice.

We granted certiorari, 522 U.S. (1997), to resolve a conflict among the Circuits over the extent to which parent corporations may be held liable under CERCLA for operating facilities ostensibly under the control of their subsidiaries. We now vacate and remand.

III

It is a general principle of corporate law deeply "ingrained in our economic and legal systems" that a parent corporation (so-called because of control through ownership of another corporation's stock) is not liable for the acts of its subsidiaries . . . (citations omitted).

. . . .

. . . Thus it is hornbook law that "the exercise of the 'control' which stock ownership gives to the stockholders . . . will not create liability beyond the assets of the subsidiary. That 'control' includes the election of directors, the making of by-laws . . . and the doing of all other acts incident to the legal status of stockholders. Nor will a duplication of some or all of the directors or executive officers be fatal." Douglas 196 (footnotes omitted). Although this respect for corporate distinctions when the subsidiary is a polluter has been severely criticized in the literature, *see, e.g., Note, Liability of Parent Corporations for Hazardous Waste Cleanup and Damages*, 99 Harv. L. Rev. 986 (1986), nothing in CERCLA purports to reject this bedrock principle, and against this venerable common-law backdrop, the congressional silence is audible. *Cf. Edmonds v. Compagnie Generale Transatlantique*, 443 U.S. 256, 266–267, 61 L. Ed. 2d 521, 99 S. Ct. 2753 (1979) ("silence is most eloquent, for such reticence while contemplating an important and controversial change in existing law is unlikely"). The Government has indeed made no claim that a corporate parent is liable as an owner or an operator under § 107 simply because its subsidiary is subject to liability for owning or operating a polluting facility.

But there is an equally fundamental principle of corporate law, applicable to the parent-subsidiary relationship as well as generally, that the corporate veil may be pierced and the shareholder held liable for the corporation's conduct when, *inter alia*, the corporate form would otherwise be misused to accomplish certain wrongful purposes, most notably fraud, on the shareholder's behalf . . . (citations omitted). . . . Nothing in CERCLA purports to rewrite this well-settled rule, either. CERCLA is thus like many another congressional enactment in giving no indication "that the entire corpus of state corporation law is to be replaced simply because a plaintiff's cause of action is based upon a federal statute," *Burks v. Lasker*, 441 U.S. 471, 478, 60 L. Ed. 2d 404, 99 S. Ct. 1831 (1979), and the failure of the statute to speak to a matter as fundamental as the liability implications of corporate ownership demands application of the rule that "in order to abrogate a common-law principle, the statute must speak directly to the question addressed by the common law," *United States v. Texas*, 507 U.S. 529, 534, 123 L. Ed. 2d 245, 113 S. Ct. 1631 (1993) (internal quotation marks omitted). The Court of Appeals was accordingly correct in holding that when (but only when) the corporate veil may be pierced,[9] may a parent corporation be charged with derivative CERCLA liability for its subsidiary's actions.

IV

A

If the act rested liability entirely on ownership of a polluting facility, this opinion might end here; but CERCLA liability may turn on operation as well as ownership, and nothing in the statute's terms bars a parent corporation from direct liability for its own actions in operating a facility owned by its subsidiary. As Justice (then-Professor) Douglas noted almost 70 years ago, derivative liability cases are to be distinguished from those in which "the alleged wrong can seemingly be traced to the parent through the conduit of its own personnel and management" and "the parent is directly a participant in the wrong complained of." Douglas 207, 208. n11 In such instances, the parent is directly liable for its own actions. *See* H. Henn & J. Alexander, Laws of Corporations 347 (3d ed. 1983) (hereinafter Henn & Alexander) ("Apart from corporation law principles, a shareholder, whether a natural person or a corporation, may be liable on the ground that such shareholder's activity resulted in the liability"). The fact that a corporate subsidiary happens to own a polluting facility operated by its parent does nothing, then, to displace the rule that the parent "corporation is [itself] responsible for the wrongs committed by its agents in the course of its business," *Mine Workers v. Coronado Coal Co.*, 259 U.S. 344, 395, 66 L. Ed. 975, 42 S. Ct. 570 (1922), and whereas the rules of veil-piercing limit derivative liability for the actions of another corporation, CERCLA's "operator" provision is concerned primarily with direct liability for one's own actions. *See, e.g., Sidney S. Arst Co. v. Pipefitters Welfare*

---

[9] There is significant disagreement among courts and commentators over whether, in enforcing CERCLA's indirect liability, courts should borrow state law, or instead apply a federal common law of veil piercing. *Compare, e.g.,* 113 F.3d at 584–585 (Merritt, J., concurring in part and dissenting in part) (arguing that federal common law should apply), *Lansford-Coaldale Joint Water Auth. v. Tonolli Corp.*, 4 F.3d at 1225 ("given the federal interest in uniformity in the application of CERCLA, it is federal common law, and not state law, which governs when corporate veil-piercing is justified under CERCLA"), *and* Aronovsky & Fuller, *Liability of Parent Corporations for Hazardous Substance Releases under CERCLA,* 24 U.S. F. L. Rev. 421, 455 (1990) ("CERCLA enforcement should not be hampered by subordination of its goals to varying state law rules of alter ego theory"), *with, e.g.,* 113 F.3d at 580 ("Whether the circumstances in this case warrant a piercing of the corporate veil will be determined by state law"), *and* Dennis, *Liability of Officers, Directors and Stockholders under CERCLA: The Case for Adopting State Law,* 36 Vill. L. Rev. 1367 (1991) (arguing that state law should apply). Cf. *In re Acushnet River & New Bedford Harbor Proceedings*, 675 F. Supp. 22, 33 (Mass. 1987) (noting that, since "federal common law draws upon state law for guidance, . . . the choice between state and federal [veil-piercing law] may in many cases present questions of academic interest, but little practical significance"). But cf. Note, Piercing the Corporate Law Veil: The Alter Ego Doctrine Under Federal Common Law, 95 Harv. L. Rev. 853 (1982) (arguing that federal common law need not mirror state law, because "federal common law should look to federal statutory policy rather than to state corporate law when deciding whether to pierce the corporate veil"). Since none of the parties challenges the Sixth Circuit's holding that CPC and Aerojet incurred no derivative liability, the question is not presented in this case, and we do not address it further.

[Ed. note: For a recent case holding that state common law should apply, see *Carter-Jones Lumber Co. v. LTV Steel Co.*, 237 F.3d 745 (6th Cir. 2001), *cert. denied sub nom. Dixie Distrib. Co. v. Carter-Jones Lumber Co.*, 121 S. Ct. 2244 (2001).]

Ed. Fund, 25 F.3d 417, 420 (CA7 1994) ("the direct, personal liability provided by CERCLA is distinct from the derivative liability that results from piercing the corporate veil") (internal quotation marks omitted). It is this direct liability that is properly seen as being at issue here.

Under the plain language of the statute, any person who operates a polluting facility is directly liable for the costs of cleaning up the pollution. *See* 42 U.S.C. § 9607(a)(2). This is so regardless of whether that person is the facility's owner, the owner's parent corporation or business partner, or even a saboteur who sneaks into the facility at night to discharge its poisons out of malice. If any such act of operating a corporate subsidiary's facility is done on behalf of a parent corporation, the existence of the parent-subsidiary relationship under state corporate law is simply irrelevant to the issue of direct liability. *See Riverside Market Dev. Corp. v. International Bldg. Prods., Inc.*, 931 F.2d 327, 330 (CA5) ("CERCLA prevents individuals from hiding behind the corporate shield when, as 'operators,' they themselves actually participate in the wrongful conduct prohibited by the Act"), *cert. denied*, 502 U.S. 1004 (1991); *United States v. Kayser-Roth Corp.*, 910 F.2d 24, 26 (CA1 1990) ("a person who is an operator of a facility is not protected from liability by the legal structure of ownership").

This much is easy to say; the difficulty comes in defining actions sufficient to constitute direct parental "operation." Here of course we may again rue the uselessness of CERCLA's definition of a facility's "operator" as "any person . . . operating" the facility, 42 U.S.C. § 9601(20)(A)(ii), which leaves us to do the best we can to give the term its "ordinary or natural meaning." *Bailey v. United States*, 516 U.S. 137, 145, 133 L. Ed. 2d 472, 116 S. Ct. 501 (1995) (internal quotation marks omitted). In a mechanical sense, to "operate" ordinarily means "to control the functioning of; run: operate a sewing machine." American Heritage Dictionary 1268 (3d ed. 1992); *see also* Webster's New International Dictionary 1707 (2d ed. 1958) ("to work; as, to operate a machine"). And in the organizational sense more obviously intended by CERCLA, the word ordinarily means "to conduct the affairs of; manage: *operate a business*." American Heritage Dictionary, *supra*, at 1268; *see also* Webster's New International Dictionary, *supra*, at 1707 ("to manage"). So, under CERCLA, an operator is simply someone who directs the workings of, manages, or conducts the affairs of a facility. To sharpen the definition for purposes of CERCLA's concern with environmental contamination, an operator must manage, direct, or conduct operations specifically related to pollution, that is, operations having to do with the leakage or disposal of hazardous waste, or decisions about compliance with environmental regulations.

B

With this understanding, we are satisfied that the Court of Appeals correctly rejected the District Court's analysis of direct liability. But we also think that the appeals court erred in limiting direct liability under the statute to a parent's sole or joint venture operation, so as to eliminate any possible finding that CPC is liable as an operator on the facts of this case.

1

By emphasizing that "CPC is directly liable under section 107(a)(2) as an operator because CPC actively participated in and exerted significant control over Ott II's business and decision-making," 777 F. Supp. at 574, the District Court applied the "actual control" test of whether the parent "actually operated the business of its subsidiary," *id.*, at 573, as several Circuits have employed it, *see, e.g., United States v. Kayser-Roth Corp., supra*, at 27 (operator liability "requires active involvement in the affairs of the subsidiary"); *Jacksonville Elec. Auth. v. Bernuth Corp.*, 996 F.2d 1107, 1110 (CA11 1993) (parent is liable if it "actually exercised control over, or was otherwise intimately involved in the operations of, the [subsidiary] corporation immediately responsible for the operation of the facility" (internal quotation marks omitted)).

The well-taken objection to the actual control test, however, is its fusion of direct and indirect liability; the test is administered by asking a question about the relationship between the two corporations (an issue going to indirect liability) instead of a question about the parent's interaction with the subsidiary's facility (the source of any direct liability). If, however, direct liability for the parent's operation of the facility is to be kept distinct from derivative liability for the subsidiary's own operation, the focus of the enquiry must necessarily be different under the two tests. "The question is not whether the parent operates the subsidiary, but rather whether it operates the facility, and that operation is evidenced by participation in the activities of the facility, not the subsidiary. Control of the subsidiary, if extensive enough, gives rise to indirect liability under piercing doctrine, not direct liability under the statutory language." Oswald 269; *see also Schiavone v. Pearce*, 79 F.3d 248, 254 (CA2 1996) ("Any liabilities [the parent] may have as an operator, then, stem directly from its control over the plant"). The District Court was therefore mistaken to rest its analysis on CPC's relationship with Ott II, premising liability on little more than "CPC's 100-percent ownership of Ott II" and "CPC's active participation in, and at times majority control over, Ott II's board of directors." 777 F. Supp. at 575. The analysis should instead have rested on the relationship between CPC and the Muskegon facility itself.

In addition to (and perhaps as a reflection of) the erroneous focus on the relationship between CPC and Ott II, even those findings of the District Court that might be taken to speak to the extent of CPC's activity at the facility itself are flawed, for the District Court wrongly assumed that the actions of the joint officers and directors are necessarily attributable to CPC. The District Court emphasized the facts that CPC placed its own high-level officials on Ott II's board of directors and in key management positions at Ott II, and that those individuals made major policy decisions and conducted day-to-day operations at the facility: "Although Ott II corporate officers set the day-to-day operating policies for the company without any need to obtain formal approval from CPC, CPC actively participated in this decision-making because high-ranking CPC officers served in Ott II management positions." *Id.*, at 559; *see also id.*, at 575 (relying on "CPC's involvement in major decision-making and day-to-day operations through CPC officials who served within Ott II management, including the positions of president and chief executive officer," and on "the conduct of CPC officials with respect to Ott II affairs, particularly Arnold Ott"); *id.*, at 558 ("CPC actively participated in, and at times controlled, the policy-making decisions of its subsidiary thorough its representation on the Ott II board of directors"); *id.*, at 559 ("CPC also actively participated in and exercised control over day-to-day decision-making at Ott II through representation in the highest levels of the subsidiary's management"). In imposing direct liability on these grounds, the District Court failed to recognize that "it is entirely appropriate for directors of a parent corporation to serve as directors of its subsidiary, and that fact alone may not serve to expose the parent corporation to liability for its subsidiary's acts." *American Protein Corp. v. AB Volvo*, 844 F.2d 56, 57 (CA2), *cert. denied*, 488 U.S. 852, 102 L. Ed. 2d 109, 109 S. Ct. 136 (1988); *see also Kingston Dry Dock Co. v. Lake Champlain Transp. Co.*, 31 F.2d 265, 267 (CA2 1929) (L. Hand, J.) ("Control through the ownership of shares does not fuse the corporations, even when the directors are common to each"); Henn & Alexander 355 (noting that it is "normal" for a parent and subsidiary to "have identical directors and officers"). This recognition that the corporate personalities remain distinct has its corollary in the "well established principle [of corporate law] that directors and officers holding positions with a parent and its subsidiary can and do 'change hats' to represent the two corporations separately, despite their common ownership." *Lusk v. Foxmeyer Health Corp.*, 129 F.3d 773, 779 (CA5 1997); *see also Fisser v. International Bank*, 282 F.2d 231, 238 (CA2 1960). Since courts generally presume "that the directors are wearing their 'subsidiary hats' and not their 'parent hats' when acting for the subsidiary," P. Blumberg, Law of Corporate Groups: Procedural Problems in the Law of Parent and Subsidiary Corporations § 1.02.1, at 12 (1983); *see, e.g., United States v. Jon-T Chemicals, Inc.*, 768 F.2d 686, 691 (CA5 1985), *cert. denied*, 475 U.S. 1014, 89 L. Ed. 2d 309, 106 S. Ct. 1194 (1986), it cannot be enough to establish liability here that dual officers and directors made policy decisions and supervised activities at the facility. The Government would have to show that, despite the general presumption to the contrary, the officers and directors were acting in their capacities as CPC officers and directors, and not as Ott II officers and directors, when they committed those acts. The District Court made no such enquiry here, however, disregarding entirely this time-honored common law rule.

In sum, the District Court's focus on the relationship between parent and subsidiary (rather than parent and facility), combined with its automatic attribution of the actions of dual officers and directors to the corporate parent, erroneously, even if unintentionally, treated CERCLA as though it displaced or fundamentally altered common law standards of limited liability. Indeed, if the evidence of common corporate personnel acting at management and directorial levels were enough to support a finding of a parent corporation's direct operator liability under CERCLA, then the possibility of resort to veil piercing to establish indirect, derivative liability for the subsidiary's violations would be academic. There would in essence be a relaxed, CERCLA-specific rule of derivative liability that would banish traditional standards and expectations from the law of CERCLA liability. But, as we have said, such a rule does not arise from congressional silence, and CERCLA's silence is dispositive.

2

We accordingly agree with the Court of Appeals that a participation-and-control test looking to the parent's supervision over the subsidiary, especially one that assumes that dual officers always act on behalf of the parent, cannot be used to identify operation of a facility resulting in direct parental liability. Nonetheless, a return to the ordinary meaning of the word "operate" in the organizational sense will indicate why we think that the Sixth Circuit stopped short when it confined its examples of direct parental operation to exclusive or joint ventures, and declined to find at least the possibility of direct operation by CPC in this case.

In our enquiry into the meaning Congress presumably had in mind when it used the verb "to operate," we recognized that the statute obviously meant something more than mere mechanical activation of pumps and valves, and must be read to contemplate "operation" as including the exercise of direction over the facility's activities. *See supra*, at 13. The Court of Appeals recognized this by indicating that a parent can be held directly liable when the parent operates the facility in the stead of its subsidiary or alongside the subsidiary in some sort of a joint venture. *See* 113 F.3d at 579. We anticipated a further possibility above, however, when we observed that a dual officer or director might depart so far from the norms of parental influence exercised through dual officeholding as to serve the parent, even when ostensibly acting on behalf of the subsidiary in operating the facility. Yet another possibility, suggested by the facts of this case, is that an agent of the parent with no hat to wear but the parent's hat might manage or direct activities at the facility. Identifying such an occurrence calls for line drawing yet again, since the acts of direct operation that give rise to parental liability must necessarily be distinguished from the interference that stems from the normal relationship between parent and subsidiary. Again norms of corporate behavior (undisturbed by any CERCLA provision) are crucial reference points. Just as we may look to such norms in identifying the limits of the presumption that a dual officeholder acts in his ostensible capacity, so here we may refer to them in distinguishing a parental officer's oversight of a subsidiary from such an officer's control over the operation of the subsidiary's facility. "Activities that involve the facility but which are consistent with the parent's investor status, such as monitoring of the subsidiary's performance, supervision of the subsidiary's finance and capital budget decisions, and articulation of general policies and procedures, should not give rise to direct liability." Oswald 282. The critical question is whether, in degree and detail, actions directed to the facility by an agent of the parent alone are eccentric under accepted norms of parental oversight of a subsidiary's facility. There is, in fact, some evidence that CPC engaged in just this type and degree of activity at the Muskegon plant. The District Court's opinion speaks of an agent of CPC alone who played a conspicuous part in dealing with the toxic risks emanating from the operation of the plant. G.R.D. Williams worked only for CPC; he was not an employee, officer, or director of Ott II, see Tr. of Oral Arg. 7, and thus, his actions were of necessity taken only on behalf of CPC. The District Court found that "CPC became directly involved in environmental and regulatory matters through the work of . . . Williams, CPC's governmental and environmental affairs director. Williams . . . became heavily involved in environmental issues at Ott II." 777 F. Supp. at 561. He "actively participated in and exerted control over a variety of Ott II environmental matters," *ibid.*, and he "issued directives regarding Ott II's responses to regulatory inquiries," *id.*, at 575. We think that these findings are enough to raise an issue of CPC's operation of the facility through Williams's actions, though we would draw no ultimate conclusion from these findings at this point. Not only would we be deciding in the first instance an issue on which the trial and appellate courts did not focus, but the very fact that the District Court did not see the case as we do suggests that there may be still more to be known about Williams's activities. Indeed, even as the factual findings stand, the trial court offered little in the way of concrete detail for its conclusions about Williams's role in Ott II's environmental affairs, and the parties vigorously dispute the extent of Williams's involvement. Prudence thus counsels us to remand, on the theory of direct operation set out here, for reevaluation of Williams's role, and of the role of any other CPC agent who might be said to have had a part in operating the Muskegon facility.

V

The judgment of the Court of Appeals for the Sixth Circuit is vacated, and the case is remanded with instructions to return it to the District Court for further proceedings consistent with this opinion.

It is so ordered.

NOTES AND QUESTIONS

1. *Bestfoods* deals with liability of parent corporations. What of successor corporations? On this matter, *see North Shore Gas Co. v. Salamon, Inc.,* 152 F.3d 642, 649–51 (7th Cir. 1998) (holding successor corporations to be liable under CERCLA):

> When Congress enacted CERCLA, it enabled the federal government to provide an efficacious response to environmental hazards and to assign the cost of that response to the parties who created or maintained the hazards. *See Anspec,* 922 F.2d at 1247. Accordingly, Congress was unlikely to leave a loophole that would enable corporations to die "paper deaths, only to rise phoenix-like from the ashes, transformed, but free of their former liabilities." *Mexico Feed,* 980 F.2d at 487; *see Betkoski,* 99 F.3d at 519. Moreover, there is no concern — at least theoretically — about punishing the successor for the acts (or omissions) of the predecessor; CERCLA is a remedial measure which is aimed only at correcting environmentally dangerous conditions. *See Smith Land,* 851 F.2d at 91. And holding the successor corporation liable for the cost of cleanup is not necessarily unfair, since the successor and its shareholders likely will have derived some benefit from the predecessor's use of the pollutant and the savings that resulted from the hazardous disposal methods. We therefore reach the same result as the other circuits that have considered this issue — that Congress intended the equitable doctrine of successor liability to

apply under CERCLA. We note, however, that while CERCLA permits successor liability, it does not require it "unless justified by the facts of each case." *Carolina Transformer*, 978 F.2d at 837; *see also Chicago Truck Drivers, Helpers and Warehouse Workers Union Pension Fund v. Tasemkin, Inc.*, 59 F.3d 48, 49 (7th Cir. 1995) ("Successor liability is an equitable doctrine, not an inflexible command. . . .").

Most circuits which have construed CERCLA to incorporate successor liability have concluded that the parameters of the doctrine should be fashioned by federal common law. *See Betkoski*, 99 F.3d at 519; *Carolina Transformer*, 978 F.2d at 837–38; *Smith Land*, 851 F.2d at 92; *see also* 980 F.2d at 487 n.9 (declining to decide whether federal common law or state law supplied the rule of decision, but noting that the district court was probably correct in relying on federal common law). Of course, the mere fact that CERCLA is a federal statute does not dictate that "the federal courts should fashion a uniform federal rule," since "frequently state rules of decision will furnish an appropriate and convenient measure of the governing federal law." *Atchison, Topeka & Santa Fe Ry. Co. v. Brown& Bryant*, 132 F.3d 1295, 1299 (9th Cir. 1997). But most circuits have decided that resort to federal common law is warranted because of the need for national uniformity with respect to CERCLA, and the possibility that parties would frustrate the aims of CERCLA by choosing to merge or consolidate under the laws of states "which unduly restrict successor liability." *Smith Land*, 851 F.2d at 91[.]

Because CERCLA does not clearly indicate that Congress intended the judiciary to formulate federal common law, the three-part test established in *United States v. Kimbell Foods*, 440 U.S. 715, 59 L. Ed. 2d 711, 99 S. Ct. 1448 (1979), determines whether federal common law is appropriate. *Kimbell Foods* requires a court to decide (1) whether the issue requires "a nationally uniform body of law"; (2) "whether application of state law would frustrate specific objectives of the federal programs"; and (3) whether "application of a federal rule would disrupt commercial relationships predicated on state law." *Kimbell Foods*, 440 U.S. at 728–29.

2. At this writing, there remains a split among the circuits on the question whether state law or federal law should control these questions of successor corporate liability. The First, Sixth, and Eleventh Circuits have opted to use state law, while the Second and Fourth apply the federal common law "substantial continuation" test. *See, e.g., United States v. Davis*, 261 F.3d 1 (1st Cir. 2001).

3. Is the federal government also at risk of liability under CERCLA or is it free from liability under the doctrine of sovereign immunity? *See* § 120(a), 42 U.S.C. § 9620 (waiving federal immunity). *See also, East Bay Municipal Utility Dist. v. U.S. Department of Commerce*, 142 F.3d 479 (D.C. Cir. 1998) (holding the waiver of § 120 to be coextensive with the substantive liability standards of CERCLA).

A NOTE ON THE SPECIAL CASE OF LENDERS

A major issue since the enactment of CERCLA was how to treat lenders. It was long understood that lenders with security interests who foreclosed on real property, and thereby secured title to that property, would by that acquisition become "owners" for purposes of CERCLA and therefore liable for clean-up costs of contaminated lands. That unsavory consequence prompted many lenders to either rue past foreclosure actions, or refuse to foreclose. That was the situation until some cases called the interpretation into question. *See, e.g., United States v. McLamb*, 5 F.3d 69 (4th Cir. 1993) (holding that an entity which took title solely to protect a security interest and then promptly divested itself of ownership was not liable as an "owner" under CERCLA).

In addition to facing liability risks in the capacity of "owner," a lender, if it was not careful, could find itself to be an "operator." How? If a lender took an affirmative hand in running a facility or managing a property in which it held a security interest, it would by that fact assume operator status and become liable under CERCLA. *See, e.g., In Re Bergsoe Metal Corp.*, 910 F.2d. 668 (9th Cir. 1990) (lenders can be liable under CERCLA as operators if they exercise managerial authority). Lenders were unhappy enough with that prospect, but the worst was yet to come. In *United States v. Fleet Factors Corp.*, 901 F.2d 1550 (11th Cir. 1990), the Court of Appeals for the Eleventh Circuit held that lenders could be liable as operators even if they had not participated in the day-to-day management of the contaminated property:

> Under the standard we adopt today, a secured creditor may incur section 9607(a)(2) liability, without being an operator, by participating in the *financial* management of a facility to a degree indicating a capacity to influence the corporation's treatment of hazardous wastes. It is not necessary for the secured creditor actually to involve itself in the day-to-day operations of the facility in order to be liable — although such conduct will certainly lead to the loss of the protection of the statutory exemption. Nor is it necessary for the secured creditor to participate in management decisions relating to hazardous waste. Rather, a secured creditor will be liable *if its involvement with the management of the facility is sufficiently broad to support the inference that it could affect hazardous waste disposal decisions if it so chose*
>
> . . . .

Id. at 1557–58 (emphasis added).

Fleet Factors engendered a spate of controversy, and a good many sleepless nights, within the banking community and in the federal government, which itself has been in the role of secured creditor with increasing frequency since the collapse of many savings and loan institutions in the late 1980s. The controversy prompted legislative efforts to protect lenders by amending CERCLA, but these initial efforts failed. *See, e.g.,* H.R. 4494, 101st Cong., 2d Sess. (1990), 136 Cong. Rec. H1505 (daily ed. Apr. 4). The EPA then instituted a rulemaking proceeding for the same purpose (*see* 56 Fed. Reg. 28,798 (1991)) but its final rule, promulgated in April 1992, was invalidated by the D.C. Circuit. *Kelly v. EPA*, 15 F.3d 1100 (D.C. Cir. 1994). Congress finally resolved the problem in the fall of 1996 by amending CERCLA. For the current state of the law, see § 101(20)(E)-(G), 42 U.S.C. § 9601(20)(E)-(G).

[b] ARRANGERS

"Arrangers" for disposal or treatment, a group which usually captures generators of hazardous materials, are liable persons under CERCLA. They are persons:

who by contract, agreement, or otherwise arranged for disposal or treatment, or arranged with a transporter for transport for disposal or treatment, of hazardous substances owned or possessed by such person, by any other party or entity, at any facility or incineration vessel owned or operated by another party or entity and containing such hazardous substances.

§ 107(a)(3), 42 U.S.C. § 9607(a)(3).

Liability attaches upon (a) arrangement for disposal or treatment of hazardous wastes, (b) at a facility which currently holds wastes of a similar type (c) from which a release has occurred and (d) for which response costs have been incurred. "Arranging for disposal or treatment" may be easier to do than one would think. In one case, the owner of a Michigan foundry site sold the foundry for a significantly discounted price. He did so because of the presence of electrical transformers containing PCBs on the site. A reviewing court found this transaction could constitute an arrangement for disposal of hazardous materials. *Sanford Street Local Development Corp. v. Textron, Inc.*, 768 F. Supp. 1218 (W.D. Mich. 1991).

CATELLUS DEV. CORP. v. UNITED STATES

34 F.3d 748 (9th Cir. 1994)

JUDGES: Before: J. CLIFFORD WALLACE, Chief Judge, HERBERT Y. C. CHOY, Circuit Judge, and WALTER T. McGOVERN,* District Judge.

WALLACE, Chief Judge:

On this appeal, we consider whether a party that sells spent automotive batteries to a lead reclamation plant may be liable under the Comprehensive Environmental Response, Compensation and Liability Act of 1980 (CERCLA), 42 U.S.C. § 9601 et seq., for the costs of cleaning up the property where lead-containing remnants of the batteries are eventually dumped. Catellus Development Corp. (Catellus) appeals from the district court's summary judgment which held that General Automotive (General) could not be made to contribute to the clean-up costs of Catellus's property under the theory that it "arranged for disposal or treatment" of a hazardous substance. The district court had jurisdiction under 42 U.S.C. § 9613(b) and 28 U.S.C. § 1331. We have jurisdiction over this timely appeal pursuant to under 28 U.S.C. § 1291. We reverse and remand.

---

* Honorable Walter T. McGovern, United States District Judge, Western District of Washington, sitting by designation. Opinion by Chief Judge Wallace.

I

General operates Grand Auto Parts Stores which receive used automotive batteries from customers as trade-ins. General's policy in disposing of these batteries had been to drive a screwdriver through the spent batteries and then sell them to a battery cracking plant operated by Morris P. Kirk & Sons, Inc. (Kirk) which extracted and smelted the lead. Kirk assumed full and complete ownership and control of the batteries.

After lead was extracted from the batteries, the left-over battery casings had to be disposed of. It was Kirk's practice to wash and crush the battery casings, load them into a truck, and then dump them. Tons of pieces of crushed battery casings were found at Catellus's property, a substantial number of which were transported from Kirk's plant. The battery casings contained lead which contaminated the property.

Catellus alleges that among the battery casings found on its property were battery casings originating from the batteries sold by General to Kirk. Catellus now seeks to recover response costs from General under CERCLA. Catellus argues that General is liable for response costs as a party who "arranged for disposal or treatment" of a hazardous substance under CERCLA § 107(a)(3), 42 U.S.C. § 9607(a)(3).

On cross-motions for summary judgment, the district court held that, as a matter of law, the facts alleged by Catellus did not constitute an arrangement for disposal or treatment by General. *Catellus Development Corp. v. United States,* 828 F. Supp. 764 (N.D. Cal. 1993). We review de novo the district court's summary judgment. *Briggs v. Sullivan,* 954 F.2d 534, 537 (9th Cir. 1992). The sole question before us is whether, viewing the facts in the light most favorable to Catellus, General arranged for treatment or disposal of a hazardous substance within the meaning of section 107(a)(3) of CERCLA.

II

Under CERCLA, a plaintiff may attempt to recover costs expended in the cleanup of a contaminated site from four distinct categories of persons. Among these are "any person who by contract, agreement, or otherwise arranged for disposal or treatment . . . of hazardous substances owned or possessed by such person, by any other party or entity, at any facility . . . owned or operated by another party or entity and containing such hazardous substances." 42 U.S.C. § 9607(a)(3) (emphasis added). At issue in this case is whether General's sale of the spent batteries to Kirk falls into this category because it constitutes an arrangement for either disposal or treatment.

"Disposal" and "treatment" are defined in CERCLA, 42 U.S.C. § 9601(29), by reference to the definitions of those terms in section 1004 of the Solid Waste Disposal Act (SWDA), 42 U.S.C. § 6903. We have explained that the term "disposal" as imported from SWDA necessarily includes the concept of "waste." *3550 Stevens Creek Associates v. Barclays Bank,* 915 F.2d 1355, 1361–62 (9th Cir. 1990) (*Stevens Creek*) (discussing the meaning of "disposal" in section 107(a)(2), but stating that the same definition applies to section 107(a)(3)), *cert. denied,* 500 U.S. 917, 114 L. Ed. 2d 101, 111 S. Ct. 2014 (1991). SWDA defines disposal as "the discharge, deposit, injection, dumping, spilling, leaking, or placing of any solid waste or hazardous waste into or on any land or water so that such solid waste or hazardous waste or any constituent thereof may enter the environment." 42 U.S.C. § 6903(3) (emphasis added). In *Stevens Creek,* we agreed with other circuits that "disposal" refers "only to an affirmative act of discarding a substance as waste, and not to the productive use of the substance." 915 F.2d at 1362. In *Stevens Creek,* for example, asbestos was not disposed of in a building when it was installed for use as insulation and fire retardant. *Id.* at 1361–62.

The definition of treatment in SWDA also necessarily includes the concept of "waste." Treatment is "any method, technique, or process . . . designed to change the . . . character or composition of any hazardous waste so as to neutralize such waste or so as to render such waste nonhazardous. . . ." 42 U.S.C. § 6903(34) (emphasis added).

Thus, General could be said to have arranged for the disposal or treatment of the spent batteries only if the spent batteries could be characterized as waste. SWDA defines solid waste as "any garbage, refuse, sludge, . . . and other discarded material." 42 U.S.C. § 6903(27). We have found this definition useful in determining whether a use made of a hazardous substance constitutes a disposal. Stevens Creek, 915 F.2d at 1361. We emphasize, however, that our reliance on the terms used in SWDA to describe the characteristics of waste does not necessarily indicate that the specific hazardous substances covered by CERCLA are limited to those set forth as solid waste in SWDA. 42 U.S.C. § 9601(14)(C).

A.

General argues that the spent batteries cannot be characterized as waste because they were being recycled and the lead extracted from them would be put to further productive use. In *Louisiana Pacific v. ASARCO, Inc.,* 24 F.3d 1565 (9th Cir. 1994) (ASARCO), we further refined what is meant by "waste" and "discarded material" for the purpose of establishing liability under section 107(a)(3) of CERCLA. *ASARCO* dealt with the sale of slag, a by-product of copper smelting, by ASARCO, through a middleman, to logging companies who would use it instead of gravel as a ballast to provide firmer ground. When the slag became too mixed with other debris, the logyards would have it hauled away as waste. ASARCO was held liable under CERCLA for heavy metal contamination from the slag at the logyards and at a landfill where the slag was eventually taken. On appeal, ASARCO argued that it could not be held liable under Washington's product liability statute for introducing into commerce an "object possessing intrinsic value" and simultaneously for "arranging for disposal" under CERCLA. We held that "[a] by-product of a metallurgical process, if sold, can be a product for purposes of one and waste for purposes of the other. This is especially so given that CERCLA is to be broadly interpreted to achieve its remedial goals." *Id.* at 1575. We focused on the fact that the slag was a "by-product [] with a nominal commercial value," and that ASARCO wanted to "get rid of" the slag. *Id.* at 1575.

ASARCO's classification of slag as both a useful product and as a waste might have been read as contradicting our statement in *Stevens Creek* that a sale of a substance is not considered a discarding of waste if a productive use is made of the substance. *See Stevens Creek,* 915 F.2d at 1362. However, *ASARCO* distinguished *Stevens Creek* by stating that it "involved products that were produced as the producers' principal business products, not by-products that the producers had to get rid of." *ASARCO,* slip op. at 4308 n.6.

Catellus argues that this statement in *ASARCO* requires us to reverse the district court because the spent batteries were by-products and nonprincipal business products. Catellus reads *ASARCO* to hold that whenever a person sells a nonprincipal business product or a by-product, the thing sold is classified as "waste" and establishes that the sale constitutes an arrangement for "disposal" or "treatment" within the meaning of section 107(a)(3).

ASARCO does not create such a broad rule. *ASARCO* did not consider whether a by-product that is intended for recycling should be classified as waste for the purpose of section 107(a)(3) liability. Rather, the facts of the case limited the scope of its statements to the situation where the by-product being sold will have to continue to be used in its identical state until it is disposed of.

Reading the statements in *ASARCO* as broadly as Catellus urges and applying them to all types of recycling would require us to ignore statements made in *Stevens Creek* regarding the definition of waste. In *Stevens Creek,* we looked to the regulations implementing SWDA to explain the scope of the term "waste" as it informs the definition of "disposal" in CERCLA. 915 F.2d at 1361 & n.13. Using SWDA regulations to interpret section 107(a)(3) is not inconsistent with our approach in *ASARCO.* In that case, our analysis relied heavily on *United States v. A&F Materials Co.,* 582 F. Supp. 842 (S.D. Ill. 1984), which itself based part of its decision on the definition of waste in SWDA regulations. *Id.* at 844.

Thus, the regulations implementing SWDA give us a more detailed discussion of when a recycled material should be considered a waste. But the question is: which regulations — the current ones or those in force at the time of the charged acts? We conclude that we are to look to the current SWDA regulations in interpreting section 107(a)(3) of CERCLA. CERCLA is a remedial statute which operates on principles of strict liability. *Stevens Creek,* 915 F.2d at 1357. We have consistently applied it to acts creating contamination far before CERCLA was enacted in 1980. *See, e.g., Jones-Hamilton Co. v. Beazer Materials & Services,* 973 F.2d 688, 691 (9th Cir. 1992) (Jones-Hamilton) (conduct occurring starting in 1970); *ASARCO,* slip op. at 4297 (conduct occurring in 1978); *Stevens Creek,* 915 F.2d at 1356 (conduct occurring in 1963). Because the CERCLA liability scheme is generally unconcerned about whether a responsible party had notice at the time the contamination occurred that it would later be required to pay the costs of clean up, it is appropriate to apply current SWDA regulations in construing section 107(a)(3) regardless of when the acts of contamination occurred.

Turning then to the regulations, they define solid waste as any discarded material which is "abandoned . . . recycled . . . or . . . inherently wastelike." 40 C.F.R. § 261.2(a)(2) (1993). However, an exception explains that certain materials to be recycled are not solid waste. "Materials are not solid wastes when they can be shown to be recycled by being: (i) Used or reused as ingredients in an industrial process to make a product, provided the materials are not being reclaimed." 40 C.F.R. § 261.2(e) (1993). The regulations define reclamation: "A material is 'reclaimed' if it is processed to recover a usable product, or if it is regenerated. Examples are recovery of lead values from spent batteries and regeneration of spent solvents." 40 C.F.R. § 261.1(c)(4) (1993) (emphasis added).

Thus, under the regulations, General's spent batteries would clearly be defined as waste. Since they were "reclaimed" they would not fall under the exception that removes some reprocessed recycled material from the definition of waste. We are convinced by the Eleventh Circuit's persuasive discussion in *United States v. ILCO Inc.,* 996 F.2d 1126, 1131 (11th Cir. 1993), that SWDA regulations reasonably classify lead components from spent batteries as waste.

Further support for our holding emerges as we look more closely at the details of the battery recycling procedure. An inescapable fact is that the leftover battery casings must be disposed of. The battery casings, like the slag in *ASARCO,* but unlike the lead plates within the casings, were not a subject of recycling. They retained their character as waste throughout and would have to be "gotten rid of," either by General, which could have cracked the batteries itself before selling the scrap lead, or as was the case here, by Kirk after it bought the entire battery. General cannot escape having the battery casings defined as a discarded material simply by selling the battery to another party who then disposed of the casings.

General argues that it did not "arrange" to dispose of the batteries because it did not control the eventual disposition of their remnants. This argument is precluded by our holding in *ASARCO.* ASARCO was not the party directly responsible for placing the slag at the logyards or at the landfills where it contaminated the ground. Rather, a middleman sold the slag to the logyards, and the logyards themselves arranged to have the slag hauled to the landfill. Slip op. at 4297. We have considered continued ownership or control of a hazardous substance to be evidence of arranging for disposal. *Jones-Hamilton,* 973 F.2d at 695. However, we have not required it. Requiring continued ownership or control for section 107(a)(3) liability would make it too easy for a party, wishing to dispose of a hazardous substance, to escape by a sale its responsibility to see that the substance is safely disposed of. Such a require-ment "would allow defendants to simply 'close their eyes' to the method of disposal of their hazardous substances, a result contrary to the policies underlying CERCLA." *United States v. Aceto Agr. Chemicals Corp.,* 872 F.2d 1373, 1382 (8th Cir. 1989). It is sufficient that the substance had the characteristic of waste, as we have defined it above, at the point at which it was delivered to another party.

B.

The district court, in addition to holding there was no disposal, also held that the sale of the spent batteries could not constitute an "arrangement for treatment" because General did not retain control over the method by which they would be treated. However, there is no special requirement in treatment cases that there be a contract specifying how treatment will take place. As with our interpretation of the arrangement for disposal provision, all that is necessary is that the treatment be inherent in the particular arrangement, even though the arranger does not retain control over its details. Thus, when General sold the batteries to Kirk there was an arrangement for treatment created. Treatment is defined as, among others, rendering waste "amenable for recovery, . . . or reduced in volume." 42 U.S.C. § 6903(34). When General sold the batteries to Kirk, it was in order that Kirk would treat the batteries by making the lead in the batteries "amenable for recovery." The processing by Kirk would also have the effect of "reducing in volume" the battery material that would have to be discarded.

However, we affirm on a different ground the district court's judgment that General could not be liable to Catellus for arranging treatment of the batteries. The statute imposes liability on "any person who . . . arranged for . . . treatment . . . by any other party or entity, at any facility or incineration vessel owned or operated by another party or entity and containing such hazardous substances." 42 U.S.C. § 9607(a)(3) (emphasis added). The statute thus creates a requirement that the treatment take place at the facility that contains the hazardous substances that are the subject of the clean up effort. None of the treatment activity arranged for by General and potentially causing contamination occurred at Catellus's property. It was the act of arranging for disposal that eventually led to the contamination of Catellus's property, according to its allegations. It is on this theory that Catellus may on remand seek to recover response costs from General.

REVERSED AND REMANDED.

NOTES AND QUESTIONS

1. In 1999, Congress enacted the Superfund Recycling Equity Act, thereby amending § 127, 42 U.S.C. § 9627, to free a good many recyclers from CERCLA liability. Recyclers who fail to meet the requirements of § 127, however, remain subject to liability, assuming their actions qualify as "disposal" or "treatment" under § 107(a)(3).

2. Can the mere presence of unexercised authority to control the activities of an arranger under CERCLA create independent arranger liability in the non-acting party? *See, e.g., Concrete Sales and Services, Inc. v. Blue Bird Body Co.,* 211 F.3d 1333 (11th Cir. 2000) (no).

3. Title I of the Small Business Liability Protection Act Act established a *municipal solid waste exemption* long sought by advocates of CERCLA reform. The exemption removes arranger liability for residential landowners, small business entities (those employing fewer than 100 persons), and small non-profit organizations (those employing fewer than 100 persons) who generate municipal solid waste. § 107(p), 42 U.S.C. § 9607(p). The exemption is unavailable if the waste in question contributes, or could contribute significantly, to the cost of clean-up, if the person has failed to comply with a governmental information request, or if the person has impeded a response or natural resource restoration action.

4. Is intent an implicit element of arranger liability? (No.)

[c] TRANSPORTERS

UNITED STATES v. WESTERN PROCESSING CO.

756 F. Supp. 1416 (W.D. Wash. 1991)

WALTER T. McGOVERN, United States District Judge

Transporter Defendants (Third-party defendants, Bayside Waste Hauling and Transfer, Inc.; Crosby & Overton, Inc.; National Transfer, Inc.; Pontius Trucking; and Widing Transportation, Inc.) move pursuant to Fed. R. Civ. P. 54(b) and 56 for dismissal of all claims against them based upon the Comprehensive Environmental Response, Compensation, and Liability Act (CERCLA), 42 U.S.C. § 9601 or Washington's Model Toxics Control Act (MTCA), RCW 70.105D.

The Transporter Defendants transported various wastes generated by others to the Western Processing site.

The Transporter Defendants argue, however, that they are not subject to liability under CERCLA or MTCA unless they selected the Western Processing site as the destination for the waste. Summary judgment should, therefore, be granted to all transporter defendants as to claims based on waste for which they did not select the Western Processing site.

Additionally, Transporter Defendants argue that under MTCA, regardless of who selected the site, there is no liability when the facility could legally receive the substances at the time of delivery.

Finally, Transporter Defendants argue that as to the four defendants who are common carriers, National Transfer, Pontius Trucking, Widing, and Bayside, rules imposing strict liability do not apply where the activity engaged in is required of the common carrier by virtue of its status as such.

Third-Party Plaintiffs The Boeing Company and American Tar Company, et al. (hereafter Boeing) oppose the motion in most of its aspects, but do concede others.

A. CERCLA Liability

1. CERCLA § 107(a)(4) Transporter Liability

CERCLA Section 107(a)(4) (42 U.S.C. § 9607(a)(4)) imposes liability on

any person who accepts or accepted any hazardous substances for transport to disposal or treatment facilities, incineration vessels or sites selected by such person, from which there is a release, or threatened release which causes the incurrence of response costs, of a hazardous substance. . . .

Transporter Defendants argue that this language imposes liability against them only if they selected Western Processing as the disposal site. Boeing argues that the Transporters are misreading this section. . . .

The ambiguity of Section 107(a)(4) is resolved by reference to comments by Senators who played a role in drafting CERCLA, the view of the U.S. EPA, and by consideration of the Section in view of the CERCLA statutory scheme.

Senators Chafee and Randolph explained that as to lawsuits against transporters, selection of the disposal destination by the transporter was necessary before liability could be imposed upon him. *See* R.M. Eddy & D.T. Riendl *Transporter Liability Under CERCLA,* 16 Envtl. L. Rep. 10244, 10251–52 (Sept. 1986). This comment was made in the context of the Senators introducing an amendment to the Resource Conservation and Recovery Act (RCRA) to limit possible citizen lawsuits against transporters and thus bring RCRA into accord with CERCLA, which, they stated requires site selection by the transporter *Id.;* 130 Cong. Rec. S9177 (daily ed. July 25, 1984).

The U.S. EPA takes the same view as the Senators. As a matter of EPA policy, transporters will not be sent notice letters nor have enforcement actions brought against them as potentially responsible parties until it has been determined that the transporter selected the disposal or treatment facility. . . .

To restrict transporter liability to those situations where transporters have selected the site for delivery of hazardous waste is equitable. "Site" in this context is used as a broad term that includes "facilities" for disposal and treatment of hazardous substances and incineration vessels. Also, the definition section of CERCLA, 42 U.S.C. § 9601(9), broadly defines "facility" to include a "site" or "area." Thus, the terms are virtually interchangeable.

The terms being interchangeable, there can be little sense in holding the transporter liable for deliveries made to facilities designated by others, but holding him liable for deliveries to "sites" only if the transporter chose the site. An interpretation that this Section meant to hold transporters liable regardless of who selected the site conflicts with the Senators' view referenced above.

Moreover, transporters have a limited role in the activity surrounding hazardous substances. They neither create nor treat the material, but are responsible for its safe carriage between the point where it is generated and where it is left for disposal or treatment. If the transporter does not select the delivery site, the transporter's connection with the material is the most attenuated among potentially responsible parties. If the transporter does select the delivery site, the transporter's role becomes a less passive one. As one who actively selected a disposal site, the transporter may more equitably be subject to liability.

This analysis harmonizes with Section 107(a)(3) concerning "generator" liability where the site selection language is not present. A generator of hazardous substances may be liable for somehow arranging the disposal or treatment of the substances, or by arranging with a transporter for taking care of the material. Thus, whether a generator selected the site or not, the generator will be liable, and site selection language is unnecessary. *Accord,* Sever, *id.* at 6–143. This is appropriate owing to the generator's role in creating the hazardous material in the first place. The transporter, on the other hand, has had no role in the creation or treatment of the material. When the transporter finally does become involved with hazardous material, there will be two alternatives: either the transporter is directed where to take the material, or the choice is left to the transporter. In the latter case, the more active role generates potential liability.

Accordingly, the motion of Transporter Defendants for partial summary judgment as to those deliveries for which they did not select the site is GRANTED.

[The next portion of the opinion, which discusses generator liability, is omitted.]

3. Effect of Common Carrier Status

Four Transporter Defendants — National Transfer, Pontius Trucking, Widing, and Bayside — are common carriers licensed and regulated by the Interstate Commerce Commission and the Washington State Utilities and Transportation Commission. As such, they argue a separate and additional basis for this motion.

They argue that as common carriers, they must accept, carry, and deliver all goods offered to them for transport within the scope of the operating authority set forth in their permits. They cannot discriminate against customers nor refuse to accept commodities that may be dangerous for transport. Thus, courts have recognized a "public duty" exception to absolute or strict liability arising from the carriage of hazardous substances. While this argument may have been or could have been part of the rationale for requiring that a transporter select the site for delivering hazardous materials before liability may attach, this argument as a complete defense to liability is not well taken.

CERCLA's liability provision begins at Section 107(a):

Notwithstanding any other provision or rule of law, and subject only to the defenses set forth in subsection (b) of this section. . . .

This Court has considered the availability of other defenses under this section and has concluded that this section precludes unenumerated defenses. *See United States v. Western Processing Co.,* 734 F. Supp. 930, 939 (W.D. Wash. 1990) (The better reasoned decisions and the majority of cases have held that the limited defenses of Section 107(b) are exclusive.) Therefore, since there are only three defenses under Section 107(b) — an act of God, and act of war, or an act or omission of a third party — and since the common carrier defense falls under none of these enumerated defenses, the Transporter Defendants may not raise it.

[The remainder of the opinion, dealing with defendants' liability under state law, and with procedural matters, is omitted.]

NOTE

1. A party may be liable as a transporter even if the material remains on the site, if the material is moved from one part of the site to another. *See, e.g., Kaiser Aluminum & Chem. Corp. v. Catellus Dev't Co.,* 976 F.2d 1338 (9th Cir. 1992). For a review of cases on CERCLA liability of transporters,

see William B. Johnson, J.D., Annotation, *Transporter Liability Under § 107(a)(4) of the Comprehensive Environmental Response, Compensation, and Liability Act (CERCLA) (42 U.S.C.A. § 9607(a))*, 112 A.L.R. 49 (2001).

Title I of the Small Business Liability Protection Act added a provision establishing, as a general matter, a *de micromis* exemption from liability for arrangers or transporters whose total contribution to an NPL site is less than 110 gallons of liquid materials or less than 200 pounds of solid materials (or such lesser or greater amounts as the EPA shall determine). § 107(o), 42 U.S.C. § 9607(o). The exemption is not available if the materials contributed significantly to costs of response or natural resource restoration actions, or if the otherwise liable party has failed to cooperate with an information request or enforcement activities or has been convicted criminally for the conduct to which the exemption would apply. § 107(o)(2), 42 U.S.C. § 9607(o)(2). Such determinations are not judicially reviewable. § 107(o)(3), 42 U.S.C. § 9607(o)(3).

[2] DEFENSES

Once *prima facie* liability is established under § 107, the matter of defenses comes into play. Three of CERCLA's defenses are found in § 107(b), 42 U.S.C. § 9607(b). First is the "act of God" defense. § 107(b)(1), 42 U.S.C. § 9607(b)(1). What is an act of God? For a definition, see § 101(1), 42 U.S.C. § 9601(1). Second is the "act of war" defense. § 107(b)(2), 42 U.S.C. § 9607(b)(2). "Act of war" is undefined in CERCLA. For an at-length judicial discussion, see *United States v. Shell Oil Co.*, 841 F. Supp. 962 (C.D. Cal. 1993).

The third, and most important, of the § 107(b) defenses is the "third party defense." § 107(b)(3), 42 U.S.C. § 9607(3). To understand this defense and its availability, it is necessary to review several statutory definitional sections, especially § 101(35), 42 U.S.C. § 9601(35), defining the term "contractual arrangement." The following decision examines the third-party defense.

(The fourth CERCLA defense is the bona fide prospective purchaser defense, which was added to the statute in January, 2002, as part of the Small Business Liability Protection and Brownfields Revitalization Act, P.L. 107-118, 42 U.S.C. § 9607(r). That provision is described in the Notes following the *Westwood* case, *infra*.)

WESTWOOD PHARMACEUTICALS, INC. v. NATIONAL FUEL GAS DISTRIB. CORP.

964 F.2d 85 (2d Cir. 1992)

OPINION: TIMBERS, Circuit Judge:

Appellant Westwood Pharmaceuticals, Inc. (Westwood) appeals from an order entered June 19, 1991 in the Western District of New York, John T. Curtin, District Judge, denying Westwood's motion for reconsideration of that portion of an order entered in the same court on May 21, 1990 denying Westwood's motion for summary judgment on its claim that appellee National

Fuel Gas Distribution Corporation (National Fuel) is liable in Westwood's action brought pursuant to §§ 107(a)(2), 113(f) and 113(g) of the Comprehensive Environmental Response, Compensation and Liability Act (CERCLA), 42 U.S.C. §§ 9607(a), 9613(f) and 9613(g) (1988) as amended by the Superfund Amendments and Reauthorization Act, Pub. L. No. 99-499, 100 Stat. 1613 (1986).

On October 14, 1988, Westwood commenced this action against National Fuel seeking to recover costs incurred in investigating and remedying chemical contamination at certain premises in Buffalo it had purchased from National Fuel's predecessor in interest, Iroquois Gas Corporation (Iroquois). Westwood moved for partial summary judgment on the liability issues presented by its CERCLA action. After the district court denied Westwood's motion for summary judgment, Westwood moved for reconsideration of its order. The district court on June 19, 1991 denied Westwood's motion for reconsideration. On August 6, 1991, at the request of Westwood, the district court amended its order to include certification for an interlocutory appeal pursuant to 28 U.S.C. § 1292(b) (1988). On November 6, 1991, a panel of our Court granted Westwood's petition for leave to appeal pursuant to § 1292(b).

On appeal, Westwood contends (1) that the mere existence of a contractual relationship, without more, between it and National Fuel precludes National Fuel from invoking the third-party defense of CERCLA § 107(b)(3); and, alternatively, (2) that CERCLA § 101(35)(C), 42 U.S.C. § 9601(35)(c), precludes National Fuel from raising the third-party defense provided for in § 107(b)(3).

For the reasons that follow, we affirm the order of the district court denying Westwood's motion for reconsideration of the district court's earlier order that denied Westwood's motion for summary judgment on the issue of National Fuel's liability under CERCLA.

I.

We shall summarize only those facts and prior proceedings believed necessary to an understanding of the issues raised on appeal.

The site which is the subject matter of this action was purchased in 1925 by Iroquois. Iroquois conducted gas manufacturing and storage operations on the land through 1951. For several years thereafter it continued to use the site for gas compression and storage. During these operations Iroquois placed or used various underground pipes and structures at the site. In 1968, Iroquois demolished certain structures on the northeast portion of the site, but left other structures on the site standing.

Iroquois sold the site to Westwood in 1972 for $60,100. Westwood demolished the remaining structures on the site and constructed a warehouse on the southern portion of the site. During these construction activities and associated soil testing, Westwood discovered various subsurface contaminants. In the instant action Westwood seeks to recover the response costs — the costs of cleaning up the contaminants — for which it claims National Fuel is liable. Westwood's complaint alleged claims pursuant to CERCLA as stated above, and related common law claims of public nuisance, private nuisance, and restitution. . . .

In its answer to Westwood's complaint, National Fuel alleged various affirmative defenses. In its order of May 21, 1990, 737 F. Supp. 1272 (W.D.N.Y. 1990), the district court, among other things, granted National Fuel's motion to dismiss Westwood's private nuisance and restitution claims; denied National Fuel's motion with respect to Westwood's CERCLA and public nuisance claims; and denied Westwood's motion for summary judgment which asserted that National Fuel was liable on its CERCLA claim.

The district court held that National Fuel had raised a triable issue of fact by contending that, under the "third-party defense" of CERCLA § 107(b)(3), it was not liable on Westwood's CERCLA claims. Section 107(b)(3) provides in relevant part:

> "There shall be no liability under subsection (a) of this section for a person otherwise liable who can establish by a preponderance of the evidence that the release or threat of release of a hazardous substance and the damages resulting therefrom were caused solely by — . . .

> "(3) an act or omission of a third party other than an employee or agent of the defendant, or than one whose act or omission occurs in connection with a contractual relationship, existing directly or indirectly, with the defendant . . . if the defendant establishes by a preponderance of the evidence that (a) he exercised due care with respect to the hazardous substance concerned, taking into consideration the characteristics of such hazardous substance, in light of all relevant facts and circumstances, and (b) he took precautions against foreseeable acts or omissions of any such third party and the consequences that could foreseeably result from such acts or omissions. . . ." (emphasis added)

National Fuel did not dispute the fact that its 1972 sales contract with Westwood was a "contractual relationship", since CERCLA § 101(35)(A) provides that "the term 'contractual relationship', for the purpose of section 9607(b)(3) of this title includes, but is not limited to, land contracts, deeds or other instruments transferring title or possession. . . ." National Fuel asserted, however, that Westwood's construction activities were not undertaken by Westwood "in connection with" the contractual relationship between National Fuel and Westwood. Furthermore, National Fuel asserted that, if in fact it placed hazardous substances at the site it exercised due care with respect to such substances and took precautions against the foreseeable acts or omissions of third persons. Specifically, National Fuel asserted that any such substances that were not eventually removed from the premises for off-site use or disposal were left inside secure subsurface receptacles. Moreover, National Fuel asserted that the structural integrity of these subsurface receptacles left at the site would not have been breached and therefore hazardous substances would not have escaped but for the unforeseeable construction activities of Westwood.

The district court held that the phrase "in connection with" in § 107(b)(3) requires that there be some relationship between the disposal/releasing activity and the contract with the defendant for a defendant to be barred from raising the third-party defense. Since it held that National Fuel had raised a triable issue of fact by contending that Westwood was the sole cause of the release or threatened release of hazardous substances at the site, the court denied Westwood's motion for summary judgment which asserted that National Fuel was liable under CERCLA § 107(a)(2).

Westwood made a motion for reconsideration of the court's decision in light of CERCLA § 101(35)(C), which was added to CERCLA when Congress enacted § 101(f) of the Superfund Amendments and Reauthorization Act of 1986. Section 101(35)(A) and (B) establish what is known as the "innocent landowner exception", which protects landowners who acquire the property after the disposal or placement of hazardous substances on it and who do not know and have no reason to know that the hazardous substances are on the property. The first sentence of § 101(35)(C) provides that "nothing in this paragraph or in section 9607(b)(3) of this title shall diminish the liability of any previous owner or operator of such facility who would otherwise be liable under this chapter."

The district court, in its order of June 19, 1991, 767 F. Supp. 456 (W.D.N.Y. 1991), reaffirmed its holding that the mere existence of a contractual relationship does not preclude a former owner from invoking the third-party defense, and rejected Westwood's contention that § 101(35)(C) forecloses a prior owner like National Fuel from asserting the third-party defense provided for in § 107(b)(3). There followed the § 1292(b) certifications referred to above.

On the issues raised by Westwood's interlocutory appeal as stated above, we affirm the district court for the reasons set forth below.

II.

[Part II of the opinion, concluding that this interlocutory appeal should be entertained by the court, is omitted.]

III.

The district court held that the phrase "in connection with" requires that there be some relationship between the disposal/releasing activity and the contract with the defendant for the defendant to be barred from raising the third-party defense of § 107(b)(3). The court stated that to hold otherwise would render the language "in connection with" superfluous, a result generally at odds with an accepted principle of statutory construction. 737 F. Supp. at 1286 (citing *Ohio Power Co. v. Federal Energy Regulatory Comm'n*, 279 App. D.C. 327, 880 F.2d 1400, 1406 (D.C. Cir.) (constructions rendering statutory language superfluous are disfavored), *reh'g and reh'g en banc denied*, 897 F.2d 540 (D.C. Cir. 1989), *rev'd on other grounds*, 111 S. Ct. 415 (1990); *National Ass'n of Recycling Indus., Inc. v. Interstate Commerce Comm'n.*, 212 App. D.C. 396, 660 F.2d 795, 799 (D.C. Cir. 1981) (same)).

Other cases considering this or similar questions also have indicated that something more than a mere contractual relationship is required. In *United States v. Hooker Chemicals & Plastics Corp.*, 680 F. Supp. 546 (W.D.N.Y. 1988), the court held that defendants' contractual relationship with the present landowner — defendants had deeded the land to the City — precluded defendant from raising the third-party defense of § 107(b)(3) since "[defendant] was able to control the acts of these subsequent purchasers because of the nature of its relationship with these defendants in this case." *Id.* at 558. In *Shapiro v. Alexanderson,* 743 F. Supp. 268 (S.D.N.Y. 1990), the court held that the contractual relationship clause of § 107(b)(3) does not embrace "all acts by a third party with any contractual relationship with a defendant. Such a construction would render the language 'in connection with' mere surplusage." *Id.* at 271. "The act or omission must occur in a context so that there is a connection between the acts and the contractual relationship." *Id.* In Shapiro, the court described the "classic scenario" in which a landowner would be precluded from asserting a § 107(b)(3) defense: when the third party is operating a landfill pursuant to a contract with the owner. *Id.*

We agree with the district court that a landowner is precluded from raising the third-party defense only if the contract between the landowner and the third party somehow is connected with the handling of hazardous substances. The result would be the same if the contract allows the landowner to exert some control over the third party's actions so that the landowner fairly can be held liable for the release or threatened release of hazardous substances caused solely by the actions of the third party. The mere existence of a contractual relationship between the owner of land on which hazardous substances are or have been disposed and a third party whose act or omission was the sole cause of the release or threatened release of such hazardous substances into the environment does not foreclose the owner of the land from escaping liability, provided that the owner satisfies the additional requirements of § 107(b)(3)(a) and (b).

IV.

Section 101(35)(A) and (B) establish the "innocent landowner exception" (also referred to as the "innocent landowner defense" or the "innocent purchaser defense"). Section 101(35)(A) provides in relevant part:

> "The term 'contractual relationship', for the purpose of section 9607(b)(3) of this title includes, but is not limited to, land contracts, deeds or other instruments transferring title or possession, unless the real property on which the facility concerned is located was acquired by the defendant after the disposal or placement of the hazardous substance on, in, or at the facility, and one or more of the circumstances described in clause (i), (ii), or (iii) is also established by the defendant by a preponderance of the evidence:

>> "(i) At the time the defendant acquired the facility the defendant did not know and had no reason to know that any hazardous substance which is the subject of the release or threatened release was disposed of on, in, or at the facility. . . .

> "In addition to establishing the foregoing, the defendant must establish that he has satisfied the requirements of section 9607(b)(3)(a) and (b) of this title."

Section 101(35)(B) further provides that the "innocent landowner exception" is available only to defendants who make appropriate inquiry, at the time of acquisition, into the previous ownership and use of the property.

Section 101(35)(C) provides that:

> "Nothing in this paragraph or in section 9607(b)(3) of this title shall
> diminish the liability of any previous owner or operator of such facility
> who would otherwise be liable under this chapter. Notwithstanding
> this paragraph, if the defendant obtained actual knowledge of the
> release or threatened release of a hazardous substance at such facility
> when the defendant owned the real property and then subsequently
> transferred ownership of the property to another person without dis-
> closing such knowledge, such defendant shall be treated as liable
> under section 9607(a)(1) of this title and no defense under section
> 9607(b)(3) of this title shall be available to such defendant."

Westwood contends that the first sentence of § 101(35)(C) precludes National Fuel — indeed, all previous owners of property on which hazardous
substances were disposed or placed — from invoking the third-party defense
set forth in § 107(b)(3). The district court held Westwood's restrictive —
though perhaps literal — reading of § 101(35)(C) to be untenable for several
reasons. First, the court held that the second sentence of § 101(35)(C) makes
it "abundantly clear" that, had Congress intended to place the defense
provided for in § 107(b) beyond the reach of a particular class of defendants,
it knew precisely how to do so. Second, it would be nonsensical for Congress
virtually to bury in § 101(35)(C) a fundamental change in the scope of
§ 107(b)(3) rather than simply to amend the language of § 107(b)(3) itself.
We hold both of these reasons to be persuasive. Logic suggests that Congress
intended § 101(35)(C) merely to circumscribe the parameters of the innocent
landowner exception set forth in § 101(35)(A) and (B), and not to abrogate
completely the right of previous owners to raise the third-party defense set
forth in § 107(b)(3).

The district court suggested a third ground for its determination that the
first sentence of § 101(35)(C) was not intended completely to bar § 107(a)(2)
defendants — prior land owners — from asserting the third-party defense.
The court stated that "the innocent-landowner" exception . . . provides an
exemption from the 'in connection with' limitation: under certain circumstances,
it will lift the extra burden normally placed on defendants who are contractually related to the allegedly responsible third party, thereby putting them in
the same position as defendants who are not." 767 F. Supp. at 460. In other
words, § 101(35) shields innocent landowners from liability for the release or
threatened release of contaminants caused solely by the act or omission of
a third party, even though the act or omission of the third party occurred "in
connection with a contractual relationship" with the innocent landowner. The
legislative history appears to support such a reading of the statute:

> "[Section 101(35)] is intended to clarify and confirm that under limited
> circumstances landowners who acquire property without knowing of
> any contamination at the site and without reason to know of any
> contamination (or as otherwise noted in the amendment) may have
> a defense to liability under section 107 and therefore should not be
> held liable for cleaning up the site if such persons satisfy the remain-
> ing requirements of section 107(b)(3). A person who acquires property
> through a land contract or deed or other instrument transferring title

or possession that meets the requirements of this definition may assert that an act or omission of a third party should not be considered to have occurred in connection with a contractual relationship as identified in section 107(b) and therefore is not a bar to the defense."

H.R. Conf. Rep. No. 962, 99th Cong., 2d Sess. 186–87, reprinted in 1986 U.S. Code Cong. & Admin. News 3279–80.

Accordingly, an innocent purchaser subsequently may contract with a third party for the removal or disposal of hazardous wastes that he discovers on his property, without surrendering the third-party defense provided by § 107(b)(3). The first sentence of § 101(35)(C) is intended merely to emphasize that other § 107(a) defendants — those who are not "innocent" under § 101(35) — are denied such an exemption. For example, non-innocent landowners cannot invoke the third-party defense when they contract for the removal or disposal of hazardous substances on their property, even if a subsequent release or threatened release of hazardous substances is attributable solely to the acts or omissions of the party with whom they contracted.

Although we agree with the district court's ultimate conclusion that "the first sentence of § 101(35)(C) limits only the application of the innocent-landowner exception, rather than both the innocent-landowner exception and the balance of the third-party defense," we believe that the district court may have erred when it stated that the first sentence of § 101(35)(C) was intended "simply to underscore that the innocent-landowner exception was designed to apply only to current owners of property — that is, § 107(a)(1) defendants — who otherwise would not qualify for the § 107(b)(3) defense." 767 F. Supp. at 460–61 (emphasis added).

The second sentence of § 101(35)(C) makes it clear that Congress intended the innocent landowner exception to allow innocent purchasers of property — i.e. purchasers who are unaware, despite appropriate inquiry, that hazardous substances have been placed or disposed of on the property — subsequently to sell the property without losing their exemption from liability caused solely by a third party "in connection with" such a sale. This is subject to several conditions: first, that such innocent purchasers either do not learn of the existence of such hazardous substances, or, if they do learn of their existence, they disclose such knowledge to the person to whom they subsequently transfer ownership of the property; second, that the innocent landowner fulfills the additional requirements of § 107(b)(3) (a) and (b) — i.e. the innocent landowner must exercise due care with respect to the hazardous substances he discovers on his property, and he must take precautions against the foreseeable acts or omissions of third parties. Indeed, the district court recognized (in apparent contradiction to its earlier statement) that "it would make little sense for Congress to provide a defense for an 'innocent' land purchaser but fail to provide corresponding protection for that same landowner when he or she becomes an 'innocent' seller. . . ." Id. at 462.

In short, we agree with the district court's holding that "nothing in either § 107(b)(3) or § 101(35) . . . precludes National Fuel as a matter of law from presenting its third-party defense." Id. at 463.

V.

To summarize:

We hold that the district court correctly held that the phrase "in connection with a contractual relationship" in CERCLA § 107(b)(3) requires more than the mere existence of a contractual relationship between the owner of land on which hazardous substances are or have been disposed of and a third party whose act or omission was the sole cause of the release or threatened release of such hazardous substances into the environment, for the landowner to be barred from raising the third-party defense provided for in that section. In order for the landowner to be barred from raising the third-party defense under such circumstances, the contract between the landowner and the third party must either relate to the hazardous substances or allow the landowner to exert some element of control over the third party's activities.

We also hold that the district court properly held that § 101(35)(C) does not entirely preclude previous landowners from invoking the third-party defense provided for in § 107(b)(3).

The order of the district court denying Westwood's motion for reconsideration of its earlier order which denied its motion or summary judgment is affirmed.

Affirmed.

NOTES

1. *Accord State of New York v Lashins Arcade Co.,* 91 F.3d. 353 (2d Cir. 1996). Query whether an innocent landowner pursuant to CERCLA could be successfully sued under common law toxic tort theory. According to one commentator, the answer is no. Charles S. Sarlo, *A Comparative Analysis: The Affirmative Defense of an Innocent Landowner versus the Prima Facie Case of a Toxic Tort Plaintiff: Can CERCLA's Innocent Landowner Provision be Used as a Defense in a Toxic Tort Suit?,* 16 Pace L. Rev. 243, 269 (1999).

2. While landowners have welcomed the innocent landowner exception, the difficulty in their view has been the "reason to know" limitation. The limitation specifies that, if a person had "reason to know" of any contamination on the property, he or she is disqualified as an innocent landowner. EPA has traditionally set a high bar on this determination. The agency has considered a defendant to have had reason to know if the defendant did not find contamination but could have.

The Small Business Liability Protection and Brownfields Revitalization Act, P.L. 107-118, added to CERCLA in January, 2002, lowered the bar on what it means to have had "reason to know." Newly added § 101(35)(B) provides that a defendant had no reason to know if he or she made all "appropriate inquiries." Making an appropriate inquiry, in turn, means meeting "standards and practices" to be established by EPA in regulations. Significantly, however, "[I]n the case of property for residential use or other similar use purchased by a nongovernmental or noncommercial entity, a facility inspection and title search that reveal no basis for further investigation shall be considered to satisfy the requirements of this paragraph." § 101(35)(B)(v), 42 U.S.C. § 9601(B)(v).

A NOTE ON THE BONA FIDE PROSPECTIVE PURCHASER ("BFPP") DEFENSE

Title II of the Small Business Liability Protection and Brownfields Revitalization Act (P.L. 107-118, January, 2002), added the fourth and final defense allowable under CERCLA. New § 107(r), 42 U.S.C. § 9607(r), entitled "Prospective Purchaser and Windfall Lien," stipulates that "bona fide prospective purchasers" of contaminated land "whose potential liability for a release or threatened release is based solely on the purchaser's being considered to be an owner or operator of a facility shall not be liable as long as the bona fide prospective purchaser does not impede the performance of a response action or natural resource restoration." This defense is akin to the innocent landowner exception to the contractual relationship limitation of the third party defense, but stands separate from it. To qualify for this defense, a person must be a "bona fide prospective purchaser." The Act defines a BFPP as a person who acquired land after all disposal has taken place and who has made "appropriate inquiries." § 101(40), 42 U.S.C. § 9601(40). "Appropriate inquiries," in turn, is defined in accordance with new § 101(35)(B). *See supra.* Moreover, as with the modification of the innocent landowner exception, "[I]n the case of property in residential or other similar use at the time of purchase by a nongovernmental or noncommercial entity, a facility inspection and title search that reveal no basis for further investigation shall be considered to satisfy the requirements of this subparagraph." § 101(40)(B)(iii), 42 U.S.C. § 9601(40)(B)(iii).

Note the distinctions between this provision and the innocent landowner exception. First, this provision applies of its own force; it is not tied to another defense. Second, while either actual knowledge or having reason to know of contamination prior to purchase disqualifies one from the benefits of the innocent landowner exception, only having reason to know (by failing to make "appropriate inquiries") disqualifies one from using the BFPP defense. In other words, a BFPP may have *actual* knowledge of past contamination and still use the defense. Congress intended this result to help out with the brownfields problem. *See infra.*

As the title of new § 107(r) indicates, this defense is coupled with a windfall lien provision. § 107(r)(2), 42 U.S.C. § 9607(r)(2). This provision allows the government to recoup response costs it may have paid out with respect to BFPP land. However, the government may not recoup more than the increase in market value, if any, directly attributable to the clean-up itself.

C. ISSUES OF LIABILITY AND DAMAGES

Actions for cost recovery are available under § 107(a), 42 U.S.C. § 9707(a). That provision specifically allows for recovery of damages for:

> (A) all costs of removal or remedial action incurred by the United States Government or a State or an Indian tribe not inconsistent with the national contingency plan;

(B) any other necessary costs of response incurred by any other person consistent with the national contingency plan;

(C) damages for injury to, destruction of, or loss of natural resources, including the reasonable costs of assessing such injury, destruction, or loss resulting from such a release; and

(D) the costs of any health assessment or health effects study carried out under section 9604(i) of this title.

In addition to cost recovery actions under § 107(a), CERCLA also makes available contribution actions under § 113(f), 42 U.S.C. § 9613(f). In the years since CERCLA's enactment, there has been a good deal of confusion regarding the interplay of these sections. Only recently has case law settled the outstanding questions.

DICO, INC. v. CHEMICAL CO.

340 F.3d 525 (8th Cir. 2003)

JUDGES: Before: BOWMAN, RICHARD S. ARNOLD and BYE, Circuit Judges.

BYE, Circuit Judge:

Dico, Inc., appeals the district court's grant of summary judgment dismissing its direct cost recovery action under the Comprehensive Environmental Response, Compensation and Liability Act of 1980 (CERCLA), 42 U.S.C. §§ 9601-9675.

Dico was compelled by the Environmental Protection Agency (EPA), pursuant to Unilateral Administrative Orders (UAO), to clean up contamination located on property it owned in Des Moines, Iowa. After incurring approximately $5.7 million in cleanup costs, Dico brought suit against Shell Oil Company, BP Products North America, Inc., Monsanto Company, Chevron Chemical Company, and Bayer Corporation (collectively "Customer Group") seeking direct recovery of those costs and any future costs or alternatively, seeking pro rata contribution. The district court dismissed Dico's direct cost recovery action holding that Dico, as a potentially responsible party (PRP), was limited to seeking contribution from the Customer Group. The district court also dismissed Dico's action for contribution because the Customer Group had entered into a judicially-approved consent degree with the EPA which included a grant of protection from other PRPs who might seek contribution. Dico appeals the district court's dismissal and we affirm.

I

In 1974, trichloroethylene (TCE) was detected in water coming from underground wells located near property owned by Dico and maintained by the Des Moines Water Works. The EPA designated the area the "Des Moines TCE Site" and placed it on the national priority list. The Des Moines TCE Site was divided into several "operable units." Operable Unit-2 ("OU-2") and

Operable Unit-4 ("OU-4") (together "OU-2/4") were within Dico's property. Each was contaminated with TCE, and OU-4 was also contaminated with herbicides and pesticides.

Dico's corporate predecessor, Di-Chem, had operated a chemical formulation business on the Dico property until the 1970s. In 1994, the EPA issued two UAOs and Dico conducted two removal actions at OU-2/4. The Customer Group conducted a third removal action pursuant to an Administrative Order on Consent (AOC). The EPA also incurred costs associated with the removal actions at OU-2/4.

In 1996, the EPA signed a Record of Decision (ROD), confirming completion of the three removal actions at OU-2/4. The Customer Group requested settlement negotiations with the government regarding the costs associated with the cleanup efforts. Pursuant to CERCLA, 42 U.S.C. § 9622(e)(3), the EPA undertook a nonbinding preliminary allocation of responsibility (NBAR) and allocated 61% of the responsibility to Dico and 39% to the Customer Group collectively. In April 1998, the EPA formally notified the Customer Group and Dico they were PRPs and provided each with copies of the NBAR and a proposed consent decree. Dico and the Customer Group were further notified that settlement with the government would provide protection from liability in the contribution action brought by Dico arising out of the same remediations. Despite repeated invitations from the government, Dico did not respond and chose not to participate in settlement negotiations. On November 2, 1998, on the eve of reaching an agreement with the Customer Group, the government reminded Dico that a final consent decree would include contribution liability protection for the Customer Group. Dico remained steadfast in its refusal to participate in the negotiations.

On November 29, 1999, the government filed an action in district court and simultaneously lodged the proposed consent decree. As required by CERCLA, 42 U.S.C. § 9622(d)(2), the consent decree was published in the Federal Register; in response to which Dico submitted objections and comments. Dico moved to intervene in the action and to consolidate it with this cost recovery/contribution action. The district court granted Dico's motion to intervene but deferred ruling on Dico's motion to consolidate the two actions.

Dico requested an evidentiary hearing arguing 1) a hearing was necessary because the government failed to provide a fair and complete record, and 2) Dico had a vested property interest in the contribution action which under the Fifth Amendment could not be "taken" without due process, i.e., an evidentiary hearing.

The district court denied Dico's request for an evidentiary hearing because Dico had been provided sufficient opportunity to supplement the record before and after the action was filed in district court. The district court also rejected Dico's due process challenge, holding Dico never had a right to contribution because its statutory contribution claim was at all times limited by 42 U.S.C. § 9613(f)(2) ("A person who has resolved its liability to the United States . . . in an administrative or judicially approved settlement shall not be liable for claims for contribution regarding matters addressed in the settlement."). The district court then granted the government's motion to enter the consent decree, and denied as moot Dico's motion to consolidate the contribution action with the action at bar. We affirmed the district court's decision on appeal. *United States v. BP Amoco Oil PLC,* 277 F.3d 1012, 1020 (8th Cir. 2002).

Thereafter, the Customer Group moved for summary judgment in this action arguing 1) CERCLA § 107(a)(1) and (a)(4)(B) barred Dico's direct action for cost recovery because Dico was a PRP, and 2) Dico's action for contribution was barred by the consent decree entered into between the Customer Group and the government. The district court granted the Customer Group's motion for summary judgment and this appeal followed. Originally, Dico appealed the dismissal of both causes of action but has subsequently abandoned its appeal of the dismissal of the contribution claim. Thus, the only issue before us is whether the district court properly dismissed Dico's direct cost recovery action.

II

This court reviews a grant of summary judgment de novo, applying the same standard as the district court[.] The Customer Group argues Dico's direct cost recovery action is barred because Dico is a PRP as defined by CERCLA, and CERCLA limits actions between PRPs to those for contribution. Dico argues CERCLA does not prohibit direct cost recovery actions between PRPs[.]

Parties incurring cleanup costs pursuant to an order from the EPA, who believe they are not responsible for the contamination, may bring a claim in federal court to recover their cleanup costs. *United States v. Dico, Inc.,* 136 F.3d 572, 574 (8th Cir. 1998). The statute provides two avenues for recovery. First, § 107 allows the government or an "innocent" private party to recover cleanup costs from PRPs through a direct cost recovery action. *See* 42 U.S.C. § 9607(a)(4) (stating PRPs "shall be liable for . . . (A) all costs of removal or remedial action incurred by the United States Government . . . [and] (B) any other necessary costs of response incurred by any other person. . . ."). Under § 107, PRPs are held jointly and severally liable for the costs of cleanup. Thus, one PRP may bear a disproportionate share of the cleanup costs. Accordingly, though CERCLA as originally drafted contained no express provision authorizing contribution claims between PRPs, courts interpreting CERCLA found such causes of action impliedly authorized. *Key Tronic,* 511 U.S. at 816 n.7.

In 1986, as part of the Superfund Amendments and Reauthorization Act (SARA), 42 U.S.C. §§ 9601-9675, Congress amended CERCLA and provided for an explicit right of contribution between PRPs under § 113(f)(1). Thereafter, courts held the express language providing for a right of contribution implied an intent to limit PRPs to claims for contribution, and to preclude actions between PRPs for direct recovery. *See, e.g., N. J. Turnpike Auth. v. PPG Indus., Inc.,* 197 F.3d 96, 104 (3d Cir. 1999) ("The Turnpike is PRP . . . and its action against other PRPs is properly characterized as a section 113 action."); *Axel Johnson, Inc. v. Carroll Carolina Oil Co.,* 191 F.3d 409, 415 (4th Cir. 1999) ("As a general rule any claim for damages made by a potentially responsible person — even a claim ostensibly made under § 107 — is considered a contribution claim under § 113."); *Bedford Affiliates v. Sills,* 156 F.3d 416, 424 (2d Cir. 1998) ("[A] party that is itself liable may recover only those costs exceeding its pro rata share of the entire cleanup expenditure, i.e., contribution under § 113(f)(1)."); *Centerior Serv. Co. v. Acme Scrap Iron & Metal*

Corp., 153 F.3d 344, 350 (6th Cir. 1998) ("Claims by PRPs . . . seeking costs from other PRPs are necessarily actions for contribution . . . governed by . . . § 113(f)."); *Pinal Creek Group v. Newmont Mining Corp.*, 118 F.3d 1298, 1306 (9th Cir. 1997) ("Under CERCLA, a PRP does not have a claim for the recovery of the totality of its cleanup costs against other PRPs, and a PRP cannot assert a claim against other PRPs for joint and several liability."); *Redwing Carriers, Inc. v. Saraland Apartments*, 94 F.3d 1489, 1496 (11th Cir. 1996) ("Redwing is a responsible party under CERCLA, and therefore, its claims against other allegedly responsible parties are claims for contribution."); *United States v. Colo. & E. R. R.*, 50 F.3d 1530, 1536 (10th Cir. 1995) (holding any claim for apportionment of cleanup costs between PRPs is a claim for contribution); *United Techs. Corp. v. Browning-Ferris Indus., Inc.*, 33 F.3d 96, 101 (1st Cir.1994) (holding plaintiffs who were by their own admission liable parties, were in effect asserting an action for contribution); *Akzo Coatings, Inc. v. Aigner Corp.*, 30 F.3d 761, 764 (7th Cir. 1994) (holding an action by one PRP against other jointly and severally liable parties is governed by section 113(f)); *Amoco Oil Co. v. Borden, Inc.*, 889 F.2d 664, 672 (5th Cir. 1989) (holding actions between two liable parties are actions for contribution).

Dico and the Customer Group clearly fall within § 107(a)(1)-(4)'s definition of a PRP. As such, any action brought by Dico against the Customer Group to recoup its cleanup costs must be for contribution. Dico, however, citing *Key Tronic,* argues its direct action is permissible under CERCLA. *Key Tronic* involved a claim for attorney's fees incurred by one PRP in connection with an action for contribution against another PRP. 511 U.S. at 811. The plaintiff sought to recover attorney's fees arguing §§ 107 and 113 impliedly provided for an award of attorney's fees to prevailing parties. In rejecting the argument, the Court described § 107 as "impliedly authorizing private parties to recover cleanup costs from *other* PRP's." *Id.* at 818 (emphasis added). Dico contends *Key Tronic* establishes the proposition that "private parties" is synonymous with "PRPs," and the direct recovery action found in § 107 is available to private parties and PRPs equally. We disagree. *Key Tronic* did not involve the issue before us; namely, whether a PRP may pursue an action for direct recovery against another PRP. Rather, *Key Tronic* dealt with whether a PRP could claim attorney's fees in a contribution action brought against another PRP. In that context, it was appropriate for the Court to use the terms "private parties" and "PRPs" together. More importantly, however, the language cited by Dico was used in reference to the implicit right to seek contribution found in § 107, *id.* at 816, 818, prior to SARA. Thus, we find no support for Dico's argument in the language of *Key Tronic.* Conversely, there is overwhelming authority among the circuits to support the Customer Group's argument that PRPs are limited to actions for contribution. Accordingly, we hold Dico may not bring an action against the Customer Group for direct recovery unless it can establish it falls within one of the enumerated defenses set out in § 107(b).

The Customer Group argues that only PRPs who qualify for one of the enumerated statutory defenses may bring an action for direct recovery against another PRP, and Dico fails to qualify for any of the defenses[.]

When one of the enumerated CERCLA defenses applies a PRP is deemed innocent; and an action between an innocent party and another PRP is not between two liable parties. *See, e.g., Morrison Enters. v. McShares, Inc.*, 302 F.3d 1127, 1133 (10th Cir. 2002) ("[A] party that can show that it is entitled to one of the defenses under § 9607(b) should be able to sue under § 9607(a); after all, such a party is not a PRP for purposes of the statute."); *accord Bedford Affiliates*, 156 F.3d at 425; *Axel Johnson, Inc.*, 191 F.3d at 416.

Dico, however, does not contend it qualifies for any of the enumerated defenses. Instead, it argues we should adopt a judicially created "innocent landowner" exception recognized in a line of Seventh Circuit and various district court cases. *See NutraSweet Co. v. X-L Eng'g Co.*, 227 F.3d 776, 784 (7th Cir. 2000) (noting an innocent landowner who did not contribute to the contamination could bring a direct recovery action); *Rumpke of Ind., Inc. v. Cummins Engine Co.*, 107 F.3d 1235, 1241-42 (7th Cir. 1997) (holding landowner who was not responsible for any of the waste entitled to sue under § 107); *AM Int'l v. Datacard Corp.*, 106 F.3d 1342, 1347 (7th Cir. 1997) (same); *Akzo Coatings, Inc.*, 30 F.3d at 764 (same); *Soo Line R.R. v. Tang Indus., Inc.*, 998 F. Supp. 889, 894-95 (N.D. Ill. 1998) (same); *Laidlaw Waste Sys., Inc. v. Mallinckrodt, Inc.*, 925 F. Supp. 624, 630-31 (E.D. Mo. 1996) (same); *Wolf, Inc. v. L. & W. Serv. Ctr.*, 1997 U.S. Dist. LEXIS 3758, No. v4: CV 96-3099, (D. Neb. Nov. 27, 1997) (holding landowner/plaintiff who alleged it did nothing to contribute to contamination allowed to proceed with § 107 action).

Section 107(a) imposes liability on PRPs "notwithstanding any other provision or rule of law, and subject only to the defenses set forth in subsection (b) of this section. . . ." (emphasis added). Thus, the plain language of the statute militates against Dico's argument. Additionally, other circuits have held any expansion of the list of defenses beyond those specifically delineated in the statute would circumvent the underlying purpose of CERCLA. See Bedford Affiliates, 156 F. 3d at 425 (declining to carve out a judicially created defense under CERCLA that Congress itself chose not to create); Axel Johnson, 191 F.3d at 416 ("If an innocent party exception [to § 107] is even possible . . . it would . . . seem prudent to limit its applicability to those who can make out one of the defenses . . . § 107 itself provides."); Morrison Enter., 302 F.3d at 1134 (holding the exception created by the Seventh Circuit does not square with the underlying purposes of CERCLA).

We need not, however, decide whether to adopt the "innocent landowner" exception because we have already concluded Dico is not an innocent landowner. In a previous installment of this litigation, *United States v. Dico, Inc.*, 266 F.3d 864, 875 8th Cir. 2001), Dico appealed the district court's finding that Dico had contributed to contamination at the Des Moines TCE Site. *Id.* at 868.

On appeal, we held "the record, taken as a whole, shows evidence in support of each basis for the District Court's conclusion that Dico released TCE on its property." *Id.* at 875. Dico's allegations of innocence notwithstanding, we will not re-examine our prior holding absent compelling circumstances — none of which are present in this appeal. *McCurry v. Tesch*, 824 F.2d 638, 640 (8th Cir. 1987).

III

The district court's grant of summary judgment is affirmed.

NOTE

PRPs may bring § 113 contribution actions in two circumstances only. First, "[a] person who has resolved its liability to the United States or a State for some or all of a response action or for some or all of the costs of such action in an administrative or judicially approved settlement" may do so. § 113(f)(3)(B), 42 U.S.C. § 9613(f)(3)(B). Second, a PRP may bring an action "during or following any civil action under section 9606 of this title or under section 9607(a) of this title." § 113(f)(1), 42 U.S.C. § 9613(f)(1). *Cooper Industries, Inc. v. Aviall Services, Inc.*, 2004 U.S. LEXIS 8271 (2004).

As indicated in *Dico, supra*, such contribution claims are limited by § 113(f)(2), 42 U.S.C. § 9613(f)(2) ("A person who has resolved its liability to the United States . . . in an administrative or judicially approved settlement shall not be liable for claims for contribution regarding matters addressed in the settlement.").

BELL PETROLEUM SERVICES, INC. v. U.S. ENVIRONMENTAL PROTECTION AGENCY

3 F.3d 889 (5th Cir. 1993)

JUDGES: Before JOLLY and DUHE, Circuit Judges, and PARKER, District Judge (Chief Judge of the Eastern District of Texas, sitting by designation)

OPINION: E. GRADY JOLLY, Circuit Judge:

The Environmental Protection Agency (EPA) seeks to recover its response costs under the Comprehensive Environmental Response, Compensation and Liability Act (CERCLA) because of a discharge of chromium waste that contaminated a local water supply. . . . We REVERSE the portion of the judgment imposing joint and several liability, and REMAND for further proceedings. Our review of the administrative record has convinced us that the EPA's decision to provide an alternate water supply was arbitrary and capricious; accordingly, we REVERSE the portion of the district court's judgment allowing the EPA to recover the costs of designing and constructing that system, and REMAND for deletion of those amounts and recalculating prejudgment interest.

I

In 1978, a citizen in the Odessa, Texas area complained about discolored drinking water. The Texas Water Commission conducted an investigation. It ultimately focused on a chrome-plating shop that was operated successively from 1971 through 1977 by John Leigh, Western Pollution Control Corporation (hereinafter referred to as Bell), and Woolley Tool Division of Chromalloy American Corporation . . . [later merged into Sequa] . . . just outside the city limits of Odessa. The investigation showed that during the chrome-plating process, finished parts were rinsed, and the rinse water was pumped out of the building onto the ground.

In 1984, the EPA designated a 24-block area north of the . . . facility as a Superfund site — "Odessa Chromium I." It authorized a response action pursuant to its authority under CERCLA § 104, 42 U.S.C. § 9604, and entered into a cooperative agreement with the State of Texas. The State was to perform a remedial investigation, feasibility study, and remedial design work for the site, with the EPA reimbursing the State for ninety percent of the costs. The remedial investigation revealed that the Trinity Aquifer, the only source of groundwater in the area, contained elevated concentrations of chromium . . . [a hazardous substance under CERCLA. Ed.].

A "focused" feasibility study (FFS) was undertaken to evaluate the need to provide an alternative water supply pending completion of the remaining portion of the feasibility study and implementation of final remedial action. The FFS concluded that the City of Odessa's water system should be extended to provide service in the Odessa Chromium I area. On September 8, 1986, the EPA Regional Administrator issued a Record of Decision (ROD), finding that city water service should be extended to the site. Pursuant to the cooperative agreement, the State, through its contractor, designed and constructed the system, which was completed in 1988.

II

In December 1988, the EPA filed a CERCLA cost-recovery action against Bell [et al] which was consolidated with an adversary proceeding the EPA had filed against Bell in Bell's bankruptcy case. The EPA sought to recover direct and indirect costs it incurred in studying, designing, and constructing the alternate water supply system.

In July 1989, the district court entered a case management order providing that the case would be decided in three phases: Phase I — liability, Phase II — recoverability of the EPA's response costs, and Phase III — "responsibility." In September 1989, the district court granted in part, and denied in part, the EPA's motion for summary judgment as to liability. In its memorandum opinion, it stated that the relative culpability of the parties and the "divisibility of liability" issues would be decided during Phase III. Although the district court ruled that CERCLA did not require the EPA to prove causation, it held an evidentiary hearing and made alternative findings and conclusions addressing causation, holding that "Leigh, Bell and Sequa caused the contamination." In March 1990, the district court granted the EPA's motion for clarification of the September 1989 summary judgment, holding that its previous opinion had provided that the defendants were jointly and severally liable. It also entered a declaratory judgment as to the defendants' liability for future response costs.

The Phase II proceeding on recoverability of response costs was handled through cross-motions for summary judgment. The district court held that the defendants had not met their burden of proving that the EPA's decision to implement an alternate water supply was arbitrary and capricious, and held that they were liable for the EPA's direct and indirect response costs, plus prejudgment interest from the date such costs were incurred.

[The District Court also granted a request for a hearing filed by Sequa and maintaining that Bell was not being required to pay its fair share of response costs. Thereafter, on July 24, 1990, the court denied relief to Sequa, holding "there was no method of dividing the liability among the defendants which would rise to any level above mere speculation, because each of the proposed apportionment methods involved a significant assumption factor, inasmuch as records had been lost, and because each of the apportionment methods differed significantly. In the alternative, it concluded that, based on equitable factors, responsibility should be divided as follows: Bell — 35%; Sequa — 35%; and Leigh — 30%."]

In December 1990, the district court entered an order approving another consent decree, pursuant to which the EPA settled its claims against Leigh for past and future costs — for $100,000.

In sum, the district court held that Sequa is jointly and severally liable for $1,866,904.19, including the costs of studying, designing, and constructing the alternate water supply system. In addition, Sequa is jointly and severally liable for all future costs incurred by the EPA in studying, designing, and implementing a permanent remedy. . . .

IV

Joint and Several Liability

Since CERCLA's enactment, the federal courts have struggled to resolve the complicated, often confusing, questions posed by the concept of joint and several liability, and its application under a statute whose provisions are silent with respect to the scope of liability, but whose legislative history is clear that common law principles of joint and several liability may affect liability. The issue is one of first impression in this Circuit.

A

Common Law: The Restatement of Torts

Although joint and several liability is commonly imposed in CERCLA cases, it is not mandatory in all such cases. *United States v. Monsanto Co.*, 858 F.2d at 171. Instead, Congress intended that the federal courts determine the scope of liability in CERCLA cases under traditional and evolving common law principles, guided by the Restatement (Second) of Torts. . . . [citations omitted].

Section 433 of the Restatement provides that:

(1) Damages for harm are to be apportioned among two or more causes where

(a) there are distinct harms, or

(b) there is a reasonable basis for determining the contribution of each cause to a single harm.

(2) Damages for any other harm cannot be apportioned among two or more causes.

Restatement (Second) of Torts, § 433A.

The nature of the harm is the key factor in determining whether apportionment is appropriate. Distinct harms — e.g., where two defendants independently shoot the plaintiff at the same time, one wounding him in the arm and the other wounding him in the leg — are regarded as separate injuries. Although some of the elements of damages (such as lost wages or pain and suffering) may be difficult to apportion, "it is still possible, as a logical, reasonable, and practical matter, . . . to make a rough estimate which will fairly apportion such subsidiary elements of damages." *Id.*, comment b on subsection (1).

The Restatement also discusses "successive" harms, such as when "two defendants, independently operating the same plant, pollute a stream over successive periods of time." *Id.*, comment c on subsection (1). Apportionment is appropriate, because "it is clear that each has caused a separate amount of harm, limited in time, and that neither has any responsibility for the harm caused by the other." *Id.*

The final situation discussed by the Restatement in which apportionment is available involves a single harm that is "divisible" — perhaps the most difficult type of harm to conceptualize. Such harm, "while not so clearly marked out as severable into distinct parts, [is] still capable of division upon a reasonable and rational basis, and of fair apportionment among the causes responsible. . . . Where such apportionment can be made without injustice to any of the parties, the court may require it to be made." *Id.*, comment d on subsection (1). Two examples of such harm are described in the comment. The first is where cattle owned by two or more persons trespass upon the plaintiff's land and destroy his crops. Although "the aggregate harm is a lost crop, . . . it may nevertheless be apportioned among the owners of the cattle, on the basis of the number owned by each, and the reasonable assumption that the respective harm done is proportionate to that number." *Id.* The second example involves pollution of a stream by two or more factories. There, "the interference with the plaintiff's use of the water may be treated as divisible in terms of degree, and may be apportioned among the owners of the factories, on the basis of evidence of the respective quantities of pollution discharged into the stream." *Id.*

Apportionment is inappropriate for other kinds of harm, which, "by their very nature, are normally incapable of any logical, reasonable, or practical division." *Id.*, comment on subsection (2). Examples of such harm are death, a single wound, the destruction of a house by fire, or the sinking of a barge. "Where two or more causes combine to produce such a single result, incapable of division on any logical or reasonable basis, and each is a substantial factor in bringing about the harm, the courts have refused to make an arbitrary apportionment for its own sake, and each of the causes is charged with responsibility for the entire harm." *Id.*

Apportionment is also inappropriate in what the Restatement describes as "exceptional" cases, "in which injustice to the plaintiff may result." *Id.*, comment h on subsection (1). For example, "one of two tortfeasors [may be] so hopelessly insolvent that the plaintiff will never be able to collect from him the share of the damages allocated to him." *Id.* Where the court deems it unjust to require the innocent plaintiff to bear the risk of one of the tortfeasors' insolvency, it may refuse to apportion damages in such a case. *Id.*

In sum, the nature of the harm is the determining factor with respect to whether apportionment is appropriate. Ultimately, the decision whether to impose joint and several liability turns on whether there is a reasonable and just method for determining the amount of harm that was caused by each defendant (or, in some cases, by an innocent cause or by the fault of the plaintiff). The question whether the harm to the plaintiff is capable of apportionment among two or more causes is a question of law. Restatement (Second) of Torts, § 434(1)(b). Once it has been determined that the harm is capable of being apportioned among the various causes of it, the actual apportionment of damages is a question of fact. *Id.,* § 434(2)(b) & comment d. . . .

CERCLA is a strict liability statute, one of the purposes of which is to shift the cost of cleaning up environmental harm from the taxpayers to the parties who benefited from the disposal of the wastes that caused the harm. *See, e.g., Chem-Dyne,* 572 F. Supp. at 805–06. "The improper disposal or release of hazardous substances is an enormous and complex problem of national magnitude involving uniquely federal interests." *Id.* at 808. Often, liability is imposed upon entities for conduct predating the enactment of CERCLA, and even for conduct that was not illegal, unethical, or immoral at the time it occurred. We recognize the importance of keeping these facts in mind when attempting to develop a uniform federal common law for CERCLA cases. We also recognize, however, that CERCLA, as a strict liability statute that will not listen to pleas of "no fault," can be terribly unfair in certain instances in which parties may be required to pay huge amounts for damages to which their acts did not contribute. Congress recognized such possibilities and left it to the courts to fashion some rules that will, in appropriate instances, ameliorate this harshness. Accordingly, Congress has suggested, and we agree, that common-law principles of tort liability set forth in the Restatement provide sound guidance. In applying those principles to this CERCLA case, we think that it will be helpful to examine briefly some of the relevant CERCLA jurisprudence. . . .

B

[At this point, the court discusses approaches taken by other federal courts to resolve questions of joint and several liability.]

Although these approaches are not entirely uniform, certain basic principles emerge. First, joint and several liability is not mandated under CERCLA; Congress intended that the federal courts impose joint and several liability only in appropriate cases, applying common-law principles. Second, all of the cases rely on the Restatement in resolving the issues of joint and several liability. The major differences among the cases concern the timing of the resolution of the divisibility question, whether equitable factors should be considered, and whether a defendant can avoid liability for all, or only some portion, of the damages. Third, even where commingled wastes of unknown toxicity, migratory potential, and synergistic effect are present, defendants are allowed an opportunity to attempt to prove that there is a reasonable basis for apportionment (although they rarely succeed); where such factors are not present, volume may be a reasonable means of apportioning liability.

With respect to the timing of the "divisibility" inquiry, we believe that an early resolution is preferable. We agree with the Second Circuit, however, that this is a matter best left to the sound discretion of the district court. . . . We therefore conclude that . . . [Restatement principles shall control and that defendant, to avoid imposition of joint and several liability, must demonstrate the amount of harm its pollution has caused] . . . [w]e nevertheless recognize that the Restatement principles must be adapted, where necessary, to implement congressional intent with respect to liability under the unique statutory scheme of CERCLA.

C

Application of Joint & Several Liability

We now turn to consider the application of these traditional and evolving common law principles of joint and several liability to the facts of this case. . . .

Our review of the record convinces us that Sequa met its burden of proving that, as a matter of law, there is a reasonable basis for apportionment. This case is closely analogous to the Restatement's illustrations in which apportionment of liability is appropriate. For example, where cattle owned by two or more defendants destroy the plaintiff's crops, the damages are apportioned according to the number of cattle owned by each defendant, based on the reasonable assumption that the respective harm done is proportionate to that number. Thus, the Restatement suggests that apportionment is appropriate even though the evidence does not establish with certainty the specific amount of harm caused by each defendant's cattle, and even though there is a possibility that only one of the defendant's cattle caused all of the harm, while the other defendant's cattle idly stood by. Likewise, pollution of a stream by two or more factories may be treated as divisible in terms of degree, and apportioned among the defendants on the basis of evidence of the respective quantities of pollution discharged by each.

As is evident from our previous discussion of the jurisprudence, most CERCLA cost-recovery actions involve numerous, commingled hazardous substances with synergistic effects and unknown toxicity. In contrast, this case involves only one hazardous substance — chromium — and no synergistic effects. The chromium entered the groundwater as the result of similar operations by three parties who operated at mutually exclusive times. Here, it is reasonable to assume that the respective harm done by each of the defendants is proportionate to the volume of chromium-contaminated water each discharged into the environment.

Even though it is not possible to determine with absolute certainty the exact amount of chromium each defendant introduced into the groundwater, there is sufficient evidence from which a reasonable and rational approximation of each defendant's individual contribution to the contamination can be made.

. . .

In sum, we conclude that the district court erred in imposing joint and several liability, because Sequa met its burden of proving that there is a reasonable basis for apportioning liability among the defendants on a volumetric basis. We therefore remand the case to the district court for apportionment.

V

Alternate Water Supply System

Sequa also challenges the EPA's decision to provide an alternate water supply (AWS) as an interim measure pending the completion of final remedial action. . . .

After thoroughly reviewing the administrative record, we conclude that the EPA's decision to furnish the AWS was arbitrary and capricious. In vain we have searched the over 5,000 pages of administrative record, and found not one shred of evidence that anyone in the area was actually drinking chromium-contaminated water. Amazingly, the EPA made no attempt to learn whether anyone was drinking the water, or whether anyone intended to utilize the AWS, until after it had made its decision to construct the AWS. One would think that surely such information was essential in order to reach an informed, rational decision as to whether an AWS was necessary, and whether it would reduce any significant threat to public health. . . .

VI

All Costs?

Having determined that the EPA's decision to implement the AWS was arbitrary and capricious, we must now decide whether the EPA nevertheless is entitled to recover its costs for designing and constructing the AWS.

The EPA takes the position that it is entitled to recover all costs — even if unreasonable or unnecessary — unless Sequa proves that such costs are inconsistent with the National Contingency Plan. The district court held that the EPA could recover all of its response costs, so long as they were not the product of "gross misconduct" by the agency.

Although we approve of the district court's attempt to impose some restraints on the EPA's ability to recover costs from private parties, we find no statutory basis for its "gross misconduct" limitation. Nevertheless, we are troubled by the implications of the EPA's position on this issue. Sequa contends that, under the EPA's interpretation, defendants will be liable even if the EPA allows a contractor to pay its officers and other employees unjustified millions and allows each of them a Rolls-Royce for transportation. Interestingly, the EPA did not attempt to refute Sequa's assertion, either in its appellate brief or at oral argument. Instead, the EPA asserts a policy reason to support its interpretation:

> "By refusing to permit defendants to defend against cost recovery actions by engaging in detailed attacks on the 'reasonableness' of individual government cost items, Congress provided an incentive to those defendants to conduct the necessary response actions themselves. Where defendants refuse to conduct the appropriate response actions, CERCLA allows the Government to undertake the response actions it deems necessary and appropriate without being constrained by the possibility that each line item of the costs of these actions will be challenged in cost recovery."

In addition, the EPA asks us to take comfort in the fact that, through internal agency audits and other forms of self-policing, costs will be controlled.

Acceptance of the EPA's position would effectively prohibit judicial review of the EPA's expenditures. In short, we would give the EPA a blank check in conducting response actions. We seriously doubt that Congress intended to give the EPA such unrestrained spending discretion. Moreover, such unbridled discretion removes any restraint upon the conduct of the EPA in exercising its awesome powers; if the EPA knows there are no economic consequences to it, its decisions and conduct are likely to be less responsible.

We do not have to decide the question in this case, however, because the only costs Sequa challenges as unreasonable and unnecessary are those associated with implementation of the alternate water supply system, a decision that we have already concluded was arbitrary and capricious. . . . Because the decision to implement an AWS was arbitrary and capricious, it is inconsistent with the NCP. Accordingly, the EPA is not entitled to recover the costs of designing and constructing the AWS.

We realize that, as a result of our decision disallowing the EPA's costs for the AWS, those costs will have to be borne by the Superfund. Although regrettable, this is the inevitable result of arbitrary and capricious EPA decisionmaking. Without knowing, or even attempting to learn, whether the AWS would serve to protect the safety and health of anyone, the EPA officiously ignored the comments of Bell and Sequa, and the results of its own remedial investigation, and stubbornly proceeded to spend over $300,000 to furnish a water supply system that was not needed, was not allowed to be used by the commercial establishments whose wells (according to the administrative record) were the only ones with chromium contamination in excess of the SDWA standards, and did very little — indeed, if anything — to reduce any perceived public health threat posed by the chromium-contaminated groundwater. We can only assume that the EPA was not concerned about the cost of the AWS, because it believed that it could recover whatever was spent from Sequa. Although the EPA's powers under CERCLA are indeed broad, Congress has not provided that private parties must pay for the consequences of arbitrary and capricious agency action. . . .

[The dissent by Parker, District Judge, is omitted.]

NOTES

1. *Accord, United States v. Monsanto Co.*, 858 F.2d 160 (4th Cir. 1988), *cert. den.*, 490 U.S. 1106 (1989). In *Monsanto*, the government was suing for response costs for cleaning a four-acre site which held over 7,000 large drums of highly dangerous chemical wastes. Citing *United States v. Chem-Dyne Corp.*, 572 F. Supp. 802 (S.D. Ohio 1983), for support, the court held, *inter alia*, that common law rules on joint and several liability were appropriate under CERCLA. Therefore:

> when two or more persons act independently to cause a single harm
> for which there is a reasonable basis of apportionment according to
> the contribution of each, each is held liable only for the portion of

> harm that he causes. . . . When such persons cause a single and indivisible harm, however, they are held liable jointly and severally for the entire harm.

Id. at 171–72. *See also Alcan-PAS*, 990 F.2d at 722 ("commingled" waste is not synonymous with "indivisible" harm); *Alcan-Butler*, 964 F.2d at 270 n.29 (same).

2. *Bell* indicated that Leigh settled for $100,000 in December, 1990, and thereafter Sequa was found in the District Court to be liable for $1.8 million. Had this court affirmed the District Court result, could Sequa then have successfully demanded contribution from Leigh towards payment of the greater liability? (No). Had the court found Leigh to be jointly and severally liable, could EPA then reopen its settlement as a matter of right to secure greater compensation from Leigh? (No).

3. How easy is it to prove harms are divisible? *See O'Neil v. Picillo*, 883 F.2d 176, 178–79 (1st Cir. 1989), *cert. den.*, 493 U.S. 1071 (1990) ("The practical effect of placing the burden on defendants has been that responsible parties rarely escape joint and several liability, courts regularly finding that where wastes of varying (and unknown) degrees of toxicity and migratory potential commingle, it simply is impossible to determine the amount of environmental harm caused by each party.").

4. What of PRPs who are jointly and severally liable? Even if each is liable for 100% of clean-up costs as a matter of law, still should not courts attempt to apportion damages on an equitable basis? The answer is yes. *See, e.g., Hemingway Transport, Inc. v. Kahn*, 993 F.2d 915, 921 n.4 (1st Cir. 1993):

> In a CERCLA contribution action among responsible parties who are jointly and severally liable, the burden of proof is less demanding, though the court nevertheless may undertake a comparable allocation of the relative responsibilities of the joint obligors. *See* 42 U.S.C. § 9613(f)(1) ("The court may allocate response costs among liable parties using such equitable factors as the court determines are appropriate."); *see also Smith Land & Improvement Corp. v. Celotex Corp.*, 851 F.2d 86, 90 (3d Cir. 1988), *cert. denied*, 488 U.S. 1029, 102 L. Ed. 2d 969, 109 S. Ct. 837 (1989). In approaching these divisibility and apportionment determinations, the courts have relied on various guideposts, including the legislative history in general, and the so-called "Gore Factors" in particular: (i) the ability of the parties to demonstrate that their contribution to a discharge, release or disposal of a hazardous waste can be distinguished; (ii) the amount of the hazardous waste involved; (iii) the degree of toxicity of the hazardous waste involved; (iv) the degree of involvement by the parties in the generation, transportation, treatment, storage, or disposal of the hazardous waste; (v) the degree of care exercised by the parties with respect to the hazardous waste concerned, taking into account the characteristics of such hazardous waste; and (vi) the degree of cooperation by the parties with Federal, State or local officials to prevent any harm to the public health or the environment. *Environmental Transp. Sys., Inc. v. Ensco, Inc.*, 969 F.2d 503, 508–09 (7th Cir. 1992) ("Gore factors"

provide a nonexhaustive but valuable roster of equitable apportionment considerations) (quoting *United States v. A & F Materials Co.,
Inc.*, 578 F. Supp. 1249, 1256 (S.D. Ill. 1984)).

5. In order to be reimbursable, remedial or removal activity must be justified
by the National Contingency Plan. *See* CERCLA, § 105, 42 U.S.C. § 9605.
The NCP establishes clean-up requirements, relying on the dictates of § 121,
42 U.S.C § 9621. These cleanup standards, as a general matter, are designed
to remove adverse impacts to human health and the environment. In determining the degree of cleanup, the NCP refers to the level of cleanup required
by other legislation, especially so-called "applicable or relevant and appropriate standards," or "ARARs." § 121(d), 42 U.S.C. § 9621(d).

To secure compensation, when EPA is a plaintiff, the clean-up must have
been "not inconsistent with" the NCP. When a private person is the plaintiff,
however, the cleanup must have been "consistent with" the NCP. § 107, 42
U.S.C. § 9607. To be "consistent," one must be in "substantial" compliance
with the standards set forth in the regulations, and must also accomplish a
"CERCLA-quality cleanup." 40 C.F.R. § 300.700(c)(3)(i). (The 1985 version of
the NCP required strict compliance. 40 C.F.R. § 300.71 (1988)). According to
the 1990 NCP, having a "CERCLA-quality cleanup" means that remedial
actions must be: protective of human health and the environment, implement
permanent solutions and alternative treatment technologies to the maximum
extent practicable, and be cost-effective; attain all ARARs; and provide
meaningful public participation. 55 Fed. Reg. 8793 (3/8/90). *See also, City of
Detroit v. Miller*, 842 F. Supp. 957 (E.D. Mich. 1994). EPA cut plaintiffs some
slack by stating that "an omission based on lack of experience with the
Superfund program should not be grounds for defeating an otherwise valid
cost recovery action, assuming the omission does not affect the quality of the
cleanup." *Id*.

Figuring out which NCP requirements apply is not always easy:

> When plaintiffs excavated the soil . . . and when they filed their
> suit in 1989, the 1985 NCP was in effect. . . . However, as defendants
> acknowledge in a footnote, the 1985 NCP has been replaced with new
> regulations known as the 1990 NCP. Although the 1985 NCP was in
> effect when Chicago Kedzie paid to have the soil excavated . . . some
> courts have held that the 1990 NCP, which became effective April 9,
> 1990, is to be applied retroactively. *See Con-Tech Sales Defined Benefit
> Trust v. Worthington Industries, Inc.*, 1991 U.S.Dist. LEXIS 14624.
> Other courts have held that the 1990 regulations apply if the response
> action was underway when the 1990 NCP became effective. *Tri-County
> Business Campus Joint Venture v. Clow Corp.*, 792 F. Supp. 984, 990
> (E.D. Pa. 1992) (if the clean-up was underway on April 9, 1990, the
> 1990 NCP applies). Other courts, in construing the regulations preced-
> ing the 1985 NCP, have held that the applicable NCP regulations are
> those promulgated at the time the response costs were incurred.
> *Artesian Water Co. v. New Castle County*, 659 F. Supp. 1269, 1294 (D.
> Del. 1985), *aff'd*, 851 F.2d 643 (3d Cir. 1988).

Gussin Enterprises, Inc. v. Rockola, 1993 U.S. Dist. LEXIS 4579, 36 Env't Rep.
Cas. (BNA) 1903 (N.D. Ill. Apr. 13, 1993) (the *Gussin* court did not decide the

issue, on the theory that violations of both the 1985 and 1990 NCPs were established).

Consistency with the NCP is generally viewed to be a question of liability, not of damages. *Artesian Water Co. v. Government of New Castle County*, 659 F. Supp. 1269 (D.C. Del. 1987) *aff'd*, 851 F.2d 643 (3d Cir. 1988). Response actions carried out in compliance with the terms of an order issued by EPA pursuant to § 106, 42 U.S.C. § 9606, or a consent decree entered into pursuant to § 122, 42 U.S.C. § 9622, are irrebuttably presumed to be consistent with the NCP. 40 C.F.R. § 300.700(c)(3)(ii).

6. In *Bell*, the court did not decide whether EPA could recover unreasonable, unnecessary or excessive costs. The issue was whether these costs are "not inconsistent with" the NCP. In fact, EPA's policy argument regarding its "gross misconduct" standard has enjoyed support in the courts:

> In *United States v. Northeastern Pharmaceutical & Chemical Co., Inc.*, 810 F.2d 726 (8th Cir. 1986), the court noted that § 107(a)(4)(A) does not refer to "all reasonable costs" but simply to "all costs," and concluded that "'all costs' incurred by the government that are not inconsistent with the NCP are conclusively presumed to be reasonable." *Id.* In *United States v. Hardage*, 982 F.2d 1436 (10th Cir. 1992), the court likewise stated that, "as long as the government's choice of response action is not inconsistent with the NCP, its costs are presumed to be reasonable and therefore recoverable." *Id.* at 1443. *Cf. United States v. R. W. Meyer, Inc.*, 889 F.2d at 1504 (emphasis added) ("to the extent cleanup actions are necessary, . . . the statute contemplates that those responsible for hazardous waste at each site must bear the full cost of cleanup actions").

> Beyond that, most courts hold that defendants have the burden of proving that EPA's costs are inconsistent with the NCP. *E.g., Hardage*, 982 F.2d at 1442; *Northeastern*, 810 F.2d at 747; *Ottati & Goss*, 630 F. Supp. at 1395; *United States v. Conservation Chemical Co.*, 619 F. Supp. 162, 186 (W.D. Mo. 1985); *United States v. Ward*, 618 F. Supp. 884, 899 (E.D.N.C. 1985). In private cost recovery actions, however, under § 107(a)(4)(B), nongovernmental entities carry the burden of showing that their response costs are necessary and consistent with the NCP. *County Line Investment Co. v. Tinney*, 933 F.2d 1508, 1512 & n.8 (10th Cir. 1991); *Northeastern*, 810 F.2d at 726.

Bell, supra, at n.22, 23.

*   *   *   *   *   *

Remedial and removal costs are not the only costs chargeable to liable persons.

UNITED STATES v. R.W. MEYER, INC.

889 F.2d 1497 (6th Cir. 1989)

Defendant, R.W. Meyer, Inc. (Meyer), appeals from a district court order granting summary judgment for plaintiff, the United States (hereinafter referred to as the Environmental Protection Agency (EPA) or the government), in this action arising under the Comprehensive Environmental Response Compensation and Liability Act of 1980 (CERCLA), as amended by the Superfund Amendments and Reauthorization Act of 1986 (SARA), 42 U.S.C. § 9601, et seq. Meyer claims that summary judgment was improper for several reasons. First, it claims that, as a matter of law, the government's indirect costs are not recoverable under CERCLA. Next, it contends that the district court erred in applying retroactively CERCLA's amendments authorizing the award of prejudgment interest. Meyer also claims that the district court erred in finding the defendants jointly and severally liable under CERCLA. Finally, Meyer argues that summary judgment was improper because numerous issues of material fact surrounded the government's claimed direct costs of removal, indirect costs, prejudgment interest, and the issue whether the government's actions were consistent with the National Contingency Plan (NCP), as required under CERCLA. Having determined that the district court's resolution of this matter was correct, we affirm. . . .

. . . The government then filed a motion for summary judgment on the issue of costs. The government sought $269,811.25 in response costs in addition to prejudgment interest on that amount. The $269,811.25 included $52,978.50 in indirect costs, costs paid to contractors, EPA direct payroll and travel expenses, and $35,473.28 in Department of Justice enforcement costs. This motion also was granted with the exception of $993 incurred for a title search and with the proviso that the parties submit further affidavits regarding the appropriate amount of prejudgment interest. *United States v. Northernaire Plating Co.*, 685 F. Supp. 1410 (W.D. Mich. 1988). After the parties stipulated to $74,004.97 as the amount of accumulated prejudgment interest, the court ordered the defendants to pay that amount to the government. On September 2, 1988, the court issued a final judgment on the government's claim. Only Meyer has appealed from that order. . . .

The government submitted to the district court extensive documentation supporting its claim that the defendants owe it $234,337.97 in EPA direct and indirect costs, plus $60,621.99 in prejudgment interest, in addition to $35,473.28 in Department of Justice costs. The requested EPA costs were allocated as follows: $22,241.69 — EPA payroll; 5,974.70 — EPA travel; 153,143.08 — various contract expenses (including $993 that ultimately was disallowed); 52,978.50 — EPA "indirect costs;" $234,337.97 — (Total) Meyer challenges the government's entitlement to recovery of indirect costs under CERCLA, claiming that administrative costs are recoverable only to the extent they are related to a removal action. Meyer concedes that recoverable expenses include "payroll costs and travel expenses of the EPA personnel directly involved with the Northernaire site removal action, and those of the Justice Department attorneys involved in this cost recovery action . . . [and] related administrative costs, as that right is recognized in reported cases." The gist of Meyer's claim is that the government impermissibly is seeking recovery of indirect administrative costs or other costs inherent in operating the Superfund generally. Meyer claims that these costs are not recoverable because they are unrelated to a given removal action at a given site. It contends that the absence of any reference to indirect costs in the statute and legislative history, in the face of the statute's explicit delineation of recoverable costs, supports its claim that indirect costs are not recoverable.

According to William Cooke, a cost accountant with EPA's Superfund Accounting Branch, the $52,978.50 in indirect costs sought by the government represents real costs that are necessary to operate the Superfund Program and to support cleanup efforts at specific sites, but that cannot be linked directly to the efforts at any one particular site. Cooke indicated that the indirect costs essentially are "overhead costs" attributable to "rent and utilities for site and non-site office space; payroll and benefits for program managers, clerical support and other administrative support staff, and pay earned by on-scene coordinators while on leave, or performing tasks not directly associated with a particular site." Cooke described such costs as inherent in all government grants and contracts and as widely recognized and understood in the business community. . . .

The court concluded that Congress intended that the government recover "all of the costs incurred in a remedial or removal action," and that the language of section 9604(b) together "with the broad remedial purpose of CERCLA, supports a liberal interpretation of recoverable costs." *Northernaire,* 685 F. Supp. at 1419. We agree with this interpretation, finding that the challenged indirect costs are part and parcel of all costs of the removal action, which are recoverable under CERCLA. Contrary to Meyer's assertions, the challenged indirect costs are attributable to its cleanup site in that they represent the portion of EPA's overhead expenses that supported the government's response action on Meyer's property. As such, the government's total response costs necessarily include both direct and indirect costs inherent in the cleanup operation. The EPA demonstrated that its indirect costs for such things as office space for EPA employees who oversee response actions represent costs incurred in support of more than one response action and that are apportioned regionally among all the response actions undertaken in a given region. William Cooke described the method of calculating and allocating indirect costs of the Superfund program to a particular response action. Essentially, the EPA determines, for each fiscal year, the total amount of EPA overhead costs at EPA headquarters and the ten regional EPA offices that support CERCLA response actions. EPA allocates part of the headquarters' overhead costs that support response actions to each of its ten regional offices. Those costs are added to each regional office's own overhead costs that support such actions. EPA then calculates an indirect cost rate for each region each fiscal year by dividing the region's total overhead costs attributable to Superfund activities, plus its share of headquarters' overhead costs, by the total number of hours billed by regional Superfund personnel in a given fiscal year. To determine what portion of its indirect costs support a particular response action, EPA multiplies the number of hours billed by certain regional personnel to a particular response action by the indirect cost rate for that fiscal year.

Finally, to determine the total indirect costs attributable to a particular response site, EPA adds the indirect costs attributed to that site for each year during which response action occurred at that site. According to the government, the $52,987.50 sought in indirect costs represents the portion of EPA overhead costs attributable to the response action on Meyer's property, which must be added to the government's direct costs to determine the EPA's total cost of the removal action. The use of direct and indirect costs in calculating total cost comports with standard accounting practices and reflects the true overall cost incurred by the government in cleaning up Meyer's property.

Given section 9607(a)'s authorization for the government to recover all costs of its removal or remedial actions, we are not persuaded that the government's indirect costs were unauthorized. Rather, to the extent cleanup actions are necessary, we are persuaded that the statute contemplates that those responsible for hazardous waste at each site must bear the full cost of cleanup actions and that those costs necessarily include both direct costs and a proportionate share of indirect costs attributable to each site. In essence then, the allocation of the indirect costs to specific cleanup sites effectively renders those costs direct costs attributable to a particular site. We are confident that had Meyer or the other defendants undertaken the cleanup operation by contracting with another company to perform the cleanup, the costs of that cleanup, whether characterized as costs, direct costs plus indirect costs, or otherwise, would include the type of indirect costs challenged here. The fact that the government's indirect costs may be higher than another entity's does not make those costs any less recoverable, particularly in view of the defendants' failure to handle the cleanup on their own. We are not persuaded that the challenged indirect costs are unrelated or unattributable to the removal action on Meyer's property and conclude that the district court properly found those costs recoverable."

[The *Meyer* court also found the SARA amendment to Section 107 of CERCLA, allowing EPA to recover prejudgment interest as part of its damages award, applied retroactively to defendants.]

NOTES AND QUESTIONS

1. *See also United States v. Rohm & Haas*, 2 F.3d 1265 (3d Cir. 1993) (EPA may not recover damages under CERCLA for its oversight costs arising in association with a private party's remedial or removal actions); *Atlantic Richfield Co. v. American Airlines*, 98 F.3d 564 (10th Cir. 1996) (a private party's payment of EPA's oversight costs is recoverable in a subsequent contribution action).

2. There is no right to recover attorney's fees in private cost recovery actions. *Key Tronic Corp. v. United States*, 511 U.S. 809, 114 S. Ct. 1960 (1994). Attorney's fees have been allowed, however, for the government. *See, e.g., United States v. Chapman*, 146 F.3d 1166 (9th Cir. 1998):

> The [*Key Tronic*] Court expressly declined . . . to determine whether attorney fees are recoverable by the government, stating "we offer no comment" on whether "enforcement activities" entitles the government to recover its attorney fees under section 107. *Id.* at 819. In dicta, the

Court noted that district courts have generally agreed that the government is entitled to recover litigation expenses including attorney fees as part of its cleanup costs. *Id.* at 817. "Congress arguably endorsed these holdings, as well, in the SARA provision redefining the term 'response' to include related 'enforcement activities.'" *Id.* at 817–818. Since *Key Tronic* was decided, only one circuit has addressed the issue of government cost recovery. In *B.F. Goodrich v. Betkoski,* 99 F.3d 505 (2d Cir. 1996), *cert. denied,* 118 S. Ct. 2318, 141 L. Ed. 2d 694 (U.S. 1997) (No. 97-241), the Second Circuit distinguished *Key Tronic* as applying only to private cost recovery actions, and held that attorney fees are recoverable by the government as response costs under CERCLA. 99 F.3d at 528. The Second Circuit analyzed the statute and determined that because "respond" is defined in 42 U.S.C. § 9601(25) to mean "remove, removal, remedy or remedial action," and these terms include "enforcement activities related thereto," "the government's recoverable response costs properly include not only the obvious costs of remediation, but also include, inter alia, attorneys' fees." *Id.* [citing to *United States v. Gurley,* 43 F.3d 1188, 1199–1200 (8th Cir. 1994) and *United States v. R.W. Meyer, Inc.,* 889 F.2d 1497, 1504 (6th Cir. 1989)].

Id. at 1174.

The *Chapman* court went on to agree with the Second Circuit's view allowing the government to recover attorneys' fees. *Id.* at 1175. The court saw "persuasive policy arguments" supporting its conclusion. *Id.* First, noted the court, Congress intended to place "ultimate financial responsibility for cleanup on those responsible for the hazardous waste[.]" *Id.* Second, "[t]he award of attorney fees to the government in this case can act as a powerful deterrent to other parties responsible for the cleanup of hazardous materials. The threat of attorney fees should encourage other parties in Chapman's position to take remedial action on their own when requested by the government. Who knows, it might even encourage responsible parties not to pollute and contaminate property in the first place[.]" *Id.*

3. Note that CERCLA damages do not cover all losses. They do not cover, for example, loss of property value and loss of quality of life. Accordingly, a plaintiff may well wish to pursue common law claims in addition to CERCLA. *See, e.g., Scribner v. Summers,* 84 F.3d 554 (2d. Cir. 1996).

4. Federal law is not alone in the hazardous waste clean-up effort. About 30 states have their own "superfunds" to both find potential clean-up sites and to effect removal and remedial actions at locations not on the federal NPL list.

D. NATURAL RESOURCES DAMAGES

Consistent with the statute's overall remedial slant, in addition to the aforementioned response costs, CERCLA makes persons liable for losses endured by the environment itself. In other words, CERCLA creates two classes of plaintiffs. Persons who have assumed response costs can be plaintiffs, of course, but the environment can be a plaintiff as well, in functional terms at least.[4]

Thus, CERCLA provides in § 107(a)(4)(C), 42 U.S.C. § 9607(a)(4)(C), that responsible parties may be held liable for "damages for injury to, destruction of, or loss of natural resources, including the reasonable costs of assessing such injury, destruction, or loss resulting from such a release." The federal government and the government of the state where the harmed resource is located are designated to receive these damage amounts on behalf of the environment. § 107(f)(1), 42 U.S.C. § 9607(f)(1). As a procedural device, CERCLA calls for the appointment of a "trustee" to assess natural resource damages and recover them from liable parties, by filing legal action where necessary. § 107(f)(2), 42 U.S.C. § 9607(f)(2).

The duty of promulgating regulations to govern this process resides in the U.S. Department of Interior. Section 301(c)(2), 42 U.S.C. § 9651(c)(2), calls for two different procedures for assessing natural resource damages. Under § 301(c)(2)(A), 42 U.S.C. § 9651(c)(2)(A), DOI was directed to create "standard procedures for simplified assessments requiring minimal field observation. . . ." Section 301(c)(2)(B), 42 U.S.C. § 9651(c)(2)(B), calls for "alternative protocols for conducting assessments in individual cases." The rules implementing these provisions became known as "Type A" and "Type B" rules, respectively. Each rule must "identify the best available procedures to determine such damages." § 301(c)(2), 42 U.S.C. § 9651(c)(2). While trustees are not obligated to follow either Type A or Type B procedures, the statute clothes any damages assessment made in accordance with Type A or Type B procedures with a rebuttable presumption of accuracy in any administrative or judicial proceeding to recover damages. § 107(f)(2)(C), 42 U.S.C. § 9607(f)(2)(C). In 1986, after many years of delay, the DOI promulgated its final Type B rules. 43 C.F.R. Part 11 (1986). In the next year, it promulgated its final Type A rules. 43 C.F.R. Part 11 (1987).

The Type A rules provide a "simplified assessment process" to determine natural resource damages for injuries that have occurred in coastal and marine environments. 43 C.F.R. § 11.41(a)(1). The assessment consists of four parts: assessment plan, injury determination, quantification, and damage determination. *Id.* at § 11.41(a)(2). The rules authorize the use of computer models as a substitute for on-site inspections to determine the extent of natural resource injuries. *Id.* at § 11.41(a)(1). This latter provision was challenged in *National Association of Manufacturers v. U.S. Department of Interior*, 134 F.3d 1095 (D.C. Cir. 1998), on the ground that computer models cannot demonstrate the causal connection between a release and an injury to the environment. The D. C. Circuit Court of Appeals rejected the contention, finding "nothing in the relevant provisions of CERCLA that requires greater proof of causation and injury than is provided by DOI's predictive computer

---

[4] Congress clearly understood the potential for releases of hazardous substance to work a devastation upon natural resources. *See, e.g.*, Report of the Senate Committee on Environment and Public Works, S. Rep. No. 96–848, at 84 (1980) (acknowledging that "the ramifications for the environment from such releases can be regional or national as well as local in scope . . . and that standardized techniques for assessing both the biological and economic damages from such releases should be developed."). Thus, it called for "an improved, fair and expeditious mechanism for dealing with natural resource damages. . . ." *Id.* at 85–86.

submodels." *Id.* at 1105. The court also found that Type A and Type B procedures could be used together when doing so would produce a more reliable damage assessment more expeditiously.

Since the Type B rules address more significant environmental injuries, they implement a somewhat more elaborate four-phase assessment process. The initial pre-assessment phase is for determining whether a problem exists at all. If a problem does exist, additional investigation takes place in the follow-up assessment plan phase. Next is the assessment phase, during which the trustee verifies that an injury to natural resources has taken place, quantifies the extent of the injury, and establishes a monetary value for the resource damage. In the final post-assessment phase, the trustee documents the whole process and presents the responsible parties with a demand for payment of damages.

The most important aspect of the Type B rules is its methodology for computing the value of a natural resource injury. In its initial rules, the DOI provided the damage award should represent "the lesser of: restoration or replacement costs; or dimunition of use values." 43 C.F.R. § 11.35(b)(2) (1987). This "lesser of" rule was challenged and overturned in *State of Ohio v. U.S. Department of Interior*, 880 F.2d. 432 (D.C. Cir. 1989), the court finding CERCLA to call for restoration whenever possible, not only when less expensive. Rather than appeal the decision, the DOI promulgated new regulations in 1994. 43 C.F.R. Part 11. The new rules incorporate the court's approach on use of the "lesser of" measure of damages. The measure of damages is now "the cost of restoration, replacement, and/or acquisition of the equivalent of the injured natural resources and the services those resources provided." Type A rules follow this valuation methodology as well. 43 C.F.R. § 11.80(b).

The regulations also state that "damages may also include, at the discretion of the authorized official, the compensable value of all or a portion of the services lost to the public for the time period from the discharge or release until the attainment of the restoration, rehabilitation, replacement, and/or acquisition of equivalent of the resources and their services to baseline." 43 C.F.R. § 11.80(b). These "compensable value" damages are similar to "rental" damages. How should these be computed? Should they include, for example, compensation for mental anguish? Do rental damages reflect the concept of environment as victim?

The trustee may select among various valuation methodologies to measure compensable value in "accordance with the public's [willingness to pay], in a cost effective manner." 43 C.F.R. § 11.83(c)(3). Among the various valuation methodologies, a trustee may select a "contingent valuation" methodology. 43 C.F.R. § 11.83(c)(2)(vii). Contingent valuation is a method, relying mainly on survey questions, for determining the value of resources which are not traded on a market. For a review of contingent valuation, see *"Ask a Silly Question . . .": Contingent Valuation of Natural Resources Damages*, 105 Harv. L. Rev. 1981 (1992).

Last, the Type B Rules give trustees considerably greater discretion in the selection of restoration plans. The rules require only that the trustee develop several options, ranging from no action to intensive action, based on "all relevant considerations." 43 C.F.R. § 11.82(d). Ten considerations specifically stated by the regulation for the trustee to consider are: (1) technical feasibility; (2) the relationship of the expected costs of the proposed actions to the expected benefits from the restoration, rehabilitation, replacement, and/or acquisition of equivalent resources; (3) cost-effectiveness; (4) the results of any actual or planned response actions; (5) potential for additional injury resulting from the proposed actions, including long-term and indirect impacts, to the injured resources or other resources; (6) the natural recovery period determined in § 11.73(a)(1); (7) ability of the resources to recover with or without alternative actions; (8) potential effects of the action on human health and safety; (9) consistency with relevant federal, state, and tribal policies; and (10) compliance with applicable federal, state, and tribal laws. *Id.*

The rules were challenged and upheld in *Kennecott Utah Copper Corp. v. United States Department of the Interior*, 88 F.3d 1191 (1996).

NOTE

Section 311 of the Clean Water Act, 33 U.S.C. § 1321, also authorizes federal and state officials to sue as public trustees to recover "any costs or expenses incurred by the Federal Government or any State government in the restoration or replacement of natural resources damaged or destroyed as a result of a discharge of oil or a hazardous substance" in navigable waters. CWA § 311(f)(4), 33 U.S.C. § 1321(f)(4). Trustees suing under § 311 of the Clean Water Act may use recovered funds "to restore, rehabilitate or acquire the equivalent of such natural resources." CWA § 311(f)(5), 33 U.S.C. § 1321(f)(5).

A NOTE ON CERCLA AND COMPREHENSIVE GENERAL LIABILITY INSURANCE

May a party liable under CERCLA nonetheless be saved by her or his comprehensive general liability ("CGL") insurance policy? (Note, of course, that the terms of an insurance policy cannot remove liability established by a sovereign enactment such as CERCLA; all it can do is transfer the liability as a matter of civil contract law to an insurer. A party found liable under § 107 remains so; insurance is just another way to meet the financial obligation). Such CGL insurance policies usually provide that "the Company will pay on behalf of the insured all sums which the insured shall become legally obligated to pay as damages because of bodily injury or property damage to which the insurance applies, cause by an occurrence. . . ."

In the early days of CERCLA, the question was whether response costs qualified as "damages" for purposes of these CGL policies. Some courts found that coverage extended, on the notion that expectations of policyholders should govern interpretation of policies. *See, e.g., Avondale Industries, Inc. v. Travelers Indemnity Co.*, 887 F.2d 1200 (2d Cir. 1989); *Independent Petrochemical Corp. v. Aetna Casualty and Surety Co.*, 944 F.2d. 940 (D.C. Cir. 1991). Others held that response costs are not legally "damages" but are restitutive, and hence equitable, in nature. *See, e.g., Maryland Casualty Co. v. Armco*, 822 F.2d 1348 (4th Cir. 1987), *cert. den.*, 108 S. Ct. 703 (1988). This holding can be surprising for the legal initiate. As aptly put by counsel in *Aerojet-General Corp. v. San Mateo County Superior Court*, 211 Cal. App. 3d 216 (1989): "If a layman, having taken out a General Comprehensive Liability policy and paid the premiums, were told that he had to be wary of a distinction between law and equity, he or she would look at one in dumb amazement and say 'What's that, again?'" In some 60 case decisions on this matter, through June, 1989, about 3/4 were decided in favor of policyholders, the remainder in favor of insurers.

The predictable result of this has been the insertion of new language in CGL policies to specifically include or exclude CERCLA-like liabilities. Having protected their flanks, insurers have now taken the offensive, offering individually "manuscripted" policies specifically taking on environmental risks, subject to due diligence and other requirements, and upon payment of hefty premiums. The policies can be useful in reducing risks associated with development of potentially contaminated properties.

A NOTE ON CERCLA REFORMS

Because of the penchant of CERCLA to impose huge financial liabilities on persons innocent of intentional or significant wrongdoing, EPA has tried to implement some administrative modifications to avert these effects. In 1993, in its so-called Round One of reforms, it focused on *de minimis* parties, those who are technically liable but only for miniscule contributions of hazardous materials. By negotiating early and apportioned settlements, EPA claims to have removed 12,000 people from the system, persons who otherwise faced substantial financial ruin because of Superfund liability. The agency similarly focused on *de micromis* parties — those with even less culpability — promising to simply remove all liability from this set of technically liable persons. Last, it undertook the practice of volunteering an "orphan share." This share is EPA's contribution to a site clean-up; by volunteering to help out, the agency claims to expedite the settlement process among PRPs and eases the burdens on those persons as well. The problem for the EPA in this regard is budgetary: in the age of reduced governmental appropriations, there are fewer dollars available to contribute as an orphan share.

The agency also increased its use of alternative dispute resolution mechanisms and, significantly, undertook action to address the "brownfields" problem. The brownfields problem is an intractable one produced by the liability scheme of CERCLA itself. In order to avoid CERCLA liability, developers often seek out pristine (i.e. "green") areas for development. EPA would prefer to see industrial development to go in at so-called brownfield sites, those previously industrial in use and perhaps still somewhat contaminated. (The term "brownfield site" is defined at § 101(39), 42 U.S.C. § 9601(39)). Accordingly, EPA has taken to negotiating prospective purchaser agreements ("PPAs"), which can result in a release from liability for those who choose to move into a brownfield. EPA's brownfields initiative received Harvard University's Innovations in Government Award in 2000.

Significantly, Congress engaged the brownfields problem in its CERCLA amendments of 2002. The new BFPP defense, *see* § 107(r), 42 U.S.C. § 9607(r), which facilitates purchase and re-use of brownfield sites, was part of this effort. *See* discussion, *supra*. The new legislation attempted as well to build on EPA's brownfields initiatives by expressly authorizing "revitalization funding" for brownfields. Section 104(k), 42 U.S.C. § 9604(k), calls for federal grants for eligible entities (the definition of which excludes business corporations, § 104(k)(1), 42 U.S.C. § 9604(k)(1)) of two sorts. Grants are available for site characterization and assessment in amounts not to exceed $200,000 for each site (although that amount can be increased under certain circumstances to as high as $350,000), § 104(k)(4), 42 U.S.C. § 9604(k)(2), and for brownfield remediation. Remediation grants can be for as much as $1 million. *Id.*

In Round Two of its administrative reforms, in June, 1994, the agency established an allocation system to help competing PRPs to better settle out their differences. The system was installed to assure that each PRP need only pay for a fair share of cleanup cost. Under the system, PRPs can make a good faith offer to EPA and agree to release all other PRPs from liability. Once EPA accepts the offer, the agency will go after nonsettling parties for outstanding cleanup costs.

Round Three began in October, 1995. In it, EPA attempted to remedy the orphan share problem. Instead of contributing cash, the agency may opt to reduce its own oversight charges (a "tiered oversight" for those PRPs who can be trusted) or waive past EPA costs. It also may choose to designate moneys taken from *de minimis* PRPs and use those funds for clean-up of the precise sites with which the *de minimis* parties were involved. In addition, the agency has enlarged the *de micromis* group: it used to be those whose contribution to a site was no greater than 0.005%; that number was doubled. In the realm of enforcement, Congress acted by adding new subsection (7) to § 122(g). § 122(g)(7), 42 U.S.C. § 9622(g)(7). Entitled "De minimis settlements," the new provision allows for expedited settlements at reduced amounts for PRPs who have an inability or limited ability to pay response costs. This provision is a codification of pre-existing EPA settlement policy. *See* EPA's "General Policy on Superfund Ability to Pay Determinations," Sept. 30, 1997, at *http://es. epa.gov.oeca/osre/970930~1.pdf.*

ONE CLEANUP PROGRAM

As EPA views it, there are at least four federal programs in place to clean the environment. The overall CERCLA effort to address NPL sites is one, the attempt to reduce the proliferation of brownfields is another, the hazardous wastes program of RCRA is a third, and the concerted effort to remediate leaking underground storage tanks is a fourth. Each of these programs differs from each of the others in significant procedural and substantive ways. Not unexpectedly, these differences complicate the lives of entities subject to these programs. Compliance with regulatory requirements can be difficult in the absolute; that compliance is made all the more difficult when programmatic requirements are numerous, difficult to discern, and internally inconsistent.[1]

---

[1] This complexity, notably, can burden EPA as well. In many enforcement contexts, EPA must choose which regulatory program to use, and having done that, nonetheless assure satisfaction with all the requirements of all applicable programs.

And that is just part of the problem. Add to these federal programs the motley array of state, tribal, and local initiatives of the same sort and you have a formidable regulatory challenge.

Not unexpectedly, the regulated community has chafed under this burden and has long pleaded for programmatic reform. Those entreaties have gone largely ignored, at least until the advent of the One Cleanup Program. Initiated by EPA, this program is an administrative attempt to bring some semblance of order to all of this, and to do so within the auspices of the existing legislative framework. As stated by an EPA official, "[A]ll of our different cleanup programs have to work together better, using the best thinking, the best technologies, the best information, the best measures of success. That's what the One Cleanup Program is all about." Statement of Marianne Horinko, Assistant Administrator, Office of Solid Waste and Emergency Response, Environmental Protection Agency. *See, http://www.epa.gov/oswer/onecleanupprogram/#vision.*

The One Cleanup Program may be a welcome effort, but at this writing it remains in its early stages. Still, EPA touts the program's virtues in one context, the cleaning of the Anacostia Watershed. The watershed, located near the nation's capital, is large (176 square miles) and suffers from numerous sources of contamination, the elimination of which is complicated by tidal flows. As part of its coordinated remediation effort, EPA convened the Anacostia Watershed Toxics Alliance, a coalition of 25 groups, agencies, and institutions. The idea was to bring together all the players who might accomplish change, and to pool technological and financial resources to that end. These resources might then be dedicated to solving this ecosystem-wide pollution problem in a process refreshingly free of judicial and administrative orders. EPA claims this effort has produced substantial gains already, including the repair of more than 6.5 miles of leaking storm sewers, the construction of sand filters to stem the flow of trash into the watershed, the installation of protective covers over 30 acres of land to reduce migration of contaminants, the removal of large amounts of coal tar, mercury, and petroleum, and the direct cleaning of more than 27,000 tons of contaminated soil and a million gallons of surface and groundwater.

Appendix One

TABLE OF ACRONYMS

AAPA	—	American Antiquities Preservation Act
AEA	—	Atomic Energy Act
AEC	—	Atomic Energy Commission
ALARA	—	as low as reasonably achievable
ALDF	—	Animal Legal Defense Fund
ANILCA	—	Alaska National Interest Lands Conservation Act
ANWR	—	Alaska National Wildlife Refuge
ARARS	—	applicable or relevant and appropriate standard
ASPCA	—	American Society for the Prevention of Cruelty to Animals
ATSDR	—	Agency for Toxic Substances and Disease Registry
AOC	—	Area of Concern
AOC	—	approximate original contour
APA	—	Administrative Procedure Act
AUM	—	animal unit month
AWS	—	alternative water supply
BACT	—	best available control technology
BANANA	—	build absolutely nothing anywhere near anything
BAT	—	best available technology economically achievable
BCF	—	bioconcentration factor
BCT	—	best conventional pollutant control technology
BDAT	—	best demonstrated available technology
BDT	—	best demonstrated technology
BFPP	—	bona fide prospective purchaser
BIA	—	Bureau of Indian Affairs
BLM	—	Bureau of Land Management
BMPs	—	best management practices
BO or BiOp	—	biological opinion
BOR	—	Bureau of Reclamation
BPT	—	best practicable control technology currently available
CA	—	corrective action
CAA	—	Clean Air Act
CAFE	—	corporate average fuel efficiency (standards)

CAMU	—	corrective action management unit
CCA	—	candidate conservation agreement
CCAA	—	candidate conservation agreement with assurances
CCL	—	Construction Completion List
CEMS	—	continuous emissions monitoring system
CEQ	—	Council on Environmental Quality
CERCLA	—	Comprehensive Environmental Response, Compensation, and Liability Act
CFCs	—	chlorofluorocarbons
CGL	—	comprehensive general liability (insurance)
CHD	—	critical habitat designation
CITES	—	Convention on International Trade in Endangered Species of Wild Fauna and Flora
CMA	—	Chemical Manufacturers Association
CMDB	—	combined metals data base
CO	—	carbon monoxide
CO_2	—	carbon dioxide
COE	—	Corps of Engineers
CWA	—	Clean Water Act
CZMA	—	Coastal Zone Management Act
DCC	—	Dormant Commerce Clause
DLA	—	Desert Lands Act
DOA	—	Department of Agriculture
DOD	—	Department of Defense
DOE	—	Department of Energy
DOI	—	Department of the Interior
DOJ	—	Department of Justice
DPS	—	Distinct population segment
EA	—	environmental assessment
ECPA	—	Electric Consumers Protection Act
EEC	—	European Economic Community
EEZ	—	exclusive economic zone
EIS	—	environmental impact statement
EJ	—	environmental justice
EPA	—	Environmental Protection Agency
EPCRA	—	Emergency Planning and Community Right-to-Know Act
EO	—	Executive Order
ERDA	—	Energy Research and Development Administration
ERP	—	equipment replacement project
ESA	—	Endangered Species Act
ESC	—	Endangered Species Committee
ESU	—	Evolutionarily significant unit
FAA	—	Federal Aviation Administration

FCLA	—	Federal Coal Leasing Amendments
FCLAA	—	Federal Coal Leasing Amendments Act
FCMA	—	Fishery Conservation and Management Act
FCZ	—	fishery conservation zone
FDA	—	Food and Drug Administration
FEA	—	Federal Energy Administration
FEMA	—	Federal Emergency Management Agency
FERC	—	Federal Energy Regulatory Commission
FIFRA	—	Federal Insecticide, Fungicide, and Rodenticide Act
FIP	—	federal implementation plan
FLPMA	—	Federal Land Policy and Management Act
FMP	—	fishery management plan
FOIA	—	Freedom of Information Act
FONSI	—	finding of no significant impact
FOOGLRA	—	Federal Onshore Oil and Gas Leasing Reform Act
FPA	—	Federal Power Act
FPC	—	Federal Power Commission
FRRRPA	—	Forest and Rangeland Renewable Resources Planning Act
FS	—	Forest Service
FTCA	—	Federal Tort Claims Act
FWCA	—	Fish and Wildlife Coordination Act
FWPCA	—	Federal Water Pollution Control Act (Clean Water Act)
FWS	—	Fish and Wildlife Service
GACT	—	Generally Achievable Control Technology
GAO	—	General Accounting Office
GATT	—	General Agreement on Tariffs and Trade
GFSZA	—	Gun-Free School Zones Act
GML	—	General Mining Law
GNP	—	gross national product
GPO	—	Government Printing Office
GSA	—	General Services Administration
H_2O	—	water
H_2SO_4	—	sulfuric acid
HAPs	—	hazardous air pollutants
HC	—	hydrocarbon
HCFCs	—	hydrochlorofluorocarbons
HCP	—	habitat conservation plan
HMTA	—	Hazardous Materials Transportation Act
HNO_3	—	nitric acid
HR	—	House of Representatives
HRS	—	Hazard Ranking System
HSUS	—	Humane Society of the United States

HSWA	—	Hazardous and Solid Waste Amendments
HWC	—	hazardous waste combustor
HWIR	—	Hazardous Waste Identification Rule
IBEs	—	Investment-backed expectations
IBLA	—	Interior Board of Land Appeals
ICC	—	Interstate Commerce Commission
ICR	—	ignitable, corrosive, reactive (hazardous wastes)
IMA	—	Intermunicipal agreement
IRM	—	Interim remedial measure
IRS	—	Internal Revenue Service
ITP	—	incidental take permit
ITS	—	incidental take statement
LAER	—	lowest achievable emission rate
lb/MMBTU	—	pounds per million British Thermal Units
LDRs	—	land disposal restrictions
LLRWPA	—	Low-Level Radioactive Waste Policy Act
LNG	—	liquified natural gas
LOS	—	Law of the Sea
LRMP	—	land and resource management plan
LULU	—	locally unwanted land use
LUST	—	leaking underground storage tank
MACT	—	maximum achievable control technology
MBTA	—	Migratory Bird Treaty Act
MCL	—	maximum contaminant level
MFASAQHE	—	Major federal action significantly affecting the quality of the human environment
mg/m^3	—	milligrams per cubic meter
MLA	—	Mineral Leasing Act
MMPA	—	Marine Mammals Protection Act
MMS	—	Minerals Management Service
MOA	—	memorandum of agreement
MOU	—	memorandum of understanding
MPRSA	—	Marine Protection, Research, and Sanctuaries Act
MSY	—	maximum sustainable yield
MTBE	—	methyl tertiary butyl ether
MUSYA	—	Multiple Use-Sustained Yield Act
NA	—	nonattainment
NAAQS	—	national ambient air quality standard
NAPAP	—	National Acid Precipitation Assessment Program
NAS	—	National Academy of Sciences
NASA	—	National Aeronautics and Space Administration
NCP	—	National Contingency Plan
NEA	—	National Energy Act
NEPA	—	National Environmental Policy Act

NESHAPs	—	national emission standards for hazardous air pollutants
NFMA	—	National Forest Management Act
NHPA	—	National Historic Preservation Act
NIMBY	—	not in my backyard
NMFS	—	National Marine Fisheries Service
NOAA	—	National Oceanic and Atmospheric Administration
NOx	—	nitrogen oxide
NPCA	—	National Park and Conservation Association
NPDES	—	National Pollutant Discharge Elimination System
NPL	—	National Priority List
NPS	—	National Park Service
NRA	—	national recreation area
NRC	—	Nuclear Regulatory Commission
NRDC	—	Natural Resources Defense Council
NSPS	—	new source performance standards
NSR	—	new source review
NWF	—	National Wildlife Federation
NWPA	—	Nuclear Waste Policy Act
NWRSIA	—	National Wildlife Refuge System Improvement Act
O_3	—	Ozone
OCS	—	outer continental shelf
OCSLA	—	Outer Continental Shelf Lands Act
OMB	—	Office of Management and Budget
OPEC	—	Organization of Petroleum Exporting Countries
ORVs	—	off-road vehicles
OSCLA	—	Outer Continental Shelf Lands Act
OSHA	—	Occupational, Safety, and Health Administration
OSM	—	Office of Surface Mining
OTA	—	Office of Technology Assessment
PA	—	preliminary assessment
PCBs	—	polycholorinated biphenyls
PETA	—	People for the Ethical Treatment of Animals
Pb	—	lead
PM	—	particulate matter
POTWs	—	publicly owned treatment works
PPA	—	prospective purchaser agreement
ppb	—	parts per billion
ppm	—	parts per million
ppq	—	parts per quadrillion
PRPs	—	potentially responsible parties
PSCs	—	public service commissions

PSD	—	prevention of significant deterioration
PSES	—	pretreatment standards for existing sources
PSNS	—	pretreatment standards for new sources
PUCs	—	public utility commissions
PUD	—	public utility district
PURPA	—	Public Utilities Regulatory Policies Act
RACM	—	reasonably available control measure
RACT	—	reasonably available control technology
RARE	—	Roadless Area Review and Evaluation
RCRA	—	Resource Conservation and Recovery Act
REA	—	Rural Electrification Administration
RFA	—	Regulatory Flexibility Act
RIA	—	regulatory impact analysis
RI/FS	—	remedial investigation/feasibility study
RMRR	—	routine maintenance, repair, and replacement
ROD	—	Record of decision
ROP	—	Rate of progress
RRA	—	Reclamation Reform Act of 1962
SARA	—	Superfund Amendments and Reauthorization Act
SCS	—	Soil Conservation Service
SDWA	—	Safe Drinking Water Act
SEC	—	Securities and Exchange Commission
SEPA	—	State environmental policy act
SHA	—	safe harbor agreement
SIH	—	substantial irreparable harm
SIP	—	state implementation plan
SLA	—	Submerged Lands Act
SMCRA	—	Surface Mining Control and Reclamation Act
SNUR	—	significant new use regulation
SO_2	—	sulfur dioxide
SO_4	—	sulfate
SPDES	—	state pollution discharge elimination system
SREA	—	Superfund Recycling Equity Act
SWDA	—	Solid Waste Disposal Act
SWMU	—	solid waste management unit
TCLP	—	toxicity characteristic leaching procedure
TDRs	—	transferable development rights
TGA	—	Taylor Grazing Act
TIP	—	tribal implementation plan
TMDL	—	total maximum daily load
TSCA	—	Toxic Substances Control Act
TSDFs	—	treatment, storage, and disposal facilities
TSS	—	total suspended solids
TTO	—	total toxic organics
TVA	—	Tennessee Valley Authority

UIC	—	underground injection control
UMTRCA	—	Uranium Mill Tailings Radiation Control Act (of 1978)
UNICEF	—	United Nations International Children's Fund
UMRA	—	Unfunded Mandates Reform Act
USTs	—	underground storage tanks
USGS	—	U.S. Geological Survey
UUD	—	unnecessary or undue degradation
VAWA	—	Violence Against Women Act
VMP	—	Vessel management plan
VOCs	—	volatile organic compounds
WRP	—	Wetlands Reserve Program
WQS	—	water quality standard

Appendix Two

CANONS OF STATUTORY INTERPRETATION

LINGUISTIC CANONS (embodying no substantive preference)

- **the whole act rule:** courts should give meaning to the entire legislative enactment
- **inclusio unius** (i.e. *expressio unius est exclusio alterius*): the inclusion of one means the exclusion of the other
- **ejusdem generis** (as of the same kind or nature): a word appearing in isolation to have a broad meaning should be construed more narrowly when considered in its setting
- **noscitur a sociis:** a word takes its meaning "by its companion"
- **pari materia** ("of the same matter"): when more than one statute relates to a subject, the statutes must be considered together
- **plain meaning:** words should be accorded their usual common meaning
- **words and phrases shall be given their ordinary grammatical and dictionary meaning**
- **technical and legal terms and words with special meanings should be given an interpretation appropriate to the context of the statute**
- **words of gender, number and tense should be read to include any other gender, number, or tense**

SUBSTANTIVE CANONS (embodying a substantive preference)

- **penal and tax statutes should be strictly interpreted**
- **it is presumed that a legislature does not enact legislation unless it intends to change the law**
- **all provisions within legislation are there for a purpose**
- **no provision should be construed to be entirely redundant**
- **specific provisions prevail over more general provisions**
- **when dealing with two pieces of legislation, later enactments prevail over earlier ones**
- **repeals are not implied**
- **a repeal of an act that itself repealed legislation does not revive the earlier legislation**

- **statutes shall be interpreted to avoid constitutional problems**
- **rule of lenity:** doubts about a criminal statute should be resolved in favor of a narrow construction
- **statutes in derogation of the common law should be strictly construed**
- **federal statutes are presumed not to preempt state law regarding matters traditionally subject to state regulation**
- **remedial statutes should be read liberally to effect their remedial purposes**
- **an interpretation of a statute made contemporaneous with its enactment is a particularly valuable guide to statutory meaning**
- **an interpretation of a similar statute by another jurisdictions is a particularly valuable guide to statutory meaning**
- **(various specific presumptions)**

CLEAR STATEMENT RULES*

- **there is a need for a clear statement to achieve a result that would raise a substantial constitutional question**
- **there is a need for a clear statement to warrant the extraterritorial application of American law**
- **there is a need for a clear statement to subject a state of the United States to suit in a federal court**

---

* There are many of these, and an exhaustive list may be impossible. The idea is that in certain contexts, legislation should be read as achieving a particular result only if an explicit statement in the text so provides. Judges should hesitate to imply meaning from a statute's design.

TABLE OF CASES

[References are to pages.]

[References are to pages.]

[References are to pages.]

[References are to pages.]

[References are to pages.]

N

[References are to pages.]

[References are to pages.]

[References are to pages.]

INDEX

[References are to page numbers.]

I–1

[References are to page numbers.]

[References are to page numbers.]

[References are to page numbers.]